management

Principles and Practices for Tomorrow's Leaders

Second Canadian Edition

management

Principles and Practices for Tomorrow's Leaders

Second Canadian Edition

Gary Dessler
Florida International University

Frederick A. Starke
University of Manitoba

PEARSON

Prentice Hall

Toronto

National Library of Canada Cataloguing in Publication

Dessler, Gary, 1942–
    Management: principles and practices for tomorrow's leaders/Gary Dessler, Frederick A.
Starke—2nd Canadian ed.

Includes index.
First Canadian ed. published 2001 under title: Management: leading people and organizations in
    the 21st century.
ISBN 0-13-120256-1

1. Management   I. Starke, Frederick A., 1942–   II. Title

HD31.D4225   2004   658.4   C2003-902727-9

0-13-120256-1

Vice President, Editorial Director: Michael J. Young
Acquisitions Editor: James Bosma
Director of Marketing (Business and Economics): Bill Todd
Senior Developmental Editor: Madhu Ranadive
Production Editor: Marisa D'Andrea
Copy Editor: Catherine Haggert
Proofreader: Dawn Hunter
Production Coordinator: Deborah Starks
Permissions Research: Sandy Cooke
Page Layout: Carolyn E. Sebestyen
Art Director: Mary Opper
Interior and Cover Design: Anthony Leung
Cover Image: Getty Images

4 5 6 7 8   12 11 10 09 08

Printed and bound in the United States of America.

Brief Contents

Contents

Part 2 Planning   131

Part 3 Organizing   231

Chapter 8   Fundamentals of Organizing   232

Chapter 9   Designing Organizational Structures   264

Part 4 Leading   333

Chapter 11   Being a Leader   334

Chapter 12 Influencing Individual Behaviour and Motivation 370

Chapter 15 Leading Organizational Change   466

Manager's Portfolio   M1

Preface

This book is more than just words. It's more than just a way to get new facts and information. It's a window into the world of what managers actually do, and a place to start learning how to be an effective manager. You can't master something just by reading about it—you've got to actually do it. That's why we emphasize the practical and applied nature of business management in this book. Events today are moving so fast, and competition is so intense, that new managers can't afford to spend months figuring out how to transfer what they learned in a book to their job. Rather, they have to "hit the ground running." They have to make decisions, write plans, mobilize employees, lead teams, and keep things under control from day one.

This second Canadian edition cuts through the fads and jargon and focuses on the important fundamentals of management. It provides students with the basic management principles and practices they'll need to succeed as managers, not just today, but tomorrow as well.

There are three important things you should know about this book. First, we believe that this management text is like no other, in that it integrates management principles with management applications and techniques. Every chapter contains practical applications, models, and checklists that all managers can use every day.

Second, it includes a Manager's Portfolio, a special **new** section containing a wealth of realistic exercises to reinforce concepts that you learn in the chapters. Once you learn the concepts, it's important to practise applying them in real management situations, so we've included a series of video-driven scenarios that allow students to practise their new management skills. Students can view the specially designed video clips on the accompanying CD-ROM and act as consultants to solve the company's problem.

Third, this book is filled with illustrative, real-life examples of how managers actually use the concepts and ideas that are presented in this book. You will never have to stop and say, "What do the authors mean by that?" or "How could I use that in practice?" Instead, we clearly explain how you can apply each idea that is presented.

Themes of the Text

Massive changes are taking place in the management of organizations today. Globalization, deregulation, and technological advances mean that today's organizations not only have to be more competitive than they have ever been before, but also must be ready to respond quickly to change if they are to thrive in this new, intensely competitive environment. To achieve this responsiveness and competitiveness, new management methods and philosophies have emerged, such as boundaryless organizations, team-based structures, internet-based managing, scenario planning, and commitment building to supplement traditional control techniques. Leading people and managing organizations in the twenty-first century will depend on maintaining open, communicative, and responsive organizations; this can only be achieved by sound management practices that recognize the critical importance of the firm's human capital. Within the planning, organizing, leading, and controlling framework, we focus on the following seven themes, which are woven into each chapter:

1. **People are part of managing.** With today's emphasis on competitiveness, team-based organizations, and being responsive, managers cannot separate their "people management" responsibilities from their strictly "managerial" ones. Thus, while planning requires the setting of goals, it also requires getting employees to accept these goals. This calls for significant leadership and motivational skills on

the part of managers. Because of the importance of people in organizations, each chapter contains a boxed insert entitled "The People Side of Managing" that explains why it is so important for managers to deal effectively with people.

2. **Managing today is technology-based and internet-based.** Everywhere you look today, companies and their managers are relying on the internet to manage their businesses more efficiently and responsively. Dell Computer Corporation, for example, lets its customers track their own products via the internet. This does more than simply make things more convenient for Dell's customers—it eliminates the need to add hundreds of customer relations representatives to handle phone calls as well as the need to house all of those people and provide them with telephone support. Many other companies are using technology to improve their performance. That's why this book contains numerous examples that describe how managers use the internet or some other form of technology to improve the performance of their organizations. For example, Chapter 14, Leading Groups and Teams, shows how companies use the internet and special groupware software packages to enable geographically dispersed team members to interact in real time, as if they were in the same room. Similarly, each chapter contains several examples of how companies are using the internet to better manage their business.

3. **Managing change is crucial.** Understanding how to manage under conditions of rapid change is critical for successful management. Managing change, therefore, is a central theme of each chapter in the text. Chapter 15, Leading Organizational Change, is completely devoted to the issue of change management, and numerous examples of managing change are presented in other chapters as well. Each chapter also contains a boxed insert focusing on "The Challenge of Change."

4. **Entrepreneurship is driving today's economies.** Many college and university graduates will work for smaller firms—managing a small business is the fourth theme of the text. Chapter 4, Managing Entrepreneurial Organizations, is a **new** chapter that focuses on the management of entrepreneurship and small business. Examples of effective management in small businesses are also found throughout the text.

5. **Diversity must be managed.** As the workforce becomes increasingly diverse, it is important for managers to recognize that diversity is a positive force rather than a negative one. Therefore, a portion of Chapter 3 (Ethics, Social Responsibility, and Diversity) is devoted to this topic. As well, each chapter contains examples that illustrate the need for techniques that effectively manage diversity.

6. **Teamwork is essential.** Work in organizations is increasingly organized not around traditional organization charts but around teams. A recent survey by the consulting firm Watson Wyatt concluded that the majority of companies depend to some extent on teams to get their work done. Given the importance of teamwork today, we emphasize the importance of teamwork as well as team-building skills. Chapter 14 is devoted to managing teams, and additional material on how to organize around teams is found in Chapter 9, Designing Organizational Structures. Each chapter contains examples of how teams can be used to improve decision making, communication, and the formulation of strategies.

7. **Managers manage globally.** Few changes in the past decade have had more impact on managers than globalization, and this trend will continue during the twenty-first century. Students are given an early introduction to the concept of globalization and to issues arising from it in Chapter 2. Because today's managers need to view all aspects of business and management from a global perspective, we also provide numerous examples of globalization in every chapter. Here are just a few of the many examples of globalization material contained in the text:

- Chapter 1, Managing in the Twenty-First Century, discusses the impact on management of changing political systems around the world, including the explosive opening of new markets with hundreds of millions of potential customers.

- Chapter 2, The Environment of Management: Canadian and Global, is entirely devoted to the impact of globalization on management. It covers the reasons why companies expand operations abroad and their strategies for doing so.

- Chapter 7, Strategic Management, discusses how companies achieve above-average growth rates by aggressively expanding into new geographic markets, both domestically and abroad.

- Chapter 13, Improving Communication Skills, emphasizes that cross-cultural communication is a fact of business life and illustrates how to communicate in different cultures.

- Chapter 16, Controlling and Building Commitment, points out that managing a globally dispersed workforce requires a particularly effective control system and a greater reliance on commitment-building efforts in order to avoid the problems that can arise when employees are far away from the company's central managers.

Management: Principles and Practices for Tomorrow's Leaders provides students in basic management/organization courses with a complete and highly applied description of essential management concepts and techniques in a very readable and understandable form. The book blends traditional management process coverage with a practical and applied management-skills emphasis that is totally unique in management textbooks today. In addition to this new and distinctive applied-skills theme, there are many other features that will help students to better understand the important activity of management.

Chapter Features

The features contained in each chapter of this text have been carefully designed to reinforce the major themes described above, and to make it easy for students to actively learn and retain what they read. Each chapter contains the following features:

Learning Objectives A list of learning objectives is found at the beginning of each chapter. This focuses students' attention on the key items in the chapter.

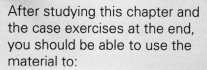

OBJECTIVES

After studying this chapter and the case exercises at the end, you should be able to use the material to:

1. Use the steps in the planning process to develop a workable plan for an organization.

2. Outline the required overall business plan and provide examples of its component functional plans.

Opening Case Each chapter begins with an interesting description of a situation facing a real organization. The information in the opening case relates to the material in the chapter. For example, the opening case in Chapter 5, Decision Making, describes the challenges facing Bell Canada Enterprises as it decides which of its businesses to emphasize so that the company can more effectively respond to changes in the competitive environment. The opening cases convey to students the dynamic environment in which managers work.

Decision Time at BCE

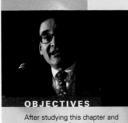

OBJECTIVES

After studying this chapter and the case exercises at the end, you should be able to use the material to:

1. Demonstrate the importance of decision making in management jobs.

2. Explain the difference between programmed and nonprogrammed decisions.

3. Describe the steps a manager must take to work through the rational decision-making process.

In April 2002, Jean Monty, the CEO of BCE Inc., unexpectedly announced that he was stepping down from his position. Michael Sabia, the new CEO, was immediately faced with a very difficult strategic decision, namely what kind of company BCE would be. Would it be a telephone company, a telecommunications company, a media company, or a New Economy company? This strategic decision was necessary because BCE had been acquiring companies in many different businesses, but several of them were not performing well. A CIBC *World Markets* research note said that BCE's strategy appeared to be in disarray.

To see why Sabia had a difficult strategic decision to make, consider the makeup of BCE in 2002. BCE had been pursuing a strategy that is often characterized by industry observers as "commerce, content, and connectivity." The *commerce* part of the equation included BCE Emergis (electronic commerce in the health and financial services industries) and CGI Group Inc. (information technology consulting). The *content* part of the equation was represented by Bell Globemedia, which includes CTV (television stations), ROBTv (business reporting), *The Globe and Mail* (a national newspaper), and Sympatico-Lycos (internet portals). The *connectivity* part of the equation included Bell Canada (telephones), Bell ExpressVu (satellite broadcasting), Teleglobe (international voice and data network), and Bell Canada International (telecom services in emerging markets).

Real-World Management Boxes Each chapter contains two boxed inserts describing how ideas discussed in the text are applied in real organizations in Canada and throughout the world. These boxes are organized into two series that run throughout the text. Each chapter contains one box for each of the following series:

- The People Side of Managing (descriptions of current management practices that demonstrate the critical importance of people in the success of organizations)
- The Challenge of Change (examples showing how important it is for managers to anticipate and effectively manage the massive changes that confront organizations worldwide)

THE PEOPLE SIDE OF MANAGING

Dream Weavers and Start-Ups

Modern start-up companies often have different characteristics than start-ups did a few years ago. In the past, entrepreneurs started their businesses from scratch and then slowly built them, brick by brick and customer by customer. Because the process was relatively slow and continuous, the entrepreneur was usually able to nurture his or her company's vision and to put all the values and systems in place that were needed to help the employees implement that vision.

Today, many start-ups are technology-based and often emerge, full-blown, out of large parent companies (or with the enormous financial backing of venture capital firms). As a result, a start-up firm—say, one born to create a new internet portal—may begin life with millions of dollars of cash and hundreds of employees, but without the traditions and values that normally go along with growing a business from scratch.

OD consultants often play the role of what one calls "dream weavers." They are asked to take all the necessary elements for success that are already in place and help pull them together into a smoothly functioning whole by working with the entrepreneur and his or her employees as a facilitator/transition agent. How exactly can OD consultants help? Here are some examples:

■ *Establish a new identity.* When a giant company spins off a new start-up, OD consultants can help the new entity establish an independent identity by working with the new team to help clarify value, vision, and mission statements.

■ *Build teams.* The new company may be staffed with people who haven't worked together before or who have little or no experience in building effective teams. The OD consultants can use their facilitation skills to create a smoothly functioning team. For example, one start-up was having a serious interpersonal communications problem. In this case, the new company's software engineers complained about each other to third parties and did poorly in one-on-one interactions. The OD consultant worked with the people involved during staff meetings to identify and address the counterproductive behaviour and facilitate teamwork.

■ *Manage cultural change.* Sometimes a new spinoff company's culture may reflect the culture of the parent firm. In one start-up, for instance, the fear of challenging the system was so ingrained that true creativity was thwarted. In this case the OD consultant was able to work with the team to help instill—through a new core value statement, new leadership and management practices, and new signs and symbols—a more risk-oriented and creative set of values.

THE CHALLENGE OF CHANGE

Going Boundaryless

Brady
www.bradycorp.com

Brady Corp., which manufactures identification and safety products, is rolling out its new boundaryless supply chain management system. The system will enable Brady's suppliers, customers, and distributors to enter and process orders seamlessly, via the internet. However, management knows that doing so demands a new organization design. For example, many orders will now come directly to production, rather than via sales/customer reps. How should Brady reorganize its sales, production, and shipping operations to best capitalize on the firm's new boundaryless supply chain?

Top management has earmarked about U.S.$50 million for the new system. However, only about a third of that money is for the technology itself. Top management is spending the rest on restructuring the firm's organization and processes. For example, Brady customer service employees used to receive orders and then pass them on to the firm's production department. Then orders would move on to shipping. The new organization structure and processes that Brady is putting in place to support the new boundaryless supply chain will be much different. Customers with simple orders will send them directly, on-line, to manufacturing. In manufacturing, Brady reengineered the operation, creating a horizontal process. One factory floor person will oversee the entire production and shipping process. Management expects the new organization and processes to cut about five steps out of the current 15-step sale-manufacturing-shipping process and to cut the processing cost of each order by a third.

Checklists These checklists provide concise summaries of specific segments of chapter material, and show students how they can actually put an idea into practice. The checklists range from self-assessments to management guidelines about how to perform a task. This new feature provides quick reference to the fundamental principles and practices successful managers use. These checklists include:

- how to develop a business plan
- how to be a better listener
- how to rate the adequacy of an organization structure
- how to conduct a new business feasibility study
- how to implement an incentive plan
- how to read an organization's culture
- how to be a transformational leader
- and many more

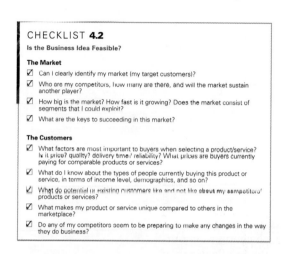

CHECKLIST **4.2**

Is the Business Idea Feasible?

The Market

☑ Can I clearly identify my market (my target customers)?

☑ Who are my competitors, how many are there, and will the market sustain another player?

☑ How big is the market? How fast is it growing? Does the market consist of segments that I could exploit?

☑ What are the keys to succeeding in this market?

The Customers

☑ What factors are most important to buyers when selecting a product/service? Is it price? quality? delivery time? reliability? What prices are buyers currently paying for comparable products or services?

☑ What do I know about the types of people currently buying this product or service, in terms of income level, demographics, and so on?

☑ What do potential or existing customers like and not like about my competitors' products or services?

☑ What makes my product or service unique compared to others in the marketplace?

☑ Do any of my competitors seem to be preparing to make any changes in the way they do business?

Key Terms In each chapter, the key terms that students should know are highlighted and defined in the text and in the margin. Key terms appear in the glossary and list the chapter in which the term is first defined.

Strategic Alliances and Joint Ventures Some firms want to diversify or integrate or expand abroad, but can't (or don't want to) use their own resources to do so. In these cases, **strategic alliances** are often the strategies of choice. They are formal agreements between two or more separate companies, the purpose of which is to enable the organizations to benefit from complementary strengths.

Joint ventures are one example of strategic alliances. For example, international airlines like Delta want to offer their passengers easier access to continuing flights and services as they travel abroad. Thus, a typical Delta passenger to France might want to transfer easily to a flight from Charles de Gaulle Airport in Paris, to a flight to Cannes. Delta could expand globally by buying or merging with a French carrier. However, many airlines instead form strategic alliances. Delta and Air France are part of the "Star Alliance." Passengers on either airline can use the other airline's facilities. The airlines derive many of the benefits of horizontal integration strategy without actually merging.

strategic alliance
An agreement between potential or actual competitors to achieve common objectives

Weblinks Web addresses given in the margin direct students to sites where they can learn more about the companies discussed in the text or gather further information about key topics.

lion in a joint venture (called Mandalay Pictures) with a major U.S. film producer. Mandalay was supposed to crank out 20 movies over the next five years. But by the middle of 2001, the venture had produced only two films: *Sleepy Hollow* (starring Johnny Depp) and *Enemy at the Gates*. The Mandalay venture has been a consistent money-loser for Lions Gate, with start-up costs and production delays being the big cause.

Lions Gate Entertainment www.lionsgate-ent. com

Examples Each chapter contains numerous examples of current management practices in Canadian and international companies. This feature helps students to understand how management ideas are put into practice. Because globalization has become such an overwhelming feature of organizations in the twenty-first century, we have included examples from Canadian, U.S., European, and Asian companies. Since the United States is such an important trading partner for Canada, we have included continuing examples from well-known U.S. firms such as General Electric, Federal Express, IBM, and Levi Strauss.

End-of-Chapter Material

Seven features are included at the end of each chapter. Each of these features is designed to help students understand the chapter material better and give them a realistic view of what management is all about. End-of-chapter features include:

Summary The material in each chapter is concisely summarized to help students understand the main points of the chapter. The summary is organized around the learning objectives listed at the beginning of the chapter.

SKILLS AND STUDY MATERIAL

SUMMARY

1. Leadership means influencing others to work willingly toward achieving objectives. Being a leader requires more than having a command of leadership theories. It also means managing organizational culture; motivating employees; managing groups, teams, and conflict; and facilitating organizational change.

2. Thinking like a leader means reviewing a leadership situation and identifying what is happening, accounting for what is happening (in terms of leadership and other behavioural science theories and concepts), and formulating leader actions.

3. The leader must provide a direction for followers. This direction may be a statement of vision, mission, or objectives, depending largely on what the leader wants to achieve and the level at which the leader is acting.

4. To be a leader one must also have the potential to be a leader. Having the right stuff (in terms of personality traits) is a foundation component. Some traits on which leaders differ from non-leaders include drive, the de-

sire to lead, honesty and integrity, self-confidence, cognitive ability, and knowledge of the business.

5. Legitimate power and authority are also elements in the foundation of leadership, because a leader without power is not a leader at all. Sources of leader power include position, rewards, coercion, expertise, and referent power or personal magnetism.

6. Leadership style or behaviours include structuring and considerate styles; participative and autocratic styles; employee-centred and production-centred styles; close and general styles; and transformational behaviour.

7. Although there are some differences in the way men and women lead, they do not account for the slower career progress of most women managers. Institutional biases such as the glass ceiling and persistent, inaccurate, stereotypes are contributing factors.

8. Situational leadership theories and the leader–member exchange theory underscore the importance of fitting the leader's style to the situation.

Critical Thinking Exercises Scenario-based questions at the end of each chapter encourage students to think more deeply about the chapter's concepts and the implications of the ideas that have been presented.

CRITICAL THINKING EXERCISES

1. As quoted in John Aram's *Presumed Superior*, affirmative action has different meanings to different people. One observer comments on the double meaning of affirmative action as a means of institutional change: "If civil rights is defined as quotas, it's a losing hand. If it's defined as protection against discrimination and efforts to promote opportunity, then it will remain a mainstream value." John Aram points out, "The dilemma is that progress on civil rights both restricts and opens opportunity. No single, definitive moral premise exists."[72]

What do you think Aram is trying to say? What aspects of HR can be related to his comments? What are your thoughts and feelings about civil rights and employment equity as they affect organizational management and jobs?

2. You are now a citizen of the twenty-first century. The rules of the job and career game appear to be changing as rapidly as machines such as ATMs replace bank tellers. You can now bank and pay bills with your computer and you can order all sorts of products over the internet, including groceries. In groups of five students, preferably from different majors, explore how you think your job choice will change in the future. Also discuss what you think the profession you are now preparing for will look like 10 years from now and 30 years from now. Be prepared to compare your discussion with that of other groups.

Experiential Exercises Experiential exercises require students to go beyond simply reading about management. In these exercises, students actually experience a situation and are thereby able to increase their understanding of the dynamics of management. Activities in these end-of-chapter exercises include asking students to think about what they would do in a certain situation, having students fill out questionnaires as a basis for discussing an important aspect of management, and working in a team with other students on various projects that generate more in-depth knowledge about management. Student recall of learning in these situations is high because they can clearly remember the experience they had while achieving the learning.

EXPERIENTIAL EXERCISES

1. Working in teams of four to five students, conduct a job analysis and develop a job description for the instructor of this course. Make sure to include a job summary, as well as a list of job duties and a job specification listing the human requirements of the job. Compare your job description with one from a website such as **www.jobdescriptions.com**.

2. Using the job description as a guide, develop a recruiting plan for the job of teaching this course, as well as a list of interview questions your team would use to screen instructor applicants for this course.

3. Working in teams of four to five students, develop a performance appraisal procedure and form for the instructor of this course.

Building Your Management Skills This new feature presents exercises that focus student attention on the practical aspects of management. Students are asked to carry out a variety of activities (for example, interviewing managers or filling out self-assessment questionnaires) which will help them better understand what management is really all about. Questions at the end of the exercises guide students in their thinking about the practical aspects of management.

BUILDING YOUR MANAGEMENT SKILLS

Planning in Action

Review the material on the planning process in this chapter. Then familiarize yourself with the planning process that was used in an organization that was working on a specific project. You may get this information by either interviewing a manager who is knowledgeable about a project in his or her firm, or by reading a detailed account of a project in a publication like *The Globe and Mail* or *Canadian Business*. In either case, your goal is to determine how the planning process was carried out in a real organization. Write up a summary of the project in enough detail that you can answer the following questions:

1. Did the organization follow the steps in the planning process that are shown in Figure 6.1? If yes, explain what was involved in each step. If no, try to account for the differences.
2. Were the steps carried out in the order shown in Figure 6.1? Were some steps skipped or repeated? Why?
3. What problems arose during the planning process? Why?

Internet Exercises These exercises encourage students to use the internet to investigate some interesting aspect of management that is relevant to the material presented in the chapter the student has just finished reading.

INTERNET EXERCISES

All industry sectors experience "ups and downs." Probably one of the most volatile sectors is biotechnology. So how do the companies in these sectors plan? Let's investigate QLT Inc., one of Canada's leading biopharmaceutical companies (www.qltinc.com) by looking at their corporate fact sheet and other information on their website.

1. Part of QLT's planning includes the preparation of forward-looking statements. What is included in these statements?
2. What uncertainties might affect QLT's planning?
3. How has QLT enhanced its planning?
4. What aspect of QLT's planning do you think has been responsible for the company's success during the sector's "ups and downs"?

Case Studies Two end-of-chapter case studies give students the opportunity to analyze an actual management situation using the material presented in the chapter to guide their thinking. At the end of each case, several questions are presented to focus student attention on certain areas of analysis.

CASE STUDY 4-2

Getting by with a Little Help from His Mother's Friends

Andrew Morris had almost everything he needed to start his Caribbean-flavoured grocery store in a New York City suburb. He had an M.B.A. from Columbia University, a business plan, and a U.S.$50 000 loan from the European American bank. However, after he negotiated the rent on a 1600 square foot retail space in Hempstead, New York, he found he did not have enough cash left for inventory, payroll, marketing, and licences. Thanks to his mother—and her friends—he was able to secure an additional U.S.$15 000 in resources, which enabled him to stock the shelves with dozens of kinds of hot sauce, curry brands, and reggae music that the growing Caribbean community craves.

Morris got the money from his mother's *susu*, a kind of club or fund developed by West Indian housewives to provide rotating credit for big-ticket household purchases. A susu, which means "partner," typically has about 20 members, most of them either relatives or close friends. Over a 20-week period every member contributes a fixed sum each week. Any time during those 20 weeks, each member is entitled to borrow an amount or *draw* to use interest-free during that time.

For example, if a 20-member susu has a set weekly contribution of $100, each member pays $100 into the fund every week, or pays a total of $2000 over twenty weeks. Each member is then also able to draw $2000 at any point during that period. Essentially the susu is a kind of planned savings program that pools money to help members of the group who need help with cash flow. The Caribbean susu is not really a unique concept; other ethnic groups have also developed informal lending networks for their members.

Andrew Morris has dipped into his mother's susu

a number of times to help his business grow. He used the money to pay a sales tax obligation, to purchase a commercial oven to cook Jamaican meat patties, to produce a special Easter promotion with traditional cheese and sweet bread sandwiches, and to expand his inventory to include unusual but popular items, such as Jamaican Chinese soy sauce. "It's a cash flow boon," Morris says. After seven years of ongoing susu support, Morris' store now has annual revenues of more than U.S.$1 million. Morris is now counting on susu support to help it expand into distributing coffee and developing a website. "It's no longer just a Christmas club," he says. "It's a way of life."

Questions

1. Andrew Morris has approached you for help. List what you believe he is doing right and doing wrong with respect to starting his business. What do you think accounts for the fact that he ran out of money before he opened, even though he had a business plan? What remedy or remedies would you suggest at this point?

2. Develop a one-page outline showing Morris how you would suggest he conduct an informal business feasibility study.

3. Lists the activity areas for which Morris should establish controls.

4. What other alternative means for obtaining financing would you recommend for Morris? What are their pros and cons when compared to continuing using his mother's susu?

You Be the Consultant A continuing case study is presented that focuses on JetBlue Airways. This feature asks students to put themselves in the place of JetBlue's managers and make decisions regarding the future direction of the company. This case material also requires students to apply the material that they have read in the chapter. Because these cases are based on information drawn from various published sources, they are meaty and realistic.

YOU BE THE CONSULTANT

jetBlue AIRWAYS

Leadership at JetBlue

It is probably not necessary to ask whether David Neeleman is an effective leader. You don't start and manage three very successful airline businesses before you're 40 if you don't have leadership skills. Particularly during the start-up period, it's the leader, by force of his or her personality and vision, who keeps the firm's employees focused. Neeleman has done this not once, but three times. As one person who knows him says, "he's low-key, and he's totally directed." One business writer, watching him make a presentation, said: "The man can be completely, utterly riveting."

However, Neeleman does not just have a "just decide and give orders" directive style. For example, at an employee orientation for new baggage handlers, he carefully explained JetBlue's philosophy, including how JetBlue can make money when the big airlines don't. He shared details about the company's plans, and answered personal questions. He spends most of his time when he flies JetBlue talking to customers and crew. He talks to flight attendants and passengers to find out their concerns and comments, and he spends time walking through the cabin helping to serve snacks. He spends time in the cockpit with the pilots, and when he is at the airport he works with the baggage handlers throwing bags.

An incident after 9/11 provides insight into Neeleman's leadership approach. He had to decide what his first response should be with respect to communicating with the flying public. Neeleman's first reaction was to draft a personal letter from him and run it as a full-page ad. However, his team thought the message was a bit too personal. Other airlines were placing ads that basically tried to convince the flying public that it was patriotic to fly and important to show that "we're not afraid to fly." Neeleman's feeling was that his personal letter was the way to go and that this was the perfect time to publicize JetBlue's low price fares. But as driven as he is as an entrepreneur, Neeleman went with his team's advice. As he says, "I'm being patient because I think the situation demands it. I have to trust the instincts of the people around me."[99]

Assignment

You and your team are consultants to Mr. Neeleman, who is depending on your management expertise to help navigate the launch and management of JetBlue. Here's what he wants to know from you:

1. Do you think I have the traits and skills to be a leader? Specifically, why or why not?

2. What leadership style did I use with respect to the decision to make our first response after 9/11? Do you think I used the right style? Use one or more of the leadership theories in this chapter to explain why you think I did or did not use the right style.

3. What do some of the other incidents in the case tell you about the other leadership styles I typically use? What you think my prevailing style is? Why?

Video Cases At the end of each of the five major parts of the text, two video cases are presented. These CBC video cases from the *Venture* program describe interesting management situations in a Canadian company. The videos help students understand the dynamic nature of management in the twenty-first century. Questions that are relevant to one or more of the chapters in the section are found at the end of each case.

VIDEO CASE 1-2

CBC

Whistleblowers

In 2002, *Time Magazine* named three female whistleblowers as "Persons of the Year" for reporting wrongdoing at the companies they worked for. Because of the publicity given to whistleblowers, many people see the activity as a noble pursuit. But it's not very glamorous when you look behind the scenes.

Just ask Joanna Galtieri, who went to the media and blew the whistle on the Foreign Affairs Department of the Canadian government. She claimed that the activities of the department were not cost-effective, and she cited the example of a Canadian diplomat who was stationed in Japan. The diplomat was supposed to be housed in a Canadian-owned residence; instead, he asked for $350 000 to rent another apartment he liked better. Galtieri says foreign affairs refused to deal with her concerns about irresponsible spending of taxpayers' money. She also claimed that her employer ostracized her in the workplace. Now, Joanna visits high schools and talks to young people about the issue of whistleblowing.

Mike Hilson, an Ontario accountant, blew the whistle on shoddy accounting practices at Philip Services, a Hamilton waste-disposal company. He knew the company was stockpiling waste but not recording the cost it would take to get rid of it. Hilson raised the issue with his boss several times, but nothing happened. The last time he raised the issue, he was fired. A few months later, he noticed that Philip Services was applying to open another landfill site near his parents' home — if the company went bankrupt, there would be no money to clean up the landfill. He sent a letter to Ontario's Minister of the Environment expressing his concerns. Soon after, he was sued for libel by Philip Services for $30 million. Hilson eventually triumphed over Philip Services. They withdrew their lawsuit and were required to pay his legal bills.

Writer Mark Wexler interviewed 200 whistleblowers and found that they were generally disillusioned with their experiences — whistleblowers think that if they speak out, somebody will do something about the problems they identify. Hilson, for example, was astonished that no one would take his comments seriously. Wexler says whistleblowers often aren't listened to, and that, if they are, less weight will be given to the charges that are being made. For example, after Hilson blew the whistle on Philip Services, the company publicized his personal problems and said he was "a troubled person."

Some people feel that strong laws are needed to protect whistleblowers. Countries that are taking that approach include the United States, South Korea, Australia, and Russia. The Liberal government of Canada promised such legislation years ago, but nothing has been done. When a reporter from *Venture* asked the Prime Minister's Office about this, she was referred to the Justice Department, who referred her to the Treasury Board, who referred her to Industry Canada. She was then referred to the Competition Bureau.

Venture then sent a formal written request to the Prime Minister's Office asking again what had happened to their campaign promise. They were referred elsewhere and the process repeated itself. When political parties are in opposition, they are proponents of whistleblowing legislation; but when they get in power, they seem to lose interest.

Joanna Galtieri's experience has caused her to become an activist on this issue. She has drafted a private member's bill which will be considered in Parliament. She doesn't think it will get very far, but it will be a vehicle to create a dialogue on this issue. Mike Hilson doesn't think that passing laws will work—he thinks it will be very difficult to change our culture so that people who speak out will be perceived as doing something useful.

Questions

1. What is whistleblowing? What are the arguments in favour of it? Are there any arguments against it?

2. Suppose a law was passed which was designed to protect whistleblowers. One provision of this law allowed for penalties like prison time for any company personnel who threatened a whistleblower. What do you think would happen?

3. "It is impossible to protect whistleblowers because the company can always claim it has done nothing wrong. By the time any proof is provided, the case

---

End-of-Text Special Material: The Manager's Portfolio

In addition to the in-chapter and end-of-chapter learning features described above, this second Canadian edition includes an exciting new learning tool—the *Manager's Portfolio*—at the end of the book. To enhance students' understanding of the key principles of management, we provide a three-level skills mastery program.

> **Learn It.** With these fill-in-the-blank exercises, students can check their knowledge of each chapter's concepts and management principles.
>
> **Practice It.** Let's go to the video! The accompanying customized CD-ROM contains special video clips. These illustrate specific management scenarios for each chapter, and thus give students a chance to apply their new knowledge and skills in solving real-life managerial problems. Gary Dessler wrote special questions and exercises to guide students in addressing the issues in the scenarios. Questions and activities are provided to guide students' understanding of how using management principles would affect this company. Self assessments and management checklists are included in the CD-ROM for additional practice.
>
> **Apply It.** The next "layer of learning" challenges students to view the process of management as a whole. Drawing on cases and exercises throughout the book, these special exercises challenge students to apply what they learned in an integrated, cross-functional way. For example: How did a leader's style inadvertently influence the plan his or her team came up with? Or, how did JetBlue's plan influence how it decided to organize?

CD-ROM Also included on the CD-ROM is an electronic copy of the entire textbook in PDF format, with links to useful websites. The CD-ROM also gives you easy access to CBC videos and cases that accompany the text.

Support Materials

Companion Website The format of our website has been updated, and includes the same great features in a more user-friendly format. Here you will find password-protected instructor's resources, as well as a student section which features true/false, multiple-choice, and internet essay questions. The CBC videos can also be found on this site. The website for Dessler and Starke's *Management: Principles and Practices for Tomorrow's Leaders*, Second Canadian Edition, can be found at **www.pearsoned.ca/dessler**.

WebCT, Blackboard, and Course Compass Online Courses This edition offers a fully developed online course for management.

PowerPoint Presentation Included on the Instructor's Resource CD-ROM, and available for faculty download on the Companion Website, this comprehensive set of PowerPoints contains over 500 colour slides. The presentation contains lecture content, as well as all of the tables and figures found in the text.

Instructor's Resource CD-ROM On a single CD, professors can find the Instructor's Manual, PowerPoint Presentation, and Test Generator. Containing all of the questions in the printed Test Item File, Test Generator is a comprehensive suite of tools for testing and assessment and allows educators to easily create and distribute tests for their courses.

Management Skills Video Video segments offer dramatizations that highlight various management skills. They allow students to see what it's like to conduct an interview, make management decisions, and more. The videos provide excellent starting points for classroom discussion and debate.

BusinessNOW Video Series Brand new to this edition, Prentice Hall is pleased to offer exciting BusinessNOW video cases. BusinessNOW is a fast-paced television newsmagazine that takes viewers on location and behind closed doors to look at interesting companies and the corporate executives who run them. These videos offer up-to-date content pertaining to the topics discussed in *Management: Principles and Practices for Tomorrow's Leaders*, Second Canadian Edition.

Instructor's Manual The Instructor's Manual is designed to guide the educator through the text. Each chapter in the Instructor's Manual includes a topic introduction, an annotated outline that includes space for the instructor's notes, and answers to all critical thinking exercises and cases, including You Be the Consultant. A video guide section provides suggested answers to the case questions for the accompanying CBC video clips.

Test Item File The Test Item File contains about 150 questions per chapter, including multiple-choice, true/false, and essay questions. Every question is page-referenced to the text and is classified as easy, moderate, or difficult to satisfy all classroom needs.

Pearson Education Canada Test Generator The Test Generator contains all of the questions in the printed Test Item File. Test Generator is a comprehensive suite of tools for testing and assessment. It allows educators to easily create and distribute tests for their courses, either by printing and distributing through traditional methods or by online delivery via a Local Area Network (LAN) server.

Self-Assessment Library Organized according to individual, group, and organizational needs, the Self-Assessment Library features self-assessment tools designed to give students insight into their skills, abilities, and interests. This electronic supplement can be packaged with your text. Please contact your Pearson Education sales representative for further details.

CBC Video Library The CBC Video Library for this text includes ten segments from CBC's program *Venture*, which accompany the CBC video cases found at the end of each part in the text. These cases focus on Canadian companies and discuss management issues from a Canadian point of view.

Acknowledgments

The authors and publishers would like to thank the following people who reviewed material for this Canadian edition:

Brent Banda, St. Francis Xavier University
Alan Chapelle, Malaspina University-College
Vic de Witt, Red River College
Janice Edwards, College of the Rockies
Robert Fournier, Red Deer College
Kristi Harrison, Centennial College
Murray Kernaghan, Assiniboine College
Fiona McQuarrie, University College of the Fraser Valley
Jacquelyn Penner, Medicine Hat College
Jeff Young, Mt. St. Vincent University

Thanks to the American reviewers whose feedback helped shape the original edition on which this text is based, and to Dr. George Puia at Indiana State University for developing some of the end-of-chapter cases. Our thanks are also due to the Prentice Hall staff in the United States who provided files and manuscript for the Canadian authors, especially Jeannine Ciliotta, the U.S. developmental editor, whose good humour, attention to detail, and efficiency in expediting the process were much appreciated.

The Canadian author would like to acknowledge the continued support from the Pearson editorial team, including James Bosma, Madhu Ranadive, Marisa D'Andrea, Catherine Haggert, and Dawn Hunter.

At Florida International University, Gary Dessler appreciates the moral support he received from all of his colleagues, including Ronnie Silverblatt, Jan Luytjes, Enzo Valenzi, and, of course, Earnest Friday and Richard Hodgetts.

Closer to home, Gary Dessler wants to acknowledge the support of his wife, Claudia, and her willingness to tolerate his disappearance for more evenings and weekends than he should have been gone while he worked on this book. However, when all of the acknowledgments are said and done, if there can be a single inspiration for a book entitled *Management: Principles and Practices for Tomorrow's Leaders*, it is his son Derek, for whom he wrote this book in as practical and useful a way as possible, and whose unswerving support was the only motivation needed.

Gary Dessler (Ph.D. business administration, Bernard M. Baruch School of Business) is Professor of Business at Florida International University. In addition to *Management: Principles and Practices for Tomorrow's Leaders,* he is the author of a number of other books, including, most recently, *Human Resource Management, Essentials of Human Resource Management,* and *Winning Commitment: How to Build and Keep a Competitive Workforce.* His books have been translated into Chinese, Russian, Indonesian, Spanish, and Portuguese, and are being used by students and managers all over the world. He has written numerous articles on employee commitment, organizational behaviour, leadership, and quality improvement, and for ten years wrote the syndicated "Job Talk" column for the *Miami Herald.*

Frederick A. Starke is an Associate Dean in the Asper School of Business at the University of Manitoba. He earned his B.A. and M.B.A. from Southern Illinois University and his Ph.D. from Ohio State University. He has been actively involved in teaching, research, and administration at the University of Manitoba. His teaching interests focus on organizational behaviour, organization theory, and decision making. He has published research articles in scholarly journals such as *Administrative Science Quarterly,* the *Journal of Applied Psychology,* and the *Academy of Management Journal.* He also writes articles for professional journals such as the *Journal of Systems Management, Information Executive,* and the *Canadian Journal of Nursing Administration.* Dr. Starke also devotes time to writing textbooks for university and community college students. His other texts, *Business* and *Business Essentials,* are used in universities and community colleges across Canada. Dr. Starke regularly presents seminars on the topics of decision making and goal setting to practising managers in both the public and private sectors.

A Great Way to Learn and Instruct Online

The Pearson Education Canada Companion Website is easy to navigate and is organized to correspond to the chapters in this textbook. Whether you are a student in the classroom or a distance learner you will discover helpful resources for in-depth study and research that empower you in your quest for greater knowledge and maximize your potential for success in the course.

Companion Website

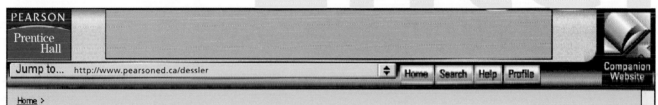

[**www.pearsoned.ca/dessler**]

PEARSON Prentice Hall

Jump to... | http://www.pearsoned.ca/dessler | Home | Search | Help | Profile | Companion Website

Home >

Companion Website

Management: Principles and Practices for Tomorrow's Leaders, Second Canadian Edition

Student Resources

The modules in this section provide students with tools for learning course material. These modules include:
- Chapter Objectives
- Multiple Choice Questions
- True and False Questions
- Essay Questions
- Key Concepts
- Links to CBC Videos and Cases

In the quiz modules students can send answers to the grader and receive instant feedback on their progress through the Results Reporter. Coaching comments and references to the textbook may be available to ensure that students take advantage of all available resources to enhance their learning experience.

Instructor Resources

The modules in this section provide instructors with additional teaching tools. Downloadable PowerPoint Presentations and an Instructor's Manual are just some of the materials that may be available in this section. Where appropriate, this section will be password protected. To get a password, simply contact your Pearson Education Canada Representative or call Faculty Sales and Services at 1-800-850-5813.

PART 1

Introduction to Managing

Part 1: Introduction to Managing provides an introduction to, and an overview of, the field of management. Managers are critical to the effective functioning of modern society, but they usually do not receive as much publicity as movie stars, politicians, or sports figures. In this section, we explain the role of managers and the fundamental importance of management. Since managers are influenced by the environment in which they work, we also examine the important environmental factors—globalization, business ethics, diversity, culture, and social responsibility—that influence them.

We begin in **Chapter 1, Managing in the Twenty-First Century**, by explaining exactly what managers do and why the study of management is so important. We describe the basic functions that all managers must perform and the different types of managers that are found in organizations. Management is an exciting career, since managers work in a rapidly changing environment that requires them to adapt to continual changes in technology, globalization, and deregulation. The **Appendix to Chapter 1** presents a brief history of the development of modern management thought.

In **Chapter 2, The Environment of Management: Canadian and Global**, we look first at the environment of management within Canada, including the key structural features of the Canadian economy that affect managers. We then move on to the international scene and examine issues such as why business firms want to sell abroad, the strategies they use to do so, the impact of global strategies on company personnel and structure, and the impact on managers, including those in an international environment. We conclude by discussing the important factors that determine the success of individuals who manage internationally.

In **Chapter 3, Ethics, Social Responsibility, and Diversity**, we examine several important but complex areas that are increasingly coming under scrutiny from employees, stockholders, government, and the general public. The focus here is on the human side of management and on what managers should know about ethics, diversity, culture, and social responsibility to effectively carry out their managerial responsibilities.

Finally, in **Chapter 4, Managing Entrepreneurial Organizations**, we explain what entrepreneurship is and why it is important in the Canadian economy. We describe what it takes to be an entrepreneur and the various ways that entrepreneurs get involved in business activity. The chapter concludes with an assessment of how entrepreneurs plan, organize, lead, and control their businesses.

Managing in the Twenty-First Century

Avon Products

After studying this chapter and the case exercises at the end, you should be able to use the material to:

1. List the specific management tasks facing a manager.

2. Identify the manager.

3. Answer the question, "Do I have what it takes to be a manager?"

4. Understand the skills that a manager must possess.

5. Explain the characteristics of the external environment that influence managers.

6. Explain how the characteristics of modern organizations influence managers.

It was November 1999, and Avon Products was in trouble. The stock market was booming, but the price of Avon stock had sagged. Fewer people were signing on as "Avon Lady" sales reps, and it was taking Avon's research and development department three years to develop new products. The whole "back end" operation—buying from suppliers, taking orders, and distributing products to local sales reps—was not automated. People still took orders by hand. One-third of the orders sent to sales reps were wrong. Sales rep motivation was down. The company's board of directors knew it had to do something.

What it did was appoint Andrea Jung as the new CEO. Could she turn the company around? As it turned out, Andrea Jung had the skills of a great manager. Within 20 months she had overhauled everything about the way Avon does business: how it advertises, manufactures, packages, and even sells its products. She started with a turnaround plan. The plan included launching a new line of businesses, developing new products, building the sales force, and selling Avon at retail stores.

Then she turned to execution. Several months after taking over as CEO she boosted Avon's research and development budget by almost 50 percent. She told R&D that its goal was to achieve a breakthrough within two years. By the end of the year, she had her product, Retroactive, an anti-aging cream that soon grossed U.S.$100 million. With the sales reps already in customers' homes, Jung saw an opportunity to expand the products they could sell. They were soon selling vitamins under Avon's new "Wellness" line. In another initiative several months later, Avon began selling a special new line in JC Penney stores.

Meanwhile Jung appointed a new chief operating officer, who helped cut U.S.$400 million in costs. Jung also turned her attention to beefing up the sales force. Under a new "Leadership" program, Avon now pays sales reps to recruit other reps. One Avon Lady says that she spends her Saturdays in front of the supermarket trying to convince people to become Avon ladies. During 2002, the number of Avon sales reps grew for the first time in years.

Other positive outcomes are evident as well. The company's stock price moved up 19 percent in 2002, product development cycles were reduced by more than 40 percent, and sales in overseas markets increased sharply, including a 30 percent increase in China.

Avon Canada
www.avon.ca

What Managers Do

Managers can have the most remarkable effects on organizations. Consider Dofasco Inc., which has emerged as an international leader on the new Dow Jones Sustainability Group Index.[1] The Index tracks the performance of the 200 leading sustainability-driven companies in 68 industry groups in 22 different countries, and Dofasco tops the steel category of the Index. To be included in the Index a company must satisfy certain criteria, including the use of innovative technology, responsible corporate governance, positive shareholder relations, industrial leadership, and social well-being. Dofasco scores well because its top managers are committed to these goals.

Dofasco
www.dofasco.ca

International examples of the impact of managers are plentiful. Louis Gerstner was appointed CEO of IBM after the company had floundered through much of the 1980s and early 1990s. It lost market share and failed to control costs, and its stock price dropped from almost U.S.$180 per share to barely U.S.$50. Within three years, Gerstner had turned the company around. He revamped the company's product line, dramatically lowered costs, changed the company's culture, and oversaw a quadrupling of IBM's stock price.[2]

Dell CEO Michael Dell created a U.S.$12-billion company in just 13 years. He did it by installing one of the world's most sophisticated direct-sales operations, by eliminating resellers' markups and the need for large inventories, and by keeping a vise-like grip on costs while dozens of his competitors were going down the drain.[3]

Managers don't just influence what happens at large corporations. Right now, managers at thousands of small businesses—restaurants, dry cleaners, motels—are running their businesses well, with courteous, prompt, first-class service, enthusiastic employees, and a minimum of problems. What would happen if the competent managers were taken out of those businesses? It would mean problems like cold food, wrinkled pants, and a dirty motel room. The majority of new businesses started this year will fail within five years, and most of those will fail because of poor management.

Business firms are not the only places where competent managers are required. Many other organizations in Canada are not businesses and do not have profit as an objective. In fact, business firms are the only organizations that do pursue a profit. All others— labour unions, churches, charities, the military, universities and community colleges, environmental groups, consumer advocate organizations, government agencies, community clubs, and professional organizations—do not pursue a profit. Yet they also need good managers if they are to reach their goals.

Whether an organization is for-profit or not-for-profit, the effect of good management is nothing short of amazing. Take an under-performing organization and install a skilled manager, and that person will soon have the enterprise humming. Conversely, take a successful enterprise that's been managed well and watch as a new, less-competent manager takes over. Supplies do not get ordered in time, employee morale drops, and bills don't get paid. One study of 40 manufacturing firms concluded that effective management was more important than factors like market share, firm size, industry average rate of return, or degree of automation.[4] Another study concluded that organizations with better managers had lower turnover rates, and higher profits and sales per employee.[5]

The "Challenge of Change" box describes the effect that a competent CEO can have on a company.

Transforming Allied-Signal

Honeywell Corporation and Allied-Signal merged in 1999, forming a new, much larger, Honeywell Corporation. The merger was made possible by the rising fortunes of Allied-Signal, which had vastly improved under its chairman and CEO, Lawrence A. Bossidy.

How did Bossidy turn Allied-Signal around? Bossidy's people skills had a remarkable effect on this huge industrial supplier of aerospace systems, automotive parts, and chemical products. He took over a troubled company that was "hemorrhaging cash." After just three years under Bossidy's guidance, Allied-Signal's profits had doubled to U.S.$708 million, and the company's market value (the total value of its shares) had more than doubled as well, to almost U.S.$10 billion.

What did Bossidy do to bring about such a dramatic transformation in just three years? Many of his changes were operational. Under his guidance the company merged business units, closed factories, reduced suppliers from 9000 to 3000, and cut 19 000 salaried jobs from the payroll. But much of what Bossidy focused on was behavioural in nature. In other words, he focused on applying his knowledge of how people, as individuals and groups, act within organizations to help bring about change. For example, in his first two months on the job he talked to thousands of employees in various company locations. He also stood on loading docks and spoke to people and answered their questions. He talked about what was wrong and what should be done to fix it.

His job, as he saw it, was not just to cut jobs and merge operations, since actions like these would have only short-term effects on profitability. In the longer run, Bossidy knew he had to excite his giant firm's many employees by promoting their ability to win, by uniting the top management team, and in general by convincing all employees that there was a tremendous need to change.

That's why Bossidy says that when he looks for managers, he looks for those who have a gift for working with and turning on employees. As he put it, "Today's corporation is a far cry from the old authoritarian vertical hierarchy I grew up in. The cross-functional ties among individuals and groups are increasingly important. There are channels of activity and communication. The traditional bases of managerial authority are eroding. In the past, we used to reward the lone rangers in the corner offices because their achievements were brilliant even though their behaviour was destructive. That day is gone. We need people who are better at persuading than at barking orders, who know how to coach and build consensus. Today, managers add value by brokering with people, not by presiding over empires."

Organization Defined

organization
A group of people with formally assigned roles who work together to achieve stated goals.

All these enterprises—Allied-Signal, Dofasco, IBM, Dell, the restaurant, the dry cleaner, and the stationery store—are *organizations*. An **organization** consists of people with formally assigned roles who work together to achieve stated goals. The fans at a Blue Jays baseball game are not an organization, since they're not there to work together to accomplish some goal. But the players on the Blue Jays team are an organization.

Many organizations are business firms, but many are not. Provincial and municipal governments are organizations, as are labour unions, charitable organizations, churches, colleges and universities, and the Canadian Forces. The federal government is also an organization, and its chief executive officer is the prime minister of Canada.

Organizations have structures. At the corner dry cleaner, for example, each employee has a specific job to do (pressing pants, cleaning clothes, dealing with customers), and the manager decides how the work will flow through the store and get done.

Whether organizations achieve their goals depends on how well they are managed. Organizations do not run themselves. Review the definition of an organization again, and you'll see why. Who makes sure that each of the employees actually knows what to do? Who makes sure that employees work together effectively? Who decides what the goals of the organization should be? The answer is: managers.

Management Defined

If you walked into a company, how could you tell who the managers were? Management expert Peter Drucker says that **management** "... is the responsibility for contribution."[6] In other words, a **manager** is someone who is responsible for accomplishing an organizational unit's goals and who accomplishes those goals by planning, organizing, leading, and controlling the efforts of other people.

This definition highlights three aspects of managerial work. First, a manager is always responsible for contribution. That means the manager is responsible for accomplishing the organization's goals. Managers may apply management theories, but management is never just theoretical. That is why Lawrence Bossidy titled his book *Execution: The Discipline of Getting Things Done.*

Second, managers always get things done through other people. The owner/entrepreneur running a small florist shop without the aid of employees is not managing. She may be an entrepreneur, but she is not a manager because she is doing all the work herself. She opens the store, places orders, handles customers, delivers the orders, and reconciles the store's books after she goes home at night. It is only when she starts hiring people and trying to get things done through them that she becomes a manager. Once she is a manager, she will have to (among other things) train new employees, motivate them to pursue the organization's goals, and put controls in place so that the person who closes the store won't "borrow" any of the day's receipts.

Some entrepreneurs—the people who start new businesses—never become managers. They either are not interested in managing others, or they are not able to do it. The same happens in big companies, too. Sometimes a great salesperson (or engineer, or mechanic, or accountant, or other technical expert) is promoted into a managerial position, but they either don't like the work, or they don't understand what is required to be successful in management.[7]

Third, managers must be able to carry out the key functions of management: planning, organizing, leading, and controlling. These four basic functions are generally referred to as the **management process**.

- *Planning* means setting goals and deciding on courses of action, developing rules and procedures, developing plans (both for the organization and for those who work in it), and forecasting (predicting or projecting what the future holds for the firm).

- *Organizing* means identifying jobs to be done, hiring people to do them, establishing departments, delegating authority to subordinates, establishing a chain of command (channels of authority and communication), and coordinating the work of subordinates.

- *Leading* means influencing other people to get the job done, maintaining employee morale, moulding company culture, managing conflicts, and communicating to relevant others in the firm.

- *Controlling* means setting standards (such as sales quotas or quality standards), comparing actual performance with these standards, and then taking corrective action as required.

Some people think that managing is easy and that anyone with half a brain can do it. After all, you will find no exotic mathematical formulas in this book, or any discussions of nuclear physics. But, if it is so easy, why do so many new businesses fail because of poor

management The process of planning, organizing, leading, and controlling other people so that organizational objectives are achieved.

manager Someone who is responsible for accomplishing an organizational unit's goals, and who accomplishes those goals by planning, organizing, leading, and controlling the efforts of other people.

management process The four key functions of management: planning, organizing, leading, and controlling.

management? Why did Kmart have to declare bankruptcy, after a new CEO turned the company in the wrong direction? The words in this book are easy to read, but don't let that lull you into thinking that anyone can be a manager, or that managing is easy.

Efficiency and Effectiveness in Management

efficiency Achieving the greatest possible output with a given amount of input.

Efficiency means achieving the greatest possible output with a given amount of input. Consider the situation at United Airlines and JetBlue. Both use identical planes (the Airbus A320) and have identical flight crews (two pilots and four flight attendants). But JetBlue's costs are significantly lower than United's on each flight. For example, United's cost to fly its plane from New York to California is U.S.$23 690, but JetBlue's cost is only U.S.$14 546. JetBlue achieves these lower costs by having lower labour costs, fewer planes, and faster turnaround time between flights.[8]

effective To achieve goals that have been set.

Although efficiency is very important, it is not enough. Managers must also be **effective**; that is, they must achieve the organizational goals that have been set. Achieving managerial effectiveness requires that managers focus on two important elements of work: the *tasks* that subordinates do, and the *satisfaction* of subordinates as they do the tasks. Effective managers have subordinates who are both productive and satisfied.

You Too Are a Manager

Managing is something that you may be called upon to do at any time. In business firms, even a non-managerial employee may pitch in and do some managing once in a while. The vice president of marketing, for example, might ask a marketing analyst to head a small team to analyze a new product's potential. Or the chief executive officer (CEO) might ask an administrative assistant to manage preparations for an end-of-season company party. Everyone who works should therefore know something about how to manage. You never know when an opportunity might arise.

Even if you aren't working at a job, you may need to exercise management skills. Let's suppose that you and some friends have decided to spend next summer in France. None of you know very much about France, so you've been elected "summer tour master" and asked to manage the trip.

You might start with *planning*. Among other things, you'll need to plan the dates your group is leaving and returning, the cities and towns in France you'll visit, the airline you'll take there and back, how the group will get around in France, and where you'll stay when you're there. You do not want to arrive at Paris's Charles DeGaulle Airport with a group of friends depending on you and not know what you're doing next.

As you think about these things, you will probably decide that you want some help. You'll want to divide up the work and create an *organization*. For example, you might put Rosa in charge of checking airline schedules and prices, Rakesh in charge of checking hotels, and Ruth in charge of checking the sights to see in various cities as well as the means of transportation between them. However, the job won't get done with Rosa, Rakesh, and Ruth simply working by themselves. Each of them will require guidance and coordination from you. Rosa obviously can't make any decisions on airline schedules unless she knows what city you're starting and ending with, and Rakesh can't schedule hotels unless he knows from Ruth what sites you'll be seeing, and when. You'll either have to schedule weekly manager's meetings or coordinate the work of these three people yourself.

Leadership could be a challenge, too. Rakesh and Ruth don't always agree, so you'll have to make sure conflicts don't get out of hand. Rosa is a genius with numbers, but she tends to get bogged down in details so you'll have to make sure she stays focused and motivated.

You will also have to make sure that the whole project stays in *control*. If something can go wrong, it will, and that's certainly the case when a group of people is travelling together. At a minimum, you'll have to make sure that all those airline tickets, hotel reservations, and itineraries are checked and checked again to make sure there are no mistakes.

What Else Do Managers Do?

Most management experts agree that "planning, organizing, leading, and controlling" don't convey the richness and complexity of what managers do. Other roles and duties also fall under the umbrella of management.

THE PEOPLE SIDE OF MANAGING

What Managers Actually Do

Henry Mintzberg of McGill University conducted a detailed study of the work of five chief executive officers and found the following:

1. Managers work at an unrelenting pace.
2. Managerial activities are characterized by brevity, variety, and fragmentation.
3. Managers have a preference for "live" action and emphasize work activities that are current, specific, and well defined.
4. Managers are attracted to the verbal media.

Mintzberg believes that a manager's job can be described as 10 roles that must be performed. The manager's formal authority and status give rise to three *interpersonal roles*: (1) *figurehead* (duties of a ceremonial nature, such as attending a subordinate's wedding); (2) *leader* (being responsible for the work of the unit); and (3) *liaison* (making contact outside the vertical chain of command). These interpersonal roles give rise to three *informational roles*: (1) *monitor* (scanning the environment for relevant information); (2) *disseminator* (passing information to subordinates); and (3) *spokesperson* (sending information to people outside the unit).

The interpersonal and informational roles allow the manager to carry out four *decision-making roles*: (1) *entrepreneur* (improving the performance of the unit); (2) *disturbance handler* (responding to high-pressure disturbances, such as a strike at a supplier); (3) *resource allocator* (deciding who will get what in the unit); and (4) *negotiator* (working out agreements on a wide variety of issues, such as the amount of authority an individual will be given).

Insight into what managers actually do can also be gained by looking at the so-called *functions* of management (planning, organizing, leading, and controlling). Consider the work of Marina Pyo, who is a publisher, school division, at Pearson Education Canada, a publisher of textbooks for elementary and secondary schools, colleges, and universities. Her job is to manage the activities that are necessary to develop resources in math and science for the Canadian elementary school market. Her work is at times intense, fragmented, rewarding, frustrating, and fast-paced. In short, she is a typical manager.

Pyo carries out the *planning* function when she drafts a plan for a new book. She is *organizing* when she develops a new organization chart to facilitate goal achievement. She is *leading* when she meets with a subordinate to discuss that person's career plans. And she is *controlling* when she checks sales prospects for a book before ordering a reprint.

Some of Pyo's activities do not easily fit into this "functions of management" model. For example, it is not clear which function she is performing when she negotiates the size of a reprint run with the manager of the sales division, or when she talks briefly with the president of her division about recent events in Pyo's area of responsibility.

Mintzberg's Managerial Roles Some years ago, Henry Mintzberg conducted a study of what managers actually do.[9] Mintzberg found that as they went from task to task, managers didn't just plan, organize, lead, and control. The boxed insert "The People Side of Managing" describes what Mintzberg found.

The Manager as Innovator Innovation is not just for scientists and engineers. One manufacturing firm uses a machine that now runs five times faster than anticipated when the firm ordered it. What accounts for the machine's super speed? The employees made more than 200 small improvements to boost its efficiency.[10] In today's fast-changing world, managers have to make sure their companies can develop new products and react quickly to change. Successful managers can't afford to just focus on designing organization charts or drawing up plans.[11] Instead, they must improve their companies' ability to be more innovative. They do this by cultivating three processes in their companies:

- *The entrepreneurial process.*[12] A study of 20 companies in Japan, the United States, and Europe found that successful managers focused much of their time and energy on getting employees to think of themselves as entrepreneurs. To do this, managers emphasized giving employees the authority, support, and rewards that self-disciplined and self-directed people need to run their operations as their own.

- *The competence-building process.* It was also found that "in a world of converging technologies, large companies have to...exploit their big-company advantages, which lie not only in scale economies but also in the depth and breadth of employees' talents and knowledge."[13] Successful managers therefore work hard to create an environment that lets employees really take charge. This means encouraging them to take on more responsibility; providing the education and training they need to build self-confidence; allowing them to make mistakes without fear of punishment; and coaching them to learn from their mistakes.[14]

- *The renewal process.* Successful managers also foster a renewal process.[15] They make sure that everyone (including themselves) guards against complacency. They encourage employees to question why they do things as they do and how they might do them differently.

Despite the importance of managing the renewal process, many Canadian executives may have trouble coming to grips with it. A study by Andersen Consulting found that 70 percent of the executives surveyed didn't see ecommerce or the internet as something worthy of a strategic initiative. And yet, 84 percent of them said that the economy will be heavily dependent on the web in a few years.[16]

Noranda
www.noranda.ca

Ernst & Young
www.ey.com

executive
The firm's top level of management.

Types of Managers

It is pretty obvious that there are different types of managers. In your college or university, there are presidents, vice presidents, provosts, deans, and department heads. There are also administrators, like human resource managers and the head of campus security.

In practice, we can differentiate managers based on their (a) *organization level* (top, middle, bottom), (b) *position* (manager, director, or vice president, etc.), and (c) *functional title* (sales manager, vice president for finance, etc.). Figure 1.1 helps to illustrate this. The managers at the top, of course, are the firm's top management. These managers are commonly called **executives**. Typical positions here are president, senior vice president, and executive vice president (in a university, you might also add "provost"). Functional titles here include chief executive officer (CEO), vice president for sales, general manager, and chief financial officer (CFO). New forms of these titles are emerging. Noranda Inc. has a vice-president of performance, and Ernst & Young has a chief knowledge officer.

middle manager
Managers immediately below the top level of managers and above lower-level managers.

Immediately below this top level (and reporting to it) may be one or more levels of **middle managers**. The positions here usually include the term "manager" or "director" in their titles. In large companies, managers usually report to directors, who in turn report to top managers like vice presidents. Examples of functional titles here include production manager, sales director, HR manager, and finance manager. The city of Mississauga has a director of organizational effectiveness.

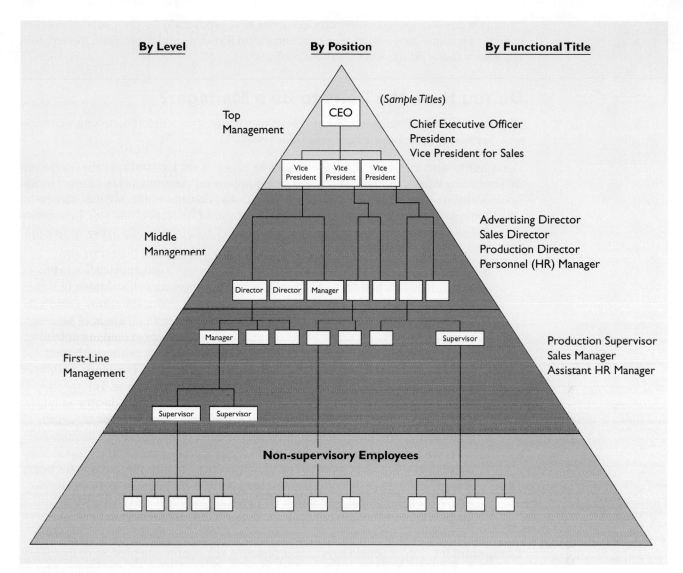

By Level   **By Position**   **By Functional Title**

Top Management

(Sample Titles)

CEO

Chief Executive Officer
President
Vice President for Sales

Vice President   Vice President   Vice President

Middle Management

Advertising Director
Sales Director
Production Director
Personnel (HR) Manager

Director   Director   Manager

First-Line Management

Manager   Supervisor

Production Supervisor
Sales Manager
Assistant HR Manager

Supervisor   Supervisor

Non-supervisory Employees

FIGURE 1.1
Types of Managers

First-line managers are on the lowest rung of the management ladder. Positions here might include "supervisor" or "assistant manager." Functional titles might include production supervisor and assistant marketing manager. Production supervisors, for example, oversee the work of assembly-line employees at organizations like Bombardier and Maple Leaf Foods.

Managers have a lot in common. They all plan, organize, lead, and control. All managers at all levels and with every functional title also spend an enormous amount of their time with people—talking, listening, influencing, motivating, and attending meetings.[17] Even chief executives (whom you might expect to be somewhat insulated from other people, up there in their executive suites) spend about three-fourths of their time dealing directly with other people.[18]

There are, however, two basic differences among managers. First, top and middle managers are in charge of other managers, while supervisors oversee the work of nonmanagers. Second, managers at different levels use their time somewhat differently. Top managers tend to spend more time on planning and setting goals (like "double sales in the next two years"). Middle managers then translate these goals into specific projects (like

first-line managers
Managers on the lowest rung of the management ladder.

"hire two new salespeople and introduce three new products") for their subordinates to execute. First-line supervisors then concentrate on directing and controlling the employees who actually do the work on these projects.

Do You Have the Traits to Be a Manager?

If you're thinking of being a manager, there's a wealth of research to help you to decide whether management is the occupation for you.

Personality and Interests Career counselling expert John Holland says that personality (including values, motives, and needs) is an important determinant of career choice. Specifically, he says six basic "personal orientations" determine the sorts of careers to which people are drawn. Research with his Vocational Preference Test (VPT) suggests that almost all successful managers fit at least one of two personality types or orientations from that group of six:

- *Social orientation.* Social people are attracted to careers that involve working with others in a helpful or facilitative way (managers as well as others like clinical psychologists and social workers would exhibit this orientation). Generally speaking, socially oriented people find it easy to talk with all kinds of people, are good at helping people who are upset or troubled, are skilled at explaining things to others, and enjoy doing social things like helping others with their personal problems, teaching, and meeting new people.[19] It's hard to be a manager if you're not comfortable dealing with people.
- *Enterprising orientation.* Enterprising people tend to like working with people in a supervisory or persuasive way in order to achieve some goal. They especially enjoy verbal activities aimed at influencing others (lawyers and public relations executives would also exhibit this orientation). Enterprising people often characterize themselves as being good public speakers, as having a reputation for being able to deal with difficult people, as successfully organizing the work of others, and as being ambitious and assertive. They enjoy influencing others, selling things, serving as officers of groups, and supervising the work of others.

Competencies Edgar Schein says career planning is a continuing process of discovery. He says each person slowly develops a clearer occupational self-concept in terms of his or her talents, abilities, motives, and values. He calls this occupational self-concept a "career anchor." Based on his study of MIT graduates, Schein concluded that managers have a strong *managerial competence* career anchor.[20] They show a strong motivation to become managers, "and their career experience enables them to believe that they have the skills and values necessary to rise to such general management positions." A management position with high responsibility is their ultimate goal.

What have these people learned about themselves that makes them think they can be good managers? They see themselves as competent in three areas: (a) *analytical competence* (the ability to identify, analyze, and solve problems under conditions of incomplete information and uncertainty); (b) *interpersonal competence* (the ability to influence, supervise, lead, manipulate, and control people at all levels); and (c) *emotional competence* (being stimulated, not exhausted, by emotional and interpersonal crises).

Achievements Research also suggests that your achievements might provide some insights. Industrial/organizational psychologists at AT&T conducted two long-term studies of managers to determine how their pre-management achievements related to their success on the job.[21] For example, those who continued their education beyond high school rose (on average) much faster and higher in management than did those who did not. Grades were important, too. People with higher grades showed greater potential for promotion early in their careers, and they rose higher in management than did those with lower grades. The quality of the school attended meant a lot more early in the person's management career than it did later. Those who had attended better-quality schools at first ranked higher as potential managers. But within several years, school quality had little effect on who was promoted.

The person's major in school also had an effect, and here there were some surprises. Managers who had majored in humanities and social sciences scored higher as potential managers and also moved faster up the corporate ladder.[22] Business administration majors ranked second, and math, science, and engineering majors ranked third. Why? At least in this study, the humanities majors scored the highest in decision making, intellectual ability, written communication skills, creativity in solving business problems, and motivation for advancement. Both the humanities/social science majors and the business majors ranked higher in leadership ability, oral communication skills, interpersonal skills, and flexibility than did the math, science, and engineering majors.[23]

Findings like these obviously don't prove that math, science, and engineering graduates will automatically have trouble if they become managers. The findings do suggest that, whatever your major, it's important for you to work on improving your decision making, creativity, and written communication skills.

Managerial Skills

The purpose of this management book is not to give you a set of ideas that you can use only until the next management fad comes along. The aim is to give you concepts and skills that will last your management lifetime. Remember that for all the new theories, what managers do today is fundamentally the same as what they have done for thousands of years. Managers who couldn't plan, organize, lead, and control would have been kicked off a pyramid job site in ancient Egypt just as quickly as they would be fired by a Canadian manufacturing firm today. This book aims to provide you with the basic concepts and skills you'll need to effectively manage in any situation. And we hope that it supplies the wisdom you'll need for knowing when and under what conditions a particular management approach is best.

Managers need many skills if they want to succeed, but three skills are particularly important: technical, interpersonal, and conceptual skills.[24]

Technical Skills

Managers must possess **technical skills** in their area of expertise. For example, accounting managers need accounting skills, sales managers should know what works and what does not work when it comes to selling, and production managers should know how the production system works. More generally, managers should know how to develop a plan, how to write a job description, and how to develop a budget.

Top managers should not get overly involved in technical issues, but sometimes they can't resist. Michael Eisner, CEO of Walt Disney Co., often attends story meetings and makes notes on movie scripts. Eisner does this because he wants to observe the company's managers in action, and because he feels ultimately responsible for the quality of the Disney's movies. Critics fault Eisner for "micromanaging" his company and say that he should focus on using his conceptual skills to develop an overall strategy for the firm.[25]

technical skills
Those skills specific to an area of expertise.

Interpersonal Skills

Managers need good *interpersonal skills*, including knowledge about human behaviour and group processes. They must also be able to understand the feelings, attitudes, and motives of others, and have the ability to communicate clearly and persuasively.[26] Tact, diplomacy, empathy, persuasiveness, and oral communications ability are all necessary in managerial jobs. Managers who possess these skills can better accomplish a wide range of daily managerial chores, such as listening attentively and sympathetically when a subordinate has a problem. Chapters 11–15 will help you learn many of these skills.

The Center for Creative Leadership studied why managers fail and came to some interesting conclusions. Some managers simply didn't do their jobs and thought more about being promoted than about doing the job they currently had.[27] However, most managers failed because they had abusive or insensitive styles, disagreed with upper management about how the business should be run, left a trail of bruised people, failed to adapt to the management culture, or didn't resolve conflicts among subordinates.

In a *Globe and Mail* study that surveyed Canadian executives, the key issue that kept senior managers awake at night was related to people. Topping the list were concerns about staffing, recruitment, retraining, and how to create and sustain employee morale. One executive noted that "people are the key to my success and the most talented ones are increasingly hard to find."[28]

Conceptual Skills

Effective leaders have more "cognitive ability," and their intelligence (and subordinates' perception of that intelligence) tends to be highly rated.[29] **Conceptual** (or cognitive) **skills** "include analytical ability, logical thinking, concept formation, inductive reasoning, and deductive reasoning."[30] Conceptual skills manifest themselves in things like good judgment, creativity, and the ability to see the "big picture" when confronted with information.

Intelligence and good judgment are not synonymous. As Lawrence Bossidy puts it, "if you have to choose between someone with a staggering IQ and elite education who is gliding along, and someone with a lower IQ but who is absolutely determined to succeed, you'll always do better with the second person."[31] Chapter 5 will help you hone your conceptual skills.

Today's Management Environment

**Microsoft
www.microsoft.com**

The modern management environment is characterized by two key facts: competition and change. Consider this interesting example: After more than 230 years of stability, Encyclopaedia Britannica was almost put out of business in the early 1990s by Microsoft's U.S.$50 Encarta CD-ROM. Suddenly, Britannica's environment became a lot more unpredictable. Today, Britannica has a new, streamlined management structure. It disbanded its door-to-door sales force and offers its encyclopedia without charge via the internet. It hopes that revenue from on-line ads and sponsorships will be enough to make the company grow again. Web designers, high-tech employees, and advertising sales reps have replaced the company's traditional door-to-door salespeople.

Canadian managers will have to cope with changes just like managers in other countries will. Al Flood, former chairman and CEO of CIBC, declared:

> This is a time of momentous change in financial services. Our industry is going through massive structural adjustments that amount to a virtual revolution in the way we do business. Incredible advances in information technology are transforming the way we deliver products and services—and require capital investments. Powerful new competitors are entering our markets. Many are financial service giants whose size and resources dwarf those of Canadian banks.[32]

**Canadian Imperial Bank of Commerce (CIBC)
www.cibc.com**

To remain competitive, the banking industry is already realizing the once-futuristic prediction that "virtual banks" would operate solely over telephone lines and in cyberspace, instead of being housed in bricks or mortar. For example, the CIBC has plans to put the infrastructure of a virtual bank in place. Although CIBC does not intend to abandon branch offices, the number will be greatly reduced (management consultants Deloitte & Touche have predicted that half of all bank branches in Canada will close by 2006).[33] In addition, transactions at branch offices have changed radically: Bank machines are the norm, and the role of traditional bank tellers has changed as a result. Currently, CIBC delivers products and services through 1140 banking centres, a national network of 4300 ATMs, telephone banking, debit and credit cards, PC banking, and the internet.

Some of the realities facing modern managers are shown in Figure 1.2. These include globalization, technological innovation, deregulation and privatization, new political systems, and changing demographics. We examine each of these briefly.

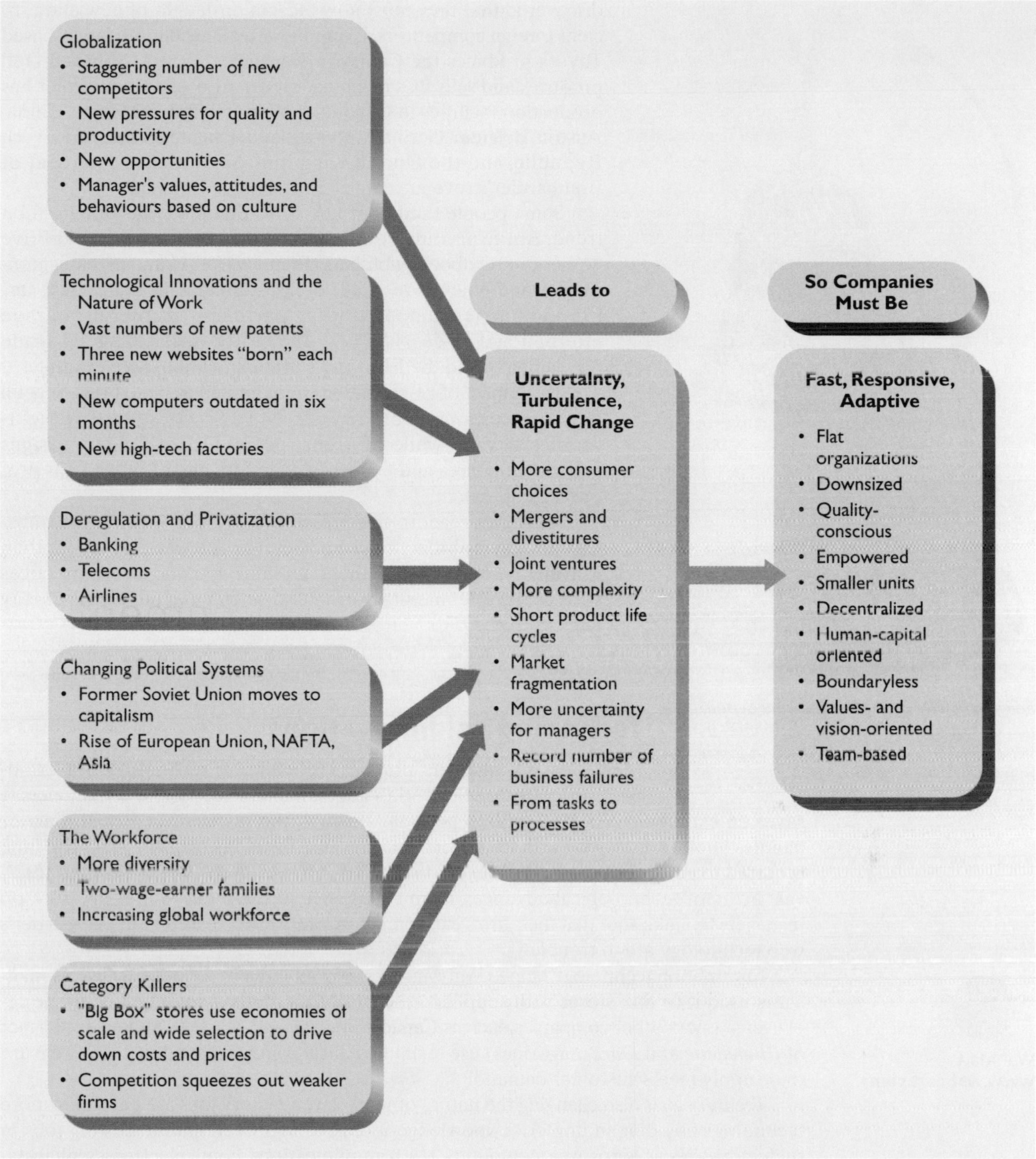

Globalization
- Staggering number of new competitors
- New pressures for quality and productivity
- New opportunities
- Manager's values, attitudes, and behaviours based on culture

Technological Innovations and the Nature of Work
- Vast numbers of new patents
- Three new websites "born" each minute
- New computers outdated in six months
- New high-tech factories

Deregulation and Privatization
- Banking
- Telecoms
- Airlines

Changing Political Systems
- Former Soviet Union moves to capitalism
- Rise of European Union, NAFTA, Asia

The Workforce
- More diversity
- Two-wage-earner families
- Increasing global workforce

Category Killers
- "Big Box" stores use economies of scale and wide selection to drive down costs and prices
- Competition squeezes out weaker firms

Leads to

Uncertainty, Turbulence, Rapid Change
- More consumer choices
- Mergers and divestitures
- Joint ventures
- More complexity
- Short product life cycles
- Market fragmentation
- More uncertainty for managers
- Record number of business failures
- From tasks to processes

So Companies Must Be

Fast, Responsive, Adaptive
- Flat organizations
- Downsized
- Quality-conscious
- Empowered
- Smaller units
- Decentralized
- Human-capital oriented
- Boundaryless
- Values- and vision-oriented
- Team-based

FIGURE 1.2
Fundamental Changes Facing Managers
A series of forces—globalized competition, technology revolution, new competitors, and changing tastes—are creating outcomes that include more uncertainty, more choices, and more complexity. The result is that the organizational winners of today and tomorrow will have to be responsive, smaller, flatter, and oriented toward adding value through people.

Globalization

Globalization refers to the tendency of firms to extend their sales, ownership, or manufacturing to new markets abroad. Firms that once competed only with local firms have

globalization
The tendency of firms to extend their sales, ownership, or manufacturing to new markets abroad.

Seagull Pewter of Pugwash, Nova Scotia, is just one of many Canadian companies that benefits from selling its products in foreign markets.

discovered that they must now face an onslaught of new and efficient foreign competitors. Examples are all around us. Japan-based Toyota produces the Camry in Kentucky, while U.S.-based Dell produces and sells PCs in China. Montreal-based Bombardier has production facilities in Canada, the United States, Mexico, China, Austria, Belgium, Germany, Switzerland, Finland, France, the Czech Republic, and the United Kingdom. More than 90 percent of Bombardier's revenue comes from outside Canada.

Some people think that U.S. firms dominate the globalization trend. But firms outside the United States own four out of five "American" textbook publishers (Prentice Hall, Harcourt, Houghton-Mifflin, and Wiley). Free trade areas—agreements that reduce tariffs and barriers among trading partners—further encourage international trade. NAFTA—the North American Free Trade Agreement—and the EU—the European Union—are examples.

The impact of globalization is not limited to large firms. Seagull Pewter Incorporated of Pugwash, Nova Scotia, sells pewter giftware worldwide, while I.P. Constructors Ltd. of Calgary designs and manufactures and exports a complete line of oil and gas processing equipment.

Managers react to this pressure in various ways. Some transfer operations abroad to take advantage of lower-cost labour than is available in Canada. Others apply new management practices such as flexible manufacturing and self-managing teams to stay competitive.

Technological Innovations

Many new management practices rely on new technology. For example, Carrier Corp.—the world's largest manufacturer of air conditioners—saves an estimated U.S.$100 million per year through the internet. In Brazil, Carrier handles all its transactions with its dealers, retailers, and installers over the web. The time required to get an order entered and confirmed has gone from six days to six minutes. A vast array of technological advances, from cellphones to the internet, put pressure on managers to make sure that their firms can compete. Competitors that can't match Carrier's web technology are in trouble.

Wal-Mart
www.walmart.com

Information technology helped Wal-Mart become an industry leader because its managers used it to link stores with suppliers to ensure that diminishing stock could be replaced at once. Other companies, such as Canada Safeway and Maclean Hunter (publisher of *Chatelaine* and *Flare* magazines) use technology as a competitive advantage to ensure that supply meets customer demand.

Technology is also changing the nature of work. Even factory jobs are becoming more technologically demanding. And knowledge-intensive high-tech manufacturing jobs in such industries as aerospace, computers, telecommunications, home electronics, pharmaceuticals, and medical instruments are replacing factory jobs in steel, auto, rubber, and textiles.[34] As Microsoft's Bill Gates put it: "In the new organization the worker is no longer a cog in a machine but is an intelligent part of the overall process." Welders at some steel jobs now have to know algebra and geometry to figure weld angles from computer-generated designs.[35]

human capital
The knowledge, education, training, skills, and expertise of a firm's workers.

Technology is not the only trend driving this change from "brawn to brains." Today two-thirds of the Canadian workforce is employed in producing and delivering services, not products. For managers, this all means a growing emphasis on "knowledge workers" and human capital.[36] **Human capital** refers to the knowledge, education, training, skills, and expertise of a firm's workers.[37] Today, "the center of gravity in employment is moving fast from manual and clerical workers to knowledge workers, who resist the command and control model that business took from the military 100 years ago."[38] Managers therefore need new, world-class management systems and skills, to select, train, and motivate these employees and to get them to work more like committed partners.

Deregulation and Privatization

During the last decade, there has been declining government involvement in business because of deregulation and privatization. **Deregulation** means a reduction in the number of laws affecting business activity and in the powers of government enforcement agencies. Deregulation simplifies the task of managing a company, because the company has increased freedom to do what it wants without government interference. Here are some examples:

- Canadian banks can now sell government securities in their branches and offer a much wider array of financial services than they could previously.
- The Canadian government no longer dictates how many airlines there will be and where and when they will be allowed to fly.
- The decision by the CRTC to allow competition among long-distance telephone companies has made long-distance calls much cheaper for Canadian customers.

Privatization refers to the process of turning formerly government-owned organizations into publicly traded businesses that pursue a profit. In the last few years, the federal government has sold many corporations it used to operate, including Canadian National Railways and Air Canada. Provincial governments have also been selling businesses; the province of Nova Scotia, for example, sold Nova Scotia Power, and the province of Manitoba sold Manitoba Oil and Gas Corp.

The privatization trend is not limited to Canada, but is a worldwide phenomenon. In Russia, Norilsk Nickel was on the brink of bankruptcy in 1998 when it was privatized. By 2001, it was one of the most profitable companies in Russia and its workers were earning more than double the typical wage of Russian workers.[39] A global survey found that privatization produced higher profits, more productivity, more long-term employment, and higher employee wages.[40] The privatization trend will likely lead to the dismantling of much of the government involvement in business that developed during the twentieth century.

deregulation
A reduction in the number of laws affecting business activity and in the powers of government enforcement agencies.

Canadian Radio-television and Telecommunications Commission (CRTC)
www.crtc.gc.ca

privatization
The process of turning formerly government owned organizations into publicly traded businesses that pursue a profit.

Air Canada
www.aircanada.ca

Changing Political Systems

As nations such as the Philippines, Argentina, Russia, and Chile join the ranks of democracy, central planning and communism are being replaced by capitalism. Such political changes have triggered the opening of new markets with hundreds of millions of potential customers. For business firms, the opportunities are enormous. But the burgeoning demand for goods and services also brings increased global competition that managers must cope with.

For example, McDonald's of Canada opened the first McDonald's outlet in Moscow in the former Soviet Union. The negotiations alone took 12 years to complete. Local supplies were unreliable, and the price of a Big Mac ($2.90) was very high in an economy where the average monthly income was less than $200. Managers struggled to overcome these difficulties during the first few years.[41] In another example, Volkswagen of Germany formed a joint venture with Škoda in the Czech Republic. The result was the building of a state-of-the-art plant in an area where labour rates were low. One of the main challenges for managers was training and motivating a workforce that had operated under a different management system for so many years.[42]

The management functions and roles outlined in this chapter vary somewhat when applied in different cultures. Management researchers have found culturally based differences in people's values, attitudes, and behaviours. For example, at the Škoda plant, managers have distinct ways of viewing the world

In the years leading up to the opening of the first McDonald's outlet in Moscow in 1990, McDonald's of Canada had to negotiate in a political environment that was not overly friendly to capitalistic ideology.

A knowledge worker: Engineer running a space shuttle heat test simulation.

ASEA Brown Boveri
www.abb.com

Future Shop
www.futureshop.ca

depending on whether they are of Czech or German origin. Because they had lived in a planned economy for many years, the Czechs didn't seem to understand the meaning of efficiency in the same way the Germans did. Over time, however, communications between the Czechs and the Germans improved, and the plant and its operations were transformed.[43]

The Workforce

The workforce is becoming more diverse as women and minority-group members increasingly participate. The labour force is also getting older, and a greater proportion of employees may work past the traditional retirement age because they do not have enough money to retire.

Most multinational firms set up manufacturing plants abroad, partly to establish beachheads in promising markets and partly to use others countries' labour forces. For example, ASEA Brown Boveri (ABB), a Swiss builder of transportation and electric generation systems, has thousands of new employees in former communist countries and has shifted many jobs from western to eastern Europe. Nortel Networks has employees in 30 different countries throughout Europe, the Middle East, and Africa.[44] Bombardier has 2000 employees in Mexico alone.[45]

Creating unanimity and human capital from such a diverse workforce won't be easy. Most managers say they encourage diversity, but most management systems—how companies recruit, screen, train and promote employees— "...will not allow diversity, only similarity."[46] Establishing management programs that turn a diverse workforce into highly skilled knowledge workers can thus be a challenge.

Category Killers

Where does an 800-pound gorilla sit? Wherever it wants to, just like category killers such as Future Shop, Wal-Mart, and Home Depot. These mammoth "big box" stores use economies of scale and wide selections to drive down costs and prices. Most small competitors—neighbourhood hardware stores, stationery stores, and bookstores, for example—can't get their costs or prices low enough. This competition squeezes out the weaker firms, unless their managers have the skills to compete.

Similarly, many smaller retail chains have been absorbed into giant chains with powerful centralized purchasing departments. When one giant chain accounts for half your company's sales, it's hard to negotiate. This squeezes manufacturers to reduce prices. Only the most efficient survive.

The Modern Organization

Periodically management writers have proposed new "paradigms," or models, that describe what the ideal approach to managing should be. For example, two decades ago McKinsey & Co. consultants Thomas Peters and Robert Waterman Jr. studied eight "excellent" companies. They concluded that these firms were excellent because of how they were managed. Managers in the firms encouraged a bias toward action; simple form and lean staff; continued contact with customers; productivity improvement via people; operational autonomy to encourage entrepreneurship; an emphasis on one key business value; a focus on doing what the company knows best; and simultaneous loose and tight controls.[47]

Rosabeth Moss Kantor studied companies like IBM, AT&T, Ford, and CBS. She concluded that fewer management levels, a greater responsiveness to change, and strategic alliances helped these firms succeed.[48] Several management theorists think that in today's fast-changing environment, the best companies are "intelligent enterprises," or "learning organizations." James Brian Quinn studied what he calls "Intelligent Enterprises." These companies depend on converting their employees "intellectual resources" (such as engineering knowledge) into services and products. Companies like these, says Quinn, must "leverage"—take maximum advantage of—their "intellectual capital" by ensuring that ideas can flow quickly among employees. Managers do this in many ways, such as by encouraging informal communications.[49]

Similarly, Peter Senge argues for creating the "Learning Organization." These are "organizations where people continually expand their capacity to create the results they truly desire,...and where people are continually learning how to learn together."[50] Among other things, learning organizations' managers encourage "systems thinking, personal mastery, building shared vision," and "team learning."

All these ideas imply that modern organizations increasingly have the following characteristics: smaller, more entrepreneurial organizational units; team-based, boundaryless organizations; empowered decision making; flatter organizational structures; knowledge-based management; an emphasis on vision; strong leadership; and technology and e-based management. Let's briefly look at each of these.

Smaller, More Entrepreneurial Organizational Units

The operating units in many companies are getting smaller. Even big firms are encouraging employees to be more like small-business entrepreneurs. For example, T. J. Rogers, president of Cypress Semiconductor, believes that large companies stifle innovation. So, when a new product must be developed, he doesn't do it within the existing corporation. Instead, he creates a separate start-up company under the Cypress umbrella. Rogers already has four successful start-ups under development.[51]

Another company that moved to smaller organizational units is Swiss electrical equipment maker ABB, which split itself into mini-units to be more responsive to customer needs. Within two years of taking over as CEO, former chairman Percy Barnevik "disorganized" the firm's 215 000 employees into 5000 mini-companies, each averaging only about 50 workers.[52] Each of the mini-companies is run by a manager and three or four lieutenants. Efficiency and responsiveness are the net results.

Cypress Semiconductor
www.cypress.com

Team-Based, Boundaryless Organizations

Managers are extending this "small is beautiful" philosophy to how they organize the work itself. Many companies today organize around small, cross-functional teams that manage themselves. GM's Saturn Corporation subsidiary is a famous example. Virtually all shop floor work is organized around work teams of 10 to 12 employees. Each team is responsible for a complete task, such as installing door units, checking electrical systems, or maintaining automated machines. The teams don't have traditional supervisors. Instead, highly trained workers do their own hiring, control their own budgets, monitor the quality of their own work, and generally manage themselves.

Many firms extend this idea to creating interdepartmental teams. Companies like these encourage free-flowing interdepartmental communication unhampered by the usual departmental boundaries. GE's former chairman Jack Welch calls this the **boundaryless organization**. To speed decision making, employees reach across the company to interact with whomever they must to get the job done.[53]

boundaryless organization
An organization that encourages free-flowing interdepartmental communication unhampered by the usual departmental boundaries.

worker empowerment
Giving front-line employees the authority they need to do their jobs so they can respond quickly to customer needs.

Empowered Decision Making

Self-managing teams can't manage themselves if they don't have the authority and training to do so. **Worker empowerment** is thus a core idea in modern management theory. Writers like Karl Albrecht say this often involves "turning the typical organization upside-down."[54] The company should put the customer—not the CEO—on top, to emphasize that every move the company makes is aimed at satisfying the customer. This requires empowering front-line employees like desk clerks at Four Seasons Hotels, cabin attendants at Air Canada, and food servers at Country Kitchen. They need the authority to respond quickly to the customers. The main purpose of managers in this "upside-down" organization is to support the front-line employees. The manager becomes more of a coach, seeing to it that employees have what they need to do their jobs.

Flatter Organizational Structures

The tall pyramid-shaped organization, with its seven or more layers of management, is disappearing. In its place, relatively flat organizations with just three or four levels prevail. Many companies, like ABB, have already cut their management layers from a dozen to six or fewer, and therefore the number of managers.[55] As the remaining managers are left with more people to supervise, they are less able to meddle in the work of their subordinates, who thus have more autonomy.

In today's organizations, says management theorist Rosabeth Moss Kanter, leaders can no longer rely on their formal authority to get employees to follow them.[56] Instead, "success depends increasingly on tapping into sources of good ideas, on figuring out whose collaboration is needed to act on those ideas, and on working with both to produce results. In short, the new managerial work implies very different ways of obtaining and using power."[57] Peter Drucker put it this way: "You have to learn to manage in situations where you don't have command authority, where you are neither controlled nor controlling."[58]

Knowledge-Based Management

Management experts say that companies today are *knowledge based*. Highly trained and educated employees apply their knowledge in a setting in which they direct and discipline their own activities.[59] This requires a new knowledge-based approach. Managers have to help employees get their jobs done by training and coaching them, removing roadblocks, and getting them the resources they need. Yesterday's manager thinks of himself or herself as a "manager" or "boss." The new manager is a "sponsor," a "team leader," or an "internal consultant." The old-style manager hoards information to build his or her personal power. The new manager shares information to help subordinates get their jobs done.[60]

An Emphasis on Vision

In companies with fewer bosses, formulating a clear vision of where the firm is heading is very important. Peter Drucker says that today's companies—staffed by professionals and other employees who largely control their own behaviour—require "clear, simple, common objectives [a vision] that translate into particular actions."[61] The vision is like a signpost. Even without a lot of supervisors to guide them, employees can steer themselves by the company's vision.

Strong Leadership

Today's managers have to be leaders and agents of change. As Jack Welch put it, "You've got to be on the cutting edge of change. You can't simply maintain the status quo, because somebody's always coming from another country with another product, or consumers' tastes change, or the cost structure does, or there's a technology breakthrough. If you are not fast and adaptable, you are vulnerable."[62]

Today's environment puts a premium on effective leadership. In a fast-changing, team-oriented environment, managers need effective leadership skills so they can motivate knowledge workers, build self-managing teams, and lead transformations like the one at ABB.

Technology and E-based Management

Moving fast means getting the information you need now, when you need it. For example, when you sit with Larry Carter, Cisco Systems' chief financial officer (CFO), you can see the whole company's activities laid out before you.[63] This is because Cisco, a manufacturer of networking hardware and software, is in the vanguard of firms using sophisticated real-time computerized financial systems to give their top executives access to data almost instantaneously. As a relatively young company (founded in 1984), Cisco "doesn't have a bunch of incompatible, old record-keeping systems gumming things up." It could therefore start with a clean slate and computerize the entire financial control system so top management can detect changes relatively quickly.[64]

Canada Post also wants to transform itself to keep pace with the electronic age. Its e-Parcel service automatically calculates the weight of a package and the distance it must travel, and allows users to keep track of deliveries. Canada Post hopes to compete with delivery-giant UPS by using the e-Parcel system to attract direct-mail clients.[65]

**Canada Post
www.canadapost.ca**

As another example, consider the Spanish retailer Zara. It doesn't need the long production runs and expensive inventories that burden competitors like The Gap because Zara operates its own internet-based worldwide distribution network, produces much of its own materials, and does much of its own manufacturing. It also has a sophisticated information technology system that lets it monitor store sales on a daily basis. As soon as it sees that a particular style is in demand at one of its worldwide stores, its "flexible manufacturing system" swings into action. It dyes the required fabric, manufactures the item, and speeds it to that store.[66]

**The Gap
www.gap.com**

An Illustration of the Modern Organization: Dell Computer

How do you build a U.S.$12-billion company in just 13 years?[67] For Dell Computer the answer meant using technology and information to "blur the traditional boundaries in the value chain among suppliers, manufacturers, and the end users."[68] What does this mean? As summarized in Figure 1.3, it basically means that there are no intermediaries like wholesalers or retailers to come between Dell and its customers and suppliers so that Dell can move much faster than it might otherwise.[69]

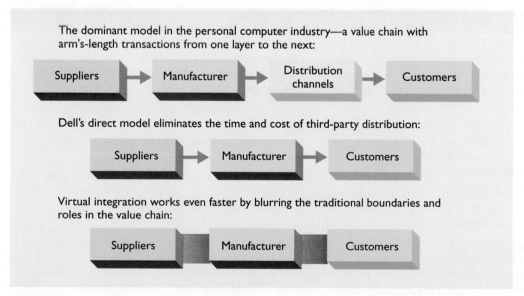

**FIGURE 1.3
The Evolution of a Faster Business Model**

For most computer companies, the manufacturing process is like a relay race: Components come in from suppliers; these components are assembled into computers; and the computers are then handed off to be distributed through wholesalers and retailers to the ultimate customers. Dell's system changes all that. For example, Dell interacts with and sells to customers directly, so it eliminates the activities of the wholesalers and retailers in the traditional distribution chain.[70]

"Virtual integration"—linking Dell with its suppliers and customers via the internet—speeds things up even more. As one example, computerized information from Dell continually updates suppliers regarding the number of components to be delivered every morning, so the "outside" supplier actually starts to look and act more like an "inside" part of Dell. Similarly, instead of stocking its own monitors, "We tell Airborne Express or UPS to come to Austin and pick up 10 000 computers a day and go over to the Sony factory in Mexico and pick up the corresponding number of monitors. And while we're all sleeping, they match up the computers and the monitors, and deliver them to the customers...of course, this requires sophisticated data exchange."[71]

The result of what Michael Dell calls "this virtual integration" of suppliers, manufacturing, and customers is a lean, efficient, and fast-moving operation that can turn on a dime if the products demanded by customers change: "There are fewer things to manage, fewer things to go wrong. You don't have the drag effect of taking 50 000 people with you.... If we had to build our own factories for every single component of the system, growing at 57 percent per year just would not be possible. I would spend 500 percent of my time interviewing prospective vice-presidents because the company would have not 15 000 employees but 80 000. Indirectly, we employ something like that many people today...but only a small number of them work for us. Their contract is with other firms.... The vast majority [of customers] think [those people] work for us, which is just great. That's part of virtual integration."[72]

SKILLS AND STUDY MATERIAL

SUMMARY

1. An organization consists of people who have formally assigned roles and who must work together to achieve the organization's goals. Organizations needn't be just business firms.

2. Organizations are run by managers. A manager is someone who plans, organizes, leads, and controls the people and the work of the organization in such a way that the organization achieves its goals.

3. Management writers traditionally refer to the manager's four basic functions of planning, organizing, leading, and controlling as the management process.

4. We can classify managers based on organizational level (top, middle, first line), position (executives, managers or directors, supervisors), and functional title (vice president of production, sales manager). All managers get their work done through people and by planning, organizing, leading, and controlling. Top managers spend more time planning and setting goals. Lower-level managers concentrate on implementing goals and getting employees to achieve them.

5. Managers play other roles such as figurehead, leader, liaison. They also engage in entrepreneurial, competence-building, and renewal processes.

6. Almost everything a manager does involves interacting with and influencing people. The bottom line is that leading people is not just another step in the management process, but also an integral part of the manager's job.

7. Managers and their organizations have to confront rapid change and intense competition. Trends contributing to this change include technological innovation, globalization, deregulation, changing political systems, category killers, the new global workforce, more service-oriented jobs, and an emphasis on knowledge work.

1. The traditional organization is usually depicted as a pyramid-shaped hierarchy with authority and decision making flowing from the top down. As this chapter points out, the changing environment demands that new forms of organization be designed. Your assignment is to graphically depict some new organizational designs. Draw the shapes you think represent the boundaryless, team-focused, and process-oriented organizations that are evolving. Then write a brief narrative describing what you have drawn and what you think the implications of your designs are for the basic management functions of planning, organizing, leading, and controlling.

2. In *The New Thing: A Silicon Valley Story* (W. W. Norton & Co., 1999), Mike Lewis relates the contrasts that are likely to frame the next century. The story focuses on how two different and powerful firms are approaching their journey. Lewis argues that Jim Clark, the founder of Netscape, is the model for the future. Clark is seen as a genius "on an endless search for some unattainable solution." Clark has a talent for anarchy that well suits him at this juncture in history. In contrast, Microsoft's Bill Gates is characterized as someone who wants the future "to look exactly like the present." Lewis characterized Microsoft as a company that doesn't want to discover the new thing, but rather to tame it. Using what you have learned in Chapter 1, speculate on which management model you think will survive and why. Will it be the world of Jim Clark or the world of Bill Gates (assuming Lewis is right about both men)? Predict what the management process might involve by the year 2020.

1. In December 1999 Air Canada won government and regulatory approval to acquire its long-time but ailing rival Canadian Airlines after a long battle for supremacy of Canada's skies. The acquisition vaulted Air Canada from 20th to 10th spot among the world's major airlines. Critics of the deal were concerned about a monopoly in the industry and price gouging. But according to the federal government, price gouging would not be tolerated. Clearly the best guarantee for reasonable airfares is viable competition. However, the government also believes that measures for dealing with pricing and predatory behaviour can be effectively enshrined in legislation. What do you think? Can legislation be effective in controlling the prices offered to customers? What has happened to the Canadian airline industry since Air Canada took over Canadian Airlines International? What do you think the future of the airline industry will be?

2. Write a short essay on the following topic: "The tasks I've performed that I most enjoyed, was proudest of, and was most successful at." (Perhaps one task includes all three areas.) Now do the same for the task you least enjoyed, were least proud of, and were least successful at. Then answer this question: Based on what you know about what managers do and what it takes to be a manager, do you think you have what it takes to be a manager?

BUILDING YOUR MANAGEMENT SKILLS

What Do Managers Do?

You can increase your understanding of management by talking to managers. Interview three managers of your choice and ask them what they do and what management is all about. Have them focus on the issue of *management* rather than on the specific tasks they carry out. Take detailed notes. After you have completed the three interviews, answer the following questions:

1. Was there agreement among the three managers as to what the manager's job involves? If so, what did they say? If not, why do you think there wasn't agreement?

2. Did the managers you interviewed talk about management in terms of the functions they performed (i.e., planning, organizing, leading, controlling) or in terms of Mintzberg's roles of management? Or both? Or neither?

3. What was the relative importance that managers attached to managing *things* versus managing *people*?

4. Overall, were the managers' comments consistent with the information provided in the chapter, or were there large discrepancies? If there were discrepancies, try to account for them.

5. What are the three most important things you learned about the nature of management as a result of your interviews?

Two of the realities facing twenty-first-century managers are globalization and technological innovation. One company that has faced these realities and achieved success is ZENON Environmental Inc. (**www.zenonenv.com**).

1. What was ZENON's vision when it was founded in 1980?

2. How did the managers at ZENON turn their vision into a viable, global company?

3. What are the key management initiatives that have made, and continue to make, ZENON a world leader in its field?

CASE STUDY 1-1

What Happened to Nortel?

In July 2000, the price of one share of Nortel stock cost $124.50. The company was flying high and was regularly called the "crown jewel" of Canada's high-tech industry. But by July 2002, the price of one share of Nortel stock cost less than $2. What in the world happened?

The most common answer given is that the high-tech industry in which Nortel operates had a catastrophically bad year and that Nortel was just one of many victims of a drastic economic downturn. There is certainly some truth to that explanation, but industry analysts say the story isn't that simple. The real explanation is found in more fundamental mistakes that the company made during the boom times of the late 1990s.

Two apparently unrelated events transpired during the late 1980s and early 1990s to set up the situation that caused Nortel such great difficulties a decade later. First, government deregulated long-distance telephone rates, causing increased competition in the telecom industry. This deregulation was largely completed by the mid-1990s. Second, the internet boom came along, and entrepreneurs saw new ways to make money in the communication business. They were successful in raising money for their new business ventures, and companies like Nortel suddenly discovered that a lot of new customers were out there who had money to spend on equipment of the type made by Nortel.

So far so good. But deregulated industries seem to follow a classic pattern: increased competition causes capital spending as firms try to achieve a larger size. But this spending inevitably causes excess capacity to develop which, in turn, virtually guarantees that price wars will occur. The price wars kill off the weakest firms, and investors become leery of lending more money to an industry that is now characterized by price wars and

weak profits. When entrepreneurs can no longer get funds, they can't order more equipment, and companies that supply such equipment see their sales dry up.

This is exactly what happened in the telecom industry. People with money eventually saw that the "New Economy" entrepreneurs were far too optimistic, so they withdrew their funds. By the first quarter of 2000, it was well known that telecom and internet firms couldn't get any more financing. In spite of that, Nortel continued to loan money to its customers so they could keep buying Nortel's equipment. Although credit sales are often seen as mandatory for a company to be competitive, sales of this type can also be very dangerous. In Nortel's case, many of the firms it loaned money to went bankrupt and therefore were no longer able to purchase equipment from Nortel. To add insult to injury, Nortel was also was unable to collect the money it was owed on loans.

Critics claim that Nortel knew all about softening demand for its products but didn't tell anyone until it unexpectedly announced in October 2001 that its sales forecasts would not be met. Once that announcement was made, it became clear that the party was over and investors began abandoning the stock. The reduced demand for the stock caused its price to drop, and investors eventually lost billions of dollars. During the good times, Nortel gave millions of dollars in stock options to employees. Giving out all these options also helped to drive down the price of the company's stock.

At its annual meeting on April 25, 2002, Nortel faced angry shareholders who said that Nortel's loss for 2001 ($27.3 billion) was the biggest financial disaster ever to hit Canada. They also didn't think it was fair that some top executives had made millions by cashing in their stock options before the price dropped.

Questions

1. Explain what each of the functions of management (planning, organizing, leading, and controlling) would mean in a company like Nortel.

2. What failures were evident at Nortel? Which functions of management were apparently carried out poorly?

3. What factors in the environment of management influenced the problems that developed at Nortel? Explain.

Nortel Networks
www.nortel.ca

CASE STUDY 1-2

Remembering the Good Times

On August 8, 2002, the Toronto Blue Jays held a recognition night honouring Pat Gillick, the team's former general manager. Paul Beeston, the former CEO was also in attendance. When Beeston and Gillick were running the show, the Blue Jays were a great success. They had 11 straight winning seasons, won five divisional titles, and won back-to-back World Series in 1992 and 1993. The SkyDome was packed with 50 000 people for every game, and fans were willing to pay twice the standard price for tickets.

Paul Beeston started as the team's first full-time accountant and rose through the ranks to become CEO in 1989. As CEO, Beeston walked a fine line between crazy kid and top-notch executive (think Tom Hanks in the movie *Big*). He was also legendary for his commitment to the team. He arrived at work between 7 a.m. and 7:30 a.m. each day and didn't take a vacation for years. Beeston handled the administration and balanced the books, while Gillick monitored the team's on-the-field performance. When fans expressed concerns about high player salaries, Beeston responded by arguing that players needed a good environment to work in.

Beeston was under constant pressure to win games and pennants. That was not a simple matter, since the club had a roster of 25 temperamental ball players. It was necessary to continually find new players through the scouting system. The team did not repeat its earlier successes in 1994 or 1995, and Beeston sent a letter to season ticket holders asking for their continued support and patience while the team tried to rebuild. He noted that it was not fun running an organization with the kinds of problems the Blue Jays had recently experienced.

Beeston was not the kind of person to give up when problems arose. In 1996, the Blue Jays acquired several new players and hope was running high that they would once again become pennant contenders. But, it hasn't happened. The team had a losing season once again in 2002. The team draws only about 20 000 fans per game and is not as popular as the Raptors basketball team.

Both Beeston and Gillick have moved on to other positions. Gillick now runs the Seattle Mariners, who won the American League's Western Division title in 2002. Beeston went on to serve as president and COO of Major League Baseball. He resigned the positions in March 2002.

Questions

1. What management skills did Paul Beeston need to be effective? How did these skills change as Beeston moved from accountant to CEO?

2. Briefly describe what each function of management involves in a position like the one Paul Beeston occupied with the Blue Jays.

3. How is being CEO of a baseball team different from being CEO of a manufacturing firm? How is it similar?

Toronto Blue Jays
www.bluejays.com

JetBlue Is Airborne

In the 20 years or so since the airline industry was deregulated, dozens of new airlines have been launched in Canada and the United States. The airline burial grounds are filled with well-known companies like Canadian Airlines International, Canada 3000, Swissair, Pan Am, Eastern, and Braniff. They simply couldn't compete in the face of the new efficiencies demanded by deregulation. Even companies that industry experts had assumed would survive—for example, United Airlines and Air Canada—have declared bankruptcy. The environment for airlines continues to be difficult.

David Neeleman stepped into this environment with plans to launch a low-cost airline. Neeleman is no industry novice; he brought to the table a 20-year record of effective management. Raised in Utah, Neeleman dropped out of college to start a travel agency in 1981. In 1984 he agreed to help another travel agent, Joan Morris, run a charter business that grew into discount airline Morris Air, which they then sold to Southwest Airlines in 1993 for U.S.$129 million in stock. Prohibited from running a U.S. airline for five years by his Southwest buyout, Neeleman headed north to help start the Canadian airline WestJet, and then headed a company that created electronic reservation systems. Meanwhile, he was making plans for a new airline.[73]

By 1998, Neeleman was speaking to investors about plans for a new airline. This presented investors with a dilemma. On the one hand, Neeleman had a 20-year record of starting and managing travel and airline businesses. On the other hand, the competition had proved deadly to many other start-ups. As one article noted, "Low fares and a cute name only kept Kiwi international airlines afloat seven years before it liquidated its assets in August 1999. And despite millions in loans from General Motors Corp., DaimlerChrysler, and the United Auto Workers, ProAir had filed for bankruptcy in September, after the federal aviation administration grounded the airline for safety and maintenance violations.[74]

There were additional aspects of Neeleman's plan that investors might have had doubts about. For example, he planned to initiate service between Fort Lauderdale, Florida, and JFK Airport in New York. That route certainly needed a low-cost competitor. However, major airlines like American and Delta were already flying the route and could be expected to respond to JetBlue by lowering their own prices. Furthermore, many customers viewed New York's JFK as congested and delay-prone and too far from the city (it takes about a half an hour more to get from JFK to New York than it does from LaGuardia). Neeleman also planned to go "first-class" and to keep costs low. He planned to buy new planes to avoid maintenance costs for the first five years or so, install leather seats (which cost more but last twice as long as regular seats), and install a TV at every seat to boost passenger comfort levels.

The question was, could he do all that and offer low-cost pricing? Some of the world's most sophisticated investors, including Chase Capital and George Soros, decided that the answer was "yes." Together, investors put together the U.S.$130 million in financing that helped launch JetBlue.

Having a great idea is one thing, implementing it is another. Now that David Neeleman had his U.S.$130 million, it was time to get his airline launched. And it turned out that he was going to have to launch JetBlue in an environment that included not just the "usual" threats like cutthroat competition, but also the 9/11 terrorist attacks, which reduced air travel by 30 percent. It was going to be a challenging few years for David Neeleman.

Assignment

You and your team are consultants to Mr. Neeleman, who is depending on your management expertise to help him navigate the launch and management of JetBlue. Here's what he wants to know from you:

1. I have the money we need to start the airline but no organization of any kind at this point. What 10 specific management tasks am I going to have to attend to during the next 12 months?

2. "He who neglects the past is doomed to repeat it." I'm a bit of a management history buff. List and briefly describe five things I can learn by studying the evolution of management thought that can help me create JetBlue.

3. List and briefly describe five environmental forces that are influencing my business.

JetBlue Airways
www.jetblue.com

Appendix

The Foundations of Modern Management

The roots of management can be traced to antiquity. Hunters banded into tribes for protection, the Egyptians used organizations to build pyramids and control the rise and fall of the Nile, and the Romans relied on organizing to build their armies and control their empire. Management is thus a very old idea (as Figure A1.1 illustrates).

Some recurring themes become apparent when we view management over the ages. First, many of the concepts we take for granted today, such as dividing employees into departments, can be traced to the earliest human organizations, including those of the Egyptians and the ancient Greeks. The close supervision and reliance on coercion and rules that management expert Peter Drucker has called "command and control" is also a product of earlier times, in particular of the militaristic organizations of Egypt and ancient Rome.

Second, we will see that the forms that organizations take and the ways that managers manage have always been a product of the time. As futurist Alvin Toffler has said (in describing nineteenth-century management):

> Each age produces a form of organization appropriate to its own tempo. During the long epic of agricultural civilization, societies were marked by low transience. Delays in communication and transportation slowed the rate at which information moved. The pace of individual life was comparatively slow. And organizations were seldom called upon to make what we would regard as high-speed decisions.[1]

So, management is also an evolutionary process. Let us now look back to the beginning of modern management theory.

| 2052 B.C. to 1786 B.C. In the Middle Kingdom of Egypt, leaders introduce the subdivision of labour into factories (if papyrus records are to be believed). | Around 59 B.C. Julius Caesar keeps people up-to-date with handwritten sheets and posters around Rome. Ever since, the greatness of leaders has been measured partly by their ability to communicate. | A.D. 1906 Sears Roebuck opens its Chicago mail-order plant. The Sears catalogue makes goods available to an entirely new audience. | 1908 William Hoover sees that automobiles will kill his business, which makes leather accessories for horse-drawn carriages. So he starts the Electric Suction Sweeper Co., creating the mass-market vacuum cleaner. | 1955 Ray Kroc likes Mac and Dick McDonald's food stand in San Bernardino, California, so much that he opens his own franchised restaurant and forms McDonald's Corp. | 1984 In his dorm room at the University of Texas at Austin, Michael Dell starts selling PCs direct and building them to order. |

FIGURE A1.1
The History of Management

The Classical Approach to Management

Management theory as we know it today is an outgrowth of the first attempts to view the management process with new and almost scientific rigour.

The Industrial Revolution

By 1750, with the advent of the Industrial Revolution, what Toffler referred to as "the long epic of agricultural civilization" was about to end. The Industrial Revolution was a period of several decades during which machine power was increasingly substituted for human or animal labour. During these years several major trends converged. Scientific and technological discoveries, including the invention of the steam engine and the use of electricity, contributed to enormous increases in productivity and output. England, generally recognized as the epicentre of the Industrial Revolution, had a stable, constitutional government, a sensitivity to laissez-faire (hands-off) economics, and a strong spirit of self-reliance. In his book *The Wealth of Nations*, Adam Smith described the division and specialization of work as a pillar of the burgeoning competitive market system.[2]

The Industrial Environment

For firms in the nineteenth century, industrialization meant emphasizing resource accumulation and company growth. Division of work and specialization required the high volume and stability that only growth could bring. Growth led to higher profits; as sales, volume, and stability increased, unit costs decreased.

But enlarged operations created new problems for entrepreneurs. They needed management techniques to run their new, large-scale enterprises. These industrialists therefore quickly adopted the structures and principles followed by managers of an earlier day, such as centralized decision making, a rigid chain of command, specialized division of work, and autocratic leadership. All of these had been born in military and religious organizations and subsequently were nurtured for thousands of years.

Frederick W. Taylor and Scientific Management

The race to accumulate resources and grow was particularly pronounced in the United States. The War of 1812 severed the United States from England economically and spurred the growth of domestic manufacturing operations. Technological advances included the steamboat, the cotton gin, the iron plough, the telegraph, the electric motor, and the expansion of a railroad and canal network that opened up new markets for producers. In turn, these new markets provided the volume that was a basic requirement for effective division of work.

Historian Alfred Chandler has pointed out that by the late nineteenth century many new industries were completing the resource-accumulation stage of their existence and beginning to move into what he calls a rationalization stage.[3] The management focus shifted from growth to efficiency. As organizations became large and unwieldy, and as competition became more intense, managers needed better ways to use the resources they had accumulated. They sought new concepts and techniques to cut costs and boost efficiency. It was out of this environment that the *classical school of management* emerged.

Frederick W. Taylor was among the first of what historians today call the "classical management writers"; he developed a set of principles that became known as *scientific management*. Taylor's basic thesis was that managers should study work scientifically to identify the "one best way" to get the job done. His framework for scientific management was based on four principles:

1. The "one best way." Management, through observation and "the deliberate gathering...of all the great mass of traditional knowledge, which in the past has been in the heads of the workmen...," finds the "one best way" for performing each job.

2. Scientific selection of personnel. This principle requires "the scientific selection and then the progressive development of the workmen." Management must uncover

each worker's limitation, find his or her "possibility for development," and give each worker the required training.

3. **Financial incentives.** Taylor knew that putting the right worker on the right job would not ensure high productivity by itself. Some plan for motivating workers to do their best and to comply with their supervisors' instructions was also required. Taylor proposed a system of financial incentives in which each worker was paid in direct proportion to how much he or she produced, instead of according to a basic hourly wage.

4. **Functional foremanship.** Taylor called for a division of work between manager and worker such that managers did all planning, preparing, and inspecting while the workers did the actual work. Specialized experts, or functional foremen, would be responsible for specific aspects of a task, such as choosing the best machine speed, determining job priorities, and inspecting the work. The worker was to take orders from each foreman, depending on what part of the task was concerned.[4]

Frank and Lillian Gilbreth and Motion Study

The work of the husband-and-wife team Frank and Lillian Gilbreth also exemplifies the techniques and points of view of the scientific management approach. Born in 1868, Frank Gilbreth passed up an opportunity to attend MIT, deciding instead to enter the contracting business. He began as an apprentice bricklayer and became intrigued by the idea of improving efficiency. By carefully studying workers' motions he developed innovations—for example, in the way bricks were stacked, in the way they were laid, and in the number of motions used—that nearly tripled the average bricklayer's efficiency.[5]

In 1904 Frank married Lillian Moller, who had a background in psychology, and together they began to develop principles and practices to analyze tasks more scientifically. In addition to using stopwatches, they developed various tools, including *motion-study principles*, to assist them in their quest for efficiency. They concluded, for example, that

1. The two hands should begin and complete their motions at the same time.

2. The two hands should not be idle at the same time, except during rest periods.

3. Motions of the arms should be made at opposite and symmetrical directions and should be made simultaneously.[6]

Therbligs, another tool used by the Gilbreths, were elemental motions like searching, grabbing, holding, and transporting. (The Gilbreths created the term *therblig* by spelling their last name backwards and transposing the *t* and *h*.) *Micromotion study* was the process of taking motion pictures of a worker doing his or her job and then running the film forward and backward at different speeds so that details of the job could be examined. Used in conjunction with timing devices, micromotion study made it possible to determine precisely how long it took to complete each component activity of a task. Performance could then be improved by modifying or eliminating one or more of these component activities.

Henri Fayol and the Principles of Management

The work of Henri Fayol also illustrates the classical approach to management and work behaviour. Fayol had been a manager with a French iron and steel firm for 30 years before writing his book *General and Industrial Management*. In it, Fayol said that managers performed five basic functions: planning, organizing, commanding, coordinating, and controlling.

He also listed a number of management principles he had found useful during his years as a manager. Fayol's 14 principles are summarized next and include his famous principle of *unity of command:* "For any action whatsoever, an employee should receive orders from one superior only."[7]

1. **Division of work.** The worker, always on the same part, and the manager, concerned always with the same matters, acquired ability, sureness, and accuracy, which increased their output.

2. **Authority and responsibility.** Authority is the right to give orders and the power to exact obedience. Distinction must be made between official authority, deriving from office, and personal authority, compounded of intelligence, experience, moral worth, and ability to lead.

3. **Discipline.** The best means of establishing and maintaining [discipline] are: good superiors at all levels; agreements as clear and fair as possible; sanctions [penalties] judiciously applied.

4. **Unity of command.** For any action whatsoever, an employee should receive orders from one superior only....

5. **Unity of direction.** There should be one head and one plan for a group of activities serving the same objective.

6. **Subordination of individual interests.** In a business, the interests of one employee or group of employees should not prevail over those of the concern.... Means of effecting it are firmness and good example on the part of superiors; agreements as far as is possible.

7. **Remuneration of personnel.** Remuneration should be fair and as far as possible afford satisfaction to both personnel and firm.

8. **Centralization.** The question of centralization or decentralization is a simple question of proportion; it is a matter of finding the optimum degree for the particular concern. What appropriate share of initiative may be left to intermediaries depends on the personal character of the manager, on his moral worth, on the reliability of his subordinates, and also on the conditions of the business.

9. **Scalar chain.** The scalar chain is the chain of superiors ranging from the ultimate authority to the lowest ranks....It is an error to depart needlessly from the line of authority, but it is an even greater one to keep to it when detriment to the business ensues.

10. **Order.** For social order to prevail in a concern, there must be an appointed place for every employee and every employee must be in his appointed place.

11. **Equity.** For the personnel to be encouraged to carry out its duties with all the devotion and loyalty of which it is capable, it must be treated with kindliness, and equity results from the combination of kindness and justice. Equity excludes neither forcefulness nor sternness....

12. **Stability of tenure of personnel.** Time is required for an employee to get used to new work and succeed in doing it well, always assuming that he possesses the requisite abilities. If, when he has gotten used to it, or before then, he is removed, he will not have had time to render worthwhile service.

13. **Initiative.** Thinking out a plan and ensuring its success is one of the keenest satisfactions for an intelligent man to experience.... This power of thinking out and executing is what is called initiative.... It...represents a great source of strength for business.

14. **Esprit de corps.** "Union is strength." Harmony, union among the personnel of a concern, is a great strength in that concern. Effort, then, should be made to establish it.

Max Weber and Bureaucratic Organization Theory

Max Weber was a contemporary of Taylor, Fayol, and the Gilbreths. His work, first published in Germany in 1921, provides further insight into the ideals of the classical management writers. Unlike most of these writers, Weber was not a practising manager but an intellectual. He was born in 1864 to a well-to-do family and studied law, history, economics, and philosophy at Heidelberg University.

During the 1920s, Weber correctly predicted that the growth of the large-scale organization would require a more formal set of procedures to administer it. At the time, managers had few principles they could apply in managing organizations. Weber therefore created the idea of an ideal or "pure form" of organization, which he called *bureaucracy*. This term did not refer to red tape and inefficiency; instead, *bureaucracy*, for Weber, was the most efficient form of organization. Weber described bureaucracy as having certain characteristics:

1. A well-defined hierarchy of authority.

2. A clear division of work.

3. A system of rules covering the rights and duties of position incumbents.

4. A system of procedures for dealing with the work situation.

5. Impersonality of interpersonal relationships.

6. Selection for employment, and promotion based on technical competence.[8]

Summary: The Classical Approach to Management

The classical approach to management generally focused on boosting efficiency. To Taylor, Fayol, Weber, and the Gilbreths, an efficiently designed job and organization were of prime importance. These writers therefore concentrated on developing analytical tools, techniques, and principles that would enable managers to create efficient organizations. Work behaviour was not unimportant to the classical writers; they simply assumed its complexities away by arguing that financial incentives would ensure motivation. As a result, intentionally or not, the classicists left the impression that workers could be treated as givens in the system, as little more than appendages to their machines. "Design the most highly specialized and efficient job you can," assumed the classicist, and "plug in the worker who will then do your bidding if the pay is right."

The Behavioural School of Management

In the 1920s and 1930s, many changes swept North America, and indeed the world. Increasing numbers of people moved from farms to cities and thus became more dependent on each other for goods and services. Factories became more mechanized and jobs became more specialized and interdependent.[9] Government became more deeply involved in economic matters, and a number of lawsuits were filed to break up industrial monopolies. Social movements developed that aimed at giving women the right to vote, establishing a minimum wage, and encouraging trade unions. Even the literature of the period became more anti-individualistic, as people questioned whether a philosophy based on hard work, individualism, and maximizing profits—the building blocks of the classical management era—might actually have some drawbacks.

The Hawthorne Studies

In 1927, the *Hawthorne Studies* began at the Chicago Hawthorne Plant of the Western Electric Company. They eventually added an entirely new perspective to the management of people at work. Three main sets of studies took place, one of which became known as the "relay assembly test studies." A group of workers was isolated and studied as a series of changes was made, such as modifying the length of the workday and altering the morning and afternoon rest breaks. Researchers noted with some surprise that these changes did not affect performance greatly, underscoring their growing belief that performance depended on factors other than physical conditions or rate of pay.

The relay assembly test studies led the researchers to conclude that the *social* situations of the workers, not just the *working* conditions, influenced behaviour and performance at work. The researchers discovered, for instance, that in countless ways, their observations had inadvertently made the workers feel that they were "special." The observer had changed the workers' situation by "his personal interest in the girls and their problems. He had always been sympathetically aware of their hopes and fears. He had granted them more and more privileges."[10]

The Hawthorne Effect These results have been codified as the Hawthorne effect. This is what happens when the scientist, in the course of an investigation, inadvertently influences the subjects so that it is not the scientist's intended changes that affect the subject's behaviour but rather the way the scientist acts. In the relay assembly test, for instance, the researchers wanted to schedule rest periods when they would be most advantageous. They therefore called a meeting during which they showed the workers their output curves and pointed out the low and high points of the day. "When asked at what times they would like to have their rest, they unanimously voted in favour of ten o'clock in the morning and two o'clock in the afternoon." Accordingly, the investigators agreed to schedule the rests at these times. In retrospect, however, the researchers concluded that the subsequent rise in employee morale and performance was due to more than just the rest breaks; it was also due to the fact that the researchers had involved the workers in the decision.

Hawthorne's Consequences The Hawthorne studies were a turning point in the study of management. As the research became more widely known, managers and management experts began to recognize that human behaviour in the workplace is a complex and powerful force. The *human relations movement*, inspired by this realization, emphasized that workers were not just givens in the system but instead also had needs and desires that the organization and task had to accommodate.

Environment, Increased Diversity, and Change

Historian Alfred Chandler has suggested that after accumulating and then rationalizing resources, managers traditionally moved to a third stage in which they attempted to better use their organizational resources by developing new products and new markets— by diversifying. In the United States and Canada, movement into this third stage was hampered in the 1930s by the Depression. However, excess production capacity did ultimately stimulate research and development. Coupled with the technological and managerial advancements that emerged in the years surrounding the Second World War, this excess capacity finally shifted most U.S. and Canadian industries into Chandler's *diversification* stage.[11]

To understand evolving management theory, it is important to recognize that this period was characterized by differentiated, complex, and rapidly changing environments. Even before the Second World War, many firms had embarked on extensive research and development to develop new products. For example, at General Electric and Westinghouse, research and development activities resulted in the manufacture of plastics as well as a variety of other products based on electronics. The automobile companies had begun to produce airplane engines, electrical equipment, and household appliances. After the war, companies in the rubber industry—such as United States Rubber and BFGoodrich, which had concentrated on tire manufacturing—entered into systematic research and development and began to market such items as latex, plastics, and flooring.

These changes in the business environment contributed to the development of management theory in several ways. First, the increased rate of change and novelty triggered by diversification meant that managers and management theorists could no longer view organizations as closed systems operating within predictable and unchanging environments.[12] Second, efficiency was no longer a manager's main concern. It was eclipsed by the drives to diversify and then to monitor the activities of previously unrelated companies. Third, the shift toward making organizations more responsive to their environments was characterized by a trend toward *decentralization*, which in essence meant letting lower-level employees make more of their own decisions. Decentralization required a new managerial philosophy: Allowing subordinates to do more problem solving and decision making meant that managers had to rely on their employees' self-control. This change (coming as it did just after Hawthorne's results were popularized) led to a new emphasis on participative, people-oriented leadership and a more behavioural approach to management.

Douglas McGregor: Theory X, Theory Y

The work of Douglas McGregor is a good example of this new approach. According to McGregor, the classical organization (with its highly specialized jobs, centralized decision making, and top-down communications) was not just a product of the need for more efficiency. Instead, it was a reflection of certain basic assumptions about human nature.[13] These assumptions, which McGregor somewhat arbitrarily classified as *Theory X*, held that most people dislike work and responsibility and prefer to be directed; that they are motivated not by the desire to do a good job but simply by financial incentives; and that, therefore, most people must be closely supervised, controlled, and coerced into achieving organizational objectives.

McGregor questioned the truth of this view and asked whether standard management practices were appropriate for the tasks faced by more modern organizations. He felt that management needed new organizations and practices to deal with diversification, decentralization, and participative decision making. These new practices had to be based on a revised set of assumptions about the nature of human beings, which McGregor called *Theory Y*. Theory Y held that people could enjoy work and that an individual would exercise substantial self-control over performance if the conditions were favourable. Implicit in Theory Y is the belief that people are motivated by the desire to do a good job and by the opportunity to affiliate with their peers, rather than just by financial rewards.

Rensis Likert and the Employee-Centred Organization

Researcher Rensis Likert's work is another example of trends in management theory during the post-war years. Likert concluded that effective organizations differ from ineffective ones in several ways. Less effective *job-centred companies* focus on specialized jobs, efficiency, and close supervision of workers. More effective organizations, on the other hand, "focus their primary attention on endeavouring to build effective work groups with high performance goals."[14] As Likert noted, in these *employee-centred companies,*

> The leadership and other processes of the organizations must be such as to insure a maximum probability that in all interactions and all relationships with the organization, each member will, in the light of his background, values and expectations, view the experience as supportive and one which builds and maintains his sense of personal worth and importance.[15]

Chris Argyris and the Mature Individual

Chris Argyris reached similar conclusions, but approached the problem from a different perspective.[16] Argyris argued that healthy people go through a maturation process. As they approach adulthood, they move into a state of increased activity, greater independence, and stronger interests, and they pass from the subordinate position of a child to an equal or superordinate position as an adult. Gaining employees' compliance by assigning them to highly specialized jobs with no decision-making power and then closely supervising them inhibits normal maturation by encouraging workers to be dependent, passive, and subordinate. It would be better to give workers more responsibility and broader jobs.

The Behaviouralist Prescriptions

Behavioural scientists like Argyris, McGregor, and Likert soon translated their ideas into practical methodologies that became the heart of the emerging field of organizational behaviour. Likert emphasized leadership style and group processes. "The low-producing managers, in keeping with the traditional practice, feel that the way to motivate and direct behaviour is to exercise control through authority."[17] In contrast, "the highest-producing managers feel, generally, that this manner of functioning does not produce the best results, that the resentment created by direct exercise of authority tends to limit its effectiveness."[18] Therefore, said Likert, "widespread use of participation is one of the more important approaches employed by the high-producing managers."[19] He found that the value of participation applied to all aspects of the job and of work, "as, for example, in setting work goals and budgets, controlling costs, organizing the work, etc."[20]

McGregor had his own prescriptions. He said that decentralization and pushing decision making down the company hierarchy should be the norm to free people from the "too-close control of conventional organization." Management should encourage job enlargement (in which the variety of tasks that an employee performs increases), so that workers' jobs become more challenging and more interesting. Participative management (which McGregor said would give employees some voice in decisions that affect them) would similarly enhance self-control. Finally, McGregor urged using management by objectives (MBO). In MBO, subordinates set goals with their supervisors and are measured on their accomplishment of these goals, thus avoiding the need for close day-to-day supervision.

Bridging the Eras: Chester Barnard and Herbert Simon

The work of Chester Barnard and Herbert Simon does not fit neatly into any one school of management theory. Their research actually spanned several schools and contributed to the development of an integrated theory of management.

The Zone of Indifference Chester Barnard used his experience as an executive to develop an important new management theory. He was the president of New Jersey Bell Telephone Company and, at various times, president of the United States Organization (the USO of the Second World War), president of the Rockefeller Foundation, and chairman of the National Science Foundation.

Barnard was the first major theorist after the Hawthorne studies to emphasize the importance and variability of the individual in the workplace. He said, for example, that "an essential element of organizations is the willingness of persons to contribute their individual efforts to the cooperative system." And he added that "the individual is always the basic strategic factor in organization. Regardless of his history or obligations, he must be induced to cooperate, or there can be no cooperation."

Barnard set about developing a theory of how to get workers to co-operate. How do you get individuals to surrender their personal preferences and go along with the authority exercised by supervisors?[21] Barnard believed the answer could be found in what he called the person's *zone of indifference*, a range within each individual in which he or she would willingly accept orders without consciously questioning their legitimacy.[22] Barnard saw willingness to co-operate as an expression of the net satisfactions or dissatisfactions experienced or anticipated by each person. In other words, organizations had to provide sufficient inducements to broaden each employee's zone of indifference and thus increase the likelihood that orders would be obeyed.

But Barnard, in a clear break with the classicists, said that material incentives by themselves were not enough: "The unaided power of material incentives, when the minimum necessities are satisfied, in my opinion, is exceedingly limited as to most men."[23] Several other classes of incentives, including "the opportunities for distinction, prestige, [and] personal power," are also required.

Gaining Compliance Whereas Barnard wrote from the vantage point of an executive, Herbert Simon was a scholar who had mastered organization theory, economics, natural science, and political science, and who went on to win the Nobel Prize in economics in 1978. Like Barnard, Simon viewed getting employees to do what the organization needed them to do as a major issue facing managers. He proposed two basic ways to gain such compliance, which can be paraphrased as follows:

Decisions reached in the highest ranks of the organization hierarchy will have no effect upon the activities of operative employees unless they are communicated downward. Consideration of the process requires an examination of the ways in which the behaviour of the operative employee can be influenced. These influences fall roughly into two categories:

First, the manager can establish in the employee him- or herself the attitudes, habits and state of mind that lead him or her to reach the decision that is advantageous to the organization. In other words, the manager somehow gets the worker to want to do the job. Or, second, the manager can impose upon the employee decisions reached elsewhere in the organization, for instance by closely supervising everything the person does.[24]

According to Simon, managers can ensure that employees carry out tasks in one of two ways. They can *impose control* by closely monitoring subordinates and insisting that they do their jobs as they have been ordered to do (using the classicists' command and control approach). Or managers can foster employee *self-control* by providing better training, encouraging participative leadership, and developing commitment and loyalty. As rapid change forced employers to depend more and more on employee initiative, fostering such self-control became a major theme in management writings.

The Quantitative School

After the Second World War, management theorists began to apply quantitative techniques to a wide range of problems. This movement is usually referred to as *operations research* or *management science* and has been described as "the application of scientific methods, techniques, and tools to problems involving the operations of systems so as to provide those in control of the system with optimum solutions to the problems."[25]

The Management Science Approach

Management science has three distinguishing characteristics. First, management scientists generally deal with well-defined problems that have clear and undisputable standards of effectiveness. They want to know, for instance, whether inventory costs have been too high and should be reduced by 20 percent, or whether a specific number of items should be produced at each of a company's plants to minimize transportation costs to customers.

Second, management scientists generally deal with problems that have well-defined alternative courses of action. A company might have four different plants from which to ship products, or various levels of product A and product B that can be produced to maximize sales revenues. The management scientist's task is to recommend a solution. Finally, management scientists must develop a theory or model describing how the relevant factors are related. Like any scientist, management scientists must understand the problem and relationships clearly enough to formulate a mathematical model.

Historian Daniel Wren points out that operations research/management science has "direct lineal roots in scientific management."[26] Like Taylor and the Gilbreths, today's management scientists try to find optimal solutions to problems. Just as Taylor and his people used scientific methods to find the one best way to do a job, management scientists used the scientific method to find the best solution to industrial problems. The difference in the two approaches is twofold. First, modern-day management scientists have much more sophisticated mathematical tools and computers at their disposal. Second, management science's goal is not to try to find a science of management as much as it is to use scientific analysis and tools to solve management problems.

The Systems Approach

The management science approach is closely associated with what is called the systems approach to management. A *system* is an entity—for example, a hospital, a city, a company, or a person—that has interdependent parts and a purpose. *Systems approach* advocates argue that viewing an organization as a system helps managers to remember that a firm's different parts, departments, or subsystems are interrelated and that all must contribute to the organization's purpose.

According to systems advocates like C. West Churchman, all systems have four basic characteristics.[27] First, they operate within an environment, which is defined as those things outside and important to the organization but largely beyond its control. For a company these include clients, competitors, unions, and governments.

Second, all systems comprise building blocks called elements, components, or subsystems. In an organization, these basic building blocks might be departments, like those for production, finance, and sales. The subsystems may also cut across traditional departmental lines. For example, the marketing subsystem might include sales, advertising, and transportation, because each of these elements has an impact on the task of getting the product to the customer.

Third, all systems have a central purpose against which the organization's efforts and subsystems can be evaluated. For example, the optimal inventory level for a firm that serves top-of-the-line customers would probably be higher than for a firm whose customers want the best buy in town and are willing to wait for shelves to be restocked.

Fourth, focusing on the interrelatedness of the subsystems (and between the subsystems and the firm's environment) is an essential aspect of systems thinking. Interrelatedness emphasizes that a manager can't change one subsystem without affecting the rest—hiring a new production manager might have repercussions in the sales and accounting departments, for instance. Similarly, managers and management theorists need to be sensitive to the way that changes taking place in industrial environments affect the organization and management of the firm.

Institutional Theory

Unlike management science, which focuses on *technical rationality*, institutional theory emphasizes *behaviour* in organizations. Some things have become entrenched ("institutionalized") not because of their technical characteristics, but for other reasons. To illustrate this point, let us examine a brief history of the typewriter.[28] Because the keys in the first typewriter (invented in 1873 by Christopher Scholes) were prone to jamming, the so-called QWERTY keyboard was developed. This keyboard (taking its name from the first six keys on the upper left) was designed to slow down typists so that the keys wouldn't jam. But by the early 1990s, technological improvements like spring-loaded keys overcame the jamming problem.

In 1932, August Dvorak invented a faster keyboard, called the DSK keyboard (Dvorak Simplified Keys). Between 1934 and 1941, typists using the DSK keyboard won top prizes at the World Typewriting Championships, and time and motion studies showed that the DSK keyboard improved productivity by 35 to 100 percent. Did this evidence cause a move away from the old QWERTY keyboard? No. You still use it today. Why? Because the QWERTY keyboard has become "institutionalized." Factors other than the technical requirements of typewriting have ensured its continued use. These factors include things like tradition (people got used to using the QWERTY keyboard and didn't want to learn a new system) and cost (companies that produced the QWERTY keyboard didn't want to pay royalties to Dvorak for his idea). The DSK keyboard is available today on word processing software. Why don't you use it?

Institutional theory helps us understand why non-rational things happen in organizations. Students who are studying for careers in management often assume that organizations are places where all decisions are rational and logical. Institutional theory helps us to have more realistic expectations about what organizations are really like.

population ecology
An approach arguing that an organization succeeds based on factors in the organization's external environment, not its internal management practices.

Population Ecology

Population ecology suggests that factors in an organization's external environment are critical in determining its success or failure. This approach implies that management may not be as important as we commonly assume. Population ecology draws an analogy between animals and organizations. Just as the number of ducks living on the Canadian Prairies is dependent on the supply of food and potholes for nesting (not on how smart the ducks are), the population of a certain type of organization expands or contracts based on the resources that are available in its environment (not on how smart its managers are).

To see how this idea works in practice, consider the research that John Usher from Memorial University conducted regarding gas stations.[29] He found that gas stations functions have changed markedly over the past 40 years. In 1959, for example, virtually all gas stations had service bays. Thirty years later, however, only 22 percent had service bays. Another 22 percent were simply gas bars, while 23 percent also had a car wash and 26 percent had a convenience store (see Figure A1.2).

The population ecology argument is this: The old service station type did not become less important because managers were ineffective. Rather, the environment changed because customers demanded certain new things from gasoline suppliers. The population ecology model says that managers had no alternative but to adapt their mode of operation to these changes in customer desires. (Of course, the managers had to be smart enough to figure out what to do!).

Strategic Choice Theory

Strategic choice theory says that managers have three important decisions to make: (1) what niche or industry the company will compete in, (2) how the organization will be designed, and (3) what performance standards will be applied. This theory summarizes much of the current thinking about management and is the basic approach to management used in this text.

Strategic choice theory also says that when managers make these important decisions, they are influenced by their personal values. For example, does the manager value predictability and control, or flexibility and change? Does the manager think that employees are merely a means to achieving organizational goals, or should organizations be a means to achieving employee goals as well? The fact is that *all* managerial decisions are influenced by managers' values.

The practice of shared farming illustrates strategic choice theory. In shared farming, a person pays a fee and is then allowed to purchase a certain amount of a farmer's environmentally friendly and organically grown vegetables. The vegetables are delivered every week to a neighbourhood depot for sharers to pick up. Sharers can also volunteer to work on the farm if they want. Many shared farms are now operating on the Canadian Prairies because the values that many people believe in (protection of the environment and avoiding pesticides) can be put into practice by getting involved in shared farming.[30]

strategic choice theory
Suggests that managers must decide what niche or industry the company will compete in, how the organization will be designed, and what performance standards will be applied.

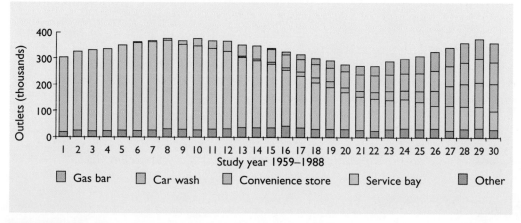

FIGURE A1.2
Change in Population Configuration of Gas Station Types

The Contingency Approach

universalist theories
Theories that propose that there is "one best way" to manage organizations and people.

Two fundamental types of theories have developed in the field of management. **Universalist theories** propose that there is "one best way" to manage organizations and people. These theories try to reduce management to certain principles that are universally applicable. They consider neither individual differences in people, nor how different situations might influence the kind of management that should be used. They take the view that a given management practice will always be effective.

contingency (situational) theories
Theories that assume that different individuals and situations require different management practices.

In contrast, **contingency (situational) theories** assume that different individuals and situations require different management practices. Although the basic management *functions* are the same in all types of organizations, the way they are *carried out* varies with the type of organization. Contingency theories were developed because managers and researchers observed that techniques or ideas that worked well in one situation often failed to work when applied in other situations. The contingency approach says, for example, that it is not very effective to manage university professors and factory workers in the same way.

The Environment of Management: Canadian and Global

Uncertainty in International Markets

Bombardier Inc. is a diversified Canadian company that specializes in transportation, recreational products, aerospace, financial, and real estate services. Bombardier is headquartered in Montreal, but its employees work in Canada, the United States, Mexico, Europe, and the Middle East. More than 90 percent of company revenues come from outside Canada. Annual sales exceed $5 billion and assets exceed $14 billion.

The company was founded in 1942 to manufacture a classic Canadian product—tracked vehicles for transportation across snow-covered terrain. Many of the original Bombardier snowmobiles that were manufactured decades ago can still be seen in remote areas of Canada. One such half-track sits on the windswept shores of Yathkyed Lake in the Northwest Territories, hundreds of kilometres from any town. It is a mute reminder of the important role Bombardier played in opening up Canada's remote North.

Bombardier has come a long way since its start. It is a major force in international aviation, having achieved that position by acquiring several aviation firms during the 1990s. In 1996, Bombardier rolled out its Global Express jet, which can fly 12 000 km at 850 km per hour. The jet is designed to capture the interest of executives who must travel long distances in the newly globalized business world.

Bombardier has done well in international aviation markets, but the competition is fierce and there is much uncertainty. In the mid-1990s, Bombardier held two-thirds of the market for regional jets, but then Brazilian rival Empresa Brasiliera de Aeronautica SA (Embraer) captured nearly half of that market. Bombardier complained to the World Trade Organization (WTO) that the Brazilian government was unfairly subsidizing Embraer, and in

OBJECTIVES

After studying this chapter and the case exercises at the end, you should be able to use the material to:

1. Describe the seven environmental factors that influence Canadian managers.

2. List the erroneous assumptions managers make when deciding to expand abroad.

3. Tell a manager why his or her company is (or is not) a suitable candidate for expanding into a specific country.

4. Evaluate your potential for global managing.

5. Specify the basic global strategy and global organization structure a manager should pursue, and why.

Bombardier
www.bombardier.com

1999 the WTO struck down Brazil's Pro-ex financing program (which gave buyers of Embraer jets reduced rates of interest). But the WTO also struck down Canada's Technology Partnership Program (TPP), saying that it, too, was an illegal export subsidy program.

In April 2000, the WTO endorsed Canada's revamped TPP program and ruled that Brazil had failed to fix its program. This was a boost for Bombardier, but then the WTO ruled that the Canadian government had given cut-rate financing to three separate buyers of Bombardier jets, and it called on the government to withdraw that financing. All of this jockeying for position by governments, the WTO, and the two jet makers has made the international competitive situation very complex.

Other problems are evident as well, most notably a drop in demand for corporate jets and reduced orders from U.S. airlines because of financial difficulties. In August 2002, when Bombardier announced that it would not make its profit projections, its stock price dropped 22 percent. In December 2002, Bombardier announced that it had hired former CN CEO Paul Tellier to re-energize the company.

In spite of all this uncertainty, Bombardier is on a mission of expansion to accelerate growth in foreign markets. It wants to

- Search for and identify new business opportunities in countries other than those in North America and Europe
- Act as an intermediary with government authorities and business communities in foreign locations
- Explore opportunities for acquisitions and strategic alliances

Other competitors are expected to loom in the market over the next few years. As it pursues its goals in the international marketplace, Bombardier will have to constantly monitor subsidies that other aviation companies receive from their governments to ensure that it does not find itself in an untenable competitive position.

The Environment of Management

As we saw in Chapter 1, the environment in which managers operate—the "world outside the company gate"—is a crucial determinant of success. Whether the environment is domestic (Canadian) or foreign (global), managers must pay attention to it and somehow cope with the challenges and opportunities it presents. Globalization in particular challenges managers and entrepreneurs to understand business activity in multiple and diverse contexts. As Bombardier's experience demonstrates, there are great opportunities and threats in both domestic and international markets. Success requires vision, creativity to deal with market challenges, and the ability to manage a global workforce.

In the age of ecommerce and technology, "going global" also requires an understanding of how to market to a diverse audience, and how to manage various international operations using the latest technology. Newfoundland-based Innova Multimedia Inc. develops educational software that it sells in China, Chile, and Jordan. Joe Wiseman, Innova's president, makes the pitch and negotiates the details via the internet as well as by travelling to meet potential clients. "When you're dealing with international markets, location is not an issue. It's not significant to the rest of the world if you're from rural Newfoundland or a city in Ontario," he says. "We can produce software here and ship it to anywhere in the world as easily as if we were in Toronto."[1]

As Canadian companies enter foreign markets, their success will depend on how effectively foreign operations are managed. In this chapter you will learn about the international business context and how to manage internationally. You will also learn about strategies for international expansion and the factors that influence a manager's decision to go global. But first, to provide some context, let's look the key features of the Canadian environment to see how it affects managerial activity. This is important, because how business is done in Canada influences our international competitiveness.

Management in the Canadian Context

In Chapter 1, we discussed several environmental factors that are generally important to managers no matter where they may work. In this section, we focus on describing the important factors in the Canadian environment. Managers must be aware of these factors and take them into account when they make decisions. Figure 2.1 shows the major external factors that influence managers operating in Canada. The circle representing the organization is broken to indicate that these environmental factors can have a big impact on managers within organizations.

There are four important observations about these environmental factors. First, managers at different levels in the management hierarchy have differing degrees of involvement with the external environment. Generally speaking, the work of managers at the upper levels of the organizational hierarchy is more directly affected by the external environment. For example, if a proposed pollution regulation will affect the firm, top managers might make representations to government and might even lobby environmental groups. Lower-level managers would not likely get involved in this kind of activity.

Second, these environmental factors may be in conflict with one another as well as with the organization. For example, employees may seek higher wages at the same time that increased competition in the market place is putting downward pressure on prices and reducing the firm's profitability. Or, owners (shareholders) may demand higher dividends at the same time that workers want increased wages.

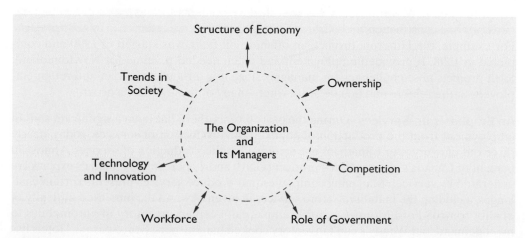

FIGURE 2.1
Environmental Factors in the Canadian Setting

Third, the importance of a specific external environmental factor varies over time, even for a given manager. For example, the vice president of human resources in a unionized manufacturing firm may serve as the head of the firm's bargaining team when the labour contract is being negotiated. At that time, the most important element of the external environment for the manager is obviously the union, but at other times, that same vice president may be more concerned with general labour market conditions that affect the company's ability to hire skilled workers.

Fourth, the environmental factors tend to work in combination with one another, and this makes their impact difficult to predict. For example, technological developments may improve the firm's competitive position, but they may also increase unemployment in society as a whole as workers are replaced with machines.

Important Characteristics of the Canadian Economy

Although Canada is the world's second-largest country in terms of area, the majority of our population resides in a narrow east-west band near the U.S. border. Canada's population is also very small by world standards (about 30 million). Both of these factors make it difficult to serve our national market effectively. Transportation costs are a major consideration in many management decisions, and the size of the country makes business travel time-consuming.

Beyond this basic point, there are five unique characteristics of the Canadian economy that affect managers' jobs. The economy is (1) resource-based; (2) made up of many one-company towns; (3) influenced by megaprojects; (4) focused on the production of services rather than the production of goods; and (5) characterized by significant foreign ownership.

Resource-Based Economy Canada's economy has historically been resource-based. This means that our main exports have been commodities like forest products, minerals, and grains. Managing resource-based companies presents a special challenge to managers because the commodities that are produced are affected by market prices, which managers can't control. Thus, if commodity prices fall, managers may have little alternative but to lay off workers.

One-Company Towns When a town is dominated by one company, unique problems exist for managers. The company may feel, for example, that it should become involved in providing community infrastructure such as roads, schools, and hospitals. Cassiar, British Columbia, was once a thriving town where employment was provided by an asbestos mine. But the town no longer exists because Cassiar Mining Corp. went bankrupt. There are many one-company towns across Canada, and in many of them employment is provided by a company that is involved in a resource-based operation like mining or forestry.

megaproject
A large-scale, costly construction or engineering project.

The Influence of Megaprojects Large-scale developments such as hydro-generating stations, pipeline construction, and offshore drilling operations are referred to as **megaprojects**. For example, the Hibernia project, an offshore oil field, was started in 1990 and completed in 1998. It provided employment and much needed revenue for Newfoundland. Such projects pose challenges for managers since it is difficult to attract and retain employees in the remote and hostile areas where many of these projects occur.

An Emphasis on Services During the past 50 years, there has been a significant shift in employment from the production of goods to the production of services. Today, nearly three out of every four Canadians are employed in the production of services. Almost 70 percent of Canada's gross national product (GNP) and 40 percent of Canada's exports are generated by services. Managing companies that produce services presents certain challenges, including the inability to store services in inventory and the increased difficulty of quality control. Ford Motor Co., for example, can keep an inventory of automobiles to meet demand, but Wendy's can't inventory cooked hamburgers. Four Seasons Hotels has a reputation for excellent service (which depends on the pleasantness and efficiency of its employees), so managers must use leadership and human-resource skills to inspire the employees to maintain that high level of service.

Foreign Ownership Many Canadian businesses, particularly large ones such as Ford Motor Co., Imperial Oil, Shell Canada, Canada Safeway, and Imperial Tobacco, are wholly or partly owned by foreign companies. Canadians who manage foreign-owned enterprises may have little real authority since important decisions are made at the foreign head office. Canadian managers may also find that when they develop a profitable operation in Canada it becomes a cash cow to be "milked" by the foreign owner.

The Ownership of Business Firms

The second environmental factor in Figure 2.1 deals with company ownership. Whoever owns a business influences the behaviour of managers in that business. There are several different categories of ownership of Canadian businesses, including individual direct owners, individual indirect owners, corporate owners, family owners, and government owners.

Individual Direct Owners Shareholders own shares in companies, but they seldom "interfere" with the managers of those companies because the owners are dispersed throughout Canada and abroad. Entrepreneurs (who operate small—and sometimes large—businesses) are also owners. The topic of entrepreneurship is discussed in Chapter 4. Employees can also own corporations through employee share purchase plans. Employee-owned corporations include Great Western Brewery (Saskatchewan), Britex Ltd. (Nova Scotia), Lar Machinerie Inc. (Quebec), and Sooke Forest Products Ltd. (British Columbia). Customers and producers may also become owners through the co-operative form of business. The Calgary Co-operative Association Ltd. and Mountain Equipment Co-operative are two of the best-known Canadian co-operatives.

Individual Indirect Owners Canadians can also become owners by contributing to mutual and pension funds that invest in business firms. Managers of mutual funds may make demands on company managers if they feel there is insufficient return on their investments. At Sherritt Gordon Ltd., for example, the board of directors was replaced and senior management ousted for this reason.

Corporate Owners Corporations can own other corporations. Instead of being accountable to thousands of shareholders, managers in owned corporations are responsible to the managers of the parent corporation. The managers in owned corporations may be closely supervised, or they may be given considerable freedom to run the business as they see fit as long as they meet the objectives that the parent corporation has set.

Family Owners Approximately one-third of the 100 largest companies in Canada are family owned. Some familiar family names are Irving (petroleum products), Ghermezian (real estate), McCain (food processing), Billes (Canadian Tire), Bombardier (transportation equipment) Bata (footwear), Sobey (supermarkets), and Weston (food manufacturing and retailing). Non-family managers face many challenges in family owned firms. They may be caught in family squabbles and asked to choose sides. Owners may also procrastinate about major expansion possibilities and succession plans, and this creates uncertainties for managers.

Government Owners Governments still own many business enterprises in Canada (although as we saw in Chapter 1 there has been a trend toward privatization). Government-owned enterprises are called Crown corporations and are owned by federal, provincial, or municipal governments. The objectives of government-owned businesses are usually service-oriented rather than profit-oriented, and managers in government-owned corporations often find that their work is more complicated and subject to political influence than work in the private sector is.

Competition

Competition between business firms in Canada is influenced by the degree of industrial concentration in the economy. **Concentration** refers to the degree to which an industry or

concentration
The degree to which an industry or the entire economy is dominated by a few large firms.

Labatt products are very recognizable since it is one of the two dominant companies in the highly concentrated brewing industry in Canada.

Labatt
www.labatt.com

the entire economy is dominated by a few large firms. In Canada, the 25 largest enterprises control more than 40 percent of all corporate assets and generate nearly 20 percent of all corporate profits.[2] This concentration is especially evident in a few industries. For example, more than 90 percent of the market for tobacco products is controlled by Imperial, Macdonald, and Rothmans Benson & Hedges, and only two companies—Molson and Labatt—dominate the Canadian brewery industry.

Managers in highly concentrated industries plan quite differently than managers do in industries where there are many competitors. In highly concentrated industries, firms behave in a similar fashion, and packaging changes and prices are copied. In less concentrated industries, however, it is impossible to keep track of all competitors or to predict their behaviour.

Although there are fewer competitors in some industries in Canada because of concentration, there are actually increasing numbers of competitors in many industries because of competition from imports. This is due to the lowering of tariff and non-tariff barriers as a result of free trade agreements. These are discussed later in this chapter. While having to compete with additional imports at home, Canadian managers are also finding opportunities to sell Canadian products in foreign markets. To be successful in exporting, managers have had to improve their skills at marketing in foreign markets by, for instance, learning foreign languages and studying foreign cultures.

A 2001 report prepared by the Canadian Manufacturers and Exporters ranked Canada last in terms of international competitiveness among the Group of Eight industrialized countries. The United States placed first, Japan second, and Germany third.[3] According to Michael Porter, a Harvard University expert on international competitiveness, Canada's competitiveness is a concern because we have been living off our rich diet of natural resources. If Canada wants to improve its competitiveness in international markets, we will have to do several things, including cut taxes, reduce government spending, increase productivity, and pay down our national debt.[4]

The Role of Government

Canadian managers must deal with government at the federal, provincial, and municipal levels. Almost every aspect of managing is influenced by government. For example, government policies influence the planning process, determine staffing practices, place constraints on how employees are treated, and stipulate what information must be disclosed when the company sells shares to the public. The introduction of the Goods and Service Tax, for example, meant that managers had to start keeping track of tax collection. For some firms, additional staff had to be hired, and detailed information on the taxes collected and any rebates requested had to be sent to the government.

The Workforce

Managers hire employees from a pool of individuals referred to as the Canadian workforce. There is a shortage of skilled workers, particularly in the trades, because neither governments nor businesses did enough during the past decade to train workers. As a result, jobs are available in areas where there are insufficient numbers of workers with the appropriate skills. Meanwhile, unemployment continues to be a problem.

The industries that employ the majority of workers today are different from those that dominated employment in Canada in the past. Employment in goods-producing industries such as mining, forestry, and manufacturing is either stable or declining. The failures of large retail operations like Woodwards, Eaton's, and Consumers Distributing, and the difficulties being experienced by firms like Nortel, have resulted in massive layoffs during the past decade. But job opportunities are expected to increase in other areas such as health care, personal and household services, professional business services, education, accommodation, printing and publishing, entertainment, and leisure services.

Managers in certain Canadian companies must also deal with unions. About 30 percent of Canadian workers belong to unions, which can influence the behaviour of both managers and employees. Although in the past relations between union and management have often been adversarial, times may be changing and these two groups are at least attempting to work together to achieve greater competitiveness. For example, to compete in the Japanese market, Mayo Forest Products, a small lumber operation, introduced a performance management system. A union member was part of Mayo's management implementation team.[5]

Managers must deal with these and many other changes that are occurring in the workforce, including the increasing participation of women, the aging of the population, and the increasing numbers of immigrants and Aboriginal peoples entering the workforce. We look at the issue of managing diversity in more detail in Chapter 3.

Technology and Innovation

Canada has a history of technological advance and innovation. For technological innovation to occur, research and development (R&D) must take place. Managers must see to it that R&D occurs because the survival of an enterprise often depends on discoveries leading to the development of new products. The production and marketing of these new products improves international trade opportunities, provides employment for Canadians, and increases the standard of living. Both government and business have been criticized for not spending enough money on R&D, despite the obvious advantages it will bring to business and the improvements it will make to the Canadian economy.

Managers must also adapt new technologies to improve productivity and quality. This involves the planning, organizing, leading, and controlling functions of management. Managing the changes will be challenging in itself. For example, managers will have to cope with displaced workers and be involved in training or relocating employees. Consumers will be affected as new products are introduced, making existing products obsolete.

Alcan
www.alcan.com

R&D in Canada is not restricted to large corporations such as Nortel, Alcan, Kodak, or CAE Industries. As we will see in Chapter 4, many inventions and innovations have been developed by small businesses in Canada.

Trends in Society

Canadian society as a whole also exerts pressures on managers because the public is not always willing to accept the actions of business people. Issues such as the accurate reporting of company profits, environmental protection, equal opportunity for women and minorities in management, and inappropriate advertising have brought criticism to business firms at various times. The general public can affect managers through government if a sufficiently large segment of society elects representatives who will support legislation to control certain business activity. In the 1970s and 1980s, for example, public concern about pollutants was expressed so widely that business firms became much more conscious of how their activities could affect air and water quality.

Consumer preferences are another expression of society's wishes. Managers must monitor such preferences, as these trends can directly affect business success. For example, in the 1980s, "yuppies" were concerned with "getting ahead" and spending money on what some might call frivolous goods. In the 1990s, however, there was increased interest in "living lightly," which means focusing on more practical products that would not negatively affect the quality of the environment.

The Importance of International Business

All of the issues discussed in the previous section are important considerations for managers. In the twenty-first century, however, Canadian managers will have to concern themselves not only with the domestic Canadian market, but also with the global market. Globalization, as explained in Chapter 1, is the tendency of firms to extend their sales, ownership, and/or manufacturing to new markets abroad. Globalization of markets is perhaps the most obvious. Bombardier, Sony, Calvin Klein, The Gap, Nike, and Mercedes Benz are some firms that market all over the world. Production is global, too. Toyota produces automobiles in Cambridge, Ontario, while Dell produces computers in China. Globalized markets and production means that globalized ownership increasingly makes more sense.

Globalization is leading to product homogenization around the world. For example, apparel manufacturer Benetton used to offer similar products in all its national markets, but then customize 20 percent of its styles to satisfy specific consumer demand in each country. Recently, it reduced the number of country-specific styles to just 5 percent to 10 percent. More and more, the collections in Toronto look like those in Milan.[6] How does "going global" effect how managers control and manage their operations? We'll look at this and related questions in this chapter.

The Language of International Business

To do business abroad, managers should know the vocabulary of international business. An **international business** is any firm that engages in international trade or investment.[7] International business also refers to those activities, such as exporting goods or transferring employees, that require the movement of resources, goods, services, and skills across national boundaries.[8] **International trade** is the export or import of goods or services to consumers in another country. **International management** is the performance of the management functions of planning, organizing, leading, and controlling across national borders. As Wal-Mart expands abroad, for instance, its managers necessarily engage in international management.

A **multinational corporation** (MNC) operates manufacturing and marketing facilities in two or more countries. Managers of the parent firm, whose owners are mostly in the firm's home country, coordinate the MNC's operations. Firms like Bombardier and Nestlé have long been multinational corporations. However, thousands of small firms are now MNCs, too.

The MNC operates in a number of countries and adjusts its products and practices to each. Sometimes, however, adjusting the global company's behaviour is easier said than done. The MNC's behaviour may still reflect its national roots. For example, when Germany's Deutsche Bank took over a British bank, the high incentive pay of the British managers created tension between them and their new German bosses.[9]

Deutsche Bank
www.db.com

Doing Business Abroad

Companies expand abroad for many different reasons, but sales expansion is most often the goal. Firms like Nortel Networks are moving resources to South America because of the relatively fast growth rate of those economies. Stable beer sales in Canada encouraged Canadian breweries such as Labatt to enter foreign markets. About 24 percent of Labatt's beer sales are outside of Canada, mainly in the United States, and Labatt is continuing to expand into other international markets.[10]

Firms also go international to seek foreign products and services that help reduce their costs. Toronto-based Bata Shoes, the world's largest manufacturer and retailer of footwear, has manufacturing plants in more than 65 countries. Many of these operations are in countries where labour and other costs are low. Sometimes high quality drives firms overseas. U.S.-based Apple Computer enlisted Sony's aid in producing parts for its new notebook computer. Companies can also smooth out sales and profit swings by going abroad. A manufacturer of snow blowers might choose to sell its products in Chile, knowing that as demand for its products drops off in the spring in Canada, it rises in Chile, where the seasons are reversed.

Margin definitions:

international business
Any firm that engages in international trade or investment.

international trade
The export or import of goods or services to consumers in another country.

international management
The performance of the management functions of planning, organizing, leading, and controlling across national borders.

multinational corporation
A firm that operates manufacturing and marketing facilities in two or more countries.

The question is, how should a company "go global"? Options include exporting, licensing, franchising, joint ventures/strategic alliances, and foreign direct investment. A typical progression of increasing global involvement is shown in Figure 2.2. Many factors—including the manager's goals and resources—determine which option is best.

Exporting

Exporting is often a manager's first choice when expanding abroad. **Exporting** is a relatively simple and easy approach. It means selling abroad, either directly to customers, or indirectly through sales agents and distributors.[11] Agents, distributors or other intermediaries handle more than half of all exports. They are generally local people familiar with the market's customs and customers.

Canadian firms are heavily involved in exporting. Abitibi-Consolidated sells newsprint and other forest products around the world, and McCain sells frozen foods. Eicon Technology of Montreal, which designs and manufactures software and hardware for corporate information systems, has won a Canada Export Award several times.[12] Some Canadian firms export more than 80 percent of their products to other countries. Almost 40 percent of all goods and services produced in Canada are exported. Canada currently ranks first among G8 countries in the proportion of its production that is exported. A more broadly based "index of globalization" (made up of measures like economic integration, political engagement, personal contact, and technology) ranks Canada seventh. Ireland ranks first because its generous tax laws encourage foreign investment).[13]

Exporting has pros and cons. It avoids the need to build factories in the host country and is a relatively quick and inexpensive way of "going international."[14] It's also a good way to "test the waters" in the host country and learn more about its customers' needs. However, transportation, tariffs, or manufacturing costs can put the exporter at a disadvantage, as can poorly selected intermediaries. Some avoid this by selling direct. L.L. Bean and Lands' End export globally via their catalogues and the internet.[15] Since the internet is basically borderless, almost any company can market its products or services directly to potential customers abroad.

But exporters can run into big problems, as Canadian lumber companies have discovered. Their difficulties are described in the "Challenge of Change" box.

Licensing

Licensing is an arrangement whereby the licensor (the exporter) grants a foreign firm the right to use intangible (intellectual) property such as patents, copyrights, manufacturing processes, or trade names for a specific period. The licensor usually gets royalties—a percentage of the earnings—in return.[16] Licensing agreements are used when a company does not want to establish a plant or a marketing network in another country. For example, Can-Eng Manufacturing, Canada's largest supplier of industrial furnaces, exports its furnaces under licensing agreements with Japan, Brazil, Germany, Korea, Taiwan, and Mexico.[17]

exporting
Selling abroad, either directly to customers, or indirectly through sales agents and distributors.

Eicon
www.eicon.com

Exporting → Licensing → Franchising → Joint ventures/ strategic alliances → Foreign direct investments

Less involvement   More involvement

FIGURE 2.2
Levels of Global Involvement

Problems in Softwood Lumber Exports

NAFTA Secretariat
www.nafta-
sec-alena.org

Canada and the United States have a long history of arguing about Canadian exports of softwood lumber to the United States, and Canadian lumber has been subject to various tariffs and duties over the past 100 years. This dispute reached a new low in March 2002, when the U.S. Commerce Department imposed a 29 percent duty on softwood lumber exported from Canada to the United States. In August 2001, the Commerce Department had imposed temporary countervailing duties, and in November 2001 added anti-dumping duties ranging from 6 percent to 20 percent.

The final decision by the United States came after months of negotiations between the two countries failed to yield an agreement. After the Commerce Department announcement, Ottawa immediately appealed the decision under the provisions of both the North American Free Trade Agreement (NAFTA) and the World Trade Organization (WTO). In July 2002, the WTO ruled against the United States on eight of nine points in the appeal. That ruling will make it harder for the United States to justify the duties against Canadian lumber, but the process of resolving the dispute will likely take many months.

In the United States, a coalition of U.S. lumber consumers also panned the new duty, saying it would raise the price of an average home by U.S.$1500, and that was not good for the industry or for people who buy homes. The U.S. Commerce Department defended the duty and said that it took the action because Canadian provinces were selling trees very cheaply to Canadian lumber companies, and this allowed the Canadian companies to sell lumber at unreasonably low prices in the United States. This, in turn, harmed U.S. lumber companies that had difficulty competing.

In 1996, Canada agreed to a five-year deal to limit lumber exports to the United States as part of a deal to head off some long-standing problems. The expiry of that deal in 2001 was what set off the current round of negotiations. In an earlier phase of the negotiations, it looked as if a temporary deal might be made that would impose export duties of up to 25 percent on Canadian softwood exported to the United States. The plan was to have the deal remain in place until Canadian provinces began charging more realistic prices for trees that they sold to private Canadian lumber companies.

At the time of the decision, the U.S. housing industry was booming, and higher priced Canadian lumber would depress that market. Eighty-four percent of Canadian lumber is exported to the United States, and Canada supplies nearly one-third of the lumber for the entire U.S. home-building market.

The duty on Canadian lumber was vigorously supported by a U.S. organization called the Coalition for Fair Lumber Imports, which represents the U.S. lumber industry. Canadian negotiators said that the Coalition was more interested in destroying the Canadian lumber industry than it was in reaching a deal on lumber duties. In commenting on the U.S. decision, Prime Minister Chrétien noted with some unhappiness that the United States wants some of our natural resources (like oil and gas), but not others (our lumber). He said that under the principle of free trade they couldn't pick and choose.

British Columbia, which accounts for half of Canada's lumber exports to the United States, was the hardest hit by the new duties. Only hours after the decision was announced, Doman Industries Ltd. announced that it would close two sawmills in British Columbia. Between August 2001 and June 2002, the B.C. lumber business laid off thousands of workers and several sawmills were closed. For the Canadian lumber industry as a whole, the duties could total as much as $3 billion, and up to 30 000 jobs could be lost. For towns like →

Campbell River, B.C., and The Pas, Manitoba, the effect could be overwhelming because a large amount of the economic activity of those towns depends on forestry.

In the wake of the U.S. decision, the Truck Loggers Association in British Columbia asked the Canadian government to give financial assistance to Canadian lumber companies. The money would be used to help them defray the cost of pursuing appeals with the WTO and NAFTA. But the Canadian government was reluctant to give financial assistance, because critics in the United States would claim that further subsidies were being given to the lumber industry.

Licensing arrangements have their pros and cons. For instance, consider a small, underfunded Canadian inventor of a new material for reducing pollution. A licensing agreement with a well-established European environmental products company could allow the Canadian firm to enter the expanding eastern European market without any significant investment. On the downside, the Canadian firm might not be able to control the design, manufacture, or sales of its products as well as it could if it set up its own facilities in Europe. It is also possible that by licensing its knowledge to a foreign firm, the Canadian firm could eventually lose control over its patented property. This is exactly what happened to Creo Products, a Vancouver-based developer and supplier of high-tech equipment for the printing industry. Creo is suing its Japanese partner, Dainippon Screen, which allegedly used its inside knowledge of Creo to develop and launch competing products.[18]

Franchising

If you've eaten in, say, McDonald's by Rome's Spanish Steps, you know that franchising is another way to do business abroad. **Franchising** is the granting of a right by a parent company to another firm to do business in a prescribed manner.[19] Franchising is similar to licensing, since they both involve granting rights to intellectual property. They are both quick and relatively low-cost ways to expand into other countries. However, franchising usually requires both parties to make greater commitments of time and money. A franchisee must generally follow strict guidelines in running the business. It must also make substantial investments in a physical plant (such as a fast-food restaurant). Licensing tends to be limited to manufacturers, while franchising is more common among service firms such as restaurants, hotels, and rental services. Maintaining the franchisee's quality can be a particular problem. For example, an early McDonald's franchisee in France had to close its restaurants when it failed to maintain McDonald's quality standards.

franchising
The granting of a right by a parent company to another firm to do business in a prescribed manner.

Joint Ventures and Strategic Alliances

A **joint venture** is "the participation of two or more companies jointly in an enterprise in which each party contributes assets, owns the entity to some degree, and shares risk."[20] Companies execute joint ventures every day. Vancouver-based Ballard Power Systems, the world leader in the development and commercialization of fuel cell power systems, has teamed with Daimler-Benz and Ford. The big Indian media company, Zee Telefilms, recently formed a series of partnerships with AOL Time Warner. The firms call their new joint venture Zee Turner. It will distribute both partners' television programs in India and neighbouring countries.[21]

A joint venture lets a firm gain useful experience in a foreign country, using the expertise and resources of a locally knowledgeable firm. Joint ventures also help both companies share the cost of starting a new operation. But, as in licensing, the joint venture partners risk giving away proprietary secrets. And joint ventures usually require sharing control.

Joint ventures can be a necessity. In China, foreign companies that want to enter regulated industries (like telecommunications) must use joint ventures with well-connected

joint venture
The participation of two or more companies jointly in an enterprise in which each party contributes assets, owns the entity to some degree, and shares risk.

Ballard Power Systems
www.ballard.com

Chinese partners. The partnership of Britain's Alcatel and Shanghai Bell to make telephone-switching equipment is an example.[22]

strategic alliance
A co-operative agreement between potential or actual competitors.

Strategic alliances are "cooperative agreements between potential or actual competitors."[23] For example, Boeing partnered with several Japanese companies to produce a new commercial jet. Also in the airline industry, the Star Alliance involves nine partners, including Air Canada, Lufthansa, and United. The airlines don't share investments but share seating on some flights, share data banks, and let passengers use alliance members' airport lounges.[24]

Star Alliance
www.staralliance.com

The point of the alliance is usually to quickly gain strengths that would otherwise take time to acquire. General Motors is using alliances to build its Asian presence. It now has minority stakes in several Asian auto manufacturers including Daewoo Motor Co., Suzuki Motor Ltd., Isuzu Motor Ltd., and Fuji Heavy Industries.[25]

Foreign Direct Investment

foreign direct investment
Operations in one country controlled by entities in a foreign country.

At some point, managers find that capitalizing on international opportunities requires substantial, direct investment. Foreign direct investment refers to operations in one country controlled by entities in a foreign country. A foreign firm might build facilities in another country, as Toyota did when it built its plant in Cambridge, Ontario. Or a firm might acquire property or operations, as when Wal-Mart bought control of the Wertkauf stores in Germany. A foreign direct investment turns the firm into a multinational enterprise. Strictly speaking, foreign direct investment means owning more than 50 percent of the operation. But in practice, a firm can gain effective control by owning less than half.

Purchases like these trigger large and small changes. For example, the Italian bank UniCredito Italiano Group purchased Boston's Pioneer Group several years ago. One of the first changes was installing an Italian espresso machine in Pioneer's offices. The Milan bank also installed video cameras and screens. Now investment managers on both sides of the Atlantic can hold videoconferences. Pioneer group managers began learning Italian. And the companies integrated their Italian and U.S. investment teams, which then went on to launch several global funds.[26]

wholly owned subsidiary
A company owned 100 percent by a foreign firm.

A wholly owned subsidiary is one owned 100 percent by a foreign firm. In the United States, Toyota Motor Manufacturing, Inc., and its Georgetown, Kentucky, Camry facility is a wholly owned subsidiary of Japan's Toyota Motor Corporation. Toys "R" Us, Inc. was the first large U.S.-owned discount store in Japan, and it is now expanding its wholly owned subsidiary there.[27] Wholly owned subsidiaries let the company do things exactly as it wants.

The "People Side of Managing" box describes one Canadian company's experience with foreign direct investment.

The Manager's International Environment

Countries differ in terms of their economic, political and legal, and socio-cultural environments. Managers ignore such differences at their peril, since they will shape managers' plans, organization, and controls.

The Economic Environment

Managers doing business abroad need to understand the economic systems of the countries in which they are doing business. This includes the level of each country's economic development, exchange rates, trade barriers, and economic integration.

The Story of McDonald's Canada in Russia

Starting a business in another country can be a huge challenge, as George Cohon, senior chairman of McDonald's Restaurants of Canada Ltd., discovered when he decided to introduce the famous fast food to Russia. In a country known for its communist ideology, the introduction of a restaurant that symbolized Western capitalism was viewed with considerable suspicion.

Negotiations began in 1976 and took 12 years to complete. The first McDonald's outlet finally opened in Moscow in 1990. However, there were several key problems that had to be solved along the way:

- Local processors could not meet McDonald's exacting standards for milk and beef, so the company had to build a huge complex to process the food that serves as the inputs for its restaurants; at the beginning, about one-half of the food items had to be imported.
- Getting inputs to the right place at the right time was a major problem in a country that had one of the worst-run agricultural sectors in the world; at one point, McDonald's workers actually had to go out and harvest potatoes.
- The idea of private enterprise was ridiculed in Russia (one critic said, "The trouble with Russia is that no one ever had a paper route").
- Russian workers had to learn to be consumer-oriented and to be polite to customers; in the beginning, western managers were brought in to provide training and direction to Russian workers.

McDonald's had to face other uncertainties as well. For example, it was not clear whether western-style food would appeal to Russians, or whether they would have enough money to purchase McDonald's hamburgers, fries, and shakes. A Big Mac is priced at $2.80, which doesn't sound like much unless you understand that the average monthly wage of Russian workers is only $200. This is equivalent to asking Canadians to pay about $35 for a Big Mac. In spite of this, demand was high from the start, and McDonald's Canada is now making profits in Russia.

The restaurant in Moscow's Pushkin Square, for example, was an instant success. It now serves about 40 000 customers per day, making it the busiest McDonald's in the world. The restaurant on the Old Arbat is the second-busiest, serving about 20 000 people per day. The three biggest restaurants in Moscow serve as much food as 30 average-sized McDonald's restaurants in North America. Cohon has since expanded operations to other Russian cities, and in 1999 there were 49 McDonald's restaurants operating in Russia.

Most of the problems that were initially encountered have now been solved. In the early days, about 80 percent of the managers were from the west. However, with the right coaching, the Russian staff gained skills and management expertise. Now only a handful of western managers remain. In addition, almost all of McDonald's ingredients are provided by 150 local businesses.

Although there are still problems with high taxes and excessive government red tape, this is a Canadian success story. It proves that opportunities exist in the global economy for Canadians who are willing to take calculated risks, who are persistent, and who are willing to adapt to local cultures and circumstances.

The Economic System Countries differ in the extent to which they adhere to a market-driven, capitalistic economic system like Canada's. For example, Hong Kong is an example of a market economy. In a pure market economy, supply and demand determines what is produced, in what quantities, and at what prices. At the other extreme, the People's Republic of China until recently was a pure command economy. Countries like these base their yearly targets on five-year plans. Then the government establishes specific production goals and prices for each sector of the economy (for each product or group of products), and for each manufacturing plant.

After taking over Hong Kong from Britain several years ago, China agreed to let Hong Kong keep its capitalist system for 50 more years. However, Beijing governs Hong Kong's political administration, and Hong Kong's legislature imposed limits on the activities of opposition political parties. Developing long-run management plans under such circumstances can be challenging.

In a **mixed economy**, some sectors of an economy have private ownership and free market mechanisms, while others are owned and managed by the government.[28] "Mixed" is, of course, a matter of degree. Although France, for example, is basically a capitalist country, it is not purely so because the government owns shares of industries like telecommunications (France Telecom) and air travel (Air France). Canada also has a mixed economy.

Economic systems in transition can trigger social instability. This occurred in Russia during the 1990s. Free-market economies require commercial laws, banking regulations, and effective, independent law enforcement and judiciary, without which business transactions are difficult. Without such a political and legal infrastructure in Russia, business owners had to cope not just with competitors, but with criminals, lax law enforcement, and the control of several industries by friends of powerful politicians. Managers taking their firms into such areas can't just be concerned with the economic system. There's the added challenge of the turbulence as the country moves from a command economy to a capitalist one.

Economic Development Countries also differ in their degree of economic development. Countries such as the Canada, the United States, Japan, Germany, France, and Italy have large, mature economies. They also have extensive industrial infrastructures. This includes telecommunications, transportation, and regulatory and judicial systems. These countries' **gross domestic products (GDP)**—the market value of all goods and services bought for final use during a period—range from about U.S.$1 trillion for Canada to U.S.$7.5 trillion for the United States.[29] Other countries, such as Mexico, are less developed.

Some countries are growing much faster than others. The growth rate of mature economies typically averages 2 percent to 4 percent per year. China, India, and Taiwan are growing at 7.5 percent, 5.0 percent, and 5.2 percent, respectively. Many companies are therefore boosting their investments in these high-growth, high-potential countries.[30]

Exchange Rates Managers engaged in international business must also juggle exchange rates. The **exchange rate** for one country's currency is the rate at which someone can exchange it for another country's currency. During the past 20 years, the value of the Canadian dollar has fluctuated a great deal in relation to the currencies of other countries, particularly the U.S. dollar. In the mid-1970s, the Canadian dollar was worth slightly more than the U.S. dollar, but in the late 1970s it started on a steady downward path. By mid-2002 the Canadian dollar was worth only U.S.$0.64. In 2003, the value of the Canadian dollar increased again to about U.S. $0.74. A drop in the value of the Canadian dollar relative to a foreign currency (say, the British pound) could have a devastating effect on a small Canadian company that suddenly found that it needed 30 percent more dollars to build a factory in Scotland.

Trade Barriers The Gap store in Paris's Passey area sells jeans that you could buy for quite a bit less in Montreal. Why is this? The answer is that trade barriers distort the prices companies must charge for their products. **Trade barriers** are governmental influences aimed at reducing the competitiveness of imported products or services. **Tariffs**, the most common trade barrier, are taxes levied on goods shipped internationally.[31] The exporting country collects export tariffs. Importing countries collect import tariffs. Countries

mixed economy
Some sectors of the economy have private ownership and free market mechanisms, while others are owned and managed by the government.

gross domestic product (GDP)
The market value of all goods and services that have been bought for final use during a period of time, and, therefore, the basic measure of a nation's economic activity.

exchange rate
The rate at which someone can exchange one country's currency for another's.

trade barriers
Governmental influences aimed at reducing the competitiveness of imported products or services.

tariffs
Taxes levied on goods shipped internationally.

through which the goods pass collects transit tariffs. Other countries impose **quotas**— legal restrictions on the import of specific goods.[32]

Non-tariff trade barriers exist too. For example, cars exported to Japan must meet a complex set of regulations and equipment modifications. Side mirrors must snap off easily if they contact a pedestrian, for example. Some countries make payments called **subsidies** to domestic producers in an attempt to make them more competitive. The payment of subsidies (or their equivalent) is a big part of the dispute between Canada and Brazil that was described in the opening case.

Economic Integration and Free Trade Free trade agreements among countries are a big part of the economic situation international managers face. **Free trade** means all trade barriers among participating countries are removed.[33] Free trade occurs when two or more countries agree to allow the free flow of goods and services. This means trade is unimpeded by trade barriers such as tariffs. **Economic integration** occurs when two or more nations obtain the advantages of free trade by minimizing trade restrictions.

Economic integration occurs on several levels. In a free trade area, member countries remove all barriers to trade among them so they can freely trade goods and services among member countries. A **customs union** is the next higher level of economic integration. Here, members dismantle trade barriers among themselves while establishing a common trade policy with respect to non-members. In a **common market**, no barriers to trade exist among members, and a common external trade policy is in force. In addition, factors of production, such as labour, capital, and technology, move freely between member countries, as illustrated in Figure 2.3.

Economic integration is taking place around the world. Back in 1957, the European Economic Community (now called the European Union, or EU) was founded by France, West Germany, Italy, Belgium, the Netherlands, and Luxembourg (see Figure 2.4). They signed the Treaty of Rome, which called for the formation of a free trade area, the gradual elimination of tariffs and other barriers to trade, the formation of a customs union, and (eventually) a common market. By 1987, the renamed European Community had added six other countries (Great Britain, Ireland, Denmark, Greece, Spain, and Portugal) and signed the Single Europe Act. This act envisages a true common market where goods, people, and money move freely among the 12 EC countries.[34] In 1995, Austria, Finland, and Sweden became the 13th, 14th, and 15th members of the EU. Figure 2.5 outlines the organizational structure of the European Union. Poland voted to join the EU in 2003, and more countries are in line for admission.

On January 1, 1999, 11 EU countries formed a European economic and monetary union (EMU). On January 1, 2002, the Union's new currency, the Euro, went into circulation. Within two to three months, it replaced the local currencies in the countries of the EMU.

In 1967, Brunei, Indonesia, Malaysia, the Philippines, Singapore, Thailand, and Vietnam organized the Association of Southeast Asian Nations (ASEAN, Figure 2.6).[35] There is also the Asia Pacific Economic Cooperation (APEC) forum. This is a loose association of 18 Pacific Rim states. Members include Australia, Chile, China, Japan, Malaysia, Mexico, Singapore, and the United States.[36] Africa similarly has several regional trading groups, including the Southern African Development Community (SADC), the Common Market for Eastern and Southern Africa (COMESA), and Economic Community of West African States (ECOWAS).

Canada, the United States, and Mexico established a North American Free Trade Agreement (NAFTA). This is the world's largest free trade market, with a total output of about $6 trillion.

The World Trade Organization (WTO) Governments work together to encourage free trade in other ways.[37] The General Agreement on Tariffs and Trade (GATT) was one example. Formed in 1947 by 23 countries, by the mid-1990s, 117 countries were participating. Among other things, GATT sponsored "rounds" or sessions at which members discussed multilateral reductions in trade barriers. The World Trade Organization (WTO) replaced GATT in 1995 and now has more than 130 members. One of the WTO's important functions is granting "most favoured nation" (or "normal trade relations") status for countries. This means that the WTO countries' "most favorable trade concessions must apply to all trading partners."[38]

quota
A legal restriction on the import of specific goods.

subsidies
A direct payment a county makes to support a domestic producer.

free trade
All trade barriers among participating countries are removed.

economic integration
Two or more nations obtain the advantages of free trade by minimizing trade restrictions.

customs union
Members dismantle trade barriers among themselves while establishing a common trade policy with respect to non-members.

common market
A system in which no barriers to trade exist among members countries, and a common external trade policy is in force that governs trade with non-members; factors of production, such as labour, capital, and technology, move freely among members.

European Union
www.europa.eu.int

Free trade area

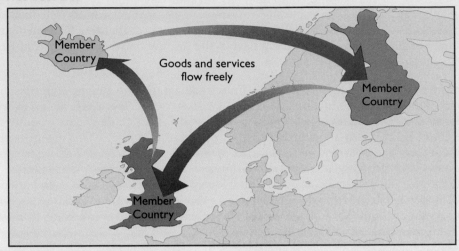

Customs union

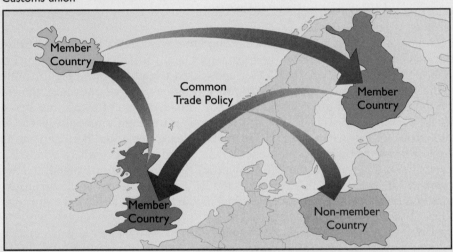

Common market

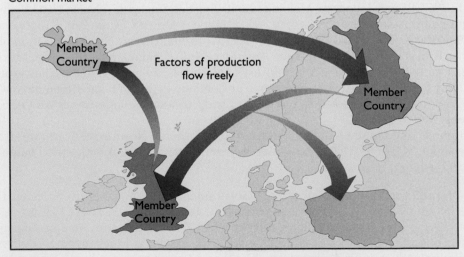

FIGURE 2.3
Levels of Economic Integration

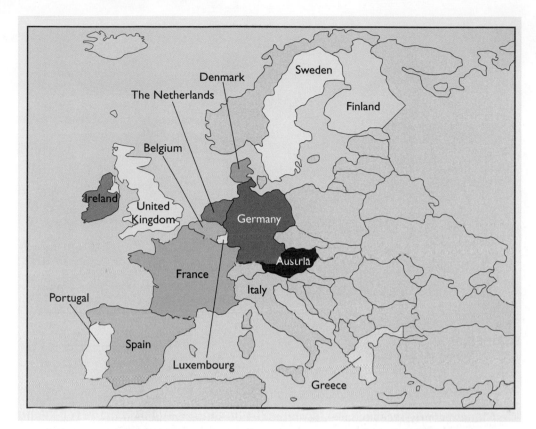

FIGURE 2.4
EU Member Countries as of 2002

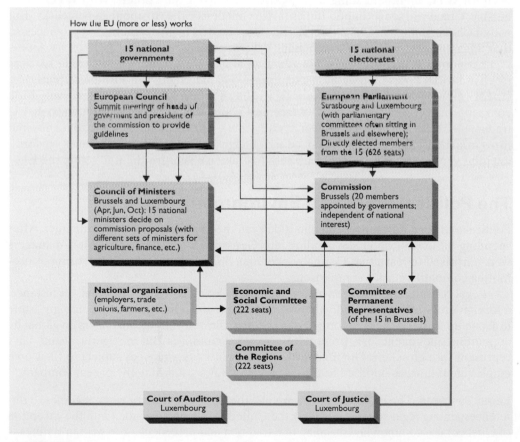

FIGURE 2.5
EU Organizational Structure

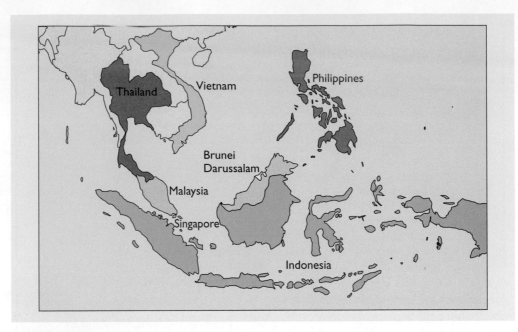

FIGURE 2.6
ASEAN Member Countries

China recently received most favoured nation status and joined the WTO. Joining means that the member nations get the benefits of normal trade relations with WTO partners but also assume the obligation of reducing their own trade barriers. However, even for WTO members, some trade barriers fall faster than others. With WTO membership, China will see its import duties on cars fall drastically (to about 25 percent).[39] But within China, Shanghai still has big "licence fees" on cars from neighbouring provinces, so that Shanghai can protect its locally built Volkswagen.

Economic integration has a big affect on managers. Stripping away trade barriers (such as tariffs) boosts competition and promotes global trade.[40] In Europe, airlines (like British Air) and telecommunications firms (like France Telecom) had relatively little competition 10 years ago. Now they face new competition from firms within their EU trading bloc (like Air France, and DeutcheTelecom). Establishing free trade zones also put firms from non-member countries at a disadvantage. Many Canadian companies are forming joint ventures with European partners, to make it easier for them to sell in the EU.

The Political and Legal Environment

Political and legal differences can blindside even the most sophisticated companies. After spending billions of dollars expanding into Germany, for instance, Wal-Mart managers were surprised to learn that Germany's commercial laws discourage advertising or promoting competitive price comparisons.

Legal considerations influence how managers expand abroad.[41] In India, for instance, a foreign investor may own only up to 40 percent of an Indian industrial company, while in Japan up to 100 percent of foreign ownership is allowed.[42] Some managers go global by appointing sales agents or representatives in other countries. But in Algeria, agents can't represent foreign sellers. Other countries view agents as employees subject to their own employment laws, as opposed to the employment laws governing the parent company.[43]

Legal Systems The examples above are just the tip of the iceberg when it comes to differences among legal systems. England, the United States, and Canada (with the exception of Quebec) use common law, meaning that tradition and precedent—not written statutes—govern legal decisions. Other countries, like France, follow a code law system, or a comprehensive set of written statutes. Some use a combination of common law and code law.

Intellectual property piracy (fake brands) can be a big problem where the legal system is inadequate or inadequately enforced. For example, Procter & Gamble reportedly estimates that about 20 percent of the products with a P&G brand sold in China are fake.[44] The same problem exists elsewhere for other brands. It is not difficult, for example, to go into a retail store in Bangkok and buy a fake Rolex watch.

International law is another factor. International law is a less-enforceable body of law, since it is embodied in treaties and other types of agreements. International law governs things like intellectual property rights, such as whether someone in Japan can reproduce Motown's music without its permission.

Political Systems International managers must be concerned not just with governmental influences on trade, but also with political risks. Sometimes the company's fate can change unexpectedly as the political winds shift in a foreign land. For example, in the mid-1990s, Coca-Cola Co. was very successful with its bottling plant in Uzbekistan. One reason, apparently, was that it opened the plant in partnership with the Uzbekistan president's son-in-law. Recently, when the president's daughter separated from her husband, the bottling company's Uzbec fortunes abruptly took a turn for the worse.[45]

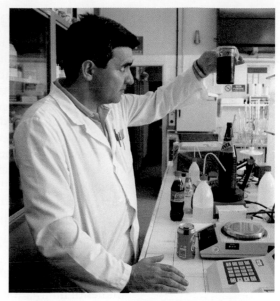

Global management can have special problems. This lab technician at a Coca-Cola plant near Verona in northern Italy tests samples after several European countries banned Coke drinks because youngsters who drank Coke produced at plants that serve Belgium became ill.

Manulife Financial Corp. experienced similar problems in Indonesia. In June 2002, the Jakarta Commercial Court declared Manulife's Indonesian operation bankrupt, even though there was no evidence that Manulife was in financial difficulty. Manulife immediately alleged that members of the Commercial Court had been bribed to make the bankruptcy decision. In July 2002, the Indonesian Supreme Court overturned the lower court's decision, and the Indonesian Justice Ministry recommended the firing of three judges in the Commercial Court.[46]

The Socio-Cultural Environment

People around the world react to situations in different ways. For example, Japanese, German, and U.S. managers tend to take different approaches when resolving workplace conflict.[47] The Japanese prefer the power approach, tending to defer to the party with the most power. Germans tend to emphasize a more legalistic, "sticking to the rules" approach. U.S. managers tend to try to take into account all parties' interests and to work out a solution that maximizes the benefits for everyone.

A country's cultural orientation influences how managers conduct business in that country. When it opened its new production plant in Valenciennes, France, Toyota had to explain to the French Labor Ministry why Toyota banned the traditional red wine at lunchtime in the company cafeteria. (The reasons given were health and working conditions).[48] On the other hand, Starbucks broke some traditions when it opened its first Tokyo store, and now has more than 300 stores in Japan. Starbucks (pronounced "STAH-buks-zu" in Japan) accomplished this by redefining (not adapting to) the way the Japanese drink coffee. Its non-smoking, bright, sofa-filled stores are in marked contrast to the dimly lit, smoke-filled stores where many Japanese traditionally drink their coffee from tiny cups. (It turned out Japanese girls preferred Starbucks' non-smoking stores, and the boys were soon following them there to socialize).[49] We will look more closely at multi-cultural issues in management later in this chapter.

Store manager Ryota Tsunoda, far right, and other employees serve customers at the opening of Starbucks' first overseas store, in Tokyo's Ginza. The Starbucks style redefined how Japanese drink coffee.

The Technological Environment

technology transfer
The transfer, often to another country, of systematic knowledge for the manufacturing of a product, for the application of a process, or for the rendering of a service; it does not extend to the mere sale or lease of goods.

Doing business abroad often involves **technology transfer**, the "transfer of systematic knowledge for the manufacture of a product, for the application of a process, or for the rendering of a service, and does not extend to the mere sale or lease of goods."[50] When Dell builds a computer factory in China, the plant's success depends on Dell successfully transferring to local managers knowledge of its sophisticated manufacturing processes.

Successful technology transfer depends on several things. It depends on having a needed and suitable technology. Social and economic conditions must favour the transfer. For example, pollution-reducing technology might be economically useless in a country where pollution reduction is not a priority. Technology transfer also depends on the willingness and ability of the receiving party to use and adapt the technology.[51] Opening a new plant, or franchising a process, requires an acceptable level of technical expertise in the receiving country. Without it, the expansion may well fail.

Distance and Global Management

Studies of international trade show that economic, political, technological, and social issues are more important than geographic distance in explaining a foreign venture's success. For example, international trade is much more likely among countries that share a common language and that belong to a common regional trading bloc. International trade is much greater among countries that formerly shared a colony-colonizer relationship (as between England and Australia). Similarly, common political systems and a common currency mean less trouble and more trade.

Nevertheless, four types of "distance" are important when a company expands abroad (see Figure 2.7): cultural distance (such as in languages and religions), administrative distance (such as absence of shared monetary or political associations), geographic distance (such as physical remoteness), and economic distance (such as differences in consumer incomes).

When expanding into specific countries, cross-border business initiatives in some industries are thus much more likely to succeed than are others (see Figure 2.8). In the textile industry, for example, geographic distance isn't nearly as important as administrative distance. Preferential trading agreements and tariffs determine whether textiles from one country are saleable in another. If you're a manager in a textile firm, you'd best take preferential trading agreements into account. Similarly, managers at Kellogg's must consider cultural distance when naming and packaging their products.

ATTRIBUTES CREATING DISTANCE			
Cultural Distance	**Administrative Distance**	**Geographic Distance**	**Economic Distance**
Different languages	Absence of colonial ties	Physical remoteness	Differences in consumer incomes
Different ethnicities; lack of connective ethnic or social networks	Absence of shared monetary or political association	Lack of a common border	Differences in costs and quality of
Different religions	Political hostility	Lack of sea or river access	• natural resources
Different social norms	Government policies	Size of country	• financial resources
	Institutional weakness	Weak transportation or communication links	• human resources
		Differences in climates	• infrastructure
			• intermediate inputs
			• information or knowledge

FIGURE 2.7
Determinants of Global Distance

Cultural Distance	Administrative Distance	Geographic Distance	Economic Distance
Linguistic ties	Preferential trading agreement	Physical remoteness	Wealth differences
		MORE SENSITIVE	
Meat and meat preparations	Gold, non-monetary	Electricity current	(economic distance decreases trade)
Cereals and cereal preparations	Electricity current	Gas, natural and manufactured	Non-ferrous metals
Miscellaneous edible products and preparations	Coffee, tea, cocoa, spices	Paper, paperboard	Manufactured fertilizers
Tobacco and tobacco products	Textile fibres	Live animals	Meat and meat preparations
Office machines and automatic data-processing equipment	Sugar, sugar preparations, and honey	Sugar, sugar preparations, and honey	Iron and steel
			Pulp and waste paper
		LESS SENSITIVE	
Photographic apparatuses, optical goods, watches	Gas, natural and manufactured	Pulp and waste paper	(economic distance increases trade)
Road vehicles	Travel goods, handbags	Photographic apparatuses, optical goods, watches	Coffee, tea, cocoa, spices
Cork and wood	Footwear	Telecommunications and sound-recording apparatuses	Animal oils and fats
Metalworking machinery	Sanitary, plumbing, heating, and lighting fixtures	Coffee, tea, cocoa, spices	Office machines and automatic data-processing equipment
Electricity current	Furniture and furniture parts	Gold, non-monetary	Power-generating machinery and equipment
			Photographic apparatuses, optical goods, watches

more sensitive ◄——————————————————————————————————► *less sensitive*

FIGURE 2.8
Industry Sensitivity to Business
The various types of distance affect different industries in different ways.

The Management Team in a Global Business

Globalization is a two-edged sword from the point of view of the manager. On the one hand, it opens up new markets and productive capabilities. On the other hand, the distances involved and factors like those described above complicate marketing, production, and staffing operations abroad.

Global Marketing

Expanding into markets abroad is often a matter of survival. In the late 1990s, Wal-Mart's total company sales rose by 16 percent, but its international sales jumped by 26 percent.[52] About 10 percent—or 135 000—of Wal-Mart's employees are outside the United States. Its website (www.walmart.com) shows how giants like Wal-Mart (and smaller firms, too) can market globally, sometimes without even leaving their home countries.

Yet expanding abroad presents marketing managers with several challenges. For many products (like Bennetton clothes) consumers' preferences in different countries are converging. However, global firms like McDonald's (which emphasize standardized products) must still fine-tune their products when they go abroad.[53] You won't find beef in McDonald's restaurants in India, but you will find sparkling water on sale on the Champs Elysees. Marketing managers expanding abroad therefore can't simply use their domestic marketing and advertising plans. They need local market research and analysis before setting new marketing plans.

Managers must avoid making the mistake of marketing their products in the same way in all countries. Marketing is culture specific, as Vancouver-based Purdy's Chocolates discovered. Already a well-known brand name in western Canada, Purdy's decided to venture into new markets in Taiwan. The company had problems getting the chocolate onto store shelves without it melting in the tropical climate; it also discovered that the rectangular package that is so common for chocolate in Canada was not well received in Taipei.[54]

Global Production

Canon
www.canon.com

Minolta
www.minolta.com

Ricoh
www.ricoh.com

Globalization of production means dispersing components of a firm's production process to locations around the globe. One aim is to support local markets abroad. Another is to capitalize on national differences in the cost and quality of production. It might, for example, be cheaper to produce in Peru than in Alberta.

Sometimes the best strategy is to integrate global production operations into a unified and efficient system of manufacturing facilities around the world.[55] For example, why ship supplies to Spain, when it's possible to support the Spain factory with supplies from the south of France? In the 1980s, each Xerox subsidiary in each country had its own suppliers, assembly plants, and distribution channels. Each country's plant managers gave little thought to how their plans fit with Xerox's global needs. This approach became untenable as Canon, Minolta, and Ricoh penetrated Xerox's Canadian, U.S., and European markets with low-cost copiers.[56]

The competitive threat prompted Xerox's senior managers to coordinate their global production processes. They organized a new central purchasing group to consolidate raw materials purchases and thereby cut worldwide manufacturing costs. They instituted a "leadership through quality" program to improve product quality, streamline and standardize manufacturing processes, and cut costs. Xerox managers also eliminated more than U.S.$1 billion of inventory costs with a computer system that linked customer orders from one region more closely with production capabilities in other regions.

Managing a global production operation is always a challenge, but the internet can help. Schlumberger Ltd., which manufactures oil-drilling equipment and electronics, has headquarters in New York and Paris but operates in 85 different countries. In most of those countries, the firm's employees are in remote locations. The company uses the internet so that engineers in, say, Dubai (on the Persian Gulf) can check email and stay in close contact with the head office at a very low cost. In addition, the field staff is able to follow research projects as easily as can personnel at the head office. Since it converted to the internet, overall communications costs have declined despite a major increase in network and information technology infrastructure spending. The main reason for the savings is the dramatic drop in voice traffic and in overnight delivery service charges (they attach complete documents to their email messages).[57]

Global Staffing

Doing business abroad also triggers global staffing issues. Setting up factories abroad requires studying employment laws in the host country, establishing a recruiting office, and ensuring the firm complies with local staffing regulations. Global staffing is very important today.[58] As we saw in the Opening Case, Bombardier has thousands of employees in Mexico. 3M produces tapes, chemicals, and electrical parts in Bangalore, India, and Hewlett-Packard assembles computers and designs memory boards in Guadalajara, Mexico.

Even the smallest expansion abroad requires a global staffing outlook. For example, sending the company's sales manager abroad for several months to close a deal means deciding how to compensate her for her expenses abroad, what to do with her house in Canada, and how to make sure she knows how to handle the cultural demands of her foreign assignment. Companies use special programs to identify and evaluate potential global managers.[59] One program at Motorola Inc. involves putting management candidates through two to three days of realistic role-playing exercises under the watchful eyes of trained psychologists. As one participant writes, "...the telephone calls, unexpected visitors and urgent tasks come so fast and furious that I quickly forget it is only a game."[60] French food firm Danone reduced the failure rate of the managers it sent to foreign countries from 35 percent to 3 percent in three years using a similar program.[61]

The Global Manager

Not everyone is competent to manage in a global arena. For one thing, global managers tend to be cosmopolitan in how they view people and the world. Webster's dictionary defines cosmopolitan as "belonging to the world; not limited to just one part of the political, social, commercial or intellectual spheres; free from local, provincial or national ideas, prejudices or attachments."[62] Global managers must be comfortable anywhere in the world, and being cosmopolitan helps them to be so.

How can you tell if you're cosmopolitan? Cosmopolitan people are sensitive to what is expected of them in any context and have the flexibility to deal intelligently and in an unbiased way with people and situations from other cultures. You needn't have travelled extensively abroad or be multilingual to be cosmopolitan, although such experiences help. The important thing is to learn about other people's perspectives and consider them in your own decisions.[63]

In addition to being cosmopolitan, global managers also have what some experts call a global brain. That means they are flexible enough to accept that, at times, their own ways of doing business are not the best. For example, Volkswagen formed a partnership with Škoda, a Czech car-maker. VW trained Škoda's managers in western management techniques. However, it followed Škoda's suggestions about how to conduct business in the Czech Republic.[64] Being willing to apply the best solutions from different systems is what experts mean by having a global brain.

Volkswagen
www.vw.com

Would Your Company Choose You as an International Executive?

What do companies look for in their international executives? One study focused on 838 lower-, middle- and senior-level managers from 6 international firms in 21 countries. The researchers studied the extent to which personal characteristics such as "sensitivity to cultural differences" could distinguish between managers who had high potential as international executives and those who didn't. Fourteen personal characteristics successfully distinguished those identified by their companies as having high potential from those identified as lower performing.

To get an initial impression of how you would rate, look at Table 2.1, which lists the 14 characteristics with sample items. For each, indicate (by placing a number in the space provided) whether you strongly agree (number 7), strongly disagree (number 1), or fall somewhere in between. The higher you score, the more likely you would have scored highly as a potential global executive in this study.[65]

Planning, Organizing, and Controlling in a Global Environment

Managing globally also complicates the management process. International management means carrying out the four management functions—planning, organizing, leading, and controlling—on an international scale.

Planning in a Global Environment

Planning means setting goals and identifying the courses of action for achieving those goals. Global planning involves dealing with some unique issues such as, "How should we balance (1) the need to provide customized products to each country in which we do business, with (2) the need to maintain standardized products worldwide so as to exploit economies of scale?"

TABLE 2.1 *Characteristics of More Successful International Managers*

SCALE	SCORE	SAMPLE ITEM
Sensitive to cultural differences		When working with people from other cultures, works hard to understand their perspectives.
Business knowledge		Has a solid understanding of our products and services.
Courage to take a stand		Is willing to take a stand on issues.
Brings out the best in people		Has a special talent for dealing with people.
Acts with integrity		Can be depended on to tell the truth, regardless of circumstances.
Is insightful		Is good at identifying the most important part of a complex problem or issue.
Is committed to success		Clearly demonstrates commitment to seeing the organization succeed.
Takes risks		Takes personal as well as business risks.
Uses feedback		Has changed as a result of feedback.
Is culturally adventurous		Enjoys the challenge of working in countries other than his or her own.
Seeks opportunities to learn		Takes advantage of opportunities to do new things.
Is open to criticism*		Appears brittle, as if criticism might cause him or her to break.
Seeks feedback		Pursues feedback even when others are reluctant to give it.
Is flexible		Doesn't get so invested in things that he or she cannot change when something doesn't work.

*Reverse scored, so 1 is "strongly agree" for this item.

Global Strategic Planning Answering the question posed above requires choosing a global strategy. Strategic planning (see Chapter 7) involves defining the mission of the business and laying out the broad strategies or courses of action the firm will use to achieve that mission. There are three basic global strategies. One is the **global integration strategy**, which means taking a centralized, integrated view of where to design and produce the company's product or service. The emphasis here is on producing, say, a standardized "world car" as efficiently as possible. The company then fine-tunes this standard car for slight differences in national tastes. The organization structure delegates less decision-making authority to local managers. Global integration assumes that market similarities and the need to be efficient are more important than the differences among the markets.

At the other extreme, the manager may decide that the differences among markets are too great to risk a standardized approach. So, the manager may choose to pursue a **host country focus strategy**. Each market here needs its own autonomous subsidiary. The managers in each country are relatively free to adapt their products or services to local tastes as they see fit. The multinational company's headquarters provides overall coordination and perhaps tries to minimize unnecessary product duplication among country subsidiaries. Some food companies, like Kellogg's, take this approach.

Many global managers try to get the best of both global strategy worlds, so they pursue a **hybrid international strategy**. Here, the manager tries to blend the efficiencies that come from integrating global production with the ability to provide each country with

global integration strategy
Taking a centralized, integrated view of where to design and produce the company's product or service.

host country focus strategy
The company gives each market its own autonomous subsidiary with headquarters providing overall coordination.

hybrid international strategy
Blending the efficiencies that come from integrating global production with the ability to provide each country with specialized products or services.

specialized products or services. The trick is to minimize excessive duplication among country units and to maximize the firm's ability to quickly transfer product innovations from one locale to another.

ABB Group Ltd. takes this hybrid approach. Local ABB units have great autonomy; however, ABB also uses the internet and information technology to make sure good ideas get fast approval and distribution. For example, if several engineers in France develop a good idea for a new process, they post their idea, with appropriate keywords, on ABB's intranet using a special template. The ABB system amounts to a private bulletin board. ABB managers and engineers worldwide use the intranet to instantaneously broadcast new ideas throughout ABB. That way, they minimize the amount of time they waste "reinventing the wheel."[66]

Figure 2.9 helps managers decide whether a global integration, host country focus, or hybrid strategy is best. For example, where the forces for local responsiveness are weak and the forces for global integration are strong, global integration is best. All countries here get more-or-less undifferentiated products. Industries fitting here include construction and mining machinery, and industrial chemicals. At the other extreme (where the forces for integration are weak and the forces for local responsiveness strong) host country focus is best. The beverages, food, and household appliances industries are examples here.

Global Feasibility Planning In general, "domestic and international strategic processes are very similar, differing only in the specifics."[67] The planning tools covered in Chapters 6 and 7 are thus quite applicable for global planning. The main difference is that companies going abroad must conduct particularly thorough feasibility studies. The reason is obvious and stems from what we discussed above. International planners must contend with a multitude of political, legal, cultural, and technological issues. Furthermore, collecting information internationally—about demographics, production levels, and so on—can be difficult, and the data are often questionable.[68]

For example, French retailer Carrefour (Wal-Mart's chief worldwide rival) conducts careful feasibility studies before entering new markets. It avoids entering developing markets—such as Russia—that don't have reliable legal systems.[69] Even in more traditional markets Carrefour won't proceed without at least a year's worth of on-site research. Carrefour doesn't make many mistakes when they enter a new market. In China, for instance, "Carrefour takes care to chop vegetables vertically—not laterally—so as not to bring bad luck to superstitious shoppers."[70]

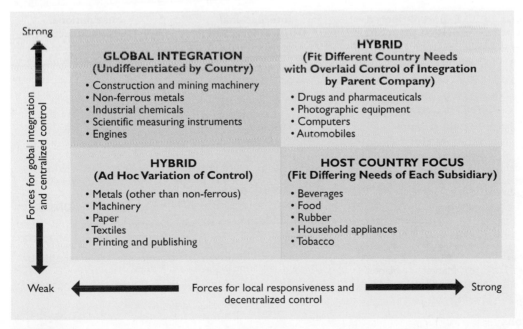

FIGURE 2.9
Environmental Influences and Global Strategy

With much less experience in the international arena, Wal-Mart's first expansions abroad did not go so smoothly. When it first opened stores in Argentina, its hardware departments offered tools and appliances wired for 110 volts, even though Argentina uses 220 volts. Similarly, Wal-Mart had to learn by trial and error that Argentine customers were in the habit of shopping at a store each day. The greater traffic meant that aisles always seemed overcrowded and floors always seemed dirty.[71] Wal-Mart adapted by making the aisles wider and installing scuff-proof floors.

Because Wal-Mart is so large, it had the resources to use trial and error instead of detailed feasibility planning and not get ruined in the process. A smaller firm runs the risk of depleting its cash and having to quickly close down.[72]

Organizing in a Global Environment

Figure 2.10 presents the typical options for organizing an international business.[73] In a *traditional* organization, each division handles its own foreign sales. In response to increasing orders from abroad, the firm may move to an *export-oriented* structure. Here, one department (often called an import-export department) coordinates all international activities such as licensing, contracting, and managing foreign sales.

In an *international* organization, management splits the company into domestic and international divisions. The international division focuses on production and sales overseas, while the domestic division focuses on domestic markets. Reynolds Metals, for instance, has six worldwide businesses, each with a U.S.-focused group and a separate international group.[74] In a *multinational* organization, each country where the firm does business has its own subsidiary. The oil firm Royal Dutch Shell is organized this way. It has separate subsidiaries for Shell Switzerland and Shell Canada (as well as many other countries).[75]

Factors That Influence Global Organization Design The organizational principles covered in Chapters 8 and 9 apply to international and domestic organizations. However, the global manager does have to address some unique issues when deciding what type of structure to choose.[76] Global strategy is one. As we'll see in Chapter 7, structure follows strategy. For example, a host country focus strategy suggests having separate subsidiaries for each locale. A global integration strategy suggests more emphasis on centralizing functions (such as product design and manufacturing) under a single manager.[77]

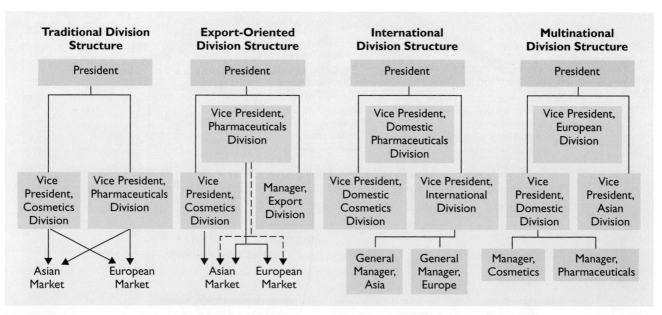

FIGURE 2.10
International Organizations
As firms evolve from domestic to multinational enterprises, their increasingly international operations necessitate a more globally oriented organization.

The company's history and its stage of internationalization will also influence how it organizes its international efforts. Thus, a company at the earliest stages of internationalization (or with few globally qualified managers) will more likely opt for running its international operations out of a headquarters "import-export" or "international" department. It's unlikely to begin its first, tentative forays into exporting abroad by reorganizing as a full-blown multinational organization. As the firm adds more foreign subsidiaries, it is more likely to move toward the multinational structure.

Top management philosophy is another factor. Some managers are more globally oriented, while some are more local (ethnocentric) in their philosophical outlooks. The manager who believes "my country's ways are best" is less likely to delegate much authority to remote local managers. Geographic distance is another consideration. Managing activities that may be thousands of kilometres away is no easy matter. The manager will have to make sure that remote operations do not slip out of control.

Controlling in a Global Environment

Several years ago, Coca-Cola had a rude surprise: Several European countries made it take its beverages off store shelves. Coke has high standards for product quality and integrity, but controlling what's happening at every plant worldwide is a challenge. Chemicals had seeped into the beverages at one of Coke's European plants.

As we'll see in Chapter 16, control means monitoring actual performance to ensure it is consistent with the standards that were set. This is hard enough when the people you're controlling are next door, but when people are thousands of kilometres apart, it can get very difficult. The other "distances" (cultural and legal, for instance) complicate it even more. The global manager has to carefully address two things: What to control, and how to control it.

Deciding What to Control Given the geographic distances involved, the global manager has to take great care in choosing the activities that will be controlled. The manager could, of course, try to micromanage everything, from hiring and firing to product design, sales campaigns, and cash management. However, too much control can smother the subsidiary. In practice, the local manager's autonomy is least for financial and capital decisions, and most for personnel decisions.[78] Production and marketing decisions tend to fall the middle. In one study of 109 Canadian, U.S., and European multinational corporations, "these firms exercised stricter financial control, and allowed greater local freedom for labor, political, and business decisions. Also, the home office of these multinational corporations made the decisions to introduce new products and to establish R & D facilities."[79]

Deciding How to Maintain Control Two things characterize the methods global managers use to maintain control. One is the use of computerized information systems. For many years Kelly Services, Inc. let its offices in each country operate with their own individual billing and accounts receivable systems. However, according to Kelly's chief technology officer, "we are consolidating our operations in all countries and subsidiaries under a standard [information system].... All our customers expect us to deliver consistent practices, metrics, and measurement. Establishing global standards is an important part of meeting and exceeding that expectation."[80]

The second characteristic is the emphasis on self-control and employee commitment. Global managers do use financial and operating reports, visits to subsidiaries, and management performance evaluations to help control their international operations.[81] However, supervisory surveillance is limited when thousands of kilometres separate boss and subordinate. Furthermore (as covered in Chapter 16), formal reports, rules, and regulations are not hard to evade. Particularly in global companies, there's wisdom in making sure employees want to do what is right and that they know what's "right" in terms of the company's values and goals.

In other words, global companies have to make sure their managers buy into "the way we do things around here."[82] These companies do this in many ways, including job rotation from country to country; multi-country management development programs; informal company sponsored events; and using teams from different countries to work on cross-border projects.

Leading and Motivating in a Multicultural Environment

Many managers are less adept at appreciating cultural differences than they think they are. When transferred abroad, they blunder into simply treating the people "there" the same as the people "here."[83] This problem is caused by the "universality assumption" of motivation, which assumes that human needs are universal.[84] U.S. researchers did much of the research on human needs and motivation, using U.S. employees. The problem is that those theories and findings don't always apply to people in other countries.

For U.S. (and perhaps Canadian) managers, the problem may exist because they don't have the same multicultural experience as people living in, say, Europe (where travel between countries is a way of life). A Chinese believing in Confucianism's emphasis on respect and obedience may react differently to autocratic leadership than would the typical Canadian. One of the biggest mistakes the international manager can make is to fail to see that "to understand why people do what they do, we have to understand the cultural constructs by which they interpret the world."[85]

values
Basic beliefs we hold about what is good or bad, important or unimportant.

Values One way people around the world differ is in terms of their values. **Values are basic beliefs we hold about what is good or bad, important or unimportant**. Values are important because they shape the way we behave. Geert Hofstede studied managers around the world and found that societies' values differ in several ways:

- *Power distance.*[86] Power distance is the extent to which the less powerful members of institutions accept and expect that power will be distributed unequally.[87] Hofstede concluded that acceptance of such inequality was higher in some countries (such as Mexico) than it was in others (such as Sweden).

- *Individualism versus collectivism.* In individualistic countries like Australia and the United States, "all members are expected to look after themselves and their immediate families."[88] In collectivist countries like Indonesia and Pakistan, society expects people to care for each other more.

- *Masculinity versus femininity.* According to Hofstede, societies differ also in the extent to which they value assertiveness (which he called "masculinity") or caring ("femininity"). Japan and Austria ranked high in masculinity, while Denmark and Chile ranked lower.

- *Uncertainty avoidance.* Uncertainty avoidance refers to whether people in the society are uncomfortable with unstructured situations in which unknown, surprising, or novel incidents occur. People in some countries (such as Sweden, Israel, and Great Britain) are relatively comfortable dealing with uncertainty and surprises. People living in other countries (including Greece and Portugal) tend to be uncertainty avoiders.[89]

Leadership in a Multicultural Environment Cultural realities like these can dramatically alter the usefulness of theories like those covered in Chapter 11 (Leadership). Consider the large differences Hofstede found in the "power distance" (inequality) that people in different cultures will tolerate.[90] Figure 2.11 lists countries with large and small power distance rankings.

Cultural differences like these have important implications for how leadership theories work abroad (or, at least, how the manager applies them). Thus, in societies where large power distances (inequalities) are an accepted way of life, participative leadership could backfire. "For example, if a superior, in a 'large power distance society' attempts to reduce the distance by acting more accessible and friendly, his or her subordinates may not willingly accept such openness."[91]

The evidence tends to support this argument. For example, studies suggest that managers in some countries (including Indonesia, Malaysia, Thailand, Turkey, and the Philippines) prefer using autocratic leadership; those in Hong Kong are less autocratic.[92]

Large	Argentina
	Brazil
	Belgium
	Chile
	Colombia
	France
	Greece
	Hong Kong
	India
	Iran
	Italy
	Japan
	Mexico
	Pakistan
	Peru
	Philippines
	Portugal
	Singapore
	Spain
	Taiwan
	Thailand
	Turkey
	Venezuela
	Yugoslavia
Power distance	
	Australia
	Austria
	Canada
	Denmark
	Finland
	Germany
	Great Britain
	Ireland
	Israel
	The Netherlands
	New Zealand
	Norway
	Sweden
Small	Switzerland
	United States

FIGURE 2.11
Country Clusters Based on Power Distance

Table 2.2 similarly suggests that leaders in some countries (including Spain, Portugal, and Greece) tend to delegate less authority than do leaders in countries like Sweden, Japan, Norway, and the United States.

Motivation in a Multicultural Environment Many of the motivation theories covered in Chapter 12 (Motivation) make implicit assumptions about peoples' needs. For example, the Maslow needs hierarchy assumes that peoples' needs form a five-step hierarchy (from basic physiological needs up to safety, belonging/affiliation, achievement, and self-actualization needs). But can the global manager assume that this is always the order in which needs motivate behaviour?

Not always. Maslow's theory emphasizes the supremacy of "self," for instance, of satisfying one's own basic needs, and of being "all you can be" (self-actualization). In other societies, peoples' needs don't necessarily revolve around "self" as much as around

TABLE 2.2　*Comparative Leadership Dimensions: Participation*

EXTENT TO WHICH LEADERS DELEGATE AUTHORITY
0 = LOW; 100 = HIGH

Sweden	75.51	Germany	60.85
Japan	69.27	New Zealand	60.54
Norway	68.50	Ireland	59.53
United States	66.23	United Kingdom	58.95
Singapore	65.37	Belgium/Luxembourg	54.55
Denmark	64.65	Austria	54.29
Canada	64.38	France	53.62
Finland	62.92	Italy	46.80
Switzerland	62.20	Spain	44.31
The Netherlands	61.33	Portugal	42.56
Australia	61.22	Greece	37.95

"social relationships." One researcher concluded that we would have to rearrange the Maslow needs hierarchy to use it in China. Social needs would come first, then physiological, then safety, and then, finally self-actualization—but, not to be "all you can be," but "to serve society."[93]

Another popular motivation theory emphasizes the importance of "the need to achieve" in motivating behaviour. Yet, an attempt by the creator of this theory to extend it to workers in India failed.[94] Similarly, "money is not an incentive everywhere—it may be accepted gladly, but will not automatically improve performance. Honor, dignity and family may be much more important. Imposing the Canadian merit system may be an outrageous blow to a respected and established seniority system."[95] Managers thus have to apply motivation theories abroad with a great deal of care.

Communications in a Multicultural Environment　Cultural differences influence communication in both obvious and subtle ways. Language barriers provide one obvious problem. A Canadian manager negotiating a deal in England can generally make himself or herself (fairly well) understood using English but might need an interpreter in France. Even where the other party speaks some English, problems can arise. For example, using a colloquialism (such as "you bet it is") may be indecipherable to the person with whom you're speaking. Furthermore, as GM discovered to its dismay, words that sound or look the same may have different meanings in different countries. Naming a car "Nova" (which means "won't go" in Spanish) is not a good idea. There are many other (often humorous) examples of how language barriers can cause problems. One airline's "Fly in Leather" slogan proved embarrassing when it translated as "Fly Naked" for the company's Latin American campaign.[96]

The problem is not just the words. As we explain in Chapter 13 (Communications), as much as 90 percent of what people "hear" isn't verbal. It is non-verbal and conveyed via facial expressions and signs and motions of one sort or another. Here is where the novice international manager can really get into trouble. Table 2.3 shows what some typical non-verbal behaviours mean in various countries. It's subtle differences like these that can make international management an adventure!

TABLE 2.3 Implications of Various Non-verbal Behaviours in Different Cultures

NON-VERBAL BEHAVIOUR	REGION	MEANING
Thumbs up	North America	A gesture of approval/OK/good job!
	Middle East	A gesture of insult
	Japan	A sign indicating "male"
	Germany	A sign for count of "one"
A finger circulating next to the ear	Argentina	A telephone
	North America	That is crazy!
A raised arm and waggling hand	North America	Goodbye
	India, South America	Beckoning
	Much of Europe	A signal for "no"
Showing the back of the hand in a V-sign	England	A rude sign
	Greece, Middle East	A sign for count of "two"
Showing a circle formed with index finger and thumb	North America	Very good!
	Turkey	Insult gesture/accusation of homosexuality
Eye contact, gazing	North America	A sign of attentiveness
	Japan	A rude behaviour/invasion of privacy
	Most Asian countries	Sign of disrespect to senior people
Widening eye	North America	An indication of surprise
	Chinese	An indication of anger
	Hispanic	Request for help
	French	Issuance of challenge
Nodding the head up and down	Western countries	A sign for agreement/yes
	Greece, Bulgaria	A sign for disagreement/no

SKILLS AND STUDY MATERIAL

SUMMARY

1. Companies can pursue several strategies when it comes to extending operations to foreign markets. Exporting is the route often chosen by manufacturers; licensing and franchising are also popular alternatives. At some point, a firm may decide to invest funds in another country. Joint ventures and wholly owned subsidiaries are two examples of foreign direct investment.

2. An international business is any firm that engages in international trade or investment. Firms are globalizing for many reasons, the three most common being to expand sales, to acquire resources, and to diversify sources of sales and supplies. Other reasons for pursuing international business include reducing costs or improving quality by seeking products and services produced in foreign countries and smoothing out sales and profit swings.

3. Free trade means that all barriers to trade among countries participating in an agreement are removed. Its potential benefits have prompted many nations to enter into various levels of economic integration, ranging from a free trade area to a common market.

4. Globalizing production means placing parts of a firm's production process in various locations around the globe. The aim is to take advantage of national differences in the cost and quality of production and then integrate these operations in a unified system of manufacturing facilities around the world. Companies also

are tapping new supplies of skilled labour in various countries. The globalization of markets, production, and labour coincides with the rise of a new type of global manager, who can function effectively anywhere in the world.

5. International managers must be able to assess a wide array of environmental factors. For example, managers must be familiar with the economic systems, exchange rates, and the level of economic development in the countries where they do business. They must be aware of import restrictions, political risks, and legal differences and restraints. Important cultural differences also affect the way people in various countries act and expect to be treated. Values, languages, and customs are examples of elements that distinguish people of one culture from those of another. The relative ease with which technology can be transferred from one country to another is an important consideration in conducting international business.

CRITICAL THINKING EXERCISES

1. Someone has said that the Mediterranean is the sea of the past, the Atlantic is the sea of the present, and the Pacific is the sea of the future. What do you think this means? Is the Pacific Rim the leading market for goods and services in the twenty-first century? Write your own version of this prediction, looking ahead to the year 3000.

2. As we look around the globe, there seems to be war or conflict on most continents. Africa continues to have internal warfare. Poverty is rampant, and disease is a major concern. Russia seems at times to be falling apart. The United Kingdom and France are boycotting each other's meat and other products. In Asia, Pakistan and India are at odds on a regular basis. Indonesia has been at odds with itself and the people of East Timor. Taiwan and China regularly exchange heated words. The United States and Canada are squabbling about duties on softwood lumber. These are just some of the world problems that are evident. How will these difficulties affect future global investment and business opportunities? How would you prepare for these problems if you wanted to expand your business abroad?

EXPERIENTIAL EXERCISES

1. You have just accepted an assignment in Russia as a marketing representative. Your company is involved in the development of biotech farming techniques and is located in Ottawa's high-tech community—where progressive agricultural techniques and a sense of social responsibility are industry trademarks. You have a week to prepare to go to St. Petersburg and then on to Moscow. Where would you begin? What impact would the political turmoil in Russia and its relationships with the former members of the USSR have on your decision? How would you go about studying the social customs? What goals would you set for yourself in terms of learning the language? How would you prepare yourself to enter the new world of Russia? What specific information would you try to get from recent immigrants from Russia? What might reading about Russia's history tell you about how to conduct business meetings there?

2. Spend several minutes using what you learned in this chapter to list 10 reasons "Why I would (or would not) be a good global manager."

3. India and China are home to approximately two-fifths of the world population. China is still a communist country, but it is developing an entrepreneurial and capitalistic economy. India is a democratic country, influenced by religion and other ancient values. In teams of four to five students, research each country's history and current situation and then answer the following questions: (a) How does religion (mainly Confucianism in China and Hinduism in India) affect managerial thinking? (b) How do you think these countries' ancient history and religions affect their respective approaches to business and the global marketplace? (c) What political issues in these regions would make them potential risks for Canadian investment?

The Context of Culture

GOAL

To help students appreciate how high-context and low-context cultures influence global business communication. Low-context cultures use explicit written and verbal messages to communicate in business and other situations. Written agreements and written messages are important. High-context cultures communicate through both explicit messages and implicit context. Interpersonal relationships, and a high level of formality and etiquette, will affect the success of the communication.

METHOD

Step 1:

A continuum of world cultures as defined by anthropologist Edward T. Hall is shown below. Use this information to develop a strategy for conducting meetings with business people in Switzerland and Japan.

Step 2:

Working in groups of four or five students, answer the following questions for each country: What should you do before you arrive in the country to increase your chance of success? If your meeting time is 1:00 p.m. on Tuesday, when should you arrive to get the best results from your meeting? What title and position should you or another member of your team hold to achieve your business goals? How would your business style and the pace of your conversation differ in each country?

Follow-up Questions

1. *Culture shock*—the inability to adapt to foreign cultures—is a problem that many Canadian business people face when they work abroad. Based on this exercise, why do you think this is a problem?

2. How can management training seminars reduce *ethnocentrism*—the tendency to judge the cultures of foreign countries by Canadian standards?

3. Japan, Arab countries, and Latin American countries are high-context cultures. Do these countries share cultural patterns? How would you adapt your business style from country to country?

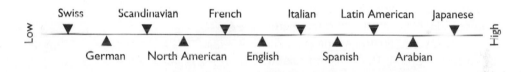

INTERNET EXERCISES

Many of today's Canadian managers can expect that their companies will not only manufacture and sell their goods in overseas markets, but will also utilize talent and resources wherever they can be found. Cultural differences affect the way people in various countries act and expect to be treated.

1. Access **www.worldbiz.com** and **www.businessculture.com**. What information do these websites provide that would help Canadian managers be successful in international business?

2. Conduct an internet search. Locate and select four publications that you consider to be important reading for Canadian managers doing business in Oman, Portugal, China, and Brazil. Explain why you chose the publications.

3. How might the Canadian Chamber of Commerce (**www.chamber.ca/newpages/aboutintnl.html**) and the Canadian Council for International Business (**www.ccib.org**) assist a Canadian manager manufacturing and selling goods in overseas markets, and hiring freelancers in foreign countries to work seamlessly with Canadian personnel via the internet?

Partnering with a German Media Giant

When Barnes & Noble was exploring ways to become more competitive in its battle with Amazon.com, there were hundreds of companies to which it could turn. Research clearly demonstrated that the cultural differences that characterize cross-border ventures made them far more complicated than domestic ones. Yet Barnes & Noble surprised competitors when it chose to form its internet joint venture with the German media giant Bertelsmann. Was Barnes & Noble mistaken to look abroad for a partner?

Bertelsmann is best known among college students for its record label and music club, BMG (both now owned by Universal), and for its "buy one, get 10 free" CD offers. With U.S.$3.9 billion in sales and nearly 65 000 employees, Bertelsmann is much more than a CD club. Its holdings include Random House, the world's largest English-language book publisher, and Offset Paperback, a firm that manufactures millions of copies of paperback books each year. Bertelsmann had also actively pursued ecommerce on its own. By the late 1990s, Bertelsmann had quietly staked out a position as the world's third-largest internet business.

To fund barnesandnoble.com, the two firms created a separate company and floated an initial public offering (IPO) to raise capital. The offering raised U.S.$421 million for the new venture, after commis-

sions and expenses, making it the largest ecommerce offering in history at that time. Since launching its on-line business in May 1997, barnesandnoble.com has become one of the world's largest ecommerce retailers. The company has successfully capitalized on the recognized brand value of the Barnes & Noble name to become the second-largest on-line retailer of books.

Questions

1. What may have motivated Barnes & Noble to partner with the German firm Bertelsmann?

2. In general terms, what advantages would Barnes & Noble gain by having an international partner?

3. With all its experience in ecommerce, why would BMG not just set up its own competitor to Amazon.com?

4. What are a few of the planning, organizing, leading, and controlling issues Barnes & Noble's managers faced in joining forces with Bertelsmann?

Barnes & Noble
www.barnesandnoble.com

Bertelsmann
www.bertelsmann.com

Ford's Response to Global Changes

Jacques Nassar, former CEO of Ford Motor Co., spearheaded a number of major initiatives aimed at making Ford more competitive globally. For example, Ford acquired the Volvo car business from AB Volvo for U.S.$6.45 billion. Ford was also considering a subtle but profound change in its strategy: The company was beginning to articulate a vision that did not include final assembly of its vehicles as a core competence.

Chairman William Clay Ford, Jr., described Ford's twenty-first-century vision as becoming the world's

leading consumer company that provides automotive products and services. Nassar was thinking of taking that vision a step further. He was considering outsourcing the final assembly of Ford cars—in other words, letting other companies actually assemble their cars.

At the same time, Ford had radically internationalized its operations. In addition to its acquisition of Volvo, Ford had acquired Aston-Martin and Jaguar. The Ford brand was already immensely popular in Europe. →

Fifty-five leading motoring journalists in Europe had selected Ford's new Focus as the 1999 European Car of the Year. However, in its manufacturing operations worldwide, Ford had continued its practice of performing the final assembly on all its autos and light trucks.

Ford had a long and proud history of manufacturing. In the early 1970s the Michigan Rouge Plant was Ford Motor Company's testament to large-scale manufacturing. Starting with iron ore and sand, the company manufactured its own steel and glass. Completed autos rolled off the assembly line, comprising almost entirely Ford-made parts. But over the decades, the business environment in which Ford operated changed dramatically. Competition in the industry became progressively more global and auto companies actively sought parts sources and assembly operations around the globe. In the tumultuous 1980s, Ford became the best-selling car in Europe, while Nissan, Honda, and Toyota captured the U.S. market.

Throughout the 1990s, Ford continued to assemble its own cars with parts from worldwide sources. In late 1999, however, Nassar signalled a potential major change in Ford's manufacturing practices. Beginning with its plant in Northeast Brazil, Ford was considering having its equipment manufacturers and parts suppliers perform vital parts of the final assembly of its cars. Under the plan, Ford would pay only for the units produced. If the Bahia Brazil plant was successful, Ford would begin outsourcing final assembly worldwide. In essence, Ford would signal that auto assembly was not one of its core activities.

Ford would not be the first auto maker to move in this direction. DaimlerChrysler and Volkswagen have already introduced similar plans.

Questions

1. What motivated Ford to become a more global manufacturing operation?

2. If Ford no longer considers assembling cars as part of its core business, on what activities should management focus its attention?

3. Why would this "outsource assembly" decision likely be made only at the highest levels of the Ford organization?

4. What specific global management problems would you see Ford encountering if it decides to let other firms assemble its cars around the world?

Ford
www.ford.com

Managing JetBlue in a Global Environment

JetBlue's route structure is basically domestic (i.e., U.S.), but that doesn't mean it can ignore its global environment. For one thing, its heavy flight schedule from New York already means that it is also advantageous to fly out of the continental United States—to Puerto Rico. On May 30, 2002, JetBlue, therefore, added three daily JFK–San Juan nonstop flights. Neeleman says that he has no plans to expand to Europe but that Canada, the Caribbean, and Mexico are possibilities sometime in the future.[97]

Furthermore, JetBlue President Barger says he would sign international code-share arrangements (which would make it easier for JetBlue's domestic passengers to switch seamlessly to flights abroad on another airline), if doing so didn't interfere with JetBlue's need for quick turnarounds. (For example, having to change JetBlue's flight schedules in such a way that they had to spend more time on the ground waiting for incoming passengers from abroad might mean longer turnaround time—and, therefore, higher costs for Jetblue.)[98]

It's not just the global aspects of its route structure that are important to JetBlue's management, but the global nature of aircraft purchases and leasing as well. Neeleman's original plan (given the U.S.$130 million or more in start-up capital) was to go directly to Airbus or Boeing to buy his firm's first aircraft. However, it turned out that neither Airbus nor Boeing could deliver all the planes the new start-up needed in the years 2000 and 2001. JetBlue therefore had to lease six Airbus A320s from a company called International Lease Finance Corp. and two more from Singapore Aircraft Leasing Enterprise. Then as JetBlue expanded (and in keeping with its desire to maintain a homogeneous fleet so that all mechanics and flight crews could more easily switch from aircraft to aircraft), JetBlue placed an order with the European aircraft manufacturer Airbus for an additional 10 A320s (the planes list for about U.S.$54 million each, but they typically sell for

less). Based on its expected needs through 2005, JetBlue will therefore end up ordering about 74 of the A320s from Europe's Airbus rather than aircraft from America's Boeing. Neeleman and his team felt that the Airbus 320 best fit their needs, given JetBlue's route structure and the Airbus's economies of operation and emphasis on technology.

Assignment

You and your team are consultants to Mr. Neeleman, who is depending on your management expertise to help navigate the launch and management of JetBlue. Here's what he wants to know from you:

1. Other start-up airlines (not JetBlue) have made the mistake of expanding abroad too soon. Make a list of five erroneous assumptions you believe these airlines' managers made in expanding abroad.

2. Neeleman says he is only interested in expanding into Mexico, Canada, or the Caribbean in the foreseeable future. Tell him why JetBlue is (or is not) a suitable candidate for expanding into each of these three areas, based on the cultural, administrative, geographic, and economic distance between that country and the U.S.

3. List the reasons why you think Neeleman might (or might not) be a good global manager.

4. Assuming JetBlue decides to expand outside the United States, briefly specify the basic global strategy the company should pursue, and why.

5. Draw an organization chart showing the basic global organization structure JetBlue should use if it begins flying to Canada, Mexico, and the Caribbean in addition to its current domestic U.S. flights.

6. What are the *non-economic* pros and cons to a company like JetBlue in placing such a large order with a foreign rather than with a domestic supplier?

Ethics, Social Responsibility, and Diversity

The Latest Flap at Cinar Corp.

Cinar Corp. produces children's shows like *Arthur*, *Caillou*, *The Adventures of Paddington Bear*, and *Wimzie's House*. The driving force behind the company had always been Micheline Charest and Ronald Weinberg, who tirelessly promoted their company to the media and to financial markets. But in March 2000, they both resigned as co-chief executives of the company amid allegations that (1) more than $100 million had been invested without proper approval from Cinar's board of directors; (2) Cinar had fraudulently obtained Canadian tax credits by putting the names of Canadians on television scripts actually written by Americans; and (3) Cinar had breached securities rules with its financial statements and other disclosure documents. All of this upheaval caused the company's stock to drop sharply in value, and Cinar was eventually delisted from both NASDAQ and the Toronto Stock Exchange. Although they are no longer executives or board members at Cinar, the two continue to hold 63 percent of the voting stock of the company.

No charges were laid in the tax fraud area, but in 2002 Charest and Weinberg were eventually fined $1 million each by the Quebec Securities Commission (QSC). They were also required to resign from the board of directors and were banned from holding directorships or voting for directors of publicly held companies in Canada.

It was originally thought that the QSC ruling would prevent Charest and Weinberg from influencing who would be appointed to Cinar's board of directors. But the QSC settlement allowed them to appoint a trustee who could nominate or vote for directors, and at Cinar's annual shareholders meeting in April 2002, trustee Robert Despres used his new-found voting clout to install directors he wanted instead of the company's proposed slate. Despres claimed that he did not represent former co-CEO's Charest and Weinberg, and was simply interested in getting a board of directors in place that would move the company forward and increase shareholder value.

The chair of Cinar's board at that meeting was Lawrence Yelin. He and CEO Barrie Usher were under fire from various people

OBJECTIVES

After studying this chapter and the case exercises at the end, you should be able to use the material to:

1. Describe the factors that influence ethics in the workplace.

2. Identify both ethical and unethical decisions.

3. Rate your own ethics level.

4. Assess and quantify the ethical culture of an organization.

5. Design a specific plan for improving ethical behaviour in a company.

6. Specify the steps a manager should take to change a company's ethical culture.

7. Design a specific diversity management plan.

because they were unsuccessful in their attempts to sell Cinar in 2001. Yelin said that it was well known that Charest and Weinberg wanted to replace the entire existing board at Cinar. Charest and Weinberg also had several disagreements with Usher about the strategy that Cinar should pursue. Despres admitted that Charest and Weinberg had suggested some names for the new board.

When problems originally arose at Cinar, Richard Finlay, chairman of the Centre for Corporate and Public Governance, offered the view that Cinar's top management and board structure were rather peculiar and likely contributed to Cinar's difficulties. The husband-wife team of Charest and Weinberg functioned as co-CEO's, one acting as president and the other chairing the board to which both reported. The corporate governance guidelines of the Toronto Stock Exchange call for a non-executive and independent director as chair of the board.

In terms of the difficulties of Cinar, Finlay thinks that the QSC failed to do its job properly because it allowed the people who were responsible for the company's troubles (Charest and Weinberg) to orchestrate its new governance regime.

What Is Ethical Behaviour?

If you are skilled at carrying out the management functions of planning, organizing, leading, and controlling, but you cannot exercise good ethical judgment, both you and your company will likely fail. Therefore, let's make sure we understand some basics about ethical behaviour.

People face ethical dilemmas every day. You might have encountered this one: Your best friend sits next to you in a large class. She has already missed several classes because she was busy doing other things, and she can't afford to miss any more sessions because attendance counts so much in the final grade. She just called to ask that you sign the class roll for her tomorrow. You know that she does have a real family emergency this time. There are 190 students in the hall, so the chance the professor will catch you is virtually zero. Should you help your best friend by signing the roll sheet for her? How can you decide?

The Meaning of Ethics

ethics
The principles of conduct governing an individual or a group.

normative judgment
A judgment that implies that something is good or bad, right or wrong, better or worse.

morality
A society's accepted norms of behaviour.

Ethics refers to "the principles of conduct governing an individual or a group"[1] and specifically to the standards you use to decide what your conduct should be. Ethical decisions always involve normative judgments.[2] A **normative judgment** implies that "something is good or bad, right or wrong, better or worse."[3] "You are wearing a skirt and blouse" is a non-normative statement; "That's a great outfit!" is a normative one.

Ethical decisions also always involve **morality**, which is society's accepted standards of behaviour. Moral standards differ from other standards in several ways.[4] They address matters of serious consequence to society's well-being, such as murder, lying, and slander. They cannot be established or changed by decisions of authoritative bodies like legislatures,[5] and they should override self-interest. Many people believe that moral judgments are never situational. They argue that something that is morally right (or wrong) in one situation is right (or wrong) in another. Moral judgments tend to trigger strong emotions. Violating moral standards may make you feel ashamed or remorseful.[6]

It would simplify things if it were always clear which decisions were ethical and which were not. Unfortunately, it is not. Ethics—principles of conduct—are rooted in morality, so in many cases it's clear what is ethical. For example, if the decision makes the person feel ashamed or remorseful, or it involves a matter of serious consequence such as murder, then chances are it's unethical. On the other hand, in some areas bribery is so widely ingrained that people don't view it as wrong. In that context, bribery may simply be how people get things done.

Good and Evil

People have asked, "what is good and what is evil?" since the beginning of time.[7] To some philosophers, the question of what is good and what is evil does not vary from situation to situation. Religious codes like the Ten Commandments reflect this absolute view. The Ten Commandments lay out what is right and what is wrong irrespective of the situation, "at all times and in all places."[8] The Greek philosopher Socrates believed in such principles. People, he said, should pursue what is good and what is true regardless of the consequences (and he was put to death as a result).

At the other extreme, some people believe that "both good and evil are relative to the conditions of the time and place, and that which is good in one place and time will be evil in another."[9] For example, most people would agree that telling the truth is good. But if a person who intends to cause harm asks you where his potential victim has gone, would telling him the truth be a good thing? Perhaps not.[10] Similarly, is it wrong to lie when doing so might help your employer to survive (and which, incidentally, might help you keep your job)?

Philosophers have names for these two points of view. A *teleologist* evaluates good or evil and right or wrong based on the consequences or results of the proposed actions. A *deontologist* (like Socrates) evaluates whether actions are good or bad, right or wrong, based on "whether or not they conform to certain principles you feel bound to obey or follow regardless of their consequences."[11] Various other positions fall between these two extremes. For example, *utilitarianism* also links right and wrong to consequences. Utilitarians believe that people should make decisions that result in the greatest total utility, that is, decisions that achieve the greatest benefit for all those affected by a decision.[12] Table 3.1 summarizes the main moral philosophies.

These points of view sometimes lead to different moral decisions. For example, consider this situation:

> You are a railroad switch operator sitting in a watchtower controlling a switch that allows trains to travel over the regular track or switches them to a siding. One morning you face a terrible dilemma. A train is travelling at high speed on the main track, and a school bus filled with 50 children has stalled on the main track. The bus driver is trying to restart the engine, but it is clear to you that the bus will not get off the track in time. On the siding track is a homeless man who has fallen down and gotten his foot caught under the rail. It's clear that he is also stuck. In 15 seconds, you must

TABLE 3.1	*A Comparison of Several Moral Philosophies*
Teleology	Stipulates that acts are morally right or acceptable if they produce some desired result, such as the realization of self-interest or utility.
Egoism	Defines right or acceptable actions as those that maximize a particular person's self-interest as defined by the individual.
Utilitarianism	Defines right or acceptable actions as those that maximize total utility, or the greatest good for the greatest number of people.
Deontology	Focuses on the preservation of individual rights and on the intentions associated with a particular behaviour rather than on its consequences.
Relativist	Evaluates ethicalness subjectively on the basis of individual and group experiences.
Virtue ethics	Assumes that what is moral in a given situation is not only what conventional morality requires, but also what the mature person with a "good" moral character would deem appropriate.

decide whether to use the switch to send the train to the siding—thereby killing the homeless man—or to do nothing and allow the train to take its normal course and thereby hit the bus and probably kill most of the schoolchildren on board.

How would each ethical theory approach the situation described above? What would you do?[13]

Ethics and the Law

One ethicist suggests viewing your ethical options as a continuum, as in Figure 3.1.

The "selfish egoists" basically say, "might makes right." These people make their decisions based on what they think they can get away with.[14] To stop (or at least slow down) these people, countries make laws. In competing with other companies, some managers voluntarily follow the law, although some powerful selfish egoists may still try to flaunt it.[15]

Other managers and professionals voluntarily adhere to the (usually) more exacting professional standards of their professions or professional associations. For example, the professional association of executive recruiters has rules regarding how long a recruiter should wait before approaching a manager that he or she placed about a new position.

Finally, there is the person who makes his or her decisions based on the highest standard of all—integrity. "The person of integrity stands as the most admired of all who value the standards of the profession. This person accepts the constraints and limitations of the profession—and more."[16]

What Influences Ethical Behaviour at Work?

Research shows that ethical (or unethical) behaviour isn't caused by any single factor. One review of the research concluded that it's not just the employee's ethics that must be considered, since even ethical employees can have their decisions influenced by *organizational* factors.[17] The *environment* is important, too. In several laboratory studies, researchers concluded that unethical behaviour was more prevalent in competitive environments and in situations in which the company rewarded such behaviour.[18] Other research similarly suggests that "ethical decisions are the result of the interaction of the person and the situation."[19] Ethical or unethical decisions are a function of the person, the company, and the pressures of the situation.

Individual Factors

Personal predispositions are certainly an important factor in ethics at work, because people bring to their jobs their own ideas of what is morally right and wrong. The individual must therefore shoulder much of the credit (or blame) for the ethical decisions he or she makes. A survey of CEOs of manufacturing firms was conducted to explain the CEOs' intentions to engage (or to not engage) in two questionable business practices: soliciting a competitor's technological secrets and making payments to foreign government officials to secure business. The researchers concluded that the CEOs' personal predispositions more strongly affected their decisions than environmental pressures or organizational characteristics.[20]

X	**Y**	**Z**	**Z+**
Selfish egoism standard	Legal standard	Professional practice standard	Integrity standard

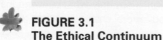

FIGURE 3.1
The Ethical Continuum

It's hard to generalize about the characteristics of ethical or unethical people, but age is clearly a factor. One study of 421 employees measured the degree to which age, gender, marital status, education, dependent children, region of the country, and years in business influenced responses to ethical decisions. (Decisions included "doing personal business on company time, not reporting others' violations of company rules and policies," and "calling in sick to take a day off for personal use.") In general, older workers had stricter interpretations of ethical standards and made more ethical decisions than younger employees. Other characteristics had no effect. Others have also found this ethical generation gap.[21]

CMA Canada surveyed accounting students and asked them to judge the acceptability of 14 business ethics scenarios. Students were asked whether things like charging higher prices in poorer areas, using cheap foreign labour, and selling unsafe products overseas were acceptable practices. Female students typically viewed the scenarios as less acceptable than did male students, and older students were more critical of questionable behaviour than were younger students.[22]

CMA Canada
www.cma-canada.org

Keep in mind that people tend to have a distorted view of how ethical they really are.[23] It's therefore easy to be lulled into a false sense of security regarding the ethics of one's actions. How would you rate your own ethics? Figure 3.2 presents a short self-assessment survey to help you answer that question.

Organizational Factors

If people did unethical things at work because of a desire for personal gain, it would be understandable (though inexcusable). The scary thing about unethical behaviour at work is that it's usually not driven by personal interests. Table 3.2 summarizes the results of one survey of the principal causes of ethical compromises, as reported by six levels of employees and managers. It's apparent that characteristics of the organization and how it's managed also influence the level of ethics.

As you can see, dealing with scheduling pressures was the number one factor in ethical lapses. For most of these employees, "meeting overly aggressive financial or business objectives" and "helping the company survive" were the other top two causes.

TABLE 3.2 *Principal Causes of Ethical Compromises*						
	SENIOR MGMT.	**MIDDLE MGMT.**	**FRONT LINE SUPV.**	**PROF. NON-MGMT.**	**ADMIN. SALARIED**	**HOURLY**
Meeting schedule pressure	1	1	1	1	1	1
Meeting overly aggressive financial or business objectives	3	2	2	2	2	2
Helping the company survive	2	3	4	4	3	4
Advancing the career interests of my boss	5	4	3	3	4	5
Feeling peer pressure	7	7	5	6	5	3
Resisting competitive threats	4	5	6	5	6	7
Saving jobs	9	6	7	7	7	6
Advancing my own career or financial interests	8	9	9	8	9	8
Other	6	8	8	9	8	9
Note: 1 is high, 9 is low						

Indicate your level of agreement with these 15 statements using the following scale:

   1 = Strongly disagree

   2 = Disagree

   3 = Neither agree or disagree

   4 = Agree

   5 = Strongly agree

1. The only moral of business is making money.	1	2	3	4	5
2. A person who is doing well in business does not have to worry about moral problems.	1	2	3	4	5
3. Act according to the law, and you can't go wrong morally.	1	2	3	4	5
4. Ethics in business is basically an adjustment between expectations and the ways people behave.	1	2	3	4	5
5. Business decisions involve a realistic economic attitude and not a moral philosophy.	1	2	3	4	5
6. "Business ethics" is a concept for public relations only.	1	2	3	4	5
7. Competitiveness and profitability are important values	1	2	3	4	5
8. Conditions of a free economy will best serve the needs of society. Limiting competition can only hurt society and actually violates basic natural laws.	1	2	3	4	5
9. As a consumer when making an auto insurance claim, I try to get as much as possible regardless of the extent of the damage.	1	2	3	4	5
10. While shopping at the supermarket, it is appropriate to switch price tags on packages.	1	2	3	4	5
11. As an employee, I can take home office supplies; it doesn't hurt anyone.	1	2	3	4	5
12. I view sick days as vacation days that I deserve.	1	2	3	4	5
13. Employees' wages should be determined according to the laws of supply and demand.	1	2	3	4	5
14. The business world has its own rules.	1	2	3	4	5
15. A good business person is a successful business person.	1	2	3	4	5

ANALYSIS AND INTERPRETATION

Rather than specify "right" answers, this instrument works best when you compare your answer to those of others. With that in mind, here are mean responses from a group of 243 management students. How did your responses compare?

1. 3.09	6. 2.88	11. 1.58
2. 1.88	7. 3.62	12. 2.31
3. 2.54	8. 3.79	13. 3.36
4. 3.41	9. 3.44	14. 3.79
5. 3.88	10. 1.33	15. 3.38

FIGURE 3.2
How Do My Ethics Rate?

"Advancing my own career or financial interests" ranked toward the bottom of the list. Thus (at least in this case), most ethical lapses occurred because employees were under pressure to do what they thought was best to help their companies. Several years ago, for example, three former CUC International executives pleaded guilty to charges of accounting fraud. The former executives said they had done so to keep the price of the company stock high.[24]

The process is insidious, and feeds on itself. As the famous investor Warren Buffett puts it, "once a company moves earnings from one period to another, operating shortfalls that occurred thereafter require it to engage in further accounting manoeuvres that must be even more 'heroic.' These can turn fudging into fraud."[25] It's this kind of evolution that may have finally tripped up Enron. As one article said at the time, "to meet the outside world's unrealistic expectations, it began to fudge the figures. To disguise liabilities, it wrapped them up in private partnerships and took them off its balance sheet. And to satisfy the wishful thinkers' insatiable demand, it brought earnings forward by selling shares and other off-balance sheet partnerships, and counting the proceeds as revenues."[26]

In 2001, Enron was one of the largest companies in the world, and Arthur Andersen was one of the world's "big five" accounting firms. One year later, Enron was in bankruptcy, and Andersen, under indictment, was fighting to stay alive. Both firms had very good managers, but that didn't do them any good. In violation of its own ethical policies, Enron let some executives set up special "off the books" partnerships. Enron then allegedly used these to hide costs and puff up revenues. Andersen, its auditor, had controls in place that questioned this dubious accounting. However, Andersen shunted off the partners that did the questioning to other jobs, apparently to help keep Enron as a client.

Having rules on the books forbidding this sort of thing does not, by itself, seem to work. For example, in 2002, charges were filed against Merrill Lynch, alleging that several of its analysts had issued optimistic ratings on stocks, while privately expressing concerns about those same stocks. The allegation was that they did so to aid and support Merrill Lynch's investment banking relationships with these companies.

Department of National
Defence
www.dnd.ca

Ethical problems do not just occur in for-profit organizations. In December 1998, allegations surfaced that members of the International Olympic Committee had received more than $1 million in improper gifts for awarding the 2002 Winter Games to Salt Lake City, Utah. A report written by Richard Pound of Montreal said that at least 16 members of the IOC had taken money illegally.[27] In 1999, Canada's Defence Department admitted that medical files of some Canadian soldiers who had served as peacekeepers in Bosnia had been tampered with, when a letter warning of potential exposure to toxic waste was removed from their files.[28]

Canadian athletes, like Mark Tewkesbury, protested against members of the International Olympic Committee after allegations surfaced that members of the IOC had received large amounts of money and gifts to influence them to pick Salt Lake City, Utah, as the site of the 2002 Winter Games.

The Influence of Top Management

Top managers (and bosses in general) react to ethical crises in different ways. When he discovered that his company was spying on Unilever, Procter & Gamble Chairman John Pepper was reportedly shocked. He ordered the campaign to stop, and he fired the managers responsible for hiring the spies. Then, he "blew the whistle" on his own company. He had P&G inform Unilever of what his firm had done. Unilever, among other things, demanded that Procter & Gamble retain a third-party auditor to make sure it does not take advantage of the documents its spies stole from Unilever's trash bins.[29]

Compare this behaviour with that at Enron. Even after an Enron vice president warned him that Enron might be an "elaborate accounting hoax," Chairman Kenneth Lay allegedly went on-line to urge the company's employees to buy Enron shares.[30]

The leader's actions may be "the single most important factor in fostering corporate behaviour of a high ethical standard."[31] The boss sets the tone for the company, and by his or her actions sends signals about what is right or wrong. A study by the American Society of Chartered Life Underwriters found that 56 percent of all workers felt some pressure to act unethically or illegally and that the problem seems to be getting worse.[32] One writer gives these examples of how supervisors knowingly (or unknowingly) lead subordinates astray ethically:

■ Tell staffers to do whatever is necessary to achieve results
■ Overload top performers to ensure that work gets done
■ Look the other way when wrongdoing occurs
■ Take credit for others' work or shift blame[33]

Ethics Policies and Codes

An ethics policy and code is one way to signal that the firm is serious about ethics.[34] For example, IBM's code of ethics has this to say about tips, gifts, and entertainment:

> No IBM employee, or any member of his or her immediate family, can accept gratuities or gifts of money from a supplier, customer, or anyone in a business relationship. Nor can they accept the gift or consideration that could be perceived as having been offered because of the business relationship. "Perceived" simply means this: if you read about it in the local newspaper, would you wonder whether the gift just might have had something to do with a business relationship? No IBM employee can give money or a gift of significant value to a customer, supplier, or anyone if it could reasonably be viewed as being done to gain a business advantage.[35]

**Canada Deposit
Insurance Corp.
www.cdic.ca**

A survey by KPMG found that two-thirds of Canada's largest corporations have codes of ethics (90 percent of U.S. firms do). The Canada Deposit Insurance Corp., for example, requires that all deposit-taking institutions have a code of conduct that is periodically reviewed and ratified by the board of directors. The Canadian Competition Bureau, the Canadian Institute of Chartered Accountants, and the Ontario Human Rights Commission all have pushed for the adoption of codes of ethics by corporations.[36]

In July 2002, the Canadian Council of Chief Executives (formerly called the Business Council on National Issues) proposed a public corporate code of conduct that was designed to prevent scandals like those at Enron from happening in Canada. Compliance with the code is voluntary.[37]

Sometimes ethics codes work, and sometimes they don't. Enron's ethical principles were widely available on the company's website. They said, among other things that "as a partner in the communities in which we operate, Enron believes it has a responsibility to conduct itself according to certain basic principles." Those values include "respect, integrity, communication and excellence."[38] In general, though, an ethical code sends a strong signal to the company's employees. One study based on structured interviews with 766 employees over a two-year period led to the following conclusions.[39]

First, "the existence of a corporate code of ethics affected both employees' ethical behavior and the perception of ethics in several ways. Respondents who worked for companies having a code of ethics judged subordinates, co-workers, themselves and especially supervisors and top managers to be more ethical than respondents employed in organizations not having a formal code of ethics. Employees in companies with an ethics code also gave higher ratings of the company's support for ethical behavior, reported higher levels of satisfaction with outcomes of ethical dilemmas, more frequently reported being encouraged to behave ethically, and felt somewhat less pressure to behave unethically than respondents from companies without an ethics code."[40]

Second, it seemed to be the mere presence of the code (rather than its content) that influenced the employees. "In fact, we found that although most respondents could not recall specific features of their company's ethics code, employees of companies having a code had very different perceptions of ethical climate and behavior than employees of companies lacking a code." Therefore, the important function of the code may be communicating the importance of appropriate behaviour, rather than educating employees about what specifically constitutes ethical behaviour.[41]

Managers around the world work with a wide range of ethical standards. Transparency International, an organization devoted to stamping out global corruption, has developed a Bribe Payers Index (BPI) that shows the likelihood that companies from various countries will pay bribes in order to get business. The 2002 BPI shows that companies from China, Taiwan, and Russia are most likely to pay bribes, while companies from Australia, Switzerland, and Canada are least likely to pay bribes.[42] As more Canadian companies do business abroad, they are finding themselves competing against companies from other countries that are not so reluctant to pay bribes in order to get business. As a result, Canadian companies risk losing business to these foreign companies.[43]

Transparency International has also developed a Corruption Perceptions Index that shows the degree of perceived corruption among public officials in various countries. Corruption is defined as the abuse of public office for private gain. The countries perceived as most corrupt are Paraguay, Nigeria, and Bangladesh.[44] The three least corrupt countries are perceived to be Finland, Denmark, and New Zealand (Canada ranks seventh). Bribery is an important element in this index as well, specifically bribe-taking by public officials. Bribery is most common in developing countries because government officials in those countries are poorly paid. In an attempt to create fairer competition among multinational companies, ministers from 29 member countries of the Organisation for Economic Co-operation and Development (OECD) agreed in 1997 to criminalize bribery of foreign public officials.[45]

Some executives are also pushing for a global corporate ethics standard under the auspices of the International Standards Organization (ISO). The ISO now provides quality (ISO 9000) and environmental (ISO 14000) standards. "We want a simple, effective way to operate internationally—one that meets all the criteria of doing business overseas, whether it's proving assurance of quality or ethical business practices," says one executive.[46] ISO ethical standards would provide a detailed list of criteria companies have to meet to prove that they do business ethically, including procedures to ensure compliance.

In spite of these initiatives, corruption and the solicitation of bribes are still the price of doing business in various countries around the world. In Albania, for instance, it's been estimated that businesses pay out bribes equal to about 8 percent of their sales (about one-third of their potential profits) as a cost of doing business.[47] In India, where many patients too poor to see doctors rely on their pharmacist for medical advice and drugs, a pharmacy owner was proud of the 29-inch colour television he received as a gift from the pharmacy company GlaxoSmithKline PLC. This particular pharmacist ordered 600 vials of one antibiotic, and 100 boxes of another—many times what he would normally order—apparently because he wanted the television.[48]

International Standards Organization (ISO)
www.iso.ch

How to Foster Ethics at Work

We've seen that there's no single cause of unethical behaviour at work, so it is not surprising that there's no simple way to prevent it. Instead, managers must take several steps to ensure ethical behaviour by their employees.[49] These include recruiting and selecting individuals who have predispositions or work histories that make them less likely to engage in unethical practices. They can also train employees to recognize ethical dilemmas and how to resolve them. And they can develop formal codes of ethical conduct and enforce them.

Activities That Foster Ethics

Researchers conclude that fostering ethics involves the managerial activities discussed next.

› **Emphasize Top Management's Commitment** Top management must be openly and strongly committed to ethical conduct, and they must constantly reinforce the values of the organization.[50]

- **Publish an Ethics Code** Firms with effective ethics programs set forth principles of conduct for the whole organization in the form of written documents.[51] Figure 3.3 summarizes six steps for effectively implementing an ethics code.

  Some firms urge employees to apply a quick "ethics test" to evaluate whether what they're about to do fits the company's code of conduct. For example, the Raytheon Co. tells employees who are faced with ethical dilemmas to ask the following questions:

  - Is the action legal?
  - Is it right?
  - Who will be affected?
  - Does it fit Raytheon's values?
  - How will it "feel" afterwards?
  - How would it look in the newspaper?
  - Will it reflect poorly on the company?[52]

- **Establish Compliance Mechanisms** Attention needs to be paid to values and ethics in recruiting and hiring, emphasizing corporate ethics in training, instituting communications programs to inform and motivate employees, and auditing to ensure compliance.[53]

- **Involve Personnel at All Levels** This can be achieved by, for example, using roundtable discussions among small groups of employees regarding corporate ethics, and surveying employee attitudes regarding the state of ethics in the firm.[54]

- **Train Employees** Training plays an important role in publicizing a company's ethical values and policies. For example, based on one survey, 89 percent of surveyed ethics officials said their companies use the new hire orientation to convey ethics codes, and 45 percent use annual refresher training. Other findings of this survey are shown in Figure 3.4.

- **Measure Results** One study of effective ethics programs found that all 11 firms used surveys or audits to monitor compliance with ethical standards.[55] The results of audits should then be discussed among board members and employees.[56] Many firms use technology to keep tabs on ethical results. We'll turn to this next.

Using Technology to Foster Ethics

Technology has been a double-edged sword for employee ethics. On the one hand, the internet may have caused a rise in the time employees spend on personal pursuits during

---

SIX STEPS TO EFFECTIVE IMPLEMENTATION OF A CODE OF ETHICS

1. Distribute the code of ethics comprehensively to employees, subsidiaries, and associated companies.

2. Assist employees in interpreting and understanding the application and intent of the code.

3. Specify management's role in the implementation of the code.

4. Inform employees of their responsibility to understand the code, and provide them with the overall objectives of the code.

5. Establish grievance procedures.

6. Provide a conclusion or closing statement, such as this one from Cadbury Schweppes:

   The character of the company is collectively in our hands. Pride in what we do is important, and let us earn that pride by the way we put the beliefs set out here into action.

FIGURE 3.3
Code of Ethics Implementation

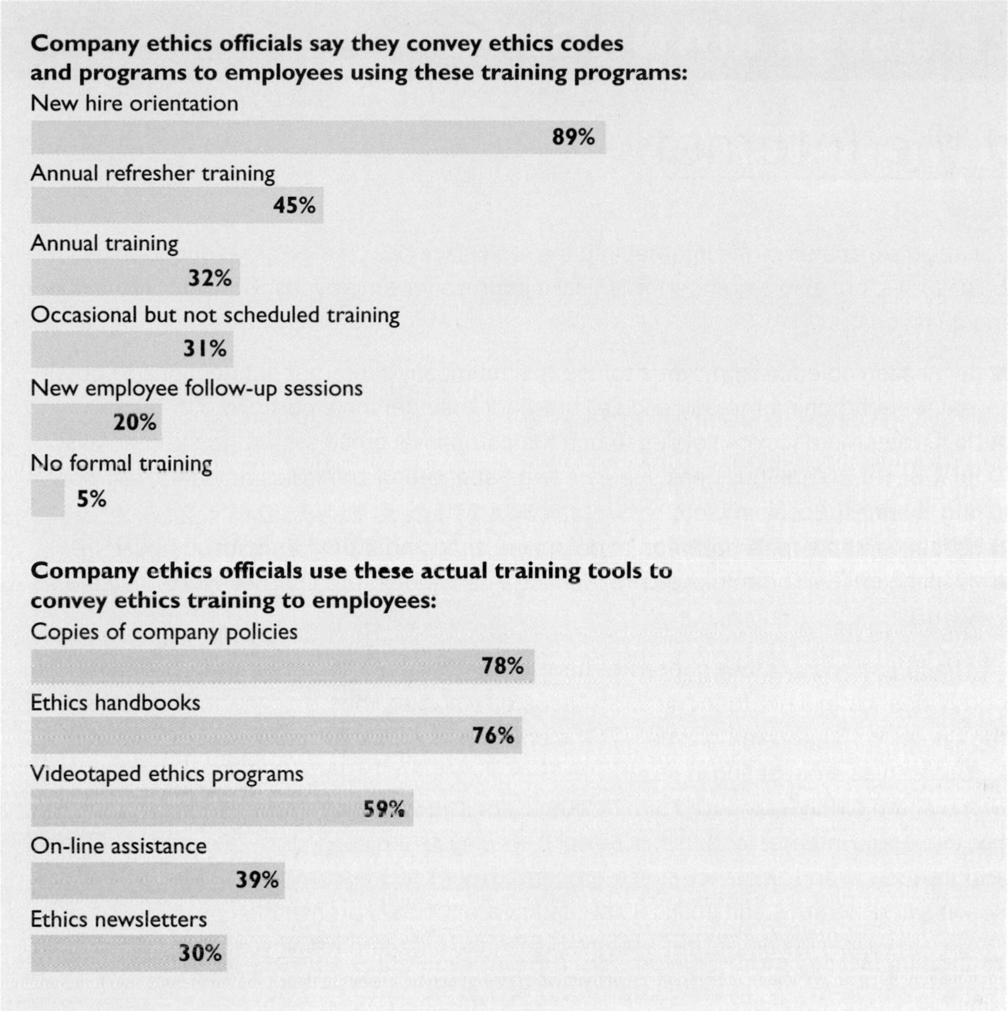

Company ethics officials say they convey ethics codes and programs to employees using these training programs:

New hire orientation

89%

Annual refresher training

45%

Annual training

32%

Occasional but not scheduled training

31%

New employee follow-up sessions

20%

No formal training

5%

Company ethics officials use these actual training tools to convey ethics training to employees:

Copies of company policies

78%

Ethics handbooks

76%

Videotaped ethics programs

59%

On-line assistance

39%

Ethics newsletters

30%

FIGURE 3.4
The Role of Training in Ethics

the day (for example, shopping on-line, sending messages to friends, etc.). UPS caught one employee using the company computer to run a personal business.

On the other hand, technology also provides the means for monitoring all kinds of potentially unethical actions. For example, Turner Broadcasting System Inc. noticed that employees at its CNN London business bureau were piling up overtime claims. CNN installed new software to monitor every web page every worker used. As the firm's network security specialist puts it, "if we see people were surfing the web all day, then they don't have to be paid for that overtime."[57] One study suggests that about 75 percent of U.S. firms now record and review some type of employee communications and/or activity, such as email, phone calls, computer files, and internet use. That's about double the 1997 figure.[58]

New software can secretly record everything your spouse, children, and employees do on-line on a particular computer. Other software lets the user find out everything your spouse, children, and employees do on-line via email. "This program works so well it's scary," says someone who has used it.[59] According to an article in *Computing Canada*, "the lack of trust demonstrated through monitoring colours the entire corporate culture of an organizations. It may create a defensive culture, which has broad and deleterious effects. If employees feel powerless, they will engage in defensive and possibly destructive behaviour. The company then responds with more restrictive rules, and a downward spiral ensues."[60] The "People Side of Managing" box gives more information on this sensitive area.

Ethics and the Internet

The rapid expansion of the internet into the workplace has created great opportunities for businesses, but also a number of ethical dilemmas for employees. Consider the following questions:

■ Is it acceptable for employees to use their company's internet connections to obtain stock quotations, or to buy and sell stock for their personal portfolios?
■ Is it acceptable for employees to use the company's email system to send emails that deal with non-business subjects (e.g., supporting political candidates, promoting charities, gossiping, etc.)?
■ Is it acceptable for employees to do on-line shopping during their lunch hour?
■ Is it acceptable for employees to look for a new job on the internet while they are at work?

These and many other questions have arisen because the internet is providing opportunities that did not formerly exist. These ethical dilemmas are the modern version of the question: "Can an employee use the company's phone for personal business?"

Companies are reacting in various ways as they try to cope with this new technology. Some seem to have accepted the inevitable and allow employees to use the company's fax, email, and internet for personal reasons, as long as the usage is of reasonable duration and frequency and does not cause embarrassment to the company. Chain letters, obscenity, and religious and political solicitation are typically prohibited.

Other companies do not set specific guidelines but warn employees that they should not expect privacy for personal matters if they use the company's email system. They also indicate that the company has the right to check on employees at any time and that employees will be disciplined if unacceptable usage occurs. And unacceptable usage does occur. One employee used his company's computer to run his own business on the side. Another employee was fired after he sent an email promoting a religious holiday to so many people that it disabled the company's email system for six hours.

What does the general public think about some of these ethical dilemmas? A poll conducted by the *Wall Street Journal* revealed the following:

■ 34 percent of those polled felt that it is wrong to use the company's email for personal business
■ 37 percent felt that it is wrong to use office equipment to help a child or spouse do school work
■ 49 percent felt that it is wrong to play computer games on office equipment
■ 54 percent said that it is wrong to do internet shopping while at work
■ 87 percent said that it is wrong to visit pornographic websites while at work

Here's another internet ethics question: Should alcohol be sold on the internet? In 2000, the liquor commissions of Manitoba, Ontario, and Quebec all began selling liquor on the internet. Some of the potential problems with selling alcohol over the internet include the following: Might delivery people inadvertently hand over liquor to a minor when delivering it? Or to someone who is already drunk? Will delivery people be tempted to take a few sips while they're delivering the goods?

Lockheed uses its intranet to help its 160 000 employees take ethics and legal compliance training on-line. Each short course addresses topics ranging from insider trading to sexual harassment. The system also keeps track of who is (and who is not) taking the required courses. Lockheed's electronic ethics software also keeps track of how well the company and its employees are doing in terms of maintaining high ethical standards.[61] For example, the program helped top management see that in one recent year, 4.8 percent of the company's ethics allegations involved conflicts of interest. It shows that it takes just over 30 days to complete an ethics violation internal investigation.[62] It also shows that several years ago, 302 Lockheed employees were sanctioned for ethical violations.

The University of British Columbia has developed a comprehensive set of on-line resources through the Centre for Applied Ethics. Business people can find information on codes of ethics, association codes of ethics, ethics institutions and organizations, publications on ethics, courses, and public sector ethics.[63]

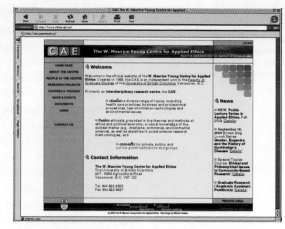

The website for the Centre for Applied Ethics at the University of British Columbia offers multiple sources of information pertaining to ethics.

Creating the Right Culture

The University of British Columbia Centre for Applied Ethics
www.ethics.ubc.ca

When it comes to ethical behaviour, it's not what you say that's important; it's what you do. Parents can talk about being ethical, but if their children see them cutting ethical corners—bringing home "free" office supplies from the office, for instance—the children may assume that "being unethical is really OK."

The same is true at work. Managers create a culture through what they do. Employees then take their signals from that behaviour and from that culture, and it influences what they do. Often, when employees do unethical things, they do so because they think they're helping the company. It's therefore important to send clear signals about what is and isn't acceptable behaviour in your company.

What Is Organizational Culture?

Organizational culture refers to the characteristic values, traditions, and behaviours a company's employees share. A *value* is a basic belief about what is right or wrong, or about what you should or shouldn't do. "Honesty is the best policy" is a value. Values are important because they guide and channel behaviour. Managing people and shaping their ethical (and other) behaviour therefore depends on shaping the values they use as behavioural guides.

Obviously, companies would like to present a positive culture to both employees and the public. But sometimes a less-than-positive culture is allowed to develop. Critics of Enron, for example, say that the company had a culture characterized by questionable financial "engineering," misstated earnings, and a practice of keeping investors in the dark about company activities.[64] In addition, top executives routinely ignored obvious conflict-of-interest guidelines. For example, employees of Enron were "encouraged" to use a travel agency operated by the sister of chairman Kenneth Lay.[65]

To an outside observer, a company's culture shows itself in several ways. You can sense it from **patterns of behaviour,** such as ceremonial events, and written and spoken comments. For example, managers and employees may engage in behaviours such as hiding information, politicking, or expressing honest concern when a colleague requires assistance.

organizational culture
The characteristic values, traditions, and behaviours a company's employees share.

patterns of behaviour
The ceremonial events, written and spoken comments, and actual behaviours of an organization's members that contribute to creating the organizational culture.

physical manifestations
Observable features of a company's culture such as written rules, office layouts, organizational structure, and dress codes.

You can also sense it from **physical manifestations**, such as written rules, office layouts, organizational structure, and dress codes.[66]

In turn, these cultural symbols and behaviours tend to reflect the firm's shared values, such as "the customer is always right" or "don't be bureaucratic." If management and employees really believe that "honesty is the best policy," the written rules they follow and the things they do should reflect this value. For example, Bata Shoes stresses that it will not be satisfied with Canada's high prices to consumers and advertises that its prices are as low or lower than those in the United States. The corporate culture enacts these values by providing competitive prices.[67]

Standards (i.e., values and beliefs) lay out what ought to be, not what is.[68] If management's stated values differ from what the managers actually value, it will show up in the managers' behaviour. You have to "Walk the talk" to set the right culture. Culture, then, reflects the firm's values and patterns of behaviour, and the values' physical manifestations (such as written rules, rewards systems, and dress codes).

Ethics and Corporate Culture

Ethical behaviour and corporate culture are closely related concepts. One does not necessarily "cause" the other, but they do feed on each other. It is true that the company's culture influences its managers' ethics, but it is also true that managers' ethics influence the culture. Suppose a university president turns a blind eye to infractions on the part of coaches regarding the regulations governing recruiting and paying athletes. The president's ethics have influenced the school's culture, but the school's culture has also influenced how it deals with ethical dilemmas.[69]

How to Create the Corporate Culture

Managers have to think through how they're going to send the right signals to their employees. They do so in the following ways.

Hewlett-Packard
Canada
www.hp.ca

● **Clarify Expectations** First, make it clear what your expectations are with respect to the values you want subordinates to follow. Publishing a corporate ethics code is one way to do this. At Hewlett-Packard Canada Ltd., the corporate culture stresses equality, open communication, togetherness, high performance, and profit sharing. Everyone wears a name tag. The practice of using first names is part of the "H-P way." The H-P way also assumes that people want to do a good job and be creative, and that they will perform well if given the proper environment in which to work.[70]

At Air Canada, managers are urging employees to pay more attention to customer service as Air Canada tries to cope with increasing competition from WestJet Airlines. In the past, Air Canada employees had a reputation among passengers as being less friendly and less helpful than employees at WestJet Airlines, and customer service hasn't been emphasized as part of the corporate culture at Air Canada like it has at WestJet.[71]

● **Use Signs and Symbols** Walk the talk. How the manager behaves does the most to create and sustain the company's culture. Magna International, a large Canadian producer of auto parts, has a strong culture. The founder, Frank Stronach, is well known for his views about working conditions, day-care centres, unions, and profit distribution (20 percent goes to shareholders, 2 percent to charities, 7 percent to R&D, 10 percent to employees, and 2 percent to Stronach).[72]

Greg Moore, vice president of audit for Tricon Global Restaurants Inc. (the parent of KFC, Pizza Hut, Long John Silver's, A&W, and Taco Bell) wants to create a culture that supports the free exchange of information. He therefore schedules "Greg Moore Days" where any employee can come into his office to share ideas or concerns. He also demonstrates the importance of open and honest communication by sharing the results of his own performance evaluations with his staff. These include not just what his superiors say about how is doing, "but also feedback from his colleagues and employees."[73]

● **Provide Physical Support** The physical manifestations of the manager's values include things like the firm's incentive plan, its appraisal system, and its disciplinary procedures. These send strong signals regarding what employees should and should not do.

● **Use Stories** Managers use stories to illustrate important company values. IBM has stories telling how its salespeople took dramatic steps (like driving all night through storms) to get parts to customers.

● **Organize Rites and Ceremonies** At JC Penney, new management employees are inducted at ritualistic conferences into the "Penney Partnership." Here they commit to the firm's ideology as embodied in its statement of core values. Each inductee solemnly swears allegiance to these values and then receives his or her "HCSC" lapel pin." These letters symbolize JC Penney's core values of honour, confidence, service, and co-operation.

JC Penney
www.jcpenney.com

Managers and Social Responsibility

Social responsibility refers to the extent to which companies should and do channel resources toward improving one or more segments of society other than the firm's owners or stockholders. Socially responsible behaviour includes creating jobs for minorities, controlling pollution, and supporting educational facilities or cultural events. The socially responsible corporation is the ethical corporation, and it applies high ethical standards to everything it does.

The phrase "social responsibility" tends to trigger images of charitable contributions and helping the homeless, but it actually refers to much more. For example, it refers to the honesty of the company's advertising, to the quality it builds into its products, and to the ethics and "rightness" of dealings with customers, suppliers, and employees. The socially responsible corporation doesn't just make charitable contributions and avoid selling dangerous products. It also does what is right.

social responsibility
The extent to which companies should and do channel resources toward improving one or more segments of society other than the firm's owners.

Ethics and Social Responsibility

In practice, the dividing line between ethics and social responsibility is sometimes difficult to draw. For example, an Eli Lilly Corp. salesperson suspected a pharmacist was diluting an Eli Lilly cancer drug before dispensing it, but said nothing. Only after a physician contacted the U.S. FBI about his concerns and implicated the salesperson did the latter admit to his suspicions. Is this an issue of ethics or of social responsibility? The answer is: It is both. Ethics (what's right or wrong) is the bedrock of socially responsible behaviour. A lawsuit has been filed against Eli Lily alleging that it did not do all it could have done to protect its users and patients.[74]

This raises an interesting question: To whom should the corporation be responsible—its customers or its shareholders? Is a company that tries to do its best only for its owners any less responsible than one that tries to help customers, vendors, and employees too? The answer depends on what you believe is the purpose of a business. Many perfectly ethical people believe that a company's only social responsibility is to its stockholders. Others disagree.

Managerial Capitalism The classic view of social responsibility is that a corporation's primary purpose is to maximize profits for its stockholders. Today, this view is most often associated with economist and Nobel laureate Milton Friedman, who has said:

The view has been gaining widespread acceptance that corporate officials and labor leaders have a "social responsibility" that goes beyond the interest of their stockholders or their members. This view shows a fundamental misconception of the character and nature of the free economy. In such an economy, there is one and only one social responsibility of business—to use its resources and engage in activities designed to increase its profits so long as it stays within the rules of the game, which is to say, engages in open and free competition, without deception and fraud....Few trends could so thoroughly undermine the very foundation of our free society as the acceptance by corporate officials of a social responsibility other than to make as much money for their stockholders as possible.[75]

Friedman says the stockholders are the company's owners, and so the firm's profits belong to them and to them alone.[76] Furthermore, stockholders deserve their profits, because these profits derive from a voluntary contract among the various corporate stakeholders (the community receives tax money, suppliers are paid, employees earn wages, and so on). Everyone gets his or her due, and additional social responsibility is unnecessary.

Stakeholder Theory An opposing view is that business has a social responsibility to serve all the corporate stakeholders affected by its business decisions. A corporate stakeholder is any group that is vital to the survival and success of the corporation.[77] As shown in Figure 3.5, six stakeholder groups are traditionally identified: stockholders (owners), employees, customers, suppliers, managers, and the local community.[78] To stakeholder advocates, being socially responsible means more than just maximizing profits.

The Moral Minimum Between the extremes of Friedman's managerial capitalism and stakeholder theory is an intermediate position. **Moral minimum** advocates agree that the purpose of the corporation is to maximize profits, but it must do so in conformity with the moral minimum. This means that the firm should be free to strive for profits so long as it commits no harm.[79] A business guided by this position would not produce exploding cigarette lighters or operate chemical plants that poison the environment, but it's also unlikely that the firm would donate money to charitable causes.

The moral minimum is not the only intermediate position between managerial capitalism and stakeholder theory. Indeed, many people would not agree with the notion that maximizing profits is acceptable as long as the company does no harm. And, while many people view managerial capitalism as a worthy goal, others would say that, in reality, ignoring the interests of non-owner stakeholders is bound to be counterproductive. The bottom line is that when it comes to being socially responsible, there are many options.

moral minimum
The theory that states that the purpose of the corporation is to maximize profits so long as it commits no harm.

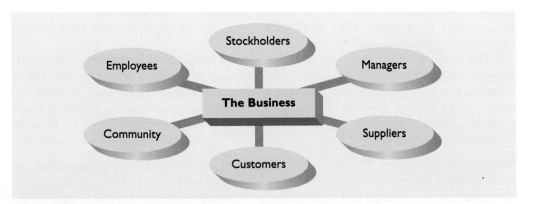

FIGURE 3.5
A Corporation's Major Stakeholders
One view of social responsibility is that a firm must consider and serve all the stakeholders that may be affected by its business decisions.

Why Are Companies Socially Responsible?

Hidden in Hong Kong's Kowloon area is the tiny headquarters of the Asia Monitor Resource Center, which monitors working conditions in China. Its aim is to uncover and publicize unacceptable working conditions in plants producing products for global firms. It hopes to thereby improve working conditions for China's factory workers.

What sorts of unethical practices does the Center report? One report alleged that some mainland Chinese people employed by Disney contractors were working up to 16 hours a day, seven days a week, and were paid little or no overtime. Another report, on China's toy industry, describes what some have called Mattel's "sweatshop Barbie" assembly lines, because of abuses including long work hours and heavy fines for workers.

Reports like these have had an impact.[80] Both Disney and Mattel now have codes of conduct. Disney has done tens of thousands of inspections of its contractors' plants to make sure they comply. Mattel has now received the certificate of workplace standards that Asia Monitor itself calls for.

In practice, how far the manager goes to be socially responsible depends on several things. It clearly depends on the manager's philosophy; that is, whether he or she believes in managerial capitalism, stakeholder theory, or the moral minimum.

Sometimes (as at Disney and Mattel) social responsibility is aided by the watchful eyes of outside monitors and pressure groups. These days, social responsibility advocates have increasingly sophisticated ways to make their positions known. For example, on St. Patrick's Day 2000, shoppers in several Home Depot stores heard the following surprising announcement: "Attention shoppers, on aisle 7 you'll find mahogany ripped from the heart of the Amazon."[81] Store managers scampered around looking for pranksters with megaphones, but there were none. It turned out that Rainforest Action Network activists had cracked the security code of Home Depot's intercom systems and were delivering the messages electronically.

All this has led some firms to reduce the decibel level of their claims of social responsiveness. Daniel Grossman, who runs toy maker Wild Planet, says he's very careful not to say his company is socially responsible, just that "we strive to be." Although he and his managers screen the factories that manufacture their toys in China, Grossman acknowledges he'd have more control over working conditions if the toys were made in North America. Economically, though, he believes doing so wouldn't be practical in the low-cost markets where he competes.[82]

Mattel
www.mattel.com

corporate social audit
A rating system used to evaluate a corporation's performance with regard to meeting its social obligations.

How to Improve the Company's Social Responsiveness

Managers improve their companies' social responsiveness by instituting policies and practices that encourage socially responsible behaviour. These include social audits, "whistle blowing," and membership in responsible advocacy groups.

The Social Audit If a firm is committed to being socially responsible, how can it ensure that it is in fact responsive? Some firms monitor how well they measure up to their aims by using a rating system called a **corporate social audit**.[83] The Sullivan Principles for Corporate Labor and Community Relations in South Africa is the classic example here.[84] The Reverend Leon Sullivan was an African-American minister and GM board of directors member. For several years during the 1970s he

"Some things, Morris, are more easily expressed through puppets."

had tried to pressure the firm to withdraw from South Africa, whose multiracial population was divided by government-sanctioned racist policies, known as apartheid. As part of that effort, Sullivan formulated the code, the purpose of which was "to guide business in its social and moral agenda in South Africa."[85]

Like all social audits, it was basically a measurement system. The code provided measurable standards by which companies operating in South Africa could be audited. For example, there were standards for non-segregation of the races in all eating, comfort, and work facilities, and "equal pay for all employees doing equal or comparable work for the same period of time."[86] In the 1990s Sullivan proposed a new code for companies returning to South Africa after apartheid had ended; this code stressed the protection of equal rights and the promotion of education and job training.

At Bombardier, corporate social commitment is an integral part of its mission. The company fulfils its social and humanitarian responsibilities primarily through the J. Armand Bombardier Foundation, a not-for-profit organization that receives funding equivalent to 3 percent of the corporation's income before taxes. Each year, in addition to funding education in the form of student bursaries and donations to colleges and universities, the foundation supports several charity and relief organizations as well as missionary work.[87]

The "Challenge of Change" box shows that there are some surprising complexities in this area that managers will be confronted with.

Whistle-Blowing Whistle-blowing refers to the activities of employees who report organizational wrongdoing. Many firms have a reputation for actively discouraging whistle-blowing, yet many arguments can be made for encouraging whistle-blowers. In a firm that adheres to the moral minimum view, for instance, whistle-blowers can help the company avoid doing harm. As one writer put it, whistle-blowers "represent one of the least expensive and most efficient sources of feedback about mistakes the firm may be making."[88] Other firms find that trying to silence whistle-blowers doesn't pay.[89] Once the damage has been done—whether it is asbestos hurting workers or a chemical plant making hundreds of people in the community ill—the cost of making things right can be enormous and might have been avoided by listening to a whistle-blower earlier.[90]

Social Responsibility Networks Some firms, such as Rhino Records, join organizations that promote socially responsible business practices and help managers to establish socially responsible programs.[91] The Social Venture Network and Businesses for Social Responsibility are examples.

Managing Diversity

The workforces of the world are becoming increasingly diverse. In Canada, the various ethnic groups that make up the population include British Isles origin (40 percent), French origin (27 percent), other European (20 percent), Aboriginal (1.5 percent), and other, mostly Asian (11.5 percent).[92] This diversity is reflected in the workforce.

In the United States, almost half of the net additions to the workforce in the 1990s were non-white, and almost two-thirds were female.[93] Similarly, it is estimated that minorities compose 8 percent to 10 percent of the workforce population in France, 5 percent in the Netherlands, and a growing proportion in Italy, Germany, and much of Europe.[94] Even Japan, while remaining a homogeneous society averse to immigration, will have to find ways to accommodate many more women in its workforce.[95]

Of all the firm's non-owner stakeholders, perhaps none has so obvious a claim on receiving socially responsible treatment as do its employees. The company is its people, and their efforts largely determine whether the company will succeed or fail. So a firm that exposes its employees to deadly toxins, for example, is the antithesis of socially responsible. Similarly, the way a company manages diversity among its employees is a measure of how socially responsible it is.

The Confusing Area of Corporate Charitable Giving

Should Canadian corporations donate money to charities, disaster relief, or social causes? A Decima Research survey found that 80 percent of Canadians think so. An Environics survey of people in 23 countries found that two-thirds of them thought that companies should contribute to the broader goals of society and that businesses were not doing enough if they simply abided by the law and provided employment.

A survey conducted by the Centre for Philanthropy found that Canadian corporations contributed less than 2 percent of all charitable revenue. Canadians think that this number is closer to 20 percent and that it should be 30 percent. The typical corporation gives less than one-half of 1 percent of its pre-tax profits to charity.

One way that corporations can be socially responsible is to give money or products when disasters strike. When 11 people died in Walkerton, Ontario, as a result of drinking contaminated water, companies such as Petro-Canada, Shoppers Drug Mart, Sobeys, and Zellers contributed products such as bleach and bottled water. Companies generally receive favourable publicity when they make contributions like these, but some people view these gifts with cynicism and are convinced the companies only do it because of the good publicity. Because some people have this view, corporations must be careful when they publicize their good works.

The sensitive nature of corporate philanthropy is illustrated by the long-running story of the Nestlé Corporation. In the 1970s, Nestlé and other makers of infant formula were trying to market their product in developing countries. Problems developed because the formula sometimes was not used properly by mothers, and their babies suffered. So activists organized a boycott of Nestlé and the United Nations began aggressively promoting breast-feeding. But when the AIDS crisis developed, it was discovered that nursing mothers who had the disease could transmit it to their infants through their milk. Infant formula was then suggested as a possible way to avoid this problem. Even though Nestlé offered to donate infant formula, long-standing suspicions of infant-formula makers meant that Nestlé's good intentions may not have been seen in a favourable light.

The terrorist attacks on the World Trade Center in 2001 also illustrate how companies must be careful when trying to do good. Some companies who donated money or products and then publicized that fact were accused of trying to take advantage of the tragedy. For example, Verizon Communications informed its customers of its charitable donations and its efforts to provide telecommunications services in Manhattan after the attacks. But some people who received that information were offended and felt that the company was trying to promote itself during a tragedy.

Verizon
www.verizon.com

Perhaps it is best for a company to make donations, but not publicize them. But that approach can also backfire. Procter & Gamble provided U.S.$2.5 million in cash and products after September 11, but did not publicize its donations. Later, the company was criticized for having done nothing to help. Honda Motor Co., which contributed generators and all-terrain vehicles for use at Ground Zero, was also denounced for having no compassion.

The complex environment in which corporate philanthropy takes place has made corporations very wary. Most large companies in Canada now have clear procedures for dealing with requests from charities and community organizations. The company first determines how much money it will give each year, usually stated as a percentage of profit. It then decides which specific organizations will receive the money and the amount each will receive. These decisions are made by the board of directors after it receives a recommendation from a committee that has been set up to consider charitable requests. Companies are increasingly taking a community-based approach to giving. They try to determine how they can create value for the community (and the company) with their donations.

managing diversity
Planning and implementing organizational systems and practices to manage people so that the potential advantages of diversity are maximized while its potential disadvantages are minimized.

Managing diversity means "planning and implementing organizational systems and practices to manage people so that the potential advantages of diversity are maximized while its potential disadvantages are minimized."[96] Managing diversity requires addressing questions like, "How much effort should a company make to employ minorities? How diverse should the company be? How much effort should managers make to manage the resulting diversity?"

Boosting Performance by Managing Diversity

Equitable and fair treatment of minorities and women is required simply on ethical (and legal) grounds, but these reasons are being overrun by changing demographics and by globalization. Today, white males no longer dominate the labour force, and women and minorities represent the lion's share of labour force growth in the foreseeable future. Globalization requires that employers hire minority members with the cultural and language skills that global companies need.

Managers are therefore striving for racial, ethnic, and gender workplace balance as a matter of enlightened economic self-interest. Managers today generally understand that they must recruit and maintain a diverse workforce to compete successfully in a global marketplace. One study found that cultural diversity contributes to improved productivity, return on equity, and market performance.[97] Here's another take on the advantages of diversity:

> What does it take to win in the global economy? A commitment to mixing people, experiences, and ideas. Companies and countries that embrace diversity to stimulate creativity will be the ones that own the future.[98]
>
> The best corporations set the pace in diversity. Their mission is to match people and needs, regardless of nationality, race, or ethnicity. Hybrid teams are the new corporate ideal.[99]

Bases for Diversity

Diversity means different things to different people. However, there is general agreement regarding its components. In one study, most respondents listed race, gender, culture, national origin, disability, age, and religion as the demographic building blocks of diversity. They are what people usually think of when they are asked what diversity means.[100]

diverse
Describes a workforce comprising two or more groups, each of which can be identified by demographic or other characteristics.

A workforce is **diverse** when it comprises two or more groups, each of whose members are identifiable and distinguishable based on demographic or other characteristics.[101] The bases upon which groups can be distinguished are numerous. However, when managers talk of diversity, they usually mean at least the following groups.[102]

■ *Racial and ethnic groups.* Asians, Aboriginal peoples, and other ethnic groups now compose a significant minority of the Canadian population. In some Canadian cities, Aboriginal peoples will account for one-fourth of all new job entrants in the next decade. Some ethnic groups are concentrated in certain cities. Asians, for example, constitute a large minority of the ethnic population in Toronto, Winnipeg, and Vancouver.

■ *Women* will represent about 48 percent of the Canadian workforce by 2005.

■ *Older workers.* The median age of the Canadian population is currently about 36 years. This is expected to rise to 50 by 2036 and reflects the rapid aging of the Canadian workforce.

■ *People with disabilities.* The Employment Equity Act of 1986 makes it illegal to discriminate against people with disabilities who are otherwise able to do the job. This act has thrown a spotlight on the

Winning with diversity: The night crew at Home Depot.

large number of people with disabilities in the workforce and has caused some companies to take specific actions to improve the work situation for people with disabilities. At Rogers Cablevision, for example, a large workplace area was completely redesigned to accommodate workers who either had vision impairments or used wheelchairs.[103]

- *Sexual orientation.* It has been estimated that 5 percent to 10 percent of the population is homosexual, which makes homosexuals a larger percentage of the workforce than some racial and ethnic minorities.[104]

Barriers in Dealing with Diversity

Unfortunately, differences like these can produce behavioural barriers that prevent collegiality and co-operation. Managers who want to manage diversity must address these barriers if they want their employees to work together productively.

Stereotyping and Prejudice Stereotyping and prejudice are two sides of the same coin. **Stereotyping** occurs when someone ascribes specific behavioural traits to individuals based on their apparent membership in a certain group.[105] **Prejudice** is a bias that results from prejudging someone based on some trait.

Most people develop lists of behavioural traits that they associate with certain groups. For example, stereotypical "masculine" traits might include strong, aggressive, and loud; "feminine" traits might include co-operative, softhearted, and gentle.[106] When someone allows traits like these to bias them for or against someone else in the absence of any facts, we say that the person is prejudiced.

Ethnocentrism **Ethnocentrism** is prejudice on a grand scale. It is the tendency to view members of one's own group as the "centre of the universe" and other social groups as less important. One study found that managers attributed the performance of some minorities less to their ability and effort and more to help they received from others; conversely, they attributed the performance of non-minorities to their own abilities and efforts.[107]

Discrimination **Discrimination** is prejudice in action. Whereas prejudice means a bias toward prejudging someone based on that person's presumed traits, discrimination means taking specific actions toward or against the person based on the person's membership in a certain group.[108] In many countries, including Canada, it is illegal to discriminate at work based on a person's age, race, gender, disability, or country of national origin. But in practice, discrimination is still a barrier to managing diversity because discrimination is often very subtle. For example, many argue that an invisible "glass ceiling," enforced by an "old boys' network" and friendships built in places like exclusive clubs, has prevented women from reaching the top ranks of management.

Tokenism **Tokenism** occurs when a company appoints a small group of women or minority-group members to high-profile positions, rather than more aggressively seeking full representation for that group. Tokenism is a diversity barrier when it slows the process of hiring or promoting more members of the minority group. Token employees often fare poorly. Research suggests, for instance, that token employees face obstacles to full participation, success, and acceptance in the company. The extra attention their distinctiveness creates magnifies their good or bad performance.[109]

Gender-Role Stereotyping Discrimination against women goes beyond glass ceilings. Working women also confront **gender-role stereotypes**, the tendency to associate women with certain (i.e., non-managerial) jobs. In one study, physical attractiveness was advantageous for female interviewees when the job was non-managerial, but when the job was managerial, there was a tendency for a woman's attractiveness to reduce her chances of being hired.[110]

How to Manage Diversity Successfully

Diversity can be a blessing or, if it is mismanaged, a curse. Bringing together people with different values and views can increase the chance that problems will be attacked in a

stereotyping
Associating certain characteristics with certain groups but not with others.

prejudice
A bias that results from prejudging someone on the basis of that person's particular trait or traits.

ethnocentrism
A tendency to view members of one's own group as the centre of the universe and to view other social groups less favourably than one's own.

discrimination
A behavioural bias toward or against a person based on the group to which the person belongs.

tokenism
Appointing a small number of minority-group members to high-profile positions instead of more aggressively seeking full representation for that group.

gender-role stereotypes
The tendency to associate women with certain (i.e., non-managerial) jobs.

richer, more multifaceted way. On the other hand, diversity can make it harder to create smoothly functioning teams.[111]

Managing diversity requires taking both legally mandated and voluntary actions. There are, of course, many legally mandated actions. For example, employers must not allow sexual harassment, and they must avoid discriminatory employment advertising (such as "young man wanted for sales position"). However, legally required steps are rarely enough to blend diverse employees into a close-knit community. Other, voluntary steps and programs are required. As shown in Figure 3.6, one diversity expert suggests the following.

Provide Strong Leadership Leaders of firms with exemplary diversity management reputations champion diversity. They take strong personal stands on the need for change; become role models for the behaviours required for the change; write a statement that defines what they mean by diversity and how diversity is important to the business; and provide financial and other support needed to implement the changes.[112]

After settling a class action suit by black employees in November 2000, Coca-Cola instituted a variety of steps aimed at improving its diversity management record. For example, it established a formal mentoring program. It also is spending U.S.$500 million to support minority suppliers.[113]

Assess Your Situation Companies can use surveys to measure current employee attitudes and perceptions toward different cultural groups in the company. Interviews with a sample of employees and managers can also be used to assess the current situation.

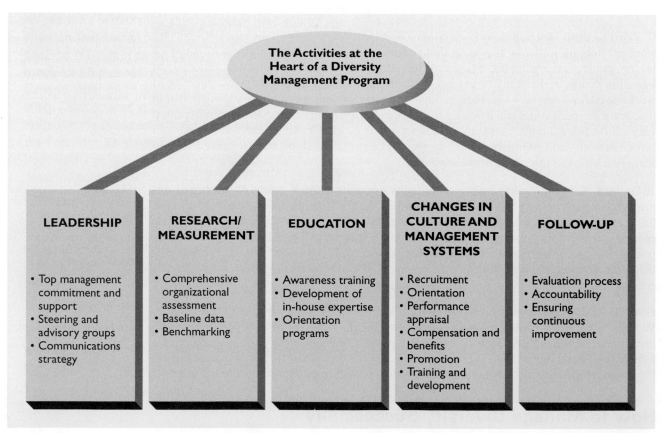

FIGURE 3.6
Activities Required to Better Manage Diversity

Provide Diversity Training and Education "The most commonly utilized starting point for...managing diversity is some type of employee education program."[114] A one- to two-day seminar involving a diverse group of employees is typical. Topics include, "What does diversity mean to you?" and "What does it mean to our organization?"[115]

After 9/11, Ford Motor Company sponsored a one-day "Islamic perspective on the events of Sept. 11th" event for hundreds of Ford employees of many faiths. Ford also supports an interfaith dialogue group and a support group for employees of Middle Eastern descent. As one Middle Eastern Ford employee said of the one-day event, "I've worked here for 15 years. I like to see my co-workers understand what Islam is about. We need...to help people understand all of this."[116]

Change the Culture and Management Systems In diversity management, "it's not what you say, it's what you do." Managers have to send the right signals. For example, six women recently filed a sexual discrimination class-action suit against Wal-Mart.[117] They claimed that they did not get the raises or promotions their male colleagues received and that they were exposed to hostile comments and actions by male employees. Wal-Mart denied any discrimination and pointed out it that has policies forbidding sexual harassment of any kind. However, some lawyers argue that it's not what Wal-Mart says, it's what it does (i.e., Wal-Mart has a policy of vigorously defending itself in such lawsuits and this could send the wrong signals). Employees may therefore conclude that Wal-Mart doesn't take sexual harassment all that seriously.

The Treasury Board of Canada, in conjunction with the Public Service Commission, implemented the Special Measures Initiatives Programme.[118] The program complemented the federal government's larger Employment Equity Program and focused on the development, advancement, and retention, as well as recruitment, of a diverse workforce. It also considered ways to change the corporate culture of organizations to support diversity. To date, several key achievements have resulted from the program:[119]

Treasury Board of Canada
www.tbs-sct.gc.ca

1. Partnership building—166 initiatives were co-funded with federal departments.

2. Internet technology—Piloted website initiatives in the Public Service Commission. website hits now range from 9000 to 11 300 per month, representing about 5 percent of the total traffic on the Public Service Commission's site.

Public Service Commission
www.psc-cfp.gc.ca

3. Accessibility—Pioneered the development of the Accessibility Self-Evaluation Test, and provided information on employment-equity and diversity-management documents, tools, and software.

4. Career consultation—Conducted 3880 career consultations with group-designated members.

One way to effectively manage diversity is to appraise supervisors based partly on their success in minimizing intergroup conflicts. Mentoring can also contribute to the success of diversity management. **Mentoring** is "a relationship between a younger adult and an older, more experienced adult in which the older person provides support, guidance, and counselling to enhance the protege's success at work and in other arenas of life."[120] It doesn't do any good to attract a diverse workforce and then leave the new people to sink or swim.[121]

mentoring
A relationship between two people in which the more experienced member provides support, guidance, and counselling to enhance the proteges success at work and in other areas of life.

Evaluate the Diversity Program Management must actively evaluate the extent to which the diversity program is achieving its goals. For example, do surveys suggest an improvement in employee attitudes toward diversity? How many employees have entered into mentoring relationships? What evidence is there that these relationships are successful?

SKILLS AND STUDY MATERIALS

1. Managers face ethical choices every day. Ethics refers to the principles of conduct governing an individual or a group. Ethical decisions always include both normative and moral judgments.

2. Being legal and being ethical are not necessarily the same thing. A decision can be legal but still unethical, or ethical but still illegal.

3. Several factors influence whether specific people in specific organizations make ethical or unethical decisions. The individual making the decision must ultimately shoulder most of the credit (or blame) for any decision he or she makes. However, the organization itself—including its leadership, culture, and incentive/compensation plan—also shapes an individual employee's behaviour.

4. Ethics policies and codes send a strong signal that top management is serious about ethics and are a sign that it wants to foster a culture that takes ethics seriously.

5. Managers take several steps to foster ethics at work: emphasizing top management's commitment, publishing a code, establishing compliance mechanisms, involving personnel at all levels, and measuring results.

6. Organizational culture refers to the characteristic traditions, norms, and values employees share. Values are basic beliefs about what you should or shouldn't do and what is and is not important.

7. Several factors contribute to creating and sustaining the corporate culture. One is a formal core values statement. Leaders also play a role in creating and sustaining culture. One of a leader's most important functions is to influence the culture and shared values of an organization. Managers also use signs and symbols, stories, and rites and ceremonies to create and sustain their companies' cultures.

8. Social responsibility is largely an ethical issue, since it involves questions of what is morally right or wrong with regard to the firm's responsibilities. People differ in answering the question, To whom should the corporation be responsible? Some say solely to stockholders, and some say to all stakeholders. Some take an intermediate position: They agree that the purpose of the corporation is to maximize profits, but subject to the requirement that it must do so in conformity with the moral minimum.

9. As the workforce becomes more diverse, it becomes more important to manage diversity so that the benefits outweigh any potential drawbacks. Potential barriers to managing diversity include stereotyping, prejudice, and tokenism. Managing diversity involves taking steps such as providing strong leadership, assessing the situation, providing training and education, changing the culture and systems, and evaluating the program.

CRITICAL THINKING EXERCISES

1. You work for a medical genetics research firm as a marketing person. You love the job. The location is great, the hours are good, and work is challenging and flexible. You receive a much higher salary than you ever anticipated. You hear via the rumour mill that the company's elite medical team has cloned the first human, the CEO. It was such a total success that you have heard that they may clone every employee so that they can use the clones to harvest body parts as the original people age or become ill. You are not sure you believe in cloning. You joined the firm because of its moral and ethical reputation. You feel that the image presented to you was one of research and development of life-saving drugs and innovative medical procedures. The thought of cloning was never on your mind, but now it must be. What would you do? What are the ethical and cultural issues involved? Do you think that managers in the United States, Japan, Sweden, Chile, or France would manage the discovery differently? Why? Do you think cloning will become even a more controversial ethical and moral issue in the future as cloning becomes part of the medical decision-making model?

2. A key to ethical perception is realizing that all people bring different views, experiences, and other relevant influences to decisions. This is particularly true in Canadian society. Read the following narratives about perception, and relate them to ethical decision-making examples in the workplace.

First narrative, by Taoist writer Lieh-tse: A man noticed that his axe was missing. Then he saw the neighbour's son pass by. The boy looked like a thief, walked like a thief, behaved like a thief. Later that day, the man found his axe where he had left it the day before. The next time he saw the neighbour's son, the boy looked, walked and behaved like an honest, ordinary boy.[122]

Second narrative, by Taoist writer Chuang-tse: An archer competing for a clay vessel shoots effortlessly, his skill and concentration unimpeded. If the prize is changed to a brass ornament, his hands begin to shake. If it is changed to gold, he squints as if he were going blind. His abilities do not deteriorate, but his belief in them does, as he allows the supposed value of an external reward to cloud his vision.[123]

1. In teams of four or five class members, research and then write about the ethical philosophies and attitudes toward business in the following nations: Russia, India, Egypt, Israel, the Congo, Norway, Saudi Arabia, and Australia. Compare and contrast their respective approaches to ethics and corporate social responsibility. Explain why there are differences.

2. You were taking a month's holiday in Europe. In your first week there, you became very ill with a recurring ailment for which you have been treated with limited success in Canada. In fact, it is a chronic condition that is inhibiting your ability to advance your career. The doctors who treated you in Europe have given you some medication that is legal there but has not been approved for use in Canada. You feel better than you have in years. Because the European drug restrictions allow this drug to be purchased across the counter without a prescription, you are able to buy a year's supply. However, you know that it is listed as an illegal drug in Canada, and you must pass through Canada customs. What would you do? What are the ethical and moral dilemmas facing you? Is there any action you can take as an individual to change the situation? If your decision is to smuggle the drug in and you are successful, what will you do in a year?

BUILDING YOUR MANAGEMENT SKILLS

What's the Right Thing to Do?

Read an article in *The Globe and Mail* or *Canadian Business* that focuses on a controversial business story (e.g., Enron, insider trading scandals, environmental pollution, wrongful dismissal, sexual harassment, etc.). In these situations, there will almost always be debate about the reasonableness of the decisions that company management made. Write a summary of the situation with enough detail in it that you can answer the following questions.

1. What do you think the different ethical viewpoints (see Table 3.1) would say was the right course of action in the situation you have described?

2. Make suggestions as to how the situation could have been handled better. When developing your suggestions, refer to each of the ideas described in the "How to Foster Ethics at Work" section of the chapter. Be specific when making these suggestions. For example, when dealing with the "emphasize top management's commitment" suggestion, indicate exactly what top management should have done to show its commitment to ethical behaviour. Likewise, when dealing with the "establish compliance mechanisms" suggestion, indicate exactly what compliance mechanisms should have been in place given the nature of the situation. Do this for all of the suggestions in the section.

3. The chapter describes three basic views of corporate social responsibility (managerial capitalism, stakeholder theory, and the moral minimum). What would each of these views say was the right course of action that should have been taken in the situation you have described? How much agreement or disagreement is there among the three positions?

INTERNET EXERCISES

Ethics and social responsibility are key elements of operating a successful organization. Bad behaviour, like bad news, travels fast; so managers have a key role in modelling and monitoring ethical and socially responsible behaviour. Their work includes creating and updating corporate policies and codes of ethics and publishing them for both public and employee use. Access Nexen's website at **www.nexeninc.com/our_commitment/corporate_governance/ code_of_ethics.asp**.

1. What is the purpose of the International Code of Ethics for Canadian Business, and what is Nexen's role?

2. Review Nexen's ethics policy. When was it last revised? What are the major topics covered under the policy? In your opinion, how does Nexen's ethics policy rate against the Guidance for Writing a Code of Ethics (**www.ethicsweb.ca/codes/**)?

3. Compare Nexen's Social Responsibility statements to those of Bombardier Inc. (**www.bombardier.com**). How do they differ in scope?

Nortel Changes Its Corporate Giving Policy

Like many companies, Nortel Networks used to make contributions to a variety of charitable organizations. It also used to match employee contributions to the United Way. But its new corporate giving strategy means no more matching contributions to the United Way and a more focused giving strategy for the contributions it does make. In the future, Nortel will focus on education efforts that have a direct relationship to its business objectives and bottom line.

Former CEO John Roth was the force behind the new policy. He believed that it makes sense for companies to fund programs that benefit them. Roth has some allies in this thinking; they argue that profit generated by a company is the property of shareholders, not corporate managers, and that shareholders should decide where it goes. Not surprisingly, Nortel's new policy has alarmed some charitable organizations, most obviously the United Way.

Nortel's new policy was developed because of concerns about the effectiveness of its traditional giving patterns. Like most major corporations in Canada, Nortel was bombarded with requests to sponsor events such as art exhibits, ballet companies, the United Way, and hospital fundraisers. But the traditional corporate citizenship model of scattering contributions among many different good causes may not be effective, so Nortel will now concentrate on three areas of giving: business fundamentals, science and technology education, and community support.

Specifically, Nortel will fund scholarships and research initiatives that link back to the company's corporate objectives. For example, $18 million will be given to establish an Institute in Advanced Information Technology at Waterloo University, and $14 million will be given to fund 7000 students in engineering and computer science. These programs benefit Nortel both directly and indirectly.

Nortel recognizes that its new approach is a departure from the traditional social responsibility model that has been evident in corporate philanthropy in Canada for many years. The company says it is "reinventing corporate citizenship for a connected world." Nortel will continue to encourage its employees to donate time and money on a voluntary basis, but the company will pursue its new strategy as well. It argues that its new approach makes sense because education benefits everyone by providing access to rewarding careers, decent wages, and opportunities for growth. It also increases the talent pool and helps industry by providing educated students.

Questions

1. In general, what are the arguments for and against corporate philanthropy?

2. What are the arguments for and against Nortel's new policy?

3. "Corporate profits are the property of shareholders and should not be given to charity." Do you agree or disagree? Explain.

Mitsubishi and Environmentalists Battle over Baja Salt Factory

Mitsubishi's proposal must have seemed like a dream to the Mexican government. Mexico has long been known for its maquiladoras—factories along the U.S.–Mexico border that produce products in Mexico for export to Canada and the United States. Although these factories had been a great help to the economy, the Mexican government wanted to see a greater diversity in Mexican manufacturing. It also needed still greater foreign direct investment.

As part of its campaign to secure more foreign investment, the Mexican government proposed a joint venture with the Japanese manufacturing giant Mitsubishi to develop the world's largest salt factory, to be located on Mexico's Pacific coast in Baja, California. Unfortunately, the proposed plant would be adjacent to the breeding habitat of the Pacific gray whale. Several environmental groups opposed the plant's location, saying the operation would ruin more than 100 square miles of coastal breeding grounds. The area is also host to abalone fishing and is a breeding ground for more than 70 animal species. Mitsubishi earned the wrath of local environmentalists when another plant it operated in Mexico proved to be responsible for the death of 94 endangered turtles.

The International Fund for Animal Welfare (IFAW) announced a campaign to boycott Mitsubishi, claiming that the salt project posed a threat to the gray whale. One month later, the money managers of 13 U.S. mutual funds announced they would no longer buy stock in Mitsubishi and urged other funds to do the same. Those funds had combined investments of nearly U.S.$14 billion.

Mitsubishi had yet to file its environmental impact study. It noted in a public response to IFAW that whale populations have risen to record levels near an existing salt facility. James E. Brumm, an executive vice president with Mitsubishi, said that the antics of environmentalists demonstrated a complete abandonment of truthfulness. He said they were using the gray whale as an icon and that didn't serve anyone's interests—not their donors, [not] the activist community as a whole, and most certainly not the whales. He also noted that IFAW had wasted resources on fundraising mailers and celebrity events that could have gone toward legitimate research, education, or conservation.

Brumm was frustrated because Mitsubishi's corporate code of ethics has a strong stance on environmental issues. Environmental responsibility is an integral part of Mitsubishi Corporation's corporate philosophy. To set forth a clearly defined framework, the company drafted its internal Environmental Guidelines for Business Activities in 1992. After four years of addressing environmental issues, the company formulated an Environmental Charter in 1996 in line with the basic concepts of the ISO 14001, the international standard for environmental management systems. This charter provides a strong base for the company to strive for further progress as a sound global enterprise.

Environmental activists noted that Laguna San Ignacio, the proposed factory site, is the last pristine Pacific gray whale nursery in the world and is part of a UNESCO World Heritage Site and the Vizcaíno Biosphere Reserve. As part of their campaign against the facility, thirty-four scientists, including nine Nobel Prize winners, have expressed opposition to the project.

Two separate scientific reports were expected to be presented concerning the salt factory. An independent, international team of scientists from the International Union for the Conservation of Nature (IUCN) was to issue a report to the World Heritage Committee Bureau. Following the IUCN publication, a two-year multidisciplinary study by some 40 scientists from prestigious Mexican universities and from the Scripps Institution of Oceanography would be completed. Unlike the IUCN project, the latter study would examine every aspect of the potential impact of a new facility—both the environmental impact and the socioeconomic impact.

In the end, Mexico responded to all the pressure by cancelling the proposed factory.

Questions

1. What should Mitsubishi's corporate position be in regard to the environment?

2. How might the initial positions taken by the different stakeholders in this case have affected their evaluation of the scientific reports?

3. Would you have done anything differently if you were Mitsubishi's CEO? Explain.

Mitsubishi
www.mitsubishi.com

Ethics, JetBlue, and the IPO

Can you trust a security analyst's recommendation, when that analyst owns tens of thousands of shares of the recommended company's stock? For many years, securities firms more or less looked the other way with respect to stocks that the analyst did or did not own. This all changed in early 2002. It was then that New York's attorney general accused Merrill Lynch's analysts of making self-serving recommendations. (One allegation went something like this: Based on email messages, some analysts were bad-mouthing the same stocks that they were recommending to the public, and they were recommending them to the public so the firm could win more investment banking business from these firms, and thereby generate more income for the security analysts). It was not a pretty scene. Merrill Lynch ended up paying a U.S.$100-million fine—although the company did not, in so doing, agree that it had done anything wrong.

Morgan Stanley was the investment banking firm that took the lead in preparing JetBlue's U.S.$125-million initial public offering of stock. When the public found out that Morgan Stanley employed an airline industry analyst who owned more than 42 000 shares of JetBlue, the discovery raised many questions. For one thing, the analyst was allegedly in violation of Morgan Stanley's new (post–Merrill Lynch) rule forbidding analysts from owning shares in companies they cover.[124] Indeed, Morgan Stanley's new rule also extends to the analyst's associates, assistants, and relatives. Analysts had until early 2002 to sell their stocks, but this analyst allegedly did not comply. So, Morgan Stanley was now in the position of being the lead underwriter trying to sell a new issue of stock in an airline in which its chief airline industry analyst held stock. Many of the customers buying the new JetBlue stock would probably turn to the analyst's recommendation in trying to decide whether to buy this new issue. The situation therefore did raise the possibility of a conflict of interest.

Of course, there are arguments pro and con. On the "con" side, would an analyst who owns stock in the company not want to see the stock go up, and therefore give that stock and overly optimistic analysis? On the other hand, would you want to buy a stock from someone who didn't think enough of it to buy it? For example, when a friend recommends a stock to you, isn't one of your first questions, "Do you own the company's shares yourself?" In other words, don't you want to make sure that that person is really committed to the company?

In any event, its analyst's ownership of the shares created complications for Morgan Stanley. It apparently could not insist that the analyst unload the shares, because there were certain contractual agreements requiring that he hold onto the shares for a particular length of time. So, why didn't Morgan Stanley simply say that they would not help JetBlue with its IPO? One outsider had this answer: "It's big money; fees are fees." In its defence, Morgan Stanley said that it was clamping many new restrictions on this analyst's stockholdings. For example, the analyst would have to "lock up" his shares (not sell them) for three years. Furthermore, he couldn't issue analyses of JetBlue stock unless he did so with an independent analyst, one who was not his subordinate. Some people were satisfied with that. Some were not.

Assignment

You and your team are consultants to Mr. Neeleman, who is depending on your management expertise to help navigate the launch and management of JetBlue. Here's what he wants to know from you:

1. List both the ethical and unethical decisions that were made by the analyst and by Morgan Stanley.

2. Provide a brief description of the ethical culture at the investment banker, Morgan Stanley.

3. Provide a one-page outline of plan for improving the ethical behaviour of the country's securities firms.

4. Tell us, what should we do now?

Managing Entrepreneurial Organizations

The Urge to Start a New Business

Thousands of new businesses are started in Canada and the United States each year by individuals who are excited about a concept that they have developed. And these concepts vary widely. Consider just three.

Ab-Original Wear. It's been a long road for Geraldine McManus, who has always wanted to open a retail store that would sell clothing with an Aboriginal theme. She finally achieved her goal in the fall of 2002, when she opened Ab-Original Wear in Winnipeg. The store sells limited edition clothing featuring Aboriginal artwork on one side and an inspirational message from a chief or elder on the other. McManus buys original artwork from local Aboriginal artists and then reproduces it on T-shirts, crew-neck shirts, and sweatshirts. The store also sells crafts made by local Aboriginal artists and miniature log cabins (that McManus makes herself from recycled wood).

McManus also plans to open a screen-printing business so that she can reproduce native artwork onto the clothing she sells. This will give her more control over production costs. She also has a goal of providing jobs for Aboriginal people, especially single mothers. She has already written a business plan for the new screen-printing business and is now looking for financing.

Ben Barry Agency. Ben Barry, 21, runs an Ottawa-based modelling business that promotes models who are considered unorthodox—various sizes and ages, different racial backgrounds, and those who have physical disabilities. Barry thinks that models should be representative of Canada's population in general and not simply be the stereotypical model body shape. His models have appeared in government advertising campaigns and on fashion runways in shopping malls. Barry works with company management to define their clientele and then chooses models who will best reflect the store's typical shoppers. His models earn $150 per hour and he receives a 20 percent commission.

He got his start when he was only 14 when he secured a modelling contract for a friend who had been told that she was too heavy

OBJECTIVES

After studying this chapter and the case exercises at the end, you should be able to use the material to:

1. Explain why you do (or do not) have the traits to be an entrepreneur.

2. List what an entrepreneur is doing right and doing wrong when starting a business.

3. List what a person did right and did wrong when buying a franchise.

4. Conduct an informal business feasibility study.

5. Recommend a start-up organization structure for a new business.

6. List the activity areas that a new business owner should be controlling.

Ben Barry Agency
www.benbarry.com

ReadyMade Magazine
www.readymademag.
com

Ace Hardware
www.acehardware.com

to be a model. He put together a dossier of her work and eventually succeeded in getting her featured in *Ottawa City Magazine*. As a teenager, Barry knew what other teens liked and disliked. He also personally knew some friends with eating disorders, and this motivated him to develop his unorthodox modelling agency.

ReadyMade Magazine. Shoshana Berger and Grace Hawthorne have started a do-it-yourself magazine for young people with a creative gene (sort of a *Martha Stewart Living* for a younger, hipper audience). The first year's editions contained advice for projects such as beds made out of meat carts, fruit bowls made out of melted LP records, and a lamp made from an old computer hard drive.

Berger and Hawthorne started ReadyMade with about U.S.$150 000 they borrowed from friends and relatives. Within a year, the magazine had a total circulation of about 50 000 and profits of U.S.$385 000. ACE Hardware, Levi's, and JVC were some of the big name advertisers in early issues. Shoshana and Grace (who are unpaid at the moment) have ended up doing much of the work themselves, including getting retailers like ACE to help circulate their magazine among potential readers.

Shoshana is immensely optimistic about ReadyMade's prospects. She and Grace are now working on brand extensions such as a book based on the same off-beat do-it-yourself theme, and they want to double circulation within a year. However, they understand that doing so will mean incurring new expenses, not the least of which is salaries. They know that you can't run a business for long staffed only with people who don't get paid.

What Is an Entrepreneur?

entrepreneur
Someone who creates new businesses for the purpose of gain or growth under conditions of risk and uncertainty.

entrepreneurship
The creation of a business for the purpose of gain or growth under conditions of risk and uncertainty.

An **entrepreneur** is someone who creates "an innovative economic organization for the purpose of gain or growth under conditions of risk and uncertainty."[1] **Entrepreneurship** "requires a vision and the passion and commitment to lead others in the pursuit of that vision [and] a willingness to take calculated risks."[2] Figure 4.1 neatly sums up the common themes in defining what being an entrepreneur is all about. In the field of management, entrepreneurs are unique. Like JetBlue CEO David Neeleman, entrepreneurs "build something of value from practically nothing."[3] Innovation, value creation, growth, and uniqueness characterize the entrepreneur's efforts.

Entrepreneurs and Small Business

Since entrepreneurs typically "create something out of nothing," it stands to reason that the companies they create usually start small (although JetBlue started with more than U.S. $100 million in initial financing). Most people therefore tend to associate "entrepreneurs" with "small businesses," although that link is, in reality a little weak. David Neeleman is certainly an entrepreneur, although the business he's running is not (and never was) very small. Conversely, someone who starts up a small dry-cleaning store and has no intention of making it grow and expand is a small-business person but not really an entrepreneur.

The Environment of Entrepreneurship

Entrepreneurs like taking risks, but that doesn't mean they are foolish. The good ones are therefore continually sizing up their opportunities and constraints in the environ-

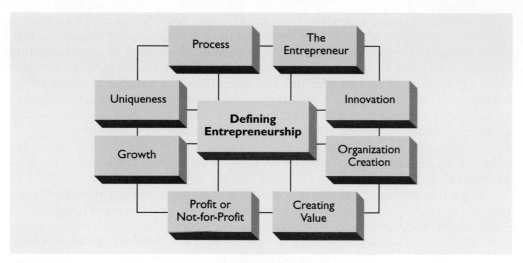

FIGURE 4.1
Common Themes in Definitions of Entrepreneurship

ment. Some environments are more conducive to entrepreneurship than are others. The level of *economic freedom* is one major consideration.[4] Some countries (and some regions within countries) make it easier to be entrepreneurial than do others. Table 4.1 shows a portion of the Heritage Foundation's index of economic freedom. For instance in Canada, Hong Kong, Singapore, New Zealand, and the United States, entrepreneurs encounter relatively few barriers in starting, financing, and growing their businesses. At the other extreme, pity the entrepreneur who wants to start a business in North Korea, Cuba, or Russia. In those countries, the combination of governmental and bureaucratic impediments and high taxes are enough to stifle new business ideas.

Heritage Foundation
www.heritage.org

TABLE 4.1	*The Index of Economic Freedom: Selected Locations*	
OVERALL RANK	**COUNTRY**	**OVERALL SCORE***
1	Hong Kong	1.45
2	Singapore	1.50
3	New Zealand	1.70
6	United States	1.80
9	United Kingdom	1.85
18	Canada	2.05
40	France	2.55
56	Mexico	2.80
68	Saudi Arabia	2.95
127	China	3.55
135	Russia	3.70
155	Cuba	4.45
156	North Korea	5.00

*Low overall score means higher economic freedom

Economic freedom means that companies in some countries also find it easier to *streamline, downsize,* and *lay off employees*, and this also affects new business creation. When a large company downsizes, many former employees return in some temporary capacity, or as vendors or contractors.[5] Downsizing is often associated with the "outsourcing" by firms of various activities, and entrepreneurial former employees create businesses to fulfill these needs. Similarly, periods of increased *economic activity* tend to be associated with increased business creation. For example, as the Canadian and U.S. economies boomed in the late 1990s, the number of businesses created jumped.

Technological advances (whether automobile, railroad, telephone, computer, or the web) also trigger bursts of business creation. Many of these inventions translate into new business ideas.

In practice, dozens of other environmental opportunities and constraints influence the budding entrepreneur's willingness and ability to create a new business. *Globalization* is one, since the opportunity to sell goods from one country to buyers in another triggers new-business creation. A short list of *other environmental factors* includes venture capital availability; technical skill level of the labour force; accessibility of suppliers; accessibility of customers; the proximity of universities; availability of lenders; accessibility of transportation; attitude of the area's population; and availability of supporting services (such as roads, electric power, and accounting firms).[6]

A study by the Global Entrepreneurship Monitor (GEM) rated Canada sixth out of 21 countries for entrepreneurial activity (Brazil ranked first). About 1 in 16 Canadians tried to start a new business in 2000.[7]

The Importance of Small Business and Entrepreneurship

As we have seen, the terms "small business" and "entrepreneurship" do not mean exactly the same thing. Nevertheless, many entrepreneurs are small-business owners who are working hard to expand their businesses. Small businesses are very important in the Canadian economy, and they can be found in every industry. Although these businesses may be "small" in terms of size, their aggregate affect on the Canadian economy is large.

Strategis, Industry Canada
www.strategis.ic.gc.ca

In terms of numbers, small business is *the* dominant type of business in Canada. Of the approximately 2.2 million businesses in Canada, 58 percent consist of self-employed individuals, while 41 percent employ fewer than 50 people. Less than 1 percent of all businesses in Canada employ more than 50 people, and less than 0.1 percent employ more than 500 people.[8] Small businesses generate more than 50 percent of Canada's gross domestic product (GDP).[9]

The contribution of small business can be measured in terms of its effects on several key elements of our economic system, but innovation is a particularly important one. History has shown that major innovations are as likely to come from small businesses as they are from big businesses. For example, small firms invented the personal computer, the stainless-steel razor blade, the transistor radio, the photocopying machine, the jet engine, the self-developing photograph, the helicopter, power steering, the automatic transmission, air conditioning, cellophane, and the ballpoint pen. Much of today's most innovative software is being written at new start-up companies such as Trilogy Software.

New small organizations generate 24 times more innovations per research and development dollar spent then do Fortune 500 organizations, and they account for over 95 percent of new and "radical" product development.[10]

What It Takes to Be an Entrepreneur

Electronic Data Systems
www.eds.com

A number of years ago, H. Ross Perot appeared on television to receive an award for his entrepreneurial activities. Someone asked Perot (who had made hundreds of millions of dollars building Electronic Data Systems Inc., and then Perot Systems Inc.) what his advice would be for people who hoped to be entrepreneurs. Perot said, "never give up, never give up, never give up." His advice highlights an interesting entrepreneurial dilemma. On the one hand, there's no doubt that tenacity is a crucial trait for entrepreneurs, since creating something out of nothing is inherently so difficult. On the other hand, at what point does one give up? Tenacity, after all, only gets the entrepreneur so far—it is only one entrepreneurial trait.

Research Findings Psychologists have studied the question of "what it takes to be an entrepreneur" with mixed results. Based on some studies of entrepreneurs, the entrepreneur's personality characteristics include self-confidence, a high level of motivation, a high energy level, persistence, initiative, resourcefulness, the desire and ability to be self-directed, and a relatively high need for economy.[11] Others argue that people high in the need to achieve are more prone to be entrepreneurs, since they like setting goals and achieving them. Yet high need for achievement people seem to be no more likely to start businesses than those with a lower need.[12] One expert concludes that the trait approach to identifying entrepreneurs has proven inadequate to explain the phenomenon of entrepreneurship.[13]

More recently, psychologists have focused on the "proactive personality" and its relationship to entrepreneurship. Proactive behaviour reflects the extent to which people "...take action to influence their environments."[14] One recent study of 107 small-business owners found some support for the notion that a proactive personality contributes to innovation in some circumstances.[15]

Other researchers focus on what they call the "dark side" of the entrepreneur. They say entrepreneurs are driven by less positive traits, such as the need for control, a sense of distrust, the need for applause, and a tendency to defend their operations.[16] This approach doesn't paint a pretty picture of how some entrepreneurs behave. With respect to the need for control, for instance, "a major theme in the life and personality of many entrepreneurs is the need for control. Their preoccupation with control inevitably affects the way entrepreneurs deal with power relationships and the consequences for interpersonal action.... An entrepreneur has a great inner struggle with issues of authority and control."[17]

Anecdotal Evidence A few behaviours do seem to consistently arise in anecdotal or case descriptions of successful entrepreneurs. *Tenacity* is one. Entrepreneurs face so many obstacles in creating a business that if they're not tenacious, they're bound to fail. For example, consider the challenges facing Asil Hero as he tries to build Broadway Digital Entertainment. Over the past few years, Hero bought the digital rights to more than 300 classic Broadway shows (including "The Glass Menagerie" with Katherine Hepburn). For now, Hero sells tapes of the shows through his internet site to theatre buffs. But he hopes to create a TV channel dedicated to Broadway.[18] Doing so will take tenacity since cable TV already has more than 600 channels, and Hero is an outsider facing giants like AOL/Time Warner. Selling old Broadway shows is not exactly "mainstream entertainment, like professional wrestling."[19]

Intensity—the drive to pursue a goal with passion and focus—is another trait that often pops up anecdotally. For example, Sky Dayton started EarthLink in the mid-1990s, and the firm is now one of the largest internet service providers.[20] Software from his new company, Boingo, will enable people with notebook computers to easily link to the web via special "Wi-Fi" hubs. What kind of person is Dayton? One friend, who watched him water surfing, says Dayton "took the sport up with a vengeance. He's as intense and fearless in water surfing as he is in business."

EarthLink
www.earthlink.net

Women and Entrepreneurship

An increasing number of women are becoming entrepreneurs. A Royal Bank of Canada study estimates that one-quarter to one-third of all businesses worldwide are owned by women and that women now account for half the increase in new businesses each year.[21] In the last decade of the twentieth century, firms led by women created jobs four times faster than the average for all Canadian companies. Women are more conservative than men in running a small business, and their failure rate is lower than that of men.[22]

Corporate Entrepreneurship

Entrepreneurship is not just for individuals. Large companies also work hard at being entrepreneurial because they understand that bureaucracy can stifle innovation.

CHECKLIST **4.1**

Should You Be an Entrepreneur?

Is entrepreneurship for you? As one gauge, take the short survey in Figure 4.2. Then answer the following questions, compliments of the U.S. Small Business Administration.

☑ *Are you a self-starter?* No one will be there prompting you to develop projects and follow through on details.

☑ *How well do you get along with different personalities?* Business owners need to develop working relationships with a variety of people including customers, vendors, staff, bankers, and professionals such as lawyers, accountants, and consultants. Will you be able to deal with a demanding client, an unreliable vendor, or a cranky employee, in the best interests of your business?

☑ *How good are you at making decisions?* Small-business owners make decisions constantly, often quickly, under pressure, and independently.

☑ *Do you have the physical and emotional stamina to run a business?* Can you handle 12-hour workdays, six or seven days a week?

☑ *How well do you plan and organize?* Research indicates that good plans could have prevented many business failures. Furthermore, good organization (not just of employees, but also of financials, inventory, schedules, production, and all the other details of running a business) can help prevent problems.

☑ *Is your drive strong enough to maintain your motivation?* Running a business can wear you down. Some business owners feel burned out by having to carry all the responsibility on their shoulders. You'll need strong motivation to make the business succeed and to help you survive slowdowns, reversals, and burnout.

☑ *How will the business affect your family?* The first few years of business start up can be hard on family life. The strain of an unsupportive spouse may be hard to balance against the demands of starting a business. There also may be financial difficulties until the business becomes profitable, which could take months or years.[23]

Respond to each of the 17 statements using the following rating scale:

    1 = Strongly disagree

    2 = Moderately disagree

    3 = Slightly disagree

    4 = Neither agree or disagree

    5 = Slightly agree

    6 = Moderately agree

    7 = Strongly agree

1. I am constantly on the lookout for new ways to improve my life.   1 2 3 4 5 6 7

2. I feel driven to make a difference in my community— and maybe the world.   1 2 3 4 5 6 7

3. I tend to let others take the initiative to start new projects.   1 2 3 4 5 6 7

4. Wherever I have been, I have been a powerful force for constructive change.   1 2 3 4 5 6 7

5. I enjoy facing and overcoming obstacles to my ideas.   1 2 3 4 5 6 7

6. Nothing is more exciting than seeing my ideas turn into reality.   1 2 3 4 5 6 7

7. If I see something I don't like, I fix it.   1 2 3 4 5 6 7

8. No matter what the odds, if I believe in something, I will make it happen.   1 2 3 4 5 6 7

9. I love being a champion for my ideas, even against others' opposition.   1 2 3 4 5 6 7

(continued)

FIGURE 4.2
Is Entrepreneurship for Me?

10. I excel at identifying opportunities.		1	2	3	4	5	6	7
11. I am always looking for better ways to do things.		1	2	3	4	5	6	7
12. If I believe in an idea, no obstacle will prevent me from making it happen.		1	2	3	4	5	6	7
13. I love to challenge the status quo.		1	2	3	4	5	6	7
14. When I have a problem, I tackle it head-on.		1	2	3	4	5	6	7
15. I am great at turning problems into opportunities.		1	2	3	4	5	6	7
16. I can spot a good opportunity long before others can.		1	2	3	4	5	6	7
17. If I see someone in trouble, I help out in any way I can.		1	2	3	4	5	6	7

SCORING KEY

To calculate your proactive personality score, add up your responses to all statements, except item 3. For item 3, reverse your score.

ANALYSIS AND INTERPRETATION

This instrument assesses proactive personality. That is, it identifies differences among people in the extent to which they take action to influence their environments. Proactive personalities identify opportunities and act on them; they show initiative, take action, and persevere until they bring about change. Research finds that the proactive personality is positively associated with entrepreneurial intentions. Your total score will range between 17 and 119. The higher your score, the stronger your proactive personality. For instance, scores above 85 indicated fairly high proactivity.

FIGURE 4.2
Is Entrepreneurship for Me?

Intrapreneurship "is the development, within a large corporation, of internal markets and relatively small autonomous or semi-autonomous business units, producing products, services, or technologies that employ the firm's resources in a unique way."[24] Intrapreneurship usually does not just mean creating products that are similar to what the company already sells. Instead, it leads to "something new for the corporation and represents, in its fullest manifestations, a complete break with the past."[25]

For example, intrapreneurship within Cisco Systems led to the creation of several spin-off companies (including Cordis Corp. and Equinox) that together produced almost U.S.$700 million for Cisco.[26] Similarly, QUALCOMM Corporation's intrapreneurial activities led to the wireless web company Handspring. Sun Microsystems' intrapreneurship helped it create and spin off several successful companies, including Caldera systems.

Intel provides another example of intrapreneurship. Several years ago it created an in-house "new business initiative."[27] "The idea for the whole thing came from our employees, who kept telling us they wanted to do entrepreneurial things..." said Intel's CEO. Although Intel is in the microprocessor business, its "new business initiative" is earmarked specifically for non-microprocessor businesses. For example, Intel engineer Paul Scagnetti came up with the idea for a handheld computer that helps people record and plan their fitness regimens. Intel gave him the funding to launch his product, the Vivonic fitness planner.

intrapreneurship
The development, within a large corporation, of internal markets and relatively small autonomous or semi-autonomous business units that produce products, services, or technologies that employ the firm's resources in a unique way.

Cisco Systems
www.cisco.com

Intel
www.intel.com

Getting Started in Business

Overcoming all the challenges that stand in the way of going "from nothing to something" requires tackling at least four main tasks along the way: Coming up with the idea for the business; deciding how to get into that business; deciding on a form of business ownership; and getting funded.

The Idea: What Business Should I Be In?

Most entrepreneurs don't come up with the ideas for their businesses by doing an elaborate analysis of what customers want. Rather, they often seem to stumble upon their ideas.[28] By far the largest proportion (between 43 percent and 71 percent) of those responding to one survey said they got their ideas for their businesses through their *previous employment*. (Thus, Ralph Lauren supposedly got his idea for the Polo line of clothes while working at Brooks Brothers). Furthermore, "in addition to providing the means to discover opportunities on which to start a business, this approach has the advantage of being much more forgiving of mistakes arising from inexperience."[29] In other words, it's smart to learn the business at someone else's expense. After work experience, *serendipity* was the source that most respondents mentioned (15 percent to 20 percent). A relative handful of respondents got their ideas from *hobbies*, or from a " *systematic search for business opportunities.*"[30]

Some business ideas do arise quite unexpectedly.[31] Consider Triumph Motorcycle Company. The original Triumph Company had been in business for years, before closing down in the 1960s. When housing developer John Bloor was looking for building sites in Coventry England, he stumbled across the shuttered Triumph factory. He decided that he didn't want to buy the factory site, but seeing the factory gave him an idea. For about U.S.$200 000, he bought the rights to the Triumph motorcycle brand name, and the company's designs and tooling. Today, a former housing developer who stumbled upon the company's factory still manages Triumph.

Triumph
www.triumph.co.uk

Methods for Getting into Business

Entrepreneurs typically get into business in several ways: through a family-owned business; by starting a business from scratch; by buying a business; or by buying a franchise.

The Family-Owned Business Perhaps the easiest way to become an entrepreneur is to be the child of an entrepreneur and take over the family business. A family-owned business "is one that includes two or more members of a family with financial control of the company."[32] Family-owned businesses in Canada (which are not necessarily small businesses) account for more than 50 percent of GDP, they employ more than half of the Canadian workforce, and they create 75 percent of all new jobs.[33]

Balancing family and business pressures is not easy. As someone once said, "you can't run a family with your head, and you can't run a business with your heart." A family is based on love, relationships, emotion, nurturing, and security, but a business demands high productivity, goal accomplishment, and the earning of profit."[34]

These issues manifest themselves in the family business in many ways. Children may fight for the right to gain control of the business. The owner may be torn between doing what's best for the business and a desire to help a child (who may not actually have what it takes) to succeed. Poor planning may worsen these problems. Many owners do little planning to help ease the burden for heirs. One survey showed that only 45 percent of the owners of family firms had selected successors. One expert suggests that the owner should prepare a kit containing items like a list of helpful advisers, the location of key documents, and advice on business strategies and on whether the survivor should sell the firm or continue running it.[35]

At a minimum, the owner of the family business should make his or her succession plans clear. "The children should know if they will take over management or if the business will be sold to an outsider. If they spend years working in the business only to find it sold to an outsider, they may have trouble finding positions in other companies."[36] The "People Side of Managing" box describes one Canadian company that experienced these classic difficulties.

Starting a New Business When most people think of "entrepreneurship," they usually think of starting a new business. It is in starting a new business that the entrepreneur supplies the spark that makes "something out of nothing" and brings a new business to life, complete with customers, suppliers, permits, accountants, lawyers, and all the paraphernalia you think of when you think about a business. Many new businesses start as a **microenterprise** that operates from the entrepreneur's home while the entrepreneur continues to work as a regular employee of another organization. The process of business creation consists of several time-sequenced steps (see Figure 4.3).

microenterprise
A business that operates from the entrepreneur's home while the entrepreneur continues to work as a regular employee of another organization.

A Divided Family

Cuddy International Corp.
www.cuddyfarms.com

Cuddy International Corp. is the largest turkey breeding and hatching company in Canada, with revenues of more than $350 million annually. It also holds the lucrative contract to supply chicken products to McDonald's. The company's founder, Mac Cuddy, is known as "the turkey king of Canada." The saga of Cuddy International is a rags-to-riches story of a brilliant entrepreneur who created a great company but then couldn't manage it. Mac Cuddy also experienced difficulty getting along with his five sons and one daughter.

In spite of the success of the business, the Cuddy family is badly divided. Gordon Pitts, the author of *In the Blood*, a book about family businesses, says that the Cuddy case is a classic example of all the things that can go wrong in a family business—a control-oriented founding father, no succession plan, untrained children who have worked only in the business, and a lack of trained and talented managers from outside the family. As a result of these problems, Cuddy International has been suffering. The company had five CEOs between 1994 and 1999, and sales have declined sharply from their former level of $500 million annually.

Mac Cuddy's sons have all worked in the business at one time or another, but Mac was always doubtful about their capabilities. He decided to bring in outsiders for the top-management positions in the company because he felt that his sons did not have the management skills to run a large company. Three of his sons—Peter, Bruce, and Brian—made several attempts to take control of the business but failed. Eventually, Mac fired Peter and Brian, and demoted Bruce. Bruce quit the business and is now a competitor to his father.

In 1997, Peter Cuddy sued the company for $11.5 million, claiming that he was not being provided with the financial information to which he was entitled. He also alleged that his father and one of his brothers were misspending company funds. He eventually dropped his lawsuit but was then sued by Cuddy International for allegedly making defamatory comments at a press conference. Oddly enough, his father is helping him set up a new snack food company.

Numerous other upheavals have occurred at Cuddy International over the years. Although the specific things that have happened may be unusually severe, the fact is that many family businesses experience the same general kinds of problems as those the Cuddy family has suffered through.

The steps listed in Figure 4.3 are very general. Before starting a business, the entrepreneur must also do some very detailed research that includes the following:

1. *List your reasons for wanting to go into business.* Some of the most common reasons for starting a business are you want to be your own boss; you want financial independence; you want creative freedom; and you want to use your skills and knowledge more fully.

2. *Determine what business is right for you.* Ask yourself, "What do I like to do with my time? What technical skills do I have? What do others say I am good at? Will I have enough money to support my family? How much time do I have to run a business? Do I have any hobbies or interests that are marketable?"

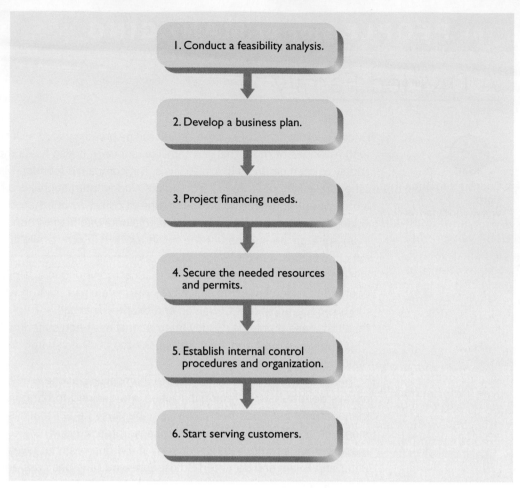

FIGURE 4.3
Steps in Creating a New Business

3. *Identify the niche your business will fill.* Conduct the necessary research to answer these questions: "What business am I interested in starting? What services or products will I sell? Is my idea practical, and will it really work? What is my competition? What is my business' advantage over existing firms? Can I deliver a better quality service? Can I create a demand for my business?"

4. *Conduct a pre-business checklist.* Now, answer these questions: "What skills and experience do I bring to the business? How will I maintain my company's business records? What insurance coverage will I need? What equipment or supplies will I need? What are my resources? What financing will I need? Where will my business be located? What will I name my business?"

Answers to these questions will help you create a detailed business plan that will serve as a blueprint for the business. The business plan spells out how you are going to operate, manage, and capitalize the proposed business.[37] We discuss the business plan later in this chapter.

Buying an Existing Business Buying an existing business is a two-edged sword. On the one hand, it reduces the entrepreneur's risks because the entrepreneur will know what the existing market is, as well as the company's revenues, expenses, and profits.

Buying a business can also mean getting into business faster and with less effort than starting a business from scratch.

On the other hand, as one cynical management consultant once put it, "there's always a reason why the business owner wants to sell, and the reason is never good." There is sometimes puffery in the revenue and profit figures the owner reports. Or, the owner may know that things are about to go wrong. The entrepreneur isn't buying just the business's assets but its liabilities as well (including problem employees).

Buying a Franchise To some extent, buying a franchise gives the entrepreneur the best of both worlds. A **franchiser** is a firm that licenses other firms to use its business idea and procedures, and to sell its goods or services in return for royalty and other types of payments. A **franchisee** obtains a licence to use a franchiser's business ideas and procedures, and which may get an exclusive right to sell the franchiser's goods or services in a specific territory. Each franchisee owns his or her **franchise** unit. The **franchising agreement** lays out the relationship between the franchiser and franchisee. The agreement creates a franchise, a franchising system, a franchiser, and a franchisee.[38]

Franchising can be a good way to get into business. The franchisee usually gets the right to start his or her business from scratch, without the problems that may be associated with buying an existing business. Yet the franchisee gets much of the start-up work done by the franchiser and generally gets a business that is based on a proven business model. Other benefits include name recognition, management training and assistance, economies in buying, financial assistance, and promotional assistance. One expert suggests looking for the following things when evaluating a franchise:

- Select a franchising company that is primarily interested in distributing products and services to ultimate customers. Franchisers like Tim Hortons and McDonald's are famous for their emphasis on providing high-quality products and services—they're not just there to sell franchises.

- Pick a franchiser that is dedicated to franchising as its primary mechanism of product and service distribution. Avoid franchisers with large numbers of company-owned stores, or who distribute their product or services through other channels, such as supermarkets.

- Pick a franchiser that provides products or services for which there is an established market demand.

- Pick a franchiser that has a well-accepted trademark.

- Evaluate your franchiser's business plan and marketing system.

- Make sure your franchiser has good relationships with its franchisees.

- Only deal with franchising companies that provides sales and earnings projections that demonstrate an attractive return on your investment.

- Meet with your accountant and lawyer and carefully review the franchising agreement. Franchisers are required to disclose essential information about the franchiser's business, but regulations vary from province to province.

The checklist in Figure 4.4 provides additional guidance for evaluating the franchise and the franchiser.

Forms of Business Ownership

In creating the business entity, the entrepreneur needs to decide what the entity's ownership structure will be. The three main forms of business ownership are the sole proprietorship, the partnership, and the corporation. As we will see, *taxation* and *liability* are big considerations in choosing an ownership form.

The Sole Proprietorship The **sole proprietorship** is a business owned by one person. The sole proprietorship is simple to start. There are no laws on setting up the sole proprietorship (although provincial, territorial, and local laws require licences and permits).

franchiser
A firm that licenses other firms to use its business idea and procedures and to sell its goods or services in return for royalty and other types of payments.

franchisee
A firm that obtains a licence to use a franchiser's business ideas and procedures, and that may get an exclusive right to sell the franchiser's goods or services in a specific territory.

franchise
A licence to use a company's business ideas and procedures and to sell its goods or services.

franchising agreement
A document that lays out the relationship between the franchiser and franchisee.

Tim Hortons
www.timhortons.com

sole proprietorship
A business owned by one person.

THE FRANCHISE

☐ 1. Did your lawyer approve the franchise contract you are considering after he or she studied it paragraph by paragraph?

☐ 2. Does the franchise call on you to take any steps that are, according to your lawyer, unwise or illegal in your province or territory, county, or city

☐ 3. Does the franchise give you an exclusive territory for the length of the franchise agreement or can the franchiser sell a second or third franchise in your terriroty?

☐ 4. Is the franchiser connected in any way with any other franchise company handling similar merchandise or service?

☐ 5. If the answer to the last question is yes, what is your protection against this second franchiser organization?

☐ 6. Under what circumstances can you terminate the franchise contract and at what cost to you, if you decide for any reason at all that you want to cancel it?

☐ 7. If you sell your franchise, will you be compensated for your goodwill, or will the goodwill you have built into the business be lost by you?

THE FRANCHISER

☐ 8. How many years has the firm offering you a franchise been in operation?

☐ 9. Has it a reputation for honesty and fair dealing among the local firms holding its franchise?

☐ 10. Has the franchiser shown you any certified figures indicating exact net profits of one or more going firms that you personally checked with the franchisee?

☐ 11. Will the firm assist you with

a. A management training program?

b. An employee training program?

c. A public relations program?

d. Capital?

e. Credit?

f. Merchandising ideas?

☐ 12. Will the firm help you find a good location for your new business?

☐ 13. Is the franchising firm adequately financed so that it can carry out its stated plan of financial assistance and expansion?

☐ 14. Is the franchiser a one-person company or a corporation with an experienced management trained in depth (so that there would always be an experienced person at its head)?

☐ 15. Exactly what can the franchiser do for you that you cannot do for yourself?

☐ 16. Has the franchiser investigated you carefully enough to assure itself that you can successfully operate one of its franchises at a profit both to it and to you?

☐ 17. Does your province have a law regulating the sale of franchises, and has the franchiser complied with that law?

YOU—THE FRANCHISEE

☐ 18. How much equity capital will you have to have to purchase the franchise and operate it until your income equals your expenses? Where are you going to get it?

☐ 19. Are you prepared to give up some independence of action to secure the advantages offered by the franchise?

☐ 20. Do you really believe you have the innate ability, training, and experience to work smoothly and profitably with the franchiser, your employees, and your customers?

☐ 21. Are you ready to spend much or all of the remainder of your business life with this franchiser, offering its product or service to your public?

YOUR MARKET

☐ 22. Have you made any study to determine whether the product or service that you propose to sell under the franchise has a market in your territory at the prices you will have to charge?

☐ 23. Will the population in the territory given to you increase, remain static, or decrease over the next five years?

☐ 24. Will the product or service you are considering be in greater demand, about the same, or less demand five years from now than today?

☐ 25. What competition exists in your territory already for the product or service you contemplate selling?

a. Non-franchise firms?

b. Franchise firms?

FIGURE 4.4
Checklist for Evaluating a Franchise

The sole proprietor usually has to register the firm's name to make sure no one else is using the name. As sole owner, the proprietor owns the firm and its profits (or losses) outright, since there are no other owners with whom to share the rewards. Sole proprietors are their own bosses. They can decide for themselves what hours to work and whether to expand their firms. Because the sole proprietor *is* the firm, he or she pays only personal income taxes on its profits. Unlike a corporation, there is no income tax on the firm as a separate entity. A sole proprietorship is also easy to dissolve. The owner needs no permission to dissolve the business.

Simple to start they may be, but the sole proprietor business form does have disadvantages. Perhaps most important, the sole proprietor has unlimited liability. **Unlimited liability** means that the business owner is responsible for any claims against the firm that go beyond what the owner has invested in the business. If the firm can't pay its debts, liability could extend to the owner's personal property (furniture, car, and personal savings). Sole proprietors therefore risk losing everything they own if their businesses go bust. Furthermore, since there are no other owners, the sole proprietorship form can limit the owner's ability to raise funds for expansion. And, similarly, there is no other owner with whom to share the management burden.

The Partnership Because of the disadvantages of the sole proprietorship, some entrepreneurs opt to form a partnership. A **partnership** is an association of two or more persons to carry on as co-owners of a business for profit. People form a partnership by entering into a partnership agreement. A **partnership agreement** is an oral or written contract between the owners of a partnership. It identifies the business and lays out the partners' respective rights and duties. The agreement states the name, location, and business of the firm. It also specifies the mutual understanding of each owner's duties and rights in running the business, the method for sharing the profits or losses, and the policies for withdrawing from the business and dissolving the partnership.

There are two basic forms of partnerships. In a *general partnership*, all partners share in the ownership, management, and liabilities of the firm. A *limited partnership* is a business in which one or more, but not all, partners (the "limited partners") are liable for the firm's debts *only to the extent of their financial investment in the firm*. This helps general partners attract investment dollars from people who do not want unlimited liability, or who do not want to get involved in managing the firm. Under the law, partners are assumed to be general partners, unless it is made known that they are limited partners.

Pentagram Design Inc. is a partnership that was originally formed in London, England, by three architects who had previously worked alone but realized that they could attract more and larger clients by working together. Partnerships are common among professionals such as accountants, doctors, architects, lawyers, and engineers because the law does not allow them to incorporate in Canada.

The partnership has several advantages. There are few restrictions on starting a partnership. A partnership permits the pooling of funds, talents, and borrowing power. The partnership also provides more chance to specialize than does the sole proprietorship. For example, the "outside person" can specialize in sales, while the "inside person" can specialize in running the business day to day. Finally, like a sole proprietorship, there's no tax on the business as distinct from the owners. The owners individually, not the firm, are taxed.

Unlimited liability is also a disadvantage of a partnership. In general partnerships, all partners have *unlimited* liability for the partnership's debts. In a partnership, this means joint liability; that is, each general partner is responsible for business debts incurred by the other partners. The general partners' combined personal property is available to the business creditors. The potential for personal disagreements is another disadvantage. As in most relationships, one must choose one's partners with great care. A partnership agreement can reduce many of the ambiguities, but disagreements can still arise over questions like how much money each partner is to invest, what their salaries will be, and the duties of each.

The Corporation A **corporation** is a legally chartered organization that is a separate legal entity apart from its owners. A corporation can sue and be sued, buy and sell property, and commit crimes and be prosecuted for them. The two most widely used methods

Jim Pattison Group
www.jimpattison.com

unlimited liability
The business owner is responsible for any claims against the firm that go beyond what the owner has invested in the business.

partnership
An association of two or more persons to carry on as co-owners of a business for profit.

partnership agreement
An oral or written contract between the owners of a partnership.

Pentagram Design Inc.
www.pentagram.com

corporation
A legally chartered organization that is a separate legal entity apart from its owners.

public corporation
One whose stock is widely held and is available for sale to the general public.

private corporation
One whose stock is held by only a few people and is generally not available for sale.

to form a corporation are federal incorporation under the Canada Business Corporations Act and provincial incorporation under any of the provincial corporations acts. A **public corporation** is one whose stock is widely held and is available for sale to the general public, while a **private corporation** is one whose stock is held by only a few people and is generally not available for sale.

The corporate form has several advantages. It is a *separate legal entity* and can issue stock certificates to shareholders as evidence of ownership. Shareholders (or stockholders) own the corporation. Each owns a part interest in the entire corporation. However, since the corporation is a separate legal entity, CN shareholders are not CN, and CN is not its shareholders. CN is like a separate "person." Banks lend money to CN, people can sue CN, and CN (not individual shareholders) hires CN's employees.

Shareholders in corporations have *limited financial liability*. This is the corporation's main advantage over sole proprietorship and partnerships. The most a shareholder can lose is what he or she paid for the shares. This makes it much easier for the company to raise money. Furthermore, because the corporation is a separate legal entity, it has permanence. The death, insanity, or imprisonment of a shareholder does not mean the end of the corporation. This also facilitates transfer of ownership. In a corporation, shareholders just sell their shares of stock to transfer ownership to someone else.

Corporations also have disadvantages. In sole proprietorships and partnerships, the owners pay the income taxes individually—the Canadian government does not separately tax them. But corporations are different. Remember, they are separate entities from their owners. The corporation thus pays taxes on its profits. If the corporation then pays cash dividends to shareholders from its after-tax profits, the shareholders must then pay personal income taxes on the dividends. So, the company's profits are subject to *double taxation*. Corporations are subject to more provincial, territorial, and federal laws and public disclosure requirements than sole proprietorships and partnerships.

Getting Funded

Generating ideas for the business, developing business plans, creating or buying the business, and deciding on a legal organization is all just a theoretical exercise if the entrepreneur can't find the money to actually start and run the business. Funding the business is therefore an issue the entrepreneur should be thinking about from the moment he or she starts thinking about creating a business.

Obviously, the amount of money that is needed will vary with the business and the situation, but the logical way to determine the amount is to produce a business plan. Develop a projection of expected first- and second-year sales. This should produce (with some research), a list of the expenses needed to support these sales, and, thus, an estimate of how much cash the business will need for the first few years.

The two basic sources of business finance are debt and equity. Equity finance represents ownership in the venture, while debt means borrowed capital.

Equity For the typical new small business, much of the initial capital traditionally comes from the founder of the business. Family and friends are usually the second-biggest source. No one knows the entrepreneur like his or her family and friends, and hopefully that familiarity translates into the faith required to help the entrepreneur start the business.

Outside equity—either from wealthy private investors or from venture capital firms—are two other possibilities. *Angels* are wealthy individuals interested in the high-risk/high reward potentials of new venture creation. *Venture capitalists* are professionally managed pools of investor money. They specialize in evaluating new venture opportunities and taking equity stakes in promising new businesses. A public offering—selling stock to the public—is usually an option open to relatively few new ventures. When the company first sells stock to outside owners, the firm has "gone public." The process is the initial public offering (IPO). Investment bankers are professionals that walk the entrepreneur through the various provincial registration requirements that enable the company to publicly offer stock.

Debt Debt, or borrowed capital, is the second main source of business finance. An entrepreneur with good personal credit and a sound business plan may be able to obtain a business loan from a chartered bank. However, banks are not in the venture capital business. Loans like these are usually guaranteed by the entrepreneur's personal assets and promise to repay.

Studies suggest that many entrepreneurs dip deeply into their personal debt-paying capacity to support the business. By one estimate, the debts of smaller businesses are divided roughly equally among (1) credit lines and loans, (2) business credit card debt, and (3) personal credit card debt.[39] Asset-based debt is a popular source of small business funds. One or more specific assets of the business serve as collateral. If the business does not pay, the lender takes the asset.

However the money is raised, the entrepreneur will have to provide a business plan and evidence that he or she can actually manage the firm. Let's therefore turn to the important topic of how entrepreneurs manage their businesses, including how they plan, organize, lead, and control their companies.

How Entrepreneurs Plan

To some people, the phrase "entrepreneurial planning" sounds inconsistent. After all, entrepreneurs get things done by being fast and innovative and by not playing by the usual rules. Therefore, doesn't the idea of thinking through the next moves run counter to the very nature of entrepreneurship?

Yes and no. Successful entrepreneurs do cut some corners and streamline the planning process, but they don't jump into business without thinking through their moves with some precision. Let's look first at strategic planning by entrepreneurs.

How Entrepreneurs Craft Strategies

Entrepreneurs do take short cuts when creating strategies for their firms. Interviews with entrepreneurs of fast-growing companies showed that they use three general guidelines in formulating strategies:[40]

1. *Screen out losers quickly.* Successful entrepreneurs know how to quickly discard ideas for new products and services that have a low potential. Their decision making tends to emphasize judgment and intuition, rather than lots of data.

2. *Minimize the resources devoted to researching ideas.* With limited resources, entrepreneurs can do only do so much planning and analysis. They then make judgment calls, sometimes based on very limited data.

3. *Don't wait for all the answers; be ready to change course.* Entrepreneurs rarely have the time or resources for the strategic planning as it is done in large companies. Entrepreneurs often don't know all the answers before they act. They introduce a product or service based on very preliminary market data. Then they quickly drop or modify the product if it doesn't click with customers.

Create Competitive Barriers Looking at entrepreneurial success stories makes it clear that entrepreneurs can and do make good use of strategic planning tools (see Chapter 7). For example, they benefit from being able to formulate a mission and vision for the firm, by being able to formulate both corporate and competitive level strategies, and by using strategic planning tools (such as SWOT or TOWS—strengths, weaknesses, opportunities, and threats).

Ask "What Business Are We In?" Chapter 7 explains that the heart of strategic planning is deciding "what business we are in." Defining the business helps the manager make all other business decisions. Managers can't intelligently choose suppliers, employees, advertising campaigns, or business partners if they don't know what business they are in. Entrepreneurs may not always do elaborate strategic analyses. However, the best ones still define their basic business with great care.

Compass Records is a case in point. Alison Brown and Garry West, both musicians, got their idea for starting Compass Records while talking before a show they were at in Stockholm.[41] Today, Compass Records is booming. Over the last seven or so years, Alison and Garry's company has released more than 100 albums, ranging from "collections of centuries-old ballads by the British folksinger Kate Rusby to an album of soukous by the Congolese singer guitarist Samba Ngo."[42]

What business is Compass Records in? Compass has built up an audience of discerning listeners by focusing like a laser on "roots" music—folk music from whatever country it may be from. As Alison Brown says, "whether we're doing Celtic or Bluegrass or singer-songwriter, it all has that common thread running through it."[43]

Sticking to that vision has taken Compass Records into some interesting musical nooks and crannies. Their first release was an album of music played on a didgeridoo, a wooden instrument from Australia. Other titles "have included sets by the progressive jazz bassist Victor Wooten, the Czech Bluegrass band Druha Trava and the neo-pop duo Swan Dive."[44] The partners may not have done a lot of strategic analysis; however, they do know exactly what business they are in.

Use the Internet Not surprisingly, the internet has been a boon to entrepreneurs because the internet lowers the barriers to entry. For example, an entrepreneur can create a virtual bookstore or other business for a fraction of the money that it would take to create a bricks and mortar version.

Today, most small businesses have their own websites. In terms of strategy, the secret of small-business web success seems to be choosing a "niche" competitive strategy. For example, Harris Cyclery is a successful New England business. Sheldon Brown, the mechanic who runs Harris Cyclery, avoids head-on competition with bigger on-line bicycle retailers by focusing on hard-to-find replacement parts. He also cultivates a competitive advantage by offering free advice over the web.[45] Ron Davis, who owns and manages a chain of apparel stores called The Shoe Horn also created a website, but he kept it highly focused. He sells dyed wedding shoes on-line.[46]

Highly focused on-line entrepreneurs can use other websites to help them promote their wares. Thanks to sites like eBay and Yahoo's small-business services, even tiny businesses can auction their products to huge audiences on-line.

The Feasibility Study: Is This Business for Me?

If a large corporation starts a new line of business or introduces a new product and the venture doesn't work out, the corporation is not likely to go bankrupt. But most entrepreneurs can't afford a big failure when they are starting out. When a person quits a job and sinks his or her (and, possibly his or her family's) life savings into a business, that entrepreneur had better be sure that the business makes sense. It is therefore important to do a feasibility study about the business idea.

At a minimum, the entrepreneur should study the market, customers, industry, and competitors. One entrepreneurship expert suggests asking the questions that appear in Checklist 4.2 when sizing up the market, customers, and industry.[47]

The Competition

"Know your enemy" is a well-known bit of military advice, but it is also applicable to entrepreneurship. With relatively few resources, entrepreneurs often blunder into situations where they don't fully understand the competition. Entrepreneurs can use the **competitive profile matrix** shown in Table 4.2 to assess their potential competitors' strengths and weaknesses. To do so, first identify the factors that are critical to success in the proposed business (for instance, price, advertising, or distribution). Next, weight their importance (weights should add up to 1.00). Then rate each competitor to identify its strengths and weaknesses, and to help answer the question, "Can we compete successfully in this industry?"

competitive profile matrix
A tool to assess the strengths and weaknesses of potential competitors.

The Business Plan

The **business plan** is the distinguishing characteristic of entrepreneurial planning. The business plan lays out what the business is, where it is heading, and how it plans to get there. Figure 4.5 summarizes the contents of a typical business plan.

business plan
A planning tool that lays out what the business is, where it is heading, and how it plans to get there.

Creating a Business Plan Creating a business plan is an important entrepreneurial activity. As with any managerial planning (see Chapters 6 and 7), developing the business plan helps the entrepreneur understand his or her options, anticipate problems, and make

TABLE 4.2 Illustrative Competitive Profile Matrix

CRITICAL SUCCESS FACTORS	WEIGHT	AVON RATING	AVON SCORE	L'OREAL RATING	L'OREAL SCORE	PROCTER & GAMBLE RATING	PROCTER & GAMBLE SCORE
Advertising	0.20	1	0.20	4	0.80	3	0.60
Product quality	0.10	4	0.40	4	0.40	3	0.30
Price competitiveness	0.10	3	0.30	3	0.30	4	0.40
Management	0.10	4	0.40	3	0.30	3	0.30
Financial position	0.15	4	0.60	3	0.45	3	0.45
Customer loyalty	0.10	4	0.40	4	0.40	2	0.20
Global expansion	0.20	4	0.80	2	0.40	2	0.40
Market share	0.05	1	0.05	4	0.20	3	0.15
TOTAL	1.00		3.15		3.25		2.80

Note: (1) The ratings values are as follows: 1 = major weakness, 2 = minor weakness, 3 = minor strength, 4 = major strength. (2) As indicated by the total weighted score of 2.8, P&G is weakest. (3) Only eight critical success factors are included for simplicity; this is too few in actuality.

tomorrow's decisions today. The entrepreneur does not want to find out six months after opening the store that labour costs are twice as high as anticipated and that the store's economics make it unlikely that the business can survive. Furthermore, the chances of getting financing without a business plan are virtually nil. No banker or financier is about to make a cash infusion without a business plan.

Experts in writing business plans underscore the importance of doing this job right. Pay particular attention to four things: clearly defining the business; providing evidence of management capabilities; providing evidence of marketing capabilities; and offering an attractive financial arrangement.[48] As one expert says, "Most entrepreneurs and small-business owners can prepare a B or B+ business plan without too much trouble. That would be fine if investors would fund B or B+ plans. Investors, however, fund only A or A+ plans...."[49]

Using Computerized Business Planning Software Software packages can facilitate this process. There are several good business planning software packages available; we use one—Business Plan Pro from Palo Alto Software—to illustrate what they do and how they're used. Business Plan Pro contains all the information and planning aids someone needs to create a business plan. It contains, for example, 30 sample plans; step-by-step instructions (with examples) for creating each part of a plan (executive summary, market analysis, and so on); financial planning spreadsheets; easy-to-use tables (for instance for making sales forecasts); and automatic programs for creating colour 3-D charts for showing things like monthly sales and yearly profits.

Business Plan Pro's Planning Wizard takes the entrepreneur "by the hand" and helps develop a business plan step by step. The result is an integrated plan, complete with charts, tables, and professional formatting. For example, click "start a plan," and the Planning Wizard presents a series of questions, including, "Does your company sell products, services, or both? Would you like a detailed or basic business plan? Does your company sell on credit?" Then, as you go to each succeeding part of the plan—such as the executive summary—the Planning Wizard shows you instructions with examples, making creating your own executive summary (or other plan section) relatively easy. As you move into the quantitative part of your plan, such as making sales and financial forecasts, the planning wizard translates your numbers into tables and charts.

INTRODUCTION
A basic description of the firm—name, address, business activity, current stage of development of the firm, and plans for the future.

EXECUTIVE SUMMARY
An overview of the entire business plan, summarizing the content of each section and inviting the reader to continue.

INDUSTRY ANALYSIS
A description of the industry the firm is competing in, focusing on industry trends and profit potential.

MANAGEMENT SECTION
A description of the management team and whether it is complete—and, if not, when and how it will be completed.

MANUFACTURING SECTION
A description of the complexity and logistics of the manufacturing process and of the firm's production capacity and current percentage of capacity use.

PRODUCT SECTION
A description of the good or service, including where it is in its life cycle (for example, a new product or a mature product); of future product research and development efforts; and of the status of patent or copyright applications.

MARKETING SECTION
A marketing plan, including a customer profile, an analysis of market needs, and a geographic analysis of markets; a description of pricing, distribution, and promotion; and an analysis of how the firm's marketing efforts are different from competitors' efforts.

FINANCIAL SECTION
Financial statements for the current year and the three previous years, if applicable; financial projections for the next three to five years; and assumptions for sales, cost of sales, cash flow, pro forma balance sheets, and key statistics, such as the current ratio, the debt/equity ratio, and inventory turnovers.

LEGAL SECTION
Form of ownership (proprietorship, partnership, or corporation) and a listing of any pending lawsuits filed by or against the firm.

FIGURE 4.5
Contents of a Good Business Plan

How Entrepreneurs Organize

At first glance, it might seem that "organizing" is not a topic that the entrepreneur would need to address in much detail. After all, what kind of organization chart does one need for managing a three-person store? However, such a conclusion would be misleading. Many small businesses have dozens or hundreds of employees, and therefore do require the sorts of organizational design techniques covered in Chapters 8 and 9. Furthermore, even the owner of a three-person business has to ensure that each person knows what to do and how their efforts interface with those of other employees.

Organizing the Small Business

In practice, new small businesses don't start off with conventional organization structures. Studies suggest they begin life with a "simple structure."[50] The entrepreneur typically works interactively with a handful of associates, making all or most decisions. At this stage of the business, it is unusual to have an organization chart.

This informality becomes counterproductive when the company grows to several dozen people. Few entrepreneurs (or anyone else for that matter) can effectively supervise so many people. At this point, an organization structure is born. The entrepreneur institutes a formal division of work among employees, including managers and a chain of command. Then, as the company grows, it may evolve into a divisional, and then a multidivisional structure. Figure 4.6 summarizes the typical structural evolution.

Netscape Communication provides an example. Between May 5, 1994 (when it started corporate life as Mosaic Communications), and March 1999 (when AOL bought it), Netscape went from nothing to a company valued at more than U.S.$10 billion. How it built its organization in such a short time provides some interesting insights into how start-up companies organize under rapidly changing conditions.[51]

Netscape began with a simple functional organization, with separate departments for activities like marketing, development, legal, and finance. However, it also provided the sort of "networked" communications that would help it avoid becoming bureaucratic. For example, management divided the technology development group into small teams of about six engineers each and gave each team a lot of autonomy. Netscape also used the internet to create a "virtual development organization." In 1994, Netscape had only 115 employees and so lacked the resources to test and debug its new browser. It therefore posted a beta version of Navigator on the internet, thus allowing users to serve as a sort of virtual quality assurance team.

As Netscape grew, management replaced its functional organization with one built around product divisions. Netscape executives did this in part because "they believed that combining the functional groups needed to build a product under a single general manager will enable the product groups to be closer to customers, to focus more effectively on specific markets and competitors, and to act more autonomously."[52] As the size of the product divisions grew, Netscape's top managers needed a more formal way to coordinate their activities. Management made various organizational changes to add more formality, such as creating a new position for "quality and customer satisfaction." The company also instituted a more systematic way of doing things, by building activities around 36-month plans.

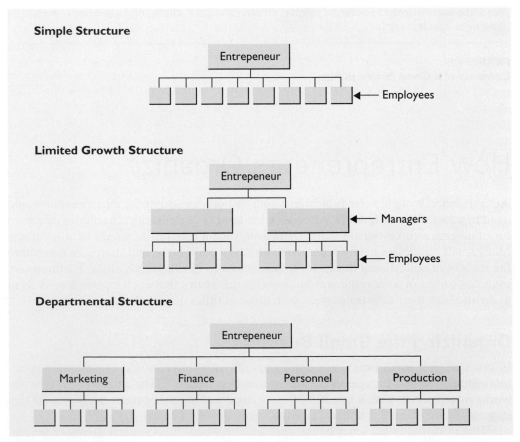

FIGURE 4.6
Illustrative Organizational Charts as a Company Grows

Staffing the Small Business

The management skills that will be covered in Chapter 10 (Staffing and Human Resource Management) apply to starting and managing a small business as much as they do to larger businesses. The entrepreneur needs to write job descriptions for the jobs in question, and have a recruiting plan showing the jobs to recruit for and how to recruit for them. The entrepreneur must also effectively interview and screen job candidates, train, appraise, and discipline the new employees, and be aware of equal employment laws.

The experience of the Duncan Group, Inc. helps illustrate this. "One day," as Melba J. Duncan recalls, "I woke up, and I knew: This is a business!"[53] After years as administrative assistant to CEOs, Duncan decided to strike out on her own. She correctly believed that top administrative/executive assistants represented an overlooked niche in the employee-search industry. Today her company successfully places administrative assistants who command salaries ranging from U.S.$55 000 to U.S.$130 000 per year.

With years as a top assistant herself, Duncan combines an understanding of what the job calls for with a comprehensive system for selecting great candidates. To send three great finalists to a client, Duncan knows she must start with a pool of 100. Her recruiters therefore work the phones "like air-traffic controllers." They also review their files and their network of contacts. An initial screening cuts the original candidate pool to about 50; these complete a 15-page questionnaire, after which they cut the pool to about 15.[54] Those 15 go through a four-hour testing and profiling process. This helps highlight their written and oral communication and clerical skills, and their management aptitude and personality. A clinical psychologist spends two days per week in Duncan's office, interviewing candidates and compiling profiles. Duncan's favourite questions for applicants are shown in Figure 4.7.[55]

HR Start-up Policies and Procedures Organizing the considerable paperwork involved with human resource management is essential. For example, just recruiting and hiring an employee might require a "notice of available position," a help wanted advertising listing, an employment application, an interviewing checklist, and a telephone reference checklist. The entrepreneur then needs an employment agreement, a confidentiality and non-compete agreement, a hiring authorization form, and an employee background verification. To keep track of the employee once he or she is on board, the entrepreneur will need—just to start—an employee change form, personnel data sheet, and daily or weekly time records. Then, there are the performance appraisal forms, notice of probation, and dozens of other, similar forms. The new business owner without these documents cannot consider his or her business to be organized.

At the Duncan Group, candidates are asked to complete a 15-page questionnaire. It's jammed with mind-benders such as "What does service mean to you?" and "What places, people, ideas, or things arouse your curiosity?" The questionnaire doesn't change, but the questions Duncan is inspired to ask during face-to-face interviews always do. Here are her current favourites, culled from the questionnaire and the interviews:

1. Describe your worst boss and best boss. ("I'm partly thinking about discretion," says Duncan. "How much are you telling me that I shouldn't know?")

2. What would a previous employer have to say about you? ("For perspective on flexibility, judgment, and maturity.")

3. What are some of the qualities that enable you to perform successfully in a support role? ("People are more important than technology in this job; of course you need both, but does the answer reveal a technician?")

4. Given the opportunity, what new activities would you try? ("Are you curious, outgoing, strong, confident? Whiners aren't good.")

5. Please write a brief paragraph on the subject of your own choosing. You may want to focus on your life, your family, your aspirations, your goals, or your achievements. ("There's nothing as important as having people's best interests at heart; I want to guide them into the right position and this answer will help me do that. I want to know they have a sense of direction. I want to know what they care about. Also, attention to detail: please, no typos!")

FIGURE 4.7
Duncan's Five Favourite Questions for Applicants

Where does the entrepreneur go to obtain the necessary HR forms and systems? For a start-up business, office supply stores such as Office Depot and Grand and Toy sell paper and pencil forms. For example, Office Depot sells packages of individual personnel forms, including an employment application, performance evaluation, and weekly expense report. However, as your company grows, it becomes increasingly unwieldy and inefficient to rely on manual HR systems. Conducting performance appraisals for a few employees and tracking the results may not be much of a problem for a small store, but for a company with 40 or 50 employees, the management time devoted to conducting appraisals can multiply into weeks. It is at about this stage that most small to medium-sized firms begin computerizing individual HR tasks.

How Entrepreneurs Lead

Small business owners face some special challenges when it comes to leading and motivating employees. Many have the type of operation that depends heavily on minimum-wage, entry-level workers, many of whom have never worked before.[56] Keeping their workers motivated while trying to manage all the other functions of a small business can be a challenge. That makes the leadership skills covered in Chapters 11 to 15 important. Knowing the right leadership style for the situation, applying a range of motivation tools (from praise to higher pay), knowing how to communicate, and being able to get the most out of the company's work teams can spell the difference between success and failure for the entrepreneur.

Motivation in Small Businesses

Steve Lauer runs eight Subway sandwich stores. He found that half his stores' turnover occurred in the first 30 days of employment. Remembering his own stress level during his first few days on the job, his first step was to get his new hires' stress levels down. He now has one of his more experienced employees periodically spend 20 hours coaching new workers.

Richard Kerley, president and CEO of Fine Host Corporation, provides another example. At any given time he has employees working in convention centres and corporate and university dining facilities, busing tables and cooking and serving food. In this highly competitive business, wages are low, but as Kerley says, "Though there may be economic restraints on what we pay them, there are no restraints on the recognition we give them." For example, the company posts workers' names in the company building to recognize good work, gives individual workers quality awards, and makes sure each employee gets a framed certificate for completing training courses.

The bottom line is that while running a smaller business may have some special challenges, the intelligent use of respect and recognition can go a long way toward motivating entry-level and low-pay workers.

Teamwork in Entrepreneurial Organizations

Entrepreneurs can make good use of the teamwork skills covered in Chapter 14. Published Image, Inc. is an example. Almost from the day he founded Published Image, Inc. and organized the shareholder newsletter process into self-managed teams, Eric Gershman had in mind the day his own position would become superfluous. His viewpoint was that employees capable of preparing their own work schedules, budgets, and bonuses shouldn't have much use for a boss. Gershman soon got his wish of working himself out of a job. After revenues doubled to more than U.S.$4 million, Standard & Poors bought his business.[57]

The Entrepreneurial Culture

Although many entrepreneurs have no trouble creating just the right culture, for others doing so can be a chore. One "dark side" of entrepreneurs is that some of them have high needs to control. This can translate into a culture of hiding and blame—hardly a desirable business culture.

This "darker" culture has potential pros and cons. It may help the entrepreneur keep things under control, but it is also the antithesis of what a small, innovative company's culture should be. Figure 4.8 sums up the preferred entrepreneurial culture. It reflects the fact that entrepreneurial activities need a risk-loving, failure-forgiving, creative, and decentralized culture to take root.

How Entrepreneurs Control

The concepts and methods of managerial control (see Chapter 16) are also applicable to entrepreneurial organizations.

What to Control?

The entrepreneur first opening his or her doors has no control infrastructure to rely on. To that person, the idea that control means "setting standards, measuring performance, and taking corrective action" (see Chapter 16) may seem a bit theoretical. The entrepreneur wants to know exactly what must be controlled.[58] The following list provides an illustrative starting point. The entrepreneur should control

- All approvals for disbursements of cash and regular accounting
- Review of cash receipts, including conciliation with the work that the firm actually did for the customer
- Reconciliation of bank statements
- Periodic review and reconciliation of inventory records
- Approval of pricing policies and exceptions
- Approval of credit policies and exceptions
- Review of all expenses and commissions
- Approval of purchasing and receiving policies
- Review of payments to vendors and employees
- Approval of signature authorities for payments (in other words, who can sign cheques?)
- Review of and changes to policies

Dimension	Traditional Organization	Entrepreneurial Organization
Strategy	Status quo, conservative	Evolving, futuristic
Productivity	Short-term focus, profitability	Short and long term, multiple criteria
Risk	Averse, punished	Emphasized and rewarded
Opportunity	Absent	Integral
Leadership	Top-down, autocratic	Culture of empowerment
Power	Hoarded	Given away
Failure	Costly	OK; teaches a lesson
Decision making	Centralized	Decentralized
Communication	By the book, chain of command	Flexible, facilitates innovation
Structure	Hierarchical	Organic
Creativity	Tolerated	Prized and worshipped
Efficiency	Valued, accountants are heroes	Valued if it helps realize overall goals

FIGURE 4.8
Organizational Culture: A Comparison

To monitor and control these and other activities, entrepreneurs need several operating reports. Control means setting targets, measuring performance, and taking corrective actions. These reports provide the tools for comparing what happened to what the entrepreneur planned. Operating reports provide insights into various facets of the company's operations. Managers typically need operating reports for activities including

- New orders and backlog (weekly, monthly)
- Shipments/sales (weekly, monthly)
- Employment (monthly)
- Inventory out of stock (weekly, monthly)
- Product quality (weekly, monthly)
- Accounts receivable aging (who owes what, and for how long?)
- Weekly overdue accounts
- Returns and allowances (monthly)
- Production (weekly, monthly)

SKILLS AND STUDY MATERIALS

SUMMARY

1. Entrepreneurship is the creation of a business for the purpose of gain or growth under conditions of risk and uncertainty. An entrepreneur is thus someone who creates new businesses under risky conditions.

2. Some environments are more conducive to entrepreneurship than others. The level of *economic freedom* is one consideration. Others include the ability to *streamline, downsize,* and *fire employees at will*, the level of *economic activity, technological advances,* the *level of innovation, globalization,* and other environmental factors including venture capital availability; technically skilled labour force; accessibility of suppliers; accessibility of customers; the proximity of universities; availability of lenders; accessibility of transportation; attitude of the area's population; and availability of supporting services (such as roads, electric power, and accounting firms).

3. A few behaviours seem to arise consistently in anecdotal/case descriptions of successful entrepreneurs. These include *tenacity* and *intensity*—the drive to pursue a goal with passion and focus.

4. Most entrepreneurs seem to stumble upon their ideas for a business. Most of those responding to one survey said they got their ideas for their businesses through their *previous employment. Serendipity* was the next source that most respondents mentioned. A relative handful got their ideas from *hobbies*, or from a *systematic search* for business opportunities.

5. In creating the business entity, the entrepreneur needs to decide what the ownership structure will be. The three main forms of business ownership are the sole proprietorship, the partnership, and the corporation. Taxation and limiting the owner's liability are always big considerations in choosing an ownership form.

6. The two basic sources of business finance are debt and equity. Equity finance represents an ownership in the venture, while debt is borrowed capital.

7. Although entrepreneurs often do develop detailed business plans to get their financing, in general they tend to abbreviate most steps of the planning process. In formulating strategies, for instance, they screen out losers quickly, minimize the resources devoted to researching ideas, don't wait for all the answers, and stand ready to change course.

8. In practice, new small businesses don't start off with conventional organization structures. The entrepreneur typically works interactively with a handful of associates, making all or most decisions himself or herself. As the firm grows, the manager institutes an organization structure and chart.

9. Small-business owners face some special challenges when it comes to leading and motivating employees. Keeping their workers motivated while trying to manage all the other functions of a small business can be a

challenge. Knowing the right leadership style for the situation, applying a range of motivation tools (from praise to higher pay), knowing how to communicate, and being able to get the most out of the company's work teams can spell the difference between success and failure for the entrepreneur.

10. The small business manager needs to be sure he or she is controlling activities crucial to the firm's viability.

These include cash disbursements and regular accounting, cash receipts, reconciliation of bank statements, review and reconciliation of inventory records, pricing policies, credit policies, all expenses and commissions, purchasing and receiving policies, payments to vendors and employees, signature authorities for payments, and changes to policies.

CRITICAL THINKING EXERCISES

1. Using the materials in this chapter, write a one-page paper on the topic, "Why I would (or would not) make a good entrepreneur."

2. Think about a business that you might like to be involved in. Then do some research on it and prepare a business plan for starting such a business (use the business plan guidelines shown in Figure 4.5).

EXPERIENTIAL EXERCISES

1. At the library or on the internet, review sales information on two popular franchises of your choice. Then, in teams of four or five students, evaluate the pros and cons of these franchise businesses, and answer the question, "Should I invest in this franchise?"

2. Assume that the dean of your business school is eager to expand the school's programs to new markets. She has

decided to try to establish a new, on-line MBA program, and she has asked you to conduct an informal, quick feasibility study. In teams of four or five students, outline what you would cover in such a study, and then explain why you believe her new program is or is not a good idea.

BUILDING YOUR MANAGEMENT SKILLS

The Entrepreneurial Perspective

An excellent way to find out about entrepreneurship is to talk to an entrepreneur. Ask your professor or some other professors to help you identify an entrepreneur or entrepreneurs who have started a business in the past five years in your local area of Canada. Contact the person and conduct an informational interview. Some questions you might want to ask are

■ What did it take to establish the business?

■ Did you have a business plan?

■ Where did you get your financing?

■ What management challenges do you face today?

■ How did you develop your human resource policies?

Also ask any other questions that specifically fit the type of business. Then prepare a paper on the major points you learned about entrepreneurship. Be ready to present your findings in class or in a small group. (You might want to do this project with two or three other students and divide the labour according to expertise.) Use references like *Inc.* or *Fast Company* (magazines that are devoted to entrepreneurship). These resources may help you find an entrepreneur or decide what questions you want to ask an entrepreneur.

Entrepreneurs have a wide range of traits that enable them to be successful. Access the website of the Centre for Entrepreneurship Education and Development (**www.ceed.info**). Read the profiles of Atlantic-Canadian Entrepreneurs at **www.ceed.info/Leadingedge/homebase/ homebase.pdf**.

1. What obstacles did these entrepreneurs encounter?
2. How did they overcome the obstacles?
3. List the traits that made these entrepreneurs successful.

CASE STUDY 4-1

What's the Catch?

Stephen Reid and Darren Gurr opened their first restaurant in 1988 in Lethbridge, Alberta. They called it Billy MacIntyre's Cattle Company. The restaurant was an immediate success, and Reid and Gurr recouped their investment in just two years. They then opened two more MacIntyre's restaurants in Calgary. They also bought a restaurant called 4th St. Rose. In the mid-1990s, they sold the MacIntyre's restaurants and used the cash to start two new upscale restaurants—Wildwood Grill and Bonterra.

In spite of all this success, Stephen Reid felt that he needed a restaurant that would really get people's attention. That's when he hit upon the idea for a swanky seafood restaurant called Catch, which is one of the most ambitious restaurant projects ever seen in Canada. After much planning and financial manoeuvring, Catch opened in 2002 in downtown Calgary. The restaurant features an American-style oyster bar on the first floor, an elegant dining room on the second floor, and a garden patio on the third. Development costs were about $560 per square foot, which is about twice what other high-end restaurants usually cost. Total development costs were well over $5 million.

In taking Catch from an idea to reality, Reid had to deal with three major problems. First, he had to find a suitable location. During his search, he discovered that the old Imperial Bank building in Calgary's financial district was available. It happened to be attached to the new Hyatt Regency, which is owned by billionaire Ron Mannix. This helped Reid with his second problem—financing. When Mannix asked Reid to share his business plan for Catch, Reid and his partner worked one entire weekend to develop one. After seeing the plan, Mannix agreed to help with the funding.

The third problem concerned staffing the key position of chef in the restaurant. Reid was able to convince Michael Noble, formerly the chef of a high-class Vancouver restaurant called Diva at the Met, to be the chef for Catch. He did so by giving Noble an equity stake in Catch. Noble was a triple-gold medal winner at the World Culinary Olympics in Berlin in 1996 and was named Chef of the Year by the Canadian Federation of Chefs and Cooks in 1999.

Reid knows that in the restaurant industry, 8 of every 10 new restaurants fail within their first two years of operation. In spite of that daunting statistic, Reid thinks his idea is a winner, and he is optimistic that his new restaurant will be a success.

Questions

1. What is the difference between an entrepreneur and a small-business owner? Is Stephen Reid a small-business owner or an entrepreneur? Or both? Explain.

2. What is franchising? Is franchising something that Stephen Reid should consider? Why or why not?

3. What are the various methods that are available for getting started in business? Which method has Stephen Reid used?

4. Explain in general terms how each of the functions of management (planning, organizing, leading, and controlling) are evident in Stephen Reid's activities.

Getting by with a Little Help from His Mother's Friends

Andrew Morris had almost everything he needed to start his Caribbean-flavoured grocery store in a New York City suburb. He had an M.B.A. from Columbia University, a business plan, and a U.S.$50 000 loan from the European American bank. However, after he negotiated the rent on a 1600 square foot retail space in Hempstead, New York, he found he did not have enough cash left for inventory, payroll, marketing, and licences. Thanks to his mother—and her friends—he was able to secure an additional U.S.$15 000 in resources, which enabled him to stock the shelves with dozens of kinds of hot sauce, curry brands, and reggae music that the growing Caribbean community craves.

Morris got the money from his mother's *susu*, a kind of club or fund developed by West Indian housewives to provide rotating credit for big-ticket household purchases. A susu, which means "partner," typically has about 20 members, most of them either relatives or close friends. Over a 20-week period every member contributes a fixed sum each week. Any time during those 20 weeks, each member is entitled to borrow an amount or *draw* to use interest-free during that time.

For example, if a 20-member susu has a set weekly contribution of $100, each member pays $100 into the fund every week, or pays a total of $2000 over twenty weeks. Each member is then also able to draw $2000 at any point during that period. Essentially the susu is a kind of planned savings program that pools money to help members of the group who need help with cash flow. The Caribbean susu is not really a unique concept; other ethnic groups have also developed informal lending networks for their members.

Andrew Morris has dipped into his mother's susu a number of times to help his business grow. He used the money to pay a sales tax obligation, to purchase a commercial oven to cook Jamaican meat patties, to produce a special Easter promotion with traditional cheese and sweet bread sandwiches, and to expand his inventory to include unusual but popular items, such as Jamaican Chinese soy sauce. "It's a cash flow boon," Morris says. After seven years of ongoing susu support, Morris' store now has annual revenues of more than U.S.$1 million. Morris is now counting on susu support to help it expand into distributing coffee and developing a website. "It's no longer just a Christmas club," he says. "It's a way of life."

Questions

1. Andrew Morris has approached you for help. List what you believe he is doing right and doing wrong with respect to starting his business. What do you think accounts for the fact that he ran out of money before he opened, even though he had a business plan? What remedy or remedies would you suggest at this point?

2. Develop a one-page outline showing Morris how you would suggest he conduct an informal business feasibility study.

3. Lists the activity areas for which Morris should establish controls.

4. What other alternative means for obtaining financing would you recommend for Morris? What are their pros and cons when compared to continuing using his mother's susu?

The Entrepreneur

jetBlue
AIRWAYS®

Just about any way you look at it, David Neeleman is your classic entrepreneur. As one friend and airline analyst put it, "he's a genius entrepreneur." Says Neeleman's second in command, "he has an uncanny knack for knowing when an opportunity is right." Neeleman's record speaks for itself. He was one of two people who started Morris Air, and then sold it for a huge profit to Southwest Airlines. Southwest bought Morris Air on the condition that Neeleman sign a five-year non-compete clause. Neeleman spent the next five years helping to start a non-competing new airline in Canada (WestJet) and a company that created an electronic reservation system. He also spent some time researching what a new, low-cost airline in the United States might look like. Thus, by the time his five-year non-compete time had run out, Neeleman had already started three very successful companies, and developed the plan for his fourth, which would turn out to be JetBlue.

You can trace Neeleman's strategy for JetBlue back to his experiences at Morris Air and Southwest Airlines. As he says, he spent part of his five-year non-compete period thinking through how to build a top-notch low-fare passenger airline. "We asked how could we create a preferred product—rather than a secondary or tertiary choice—and do that at the lowest cost?" Several of JetBlue's basic operating policies stem from Neeleman's earlier experiences. For example, at Morris Air, he was one of the airline industry's first executives to implement paperless electronic tickets. He was also one of the first to encourage telecommuting, with many of Morris's reservation agents working from their homes. From the outset, he knew he wanted his new airline to "offer a superior product with everyday low fares." His original plan therefore called for new planes, strong financing, high utilization, fleet homogeneity, great pricing, and experienced management. As he put it, "we're Southwest with seat assignments, leather seats and television." With a strong plan and years of success in creating value for his investors, it's probably not surprising that Neeleman was able to raise about U.S.$160 million, making his new airline the best financed new airline in history. His investors included J.P. Morgan Partners, Soros private equity partners, and Weston Presidio capital, all top financiers. He soon followed that up with an initial public offering that raised more than U.S.$100 million more and helped pay back several of his initial investors.

Neeleman exhibits some of the traits most people would associate with successful entrepreneurs, as well as some they might not. He is a college dropout, as well as "a Mormon with nine kids who won't sip coffee, much less chain smoke cigarettes and toss back the Wild Turkey." He doesn't spend much time partying and says his only hobby (other than spend-ing time with his family) is reading history books. Neeleman self-mockingly told one reporter that he sometimes thinks he has "attention deficit disorder," apparently because he is so quick to move from one idea to another. On the other hand, friends and associates describe him as highly focused. "He's low-key, and he's totally directed..." says one associate. One reporter, after watching him lead an orientation session for new employees, described him as "completely, utterly riveting."

So far, according to virtually all reports, JetBlue has avoided the sorts of poor service and/or spotty performance problems that have tripped up some other start-up airlines. However, some airline industry analysts have expressed some concerns. At the moment, for instance, JetBlue's profitability is high in part because, with brand-new airplanes, it has no maintenance costs—the maintenance is provided as part of the original purchase price of the aircraft. Furthermore, now that JetBlue is on the radar screen of major airlines like American and United, they are more aggressively resisting JetBlue's incursions onto their turf. Employees at Southwest Airlines (which, remember, served as part of the model for JetBlue) have recently been much more vocal about getting a bigger share of the "pie" from Southwest management. Furthermore, Neeleman has said, staying "small" (in terms of maintaining JetBlue's enthusiastic entrepreneurial culture) is "our greatest challenge as we move forward." That will mean maintaining good compensation (including the company's profit-sharing and stock purchase plan), as well as doing whatever else is necessary to keep employees happy and focused on customer service and high productivity.

Assignment

You and your team are consultants to Mr. Neeleman, who is depending on your management expertise to help navigate the launch and management of JetBlue. Here's what he wants to know from you:

1. In what ways does Neeleman fit the stereotype of the "typical" entrepreneur? In what ways does he differ? Would you say that he has the traits to be an entrepreneur? Why or why not?

2. List in outline form the things you think Neeleman did right and did wrong with respect to starting JetBlue.

3. Based on what you know, what are Neeleman and his team doing to maintain an entrepreneurial culture at JetBlue? What else would you suggest that they do?

Border Security

What if you're a Canadian company and the success of your business depends on getting across the border into the United States? The answer used to be "No problem," but things have drastically changed since 9/11. Although Canada and the United States have long been famous for having the "longest undefended border in the world," world events have changed all that. A simple business trip to the United States isn't certain anymore, particularly for managers who live in Canada but who originally came from Iran, Iraq, Libya, Syria, or Sudan (anyone born there arouses the suspicions of U.S. border guards). All sorts of Canadian citizens and landed immigrants are now being denied entry to the United States, and the United States is claiming that Canada's security measures are insufficient to stop terrorists.

All of this has had a major impact on Canadian businesses, who have discovered that they have to decide who on staff is "good to go" to the United States. Bob Whitehorse, a vice-president at Vancouver-based Westower, has to screen staff to determine if they will have trouble crossing the border to work on communication towers in the U.S. Ramin Safavy is a Canadian citizen who was born in Iran. He used to be a frequent visitor to the United States, but he hasn't travelled there lately, and his customers don't know why. Someone else from his firm now goes to the United States to do what he used to do.

U.S. officials says they will do everything they can to respect Canadian citizens, but the fact is that anyone born in the five countries noted above may have trouble getting jobs with Canadian firms because they can't travel to the United States. Ben Trister, a lawyer that Canadian companies often ask for advice, says that some U.S. border employees behave badly just because they have a badge and like to push people around. Trister is heading up a committee that is trying to keep the border as open as possible, but he is also hiring more staff as corporate clients increasingly come to him with their travelling headaches.

Problems are also created for Canadian companies because the border-crossing rules can change unexpectedly as a result of the latest directive from Washington. For example, Canadian businesses have recently discovered that if one of their employees had a minor brush with the law many years ago, that employee may now be barred from entering the United States at all. Formerly, Canadians with minor criminal records were once able to cross the border easily, but no longer. Since 9/11, governments have been linking up databases to more closely check the status of individuals crossing the border. A person who was caught crossing the border with a small amount of marijuana years ago now can't get into the United States. There may be thousands of Canadians in this situation.

Because of the extra scrutiny that is evident at border crossings, it is not enough for Canadian companies to simply know the rules. They must also know their employees and their backgrounds. Canadian companies are becoming increasingly frustrated by the new rules since many of them are very involved in exporting to the United States, and it is important that Canadian employees go to the United States to work the market. Canadian companies feel that they have been made the "front line of defence" in the war against terrorism that is being waged by the United States.

Questions

1. List and describe the various "international environments" that Canadian managers must cope with. Which are the most relevant ones in this case? Explain.

2. Briefly explain what is involved in each of the *functions* of management. Which functions are most important in dealing with this situation? Why?

3. Briefly explain what is involved in each of the *skills* of management. Which ones are most important in this situation? Why?

4. Read the material on crisis management and contingency planning in Chapter 6. How are these concepts relevant in this situation? Develop a contingency plan for the border security issue described in this video.

5. Canadian firms that export to the U.S. have experienced problems at the border because of increased security that has been instituted since 9/11. What alternatives to exporting might Canadian firms consider? How would these alternatives help them avoid border problems? What are the pros and cons of each of these alternatives?

Video Resource: "Border Security," *Venture* #854 (November 17, 2002).

Whistle-blowers

In 2002, *Time Magazine* named three female whistle-blowers as "Persons of the Year" for reporting wrong-doing at the companies they worked for. Because of the publicity given to whistle-blowers, many people see the activity as a noble pursuit. But it's not very glamorous when you look behind the scenes.

Just ask Joanna Galtieri, who went to the media and blew the whistle on the Foreign Affairs Department of the Canadian government. She claimed that the activities of the department were not cost-effective, and she cited the example of a Canadian diplomat who was stationed in Japan. The diplomat was supposed to be housed in a Canadian-owned residence; instead, he asked for $350 000 to rent another apartment he liked better. Galtieri says foreign affairs refused to deal with her concerns about irresponsible spending of taxpayers' money. She also claimed that her employer ostracized her in the workplace. Now, Joanna visits high schools and talks to young people about the issue of whistle-blowing.

Mike Hilson, an Ontario accountant, blew the whistle on shoddy accounting practices at Philip Services, a Hamilton waste-disposal company. He knew the company was stockpiling waste but not recording the cost it would take to get rid of it. Hilson raised the issue with his boss several times, but nothing happened. The last time he raised the issue, he was fired. A few months later, he noticed that Philip Services was applying to open another landfill site near his parents' home — if the company went bankrupt, there would be no money to clean up the landfill. He sent a letter to Ontario's Minister of the Environment expressing his concerns. Soon after, he was sued for libel by Philip Services for $30 million. Hilson eventually triumphed over Philip Services. They withdrew their lawsuit and were required to pay his legal bills.

Writer Mark Wexler interviewed 200 whistle-blowers and found that they were generally disillusioned with their experiences — whistle-blowers think that if they speak out, somebody will do something about the problems they identify. Hilson, for example, was astonished that no one would take his comments seriously. Wexler says whistle-blowers often aren't listened to because the public is skeptical of their claims.

When confronted with a whistle-blower's claim, companies may embark on an aggressive campaign to discredit the whistle-blower. This can include attacking the whistle-blower's character; if this is successful, the whistle-blower will appear to have no credibility and less weight will be given to the charges that are being made. For example, after Hilson blew the whistle on Philip Services, the company publicized his personal problems and said he was "a troubled person."

Some people feel that strong laws are needed to protect whistle-blowers. Countries that are taking that approach include the United States, South Korea, Australia, and Russia. The Liberal government of Canada promised such legislation years ago, but nothing has been done. When a reporter from *Venture* asked the Prime Minister's Office about this, she was referred to the Justice Department, who referred her to the Treasury Board, who referred her to Industry Canada. She was then referred to the Competition Bureau.

Venture then sent a formal written request to the Prime Minister's Office asking again what had happened to their campaign promise. They were referred elsewhere and the process repeated itself. When political parties are in opposition, they are proponents of whistle-blowing legislation; but when they get in power, they seem to lose interest.

Joanna Galtieri's experience has caused her to become an activist on this issue. She has drafted a private member's bill which will be considered in Parliament. She doesn't think it will get very far, but it will be a vehicle to create a dialogue on this issue. Mike Hilson doesn't think that passing laws will work—he thinks it will be very difficult to change our culture so that people who speak out will be perceived as doing something useful.

Questions

1. What is whistle-blowing? What are the arguments in favour of it? Are there any arguments against it?

2. Suppose a law was passed which was designed to protect whistle-blowers. One provision of this law allowed for penalties like prison time for any company personnel who threatened a whistle-blower. What do you think would happen?

3. "It is impossible to protect whistle-blowers because the company can always claim it has done nothing wrong. By the time any proof is provided, the case will be forgotten and the whistle-blower will likely have been fired. Therefore, whistle-blowers shouldn't bother." Do you agree or disagree? Explain your reasoning.

Source: "Corporate Whistleblowers," *Venture* #861 (January 5, 2003).

PART 2 Planning

Part 2: Planning provides an overview of the planning function. It includes a description of the planning process, an analysis of strategic planning, and an in-depth look at the essence of management—decision making. In the opening cases of Chapters 5, 6, and 7, you will read about Michael Sabia (CEO at BCE), Frank Giustra (former CEO at Lions Gate Entertainment), and Edgar Bronfman, Jr. (former CEO of Seagrams) and how the decisions they made have affected their companies and the people who work there.

We begin in **Chapter 5, Decision Making**, by describing the different types of decisions that managers are called upon to make, the rational decision-making process, and several decision making techniques that are available to managers. We also make suggestions as to how managers can make better decisions and how they can use groups in decision making. The **Appendix to Chapter 5** explains several popular quantitative techniques that are used by managers to improve their decision making.

Next, in **Chapter 6, The Planning Process**, we describe the planning process and the central role that managers play in it, the importance of goal setting in management, the various types of plans that managers create, and the management by objectives approach.

Finally, in **Chapter 7, Strategic Management**, we describe the important process of strategic decision making. These decisions have a major impact on the firm because they determine what kinds of activities the firm will pursue and what kind of company it will be. The specific strategic options that are available to managers at various levels in the firm are also explained.

Decision Making →

Decision Time at BCE

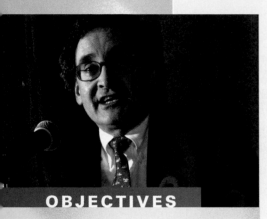

After studying this chapter and the case exercises at the end, you should be able to use the material to:

1. Demonstrate the importance of decision making in management jobs.

2. Explain the difference between programmed and nonprogrammed decisions.

3. Describe the steps a manager must take to work through the rational decision-making process.

4. Apply the suggestions for making better decisions to a real problem.

5. Develop a decision matrix for solving a management problem.

6. Avoid the decision traps that managers face.

7. Understand how to use groups more effectively in the decision-making process.

In April 2002, Jean Monty, the CEO of BCE Inc., unexpectedly announced that he was stepping down from his position. Michael Sabia, the new CEO, was immediately faced with a very difficult strategic decision, namely what kind of company BCE would be. Would it be a telephone company, a telecommunications company, a media company, or a New Economy company? This strategic decision was necessary because BCE had been acquiring companies in many different businesses, but several of them were not performing well. A CIBC *World Markets* research note said that BCE's strategy appeared to be in disarray.

To see why Sabia had a difficult strategic decision to make, consider the makeup of BCE in 2002. BCE had been pursuing a strategy that is often characterized by industry observers as "commerce, content, and connectivity." The *commerce* part of the equation included BCE Emergis (electronic commerce in the health and financial services industries) and CGI Group Inc. (information technology consulting). The *content* part of the equation was represented by Bell Globemedia, which includes CTV (television stations), ROBTv (business reporting), *The Globe and Mail* (a national newspaper), and Sympatico-Lycos (internet portals). The *connectivity* part of the equation included Bell Canada (telephones), Bell ExpressVu (satellite broadcasting), Teleglobe (international voice and data network), and Bell Canada International (telecom services in emerging markets).

The economic performance of these diverse holdings has varied widely. Bell Canada is the most successful and will continue to provide steady cash flow to the company. CGI Group is also doing well. But there are problems in each of the other areas. BCE Emergis, for example, has had difficulty reaching revenue projections because new customers simply haven't materialized. In spite of that, Sabia says that BCE is very committed to making Emergis a success. The same sorts of problems exist with Teleglobe and BCI. Bell Globemedia is also losing money, partly because of a slump in advertising.

Former CEO Jean Monty's strategy was to take money earned in the reliable Bell Canada part of the business and use it to acquire other New Economy businesses, some of which would likely grow very fast and make a lot of money for BCE. Monty's leadership style was active and decisive. He would analyze a situation, then take action. For example, in 2000 he decided to sell BCE's stake in Nortel Networks, which BCE had owned since 1957. His timing was perfect. BCE received a huge windfall when it sold its shares for $90 a share (by mid-2002, Nortel was trading for less than $1 a share).

But decisive action does not guarantee success. In 2000, BCE bought a 77 percent stake in Teleglobe for $7.4 billion as part of its "convergence" strategy to bring together various media in one organization. By 2002, however, Teleglobe was essentially worthless because of a glut in the market, and even though BCE considered Teleglobe a "core holding," it was cut loose. Teleglobe became known as "Monty's folly" in investment circles. Soon after being dropped by BCE, Teleglobe sought bankruptcy protection.

Monty saw BCE as a growth company, not a stodgy utility, and took the lead in getting BCE into wireless, high-speed internet and electronic commerce. His actions were a continuation of a long series of diversification decisions. Between 1980 and 2000, for example, BCE invested in TransCanada Pipelines (oil and gas), Quebecor (media and printing), Montreal Trustco (financial services), and BCE Developments (real estate). These ventures were generally unsuccessful, and some of them generated large losses ($440 million in the case of BCE Developments).

Given all that has happened in the past, Michael Sabia has some major strategic decisions to make. Diversification does not seemed to have worked very well for BCE, and some industry analysts are now saying that Sabia should forget diversification and focus on the telephone utility business. If he does that, BCE might be able to both dominate the market and generate a lot of profit.

Observers didn't have long to wait for Sabia's decision. In July 2002, BCE announced that it planned to repurchase 20 percent of Bell Canada from SBC Communications (which it had sold to SBC in 1999 for $5.1 billion). Michael Sabia said that BCE will concentrate on Bell, while other holdings will be reviewed to determine how they help the phone utility.

BCE
www.bce.ca

BCE Emergis
www.emergis.com

CGI Group
www.cgi.com

Understanding Decision Making

We all continually face the need to choose—the route to school, the job to accept, who to marry, or, in the case of Michael Sabia at BCE, which corporate strategy to pursue. A **decision** is a choice from among the available alternatives. **Decision making** is the process of developing and analyzing alternatives and making a choice.

Most decisions are prompted by problems. A *problem* is a discrepancy between a desirable situation and an actual situation. For example, if you need $50 for a show and you only have $10, you have a problem. A decision doesn't necessarily involve a problem, although this is often the case. On the other hand, problem solving always involves making decisions, so we'll use the terms "decision making" and "problem solving" interchangeably in this book. *Judgment* refers to the cognitive or "thinking" aspects of the decision-making process.[1] We'll see in this chapter that the decision-making process is often subject to distortions and biases, precisely because it is usually a judgmental, not a purely mechanical, process.

decision
A choice from among the available alternatives.

decision making
The process of developing and analyzing alternatives and making a choice.

As noted at the end of Chapter 3, we've focused to this point on the things that surround and influence what managers do: specifically, on outside and inside forces such as globalization, deregulation, values, culture, and ethics. Now, in Chapter 5, we begin a more detailed discussion of what managers actually do. Since making good decisions underlies just about everything we do, we've turned first to making decisions.

Decisions and the Management Process

Decision making is at the heart of what managers do. Planning, organizing, leading, and controlling are the basic management functions. However, as illustrated in Table 5.1, each of these calls for decisions to be made—which plan to implement, what goals to choose, and which people to hire, for instance.

Every manager on the company's business team makes decisions. This is illustrated in Table 5.2. The accounting manager decides what outside auditing firm to use, and how many days a customer can be allowed to wait before it pays its bills. The sales manager decides which sales representatives to use in each region, and which advertising agency to hire.

The production manager chooses between alternative suppliers and decides whether to recommend building a new plant. Nearly everything a manager does brings him or her to a decision that must be made.

Two Basic Types of Decisions

Any decision a manager makes can be classified as either a *programmed decision* or a *non-programmed decision*. The two differ in the extent to which the decision must be handled as a completely new situation.[2]

Programmed Decisions Luckily for managers, not every decision must be handled as a brand new situation. Instead, many decisions can be classified as programmed decisions. **Programmed decisions** are repetitive and routine and can be solved through mechanical procedures such as by applying rules. For example, to expedite the refund process, a department store may use this rule: "If the customer returns a jacket, you may give that person a refund if the tag is not removed, if the jacket is not damaged, and if the pur-

programmed decision
A decision that is repetitive and routine and that can be solved through mechanical procedures such as by applying rules.

TABLE 5.1	*Decisions in the Management Functions*
MANAGEMENT FUNCTION	**TYPICAL DECISIONS MANAGERS FACE**
Planning	What are the organization's long-term objectives?
	What strategies will best achieve these objectives?
	What should the organization's short-term objectives be?
	How difficult should individual goals be?
Organizing	How many subordinates should I have report directly to me?
	How much centralization should there be in the organization?
	How should jobs be designed?
	When should the organization implement a different structure?
Leading	How do I handle employees who appear to be low in motivation?
	What is the most effective leadership style in a given situation?
	How will a specific change affect worker productivity?
	When is the right time to stimulate conflict?
Controlling	What activities in the organization need to be controlled?
	How should these activities be controlled?
	When is a performance deviation significant?
	What type of management information system should the organization have?

TABLE 5.2 Some Decisions Business-Team Managers Make

MANAGER	EXAMPLES OF DECISIONS THESE MANAGERS FACE
Accounting manager	What accounting firm should we use? Who should process our payroll? Should we give that customer credit?
Finance manager	What bank should we use? Should we sell bonds or stocks? Should we buy back some of our company's stock?
Human resource manager	Where should we recruit for employees? Should we set up a testing problem? Should I advise settling the employment equity complaint?
Production manager	Which supplier should we use? Should we build the new plant? Should we buy the new machine?
Sales manager	Which sales rep should we use in this district? Should we start this advertising campaign? Should we lower prices in response to our competitor's doing so?

chase was made within the past two weeks." Other examples include the personnel at the University of Calgary deciding how to register students each fall, Canada Customs and Revenue determining an appropriate auditing procedure for income tax returns, and Kasba Lake Lodge in the Northwest Territories deciding how to schedule float plane flights to bring tourists to the lodge each Saturday.

Up to 90 percent of management decisions are programmed.[3] In many universities, for example, the question of which students to admit is made by mathematically weighting each candidate's test scores and grades. In most companies, the calculation of overtime pay and weekly payroll benefits is made by computer software. In fact, the advent of computers has dramatically boosted the number of decisions that can now be "programmed." For example, when your credit card is "swiped" at a point of purchase, the decision to accept it is generally computerized. The decision is referred to a credit manager only if your credit limit has been reached. It makes sense for managers to try to determine whether particular decisions can be programmed, and if so, the decisions can be left to subordinates.

Non-Programmed Decisions In contrast, **non-programmed decisions** are unique and novel. The Toronto Stock Exchange made a non-programmed decision when it decided to install state-of-the-art equipment for tracking stock transactions, as did IBM when it decided to enter the home computer market. Algonquin College made a non-programmed decision when it decided to introduce a new program of studies for students, and the province of Manitoba did the same when it imposed border duties on liquor purchased in the United States.

Non-programmed decisions are generally "...the kinds of [major] decisions which managers are paid to address...."[4] They rely on judgment and focus on the firm's long-term strategic development and survival. With the big and unexpected changes of the past few years—deregulation, global competition, and downsizings, for instance—such decisions are increasingly common. Table 5.3 compares programmed and non-programmed decision making.

Top-level managers tend to face more non-programmed decisions, while lower-level managers face more programmed ones, as illustrated in Figure 5.1. Lower-level managers tend to spend more time addressing programmed decisions, such as "How many employees should I put on the assembly line today?" Top managers face more decisions like "How should we respond to our competitor's moves?"

non-programmed decision A unique and novel decision that relies on judgment.

Toronto Stock Exchange
www.tse.com

Algonquin College
www.algonquinc.on.ca

TABLE 5.3 *Comparing Programmed and Non-programmed Decisions*

	PROGRAMMED	NON-PROGRAMMED
Type of decision	Programmable; routine; generic; computational	Non-programmable; unique; innovative
Nature of the decision	Procedural; predictable; well-defined information and decision criteria	Novel; unstructured; incomplete channels of information; unknown criteria
Strategy	Reliance on rules and computation	Reliance on principles; judgment; general problem solving
Decision-making techniques	Management science; capital budgeting, computerized solutions, rules	Judgment; intuition; creativity

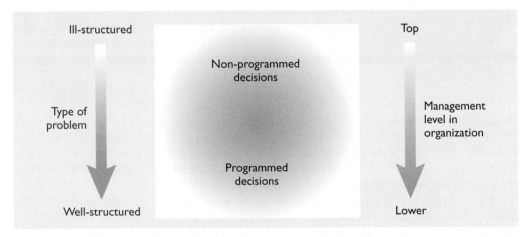

FIGURE 5.1
Types of Decisions Managers Face
Top managers tend to confront more ill-structured, ambiguous situations and so make more non-programmed decisions; lower-level managers tend to confront more structured situations and make more programmed decisions.

Decision-Making Models

Assume that you own a retail store, and you are trying to decide which of several trucks to buy for deliveries. How would you make this decision? Would you identify all your options, and then carefully weigh the advantages and disadvantages of each? Perhaps. Perhaps not. There are two main schools of thought (or "models") regarding how people make decisions.

The Classical Approach

The idea that managers are fully rational has a long and honourable tradition in economic and management theory. Classical economists needed a simplified way to explain economic phenomena, like how demand affects prices. Their solution was to accept a number of assumptions about how managers made decisions. Specifically, they assumed that the rational manager

1. Had complete or "perfect" information about the situation, including the full range of goods and services available on the market and the exact price of each good or service.

2. Could perfectly define the problem and not be confused by symptoms or other obstacles.

3. Could identify all criteria and accurately weigh all of the criteria according to certain preferences.

4. Knew all alternatives and could assess each against each criterion.

5. Could accurately calculate and choose the alternative with the highest perceived value and could therefore be expected to make an "optimal choice."[5]

The Administrative Approach

You know from your own experiences that these assumptions leave something to be desired. Does anyone really (even with the internet) ever have perfect knowledge of all the options? Do they really, unemotionally, analyze every single option? Not likely.

"It was precisely this kind of indecisiveness that got us into trouble in the first place!"

Herbert Simon and his associates proposed a decision-making model they thought better reflects these realities. They agreed that decision makers try to be rational, but pointed out that such rationality is, in practice, subject to many constraints: "The number of alternatives [the decision-maker] must explore is so great, the information he would need to evaluate them so vast, that even an approximation to objective rationality is hard to conceive...."[6]

You may have experienced the situation where, faced with too many final exams and other pressing problems, you have said, "I can't take this any more!" You are not alone. In one classic series of studies, participants were required to make decisions based on the amount of information transmitted on a screen. Most people quickly reached a point of "information overload" and began adjusting in several ways. Some omitted or ignored some of the information; others began making errors by incorrectly identifying some of the information; others gave only approximate responses (such as "about 25" instead of "24.6"). Based on a review of a lot of evidence like this, one expert concluded that "even the simplest decisions...rapidly overwhelm human cognitive capabilities."[7]

Simon argues that "bounded rationality" more accurately represents how managers actually make decisions.[8] **Bounded rationality** means that managers' decisions are only as rational as their unique values, capabilities, and limited capacity for processing information permit them to be. There are two main implications of bounded rationality. The first concerns the manager's search for solutions. The classicist's "rational" manager is an optimizer who continues to review potential solutions until the optimal one is found. By contrast, Simon's "administrative man" **satisfices**, that is, looks for solutions until a satisfactory one is found.

For example, suppose you are going fishing in northern Canada. You arrive in Rankin Inlet only to discover that your fishing rods were lost by the airline. The float plane that will take you out to the fishing lodge is going to leave in one hour, so you rush into town and buy a couple of fishing rods at the Northern Store (thankful that they even have fishing rods in stock). This decision is not optimal in terms of money spent or in terms of the equipment you purchased, but it does allow you to reach your fundamental goal of fishing.

Optimal solutions are searched out only in exceptional cases.[9] The "People Side of Managing" box describes another example of satisficing.

The second implication is that many biases and decision traps lie in wait for unsuspecting managers. Wise managers are therefore advised to consciously take their values, biases, and capabilities into account before making decisions. Keeping these points in mind, let's look now at an ideal decision-making process.

bounded rationality
Managers' decisions are only as rational as their unique values, capabilities, and limited capacity for processing information permit them to be.

satisfice
To look for solutions until a satisfactory one is found.

So Many Decisions, So Little Time

Perhaps the best way to illustrate "decision making: how it should be versus how it is" is with an example. This one is from Dominic Orr, president and CEO of Alteon WebSystems Inc. Ask him what his main management problem is, and he responds that he has to make choices every day about competitive strategy and product development. He needs to make decisions that he can trust without wasting valuable time. He knows that fast execution and fast delivery are easy, but that fast decision making is harder.

Young industries and start-ups are constantly changing, which means that even day-to-day decisions take on huge strategic importance. Therefore, making high stakes decisions as a team is important. But there is no time for endless debate or for office politics.

So how do they actually make decisions at Alteon? Management focuses on collecting as many facts as quickly as possible, and then decides on what appears to be the best (but not necessarily the perfect) solution. In Alteon's decision-making process, the people element is particularly important. The goal is to encourage lively debate while avoiding dysfunctional, personal comments. There is no room for "silent disagreement," and getting personal is out-of-bounds. The goal is to make each major decision in a single meeting. People arrive with a proposal or a solution—and with the facts to support it. After an idea is presented, the floor is open to objective critique of the ideas. If the idea doesn't stand this scrutiny, managers move on to another idea with no hard feelings. The idea is judged, not the person who came up with it. There is no real attempt to regulate how people feel. When intense conflict occurs, it is taken as a sign that progress is being made, not a sign that the discussion is out of control. Individuals can act as referees by asking certain focus questions such as "Is this good for the customer?" or "Does it keep our time-to-market advantage impact?" By focusing relentlessly on the facts, managers are able to see the strengths and weaknesses of an idea clearly and quickly.

The Decision-Making Process

There are five major steps in the ideal decision making process (see Figure 5.2). Given the points made above, it is obvious that this ideal will not always be achieved, either by managers in organizations, or by individuals making their own personal decisions.[10]

Step 1—Define the Problem

Identifying or defining the problem is trickier than it may appear. Common mistakes include emphasizing the obvious and being misled by symptoms.[11] Here is a classic example that demonstrates these mistakes. Workers in a large office building were upset because they had to wait so long for an elevator. The owners called in a consulting team and told them the problem was that "the elevators were running too slowly." If you accept this definition of the problem, then all the solutions are expensive. The elevators were running about as fast as they could, so speeding them up was not an option. You could ask the workers to stagger their work hours, but that could cause more animosity than the slow-moving elevators. Adding more elevators would also be very expensive.

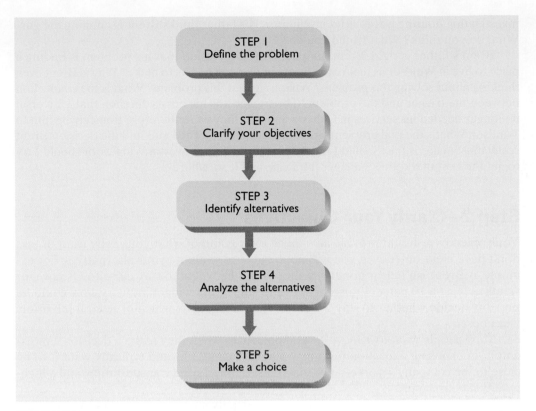

FIGURE 5.2
Steps in the Decision-Making Process

The point is that the alternatives you identify and the decisions you make reflect how you define the problem. What the consultants actually did in this case was define the problem as, "the workers are upset because they have to wait for an elevator." The consultants decided on a relatively inexpensive solution: install full-length mirrors by each bank of elevators so the workers could admire themselves while waiting. The complaints virtually disappeared. The moral of the story is this: Never take the statement of the problem for granted.

How to Define the Problem The consultants' clever solution illustrates the first (and perhaps most important step) in defining problems: Always ask, "What triggered this problem?" Doing so will help guide you to more accurately define it. Luckily for the building owners, the consultants asked themselves, "What triggered the problem?" The answer, of course, was the workers' complaints, which were triggered by the frustration of having to wait for an elevator. The problem then became: How do we reduce or eliminate frustration with having to wait?

There are some useful hints to keep in mind here.[12] Start by writing down your initial assessment of the problem. Then, dissect it. Ask, What triggered this problem (as I've assessed it)? Why am I even thinking about solving this problem? What is the connection between the trigger and the problem? That's how the consultants approached defining the problem, and how you should, too.

Now consider another example. Brent has had a job as marketing manager for Universal Widgets, Inc. for about five years and has been happy with his job and with the company. However, the recent recession wreaked havoc with the company's business, and it had to cut about 10 percent of the staff. Brent's boss gave him the bad news: "We like the work you've been doing here, but we're closing the Oshawa office. We want you to stay with Universal, though, so we found you a similar position with our plant in Windsor." Brent is thrilled. As he tells his parents, "I have to move to Windsor, but at least I still have a job. The problem is, where should I live?" He immediately starts investigating housing possibilities in Windsor. His father thinks Brent is jumping the gun. What do you think? What would you do?

Brent's father is right. Brent jumped to the conclusion that his problem is finding a place to live in Windsor. Is that really the main decision he has to make? Why is Brent even thinking about solving this problem? What triggered this problem? What is the connection between the trigger and the problem? The trigger was his boss's decision that Universal no longer needed his services in Oshawa and that they were therefore transferring him to Windsor. What's the real problem Brent must face here? The issue, and the decision Brent really must make, is this: Should I move to Windsor with Universal Widgets, or should I try to get the best marketing manager job I can, and if so, where?[13]

Step 2—Clarify Your Objectives

Your objectives should provide an explicit expression of what you really want. If you don't have clear objectives, you will not be able to evaluate your alternatives. For example, if Brent isn't clear about whether or not he wants to stay close to Oshawa, or wants at least a 10 percent raise, or wants to stay in the widget industry, how could he possibly decide whether to stay with Universal Widgets, or which of several job offers were best?

Most people want to achieve several objectives when they make a decision. For example, in choosing a location for a new plant, a manager would typically want it to be close to the company's markets, raw materials supplies, good transportation, and a high-quality labour supply.

Football coach Vince Lombardi once reportedly summed up his decision-making philosophy by saying, "Winning isn't everything. It's the only thing." However, most people don't have the luxury of focusing on just a single objective. When deciding on a new laptop computer, you may want to get the most memory, portability, and reliability you can for the price. You'd buy the one that, on balance, best satisfies all these objectives. You'd try to avoid the trap of making your decision based on just one factor like price.

How to Clarify Objectives It's easy to improve your objectives-setting skills. Here is a useful five-step procedure.[14] First, write down all the concerns you hope to address through your decision. Don't worry about repetition. Looking at the same concern in different ways may help you clarify what your concerns really are. Some people compose a wish list. The idea here is to make a comprehensive list of everything you hope to accomplish with your decision. Brent's concerns include affecting his long-term career; enjoying what he's doing; living close to a large urban centre; and earning more money than he earns now.

Second, convert your concerns into specific, concrete objectives. Your objectives should be measurable. Brent's concerns translate into getting a job that puts him in a position to be senior marketing director within two years; is with a consumer products company (and preferably in the widgets industry); is within a one-hour drive of a city with a population of at least one million people; and pays at least $1200 per week.

Third, separate ends from means to establish your fundamental objectives. Zero in on what you really want. One way to do this is to ask, several times, "why?" So, for example, Brent asks himself, "Why do I want to live within one hour drive of a city with a population of at least one million people?" Because he wants to make sure he can meet many other people his own age, and because he enjoys what he sees as big city benefits such as museums, theatre, and opera. This helps clarify what Brent really wants. A smaller town might do, if the town has the right demographics and cultural attractions.

Fourth, clarify what you mean by each objective. For example, "getting a raise" would be a fuzzy objective. Brent has already clarified what he means by his financial objective. He wants to "earn at least $1200 per week."

Fifth, test your objectives to see whether they capture your interests. This is your reality check. Brent carefully reviews his full list of final objectives to make sure they completely capture what he wants to accomplish by his decision.

Step 3—Identify Alternatives

Choice is necessary for effective decision making. When you have no choice, there really isn't any decision to make, except perhaps to "take it or leave it." Wise managers therefore ask, "What are my options?" Decision-making experts call alternatives "the raw material of decision making." They say alternatives represent "the range of potential choices you'll have for pursuing your objectives."[15]

How to Identify Alternatives There are several ways to generate good alternatives. First, remember that this is essentially a creative process. Start by the trying to generate as many alternatives as you can yourself. Then, expand your search, by asking other people, including experts. One useful technique is to look at each of your objectives and ask, "How?" For example, Brent might ask, "How could I get a position that would lead to a marketing director's job within two years?" One alternative is to take a senior marketing manager's job. Another might be to go after the senior director's job right away. Let's assume that Brent has used this process and has generated several feasible alternatives. He can take the Windsor Universal Widget job. Or he can leave the company. If he leaves, his search for alternatives turns up four other possibilities: a job with a dot-com as senior manager in Oshawa, a marketing director's job in Detroit, and two other marketing manager jobs, one with a pet food company in Peterborough, and one with Nokia in Washington, D.C.

Step 4—Analyze the Alternatives

How does each alternative stack up, given your objectives? Should Brent stay with Universal, or should he seek his fortune with another company? If so, which company? To carry out this step properly, keep in mind that you make decisions today, but you feel them tomorrow. You buy a computer today, and tomorrow you discover that it doesn't really satisfy your needs, because your memory requirements are now higher. Suppose Brent decides today to stay with Universal. Then, he finds out next year that his prospects of promotion are almost nil, because they already have two Windsor marketing directors, and neither one plans to leave. "If only I'd thought of that," Brent would say.

One expert says, "This is often the most difficult part of the decision-making process, because this is the stage that typically requires forecasting future events."[16] As we've seen, classical economists assumed decision makers faced completely rational conditions, and could therefore precisely assess the potential consequences of choosing each alternative. However, such perfect conditions rarely exist. Brent needs a practical way to compare each of his options and how they will impact each of his basic objectives.

How to Analyze the Alternatives Your job is to think through, for each alternative, what the consequences of choosing that alternative will be for each of your objectives. Here is a basic process you can use.[17] First, mentally put yourself into the future. For example, imagine that you bought that new computer, and that you're actually using it now, six months later. How do you like it? Has anything changed in your life that should have influenced your decision six months ago? Of course, looking into the future isn't something that most people find very easy, but it's a crucial analytical skill.

Second, eliminate any clearly inferior alternatives. For example, if Brent does his homework and thinks through the consequences of each of his alternatives, it should be obvious that his prospects for promotion to marketing director are virtually nil if he stays with Universal Widgets. Therefore, why even continue considering this alternative? He crosses it off his list.

Third, organize your remaining alternatives into a consequences table. A consequences table lists your objectives down the left side of the page and your alternatives along the top. In each cell of the matrix, put a brief description that shows the consequences of that alternative for that objective. This provides a concise, birds-eye view of the consequences of pursuing each alternative. Now, let's return to Brent's problem again. He started with five alternatives and four basic objectives. Figure 5.3 illustrates these, as well as the consequences he sees for each.

Step 5—Make a Choice

Your analyses are useless unless you make the right choice. Under perfect conditions, making the right choice should be straightforward. Simply review the consequences of each alternative, and choose the alternative that maximizes your benefits. But in practice, as you know, making a decision—even a relatively simple one like choosing a computer—usually can't be done so accurately or rationally.

So, which alternative should Brent choose? He starts by doing some research. He learns there are two marketing directors at the Windsor plant, and so the prospects of a promotion are virtually nil; he discards that option. That leaves four options—the dot-

Objective / Alternative	Senior marketing director in two years	Consumer products company	One-hour drive from major city	Earn at least $1200 per week
Marketing manager, Universal Widgets, Pittsburgh	Little or no possibility—eliminate this option	NA (Eliminated)	NA (Eliminated)	NA (Eliminated)
Senior manager, dot-com, Oshawa	High probability—if company survives that long	Consumer-oriented, but does not really sell products	Yes, excellent	$1250 plus stock options
Marketing director Ford, Detroit	Moderate possibility—bigger company, longer climb	Yes, but not as interesting as selling widgets—I may get bored	Yes	$1100 plus great benefits
Marketing manager, pet foods, Peterborough	High probability—small, growing company with little marketing expertise now	Yes, but not quite as interesting as selling widgets	Yes	$1200
Marketing manager, Nokia, Washington D.C.	Fairly high probability—fast-growing company	Yes—exciting industry	Yes—exceptional cultural attractions, and demographics	$1200

FIGURE 5.3
Consequences Table

com in Oshawa, and jobs at Ford in Detroit, pet foods in Peterborough, and Nokia in Washington, D.C. How would you proceed if you were Brent?

He reviews his consequences matrix. For three of the jobs—the dot-com, Ford, and pet foods—his research (and intuition) suggests they probably lack the direct interaction with consumers and consumer products that he prefers. Senior director would also probably take more than two years at Ford, which in 2002 was suffering some reversals. He asks himself where he'll be six months from now if he takes the dot-com job and is dissuaded by the high failure rate of dot-coms: six months from now, he might well be out of a job.

Based on his decision matrix, the pet food and Nokia jobs look like the clear favourites. The pet food job is a real possibility. In terms of senior director, it's a good career move, however, he's a little less enthusiastic about the pet food business, although it scores a bit higher. Brent has a good feeling about the Nokia job. It satisfies his objectives, and his research suggests living costs in Washington, D.C., are comparable to Oshawa. He's excited about the cellphone business. Looking down the road, he sees this industry's fast growth opening many new options for him. He can definitely see himself living in Washington, so he takes the job.

A Cautionary Note: Organizational Politics and Managerial Decision Making

Organizational politics refers to the activities that individuals in organizations pursue as they try to achieve their own desired outcomes. Organizational politics is evident in all organizations to varying degrees, and it may have a significant impact on some of the decisions that managers make. This means that the "ideal" five-step decision-making process is often distorted as managers pursue their own interests, or when they try to prevent someone else from pursuing their interests. Organizational politics may or may not lead to "bad" decision outcomes, but it definitely influences the ideal decision-making process.

organizational politics
The activities that individuals in organizations pursue as they try to achieve their own desired outcomes.

How to Make Better Decisions

Some people assume that good decision-making ability is like having a good singing voice: you either have it or you don't. However, that's not quite true. Just as you can improve your voice with training, you can also improve your decision-making skills if you make an effort. In this section, we make several suggestions to help you improve your decision-making skill. Let's look first at creativity.

creativity The process of developing original, novel responses to a problem.

Be Creative

Creativity—the process of developing original, novel responses to a problem—plays a big role in making good decisions. It is essential for decision-making activities like framing the problem and developing new alternatives. Remember the consultant's creative redefinition of the "slow-moving elevators" problem. Creativity *can* be cultivated, as shown in the "Challenge of Change" box. Here are some additional suggestions.

Check Your Assumptions Decision-making barriers like anchoring and psychological set (see p. 151) can be avoided in part by forcing yourself to check your assumptions. Look at the problem of the nine dots in Figure 5.4. Your assignment is to connect all the dots using only four straight lines, and to do so without lifting your pen from the paper. Psychological set, the ten-

Boosting creativity: Making sure meeting rooms are well equipped for helping participants exercise creativity.

Nurturing Creativity at Hallmark Cards Inc.

Hallmark Cards
www.hallmark.com

When you're in the business of developing greeting cards, you simply must encourage employee creativity. That's exactly what Hallmark Cards Inc., the world's largest greeting card company, does. Consider the experience of Robert Hurlburt, a 17-year employee. He was given a three-month sabbatical to do whatever he wanted to develop his creative spark. He chose to learn pottery. Although his pottery will probably never be sold commercially, Hallmark hopes that when he returns to his regular duties, the company will see a return in terms of increased creativity. Hallmark's biggest competitor, American Greetings Inc., has similar programs for its employees.

The sabbatical program is available to many writers and artists at Hallmark. And it is not the only program available. Other creativity-enhancing ideas include having workers get together away from the workplace to exchange ideas, giving workers free movie passes, sending workers overseas to absorb new cultures, and having retreats far away from the head office where employees do fun activities like building bird houses. The wackiest extreme is found in the Shoebox Cards division, where teams of writers and editors start their day by watching videotapes of popular TV shows like David Letterman. They also look at magazines and have exercise sessions during the day.

But there are serious business goals behind all these creativity-enhancing activities. The Shoebox group, for example, is expected to develop 70 new greeting cards each week. To achieve that goal, they usually have to develop at least 150 ideas. At the end of each day, new greeting-card ideas are screened at a meeting led by the senior editor. He or she reads each card aloud and then, based on the reaction of the group, either accepts or rejects it.

The success of each card that actually makes it to the market is assessed through surveys and information gathered from store cash registers. Therefore, each employee knows how well his or her card ideas are selling.

dency to take a rigid view of a problem, may be the decision-making barrier at work here. Most people tend to view the nine dots as a square, but this of course limits the solutions.

Figure 5.5 shows one creative solution. The key to this solution is breaking through your assumptions about how the problem needs to be solved. In fact, there is no way to connect all of the dots with just four lines as long as you make the assumption that the nine dots are a square. One managerial decision-making expert refers to creativity as, in essence, "...an assumption-breaking process."[18] Now try to solve the problem in Figure 5.6. Remember: Always check your assumptions.

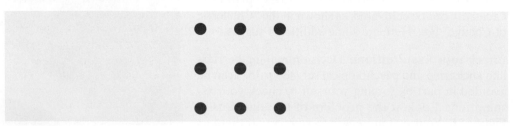

FIGURE 5.4
Looking at the Problem in Just One Way

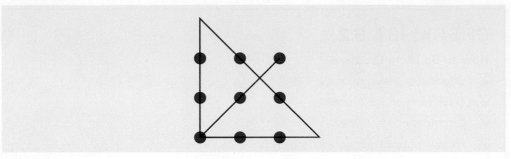

FIGURE 5.5
The Advantage of Not Just Looking at the Problem in One Way

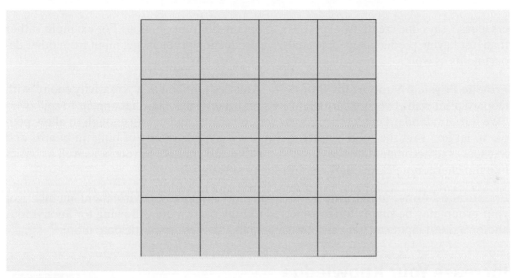

FIGURE 5.6
Using Creativity to Find a Solution
How many squares are in the box? Now, count again. Only 16? Take away your preconception of how many squares there are. Now, how many do you find? You should find 30!

Think Through the Process Forcing yourself to think through the decision and each of its consequences, as if you were actually there experiencing them, can also help you be more creative. Consider this problem: An extraordinarily frugal person named Joe can make one whole cigar from every five cigar butts he finds. How many cigars can he make if he finds 25 cigar butts? Before you answer "five," think through Joe's cigar-making process, step by step. There he sits on his park bench, making (and smoking) each of his five cigars. As he smokes each cigar, he ends up with one new cigar butt. Thus, in smoking his five hand-made cigars, Joe ends up with five new butts, which of course he combines into his sixth, and in this case final, whole new cigar.[19]

This problem illustrates how "process analysis" can boost creativity and insight. Process analysis means solving a problem by thinking through the process involved from beginning to end, imagining what actually would happen at each step.[20] In this case, process analysis meant envisioning Joe sitting on his park bench, and thinking through each of the steps he would take as if we were there. By using process analysis to look over his shoulder in this way, we boosted our creativity and discovered that he made a sixth cigar.

Get More Points of View When it comes to creativity, more points of view are usually better than fewer, and diverse points of view are better than homogeneous ones. "Creativity works better when you have a group of three or four than it does with one, because you have the synergistic effect where people are working with each other, building on oth-

America Online
www.aol.com

ers ideas," says one creativity expert. Try to obtain different opinions. For example, rather than just having production people analyze a production problem, get input from other departments as well.

Provide Physical Support for Creativity America Online has a "creativity room" with leopard print walls, oversize cartoon murals, and giant paint cans that appear to spill over. "We felt the standard conference rooms weren't casual and comfy enough to allow people to let go," says the room's creator. Similarly, provide plenty of bulletin boards and flat spaces to accommodate the decision-making and creativity process, as well as basics like flip charts, note cards, markers, and sticky notes.

Encourage Anonymous Input Even in the most supportive environment, members of your group may be simply too introverted to fully participate. Allowing for anonymous and/or written input can help encourage people like these to participate more.[21]

Increase Your Knowledge

"Knowledge is power," someone once said, and that's particularly true when it comes to making decisions. Even the simplest decisions—mapping your route to work in the morning or deciding which cereal to buy, for instance—become problems if you lack basic information, such as the distances involved or the costs of each of the various products. And making major, more complex life decisions of course depends even more on what you know about the situation. For example, Ed was a medical doctor who practised for many years in one location. He then accepted a job with a group of young doctors in another province, only to find that what he was expected to do and the hours he had to work were not at all what he had anticipated. After less than a year of being run ragged he had to leave, albeit as a wiser man. Knowledge is power, and the more you know about the elements of the decision before you make that decision, the better the decision will be. Increasing your knowledge will increase your ability to carry out the steps in the rational decision-making process (for example, by being aware of more alternatives).

That's easy to say, of course, but how do you go about getting the knowledge you require? There are several things you can do. First, ask, ask, ask. In formulating your questions, always keep the six main "question" words in mind: Who, What, Where, When, Why, and How. Then, even for a smaller decision like buying a used car, make sure to do your research. Who is selling the car, and who has owned it? What do similar cars sell for? What, if anything, is wrong with this car? Where has it been serviced? Why does the owner want to sell it? How well has the car been maintained? And how much does the owner want to sell it for? Think of how much trouble Dr. Ed could have saved himself if he had asked his prospective partners a few incisive questions about the job!

Second, get experience. For many endeavours, there's simply no substitute for getting some experience. That's certainly true on a personal level: Many students find that interning in a job similar to the occupation they plan to pursue can help enormously in clarifying whether that's the right occupation for them. And it's certainly true when it comes to managing organizations. In Chapter 2 we saw that some companies expand abroad by opening their own facilities, while others enter into joint ventures. What do you think determines which route a company's managers choose? It turns out that experience has a lot to do with it. Multinational corporations that already have a great deal of experience in doing business in a particular country generally opt for full ownership of foreign affiliates. Less experienced companies tend to establish joint ventures in foreign markets, in part so they can get the necessary expertise.[22]

Use Your Intuition

Intuition is a cognitive process whereby a person instinctively makes a decision based on his or her accumulated knowledge and experience. Consider this illustrative story: A fire commander and his crew encounter a fire at the back of a house. The commander leads his team into the building. Standing in the living room, they blast water onto the smoke and flames, which appear to be consuming the kitchen. Yet, the fire roars back and continues to burn. The fire's persistence baffles the commander. His men douse the "kitchen fire" again, and the flames subside. But then they flare up with an even greater intensity. The firefighters retreat a few steps to regroup. Suddenly, an uneasy feeling grips the commander. His intuition (which he calls his "sixth sense") tells him to vacate the house. He orders everyone to leave. Just as the crew reaches the street, the living room floor caves in. The fire was in the basement, not the kitchen. Had they still been in the house, the men would have plunged into an inferno.[23]

As this story shows, we reach intuitive decisions by quickly (and, often, unthinkingly) comparing our present situation to situations we've encountered in the past. In his study of firefighters, Klein found that they accumulate experiences and "subconsciously categorize fires according to how they should react to them."[24] The fire commander did exactly that. The fire, based on his experience, just didn't make sense. Why? Because it wasn't up ahead in the kitchen, but below, in the basement. The floor muffled the sounds of the fire and retarded the transfer of heat. The commander, standing with his men in the living room, felt that something was wrong. The "kitchen fire" seemed too quiet and too cool. His intuition saved the day.

In many ways, intuition is the opposite of systematic decision making. Systematic decision makers take a logical, step-by-step approach to solving a problem, while intuitive decision makers use more of a trial-and-error approach, disregarding much of the information available and rapidly bouncing from one alternative to another to get a feel for which seems to work best.[25] One study that compared "systematics" and "intuitives" found that the former systematically searched for information, and thoroughly evaluated all alternatives, while the latter sought information non-systematically, and then quickly evaluated just a few favoured alternatives. The intuitive approach usually worked best.[26] The lesson here seems to be that working through all the options is fine if time permits. However, don't get bogged down in the process: It's often best to follow your instincts and "just do it," as Nike says.[27]

You can usually tell when a decision fits with your inner nature, for it brings an enormous sense of relief. Good decisions are the best tranquilizers ever invented; bad ones often increase your anxiety.[28] The psychiatrist Sigmund Freud made this interesting observation on making decisions:

> When making a decision of minor importance I have always found it advantageous to consider all the pros and cons. In vital matters, however, such as the choice of a mate or a profession, the decision should come from the unconscious, from somewhere within ourselves. In the important decisions of our personal life, we should be governed, I think, by the deep inner needs of our nature.[29]

That's the good news about intuition. But intuition also has limitations. For one thing, human nature can easily cloud our decision making.[30] For example, people tend to take higher than normal risks when they want to recover a loss. They also tend to be overconfident, particularly about areas they know little about.[31] An executive with a manufacturing company led his firm into a disastrous expansion into Asia in the face of negative evidence. After discussing the opportunity with his executive staff and consultants, rational analysis indicated it was a very risky venture. The market data looked barely favourable, and the political and cultural factors were huge unknowns. Yet, the overconfident executive blundered ahead. What would you have done if you were in his shoes?[32]

We can measure intuitiveness. The short test in Figure 5.7 provides an approximate reading on whether you are more rational (systematic) or intuitive in your decision making.[33]

Weigh the Pros and Cons

It's often useful to quantitatively weigh the merits of each option as well. Doing so can help you size up your options and take into consideration the relative importance of each objective. For example, in buying a car, price may be more important than style, and style may be more important than dealer quality (since you can always have it serviced somewhere else). Weighing the pros and cons lets you quantify such realities. The process provides another perspective on your options, by supplementing more subjective analyses of the situation. It's helpful here to use a decision matrix like the one in Figure 5.8.

Don't Overstress the Finality of Your Decision

In making your choice, remember that few decisions are forever.[34] There is more reversibility in decisions than we realize. It is true that some strategic decisions are hard to reverse. In 2002, when Ford decided to stop producing the Taurus in one of its plants and to make their new "Cross-Trainer" SUV instead, it was a decision the company would have to live with for several years. And when BCE unwisely invested billions of dollars in Teleglobe, it had to cope with the consequences later. However, most decisions aren't this dramatic, and even if you make a bad decision it's probably not the end of the world. So, don't become frozen with an unrealistic fear that a decision can't be changed or modified.

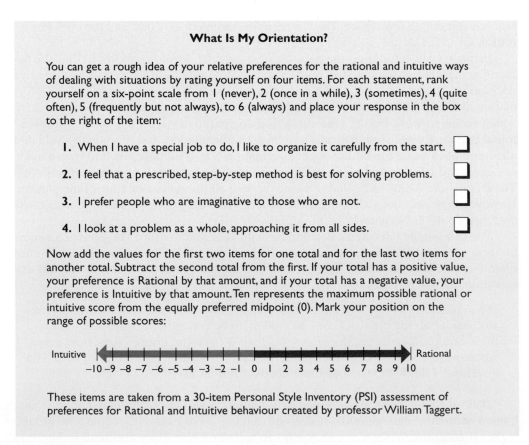

What Is My Orientation?

You can get a rough idea of your relative preferences for the rational and intuitive ways of dealing with situations by rating yourself on four items. For each statement, rank yourself on a six-point scale from 1 (never), 2 (once in a while), 3 (sometimes), 4 (quite often), 5 (frequently but not always), to 6 (always) and place your response in the box to the right of the item:

1. When I have a special job to do, I like to organize it carefully from the start. ☐

2. I feel that a prescribed, step-by-step method is best for solving problems. ☐

3. I prefer people who are imaginative to those who are not. ☐

4. I look at a problem as a whole, approaching it from all sides. ☐

Now add the values for the first two items for one total and for the last two items for another total. Subtract the second total from the first. If your total has a positive value, your preference is Rational by that amount, and if your total has a negative value, your preference is Intuitive by that amount. Ten represents the maximum possible rational or intuitive score from the equally preferred midpoint (0). Mark your position on the range of possible scores:

Intuitive ◄─┼─► Rational
　　　　　−10 −9 −8 −7 −6 −5 −4 −3 −2 −1　0　1　2　3　4　5　6　7　8　9　10

These items are taken from a 30-item Personal Style Inventory (PSI) assessment of preferences for Rational and Intuitive behaviour created by professor William Taggert.

FIGURE 5.7
Are You More Rational or More Intuitive?

Harold's Objectives	Relative importance of each objective	Marketing manager, Universal Widgets, Pittsburg*	Senior manager, dot-com, Oshawa*	Marketing manager, Ford, Detroit*	Marketing manager, pet foods, Peterborough*	Marketing manager, Nokia, Washington DC*
Marketing director in two years	0.50	1	2	2	5	4
Consumer products company	0.20	5	2	3	3	5
One-hour drive from major city	0.15	5	5	5	5	5
Earn at least $1200 per week	0.15	3	4	3	4	4
	1.00	Sum= 2.70**	2.55	2.80	4.10	4.35

* 1 is low, 5 is high. ** 1 × 0.50 + 5 × 0.20 + 5 × 0.15 + 3 × 0.15 = 2.20

Note: Rate each alternative on how well it achieves each of your objectives (such as with a 1-5). Then multiply that rating by the objective's importance score to get a numerical weighted score for each alternative.

FIGURE 5.8
Decision Matrix

It is, however, important to know when to quit. Once you have made a decision, stick with it if you believe you're on the right track. But be open to data that show that it's time to change your decision.

Avoiding Decision-Making Traps

Don't let the apparent rationality of the decision-making process mislead you. Embedded in the decision-making terrain are a series of traps waiting to catch the unsuspecting manager. The unnerving thing is that the manager probably won't even realize what's happened. In this section, we look at several decision-making traps—decision-making shortcuts, perceptual biases, inaccurate framing of the problem, anchoring, psychological set, organizational barriers, and escalation of commitment.

Decision-Making Shortcuts

People have their own instinctive way of "programming" many of the decisions they have to make. They do this by using **heuristics**, or decision-making shortcuts (also called "rules of thumb"). For example, a mortgage lender might use the heuristic that "people should not spend more than 30 percent of their gross monthly income for mortgage payments and other house-related expenses."[35]

heuristics
Decision-making shortcuts.

CHECKLIST **5.3**

How to Make Better Decisions

☑ Be creative.

☑ Increase your knowledge.

☑ Use your intuition.

☑ Weigh the pros and cons.

☑ Don't overstress the finality of your decision.

Managers consciously or unconsciously apply heuristics all the time. For example, in the 1990s and early 2000s, Tyco International then-CEO Dennis Kozlowski reviewed hundreds of potential acquisitions every year. Carefully analyzing each of them was too time-consuming. He streamlined his decision process by using two decision rules. He only considered deals that were (1) friendly (no hostile takeovers), and (2) would immediately add to Tyco's earnings.[36]

Heuristics manifest themselves in many ways. For example, a manager might predict what a subordinate's performance will be, based on that person's similarity to others with the same ethnic background that the manager has known. Another shortcut involves basing decisions on what happened most recently. Based on 150 interviews with decision-makers, one researcher concludes, "relatively few decisions are made using analytical processes such as generating a variety of options and contrasting their strengths and weaknesses." Instead, most people tend to use cognitive shortcuts.[37]

Perceptual Biases

perception
The selection and interpretation of information we receive through our senses and the meaning we give to the information.

Perception is the selection and interpretation of information we receive through our senses and the meaning we give to the information. Many things, including our individual needs, influence how we perceive a stimulus. A thirsty person in the desert may perceive faraway heat waves as a mirage, whereas a rescuer sees nothing but sand. In organizations, a person's prior experiences and position in the company can have a big effect on how the person perceives a problem and reacts to it.

In a classic study of this phenomenon, 23 executives who were employed by a large manufacturing firm, were asked to read a business case.[38] The researchers found that a manager's position influenced how he or she defined the most important problem facing the company. For example, five of six sales executives thought that the most important problem was a "sales problem." "Organizational problems" were mentioned by four out of five production executives, but by only one sales executive and no accounting executives. It was clear that the managers' experiences and functional roles moulded and influenced how they perceived the problem. The managers looked at the same data but interpreted it differently, and each would probably have taken action based on his or her own view of the problem.

Inaccurate Framing of the Problem

Misdefining the problem may be the biggest barrier to making good decisions. Remember how much money the building owners would have wasted if their elevator consultants had accepted at face value the owners' claim that the problem was "slow-moving elevators!" Here's how three decision-making experts put it:

> The greatest danger in formulating a decision problem is laziness. It's easy to state the problem in the most obvious way, or in the way that first pops into your mind, or in the way it's always been stated in the past. But the easy way isn't necessarily the best way.[39]

In other words, managers need to work hard to understand what the "problem" really is. Care to test your framing skills? Since you should be an expert at solving "mirror" problems by now, here's another one for you. You just bought a new but small apartment, and you'd like to make it look roomier. On your right as you enter is a three-metre-wide closet with a set of two bifold doors. Mirrors make a room look bigger, so your significant other has suggested you have mirrors mounted on the door panels. Unfortunately, the estimates you've gotten so far are much too high. So, you are about to give up. But first you ask, "Did I frame the problem correctly?" Well, probably not. What did you do wrong? For one thing, you've defined the problem as "How do we mount mirrors on the door panels?" Even if we assume that mirroring the closet is the best way to make your apartment look roomier, why limit yourself to accomplishing that by *mounting* mirrors on the closet doors? You don't really care if you *mount* mirrors there, do you? The problem really is this: "What's the best way to put mirrors where we now have closet doors?" A quick trip to your local building supply store uncovers a set of inexpensive sliding-door mirror panels that will replace your bulky doors, and that slide back and forth on a track you install yourself. Total cost: one-half the previous estimates.

Anchoring

Errors in framing are sometimes caused by **anchoring**, which means unconsciously giving disproportionate weight to the first information you hear.

<!-- margin glossary -->**anchoring**
Unconsciously giving disproportionate weight to the first information you hear.

Anchors pop up in the most unexpected ways. Let's say you're selling your car, which you know is worth about $10 000. Joe has responded to your classified ad; when he arrives he offhandedly remarks that the car is only worth about $5000. What would you do? On the one hand, you know that Joe is probably just positioning himself to get a better deal, and you know that $5000 is absolutely ridiculous. On the other hand, Joe is the only game in town at the moment (one other person called but never showed up) and you don't really feel like spending any more weekends placing ads and waiting around for buyers who don't show up. So, you start bargaining with Joe: He says $5000, you say $10 000, and before you know it you've arrived at a price of $8000, which Joe graciously points out is "better than splitting the difference" from your point of view. What happened here? Without realizing it, you gave disproportionate weight to Joe's "offhand" comment, and your decision making (and bargaining) from that point on revolved around his price, not yours. (What should you have done? One response might have been "$5000? Are you *kidding*? That's not even in the *ballpark*!" It might not have worked, but at least you'd have loosened that subliminal anchor, so the bargaining could have been on your terms, not his.)

Psychological Set

The tendency to focus on a rigid strategy or point of view is called *psychological set*.[40] This mental trait can severely limit a manager's ability to think of alternative solutions. A classic example was presented in Figure 5.4. Your assignment was to connect all nine dots with no more than four straight lines running through them, and to do so without lifting your pen from the paper.

Organizational Barriers

All too often it's the company itself—how it's organized, or its policies and procedures, for instance—that undermine employees' ability to make good decisions. You've probably experienced that yourself. For example, you ask a salesperson at a department store to make a simple change and you're told, "You'll have to get that approved first by customer service." Microsoft went through a major reorganization in 1999, in part to ensure that lower-level managers could make more decisions themselves, without having to refer to Bill Gates.

In a recent study, nearly two-thirds (62 percent) of 773 hourly workers surveyed said their organizations were operating with half or less than half the employee brain power available to them. This observation was shared by 63 percent of the 641 managers who responded to the survey. About 40 percent of all employees listed "organizational politics" as one of the three big barriers to effective thinking in their firms. Time pressure and a lack of involvement in decision making were the other two big barriers. Less important barriers included lack of rewards, lack of skills, procedures/work rules/systems, lack of training, and unclear job expectations. Obviously managers can undermine decision making in many ways if they aren't careful.

Escalation of Commitment

<!-- margin glossary -->**escalation of commitment**
The situation in which a manager becomes increasingly committed to a previously chosen course of action even though it has been shown to be ineffective.

Escalation of commitment refers to the situation in which a manager becomes increasingly committed to a previously chosen course of action even though it has been shown to be ineffective. A good example of this is Expo '86, the world's fair held in British Columbia. When the project was first conceived, the deficit was projected at about $56 million. Over the next few years, the projected deficit kept rising, until it was more than $300 million. In spite of this, the project went forward.

There are various reasons why supposedly rational managers get into difficulties like these: because they are success-oriented, they are motivated to defend their initial decision; they are reluctant to admit they made a mistake; they fear that their career will be harmed if their project fails; or they believe that they simply haven't worked hard enough to ensure the success of the project. Managers can avoid overcommitment by setting specific goals ahead of time that deal with how much time and money they are willing to expend on the project. The existence of specific time and money goals makes it harder for the manager to interpret unfavourable news in a positive light.

CP Rail
www.cpr.ca

DaimlerChrysler
www.daimlerchrysler.
com

group
Two or more persons who interact together for some purpose and in such a manner that each person influences and is influenced by each other person.

cohesiveness
The attraction of the group for its members.

norms
The informal rules that groups adopt to regulate and regularize members' behaviour.

Using Groups to Make Better Decisions

In organizations, decisions can be made by one person or by a group of people working together. Laurent Beaudoin, Executive Chairman of the Board at Bombardier, is an autocrat who does not share power, so there is little group decision making at that firm.[41] At CP Rail, by contrast, an executive committee makes major decisions affecting the firm.[42]

Groups at Work

Whether they are called work groups, teams, or committees, groups accomplish much of the work in organizations. Since we've focused on individual decision making up to now, it's important that we turn our attention to using the power of groups to make better decisions.

Although we'll discuss groups in more detail in Chapter 14, some working definitions are in order now. A **group** is two or more persons who interact together for some purpose and in such a manner that each person influences and is influenced by each other person. Thus the board of directors of Inco is a group, as is the work team that installs the dashboards in DaimlerChrysler's vans at its Windsor, Ontario, plant. Groups are important at work in part because of the effect they have on their members. For example, pressure by other group members can cause a member to raise or lower his or her output. In turn, the extent to which a group can influence its members depends on several things, including the **cohesiveness** of the group—the attraction of the group for its members—and on the group's **norms**—the informal rules that groups adopt to regulate and regularize members' behaviour.[43]

Pros and Cons of Group Decision Making

You probably have found from your own experience that groups to which you belong can and do influence how you behave and the decisions you make. It is therefore not surprising that having groups make decisions has its pros and cons. These pros and cons are summarized in Figure 5.9.

Advantages of Using Groups to Make Decisions The old saying that "two heads are better than one" can be true when you bring several people together to make a decision. Pooling the experiences and points of view of several people can lead to more points of view regarding how to define the problem, more possible solutions, and more creative decisions in general. Groups that analyze a problem and come up with their own decisions also tend to "buy into" those decisions; this acceptance boosts the chance that the group will work harder to implement the decision once it's put into effect.[44] Overall,

Better decisions sometimes result from consultation with others, particularly if they are more knowledgeable or more experienced in dealing with similar problems.

PROS	CONS
• "Two heads are better than one" • More points of view • Fosters acceptance • Group may work harder to implement decisions	• Pressure for consensus • Dominance by one individual • Escalation of commitment: pressure to "win your point" • More time consuming • Groupthink

FIGURE 5.9
Summary of Pros and Cons of Using Groups to Make Decisions

groups can better cope with the problems of anchoring, psychological set, and perceptions because of the various perspectives that individuals in groups bring to the decision-making process.

Disadvantages of Using Groups to Make Decisions Although group-decision-making advocates say that "two heads are better than one," detractors reply that "a camel is a horse put together by a committee." This is a reference to the fact that using a group can sometimes actually short-circuit or distort the decision-making process.

Several things can go wrong when groups make decisions. The desire to be accepted tends to silence disagreement and to favour consensus, a fact that can actually reduce creative decisions instead of enhancing them.[45] In many groups, a dominant individual emerges who effectively cuts off debate and channels the rest of the group to his or her point of view. Escalation of commitment can be a problem, too. When groups are confronted by a problem, there is often a tendency for individual members to become committed to their own solutions; the goal then becomes winning the argument rather than solving the problem. Groups also take longer to make decisions. The process can therefore be inherently more expensive than having an individual make the decision.

One of the hazards of a cohesive work group is the phenomenon known as "groupthink."[46] **Groupthink** occurs when members of a group voluntarily suspend their critical-thinking abilities and repress any conflict and disagreement that could challenge group solidarity. Groupthink is a problem because it suppresses minority opinions and unpopular views, both of which can help the group to critically examine its decision-making processes. Eight symptoms of groupthink have been identified (see Table 5.4). When these symptoms are evident in the group, the likely outcome is poor development and analysis of alternatives, a poor choice of decision, a failure to consider the difficulties in implementing the decision, and a failure to re-examine the assumptions that were used to make the decision.

Groupthink can occur in any highly cohesive group. It has been observed in business firms that made poor competitive decisions, and in not-for-profit organizations that adopted inappropriate strategies. Groupthink is probably best known because of some spectacular examples of poor decision making. In the case of the space shuttle *Challenger*, for example, engineers warned that the air temperature on the morning of the rocket launch was low enough to cause hardening of "O-rings," which could cause hot gases to escape from the fuel tank and cause an explosion. But these warnings were ignored by NASA management, who felt pressure to stay on schedule for the launch, and the engineers did not pursue the issue. So, the shuttle was launched and seven astronauts died when the O-rings failed. The likelihood that groupthink will develop can be reduced if certain strategies are adopted (see Table 5.5). These strategies require that group members accept the view that conflict and disagreement—while time-consuming and perhaps uncomfortable—must be encouraged if bad decisions are to be avoided. Legitimizing dissent is the underlying theme of the strategies listed in Table 5.5.

groupthink
Occurs when members of a group voluntarily suspend their critical-thinking abilities and repress any conflict and disagreement that could challenge group solidarity.

NASA
www.nasa.gov

TABLE 5.4 Symptoms of Groupthink

SYMPTOMS	EXPLANATION
1. Illusion of invulnerability	Group members believe that they are invulnerable to any actions that opponents or competitors might take.
2. Rationalization	Group members develop rationalizations to reassure themselves that the decision they made was the right one.
3. Moralization	Group members believe that their chosen course of action is "right" and is therefore justified.
4. Stereotyping	Group members view the enemy or competition as evil, incompetent, weak, or ineffective.
5. Pressure	Group members apply pressure to anyone in the group who expresses doubts about the group's illusions.
6. Self-censorship	Group members say nothing about their misgivings and minimize the importance of their own decisions.
7. Illusion of unanimity	Group members have the feeling that they alone have doubts about the wisdom of the decision and that everyone else in the group is in favour of it.
8. Mindguards	Some group members take it upon themselves to protect other group members from negative information that might jolt the group out of its complacency.

TABLE 5.5 Remedies for Groupthink

REMEDIES	EXPLANATION
1. Legitimize dissent	The group leader should assign the role of critical evaluator to every member of the group.
2. Stress impartiality	The leader should adopt an impartial stance on major issues instead of stating preferences at the outset.
3. Divide group into subgroups	The group should be divided into subgroups that meet separately and then come together to work out their differences.
4. Consult constituents	Each member should be required to discuss the group's tentative consensus with members of the unit he or she represents.
5. Consult outside experts	Outside experts should be invited to meetings to give their views and to challenge the views of group members.
6. Assign devil's advocate role	The devil's advocate role should be assigned on a rotating basis to group members.
7. Assess warning signals	One or more sessions should be devoted to assessing the warning signals from enemies or competitors.
8. Give "last chance" opportunity	After a tentative consensus has been reached a "last chance" meeting should be held to allow group members to express any doubts they may have.

Tools for Improving Group Decision Making

The manager's job is to use groups in such a way that the advantages of group decision making outweigh the disadvantages. For this there are several group decision-making tools in the manager's tool box.[47]

Brainstorming **Brainstorming** is one way to amplify the creative energies of a group. It has been defined as a group problem-solving technique whereby group members introduce all possible solutions before evaluating any of them.[48] The technique is aimed at encouraging everyone to introduce solutions without fear of criticism; it uses four rules: (1) avoid criticizing others' ideas; (2) share even wild suggestions; (3) offer as many suggestions and supportive comments as possible; and (4) build on others' suggestions to create your own.[49] Interestingly, brainstorming can produce more creative solutions even if group members feel too inhibited to make wild suggestions.[50]

Brainstorming is not without shortcomings. In fact, studies during the 1960s and 1970s consistently showed that brainstorming actually produced fewer and lower-quality ideas than did individuals working alone. But a new, high-tech variation of brainstorming—**electronic brainstorming**—overcomes these problems by having group members type ideas into a computer. These ideas then show up simultaneously on the computer screens of other group members. Studies of electronic brainstorming show that performance increases as group size increases. As well, the problems of production blocking (not everyone in the group can talk at once, and people forget ideas because they can't immediately express them) and evaluation apprehension (fear of having your idea ridiculed) are almost completely eliminated in electronic brainstorming.

Executives from Metropolitan Life who gathered at Queen's University spent their time seated side-by-side in front of microcomputers. They typed in ideas for how their firm could improve operations. The company's vice president estimated that the managers accomplished in one day what would normally have taken five days using traditional methods. Many other Canadian firms are also using electronic brainstorming. In fact, IBM Canada, Royal Trust, and Sears Canada have set up their own electronic meeting rooms.[51]

Devil's-Advocate Approach One way to guard against the tendency for one group member's efforts to stifle debate is to formalize the process of criticism. In the devil's-advocate approach, an advocate defends the proposed solution while a "devil's" advocate is appointed to prepare a detailed counter-argument listing what is wrong with the solution and why it should not be adopted.

The Delphi Technique The Delphi technique maximizes the advantages of group decision making while minimizing its disadvantages. Basically, the opinions of experts who work independently are obtained, with the expert's written opinions from one stage providing the basis for the experts' analyses of each succeeding stage. In a typical Delphi analysis, the steps are as follows: (1) a problem is identified; (2) experts' opinions are solicited anonymously and individually through questionnaires (for example, on a problem such as, "What do you think are the five biggest breakthrough products our computer company will have to confront in the next five years?"); (3) the experts' opinions are then analyzed, distilled, and resubmitted to other experts for a second round of opinions; (4) this process is continued for several more rounds until a consensus is reached.

This can obviously be a time-consuming process; on the other hand, as in electronic brainstorming, problems like groupthink can be reduced by eliminating face-to-face meetings.

The Nominal Group Technique The nominal group technique is a group decision-making process in which participants do not attempt to agree as a group on any solution, but rather meet and secretly vote on all the solutions proposed after privately ranking the proposals in order of preference.[52] It is called the "nominal" group technique because the "group" is a group in name only: Members vote on solutions not as a group but individually. The process is this: (1) each group member writes down his or her ideas for solving the problem at hand; (2) each member then presents his or her ideas orally and the ideas are written on a board for the other participants to see; (3) after all ideas have been presented, the entire group discusses all ideas simultaneously; (4) group members individually and secretly vote on each proposed solution; and (5) the solution with the most individual votes wins.

The Stepladder Technique The stepladder technique also aims to reduce the potentially inhibiting effects of face-to-face meetings. Group members are added one by one at

brainstorming
A group problem-solving technique whereby group members introduce all possible solutions before evaluating any of them.

electronic brainstorming
A form of brainstorming in which group members type ideas into a computer.

Metropolitan Life
www.metlife.com

IBM Canada
www.ibm.com/ca

Sears Canada
www.sears.ca

each stage of the process so that their input is untainted by the previous participants' points of view. The process involves these steps: (1) individuals A and B are given a problem to solve and each produces an independent solution; (2) A and B meet and develop a joint decision, then meet with C, who had independently analyzed the problem and arrived at a decision; (3) A, B, and C jointly discuss the problem and arrive at a consensus decision, then are joined by D, who has individually analyzed the problem and arrived at his or her own decision; (4) A, B, C, and D arrive at a final group decision.[53]

How to Lead a Group Decision-Making Discussion

The person leading the group discussion can have a big effect on whether the group's decision is useful. If a committee chairperson monopolizes the meeting and continually shoots down others' ideas while pushing his or her own, it's likely that other members' points of view will go unexpressed. An effective discussion leader has a responsibility to do the following:

1. **Ensure that all group members participate.** As a discussion leader, it is your responsibility to ensure that all group members actively participate in the discussion by having an opportunity to express their opinions. Doing so can help ensure that different points of view emerge and that everyone "takes ownership" of the final decision.

2. **Distinguish between idea generation and idea evaluation.** Studies conclude that evaluating and criticizing proposed solutions and ideas actually inhibits the process of generating new ideas. Yet in most group discussions, there's a tendency for one person to present an alternative and for others to begin immediately discussing its pros and cons. As a result, group members quickly become apprehensive about suggesting new ideas. Instituting brainstorming rules—in particular, forbidding criticism of an idea until all ideas have been presented—can be useful here.

3. **Do not respond to each participant or dominate the discussion.** Remember that the discussion leader's main responsibility is to elicit ideas from the group, not to supply them. As a discussion leader, you should therefore work hard to facilitate a free expression of ideas and to consciously avoid dominating the discussion.

4. **See that the effort is directed toward overcoming surmountable obstacles.** In other words, focus on solving the problem rather than on discussing historical events that cannot be changed. For example, some discussion groups make the mistake of becoming embroiled in discussions concerning who is to blame for the problem or what should have been done to avoid the problem. Such discussions can't lead to solutions, because the past can't be changed. Instead, as a discussion leader, your job is to ensure that the group focuses on obstacles that can be overcome and on solutions that can be implemented.[54]

SKILLS AND STUDY MATERIAL

SUMMARY

1. A decision is a choice from among available alternatives. Decision making is the process of developing and analyzing alternatives and making a choice.

2. Decisions can be either programmed (repetitive and routine) or non-programmed (unique and novel). Non-programmed decisions require more intuition and judgment of decision makers.

3. Rational decision making assumes ideal conditions such as accurate definition of the problem and complete knowledge about all relevant alternatives and their values. The rational decision making process involves five steps: define the problem, clarify your objectives, identify alternatives, analyze the alternatives, and make a choice.

4. In reality, decision making is influenced by differences in managers' abilities to process information, their reliance on heuristics or shortcuts, inaccurate framing of the problem, anchoring, escalation of commitment, psychological set, and factors in the organization.

5. "Bounded rationality" describes decision making in reality and often implies satisficing, or accepting satisfactory (as opposed to optimal) alternatives.

6. Guidelines for making better decisions include (1) *be creative* (be willing to make novel responses to problems), (2) *increase your knowledge* (make sure you have all relevant information before making a decision), (3) *use your intuition* (consult your inner feelings, especially when making important decisions), (4) *weigh the pros and cons* (use the decision matrix to help with this), and (5) *don't overstress the finality of your decision* (be willing to change your mind if it becomes necessary).

7. A group consists of two or more persons who interact for some purpose and who influence each other in the process. Group decision making can result in the pooling of resources and strengthened commitment to the decision. Tools for better group decisions include brainstorming, the devil's advocate approach, the Delphi technique, the nominal group technique, and the stepladder technique.

CRITICAL THINKING EXERCISES

1. To paraphrase philosopher Bertrand Russell, there are two kinds of workers: those who roll the rock up the hill and those who tell them to do so. Since you are probably in college or university as you read this textbook, let's assume that you want to be the one giving the directions (the brain work) rather than rolling the rock (the brawn work). The brain-based economy reinforces the necessity of education if you want neither to roll the rock up the hill nor have it roll down on you. Times are continually changing. As a result, there are many things you need to know as a manager to make good decisions. How do you think managerial decision making is different in a brain-based economy than in an industrial or brawn-based one? What are the most important factors or variables that go into making managerial decisions in the twenty-first century? What do you think decision making will be like in the year 2100? Will the rational model prevail or will some form of creativity and innovation displace the time-honoured tradition of Western thought and Descartes' dictum: "I think, therefore I am"? Be prepared to discuss these questions in class.

2. In his provocative book *Managing as a Performing Art*, Peter Vaill argues that there are seven myths in managing organizations. Three of these are as follows.

The myth of a single person called "the manager" or "the leader." Vaill contends that all kinds of people without the title or power have opportunities for management and leadership in modern organizations.

The myth that what the leader leads and the manager manages is a single, free-standing organization. Vaill states that thinking of organizations as singular things allows us to ignore the fact that they are a part of their environment and therefore must be aware of their impact on that environment.

The myth of rational analysis as the primary means of understanding and directing organizations. Intuition is important; change is so constant and discontinuous that we must be creative constantly, and there is much mystery in our decisions today.

Analyze and discuss the points made by Vaill in light of what you now know about decision making and organizations.

EXPERIENTIAL EXERCISES

1. The world is becoming more competitive every day. Management expert Rosabeth Moss Kanter uses an analogy of *Alice in Wonderland"* in *When Giants Learn to Dance* to explain her perspective on the "game of change" that managers find themselves playing.

To some companies, the contest in which they are now entered seems increasingly less like baseball or other traditional games and more like the croquet game in *Alice in Wonderland*—a game that compels the player to deal with constant change. In that fictional game, nothing remains stable for very long, because everything is alive and changing around the player—an all-too-real condition for many managers. The mallet Alice uses is a flamingo, which tends to lift its head and face in another direction just as Alice tries to hit the ball. The ball, in turn, is a hedgehog, another creature with a mind of its own. Instead of lying there waiting for Alice to hit it, the hedgehog unrolls, gets up, moves to another part of the court, and sits down again. The wickets are card soldiers, ordered around by the Queen of Hearts, who changes the structure of the game seemingly at whim by barking out an order to the wickets to reposition themselves around the court.

Substitute technology for the mallet, employees and customers for the hedgehog, and everyone else from government regulators to corporate raiders for the Queen of Hearts, and the analogy fits the experience of a growing number of companies.

Divide the class into teams of five to seven people. Assign one of the following companies to each group: Microsoft, Nortel, GM Canada, Levi Strauss, Home Depot, Johnson &Johnson, Cott Cola, McDonald's, Canadian National Railways, Corel Corp., Air Canada, Four Seasons Hotels, Maclean-Hunter, and Hudson's Bay Company. Each group should research its company, applying the *Alice in Wonderland* analogy, and generate a two- to three-page analysis to be presented in class describing examples of how the analogy applies and how it affects organizational decision making.

2. As a team, analyze the following story by Taoist thinker Chuang-tse:

While sitting on the banks of the P'u River, Chuang-tse was approached by two representatives of the Prince of Ch'u, who offered him a position at court. Chuang-tse watched the water flowing by as if he had not heard. Finally, he remarked, "I am told that the Prince has a sacred tortoise, over two thousand years old, which is kept in a box, wrapped in silk and brocade." "That is true," the officials replied. "If the tortoise had been given a choice," Chuang-tse continued, "which do you think he would have liked better—to have been alive in the mud, or dead within the palace?" "To have been alive in the mud, of course," the men answered. "I too prefer the mud," said Chuang-tse. "Good-bye."

In our rapidly changing world, we must all make a number of decisions as to how we want to live our lives. As a class project, research decision making as it relates to career choices and life choices.

Creative Decision Making

You probably belong to several different groups (perhaps a student group, a church group, a community group, a sports group, etc.). Each one of these groups is likely to have at least one problem that it is trying to resolve but hasn't yet found a solution to. Use the material in this chapter to help your group develop a creative solution to its problem. Answer the following questions:

1. Use the checklist "How to Be More Creative" to help your group solve its problem. Make sure that you fully explore each of the suggestions on the checklist. For example, for the "check your assumptions" suggestion, describe exactly what assumptions have

been made, given the problem. Then explain how different assumptions might lead to a solution. Likewise, for the "get more points of view" suggestion, explain exactly how you would do that (including who you would ask outside the group). Address all of the suggestions on the list and develop specific recommendations.

2. Did you observe any resistance to your suggestions about the process of creative decision making? If yes, why do you think there was resistance? How would you deal with the resistance you encountered? (*Hint:* Look at the material in Chapter 15.)

INTERNET EXERCISES

The quality and timing of management decisions can have a radical effect on the success, failure, or mediocrity of a company. You don't have to read too many business journals and newspapers to find examples of poor decision making and its effects.

1. In early April 2003, Air Canada (**www.aircanada.ca**) announced it was seeking protection from creditors. Accusations of mismanagement of the former Canadian Crown corporation were levelled. Research the Air Canada situation to find out what went wrong and why (**www. nationalpost.com**; **www.nationalpost.com/financialpost/**; **www.businessweek.com**; **www.canadianbusiness.com**; **www.globeandmail.com**).

2. Nortel Networks Inc. (**www.nortel.ca**) has also experienced major setbacks. Were these due to poor management decisions? Research the Nortel Networks situation to find out what went wrong and why. Is there any correlation between the management decisions at Air Canada and those at Nortel?

3. The Elephant & Castle Group (**www.elephantcastle.com**) had pub roots and then expanded into what it thought was the lucrative restaurant market (Alamo restaurants). Research what went wrong and why. Are there any similarities in the management decisions made at Air Canada, Nortel, and the Elephant & Castle? Are there any lessons that managers can learn from these three companies' experiences?

Finally! A Decision on Voisey's Bay

On June 11, 2002, the government of Newfoundland and Labrador and Inco Ltd. agreed on a deal to develop a mine at Voisey's Bay in Labrador. One month earlier, the Labrador Inuit Association and Labrador's Innu Nation had endorsed agreements with Inco regarding the nickel development project. Those agreements specified how the Aboriginal groups would benefit from revenue sharing, environmental protection, hiring quotas, and job training. The various agreements create thousands of jobs in Newfoundland and Labrador, and will guarantee economic growth for Canada's poorest province.

The road to development of Voisey's Bay has been long and hard. The story is complicated, and it demonstrates how unforeseen events can make organizational decision making difficult.

The story began in 1993, when two diamond prospectors stumbled upon one of the world's richest nickel finds in the rolling hills of northeast Labrador. In 1996, Inco decided to buy controlling interest in the site for $4.3 billion. Unfortunately, once Inco gained control of the deposit, things began to go wrong. Among other things, the price of nickel dropped, and so did Inco's stock price.

In 1997, Inco announced that it would have to delay development of the site because of a time-consuming and expensive environmental review process. The government of Newfoundland and Labrador had also gotten into the act by demanding that Inco build a smelter in the province to smelt the ore it mined. The Innu Nation was also demanding a 3 percent smelter royalty and a guarantee that the mine would be in operation for 25 years.

By 1999, though, things were looking up. Nickel prices (and Inco's stock price) had increased sharply, and Inco returned to the bargaining table with provincial politicians to try to work out an agreement. With its improved financial condition, Inco was now apparently willing to talk about building the smelter in Newfoundland and Labrador after all. But in February 2000, Inco announced the closing of its Newfoundland and Labrador office because it had been unable to reach an agreement with the provincial government.

At the annual shareholders meeting in April 2000, angry shareholders focused on the stalled Voisey's Bay project and the possibility of a strike by 3500 workers at Inco's Sudbury operations. Also present at the meeting was a group of Indonesian villagers who expressed concerns about growing social problems and unemployment difficulties near one of Inco's properties in their country.

In June 2001 negotiations with Newfoundland and Labrador resumed again, and by October 2001 the Newfoundland and Labrador minister of mines and energy announced that most of the issues that were holding up development of Voisey's Bay had been resolved. Inco was more cautious in its interpretation of the negotiations. It said that it was facing an unexpected decline in its business because the terrorist attacks in New York had caused a slowdown in the world's economies.

At Inco's annual meeting in April 2002, CEO Scott Hand said he hoped to reach an agreement with Newfoundland and Labrador by June 2002. Newfoundland and Labrador Premier Roger Grimes seemed less optimistic in a CBC Radio broadcast. He said he didn't have the same level of confidence that a deal was close. The continuing point of contention was how much of the ore mined in Newfoundland and Labrador would also be processed there.

But finally the agreement was reached. The Voisey's Bay mine will become operational in 2006, and the new smelter will be built in Argentia in 2011.

Questions

1. What criteria did Inco managers likely use when they originally decided to spend $4.3 billion to gain control of the Voisey's Bay nickel deposit?

2. Did Inco make a rational decision when they bought Voisey's Bay? Explain.

3. In 1996, did it look like Inco had made a good decision? How good did this decision look in 1998? in 2000? in 2002?

4. Given all that has happened, was Inco's decision to buy Voisey's Bay a good one? Is there a difference between a "good" decision and a "rational" decision?

Inco
www.incoltd.com

Make a Decision Now!

"Rama, you've got a problem, and you've got to make a decision immediately about how to straighten it out," said Pat McGlothin, manager of distribution for the *Daily Harold*. McGlothin was speaking to Rama Chakalas, the supervisor of the truck drivers who delivered the newspapers to the carrier drop-off stations and to newsstands in the surrounding towns. There were 25 drivers who put hundreds of kilometres per day on the trucks.

The conversation between McGlothin and Chakalas continued:

McGlothin: I've been watching the maintenance costs on the trucks and right now our costs are up 20 percent over last year. That's a big jump.

Chakalas: Well, maybe a different maintenance program is being carried out on the trucks and that has increased the expense.

McGlothin: No, that can't be it. I've already talked to the maintenance supervisor and he says that they're doing what they've always done. That means your drivers are responsible for the increased costs. What are you going to do about it?

Chakalas: I'm not sure.

McGlothin: What do you mean, you're not sure? The facts speak for themselves. You certainly can't argue with the facts, can you?

Chakalas: I'm not trying to argue with the facts. I'd like to do some additional checking to see what might be causing the problem before I make any hasty decisions.

McGlothin: I can't see what additional checking there is to do. We've got to get this thing resolved quickly or the VP is going to have us on the carpet. I'll bet he's already seen the cost figures, so it won't be long before I'm called in to explain them. I want you to do something now!

Chakalas: That's putting a lot of pressure on me. I think it would be better to look into this more carefully instead of making a snap decision.

McGlothin: I want a decision by tomorrow at noon!

Chakalas: I'll do my best.

Questions

1. What kind of decision does Rama Chakalas have to make (crisis, opportunity, or problem)? Is this a programmed or non-programmed decision? Give reasons for your answer.

2. Which step in the rational decision-making process is Pat McGlothin failing to consider?

3. What difficulties are likely to arise in this situation as a result of failing to consider this key step?

4. If Chakalas is allowed to follow the rational model, how should he proceed?

Which Routes to Fly?

As an experienced airline manager, David Neeleman knows there are no more important decisions he has to make than those concerning the routes JetBlue will fly. The right decision will maximize ridership and minimize competitive retaliation, by offering low-cost flights that competitors aren't now providing. The wrong decision will confront Neeleman's fledgling airline with fast and sure competitive retaliation, in which case JetBlue could be out of business before it really takes off.

The first and biggest route decision probably revolved around whether to choose New York's JFK as his first major gateway. There was a time when JFK was actually the headquarters for several U.S. airlines, but most moved on to other cities and airports where costs were lower and spaces were easier to come by. From JetBlue's point of view, JFK has several advantages. It is in the middle of one of the ten busiest air passenger markets in the United States. New York's political leaders badly wanted a low-cost airline for their state that would help reduce the cost of flying from the New York City area to upper New York State. And, although JFK did have many delays, it actually was less busy than the New York's other major airport, LaGuardia, for the time slots JetBlue was looking at.

Neeleman and his team considered other airport alternatives. At Boston's Logan Airport, for instance, Neeleman says, "No one will give us gates." In other words, there's so much competition from American Airlines and US Airways that JetBlue can't get the gates it needs, even though, according to Neeleman, the gates at Logan are now underutilized.

In terms of what he looks for in choosing routes, Neeleman says one thing his company must watch out for is spreading itself too thin. Spreading his flights among too many destinations runs the risk of lowering the utilization rate of each plane—there'd be too much downtime, without enough passengers on each route. As he says, "I just want passengers on the planes." The basic idea, therefore, is to go into a few major gateways, like JFK, and to use the traffic and population base around these gateways to fly into smaller cities that are not adequately served by low-cost airlines. For example, he wants to fly passengers from JFK to Buffalo, New York, and Fort Lauderdale (instead of Miami). The problem is, "Where should JetBlue fly next?"

Getting the slots (the permissions to fly in and out at specific times) at a busy airport like JFK is not going to be easy. He set up a lobbying operation in Washington, D.C., in order to help convince New York's congressional delegation that cities like Buffalo, Syracuse, and Rochester needed JetBlue's low-cost alternative flights from New York City. In turn, New York congressional members will have to work on convincing the Department of Transportation that the needs of New Yorkers (and JetBlue) are important enough to put JetBlue's interest ahead of those of major airlines like American and USAir.

Getting the slots doesn't mean JetBlue is home free. For example, it was able to obtain numerous arrival and departure slots at California's Long Beach airport. However, those slots came with the condition that they must all be utilized within several years. American Airlines is already battling to take over some of those slots and is lowering prices to Long Beach, and increasing incentives (such as adding more frequent-flier miles for those who fly there from JFK). In the not too distant future, Neeleman also would like to see JetBlue fly to cities in Canada and Mexico.

Assignment

You and your team are consultants to Mr. Neeleman, who is depending on your management expertise to help navigate the launch and management of JetBlue. Here's what he wants to know from you:

1. Accurately spell out what triggered the route-decision problems stated in the case.

2. List at least four ways that Neeleman can define the "Where should we fly next" problem, and then choose the best alternative.

3. Propose at least five objectives for Neeleman, who must make the decision regarding routes and gateways.

4. Propose at least four alternatives to solve the situation. Develop a consequences matrix for the situation.

5. Develop a decision matrix for the position.

Appendix

Quantitative Decision-Making Tools

Many decisions (particularly programmed ones) lend themselves to solution through quantitative analysis. Here are several popular quantitative decision-making techniques.

Break-Even Analysis

break-even analysis
A decision-making aid that enables a manager to determine whether a particular volume of sales will result in losses or profits.

In financial analysis, the break-even point is that volume of sales at which revenues equal expenses and there is neither a profit nor a loss. **Break-even analysis** is a decision-making aid that enables a manager to determine whether a particular volume of sales will result in losses or profits.[1]

Break-Even Charts

Break-even analysis makes use of four basic concepts: fixed costs, variable costs, revenues, and profits. Fixed costs (such as for plant and machinery) are costs that basically do not change with changes in volume. In other words, you might use the same machine to produce 10 units, 50 units, or 200 units of a product. Variable costs (such as for raw material) do rise in proportion to volume. Revenue is the total income received from sales of the product. For example, if you sell 50 dolls at $8 each, then your revenue is 8×50 or $400. Profit is the money you have left after subtracting fixed and variable costs from revenues.

break-even chart
A graph that shows whether a particular volume of sales will result in profits or losses.

A **break-even chart** is a graph that shows whether a particular volume of sales will result in profits or losses (see Figure A5.1). The fixed-costs line is horizontal, since fixed costs remain the same regardless of level of output. Variable costs, however, increase in proportion to output and are shown as an upward-sloping line. The total-costs line is equal to variable costs plus fixed costs at each level of output.

break-even point
The point at which the total-revenues line crosses the total-costs line.

The **break-even point** is the point at which the total-revenues line crosses the total-costs line. Beyond this point (note the shaded area in Figure A5.1), total revenues exceed total costs. In this example, an output of about 4000 units is the break-even point. Above this, the company can expect to earn a profit. But if sales are fewer than 4000 units, the company can expect a loss.

Break-Even Formula

The break-even chart provides a picture of the relationship between sales volume and profits. However, a chart is not required for determining break-even points. Instead, you can use a formula:

$$P(X) = F + V(X)$$

where

F = fixed costs
V = variable costs per unit
X = volume of output (in units)
P = price per unit

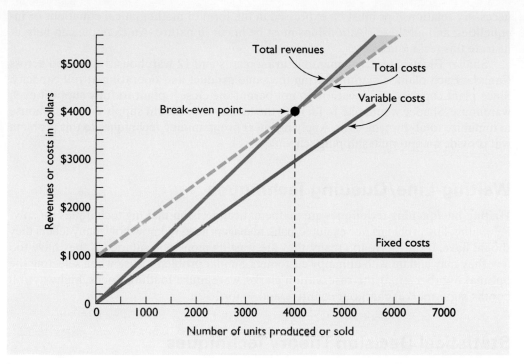

FIGURE A5.1
A Break-Even Chart
The break-even point is that number of units sold at which total revenues equal total costs.

Rearranging this formula, the break-even point is $X = F/(P - V)$. In other words, the break-even point is the volume of sales where total costs equal total revenues. If, for example, you have a product in which:

> F = fixed costs = $1000
> V = variable costs per unit = $0.75
> P = price per unit = $1 per unit

then the break-even point is $1000/($1 - $0.75) = 4000 units.

Linear Programming

Break-even analysis is only one of many decision techniques. Decision-science techniques are a second category of programmed decision-making aids, all of which are distinguished by their reliance on mathematics. For example, **linear programming** is a mathematical method used to solve resource allocation problems. These arise "whenever there are a number of activities to be performed, but limitations on either the amount of resources or the way they can be spent."[2] For example, linear programming can be used to determine the best way to

- distribute merchandise from a number of warehouses to a number of customers
- assign personnel to various jobs
- design shipping schedules
- select the product mix in a factory to make the best use of machine and labour hours available while maximizing the firm's profit
- route production to optimize the use of machinery

For managers to apply linear programming successfully, the problem must meet certain basic requirements: There must be a stated, quantifiable goal, such as "minimize total shipping costs"; the resources to be used must be known (a firm could produce 200 of one item and 300 of another, for instance, or 400 of one and 100 of another); all the

linear programming
A mathematical method used to solve resource allocation problems.

necessary relationships must be expressed in the form of mathematical equations or inequalities; and all these relationships must be linear in nature. An example can help illustrate this technique:

Shader Electronics has 5 manufacturing plants and 12 warehouses scattered across Canada. Each plant is manufacturing the same product and operating at full capacity. Since plant capacity and location do not permit the closest plant to fully support each warehouse, Shader would like to identify the factory that should supply each warehouse to minimize total shipping costs. Applying linear programming techniques to this problem will provide an optimum shipping schedule.

Waiting-Line/Queuing Techniques

Waiting-line/queuing techniques are mathematical decision-making techniques for solving waiting-line problems. For example, bank managers need to know how many tellers they should have. If they have too many, they are wasting money on salaries; if they have too few, they may end up with unhappy customers. Similar problems arise when selecting the optimal number of airline reservation clerks, warehouse loading docks, highway toll booths, supermarket checkout counters, and so forth.

Statistical Decision Theory Techniques

Statistical decision theory techniques are used to solve problems for which information is incomplete or uncertain. Suppose a shopkeeper can stock either brand A or brand B, but not both. She knows how much it will cost to stock her shelves with each brand, and she also knows how much money she will earn (or lose) if each brand turns out to be a success (or failure) with her customers. However, she can only estimate how much of each brand she might sell, so her information is incomplete. Using statistical decision theory, the shopkeeper would assign probabilities (estimates of the likelihood that the brand will sell or not) to each alternative. Then she could determine which alternative—stocking brand A or brand B—would most likely result in the greatest profits.

Three Degrees of Uncertainty

Statistical decision theory is based on the idea that a manager may face three degrees of uncertainty in making a decision. Some decisions are made under conditions of **certainty**. Here, the manager knows in advance the outcome of the decision. From a practical point of view, for example, you know that if you buy a $50 Canada Savings Bond, the interest you will earn to maturity on the bond is, say, 6 percent. However, managers rarely make decisions under conditions of certainty.

At the opposite extreme, some decisions are made under conditions of **uncertainty**. Here, the manager cannot even assign probabilities to the likelihood of the various outcomes. For example, a shopkeeper may have several new products that could be stocked but no idea of the likelihood that one brand will be successful or that another will fail. Conditions of complete uncertainty are also relatively infrequent.

Most management decisions are made under conditions of **risk**. In these situations, the manager can at least assign probabilities to each outcome. In other words, the manager knows (either from past experience or by making an educated guess) the chance that each possible outcome (such as product A being successful or product B being unsuccessful) will occur.

Decision Trees

A **decision tree** is one technique for making a decision under conditions of risk. With a decision tree like the one shown in Figure A5.2, an expected value can be calculated for each alternative. **Expected value** equals the probability of the outcome multiplied by the benefit or cost of that outcome.

For example, in Figure A5.2 it pays for our shopkeeper to stock brand B rather than brand A. Stocking brand A provides a 70 percent chance of making an $800 profit, so the shopkeeper has to balance this $560 profit she could make against the possibility of a $90 loss (30 percent 3 possible loss of $300). The expected value of stocking brand A is thus $470. However, the expected value of stocking brand B is a relatively higher $588.

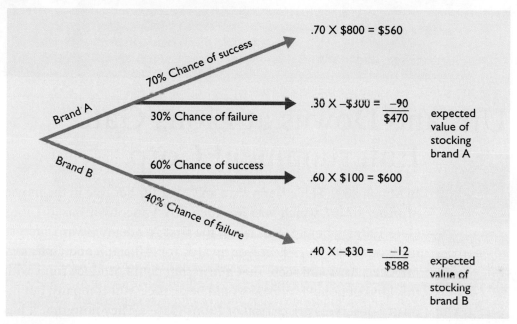

FIGURE A5.2
Example of a Decision Tree
The expected value of each alternative is equal to the chance of success or failure multiplied by the expected profit or loss.

The Planning Process →

6

Ups and Downs at Lions Gate Entertainment Corp.

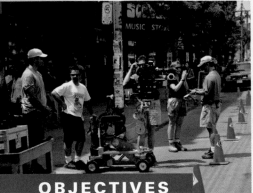

OBJECTIVES

After studying this chapter and the case exercises at the end, you should be able to use the material to:

1. Use the steps in the planning process to develop a workable plan for an organization.

2. Outline the required overall business plan and provide examples of its component functional plans.

3. Express the plans in descriptive, graphical, and financial formats.

4. Explain what a manager did right (and wrong) with respect to setting goals for subordinates.

5. Explain the forecasting tools you think a manager should use and why.

In March 2002, Halle Berry won an Oscar for her role in the movie *Monster's Ball*, which was produced by Vancouver-based Lions Gate Entertainment. This is not the first Academy Award success for Lions Gate; in 1999, it won awards for *Affliction* and *Gods and Monsters*. It would seem that a firm that could produce films with this kind of popular appeal would be a successful company, but industry observers are critical of Lions Gate's. They note that it has failed to capitalize on the media buzz it has generated with its high-profile Academy Award wins. They also point out that the company's profit potential has never been realized and that its stock price will continue to languish in the $3 to $5 per share range until major strategic changes are made in the company.

Lions Gate was started in 1997 by Frank Giustra, who had been a mining promoter but who abandoned that business and raised $120 million to acquire a studio and film production and film distribution companies. Like its U.S. competitors, Lions Gate employs an integrated media model; that is, it has a series of operating divisions (motion pictures, television, animation, and studio facilities) that can deliver stand-alone products or provide support services to each of its other divisions.

Originally, the strategy was to make low-budget films that would turn a profit even if they didn't attract the kind of attention that major films do. For example, *American Psycho* grossed just U.S.$15 million, which is only a fraction of what a blockbuster movie would generate, but since it cost only $8 million to make, it was still profitable for Lions Gate. The original strategy also meant imitating the best existing structures that other companies were using, and using external resources to make up for Lions Gate smaller size.

But somewhere along the line the original strategy changed. To help it produce and distribute class-A feature films (larger budget films with international distribution), Lions Gate invested $50 million in a joint venture (called Mandalay Pictures) with a major U.S. film producer. Mandalay was supposed to crank out 20 movies over the next five years. But by the middle of 2001, the venture had produced only two films: *Sleepy Hollow* (starring Johnny Depp) and *Enemy at the Gates*. The Mandalay venture has been a consistent money-loser for Lions Gate, with start-up costs and production delays being the big cause.

Jon Feltheimer, formerly president of Columbia TriStar Television, was hired in 2000 as the CEO of Lions Gate. His job was to improve Lions Gate's balance sheet and its stock price. He quickly developed a plan to resolve the company's problems, first by getting a $200 million line of credit and then floating a $33 million preferred share offering. The money was to be used to acquire other companies so that Lions Gate could gain the size necessary to compete with the industry giants. By mid-2000, Lions Gate had acquired Trimark Holdings (best known for its action and horror movies) and CinemaNow (a website where people watch films on-line).

But there have been few additional acquisitions since then, and investor confidence has waned. Because Lions Gate stock price is so low, it will have to offer cash as an incentive in further acquisitions, but it doesn't have much cash.

Industry sources think that Lions Gate will not survive as a stand-alone company and that it will eventually be bought out by a bigger filmmaker.

Lions Gate
Entertainment
www.lionsgate-ent. com

Mandalay Pictures
www.mandalay.com/ main.html

The Nature and Purpose of Planning

Planning is something we all do every day. For example, if you are like most readers of this book, you're probably reading it as part of a management course. Chances are the course is part of your program of studies. This program is a plan. It identifies your goal (say, getting a business degree in two years), and it identifies how you will reach that goal (by specifying the courses you'll need to graduate). **Plans** are devices that answer questions such as these: What will we do? When will we do it? Who will do it? How much will it cost?[1]

All plans specify or imply goals (such as "increase sales by 10 percent"), and courses of action (such as "hire a new salesperson and boost advertising by 20 percent"). Plans are therefore methods for achieving a desired result. **Goals**, or **objectives**, are specific results you want to achieve. **Planning** is thus "the process of establishing objectives and courses of action, prior to taking action."[2]

Your own plans do not end with earning the degree. You also have a broader goal, a vision of where you're headed in life. Your degree is likely just one step in a longer-term plan. For example, suppose you dream of running your own consulting firm by the time you are 35. You therefore ask yourself, "What must I do to achieve this goal?" The answer may be to work for a nationally known consulting firm, thus building up your experience and your reputation in the field. So here is your plan: Take this course to get the degree, get the degree to get the consulting job, and then work as a consultant to achieve your dream. You are well on the way to setting up "Business Consultants Ltd."

plan
A method for doing or making something, consisting of a goal and a course of action.

goal
A specific result to be achieved; the end result of a plan.

objective
A specific result toward which effort is directed.

planning
The process of setting goals and courses of action, developing rules and procedures, and forecasting future outcomes.

What Planning Involves

Planning really means making tomorrow's decisions today. Planning requires choosing goals and the courses of action to achieve them. Therefore, when you make a plan, you're actually deciding now what you are going to do in the future. In that sense, a plan is simply a set of current decisions that will allow you to achieve a future goal.

Suppose you are planning a vacation to Paris. Your plan might consist of the following decisions (among others): The date you leave; how you plan to get to the airport; your airline and flight; the airport of arrival; how you'll get into downtown Paris; your hotel; and a fairly detailed itinerary (or plan) for each day you're in Paris.

Suppose you don't decide ahead of time (plan) how you're getting to or from the airport, or what you'll be doing each day in Paris. What will happen? Maybe nothing. More likely, you'll have to make many last-minute decisions under stressful conditions. Instead of arranging to have a friend take you to the airport, you may be scrambling to find a cab. Instead of researching and pricing your transportation alternatives ahead of time, you may find yourself at Charles de Gaulle Airport, tired and faced with a bewildering variety of buses and cabs. And instead of deciding ahead of time, in the comfort of your home (and with all your guidebooks) what you'll do each day, you may waste several hours each day deciding what to do, finding out what is open, or drifting aimlessly through the Paris streets (which might be OK with some people).

What Planning Accomplishes

Planning has real benefits: First, it allows you to *make your decisions ahead of time*, in your home (or office), and with the luxury of having the time to research and weigh your options. It also helps you *anticipate the consequences* of various courses of action and to think through the practicality and feasibility of each, without actually having to commit the resources to carry out that course of action.

Planning also provides *direction and a sense of purpose*. "If you don't know where you're going, any path will get you there," the Mad Hatter tells Alice as she stumbles into Wonderland. The same is true for all your endeavours. Knowing ahead of time that your goal is to own a consulting firm provides a sense of direction and purpose for all the career decisions you have to make, such as what to major in and what experience you'll need along the way. Someone once said, "The world parts, and makes a path for the person who knows where he or she is going."

R. R. Donnelley
www.rrdonnelley.com

A plan also therefore provides a *unifying framework* against which to measure decisions, and thus helps you avoid piecemeal decision making (decisions that are not consistent with your goal or with each other). For example, R. R. Donnelley & Sons Company (owned by Quebecor) is in the business of printing documents and other materials for a broad range of clients including investment bankers. The company is a leading printer of books, magazines, and catalogues, and is one of the world's largest managers and distributors of books in electronic form.[3] Donnelley's planning led its managers to anticipate a demand caused by the globalization of its customers. The company therefore invested heavily in advanced technology and a worldwide electronic network. Now, with the help of satellites, R. R. Donnelley can print a securities prospectus simultaneously in many locations around the globe.[4]

It would have been wasteful for R. R. Donnelley to spend its investment dollars building more printing factories in its home country (the United States). The globalization of its customers demanded—and technological advances made possible—the transmitting and creating of documents via satellite around the globe. Its plan for doing so helped ensure that the firm channelled its resources toward those desired results and avoided activities— such as building unneeded domestic printing plants—that were inconsistent with its overall direction.

Planning's benefits don't stop there. Management theorist Peter Drucker says that planning also helps *identify potential opportunities and threats* and reduce long-term risks.[5] For example, R. R. Donnelley's planning process helped identify the opportunity for satellite-based global printing.

Finally, planning *facilitates control*. Control means ensuring that activities conform to plans, and planning is an important part of control. Thus, a company's plan may specify that its profits will double within five years. This goal becomes the standard against which to measure, compare, and control managers' performance. "Planning" and "control" are sometimes called the Siamese twins of the management process. You can't have controls without a plan; and it's useless to have a plan if you don't monitor how you're doing.

The Management Planning Process

You may not have thought about it, but you already know quite a lot about the management planning process. Consider the five steps you might take to plan a career. (1) Set a career goal, such as "work as a management consultant." (2) Analyze the situation to assess your skills and to determine your prospects. (3) Determine your alternative courses of action, that is, the various paths you might follow (college or university major, summer experiences, etc.) to reach your goal. (4) Evaluate these various paths, and finally (5) formulate and implement your plan (including a budget). It's a logical process and one that parallels how you would make any decision.

These five steps are the heart of the management planning process and are summarized in Figure 6.1. It doesn't matter whether you are planning your career, or a trip to France, or how you're going to market your firm's new product. The basic process always involves setting objectives, analyzing the situation, determining alternative courses of action, evaluating those options, and then choosing and implementing your plan.

The process is the same when managers plan for their firms, with two small differences. First, there's usually a hierarchical aspect to the planning: Top management approves a long-term plan, and each department creates its own budgets and other plans to fit and to contribute to the company's long-term plan. Second, the process may involve much interaction and give-and-take among different departments and organizational levels. In other words, corporate planning in practice is iterative: Top management formulates its plans at least in part based on upward feedback from the departments, and the departments in turn draft plans that make sense in terms of top management's plan. Let's look at this process more closely.

The Planning Hierarchy

As you can see from this discussion, the final step in Figure 6.1 is not really the final step. It's really just the start for round 2, because top management's goals then become the

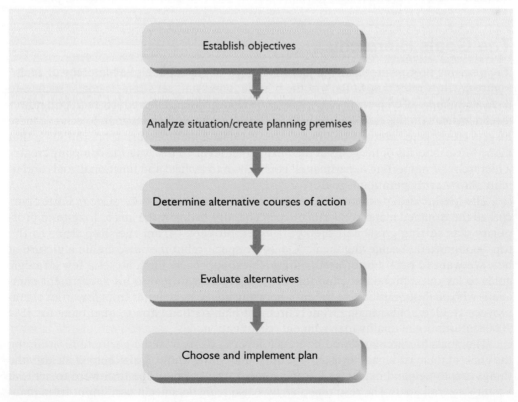

FIGURE 6.1
The Planning Process

targets for which the departments craft derivative plans. In other words, the planning process produces a hierarchy of plans. This hierarchy includes (1) the company-wide plan and goals, and (2) various levels of subsidiary units' derivative plans and objectives, each of which contributes to achieving the goals of the next higher unit's plans. A hierarchy of plans evolves.

Sunbeam
www.sunbeam.com

Several years ago, the management of Sunbeam Corporation decided to drive down costs by at least 20 percent by shrinking the firm. What evolved was a top-management plan to reduce the number of employees by half, roll out 30 new products per year, and shrink the number of factories and warehouses from more than 40 to just 13. With that planning framework as a guide, lower-level managers made plans for their departments. Managers for each product group had to formulate and receive approval for plans for which products they wanted to add and which they wanted to drop. The production head had to craft plans showing which plants would be closed to meet the goal.

Then, third-level managers needed operational plans. For example, once the HR manager knew which plants were closing, she would need operational plans for handling the dismissals. And plant managers would need specific monthly production plans, once they knew the targets top management had set for their facility. The result was a hierarchy of plans. Managers at each level devised plans of increasing specificity (and of shorter time horizon) from the top of the firm to the bottom.

The planning process may take up to a year. In some companies, top management and the board formulate a few strategic themes at the start of the year. The divisions then complete reviews of their current businesses in April and forward these to corporate planning. In June, the board adopts a set of planning assumptions and guidelines prepared by the corporate planning department. At the same time, the planning group might be preparing financial forecasts, again based in part on projections from the divisions.

At some point, the board of directors reviews and sets the firm's financial objectives, and then these goals are sent to each business unit. The units then use these financial targets (as well as the firm's strategic guidelines) to prepare their own plans. They submit these for approval a few months later. Once adopted, top management monitors progress, perhaps via quarterly reports from the operating units. Once the divisions receive approval for their plans, departments can develop shorter-term tactical and operational plans.

The Goals Hierarchy

The planning process produces not just a hierarchy of plans, but also a hierarchy of goals.[6] Figure 6.2 illustrates this. At the top, the president and staff set strategic goals (such as to have a minimum of 55 percent of sales revenue from customized products by 2006). Lower level managers (in this case, starting with the vice presidents) then set goals to achieve these targets (such as to "convert building C to customized manufacturing operations") that make sense in terms of the goals at the next higher level. In this way, the company creates a hierarchy of supporting departmental goals, down to tactical and functional goals and finally short-term operational goals.

The hierarchical planning process needn't be complicated. When Gregg Foster purchased the troubled metal-converting Elyria Foundry, he knew the key to long-term prosperity was setting goals and then getting employees—from the shop floor to the top—committed to achieving them. "Goals are specific, but they also create a picture of how we want to be."[7] Foster used a hierarchical approach. First, he set a few strategic goals to lay out a broad direction for the firm. He next turned to his department managers, who each submitted five to ten supporting goals. Next, input from lower-level employees yielded goals ranging from retirement plan participation to qualifying for ISO 9000 (international quality management) certification.

The goals hierarchy showed how each level's efforts would contribute to attaining the goals at the next higher level and for the foundry as a whole. It also helped identify the things employees and managers felt the company had to fix if the firm were to achieve Foster's overall goals. The resulting plan was also realistic, since it used input from managers and employees who were actually "at ground level," doing the job on a day-to-day basis. We'll discuss how to set goals in more detail later in this chapter.

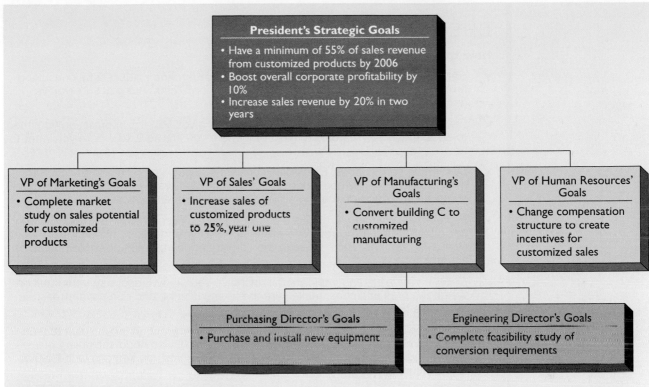

President's Strategic Goals

- Have a minimum of 55% of sales revenue from customized products by 2006
- Boost overall corporate profitability by 10%
- Increase sales revenue by 20% in two years

VP of Marketing's Goals

- Complete market study on sales potential for customized products

VP of Sales' Goals

- Increase sales of customized products to 25%, year one

VP of Manufacturing's Goals

- Convert building C to customized manufacturing

VP of Human Resources' Goals

- Change compensation structure to create incentives for customized sales

Purchasing Director's Goals

- Purchase and install new equipment

Engineering Director's Goals

- Complete feasibility study of conversion requirements

Note: A hierarchy of goals like this is one important by-product of the planning process. This figure shows some (not all) of the supporting goals that need to be formulated to help achieve the company's overall goal of having a minimum of 55 percent of its sales revenue from customized products by 2006.

FIGURE 6.2
Hierarchy of Goals

Who Does the Planning?

Who actually does the planning depends on the size of the firm. In a small business the entrepreneur will do most of the planning himself or herself. This would likely involve informally bouncing around ideas with several employees, or using business planning software.

In large firms there may be a central corporate planning group whose role is to work with top management and each division to solicit, challenge, and refine the company's plan. Over the past few years, many firms have decentralized their planning.[8] Today, the main planners even in big firms are not headquarters specialists. Instead, they are the firms' product and divisional managers, perhaps aided by small headquarters advisory groups. The assumption is that the line managers are in the best position to sense changes in customer, competitive, and technological trends and react to them.

Where headquarters groups do exist, they usually perform the following activities:

- Compile and monitor all planning-related data such as data on each division's progress toward its goals and financial targets
- Conduct competitor and market research
- Provide divisional planners with training in the techniques they could or should be using
- Devise company-wide planning reports and forms (so division plans are comparable in the information they provide)

The Business Plan and Its Components

Whether it's a tiny firm or BCE, it's never accurate to refer to the company's "plan." Every firm has not one but a hierarchy of plans. There's typically an overall plan guiding the business and many subsidiary plans laying out the methods each sub-unit is to follow if the firm is to achieve its overall goals.

We can illustrate this with an example. Assume you are now the owner-president of your own company, Acme Consulting. Your business is growing, and you see the potential (several years down the road) of selling your firm to a major consulting or accounting firm for a great deal of money. Accomplishing this will take a lot of effort over several years. However, you have several immediate challenges. First, you'll need bank financing to support the expansion of services you anticipate over the next five years. Second, you need a business plan because no bank will lend you money without seeing such a plan. You also need the business plan to provide you and your colleagues with a roadmap that spells out what they're expected to do, as well as when, how, and at what cost.

That last point bears repeating: In business, you must decide today what you want to be doing tomorrow. If selling Acme means that you must have $2 million in sales at the end of five years, then you must plan today how you will achieve that goal. That means stating what kinds of clients you need to add, how you are going to market your services, what people you need to hire, and so forth. What you plan to do should generally guide your actions. You can't build a $2-million business without a plan, any more than you would try to get a degree without thinking through your major, your program of studies, and how you intend to pay for it all. How else would you know what courses to take each term?

The Components

To be successful in building Acme Consulting, you will need an overall business plan as well as plans for each of the key areas in your company. These are described in the following paragraphs.

The Business Plan The company's **business plan** provides a comprehensive overview of the firm's situation today, and of company-wide and departmental goals and plans for the next three to five years. Managers often use the term "business plan" in relation to smaller businesses, and particularly to the sort of plan that investors or lenders want to see before providing money to the firm. However, small businesses don't have a monopoly on business plans. Companies like WestJet, Microsoft, or Canadian Pacific will have a version of a comprehensive plan like this, although they may label it their "long-term" or perhaps "strategic" plan.

There are no rigid rules regarding what such plans must contain. Of particular importance are that plans have been developed for the major departments in the company (marketing, production, human resources, and finance).

business plan
A plan that lays out what the business is, where it is heading, and how it plans to get there.

The Marketing Plan To have a successful business, you must have customers. And to have customers, you must have a plan for marketing your products or services to them. Acme may have the best consultants in the province, but if potential clients don't know of its existence, its business prospects are limited. The **marketing plan** specifies the nature of your product or service (for instance its variety, quality, design, and features), as well as the approaches you plan to take with respect to pricing and promoting the product or service, and getting it sold and delivered to your target customers. (Marketing managers call these "the four Ps"—product, price, promotion, and place).

Marketing plans can range from simple to complex. Some marketing plans are quite comprehensive. Figure 6.3 demonstrates the contents of one such plan. It includes an analysis of the markets as they stand now, as well as detailed product, pricing, promotional, and distribution plans and budgets for realizing those plans.

marketing plan
A plan that specifies the nature of your product or service, as well as the approaches you plan to take with respect to pricing, promotion, and place.

Section	Purpose
Executive summary	Presents a brief summary of the main goals and recommendations of the plan for management review.
Current marketing situation	Describes the target market and company's position in it, including information about the market, product performance, competition, and distribution. This section includes
	• A *market description* that defines the market and major segments, then reviews customer needs and factors in the marketing environment.
	• A *product review* that shows sales, prices, and gross margins of the major products in the product line.
	• A review of *competition*, which identifies major competitors and assesses their market positions and strategies.
	• A review of *distribution*, which evaluates recent sales trends and other developments in major distribution channels.
Threats and opportunity analysis	Assesses major threats and opportunities that the product might face.
Objectives and issues	States the marketing objectives that the company would like to attain during the plan's term and discusses key issues that will affect their attainment.
Marketing strategy	Outlines specific strategies for each marketing mix element and explains how each responds to the threats, opportunities, and critical issues spelled out earlier in the plan.
Action programs	Spells out how marketing strategies will be turned into specific action programs that answer the following questions: *What* will be done? *When* will it be done? *Who* is responsible for doing it? *How* much will it cost?
Budgets	Details a supporting marketing budget that is essentially a projected profit-and-loss statement.
Controls	Outlines the control that will be used to monitor progress.

FIGURE 6.3
Outline of a Marketing Plan

Your marketing plan for Acme may not be so comprehensive. It might start with a market analysis that projects the potential growth of each segment of your potential market—North American high tech, European high tech, Latin America, and Other. Figure 6.4 shows this part of your plan.

Figure 6.5 shows the product, pricing, and sales forecast portions of your marketing plan. You would also want to include summaries of how you plan to promote and distribute your product or service. Like any plan, your marketing plan should show what will be done, when it will be done, who is to do it, and how much it will cost and/or produce in revenues.

The Personnel/Management Plan To serve its customers, Acme will need consultants, managers, and secretarial staff. Your **human resources plan** needs tend to reflect your sales projections. The projected number of clients and amount of planned consulting will help determine how many consultants you'll need at each stage of the plan. This will in turn determine your needs for clerical and management staff.

Figure 6.6 summarizes your personnel plan, in financial terms. You might also want to accompany this with a detailed monthly schedule showing what sorts of people you'll be hiring, and when. You might supplement this with a detailed breakdown showing the specific duties of each employee and what their skills and experience should be.

The Production/Operations Plan Implementing your marketing plan will require adequate productive assets. This is perhaps most obvious in manufacturing firms. For example, it takes factories and machines to assemble PCs, and PC sellers like Mind Computer Products and Dell must therefore plan for how they will meet projected demand for PCs. They will have to decide, well in advance, how to support projected manufacturing needs.

Some **production plans** are decidedly more short-term. Since Acme is a service business, Figure 6.7 simply shows Acme's projected sales by type of service for January and February, 2003. (A manufacturing firm might also create a weekly Master Planning Schedule to lay out its weekly production plans, showing how much it will produce of each product.) Acme may also use a **Gantt chart** (see Figure 6.8 on page 176) to plan and thus better gauge how many days of factory time each order will take.

human resources plan
A plan that projects personnel needs based on sales projections.

Dell
www.dell.ca

production plan
A plan that shows how projected manufacturing needs will be supported.

Gantt chart
A production scheduling chart that plots time on a horizontal scale and generally shows, for each product or project, the start and stop times of each operation.

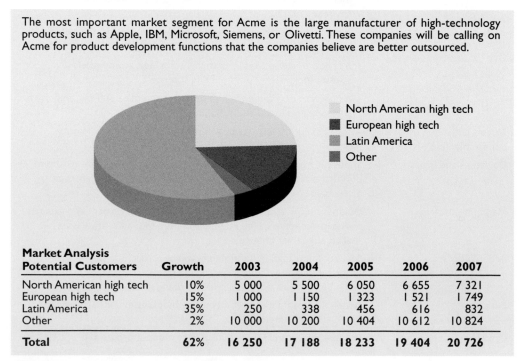

The most important market segment for Acme is the large manufacturer of high-technology products, such as Apple, IBM, Microsoft, Siemens, or Olivetti. These companies will be calling on Acme for product development functions that the companies believe are better outsourced.

- North American high tech
- European high tech
- Latin America
- Other

Market Analysis Potential Customers	Growth	2003	2004	2005	2006	2007
North American high tech	10%	5 000	5 500	6 050	6 655	7 321
European high tech	15%	1 000	1 150	1 323	1 521	1 749
Latin America	35%	250	338	456	616	832
Other	2%	10 000	10 200	10 404	10 612	10 824
Total	**62%**	**16 250**	**17 188**	**18 233**	**19 404**	**20 726**

FIGURE 6.4
Market Analysis of Acme's Potential Market Segments

Acme Consulting won't have to worry about factories, but it will require productive assets such as office space, computers, and communications systems. You'll have to project these needs on a monthly basis (probably as a function of human resources needs), and then

Product
Acme will focus on three geographical markets (North America, Europe, and Latin America) and in limited product segments (personal computers, software, networks, telecommunications, personal organizers, and technology-integration products).

The target customer is usually a manager in a larger corporation and occasionally an owner or president of a medium-sized corporation in a high-growth period.

Pricing
Acme Consulting will be priced at the upper edge of what the market will bear, competing with the name-brand consultants. The pricing fits with the general positioning of Acme as providing high-level expertise. Consulting should be based on $5000 per day for project consulting, $2000 per day for market research, and $10 000 per month and up for retainer consulting.

Sales Forecast
Sales forecasts as follows:

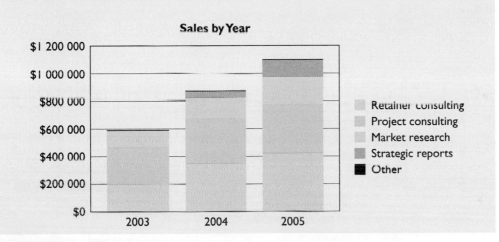

FIGURE 6.5
Product, Pricing, and Sales Forecasts: Marketing Plan Components

Personnel	2003	2004	2005
Partners	$144 000	$175 000	$200 000
Consultants	$0	$50 000	$63 000
Editorial/graphic	$18 000	$22 000	$26 000
VP marketing	$20 000	$50 000	$55 000
Sales people	$0	$30 000	$33 000
Office manager	$7 500	$30 000	$33 000
Secretarial	$5 250	$20 000	$22 000
Other	$0	$0	$0
Total Payroll	$194 750	$377 000	$432 000
Total Headcount	7	14	20
Payroll Taxes and Benefits	$27 265	$52 780	$60 480
Total Payroll Expenditures	$222 015	$429 780	$492 480

FIGURE 6.6
Personnel Plan

Sales by Consulting Service	January	February
Retainer Consulting - Projects	$9 000	$9 000
Project Consulting - Projects	$12 300	$14 200
Market Research - Projects	$6 700	$7 800
Strategic Reports - Projects	$17 000	$22 000
Total Sales	**$45 000**	**$53 000**

FIGURE 6.7
Sales Forecast by Service: Two-Month Sales Plan for Acme Consulting, 2003
Since Acme is a service business, its "production plan" simply shows projected sales by type of service.

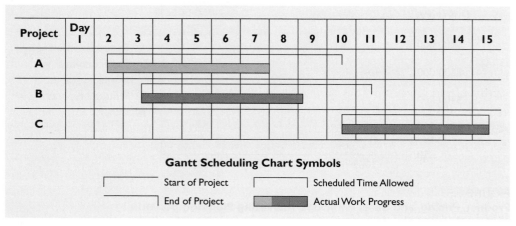

FIGURE 6.8
Gantt Scheduling Chart for Acme *Strategic Report* Projects, January 15, 2003
This Gantt chart helps Acme's managers plan their consultants' time and to keep track of each project's progress. Similar Gantt charts help managers in factories plan machine usage for building different products.

convert these needs to dollars and cents. You may also be able to make use of production planning tools like the Gantt chart, for instance to help you visualize how much of your firm's capacity each consulting job you have will consume.

The Financial Plan "What's the bottom line?" is the first question many managers and bankers ask. The question underscores a truism about business and management. At the end of the day, most of your plans, goals, and accomplishments will end up expressed in financial terms. The **financial plan** is the document that combines the various individual financial plans required to manage the business.

Figure 6.9 shows part of Acme's financial plan. This includes a projected (or "pro forma") profit and loss statement. The "P&L" shows the revenue, cost, and profit (or loss) implications of Acme's business, marketing, production, and personnel plans. The P&L says this: If your plans work out as you anticipate, these are the revenues, costs, and profits or losses you should produce each month (or quarter, or year). It shows you the bottom line.

financial plan
The document that combines the various individual financial plans required to manage the business.

Pro Forma Profit and Loss (Income Statement)	2003	2004	2005
Sales	$592 000	$875 000	$1 100 000
Direct Cost of Sales	$159 000	$219 000	$289 000
Other	$0	$0	$0
Total Cost of Sales	$159 000	$219 000	$289 000
Gross Margin	$433 000	$656 000	$811 000
Gross Margin %	73.14%	74.97%	73.73%
Operating expenses:			
Advertising/Promotion	$36 000	$40 000	$44 000
Public Relations	$30 000	$30 000	$33 000
Travel	$0	$0	$0
Miscellaneous	$0	$0	$0
Payroll Expense	$194 750	$377 000	$432 000
Payroll Taxes and Benefits	$27 265	$52 780	$60 480
Depreciation	$3 600	$0	$0
Leased Equipment	$18 000	$7 000	$7 000
Utilities	$0	$12 000	$12 000
Insurance	$0	$2 000	$2 000
Rent	$0	$0	$0
Other	$0	$0	$0
Contract/Consultants	$0	$0	$0
Total Operating Expenses	$423 615	$587 780	$708 480
Profit Before Interest and Taxes	$9 385	$68 220	$102 520
Interest Expense Short-Term	$1 800	$6 400	$10 400
Interest Expense Long-Term	$5 000	$5 000	$5 000
Taxes Incurred	$646	$14 205	$21 780
Net Profit	$1 939	$42 615	$65 340
Net Profit/Sales	0.33%	4.87%	5.94%

FIGURE 6.9
Acme Consulting Profit and Loss

Planning Tools

Managers need a way to convert business, marketing, production, personnel, and financial plans into concrete goals their subordinates must achieve. Many use the executive assignment action plan for documenting the goals and plans emerging from this hierarchical business planning process. Table 6.1 shows an example. Its purpose is to link management's goals at one level to the derivative plans at the next level down.[9]

Table 6.1 spells out each executive's assignment for carrying out the overall plan. In this case, one long-term top-management goal is to "have a minimum of 55 percent of sales revenue from customized products by 2006." The action plan summarizes the targets each department needs to achieve if that long-term goal is to be met. Thus, the vice president of marketing is to "complete market study on sales potential for customized products" within one year. The vice president of manufacturing is to "convert building C to customized manufacturing operation" within a year.

Each vice president's assigned goals then become the target for which they must develop their own plans. Table 6.2 illustrates this. Here the manufacturing vice president's goal of

TABLE 6.1 Executive Assignment Action Plan for Achieving Long-Term Objective

Long-Term Objective: Have a minimum of 55 percent of sales revenue from customized products by 2006.

EXECUTIVE ASSIGNMENTS/ DERIVATIVE OBJECTIVES	ACCOUNTABILITY		SCHEDULE		RESOURCES REQUIRED			FEEDBACK MECHANISMS
	Primary	Supporting	Start	Complete	Capital	Operating	Human	
1. Complete market study on sales potential for customized products	VP Marketing	VP Sales	Yr 1	**Year 1**		$10 000	500 hrs	Written progress reports
2. Revise sales forecasts for Years 1, 2, and 3 to reflect changes	VP Sales	VP Marketing		**Year 1**			50 hrs	Revised forecasts
3. Convert building C to customized manufacturing operation	VP Mfg	VP Engineering VP Admin	Yr 1	**Year 2**	$500 000	$80 000	1100 hrs	Written progress reports
4. Change compensation structure to encourage customized sales	VP HR	VP Sales	Yr 1	**Year 1**		$50 000	100 hrs	Revised structure report
5. Train sales staff in new technology	Director of Training	VP Sales	Yr 2	**Year 2**		$50 000	1000 hrs	Training plan reports
6. Expand production of customized products —to 25 percent —to 30 percent —to 40 percent —to 50 percent to 55 percent	VP Mfg	VP Engineering	Yr 1	**Year 2** **Year 2** **Year 3** **Year 3**		Budgeted	Budgeted	Production reports
7. Increase sales of customized products —to 25 percent —to 30 percent —to 40 percent —to 55 percent	VP Sales	VP Marketing	Yr 1	**Year 2** **Year 2** **Year 3** **Year 3**				Sales reports
8. Revise sales forecasts	VP Sales	VP Marketing		**Year 3**				Revised forecasts

Note: This executive assignment action plan shows the specific executive assignments required to achieve top management's long-term objective: "Have a minimum of 55 percent of sales revenue from customized products by 2006."

"converting building C to customized manufacturing" is the goal for which she'll have to craft a supporting plan. For instance, converting building C will entail completing a feasibility study and purchasing and installing new equipment. In this way, the Executive Assignment Action Plan helps ensure coordinated, purposeful effort by the management team.

No single person can formulate and implement a strategy for a complex organization.[10] Creating a cohesive top-management team including the CEO and his or her subordinate officers is necessary if a firm is to implement its plans and achieve its goals. Planning experts list several reasons why top-management teamwork is crucial for success:[11]

■ The CEO has a complex coordination task and cannot be effective without working closely with the people who are in charge of the company's major activities (such as functions, products, or regions).

TABLE 6.2 Action Plan for Specific Executive Assignment

Executive Assignment: Convert building C to customized manufacturing operation by 2006.

ASSIGNMENTS/ DERIVATIVE OBJECTIVES	ACCOUNTABILITY		SCHEDULE		RESOURCES REQUIRED			FEEDBACK MECHANISMS
	Primary	Supporting	Start	Complete	Capital	Operating	Human	
1. Complete feasibility study on conversion requirements	Director Engineering	VP Engineering	Yr 1	**Year 1**		$10 000	100 hrs	Written progress reports
2. Complete converted production line design and equipment specifications	Director Engineering	VP Engineering		**Year 1**		$50 000	500 hrs	Design review meetings
3. Purchase and install new equipment	Purchasing	VP Mfg	Yr 1	**Year 1**	$400 000		100 hrs	Written progress reports
4. Modify existing equipment	VP Mfg	VP Engineering	Yr 1	**Year 1**	$100 000	$10 000	100 hrs	Written progress reports
5. Train production staff	Director of Training	VP Mfg	Yr 1	**Year 1**		$10 000	300 hrs	Training plan reports
6. Initiate customized production line	VP Mfg	VP Engineering				Budgeted	Budgeted	Production reports
7. Increase production of customized products —to 25 percent —to 30 percent —to 40 percent —to 50 percent to 55 percent	VP Mfg	VP Engineering	Yr 1	**Year 2** **Year 2** **Year 3** **Year 3**		Budgeted	Budgeted	Production reports
8. Reassess future production capacity	VP Mfg	VP Engineering		**Year 3**				Production forecast

Note: This action plan shows the subsidiary assignments required to achieve the specific executive assignment: "Convert building C to customized manufacturing operations by 2006."

- The CEO's subordinate officers usually possess greater expertise about the operating components of the organization and their own fields of expertise than does the CEO.
- The team members can be more understanding of and supportive of the CEO's strategic decisions if they have a voice in shaping those decisions. Teamwork among the members of the top-management team enhances communication and coordination among them.
- Technical and administrative innovations will be more likely when team members have more opportunity for cross-functional communication.

Most CEOs therefore spend considerable time moulding their subordinates into a cohesive team. Former Chairperson and CEO Stephen Wolf of United Airlines reportedly worked closely on a daily basis with the executives in charge of areas like finance, marketing, and employee relations.[12]

Types of Plans

It should be apparent from the material presented so far that plans come in a variety of types and formats. For example, plans differ in their functional orientation. They range from comprehensive, overall business plans to functionally specialized marketing, production, personnel, and financial plans.

You can express your own plans in a variety of *formats*. **Descriptive plans**, like your program of studies, or the marketing plan in Figure 6.3, state in words what is to be achieved, by who, and when and at what cost. Plans stated in financial terms are **budgets**. **Graphic plans** like those in Figures 6.4 and 6.8 show what is to be achieved, and how and when, in the form of charts or in graphical networks.

Plans also differ in the *time span* they cover. Top management usually engages in long-term (three- to five-year) business or **strategic planning**. For example, the planning process for Bombardier's Global Express executive jet started in 1991, but the product was not available for sale until 1996. Middle managers focus on developing mid-term tactical plans (two to three years' duration). **Tactical plans** (sometimes called functional plans) pick up where strategic plans leave off. These are your firm's marketing, production, and personnel plans. They show each department's role in helping carry out the company's overall strategic plan. First-line managers focus on short-term **operational plans**. This means they focus on detailed, day-to-day planning. The Gantt chart in Figure 6.8 helps show exactly which workers the supervisor plans to assign to which machines or exactly how many units will be produced on a given day.

Finally, some plans are made to be used once, and others over and over. Some plans are **single-use plans** that present all the steps in a major one-time project in an orderly fashion. Your program of studies is such a plan. Single-use plans are often developed in response to a crisis. The United Nations' plan to enter Kosovo and keep the peace in 1999 was a single-use plan. The Canadian Imperial Bank of Commerce (CIBC) had 2000 people working in a building next to the World Trade Center when it was attacked by terrorists on September 11, 2001. Immediately after the first plane hit the north tower, the CIBC employees were evacuated with no loss of life. By the afternoon of September 11, CIBC managers were already meeting to develop a plan to allow them to continue working despite the loss of their workplace.[13]

In contrast, managers design **standing plans** to be used as the need arises.[14] Like all plans, standing plans are methods, formulated beforehand, for doing or making something. They are all decisions you make today, to guide decision making tomorrow. Like all plans, they specify (or imply) what's to be accomplished, when, by who, and at what cost.

Policies, procedures, and rules are examples of standing plans. **Policies** set broad guidelines. For example, it might be the policy at Holt Renfrew to sell only high-fashion apparel. How is this a "plan"? Because it shows all of the firm's apparel buyers what general course of action they should follow in choosing merchandise to buy for their stores.

Procedures spell out what to do if a specific situation arises. For example, "Before refunding the customer's purchase price, the salesperson should carefully inspect the garment and then obtain approval for the refund from the floor manager." Finally, a **rule** is a highly specific guide to action. For example, "Under no condition will the purchase price be refunded after 30 days." Managers usually write standing plans like procedures or rules so that the goal or purpose is implied but clear.

Contingency Planning

Managers have no guarantee that future outcomes will be favourable, but they can at least develop plans for what to do if they are unfavourable. **Contingency planning** involves identifying possible future outcomes and then developing a plan for coping with them. Air Canada has an elaborate contingency plan for its airplanes. Its Systems Operations Control (SOC) continuously tracks all of the company's aircraft. If a snowstorm develops, for example, the SOC goes into action to ensure that Air Canada's planes do not get stranded at snowed-in airports.[15] Manitoba Telephone System developed a contin-

descriptive plan
A plan that states what is to be achieved and how.

budget
A financial plan that shows financial expectations for a specific period.

graphic plan
A plan that shows graphically or in charts what is to be achieved and when.

strategic planning
Identifying the current business of a firm, the business it wants for the future, and the course of action or strategy it will pursue.

tactical plan
A plan that shows how top management's plans are to be carried out at the departmental, short-term level.

operational plan
A short-term plan that shows the detailed daily steps of business operations.

single-use plan
A plan made to be used once.

standing plan
A plan established to be used repeatedly, as the need arises.

policy
A standing plan that sets broad guidelines for the enterprise.

procedure
A plan that specifies how to proceed in specific situations that routinely arise.

rule
A highly specific guide to action.

contingency planning
Identifying possible future outcomes and then developing a plan for coping with them.

gency plan that involved getting customers to sign long-term leasing agreements so that MTS wouldn't be negatively affected when it lost its monopoly because of deregulation in the telephone industry.[16] After the terrorist attacks in New York, many companies began thinking of contingency plans in a much different light.

Now, back to your attempts at planning for Acme Consulting. You are sitting there trying to decide how to create the plan you'll need to get Acme financed and to provide direction for the next few years. Where would you start? The basic thing to remember is this: *There is nothing mysterious about what a plan is.* Any plan, in essence, simply answers four questions: What are you going to do? When are you going to do it? Who is going to do it? What will the cost of implementing the plan be? You may lay out your plan in terms of words or graphs or budgets.

The planning process is equally straightforward: Set an objective; develop your forecasts and planning premises; determine what your options are; evaluate your alternatives; choose your plan and implement it; then go to level two. You'd probably want to start your Acme plan at the end and work back. What is your objective? To sell Acme in about five years. What do you have to do over the next five years to accomplish that? You have to get Acme up to about $2 million is sales. To do that, you're going to have to increase sales revenue from its current level of (let's say) $80 000 to $2 million. How will you do that? Here's where your analyses and forecasts come in handy. You've got a great many options. However, let's say you decide to focus on adding four types of clients over the next five years: North American high tech, European high-tech, Latin America, and Other.

That provides a basic outline for your overall business plan. Now you can draft a marketing plan that lays out your basic product, price, promotion, and place plans for the next few years. Decide what that means in terms of how many and what sorts of personnel you'll have to hire and train. Project what your plans to this point mean operationally, in terms of the computers, phones, office space, and supplies you'll need. Produce a financial plan that lays out in dollars and cents what each element of your plan (advertising, rent, PCs, personnel, and so on) will cost and what that should mean in terms of profits or losses. Use the executive action plan to formalize the goals for your managers. Complete your plans with a set of policies and procedures (how do we pay accounts receivables, how do we interview applicants and check references, and so on). You may decide to use an off-the-shelf software package like PoliciesNow! (from Knowledgepoint) to help you here.

Then, perhaps you can move to level three. Each year, put together short-term plans (or at least budgets). These show in some detail what you expect each group in Acme to be doing each month. For example, they show what (how many clients and so forth) your North American high-tech consultants should be working on in June and when you expect to have to go to the bank to draw down some of your financing. You've thus produced a set of long- and short-term goals for you and your colleagues. Let's now look more closely at how to set objectives or goals.

Manitoba Telephone System
www.mts.mb.ca

Knowledge Point
www.knowledgepoint.com

How to Set Objectives

As a manager, you can always expect to be judged on the extent to which you have achieved your unit's goals. Whether you're in charge of a door assembly team or all of Toyota, you are expected to move the unit ahead, and this means visualizing where the unit must go and helping it get there. At CN, for example, Paul Tellier set an objective of sharply reducing CN's operating ratio (the amount of money it costs to generate $1 of revenue) so that CN could effectively compete with U.S. railroads. When Anthony Comper became CEO of the Bank of Montreal, he set an objective to increase the bank's return on equity from 15 percent to nearly 20 percent.

CN
www.cn.ca

Organizations exist to achieve some purpose, and if they fail to move forward and achieve their aims, to that extent they have failed. As Peter Drucker put it, "There has to be something to point to and say, we have not worked in vain."[17]

How to Put SMART Goals into Words

Goals should be "SMART," that is, they should be *specific* (clearly state the desired results), *measurable* (answer the question "How much?"), *attainable* (managers are able to achieve them), *relevant* (clearly focused on important company needs), and *timely* (reflect deadlines and milestones).[18]

Planning expert George Morrisey presents a four-point model to use in actually expressing what the goal should be (see Table 6.3). The table also contains examples of how to properly express goals.

In practice, the areas for which managers can set goals are practically limitless. A partial list includes the following:

1. Market standing
2. Innovation
3. Productivity
4. Physical and financial resources
5. Profitability
6. Managerial performance and development
7. Worker performance and attitude
8 Public responsibility[19]
9. Market penetration
10. Future human competencies
11. Revenue/sales
12. Employee development
13. New product/service department
14. New/expanded market development
15. Program/project management
16. Technology
17. Research and development
18. Customer relations/satisfaction
19. Cost control/management
20. Quality control/assurance
21. Productivity
22. Process improvement
23. Production capability/capacity
24. Cross-functional integration
25. Supplier development/relations
27. Unit structure (reorganization)[20]

One thing that's clear is that setting goals just for "profit maximization" is not enough. Economic theory assumes that managers try to maximize profits, but as we saw in the previous chapter, managers are more likely to satisfice than to maximize. As well,

TABLE 6.3 *Model and Examples of Well-Stated Objectives*

MORRISEY'S FOUR-POINT MODEL

To (1) (*action verb*)	(2) (single measurable *result*)
by (3) (*target* date/time span)	at (4) (*cost* in time and/or money)

EXAMPLES OR OBJECTIVES THAT FOLLOW THE MODEL

- To (1, 2) complete the Acme project by (3) December 31 at a (4) cost not to exceed $50 000 and 500 work hours.

- To (1) decrease the (2) average cost of sales by a minimum of 5 percent, effective (3) June 1, at an (4) implementation cost not to exceed 40 work hours.

- To (1, 2) release product A to manufacturing by (3) September 30 at a (4) cost not to exceed $50 000 and 5000 engineering hours.

- To (1) reduce (2) average turnaround time on service requests from eight to six hours by (3) July 31 at an (4) implementation cost of 40 work hours.

telling managers that their goal is to maximize profits would not provide them with much guidance, nor would it make much sense. Remember that managers need goals in areas that are relevant to their responsibilities. Setting goals for areas like market penetration and customer service is therefore the only practical way of ensuring that each manager's goals and actions will in fact contribute to boosting profits.

How to Set Motivational Goals

You know from your own experience that some goals simply cannot be achieved. You might be the best marathon runner in the world, but you'd view the goal of running the Montreal Marathon in 42 minutes as so unrealistic that even a $10-million prize would not motivate you to try it. The point is that goals are only useful to the extent that employees are motivated to achieve them. What is it about the goal or how it is set that makes it "motivational"? **Goal-setting studies** provide useful insights into setting motivational goals. Four steps should be taken.

goal-setting studies
Organizational behaviour research that provides useful insights into how to set effective goals.

Assign Specific Goals Employees who are given specific goals perform better than those who are given "do your best" goals. One study analyzed the productivity of truck drivers whose job was to load logs and drive them to the mill.[21] It was discovered that the truckers often did not fill their trucks to the maximum legal net weight. The researchers believed this happened largely because the workers were simply urged to "do their best" when it came to loading the truck.

The researchers therefore arranged to communicate a specific loading goal ("94 percent of a truck's net weight") to each driver. Performance jumped markedly as soon as the truckers got their specific goals, and it generally remained at this much higher level. This and other evidence shows that setting specific goals with subordinates, rather than setting no goals or telling them to "do their best," improves performance in a wide range of settings.[22]

Assign Measurable Goals Goals[23] should be stated in quantitative terms, and they should include target dates or deadlines. Goals set in absolute terms (such as "an average daily output of 300 units") are less confusing than goals set in relative terms (such as "improve production by 20 percent"). If measurable results are not readily available, then something like "satisfactorily attend workshop" or "satisfactorily complete degree" is the next best thing. In any case, target dates or deadlines should always be set.

Assign Challenging but Achievable Goals Goals should be challenging, but not so difficult that they appear impossible or unrealistic (remember that 42-minute marathon).[24] Particularly in areas such as sales management, where immediate and concrete performance is obvious and highly valued, goals consistent with past sales levels are widely used.[25] When is a goal "too difficult"? One expert says,

> A goal is probably too easy if it calls for little or no improvement in performance when conditions are becoming more favourable, or if the targeted level of performance is well below that of most other employees in comparable positions. A goal is probably too difficult if it calls for a large improvement in performance when conditions are worsening, or if the targeted level of performance is well above that of people in comparable positions.[26]

Encourage Participation Throughout your management career you'll be faced with this decision: Should I just tell my employees what their goals are, or should I let them participate in setting their goals? Sometimes, of course, the situation is out of your hands. You've been given a target to reach (like DaimlerChrysler's "cut costs by $3.1 billion"), and your employees will simply need to do it. Most of the time, though, you will have some discretion, and the research suggests that participation can be a good thing. Here is what you need to know about participation.

- Employees who participate in setting goals actually perceive themselves as having had more impact on setting those goals than do employees who just get their goals from their managers.[27]

- Participatively set goals tend to be higher than the goals the supervisor would normally have assigned.[28]
- When participatively set goals are more difficult than those assigned, the employees don't perceive them as such.[29]
- Participatively set goals do not consistently result in higher performance than assigned goals, nor do assigned goals consistently result in higher performance than participatively set ones. It is only when the participatively set goals are more difficult than the assigned ones that the participatively set goals produce higher performance. It's the fact that the goal is more *difficult*, not that it was participatively set, that explains the higher performance.[30]

The last point is usually the key. Participatively set goals do tend to be higher, so there's usually a value in discussing the goals with your employees before they are set. The resulting goals will probably be both more difficult and more accepted. And there is an added benefit. Most people aren't crazy about taking orders. Simply telling an employee what his or her goal is may therefore trigger at least some low-level resistance. Participation creates a sense of ownership in the goals and can reduce resistance.[31]

Using Management by Objectives

management by objectives (MBO)
A technique in which the supervisor and subordinate jointly set goals for the latter and periodically assess progress toward those goals.

Investors Group
www.investorsgroup.com

How do you translate the goals of the company and its departments into specific, meaningful goals for each employee? For the company's managers, the executive action plan is one alternative. **Management by objectives** (MBO) is another. MBO is a technique in which the supervisor and subordinate jointly set goals for the latter and periodically assess progress toward those goals. Managers use MBO to facilitate setting organization-wide goals and to set goals for subsidiary units and their employees. A manager may engage in a modest MBO program by setting goals with his or her subordinates and periodically providing feedback. However, MBO usually refers to a comprehensive organization-wide program and is usually reserved for managerial and professional employees.

Investors Group Financial Services uses MBO to motivate its sales force in selling financial services. The MBO process begins when the vice president of sales develops general goals for the entire sales force. This sets the stage for Planning Week, which is held annually at regional centres across Canada. During Planning Week, sales representatives review their past accomplishments and set financial goals for the coming year.[32]

Peter Drucker, the creator of MBO, emphasizes thinking of it as a philosophy, not as a rigid sequence of steps. The point, he says, is that "the goals of each manager's job must be defined by the contribution he or she has to make to the success of the larger unit of which they are part." In general, the MBO process consists of five steps:

1. *Set organization goals.* Top management sets strategic goals for the company.

2. *Set department goals.* Department heads and their superiors jointly set supporting goals for their departments.

3. *Discuss department goals.* Department heads present department goals and ask all subordinates to develop their own individual goals.

4. *Set individual goals.* Goals are set for each subordinate, and a timetable is assigned for accomplishing those goals.

5. *Give feedback.* Supervisor and subordinate meet periodically to review the subordinate's performance and to monitor and analyze progress toward his or her goals.[33]

MBO has certain advantages. Corporate planning tends to be hierarchical anyway, so using MBO provides a process for working through how the goals at each level will relate to those above and to those below. It also taps the advantages of participation, which we listed above. But MBO is also time-consuming. These programs often involve numerous meetings among employees and supervisors, and then extensive documentation of each person's goals in various electronic or hard-copy formats. It is good to remember that MBO's aim is simply to integrate the goals of the individual, of the unit in which the individual works, and of the company as a whole.[34]

Forecasting and Developing Planning Premises

People base their plans—whether for careers, trips to Paris, or cutting costs at DaimlerChrysler—on premises or assumptions they make about the future. Students choose careers based in part on the projected future demand for workers in particular occupations. People reduce their travel to areas hit by terrorist threats. DaimlerChrysler cut costs because forecasts showed it couldn't survive with the losses it was going to sustain if it kept up its current rate of expenditures. Wal-Mart expanded to Europe because it forecast a burgeoning market for low-cost consumer goods there.

Managers use several techniques to produce the premises on which they build their plans. These include forecasting, marketing research, and competitive intelligence.

Forecasting

To **forecast** means to estimate or calculate in advance or to predict.[35] In business, forecasting often starts with predicting the direction and magnitude of the company's sales. Errors in forecasting can cause major problems. In 1989 the Ontario Workers' Compensation Board forecast that its unfunded liability (the difference between its assets and the future costs of worker compensation claims already on the books) would be reduced to zero by the year 2007. In 1993 the Board made a new prediction: The unfunded liability would be $50 billion by the year 2014! Ontario Hydro has also made some wildly inaccurate forecasts. In the 1960s it predicted that it would need 80 000 megawatts of capacity by 2000; the actual number was closer to 30 000 megawatts.[36]

Managers use either quantitative or qualitative sales forecasting methods (or a combination of the two). **Quantitative forecasting** uses statistical methods to examine data and find underlying patterns and relationships. **Qualitative forecasting** emphasizes human judgment.

Quantitative Methods Quantitative methods include time-series methods and causal models. These methods produce forecasts by assuming that past relationships will continue into the future. A **time series** is a set of observations taken at specific times, usually at equal intervals. Examples of time series are the yearly or monthly gross domestic product of Canada over several years, a department store's total monthly sales receipts, and the daily closing price of a share of stock.[37]

forecast
To estimate or calculate in advance or to predict.

quantitative forecasting
A type of forecasting in which statistical methods are used to examine data and find underlying patterns and relationships; includes time-series methods and causal models.

qualitative forecasting
Predictive techniques that emphasize human judgment.

time series
A set of observations taken at specific times, usually at equal intervals, to identify fundamental patterns.

If you plot time-series data on a graph for several periods, you may note various patterns. For example, if you were to plot monthly sales of air conditioning units, you would find seasonal increases in late spring and summer, and reduced sales in the winter months. For some time series, you may see an irregular pattern, such as a sudden blip on the graph that is caused by an unusual event. For example, airline ticket sales plummeted for a time after the World Trade Center tragedy in September 2001. The basic purpose of time-series forecasting methods is to remove irregular and seasonal patterns and to allow managers to identify fundamental trends.

Sometimes, though, simply tracking activity over time is not enough. Instead, managers may need to understand the causal relationship between two variables. For example, the sales department at General Motors needs to know the causal relationship between car sales and an indicator of economic activity, like disposable income. If you can discover a causal relationship between one factor, such as car sales, and a second, more predictable, factor, such as disposable income, you can use that relationship to forecast your sales.[38] **Causal methods** develop a forecast based on the mathematical relationship between a company factor and those variables that management believes influence or explain the company factor.[39] **Causal forecasting** estimates the company factor (such as sales) based on other factors (such as advertising expenditures or level of unemployment). Managers use statistical techniques such as correlation analysis (which shows how closely the variables are related) to identify the necessary relationships.

U.S.-based Rack Room Shoes has more than 340 stores, and opens 20 to 40 new stores per year. For many years, the firm's real estate committee made site location decisions subjectively. The committee consisted of the firm's president, chief financial officer (CFO), and vice presidents for store operations and real estate. When the firm hired Chris Kochan as its new market research manager, his first job was to create a sales forecasting model to improve the accuracy of location decisions. Based on Rack Room's historical sales experience, Kochan was able to correlate sales to demographics. Today, various services make it easy to identify demographics by zip code or postal code. Kochan's sales forecasting model therefore enables Rack Room to predict how much sales volume a new store might generate if placed in a particular zip code. As Kochan says, "Our forecasts now come within 20 percent of actual sales about 75 percent of the time. The gut-feel approach was within 20 percent of actual sales only 34 percent of the time."[40]

Some firms use the internet to improve their sales forecasts. For example, Coors Brewing Company's distributors can use the firm's new CoorsNet.com extranet to place orders and to help analyze the impact of advertising and other promotional activities. Because it takes about eight weeks to produce, package, and ship a barrel of beer, "forecasting demand is a huge problem for these folks" says one supply chain consultant.[41] "So many times, they are reacting instead of planning ahead. What happens is that they make distributors order too far in advance, and they aren't ready to quantify how much they need to order."

Coors expects its new internet-based system to improve performance because Coors will be able to receive real-time orders. Its distributors should be able to predict more accurately how advertising campaigns and other promotional events will affect sales. Wal-Mart is another firm that uses sophisticated technology to forecast sales, as the box "Demand Forecasting at Wal-Mart" shows.

The term "**supply chain**" refers to all of the production facilities, distribution centres, retail outlets, employees, and information that must work together to get goods and services from producers to consumers. The idea of **supply chain management** is to integrate customer, supplier, and distributor into one boundaryless process.

For example, each time a customer buys a size 30 pair of Levi 501 jeans at Wal-Mart, a message moves electronically from the point-of-sale cash register to Levi's. The replenishment process thus becomes virtually automatic and just-in-time. With this system, Wal-Mart does not need to keep large quantities of 501 jeans in the store or local warehouse because Levi's knows, on a real-time basis, how many size 30 jeans are needed in each store and sends them directly. Think of how much money Wal-Mart saves by stripping its supply lines of the need for costly inventories.

Boundaryless, internet-based supply chain systems integrate all components of the supply chain, such as the customer, supplier, manufacturer, and shipper. To a large extent,

causal methods
Forecasting techniques that develop projections based on the mathematical relationship between a company factor and the variables believed to influence or explain that factor.

causal forecasting
Estimating a company factor (such as sales) based on other influencing factors (such as advertising expenditures or unemployment levels).

Rack Room Shoes
**www.rackroomshoes.
com**

supply chain
All the production facilities, distribution centres, retail outlets, employees, and information that must work together to get goods and services from producers to consumers.

supply chain management
The integration of the activities that procure materials, transform them into intermediate goods and final products, and deliver them to customers.

Demand Forecasting at Wal-Mart

Wal-Mart has what is probably the most sophisticated information technology system in all of retailing, and it uses that system to give its customers what they want, while squeezing every bit of extraneous cost from its operation.

Wal-Mart's data warehouse collects information on things like sales, inventory, products in transit, and product returns from Wal-Mart's 3000 stores. These data are then used to help Wal-Mart's managers analyze trends, understand customers, and more effectively manage inventory. As one example, Wal-Mart is implementing a new demand-forecasting system. Its data warehousing tracks the store-by-store sales of 100 000 products. This powerful system lets Wal-Mart managers examine the sales of individual items for individual stores, and also creates seasonal profiles for each item. Armed with this information, managers can more accurately plan what items will be needed for each store and when.

Wal-Mart is also teaming with vendors like Warner-Lambert to create an internet-based collaborative forecasting and replenishment (CFAR) system. Wal-Mart collects data (on things like sales by product and by store, and seasonal trends) for its sales of Warner-Lambert products. Managers at Wal-Mart and Warner-Lambert then collaborate to develop forecasts for sales by store for Warner-Lambert products, such as Listerine. Once Warner-Lambert and Wal-Mart planners decide on mutually acceptable figures, a purchase plan is finalized and sent to Warner-Lambert's manufacturing planning system. So far, CFAR has helped cut the supply cycle time for Listerine from twelve weeks to six. That means less inventory, lower costs, and better buys for Wal-Mart customers.

This photo shows the interior of a new Wal-Mart in Bristol, UK, the first 24-hour superstore in Bristol

firms like Wal-Mart do not have to depend on short-term sales forecasts. They can make their supply and production decisions based on actual demand.

Information is the foundation of any forecast, and the usefulness of information depends on the accuracy and sensitivity of a company's control systems. Consider the situation in the computer software business. Toward the end of 2000, many analysts were predicting that sales of software were going to rise dramatically. But when the CEO of Siebel Systems (a firm that sells sales management software) looked at his computer screen filled with various types of sales reports, he concluded that those optimistic estimates were wrong. By February 2001, he could see that customers were scaling back orders, and that many contracts that were supposed to close weren't getting signed. His firm's special sales-control software gave him enough time to change his plans and take evasive action. He dramatically reduced expenses, increased pressure on the sales force, and supplemented the sales force with special executive-led teams to focus on big-ticket customers. In an otherwise bleak year for software makers, Siebel Systems' revenues were up 84 percent, while its profits more than doubled.[42]

Qualitative Forecasting Methods Qualitative forecasting tools emphasize human judgment. They gather—in as logical, unbiased, and systematic a way as possible—all the information and human intelligence that can be brought to bear on the factors being forecast.[43] Table 6.4 lists some expert qualitative forecasts that didn't quite work out.

In spite of dramatic errors like those listed in Table 6.4, you should not underestimate the value of qualitative forecasting. It's true that hard data and numbers are usually very important in developing adequate plans. However, it's also true that if you want realistic plans, there's usually no substitute for a human analysis of the situation and of its possible consequences. Quantitative tools are also not helpful when data are scarce, such as for a new product with no sales history.[44] And quantitative tools are of little use in dealing with unforeseeable, unexpected occurrences. Yet it is unexpected occurrences that often have the most profound effects.

Consider what happened to British Airways. For years it built its plans—hiring, advertisements, schedules, and aircraft seat configurations—around the basic idea of catering to business travellers. September 11 changed all that. With the fall-off in business travel, British Airways had to quickly revise its plans. By the end of 2001, it had cancelled flights on ten routes, sold airplanes, and embarked on a new plan to attract budget passengers to its European networks. Sometimes, great uncertainty makes the human, subjective side of planning more important.[45]

On the other hand, basing plans solely on subjective sales forecasts can be perilous. During the summer of 2000, Nortel Networks Corp. planned to meet "explosive customer demand" by spending almost $2 billion to boost production and by adding 9600 jobs.[46] Throughout 2000, Nortel executives questioned their largest customers to compile sales estimates. Unfortunately, those subjective estimates were way off. Nortel's CEO later found that some of his largest customers were telling him Nortel had to gear up to ship them more equipment, even as diminishing demand was making it harder for them to pay for that equipment.

Nortel did have professional researchers helping it compile forecasts, but the researchers relied heavily on feedback from the firm's sales force, and these sales force estimates simply reflected the customers' overly optimistic estimates. By June 2001, Nortel had announced it would lose $19 billion in that quarter alone and fire 10 000 people, over and above the 20 000 jobs it had already cut. The same thing happened at Cisco Systems. In early 2001, Cisco Systems customers were saying they needed more of the firm's networking equipment. However, it soon became obvious that the customers—thousands

---

TABLE 6.4 *Expert Predictions That Went Amiss*

1. "There is no reason for any individual to have a computer in their home." (Ken Olson, 1977, president of Digital Equipment Corporation, speaking at the convention of the World Future Society)

2. "Man will never reach the moon, regardless of all future advances." (Dr. Lee DeForest, inventor of the auditron tube, quoted in *The New York Times*, 25 February 1957; early in his career, DeForest had been told that the auditron tube was a scientific impossibility)

3. "The radio craze will die out in time." (Thomas Edison, 1922)

4. "I cannot imagine any condition which would cause a ship to founder. Modern ship-building has gone beyond that." (Captain Edward J. Smith, 1906, future commander of the *Titanic*)

5. "Man will not fly for 50 years." (Wilbur Wright, to his brother Orville, in 1901)

6. "The horseless carriage is at present a luxury for the wealthy, and although its price will probably fall in the future, it will never, of course, come into as common use as the bicycle." (*Literary Digest*, October 14, 1899)

7. "Well-informed people know it is impossible to transmit the voice over wires and that were it possible to do so, the thing would be of no practical value." (Editorial in the *Boston Globe*, 1865, commenting on the arrest of Joshua Coopersmith for fraud as he attempted to raise funds for work on a telephone)

of dot-coms—were either overly-optimistic or just plain wrong. Cisco's inventory ballooned, and the firm had to reduce the value of the inventory by more than $2 billion.[47]

Qualitative forecasts are valuable when used correctly. For example, the **jury of executive opinion** technique involves asking a "jury" of key executives to forecast sales for, say, the next year. Each executive receives data on forecasted economic levels and anticipated corporate changes. Each jury member then makes an independent forecast. Differences are reconciled by the president or at a meeting of the executives.

The **sales force estimation method** gathers the opinions of the sales force regarding what they think sales will be in the forthcoming period. Each salesperson estimates his or her next year's sales, usually by product and customer. Sales managers then review each estimate, compare it with the previous year's data, and discuss changes with each salesperson. The sales manager then combines the separate estimates into a sales forecast for the firm.

Forecasting is not limited to predicting company sales. It can also be used to predict how technological changes will affect a company, how changing demographics will affect a company's workforce, or how changing sales levels will determine the firm's financial requirements.

Marketing Research

Forecasting tools can help managers explore the future and thereby develop better planning premises. But there are times when, to formulate plans, managers want to know not just what may happen in the future, but also what customers are thinking today. **Marketing research** refers to the procedures used to develop and analyze customer-related information that helps managers make decisions.[48]

Harlequin Enterprises Ltd., which started in Winnipeg in 1949, is the leading company in the romance novels industry. When deciding whether to enter a foreign country, Harlequin does market research to determine whether a distribution system is in place, whether there is access to TV and print media (so that demand can be stimulated through advertising), and whether the company will be able to convert local currency into Canadian dollars.[49]

Marketing researchers depend on two main types of information. One source is **secondary data**, or information collected or already published. Good sources of secondary data include Statistics Canada, the internet, libraries, trade associations, company files and sales reports, and commercial data, for instance from companies such as A. C. Nielsen. **Primary data** refer to information specifically collected to solve a current problem. Primary data sources include mail and personal surveys, in-depth and focus-group interviews, and personal observation such as watching the reactions of customers who walk into a store.[50]

Competitive Intelligence

Developing useful plans requires knowing as much as possible about what competitors are doing or are planning to do. **Competitive intelligence (CI)** is a systematic way to obtain and analyze public information about competitors. This sounds (and is) a lot like legalized spying, and it has become much more popular over the past few years.

CI practitioners use various tools to discover what clients' competitors are doing. These include keeping track of existing and new competitors by having specialists visit their facilities, hiring their workers, and questioning their suppliers and customers. CI firms also do extensive internet searches to unearth information about competitors, as well as mundane searches like reading stock analysts' reports on the competitors' prospects. CI consulting firms use former prosecutors, business analysts, and former RCMP employees to ferret out the sorts of information you might want to know before entering into an alliance with another company, or before deciding to get into a specific business.

jury of executive opinion
A qualitative forecasting technique in which executives are given pertinent data and asked to make independent sales forecasts, which are then reconciled in an executive meeting or by the company president.

sales force estimation method
A forecasting technique that gathers and combines the opinions of the salespeople on what they predict sales will be in the forthcoming period.

marketing research
The procedures used to develop and analyze current customer-related information to help managers make decisions.

secondary data
Information that is already collected or published.

primary data
Information specifically collected to solve a current problem.

competitive intelligence (CI)
A systematic way to obtain and analyze public information about competitors.

Focus groups, in which a moderator leads a group of typical consumers in a discussion or trial of the firm's products, are a good source of primary data. Sometimes, as here, special rooms equipped with one-way observation windows allow the process to be videotaped unobtrusively.

CI firms can be quite useful because they help client companies learn more about competitors' strengths and vulnerabilities, product strategies, investment strategies, and financial capabilities. Other CI services include evaluating the capabilities, weaknesses, and reputation of potential or existing joint-venture partners; identifying the major players in a new market or industry the firm is thinking of entering; and helping planners boost sales opportunities (for example, by identifying the decision makers who actually do the purchasing and the critical factors they look for in vendors).

The Internet and CI The internet has turned out to be a gold mine for competitive intelligence investigations. Amazon.com recently used this approach after discovering that Barnes & Noble had just listed three new product category tabs on its homepage. Amazon.com hired a competitive intelligence firm to review the site and to analyze Barnes & Noble's web activity with internet service providers. Amazon thereby found out that only one of the new BarnesandNoble.com product tabs was popular with shoppers.

Unearthing competitive intelligence over the web is easier than you might think. Suggestions for doing so include the following:[51]

- Use a search engine such as AltaVista (**altavista.com**) to get a list of all the web pages your competitor has opened on the internet by typing in **url://companyname.com**.

- Find all the websites linked to your competitor's site by typing in **link://www. companyname.com**.

- Comb through your competitor's website looking for information on things like the firm's business goals.

- If your competitor is publicly traded, carefully review its investor relations site. This contains public information (like quarterly profits reports and unusual expenses) required by law, and conveniently located in one place.

- On the website, review your competitor's press releases; these may provide insights into potential problems, like those indicated by restructuring plans.

- Carefully review your competitor's listed job openings. For example, is one of its product lines listing many new job openings? That might point to an expected expansion.

- Check out message boards and chat rooms dedicated to the company. These often contain customer and/or employee complaints that provide insights into the firm's strengths and weaknesses.

Ethics and CI Is using the internet to unearth competitive intelligence ethical? As long as the firm publicly lists the information on the web, using it is roughly comparable to walking through a competitor's store to see what he or she is up to. However, you cross the line, says one ethics expert, if you anonymously pry private information from unsuspecting competitors.[52]

Even respected firms have stepped over the line. We saw in Chapter 3 that Procter & Gamble's competitive intelligence managers allegedly hired outsiders to gather information on Unilever's hair care products. These outsiders (P&G now calls them "rogue operators") engaged in dubious activities like digging through Unilever's dumpsters on Unilever's private property and misrepresenting themselves to Unilever employees. When Procter & Gamble's CEO discovered the operation, he reported it to Unilever.[53] Managers obviously must publicize and apply rigid ethical standards when using CI.

A Final Word: There's No One Best Planning Process

Planning can sometimes be more trouble than it's worth. Even for something as simple as a trip to Paris, blind devotion to the plan could cause you to miss a great last minute opportunity. In a business, such inflexibility can be deadly. For example, department stores would have been foolish to ignore the possibility of internet catalogue sales, just because the word "internet" didn't appear in their long-term plans in the late 1990s.

THE PEOPLE SIDE OF MANAGING

People Versus Systems in Planning

The Norton Company, a manufacturer of industrial abrasives, prided itself on its sophisticated planning systems. It eagerly adopted the newest planning systems as they became available. For example, it was a pioneer in the use of profit impact of market strategies (PIMS). Top management at Norton used information provided by its planning systems to screen acquisitions in their search for profitable growth. In spite of this well-organized planning activity, the expectations of Norton's shareholders and managers were often not met, and the company was eventually absorbed by the French firm Compagnie de Saint-Gobain.

During the same general time period, Norton's chief competitor was Minnesota Mining and Manufacturing (3M). Unlike Norton, 3M achieved many of its growth and diversification goals, yet it never put a lot of emphasis on formal planning systems. Instead of exercising top-down management planning and control, the top management of 3M focused on nurturing the innovative ideas that engineers, salespeople, and other employees came up with. By doing this, they built a company that has become legendary for introducing successful new products.

In the 1940s, Norton and 3M were similar in size, but by the time Norton was acquired by the French firm, 3M's sales were eight times the sales of Norton. 3M achieved great success in planning through *people*, while Norton tried to do it through *systems*. 3M did, of course, have a planning and controlling system, but it was flexible. For example, individuals were encouraged to present new-product ideas directly to management and to discuss these ideas with them. Top managers saw their roles not as directing and controlling subordinates, but as supporting their initiatives.

3M
www.3m.com

The 3M planning model, which is centred on entrepreneurship and initiative, is essential in today's globalized business environments. Yet many large corporations seem to be using the same complex and impersonal approach to planning that Norton used. It seems likely that in the future these traditional planning systems will not work well in environments where the key elements are knowledge and quick response time.

In one study of 20 large firms that have been particularly successful in strategic planning, it was found that top managers downplayed their decision-making role and instead delegated more responsibility to middle managers who knew the market much better. In these companies, planning systems are viewed as only one element in successful planning, and lower-level managers are empowered to make important decisions.

The emphasis in these successful companies is not on top-down control, but on making sure that managers clearly understand company objectives. Top management has discovered that when people know what the objectives are, they try hard to achieve them. At ISS, International Service Systems, for example, cleaning-team supervisors are provided with financial information about individual cleaning contracts. Thus, the supervisors are self-motivated to take action to increase their efficiency and effectiveness.

Inflexibility isn't the only potential problem. The plan is only as good as its implementation, and it is worthless if top management can't coax managers to actually do things differently. Some managers go too far in the opposite direction by naively insisting on counterproductive changes to their division managers' proposed plans. As one planning expert says, top managers have only limited time to devote to analyzing the plans of the firm's separate businesses, so "the potential for misguided advice is high, especially in diversified companies."[54] The more unpredictable things are, the more likely it is that poor advice will be followed.

When planning, managers must not overemphasize the planning *system* at the expense of the people who are actually doing the planning. The "People Side of Managing" box demonstrates this important point.

The bottom line is that a planning process that works for one firm won't necessarily work for another. A good planning process

> ...is not a generic process but one in which both analytic techniques and organizational processes are carefully tailored to the needs of the businesses as well as to skills, insight, and experiences of senior corporate managers. A mature electrical-products business, for example, has different planning needs than a fast growing entertainment business or a highly cyclical chemicals business.[55]

Granada Group
www.granadamedia.com

Each company needs a planning process that's right for it. Perhaps the most important question here is what the manager wants the planning process to achieve. For example, Granada (a British conglomerate with businesses in television broadcasting, hotels, catering, and appliances), prides itself in pushing its managers to find new business opportunities. Therefore, its planning process deliberately discourages managers from comparing or benchmarking their financial results to those of competitors. When you do that, "you lock yourself into low ambitions" the CEO says.[56] Instead, Granada's planning process challenges its managers to find ways to achieve huge leaps in their divisions' sales and profitability. "Planning [at Granada] is about raising ambitions and helping businesses get more creative in their search for ways to increase profits."[57]

Dow Chemical
www.dow.com

At the other extreme, a company like Dow Chemical Corporation operates in a relatively tranquil and cost-conscious environment. Dow's planning process aims to find small, incremental improvements in processing costs since costs are crucial in the slow-growth chemicals industry. The planning process at Dow is therefore relatively formal, analytical, comparative, and numbers-oriented. The point, again, is that managers must decide what they want to achieve with their planning before establishing a planning process.

SKILLS AND STUDY MATERIAL

SUMMARY

1. Plans are methods formulated for achieving desired results. Planning is the process of establishing objectives and courses of actions before taking action. Plans differ in format, timetable, and frequency.

2. The management planning process consists of a logical sequence of five steps: establish objectives; conduct situation analysis; determine alternative courses of action; evaluate alternatives; and choose and implement the plan. In practice, this produces a planning hierarchy because top-management's goals become the targets for which subsidiary units must formulate derivative plans.

3. Most companies have moved from centralized to decentralized planning in the past few years, in part to place the planning responsibility with the product and divisional managers who are probably in the best position to understand their customers' needs and competitors' activities. Central planning units in larger companies, though dramatically downsized, still carry out important planning activities such as competitor and market research, communicating company-wide objectives, and providing planning-related consulting services to the divisions.

4. Because managers are appraised on the extent to which they achieve assigned objectives, setting objectives is an essential management skill. The areas for which objectives can be set are virtu-ally limitless, ranging from market standing to innovation and profitability.

5. Goal-setting studies suggest these guidelines: assign goals that are specific, measurable, achievable, relevant, and timely (SMART); also, encourage participation when assigning the goals, where feasible.

6. In setting goals, managers need to distinguish among an area to be measured, a yardstick, and an objective; they also must specify what is to be done, and at what cost or in what time period. Management by objectives can be used to create an integrated hierarchy of goals throughout the organization.

7. Among the techniques for developing planning premises are forecasting, marketing research, and competitive intelligence. Forecasting techniques include quantitative methods such as time-series analysis and causal methods. Qualitative forecasting methods such as sales-force estimation and jury of executive opinion emphasize human judgment.

CRITICAL THINKING EXERCISES

1. Consider an ancient country with a long tradition of religious philosophy, an ethic of hard work, and strong warrior instincts. Imagine this country—with 1.2 billion consumers—emerging into the world marketplace almost overnight. Many of its citizens have a per capita income of only $500, but economists estimate that as many as 200 million middle-class consumers have disposable income to spend on a variety of products. There are believed to be at least one million millionaires in this socialistic-capitalistic country. Many Canadians are concerned with the civil and intellectual rights of the people of this country, which has imposed government sanctions on demonstrators and has a history of human-rights violations. The country, of course, is the world's largest: China. There is great potential and opportunity for business here. However, there are also threats. Using the concepts presented in this chapter, explain how you would go about developing a plan for doing business in China for the next five years. (Assume that you are a manager in a consumer products company, and that your firm sells low-priced goods such as candy.)

2. The internet is increasingly a part of our lives. We can bank with it; shop for groceries, cars, and homes; go to college or university; be our own travel agents; research topics; talk with others in chat rooms; and employ it for a host of other uses. The long-term implications of the internet are amazing. The internet can provide a much more flexible and convenient lifestyle for many. But there are potential downsides. What happens to all the jobs that are displaced by technology? For example, many of us have not been into a bank for years because we use ATMs. Now we can bank over the internet from home. We can pay bills. We can shop and have goods delivered. Critical questions arise in terms of the planning and setting of objectives for companies, individuals, and society. What will happen to displaced workers? Will there be enough jobs for everyone? What about those who are not technologically literate or do not own a computer? What about the monthly service charges for the internet for those who cannot afford to use the service? Use the concepts and techniques in this chapter to write an essay that explains how the internet will affect the planning process in business firms.

1. One of the chronic complaints of employers about prospective employees, especially those just out of universities who have limited work experience, is that they don't have well-honed presentation skills. A recent issue of *Fast Company* outlined an eight-point program for presentations guaranteed to keep your listeners on the edge of their seats.[58] The eight points are as follows.

   1. Incite, don't just inform. Effective presentations don't end with nodding heads and polite applause, they end with action.

   2. Don't talk to strangers. Know your audience by doing research before the presentation.

   3. First (and last) impressions are everything. The two most important parts of your presentation are the first 30 seconds and the last 15 seconds.

   4. Simpler is better. Make your presentations short and candid.

   5. Perform, don't present. The impact of a typical presentation is 55 percent visual (how you look), 38 percent vocal (how you talk), and only 7 percent verbal (what you say). In other words, you don't deliver presentations, you perform them.

   6. The show must go on. Concentrate on the performance factor.

   7. There's one in every crowd. That is, there is always a hostile member you must handle. The first rule is to disagree without being disagreeable, and don't pick a fight.

   8. Practise, practise, practise.

   Select a topic from this chapter on planning and prepare a five-minute presentation, following the rules outlined here. Be ready to give your presentation to your class.

2. You are the chancellor of a major Canadian university. You know that with an increasing number of high-school students deciding to go to university and with the continuing immigration into the province that the university system could be swamped by the year 2010. The provincial legislature has allocated only limited funds for introducing technology into every classroom. Some faculty members are not as computer literate as their students, and this situation may worsen as the years go by. The first-year students of 2010 are likely to be more technologically sophisticated than the current students are. The world of technology seems to grow geometrically in terms of the knowledge you need to understand and effectively use computers. You have quite a planning challenge. Outline how you would use the information provided in the chapter about planning and setting objectives to formulate a plan for the university. Assume that there is increased funding, along with increased pressures to educate a larger percentage of the population as 2010 approaches.

BUILDING YOUR MANAGEMENT SKILLS

Planning in Action

Review the material on the planning process in this chapter. Then familiarize yourself with the planning process that was used in an organization that was working on a specific project. You may get this information by either interviewing a manager who is knowledgeable about a project in his or her firm, or by reading a detailed account of a project in a publication like *The Globe and Mail* or *Canadian Business*. In either case, your goal is to determine how the planning process was carried out in a real organization. Write up a summary of the project in enough detail that you can answer the following questions:

1. Did the organization follow the steps in the planning process that are shown in Figure 6.1? If yes, explain what was involved in each step. If no, try to account for the differences.

2. Were the steps carried out in the order shown in Figure 6.1? Were some steps skipped or repeated? Why?

3. What problems arose during the planning process? Why?

All industry sectors experience "ups and downs." Probably one of the most volatile sectors is biotechnology. So how do the companies in these sectors plan? Let's investigate QLT Inc., one of Canada's leading biopharmaceutical companies (**www.qltinc.com**) by looking at their corporate fact sheet and other information on their website.

1. Part of QLT's planning includes the preparation of forward-looking statements. What is included in these statements?
2. What uncertainties might affect QLT's planning?
3. How has QLT enhanced its planning?
4. What aspect of QLT's planning do you think has been responsible for the company's success during the sector's "ups and downs"?

CASE STUDY 6-1

A Planner Outstanding in His Field

Gerhard Kreuger is the owner and wine maker at Kreuger Wines Inc. at Niagara-on-the-Lake. As he walks among the neat rows in his vineyard, he thinks about last summer (not a good one). The weather was unseasonably cool in the spring of 2002, then there was too much rain in June, and finally a hailstorm wiped out about half his crop in August. But he also remembers that for three years running before that, the weather co-operated and he had bumper crops.

Kreuger accepts that he can't control the weather, so he spends his time working on the things he can control. He recently merged with another smaller winery, and this will give him access to the other winery's chain of retail outlets. Kreuger has also purchased an additional grape press and fermenter in Europe so that he can increase production of his award-winning wine (one of his wines won a Grands Prix d'Honneur at the 1998 VinExpo in France, which is equivalent to an actor winning an Academy Award).

Good news like this is something of a surprise. Just a few years ago, there was much doom and gloom in the industry because of the move toward free trade. When the free trade agreement first took effect, the price differentials between Canadian and foreign wines were eliminated. It was thought that this might destroy the Canadian wine industry. And, in fact, the market share of Canadian firms did decline, vineyard hectarage was reduced, and some vintners went out of business. But the increased competition forced the remaining firms to increase product quality, and in so doing, find new markets for Canadian wine.

The quality improvements have occurred because *vitis labrusca*, the native North American grapevine,

has been banned from table wines. It has been replaced with *vitis vinifera*, a higher-quality and more delicate stock. Canadian wineries can get far more dollars per tonne for *vinifera* than they can for *labrusca*, but replanting all the vineyards is expensive and time-consuming. It take five years to get a new *vinifera* crop into production, and five to seven more years to recover initial investment costs. Bad weather along the way can extend the time even further.

Other uncertainties continue to create problems for the Canadian wine industry. The Canadian industry's share of the world market has declined, and the quota program in British Columbia that ensured that wineries would purchase the entire grape crop from provincial growers was phased out in 1995. Buyers are now able to purchase wine juice from foreign producers if they wish. And consumers are still not convinced that Canadian wine has the quality that French or California wines do.

All of these uncertainties create planning dilemmas for Gerhard Kreuger.

Questions

1. How is the planning process in the wine industry different than that in an industrial firm? How is it similar?
2. What kinds of contingency plans are necessary in the wine business?
3. In what areas of the wine business should plans be made, and over what time frames should the plans extend?

Opening the Hollywood Knitting Factory

You don't raise $5 million and run a successful, growing business for more than 10 years unless you know where you're going. But when it comes to making detailed business plans, managers at KnitMedia—a company that runs jazz clubs in several cities—still have some doubts. For example, when asked if the company does much planning, Michael Dorf, the firm's CEO, replies: "Sure, we actually are, you know, starting to use, well, budgets—I can't even say it because it's so hard for me to adhere to them, but, you know, we are using budgets to some extent. [In fact] every so often, I put together the business plan and I talk with every team member and try and consolidate all our ideas and our plans. [However,] it's difficult to be very fast-moving, especially at internet speeds, if everything has to be constricted to a pure schedule and plan."

In fact, Dorf's dilemma is often the dilemma that all start-ups (and especially technology-oriented start-ups) face every day. As he says, KnitMedia's managers have to adapt very quickly to stay ahead of the competition, and it's not easy to do that if every step was decided several months or years ago.

Alan Fried, KnitMedia's chief operating officer, makes much the same point. As he says: "I mean, we are very much a media company and as some of the clichés around go, internet years happen much quicker than calendar years. And if you have to move so fast, you have to move fast because if you're thinking of it, somebody else's thinking of it and first player advantage means a lot. So, sometimes we don't have the good fortune to just sort of sit down and plan everything. [What we do, though] is have an idea, and we have some meetings about it and we just move where I think we have to." That way, the company is always moving in the new direction even though it doesn't have a rigid, predetermined plan.

The problem is, Dorf and his team are not entirely convinced that this more or less seat-of-the-pants approach to planning is necessarily the best, although it's certainly worked so far. Furthermore, as more people invest money in the business, it's become increasingly important to develop formal plans so others will know where you're planning on going.

Questions

The management team has approached you to help it formalize KnitMedia's planning process. Use what you learned in this chapter to answer the following questions.

1. At a minimum, what sorts of plans do you think they should develop and use at KnitMedia? Why?

2. Their immediate task is opening the new Hollywood, California, club. What forecasting tools do you suggest they use? Provide them with an outline of an executive assignment action plan that they can use to guide them in opening that location.

3. Is it possible for them to assign specific goals to department managers even though they don't have a formal planning process? If so, how?

Planning in the Face of Uncertainty

David Neeleman attributes much of JetBlue's initial success to the fact that he and his team stuck closely to his original concept and plan. As Neeleman says, "we're Southwest with seat assignments, leather seats, and television." The foundations of his original plan called for strong financing, fleet homogeneity (so maintenance people and pilots and flight service crews can easily switch from plane to plane), high fleet utilization, attractive pricing, and experienced management.

To a large extent, things are working according to plan. JetBlue is flying about 80 percent full, versus an industry average of about 68 percent. JetBlue is also profitable, an impressive feat given the fact that virtually all its competitors are racking up losses. Although its fleet of brand-new Airbus A-320 jets meant higher purchase and/or leasing costs, they are also much less expensive to fly. They burn less fuel and require virtually no expenditures on heavy maintenance (Airbus warranties them for the first few years). As Neeleman says, "the way to have low costs is to buy brand-new airplanes."

However, a plan is only as good as the assumptions it's based on, and no manager is ever dealing with an entirely predictable future. On the one hand, some things have worked in JetBlue's favour. For example, right after JetBlue began flying out of JFK airport in New York, LaGuardia airport (also in New York) was hit with months of record delays, making JFK a more attractive alternative. Furthermore, Neeleman's most basic assumption—that there was a huge, pent-up demand for flights from places like Fort Lauderdale to JFK on a low-cost airline with new planes and top-quality service—proved very accurate.

On the other hand, many other things were impossible to predict. No one, for instance, expected the 9/11 attacks, or the decline in air travel that followed. And, although competition was to be expected, even JetBlue's managers were surprised by the aggressiveness of some of their competitors. For example, in a February 22, 2002, letter to Chris Kunze, the manager of Long Beach, California airport, American Airlines pointed out that JetBlue was using few of its slots at the airport and that "it is important that American receive (4) slots so that another air carrier cannot deprive us of the right to operate at Long Beach." Under the terms of its agreement, JetBlue has several years before it must fully utilize its slots. However, American Airlines can file suit to try to win some of those slots and thereby compete head-to-head with JetBlue.

Soaring oil prices and a slowing economy didn't help JetBlue in 2001–2002 either. One problem small airlines can't hedge against is rising fuel costs, since they haven't the financial wherewithal to do so. The big carriers can. As someone who ran a company that developed and marketed airline scheduling and reservation forecasting systems, Neeleman is well positioned to understand how to develop sophisticated forecasting systems. However, those sophisticated scheduling and reservation systems require several years experience on which to build their forecasts. Neeleman and his team therefore have to make decisions (like how many planes to add to particular routes and what fares to charge) more on instinct than on quantitative techniques. As the firm's chief financial officer put it, "the peak last Christmas was far deeper, stronger, and longer than expected. This year there'll be fewer discounts." Partly as a result of all this uncertainty, JetBlue, which is still in strong financial condition, was quickly accumulating debt as late as 2002.

Assignment

You and your team are consultants to Mr. Neeleman, who is depending on your management expertise to help him navigate the launch and management of JetBlue. Here's what he wants to know from you now:

1. From what you know, how well did my team and I do in applying effective planning procedures? Please list what we did right, and wrong.

2. Develop an outline of a business plan (just the main heading, please), including the component functional plans we will need for the company as a whole.

3. Give me examples of how JetBlue can use descriptive plans, graphical plans, and financial plans.

4. List four forecasting tools you think we should apply, and explain why.

Strategic Management

CHAPTER 7

OBJECTIVES

After studying this chapter and the case exercises at the end, you should be able to use the material to:

1. Develop a workable strategic plan for an organization using SWOT analysis.

2. Identify a company's current corporate strategies and list its strategic options.

3. Develop a vision and mission statement for a company.

4. Accurately identify a company's "core competencies."

5. Explain each of the strategy planning tools you think the CEO should use and why.

The French-Canadian Connection: Vivendi and Seagram

Vivendi Universal is a French media and utilities conglomerate that is having difficulty coming up with a successful corporate strategy. Former CEO Jean-Marie Messier originally had a grand vision of creating a global media and telecom company that would send music, television, and other entertainment content directly to consumers via wireless and cable. But the strategy didn't work, and by mid-2002 the company was thinking about splitting off its recently acquired telecom and entertainment interests and keeping the more stable utilities.

A fabled Canadian family—the Bronfmans—became Vivendi's largest shareholder when Seagram's was sold to Vivendi in 2000. Vivendi handed over stock worth about $75 per Seagram share, which was well above the high $40-range that Seagram stock was trading at just prior to the sale. As part of the deal, Edgar Bronfman Jr. became Vivendi's vice-chair and was supposed to co-lead the company. But Messier soon became dominant, and Bronfman resigned in December 2001.

In July 2002, Messier was ousted as CEO of Vivendi. In an interview published in the French magazine *Le Point*, Messier said that Charles Bronfman—a key shareholder—had never believed in Messier's vision for the company and wanted to take back control of the company. Vivendi's stock lost more than half its value during 2001, and the Bronfman family may have lost between $1 billion and $2 billion as a result. The ousting of Messier is likely related to those losses.

Prior to its sale to Vivendi, Seagram was a famous Canadian company. Sam Bronfman started Seagram's in the 1920s and sold liquor by mail order. His son, Edgar Bronfman Sr., became CEO in 1957. Until the early 1990s, Seagram's focused largely on the production of wine, distilled spirits, and orange juice. But by the mid-1990s, Edgar Bronfman Jr. was CEO and he began making some dramatic strategic moves away from traditional products and toward the high-risk entertainment business.

Some of his decisions were startling. For example, he paid more than $2 billion for 15 percent of Time Warner in 1993, but then sold those shares as well as a large block of DuPont shares that Seagram had held for many years. In 1995, he bought MCA Inc. (now Universal) for $5.7 billion. In 1998, he spent $10.6 billion to acquire Polygram, a company whose artists are as diverse as Elton John, U2, and The Three Tenors. With the acquisition of Polygram, Seagram instantly became the world's largest music company.

Critics of Bronfman noted that the DuPont stock that he sold for $8.8 billion in 1995 was worth $20 billion in 1998. But in 1999, Bronfman countered these critics by noting that Seagram stock was at its highest level in a year and that an investment in Seagram made at the same time it sold off its DuPont stock was worth more than an investment made in DuPont.

The strategic direction of Vivendi is uncertain at the moment. What is certain is that one of Canada's largest and most famous companies has suddenly disappeared.

Vivendi Universal
www.vivendiuniversal.com

Strategy and Strategic Planning

The plans you designed for Acme Consulting in Chapter 6 assume one crucial thing: that you know what business Acme is in. If your business goal was to provide computer systems consulting for high-tech firms, that would determine what kinds of consultants you hire, the clients you pursue, the way you market your services, and how much money you need to run your business. However, if you decided that the goal of your business was to provide accounting services to grocery stores, most of your plans would change. The bottom line is this: You have to be able to answer the question "What business are we in?" before you can do any business planning. You'll need a strategy for your company. You'll then build all your plans on that foundation.

The same logic applies to your personal planning. To see why, consider your own career plans. Defining your occupational "business" as "management consultant" will lead you to make short-term plans regarding which college or university to attend and which courses to take. These might be vastly different than if you had decided to be a dentist. Knowing the "business" you want to be in provides a path and a sense of direction for everything you do. Without it, your career may simply drift. You have to decide what business you are in before you can develop the rest of your plans.

Peter Drucker says that top management's primary task is thinking through the mission of the business, that is, asking the question, "What is our business and what should it be? This leads to the setting of objectives, the development of strategies and plans, and the making of today's decisions for tomorrow's results."[1] Knowing that they're running the world's low-cost leader retail chain provides Wal-Mart managers with a clear sense of what they must do: Expand their satellite-based logistics system; open more stores in relatively low-cost locations; and drive down apparel manufacturing costs. Could they make decisions like these if they did not know the business they were in? The answer is no.

A **strategy** is a comprehensive and integrated plan that states how the organization will use its resources in the pursuit of its mission and objectives. **Strategic planning**—the subject of this chapter—is a process that involves defining the mission of the business and laying out the broad strategies or courses of action the firm will use to achieve that mission. Since you can't do any business planning if you don't know how to strategically plan, in this chapter we focus on strategic planning.

Strategic planning is a type of planning and thus has a lot in common with the planning process described in Chapter 6. Both involve assessing your situation today and

strategy
A comprehensive and integrated plan that states how the organization will use its resources in the pursuit of its mission and objectives.

strategic planning
A process that involves defining the mission of the business and laying out the broad strategies or courses of action the firm will use to achieve that mission.

predicting the future; both involve setting objectives; and both involve crafting courses of action to get you from where you are today to where you want to be tomorrow.

But, strategic planning is in a class of its own. For one thing, it relies on special tools and techniques. For another, it's often highly subjective. Tom Peters, a management guru, reportedly once offered $1000 to the first manager who could demonstrate that he or she had created a successful strategy from a planning process.[2] His point was that a careful planning process may actually produce worse, not better, strategic plans.

How could this be? The problem is that strategic planning is a very creative, judgmental process. Unlike shorter-term plans (What courses should I take this term?), strategic planning (What occupation is best for me?) requires looking far ahead and using insight and creativity to make sense of many imponderables. For your personal strategic plan, these might include: Will I be a good consultant? Will I enjoy that career? Will there be enough jobs in five years to make being a consultant worthwhile? Two experts put it this way: "Planning processes are not designed to accommodate the messy process of generating insights and molding them into a winning strategy."[3]

The techniques in this chapter can help make you a better strategic planner. However, don't let them mislead you into believing that strategic planning is a simple mechanical process. Rather, insight and creativity always play a big role.

The Strategic Management Process

Strategic planning is the process of identifying the business of the firm today as well as what the business of the firm will be in the future. It then requires identifying the course of action the firm should pursue. To do this, managers must consider the opportunities that are available, the threats to success that exist, and the firm's strengths and weaknesses. The strategic plan specifies with whom the firm will compete, and how it will compete with them.

Strategic planning is part of the firm's strategic management process. It includes evaluating the firm's internal and external situation, defining the business and developing a mission, translating the mission into strategic goals, and crafting a strategy or course of action to move the organization from where it is today to where it wants to be. **Strategic management** also includes the implementation phase. It is the process of identifying and executing the organization's mission, by aligning the organization's internal capabilities with the external demands of its environment.[4] All of this may sound complicated, but the basic idea is pretty simple: Decide what business you're in now, and which one(s) you want to be in in the future; formulate a strategy for getting there; then execute your plan.

The strategic management process consists of several related steps (see Figure 7.1). Let's examine each one.[5]

strategic management
The process of identifying and executing the organization's mission by matching the organization's capabilities with the demands of its environment.

Step 1: Define the Business and Its Mission

The fundamental strategic decisions managers face are these: "Where are we now, in terms of the business we're in?" and "What business do we want to be in, given the opportunities and threats facing us, and our internal strengths and weaknesses?" Once the answers to these questions are clear, the company can then choose strategies such as buying competitors or expanding overseas to get it from where it is today to where it wants to be tomorrow. Making these decisions involves analyzing the company's strategic situation (we'll discuss how to do that later in this chapter).

Defining the firm's "business" is trickier then it might appear. Ferrari and Toyota both make cars. However, Ferrari specializes in high-performance cars, and its competitive advantage depends on high-speed performance. Toyota produces a range of cars, and its competitive advantage depends on cost-efficient production and a strong dealer network. So we can't simply say they're "both in the car business." Doing so would not provide the degree of specificity managers need to decide what kind of cars to produce or how to market them.

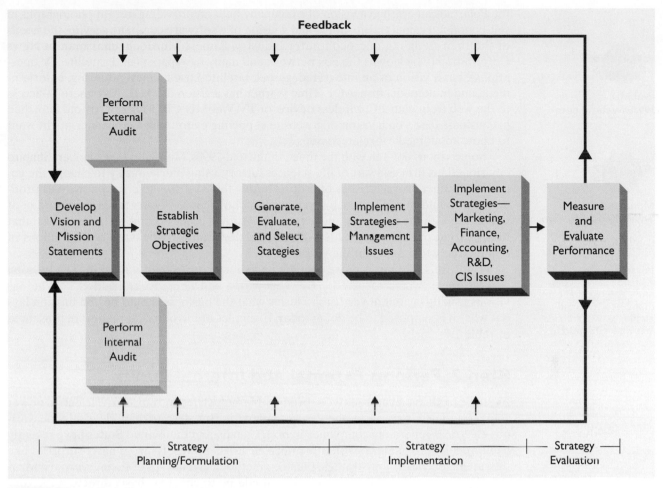

FIGURE 7.1
A Comprehensive Strategic Management Model

Consider another example. At first glance, Wal-Mart and Kmart might seem to be in the same business. Wal-Mart, however, distinguished itself from Kmart by at first concentrating its stores in small southern towns in the United States and by building a state-of-the-art, satellite-based distribution system. Kmart opened stores throughout the United States, where it had to compete with a great many other discounters, often for expensive, big-city properties.

Defining a company's business thus involves more then just deciding what broad industry it is in. Even in the same industry, companies differ in their *product scope*, or in the range and diversity of products they sell. They differ in the extent to which they are *vertically integrated*, or in the degree to which they produce their own raw materials, or distribute their own products. They also differ in *geographic scope*; some firms operate just locally, while others may operate province-wide, nationally, or globally. Companies also differ in how they compete: Volvo builds cars for safety, while Ferrari stresses speed. Timex and Rolex both produce watches, but Timex sells to low-cost department and discount stores, while Rolex sells high-quality, high-fashion watches only in selected jewellery stores.

Management experts use the terms vision and mission to help define the company's current and future business. Vision tends to be the broader and more future-oriented of the two. The company's **vision** is a "general statement of its intended direction that evokes emotional feelings in organization members."[6]

Carrier Canada is a leading supplier of residential and commercial heating and cooling equipment. The company is committed to the vision of being "the biggest and the best." This vision is realized by constantly reminding all stakeholders, especially employees, of Carrier's objectives and the need to perform better. Dr. Edwin Land, who invented

Ferrari
www.ferrari.com

Timex
www.timex.com

Rolex
www.rolex.com

vision
A general statement of an organization's intended direction that evokes emotional feelings in its members.

WebMD
www.webmd.com

Monsanto
www.monsanto.com

mission
A broad outline of the firm's purpose that communicates "who the organization is, what it does, and where it's headed."

the Polaroid camera, had a vision of a company built on providing instant photographs in self-contained cameras. Bill Gates had a vision of a software company serving the needs of the then-fledgling microcomputer industry. Rupert Murdoch, chairman of News Corporation (which owns the Fox network and many newspapers and satellite TV operations), has a vision of an integrated, global, satellite-based, news-gathering, entertainment, and multimedia firm. AOL-Time Warner has a vision of "AOL Anywhere"—access to the web from your PC, wireless device, or TV. WebMD CEO Jeffrey Arnold launched his business based on a vision of a website supplying everything a consumer might want to know about medical-related issues.[7]

Some visions don't fit with the times. In the mid-1990s, Monsanto CEO Robert Shapiro envisioned his firm as a sort of life sciences factory, using biochemistry to change the genetic and other characteristics of crops. He saw this as a way to create new food products that could, for instance, lower people's cholesterol.[8] Unfortunately, the idea of tampering with the chemistry and genetic structure of crops became so controversial that Monsanto has now largely tabled the idea. Unfortunately, Monsanto spent millions of dollars trying to implement the vision.

The firm's mission is more specific and shorter-term than its vision. The **mission** "serves to communicate 'who we are, what we do, and where we're headed.'"[9] Whereas visions usually lay out in very broad terms what the business should be, the mission lays out what it is supposed to be doing today. Examples of mission statements are presented in Table 7.1.

Step 2: Perform External and Internal Audits

Events can throw even relatively predictable industries into disarray. Electric power sources and needs are supposedly easy to plan for. But, despite their clear mission, various electrical generating companies in both Canada and the United States have recently had difficulty providing consistently priced electrical power. To avoid nasty surprises like this, managers base their strategic plans on methodical analyses of their external and internal situations. The point of your plan should be to choose a basic direction for your firm that makes sense, in terms of the external opportunities and threats you face, and the internal strengths and weaknesses you possess. For this, special tools are required. We'll learn how to use strategic analysis tools later in this chapter.

strategic, or long-term, goals
Goals that specify exactly what the mission means in terms of how many and what specific types of actions need to be taken.

Step 3: Translate the Mission into Strategic Goals

Operationalizing the firm's mission for its managers is a key activity. To do this, the firm's managers need **strategic**, or **long-term, goals**. These goals will specify, for example, ex-

---

TABLE 7.1 *Examples of Mission Statements*

Bell Canada's mission is to be a world leader in helping communicate and manage information.

Transit Windsor is a company that provides public transportation for the City of Windsor and adjacent areas. Its mission is to continually improve public transportation services for the people of Windsor at a reasonable cost to both the customer and the taxpayer.

The business mission of **Atco Ltd.** is to achieve an international reputation for excellence by providing products and services to the energy and resource industries and to invest principally in energy-related assets in North America.

Noverco is a Quebec public company with a North American vocation. It was formed with the purpose of acquiring, financing, and managing large-scale companies, which will afford its shareholders solid guarantees for the future and excellent rates-of-return, in various activities principally related to the energy field.

The business mission of **Investors Group** is to satisfy clients in need of general and comprehensive financial planning. Through product development and a well-trained sales distribution organization, investors will assist in implementing financial plans and providing effective ongoing service.

actly what the mission means in terms of how many and what specific types of actions need to be taken.

When new CEOs take over, they often state very explicit strategic goals. For example, when Anthony Comper became CEO of the Bank of Montreal in 1999, he indicated that he wanted the bank to achieve a return on equity (ROE) of 18 percent to 20 percent over the next four years. (The bank had only been achieving an ROE of about 15 percent.) To achieve this goal, he decided that the Bank of Montreal should focus its capital on lines of business that had a high profit margin, such as residential mortgages and small-business loans, and get out of lines of business that made only a marginal return, like corporate lending.[10] When Wallace McCain took control of Maple Leaf Foods Inc., he

"Never choose a mission statement on a dark, rainy day."

set three strategic goals: to make Maple Leaf a bigger company through acquisitions, to build larger animal-processing plants, and to cut labour costs.[11]

Step 4: Formulate a Strategy to Achieve the Strategic Goals

The firm's strategy is a bridge connecting where it is today with where it wants to be tomorrow. The question is, "Exactly how do we get from here to there?" A strategy is a course of action. It shows how the enterprise will move from the business it is in now to the business it wants to be in (as stated in its vision, mission, and strategic goals), given its opportunities and threats and its internal strengths and weaknesses. For example, many years ago Wal-Mart decided to pursue the strategic goal of moving from being a small, southern U.S.–based chain of retail discount stores to becoming the national leader (in terms of market share) in low-cost merchandise. To accomplish this, Wal-Mart chose several strategies. One was to pursue a low-cost leader strategy by reducing distribution costs and minimizing inventory and delivery times through a satellite-based distribution system. We'll discuss the various strategies a firm might pursue later in this chapter.

Step 5: Implement the Strategy

Strategy implementation means translating the strategy into actions and results—by actually hiring (or firing) people, building (or closing) plants, and adding (or eliminating) products and product lines. Strategy implementation involves applying all the management functions: planning, organizing, leading, and controlling.

When CIBC needed a top executive who could effectively execute a strategy to improve its operations, it chose John Hunkin.[12] He was seen by some as a risk taker, but he is not reckless. Rather, he takes calculated risks. He decided to focus the activity of CIBC on wealth management and ecommerce. The overall strategy will be to have less emphasis on the wholesale side of banking (for example, brokerages) and more emphasis on the retail side (for example, branch banking).

Employees can't and won't implement strategies that they don't buy into. Top companies therefore craft strategies whose basic principles are easy to communicate. Figure 7.2 illustrates this. For example, the essence of Dell's strategy has always been "be direct." Wal-Mart's strategy boils down to the familiar "low prices, every day."

A knowledge of and a commitment to the strategy help ensure that employees make decisions that are consistent with the company's needs. For example, the executive team's deep understanding of Nokia Corp.'s strategy helps explain how the firm can make thousands of decisions each week so coherently.[13]

strategy implementation
Translating the strategy into actions and results.

Step 6: Evaluate Performance

Strategies don't always work out. For example, when General Motors recently sold the last of its Hughes Electronics assets, it was the end of a strategy put in place more than a

COMPANY	STRATEGIC PRINCIPLE
America Online	*Consumer connectivity first—anytime, anywhere*
Dell	*Be direct*
eBay	*Focus on trading communities*
General Electric	*Be number one or number two in every industry in which we compete, or get out*
Southwest Airlines	*Meet customers' short-haul travel needs at fares competitive with the cost of automobile travel*
Vanguard	*Unmatchable value for the investor-owner*
Wal-Mart	*Low prices, every day*

FIGURE 7.2
Strategies in Brief

General Motors
www.gm.com

decade earlier. In the 1980s, GM had bought both Electronic Data Systems and Hughes Electronics with the idea of using these technology firms to automate and reinvigorate their automobile production and sales. GM did make a big profit when they sold those two companies years later. However, many believe that the acquisitions were actually such a distraction that they helped push GM's market share down in the interim, from about 60 percent to 28 percent.[14] Similarly, Procter & Gamble sold its remaining food businesses— Jif, Crisco, and Folgers coffee—because management wanted to focus more on household and cosmetics products.[15]

Managing strategy is thus an ongoing process. Competitors introduce new products, technological innovations make production processes obsolete, and societal trends reduce demand for some products or services while boosting demand for others. Managers must be alert to opportunities and threats that might require modifying or totally redoing their strategies. And they must be alert to problems that may be hampering their efforts to implement the current plan.

Strategic control keeps the company's strategy up to date. It is the process of assessing progress toward strategic goals and taking corrective action as needed. Ideally, this is a continuing process. Management monitors the extent to which the firm is meeting its strategic goals, and asks why deviations exist. Management simultaneously scans the firm's strategic situation (competitors, technical advances, customer demographics, and so on) to see whether it should make any strategic adjustments. Strategic control addresses several important questions: Are all the resources of the firm contributing as planned to achieving our strategic goals? What is the reason for any discrepancies? Do changes in our strategic situation suggest that we should revise our strategic plan?

 # Types of Strategies

corporate-level strategy
A plan that identifies the portfolio of businesses that compose a corporation and how they relate to each other.

competitive strategy
A strategy that identifies how to build and strengthen the business's long-term competitive position in the marketplace.

There are three main types of strategies (see Figure 7.3). Many companies consist of a portfolio of several businesses. For instance, Disney includes movies, theme parks, and the ABC TV network. These companies need a **corporate-level strategy** that identifies the portfolio of businesses that compose the corporation and the ways in which these businesses fit together.

The question, then, is "How will each of these portfolio businesses compete?" Each of these separate businesses needs a business-level or **competitive strategy** that identifies how to build and strengthen the company's long-term competitive position in the marketplace.[16] It identifies, for instance, how Disney films will compete with Warner films (e.g., Disney has historically differentiated itself with G-rated movies).

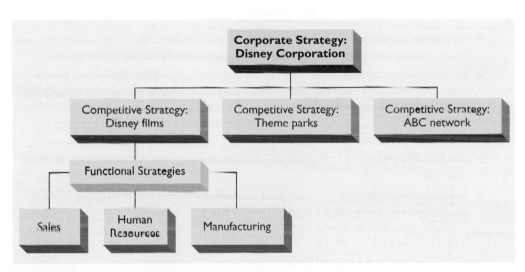

FIGURE 7.3
Relationships Among Strategies in Multiple-Business Firms
Companies typically formulate three types of strategies: Corporate strategies, business-level/competitive strategies, and functional strategies.

Each business (such as Disney Films) in turn comprises departments, such as production, marketing, and HR. **Functional strategies** identify the basic courses of action each functional department will pursue to contribute to attaining the business's competitive goals. Thus, Disney Film's production strategy might include guidelines regarding the types of stories that are acceptable and how directors should film them. We'll look at each type of strategy in turn.

functional strategy
The overall course(s) of action and basic policies that each department is to follow in helping the business accomplish its strategic goals.

Corporate-Level Strategies

Every company must decide the number of businesses in which it will compete and the relationships that will exist among those businesses. In other words, they must have a corporate-level strategy. Companies can pursue one or more of the following corporate-level strategies when deciding what businesses to be in and how these businesses should relate to one another.

Concentration With a **concentration strategy**, the company offers one product or product line, usually in one market. Firms with single business strategies include McDonald's, KFC, and WD-40 Company. Canadian National Railways has pursued a concentration strategy by acquiring Illinois Central and trying to acquire Burlington Northern Santa Fe. CN is now a railroad giant in North America, with more than 80 000 km of track and more than U.S.$18.5 billion in annual revenue.[17]

The main advantage here is that the company can concentrate on the one business it knows well. This should allow it to do that one thing better than competitors. The main disadvantage is the risk inherent in putting all of one's eggs into one basket. Thus, if for some reason hamburgers fall out of favour, McDonald's might find itself with no backup businesses. Concentrators must therefore always watch for signs of decline. After years of concentrating on the hamburger franchise business, McDonald's tried unsuccessfully to diversify into franchising children's play areas in covered shopping malls. Harley Davidson, on the other hand, successfully diversified from motorcycles into clothing, restaurants, and finance.

Concentration can also leave the firm open to wide seasonal or cyclical swings in earnings, as demand for the company's product or service ebbs and flows. Adding a line of lawnmowers can help a snowmobile maker even out its yearly production. Concentrating on a single line of business doesn't mean the firm can't or won't try to grow. Some traditional concentrators like Coca-Cola have achieved very high growth rates through concentration. They do this in one of four ways:[18]

- **market penetration**—This means taking steps to boost sales of present products by more aggressively selling and marketing into the firm's current markets.
- **geographic expansion**—*The Wall Street Journal* has achieved above-average growth rates while concentrating on its traditional business by aggressively expanding into new geographic markets, domestic and overseas. Companies like Midas Muffler, McDonald's, and Wal-Mart have also grown through geographic expansion.
- **product development**—This means developing improved products for current markets.
- **horizontal integration**—This means acquiring ownership or control of competitors in the same or similar markets with the same or similar products. In 2002, Tricon Global Restaurants Inc.—which already owned Pizza Hut, KFC, and Taco Bell—purchased Long John Silver's and A&W. It also changed its corporate name to YUM Brands Inc.[19]

Vertical Integration **Vertical integration** means owning or controlling the inputs to the firm's processes (backward integration) or the channels through which it distributes its products or services (forward integration). Polo, Ralph Lauren, and Levi's have integrated forward by opening their own retail stores.

Some firms vertically integrate because that's what their customers want. For example, many electronic devices (including cell phones) aren't built by the firms whose names appear on the products. Instead, huge contract manufacturers like Solectron, and Flextronics assemble them. In turn, these contract manufacturers are vertically integrating. They're buying up design and even shipping firms, because they are trying to provide "cradle-to-the-grave" services from designing to final shipping to customers.[20]

Diversification **Diversification** is a strategy of expanding into related or unrelated products or market segments.[21] Diversification helps the firm avoid the problem of having all its eggs in one basket by spreading risk among several products or markets. However, diversification adds a new risk. It forces the company and its managers to split their attention and resources among several products or markets. To that extent, diversification may undermine the firm's ability to compete successfully in its chosen markets.

concentration strategy
The firm offers one product or product line, usually in one market.

Midas Muffler
www.midas.com

market penetration A growth strategy to boost sales of present products by more aggressively permeating the organization's current markets.

geographic expansion A strategic growth alternative of aggressively expanding into new domestic and/or overseas markets.

product development The strategy of improving products for current markets to maintain or boost growth.

horizontal integration Acquiring ownership or control of competitors who are competing in the same or similar markets with the same or similar products.

vertical integration A growth strategy in which a company owns or controls the inputs to its processes and/or its distribution channels.

diversification A strategy of expanding into related or unrelated products or market segments.

A firm can diversify in several ways. **Related diversification** means diversifying into other industries in such a way that a firm's lines of business still possess some kind of fit.[22] For example, CN diversified into trucking, an activity that is clearly related to railway operations. Campbell's Soup purchased Pepperidge Farm Cookies because it felt that Pepperidge's customer base and channels of distribution were a good fit with its existing customers. Maple Leaf Gardens Ltd., which already owned a professional hockey team (the Toronto Maple Leafs), acquired a professional basketball team (the Toronto Raptors). When women's-wear maker Donna Karan expanded into men's clothing, that was also related diversification. British Telecom recently took steps aimed at adding television to its telephone and internet services.[23]

Conglomerate diversification, in contrast, means diversifying into products or markets not related to the firm's present businesses or to one another. For example, Bell Canada decided to diversify by forming BCE Inc., which then acquired interests in such unrelated businesses as trust companies, pipelines, and real estate. Getty Oil diversified into pay television. Conglomerate diversification is not as popular as it was 20 years ago. Businesses are now focusing their attention on a few core activities. For example, TransCanada Pipelines Ltd. got rid of its chemical division, and Alcan divested itself of its non-core businesses so it could focus on aluminum production.

Amazon.com has pursued both related and conglomerate diversification. It originally specialized in selling books over the Net. It then expanded its offerings to music and electronics. Recently it formed partnerships with companies like Toys "R" Us to manage these companies' internet-based sales. And, Amazon.com recently formed a partnership with Disney to display show times, advertisements, and movie reviews.[24]

Status Quo Strategies   Sometimes the manager will assess the situation and decide that no change in strategy is advisable. A stability or status-quo strategy is a more conservative approach. It assumes the organization is satisfied with its rate of growth and product scope. Operationally, this means maintaining its present strategy and continuing to concentrate on its present products and markets. Status quo is one corporate strategy pursued by the company that makes WD-40. It rarely advertises or aggressively pursues increased market share.

Investment Reduction Strategies   Sometimes it turns out that the firm's reach exceeds its grasp. In that case, investment reduction and defensive strategies may be called for. They are reactions to over-expansion, ill-conceived diversification, or some other financial emergency. They involve reducing the company's investments in one or more of lines of business. **Retrenchment** means the reduction of activities or operations. For example, in the 1980s Federal Industries was a conglomerate with interests in trucking, railways, metals, and other product lines, but it has now retrenched and focused on a much more limited set of products and customers.

Levi Strauss suffered a dramatic loss of market share and closed many of its U.S. clothing plants. IBM engaged in a massive retrenchment effort, dramatically reducing (downsizing) the number of its employees and closing many facilities. **Divestment** usually denotes the sale of a viable business, while liquidation denotes the sale or abandonment of a non-viable one.

Strategic Alliances and Joint Ventures   Some firms want to diversify or integrate or expand abroad, but can't (or don't want to) use their own resources to do so. In these cases, **strategic alliances** are often the strategies of choice. They are formal agreements between two or more separate companies, the purpose of which is to enable the organizations to benefit from complementary strengths.

Joint ventures are one example of strategic alliances. For example, international airlines like Delta want to offer their passengers easier access to continuing flights and services as they travel abroad. Thus, a typical Delta passenger to France might want to transfer easily to a flight from Charles de Gaulle Airport in Paris, to a flight to Cannes. Delta could expand globally by buying or merging with a French carrier. However, many airlines instead form strategic alliances. Delta and Air France are part of the "Star Alliance." Passengers on either airline can use the other airline's facilities. The airlines derive many of the benefits of horizontal integration strategy without actually merging.

related diversification
A strategy of expanding into other industries or markets related to a company's current business lines, so that the firm's lines of business still have some kind of fit.

conglomerate diversification
Diversifying into other products or markets that are not related to a firm's present businesses.

Amazon
www.amazon.com

retrenchment
The reduction of activities or operations.

divestment
Selling the individual businesses of a larger company.

strategic alliance
An agreement between potential or actual competitors to achieve common objectives.

Joint ventures involve joint ownership and operation of a business. As the cellphone market became increasingly competitive, some firms began creating joint ventures. For example, Ericsson and Sony now jointly produce and market cellphones, while Japan's NEC Corp. and Matsushita have discussed a similar alliance. Similarly, joint ventures are central to the strategy of textile maker Frisby Technologies. To help move the firm into Europe, Frisby formed a joint venture there with Schoeller textiles. It then signed another partnership with Reh Band, a manufacture of a sports brace in Sweden. Information technology is facilitating global partnerships like these. As Duncan Russell, Frisby's president says, "the internet era has helped usher in global partnerships because of the ease and speed of communication."[25]

The internet is making competitors' alliances much more common. For example, General Motors, Ford, and Chrysler together created an on-line exchange to help automate their procurement processes.[26] Suppliers—particularly suppliers of commodity products like gaskets, and spark plugs—use the exchange to review the buyer's product specifications, and to bid on the various projects. Other competitors creating exchanges include forest products producers Georgia-Pacific and International Paper, and department store chains Sears and Carrefour.

The Virtual Corporation The virtual corporation, which is a modern version of the strategic alliance, is "a temporary network of independent companies (suppliers, customers, even rivals) linked by information technology to share skills, costs, and access to one another's markets."[27] Virtual corporations don't have headquarters' staffs, organization charts, or the organizational trappings that we associate with traditional corporations. In fact, they generally aren't corporations at all, in the traditional sense of common ownership or a chain of command. Instead, they are networks of companies, each of which lends the virtual corporation/network its special expertise. Information technology (computer information systems, fax machines, electronic mail, and so on) enables the virtual corporation's far-flung company constituents to stay in touch and make their contributions.[28]

Successful virtual corporations rely on trust and on a sense of "co-destiny." This means recognizing that the fate of each partner and of the virtual corporation's whole enterprise is dependent on each partner doing its share.[29] For example, when start-up company TelePad came up with an idea for a handheld, pen-based computer, a virtual corporation was how it breathed life into the idea. An industrial design firm in California designed the product, Intel engineers helped with engineering details, several firms helped develop software for the product, and a battery maker helped produce the power supply.[30] (Unfortunately, the idea didn't work out as planned and TelePad went out of business.)

Elance
www.elance.com

The internet is enabling more firms and people to work together through virtual arrangements. For example, the website Elance lets freelance consultants and graphic designers sell their services to businesses by allowing them to post information about their skills and fees.[31] Graphic designer Serena Rodriguez gets about 10 percent of her business through that site. She works on projects, virtually, long distance, without seeing or being a formal part of firms like pharmaceuticals manufacturer Merck.

Competitive Strategies

Whether a company concentrates on a single business or diversifies into a dozen or more, each of those businesses needs a competitive strategy. Professor Michael Porter defines competitive strategy as a plan to establish a profitable and sustainable competitive position against the forces that determine industry competition.[32] A competitive strategy specifies how the company will compete. Wal-Mart competes based on low cost, while Mercedes Benz competes on high quality.

Without a clear competitive strategy, customers don't know what to make of your product or service. For example, when Marriott International Inc. bought the Renaissance hotel chain, "nobody knew what to do with [Renaissance]," according to one Marriott senior vice president. The problem was, Renaissance didn't have the clear brand image it needed to differentiate it from other hotel chains. As a result, it really couldn't compete effectively against the likes of the Marriott and Starwood Hotels chains. After many focus groups and consultations, Marriott decided to turn Renaissance into a chain of chic, up-market hotels. Marriott recently built 15 new Renaissance hotels that fit that image, and is renovating existing hotels.[33]

Firms generally pursue one of three competitive strategies: cost leadership, differentiation, or focus.[34]

Cost Leadership Most firms try to hold down costs, but a **cost leadership** competitive strategy goes beyond this. A business that pursues this strategy aims to be the low-cost leader in an industry. It does this by pursuing absolute cost advantages from all possible sources. Wal-Mart is the classic industry cost leader. It minimizes distribution costs through a satellite-based distribution system linked to suppliers, its stores are plain, and it negotiates the lowest prices from suppliers.

Pursuing a cost leadership strategy requires a tricky balance between pursuing lower costs and maintaining acceptable quality. WestJet Airlines, for instance, keeps its cost per passenger mile below those of most other major airlines while still providing service as good as or better than that of its competitors. Managers who maintain exceptionally high employee morale help explain such performance.

Differentiation Most firms would love to have a "monopoly." Then, they could offer something buyers can get only from them. This is generally not possible, but for many firms, a differentiation strategy is the next best thing. With a **differentiation strategy**, a firm seeks to be unique in its industry along some dimensions that are valued by buyers.[35] In other words, it picks one or more attributes of the product or service that its buyers perceive as important, and then positions itself to meet those needs better than its competitors.

As anyone who watches television knows, there's no end to the ways you can try to differentiate your product. In practice, the dimensions along which you can differentiate range from the "product image" offered by cosmetics firms, to concrete differences such as the product durability emphasized by Caterpillar. Volvo stresses safety, Apple Computer stresses usability, and Mercedes-Benz emphasizes quality.

Focus A business pursuing a **focus strategy** selects a narrow market segment and then builds its competitive strategy on serving the customers in that niche better or more cheaply than its competitors. Differentiators (like Volvo) and low-cost leaders (like Wal-Mart) are generalists when it comes to the market. They tend to aim their business at all or most potential buyers.

The basic reason to be a focuser is so you can specialize. Therefore, the manager must ask this: By focusing on a narrow market, can we provide our target customers with a product or service better or more cheaply than our generalist competitors? If the answer is "yes" (and if the market is big enough), it may pay to focus. A Pea in the Pod Inc., a chain of maternity stores, focuses on selling stylish clothes to pregnant working women. By specializing in "working woman maternity clothes," the company can provide a wider range of such clothes to its target customers than can generalist competitors like The Bay, Zellers, or Wal-Mart. Other focusers are E.B. Eddy Forest Products Ltd. and Fraser Inc., both of which focus on producing the high-quality, durable, lightweight paper that is used in Bibles.

The Five Forces Model How a company competes depends on the intensity of the competition in its industry. Years ago when competition was not so keen in the auto industry, GM was not very concerned with competing on cost and quality. As competition increased, GM had to seek ways to compete more effectively. They needed to fine-tune their competitive strategies.

To formulate a competitive strategy, the manager should understand the company's competitive situation. For example, how intense are the rivalries among the industry's competitors? On what basis do the firms compete? Based on that

cost leadership strategy
A strategy to be the low-cost leader in an industry.

differentiation strategy
A firm picks one or more attributes of a product or service that its buyers perceive as important and then positions itself to meet those needs better than its competitors.

focus strategy
A strategy in which a business selects a narrow market segment and builds its strategy on serving those in its target market better or more cheaply than its generalist competitors.

A Pea in the Pod
www.peainthepod.com

This Pea in the Pod store serves a narrow market better than its generalist competitors.

analysis, the manager must find a sustainable ~~competitive advantage,~~ a basis on which to ~~identify a relative superiority over competitors.~~ Wal-Mart's satellite system is a main source of its competitive advantage. WestJet has a unique management system that helps it minimize aircraft turnaround time and thus keep its costs lower than its competitors. Managers should strive to find a competitive advantage for their firms. Like moats protecting a castle, these can help stop or delay new competitors from entering the marketplace battle.

~~Michael Porter's five-forces model~~ is one tool managers can use to analyze their competitive situations and to think through what their competitive advantages should be. Using the model means understanding the five main forces moulding the competitive intensity in an industry (see Figure 7.4). The model helps managers systematically study each of these five sources of competitive pressure, and we'll discuss them next.[36]

~~Threat of Entry~~ Competition can arise from new competitors entering or changing the industry. For example, the competitive landscape for Encyclopaedia Britannica changed dramatically when Microsoft introduced Encarta. Suddenly the market for hardcopy encyclopedias plummeted. The more easily new competitors can enter the business, the more intense the competition, and, to that extent, the more unattractive the industry is. Industries differ in their ease-of-entry. Some industries are so capital-intensive that only the wealthiest companies can even contemplate entering them. For example, the average person couldn't start an automobile manufacturing business, but most anyone could start a lawn-care service.

~~Rivalry Among Existing Competitors~~ Some industries are more warlike then others. Rivalry among existing competitors manifests itself in tactics like price competition, advertising battles, and increased customer service.[37] For many years, the rivalry among chartered accounting firms was low-key. It is now quite cutthroat. This has prompted most of these firms to cut costs, to offer special pricing plans to clients, and to merge. It has also driven them to find new ways to distinguish themselves from their competitors (in other words, to revamp their competitive strategies).

~~Pressure from Substitute Products~~ Substitute products perform the same or similar functions. For example, frozen yogourt is a substitute for ice cream, and synthetics are a substitute for cotton. The more substitute products, then, the more competitive the industry.

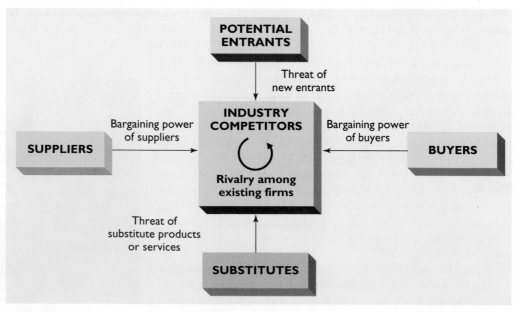

FIGURE 7.4
Forces Driving Industry Competition

Buyers' Bargaining Power Toyota and Wal-Mart have a lot of clout with their suppliers. In general, when the products are standard or undifferentiated, and when buyers face few costs when they switch suppliers, then buyers tend to have more power.

Suppliers' Bargaining Power Suppliers can influence an industry's competitive intensity and attractiveness by threatening to raise prices or reduce quality. Suppliers tend to have greater bargaining power when there are only a few of them. In a famous lawsuit, the U.S. government claimed that Microsoft exerted tremendous power as the only Windows supplier.

Managers use five forces analysis to help them decide which industries are (or are not) intensely competitive. This will help them to decide which industries they should enter or leave. Figure 7.5 illustrates this. The internet has made many industries much more competitive. For example, by making it easier for consumers of airline tickets to compare prices, it shifted the bargaining power toward the consumers. Similarly, since everyone everywhere can now easily compare the prices and pros and cons of each product or service, the net turned a wide range of products and services into commodities by reducing price differences among competitors. The ability to inexpensively create, say, a bookstore on the web, means the internet helps create many "new entrants" and "substitution" threats.

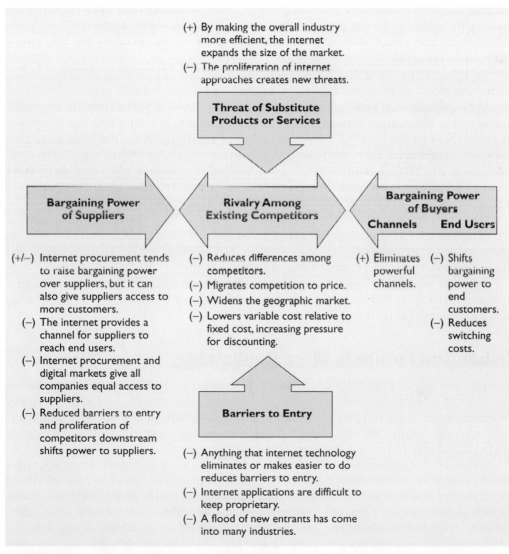

FIGURE 7.5
How the Internet Influences Industry Structure

Functional Strategies

functional strategy
The overall course(s) of action and basic policies that each department is to follow in helping the business accomplish its strategic goals.

A **functional strategy** lays out a department's basic operating policies. Functional strategies flow from and must make sense in terms of the firm's competitive strategy. We have seen that Wal-Mart competes as the industry's low-cost leader. To implement this competitive strategy, it formulated departmental functional strategies that made sense for moving Wal-Mart toward its desired competitive position. For example, the distribution department pursued a strategy (satellite-based warehousing) that ultimately drove down distribution costs to a minimum. The company's land development department found locations that fit the firm's customer profile and kept construction costs to a minimum. The merchandise buyers found sources capable of providing good-quality merchandise at the lowest possible prices.

Strategic Planning Methods

Managers don't craft strategic plans in a vacuum; rather, their plans reflect an intelligent analysis of the strategic situations that they face. The aim, you'll recall, is to devise strategies that balance the firm's external opportunities and threats with its internal strengths and weaknesses. The strategy should capitalize on evolving opportunities and address the potential threats. For this, the manager must understand the trends that are driving the industry. At the same time, the strategy must be achievable. It should capitalize on the company's strengths. And it should avoid—or compensate for—the firm's current weaknesses.

In this section, we'll discuss the tools managers use for creating their strategies. Although tools like these are important, do not assume that strategic planning is or ever could be a mechanical process. Insight and creativity play vital roles. They are especially important at the strategy formulation stage. A *Fortune* article relates how the 17 companies that topped the Fortune 1000 in shareholder return one year did so in large part based on insightful and creative strategies. The article noted that "While many of its competitors in the biotech industry let the disease lead them to the science, Amgen stays ahead by taking the opposite approach. It develops its drugs by identifying areas of promising research that may lead to breakthrough products."[38]

The creativity-boosting methods discussed in Chapter 5 are useful here. One strategy expert suggests having the top-management team spend several hours brainstorming all the possible forces that might influence the firm.[39] Other firms use the Delphi method and have experts develop alternative future scenarios.

Strategic planning always involves predicting the future, but some futures are more predictable than others. This means that managers must adjust their strategic analysis methods to the needs of the situation.

When the Future Is More Predictable

Imagine you are the president of Air Canada. You need a strategy to deal with the possible entrance of a low-cost, no-frills airline (like WestJet) into one of your major markets. What strategies might you pursue? Options include introducing a low-cost Air Canada service, surrendering the low-cost niche to the new entrant, or competing more aggressively on price and service to drive the entrant out of the market.[40]

What kind of information would you need to make your decision? Generally, you'd need the type of information provided by traditional planning tools. For example, you'd need market research on the size of the different markets, on the likely responses of customers in each market segment to different combinations of pricing and service, and competitive information about the new entrant's competitive objectives. There are also traditional strategic planning tools you might use. These include SWOT analysis, environmental scanning, benchmarking, the TOWS matrix, and portfolio analysis. Let's look at each of these.

SWOT Analysis The company's strengths, weaknesses, opportunities, and threats (SWOT) loom large in any strategic analysis. Strategic planning involves identifying the strategic actions that will balance the firm's strengths and weaknesses with its external opportunities and threats. Managers want to take advantage of opportunities while capitalizing on the firm's strengths. They want to anticipate and make accommodations for threats and reduce (or avoid) businesses that might be affected by the firm's weaknesses.

Opportunities might include the possibility of serving additional customers in the face of weakening competition, or the chance to enter foreign markets due to falling trade barriers. Threats might include the likely entry of new lower-cost foreign competitors, rising sales of substitute products, and slowing market growth. Strengths might include adequate financial resources, economics of scale, and proprietary technology. Weaknesses include lack of strategic direction, obsolete facilities, and lack of managerial depth and talent.

Managers use **SWOT analysis** (see Figure 7.6) to consolidate information regarding their firm's internal strengths and weaknesses and external opportunities and threats. SWOT analysis serves two purposes: (1) it supplies illustrative generic opportunities, threats, strengths, and weaknesses to guide the manager's analysis, and (2) it provides a standardized four-quadrant format for compiling the company's situational information.

Environmental Scanning **Environmental scanning** is the process of gathering and compiling information about environmental forces that might be relevant to the firm's strategic planners. Managers traditionally scan six key areas (see Figure 7.7) to identify opportunities or threats to list in their SWOT analyses.

1. **Economic trends.** These relate to the level of economic activity and to the flow of money, goods and services. For example, in 2002, there was great uncertainty about the economy. What opportunities and threats would such uncertainty imply for business people thinking of expanding in Canada and abroad?

2. **Competitive trends.** These involve actions that have been (or may be) taken by current and potential competitors. For example, Microsoft's move into internet browsers helped push Netscape into the waiting arms of AOL, which acquired it.

3. **Political trends.** These are factors related to actions of local, national, and foreign governments. For example, Imperial Tobacco must monitor trends in the regulation of cigarette smoking around the globe, and most cigarette firms have diversified into other businesses as regulations became more widespread.

4. **Technological trends.** These relate to the development of new or existing technology, including electronics, machines, tools, and processes. From 1998 to 2000, many firms invested heavily by expanding into areas that utilized the internet; others, such as Disney, held back, wisely predicting that the dot-com bubble would soon burst.

SWOT analysis
A strategic planning tool for analyzing a company's strengths, weaknesses, opportunities, and threats.

environmental scanning
The process of gathering and compiling information about environmental forces that might be relevant to the firm's strategic planners.

POTENTIAL STRENGTHS	POTENTIAL WEAKNESSES
• Market leadership	• Large inventories
• Strong research and development	• Excess capacity for market
• High-quality products	• Management turnover
• Cost advantages	• Weak market image
• Patents	• Lack of management depth

POTENTIAL OPPORTUNITIES	POTENTIAL THREATS
• New overseas markets	• Market saturation
• Falling trade barriers	• Threat of takeover
• Competitor's failure	• Low-cost foreign competition
• Diversification	• Slower market growth
• Economic recovery	• Growing government regulation

FIGURE 7.6
Example of a Company's Strengths, Weaknesses, Opportunities, and Threats

Economic Trends
(such as recession; inflation; employment; monetary policies)

_____
_____
_____
_____

Competitive Trends
(such as competitors' strategic changes; market/customer trends; entry/exit of competitors;
new products from competitors)

_____
_____
_____
_____

Political Trends
(such as national/local election results; special interest groups; legislation; regulation/
deregulation)

_____
_____
_____
_____

Technological Trends
(such as introduction of new production/distribution technologies; rate of product
obsolescence; trends in availability of supplies and raw materials)

_____
_____
_____
_____

Social Trends
(such as demographic trends; mobility; education; evolving values)

_____
_____
_____
_____

Geographic Trends
(such as opening/closing of new markets; factors affecting current plant/office facilities;
location decisions)

_____
_____
_____
_____

FIGURE 7.7
Worksheet for Environmental Scanning

5. Social trends. These reflect the way people live and the nature of the people in a society, including what they value. In Canada, for example, the proportion of people who are Asian or Aboriginal is rising. What impact might such trends have on major advertising companies and on makers of consumer products?

6. Geographic trends. These relate to climate, natural resources, and so forth. The possibility of global warming, for example, may mean a gradual northward expansion of agriculture on Canada's Prairies. Conversely, a cooling trend in Florida would mean a reduced possibility of continuing to grow oranges there.

Managers actually "scan" in several ways. Some have employees monitor key areas by scouring publications like *The Globe and Mail* and *The Wall Street Journal*, as well as the internet, consultants' reports, information services, and industry newsletters. Others use consultants called environmental scanners. These experts read and abstract a variety of publications to search for environmental changes that could affect the client firm. Some firms set up internet news services to continually and automatically screen thousands of news stories and provide precisely the types of stories in which they're interested.

Benchmarking   Sometimes a company must build its strengths or reduce its weaknesses to become a stronger competitor. To do so, the manager first wants to discover how his or her firm compares to other firms. For example, why create a new way to handle customer inquiries, when L.L. Bean already has a world-class system for doing so? Benchmarking is the process through which a company learns how to become the best in some area by carefully analyzing the practices of other companies that already excel in that area (best-practices companies). For example, Toronto Hospital gathered performance data on 26 indicators from various Canadian hospitals so that it could determine how well it was performing compared to other organizations in the health care industry.[41] Executives from Ford, Chrysler, and General Motors frequently tour Toyota manufacturing facilities as they try to figure out how Toyota makes cars so efficiently.

The basic benchmarking process typically follows several benchmarking guidelines (See Checklist 7.2).

The TOWS Matrix   The TOWS matrix helps managers answer the question, "What are the strategies—the courses of action—we can pursue, given our firm's opportunities and threats, and strengths and weaknesses? The TOWS matrix picks up where SWOT analysis, scanning, and benchmarking leave off. Figure 7.8 shows a TOWS matrix for a large cinema company. You fill in the TOWS by first filling in the opportunities, threats, strengths, and weaknesses from your environmental scan, benchmarking, and SWOT analysis. You then develop four possible sets of strategies. SO strategies capitalize on your strengths to take advantage of your opportunities. WO strategies capitalize on opportunities to overcome your weaknesses. ST strategies use your strengths to address impending threats. And WT strategies aim to both reduce your weaknesses and address your threats.

Portfolio Analysis: The BCG Matrix   Most firms (especially large ones) are in several businesses at once. For example, Pepsico has pursued corporate strategies of diversification and vertical integration, and now has business divisions for things like Pepsi-Cola, Frito-Lay, and Quaker. How do you decide which businesses to keep in (or drop from) a portfolio? Managers use portfolio analysis tools like the BCG (for Boston Consulting Group)

The Globe and Mail
www.theglobeandmail. com

The Wall Street Journal
www.wsj.com

benchmarking
The process through which a company learns how to become the best in some area by carefully analyzing the practices of other companies that already excel in that area.

TOWS matrix
A strategic planning tool that presents possible strategies for addressing the firm's strengths, weaknesses, opportunities, and threats.

CHECKLIST **7.2**

How to Benchmark

☑ Focus on a specific problem and define it carefully. The problem might be, "What order-fulfillment processes do best-practices companies use in the mail-order business?" Here, managers often analyze L.L. Bean's order taking and fulfillment system. Most experts view it as a best-practice company for the way it expeditiously handles customers' questions and fulfills orders.

☑ Use the employees who will actually implement those changes to identify the best-practices companies and to conduct on-site studies. Employees often have a better insight into specific aspects of the business. Their participation can help ensure their acceptance of the changes.

☑ The study of best practices is a two-way street, so be willing to share information with others.

☑ Avoid sensitive issues such as pricing, and don't look for new product information.

☑ Keep information you receive confidential.

	STRENGTHS—S	WEAKNESSES—W
	1. Located in large population centres 2. Positive cash flow three years running 3. Double the industry concession sales rate 4. Many cost-cutting measures in place 5. Upgraded audio in many places 6. Profitable in Canada	1. Poor labour relations 2. Current ratio of 0.25 3. Flat operating cost through falling revenue 4. Triple the G&A expenses of Carmike 5. Significant losses in the United States 6. Management concentrating on market share 7. Restrictive covenants set by lenders
OPPORTUNITIES—O 1. Approached by most major chains for potential merger 2. Opening economies in Eastern Europe 3. Rebounding attendance (up 6.4%) 4. Videotape industry worth estimated $18 billion vs. $6.4 billion for movie theatres 5. Foreign per capita income growth outpacing the United States	**SO STRATEGIES** 1. Open theatres in Eastern Europe (S1, O2, O5)	**WO STRATEGIES** 1. Pursue merger with American Cinemas (O1, O2, W3, W4, W5, W6)
THREATS—T 1. 80% of all households own VCRs 2. Aging population 3. Dependence on successful movies 4. Switch from bid to allocation for licences 5. Seasonality for movie releases 6. Increased competition in exhibition	**ST STRATEGIES** 1. Open 50 video rental stores in 10 markets (S1, S6, T1, T3, T5) 2. Construct 20 multidimensional entertainment complexes (S1, T3, T5, T6)	**WT STRATEGIES** 1. Reduce corporate overhead (W3, W4, T3, T5, T6) 2. Divest U.S. operations (W2, W3, W4, W5, W6, T6)

FIGURE 7.8
Cineplex Odeon TOWS Matrix

matrix to help them decide. The BCG helps managers identify the relative attractiveness of each of a firm's businesses.

The BCG assumes that a business's attractiveness depends on two things: the growth rate of the business and the market share the business has. These two factors are used to map growth rate and relative competitive position (market share) for each of the company's businesses (see Figure 7.9). "Stars" are businesses in high-growth industries in which the company has a high relative market share. For example, Intel's microprocessor business has a high growth rate and Intel has a relatively high market share. Star businesses usually require large infusions of cash to sustain growth, but their strong market positions help them generate the needed cash.

"Question marks" are businesses in high-growth industries, but with low market shares. These business units face a dilemma: They are in attractive high-growth industries, but they have such low market shares that they can't fend off larger competitors. A

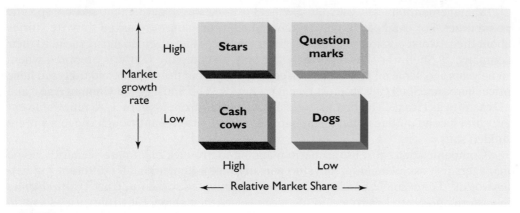

FIGURE 7.9
BCG Matrix
Once the position of each of the company's businesses is plotted, a decision can be made regarding which businesses will be cash sources and which will be cash users.

company must either divert cash from its other businesses to boost the question mark's market share or get out of the business.

"Cash cows" are businesses in low-growth industries that enjoy high market shares. Being in a low-growth, unattractive industry argues against making large cash infusions into these businesses. However, their high market share generally allows them to generate high sales and profits for years, even without much new investment. Cash cows help drive a firm's future success. Kodak's consumer film unit is a classic cash cow. Although the market is shrinking, Kodak has a commanding market share. In one recent year, Kodak was therefore able to generate more than U.S.$1 billion in cash flow to help nurture growth businesses like digital photography.[42]

"Dogs" are low-market-share businesses in low-growth, unattractive industries. Having a low market share puts the business in jeopardy relative to its larger competitors. As a result, dogs can quickly become "cash traps," absorbing cash to support a hopeless and unattractive situation. Managers usually sell them to raise cash for stars and question marks.

When the Future Is Less Predictable

Difficult-to-predict events can have profound effects on a company's business. Late in 2001, most airlines had elaborate SWOT, TOWS, and BCG-type planning models showing how they would respond if two or more of their competitors decided to merge, or if a new competitor entered one of their markets. What most of them didn't have was a plan to deal with a massive terrorist attack, or with the human and economic consequences of such a disaster. Yet, it was just such an attack that moulded the future course of the airline business after September 11.

Many firms use the scenario planning method in an attempt to deal with unpredictable future events. Scenario planning involves imagining alternative futures. **Scenario planning** tries to answer two kinds of questions: (1) how might some hypothetical situation come about, and (2) what alternatives exist for preventing (or facilitating) the process?[43]

Shell Oil has long used this approach.[44] As one of its officers said, "The Shell approach to strategic planning is, instead of forecasting, to use scenarios, which are 'stories' about alternative possible futures. These stories promote a discussion of possibilities other than the 'most likely' one, and encourage the consideration of 'what-if' questions."[45]

scenario planning
A hypothetical sequence of events constructed for the purpose of focusing attention on causal processes and decision points and thereby helping the manager anticipate events and thus create plans for them.

Kodak's digital camera, PalmPix, at its debut in 2000 at the world's largest computer trade fair.

Management typically asks the planners to produce scenarios that address specific possibilities. For example, in one exercise, Shell's planners were asked to write stories about their "worst possible nightmares, given the forces they deemed most crucial to their company."[46] Shell was thus reportedly the only oil company that was prepared when, some years ago, some oil producers took control away from the oil firms and triggered huge price increases. Shell calls its most recent scenarios "The Spirit of the Coming Age," and "Dynamics as Usual." The first foresees a gradual shift from fossil fuels to renewable energy; the second outlines what might happen if a technical breakthrough triggers a more sudden shift.

Companies don't just use scenario planning to produce nightmare scenarios. Some managers just ask planners to develop narratives of a fundamentally different but better world.[47] For example, one Austrian insurance firm used scenarios to anticipate changes in eastern and central Europe and to enter new markets there. Electrolux uses scenario planning to spot new consumer markets, and Krone, a wiring and cable supplier in Berlin, uses scenario planning to develop new product ideas.

One obvious reason to do scenario planning is to shake management out of its traditional ways of thinking. The scenario planning process should therefore force managers to "think outside the box." It should do this by confronting them with new and innovative possibilities and with the implications of these possibilities. The "Challenge of Change" box gives an example of how scenario planning works.

THE **CHALLENGE** OF **CHANGE** ⇒ ⇒ ⇒

Developing a New Corporate Strategy

Your cousin Jim, who owns a small travel agency in Mississauga, Ontario, has just come to you with your first-ever consulting assignment. He needs a strategic plan, and he needs it fast. It is March 2002, and Air Canada has just eliminated sales commissions on most ticket sales. Many airlines, including Air Canada, now want to sell tickets themselves, preferably over the internet. Your cousin is going to have to start charging his customers to book tickets for them, and he fears that he may lose half his clientele. So, he needs a new strategic plan. He calls you and asks "Where would you start?"

This is your opportunity to apply what you've learned about strategic planning.

You first ask him about his current situation. He says that about a third of his business comes from corporate clients, who use him to schedule trips for employees. Another third comes from selling tour packages to places like Disney World and the Caribbean. The final third comes from selling cruises, mostly to the Caribbean. Ten percent of his business comes in over the internet. The rest (all local) is from past clients and from word-of-mouth.

Jim is not sure he has any huge competitive advantage. However, he does have a fine reputation. And, he has exceptionally good relationships with the firms that package the tours he sells. He has six employees and earns about $60 000 for himself each year, after paying all expenses.

You interview him, speak with travel associations, and do some internet and library research to create a situational analysis for his industry. (Luckily, you find that several stock-brokerage firms have already published their own travel industry analyses for their clients). You use the environmental scan and SWOT to compile what you find. In brief, you find that *opportunities* include a fast-growing cruise market; more retirees looking for tours; and a booming business for selling travel services via the net. *Threats* include airlines con- →

tinuing to squeeze travel agents; growing competition among agents to sell cruises; and more consolidation, with big firms gobbling up smaller firms and some specializing in servicing corporate clients. *Strengths* of Jim's firm include a good list of clients; good relationships with tour packagers; a successful website; and six very loyal and competent employees. *Weaknesses* include too small a scale to adequately serve the corporate clients (who require a great deal of time and attention); inadequate funds to advertise; and a diminishing source of revenues, now that airlines are cutting commissions.

You compile all this in a TOWS matrix. Two of the many possible strategies you come up with are an "SO" strategy (where you use your strong relationship with tour packagers to take advantage of the opportunity to sell more tours to retirees), and a "WO" strategy (where you form one or more joint ventures with retirees' associations to split the cost of advertising your tours to their members).

You also do a BCG analysis. For Jim's firm, the "corporate" travel business is basically a cash cow. He has a decent market share, however, companies are cutting back—using, for example, more videoconferencing—so the market isn't growing. Both the cruise and tour businesses fall in the "question mark" quadrant. Jim has a decent market share here, and both markets are growing fast. Perhaps he can reduce his corporate business market efforts and use the revenues the existing corporate clients generate to expand his cruise and tour efforts.

So, you make a suggestion. In terms of *corporate strategy*, Jim should start to concentrate more on the cruises and tours. He should use his strong relationship with tour packagers to take advantage of the opportunity to sell more tours to retirees. He should try to sign exclusive sales agreements with the tour packagers for the Mississauga area. He could also form joint ventures with one or more local and national retirees' association to split the cost (and revenues) of advertising cruises and tours. He should keep his current corporate clients for now, but gradually phase out this part of his business.

Your suggested *competitive strategies* include differentiation (for now) and focus (probably, in the near future). He should *differentiate* the firm by offering exclusive tour packages in the Mississauga area from these particular tour packagers. And, he should consider moving to a *focus* strategy, in which the travel agency starts to focus on the Mississauga area retiree market and its needs.

Next, he should set out a few specific *goals*: revenues next year from each business line; how many tour packagers to sign agreements with, and by when; and how many retirees' associations to form joint ventures with, and by when. Jim is now set to embark on his new strategy.

Managers should keep the following scenario planning principles in mind as they use this tool:

1. Scenarios only have value to the extent that they inform decision makers and influence decision making.

2. Scenarios only add value to decision making when managers and others use them to systematically ask questions about the present and the future, and to guide how they go about answering the questions.

3. In developing scenarios, the emphasis must be on identifying, challenging, and refining the substance of managers' mindsets and knowledge.

4. Alternative projections about a given future must challenge managers' current mental models by creating tension among ideas, hypotheses, perspectives, and assumptions.

5. The dialogue and discussion triggered by the consideration of alternative futures should directly affect managers' knowledge.

6. Scenarios should include enough indicators so managers can track how the future is actually evolving. In this way, the learning and adaptations stimulated by the scenarios are continual.[48]

Strategic Planning in Practice

When doing strategic analysis, managers invariably face a dilemma: Given their firm's opportunities and threats, and their strengths and weaknesses, should they simply "fit" their capabilities to the opportunities and threats that they see, or, should they "stretch" well beyond their capabilities to take advantage of an opportunity? Let's examine this debate.

Achieving Strategic Fit

Strategic planning expert Michael Porter emphasizes the "fit" point of view. He says that all the firm's activities must fit its strategy, and that the firm's functional strategies should support its corporate and competitive strategies. "It's this 'fit' that breathes life into the firm's strategy."[49] Let's look at two examples—Interprovincial Pipelines of Edmonton and WestJet of Calgary. Interprovincial Pipelines operates the largest petroleum pipeline system in Canada and the United States. The company wanted to expand its business beyond simply transporting liquid hydrocarbons; it also wanted to be the industry leader by being proactive in safety and environmental protection. To achieve these long-term goals, Interprovincial implemented several strategies:

- identifying and developing key growth areas
- increasing efficiency and effectiveness through continuous improvement programs
- improving relations with shippers
- working with regulators to create a more positive regulatory climate
- ensuring that the company's human resources were appropriately trained to achieve the company's objectives

All of these strategies work together to facilitate the goal of being the industry leader. The company also recognizes that its continued success depends on recognition of the company's people and equipment as key assets.[50]

WestJet is modelled after U.S.-based Southwest Airlines, which pioneered cheap air travel. WestJet's strategy is to appeal to price-sensitive travellers who make up the so-called "VFR" market (visiting friends and relatives). By setting prices very low (as low as one-sixth of what Air Canada charges), WestJet believed it could entice many more people to fly a commercial airline. In fact, the travel market in western Canada has doubled on the routes that WestJet flies.

WestJet's low-price, no-frills style fits well with its strategy of occupying a specific niche in the Canadian air travel market. The company has been successful almost from the day it started. Although it is tiny compared to industry giant Air Canada, it is a fearsome competitor because it has a very low cost structure that allows it to make a profit even though it offers ultra-cheap fares.[51]

Strategy as Stretch and Leverage

Strategy experts Gary Hamel and C. K. Prahalad caution against becoming too enamoured with the notion of strategic fit.[52] They agree that every company "must ultimately effect a fit between its resources and the opportunities it pursues," however, they argue that being preoccupied with fit can limit growth.[53] They therefore argue for "stretch." They say that **leveraging resources**—supplementing what you have and doing more with what you have—can be more important than just fitting the strategic plan to current resources.

They note, for example, "If modest resources were an insurmountable deterrent to future leadership, GM, Phillips, and IBM would not have found themselves on the defensive with Honda, Sony, and Compaq."[54] Similarly, Kmart would not have found itself over-

leveraging resources
To gain a competitive edge by concentrating a company's resources on key strategic goals or competencies.

THE PEOPLE SIDE OF MANAGING

It's the People That Make the Strategy Work

Although strategic tools like scenario planning are important in strategic planning, as a practical matter the people side of managing is crucial, too. One survey of 9144 employees illustrates this. The results showed that the vast majority understood their employers' goals (83 percent) and their own job responsibilities (87 percent), both important factors in getting employees to co-operate in carrying out the firm's strategies. Yet fewer than half of the employees (43 percent) said they were given the skills and training and information they needed to achieve their goals. The problem, of course, is that having a strategy that's widely known and accepted is of little use if the employees don't have the ability to implement it.

Smart companies know that and are doing something about it. In companies like Motorola, Saturn, and 3M, employees average between 40 and 80 hours per year of training. And many companies practice "open-book management," which means keeping all employees continually informed about the company's financial and other situations so that the employees are, in a real sense, treated like partners.

In other words, the CEOs of most successful companies today understand that creating a brilliant strategy is only half the work. The ability of WestJet, for example, to keep costs down by turning aircraft around in half the time it takes competitors is not the result of special equipment or methods. Instead, it's the work of highly motivated managers and employees who believe in WestJet's low-cost strategy and who have the skills and wherewithal to implement it.

Managers must accurately define their core competencies. Several years ago, Circuit City managers decided to start the CarMax chain to sell top-of-the-line used cars. Between 1993 and 1998, they opened 23 CarMax stores in seven U.S. states. With more store openings planned, it suddenly became apparent that their strategy wasn't working because new car prices were holding steady. What prompted Circuit City to enter the used car business in the first place? Some argue it's because they did not define their core competency accurately. Management may have felt that their core competency was not "selling televisions and other electronics" but "operating super-efficient megastores with sophisticated distribution systems." If so, they may have been mistaken.[55]

Starbucks recently ran into a similar situation, with its ill-fated foray into serving sandwiches. The idea was to have prepackaged high-quality sandwiches that employees packaged fresh each morning at a central location and then to sell them in the stores throughout the day. But customers wanted fresh sandwiches, not prepackaged ones, and the typical Starbucks isn't set up to make sandwiches. Today, Starbucks is back to selling mostly coffee. As founder and CEO Howard Schultz put it, "We recognize more than ever our core competency is roasting and selling the best coffee in the world."[56]

taken by Wal-Mart. Companies, they say, can leverage their resources by concentrating them more effectively on key strategic goals. For example, Wal-Mart focused its relatively limited resources on building a satellite-based distribution system and gained a competitive advantage that helped it overtake Kmart.

The Strategic Role of Core Competencies According to Hamel and Prahalad, it's the firm's "core competencies" that it should leverage. They define **core competencies** as "the collective learning in the organization, especially [knowing] how to coordinate diverse production skills and integrate multiple streams of technologies."[57] Canon Corporation provides one example. Over the years it developed three core competencies: precision mechanics, fine optics, and microelectronics. These competencies reflect collective learning and skills that cut across traditional departmental lines; they are dispersed throughout the company, ready to be drawn upon by Canon. They are the end result of how Canon has hired, trained, and nurtured its employees.

Canon builds its new businesses on these core competencies. It starts by drawing on its core competencies to produce core component products like miniature electronic controls and fine lenses. Then it builds products and businesses—digital cameras, laser printers, and fax machines—around these core products.

Growing its businesses and products out of a few core competencies makes it easier for Canon to quickly change its product mix. Regardless of how the demand for products shifts, Canon's "assets" aren't in its products but in its core competencies (precision mechanics, fine optics, and microelectronics). If Canon's managers sense changes in customer demand, they can reach across departmental lines to marshal these core competencies. Suppose the managers sense the need for a new consumer electronic product, like a tiny camera to take PC-based pictures. Its managers can "harmonize know-how in miniaturization, microprocessor design, material science, and ultra thin precision casting—the same skills it applies in its miniature card calculators, pocket TVs, and digital watches—to design and produce the new camera."[58]

Companies can get into trouble if they try to go beyond their core competencies. Arrow Manufacturing Inc. of Montreal had a core competency in making men's belts, but when it tried to enter the luggage business, it ran into problems. Arrow discovered that although both products were made of leather, the similarity ended there. To sell luggage required large amounts of space for inventory, as well as a new sales force. After losing money in the luggage business, Arrow returned to its core competency of making belts.[59]

core competencies
The collective learning in the organization, especially the knowledge of how to coordinate diverse design and production skills and integrate multiple streams of technologies.

SKILLS AND STUDY MATERIALS

SUMMARY

1. A primary task of top management is to think through the mission of the business and ask, "What is our business, and what should it be?" Strategic management is the process of identifying and pursuing the organization's mission by aligning its internal capacity with the external demands of the environment.

2. There are five steps in the strategy management process: define the business and develop a mission; translate the mission into strategic objectives; formulate a strategy

to achieve the strategic objectives; implement the strategy; and evaluate performance and initiate corrective adjustments as required. Strategic planning includes the first three steps of this process.

3. There are three main types of strategies. The corporate-level strategy identifies the portfolio of businesses that in total will compose the corporation and the ways in which these businesses will relate; the competitive strategy identifies how to build and strengthen the business's

long-term competitive position in the marketplace; and functional strategies identify the basic courses of action that each department will pursue to contribute to the attainment of its goals.

4. Each type of strategy contains specific standard or generic strategies. Generic corporate strategies include concentration, market penetration, geographic expansion, product development, horizontal integration, vertical integration, and diversification, as well as status quo and retrenchment strategies.

5. Generic competitive strategies include being a low-cost leader, differentiator, or focuser. Formulating a specific competitive strategy requires understanding the competitive forces that determine how intense the competitive rivalries are and how best to compete. The five

forces model helps managers understand the five big forces of competitive pressure in an industry: threat of entry, intensity of rivalry among existing competitors, pressure from substitute products, bargaining power of buyers, and bargaining power of suppliers.

6. Creating strategic plans involves identifying environmental forces, formulating a plan, and creating implementation plans. Useful techniques include SWOT analysis, environmental scanning, benchmarking, portfolio analysis, and scenario planning.

7. Implementing the organization's strategy involves several activities, among them achieving strategic fit, leveraging the company's core competencies, and effectively leading the change process.

CRITICAL THINKING EXERCISES

1. You have just been appointed to a strategic planning committee for Apple Computer. You know that in the late 1990s the company had been having a difficult time with its strategies. Do some research on the history of Apple by reading articles in *The Globe and Mail*, *Fortune*, and *Business Week*. Using this information, apply the ideas, concepts, and approaches discussed in this chapter to develop a strategic plan for Apple.

2. You are a strategic planner for GM. In the late 1990s you observed the merger of DaimlerChrysler. Soon

after the merger, the Germans took greater control of the company and put some Chrysler people off the board of directors. Rumour has it that the cultures of the two companies have not completely merged. Now there is a rumour that Ford and Toyota are thinking of merging. What would you recommend that GM do? Using the concepts presented in the chapter, analyze the situation and make recommendations to the GM board.

EXPERIENTIAL EXERCISES

1. With three to four other students in the class, form a strategic management group for your college or university. In a two-hour period, identify what "business" your college or university is in, where it is in terms of implementing a strategy, and where it needs to be strategically headed. Prior to meeting to develop your plan, look at what your college or university has developed in the way of a strategic plan by interviewing some administrators, faculty members, and students about their knowledge of the strategic plan. From the information gathered, prepare some strategic alternatives for the other students to discuss in a class brainstorming session.

2. You are the newest member of the design team for a major toy manufacturer. You just saw a program on A&E that identified the most popular toys of the last century. The top five were, in ascending order, Playdoh, Lionel trains, Barbie, the crayon, and the yo-yo. Your job is to design a new toy that could be the top toy of the twenty-first century. In a team of four to five students, formulate a strategy for developing, designing, advertising, marketing, and evaluating such a toy.

BUILDING YOUR MANAGEMENT SKILLS

Obtain a copy of the strategic plan for your university or community college. Read the strategic plan and then answer the following questions:

1. To what extent does the strategic plan follow the steps in the strategic planning process that are described in the chapter? Note any inconsistencies and try to determine why they might exist.

2. Review Porter's five forces model. Explain how each of the forces in Porter's model apply to your school's situation.

3. Is strategic planning as important for a university or a community college as it is for a business firm? Why or why not?

Managers have to continually develop innovative corporate strategies to ensure that their companies remain competitive and survive in the global marketplace. Apple Computer Inc. and the Olivetti Group are two corporations that have had to change and adapt over time to ensure their survival.

1. Identify the similar challenges faced by Apple and Olivetti (**www.apple-history.com**; **www.theapplemuseum.com**; **www.olivetti.com**). Were these challenges faced at the same times in history? If not, explain the historical context of the challenges.

2. What corporate strategies did Apple's and Olivetti's managers develop and institute to ensure that their companies remained competitive and viable?

3. Perform a SWOT analysis on both companies.

CASE STUDY 7-1

More Upheaval in the Airline Industry

Most people thought that the upheavals in the domestic airline business would cease after Air Canada bought out its long-time competitor Canadian Airlines International (CAI). But it hasn't turned out that way. Instead, the industry is experiencing a host of new changes.

Throughout the 1990s, Air Canada and Canadian Airlines International were locked in a bitter competitive struggle for supremacy in the domestic airline market. CAI, which was continuously on the brink of bankruptcy, was finally bought by Air Canada in 2000. After that purchase, Air Canada controlled about 80 percent of all domestic air traffic. Consumers and government officials were worried that Air Canada's dominance would not be good for competition and that consumers would have to pay higher prices for reduced services. This worry intensified after Canada 3000 went bankrupt.

After Canada 3000 went out of business, Air Canada CEO Robert Milton claimed that the void had been filled by U.S. charter companies and Toronto-based Skyservice Airlines Inc. But discount airline owners didn't believe him and moved quickly to fill niche markets in the vacation business. Barry Lapointe and Jacques Cimetier launched Vacances Air Columbus to fly to sunshine destinations from Quebec, and Conquest Vacations launched domestic service in 2001. Other new start-up airlines include Jetz (for sports teams and corporate executives), Zip Air (operating in western Canada), and Jazz (a regional airline). All of these latter airlines are subsidiaries of Air Canada.

Air Canada's big headache is WestJet, an airline that started up in 1996. WestJet's strategy is to sell tickets at bargain prices, offer good customer service, keep costs down by running a low-cost operation, and fly short-haul trips to carefully chosen markets. Using this strategy has allowed WestJet to achieve a much higher level of productivity per worker than Air Canada. One telling statistic is this: WestJet operates with fewer than 60 people per aircraft, while Air Canada uses more than 140.

WestJet has aggressive growth plans, and it added eight planes to its fleet in 2002. It is also expanding into new markets, including Toronto, Montreal, Halifax, and St. John's. During 2001, WestJet's business was up 53.9 percent, while Air Canada's was down 2.1 percent. WestJet's strategy is working, and it is making lots of money while Air Canada continues to struggle.

Robert Milton, the CEO of Air Canada, says that the domestic airline business has fundamentally changed in the last few years, and that Air Canada's traditional business model can no longer generate profits. Air Canada's bankruptcy in 2003 showed this very clearly. The "no-frills" approach used by WestJet appears to be the wave of the future. Other individuals have come to the same conclusion and are starting up new companies so they can get a piece of the action. For example, in 2002 Michel Leblanc, who made Royal Airlines profitable before it was bought out by Canada 3000, started a new company called Jetsgo. It offers flights from Toronto to Winnipeg; Vancouver; Sydney, Nova Scotia; and Stephenville, Newfoundland and Labrador.

Leblanc's company is not the only new one. CanJet, which focuses on Central and Atlantic Canada, started operations in mid-2002. Air Canada introduced its own new airline called Tango in November 2001. It is designed to lower Air Canada's high labour costs and win back the market share Air Canada has lost to WestJet in recent years. Tango represents 10 percent of Air Canada's domestic capacity and was already using 21 aircraft to serve 23 cities in the summer of 2002.

The start up of so many new airline companies is not the only change evident in the airline industry. Another major change involves commissions for travel agents. Historically, the airlines paid travel agents up to $70 for each ticket they booked. But airlines were looking for ways to cut costs, and travel agent commissions were a tempting target. Early in 2002, several U.S. airlines announced that they were no longer going to pay commissions to travel agents for booking tickets. Air Canada decided to stop paying commissions on April 22, 2002. This change will cause many travel agencies to go out of business and will force others to start charging customers for a service that used to be provided free. Travel agents are now charging up to $100 to book a ticket.

It appears that the only constant in the airline business is change.

Questions

1. Briefly describe the six steps in the strategic management process. Identify the decisions that Air Canada and WestJet made for each of the steps, and how these decisions were either similar or different.

2. What is the difference between corporate-level strategy and competitive strategy? Compare and contrast the corporate-level and competitive strategies that have been adopted by Air Canada and WestJet.

3. Explain how each of the factors in Porter's five forces model has affected Air Canada and WestJet.

4. Do a SWOT analysis for Air Canada and WestJet.

WestJet
www.westjet.com

CASE STUDY 7-2

It's a "Good Thing" to Have a Well-Known Brand Name

Very few new companies begin the initial public offering (IPO) stage of their history with the brand identity of Martha Stewart Omnimedia (MSO). On the day of her company's IPO, Martha Stewart came to Wall Street to serve croissants, muffins, and scrambled egg brioches to startled traders on the floor of the stock exchange. By the end of the day, Stewart's small company (only 385 employees) had raised U.S.$2.3 billion in working capital. The question is, with its newfound capital, does MSO have the strategy required to gain and sustain competitive success?

Stewart describes her firm as a leading creator of how-to content and related products and services for homemakers and other consumers. The firm's prospectus makes clear that MSO intends to leverage the well-known Martha Stewart name to gain access to key promotional and distribution channels.

Stewart's business is built around seven core content areas: home, entertainment and cooking, gardening, crafts, holidays, keeping, and weddings. For each of these areas, the MSO team puts together a library of articles, books, television programs, newspaper columns, radio segments, and products. The firm has two strategic objectives:

■ Provide original how-to content and information to as many consumers as possible.

■ Turn consumers into doers by offering them the information and products they need for do-it-yourself ingenuity, the "Martha Stewart way."

MSO distributes its content through a broad media platform that includes two magazines, an Emmy Award-winning television program, a weekly TV segment on *CBS This Morning*, a daily cable TV program, a weekly syndicated newspaper column, a radio program, periodic primetime television broadcasts, and (to date) 27 how-to books. Stewart's two magazines alone, *Martha Stewart Living* and *Martha Stewart Weddings*, have an estimated readership of 9.9 million per month. MSO also has a website that now boasts close to 1 million registered users.

In addition to its impressive communication outlets, the company also has created what it calls its "omni-merchandising" platform. The platform consists of products with the Martha Stewart name. At the time of the IPO, the company had more than 2800 distinct variations of products, including bed and bath products, interior paints, craft kits, outdoor furniture, and garden tools, as well as a line of branded products sold at Kmart. Products are also marketed through national department stores, the upscale catalogue *Martha by Mail*, and the on-line store.

Although Stewart's brand name has given her firm a great start, to sustain advantage MSO plans to position itself as "a leading authority across key categories of domestic arts." To accomplish this goal, the firm plans to capitalize on what it sees as a number of key strengths besides its brand name: a highly experienced team of creative and business personnel; strong relationships with key distribution, fulfillment, and marketing channels; an extensive research and development process; and an extensive library of high-quality products and designs.

The firm is not comfortable resting on its existing reputation but has very specific strategies to build revenue over the next few years. These strategies include plans to expand the company's merchandising along its core content lines, amortize the cost of developing high-quality content by sharing it across media and merchandising platforms, exploit the revenue potential of the internet, and cross-sell and promote its brands.

One of MSO's strategies is somewhat controversial. The firm has publicly stated that it plans to "evolve our brands through team-based content and reduce dependence on our founder." Some analysts feel it is dangerous to remind the market of Stewart's mortality since so much of the promotional strategy depends on her many media appearances. The company has taken out a U.S.$67-million life insurance policy to reduce its exposure to risk in the event that it loses Stewart for any reason. This move has also made some investors edgy. At age 58, Stewart is only 7 years away from the time the average person retires. To signal her commitment to the firm, Stewart has signed a five-year contract. Currently, Martha Stewart owns 70 percent of the outstanding shares of MSO.

Consumer companies generally face tremendous pressure. First, consumer preferences can be unpredictable. Fads like Furbys and Pokémon are nearly impossible to predict. There has also been significant consolidation in retail distribution channels. The risk here is that in losing one key distributor, MSO could lose several chains of stores. Further, MSO's competitors will not sit still. Each will work to find ways to throw MSO off track.

Stewart's new publicly traded firm was originally off to a great start. She clearly had a well-known brand name, and her slogan, "It's a good thing," is memorable. Now, MSO will have to move past image and slogans to the difficult task of effectively implementing strategy. This may be difficult given the negative publicity Martha Stewart received in the summer of 2003, when she was indicted on several counts of illegal behaviour. When this was publicized, the share price of Stewart's company dropped dramatically.

Questions

1. Which of the generic corporate strategies seems best to describe MSO? What competitive strategy does it seem to be pursuing for most of its lines?

2. Based on what you know about MSO or can find out, to what extent do the firm's activities seem to reflect a well-thought-out policy of strategic fit?

3. Perform a brief SWOT analysis for MSO.

4. Based on your results from question 2, have Stewart and her team positioned MSO so that it can gain and sustain a competitive advantage? Why or why not?

Martha Stewart Omnimedia
www.marthastewart.com

JetBlue: A Winning Strategy

In the intensely competitive airline industry, you'd better have the right strategy or it doesn't pay to open for business. Since the commercial airline business has been deregulated, dozens of Canadian and U.S. airlines have gone out of business, either because they had the wrong strategy, or less-than-competent management, or both.

In terms of its corporate level strategy, JetBlue's plan wasn't that different from the plan followed by other industry start-ups. Its management stuck to the airline business and (in terms of geography) started small, with several flights between just a few cities. It gradually pursued a geographic expansion strategy, and contemplated new routes to U.S. and Canadian cities. The basic idea is to take care of all of its airplane servicing in-house, but for now contractors at some airports (such as JFK in New York) handle JetBlue's servicing.

It is with respect to its competitive strategy that JetBlue really distinguished itself. Most companies opt to be either a differentiator, a low-cost leader, or a focuser. In the airline industry, for instance, American Airlines tries to be a differentiator by doing things like offering its passengers strong internet support and a strong frequent-flier program. WestJet is a low-cost leader. Every decision WestJet makes—from the routes it chooses to the planes it flies—is aimed at minimizing costs so it can pass the savings onto passengers. Other airlines (such as the small airlines that specialize in emergency medical evacuations) focus on serving very specific niche markets.

In terms of competitive strategy, JetBlue seems to be following a hybrid approach. It seeks to combine the advantages of being a low-cost leader with the kind of high-quality service you'd expect to find only on major, differentiator airlines such as Air Canada and American Airlines. JetBlue keeps cost down by flying new, low-maintenance planes, eliminating meals, training teams of employees to turn aircraft around quickly, and flying only one type of aircraft so that all pilots and crew can easily switch from plane to plane. At the same time, JetBlue aims to provide, not "cut-rate," but top-notch service for its passengers (for example, leather seats, each with its own TV monitor). JetBlue's Airbus seats are also wider than most Boeing economy class seats.

Managers carefully select and train employees to provide upbeat, courteous service. As with the majors, passengers flying JetBlue get reserved seats. (You don't get your seat assignment at the airport, as on some low-cost airlines, such as Tango and Southwest). And, while JetBlue eliminated meals, it does provide baskets of unlimited snacks (including blue potato chips, made from "natural blue potatoes").

This competitive strategy has worked well so far, but the competition is becoming much more fierce. When JetBlue was "not on the radar screens" of competitors, it had the low-cost flights from some airports pretty much to itself. However, its own success has increased the attention that it is getting from its competitors. David Neeleman therefore knows that he's going to have to monitor events very carefully to make sure, among other things, that his "quality service/low-cost" hybrid competitive strategy doesn't become difficult to maintain.

Assignment

You and your team are consultants to Mr. Neeleman, who is depending on your management expertise to help navigate the launch and management of JetBlue. Here's what he wants to know from you:

1. Develop a vision and mission statement for JetBlue.
2. On a single sheet of paper, write the outline of a workable strategic plan for JetBlue.
3. Identify JetBlue's current corporate strategies, and list its strategic options.
4. Identify JetBlue's core competencies.
5. List the strategic planning tools you think JetBlue should use and explain why.

Scenario Planning

These are uncertain times for businesses, and companies are trying hard to stay ahead of sudden, unpleasant surprises. Scenario planning is one tool that companies use to try to stay prepared for the future. It involves asking how some hypothetical situation could come about and what alternatives exist for coping with the situation. Scenario planning means spending time and money imagining things that *might* happen. The Royal Bank of Canada and Finning are just two companies that use scenario planning. At companies like these, managers are asked to contemplate scenarios that are actually unlikely, but that, if they happened, would seriously threaten the company.

Many business firms are exploring alternatives to traditional forecasting techniques, but some of the most ground-breaking work has been done at oil companies. As far back as the 1970s (when oil shortages were common), Shell Oil executives wondered what would happen if there were too much oil. So, they asked all of their divisions around the world to think about what would happen to the company if an oil glut developed. In fact, an oil glut did occur in the 1980s and prices dropped. During that period, Shell moved up from the seventh position to the second position in the world oil business, cut its inventories, and saved $2 billion. A lot of the credit was given to the managers who had used scenario planning to think about an unlikely outcome like an oil glut.

The idea in scenario planning is *not* to pick one specific scenario, but rather to consider a variety of possibilities. As one executive says, "If you can think of a scenario that will put you out of business, you should think about how you would cope with it. You should be ready to change plans if one of your worst nightmares comes true."

Scenario planning isn't just for oil companies. Vancouver-based Finning also does scenario planning. It asks questions like "What if a price war broke out? How would we respond?" The idea is to avoid being blindsided. Finning is spending $750 million to buy an equipment rental company because various scenarios pointed them in the direction of renting equipment rather than buying it.

Mike Walsh is an entrepreneur who is betting that scenario planning is going to be a big deal before long. He has developed software for scenario planning and is currently using it to help government agencies make decisions. He thinks that private sector companies will also be willing to pay for this software.

Some people don't want to think about the difficulties of planning in an uncertain world. Others argue that when situations are very uncertain, planning does not make sense. But the fact is that planning becomes even more crucial as uncertainty increases, so more and more companies are likely to adopt scenario planning. John Aitken, the vice president of risk analysis at the Royal Bank, says that the trick is to find a tool that helps you cope with uncertainty. The more often turmoil defeats traditional planning, the more likely it is that companies will use scenario planning.

Questions

1. What are the steps in the basic planning process? Where does scenario planning fit in to the basic planning process?

2. How is contingency planning different from scenario planning? How is it similar?

3. What are the benefits of planning? How do these relate to scenario planning?

4. What is the difference between qualitative and quantitative planning techniques? Where does scenario planning fit into this scheme?

5. Consider this statement: "When a situation is very uncertain and unpredictable, it doesn't make any sense to waste time planning." Do you agree or disagree? Explain.

Video Resource: "Scenario Planning," *Venture* #824, (April 24, 2002).

Spin Master Ltd.

In 1993, Anton Rabie and a couple of friends from business school began manufacturing the Earth Buddy—a sawdust and grass-seed-filled novelty that competed with products like Chia Pet. The firm had some early successes selling Earth Buddies to large Canadian retail operations like Zellers. Then the U.S. retail giant Kmart indicated that they would like to place an order for half a million units. Although Anton did not have a firm purchase order in hand, he decided to take the risk and began manufacturing hundreds of thousands of Earth Buddies in the hope that Kmart would actually send in an order. To achieve the production volume that was required, Anton had to hire an additional 140 people and had to manage a production system that was producing at a far higher level than anything the company had experienced before.

What has happened to Anton's company since 1993? Well, the news is very positive. The company eventually got the Kmart order and made $500 000 profit from it. By the end of 1998, the company—now called Spin Master Ltd.—was selling several different lines of toys, and its annual sales had reached the $10 million mark. During December 1998, Spin Master had another mega-Christmas-hit toy on its hands, and Anton was scrambling to try to fill orders from retailers across North America who were desperate to stock the product on their shelves. The product was Air Hogs, a toy plane powered by compressed air that is manufactured in China. Spin Master never planned for a toy that would be so in demand, so the company has had to dramatically increase output at the Chinese factory where it is made.

In February 1999 Spin Master took part in the Toy Fair in New York City. The idea was to push the toys that Spin Master was selling and to look for new toy ideas. The latest product (an obvious extension of Air Hogs) is an air-pressure-powered toy car, which Spin Master demonstrated to retailers at the Toy Fair.

Wal-Mart, Toys 'R' Us, and Price-Costco all expressed a lot of interest in the various air-powered toys that Spin Master has available.

Yet another twist has developed. Spin Master is now looking at a water-powered rocket that uses the same basic propulsion idea as the air-powered cars and airplanes. Toys 'R' Us thinks it can sell a couple of million units of the water-powered rocket. It wants a partnership with Spin Master and will commit to an Air Hogs toy section in its retail outlets. Sales for these products could reach $50 million to $60 million. That scale would be far greater than anything Spin Master has seen so far. Anton's dream is to have an Air Hogs section in every toy store.

In December 1999, Spin Master produced yet another hit toy. This one was called finger bikes, which are miniature (collectible) models of real bikes. Anton Rabie is always looking for that next hit toy product. So far, he has been very successful.

Questions

1. Is Anton Rabie making programmed or non-programmed decisions? Explain.

2. Describe the three activities that are required in the strategic planning process. What kinds of things would Anton Rabie need to do at Spin Master Ltd. to complete these steps?

3. Explain the concept of environmental scanning and the six key factors in the environment of business firms. Which of these factors are likely to be most important for Spin Master Ltd.?

4. Six different corporate-level strategies are described in the text. Which of these strategies best describes Spin Master's approach? Explain.

Video Resource: "High Flyers," *Venture* #739 (February 15, 2000).

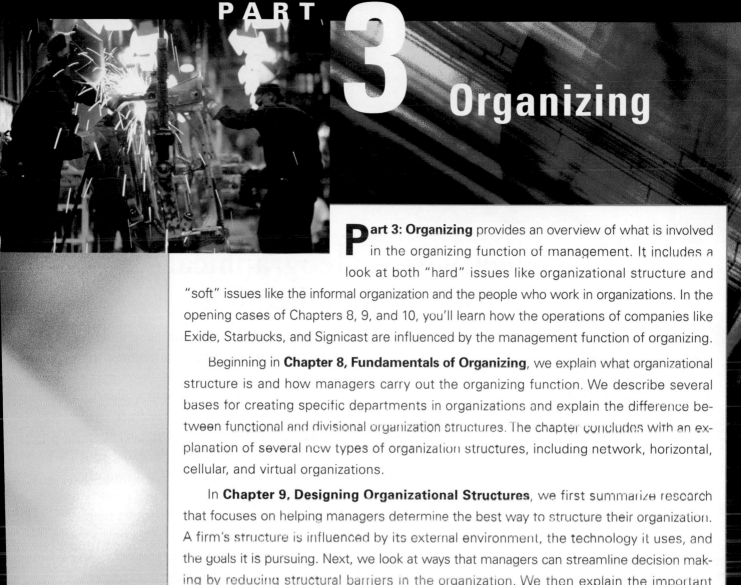

PART 3 Organizing

Part 3: Organizing provides an overview of what is involved in the organizing function of management. It includes a look at both "hard" issues like organizational structure and "soft" issues like the informal organization and the people who work in organizations. In the opening cases of Chapters 8, 9, and 10, you'll learn how the operations of companies like Exide, Starbucks, and Signicast are influenced by the management function of organizing.

Beginning in **Chapter 8, Fundamentals of Organizing**, we explain what organizational structure is and how managers carry out the organizing function. We describe several bases for creating specific departments in organizations and explain the difference between functional and divisional organization structures. The chapter concludes with an explanation of several new types of organization structures, including network, horizontal, cellular, and virtual organizations.

In **Chapter 9, Designing Organizational Structures**, we first summarize research that focuses on helping managers determine the best way to structure their organization. A firm's structure is influenced by its external environment, the technology it uses, and the goals it is pursuing. Next, we look at ways that managers can streamline decision making by reducing structural barriers in the organization. We then explain the important concept of coordination and what managers can do to coordinate the various tasks that must be completed. We conclude by describing the nature of authority and how managers can effectively delegate authority.

This section concludes with **Chapter 10, Staffing and Human Resource Management**, which focuses on the process of mobilizing people—the most valuable asset in an organization. We discuss the key elements in human resource management, including planning for human resources, staffing the organization, developing and compensating the workforce, and providing human resource services.

Fundamentals of Organizing

OBJECTIVES

Product Versus Geographical Departmentalization

Exide Corp. is the world's largest producer of automotive and industrial batteries. In 2000, the company introduced a major structural change in an attempt to reverse a trend of decreasing profitability. The change involved shifting from geographical to product departmentalization. Previously, Exide's structure consisted of about ten "country organizations." The head of each country organization had considerable latitude to make decisions that were best for that person's country. It also meant that each country manager focused on products that were marketable in that country. But geographical departmentalization also motivated country managers to export into each other's territory and to undercut one another's prices. Thus, Exide was competing against itself on price. As Exide then-CEO, Robert Lutz, said, "the guys were poking each other in the eye."

So, the company decided to introduce product departmentalization. Global business units were formed to oversee the company's various product lines such as car and industrial batteries. The focus would now be on products, not on geography. But before long it was clear that the new system had problems of its own. For example, when Exide made an acquisition, some top executive got upset when their unit was made subordinate to the newly acquired unit. It wasn't long before Exide was tinkering with its organization chart again.

Exide's experience is typical of companies that are trying to answer a fundamental organizing question: Is it better to organize by products or by geography? The answer? Either approach can cause problems if taken to an extreme. If a company organizes by product, it can standardize manufacturing, introduce new products around the world faster, and eliminate overlapping activities. But if too much emphasis is placed on product and not enough on geography, a company is likely to find that local decision making is slowed, pricing flexibility is reduced, and products are not tailored to the needs of a specific country's customers.

Ford Motor Co. experienced exactly these problems when it decided to move toward the product model. It combined its functional departments and its geographical areas into one global product-based automotive operation. Although the reorganization saved the company U.S.$5 billion in its first few years of operation, Ford's market share declined from 12.7 percent in 1995 to 8.8 percent in 2000. This is precisely what we would expect to happen when too much emphasis is placed on product departmentalization. Ford responded to this drop in market share by giving executives in various regions more authority to decide what types of vehicles were best for their local market. In other words, it moved back a bit toward the geographical model.

Procter & Gamble also had problems after it replaced country organizations with global business units that were organized around product categories like paper goods, feminine protection, and beauty care. The reorganization was introduced by new CEO Durk Jager in an attempt to globalize P&G brands like Tide, Pampers, and Crest. But the reorganization caused great upheaval within the company as thousands of employees shifted into new jobs. As many as half of all company executives took on new roles. In addition, the company's announcement that it planned to cut 15 000 jobs worldwide alarmed many employees. CEO Jager left the company just 17 months into his job.

It's not easy to strike the proper balance between geographical and product departmentalization.

Exide
www.exideworld.com

Procter and Gamble
www.pg.com

Organizing and Organizational Structure

Organizing means arranging activities in such a way that they systematically contribute to the company's goals. It is the manager's job to decide how to divide the work, who does what, who reports to whom, and how to coordinate the organization's various activities. **Organizational structure** refers to the pattern of formal relationships that exists among groups and individuals in an organization. Every organization, regardless of size or function, has a structure. Organizational structure has several important dimensions: *formalization* (the number of written job descriptions, policies, and procedures that guide employee behaviour), *centralization* (how much authority is held at the various management levels in the organization), *complexity* (the number of distinctly different job titles and departments in an organization), and *specialization* (the breaking down of complex tasks into simple ones).

organizing
Arranging activities in such a way that they systematically contribute to the company's goals.

organizational structure
The pattern of formal relationships that exists among groups and individuals in an organization.

From Planning to Organizing

The organization should grow out of a plan. Consider the experience at Starbuck's. When it was small, its strategy was to offer high-quality coffee drinks through small, specialized, local coffee houses. This plan suggested the main jobs for which CEO Howard Schultz had to hire lieutenants (for example, for store management, purchasing, and finance and accounting). Departments then grew up around these tasks. As Schultz's plan evolved,

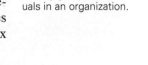
Starbucks
www.starbucks.com

so did his organization design. As Starbuck's expanded across the United States and Canada, and then overseas, he established regional divisions to oversee the stores in each area. Today, with Starbucks coffee also sold to airlines, bookstores, and supermarkets, the company's structure includes new departments to sell to and service the needs of these new markets. Schultz's organization grew out of his plan; in other words, structure follows strategy.

This structure-strategy link should always apply. Let's return to the management task we first tackled in Chapter 1—your assignment as summer tour master. As you recall, your organization's strategic mission is to plan, organize, and execute a successful trip to France. What division of labour does that imply? One way to organize (and the one we chose in Chapter 1) is to break the job into the main functions you need performed. So we put Rosa in charge of airline scheduling, Rakesh in charge of hotels, and Ruth in charge of city sites.

How would you organize if your strategic mission were different? Suppose next year your friends put you in charge of simultaneously planning several trips—to England, Sweden, and the south of France. Your organization's strategic mission has therefore changed, too. It is now to plan, organize, and execute three successful trips, and to do so more or less simultaneously. How would you organize now? Perhaps you'd put each of last year's trusted lieutenants in charge of a country (say, Rosa for England, Rakesh for Sweden, and Ruth for the South of France). You'd then have a sort of "regional" organization. Each lieutenant might in turn hire friends to arrange for airline tickets, hotels, and sights to see. Again, the tasks you need done, and thus how you organize, have flowed logically from your plan.

Authority and the Chain of Command

The usual way of depicting the formal organization is with an organization chart, such as the one shown in Figure 8.1. **Organization charts** include the title of each manager's position and, by means of connecting lines, show who is accountable to whom and who has authority for each area. The organization chart also shows the **chain of command** (sometimes called the *scalar chain* or the *line of authority*) between the top of the organization and the lowest positions in the chart. The chain of command represents the organization's hierarchy of authority. Put another way, it shows the path a directive should take in travelling from the president to employees at the bottom of the organization chart or from employees at the bottom to the top of the organization chart.

Authority is a central concept in organizations; it refers to a person's legal right or power. In a corporation, authority stems from the owners/stockholders of the company. They elect a board of directors and authorize the board to represent the owners' interests;

organization chart
A chart that shows the structure of the organization including the title of each manager's position and, by means of connecting lines, who is accountable to whom and who has authority for each area.

chain of command
The path that a directive and/or answer or request should take through each level of an organization; also called a scalar chain or the line of authority.

authority
A person's legal right or power.

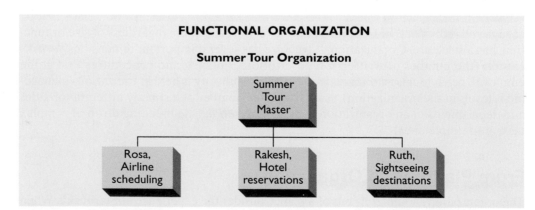

FUNCTIONAL ORGANIZATION

Summer Tour Organization

FIGURE 8.1
Functional Departmentalization
This chart shows a *functional* organization, with departments for basic functions like scheduling, reservations, and sightseeing.

therefore, the owners, through the board, are at the top of the chain of command. The board's main functions are to choose the top executives, to approve strategies and long-term plans, and to monitor performance to make sure that management is protecting the owners' interests. The board then delegates to the CEO the authority to actually run the company—to develop plans, to hire subordinate managers, and to enter into agreements (we discuss delegation in more detail in Chapter 9). This is how an organization chart and chain of command evolve.

Line and Staff Authority

In organizations, a distinction is made between line and staff authority. **Line managers** (like the president, production manager, and sales manager) have line authority. This means they are in charge of essential activities, such as sales or production, and can issue orders down the chain of command. **Staff managers** have staff (or advisory) authority, that is, they generally cannot issue orders down the chain of command (except within their own departments). They can only assist and advise line managers. Line managers run line departments, while staff managers run staff departments.

The HR manager is a good example of a staff manager. An HR manager can *advise* a production supervisor regarding the types of selection tests to use, but the HR manager cannot *order* the supervisor to hire a particular employee. On the other hand, the production supervisor's boss—the production manager—could issue such orders.

There is an exception to this rule: A staff manager may also have functional authority. **Functional authority** means that staff managers can issue orders to line managers within the very narrow limits of the staff manager's special expertise. For example, in some companies, no screening tests can be administered without the HR manager's approval. That manager then has functional authority with regard to the use of screening tests.

Some small organizations use only line managers, but most large ones have both line managers and staff managers. These are called **line-and-staff organizations.** Typical line positions include the CEO, and the managers for sales and production. Typical staff positions include the managers for marketing research, accounting, security, quality control, legal affairs, and human resources.

In Figure 8.2, the line managers are represented by solid lines and the staff managers are represented by dotted lines. In the Canadian Forces, for example, the line officers are the ones who actually engage in battle. The staff officers perform functions like military intelligence that support the activities of the line officers. At Iron Ore of Canada, the line managers oversee the extraction and marketing of iron ore. Staff managers (for example, safety officers) support the line managers by making sure that the mines are safe so that production operations can be carried out.

We can distinguish between line and staff managers if we keep in mind the goals of the particular organization. At Aluminum Company of Canada, the director of personnel is a staff manager because the personnel department supports the primary functions of producing and marketing aluminum. However, at an employment agency like Office Overload, the director of personnel is a line manager because the primary goal of that firm is to provide personnel to other firms. The legal staff at Canadian National Railways are staff people, but at a law firm like Shewchuk & Associates, they are line people.

Types of Staff Four distinct types of staff are found in organizations. **Personal staff** assist specific line managers but generally lack the authority to act for them in their absence. For example, the "assistant to the president" carries out a variety of jobs as directed by the president but does not have authority over the vice presidents. **Advisory staff** advise line managers in areas where these staff have particular expertise. For example, the legal department may advise marketing on patents. **Service staff** provide specific services to line managers. For example, the HR department interviews and tests prospective employees for various line departments. **Control staff** are responsible for controlling some aspect of the organization. A quality control inspector at Chrysler's Windsor plant is an example of control staff.

line manager
A manager who is (1) in charge of essential activities such as sales and (2) authorized to issue orders to subordinates down the chain of command.

staff manager
A manager without the authority to give orders down the chain of command (except in his or her own department); generally can only assist and advise line managers in specialized areas such as human resources management.

functional authority
Staff managers can issue orders to line managers within the very narrow limits of the staff manager's special expertise.

line-and-staff organization
An organization with both line and staff managers.

personal staff
Employees who assist specific line managers but lack the authority to act for them in their absence.

advisory staff
Employees who advise line managers in areas where these staff have particular expertise.

service staff
Staff who provide specific services to line managers, such as interviewing new applicants.

control staff
Staff who are responsible for controlling some aspect of the organization, such as quality control.

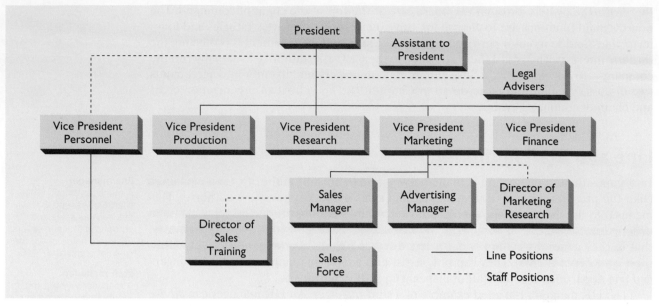

FIGURE 8.2
Typical Line-Staff Structure in a Production-Oriented Organization

The Informal Organization and Organizational Politics

informal organization
The network of interpersonal relationships and the informal way of doing things that inevitably develops in organizations.

Organizations are not always what they appear to be as depicted in their formal organization charts. One thing the organization chart does not show is the **informal organization**, which is the network of interpersonal relationships and the informal way of doing things that inevitably develops in organizations. At the New York Metropolitan Opera, for example, musicians and singers play poker during the intermissions. Hands are played quickly, with most pots in the $30–$40 range. Luciano Pavarotti, the famed tenor, once played and lost big.[1]

The existence of the informal organization means that a salesperson might call the plant manager to check the status of an order. Doing so is quicker than adhering to the chain of command, which might involve having the salesperson ask the sales manager, who in turn checks with the plant manager. The organization chart may show the president's assistant as a secretary, but as the president's gatekeeper, he or she may wield enormous influence. Effective managers know that they must exercise some healthy skepticism when reviewing a company's organization chart.

As we saw in Chapter 5, managers must also be aware of a related concept called organizational politics. Organizational politics is universal and inevitable, and it influences everything that goes on in organizations. In a study of 428 Canadian managers, 60 percent of them said that most casual talk at work was political in nature, and 70 percent said that political behaviour was common in their organizations. They also felt that managers had to be good politicians to get ahead in their organization.[2]

Because many managers feel that organizational politics is bad, they either try to ignore it or suppress it. But this approach is doomed to failure because the forces that encourage politics are so strong. These forces include *self-interest* (each person looks out for their own best interests), *limited resources* (not everyone can have what they want), and *conflicting goals* (different individuals have different visions about what the organization should do). Generally speaking, people are motivated to do things that will benefit them, but some people do not care whether their actions will have a negative effect on others. For example, consider the following situation.

Tom reports to the vice president of marketing of a large company. He is aggressive and considers himself top management material. By ingratiating himself with the vice president's secretary, he discovers that the vice president is often out of the office, apparently on matters unrelated to his work. Tom informally presents this "evidence" to certain key members of the board of directors (who just happen to belong to the same country club as Tom's father). Two months later, the vice president is fired and Tom is chosen as his replacement.

Situations like this are not uncommon, yet many managers think that they need not concern themselves with these types of things, and that if they just focus on doing a good job, they will be rewarded. Although good performance is necessary for advancement, it is not sufficient. What is also required is sensitivity to the importance of the informal organization and organizational politics. Managers who are insensitive to these informal issues often find that they have difficulties in the formal organization.

Departmentalization: Creating Departments

Every enterprise must carry out many activities to accomplish its goals. In a company, these activities might include manufacturing, selling, and accounting. In a city, they might include fire, police, and health protection. In a hospital, they might include nursing, medical services, and radiology. **Departmentalization** is the process by which the manager groups the enterprise's activities together and assigns them to subordinates; it is the organization-wide division of work. The departments—the logical groupings of activities—may also be called divisions, units, or sections, or some other similar term.

In any endeavour, the manager has to ask, "How should I divide up the work that needs to be done?" The student who takes over the student newspaper as editor-in-chief must decide (based on what he or she plans to accomplish) how to divide up the work, perhaps by appointing associate editors for advertising, production, and editorial, and letting these people grow their own departments.

Deciding the activities around which you should organize departments may not be simple. As editor-in-chief, should you organize around functions like editing, production, and sales? Or, should you appoint one lieutenant for each quarterly issue you plan to publish, and let each of these people recruit their own production, editorial, and advertising people? In managing your summer overseas tour, should you organize your people around functions such as airline scheduling and hotels, or around places such as England and the south of France? In a company, should you organize departments for sales and manufacturing? Or should there be separate departments for industrial and retail customers, each of which will then have its own sales and manufacturing units? Many options are available, each with pros and cons. The decision usually depends more on experience, logic, and common sense than on some rigid formula. Let's discuss the traditional alternatives first. Then, in Chapter 9, we'll look more closely at the factors that determine how you organize.

Organizing Departments Around Functions

Functional departmentalization is the simplest and most obvious way to organize. It means grouping activities around the enterprise's core functions, like manufacturing, sales, and finance. Figure 8.3 shows the organizational structure for the ABC car company. At ABC, each department is organized around a different business function—sales, finance, and production. The directors report to the president and carry out the sales, finance, and production functions.

The "functions" are not necessarily limited to functions such as sales and finance. In a university, the functions typically include academic affairs, business affairs, and student affairs. Banks typically have functional departments for operations, control, and loans.

departmentalization
The process by which the manager groups the enterprise's activities together and assigns them to subordinates.

functional departmentalization
Grouping activities around the enterprise's core functions.

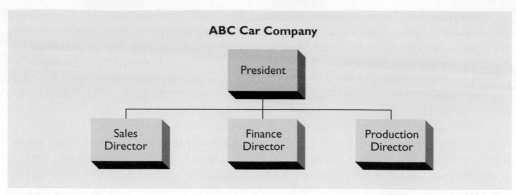

ABC Car Company

President

Sales Director · Finance Director · Production Director

FIGURE 8.3
Functional Departmentalization at ABC

Your group going to France might have one person in charge of transportation, one in charge of hotels, and another in charge of sightseeing. The basic idea of functional departmentalization is to group activities around the core functions the enterprise must carry out.

Advantages Organizing departments around functions has several advantages:

1. It is simple, obvious, and logical to build departments around the basic functions in which the enterprise must engage.

2. Functional departments are specialized departments. Departments for areas like sales, production, and finance do the same (functional) job for all the firm's products or services. This can mean economies of scale—for instance, the company can afford larger plants and efficient equipment.

3. It minimizes duplication of effort. There is only one production department (and marketing and finance department) for all the company's products.

4. It can simplify executive hiring and training. The duties of the managers running these departments are specialized (a manager may specialize in finance or production, for instance); the enterprise therefore needs fewer managers who must administer several functions at once.

5. It can facilitate top management control. Functional department managers tend to focus on just the activities that concern their own specialized functions. They often have to rely on their boss to coordinate their efforts. This makes it easier for that boss to maintain an iron grip on what's happening in the organization.

Disadvantages Functional organization also has the following disadvantages:

1. It increases the coordination required of the executive to whom the functional department heads report. Responsibility for the enterprise's overall performance for all products and services rests on the shoulders of one person, usually the CEO. The CEO may be the only one in a position to coordinate the work of the functional departments, each of which is only one element in producing and supplying the company's products or services. This may not be a problem in a small business or when a firm has just one or two products. But as size and diversity of products increase, the job of coordinating, say, production, sales, and finance for many different products may prove too great for one person. The enterprise could then lose its responsiveness.

2. It may reduce the firm's sensitivity to and service to the customer. For example, if a department store was organized nationally around the functions of merchan-

dising, purchasing, and personnel, all its Canadian stores might tend to get the same products to sell, even if the customers' tastes and needs in Vancouver were different from those in Moncton.

3. Because it fosters an emphasis on specialized managers (finance experts, production experts, and so forth), it produces fewer general managers. This can make it more difficult to cultivate managers with the breadth of experience required for general management jobs like CEO.

Functions Versus Divisions Managers traditionally have two basic choices when it comes to organizing departments. They can organize departments around functions, as we've just seen, or they can organize departments around "self-contained" divisions or purposes. For example, an editor-in-chief can appoint functional department heads for editing, production, and ads. Or, departments can be organized around some self-contained purpose, such as by appointing editors for each of the paper's three upcoming editions—fall, spring, and summer. This would be a self-contained, divisional arrangement because the spring editor, for example, would have within her department her own editorial, production, and advertising editors. This organization structure would be a **divisionalized** one.

There are four varieties of divisional, self-contained arrangements—by product, customer, marketing channel, and territory.

Organizing Departments Around Products

With **product departmentalization,** the manager organizes departments around the company's products or services, or for each family of products or services. The editor-in-chief who decided to appoint lieutenants for each of the paper's three editions was organizing around products since each edition is an identifiable product. Department heads in this arrangement are generally responsible for both producing and marketing the product or service. As with the spring edition editor, they have all the resources in their units (in this case editorial, production, and advertising editors) to get the entire product or service (the spring edition) produced and on the market.

The divisional organization in Figure 8.4 is typical. Here the CEO organized the firm's top-level departments so that each contains all the activities required to develop, manufacture, and sell a particular product (skin care, vitamins, drugs). The general manager of each division has functional departments—for production, sales, and HR—reporting to him or her. Each of these product divisions is self-contained. Each controls all the resources required to create, produce, and supply its product or products.

At Nortel Networks, former CEO Jean Monty reorganized the company into four divisions—public carrier networks (the phone companies); broadband networks (cable-TV companies and all of the long-distance companies that have sprung up since deregulation); enterprise networks (internal communication for government agencies and business firms); and wireless networks. Splitting the company into four divisions is one way to ensure that customers are not ignored. It also helps Nortel find out what customers think of the company and the products and services it produces.[3]

Advantages Divisionalization (whether by product, customer, territory, or marketing channel) has several advantages.

1. Since the product or service gets the single-minded attention of its own general manager, customers may get better, more responsive service. A general manager oversees all the functions required to produce and market each particular product or service. That general manager's division "specializes" in that product or service. Furthermore, the division manager need not rely on research, manufacturing, or sales managers who are not within that division. The net effect should be that the product or service (and its customers) get focused, more responsive attention with

---

divisionalized structure
A form of organization in which the firm's major departments are organized so that each one can manage all or most of the activities needed to develop, manufacture, and sell a particular product or product line.

product departmentalization
The firm's departments are organized around the company's products or services.

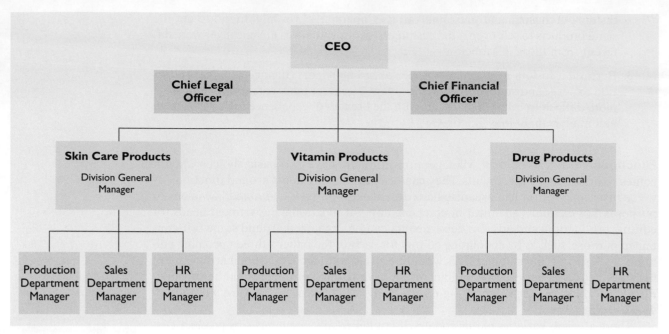

FIGURE 8.4
Divisional Organization for a Pharmaceuticals Company

this type of organization than they would in a functional organization (in which, for instance, the same sales manager must address the needs of multiple products).

2. It's easier to judge performance. If a division is (or is not) doing well, it is clear who is responsible, because one general manager is managing the whole division. This may in turn better motivate the general manager.

3. It develops general managers. Divisions can be good training grounds for an enterprise's executives, because they are "miniature companies" that expose managers to a wider range of functional issues.

4. It reduces the coordination burden on the company's CEO. In Figure 8.4, imagine if the CEO had to coordinate the tasks of designing, producing, and marketing each of the company's many products. The CEO would face an enormous diversity and number of problems. This is a mean reason why virtually all very large companies, as well as many small ones with diverse products and customers, divisionalize.[4]

Intuit
www.intuit.com

Here is how Bill Harris, then executive vice president of software company Intuit, explained his firm's reorganization:

...it was becoming clear that the bigger we got, the more being organized by functions was a liability.... The executive team had become a real bottleneck. We needed a new structure [and decided] to bust the organization apart. [Our new CEO] created eight business units, each with its own general manager and customer mission. The basic goal was to flatten the organization and fragment the decision-making process. Each business unit would be the size that Intuit had been a few years ago, and each would focus on one core product or market.

The reorganization was effective. Top management previously made or approved most product-related decisions. Now they leave these decisions to the business units, and within these units, the managers usually leave these decisions to individual product teams. With smaller, product-oriented divisions that are closer to their customers, Intuit is now more responsive and effective at serving its customers, and at responding to and managing change.[5]

Disadvantages Organizing around divisions can also produce disadvantages:

1. It creates duplication of effort. Being self-contained is a two-edged sword. The very fact that each product-oriented unit is self-contained implies that each unit has its own production plants, sales force, and so on.

2. It may diminish top management's control. At Intuit, the business units now make decisions that top management used to make. With top management making fewer of the day-to-day decisions, the business units have more autonomy. The net effect is that top management tends to have less control over day-to-day activities in divisionalized firms. A division might, for instance, run up excessive expenses before top management discovers that there is a problem. Striking a balance between providing each division with enough autonomy, while maintaining top management control is the central issue in organizing in this way.

3. It requires more managers with general management abilities. Each product division is a miniature company, with its own production plant, sales force, personnel department, and so forth. This means these firms must work diligently to identify and develop managers with general management potential.

4. It can breed compartmentalization. One problem with any type of divisionalization is that establishing semi-autonomous units can inhibit the spread of innovation from one division to another.

This latter problem occurred at toiletries marketer Caswell Massey. For many years, the firm had been organized around "marketing channels," with their catalogue, retail, and wholesale channels run as separate businesses. CEO Ann Robinson says that the various channels were oblivious to what the others were doing. "Retail wasn't listening to catalogue and vice versa. The items featured on the catalogue's cover were not necessarily in the store window. There was little synergy between brands." Part of her solution was to start marketing Caswell Massey's products on a more unified basis, coordinating the marketing effort among the channels.[6]

Organizing Departments Around Customers

Customer departmentalization is used when an organization wants to focus on the needs of specific types of customers. A firm selling electronics equipment might departmentalize on the basis of consumer, government, and industrial buyers (see Figure 8.5).

The advantages and disadvantages of customer departmentalization parallel those of product departmentalization. For example, with one manager and unit focused on the customer, customers can expect faster, more satisfactory service than they'd get with a functional structure, particularly when customers' needs are diverse.

As with product departmentalization, duplication of effort may also occur here. The company may have several production plants instead of one and several sales managers, each serving the needs of specific customers. This may reduce overall corporate efficiency.

customer departmentalization
Generally self-contained departments are organized to serve the needs of specific groups of customers.

Organizing Departments Around Marketing Channels

With **marketing-channel departmentalization**, management organizes the departments around each of the firm's marketing channels (instead of products or customers). A **marketing channel** is the conduit (wholesaler, drugstore, grocery, or the like) through which a manufacturer distributes its products to its ultimate customers. That is how Caswell Massey was organized.

This approach is slightly different from customer departmentalization (see Figure 8.6). Customer-oriented departments (such as for industrial customers, retail customers, and municipal customers) traditionally market and manufacture their own products for their customers. Marketing-channel departments typically market the same product (such

marketing-channel departmentalization
An arrangement in which departments of an organization focus on particular marketing channels, such as drugstores or grocery stores.

marketing channel
A conduit through which a manufacturer distributes its products to its ultimate customers.

as Ivory soap) through two or more channels (such as drug stores and grocery stores). Management therefore usually chooses one department to manufacture the product for all the marketing-channel departments.

Managers use this structure when it's important to cater to each marketing channel's unique needs. For example, Revlon sells through department stores and discount drugstores, and the demands of these two channels are quite different. The department store may want Revlon to supply specially trained salespeople to run concessions in its stores, while the discount druggist may just want quick delivery and minimal inventory. Putting a manager and department in charge of each channel helps ensure that Revlon meets these diverse needs quickly and satisfactorily. As in product and customer departmentalization, the resulting duplication—in this case, of sales forces—is the main disadvantage. Better serving the marketing channel's needs is the main advantage.

Organizing Departments Around Geographic Areas

With **geographic,** or **territorial, departmentalization**, the manager establishes separate departments for each of the territories in which the enterprise does business. Each divi-

Revlon
www.revlon.com

geographic (territorial) departmentalization
An arrangement in which managers establish separate departments for each of the territories in which the firm does business.

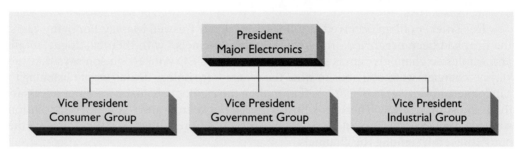

 FIGURE 8.5
Departmentalization by Customer

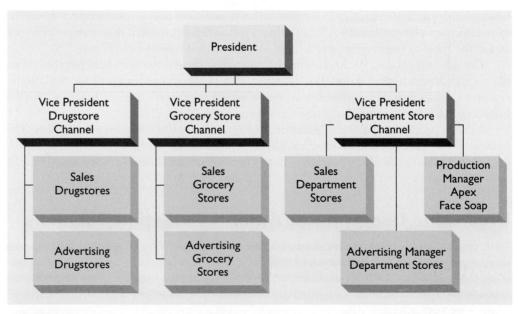

 FIGURE 8.6
Marketing-Channel Departmentalization
With marketing channels, the main departments are organized to focus on particular marketing channels, such as drugstores and grocery stores. **Note:** Only the department store channel produces the soap, and each channel may sell to the same ultimate consumers.

sion may have its own production, sales, and personnel activities. For example, the Personal Services Division of Montreal Trust is organized around four regions—Atlantic, Quebec, Central, and BC/Western regions. Regional vice presidents in the marketing function at Air Canada are organized into western, central, eastern, Atlantic Canada, United States, and European regions.

Again, the advantages and disadvantages parallel those of product or customer departmentalization. Geographic departmentalization can help ensure quick, responsive reaction to the needs of the company's clients. On the other hand, it may also lead to duplicate production and other facilities, and compartmentalization of knowledge.

Organizing geographically grew in popularity as firms expanded across national borders. Years ago, when relatively limited communications made it difficult to take the pulse of consumer needs or monitor operations abroad, it made sense to let local managers run their regional or country businesses as more or less autonomous companies. However, two trends are making this structure less popular today. First, information technology is reducing the impediments to cross-border communication. Internet-based videoconferencing, email, fax, and computerized monitoring of operations means that executives in Canada can now easily keep their finger on the pulse of operations around the world.

Second, global competition is so intense that firms can't afford to miss an opportunity to quickly transfer product improvements from one region to another. For example, if a company's Japan office discovers a new way to formulate a product or service, the company will want to make sure the improvement is also quickly applied to the firm's other international operations. A geographic structure, with its relatively compartmentalized country divisions, may hamper such dissemination of ideas.

Many firms are therefore switching from geographic to product organizations (review chapter opening case on p. 232). Heinz CEO William Johnson said he was ending the company's system of managing by country or region.[7] Instead, Heinz will organize by products or categories; managers in the United States will then work with those in Europe, Asia, and other regions to apply the best ideas from one region to another. Procter & Gamble also has a new organization. The new structure eliminates its four regional business units; seven new executives each manage product groups like baby care, beauty, and fabric and home care for all regions. The company believes the reorganization will speed decision making and send products to market faster.[8]

Heinz
www.heinz.com

When John Hunkin became the CEO of the Canadian Imperial Bank of Commerce (CIBC), he immediately began to reorganize the bank, cut costs, and flatten the management structure. At CIBC, there have been two distinct parts of the business—the conservative and traditional retail/commercial banking side, and the more volatile investment banking side. Hunkin wanted to break down the walls between these two areas. He did so by drawing on managers from both areas in his new plans. CIBC is now organized around product lines like other Canadian banks.[9]

The U.S. Immigration and Naturalization Service (INS) had a similar problem. Organized geographically, it was apparent after 9/11 that the geographically compartmentalized INS was not focusing enough on functions like immigration enforcement. Each area INS manager had his or her own applications processing and enforcement units, and there was relatively little focus on enforcement at the national level. The government felt it needed a stronger and more concerted national emphasis on functions like enforcement. Therefore, one of the internal INS reorganizations under consideration was a move from geography to functions. Functions would include immigration services (for processing applications) and immigration enforcement (such as guarding borders).[10]

Creating Matrix Organizations

Sometimes managers want to leave employees in, say, their specialized functional departments, but also have those employees focus on particular projects, products, or customers. This can be accomplished by using a matrix organization. A **matrix organization** is an organization structure in which employees are permanently attached to one department but simultaneously have ongoing assignments to project, customer, product, or geographic unit heads.[11]

matrix organization
An organization structure in which employees are permanently attached to one department but simultaneously have ongoing assignments to project, customer, product, or geographic unit heads.

The project management form of organization is widely used for the construction of large ships like this icebreaker.

Figure 8.7 illustrates this concept. Management organized the firm's automotive products division functionally, with departments for production, engineering, and personnel. However, in this case, each of the firm's big customers had special new-product needs that required attention. Management therefore established three product groups—one for the Ford project, one for the Chrysler project, and one for the GM project. Each of these product groups has its own product manager, or project leader. One or more employees from each functional department (like production and engineering) is temporarily assigned to each project. Employees report to both their functional and customer-product heads.

Vancouver Shipyards specializes in the custom building and repair of icebreakers, research vessels, ferries, tugs, and barges. Construction periods for ships vary from four months to two years. Each ship is treated as a project that is overseen by a project manager (PM). The PM is responsible for devel-

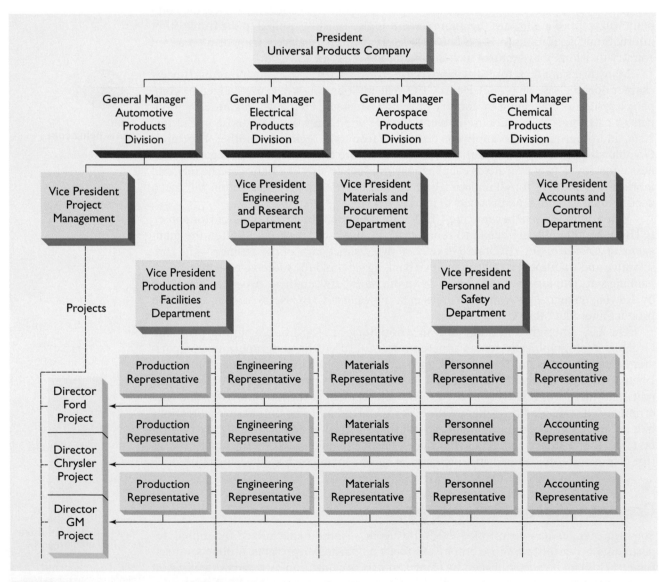

FIGURE 8.7
Matrix Departmentalization
With a matrix organization, a project structure is often superimposed over a functional organization.

oping the master schedule for the building of the ship. The workers that actually build the ship report to their own line supervisor. If the supervisor and the PM disagree about something, they can appeal to their common superior (the superintendent). If the disagreement is about how many workers should be assigned to the project, the PM usually prevails, but if the disagreement is about something like trade practices, the supervisor usually prevails.[12]

Another example of matrix management is described in the "People Side of Managing" box below.

The matrix organization is used extensively by Canadian firms, although it is much less common than the functional structure. It is very likely to be used in the construction of hydroelectric generating stations like those developed by Hydro-Québec on the La Grande River and those developed by Manitoba Hydro on the Nelson River. When the generating station is complete, it becomes part of the traditional structure of the provincial hydroelectric utility.

In some firms, the matrix structure is combined with customer and geographic departmentalization.[13] For example, many banks are organized geographically, with separate

Hydro-Québec
www.hydroquebec. com

Manitoba Hydro
www.hydro.mb.ca

The project organization structure is typically used in construction projects like the Nelson River hydro-electric generating station in northern Manitoba.

officers and employees attached to the bank's offices in France or the United Kingdom. Employees in each region simultaneously report to project heads for major customers. Thus, project heads for, say, IBM lead teams (comprising of bank employees from each country) who concentrate on the local and worldwide financial interests of IBM. Bank employees in each country report to both their country managers and their project managers.

J.P. Morgan uses a matrix structure. Managers around the world answer to two bosses: their regional head and the head of their product area. For example, a J.P. Morgan investment banking manager in Mexico City would report to both her investment banking head back in New York, and to Eduardo Cepeda, who heads J.P. Morgan's Mexico City office.[14]

Some matrix organizations are more permanent than others. Sometimes temporary project managers just provide coordination across functional departments for some project or customer. Other firms add a permanent administrative system (including, for instance, project employee appraisal forms) to help emphasize the project's importance.[15] Many firms (including Citicorp, TRW Systems, NASA, UNICEF, and various accounting, law, and security firms) have used matrix management successfully.[16]

Advantages and Disadvantages To some extent, matrix management provides the best of both worlds. It gives employees the stability and benefits of belonging to permanent departments. And it gives the firm most of the advantages of having units and employees focused on specific projects, products, or customers. Thus, the J.P. Morgan investment banker can continually tap the expertise of her investment banking colleagues, while also focusing on the needs of her local Mexico City clients.

However, matrix organization also has some special drawbacks:

- *Confusion.* Having two bosses can cause confusion. Dual reporting lines are appropriate only "for complex tasks and uncertain environments" where ambiguity is a reasonable price to pay for dealing with rapid change.[17]

- *Power struggles and conflicts.* The issue of "who's in charge of what" tends to be more ambiguous in matrix organizations. Therefore, struggles between the managers who head the functional and project groups may be more common than in traditional organizations.

- *Lost time.* Matrix organizations tend to have more inter- and intra-group meetings, which can be time-consuming.

- *Excessive overhead.* Matrix organizations may raise costs, because hiring dual sets of managers (functional and project) raises overhead.

Departmentalization in Practice: A Hybrid

In practice, most organizations use multiple bases of departmentalization. No one form of departmentalization meets the needs of all firms as diverse as Bell Canada, Bristol Aerospace, Canada Customs and Revenue Agency, The Bay, or Saskatchewan Telephones. The organization of a firm illustrates how multiple bases of departmentalization can be used within one organization (see Figure 8.8). At the top (divisional) level, departments are organized mainly on the basis of the customers the firm sells to. Within the personal services division, functional departmentalization is used, while the branch offices in the personal services division are departmentalized on a territorial basis.

Managers mix the types of departmentalization for three reasons. One is hierarchical. If the top-level departments are based on, say, products, then each product department will probably have subsidiary departments for functions like sales and manufacturing.

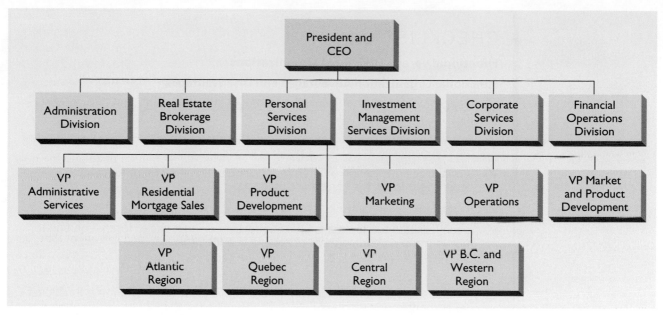

FIGURE 8.8
Combination Departmentalization

The second is efficiency. Product, customer, and territorial departments tend to result in duplicate sales, manufacturing, and other functional departments. One way to minimize this source of inefficiency is to have a single production department serving multiple customer departments.

The third is common sense. Departmentalizing is still more an art then a science. Managers don't arrive at organization structures through a mathematical formula. A variety of factors including what management plans to achieve and the unique needs of the firm's customers, territories, and products all influence the decision.

Now, let's return to your summer tour organization and apply these ideas. Assume that your summer tour organizing fame has spread, and more of your friends want to join your tours. You're now heading into your third summer tour. What started as a simple first-year mission—to plan, organize, and execute a successful trip to France—has blossomed into much more. You now have tour groups going to France, England, Greece, Hong Kong, Nepal, and Japan, and they're all leaving at about the same time. You stand to personally earn almost $20 000 if all goes well. However, you have to decide how you should organize and who should do what.

As you will recall, organizing your first summer tour was relatively straightforward. You broke the task into the main functions you needed performed. You therefore put Rosa in charge of airline scheduling, Rakesh in charge of hotels, and Ruth in charge of city sites. The second year's tour got more complicated. You were now in charge of simultaneously planning several trips (to England, to Sweden, and to the south of France). You decided on a divisional allocation of duties. You put each of last year's trusted lieutenants in charge of a country (Rosa for England, Rakesh for Sweden, and Ruth for the south of France). You had a regional organization. Each lieutenant in turn hired people to arrange for airline tickets, hotels, and sights to see. But how should you arrange your now much-more-complicated worldwide tours?

One way to decide is to determine how last year's regional organization worked. From your point of view, the organization was good, but not perfect. Everyone was happy with his or her vacation, which is certainly your main criterion. Rosa, Rakesh, and Ruth each did a fine job of seeing to it that everything went smoothly within each of "their" countries. However, there were two problems. First, Rosa, Rakesh, and Ruth were so on top of the detailed planning for their countries that you felt you were often out of the loop. The advantage was, they did their own planning without using up much of your time, but that

CHECKLIST 8.1

Functional Versus Divisional Organizations

Functional Organization Advantages and Disadvantages:

- ☑ It is simple, obvious, and logical to build departments around the basic functions that the enterprise must carry out.

- ☑ Functional departments are specialized. This can mean economies of scale since the company can afford larger plants and efficient equipment.

- ☑ It minimizes duplication of effort. For example, there is one production department for all the company's products.

- ☑ It can simplify executive hiring and training.

- ☑ It can facilitate the top manager's control by making it easier for that person to maintain an iron grip on what's happening in the organization.

But,

- ☑ It increases the coordination workload on the executive to whom the functional department heads report.

- ☑ It may reduce the firm's sensitivity to and service to the customer.

- ☑ It produces fewer general managers.

Divisional Organization Advantages and Disadvantages:

- ☑ Because the product or service gets the single-minded attention of its own general manager and unit, its customers may get better, more responsive service.

- ☑ It's easier to judge performance.

- ☑ It develops general managers.

- ☑ It reduces the coordination burden for the company's CEO.

But,

- ☑ It duplicates efforts.

- ☑ It may diminish top management's control. A division might, for instance, run up excessive expenses before top management discovers there's a problem.

- ☑ It requires more managers with general management abilities.

- ☑ It can breed compartmentalization Establishing semi-autonomous units can inhibit the spread of innovation from one division to another.

---

was a disadvantage, too. If they had gotten you more involved, you'd have scheduled more time in London, and less in Oxford, for instance.

Second, there was a lot of compartmentalized decision making by country. For example, instead of everyone buying discounted tickets via London from British Air, Rosa, Rakesh, and Ruth each made their own plane reservations. They ended up spending a lot more then they would have if ticket purchasing had been a separate, specialized function.

What does this tell you about how to organize for the upcoming worldwide tours? What would you do? Going back to a pure functional structure doesn't seem to be the way to go. You would like to supply some oversight for each country's plans, and make suggestions when they're relevant. However, getting into the nitty-gritty of coordinating the travel plans to and within five different countries would exceed your knowledge, time, and capabilities. On the other hand, going back to a pure divisional organization, by country, won't work either. You want to be able to exercise more oversight regarding the details of each country manager's plans than you did last year. And someone must ensure that your groups can use their total buying power to get the best possible deal on the tickets.

Organizationally, you decide to make three changes. First, you appoint experienced people from last summer's tour to head up each of the tours to France, England, Greece, Hong Kong, Nepal, and Japan. You therefore have a regional division structure. Second, you appoint Ruth, who's done a stellar job the past two years, to head up a separate Shared Services Department. She and her assistant will do all the actual negotiating and purchasing of airline, hotel, and other travel services for all the tours. Figure 8.9 shows your new organization chart. Third, you institute a new formal planning system. Henceforth, the country tour division heads need to work out detailed daily itineraries and submit them to you (and Ruth) for approval by March 1. That gives you an opportunity to fine-tune each itinerary. And, once you approve the plans, Ruth can get the best prices on air, hotel, and travel services. Your worldwide tours organization is off and running.

Tall and Flat Organizations and the Span of Control

Establishing departments is not the only organizational task the manager faces. Managers also have to decide what their span of control is going to be. That will in turn determine whether the organization has a "flat" or "tall" shape.

The Span of Control

The **span of control** is the number of subordinates reporting directly to a supervisor. In the country-based geographic organization shown in Figure 8.10, the span of control of the country general manager is 13. There are 6 business managers, 5 directors, 1 innovation manager, and 1 manufacturing manager.

The average number of people reporting to a manager determines the number of management levels in the organization. For example, if an organization with 64 workers to be supervised has an average span of control of 8, there will be 8 supervisors directing the workers and 1 manager directing the 8 supervisors (a flat organization). If, on the other hand, the span of control is 4, the same number of workers would require 16 supervisors. The latter would in turn be directed by 4 managers. These 4 managers would in turn be directed by 1 manager (a tall organization).

Tall Versus Flat Organizations

Whether "tall" or "flat" is best has long been a matter of debate. Classic management theorists such as Henri Fayol said that tall organizational structures (with narrow

span of control
The number of subordinates reporting directly to a supervisor.

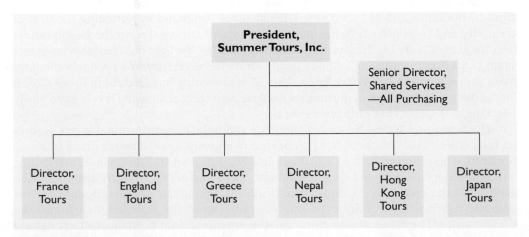

FIGURE 8.9
The New Summer Tour Organization

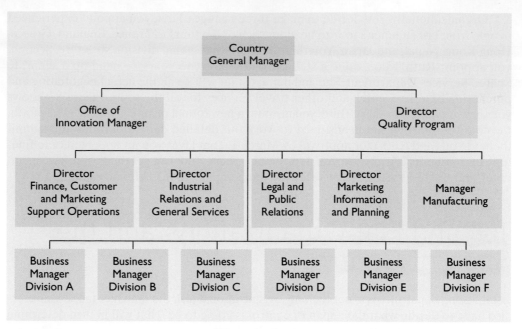

FIGURE 8.10
Spans of Control in Country-Based Organizations
In this chart, the span of control of the general manager is 13: 6 business managers, 5 directors, 1 innovation manager, and 1 manufacturing manager.

spans of control) improved performance by guaranteeing close supervision.[18] The thinking was that having six to eight subordinates was ideal, since beyond that it became increasingly difficult to monitor and control their behaviour. The counter-argument is that flat is better. Flat means wide spans, which means less meddling with (and a more motivational experience for) subordinates. Some believe that a tall organization slows decisions because each decision must pass through more people at more levels.

Current thinking seems to be that flat is better.[19] Flattening a firm cuts out levels and managers, and to that extent may save the company money. There is also the view that eliminating layers pushes decisions closer to the customer, so flat firms may make faster, more responsive decisions. Having wider spans also implies that the manager monitors subordinates less, and this is more practical today, with the trend toward highly trained and empowered employees.

General Electric
www.ge.com

The classic example of "flattening" occurred in the late 1980s. GE's new CEO at the time, Jack Welch, believed he had to make dramatic organizational changes. He had climbed the ranks and had seen how GE's chain of command was draining the firm of creativity and responsiveness. Business heads needed approval from the headquarters staff for almost every big decision they made. In one case, the light bulb business managers spent U.S.$30 000 producing a film to demonstrate the need for some production equipment they wanted to buy. Welch knew that GE was wasting hundreds of millions of dollars and missing countless opportunities because managers at so many levels were busily checking and rechecking each others' work.

The first thing Welch did was to eliminate redundant organizational levels. Before he took over, "GE's business heads reported to a group head, who reported to a sector head, who reported to the CEO. Each level had its own staff in finance, marketing, and planning, checking and double checking each business."[20] Welch disbanded the group and the sector levels, thus dramatically flattening the organizational chain of command. When he was done, no one stood between the business heads and the CEO's office. The effect was to eliminate the organizational bottlenecks they caused (and the salaries of almost 700 corporate staff). The "new" GE was much leaner and more responsive.

Network-Based Organizations

Classical organizations (like the pre-Welch GE) stressed the wisdom of "sticking to the chain of command." Each employee had a position and specific people with whom he or she could communicate. This arrangement usually worked well, as long decisions didn't have to be made very fast. There was plenty of time for each problem and solution to be analyzed and reanalyzed as it worked its way up and down the chain of command.

Some of today's organizations would shock the classicists. Not only is "sticking to the chain of command" not a high priority; these companies actually encourage almost everyone to communicate with almost everyone else, as long as getting the job done requires doing so. In terms of organization structure, these companies are networked. An **organizational network** is a system of interconnected or co-operating individuals.[21] Through various devices, these firms encourage communications to flow freely without respect to departmental or organizational level.

organizational network
A system of interconnected or co-operating individuals.

We'll look at six such arrangements here: informal, formal, and electronic organizational networks, team-based and horizontal organizations, and federal organizations. They all share the same core idea: To link employees from different functions, departments, levels, and geographic areas so they can communicate and get their jobs done through relatively free-flowing, interactive communications.[22]

Network Organizations

The idea that communications in any organization sticks only to the formal chain of command was always, of course, a naive notion. If a sales manager needs to know the status of an order, chances are the request will go directly to the plant manager instead of being funnelled through the chain of command. This is an example of the **informal organizational network**. Informal organizational networks consist of co-operating individuals connected only informally. They share information and help solve each other's problems based on personal knowledge of each other's expertise. Thus, if a Shell Latin America sales manager needs an introduction to a new client, she might call a Shell Zurich manager she knows, who has a contact at the client firm.

informal organizational network
Informal relationships between workers that help get work accomplished.

Networks like these arise spontaneously, but firms today also nurture them. They do this by helping to develop the personal relationships on which they depend. Some build personal relationships through international executive development programs. They bring managers from around the world to work together in training centres. Moving managers from facility to facility around the world is a similar approach.

> [International mobility] has created what one might call a "nervous system" that facilitates both corporate strategic control and the flow of information throughout the firm. Widespread transfers have created an informal information network, a superior degree of communication, and mutual understanding between headquarters and subsidiaries and between subsidiaries themselves, as well as a stronger identification with the corporate culture, without compromising the local subsidiary cultures.[23]

A **formal organizational network** is a group of managers assembled by the CEO and the senior executive team. The members are drawn from across the company's functions, business units, and geography, and from different levels of the hierarchy. The number of managers involved almost never exceeds 100 and can be fewer than 25—even in global companies with tens of thousands of employees.[24]

formal organizational network
A recognized group of managers or other employees assembled by the CEO and the other senior executive team, drawn from across the company's functions, business units, geography, and levels.

Figure 8.11 represent a typical formal network. Note the number of organizational levels and departments represented by the blue boxes. Management decides what tasks it needs a network for and then assigns employees from various departments, levels, and locations to the formal network.

At one railroad, 19 middle managers from various departments and levels constitute the firm's Operating Committee, which helps make most of the firm's key operating decisions. The Operating Committee is a formal network. Members meet for several hours on Monday mornings to review and decide on tactical issues (delivery schedules and

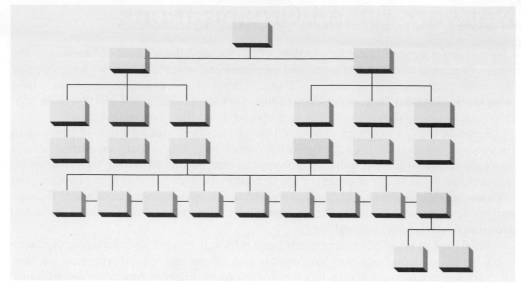

FIGURE 8.11
How Networks Reshape Organizations for Results
The members of a formal network may be selected from various departments and organizational levels.

Electrolux
www.electrolux.com

prices, for instance) and work on longer-term issues such as five-year business plans.[25] However, as an informal network, they also communicate continuously during the week to monitor operations activities across their departments.

Electrolux provides another example. When Leif Johansson took over, Electrolux included 20 products, numerous acquired companies, and more than 200 plants in many countries. Each presented unique market positions, capabilities, plant capacity, and competitive situations. Johansson knew he had to create strengths across functional and geographic borders if he were to derive maximum economies of scale from the multiproduct, multiplant, multinational operation. Abandoning local brands would jeopardize existing distribution channels and customer loyalty. How could Johansson capitalize on the benefits of Electrolux's multicountry scale while maintaining local brand autonomy?

He created a formal network comprising managers from various countries and he charged the network with coordinating cross-border operations. That way, local managers still had wide authority to design and market local brands. But the formal network helps provide the overall multinational and multiproduct coordination in areas like production and inventory management that helped Electrolux obtain economies of scale.[26]

International alliances often depend on formal networks. For example, a formal network manages the day-to-day operations of the Global One telecommunications joint venture, led by Sprint, Deutsche Telecom, and France Telecom. The formal network consists of employees serving 65 countries, and functioning as one company to serve the global telecommunications needs of the Global One alliance.[27]

electronic networking
Networking through technology-supported devices such as email, videoconferencing, and collaborative computing software.

Information technology has been a boon to organizational networking. Collaborative computing, the internet, and PC-based videoconferencing have given rise to **electronic networking**. This is networking through technology-supported devices such as email, videoconferencing, and collaborative computing software like Lotus Notes.

Electronic networking supports the firm's informal and formal networks. For example, PricewaterhouseCoopers' 18 000 accountants stay connected via electronic bulletin boards. Thus, a Dublin employee with a question about dairy plant accounting might have her question answered by a networked colleague half a world away.[28] Collaborative group decision support system packages (like Lotus Notes) provide another example.[29] One, called IP Team 3.0, includes tools that automate and document the making of engineering decisions.[30] One key feature is that it integrates suppliers and contractors into the

PricewaterhouseCoopers
www.pwcglobal.com

product development cycle. It lets a geographically dispersed group from the company and its suppliers work together to develop a product, and then automates the bidding procedure.[31] OneSpace is another. It allows several design teams "to collaborate over the internet and across firewalls in real-time by working directly on the 3D solid model."[32]

Team-Based Organizations

You know from your own experience that teams don't typically communicate though a chain of command. As the Toronto Raptors work the ball down the court, they are not about to stop for committee meetings. Instead, they continuously interact visually and audibly with each other, as they pursue their goal of getting a basket. On the court, passing the ball from one to another, the Raptors are organizationally a mini-network.

Many firms similarly apply the logic of organizational networking on a micro basis. They do this by organizing individual activities around self-managing work teams. A **team** is a group of people who work together and share a common work objective.[33]. For example, when Tim Adlington became the new operations manager at the Black Diamond cheese factory in Ontario, he decided to run every department with employee teams that would be organized to address problems such as waste reduction, productivity, excessive rework, lost time for accidents, and customer returns.[34] Under this system, managers became facilitators rather than order-givers. Managers who used to spend all of their time watching workers to ensure they did what they were supposed to do now spend most of their time facilitating and organizing work, and chairing meetings that are designed to improve operations.

In firms like these, teams are responsible for an entire body of work, such as building a jet engine from start to finish. Since they're a team, the individual team members are "networked," that is, they are continually in touch with and interacting with each other. A GE jet engine plant in Durham, North Carolina illustrates how this works. More then 170 employees work there, as members of small, self-managing teams. There's only one manager—the plant manager.[35] The plant doesn't have a conventional organizational hierarchy or chain of command. The well-trained teams manage their own activities.

The Building Blocks of Team-Based Organizations[36] The GE plant illustrates the basic characteristics of the team approach. Traditional firms organize with individuals, functions, or departments as the basic work units or elements. This is evident in the typical organization chart, which shows separate boxes for each functional department and perhaps separate tasks for individual workers at the bottom of the chart.

Team-based organizations are different. Here the team is the basic work unit. Employees work together in teams and do much of the planning and decision making you'd often expect a firm's supervisors to do. The teams in a plant like GE's are responsible for receiving materials, installing parts, and dealing with vendors who ship defective parts. The teams have more authority and replace many (or most) of the supervisors in a traditional firm's chain of command. The result is a flat organization in which teams of employees report to a relative handful of traditional managers.

At Johnsonville Foods, the CEO organized most of the firm's activities around self-managing, 12-person work teams. These teams are responsible for operating and maintaining the firm's packaging equipment. Typical team duties include the following:

- Recruiting, hiring, evaluating, and firing (if necessary) team members
- Conducting quality-control inspections, subsequent troubleshooting, and problem solving
- Establishing and monitoring quantitative standards for productivity and quality
- Suggesting and developing prototypes of possible new products and packaging[37]

Chesebrough Ponds replaced a functional organization with a structure built around self-directed teams, and the teams now run the plant's four production areas. Team members make employee assignments, schedule overtime, establish production times and changeovers, and even handle cost control, requisitions, and work orders. They are also solely responsible for quality control under the plant's Continuous Quality Improvement

team
A group of people who work together and share a common work objective.

Black Diamond
www.blackdiamond.ca

Challenge. Quality acceptance is now 99.25 percent. Annual manufacturing costs are down U.S.$10.6 million; work-in-process inventory has been reduced 86 percent; and total inventory is down 65 percent.[38]

horizontal corporation
A structure that is organized around customer-oriented processes performed by multidisciplinary cross-functional teams rather than by formal functional departments.

reengineering
Combining several specialized jobs into more enlarged jobs, and giving employees added authority to perform these newly enlarged jobs.

Ryder
www.ryder.com

Horizontal Corporations Horizontal corporations are special team-based organizations. The difference here lies in the tasks around which management organizes the teams. As illustrated in Figure 8.12, the horizontal corporation consists of multidisciplinary teams performing customer-oriented processes, such as new-product development, sales fulfillment, and customer support. In a traditional firm, a process like sales fulfillment might look something like a relay race. The order comes into the sales department, which processes it and hands it off to manufacturing, which hands it off to shipping. In a horizontal organization, one multidisciplinary "sales fulfillment team" is responsible for the entire process. Working together, they receive the order, and then produce it and make sure it's shipped.

Organizing teams to perform customer-oriented processes that may slice through many steps and functions requires reengineering the company's processes. Reengineering means "the fundamental rethinking and radical redesign of businesses processes, to achieve dramatic improvements in...cost, quality, service, and speed."[39] In practice, reengineering typically involves combining several specialized jobs into more enlarged jobs and giving employees added authority to perform these newly enlarged jobs. The basic idea is to have one tightly integrated multidisciplinary team that works in unison on all the formerly discrete steps in the process. Defining the firm's core processes is the essence of creating a horizontal corporation (see Figure 8.13). Managers organize one or more teams around each of these processes. Once the process teams are in place, the firm can eliminate most functional departments and organizational levels.

These "horizontal" process units don't run themselves. As Michael Hammer (a developer of reengineering and of process organization) put it, "the most visible difference between a process enterprise and a traditional organization is the existence of process owners. Senior managers with end-to-end responsibility for individual processes, process owners are the living embodiment of the company's commitment to its processes."[40]

An example can help illustrate what is involved. At Ryder Systems, purchasing a vehicle for subsequent leasing by Ryder required as many as 17 handoffs, as the relevant documents made their way from one department to another. Since such handoffs occurred both horizontally and vertically, the amount of time and energy wasted was enormous. Ryder corrected the situation by reengineering the vehicle purchase process. Now, a single multi-specialist "horizontal" vehicle purchase team handles all the tasks in the vehicle-

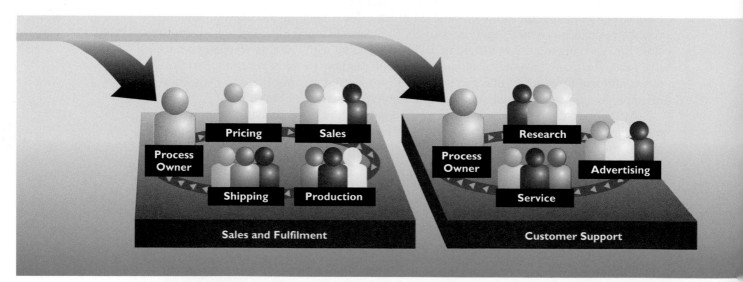

FIGURE 8.12
The Horizontal Corporation
In the horizontal corporation the work is organized around cross-functional processes with multifunction teams carrying out the tasks needed to service the customer.

purchasing process. By organizing these teams, Ryder was able to dramatically streamline each customer's vehicle purchase process. Each corporate customer had its order assigned to and quickly processed by a single team. The old procedure would have involved handing the customer's file from the sales department to the credit department, and so on. In the new organization, a single multidisciplinary team handles the whole transaction. As at Ryder, horizontal organizations typically eliminate functional departments, instead sprinkling functional specialists throughout the key process teams.[41] Another example of major changes is described in the "Challenge of Change" box.

Federal-Type Organizations

Exam

Some companies are not companies in the traditional sense, but are networks of several firms and entities, all working toward the same aim. In **federal organizations** (as in federal governments), power is shared among a central authority and a number of independent but constituent units, and the central unit's authority is intentionally limited.[42] The federal approach lets a company accomplish something it might not be able to accomplish in any other way. Thus, it might enable a tiny firm with a great idea for a new product to quickly marshal the resources it needs, by letting several independent companies each work on a piece of the project.[43] Let's look at two examples of federal organizations.

federal organization
An organization in which power is distributed among a central unit and a number of constituents, but the central unit's authority is intentionally limited.

Cellular Organization Consider the **cellular organization** at TCG, which develops a wide variety of products such as portable and handheld data terminals.[44] It is organized around 13 individual small firms, and "Like a cell in a large organism, each firm has its own purpose and ability to function independently, but shares features and purposes with all of its sister firms."[45] Figure 8.14 shows how TCG's "cellular" structure operates.

cellular organization
A structure in which independent companies or self-managing teams (cells) are self-sufficient and perform specialized functions. Each cell contributes to the overall functioning of the company.

Each of TCG's individual (but TCG-owned) firms continually searches for new product and service opportunities. When it finds an attractive opportunity, it incubates it. Then, when the new product shows concrete progress, the initiating firm acts as project leader for what TCG calls its "triangulation" process. Triangulation means that the initiating firm creates and leads a three-way partnership consisting of (1) one or more TCG firms, (2) an external joint venture partner, and (3) a principal customer for the product or service.[46] The triangulation process and mutual support among the 13 TCG firms help make TCG more than the sum of its parts. Its firms learn from one another, have access to one another's customers and resources, and help to capitalize and fund one another's projects.

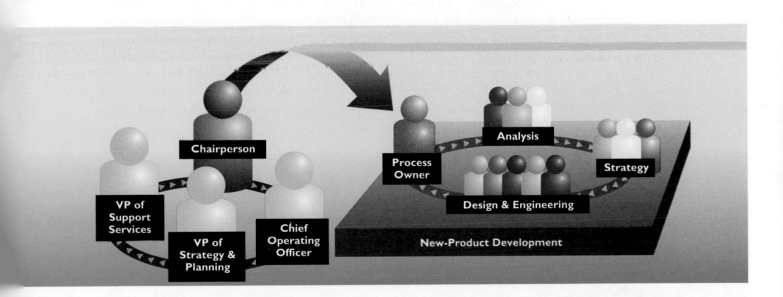

| Identify strategic objectives. | Analyze key competitive advantages to fulfill objectives. | Define core processes, focusing on what's essential to accomplish your goals. | Organize around processes, not functions. Each process should link related tasks to yield a product or service to a customer. | Eliminate all activities that fail to add value or contribute to the key objectives. |

FIGURE 8.13
How to Create a Horizontal Organization
Creating a horizontal organization involves several steps, starting with determining the firm's strategic objectives, and including flattening the hierarchy and using teams to accomplish the work.

THE **CHALLENGE** OF **CHANGE**

Going Boundaryless

Brady
www.bradycorp.com

Brady Corp., which manufactures identification and safety products, is rolling out its new boundaryless supply chain management system. The system will enable Brady's suppliers, customers, and distributors to enter and process orders seamlessly, via the internet. However, management knows that doing so demands a new organization design. For example, many orders will now come directly to production, rather than via sales/customer reps. How should Brady reorganize its sales, production, and shipping operations to best capitalize on the firm's new boundaryless supply chain?

Top management has earmarked about U.S.$50 million for the new system. However, only about a third of that money is for the technology itself. Top management is spending the rest on restructuring the firm's organization and processes. For example, Brady customer service employees used to receive orders and then pass them on to the firm's production department. Then orders would move on to shipping. The new organization structure and processes that Brady is putting in place to support the new boundaryless supply chain will be much different. Customers with simple orders will send them directly, on-line, to manufacturing. In manufacturing, Brady reengineered the operation, creating a horizontal process. One factory floor person will oversee the entire production and shipping process. Management expects the new organization and processes to cut about five steps out of the current 15-step sale-manufacturing-shipping process and to cut the processing cost of each order by a third.

TCG has found that, to be effective, each "cell" must follow three principles. First, each firm must accept its entrepreneurial responsibilities, aggressively identify new project opportunities, and pursue customers. Second, each must be self-contained and function with "both the ability and freedom" to respond quickly and creatively to customer and partner needs. Third, each firm must have the responsibility to be profitable and to have the opportunity to invest in (and even own stock in) the other TCG firms.

Virtual Organizations It often happens that a company has to organize substantial resources to accomplish some big project, but can't afford the time or expense of acquiring and owning those resources itself. For many firms, the answer (as we first saw in Chapter 7)

| Cut function and staff departments to a minimum, preserving key expertise. | Appoint a manager or team as the "owner" of each core process. | Create multidisciplinary teams to run each process. | Set specific performance objectives for each process. | Empower employees with authority and information to achieve goals. | Revamp training, appraisal, pay, and budgetary systems to support the new structure and link it to customer satisfaction. |

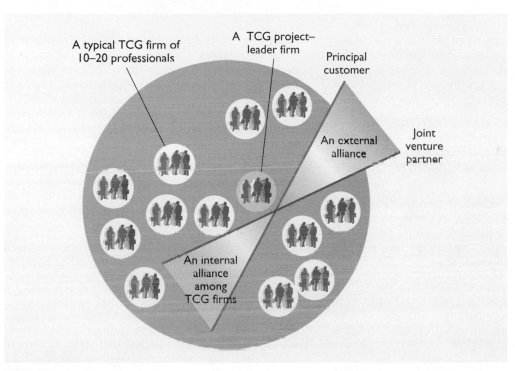

FIGURE 8.14
TCG's Cellular Organization

is a **virtual corporation**, "a temporary network of independent companies—suppliers, customers, perhaps even rivals—linked by information technology to share skills, costs, and access to one another's markets."[47] Virtual corporations are not corporations in the traditional sense. Rather, they are networks of companies, each of which brings to the virtual corporation its special expertise.

Virtual organizations have two main features. First, they depend on alliances and partnerships with other organizations.[48] A virtual organization is a collection of enterprises tied together through contractual and other means, such as partial ownership arrangements. Included under the general heading of virtual organizations are joint ventures, strategic alliances, minority investments, consortia, coalitions, outsourcing, and franchises.[49]

Second, corporate self-interest, not authority, generally keeps everyone in line. In traditional organizations, the employees who actually do the work are supposed to follow orders. In virtual organizations, it's not the company's employees who are doing the work, but the principals and employees of its virtual partners. Giving orders and relying on a chain

virtual corporation
A temporary network of independent companies linked by information technology to share skills, costs, and access to one another's markets.

of command is usually not too helpful in this kind of situation. Instead, the trick is to pick competent and reliable partners, and to provide for equitable incentives.[50] Responsibility and self-interest then hopefully keep all partners in line.

SKILLS AND STUDY MATERIAL

SUMMARY

1. Organizing is the arranging of an enterprise's activities in such a way that they systematically contribute to the enterprise's goals. An organization consists of people whose specialized tasks are coordinated to contribute to the organization's goals.

2. Departmentalization is the process through which an enterprise's activities are grouped together and assigned to managers. Departments can be grouped around functions, products, customer groups, marketing channels, or geographic areas.

3. A matrix organization, or matrix management, is defined as an organization in which one or more forms of departmentalization are superimposed on an existing one. In practice, most enterprises are hybrids and use several forms of departmentalization.

4. Many companies are adopting flatter structures in an effort to eliminate duplication of effort, inspire creativity, and increase responsiveness. The span of control in a company is the number of subordinates reporting directly to a supervisor.

5. Authority is the right to take action, to make decisions, and to direct the work of others. Managers usually distinguish between line and staff authority. Departments could not be organized without delegation, which is defined as the pushing down of authority from superior to subordinate. In a decentralized organization, authority for most decisions is delegated to the department heads.

6. Many firms superimpose organizational networks over existing structures. A network is a system of interconnected or cooperating individuals. It can be formal or informal, and it can be electronically based. The basic idea is to link managers from various departments, levels, and geographic areas so they form a multidisciplinary team whose members communicate across normal organizational boundaries.

7. Taken to its logical conclusion, a networked organization results in a boundaryless organization in which managers have taken the steps required to pierce the organizational boundaries that often inhibit networked communications and decision making.

8. The horizontal corporation is a structure organized around basic processes such as new-product development, sales fulfillment, and customer support. Everyone works together in multidisciplinary teams, with each team assigned to perform one or more of the processes.

9. Federal organizations are organizations in which power is distributed between a central unit and a number of a constituent units, but the central unit's authority is intentionally limited; virtual organizations and cellular organizations are two examples. A virtual organization is a collection of independent enterprises tied together by contracts and other means, such as partial ownership arrangements. In a cellular organization, small independent companies are the basic building blocks, and while each is self-sufficient, they all contribute to each other's and to the parent firm's success.

CRITICAL THINKING EXERCISES

1. Organizations and how managers structure them to accommodate a changing set of circumstances are increasingly important to company survival. New organizational models are required. In less turbulent times, the bureaucracy with its top-down control and hierarchically arranged roles and authority was relatively efficient and effective. With the advent of the global economy, constantly changing technology, and immense competitive pressures, most managers are looking for a way to more efficiently and effectively structure the flow of work in their organizations. One of the most frequently touted means is the use of groups or teams. Warren Bennis's and Patricia Ward Biederman's *Organizing Genius: The Secrets of Creative Collaboration* (Addison-Wesley, 1997)

explores the workings of famous collaborations from what they call "Troupe Disney" to the Manhattan Project. Their thesis is "None of us is as smart as all of us." They come to a number of interesting conclusions, including the following: Greatness starts with superb people; great groups and great leaders create each other; every great group has a strong leader; leaders of great groups love talent and know where to find it; and great groups see themselves as winning underdogs and always have an enemy. To survive in this millennium, we can speculate that all our brainpower and creativity will be needed. Given the structures discussed in the chapter and the information about needing teams-based organizations in *Organizing Genius*, design a new structure for a company in the following industries: retail sales, the aerospace industry, hospitals, auto manufacturing, and construction.

2. Think about the university or college you are attending. How is it organized? Could it be organized more efficiently, using the concepts discussed in this chapter? How would you reorganize your school to be more effective and efficient for all stakeholders?

3. The book *Creative Organization Theory*, by Gareth Morgan, offers a series of mind-stretchers, including the following one:

Conventional texts on management often define organizations as groups of people united by a common goal. This kind of definition eliminates almost all the interesting features of organizations in practice. They are rarely so rational and so united as the definition suggests. How would you define an organization?

EXPERIENTIAL EXERCISES

1. Colleges and universities are interesting places from an organizational viewpoint because the employees (the faculty members) tend to make so many of the decisions. It is common, for example, to have faculty members elect the senate, which in turn makes many major decisions. Similarly, the students evaluate the teaching skills of faculty members and elect their own student governments. Some critics say this is like "letting the inmates run the asylum." And, in fact, criticism of universities and colleges has increased during the last few years. With more schools going on-line, students also have more educational choices. As a result, schools are scrambling to cut costs and increase efficiency.

Form teams of four to five students and answer the following questions:

a. Draw an organization chart for your college or university. What type(s) of departmentalization does it use? How would you show, on the chart, the authority exercised by the faculty and faculty committees (teams)?

b. The chapter says that having a network structure tends to speed decisions. However, some people think that colleges and universities *are* networked, but still the most "bureaucratic" organizations they've ever dealt with. To what extent, and in what way, is your school "networked?" Do you consider it bureaucratic? If so, what explains why a networked organization produces such bureaucracy?

c. How would you reorganize your school if "streamlining and more efficiency" were your goals?

2. You have been hired to reorganize and redesign ABC Corporation, which has had a single product line, women's dress shoes, for over four decades. It is a traditional tall organization with authority at the top (the CEO is a former designer) and a functional structure of sales, design, marketing, human resources, customer relations, finance and accounting, and production. Lately, sales have been falling off because styles in women's shoes have changed. Using the information provided in the chapter, propose how a new organization might help avoid further dips in sales.

BUILDING YOUR MANAGEMENT SKILLS

What's Really Important

The formal structure of an organization does not explain all of the interactions and relationships that are important. In fact, many managers would say that the formal organization structure is not nearly as important as the network of *informal* relationships that inevitably develop in organizations. These, in turn, can cause organizational politics to be very important in many situations. To get a better understanding of this important phenomenon, ask a manager how important organizational politics is in the practice of management. Also ask the manager to describe in detail an incident from the manager's work where organizational politics influenced an important decision that was made. Make sure that the incident is described in sufficient detail by the manager so that you can understand the key elements in the incident. Then ask the manager the following questions:

1. In general, why does organizational politics occur in organizations?

2. In the situation that the manager described, why was politics a part of the decision?

3. Is politics harmful or beneficial to *organizations* ? Is it harmful or beneficial to *individuals* in the organization?

4. Should steps be taken to reduce to reduce the incidence of organizational politics? Why or why not?

Carefully consider what you have learned about organizational politics in the workplace as a result of talking to the manager. Write down five practical guidelines that you can use in your work to help you deal with the reality of organizational politics.

INTERNET EXERCISES

Rona Inc. operates 540 stores in all regions of Canada. RONA is a leading distributor and retailer in hardware, home improvement and gardening products. Visit its website at **www.rona.ca**.

1. How is Rona Inc. structured today? How is the chain of command organized?

2. What challenges do you think Rona faces as a result of its organizational structure?

3. Compare and contrast Rona's organizational structure with that of Watkins Incorporated (**www.watkinsonline.com**). What are the strengths and weaknesses of each structure?

CASE STUDY 8-1

Jersak Holdings Ltd.

Vaclav Jersak was born in Prague, Czechoslovakia, in 1930. His family had long been active in the retail trade in that city. The Jersak family was very close, but the 1930s and 1940s were a time of great turbulence in central Europe. In 1938, Hitler's troops invaded Czechoslovakia and five years of war followed. After the war, Czechoslovakia came under the influence of the Soviet Union, and capitalistic ventures that had been such an integral part of the Jersak family were severely restricted. By the early 1960s, there were some hints of a return to a more capitalistic economy. To Jersak's dismay, these were snuffed out by the Soviet Union's invasion of Czechoslovakia in 1968.

The invasion was the last straw for Jersak, who had felt for some years that the environment for private business activity was very poor. At age 38, he decided to leave Czechoslovakia for a better life in Canada. He arrived in Toronto in December 1968, determined to apply his entrepreneurial talents in a more promising business environment.

Jersak quickly discovered the freedom that entrepreneurs had in Canada. He started a small gas station, and over the next three years he opened several more. In 1971, he purchased a franchise of a major fast-food outlet, and by 1977 he owned four fast-food restaurants. His entrepreneurial instincts led him into a wide variety of business operations after that. From 1977 to 1991, he expanded his activity into the manufacture of auto parts, microcomputers, textiles, and office furniture. He purchased five franchises of a retail auto parts store, two automobile dealerships, and a carpet business that sells to both residential and commercial users. A mining company, a soft drink bottling plant, and a five-store chain of shoe stores are also part of Jersak Holdings Ltd.

As each new business venture was added, Jersak hired a person to manage the operating company. He also added individuals with expertise in accounting, finance, marketing, and production in his head office. Currently, Jersak Holdings Ltd. contains 17 operating companies, each headed by a manager (see Figure →

8.15). Employment ranges from five to ten people in each company.

Head office staff make most of the strategic decisions in the firm. Jersak and the other top executives have frequent informal meetings to discuss matters of importance to the firm. Discussions usually continue until a consensus is reached on a course of action. The operating managers are expected to put into practice the strategic plans that are made at head office.

As Vaclav Jersak looks back on the last 35 years, he feels a great sense of satisfaction that he has accomplished so much. He has been thinking of retiring, but he is not sure how well the company will perform once he is gone. He recognizes that the top management group operates smoothly because the people have worked together for many years. But he feels that areas of authority should be more clearly defined so that when changes occur in top management because of retirements, the new people will know exactly what they are responsible for.

Some of Jersak's business acquaintances are of the view that he should delegate considerably more authority to the managers of the operating companies. In effect, they recommend that he turn these operating managers into presidents of their own firms, each of them being responsible for making a profit in their particular enterprise. His acquaintances point out that giving the managers of the operating companies this level of responsibility will motivate them to achieve much more than they do now. Also, it should motivate the employees in these firms because they will have more discretion as well. Jersak sees some real benefits in this approach, but worries that the current managers of the operating companies haven't had much experience in making important decisions. He also fears that head office will lose control of the operating companies. Jersak feels that it is important for head office staff to know some of the details of each operating company. Without this knowledge, he feels that the head office staff will be unable to make good decisions regarding the operating companies.

Other friends of Jersak argue that the time has come to centralize control at head office because the firm has gotten so large and is so diverse. Only in this way, they argue, will top management be able to effectively control all of the activities of Jersak Holdings Ltd.

Jersak is uncertain about what to do, but he feels he must do something to ensure that his life's work will not disappear when he retires.

Question

1. What problems are evident in the current organizational structure of Jersak Holdings Ltd.? Design a new organization chart for the company that will solve these problems.

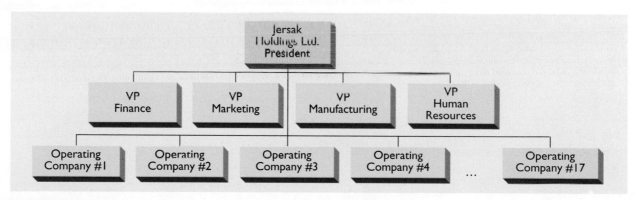

FIGURE 8.15
Organization of Jersak Holdings Ltd.

Organizing at Greenley Communications

Louis Greenley was facing a difficult decision. His company, Greenley Communications, was a diversified communications company that operated primarily in western Canada. The firm owned and operated newspapers and radio and television stations. For years there had been an "invisible wall" between the print operations and television.

The existing structure focused on organizing by industry; that is, there was a newspaper division, a radio division, and a television production division. Each division had its own bookkeeping, sales, marketing, operations, and service divisions. Accounting and financial management were handled at the corporate level.

In the newspaper division, there was a clear distinction between the news and the financial sides of the business. Coming from a family of journalists, Greenley was always concerned that the sale of advertising to local clients would influence the paper's coverage of the news. For example, editors might ignore potential stories if they reflected negatively on an advertiser.

The vice president of broadcast operations, Greenley's television arm, recently proposed that the organization be restructured along geographical lines. This would allow regional managers to have a single sales force that could sell advertising in any form: print, radio, or TV. The approach had some appeal. There was significant geographic overlap at Greenley because the company tended to own multiple properties in the same region. Certainly there would be savings in personnel, as the company would need a far smaller sales staff.

Questions

1. What factors should influence Greenley's decision to restructure?

2. What risks does the proposed restructuring create?

3. If you were Greenley, what choice would you make? Why?

JetBlue's Basic Organization

An airline like JetBlue has basic tasks it must attend to, and so it has organized a number of departments. These departments include flight operation (pilots); in-flight (flight attendants); reservations; systems operations (the dispatchers that work with the pilots to determine flight paths); technical operations (mechanics, engineers, quality control), human resources; finance/accounting/treasury; airport (customer service); security; marketing; sales; public relations and communications; information technology; real estate and facilities; legal; and safety. In addition to its CEO and president, JetBlue also has vice presidents for reservations management (in charge of a group determining aircraft load factors and what to charge for each ticket); and vice presidents for planning and scheduling.

Although the company obviously has an organization, it has no published organization chart. There are several reasons for this, according to the company's head of HR. For one thing, JetBlue wants to avoid the sense of bureaucracy that often arises when employees start getting preoccupied with organization charts. Furthermore, he points out that "we've been very fluid," and after growing from zero employees to 3200 in less than three years, the reality is that any published organization chart is quickly out of date. There are also some practical, competitive reasons for not publishing the chart. For example, why spend time and effort recruiting, selecting, and hiring the best employees and then make it easy for competitors to recruit those employees from you by showing the other firms who's in charge of what at your company?

Internally, however, employees do have access to the sort of information you'd normally expect on an organization chart. For instance, JetBlue does have, as noted above, departments with specific responsibilities. These departmental assignments and the employees in them are available to JetBlue employees on the company's intranet in the form of a spreadsheet. So, if an employee has a question regarding, say, accounts receivables, he or she can check the JetBlue intranet in order to find the right person to talk to. However, while the company currently deemphasizes organization charts, there's no doubt that as JetBlue grows in size, it will need more structure, and may well move toward a more conventional organization chart-based structure.

Assignment

You and your team are consultants to Mr. Neeleman, who is depending on your management expertise to help navigate the launch and management of JetBlue. Here's what he wants to know from you:

1. Based on the information in this case and on information you can obtain from the JetBlue website, develop a workable organization chart for the company.

2. List the pros and cons of JetBlue's current approach to organizing and particularly its emphasis on avoiding formal organization charts.

3. Based on the information in this case and on anything else you know about JetBlue, show specifically, in chart and narrative form, how the company could install a network organization.

4. Given JetBlue's current organization and list of departments, what specifically would you recommend if the company wanted to reorganize its tasks around "horizontal organizations"?

Designing Organizational Structures

Strategy and Structure

OBJECTIVES

After studying this chapter and the case exercises at the end, you should be able to use the material to:

1. Explain what the situation calls for in terms of organizing the firm's lines of authority; departmentalization; degree of specialization of jobs; delegation and decentralization; and span of control.

2. Design an organization structure for a company.

3. Reorganize a company's current structure to that of a learning organization.

4. Explain what a company is now doing wrong with respect to achieving coordination, and explain how you would correct the situation.

5. Explain what a manager is doing wrong with respect to delegating authority, and explain how the problem can be rectified.

Starbucks Coffee buys and roasts high-quality coffee beans and sells them at its retail outlets. It also sells freshly brewed coffee, pastries, confections, and coffee-related equipment at company-owned retail outlets. Starbucks is a familiar sight to mall-cruising Canadians.

The company's objective is to become the most recognized and respected brand in the world. Indeed, it is difficult to escape Starbucks. The company has 4247 outlets across Canada and the United States, and the Starbucks Coffee International division operates stores in Japan, China, Kuwait, Taiwan, New Zealand, Malaysia, Singapore, and the Philippines. As of 2002, Starbucks had a total of 5689 outlets in 28 countries. It was identified as one of the world's fastest growing brand names in a *Business Week* survey in 2002.

Howard Schultz, head of Starbucks Corporation, knows that organizing the company is no easy task. Employees must be trained to be café managers (who know, for example, that every espresso must be pulled within 23 seconds or be thrown away). There is also a department to sell coffee to United Airlines and supermarkets. A way must also be found to manage stores in the Philippines and Beijing. How to organize is, therefore, not an academic issue to Howard Schultz.

An organization should grow out of a plan. When Starbucks was starting out, its strategy was to offer high-quality coffee drinks through small, specialized, local coffee houses. This plan suggested the main jobs for which Schultz had to hire lieutenants—for store management, purchasing, finance, and accounting. Departments then grew up around these tasks.

Starbucks' strategy is now to open 5000 more outlets in Europe, Asia, and Central America by 2005. To facilitate this geographic expansion, the company's organization design has been changed and Schultz has established regional divisions to oversee the stores in each geographic area. Today, Starbucks coffee is also sold to airlines, bookstores, and supermarkets, so the company's structure includes new departments to sell to these new markets.

What Schultz has discovered is that the organization's structure is determined by its plan. Stated another way, strategy determines structure.

Starbucks
www.starbucks.com

The Factors That Determine How to Organize

Organizing is part art and part science. Based on experience, knowledge, and common sense, managers decide (keeping their plans in mind) what they want their organizations to do.

There is considerable scientific knowledge managers can apply. In this chapter, we'll discuss research findings and knowledge that managers can use to help them answer the question, "How should we organize?" This knowledge fits under the title *organization theory*. This is the body of knowledge used to explain and predict how to organize an enterprise.

The Classical Approach

Recall (from Chapter 1) that management and organization theory got it start just over 100 years ago. Industrialization was spreading rapidly, and entrepreneurs focused on making their firms as big as possible. Size meant economies of scale, which meant increased efficiency and lower costs, which meant more sales and more profits. Entrepreneurs needed rational management methods to run their new, large-scale enterprises. They turned to the classical writers, like Taylor, Weber, and Fayol.

Henri Fayol and the Principles of Management The work of Henri Fayol illustrates the classical approach to organizing. In his book *General and Industrial Management*, Fayol outlined a list of management principles he had found useful during his years as a manager. Most of these principles addressed how to organize. They included principles like "division of work" (the worker always worked on the same part), "unity of command" (an employee should receive orders from one superior only), "unity of direction" (there should be one head and one plan for a group of activities serving the same objective), "scalar chain" (the path of authority from the ultimate authority to the lowest ranks), "order" (there must be an appointed place for every employee, and every employee must be in his or her appointed place), and "esprit de corps" (harmony among the personnel of a business is a great strength).[1]

Fayol was a practical person and knew that these principles were not unbendable. He was savvy enough to know that there are times when sticking to the chain of command, for example, results in slow decisions and slow responses. Fayol therefore said that orders and inquiries should *generally* follow the chain of command, but in very special circumstances, a "bridge" of communication could occur, say, between a salesperson and a production supervisor, if a decision was required at once. For the most part, though, the classical emphasis was on a more centralized, functional, "stick to the chain of command" approach. The resulting organizations were quite militaristic and rigid.

A Changing Environment

Prescriptions worked well in the environment of Fayol's time. Competition was local, not global, and new-product introductions were relatively slow. Consumers were less demanding, and things didn't change too fast. Organizing by giving employees specialized jobs and making them stick to the chain of command therefore worked well. But over time, as the number of unexpected problems and issues became less manageable (for example, new competitors, new products, technological innovations), the classical-type organization got overloaded and errors started to mount.

To see how changes affect a business firm, assume for the moment that your family owns a small chain of supermarkets in Ontario. For many years, your traditional structure (a fairly large central staff of produce and food buyers, a layer of regional managers, a layer below that of store managers, each with two or three layers of department managers), worked well, in part because things weren't changing very quickly. You've had basically the same competitors for the past 30 years, and you all sold more or less the same line of products. You all used more or less the same technology—telephones, fax machines, and personal computers. No one was a lot more efficient than anyone else, no one was introducing new technologies, and everyone was selling at about the same prices, since they all had about the same costs. You were kept quite busy, but you didn't have to make a lot of split-second decisions. Nor did you face a lot of unforeseen events. Life was good.

But now things are changing. Two of your competitors just merged and became the new number one chain, and that firm is building superstores complete with pharmacies. They can also now consolidate backroom operations (functions like accounting and purchasing) that will drive down their costs and prices. As if that weren't enough, you just read that Wal-Mart is building a superstore right outside of town, as is Costco. You know that with their super-efficient satellite-based distribution systems, costs and prices are going to fall even more. The decision-making pace is picking up.

Suddenly, managers are coming to you with emergencies, with complaints, and with problems they want you to solve. They can no longer wait weeks for your office to make or approve a decision. You're going to have to make your whole organization structure a lot smarter and faster-moving than it's ever been before. You can't afford to have so many people passing requests for decisions up and down the chain of command like some kind of relay race. You've got to streamline your organizational structure and reorganize. You have to make it easier for decisions to get made.

But what changes are you going to introduce? Should you let your store managers make more decisions themselves? Should you set up regional divisions? Should you give your store managers more support staff? What would you do, and what body of knowledge can you draw on?

Organization and Environment: The Burns and Stalker Study

There is some research evidence you can use to help you decide what to do. Experts in the United Kingdom conducted some of the earliest and still best research in this area. Tom Burns and G. M. Stalker conducted one particularly astute research program.[2] They saw that the world faced by classical management experts like Fayol was much more sedate than that faced by modern managers. The classical experts' environment, said Burns and Stalker, has several distinguishing characteristics. Demand for the organization's product or service is stable and predictable; there is an unchanging set of competitors; and technological innovation and new product developments are evolutionary rather than revolutionary, so managers can make the required modifications at a leisurely pace.

Burns and Stalker studied a textile mill that operated in such a "stable" environment. To be successful, this firm had to minimize costs and stress efficiency. Its existence depended on keeping unexpected occurrences to a minimum, so as to maintain steady, high-volume production runs. This firm had a very militaristic (Burns and Stalker called it "mechanistic") organization structure. **Mechanistic organizations**, they said, are characterized by close adherence to the chain of command; a functional division of work; highly specialized jobs; use of the formal hierarchy for coordination; and detailed job descriptions that provide a precise definition of rights, obligations, and technical methods for performing each job. The mechanistic organization fit the needs of the stable environment.

mechanistic organization An organization structure characterized by close adherence to the established chain of command, highly specialized jobs, and vertical communications.

A mechanistic organization: Toyota truck assembly line.

Burns and Stalker also studied firms that had to compete in fast-changing, "innovative" environments. In these environments, demand for the organization's product or service can change drastically, sometimes overnight, as competitors introduce radically improved products. Sudden, unexpected changes occur in the nature of the organization's competitors, and an extremely rapid rate of technological innovation and new product development is common.[3]

Several electronics firms were competing in just such an environment. Their survival depended on being able to introduce innovative electronic components. They had to be alert for innovations by competitors. In this environment, creativity, fast decisions, and entrepreneurial activities were crucial. These firms had therefore developed new types of responsive, flexible, networked organization structures to fit these new demands. Burns and Stalker called them "organic" organizations.

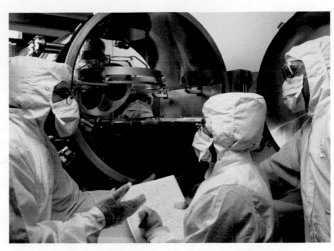

An organic organization: Microelectronic Research Center, making chips.

These **organic organizations** are the antithesis of mechanistic organizations. Managers organize organic structures for speed, not for efficiency. For example, managers here don't insist employees "follow the rules" or stick to the chain of command. They also decentralize decision making, by letting more decisions get made further down the chain of command. Jobs and departments are less functionally specialized.[4] Organic firms tended to have divisional, rather then functional structures. Employees here don't view job responsibility as a limited field of rights and obligations. Employees don't respond to requests by saying, "That's not my job." And, there is an emphasis on networked rather than vertical communication and on consultation rather than command. Table 9.1 summarizes the features of organic and mechanistic organizations.

organic organization
An organizational structure characterized by flexible lines of authority, less specialized jobs, and decentralized decisions.

In terms of organizational structure, we can summarize the Burns and Stalker findings as follows:

1. *Lines of authority.* In mechanistic organizations, the lines of authority are clear and everyone closely adheres to the chain of command. In organic organizations, employees' jobs are always changing, and the lines of authority are not so clear. Here

TABLE 9.1   *Features of Organic and Mechanistic Organizations*

CHARACTERISTICS	TYPE OF ORGANIZATION	
	MECHANISTIC	**ORGANIC**
Type of environment	Stable	Innovative
Comparable to	Classical organization	Behavioural organization emphasis on self-control
Adherence to chain of command	Firm	Flexible—chain of command often bypassed
Type of departmentalization	Functional	Divisional
How specialized are jobs?	Specialized	Unspecialized—jobs change daily, with situation
Degree of decentralization	Decision making centralized	Decision making decentralized
Span of control	Narrow	Wide
Type of coordination and communications	Hierarchy and rules, chain of command	Committees, liaisons, and special integrators, networking

there is less emphasis on sticking to the chain of command. Employees simply speak directly with the person who can solve the problem.

2. *Departmentalization.* In mechanistic organizations (with their emphasis on efficiency), functional departmentalization prevails. In organic organizations (where flexibility is the rule), a product/divisional type of departmentalization prevails.

3. *Degree of specialization of jobs.* In mechanistic organizations, each employee has a highly specialized job at which he or she is expected to become an expert. In organic organizations, "job enlargement" is the rule.

4. *Delegation and decentralization.* Mechanistic organizations centralize most important decisions. Lower-level employees in organic organizations tend to make more important decisions, so these firms are more decentralized.

5. *Span of control.* The span of control is narrow in mechanistic organizations, and there is close supervision. Spans are wider in organic organizations, and supervision is more general.

Organization and Technology: The Woodward Studies

British researcher Joan Woodward found that a firm's production technology (the processes it uses to produce its products or services) affects how management should organize the firm. Woodward and her associates spent months analyzing volumes of data on each company's history and background, size, and policies and procedures. Surprisingly, none of these factors seemed to explain why some successful firms had classic, mechanistic structures while others were more networked and organic.

In search of an answer, Woodward decided to classify the companies according to their production technologies. Unit and small batch production firms produced one-at-a-time prototypes and specialized custom units (like fine pianos) to customers' requirements. They therefore had to be very responsive to customer needs. Large batch and mass production firms produced large batches of products on assembly lines (like automobiles). They emphasized efficiency. Process production firms produced products (such as paper and petroleum products) through continuously running facilities. Here, highly trained technicians had to be ready to respond at a moment's notice to any production emergency.

Once the research team classified the firms this way, it became obvious that a different type of organizational structure was appropriate for each type of technology. Table 9.2 summarizes Woodward's findings. Note that networked, organic structures were usually best in the unit and in process production firms, while mass production firms usually did best with mechanistic structures. The reason may be this: When responding fast is paramount, organic structures do best. For pure efficiency and when demand is more predictable, classical, mechanistic structures seem to do best.

We can summarize the Woodward findings as follows:

1. *Lines of authority.* The lines of authority and adherence to the chain of command are rigid in mass production firms but more informal and flexible in unit and process production firms.

2. *Departmentalization.* There is functional departmentalization in mass production firms and product departmentalization in unit and process production firms.

3. *Degree of specialization of jobs.* Jobs are highly specialized in mass production firms and less so in unit and process production firms.

4. *Delegation and decentralization.* Organizations tend to be centralized in mass production firms and decentralized in unit and process production firms.

5. *Span of control.* Unit and process production firms have smaller supervisory level spans of control than do mass production firms.

TABLE 9.2 *Summary of Woodward's Research Findings*			
	UNIT AND SMALL-BATCH FIRMS (EXAMPLE: CUSTOM-BUILT CARS)	**LARGE-BATCH AND MASS PRODUCTION (EXAMPLE: MASS-PRODUCED CARS)**	**PROCESS PRODUCTION (EXAMPLE: OIL REFINERY)**
Chain of command	Not clear	Clear	Not clear
Span of control	Narrow	Wide	Narrow
Departmentalization	Product	Function	Product
Overall organization	Organic	Mechanistic	Organic
Specialization of jobs	Low	High	Low

Note: Summary of findings showing how production technology and organization structure are related.

Synthesis: A Contingency Approach to Organizing

The research described above suggests that different organizational structures are appropriate for, and contingent on, different tasks. At one extreme are organizations for dealing with predictable, routine tasks. In these situations, management wants to emphasize efficiency, and successful organizations tend to be mechanistic. They stress adherence to rules and to the chain of command, are highly centralized, and have a more specialized, functional departmentalization.

At the other extreme, some organizations continually face the need to invent new products and respond quickly to changes. Here, management must emphasize creativity and entrepreneurial activities, and to encourage these activities such organizations tend to be organic. They do not urge employees to "play by the rules" or to stick closely to the chain of command. Similarly, decision making is pushed down lower in the chain of command (more decentralized), and jobs and departments are less specialized.

Organizing: Always Keep Your Goals in Mind

These research findings illustrate an important management principle: The manager's goals should guide how he or she organizes. In other words, "structure follows strategy." For example, boosting efficiency typically suggests (as Woodward found) one structural approach, while being able to react quickly to customers' concerns suggests another.

There are many contemporary examples of how the manager's goals drive how companies are organized. For example, in March 2002—six months after 9/11—it was reported that the U.S. Immigration and Naturalization Service had mailed pilots' visas for two accused World Trade Center pilots to the school in Florida where they had learned to fly. Why was no one at INS exercising any oversight on matters like this? This problem was partly organizational. INS and Border Patrol were part of the Justice Department, while Customs was in the Treasury Department. This organization thus split the critical enforcement function between two departments, Justice, and Treasury. This made sense years ago, when the main goal for Customs was ensuring that tariffs were paid. However, today, security plays a much bigger role. The homeland security team therefore recommended merging Customs with INS and the border patrol. Doing so would consolidate their enforcement capabilities, and thus help achieve the new goal of better protecting the country's borders.

Another example: When new CEO Louis Gerstner arrived at IBM in the 1990s, he found the firm preoccupied with its organization charts. As one writer described them, "these foldout charts were minor masterpieces of craftsmanship and printing, an intricate latticework of lines, color-coded boxes and asterisks. Lovely to behold, they recalled

IBM
www.ibm.com

the engineering drawings of Leonardo Da Vinci, according to one executive. Producing them was a cottage industry within IBM, and thousands of them were pinned on the office walls of its workers."[5] Gerstner wanted IBM to be much more competitive and much more customer-oriented. Therefore, one of his first moves was to eliminate the firm's preoccupation with organization charts. He told his employees that anyone asking for organization charts was focusing on the wrong thing and that in the future the important thing was building IBM from the customer back, not from the company out.

The "Challenge of Change" box describes another example of how goals influence organization structure.

Organizing: Use Logic and Common Sense

In the final analysis, there is no simple answer to the question "How should we organize?" Organizing is still basically an art, and although you must start by using logic and common sense, the organizing process often tends to be one of continual fine-tuning, even in the largest firms. For example, a persistent issue is whether to organize around products, functions, or geographic areas. The problem (as we saw in Chapter 8) is that all of these organization schemes have pros and cons:

> ...in the product model, businesses can reap efficiencies by standardizing manufacturing, introducing product around the world faster, coordinating prices better, and eliminating overlapping plans. Yet, companies typically find that tilting too far away from a geographic model slows their local decision making, reduces their pricing flexibility and can impair their ability to tailor products to the needs of specific customers.[6]

Goals, environment, and technology are important, but there are so many complexities that there's often no simple answer. Review the opening case in Chapter 8, and you can clearly see how goals, environment, and technology influenced the restructuring decisions that were made at Exide, Ford, and Procter & Gamble.

Summary of Factors That Determine Organization Structure

1. *Environment.* In terms of structural dimensions such as lines of authority, departmentalization, degree of specialization of jobs, delegation and decentralization, and span of control, innovative, fast-changing environments tend to require more adaptive, organic structures; placid, slowly changing environments tend to favour classical, mechanistic structures.

2. *Technology.* In terms of structural dimensions such as lines of authority, departmentalization, degree of specialization of jobs, delegation and decentralization, and span of control, unit and continuous production processes tend to favour organic structures. Mass production processes favour mechanistic structures.

3. *Goals.* "What are the main goals we want to achieve via this organization?" When INS and Custom's goals evolved, after 9/11, from taxes to security, that goal virtually mandated reorganizing those two department's enforcement units into a single more powerful unit.

4. *Logic and common sense.* It is impossible to predict every problem that may arise. At Ford, for instance, a sensible global functional structure undermined local decision making. Competency of management talent, shared values, degree of inter-unit "politicking," and adequacy of the firm's compensation plans are a few of the other things that influence a structure's success. This means that managers have to use logic and common sense when organizing and to fine-tune the organization structure as needed.

How Goals Influence Organization Structure

When General Motors created the Saturn Car Company in the mid-1980s, it wanted to learn more about and adopt Japanese production methods like teamwork. GM therefore created Saturn as an autonomous division: what GM called "a new kind of car company." The autonomy meant some extra duplication and inefficiencies, but it allowed Saturn to nurture their "Japanese" approach to building cars.

Fast forward to 2001. Now, GM's goals had changed. Saturn had been losing money for several years, small cars were no longer as popular, and GM, like most car manufacturers, had already adopted all of the Japanese methods they wanted to adopt. When GM's goals for Saturn changed, GM also changed the Saturn organization, as Figure 9.1 illustrates. In January 1991, Saturn was a separate division, and its president, Richard LeFauve, reported directly to GM's president. With the reorganization in August 2001, management absorbed Saturn into the giant GM structure, and Saturn is no longer an autonomous division. Its president, Annette Clayton, now reports to 1 of 28 GM vice presidents, and is, essentially, the Saturn factory manager.

Other structural changes are also evident. Now, instead of reporting to the Saturn president, Saturn's chief designer, engineering vice president, and marketing vice president all report to the corresponding General Motors vice presidents. The point is this: When managers organize, they have to start by asking what they want to achieve. Those goals should guide how they organize. The organization structure is only a means to an end and must reflect what the firm is trying to do.

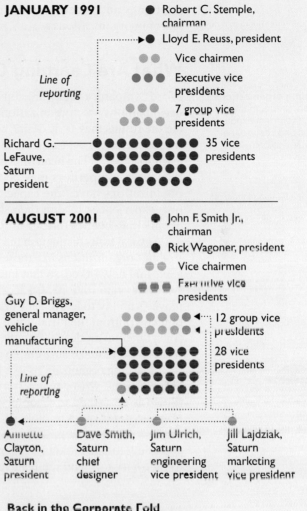

Back in the Corporate Fold
Saturn's president once reported to GM's president and oversaw the entire Saturn operation. Now, the Saturn president reports to a GM vice president and runs its factories. Design, engineering and marketing report to other GM executives.

FIGURE 9.1
Back in the Corporate Fold

How to Create Learning Organizations

Suppose a company does something new like tapping into an on-line marketplace and linking the firm through the web with suppliers and customers. This sounds like a great idea (and sometimes it is), but this company failed to get good results with this new idea. Why? Because it didn't reorganize as a "learning organization." The company joined the on-line marketplace to get instant, best prices. However, it continued to make its purchasing decisions centrally, once or twice a month. It does little good to have lower-level managers monitoring real-time changes in the prices of your company's supplies when those actually making the purchasing decisions don't learn of the prices or make the decisions until two weeks later. Trends like boundaryless decision making, deregulation, globalization, and information technology all mean that companies have to be much faster at learning things and reacting to them than they've ever been before. They have to become learning organizations.

What Are Learning Organizations?

learning organizations
Organizations that learn from their own experiences and change their activities to be more effective.

More companies today are converting themselves into learning organizations. **Learning organizations** are "organizations where people continually expand their capacity to create the results they truly desire, where new and expansive patterns of thinking are nurtured, where collective aspiration is set free, and where people are continually learning how to learn together."[7] The head of planning for Royal Dutch/Shell says, "the ability to learn faster than your competitors may be the only sustainable competitive advantage."[8] Learning organizations have "the capacity to adapt to unforeseen situations, to learn from their own experiences, to shift their shared mindsets, and to change more quickly, broadly, and deeply than ever before."[9]

Several traits distinguish the learning organization from the classical, mechanistic, "controlling" organizations like those prescribed by Fayol. Learning organizations tend to be organic and networked, so that information can flow, almost instantly, anywhere it is needed. Learning organizations also accentuate personal mastery—the idea of developing each employee's ability to learn. They are organized and managed to encourage employees to continually confront their traditional and deeply ingrained assumptions and ways of doing things (their "mental models"); employees don't just take things for granted. And top management works hard to make sure employees understand the firm's overarching shared vision.[10]

Nokia
www.nokia.com

Learning organizations like Brady Corp. use formal or informal networks; team-based organizations; virtual teams; horizontal, process-oriented structures; or federal-type structures (as described in Chapter 8) to make sure that the people who need the information can get it quickly. Nokia's network structure helps account for much of the firm's wireless phone success. There is such a deemphasis on the organization chart at Nokia that, according to one Nokia HR manager, "people who join Nokia spend a few months trying to figure it out... You really have to figure out a network of people to get things done."[11]

How to Abolish Organizational Boundaries

Anyone who has tried to register for a full course or return an item without a receipt knows that traditional organizations have boundaries. Vertically, the chain of command implies authority boundaries. The president gives orders to the vice president, who gives orders to the managers, and so on down the line. There are also horizontal or departmental boundaries. Some call this the "silo" approach to organizing. The whole firm consists of departmental silos. The production department has its own responsibilities and point of view, the sales department has its own, and so on. And there's often not much enthusiastic interaction among them.[12]

boundaryless organization
An organization in which the widespread use of teams, networks, and similar structural mechanisms means that the boundaries that typically separate organizational functions and hierarchical levels are reduced and made more permeable.

It hardly pays to network an organization or to create horizontal team-based structures if boundaries like these stand in the way of information flow. Networking and creating true learning organizations assumes you can abolish some or all of these boundaries. In a **boundaryless organization**, management strips away the "walls" that typically separate organizational functions and hierarchical levels.[13] Doing so begins with understanding what the four main boundaries are (see Figure 9.2).

authority boundary
The boundary at which superiors and subordinates always meet.

The Authority Boundary Bosses and subordinates in every company deal with an **authority boundary**. This boundary represents the authority differentials caused by the com-

Authority Boundary	**"Who is in charge of what?"** ➡	How to lead but remain open to criticism. How to follow but still challenge superiors.
Task Boundary	**"Who does what?"** ➡	How to depend on others you don't control. How to specialize yet understand other people's jobs.
Political Boundary	**"What's in it for us?"** ➡	How to defend one's interests without undermining the organization. How to differentiate between win-win and win-lose situations.
Identity Boundary	**"Who is—and isn't—'us'?"** ➡	How to feel pride without devaluing others. How to remain loyal without undermining outsiders.

FIGURE 9.2
The Four Organizational Boundaries that Matter
In setting up a boundaryless organization, four boundaries must be overcome, but doing so means dealing with the resulting tensions.

pany's chain of command. But, therein lies the problem. To achieve the openness required of a team-based or network structure, just issuing and following orders "is no longer good enough."[14] For example, a manager in a formal network who happened to be a vice president would inhibit the network's effectiveness if she demanded the right to give orders based solely on the fact that she was the network's highest-ranking person. A network should rely more on knowledge and expertise than formal authority.

Piercing an authority boundary requires that bosses know how to lead while still welcoming criticism; they must also learn how to accept "orders" from lower-ranking employees who happen to be experts on the problem at hand. Subordinates must learn how to follow but still challenge superiors if necessary.

The Task Boundary Employees have a tendency to focus on their own individual tasks. Managing this **task boundary** means getting employees to rid themselves of the "It's not my job" attitude. More and more jobs today call for a coordinated team effort. Employees therefore have to understand that, "...while focusing primarily on their own task, they must also take a lively interest in the challenges and problems facing others who contribute in different ways to the final product or service."[15]

The Political Boundary Organizational politics can also present a barrier. Here, individuals or groups scheme to advance their own interests, often at the expense of the firm's. Two managers may be quietly politicking for the same promotion, for instance. The result of such opposing agendas can be a conflict at the departments' **political boundary**.

Realistically, employees are always going to ask, "What's in it for us?" even in boundaryless organizations. Still, the manager should encourage them to take a more collegial, consensus-oriented approach, and to "walk the talk" while doing so. The aim should be to have employees defend their own interests, without undermining the best interests of the team, network, or organization.

task boundary
The boundary defining how employees from different departments feel about "who does what" as the necessary work is divided up.

political boundary
The boundary defining what different departments want, based on who will benefit from an activity and who will not.

identity boundary
The boundary identifying those who share values and experiences from those who do not.

The Identity Boundary Everyone identifies with several groups—for instance with one's family, school, department, profession, and company. The **identity boundary** means that we tend to identify with groups with which we have shared experiences and with which we believe we share fundamental values. The problem arises because we tend to trust those with whom we identify but distrust others. Distrust can undermine the free-flowing co-operation that networked or team-based organizations require.

The basic solution here is to expand the size of the "group" with which the employee identifies. For example, emphasize that although team spirit may be laudable, employees must avoid "devaluing the potential contribution of other groups."[16] Similarly, make it clear to new employees that you expect them to identify first with the company and its goals, not just with their own departments or work crews.

Abolishing boundaries is not just an academic exercise.[17] For example, IBM has eight laboratories worldwide, employing about 3000 researchers. The labs generated U.S.$1.3 billion in licensing revenues in one recent year. Why are they so productive? Many believe it's because IBM takes a boundaryless approach to developing and implementing its innovations. Abolishing IBM's new product development boundaries took a great deal of effort. As IBM's senior vice president for research put it, "The development side is highly disciplined, with a lot of checkpoints, tests, and milestones... The research side is the exact opposite; it's much more freewheeling. Left unattended, such differences could create barriers and impede the development and commercialization of new products."

However, that hasn't happened because IBM was able to eliminate the barriers between the research and development groups. Although they're still separate departments, their efforts are more like those of a joint venture group. By working conscientiously to reduce the disruptive barriers created by the authority, task, political, and identity boundaries, IBM has been able to blend the work of two very different departments into a collaborative, team-like effort.

Streamlining Organizational Decision Making

Firms do not become learning organizations in one large step. For example, GE did not go from "bureaucratic" to "boundaryless" overnight. Rather, it moved incrementally, first streamlining its organization structure in a series of specific organizational moves. These moves included the following.

downsizing
Dramatically reducing the size of a company's workforce.

Downsize As globalization and deregulation increased the intensity of competition, many firms downsized. **Downsizing** means dramatically reducing the size of a company's workforce.[18] For example, faced with dwindling demand, Ford Motor Company, several years ago, cut well over 10 000 white-collar jobs as a way of reducing expenses.

Reduce Management Layers Reducing management layers is another popular way to help streamline an organization. Eliminating layers ("flattening" the chain of command) can reduce costs and boost productivity by cutting the total salary bill. It may also speed decision making by reducing the number of people whose approvals and reviews are required and by letting people "on the ground" actually make the decisions.

Rosenbluth International
www.rosenbluth.com

Establish Mini-Units When it comes to streamlining, many managers have concluded that "smaller is better." They advocate splitting companies into mini-companies. Many firms have taken this route. At Intuit, the new CEO broke the company into eight separate businesses, each with its own general manager and mission.[19] Hal Rosenbluth fragmented Rosenbluth International into more than 100 business units, with each focused on specific regions or clients.[20] Note that fragmentation is no panacea. Splitting resources among several smaller units may mean the company won't have the concentrated firepower it needs to effectively compete. That's why Japan Telecom recently said it was merging three of its wireless units into a fourth, which it called J-phone Communications Company. It hopes that by consolidating its wireless resources, it will be better positioned to compete with Japanese market leaders like DoCoMo.

Cultivating Personal Mastery

You can't create a learning organization just by tinkering with the organization chart. If employees don't want to learn, or are reluctant to express their views, it's not likely that even the most streamlined, boundaryless, networked organization will make them do so. It takes something more, including the following.[21]

Provide Continual Learning Opportunities Learning organizations offer extensive opportunities for on- and off-the-job training. This increases every employee's personal mastery with respect to what he or she knows and how quickly he or she can learn it.

Foster Inquiry and Dialogue Make people feel safe to share openly and take risks. Set the right culture. Make sure that all the company's systems and procedures, and all the signals managers send, encourage open inquiry and dialogue.

Establish Mechanisms to Enhance Environmental Awareness This will ensure that the organization is continually aware of and can interact with its environment. For example, encourage formal and informal environmental scanning activities, and establish more boundaryless supply chain–type relationships.

How to Achieve Coordination

We have seen that departmentalization is the process through which managers divide up the total work to be done. At STO, you assigned jobs to Rosa, Rakesh, and Ruth. However, dividing the work is only part of the organizational job facing the manager. The very process of dividing the work suggests that the manager must make provisions to ensure that the work is then coordinated. What good would it do if Rosa got airline tickets that weren't coordinated with Rakesh's hotel reservations or with Ruth's sightseeing plans? The only way their efforts (and the trip) will work is if Rosa's, Rakesh's, and Ruth's activities are coordinated.

Coordination is important for all kinds of organizations. Wescam Inc. of Ontario makes cameras that are designed to give good-quality pictures even when filming is done from unsteady objects like helicopters, boats, and cars. (Wescam cameras were used in the helicopters that filmed the police chasing O.J. Simpson down a Los Angeles freeway.) In recent years, the company has grown by acquiring several other firms. For Wescam to be effective, it must coordinate the work of these newly acquired firms so that corporate objectives are achieved.[22] The same is true for Abitibi-Consolidated, which was created by the merger of Abitibi-Price and Stone Consolidated. CEO Ronald Oberlander had to oversee the integration of the two companies into one effective unit.[23]

Wescam
www.wescam.com

Abitibi-Consolidated
**www.abitibi
consolidated.com**

Coordination Defined

Coordination is the process of achieving unity of action among interdependent activities. Coordination is required whenever two or more interdependent individuals, groups, or departments must work together to achieve a common goal. In companies, departmentalization creates differentiated jobs, such as managers for production and for sales, or for product A and product B. Somewhere along the line the work of these people must be coordinated so that the company achieves its goals.

coordination
The process of achieving unity of action among interdependent activities.

Methods for Achieving Coordination

There are many ways to coordinate activity. For example, at STO you could coordinate the work of Rosa, Rakesh, and Ruth by having the three meet twice a week to discuss their progress and to fine-tune their plans. Or, you could coordinate their efforts yourself by using the chain of command and by speaking with each of them several times a day to make sure that all their work fits logically together. Let's look at the basic techniques managers use to achieve coordination.[24]

mutual adjustment
Achieving coordination through face-to-face interpersonal interaction.

Use Mutual Adjustment ~~Mutual adjustment~~ means ~~achieving coordination by relying on face-to-face interpersonal interaction~~. This is an obvious and widely used approach. In simple situations (such as two people moving a heavy log), you could achieve coordination by having one person count "one, two, three, lift," at which time both people lift the log in unison. Mutual adjustment is often the technique of choice in the most complex situations, too. Thus, a special forces squad may carefully follow the chain of command when planning their attack. But when they hit the ground, most coordination will likely take place through a real-time process of mutual adjustment. The soldiers will continually interact with and respond to one another as they meet with unanticipated problems. Today's networked organizations facilitate just this type of mutual adjustment by letting employees throughout the firm freely interact, without the usual structural constraints of authority and other organizational boundaries.

Formalize (Rules and Procedures) Rules and procedures are useful for coordinating routine, recurring activities. They specify what course of action each employee should take if a particular situation should arise. Thus, a restaurant manager could have a rule that "tables will be cleared as soon as customers finish eating." This ensures that the work of the wait staff and busers is coordinated.

Standardize Standardization helps ensure that the components fit together properly. Ford builds cars from standardized parts, so that the parts all slide into place as the car moves down the assembly line. Professors give standardized tests, so that the results among students are comparable. Managers also use standardization to achieve coordination. They standardize three things—goals, skills, and values—to help ensure that coordination takes place. Setting specific goals is one way to achieve this. For example, as long as the sales, finance, and production managers attain their assigned goals, the president can be reasonably sure that there will be enough financing and production capacity to meet the sales target.

Managers also standardize skills. Imagine the culinary chaos if wait staff don't know how to process customers' orders, busers don't know when to clean tables, and chefs can't cook. Nothing will go right. Firms therefore spend millions each year training workers. Each team member knows how his or her efforts fit with the others and how to proceed. This means less coordination work for the team's immediate supervisor.[25]

Unilever
www.unilever.com

Many companies try to standardize values among employees. Every year, Unilever gives about 150 of its worldwide managers temporary assignments at corporate headquarters.[26] This helps give the visiting managers a strong sense of Unilever's values. As one of its managers put it, "The experience initiates you into the Unilever club and the clear norms, values, and behaviors that distinguish our people—so much so that we really believe we can spot another Unilever manager anywhere in the world."[27] This helps to ensure that, wherever they are around the world, Unilever managers' actions are consistent with Unilever's values.

Exercise Direct Supervision (Use the Chain-of-Command) Direct supervision achieves coordination by having one person coordinate the work of others, issuing instructions and monitoring results.[28] In other words, "Let's ask the boss." When problems arise that the rules or procedures don't cover, subordinates bring the problem to the manager. In addition to using rules and mutual adjustment, all managers use the chain of command in this way to achieve coordination.

Divisionalize Functional departmentalization creates heavy coordination demands on top management. This is because the work of the functional departments (like sales and production) is both specialized and interdependent. Someone must make sure to coordinate the departments' efforts. Divisionalizing reduces interdependence and reduces the president's coordination burden. The president puts a manager in charge of a self-contained operation. These managers coordinate their own operations. The divisions are relatively independent. Thus, the president can coordinate less, and strategically plan more. In the case of STO, that's one reason to appoint separate country tour heads for each destination country and to let them coordinate all the tourist activities in their assigned countries.

Appoint Staff Assistants Coordinating can be demanding from the point of view of the person in charge. He or she must monitor the activities of the subordinate departments, and analyze and address questions from lieutenants. Some managers hire staff assistants to help with these tasks. When subordinates bring a problem to the manager, the assistant can compile information about the problem, research it, and offer advice. This effectively boosts the manager's ability to handle problems and coordinate the work of his or her subordinates.

Appoint Liaisons When the volume of contact between two departments grows, some firms use special liaisons to facilitate coordination. For example, the sales department manager might appoint a salesperson to be his or her liaison with the production department. This liaison stays in the sales department but travels frequently to the factory to learn as much as possible about the plant's production schedule and the status of various orders. Then only deviations come to the manager's attention.

Appoint Committees One way to make sure a project like your France trip is coordinated is to have Rosa, Rakesh, and Ruth meet with you before making any final decisions on the trip. Similarly, many firms achieve coordination by appointing interdepartmental committees, task forces, or teams. These usually comprise representatives of the interdependent departments. They meet periodically to discuss common problems and ensure interdepartmental coordination.

Organize Independent Integrators An **independent integrator** is an individual (or group) that coordinates the activities of several interdependent departments.[29] Integrators differ from liaisons in that integrators are independent of the departments they coordinate. They report to the manager who oversees those departments.

> **independent integrator**
> An individual or group that coordinates the activities of several interdependent departments but is independent of them.

Determinants of Coordination

What determines whether the manager uses committees, liaisons, integrators, or some other device to achieve coordination? Much of what we know about how to coordinate stems from a classic study by Paul Lawrence and Jay Lorsch.[30] The basic question they addressed was, "What kind of organization does it take to deal with various economic and market conditions?" They studied companies in the plastics, food, and container industries. These industries displayed differences in the speed with which they were changing, and, in particular, in their rates of technological change.

Lawrence and Lorsch focused on what they called differentiation and integration. **Differentiation** referred to the degree to which there were differences in the structures, interpersonal orientations, goals, and time orientations of the employees in each of the departments. **Integration** basically meant coordination, "the process of achieving unity of effort among the various subsystems in accomplishing the organization's tasks."

They discovered three things.

> **differentiation**
> The degree to which there are differences in the structures, interpersonal orientations, goals, and time orientations of employees in different departments.

> **integration**
> The process of achieving unity of effort among the various subsystems in accomplishing the organization's tasks.

- Plastics and food firms faced a lot more uncertainty then did the container firms. Container firms had to construct plants years in advance near customers like Pepsi, so they had to be able to predict demand fairly far in advance. There was much more unexpected change in the plastics and foods industries.

- The rapid technological change and uncertainty facing the plastics and food firms was associated with differences among departments. For example, the plastics firms' marketing and research and development departments had to be forward-looking, while their manufacturing departments had to concentrate on being efficient today. On the other hand, all the departments in the container firms tended to face more similar, predictable, less-changing tasks.

- The degree of differentiation among departments influenced how the companies achieved coordination. Departments in the container firms (who faced similar tasks) were less differentiated and used traditional inter-departmental coordination techniques, like having managers stick to the chain of command, and relying on rules and procedures. Departments in the plastics and food firms (which faced more disparate tasks) were different in how they organized and viewed the world. These differences made it harder to achieve coordination. Plastics firms therefore organized special "independent integrator" coordinating units.

How to Organize to Reduce Inter-Unit Conflict

line–staff conflict
Disagreements between a line manager and the staff manager who is giving him or her advice.

Because differences among departments can cause conflict to develop among them, some thought has to be given to how coordination will be affected. Opposing parties may put their own aims above the company's, and the time they could have used productively evaporates as people hide information and jockey for position. **Line–staff conflict** is a typical example. Conflict might result when line managers feel staff managers are encroaching on their prerogatives, or when staff managers feel line managers are ignoring good advice. Or conflict might stem from personality differences. One recent study concluded that "staff personnel were more modest and accurate in their self-assessment, while line managers were more service oriented but significantly weaker at relationships, openness to new ideas, demonstrating respect, and adaptability to change."[31]

Interdepartmental conflict isn't necessarily counterproductive; sometimes it's best to have a healthy airing of an issue's pros and cons. However, good or bad, you want to manage such conflict effectively. In terms of the organization's structure, conflict can be managed as described below.

Appeal to Power and the Supervisor The traditional[32] way to resolve a conflict is to appeal to the boss. One study found that even in decentralized firms, the CEO's power was the most widely used way of solving disagreements. The CEO did this either through decree, or by acting as mediator or arbitrator.[33]

pooled interdependence
Departments in an organization can each work separately on their contribution to organizational effectiveness.

Reduce Interdependencies Conflicts rarely arise among groups not required to work together. Therefore, one way to reduce conflict is to reduce the required interdepartmental interdependencies. James Thompson distinguished three levels of interdependencies—pooled, sequential, and reciprocal—as shown in Figure 9.3.[34] **Pooled interdependence** exists when the various departments in an organization can each work independently to make their contribution to overall organizational effectiveness. For example, in a franchising operation like Midas Muffler or 7-Eleven, each store makes an independent contribution to the profit of the total corporation.

CHECKLIST 9.1

How to Achieve Coordination

☑ Devices for achieving coordination include mutual adjustment, rules, standardization, direct supervision, divisionalization, the appointment of liaisons, staff assistants, committees, and the organization of independent integrators.

☑ The work of Woodward and Burns and Stalker suggests that when things are changing fast, there should be more emphasis on devices like mutual adjustment, networked organizations, the standardizing of shared values, and divisionalization. More routine situations favour "sticking to the chain of command" and relying more on rules and standardization.

☑ The work of Lawrence and Lorsch suggests that companies whose departments face differentiated tasks may need special independent integrator departments to achieve coordination. Where all the departments face similar, relatively slow-moving demands, rules, procedures, and adhering to the chain of command are effective.

☑ However, it is always a matter of degree. For example, companies operating in fast-changing conditions still use rules, the chain of command, and committees, at least to some degree. Those operating in more placid and unchanging environments still use mutual adjustment and shared values to some degree.

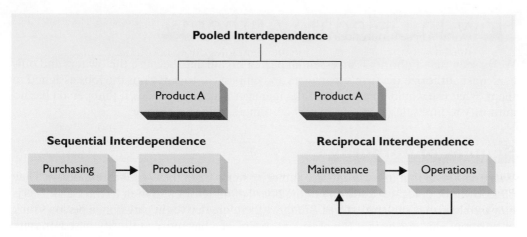

FIGURE 9.3
Types of Interdependence

Sequential interdependence exists when work must be completed in a specific way and when the output of one individual or department becomes the input for another individual or department. At Ford Motor of Canada, for example, the output of the radiator subassembly becomes the input for the main production line. Sequential interdependence requires a higher level of coordination than pooled interdependence.

Reciprocal interdependence exists when individuals and departments must deal with work continually flowing back and forth until the job is completed. For example, at Victoria Hospital, surgeons, anaesthetists, x-ray technicians, nurses, and other specialists work together as a team to complete a complicated surgery. At Air Canada, the output of the maintenance unit becomes an input for operations, and the by-product of operations is an input for maintenance. Reciprocal interdependence is the highest level of interdependence.

Reducing interdependencies reduces the potential for conflict, so one obvious structural way to manage conflict is to reduce such interdependencies. This can be done by moving from reciprocal to sequential and finally to pooled interdependence. For example, if conflict between sales and production in a functionally organized company is out of hand, reorganize around divisional departments. Let each product division manager have his or her own smaller, more dedicated sales and production units.

Exchange Personnel Sometimes it helps to see things from the other side's point of view. Conflict theorists therefore advise having conflicting groups trade personnel for a specific time.[35] In one study, 62 three-person groups of students each acted as either a "manufacturing" or a "wholesaler" of medical instruments. Their goal was to get agreement on the selling price and quantity of these instruments. Thirty minutes into the bargaining session, a random selection of groups got a memo that said the chief executive officers of each firm had decided to undertake a temporary exchange of personnel. The "manufacturer's salesperson" and "wholesaler's purchasing agent" traded positions for 30 minutes. Then, when 20 minutes had elapsed, the "salesperson" and the "purchasing agent" returned to their "home" companies. The bargaining then continued until the trial ended. The researchers concluded that the exchange of personnel helped to reduce conflict and speed agreement.

sequential interdependence
The output of one individual or department becomes the input for another individual or department.

reciprocal interdependence
The highest level of interdependence, when work continually flows back and forth until the job is completed.

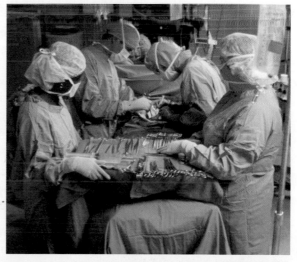

This surgical team illustrates the concept of reciprocal interdependence. The work of each member of the team must be highly coordinated with that of the other members in order for the surgery to be successful.

How to Delegate Authority

We've seen that authority is an essential part of organizing, because the owners and officers must authorize the firm's managers and employees to carry out the jobs assigned to them. What use would it be to put a sales manager in charge of sales, if that person has no authority to hire salespeople or to visit customers or to close a sale?

Sources of Authority

We've also seen that in corporations, authority stems from the owner-stockholders. They pass down (or delegate) authority to the board of directors, and then to the CEO. This is how the chain of command evolves. Authority therefore derives in part from a person's rank or position. This means that the president of EnCana has more authority based on rank than does one of the senior vice presidents.

Authority can also stem from other sources. Some people have authority because of personal traits, such as intelligence or charisma: People defer to and follow their instructions because of the power of their personalities. Others have authority because they are experts in an area, or have knowledge that requires others to depend on them.

Some astute management writers argue that, regardless of the source, authority always depends on subordinates' acceptance of supervisors' orders. Theorist Chester Barnard was an early proponent of this view. Barnard argued that for orders to be carried out, they must lie within a subordinate's "zone of acceptance," in other words, they must be viewed as acceptable. Getting employees' acceptance is increasingly important today, given the emphasis on empowered workers and team-based organizations.

The Principles of Delegation

delegation
The act of pushing down authority from supervisor to subordinate.

Organizing departments would be useless without **delegation**, which is the pushing down of authority from supervisor to subordinate. The assignment of responsibility for some department or job traditionally goes hand in hand with the delegation of authority to get the job done. It would be inappropriate, for example, to assign a subordinate the responsibility for designing a new product and then deny him or her the authority to hire designers to create the best design.

A well-known management saying is, "you can delegate authority, but you cannot delegate responsibility." The CEO is ultimately responsible for whatever occurs in the organization. Similarly, any manager is ultimately responsible for ensuring that the job he or she is in charge of gets done properly. It's a feeble excuse to say, "But I put that person in charge, and he didn't do it." Because the person doing the delegating always retains the ultimate responsibility, delegation of authority always entails the creation of accountability. Subordinates become accountable (answerable) to the supervisor for the performance of the tasks assigned to them, particularly if things go wrong. The boss may fire or discipline the subordinate who fails to do a job properly, however, the boss is still, strictly speaking, responsible for all that goes wrong (or right).

Managers are people who get things done through others, and so knowing how to delegate is a crucial management skill. Principles for delegating include the following.[36]

Clarify the Assignment First, make it clear what you want your subordinate to accomplish, the results you expect, and by when you want those results. Frequently, when employees don't perform up to par, it is not because they're not motivated, but because they're not sure what you expect them to do.

Delegate, Don't Abdicate Shortly after assuming the CEO position at Motorola, Chris Galvin sat in on several meetings with the company's mobile phone group. At that time, the group was working on a new phone (code-named Shark) for Europe. Galvin knew that Europeans preferred light, inexpensive phones, so he asked whether the market data supported the idea that the relatively heavy Shark would appeal to customers. The manager said "yes," and that's reportedly where Galvin left it. He didn't follow up or dig

Motorola
www.motorola.com

deeper. He let his managers move ahead and launch the product, which subsequently failed.[37] The moral is this: Never delegate without challenging your employees, or without thinking through how you're going to monitor their results. Just giving a person a job and not following up is abdication, not delegation.

Know What to Delegate Larry Bossidy, the executive who turned AlliedSignal around and helped it merge with Honeywell, says there is "one job no CEO should delegate," and that is finding and developing great leaders.[38] Bossidy spent approximately one-third of his time the first two years hiring and developing leaders. That's a lot of time for a CEO to give to any single task, but it was essential. He knew he had to quickly build a strong management team.

In Bossidy's case, finding and developing great leaders was "one job no CEO should delegate." For a manager in a different company and at a different level, there will be other tasks that you cannot (or should not) delegate. These are the tasks—such as actually checking and paying for the tickets for your trip to France—that are too important for the unit's well-being to be assigned to a subordinate.

Honeywell
www.honeywell.com

Specify the Subordinate's Range of Discretion You should give subordinates enough authority so that they can successfully do the task, but not so much that their actions can have adverse effects outside of the areas for which you have made them responsible. For example, if you want to delegate the task of doing the research for finding the best airline tickets for France, tell Rosa that you are authorizing her to check the internet and make the calls necessary to accomplish that task. Do not leave her with the impression that she has the authority to actually commit you to buying the tickets. Decide up front how much discretion you want the person to have. The range from low to high discretion is as follows:

"Wait to be told what to do."

"Ask what to do."

"Recommend, then take action."

"Act, then report results immediately."

"Take action, and report only routinely."

Authority Should Equal Responsibility A basic principle of management is "authority should equal responsibility." The person should have enough authority to accomplish his or her task.

Make the Person Accountable for Results Make it clear to subordinates that they are accountable to you for results. This means that there must be predictable and acceptable measures of results.

Beware of Backward Delegation A famous *Harvard Business Review* article is titled "Who's Got the Monkey?" It explains what happens to an unsuspecting manager whose subordinate comes into his office to discuss a problem. The subordinate says, "I have a problem with the job you gave me to do." After a few minutes of discussion, the manager, pressed for time, says "I'll handle it." Like a monkey, the job has jumped from the subordinate's back to the manager's. When confronted with this situation, suggest some solutions, or insist that your subordinate take the initiative in solving the problem. Do not unthinkingly let the task you delegated bounce back to you.

Bank of Nova Scotia
www.scotiabank.com

Centralization and Decentralization

In every organization, management must decide how authority will be distributed throughout the hierarchy. **Centralization** exists when top management makes all decisions regarding the hiring and firing of personnel, the purchasing of equipment and supplies, and other key decisions. Lower-level managers and workers do what is required to ensure that top-level decisions are followed. For example, Cedric Ritchie, the former CEO of the Bank of Nova Scotia, knew all details of the bank's operations and made many

centralization
When top management makes all key decisions and lower-level managers and workers do what is required to ensure that top-level decisions are followed.

decentralization
When the right to make decisions is pushed down to the middle and lower levels of the management hierarchy.

**Bank of Montreal
www.bmo.com**

decisions that CEOs of other banks delegate to subordinates. Most Japanese business firms are very centralized, and their overseas managers do not have much discretion.

Decentralization exists when the right to make decisions is pushed down to the middle and lower levels of the management hierarchy. When Paul Tellier became president and CEO of Canadian National Railways, he introduced many changes that were designed to return the railroad to profitability. One of these changes involved decentralizing the organization because it was too head-office oriented.[39] At the Bank of Montreal, bank branches have been organized into "communities" of branches in a specific geographical area. Each community is managed by an area manager who actually works close to the branches in that community. This allows the Bank of Montreal to respond quickly and intelligently to the needs of local customers.[40]

When managers say "decentralize," they are often referring to the extent to which employees must channel all their communications through the CEO.[41] For example, must the finance, production, and sales managers communicate with each other only through the CEO, or can they communicate directly when arriving at a joint decision? The more they are required to channel communications through the CEO, the more centralized the firm. The more managers can communicate directly with one another, the more decentralized the firm.

In practice, a decentralized organization is one in which authority for most departmental decisions is delegated to the department heads, while control for major company-wide decisions is maintained at the headquarters office. Managers may organize decentralized companies around product, customer, or geographic divisions. However, managers usually use the term "decentralized" in conjunction with product divisions. Managers of product divisions often run what amounts to their own miniature companies. They have the authority to make most decisions that have anything to do with their products, with little or no communication with the firm's CEO. However, the CEO retains authority over major, company-wide decisions.

You can't have a decentralized company without effective, centralized controls because without them, you would have chaos. Consider the problems Arthur Andersen had auditing Enron's books a few years ago. Andersen's Houston office apparently wanted to take a particularly aggressive approach to letting Enron account for some transactions. Andersen Worldwide had a special, centralized Professional Standards Group (PSG) at its Chicago headquarters that apparently told the local Andersen managers in Houston not to do that. It appears someone at Andersen in Houston may have approved the transaction anyway. Managers at Andersen Worldwide had decentralized most decisions to its branches, with the understanding the branches would abide by the Professional Standards Group's centralized oversight and control. In this case, those controls may not have been adequate. Local managers overrode the PSG's decision.[42] This led to the bankruptcy of Andersen.

In practice, decentralization therefore must always represent a balance between delegated authority and the centralized control of essential functions. On the one hand, division managers get the autonomy and resources they need to quickly service local customers. On the other hand, headquarters maintains the control it needs, by centralizing major decisions regarding activities like capital appropriations, incoming cash receipts, and setting profitability goals. The art is in delegating enough to get the job done while centralizing (or retaining) enough authority and tight enough control over the right activities so that you avoid gross deviations.

Why Should a Company Decentralize? A study by economic historian Alfred Chandler helps answer this question.[43] Chandler analyzed the histories of about 100 large industrial enterprises. He got information from annual reports, articles, government publications, and from interviews with senior executives. Chandler wanted to discover why some companies had adopted decentralized, divisionalized organizational structures, while others had remained functionally departmentalized. Chandler concluded that "structure follows strategy," or that a company's organizational structure has to fit its strategy. He said:

> The prospect of a new market or the threatened loss of a current one stimulated [strategies of] geographical expansion, vertical integration, and product diversification... [In turn] expansion of volume...growth through geographical dispersion...[and finally] the developing of new lines of products...brought the formation of the divisional structure.[44]

Westinghouse
**www.westinghouse.
com**

This was an important insight. A diversification strategy at firms like GE led to multiple product lines for these firms. This meant that they had to manage an increasingly diverse range of products and an increasingly diverse range of customers. Having to deal with so many products and customers made the firms' original (functional) structures obsolete. The comments of one early Westinghouse executive neatly summarize this:

> All of the activities of the company were [originally] divided into production, engineering, and sales, each of which was the responsibility of a vice president. The domain of each vice president covered the whole diversified and far-flung operations of the corporation. Such an organization of the corporation's management lacks responsiveness. There was too much delay in the recognition of problems and in the solution of problems after they were recognized.[45]

The steel industry was at the other extreme. Here the strategy was to concentrate on one product, and the main strategic goal was boosting efficiency. These CEOs had little concern about multiple products. In fact, the duplication inherent in setting up separate product divisions would have been inefficient. These companies generally stayed functionally departmentalized.

In sum, "structure follows strategy." Diversification required serving the diverse needs of many product lines and customers, and forced managers to organize around decentralized divisions. But concentrating on one product and on being efficient led managers to stay with the functional structure.

What Should Be Decentralized? One useful rule is this: Decentralize decisions that will affect just one division or area and that would take a great deal of time for you to make. Centralize decisions that could adversely affect the entire firm and that you can make yourself fairly expeditiously. So, for STO, you would likely decentralize the ticket research, but centralize the actual purchase. The "People Side of Managing" box gives further insight into this issue.

Sometimes firms re-centralize one or more of their departments. For example, before the merger, most of AOL's and Time Warner's separate units carried out their own marketing efforts. After the merger, AOL Time Warner needed a more centralized approach, so it created a new central Global Marketing Solutions Group. This unit now markets and sells ads for all AOL Time Warner's on-line, magazine, and television media properties. This helps it accomplish one of the main goals of the AOL Time Warner merger. That is, management wanted to enable advertisers to create special types of promotions that they could market simultaneously through multiple AOL Time Warner media properties, including on-line, magazine, and television. Re-centralizing marketing helped them do that.[46]

AOL Time Warner
**www.aoltimewarner.
com**

Decentralization at Cirque du Soleil

Cirque du Soleil
**www.cirquedusoleil.
com**

Cirque du Soleil, producer of international travelling circuses, is headquartered in Montreal. It has 2100 employees worldwide and offices in Amsterdam, Las Vegas, and Singapore. Employees are from 40 different countries and speak more than 15 languages. Two-thirds of the employees work outside Montreal. It has simultaneous, multiple tours. How does the company manage an operation like that? The answer is, they decentralize.

Each tour is like a separate, small-town circus. Everyone works for Cirque du Soleil, but most of the 2100 employees travel with the local, geographic-division tours. Management decentralizes decisions on matters like human resources to the separate tour managers (since employment law, for example, can vary drastically from country to country). Management centralizes other decisions, such as those dealing with major investments. The company maintains a sense of central unity through its strong culture of shared values and beliefs. It posts jobs on the internet, and employees write the company newspaper. Members of the Las Vegas finance department videotape themselves on the job and swap tapes with the casting crew in Montreal to keep the community feeling. The result is the ability to take advantage of Cirque du Soleil's size, while keeping the separate tours more like small family businesses.

A Cirque du Soleil troupe in action.

SKILLS AND STUDY MATERIALS

SUMMARY

1. Managers can make a number of basic structural changes to make their organizations operate more responsively. Simplifying or reducing structure by reducing layers of management, creating mini-units, reassigning support staff, and widening spans of control are alternatives.

2. Research suggests that different organizational structures are appropriate for, or contingent on, different tasks. Routine, efficiency-oriented tasks seem best matched with mechanistic organizational structures. At the other extreme, rapid change and technological innovation seem more suited to organic structures.

3. Learning organizations are organic, networked organizations that encourage employees to learn and to confront their assumptions. They share a common vision so that they have the capacity to adapt to unforeseen situations, to learn from their own experiences, to shift their shared mindsets, and to change more quickly, broadly, and deeply than ever before.

4. Managers can make a number of basic structural changes to make their organizations operate more responsively. Simplifying or reducing structure by reducing layers of management, creating mini-units, reassigning support staff, and widening spans of control are examples.

5. In boundaryless organizations, management breaks down the "walls" that separate various departments so that activities are better coordinated. The four boundaries that must be dealt with are the authority, task, political, and identity boundaries.

6. Coordination is the process of achieving unity of action among interdependent activities. It is required when two or more interdependent entities must work together to achieve a common goal. Techniques for achieving coordination include mutual adjustment; the use of rules or procedures; direct supervision; departmentalization;

the use of a staff assistant, a liaison, a committee, or independent integrators; and the standardization of targets, skills, or shared values.

7. Authority is the right to take action, to make decisions, and to direct the work of others. Managers usually distinguish between line and staff authority. Departments could not be organized without delegation, which is defined as the pushing down of authority from superior to subordinate. In a decentralized organization, authority for most decisions is delegated to the department heads.

8. Principles of delegation include (a) delegate authority but not responsibility, (b) clarify the assignment, (c) delegate, don't abdicate, (d) know what to delegate, (e) specify the subordinate's range of discretion, (f) authority should equal responsibility, (g) make the person accountable for results, and (h) beware of backward delegation.

9. Decentralized organizations are those in which authority for most departmental decisions is delegated to the department heads, while control for major company-wide decisions is maintained at headquarters. Managers usually use the term "decentralized" in conjunction with product divisions.

CRITICAL THINKING EXERCISES

1. This chapter introduced new organizational structures that have been created to deal with accelerated changes in technology and the environment. Here are two examples that illustrate some of those structures.

   ■ At American Express, a program called "One Enterprise" led to a range of projects where peers from different divisions worked together on cross-marketing, joint purchasing, and co-operative product and market innovation. Employees' rewards were tied to their One Enterprise efforts. Executives set goals and could earn bonuses for their contributions to the results of other divisions.

   ■ At Alcan, managers and professionals from line divisions formed screening teams to consider new-venture proposals to aid the search for new uses and applications for its core product, aluminum. A venture manager chosen from the screening team took charge of concepts that were good enough, drawing on Alcan's worldwide resources to build a new business. In one case of global synergy, Alcan created a new product for the Japanese market using Swedish and U.S. technology and Canadian manufacturing capacity.

   What types of organizational restructuring are illustrated by the above examples?

2. Max Weber, the German sociologist, is considered by most to be the "Father of the Mechanistic or Bureaucratic Organization." Writing in the late nineteenth and the early twentieth century, Weber was analyzing the start of what 1990s management expert Charles Handy has called "The Century of Organizations." For Weber it was a time when the new revolution of large-scale organizations would emphasize the importance of authority in the system: "In the past the man has been first, in the future the system must be first." What do you think Weber meant by that statement? How would he see the new revolution of today's boundaryless organizations? How might today's new structures change the relationship between the system and the human beings?

3. New organizational structures are all around us. Teams largely manage some companies, such as Whole Food Markets. At Whole Foods Markets, the financial books are open to all, teams hire and fire team members, and they measure every aspect of performance. At Southwest Airlines, a team spirit that involves cross-training and employee input is deeply valued by the management. UPS management took its company public in November 1999, making its employees—most of whom own stock in the company—wealthier. Some organizations are virtual. Some are primarily made up of telecommuters who never come to the office. Many businesses are merging into giant corporations: Think of DaimlerChrysler. With such trends in mind, describe what you think will be the typical organization of the twenty-first century.

1. In *The Horizontal Organization*, Frank Ostroff argues that the vertical organizational design is outdated and that the horizontal organization is the organization of the future. The vertical organization has inherent shortcomings in our competitive, technological, and workforce environment. Among the shortcomings are (1) its internal focus on functional goals rather than an outward-looking concentration on delivering value and winning customers; (2) the loss of important information as knowledge travels up and down the multiple levels and across the functional departments; (3) the fragmentation of performance objectives brought about by a multitude of distinct and fragmented functional goals; (4) the added expense involved in coordinating the overly fragmented work and departments; and (5) the stifling of creativity and initiative of the workers at lower levels. Ostroff sees the horizontal corporation as the structure for today and the future. Among the reasons given are that (1) horizontal organizations organize around cross-functional core processes, not tasks or functions; (2) they install process owners or managers who will take responsibility for the core process in its entirety; (3) teams, not individuals, are the cornerstone of the organizational design and performance; and (4) they empower people by giving them the tools, skills, motivation, and authority to make decisions essential to the team's performance. Working in teams of four to five students, list the organizations (including student groups) in which you've worked that you would consider vertical or horizontal organizations. What makes you say they were vertical or horizontal? What were your experiences, in terms of getting things done, and problems that arose? List five ways vertical and horizontal organizations differ in how they achieve coordination.

2. There is a new system of organizing—called "open book management"—that gets every employee thinking like a businessperson; that is, like a competitor.[47] In a nutshell, open-book management is a way of running a company that gets everyone to focus on helping the business make money. There are three essential differences between this approach and conventional approaches to management: (1) every employee sees—and learns to understand—the company's financial records, along with all of the other numbers that are critical to tracking the business' performance; (2) employees learn that, whatever else they do, part of their job is to move those numbers in the right direction; and (3) employees have a direct stake in the company's success: If the company makes a profit, they get a share; if it doesn't, they don't.

   You work for an old-line industrial firm with a mechanistic organizational structure that has been managed by basically the same management team for the last 30 years. The company has developed a paternalistic culture where employees are expected to do their jobs but not to question the whys and wherefores. Financial data, including salaries and compensation packages, are kept secret. In fact, if you share information about your pay with others, you may be fired. Your competitors seem to have a very motivated workforce and aggressive sales and marketing people, as well as technologically sophisticated products. As the newest member of the management team, you are very interested in introducing new ideas (like those discussed in this chapter) about organizational design, including open-book management.

   Your assignment is to write a brief report on how you would introduce these new concepts into this organization. The report should only be two pages and should outline the issues and your recommendations based on concepts from the chapter. You should be ready to present your report either to a group in class or to the whole class.

3. Since you are in college or university to learn, it is reasonable to assume that your school in general, and your management class in particular, are "learning organizations." In teams of four to five students, answer the following questions:

   a. If you were the "manager" taking over this class, what would you say are the main goals you want the class to achieve?

   b. Based on that, what are the main tasks the class's organization must perform?

   c. Draw the organization chart of the class as it is now. Then, list five things you would do to reorganize the class as a learning organization.

   d. To what extent is the class subject to the various "boundaries" discussed in this chapter?

BUILDING YOUR MANAGEMENT SKILLS

Understanding Coordination

Review the section in the chapter entitled "Methods for Achieving Coordination." Then interview a manager who is responsible for the production of a physical product or a service. Ask the manager to describe in detail how the production of the physical product or service is actually achieved and what kinds of interactions are necessary between various departments and individuals to successfully produce the product or service. (Keep in mind the various methods for achieving coordination as you ask the manager questions, but do not ask the manager what kinds of coordination methods are used. Ask questions in such a way that you will be able to make an assessment of coordination methods later. Make sure you understand the structure of the organization and the way that various groups work together. Take detailed notes during the interview.)

After the interview, review your notes and answer the following questions:

1. Which of the coordination methods described in the chapter did the manager rely upon?

2. Which coordination methods were mentioned most frequently?

3. Why were some coordination methods not used?

4. Were some coordination methods likely used, even though the manager didn't mention them? Why would this be so?

5. What kind of interdependence (pooled, sequential, or reciprocal) was used in the production process? Give an example.

INTERNET EXERCISES

Employee empowerment is a major consideration for many of today's managers. When implemented, it changes the structure of an organization and encourages "front-line" employees to make decisions, seek new solutions to problems, and so on. Three Canadian companies that have adapted their organizational structures to enhance employee empowerment are IMS Health Canada (**www.imshealthcanada.com**), EnCana (**www.encana.com**), and Oneida Canada Ltd. (**www.oncida.com**).

1. How does the organizational structure change when a company empowers its employees to make decisions, seek new solutions to problems, and find new and better methods of doing their work?

2. Based on your internet research of IMS Health Canada, EnCana, and Oneida, what are the advantages and disadvantages of employee empowerment? Further reference: See "Power to the People," by David Hogg, *CMA Magazine*, May 1993, at **www.highperformancesolutions.ca/resources_articles.htm.**

3. Based on your internet research, what challenges face managers who empower their employees?

CASE STUDY 9-1

Should Brascan Change Its Structure?

Toronto-based Brascan is one of Canada's few remaining conglomerates, that is, a company that owns a diverse group of other companies. Brascan owns Noranda Inc. (mining), Nexfor Inc. (paperboard), Brookfield Properties Corp. (real estate), Great Lakes Power, Inc. (hydroelectric generation), Trilon Financial Corp. (financial services), and two Brazilian cattle ranches that it bought very cheaply when the Brazilian currency collapsed.

In the 1980s, the conglomerate model was very popular, but it is now out of favour because markets like so-called "pure-play" companies that focus on a single industry. Investors have been unhappy with Brascan's reluctance to give up the conglomerate strategy and have essentially attached a "holding company discount" to its stock price. This has occurred in spite of the fact that Brascan has regularly been profitable.

Revenue for the three months ended March 31, 2002, was $1.1 billion, and profits were $102 million.

Until 2002 Jack Cockwell was the CEO of Brascan. He was a legendary bargain hunter whose strategy was to buy undervalued companies. In the early 1990s, he took $20 million of Seagram Co. Ltd. stock owned by Peter and Edward Bronfman and parlayed it into Canada's most powerful and controversial conglomerate—Edper Group. But when real estate prices dropped, Edper faced bankruptcy because it was unable to pay its debts. The company sold assets to stay alive and by the mid-1990s had sold nearly $5 billion in assets and had raised $6.6 billion in new financing. It was renamed Brascan in 2000.

Brascan's strategy of continuing to emphasize "old economy" businesses has been criticized by industry observers as out-of-date and ineffective. Brascan's →

stock price performance has lagged behind that of the S&P/TSX index since 1998, leading various business commentators to suggest that Brascan be split up into separate companies because in total they would be worth more than Brascan is worth now. But Cockwell remained committed to the conglomerate strategy and rejected many break-up proposals.

In 2002 Cockwell was succeeded by Bruce Flatt, who says that he will do whatever it takes to deliver value for shareholders. After being appointed CEO, Flatt said that his strategy calls for Brascan to focus on just three core businesses: real estate, hydroelectricity, and financial services. He said that he would not sell resource companies like Noranda or Nexfor during a time of cyclical downturn, but he did not rule out selling them at a later date.

Flatt says that assets must meet a threshold return or they won't be kept. He wants to achieve a 15 percent annual growth in sustainable cash flow and a 20 percent cash return on equity. These goals may be achievable in real estate, financial services, and power generation, but not in highly cyclical businesses like mining and paperboard. This may mean that Noranda and Nexfor may be sold. In fact, Brascan has already sharply reduced its emphasis on resource-based assets (which accounted for 60 percent of Brascan's assets in 1997 but less than 10 percent in 2002).

Questions

1. What is the difference between a "mechanistic" and "organic" organization? Which seems most likely at Brascan? Why?

2. What different kinds of environments do each of the various units of Brascan face? What does the nature of these environments imply about the extent to which each unit is mechanistic or organic?

3. What does the phrase "structure follows strategy" mean in general terms? What does it mean for Brascan?

4. What is a "learning organization?" Do you think Brascan is a learning organization? Explain.

5. How are decentralized organizations different from centralized ones? Is Brascan likely to be a centralized firm or a decentralized one? Explain.

6. How is Bruce Flatt's view of the organization different from that of former CEO Jack Cockwell? What does this imply about the future structure of Brascan? What does it imply about the level of centralization or decentralization?

Brascan
www.brascancorp.com

CASE STUDY 9-2

W. L. Gore & Associates: Structuring for Continuous Change

Would you offer someone a high-salary position without knowing what job they would do? W. L. Gore & Associates does. It is one of the many unusual practices that have helped Gore, makers of the waterproof fabric GORE-TEX, to be repeatedly named to the *Fortune* list of 100 best companies to work for, most recently ranking as the 11th best firm. The firm's annual revenues exceed U.S.$1 billion, and it operates in 45 countries (but employs only 6100 people).

Gore operates a high-tech company in a market (textiles) that is traditionally low-tech. As a high-tech company, Gore must be prepared to change rapidly when the market changes. To do this, Gore's structure and processes are distinguished by three unique characteristics: sponsors rather than bosses, a "lattice" organization, and the "waterline principle."

Gore sees the way it organizes and works as one of the things that sets it apart from its competitors. Gore militates against bureaucracy and sees hierarchies as the enemies of innovation. Gore hires "associates" (not employees) into general work areas. When hired, these employees don't have specific job titles →

or positions. With the help of their Gore sponsors (bosses), associates select and commit to projects that seem to match their skills and interests. One of the sponsors' jobs is to help associates find a place in Gore that will offer personal fulfillment and maximize their contribution to the enterprise. Gore does not assign managers. In the company's view, leaders are people who have followers. If the organization is left on its own, leaders will emerge naturally, by demonstrating the character, knowledge, and skills that attract followers. To become a leader at Gore, you need to perform in a way that attracts followers.

This self-selecting process leads to what Gore calls the lattice organization, where there are no chains of command, and decision making is delegated to the point where the decision must be made. It is assumed that employees are sufficiently concerned about the good of the organization to make good decisions on behalf of the organization. Gore's lattice has no pre-established channels of communication, either. New associates are coached by their sponsors to communicate directly with one another. Associates work in multidisciplinary teams and are accountable to each other. The goal of this innovative structure is to unleash the creative potential of all of the associates, thus allowing Gore to become a truly innovative company.

The "waterline principle" is cited by many as a key to Gore's successful ability to adapt. The company is viewed as a ship. Holes above the waterline are unattractive (not deadly), but holes below the waterline will sink the ship. If you are a Gore associate and you see an action or event that could hit Gore below the waterline, then it is your individual responsibility to do something, even if the event or action happens outside your department or area. Failing to act on a waterline issue would earn you a severe reprimand from your peers, the other associates. After all, it is the role of every employee to protect the ship.

With these principles firmly in place, Gore has been able to be remarkably flexible, to change constantly to meet the needs of current and future clients. The results of Gore's structure and processes have been impressive. Its world-renowned fluoro-polymer technology has allowed it to extend the product line far beyond the well-known GORE-TEX brand. The same technology has allowed the company to produce Glide, a nonstick dental floss, and Elixir, a corrosion-resistant guitar string. Lesser-known but equally impressive products, including next-generation materials for printed circuit boards and fibre optics, and new methods to detect and control environmental pollution, are marketed in the industrial sector. Gore has also been recognized for its work in advancing the science of regenerating tissue destroyed by injuries.

The Company's founder, Bill Gore, originally articulated the company's unique structure and culture. To Gore, the company would be successful only if it could create an environment that was naturally conducive to the highest levels of innovation and productivity. Gore envisioned associates making a commitment to four basic principles: fairness to each other and everyone they came in contact with; freedom to encourage, help, and allow other associates to grow in knowledge, skill, and scope of responsibility; the ability to make one's own commitments and keep them; and consultation with other associates before undertaking actions that could affect the reputation of the company by hitting it "below the waterline."

Questions

1. In what ways is Gore's lattice structure similar to the structures discussed in this chapter?

2. In what ways does Gore's lattice structure make it better suited to change?

3. Gore asserts that its structure makes it more innovative. Could a traditionally structured company be as innovative as W. L. Gore & Associates? Why or why not?

4. What difficulties might you encounter if you tried to apply Gore's structural principles to an existing company?

W. L. Gore
www.gore.com

Coordinating JetBlue

JetBlue does not publish a formal organization chart. Indeed, it tries to minimize employees' preoccupation with organization charts to maintain its "think small," start-up, entrepreneurial culture. However, in an industry in which safety is always the main concern, the company has had to take steps to ensure that the work of all its departments is coordinated and that "the left hand knows what the right hand is doing."

JetBlue accomplishes this coordination in a variety of ways. It holds monthly meetings within each department at which employees are kept apprised of what their colleagues are doing. Within departments such as human resources, there are also weekly meetings (e.g., between the recruiting and training groups) to address questions such as training schedules and what open jobs the company is trying to fill (typically there are more than 100 jobs open at any time). There is a conference call every morning, in which all general managers and corporate managers participate, and any JetBlue employee can listen in. This daily phone conference addresses problems and issues that may have arisen during the previous 24 hours, such as weather problems, unusual events, and the status of the company's aircraft. The company also holds monthly officers meetings.

One of JetBlue's underlying themes is that if it treats its people right, they will perform in a way that creates prosperity for them and the company. The company therefore organizes the agenda for these monthly officers meetings around what it calls the "3-Ps"—people, performance, and prosperity. JetBlue is also considering formalizing these monthly meetings at the next organizational level down and having its directors meet at monthly meetings.

Given the company's rapid growth and successful financial performance, its organizational arrangements seem to be working well. However, management is still considering the need to reorganize, and, in particular, to institute a more structured approach than it now uses. The company's growth seems to demand doing so. For example, not too long ago there was a three-person benefits group within the HR department, where each employee tackled any benefits issues that came his or her way. The department is now up to five employees with a manager, and it has become necessary to divide the benefits

work in a more formal manner and to assign specific tasks to each benefits employee.

It is also important to institute a more structured approach because the amount of work that managers need to do is now considerably more than it was just six months or year ago, given the company's rapid growth. Management knows that much of its success is a direct result of the fact that senior managers—including the CEO, president, and head of HR—spend a great deal of their time out in the field, speaking with customers and employees. Even working 80-hour weeks, that doesn't leave much time for them to tackle the day-to-day technical aspects of their jobs. One way to deal with that is to add more subordinates and delegate specific tasks to them.

The bottom line is that JetBlue is going to have to take the sorts of steps that leave them open to possibly adding some "bureaucracy" to their organization (such as putting more emphasis on organization charts, delegating specific duties, and a chain of command), while at the same time trying hard to maintain its small-company, entrepreneurial culture.

Assignment

You and your team are consultants to Mr. Neeleman, who is depending on your management expertise to help navigate the launch and management of JetBlue. Here's what he wants to know from you:

1. Based on what you know about the airline industry and JetBlue's environment, where, on a continuum, would you say they should be (in terms of Burns and Stalker's mechanistic and organic types of organizations) with respect to lines of authority; departmentalization; degree of specialization of jobs; delegation and decentralization; and span of control?

2. Explain what the company is doing right and wrong with respect to achieving coordination, and explain how you would improve the situation in light of findings like those of Lawrence and Lorsch.

3. Based on what you know about JetBlue, list the specific things you would do to reorganize the company from its current structure to that of a "learning organization."

4. Design an organization structure for JetBlue.

Staffing and Human Resource Management

Human Resource Strategy at Signicast

Signicast Corporation produces metal parts from a casting process. Workers use wax moulds to create ceramic moulds, which they in turn use to cast the metal parts. To compete, the firm knew it had to reinvent itself, by building a new, highly automated plant about 45 kilometres away from its current location. But it discovered that new automation technology required a new kind of employee. The question was, how should Signicast select, train, and organize the employees so the new plant would be a success? Management knew that to implement its strategy, it needed to apply modern staffing and human resource management concepts and techniques.

At Signicast, HR's involvement began at the plant design stage. HR people invited employees from the existing facility to participate in planning and design meetings. They solicited suggestions on matters ranging from how to design a new piece of equipment to the workflow in the new plant. Employees would first come up with suggestions, and management would implement the ideas and then check back with employees for confirmation that things were working well.

HR's role in the building of this new plant was apparent in other ways. As the new plant began taking shape, HR had to select and train the new workforce. Since the new automated plant would produce parts almost five times faster than the old plant, there was little time for rework. The new plant employees would therefore have to be given more responsibility to ensure that quality was maintained. They would also have to be more highly trained and carefully selected than their counterparts at the old facility.

The new plant's selection standards were thus tighter. At the old plant, for example, no specific prior experience was required—the only hiring requirements were a high school diploma and a good work ethic. The 135 employees at the new plant would require the same high school degree and work ethic *plus* a team orientation, good trainability, good communication skills, and a willingness to do varied jobs over a 12-hour shift. HR also had to create a cross-training program so that employees could do each other's

OBJECTIVES

After reading the chapter and the case studies at the end, you should be able to use the material to.

1. Write a job description for a specific job.

2. Lay out a recruiting plan for a job, showing specifically how you would recruit for the position.

3. Explain what a manager can do wrong in interviewing, training, and disciplining employees, and what the manager should do to correct any shortcomings.

4. Explain what a manager is doing that may cause legal problems with human rights legislation, and what the manager should do to correct any shortcomings.

Signicast Corp.
www.signicast.com

jobs, so that they would not get bored or tired during their 12-hour shifts. A new compensation plan was instituted that paid workers not just for performance, but also for knowledge and for the number of jobs at which they became competent. HR therefore played a crucial role in implementing Signicast's expansion strategy.

That's basically what Signicast's managers did in designing and opening the new Signicast plant. The firm's expansion and the concepts underlying the design of its new plant weren't simply the outcome of discussions among the firm's top executives and production managers. Instead, these managers wisely recognized that even the most sophisticated computerized equipment was useless unless they had the sorts of skilled and motivated employees who could take advantage of this new technology. The firm thus involved its HR managers at every step of the expansion process. That is the essence of strategic human resource management.

The Strategic Role of Human Resources Management

human resources management (HRM)
All the activities that are necessary to acquire, train, appraise, and pay the organization's employees.

We saw in Chapters 8 and 9 that organization charts don't show what employees actually do, or what kinds of skills they need to do their jobs. So, we now turn to the issue of how to actually fill the various positions in organizations with qualified people. **Human resource management (HRM)** includes all the activities that are necessary to acquire, train, appraise, and pay the organization's employees.

Most large firms have HR departments with their own human resource managers. However, all managers are HR managers because they all get involved in recruiting, interviewing, selecting, training, and appraising employees. All managers therefore need staffing skills to do these things. Figure 10.1 shows this step-by-step HR process. As well, managers must be knowledgeable about a variety of legislation that governs the relationship between employees and the organizations they work for. We'll focus on each set of skills in the rest of this chapter.

Human Resource Management as a Strategic Partner

Managers used to view the HR function as strictly operational, arguing, for instance, that HR involves "putting out small fires—ensuring that people are paid on the right basis; that

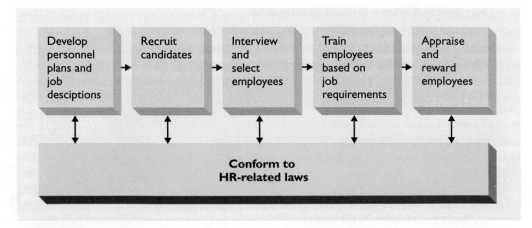

FIGURE 10.1
The Basic HR Process

a job advertisement meets the newspaper deadline; and a suitable supervisor is recruited for the night shift by the time it goes ahead..."[1] Over the last decade or so, however, there has been a big change in how companies view the HR function. Managers know that in today's flattened, downsized, and high-performing organizations, trained and committed employees—not machines—are the firm's competitive key. All firms have access to the same high-tech machines and devices today, so that isn't likely to be a source of competitive advantage. Rather, it's the employees who use those machines who set their firms apart. Employees are their firms' best competitive advantage.

If that is true, then the function responsible for acquiring, training, appraising, and compensating employees must play a bigger role in the firm's strategic success. This has led to a new field of study, known as **strategic human resource management**. Strategic human resource management is the process of aligning the firm's human resource management goals and policies with the strategic goals of the enterprise to improve business performance. Ideally, HR and top management work as one to craft the company's business strategy. That strategy then shapes specific HR policies such as where to recruit, who to hire, and how much to pay.

strategic human resource management
The process of aligning the firm's human resource management goals and policies with the strategic goals of the enterprise to improve business performance.

Writing Job Descriptions and Recruiting Employees

Staffing, in its narrowest sense, means filling a firm's open positions. As shown in Figure 10.2, this encompasses job analysis, recruiting, selecting, and training employees.

Job Analysis

Developing an organization chart creates jobs the firm must fill. **Job analysis** is the procedure through which managers determine the duties of the job and the kinds of people (in terms of skills and experience) that should be hired for the job.[2] This information is then used to develop a **job description** (a list of duties showing what the job entails) and **job specification** (a list of the skills and aptitudes sought in people hired for the job). It's not possible to know what kinds of people to recruit or select, or how to train them, if you don't understand the jobs they have to do. The job description, as shown in Figure 10.3, identifies the job, provides a brief job summary, and then lists specific responsibilities and duties.

staffing
Filling a firm's open positions.

job analysis
The procedure through which managers determine the duties of the job, and the kinds of people (in terms of skills and experience) that should be hired for the job.

job description
A list of duties showing what the job entails.

job specification
A list of the skills and aptitudes sought in people hired for the job.

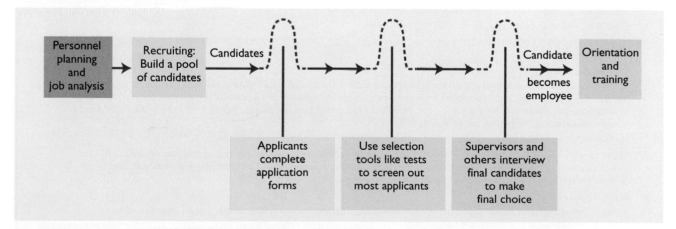

FIGURE 10.2
Steps in the Recruitment and Selection (Staffing) Process
The recruitment and selection process is a series of hurdles aimed at selecting the best candidate for the job.

OLEC CORP.
Job Description

Job Title: Marketing Manager
Department: Marketing
Reports To: President
Prepared By: Michael George
Prepared Date: April 1, 2004
Approved By: Ian Alexander
Approved Date: April 15, 2004

SUMMARY

Plans, directs, and coordinates the marketing of the organization's products and/or services by performing the following duties personally or through subordinate supervisors.

ESSENTIAL DUTIES AND RESPONSIBILITIES include the following. Other duties may be assigned.

Establishes marketing goals to ensure share of market and profitability of products and/or services.

Develops and executes marketing plans and programs, both short and long range, to ensure the profit growth and expansion of company products and/or services.

Researches, analyzes, and monitors financial, technological, and demographic factors so that market opportunities may be capitalized on and the effects of competitive activity may be minimized.

Plans and oversees the organization's advertising and promotion activities including print, electronic, and direct mail outlets.

Communicates with outside advertising agencies on ongoing campaigns.

Works with writers and artists and oversees copywriting, design, layout, paste-up, and production of promotional materials.

Develops and recommends pricing strategy for the organization that will result in the greatest share of the market over the long run.

Achieves satisfactory profit/loss ratio and share of market performance in relation to preset standards and to general and specific trends within the industry and the economy.

Ensures effective control of marketing results and that corrective action takes place to be certain that the achievement of marketing objectives are within designated budgets.

Evaluates market reactions to advertising programs, merchandising policy, and product packaging and formulation to ensure the timely adjustment of marketing strategy and plans to meet changing market and competitive conditions.

Recommends changes in basic structure and organization of marketing group to ensure the effective fulfillment of objectives assigned to it and to provide the flexibility to move swiftly in relation to marketing problems and opportunities.

Conducts marketing surveys on current and new product concepts.

Prepares marketing activity reports.

SUPERVISORY RESPONSIBILITIES

Manages three subordinate supervisors who supervise a total of five employees in the Marketing Department. Is responsible for the overall direction, coordination, and evaluation of this unit. Also directly supervises two non-supervisory employees. Carries out supervisory responsibilities in accordance with the organization's policies and applicable laws. Responsibilities include interviewing, hiring, and training employees; planning, assigning, and directing work; appraising performance; rewarding and disciplining employees; addressing complaints and resolving problems.

QUALIFICATIONS

To perform this job successfully, an individual must be able to perform each essential duty satisfactorily. The requirements listed below are representative of the knowledge, skill, and/or ability required. Reasonable accommodations may be made to enable individuals with disabilities to perform the essential functions.

EDUCATION and/or EXPERIENCE

Master's degree (M.A.) or equivalent; or four to ten years related experience and/or training; or equivalent combination of education and experience.

LANGUAGE SKILLS

Ability to read, analyze, and interpret common scientific and technical journals, financial reports, and legal documents. Ability to respond to common inquiries or complaints from customers, regulatory agencies, or members of the business community. Ability to write speeches and articles for publication that conform to prescribed style and format. Ability to effectively present information to top management, public groups, and/or boards of directors.

MATHEMATICAL SKILLS

Ability to apply advanced mathematical concepts such as exponents, logarithms, quadratic equations, and permutations. Ability to apply mathematical operations to such tasks as frequency distribution, determination of test reliability and validity, analysis of variance, correlation techniques, sampling theory, and factor analysis.

REASONING ABILITY

Ability to define problems, collect data, establish facts, and draw valid conclusions. Ability to interpret an extensive variety of technical instructions in mathematical or diagram form.

FIGURE 10.3
Sample Job Description

There is no standard format for writing a job description. However, most descriptions contain sections that cover the following items:

- Job identification
- Job summary
- Responsibilities and duties
- Authority of incumbent
- Standards of performance
- Working conditions
- Job specification (the human requirements of the job)

Managers can use a **job analysis questionnaire** (see Figure 10.4) to ascertain a job's duties and responsibilities. It requires employees to provide detailed information on what they do by briefly stating their main duties in their own words, describing the conditions under which they work, and listing any permits or licences required to perform duties assigned to their positions. Supervisors and/or specialists from the company's HR department then review this information. They then question the employee and decide exactly what the job does—or should—involve. Checklist 10.1 provides typical questions that are asked.

Most employers still write their own job descriptions, but more and more are turning to the internet. One site, **www.jobdescription.com**, illustrates why. The process is simple. Search by alphabetical title, keyword, category, or industry to find the desired job title. This leads you to a generic job description for that title—say "computers & EDP systems sales representative." You can then use the wizard to customize the generic description for this position. For example, you can add specific information about your organization, such as job title, job codes, department, and preparation date. And you can indicate whether the job has supervisory abilities and choose from a number of possible desirable competencies and experience levels.[3]

Personnel Planning

Job analysis is part of personnel planning. **Personnel planning** is the process of determining the organization's future personnel needs, as well as the methods to be used to

job analysis questionnaire
A form used by managers to determine the duties and functions of a job through a series of questions that employees answer.

Job Descriptions
www.jobdescription. com

personnel planning
The process of determining the organization's future personnel needs, as well as the methods to be used to fill those needs.

CHECKLIST **10.1**

Job Analysis Questions to Ask

- ☑ What is the job being performed?
- ☑ What are the major duties of your position? What exactly do you do?
- ☑ What are the education, experience, skill, and (where applicable) certification and licensing requirements?
- ☑ In what activities do you participate now?
- ☑ What are the job's responsibilities and duties?
- ☑ What are the basic accountabilities or performance standards that typify your work?
- ☑ What are your responsibilities?
- ☑ What are the environmental and working conditions involved?
- ☑ What are the job's physical demands? its emotional and mental demands?
- ☑ What are the health and safety conditions?
- ☑ Does the job expose you to any hazards or unusual working conditions?

Job Analysis Information Sheet

Job Title _____ Date _____

Job Code _____ Dept. _____

Superior's Title _____

Hours worked _____ AM to _____ PM

Job Analyst's Name _____

1. **What is the job's overall purpose?**
_____

2. **If the incumbent supervises others,** list them by job title; if there is more than one employee with the same title, put the number in parentheses following.
_____

3. **Check those activities** that are part of the incumbent's supervisory duties.
- ☐ Training
- ☐ Performance appraisal
- ☐ Inspecting work
- ☐ Budgeting
- ☐ Coaching and/or counselling
- ☐ Others (please specify) _____

4. **Describe the type and extent of supervision** received by the incumbent.
_____

5. **JOB DUTIES:** Describe briefly WHAT the incumbent does and, if possible, HOW he/she does it. Include duties in the following categories:

   a. daily duties (those performed on a regular basis every day or almost every day)
   _____

   b. periodic duties (those performed weekly, monthly, quarterly, or at other regular intervals)
   _____

   c. duties performed at irregular intervals
   _____

6. Is the incumbent performing duties he/she considers unnecessary? If so, describe.
_____

7. Is the incumbent performing duties not presently included in the job description? If so, describe.
_____

8. **EDUCATION:** Check the box that indicates the educational requirements for the job (**not** the educational background of the incumbent).

- ☐ No formal education required
- ☐ High school diploma (or equivalent)
- ☐ 4-year college or university degree (or equivalent) (specify:)
- ☐ Professional licence (specify:)
- ☐ Eighth grade education
- ☐ 2-year college degree (or equivalent)
- ☐ Graduate work or advanced degree

FIGURE 10.4
Job Analysis Questionnaire for Developing Job Descriptions
Use a questionnaire like this to interview job incumbents, or have them fill it out.

fill those needs. It involves developing job descriptions and specifications to determine what sorts of people it will need to staff, say, a new department. And, it involves deciding ahead of time where those new employees will come from (within or outside the company's employee pool) and how to train them.

9. **EXPERIENCE:** Check the amount of experience needed to perform the job.

☐ None ☐ Less than one month

☐ One to six months ☐ Six months to one year

☐ One to three years ☐ Three to five years

☐ Five to ten years ☐ More than ten years

10. **LOCATION:** Check location of job and, if necessary or appropriate, describe briefly.

☐ Outdoor ☐ Indoor

☐ Underground ☐ Pit

☐ Scaffold ☐ Other (specify)

11. **ENVIRONMENTAL CONDITIONS:** Check any objectionable conditions found on the job and note afterward how frequently each is encountered (rarely, occasionally, constantly, etc.)

☐ Dirt ☐ Dust

☐ Heat ☐ Cold

☐ Noise ☐ Fumes

☐ Odours ☐ Wetness/humidity

☐ Vibration ☐ Sudden temperature changes

☐ Darkness or poor lighting ☐ Other (specify)

12. **HEALTH AND SAFETY:** Check any undesirable health and safety conditions under which the incumbent must perform, and note how often they are encountered.

☐ Elevated workplace ☐ Mechanical hazards

☐ Explosives ☐ Electrical hazards

☐ Fire hazards ☐ Radiation

☐ Other (specify)

13. **MACHINES, TOOLS, EQUIPMENT, AND WORK AIDS:** Describe briefly what machines, tools, equipment, or work aids the incumbent works with on a regular basis:

_____

14. Have concrete work standards been established (errors allowed, time taken for a particular task, etc.)? If so, what are they?

_____

15. Are there any personal attributes (special aptitudes, physical characteristics, personality traits, etc.) required by the job?

_____

16. Are there any exceptional problems the incumbent might be expected to encounter in performing the job under normal conditions? If so, describe.

_____

17. Describe the successful completion and/or end results of the job.

_____

18. What is the seriousness of error on this job? Who or what is affected by errors the incumbent makes?

_____

19. To what job would a successful incumbent expect to be promoted?

[**Note:** This form is obviously slanted toward a manufacturing environment. but it can be adapted quite easily to fit a number of different types of jobs.]

FIGURE 10.4
(continued)

personnel replacement charts
Company records showing present performance and promotability of inside candidates for the most important positions.

Many employers use **personnel replacement charts** (Figure 10.5) to keep track of inside candidates for their most important positions. These show the present performance and promotability for each potential replacement for important positions. As an alternative, a position replacement card can be used. A card is made up for each position showing possible replacements as well as present performance, promotion potential, and training required by each possible candidate. Thanks to computers, personnel planning is increasingly sophisticated. Many firms maintain data banks containing information on hundreds of traits (like special skills, product knowledge, work experience, training courses, relocation limitations, and career interests) for each of their employees.

Employee Recruiting

recruiting
Attracting a pool of viable job applicants.

Once you know the jobs that must be filled, **recruiting**—attracting a pool of viable job applicants—becomes very important. If you have only two candidates for two openings, you may have little choice but to hire them. But if many applicants appear, you can use techniques like interviewing and testing to hire the best. Managers recruit candidates in various ways.

Current employees are one logical option. Filling open positions with inside candidates has both pros and cons. On the plus side, employees see that the firm rewards competence, which may in turn enhance morale and performance. Inside candidates are also known quantities in terms of performance and skills, and are more likely committed to the company and its goals. However, employees who unsuccessfully apply for jobs may become demoralized. And when an entire management team has come up through the ranks, there may be a tendency to maintain the status quo when innovation is required.

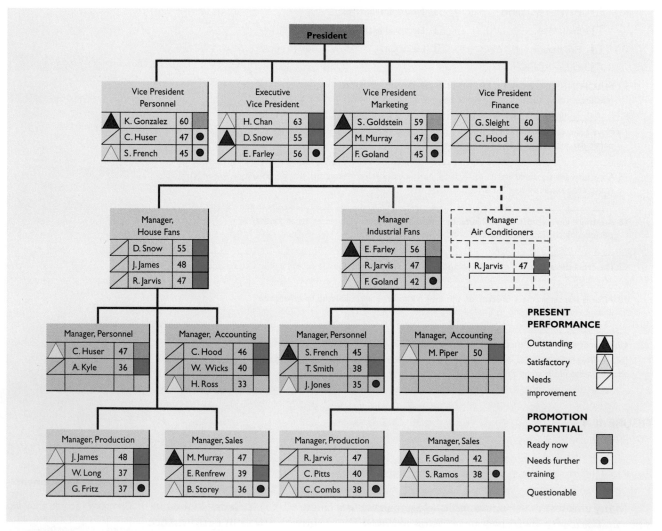

FIGURE 10.5
Management Personnel Replacement Chart

Promotion from within generally requires job posting.[4] **Job posting** means publicizing the open job to employees (often by literally posting it on bulletin boards and intranets) and listing the job's attributes, like qualifications, supervisor, working schedule, and pay rate. Some union contracts require job posting to ensure that union members get first choice of new and better positions. Job posting can be a good practice, even in non-union firms, if it facilitates the transfer and promotion of qualified inside candidates.[5]

Advertising Advertising is a major way to attract applicants. The main issue here is selecting the best advertising medium, be it the local paper, *The Globe and Mail*, a technical journal, or the internet.

The Internet A large and fast-growing proportion of employers use the internet as a recruiting tool. Managers use internet recruiting in numerous ways. A Boston-based recruiting firm posts job descriptions on its web page. NEC Electronics, Unisys Corp., and LSI Logicorp have all posted internet-based "cyber fairs" to recruit for applicants.[6]

Employment Agencies An **employment agency** is an intermediary whose business is to match applicants with jobs. There are three basic types. Public employment agencies, often called job service or unemployment service agencies, exist in every province. They are good sources of blue-collar and clerical workers, and some firms also use them for professional and managerial-level applicants. Not-for-profit employment agencies like professional and technical societies help their members find jobs. Private employment agencies charge the employer a fee for each applicant they place. These agencies are important sources of clerical, white-collar, and managerial personnel. Checklist 10.2 shows the points managers should keep in mind when dealing with employment agencies.

Contingent Workers and Temporary Help Agencies Employers often supplement their permanent workforce by hiring **contingent,** or **temporary, workers,** often through temporary help employment agencies. Also known as part-time or just-in-time workers, the contingent workforce is big and growing. Such workers are broadly defined as workers who don't have permanent jobs.[7]

The contingent workforce isn't limited to clerical or maintenance staff. People often find temporary work in engineering, science, or management support occupations. And growing numbers of firms use temporary workers as short-term chief financial officers, or even chief executive officers. For example, the CFO of Frantic Films, a Winnipeg-based special effects company, is a contingent worker.

<aside>
job posting
Publicizing the open job to employees and listing the job's attributes.

NEC Electronics
www.nec.com

employment agency
An intermediary whose business is to match applicants with jobs.

contingent (or temporary) worker
A temporary worker hired by an employer to fill short-term needs; not a permanent full-time or part-time employee.
</aside>

CHECKLIST **10.2**

How to Use an Employment Agency

☑ Give the agency an accurate and complete job description. The better it understands the job you want filled, the greater the likelihood it will produce a reasonable pool of applicants.

☑ Tests, application blanks, and interviews should be a part of the agency's selection process. They should not just rely on subjective evaluations.

☑ Periodically review data on candidates accepted or rejected by your firm and by the agency. Check on the effectiveness and fairness of the agency's screening process.

☑ It feasible, develop a long-term relationship with one or two agencies.

☑ Screen the agency. Check with other managers. Find out which agencies have been the most effective at filling the sorts of positions you need filled. Do they have the qualifications to understand the sorts of jobs for which you are recruiting? What is their reputation in the community?[8]

Executive Recruiters **Executive recruiters** (also called headhunters) are agencies retained by employers to look for top management talent, usually those earning $70 000 and up. They have extensive contacts and a file of potential recruits, and are adept at contacting qualified employed candidates who aren't looking to change jobs. They can also keep the client firm's name confidential until late in the search process. The recruiter saves management time by advertising the position and screening what could turn out to be hundreds of applicants. Digging up the initial "long list" of candidates used to take months, but that's not practical anymore. Most search firms are therefore creating internet-linked computerized databases[9] which can create a long list of candidates at the push of a button.[10]

Walk-ins and Referrals Walk-ins—people who apply directly at the office—are a major source of applicants, particularly for hourly paid workers. Encouraging walk-ins may be as simple as posting help-wanted signs on the door. Some firms use printed announcements of openings and requests for *referrals* in the company's newsletter, intranet, or on bulletin boards. Of the firms responding to one survey, 40 percent said they use employee referral systems and hire about 15 percent of their employees through referrals. A cash award for referring hired candidates is the most common incentive. Some experts contend that the most effective recruiting method is to encourage existing employees to refer qualified friends and colleagues.[11] Recruiting high-tech employees is especially amenable to such programs.

University and College Recruiting Sending employers' representatives to university and college campuses to pre-screen applicants and create an applicant pool from the graduating class is an important source of management, professional, and technical employees. One study of 251 staffing professionals concluded that firms filled about 38 percent of all externally filled jobs requiring a university or college degree with new grads.[12]

Many students get their jobs through internships. Employers can use interns to make useful contributions, while evaluating them as possible full-time employees. Internships can be win-win situations for both students and employers. For students, it may mean being able to hone business skills, check out potential employers, and learn more about their occupational likes (and dislikes).

Marriott
www.marriott.com

Recruiting a More Diverse Workforce Recruiting a diverse workforce isn't just socially responsible; it's a necessity. Tools here include diversity data banks, word-of-mouth, and minority-oriented applicant sources. Marriott International hired 600 welfare recipients under its Pathways to Independence program. The heart of the program is a six-week pre-employment training program that teaches work and life skills "designed to rebuild workers' self-esteem and instill positive attitudes about work."[13]

Many companies are actively recruiting older workers, minorities, and women in an attempt to make the workforce more diverse.

Changing demographics will influence managers as they recruit a diverse workforce. The rapid increase in the number of women, people with disabilities, and Aboriginal people in the labour pool means that managers will have to use recruiting strategies that are different from the ones they have traditionally used to hire white males. The large number of immigrants that have entered Canada during the last 20 years is another source of diversity in the workforce. During the 1980s, one million immigrants entered Canada, and in the 1990s, two million more entered. The incorporation of many of these immigrants into Canadian businesses will further increase the diversity of the workforce.

The rapid aging of the Canadian population is another factor that human resource professionals must deal with. In 1981, the most populous age bracket in Canada was the 15–24 age. By 2006, the largest group will be the 40–49 bracket, and by 2031 the largest group will be those aged 70–74. These are dramatic changes and will provide both challenges and opportunities to business firms. On the one hand, an aging workforce raises issues of retirement and health care for companies, but it also presents an opportunity to maintain a workforce that is very experienced.

Interviewing and Selecting Employees

Once they have a pool of applicants, managers turn to selecting the best one. Here they use several screening techniques—application forms, tests, interviews, and reference checks—to assess and investigate an applicant's aptitudes, interests, and background. The manager then chooses the best candidate, given the job's requirements. Employee selection is important because your own performance as a manager hinges on your subordinates' performance. A poor performer drags a manager down, and a good one enhances the manager's and the firm's performance.

Screening applicants is expensive, so it is important to do it right. Hiring a manager who earns $60 000 a year may cost as much as $40 000 or $50 000, including search fees, interviewing time, and travel and moving expenses. The cost of hiring even non-executive employees can be $3000 to $5000 or more.

Application Forms

For most employers, the **application form** is the first step in the selection process (although some firms first require a brief pre-screening interview.) The application is a good way to quickly collect verifiable historical data from the candidate. It usually includes information about such areas as education, prior work history, and hobbies (see Figure 10.6).

In practice, most organizations need several application forms. For technical and managerial personnel, the form may require detailed answers to questions concerning education and experience. The form for hourly factory workers might focus on the tools and equipment the applicant has used.

Testing for Employee Selection

A **test** is a sample of a person's behaviour. Employers use tests to predict success on the job. About 45 percent of 1085 companies surveyed by the American Management Association tested applicants for basic skills (defined as the ability to read instructions, write reports, and do arithmetic at a level adequate to perform common workplace tasks).[14] Another survey concluded that 38.6 percent of companies said they performed psychological testing on job applicants, ranging from tests of the applicants' cognitive abilities to "honesty testing."[15] Try the short test in Figure 10.7 to see how prone you might be to on-the-job accidents.

Although popular, there are many legal and ethical constraints on the use of tests. It is useless (and often illegal) to use a test that lacks validity or reliability. Test *validity* answers the question "does this test measure what it is supposed to measure? In practical terms, this means that a test should predict actual performance on the job. *Reliability* refers to a test's consistency. For example, if a person scores 90 on an intelligence test on Monday and 130 on Tuesday, you probably wouldn't have much faith in the test's reliability.

Types of Tests Many types of tests are available. Employers use intelligence (IQ) tests like the Stanford-Binet or the Wechsler or Wonderlic to measure general intellectual abilities. For some jobs, managers are also interested in testing other abilities. The Bennett Test of Mechanical Comprehension (see Figure 10.8) helps assess an applicant's understanding of basic mechanical principles. It is useful for predicting success on a job such as machinist or engineer. Other tests measure personality and interests. For example, you probably wouldn't hire someone for an entry-level job as an accounting clerk if he or she

APPLICATION FOR EMPLOYMENT

Position being applied for	Date available to begin work

PERSONAL DATA

Last name	Given name(s)

Address	Street	Apt. No.	Home Telephone Number
City	Province	Postal Code	Business Telephone Number

Are you legally eligible to work in Canada? ☐ Yes   ☐ No

Are you 18 years or more and less than 65 years of age? ☐ Yes   ☐ No

Are you willing to relocate in Ontario? ☐ Yes ☐ No	Preferred location

To determine your qualification for employment, please provide (below and on the reverse) information related to your academic and other achievements including volunteer work, as well as employment history.
Additional information may be attached on a separate sheet.

EDUCATION

SECONDARY SCHOOL ■	BUSINESS, TRADE OR SECONDARY SCHOOL ■
Highest grade or level completed	Name of course Length of course
Type of certificate or diploma obtained	Licence, certificate, or diploma awarded? ☐ Yes ☐ No

COMMUNITY COLLEGE ■	UNIVERSITY ■
Name of program Length of program	Length of course Degree awarded ☐ Pass ☐ Yes ☐ No ☐ Honours
Diploma received ☐ Yes ☐ No	Major subject
Other courses, workshops, seminars	Licences, certificates, degrees

Work-related skills

Describe any of your work-related skills, experience, or training that relate to the position being applied for.

FIGURE 10.6
Sample Application Form

CHECK YES OR NO   YES   NO

1. You like a lot of excitement in your life.

_____

2. An employee who takes it easy at work
   is cheating on the employer.

_____

3. You are a cautious person.

_____

4. In the past three years, you have found yourself
   in a shouting match at school or work.

_____

5. You like to drive fast just for fun.

_____

Analysis: According to John Kamp, an industrial psychologist, applicants who answered no, yes, yes, no, no to questions 1, 2, 3, 4, and 5 are statistically likely to be absent less often, to have fewer on-the-job injuries, and, if the job involves driving, to have fewer on-the-job driving accidents. Actual scores on the test are based on answers to 130 questions.

FIGURE 10.7
Sample Test

had no measurable interest in working with numbers.[16] Most of us have had some experience dealing with service people who are obviously not psychologically suited for such jobs. A personality test might have screened them out.

Assessment Centres In an **assessment centre**, candidates spend two or three days performing realistic management tasks while expert appraisers observe them and draw conclusions about each candidate's potential.[17] The centre's activities might include individual presentations, objective tests, interviews, and participation in management games.

Video Assessment **Video assessment** involves showing job applicants videos of realistic work situations (portrayed by actors) and then asking the applicants to choose a course of action.[18] For example, one scenario might show an assistant to a department manger who is trying to convince the supervisor of the word-processing pool to give his job top priority because the boss wants some last-minute changes made in a report. At the end of each scenario, the viewers choose one of four courses of action to resolve the problem shown in the video. The test administrator then uses the computer to score candidate choices (much like a university or college instructor would grade student exams).

Video assessment is fast, reliable, and relatively inexpensive. It gives management greater insight into employee strengths and weaknesses before they are hired, and this can help the company solve long-standing problems like high turnover. Firms using video assessment include Weyerhaeuser, Reebok, Nortel, and B.C. Hydro.

Computerized Testing This type of testing is increasingly replacing conventional paper and pencil and manual testing. In one large manufacturing company, experts developed a computerized testing procedure for selecting clerical personnel.[19] They developed eight test components to represent actual work performed by secretarial personnel, such as maintaining and developing databases and spreadsheets, and handling travel arrangements. For the "word processing" test, applicants had three minutes (monitored by the computer) to type as much of a letter as possible. The computer recorded and corrected the manuscript. For the "travel expense form completion" test, applicants had to access the

assessment centre
An approach to selection in which candidates spend two or three days performing realistic management tasks under the observation of expert appraisers.

video assessment
An approach to selection that involves showing job applicants videos of realistic work situations and then asking the applicants to choose a course of action.

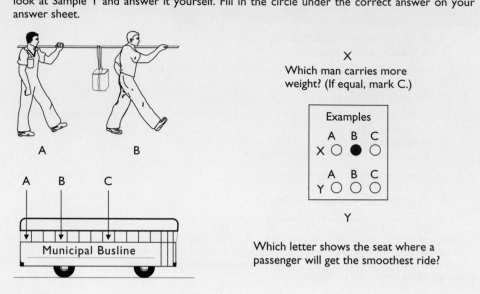

Look at Sample X on this page. It shows two men carrying a weighted object on a plank, and it asks, Which man carries more weight? Because the object is closer to man B than to man A, man B is shouldering more weight; so blacken the circle under B on your answer sheet. Now look at Sample Y and answer it yourself. Fill in the circle under the correct answer on your answer sheet.

X
Which man carries more weight? (If equal, mark C.)

Examples

A B C
X ○ ● ○

A B C
Y ○ ○ ○

Y

Which letter shows the seat where a passenger will get the smoothest ride?

FIGURE 10.8
Bennett Test of Mechanical Comprehension, Example
Human resource managers often use personnel tests, like this one, to measure a candidate's skills and aptitudes.

database file, use some of the information there to compute quarterly expenses, and transfer this information to the travel expense form.

Interviews

The **interview** is probably the most widely used selection device, and it would be very unusual for a manager to hire a subordinate without at least a brief personal interview. The problem is that although almost everyone gets a job interview, the traditional interview format may not produce very reliable information. A new technique called **behaviour-based interviewing** shows some promise in overcoming these problems (see the "People Side of Managing" box).

Guidelines that will help both interviewers and interviewees get more useful information from interviews are summarized in Table 10.1 and discussed below.[20]

Guidelines For Interviewers

Plan the Interview Begin by reviewing the candidate's application and résumé, and note any areas that are vague or may indicate strengths or weaknesses. Review the job specification. Start the interview with a clear picture of the traits of an ideal candidate.

Structure the Interview The main problem with most interviews is that they are far too informal. The interviewer gives little thought to the sorts of questions that might actually differentiate among the applicants. And the whole process is one in which subjectivity rules, with hard-to-measure or easy-to-fake questions like "What are your main strengths?" playing too big a role. Therefore, rather than the usual subjective questions, ask ones that are clearly relevant to success on the job.

Behaviour-Based Interviewing

Behaviour-based interviewing assumes that your past behaviour is a pretty good predictor of your future behaviour. Specifically, it assesses how you reacted to difficult and/or important job situations in the past and assumes that these are a good indicator of how you will react to similar job situations in the future. The approach can be used to test for technical skills (e.g., accounting, welding, computer programming, etc.), management skills (e.g., organizing, motivating others, communicating, etc.), and individual skills (e.g., dependability, discipline, ability to work on a team, etc.).

Instead of asking a traditional interviewing question like "Do you often take the initiative?" behaviour-based interviewing asks "Tell me about a situation where you became aware of a problem. What did you do?" Asking questions like this one focuses the interview much more on your behaviour than on what you say you would do if the problem arose in the future. Other typical questions that interviewers ask in behaviour-based interviewing are as follows:

- Think of a time when you were asked to analyze information and then make a specific recommendation. What kind of reasoning and thought processes did you use?
- Think of a time when you had to deal with a customer that you thought was being unreasonable. How did you deal with that person?
- Think of a time when you had to cope with a major change in your job. What did you do?
- Think of a time when you had to work with a person who was not "pulling their weight." What, if anything, did you do?

Behaviour-based interviewing requires the person who is interviewing candidates to first identify the characteristics, skills, and behaviours that are important in the job that needs to be filled. The interviewer then constructs open-ended questions that will determine whether the interviewee possesses those characteristics, skills, and behaviours.

Behaviour-based interviewing is becoming more common because companies are facing increasingly competitive environments. These competitive environments have meant downsizing, which places increasing demands on the workers who remain. There is also more emphasis on working in teams. These changing work situations have motivated companies to be much more focused in their hiring because they want workers who are more skilled and motivated than previously.

The increasing use of behaviour-based interviewing means that you are likely to be exposed to it at some point in your job search. What should you do to prepare for a behaviour-based interview? The main thing is to think about the job you are interviewing for and the skills that will be required to do it. Try to tell an interesting story (from a previous paid or volunteer position) that succinctly describes a situation you faced, the actions you took, and the outcome that resulted from your actions. If the outcome was good, the interviewer will likely be favourably impressed with your logical thinking and actions. Even if the outcome wasn't so good, you can indicate what you learned from the experience and how that experience will benefit your new employer.

TABLE 10.1 *Guidelines for Interviewers and Interviewees*

FOR INTERVIEWERS	FOR INTERVIEWEES
1. Plan the interview.	1. Prepare.
2. Structure the interview.	2. Make a good first impression.
3. Emphasize situational questions.	3. Uncover the interviewer's real needs.
4. Establish rapport.	4. Relate your answers to the interviewer's needs.
5. Ask questions.	5. Think before answering.
6. Delay your decision.	6. Watch your non-verbal behaviour.
7. Close the interview.	

Emphasize Situational Questions Situational questions make the applicant explain how he or she would handle a hypothetical situation, such as "If you were a supervisor here, what would you do if one of your subordinates came in consistently late?" or "What program would you use to design this website?" Also ask job-relevant questions about the applicant's past behaviour. For example (if the job requires making cold calls), "Tell me about a time when you had to make an unsolicited sales call. How did you do it? What happened? What was the result?" Ask relevant "background" questions like "What work experiences, training, or other qualifications do you have for working in a team work environment?" Job knowledge questions are important too, for instance, "What factors should you consider when developing a TV advertising campaign?"

Interviews based on a structured guide (see Figure 10.9), usually result in the best interviews.[21] At a minimum, write out your questions prior to the interview.

Establish Rapport The main purpose of the interview is to find out about the applicant, and to do this it's helpful to put the person at ease. Greet the candidate and start by asking a non-controversial question—perhaps about the weather or the traffic conditions that day. As a rule, all applicants—even unsolicited drop-ins—should receive friendly, courteous treatment, not only on humanitarian grounds, but also because your reputation is on the line.

Ask Questions Try to follow your structured interview guide or the questions you wrote out ahead of time. Some suggestions for asking questions include

- Avoid questions that the candidate can answer with a simple yes or no.
- Don't put words in the applicant's mouth or telegraph the desired answer (for instance, by nodding or smiling when the right answer is given).
- Don't interrogate the applicant as if the person were a criminal, and don't be patronizing, sarcastic, or inattentive.
- Don't monopolize the interview by rambling, or let the applicant dominate the interview.
- Listen to the candidate and encourage him or her to express thoughts fully.
- Don't just ask for general statements about a candidate's accomplishments; also ask for examples.[22] If the candidate lists specific strengths or weaknesses, follow up with, "What are specific examples that demonstrate each of your strengths?"

Delay Your Decision Interviewers often make snap judgments even before they see the candidate, perhaps based on the application or résumé. Keep a record of the interview, and review it afterward. Make your decision then.[23]

CANDIDATE RECORD NAP 100 (10/77)

CANDIDATE NUMBER | NAME (LAST NAME FIRST) | COLLEGE NAME | COLLEGE CODE

| | U 921 |
(1–7) | (8–27) | | (28–30)

INTERVIEWER NUMBER
| 0 |
(33–40)

INTERVIEWER NAME

SOURCE (41)
Campus ☐ C
Walk-in ☐ W
Intern ☐ I
Agency ☐ A

RACE (42)
White ☐ W
Black ☐ B
Asian ☐ A
Hispanic ☐ H
Native Am. ☐ NA

SEX (43)
Male ☐ M
Female ☐ F
Init.
Cont.
Date

DEGREE (53)
Bachelors ☐ B
Masters ☐ M
Law ☐ L
Majors

AVERAGE
(A = 4.0)
Overall ☐☐ (54–55)
Acctg. ☐☐ (56–57)

CLASS STANDING (59–59)
Top 10% ☐ 10
Top 25% ☐ 25
Top Half ☐ 50
Bottom Half ☐ 75

CAMPUS INTERVIEW EVALUATIONS

ATTITUDE – MOTIVATION – GOALS

POOR ☐   AVERAGE ☐   GOOD ☐   OUTSTANDING ☐

(POSITIVE, CO-OPERATIVE, ENERGETIC, MOTIVATED, SUCCESSFUL, GOAL-ORIENTED)
COMMENTS:

COMMUNICATIONS SKILLS – PERSONALITY – SALES ABILITY

POOR ☐   AVERAGE ☐   GOOD ☐   OUTSTANDING ☐

(ARTICULATE, LISTENS, ENTHUSIASTIC, LIKEABLE, POISED, TACTFUL, ACCEPTING, CONVINCING)
COMMENTS:

EXECUTIVE PRESENCE – DEAL WITH TOP PEOPLE

POOR ☐   AVERAGE ☐   GOOD ☐   OUTSTANDING ☐

(IMPRESSIVE, STANDS OUT, A WINNER, REMEMBERED, LEVELHEADED, AT EASE, AWARE)
COMMENTS:

INTELLECTUAL ABILITIES

POOR ☐   AVERAGE ☐   GOOD ☐   OUTSTANDING ☐

(INSIGHTFUL, CREATIVE, CURIOUS, IMAGINATIVE, UNDERSTANDS, REASONS, INTELLIGENT, SCHOLARLY)
COMMENTS:

JUDGMENT – DECISION-MAKING ABILITY

POOR ☐   AVERAGE ☐   GOOD ☐   OUTSTANDING ☐

(MATURE, SEASONED, INDEPENDENT, COMMON SENSE, CERTAIN, DETERMINED, LOGICAL)
COMMENTS:

LEADERSHIP

POOR ☐   AVERAGE ☐   GOOD ☐   OUTSTANDING ☐

(SELF-CONFIDENT, TAKES CHARGE, EFFECTIVE, RESPECTED, MANAGEMENT MINDED, GRASPS AUTHORITY)
COMMENTS:

CAMPUS INTERVIEW SUMMARY

INVITE (Circle)
Yes   No
DATE AVAILABLE

AREA OF INTEREST (Circle)
AUDIT   TAX
MCS   ABC
OTHER

SEMESTER HRS.
Acct'g.
Audit
Tax

OFFICES PREFERRED:
No. 1
No. 2
No. 3

SUMMARY COMMENTS:

FIGURE 10.9
Structured Interview Form for College Applicants

Close the Interview Toward the end of the interview, leave time to answer any questions the candidate may have and, if appropriate, to promote your firm to the candidate. Tell the applicant whether there is an interest in him or her and, if so, what the next step will be. Make rejections diplomatically, with a statement like, "Although your background is impressive, there are other candidates whose experience is closer to our requirements."

Guidelines For Interviewees

Prepare Before the interview, learn all you can about the employer, the job, and the people doing the recruiting. Look through business periodicals and websites to find out what is happening in the company and industry.

Make a Good First Impression Most interviewers make up their minds about the applicant during the early minutes of the interview. Bad first impressions are almost impossible to overcome.

Uncover the Interviewer's Real Needs Avoid giving long answers to questions until you know the interviewer's needs. First determine what the person is looking for and what problems he or she needs solved. Sample questions you can ask include the following:

- Would you mind describing the job for me?
- What's the first problem you'd want me to address?
- Could you tell me about the people who would be reporting to me?
- Do you have a written job description for this position?
- How would you define the company's management philosophy?

Relate Your Answers to the Interviewer's Needs Start by saying something like, "One of the problem areas you've said is important to you is similar to a problem I once faced." Then state the problem, describe your solution, and reveal the results.

Think Before Answering Answering a question should be a three-step process: pause, think, speak. Pause to make sure you understand what the interviewer is driving at, think about how to structure your answer, and then speak.

Watch Your Non-verbal Behaviour In most interviews, the interviewee's non-verbal behaviour broadcasts as much about the person as what the person says. Maintain eye contact. Speak with enthusiasm, nod agreement, and remember to take a moment to frame your answer (pause, think, speak) so that you sound articulate and fluent.[24]

Other Selection Techniques

Managers use several other selection techniques to screen applicants. These include background investigations, honesty tests, and health tests.

Background Investigations Employers should verify the applicant's background information and references.[25] This is necessary to corroborate the information the candidate provides, and to uncover other, potentially damaging information (about an unrevealed conviction, for instance). Most employers at least make telephone inquiries. The rest use sources like commercial credit-checking agencies and reference letters.

The most commonly verified background areas are legal eligibility for employment (to comply with immigration laws), dates of prior employment, military service (including discharge status), education, and identification (including date of birth and address).[26] Most companies at least try to verify an applicant's current or previous position and salary with the current employer by telephone. Others call current and previous supervisors to discover more about the person's motivation, technical competence, and ability to work with others. Some employers also get background reports from commercial credit-rating companies. This can provide information about an applicant's credit standing, indebtedness, reputation, character, and lifestyle. Others use special pre-employment information services. These firms use internet and computerized databases to access and accumulate information about matters such as applicants' compensation histories, credit histories, driving records, and conviction records.

Honesty Testing Many employees work in jobs for which honesty is crucial—as bank tellers or cashiers, for instance—and so paper-and-pencil "honesty testing" is a mini-industry.[27] Questions such as, "Have you ever made a personal phone call on company time?" assess a person's tendency to be honest. Experts initially questioned the validity of tests like these, but the consensus today is that they can predict which applicants may be dishonest. However, in practice, detecting dishonest candidates involves not just tests, but also comprehensive anti-theft screening procedures. The following checklist summarizes what the manager can do here.

Health Exams The selection process often ends with a physical examination and possibly a drug screening test. Employers use the medical exam to confirm that the applicant qualifies for the physical requirements of the position and to discover any medical limitations that should be taken into account. By identifying health problems, a physical exam can also reduce absenteeism and accidents and detect communicable diseases that may be unknown to the applicant.

Because drug use can be a serious problem at work, many companies use drug tests, even though they are increasingly coming under fire for doing so. In 1998, for example, the Ontario Divisional Court decided that Imperial Oil's drug policy—which included pre-employment drug testing that made offers of work conditional on a negative result—was unlawful because Imperial failed to prove that a positive drug test would indicate a failure to perform essential duties. Imperial's policy also required random drug and alcohol testing, but that was also judged to be discriminatory because the company could not prove that such testing was necessary to deter alcohol or drug impairment on the job.[30]

Toronto Dominion Bank wanted to give drug tests to all new employees because it felt that drug use was a growing problem in society and because it wanted to have the public's trust. But a federal court ruled that TD Bank's policy was discriminatory and that it was not related closely enough to job performance.[31]

Orienting and Training Employees

Once employees are hired, they must be prepared to do their jobs; this is the purpose of orientation and training. Most people have had experience with inadequately trained personnel: The waiter who doesn't say "hello," or the drycleaner that doesn't properly press your jacket. Designing and implementing training programs are essential managerial activities. Do not underestimate their importance. It is futile to carefully select new employees and then to put them on their jobs with little or no training.

Orienting Employees

Employee **orientation** means providing new employees with basic information on things like work rules and vacation policies. In many companies, employees receive a hardcopy

orientation
Providing new employees with basic information on things like work rules and vacation policies.

training program
The process of providing new employees with information they need to do their jobs satisfactorily.

on-the-job training
Training in which a person learns a job while her or she is working at it.

off-the-job training
Training that is performed at a location away from the work site.

or internet-based handbook that contains this information. Orientation aims to familiarize the new employee with the company and his or her co-workers; provide information about working conditions (coffee breaks, overtime policy, and so on); explain how to get on the payroll and how to obtain identification cards; what the working hours are; and generally reduce the jitters often associated with starting a new job. Given that companies spend a lot of money recruiting new employees, it would seem likely that they would also pay attention to orientation. But a recent survey by RHR International of Toronto found that companies often do very little to orient new managers to their positions, and that 30 percent to 40 percent of new hires either quit, significantly under-perform, or get fired within a year of hiring. Figure 10.10 outlines a typical orientation program.

Training Employees

Orientation is usually followed by a **training program**, one aimed at ensuring that the new employee has the basic knowledge required to perform the job satisfactorily. Some companies find that they must retrain their current employees because of changes in products and markets. When Honeywell Ltd.'s Scarborough, Ontario, plant won a mandate to export to the United States and Europe, the plant had to become more competitive. To achieve this goal, the company offered training opportunities to its workers. When it offered 30 spaces in after-work classes in English as a second language, it received 130 applications. Two hundred applications were received for a computer awareness course, and 60 people signed up for a course designed to increase the workers' ability to work in teams.[33]

On-the-job training occurs while the employee is actually at work. Ford Motor of Canada trained 140 workers for a year to work in a new aluminum casting plant in Windsor, Ontario. Because workers needed to know many jobs, they needed a lot of training. Much on-the-job training is unplanned and informal, as when one employee shows another how to use the new photocopier.

Off-the-job training, by contrast, is performed at a location away from the work site. For example, refresher courses are offered for managers of McDonald's Canadian restaurants at the Canadian Institute of Hamburgerology. Second Cup Ltd., Canada's largest retailer of specialty coffee, runs Coffee College, where franchisees and managers learn a lot of details about coffee. They also learn how to hire workers, keep the books, detect employee theft, and boost Christmas sales.[34] At Toronto Plastics Ltd., machine operators must continually assess the performance of their equipment as part of a new emphasis on statistical process control. To help the employees do a better job, the company trained 75 machine operators in statistics and mathematics.[35]

Statistics Canada reports that 16 percent of Canadian adults cannot read the majority of written materials they encounter in everyday life, and that 22 percent do not have the reading skills to deal with complex instructions. Companies like Nortel Networks and CCL Custom Manufacturing are finding that they have to train workers because the equipment they must use is increasingly complex.[36] A study by the Conference Board of Canada found that, on a per-employee basis, large Canadian companies spend only half as much on training as U.S. firms do. And U.S. firms, in turn, spend only a fraction of the amount that Japanese firms spend.[37]

Other activities that come under the general heading of training and orientation are *mentoring* (helping younger managers learn the ropes and benefit from the experiences of older

Toyota's Lexus sales staff use a computerized simulation called Fact Lab for sales training. A simulation test shows four digital images of sales scenarios.

Second Cup Ltd. runs Coffee College, where recruits learn about all aspects of the retail coffee business.

UCSD Healthcare   **NEW EMPLOYEE DEPARTMENTAL ORIENTATION CHECKLIST**
(Return to Human Resources within 10 days of hire)

NAME:	HIRE DATE:	SIN:	JOB TITLE:
DEPARTMENT:	NEO DATE:	DEPARTMENTAL ORIENTATION COMPLETED BY:	

TOPIC	DATE REVIEWED	N/A
1. HUMAN RESOURCES INFORMATION		
a. Departmental Attendance Procedures and UCSD Healthcare Work Time & Attendance Policy	a. _____	☐
b. Job Description Review	b. _____	☐
c. Annual Performance Evaluation and Peer Feedback Process	c. _____	☐
d. Probationary Period Information	d. _____	☐
e. Appearance/Dress Code Requirements	e. _____	☐
f. Annual TB Screening	f. _____	☐
g. Licence and/or certification Renewals	g. _____	☐
2. DEPARTMENT INFORMATION		
a. Organizational Structure-Department Core Values Orientation	a. _____	☐
b. Department/Unit Area Specific Policies & Procedures	b. _____	☐
c. Customer Service Practices	c. _____	☐
d. CQI Effort and Projects	d. _____	☐
e. Tour and Floor Plan	e. _____	☐
f. Equipment/Supplies	f. _____	☐
• Keys Issued	_____	☐
• Radio Pager Issued	_____	☐
• Other _____	_____	☐
g. Mail and Recharge Codes	g. _____	☐
3. SAFETY INFORMATION		
a. Departmental Safety Plan	a. _____	☐
b. Employee Safety/Injury Reporting Procedures	b. _____	☐
c. Hazard Communication	c. _____	☐
d. Infection Control/Sharps Disposal	d. _____	☐
e. Attendance at Annual Safety Fair (Mandatory)	e. _____	☐
4. FACILITES INFORMATION		
a. Emergency Power	a. _____	☐
b. Mechanical Systems	b. _____	☐
c. Water	c. _____	☐
d. Medical Gases	d. _____	☐
e. Patient Room	e. _____	☐
• Bed	_____	☐
• Headwall	_____	☐
• Bathroom	_____	☐
• Nurse Call System	_____	☐
5. SECURITY INFORMATION		
a. Code Triage Assignment	a. _____	☐
b. Code Blue Assignment	b. _____	☐
c. Code Red – Evacuation Procedure	c. _____	☐
d. Code 10 – Bomb Threat Procedure	d. _____	☐
e. Departmental Security Measures	e. _____	☐
f. UCSD Emergency Number 6111 or 911	f. _____	☐

This generic checklist may not constitute a complete departmental orientation or assessment. Please attach any additional unit specific orientation material for placement in the employee's HR file.

I have been oriented on the items listed above_____

FIGURE 10.10
New Employee Departmental Orientation Checklist

managers), *networking* (improving informal interactions among managers), and *management development programs* (training managers to be more effective in their work). The "Challenge of Change" box describes one company's management development efforts.

Training is one of the things that distinguishes superior companies from inferior ones. Superior firms invest much time and money training employees.[38] For example, why do you think the coffee always tastes good at Starbucks? It's not just the beans; it's the training. "Brewing the perfect cup" is one of five classes that all Starbucks employees take during their first six weeks on the job.[39] They learn that they must steam milk at temperatures of at least 150°F; that orders are "called out," (such as "triple-tall nonfat mocha"); and that coffee should never sit on the hot plate for more than 20 minutes.

Employee Development at EnCana

EnCana
www.encana.com

In 2002, shareholders at Alberta Energy Company Ltd. and PanCanadian Energy Corp. approved a merger of the two companies. The new entity—called EnCana—is one of the largest independent oil and gas producers in the world.

Because of what it does, EnCana employs a lot of technical specialists like geologists, engineers, and accountants. When it took a close look at how well it was training its employees, it discovered that although it was providing ample technical training, it was providing very little management training to people who worked their way up from these technical positions into management positions. They were therefore not trained to lead and motivate other workers.

Terry Lawrence, the vice president of human resources, started out as a reservoir engineer (a person who evaluates the amount of oil underground). He came to the realization that many of the managers in the company really didn't know anything about management. And before they were promoted to management, the company sometimes didn't even check to see whether they had people skills, a crucial element in leadership success.

To remedy these problems, the company established the PanCanadian Management Institute in co-operation with the University of Calgary. At the Institute, executives receive basic training in management. Lawrence says that employees think that the training they receive is a very good experience. They not only improve their performance and take on more challenges, the training itself is a reward and recognition. As such, it is very motivating.

The company also sends employees to other executive development programs such as the Banff School of Management and the Niagara Institute Leadership Development Program. Lawrence has taken some training himself and has attended an intensive two-week course in strategic human resources at the University of Michigan. The company spends 5 percent to 7 percent of its operating budget on training, compared to the Canadian average of 2 percent to 3 percent.

In addition to training people with managerial potential, EnCana also trains employees who make a difference in the technical side of the business. Lawrence recognizes that the best engineers and geologists are not necessarily the best managers.

Since the oil and gas that EnCana produces looks just like the oil and gas produced by competitors, the company has to distinguish itself on the basis of the quality of the decisions its managers make. It therefore plans to put all of its employees, especially those identified as having "high potential," through training programs that will prepare them for the rapid changes ahead.

Training programs typically involve the following steps:

Step 1—Identify the specific job performance skills needed, analyze the skills and needs of the prospective trainees, and develop specific, measurable knowledge and performance objectives.

Step 2—Compile and produce the training program content, including workbooks, exercises, and activities.

Step 3—Work out the "bugs" in the training program by presenting it to a small representative audience.

Step 4—Implement the program by actually training the targeted employee group.

Step 5—Assess the program's success or failure.

Most managers do not create their own training materials, since many materials are available on- and off-line. For example, the professional development site **Click2learn.com** offers a wide range of web-based courses employees can take on-line. Many firms provide turnkey training programs on various topics. The programs include a training leader's guide, self-study book, and a video for improving skills in areas such as customer service, documenting discipline, and appraising performance.

Much training today is technologically advanced. For example, instead of sending new rental agents to week-long, classroom-based training courses, Value Rent-a-Car now provides them with interactive, multimedia-based training programs utilizing CD-ROMs. These help agents learn the car rental process by walking them through various procedures, such as how to operate the rental computer system.[40]

Internet Learning Portals Many firms are creating their own internet-based learning portals for their employees. These let the company contract with training content providers, which offer their training content to the firm's employees via the portal. ADC Telecommunications installed such a system. ADC supplies equipment and services for broadband communications and has 16 000 employees worldwide. The firm's training department concluded that its existing instructor-led training was not meeting its needs. The company decided that the solution was to deliver training programs on-line. To accomplish this, ADC turned to Click2learn. Click2learn installed a version of its standard portal for ADC. As one ADC manager put it, "our Click2learn learning site gives ADC personnel access to the wide variety of on-line courses available on the learning network...and all displayed in a way that makes it easy for users to find what they're looking for. And with a pay-as-you-go model, we're only paying to train those who need it."[41]

Appraising and Compensating Employees

Once employees are recruited, hired, oriented, and trained, the manager turns to appraising their performance and to providing for their compensation and working conditions.

Employee Appraisal

performance appraisal
Evaluating an employee's current or past performance in relation to the performance standards for the position.

Performance appraisal means evaluating an employee's current or past performance in relation to the performance standards for the position. You've probably already had experience with performance appraisals. For example, most colleges and universities ask students to rank instructors on scales like the one shown in Figure 10.11.

Probably the most familiar performance appraisal method involves using a graphic rating scale. This lists several job characteristics (like quality of work) and provides a rating scale (from outstanding to unsatisfactory), along with short definitions of each rating. The form in Figure 10.12 is relatively objective because it calls for numerical ratings. However, it also provides space for more subjective examples of particularly good or particularly bad employee performance.

Some firms dispense with graphic forms and use the *critical incidents method* instead. Here, the manager compiles brief examples of the employee's good or bad performance, and then uses these to support the person's appraisal and to identify development needs.

The *forced distribution method* is similar to grading on a curve. With this method, you place predetermined percentages of ratees into performance categories. For example, you may decide to distribute employees as follows: 15 percent high performers, 20 percent high average performance, 30 percent average performers, 20 percent low average performers, and 15 percent low performers. Sun Microsystems recently began forced ranking of all its 43 000 employees. Managers appraise employees in groups of about 30, and 10 per-

Sun Microsystems
www.sun.com

This questionnaire is designed to improve teaching effectiveness. Please do not sign your name—participants are to remain anonymous.

Rate your instructor on each item. The highest rating (10) reflects exceptional teaching, while the lowest (1) indicates very poor teaching. Use the rating that most clearly expresses your view.

Use the blank lines for any additional qualities you would like to rate.

Instructor _____   Course _____

Semester _____   Academic Year _____

Exceptional				Good				Very Poor		Don't Know
10	9	8	7	6	5	4	3	2	1	X

_____ Do the course objectives reflect the lesson assignments?

_____ Are the instructing methods used by the teacher effective?

_____ Is the instructor competent in the subject matter?

_____ Are the classes organized and well-planned?

_____ Are the classes designed to challenge and stimulate?

_____ Does the instructor welcome differing viewpoints?

_____ Does the instructor show interest in helping you in and out of class?

_____ Rate the fairness and effectiveness of the grading system employed by the instructor.

_____ Does the instructor show genuine interest in the subject matter?

_____ _____

_____ _____

FIGURE 10.11
An Example of a Teaching Appraisal by Students

cent of each group gets 90 days to improve. If they're still in the bottom 10 percent in 90 days, they get a chance to resign and take severance pay. Some decide to stay, but if it doesn't work out, the firm can dismiss them without severance.[42]

Many experts and managers don't like the potential "ruthlessness" of this approach. For example, the newly hired HR vice president at Electronic Data Systems abruptly left when the CEO instituted a plan like this despite employee resistance. Instituting such a system played a role in the quick demise of Jacque Nasser as Ford CEO. Experts like W. E. Deming argue this system fosters fear and is unfair. The basic argument is that performance is more often a product of the person's training and of the company's support, and that employees therefore shouldn't be summarily dismissed for poor performance. Deming recommends, among other things, using "360-degree feedback" and having employees sign performance contracts laying out the steps they and the company will take to get the person's performance back up to par.

With **360-degree feedback**, the employee's peers, supervisors, subordinates, and customers complete appraisal surveys.[43] These take many forms, but (for managers) often include supervisory skill items such as "returns phone calls promptly, listens well," and "my manager keeps me informed."[44] Computerized systems compile the feedback into individualized reports for the ratee.[45] The feedback is generally used for training and development, rather than for deciding pay raises.[46] One study found that 29 percent of employers used 360-degree feedback and another 11 percent plan to implement it.[47]

360-degree feedback
An appraisal system where the employee's peers, supervisors, subordinates, and customers complete appraisal surveys, which are compiled into individualized reports for the ratee.

The Appraisal Interview An appraisal typically culminates in an appraisal interview. It is safe to say that most people do not look forward to these interviews. Few people like to receive—or give—negative feedback. Checklist 10.5 summarizes a suggested approach for conducting appraisal interviews.

Performance Appraisal for:

Employee Name_____ Title _____

Department_____ Employee Payroll Number _____

Reason for Review: ☐ Annual ☐ Promotion ☐ Unsatisfactory Performance
 ☐ Merit ☐ End Probation Period ☐ Other _____

Date employee began present position _____ / _____ / _____

Date of last appraisal _____ / _____ / _____ Scheduled appraisal date _____ / _____ / _____

Instructions: Carefully evaluate employee's work performance in relation to current job requirements. Check rating box to indicate the employee's performance. Indicate N/A if not applicable. Assign points for each rating within the scale in the corresponding points box. Points will be totalled and averaged for an overall performance score.

RATING IDENTIFICATION

O – Outstanding – Performance is exceptional in all areas and is recognizable as being far superior to others.

V – Very Good – Results clearly exceed most position requirements. Performance is of high quality and is achieved on a consistent basis.

G – Good – Competent and dependable level of performance. Meets performance standards of the job.

I – Improvement Needed – Performance is deficient in certain areas. Improvement is necessary.

U – Unsatisfactory – Results are generally unacceptable and require immediate improvement. No merit increase should be granted to individuals with this rating.

N – Not Rated – Not applicable or too soon to rate.

GENERAL FACTORS	RATING	SCALE	SUPPORTIVE DETAILS OR COMMENTS
1. **Quality** – The accuracy, thoroughness, and acceptability of work performed.	O ☐ V ☐ G ☐ I ☐ U ☐	100–90 90–80 80–70 70–60 below 60	Points ☐
2. **Productivity** – The quantity and efficiency of work produced in a specified time.	O ☐ V ☐ G ☐ I ☐ U ☐	100–90 90–80 80–70 70–60 below 60	Points ☐
3. **Job Knowledge** – The practical/technical skills and information used on the job.	O ☐ V ☐ G ☐ I ☐ U ☐	100–90 90–80 80–70 70–60 below 60	Points ☐

(continued)

FIGURE 10.12
Performance Appraisal Chart
This is a page from a typical performance appraisal form. Supervisors use it to rate the employee's performance on factors like quality and productivity.

Do Performance Appraisals Work? Managers usually assume that performance appraisals lead to increased worker productivity. But there has always been a nagging concern that performance appraisals may work only for the people who are top performers, and that appraisals simply deflate the sense of self-worth of everyone else. A survey of more than 2000 Canadian workers found the following:

4. Reliability – The extent to which an employee can be relied upon regarding task completion and follow up.	O ☐ V ☐ G ☐ I ☐ U ☐	100–90 90–80 80–70 70–60 below 60	Points		
5 . Availability – The extent to which an employee is punctual, observes prescribed work break/meal periods, and the overall attendance record.	O ☐ V ☐ G ☐ I ☐ U ☐	100–90 90–80 80–70 70–60 below 60	Points		
6. Independence – The extent of work performed with little or no supervision.	O ☐ V ☐ G ☐ I ☐ U ☐	100–90 90–80 80–70 70–60 below 60	Points		

CHECKLIST 10.5

How to Conduct an Appraisal Interview

☑ Prepare for the interview. Assemble the data, study the person's job description and performance, and give the person at least a week's notice to review his or her work.

☑ Be direct and specific. Talk in terms of objective work data. Use examples such as absences, tardiness, quality records, and inspection reports.

☑ Don't get personal. Don't say "you're too slow in producing those reports." This will only trigger the employee's defensiveness. Instead, try to compare the person's performance to a standard ("these reports should normally be done within ten days").

☑ Encourage the person to talk. Stop and listen to what the person is saying: ask open-ended questions such as, "What do you think we can do to improve the situation?" Use encouragements such as "Go on," or "Tell me more."

☑ Don't tiptoe around. Make sure the person leaves the appraisal knowing exactly what he or she is doing right and wrong.

- 81 percent did not think there was a clear link between their performance and their pay[48]
- 61 percent felt that appraisals were not helpful in improving their performance
- 58 percent said that appraisals were not timely
- 53 percent felt that managers did not express goals clearly
- 43 percent thought that their performance was not rated fairly
- 40 percent of employees did not understand the measures that were used to evaluate their performance

Performance appraisals can cause stress for both managers and employees. Although performance appraisals should probably not be done away with, certain improvements are

compensation All work-related pay or rewards that go to employees.

fixed salary Compensation based on an agreed rate for a set period of time.

hourly wage Compensation based on a set hourly pay rate for work performed.

incentive program Any program in which a company offers its workers additional pay over and above the normal wage or salary level to motivate them to perform at a higher-than-normal level.

financial incentive Any financial reward that is contingent on performance.

commission A financial reward in proportion to the items or services an employee sells.

piecework A standard sum for each item the worker produces.

merit pay A salary increase awarded to an employee based on individual performance.

bonus A one-time financial payment.

gain-sharing plan An incentive program in which employees receive a bonus if the firm's costs are reduced because of greater worker efficiency and/or productivity.

profit-sharing plan An incentive program in which employees receive a bonus depending on the firm's profits.

Palliser Furniture
www.palliser.com

employee benefits Supplements to pay based on working for the organization.

necessary. Perhaps the key improvement is more effective communication between managers and their subordinates. Improving communication opens the door for increased understanding between managers and their subordinates, increased goodwill on the part of employees toward the company, and increased commitment and effort on the part of employees.

Compensation

Compensation refers to all work-related pay or rewards that go to employees, including direct financial payments in the form of wages, salaries, incentives, commissions, and bonuses, and indirect payments in the form of financial fringe benefits like employer-paid insurance and vacations.[49]

A **fixed salary** or an **hourly wage** is the centrepiece of most employees' pay. For example, clerical workers usually receive hourly, or daily, wages. Some employees—managerial, professional, and often secretarial—are salaried (i.e., they are paid by the week, month, or year).

The compensation that top managers receive can be controversial, particularly if they receive large salaries even when their companies are losing money. A 2002 *Globe and Mail* survey showed that executive compensation at 100 of the largest companies on the Toronto Stock Exchange rose 54 percent during 2001. This large increase occurred during the same year that a sharp drop in overall company profits was reported. Companies like Celestica, Shaw Communications, and Ballard Power Systems all lost money, but their CEO's were paid millions of dollars in salaries and bonuses.[50] A survey of 1000 Canadians conducted by GPC International found that 67 percent of the respondents felt that top executives are overpaid.[51] Some top managers did indeed make very large totals (salary plus bonuses) during 2001. These included David O'Brien, Fairmont Hotels & Resorts ($83 million); Frank Stronach, Magna International ($55 million); and Gerald Schwartz, Onex ($49 million).[52]

In spite of the concern being expressed about how much money top executives are paid, Canadian workers on average do not appear to be particularly unhappy with their own pay. Aon Consulting interviewed 2000 workers and asked them whether their organization had met their expectations in the area of pay and benefits. A majority of respondents (69 percent) indicated that their expectations had been met or exceeded, while a minority (31 percent) said their expectations had not been met.[53]

Incentive Programs **Incentive programs** are special pay programs designed to motivate high performers. A **financial incentive** is any financial reward that is contingent on performance (often called "pay for performance"). Salespeople get financial incentives called **commissions**, generally in proportion to the items or services they actually sell. Production workers may receive a financial incentive called **piecework**, which is a standard sum for each item the worker produces. Many employees periodically receive **merit pay** or a merit raise, which is a salary increase awarded to an employee based on individual performance. Merit pay differs from a **bonus**, which is a one-time financial payment. We discuss incentives further in Chapter 12.

Some incentive programs apply to all employees in a firm. **Gain-sharing plans** distribute bonuses to all employees in a company based on reduced costs from working more efficiently. Palliser Furniture Ltd. introduced a gain-sharing plan that rewards employees for increasing production. Any profit resulting from production above a certain level is split 50-50 between the company and the employees.[54]

Profit-sharing plans are based on profit levels in the firm. Profits earned above a certain level are distributed to employees. Stock ownership by employees serves as an incentive to lower costs, increase productivity and profits, and thus increase the value of the employee's stock.

Employee Benefits

Employee benefits are supplements to pay based on working for the organization. The Aon Consulting study also asked respondents to indicate how important benefits were in keeping them with their current employer. Eighty-four percent of the respondents said that benefits were "important," "very important," or "critical." Most employees (74 percent) said that their expectations about benefits were being met by their organization.[55]

Employee benefits typically include life insurance, vacation, pension, and education plans. Many of these benefits are legally mandated. For example, under federal law, **employment insurance** is paid to workers who lose their jobs through no fault of their own. The funds come from a tax on the employer's payroll. **Workers' compensation**, another legally mandated benefit, is a payment aimed at providing income and medical benefits to victims of work-related accidents or their dependents, regardless of fault. Payments made to the Canada Pension Plan are another federally mandated benefit, paid for by a tax on an employee's salary or wages.

As the range of employee benefits has grown, so has concern about containing their cost. Businesses are therefore experimenting with a variety of procedures to cut benefit costs while maintaining the ability to attract, retain, and maintain the morale of employees. One approach is the use of **cafeteria benefits**. These plans provide a set dollar amount in benefits and allow employees to pick among alternatives. For example, employees at Toyota's Cambridge, Ontario, plant are given the opportunity once each year to structure their benefits packages. They can give more weight to dental coverage if they have young children, or to life insurance or disability coverage, depending on their circumstances.[56] At companies like Canada Life Assurance and KPMG Canada, employees actually have the option of taking their benefit dollar figure as cash.[57]

The Aon Consulting study found that flexible benefits are important to employees. When respondents were asked to rank six different benefits techniques (e.g., stock purchase plan, cash bonus based on performance), the top-ranked item was flexible benefits.[58]

More and more firms are using "temporary" workers on a long-term basis. Since they are not covered by most companies' benefits plans, temporary workers allow businesses to keep staff levels high and benefits costs low.

employment insurance
A benefit paid to workers who lose their jobs through no fault of their own; the funds come from a tax on the employer's payroll.

workers' compensation
A payment aimed at providing income and medical benefits to victims of work-related accidents or their dependents, regardless of fault.

cafeteria benefits
Benefit plans that provide a set dollar amount in benefits and allow employees to pick among alternatives.

Retirement

Some employees are ready for retirement much earlier than others. But because most retirement plans are based on an employee's age, some workers who should retire earlier stay on the job while others, who are still useful workers, leave before they would like to. This policy is short-sighted. A compromise is to grant year-to-year extensions to productive employees who want to continue working but who have reached retirement age. Recently several workers in different locations across Canada have successfully challenged mandatory retirement rules. Their employers must now allow them to work even though they are past the traditional retirement age of 65.

In spite of these developments, Canadians generally are retiring earlier than they used to. In the period 1976–1980, for example, the median retirement age in Canada was 64.9 years, but in the period 1991–1995 that figure dropped to 62.3 years.[59] Two other interesting facts: Workers over age 65 are nearly four times as likely to die from work-related causes than younger workers, and older workers have double the health care costs that workers in their forties do.[60]

Discipline, Grievances, and Dismissal

Discipline means applying a penalty to subordinates, usually when they violate a rule. A company should have clear rules (such as "No smoking allowed when dealing with customers"), as well as a series of progressive penalties that all employees know the firm will enforce if the rule is broken. In assessing the need for discipline, some supervisors follow the so-called FRACT model: Get the *Facts*, obtain the *Reason* for the infraction, *Audit* the records, pinpoint the *Consequences*, and identify the *Type* of infraction before taking remedial steps. Some use discipline without punishment. This involves giving an employee an oral reminder if he or she breaks a rule and then a written reminder if it occurs again. The person gets a paid, one-day "decision-making leave" if another incident

discipline Applying a penalty to subordinates, usually when they violate a rule.

occurs in the next few weeks. If the rule is broken again, a dismissal may be in order. Effective discipline guidelines are shown in Checklist 10.6.

grievance
A complaint an employee lodges against an employer.

A **grievance** is a complaint an employee lodges against an employer, usually regarding wages, hours, or some condition of employment like supervisory behaviour. Most union contracts contain a grievance procedure whereby the employer and the union determine whether there has been a violation of some clause in the contract. For example, a terminated employee might file a grievance stating that the supervisor had issued no warnings as was called for in the union agreement and that the firing was therefore unwarranted. Grievance steps typically include discussing the problem with a supervisor, and then referring the matter to the department head, the personnel department, and finally the head of the unit. Many non-union companies voluntarily offer grievance procedures. One way to avoid grievances is to adhere to disciplinary guidelines like those listed in the checklist below.

dismissal
The involuntary termination of an employee's employment with the firm.

Dismissal—the involuntary termination of an employee's employment with the firm— is the most dramatic disciplinary step an employer can take toward an employee. The dismissal must be just (sufficient cause should exist for it), and it should occur only after all reasonable steps to rehabilitate or salvage the employee have failed. However, there are undoubtedly times when immediate dismissal is required—such as for gross insubordination.

Companies must be very careful when dismissing employees. A general manager at Jumbo Video Inc., who was fired when he refused to take a pay cut, was awarded more than $226 000 in damages. The manager had earlier signed a contract containing certain stipulations that the company later tried to void because of financial problems. The judge ruled that the company had reneged on the contract.[61]

Canada Labour Code
http://laws.justice.gc.ca/en/L-2

Legislation on unjust dismissal in the Canada Labour Code requires the company to prove that it had "just cause" in firing the person. However, some strange rulings have been handed down. One Canadian Imperial Bank of Commerce employee was fired because of the people she associated with while she was not at work. Police burst into her apartment at precisely the same time that five men were dividing the money from a CIBC robbery. A Labour Canada adjudicator ruled that CIBC did not have "just cause" to fire her because she hadn't actually done anything wrong herself. A supervisor at another bank got her job back even after she admitted that she had planned to steal customers' money.[62]

CHECKLIST **10.6**

Guidelines for Disciplining an Employee

☑ Make sure the evidence supports the charge of employee wrongdoing.

☑ Protect employees' due process rights.

☑ Warn employees ahead of time of the disciplinary consequences.

☑ The rule that the person allegedly violated should be "reasonably related" to the efficient and safe operation of the work environment.

☑ Fairly and adequately investigate the matter before administering discipline.

☑ The investigation should produce substantial evidence of misconduct.

☑ Apply rules, orders, or penalties even-handedly.

☑ Make sure the penalty is reasonably related to the misconduct and to the employee's past work history.

☑ Maintain the employee's right to counsel.

☑ Don't rob subordinates of their dignity during the process.

☑ Remember that the burden of proof is on you.

☑ Get the facts. Don't base your decision on hearsay or on your "general impression."

☑ Don't act while angry.

Understanding HR's Legal Framework

More than any other management function, personnel is subject to numerous constraints in the form of federal and provincial laws. These laws affect recruiting practices, how employees are paid, sexual harassment, employee health and safety, labour-management relations, and employment laws in general. Each of these areas is discussed in this section.

Recruiting

When recruiting, firms must be careful not to violate anti-discrimination laws. The key federal anti-discrimination legislation is the **Canadian Human Rights Act** of 1977. The goal of this act is to ensure that any individual who wants to obtain a job has an equal opportunity to compete for it. The act applies to all federal agencies, federal Crown corporations, any employee of the federal government, and business firms that do business interprovincially. Even with such wide application, the act affects only about 10 percent of Canadian workers; the rest are covered under provincial human rights acts.

The Canadian Human Rights Act prohibits a wide variety of practices in recruiting, selecting, promoting, and dismissing personnel. The act specifically prohibits discrimination on the basis of age, race and colour, national and ethnic origin, physical disability, religion, gender, marital status, or prison record (if pardoned). Some exceptions to these blanket prohibitions are permitted. Discrimination cannot be charged if a blind person is refused a position as a train engineer, bus driver, or crane operator. Likewise, a firm cannot be charged with discrimination if it does not hire a deaf person as a telephone operator or as an audio engineer.

These situations are clear-cut, but many others are not. For example, is it discriminatory to refuse women employment in a job that routinely requires carrying objects that weigh more than 50 kilograms? Ambiguities in determining whether discrimination has occurred are sometimes dealt with by using the concept of "**bona fide occupational requirement**." An employer may choose one person over another based on overriding characteristics of the job in question. If a fitness centre wants to hire only women to supervise its women's locker room and sauna, it can do so without being discriminatory because it established a bona fide occupational requirement.

Even after referring to bona fide occupational requirements, other uncertainties remain. Consider three cases: Would an advertising agency be discriminating if it advertised for a male model about 60 years old for an advertisement that is to appeal to older men? Would a business firm be discriminating if it refused to hire someone as a receptionist because the applicant was overweight? Would a bank be discriminating because it refused to hire an applicant whom the human resources manager felt would not "fit in" because of the person's appearance?

We might speculate that the advertising agency is not discriminating, the business firm might or might not be discriminating, and the bank could probably be accused of discrimination, but we can't be sure. The human rights legislation cannot specify all possible situations; many uncertainties remain over what the law considers discriminatory and what it considers acceptable. Nevertheless, the spirit of the legislation is clear, and managers must try to abide by it.

Enforcement of the federal act is carried out by the **Canadian Human Rights Commission**. The commission can either respond to complaints from individuals who believe they have been discriminated against, or it can launch an investigation on its own if it has reason to believe that discrimination has occurred. During an investigation, data are gathered about the alleged discriminatory behaviour and, if the claim of discrimination is substantiated, the offending organization or individual may be ordered to compensate the victim.

Each province has also enacted human rights legislation to regulate organizations and businesses operating in that province. These provincial regulations are similar in spirit to the federal legislation, with many minor variations from province to province. All provinces prohibit discrimination on the basis of race, national or ethnic origin, colour, religion, sex, and marital status, but some do not address such issues as physical disabilities, criminal record, or age. Provincial human rights commissions enforce provincial legislation.

The **Employment Equity Act** of 1986 addresses the issue of discrimination in employment by designating four groups as employment disadvantaged—women, visible minorities, Aboriginal people, and people with disabilities. Companies covered by the act are required to publish statistics on their employment of people in these four groups. The Bank of Montreal, which won a prestigious award for promoting women's careers, has introduced initiatives such as flexible working hours, a mentoring program, a national career information network, and a gender awareness workshop series.[63]

Companies are increasingly making provisions for employees with disabilities. At Rogers Cablevision, a large workplace area was completely redesigned to accommodate workers who either had vision impairments or used wheelchairs. Special equipment was also installed—a large print computer for workers with partial sight and a device that allows blind workers to read printed materials.[64]

Comparable Worth

In spite of recent advances, women, on average, still earn only about three-quarters of what the average man earns. *Single* women, however, earn 99 percent of what single men earn. Although improvements are evident, progress is slow in this area, and most top jobs in the public and private sector continue to be held by men.[65] Women have also had difficulty moving out of low-paying jobs. A Statistics Canada report showed that one-third of the men who had low-paying jobs had been able to get a better paying job, but that only 17 percent of the women were able to do so. Only 12 percent of *single-parent women* were able to get a better paying job.[66]

Comparable worth is a legal concept that aims at paying equal wages for jobs that are of comparable value to the employer. This might mean comparing dissimilar jobs, such as those of nurses and mechanics or secretaries and electricians. Proponents of comparable worth say that all the jobs in a company must be evaluated and then rated in terms of basic dimensions such as the level of skill they require. All jobs can then be compared based on a common index. People in different jobs that rate the same on this index would be paid the same. Experts hope that this will help to reduce the gap between men's and women's pay.

Critics of comparable worth say that it ignores the crucial issue of supply and demand aspects of labour and that forcing a company to pay people more than the open market price for their labour (which may happen in jobs where there is a surplus of workers) is not economically sound. A study prepared for the Ontario Ministry of Labour estimated that it would cost approximately $10 billion for the public and private sectors in Ontario to establish equitable payment for jobs of equal value. Yet the cost defence cannot be easily used. In 1999, the Canadian Human Rights Tribunal ruled that the federal government must pay a total of more than $3 billion to thousands of civil servants because it discriminated against workers in female-dominated job classifications. About 85 percent of these workers were women.

Sexual and Personal Harassment

Sexual harassment doesn't simply mean insisting on sexual favours in return for some reward, as many people believe. It also includes unwelcome sexual advances, requests for sexual favours, and other verbal or physical conduct of a sexual nature that occurs under conditions including the following:

- when such conduct is explicitly or implicitly a term or condition of an individual's employment
- when submission to, or rejection of, such conduct by an individual is used as the basis for employment decisions affecting the individual
- when such conduct has the purpose or effect of unreasonably interfering with an individual's performance or creating an intimidating, hostile, or offensive

Employment Equity Act
Federal legislation that designates four groups as employment disadvantaged: women, visible minorities, Aboriginal people, and people with disabilities.

Employment Equity Act
http://laws.justice.gc.ca/en/E-5.401

comparable worth
A legal concept that aims at paying equal wages for jobs that are of comparable value to the employer.

Canadian Human Rights Tribunal
www.chrt-tcdp.gc.ca

sexual harassment
Unwelcome sexual advances, requests for sexual favours, and other verbal or physical conduct of a sexual nature.

work environment. In other words, if it makes the other person feel uncomfortable, it may be sexual harassment.

Managers cannot be complacent about the activities of employees toward one another, and they must remember that the Canadian Human Rights Act takes precedence over any policies the company might have developed in this area. If a manager or a co-worker is found guilty of sexual harassment, the company is also liable, even if it didn't condone or know about the behaviour. The most reasonable and prudent course of action for a company to take is to establish a clear policy against sexual harassment and then to enforce that policy vigorously.

Canadian Courts are becoming increasingly strict when determining what constitutes sexual harassment. In 2002, the Ontario Court of Appeal overturned a lower court ruling that a manager had been wrongfully dismissed. The Court of Appeal found that the manager (who was fired after several female co-workers complained that he had sexualized the work environment) had not been wrongfully dismissed. This decision, as well as others, shows that sexual harassment suits are being taken very seriously.[67]

Dealing with Sexual Harassment at Work There are a number of steps that employers and individuals can take to avoid or deal with sexual harassment when it occurs (see Table 10.2).

Sexual harassment is not the only type of harassment that exists in the workplace. **Personal harassment** involves activities like verbal assaults, bullying, ridiculing, or any other actions that make the workplace stressful for the target of the harassment. A company may be liable even if one employee is harassing another. At Levac Supply Ltd. of Kingston, Ontario, one employee harassed another over many years. A board of inquiry

personal harassment
Activities like verbal assaults, bullying, ridiculing, or any other actions that make the workplace stressful for the target of the harassment.

TABLE 10.2   *Dealing with Sexual Harassment*

WHAT THE EMPLOYER SHOULD DO	WHAT EMPLOYEES SHOULD DO
1. Take all complaints about harassment seriously.	1. Make a verbal request to the harasser and the harasser's boss that the unwanted overtures cease because the conduct is unwelcome.
2. Issue a strong policy statement condemning such behaviour.	2. Write a letter to the harasser providing a detailed statement of the facts and a statement that the employee wants the harassing activities to end immediately (the letter should be delivered in person and, if necessary, a witness should accompany the employee),
3. Inform all employees about the policy prohibiting sexual harassment and of their rights under the policy.	3. Report the unwelcome conduct and unsuccessful efforts to get it to stop to the harasser's manager or to the HR director (or both), verbally and in writing.
4. Establish a complaint procedure so that employees understand the chain of command when it comes to filing and appealing sexual harassment complaints.	4. Finally, consult an attorney about suing the harasser and possibly the employer.
5. Establish a management response system that includes an immediate reaction and investigation by senior management when charges of sexual harassment are made.	
6. Begin management training sessions with supervisors and increase their awareness of the issues.	
7. Discipline managers and employees involved in sexual harassment.	

ruled that the company was jointly responsible for the harassment with the employee who had done the harassing. The employee who was harassed received a settlement of $448 273.[68]

Employee Health and Safety

Employee **health and safety programs** help to reduce absenteeism and turnover, raise productivity, and boost morale by making jobs safer and more healthful. In Canada, each province has developed its own workplace health and safety regulations. The purpose of these laws is to ensure that employees do not have to work in dangerous conditions. These laws are the direct result of the undesirable conditions that existed in many Canadian businesses at the close of the nineteenth century.

Government regulations about employee safety are getting stricter. Ontario, which loses more than seven million working days yearly because of on-the-job injuries, has passed amendments to the Ontario Occupational Health and Safety Act. Officers and directors of companies are now held personally responsible for workplace health and safety and are subject to punishment by jail terms and fines for permitting unsafe working conditions.[69]

Some industrial work—logging, construction, and mining—can put workers at risk of injury in obvious ways. But other work, such as typing or lifting, can also cause painful injuries. Repetitive strain injury is becoming much more common. At Cuddy Food Products (the sole supplier of poultry products to McDonald's), as many as 44 workers per month became disabled from repetitive strain injury. The company instituted a plan to redesign how workers performed their jobs and trained people to avoid injuries. During one nine-month period after the training, not a single repetitive strain injury was reported. At CP Rail, injuries were reduced 50 percent when employees did 10 minutes of warm-up exercises before beginning work.[70]

The Ontario Occupational Health and Safety Act is typical of current legislation in Canada. It requires that all employers ensure that equipment and safety devices are used properly. Employers must also show workers the proper way to operate machinery. At the job site, supervisors are charged with the responsibility of seeing that workers use equipment properly. The act also requires workers to behave appropriately on the job. Employees have the right to refuse to work on a job if they believe it is unsafe, and a legal procedure exists for resolving any disputes in this area.

In most provinces, the Ministry of Labour appoints inspectors to enforce health and safety regulations. If the inspector finds a sufficient hazard, he or she has the authority to clear the workplace. Inspectors may come to a firm unannounced to conduct an inspection.

Safety in Practice Companies can take a number of steps to improve the safety and health of their workforces. Examples include the following:

- *Reduce unsafe conditions that can lead to accidents*. This is an employer's first line of defence. For example, is material piled in a safe manner? Are there safety feet on straight ladders? Do stairways have guardrails?

- *Hire safety-prone people*. Employee selection and testing can be used to hire people who are less likely to have accidents, particularly on accident-prone jobs like driving heavy equipment. For example, psychological tests—especially tests of emotional stability—have been used to screen out accident-prone taxi drivers.[71] Similarly, tests of muscular coordination are important for jobs such as lumberjack, and tests of visual skills are important for drivers and employees operating machines.

- *Emphasize safety*. Use safety posters and continual reminders from top management that safety is paramount.

- *Use training to improve safety*. Safety training, such as instructing employees in safe practices and procedures and warning them of potential hazards, can help employees act more safely at work.

- *Set specific loss-control goals*. Analyze the number of accidents and safety incidents and then set specific safety goals to be achieved, for instance, a maximum for time lost due to injuries.

- *Formulate and enforce safety rules.* Set specific safety rules, such as "Safety hats must be worn in construction area," and "Oil spills must be wiped up promptly," and actively enforce these rules.
- *Conduct safety and health inspections regularly.* Similarly, investigate all accidents and "near misses" and have a system in place to allow employees to notify management about hazardous conditions.

Labour–Management Relations

Under the laws of Canada and many other countries, workers are permitted to organize into **labour unions**—groups of individuals working together to achieve job-related goals such as higher pay, shorter working hours, and better working conditions. In Canada, Privy Council Order 1003 recognizes the right of employees to bargain collectively, prohibits unfair labour practices on the part of management, establishes a labour board to certify bargaining authority, and prohibits strikes except in the course of negotiating a collective agreement. Each province also has a labour relations act that regulates labour activity within the province.

labour unions
Groups of individuals working together to achieve job-related goals such as higher pay, shorter working hours, and better working conditions.

Other Employment Law Issues

The **Canada Labour Code** is a comprehensive piece of legislation that applies to the labour practices of firms operating under the legislative authority of Parliament. The code sets out guidelines in areas such as fair employment practices, vacations and holidays, employee safety, and industrial relations regulations. It also addresses the issue of child labour. In Canada, for example, young people under the age of 17 may work, but only if (a) they are not required to attend school under the laws of their province, and (b) the work is not likely to endanger their health or safety. No one under the age of 17 is permitted to work between 11 p.m. and 6 a.m.

Canada Labour Code
A comprehensive piece of legislation that applies to the labour practices of firms operating under the legislative authority of Parliament.

SKILLS AND STUDY MATERIAL

SUMMARY

1. Human resources management is the management function devoted to acquiring, training, appraising, and compensating employees. As workers become more fully empowered, the HR function has grown in importance.

2. Staffing—filling a firm's open positions—starts with job analysis and personnel planning. Recruiting—including the use of internal sources, advertising, employment agencies, recruiters, referrals, university and college recruiting, and recruiting a more diverse workforce—is then used to create a pool of applicants.

3. With a pool of applicants, the employer can turn to screening and selecting, using one or more techniques—including application blanks, interviews, tests, and ref-

erence checks—to assess and investigate an applicant's aptitudes, interests, and background. To be effective, an interviewer must plan the interview (familiarize yourself with the applicant's qualifications), establish rapport (put the applicant at ease), ask questions (follow questions you have prepared ahead of time), close the interview (on a positive note), and review the interview (consult the notes that you took during the interview).

4. Once employees have been recruited, screened, and selected, they must be prepared to do their jobs. This is the role of employee orientation and training. Orientation means providing new employees with basic information about the employer, while training ensures

that the new employee has the basic knowledge required to perform the job satisfactorily.

5. Once they are on the job, employees are appraised.

6. Employee compensation refers to all work-related pay or rewards that go to employees. It includes direct financial payments in the form of wages, salaries, incentives, commissions, and bonuses, and indirect payments in the form of financial fringe benefits like employer-paid insurance and vacations.

7. In disciplining employees, managers should be sure they have all the facts and that the discipline is defensible and fair.

8. In hiring, training, compensating, and/or dismissing workers, managers must obey many laws. Equal employment opportunity and equal pay laws forbid discrimination other than that based on legitimate job requirements. Controversy over what constitutes discrimination in paying men and women who hold different jobs is a current issue. Managers are also required to provide employees with a safe working environment.

CRITICAL THINKING EXERCISES

1. As quoted in John Aram's *Presumed Superior*, affirmative action has different meanings to different people. One observer comments on the double meaning of affirmative action as a means of institutional change: "If civil rights is defined as quotas, it's a losing hand. If it's defined as protection against discrimination and efforts to promote opportunity, then it will remain a mainstream value." John Aram points out, "The dilemma is that progress on civil rights both restricts and opens opportunity. No single, definitive moral premise exists."[72]

    What do you think Aram is trying to say? What aspects of HR can be related to his comments? What are your thoughts and feelings about civil rights and employment equity as they affect organizational management and jobs?

2. You are now a citizen of the twenty-first century. The rules of the job and career game appear to be changing as rapidly as machines such as ATMs replace bank tellers. You can now bank and pay bills with your computer and you can order all sorts of products over the internet, including groceries. In groups of five students, preferably from different majors, explore how you think your job choice will change in the future. Also discuss what you think the profession you are now preparing for will look like 10 years from now and 30 years from now. Be prepared to compare your discussion with that of other groups.

EXPERIENTIAL EXERCISES

1. Working in teams of four to five students, conduct a job analysis and develop a job description for the instructor of this course. Make sure to include a job summary, as well as a list of job duties and a job specification listing the human requirements of the job. Compare your job description with one from a website such as **www.jobdescriptions.com**.

2. Using the job description as a guide, develop a recruiting plan for the job of teaching this course, as well as a list of interview questions your team would use to screen instructor applicants for this course.

3. Working in teams of four to five students, develop a performance appraisal procedure and form for the instructor of this course.

BUILDING YOUR MANAGEMENT SKILLS

Writing a Job Description

Fill out the job analysis questionnaire (Figure 10.4) for a job that you currently hold or that you have recently held. Based on the information you provide in the questionnaire, write a job description for your job. When writing the job description, make sure that you consider all the questions in the job analysis checklist. After you have completed the job description, go to the **www.jobdescription.com** website and try to find a job like the one you are trying to describe. To what extent does the website make your work easier?

One year HSBC Bank Canada (**www.hsbc.ca**) entered a team of 1300 runners, almost 50 percent of the bank's employee pool, for the corporate division of Vancouver's 10-km Sun Run. Organizations such as HSBC recognize the importance of workplace wellness to the health of the corporation.

1. What policies and programs has the bank explored and implemented to help employees reach and maintain a healthy balance of work and home life? Further reference: **http://labour.hrdc-drhc.gc.ca/worklife/hsbc-en.cfm**.

2. Delta Hotels was the first hotel company in the history of Canada to win the National Quality Institute's Award for Excellence (**http://labour.hrdc-drhc.gc.ca/worklife/deltahotels-en.cfm**). What key elements are responsible for Delta creating a healthy culture for its staff?

3. Compare and contrast the management initiatives taken by HSBC Canada and Delta Hotels. Identify which initiatives you find most attractive and why.

CASE STUDY 10-1

What About Contracting?

Years ago, when people thought about a career, they usually thought of going to work full time for a company and, if they liked it, staying at that company for many years. Even if a person didn't stay at one firm, the idea still was that she or he would work full time for a company for a least a few years.

But times are changing. A growing number of workers are becoming contract workers or freelancers—individuals who contract with a company for a set period of time, usually until a specific project is completed. After the project is finished, the contract worker moves on to another project in the firm, or to another firm altogether. Statistics Canada estimates that 30 percent of working adults do contract work.

Why is contracting work becoming so common? As the economic situation has become more uncertain, an increasing number of companies are using contract workers to avoid making long-term financial commitments. Playdium Corp., which operates virtual-reality entertainment centres, uses contract employees for a variety of purposes: to fill in for regular employees who call in sick, to replace those who are on maternity leaves, and to meet changes in seasonal demand for its products. Most of Playdium's contractors work for three to four months.

Competitive pressures are also forcing firms to reduce their costs and increase their productivity. The current buzzword is "flexibility," which can often be achieved by hiring contract workers to solve specific company problems. This allows a firm to maintain a minimum number of full-time workers and supplement them with contractors. Recent advances in information technology have also facilitated contract work, since workers do not necessarily have to be at the workplace to do their jobs.

Companies also hire contractors to save money (contract workers may cost companies 10 percent less than permanent staff). For one thing, they don't have to pay Canada Pension Plan or Employment Insurance premiums. But pressures are building to change this—in 1994, Saskatchewan became the first province in Canada to require companies to pay contract and part-time workers at least some benefits.

Ray Sherwood is the chief financial officer (CFO) for Winnipeg-based Frantic Films, a firm that produces historical television series and special effects for movies. As CFO, he closely watches cash flows, generates financial projections, and generally ensures that the company achieves its short- and long-term financial goals. Sherwood is a contract worker who started with Frantic Films in May 2002. He receives payment for his services, but he receives no other fringe benefits. His contract is reviewed each year. Frantic Films requires about 70–80 percent of his time. Sherwood also presents seminars on accounting and finance topics to managers in both public- and private-sector companies on a contract basis.

After graduating with a bachelor's of commerce degree, Sherwood worked in the banking industry for a few years, then switched to being a contract worker. This includes working as a financial officer for Credo Entertainment and VZS Films, as well as performing sessional lecturer work at the University of Manitoba, the University of Winnipeg, and Red River College.

Sherwood is very happy about being a contract worker. He says that he is an entrepreneurial, risk-taking sort of person and he likes the flexibility and independence that contract work offers. He also says that contractors that "put all their eggs in one basket" and only work for one company can be exposed to higher risk than those who have client diversification.

Sherwood recognizes that as a contract worker he does not get certain benefits (for example, a pension), and that he may be foregoing promotions that he might get if he were an employee, but he feels that the benefits of contract work clearly outweigh the costs. He points out that in today's uncertain economic environment, there is really very little job security even for regular employees. With this in mind, he feels that he does not give up much to be a contract worker. In the long term, he wants to continue working with Frantic Films through his consulting company and provide financial expertise to other clients on a contract basis.

Why are people willing to work on a contract basis if they don't receive the benefits that full-time workers get? Some do contract work simply because they can't get full-time work with one company, but others, like Ray Sherwood, do it by choice. Accomplished contract workers can control their own destiny, make above-average incomes, and have a strong sense of flexibility and freedom. Contractors can also offer new ideas and fresh perspectives to companies.

While companies often contract out the work of technical or professional employees, the management of various *functions* may also be contracted out. Some years ago, the Halifax District School Board contracted out the management of custodial services for the district's 42 schools to ServiceMaster Canada Ltd. Manpower Temporary Services managed a packaging department for a pharmaceutical firm that sometimes numbers as many as 130 people, and sometimes as few as 70, depending on demand. A Manpower manager is on site at the pharmaceutical firm; she recruits the temporary workers, does some of the necessary training, conducts performance appraisals of temporary workers, and handles the payroll.

With the massive layoffs that have been evident in recent years, workers are beginning to realize that large firms do not necessarily provide job security. Rather, security comes from having confidence in your own knowledge and skills, and marketing yourself in innovative ways. There are both positive and negative aspects to the idea of non-standard work. From the worker's perspective, those with marketable skills will find that non-standard work will result in high pay and satisfying work. For those without marketable skills, non-standard work will likely mean part-time work in low-paying service jobs. Those individuals who lack either the ability or interest to capitalize on non-standard work could find uncertainty in their careers.

From the organization's perspective, reaching a conclusion about the value of non-standard work means weighing the value of long-term employee loyalty and commitment against the benefits of the increased flexibility that is possible with contract workers.

Questions

1. What kind of people are most likely to want contract work?

2. What are the pros and cons of contract work from the individual's perspective? From the organization's perspective?

3. Is it unethical to hire contract workers to avoid paying company benefits to them?

CEO Succession Planning at American Express

American Express is one of the largest diversified financial and network service companies in the world. Since its founding in 1850, it has been a leader in global markets in charge and credit cards, travel and vacation services, financial planning, investment products, insurance, and international banking. Being one of the largest service firms in the world also makes American Express one of the most visible. Changing the top leader in a company like this can be a traumatic event. Investors and senior managers come to rely on the consistency of leadership in dynamic or uncertain markets. That is certainly true for American Express.

Typically, when looking for a replacement CEO, companies take into account the candidate's experience, track record (how successful the potential CEO was in managing complex tasks in a dynamic environment), and experience with the industry, among other factors. In choosing a new CEO, firms often emphasize consistency. Firms use several methods to attain consistency. Having a replacement management team in place for a number of years prior to the CEO change, allowing the financial community to become familiar with the potential CEO's work, appointing a new CEO prior to the departure or retirement of the current CEO, or asking the CEO to remain with the company as a chair or vice chair of the board to assure continuity of leadership. Of course, the board of directors is intimately involved in the decision.

In the case of American Express, CEO Harvey Golub announced his retirement in 1999, saying Division President Ken Chenault would accept the position of CEO in 2001. In his letter to employees, Golub asserted:

> In a sense, there is no ideal time for retirement. There is always more to do, always more challenges to meet, always opportunities to capitalize on and problems to deal with. Nonetheless, succession planning is a critical part of good corporate governance for any company and its board of directors. Indeed, I believe the most important task for any CEO is to ensure the seamless transition of executive authority. This is a process that we began at American Express several years ago with Ken's appointment as president and chief operating officer. Today's announcement is the next step in this process.

Golub also announced that the company would immediately begin to expand Chenault's range of responsibilities. He noted that customers, employees, investors, and suppliers would know that in dealing with Chenault, they were dealing with the next CEO of the company.

One of the key issues in the American Express decision to go with an inside candidate was to maintain a continuity of strategy. Golub's leadership team envisioned several major strategic tasks, among them to

- develop and implement a compelling internet strategy
- accelerate growth at American Express Financial Advisors
- recognize that in the future regulations that kept banks from offering both Visa/MasterCard and American Express were likely to be overturned

The ultimate decision about who would be the new CEO was placed in the hands of the American Express board of directors. The board consists of 14 individuals—2 from American Express and 12 outside directors from a variety of perspectives and backgrounds.

Questions

1. Given its critical issues, would American Express be better served by promoting from within, or hiring a CEO from outside the company? Why?

2. To what extent does Amex seem to have adhered to the recruitment and selection process as outlined in this chapter? How was the Amex process similar? How was it different?

3. Should the board accept Golub's recommendation that Chenault succeed him as CEO?

4. What are the strengths and weaknesses of Golub's succession plan for American Express?

American Express
www.americanexpress.com

JetBlue: Staffing the Blue Skies

When airline passenger traffic declined after September 11, most airlines responded predictably, by dramatically downsizing their staffs. Throughout the industry, company after company laid off employees as passenger traffic declined and the airlines cut flights.

David Neeleman and his management team bucked the industry trend.[73] Neeleman's first reaction was to not lay off any of JetBlue's 2000 employees. It wasn't easy. "We are probably carrying half as many (passengers)," as one JetBlue spokesperson said.[74] Neeleman's decision reflects his approach to human resource management. JetBlue's management team works hard to make sure that it has highly qualified, people-oriented employees and that those employees like what they do and how they're treated. JetBlue's managers believe that one of the best ways to keep service standards up is to make sure the employees who are providing that service enjoy what they're doing and love dealing with people.

JetBlue's HR process starts by hiring the right people in the first place. As David Neeleman says, "It's really focused on whether or not you like people."[75] How does JetBlue make sure it hires people who like people? One way is by asking applicants the right questions. For example the company will ask prospective employees to tell it about a specific time in their past work experience when they did something out of the ordinary for their job description and helped someone. One of JetBlue's best flight attendants is a 60-year-old retired firefighter. His answer to the interview question was, "I was in a burning building, and some of my guys were inside, and the building was coming down, and I had to go in to get them out of there." The man was hired on the spot.

At an airline like JetBlue, keeping costs down means having highly committed employees, ones who are willing to pitch in when the plane comes in—to make sure bags are loaded, passengers embark, and that the airplane gets turned around as quickly as possible. JetBlue's employment interviewers therefore look for employees who are used to pitching in; they want employees "who aren't regimented to the point where they say, 'That's not my job; that's your job.'"[76] At JetBlue, when the plane comes in, every employee—from the CEO, to marketing executives, to the pilots—is expected to help get the plane turned around and out as fast as possible.

Therefore, anyone who's not willing to pitch in and get his or her hands dirty need not apply.

JetBlue also takes a non-traditional approach to the way it hires and manages its telephone reservations agents. Here, flexibility is the rule. For example, instead of being crammed into office cubicles answering phones all day, JetBlue's 350 reservationists work out of their homes.[77] That approach has a double-barrelled benefit. "It's efficient for us," says JetBlue's manager for corporate communications, since JetBlue saves on office space. "But it also allows people to have a job and be able to pick their kids up from school." Partly because of that flexibility, JetBlue's reservationist turnover rate is less than 1 percent.

JetBlue extends its flexible staffing approach to its flight attendants. For example, it has the JetBlue Friend's Crew program. In this program, JetBlue hires two people to share a schedule. The two friends interview together. If JetBlue hires them, it gives them a flight schedule and leaves it to them to decide who works when. JetBlue doesn't care who shows up for the flight, as long as one of them does. For example, one JetBlue Friend's Crew is a mother–daughter duo. They share a flight schedule and the daughter's childcare responsibilities.

Assignment

You and your team are consultants to Mr. Neeleman, who is depending on your management expertise to help navigate the launch and management of JetBlue. Here's what he wants to know from you:

1. Write a job description for the positions of reservations agents and JetBlue Friend's Crew member.

2. Provide me with a recruiting plan for the jobs of reservations agents and JetBlue Friend's Crew Member. Please make sure to tell me specifically how you would recruit for these employees.

3. Explain what we are doing right and wrong with respect to interviewing for our positions now and what, if anything you think we should do to improve our process. Please be sure to provide me with at least five specific questions we should be asking prospective flight attendants and also five questions for reservation clerks.

Stress at Work

Increasingly people are having trouble balancing the demands of home and job. Downsizing means fewer people to do the same amount of work, so Canadian workers are under more pressure than ever before. Linda Duxbury, an HRM consultant, asked 33 000 Canadians to complete a questionnaire about their work. Among other things she found that

- most people are working 50 hours or more per week
- absenteeism costs the Canadian economy $3 billion per year
- 60 percent of workers report high levels of stress
- one-third of workers report depression

Employers need to help employees find a balance between work and home life. Although lots of corporations (particularly the large ones) have worker-friendly policies, they often don't encourage workers to use them. There is a disconnect between talk and action, with many organizations paying only lip service to their policies. Managers who are supportive of the idea of balancing work and home life say that businesses must do what is right for the long-term health of the workforce. They also recognize, however, that it may be difficult to achieve the ideal. But some progress is being made. Canadian workers are jumping at the chance for extended maternity leave, and compassionate leave is increasingly being offered to people who are caring for family members who are ill.

The real challenge is getting both managers and workers to understand that it is *productivity* that is important, not just putting in "face time" at work. Pressure to be at work for long hours can increase stress, and stress negatively affects productivity because stressed people make mistakes. At Davies-Howe Partners, the emphasis is on employees getting their jobs done in a relaxed work environment, not on how much time they spend at work. The company has found that the quality of work is better if the work environment is relaxed.

The Blair government in the United Kingdom launched a program called Opportunity 2000 after it realized that the long hours worked by the British labour force hadn't yielded much (the United Kingdom is the least productive nation in the European Union). The government also has a "Challenge Fund" to help employers make the workplace a happier place.

One way to achieve a better balance between work and home life is to offer employees flexible working hours (including allowing them to work at home for part of each week). British Telecom has 3000 home workers and their productivity is higher than their office-bound colleagues. These employees take less sick leave, and the company has saved $25 million with the program. Another company had a problem with absenteeism. It received a government grant to pay for a research project that yielded advice on how to deal with the problem of staff being stressed with elder care. The solution was to give the staff emergency paid leave to sort out their elder-care problems. Now, staff members don't phone in sick as much as they used to, and they are away from work for only as long as it takes them to solve the crisis at hand. The average employee takes only one "emergency day" a year, and this has saved the company $600 000 per year.

New graduates are increasingly asking what the flexible working options are. A recent UK study found that two out of three workers would rather have flexible work hours than win the lottery. New legislation in the United Kingdom gives parents with children under six the right to request flexible working hours. The road to workforce utopia is a long one, but perhaps the march has started.

Questions

1. What is the relationship between downsizing and stress?

2. Read the section in Chapter 12 entitled "Motivating in Action: Ten Methods for Motivating Employees." Which of the methods described there do you think are the most useful in focusing employee attention on productivity? Why? Which are most useful in terms of reducing the stress that employees may feel? Why?

3. If managers hope to have employees who are productive and happy, they must carry out several human resource management tasks. Briefly describe each of these tasks, and then indicate how effective management of them will reduce employee stress and increase employee productivity.

4. Explain how a matrix organization structure might cause employee stress. How might other structural elements (e.g., span of control) cause employees to feel stressed?

Video Resource: "Work-Life Balance (Special Edition)," *Venture* # 863 (January 19, 2003).

Downsizing

For the last 15 years or so, companies have pursued a strategy of downsizing in an attempt to cope with increasingly competitive markets. Middle managers are often downsized because they don't get big severance packages when they are let go, and it is often not clear what will be lost when they are gone.

One thing, however, has become clear about downsizing: it seems to cause an increase in employee fraud. Why? When a company lets go a lot of middle managers, there are simply fewer managers left to check the work of other employees. Opportunities for fraud therefore increase. Also, with fewer managers, the remaining managers have more power, and they can more easily engage in fraud.

Because companies lose an important fraud-detecting capability when they lay off middle managers, they often hire private detectives to ferret out fraud. Consider what happened at a company that had two managers handling rent cheques on buildings it owned. After one manager was laid off to save money, it was not too long before the remaining manager began cheating the company. Apartments that were shown as vacant on the books actually had tenants, and the rent cheques were directed into the manager's pocket. The company lost more in the fraud than they saved from the salary of the manager who was laid off.

Many companies are surprised when layoffs lead to increased fraud, assuming "it couldn't happen to me." It has reached the point where insurance companies now are worried because policyholders are making big claims. With fewer middle managers on the job, any fraudulent activity is likely to go undetected for longer periods, costing the company more money. Increasingly, insurance companies are pressuring their clients to resolve their fraud problems.

Fraud isn't the only difficulty associated with downsizing. Because a level of supervision is often removed in downsizing, employees may not be able to work as effectively afterward. One Ontario shipbuilding company found that productivity dropped after downsizing because there were no longer enough supervisors to provide proper management for workers.

Employee morale also takes a beating during downsizing. Employees who survive downsizing wonder if they're going to be next and spend a lot of time and energy worrying about losing their jobs. Downsizing usually means more work for those who remain, but they are reluctant to let go of any work for fear that they will appear dispensable.

Why don't companies avoid all these problems and simply hire back some of the middle managers they laid off? The answer is simple: competition. With the move toward "lean and mean" companies, the pressure is on to operate with as few personnel as possible, even when it is common sense that some unanticipated negative outcomes may result.

Questions

1. What is downsizing? What unanticipated negative consequences can arise because of downsizing?

2. What is the span of control? How might downsizing affect the span of control in a company?

3. What can managers do to reduce the chance that employees who remain after downsizing do not engage in fraudulent behaviour?

4. "A company that is profitable does not need to engage in downsizing." Do you agree or disagree? Explain.

Video Resource: "Revenge of the Middle Managers," *Venture* #724 (October 12, 1999).

PART 4 Leading

Part 4: Leading provides an overview of the "people" side of management. It considers what effective leadership involves, how to successfully motivate and communicate with subordinates, how to gain the benefits of teams, and how to lead organizational change.

We begin in **Chapter 11, Being a Leader**, by noting the importance of leadership and explaining how to think and act like a leader, the importance of understanding the foundations of leadership, and how to provide a vision for subordinates.

Next, in **Chapter 12, Influencing Individual Behaviour and Motivation**, we begin by explaining how individual differences complicate the manager's job and how factors like personality, perception, attitudes, abilities, and job satisfaction affect employee performance. We then present several important motivation theories that help leaders understand and motivate employees. We conclude by making several very practical suggestions about how to actually motivate employees in the workplace.

In **Chapter 13, Improving Communication Skills**, we explain the basic communication process and what a manager must know about communicating to be an effective leader. We also describe the interpersonal and organizational barriers to communication and how to overcome them. The chapter concludes with a discussion of the impact of technology on communication.

In **Chapter 14, Leading Groups and Teams**, we first examine the concept of groups, group norms, and group cohesiveness. We describe the various kinds of teams that are found in organizations and make specific practical suggestions on how to build effective teams. We conclude by describing the kinds of behaviours and attitudes managers must exhibit in order to be effective when leading teams and the group dynamics the leader should take into account when building and leading productive teams.

In **Chapter 15, Leading Organizational Change**, we describe the need for change in organizations, why people resist change, and practical suggestions for helping managers lead change in their organizations. The chapter also examines the topics of conflict and organization development, and how these areas relate to organizational change.

Being a Leader

Leadership at WestJet

Clive Beddoe is the CEO of WestJet Airlines, which started operations on February 29, 1996. The company's strategy is to sell tickets at bargain prices, offer good customer service, keep costs down by running a low-cost operation, and fly short-haul trips to carefully chosen markets. In just a few short years, WestJet's fleet has grown dramatically and so have its annual revenues. Its share price immediately after its initial public offering (IPO) in 1999 was U.S.$10 per share; by mid-2002, the price per share was U.S.$30.

How has WestJet achieved these remarkable results in an era when most commercial airlines are having financial difficulty? Ted Larkin, an analyst with HSBC Securities says the answer is simple: "WestJet operates an airline in a non-traditional manner and achieves non-traditional results." A more specific answer is that WestJet has a CEO who knows how to lead and motivate employees.

Beddoe has encouraged a corporate culture that aligns the interests of the employees with those of the company. He recognizes that in the commercial airline business it is difficult to closely manage employees because they are spread out all over the country as they work in various airports and on the airplanes. Therefore, he has encouraged people to manage themselves. WestJet gives a lot of latitude to workers to perform their jobs. This strategy means fewer layers of supervisors and a much higher level of productivity per worker.

Beddoe isn't so naive as to assume that workers will automatically be motivated to take ownership of their job. He realizes the value of incentives in motivating employees, so WestJet has instituted a profit-sharing plan that motivates employees to focus on corporate profitability. The plan works as follows: If WestJet's profit margin is, say, 10 percent, then 10 percent of net income is given to employees (prorated by salary). If the profit margin is 15 percent, employees get 15 percent, and so on up to a maximum of 20 percent. WestJet pays salaries that are slightly lower than the industry average, but when the profit sharing benefit is added in, employees are better off than other workers in the industry.

Beddoe has also introduced a stock option plan for employees. For every dollar an employee invests, the company matches that amount. This means that employees are able to buy shares of stock in WestJet at half the going market price. Therefore, it isn't surprising that 83 percent of employees own shares in the company. The employees who bought shares before the (IPO) now have an impressive portfolio. Some flight attendants, for example, now own more than U.S.$400 000 in stock, and some WestJet pilots are millionaires.

Beddoe's strategies are working: WestJet operates with fewer than 60 people per aircraft, while rival Air Canada uses more than 140 per aircraft. The culture at WestJet is also quite different from the culture at Air Canada. When WestJet employees fly on their own airline, they stick around after the flight lands to help clean up. This teamwork culture keeps the lid on costs, something that Air Canada continually has trouble with.

WestJet receives more than 3000 résumés each week from people who want to join the company. Most of these people do not currently work in the airline industry. Beddoe views that positively, saying that it's important to hire people who have new ideas and a new vision. WestJet is particularly interested in applicants who are enthusiastic and have a sense of humour, because Beddoe thinks that everyone should have fun while working.

WestJet
www.westjet.com

What Do Leaders Do?

Managers know that even after plans are set and the organization and employees are in place, nothing will happen without leadership. Leadership breathes life into the manager's plans and organization by translating those plans into action. In any company conflicts must be resolved, employees motivated, and organizational values set if the plans are to become results. Doing so requires leadership. Leading is thus the third main function in the management process. The first two, planning and organizing, are useless without it.

Leadership involves the distinctly behavioural and interpersonal aspect of what managers do. In the previous two parts of this book we've covered the management functions of planning and organizing. Now we turn to the concepts and skills involved with actually influencing the organization's employees to implement the company's plans.

The Leadership Function in the Management Process

Leadership means influencing others to work willingly to achieve the firm's objectives. But it also means something more. Managers also use "leading" as an umbrella term, to cover all or most of the behavioural (or people-oriented) things managers do. That's why Part IV of this book is called leading. It covers all the manager's people-oriented tasks, like motivation, communication, groups, conflict, and change.[1]

The knowledge contained in this chapter—Being a Leader—is therefore only part of what managers/leaders must know about leading. To really become an effective leader, you'll also need to understand the material in Chapters 12 to 15. These chapters contain a wealth of information about leadership and behavioural science concepts and skills. After studying them, you'll be able to apply the right skill in the right situation. One word of encouragement: Don't be overwhelmed by the number of leadership concepts and skills that you'll read about in Part 4. Instead, think of each as a tool in your leadership toolbox, each useful in its way and under the right conditions for leading your employees.

leadership
Influencing others to work willingly to achieve the firm's objectives.

Studying Leadership

The question "What makes some leaders more effective than others?" has perplexed and fascinated organizational experts for hundreds of years. Machiavelli, a shrewd adviser to kings and princes, addressed the question 400 years ago, and the Bible has many references to the actions leaders should take to be more effective. Medieval kings, Louis IV, pharaohs, and even the earliest "team leaders" who led their bands of cave dwellers across the plains must have asked themselves, "What makes some leaders more effective than others?"[2]

Although it's an age-old question, it has only been in the past 60 or so years that experts have made a systematic effort to find out what makes some leaders more effective than others. The current thinking, in brief, is this: effective leadership reflects a balance of leader traits, skills, and leadership styles that are combined in a way that's right for the situation. Leadership, in other words, reflects who we "are" (in terms of traits and skills) and how we behave (our leadership style) in particular leadership situations. The three main approaches to studying leadership have been to focus either on (1) the leader's traits and skills, (2) the leader's behaviour, or (3) how the situation influences what type of leader is best. We'll look at these three main approaches in this chapter.

The Traits and Skills of Leaders

The idea that leaders have certain traits or skills that distinguish them from non-leaders is not new. In fact, it is an idea that probably resonates with most people, since it's something we've all had some experience with. Who hasn't had a classmate whose charisma and decisiveness made him or her stand out as "the most likely to succeed"? Who hasn't had a boss whose intelligence and authority and empathy made us want to follow that person? On the other hand, who hasn't worked for someone whose traits or skills—perhaps indecisiveness, lack of confidence, or dishonesty—would make us vote them "the worst leader I've ever met."

Early researchers believed that if they studied the personality and intelligence of great leaders, they would uncover the combination of traits and skills that made these people great.

In thinking about what it is about leaders that determines their leadership effectiveness, experts usually don't just focus on leadership traits; they talk about both traits and skills. **Traits** (such as intelligence or self-confidence) are more or less unchanging characteristics of the person that predispose them to act in a particular way. **Skills** refer to the ability to carry out some task in an efficient manner.[3] Skills may be technical (knowing how to program a computer), interpersonal (being able to empathize with other people), or conceptual (being able to solve complex problems). Thus, when we think of leaders, we typically think of both their traits and skills.

What Are the Leadership Traits and Skills?

Early trait research typically asked leaders to describe their leadership traits, or administered personality inventories to leaders to assess their traits. Researchers found that specific traits related to leader effectiveness in some situations but not in others. No traits seemed to relate to effective leadership in a variety of different studies and situations. The trait approach was therefore out of style for many years in the mid-twentieth century.

Gradually, however, the trait approach has come back into vogue. For example, after reviewing 163 studies of leadership traits, professor Ralph Stogdill put it this way:[4]

> The leader is characterized by a strong drive for responsibility and task completion, vigor and persistence in pursuit of goals, venturesomeness and originality in problem solving, drive to exercise initiative in social situations, self-confidence and sense of personal identity, willingness to accept consequences of decision and action, readiness to absorb interpersonal stress, willingness to tolerate frustration and

traits
More or less unchanging characteristics of the person that predispose them to act in a particular way.

skills
The ability to carry out some task in an efficient manner.

delay, ability to influence other person's behavior, and capacity to structure social interaction systems to the purpose at hand.

Table 11.1 summarizes the leadership traits and skills Stogdill concluded were important. Recent research suggests that there are six traits or skills on which leaders differ from non-leaders.[5] These include drive, the desire to lead, honesty and integrity, self-confidence, cognitive ability, and knowledge of the business.

Leaders Have Drive Leaders are action-oriented people with a high desire to achieve. They get satisfaction from successfully completing challenging tasks. Leaders are more ambitious than non-leaders. They have high energy because "working long, intense work weeks (and many weekends for many years) requires an individual to have physical, mental, and emotional vitality."[6] Leaders are also tenacious and better at overcoming obstacles than are non-leaders.

Leaders Are Motivated to Lead Leaders are motivated to influence others. They prefer to be in leadership rather than subordinate roles, and they willingly shoulder authority. In turn, other traits seem to drive the motivation to lead. For example, there is evidence that whether a person is motivated to lead depends on his or her extraversion, agreeableness, conscientiousness, openness to experience, and emotional stability. Some psychologists call these "The Big 5" traits, because they are an important foundation of personality.[7]

Leaders Have Honesty and Integrity If your followers can't trust you, why should they follow you? Studies have found that people tend to rate leaders as more trustworthy and reliable in carrying out responsibilities than they do followers.[8]

Leaders Have Self-Confidence As two experts say, "Self-confidence plays an important role in decision making and in gaining others' trust. Obviously, if the leader is not sure of what decision to make, or expresses a high degree of doubt, then the followers are less likely to trust the leader and be committed to the vision."[9]

TABLE 11.1 *Traits and Skills Differentiating Leaders from Non-leaders*

TRAITS	SKILLS
Adaptable to situations	Clever (intelligent)
Alert to social environment	Conceptually skilled
Ambitious, achievement oriented	Creative
Assertive	Diplomatic and tactful
Co-operative	Fluent in speaking
Decisive	Knowledgeable about the work
Dependable	Organized (administrative ability)
Dominant (power motivation)	Persuasive
Energetic (high activity level)	Socially skilled
Persistent	
Self-confident	
Tolerant of stress	
Willing to assume responsibility	

Leaders Have Cognitive Ability The leader is the one who must pick the right direction and then put the mechanisms in place to get there. The leader's intelligence and decision making ability, and the subordinates' perceptions of those abilities, are therefore important leadership traits.[10]

CN
www.cn.ca

Leaders Know the Business Generally speaking, effective leaders are knowledgeable about the company and the industry. Their information helps them make informed decisions and anticipate the implications of those decisions.[11] However, there are exceptions. Paul Tellier, who became CEO of Canadian National Railways after much experience in the public sector, was instrumental in making CN one of the most efficient railroads in North America.

Power and Leadership

Perhaps you've had the unfortunate experience of being in charge of something, only to find that your subordinates ignore your instructions. A leader without power is really not a leader at all, since he or she has zero chance of influencing anyone to do anything. Skilful leaders know that they must have a power base, and they know how to build one.

Sources of Power As a leader, your power can derive from several sources. It most commonly stems from the position you hold. It also stems from your authority to reward employees who do well and to punish those who don't. You may have expert power and have such expertise that people do what you ask because they want the job done right. You may possess referent power (people look up to you because you are a fine person), and people will follow you because of that. You may control information that other people need, and that will give you power because you are a "gatekeeper." Several different sources of power are summarized in Table 11.2.

Some sources of power seem more legitimate than others, and some management writers have taken interesting positions on this topic of power. Here's how the sixteenth-century Italian writer Niccolò Machiavelli, summed this up in his book *The Prince*:

> One ought to be both feared and loved, but as it is difficult for the two to go together, it is much safer to be feared than loved. For love is held by a chain of obligation which, men being selfish, is broken whenever it serves their purpose; but fear is maintained by a dread of punishment which never fails.

Command and Control? Because power is partly in the eye of the beholder, it is not absolute. Chester Barnard wrote that managers are essentially powerless unless their followers grant them the authority to lead.[12] It usually doesn't matter how much power you have (or think you have). What matters is how much power your followers are willing to accept. If your subordinates think you're a great leader (for whatever reason), that may be all that matters. Conversely, if they don't (for whatever reason), your commands may be essentially ignored. You must therefore give some thought to how you're going to convince your followers that you have the right to lead them.

The issue of power is especially tricky in today's "empowered" organizations. Managers increasingly organize around self-managing teams where employees control their own activities. Influencing people to get their jobs done by relying too heavily on your own formal authority is therefore a dubious tactic today. The "command and control" approach to leadership is increasingly giving way to a more collegial system in many situations.

This is even true in some situations where you'd least expect it. For example, General Peter Schoomaker is former commander in chief of the U.S. Special Operations Command (which includes the Army's Delta Force, the Green Berets, the Rangers, and the Navy Seals). He argues that the traditional military way of issuing orders that soldiers obey unquestioningly is often an outmoded, inaccurate, and dangerous model for leadership today.[13] That's because the armies (and companies) that win today will be those that marshal "creative solutions in ambiguous circumstances," such as diffusing ethnic tensions, delivering humanitarian aid, and rescuing civilians trapped in overseas uprisings. In situations like these, "everybody's got to know how to be a leader."[14]

TABLE 11.2 *Sources of Power*

TYPE OF POWER	DEFINITION	EXAMPLE
1. Reward power	Person A has the ability to control the rewards that Person B receives.	Dindar Singh, who needs money, agrees to do a job for Vijay Prasad, who promises to "make it worth Singh's while."
2. Coercive power	Person A has the ability to determine the punishments that Person B receives.	Julie Parish gives her purse to a man who threatens to harm her if she does not comply.
3. Referent power	Person B does what Person A wants because Person B admires Person A.	Menno Friesen takes the advice of his pastor on a personal matter because he admires the pastor.
4. Expert power	Person A possesses some expert knowledge that Person B needs.	June Bielaczka, a manager in one department of a firm, follows the advice of John Kordic, an engineer in another department, because Kordic is the acknowledged expert on the problem facing Bielaczka.
5. Information power	Person A has information that convinces Person B to pursue a course of action desired by Person A.	Jonah Etah pays money to a blackmailer in return for that person not revealing embarrassing information about Jonah.
6. Persuasive power	Person A is able to convince Person B to take a certain course of action by making logical arguments.	Jonathan Etheridge convinces Henry Hill to support a warehouse expansion decision because of increased demand for the company's product.
7. Legitimate power	Person B believes that Person A has the "right" to give orders.	Alex Osig picks up a visitor from head office because his manager, Marion Hill, told him to do so.

Beyond the Leadership Foundations Having power and the right skills and traits won't guarantee that you'll be a successful leader. They are only a precondition. Having them gives you leadership potential.[15] As Kirkpatrick and Locke note, "Traits only endow people with the potential for leadership. To actualize this potential, additional factors are necessary."[16] The leader must also engage in the behaviours required to get people moving in the desired direction. This brings us to the issue of leadership behaviour.

Leader Behaviours

Consider the following sentiments:

"I wouldn't work for him again if he were the last person left on earth."

versus

"I'd follow her through a burning building if she asked."

What is it about a leader that triggers such emotions? Researchers have spent years trying to explain how leadership behaviour relates to leadership effectiveness. The basic assumption underlying most of these studies is that leaders perform two main functions—accomplishing the task and satisfying the followers' needs.

This assumption makes a great deal of sense. The task-oriented functions of a leader include making it clear to subordinates what they must do and then making sure they focus on doing it. The social or people-oriented leadership role is to reduce tension, make the job more pleasant, boost morale, and crystallize and defend the values, attitudes, and beliefs of the group. A number of specific leadership styles and schools of thought are associated with these basic task and people dimensions.[17]

Structuring and Considerate Styles

Research aimed at studying leader behaviour was carried out at the Bureau of Business Research at the Ohio State University. The research team developed a survey called the Leader Behaviour Description Questionnaire (LBDQ), which was then further refined by subsequent researchers.[18] The two leadership styles it measures—consideration and initiating structure—are as follows:[19]

Consideration (C) The leader behaves in a way that indicates mutual trust, friendship, support, respect, and warmth. (Example: "The leader is friendly and approachable.")

Initiating Structure (IS) The leader organizes the work to be done and defines relationships or roles, the channels of communication, and the ways of getting jobs done. (Example: "The leader lets group members know what is expected of them.")

The researchers' basic question was, "Which of these styles makes a leader more effective? That people are more satisfied when they have considerate leaders is not in doubt. The findings led Gary Yukl to conclude, "in most situations, considerate leaders will have more satisfied subordinates."[20] Subordinate satisfaction, while important, is only part of the story. High performance is also essential. Here, considerate leadership is not always the solution. Many considerate leaders had low performing groups.

Leaders high in IS often don't fare much better. They often have high performing groups. However, in one representative study, structuring activities by the leader seemed to trigger employee grievances. Thus, being task-oriented seems to produce low morale.

What explains such inconclusive findings? First, as we'll see in the next section, the style that's right for one situation might be wrong in another. You might need one style for leading a research team and another for leading a group of soldiers in battle. Second, it's usually not one style or the other but a balance that works best. For example, the Ohio State researchers found that IS behaviour did not trigger grievances (reduce morale) for those leaders who were also very considerate.[21]

In practice, balance means that leaders have to avoid what is called "country club" management—all consideration and no focus on the work.[22] Showing respect for employees, keeping them happy, providing support, and generally being considerate of their material and psychological needs is certainly important. But setting goals and getting things done is what the leader is there to do. Great leaders balance supportiveness with a clear expectation that employees are there to get their jobs done.

employee-oriented leaders
Leaders who focus on the individuality and personality needs of their employees and emphasize building good interpersonal relationships.

job-centred leaders
Leaders who focus on production and the job's technical aspects.

© 1998 Randy Glasbergen.

"When the boss isn't around to watch us, he loads up this screen saver."

Participative and Autocratic Styles

While the Ohio State researchers were working with their LBDQ, a research team at the University of Michigan was conducting a parallel series of leadership style studies. They identified two leadership styles: **employee-oriented leaders** (who focused on the individuality and personality needs of their employees and emphasized building good interpersonal relationships) and **job-centred leaders** (who focused on production and the job's technical aspects).

The most effective leaders were those who focused their attention on both the human aspects of their subordinates' problems and on building effective work groups with high performance goals.[23] Other University of Michigan researchers studied what they termed close and general leadership styles. **Close supervision** is at "one end of a continuum that describes the degree to which a supervisor specifies the roles of subordinates and checks up to see that they comply with these specifications." The **laissez-faire leader** who follows a completely hands-off policy with subordinates is at the other extreme, while a **general leader** is toward the middle of the continuum.

It is clear that most people don't like being closely supervised, since close supervision was usually associated with lower employee morale.[24] Yet, in practice, knowing when to put your foot down, and when to back off, is a continuing leadership dilemma. For example, after the 9/11 attacks, Greg Malever, CEO of Lanta Technology Group, tried to be sensitive to his employees' new anxieties.[25] But when an employee brought a TV to work so he could watch the news all day, the CEO felt he'd gone too far. "He just plugged into the wall and pulled up the rabbit ears... I marched over to his office and told him to turn it off. Enough is enough." Some managers are even more aggressive. The CEO of the Italian luxury goods company Prada is sometimes called Toscanaccio, or "rough Tuscan."[26] On one occasion, he became angry because some employees were not parking in their assigned factory parking spots. He then walked through the lot smashing their headlights. He says he paid their repair bill, but that from that point on, the employees parked in their assigned spots.

Although the Michigan researchers found that close supervision seemed to undermine morale, they found no consistent relationship between closeness of supervision and employee performance. Some "close" leaders had high performing groups, some did not. It was apparent that in some situations, employees did need to have a supervisor specify their roles and carefully check up on them if the work was to get done right. Findings like these further underscored the notion that leaders had to adjust their styles to fit the task.

Participative and autocratic styles roughly parallel the basic "people" and "task" dimensions noted earlier. However, they focus on the extent to which the leader lets the followers make decisions themselves, rather then unilaterally making the decisions for them. Faced with the need to make a decision, autocratic leaders solve the problem and make the decision alone, using the information available at the time.[27] Laurent Beaudoin of Bombardier Inc. was often cited in the business press as being an autocratic.[28] Former Prime Minister Brian Mulroney was seen as an all-powerful leader who cracked the whip to make everybody jump.[29]

At the other extreme, participative leaders share the problem with subordinates as a group. Then, together they and their groups generate and evaluate alternatives and try to reach consensus on a solution. Charles Hantho (Dominion Textile) and Bob Hamaberg (Standard Aero) were often cited as participative leaders.[30]

Some experts view participation as a continuum (see Figure 11.1).

Encouraging employees to make and implement decisions affecting their jobs has advantages, and much research supports the wisdom of doing so. For example (as explained in Chapter 6), employees who participate in setting goals tend to set higher goals than the

close supervision
A leadership style involving close, hands-on monitoring of subordinates and their work.

laissez-faire leader
A leader who follows a completely hands-off policy with subordinates.

general leader
A leader who takes a middle-ground approach between close supervision and laissez-faire leadership.

Lanta Technology Group
www.lanta.com

Bombardier
www.bombardier.com

Standard Aero
www.standardaero.com

AUTOCRATIC
The leader makes the decision alone.

CONSULTATION
The leader asks the followers for their opinions and then makes the decision by him or herself.

JOINT DECISION
The leader and followers discuss the problem and make the decision together.

DELEGATION
The leader gives the individual or group the authority and responsibility to make the decision themselves.

FIGURE 11.1
The Participation Continuum

supervisor would normally have assigned.[31] Participation also brings more points of view to bear and can improve the chances that participants will "buy into" the final decision.

Consider what happened when former Ford CEO Jacque Nasser tried to force through his new performance appraisal system. His felt that about 5 percent of managers should get a "C" performance grade each year and that two consecutive "C's" would mean dismissal. He instituted his new system unilaterally, without checking with the managers. A bit of participatory decision-making would have revealed how deeply his employees (and their union) resented the new system. The board soon forced Nasser out as CEO, in part due to the antagonism (and litigation) he triggered with the new system.

Nasser was trying to propel Ford to a higher level of excellence and believed that the new appraisal system would help him to do that. He set a direction and tried to get his employees moving in that direction. Isn't that what leaders are supposed to do? Yes, but as one historian put it, "Leadership is always about advancing an agenda, and you aren't likely to achieve that without empathy for other viewpoints."[32] Yet, in practice, there are obviously situations (like a sinking ship) where autocratic behaviour is exactly what's called for. Here, too (as with knowing when to use close supervision or some other leadership style), it seems great leaders know how to adjust their style to the needs of the situation.

Are There Gender Differences in Leadership Styles?

Although the proportion of women in management jobs has risen to almost 40 percent, barely 2 percent of top management jobs are held by women.[33] Most women managers are having trouble breaking into the top ranks. Why? The evidence suggests that it's *not* due to some inherent inability of women to lead (keep in mind such leaders as Elizabeth I, Joan of Arc, and Margaret Thatcher). In fact, the most recent research shows that men and women don't actually manage any differently. A study of 229 small business owners found that both male and female managers *talk* as if they lead according to gender stereotypes, but they actually *behave* in much less gender-specific ways.[34]

So, why are women so poorly represented at upper levels of management? The answer seems to be institutional biases and persistent, if inaccurate, stereotypes. We can summarize the more relevant research findings as follows.

Glass ceiling institutional biases explain part of the problem: Women often simply don't get access to the same "old boy's network" their male colleagues so easily draw on. Persistent, inaccurate stereotypes are another problem. Managers tend to identify "masculine" (competitive) characteristics as managerial and "feminine" (co-operative and communicative) characteristics as non-managerial.[35] Women tend to be seen as less capable of being effective managers than men. Other stereotypes are that women managers fall apart under pressure, respond impulsively, and have difficulty managing their emotions.[36]

But such stereotypes don't hold up under scrutiny. Studies suggest few measurable differences in the leadership behaviours women and men use on the job. Research shows that women managers are somewhat more achievement-oriented, while men are more candid with co-workers.[37] In one study, the only gender differences found were that women were more understanding than men.[38] Women and men who score high on the need for power (the need to influence other people) tend to behave more like each other than like people with lower power needs.[39]

How do women managers rate when compared with men? On the job and in job-like work simulations, women managers perform similarly to men. In actual organizational settings, "women and men in similar positions receive similar ratings."[40] In an assessment centre (where managers perform realistic leadership tasks such as leading problem-solving groups and making decisions), men and women managers performed similarly. Only in several off-the-job laboratory studies did men score higher in performance.[41]

There was one interesting difference, though. Women often scored higher on measures of patience, relationship development, social sensitivity, and communication. These may be precisely the skills that managers will need to manage diversity and the empowered members of self-managing teams.[42]

Transformational Leadership Behaviour

As we saw in Chapter 9, moving from mechanistic to learning-type organizations is not an easy task. Boundaries must be erased between the organization's departments and levels, new formal, informal, and electronic network-based structures installed, and the culture and systems changed so that employees are open and willing to learn. Creating a new company like this from an old one can require a major transformation. Nasser's experience at Ford illustrates what happens when the leader is unable to exercise the leadership needed to transform the organization.

In a book entitled *Leadership*, James MacGregor Burns argues for a new type of leadership style.[43] He says that leadership behaviour is either transactional or transformational.[44] **Transactional behaviours** are "largely oriented toward accomplishing the tasks at hand and at maintaining good relations with those working with the leader [by exchanging promises of rewards for performance]."[45] Leader behaviours like initiating structure and consideration, he suggests, are based on quid pro quo "you do something for me, and I'll do something for you" transactions (for example, "You do this, and you'll get a raise").

What Transformational Leaders Do Burns says the transactional style doesn't work when employees must be inspired to make a major change. Today, leaders must transform their companies, often in a very short time frame, and Burns says that transformational leaders are needed to achieve these massive changes. "**Transformational leadership** refers to the process of influencing major changes in the attitudes and assumptions of organization members and building commitment for the organization's mission, objectives and strategies."[46] Transformational leaders are those who bring about "change, innovation, and entrepreneurship."[47] They are responsible for leading a corporate transformation that "recognizes the need for revitalization, creates a new vision, and institutionalizes change."[48] The "Challenge of Change" box describes one such transformational leader.

Transformational leaders have the knack for inspiring their followers to want to make the change and to throw themselves into doing so. They encourage—and get—performance beyond expectations by formulating visions and then inspiring subordinates to pursue them. In so doing, transformational leaders cultivate employee acceptance and commitment to those visions.[49] They "attempt to raise the needs of followers and promote dramatic changes in individuals, groups, and organizations."[50] For example, when Ted Newall took over as head of Alberta-based Nova Corporation in 1991, it was losing hundreds of millions of dollars a year. He conveyed his belief in the company to employees in a very dramatic way: He refused a salary and accepted only stock options and shares of Nova's stock as his compensation. Everyone knew that if the firm didn't make money that Newall would be working for nothing. By 1996, Newall was the highest-paid executive in the petroleum industry.[51]

As we saw in the boxed insert, Rick George of Suncor is another transformational leader. He turned the company around by making peace with environmentalists, convincing employees that the company had a future, and improving the company's antiquated technology. The changes he introduced improved employee morale and increased the company's stock price.[52]

Perhaps you've worked with such a person. From the vantage point of their followers, transformational leaders come across as charismatic, inspirational, considerate, and stimulating:[53]

- *Charismatic.* Employees often idolize and develop strong emotional attachments to them. Charisma isn't an either-or thing; it depends on both the leader and the followers. Just as "beauty is in the eye of the beholder," so is charisma. "Most [charismatic leadership] theorists now view charisma as the result of follower perceptions and attributions influenced by actual leader traits and behaviour, by the context of the leadership situation, and by the individual and collective need of the followers."[54]

- *Inspirational.* "The [transformational] leader passionately communicates a future idealistic organization that can be shared. The leader uses visionary expla-

transactional behaviours
Leadership actions that focus on accomplishing the tasks at hand and on maintaining good working relationships by exchanging promises of rewards for performance.

transformational leadership
The leadership process that involves influencing major changes in the attitudes and assumptions of organization members and building commitment for the organization's mission, objectives, and strategies.

Leading Transformational Change at Suncor

Suncor is a major oil company that is best known for its pioneering work in extracting crude oil from the tar sands near Fort McMurray, Alberta. The oil business in general has a reputation for being environmentally unfriendly, and for many years Suncor was part of that image. The company experienced toxic fires at its mine, pollution leaks into the Athabasca River, worker deaths, and low employee morale as it tried to make a go of the difficult tar sands mining process.

But then Rick George became president and CEO in 1991, and things started changing. Over the next decade, Suncor became a high-performing company in two critical areas. First, the production of oil increased dramatically and has now reached 225 000 barrels a day (George wants to eventually achieve 500 000 barrels a day). The price of the company's stock has gone from under $5 per share to more than $50 per share, and employee morale is way up. The company added eight billion barrels of oil reserves in 1994 and workers now see a long-term future for the company.

Second, Suncor has become the standard in the industry for environmentally sound mining practices. When George took over, Suncor was one of Canada's top polluters (primarily benzene and sulphur dioxide). When he announced that Suncor would develop a new mine, environmentalists objected and threatened to block development by holding public hearings. The objection was partly based on the fact that tar sands oil produces 17 percent more pollution per barrel than conventional oil does. To everyone's surprise, George bargained directly with environmentalists and reached an agreement that saw Suncor promise no increases in greenhouse gas emissions and actual reductions in other noxious fumes. Both sides won this fight: the environmentalists got tougher air quality controls than Alberta's regulators would have imposed, and Suncor got its new mine up and running two years earlier than it otherwise would have. Since the opening of the mine, benzene and sulphur dioxide discharges have dropped by more than 75 percent.

How did George achieve these two apparently contradictory goals?

nations to depict what the employee work group can accomplish."[55] Employees are then motivated to achieve these organizational aims. The transformational leader "provides vision of what lies ahead."[56] The "People Side of Managing" box on page 346 describes what one leader did to motivate employees.

■ *Considerate.* Transformational leaders treat employees as individuals and stress developing them in a way that encourages the employees to become all they can be. Employees are treated as individuals rather than just as a member of the group.

■ *Intellectually stimulating.* Transformational leaders "encourage employees to approach old and familiar problems in new ways."[57] This enables employees to question their own beliefs and use creative ways to solve problems by themselves. These leaders show employees how to think about problems in new ways.

Using Transformational Leadership The evidence suggests that a transformational leadership style is not just for leaders who want to build learning organizations or to implement

- He made sure that employees knew his motto: "Increase production, reduce costs, and reduce the environmental footprint."
- He gave orders to senior management to benchmark and become more competitive.
- He hired the best people he could find.
- He overhauled the company's antiquated technology and brought production costs down from $19.50 per barrel of oil to $16 per barrel.
- He confronted the low morale facing the company's employees by ensuring the long-term future of Suncor in the tar sands.
- He took the company public and moved its head office to Calgary.
- He set goals for financial performance with senior staff to double shareholder value every five years (Suncor has consistently exceeded that goal).
- He gave bonuses for good performance (the company's 3300 employees shared a $107 million bonus in February 2002).
- He interacts regularly with environmentalists so that he knows their concerns and they know his.

Rick George, president and CEO of Suncor.

Suncor has made the Dow Jones Sustainability Index for three years running. It is also getting into alternative energy sources. Because that is costly, Suncor has joined a coalition of corporate, municipal, and green groups and secured $200 million in incentives for developing wind power. Regulatory hurdles and poor cost returns continue to make wind and solar power projects economically questionable, but Suncor has built six wind turbines in Gull Lake, Saskatchewan, that are powering 6000 homes.

Michael Jantzi Research Associates Inc., a Toronto firm that analyzes ethical investments, says that when George arrived at Suncor, the company was at the bottom of the oil and gas list in terms of corporate performance, but now it is at the top. Jantzi says that this shows how social and environmental issues can go hand in hand with financial success.

Suncor
www.suncor.com

major organizational changes. Transformational leadership can also help produce day-to-day change. For example, one study found that successful champions of relatively small-scale technological change (leading the introduction of a new product, for instance) used more transformational leader behaviours than did less successful champions.[58] Another study[59] found that high-performing managers in an express delivery firm used significantly more transformational leader behaviours[60] than did less successful managers.[61] Other findings suggest that transformational leadership is more closely associated with leader effectiveness and employee satisfaction than are transactional styles such as general or laissez-faire leadership.[62] All leaders are responsible for moving their followers forward. To that extent, it appears that most can benefit from transformational-type leadership behaviours.

Can managers be trained to be more transformational? The results of one study suggest that the answer is "Yes." The study took place at one of the five largest Canadian banks. The managers of the 20 branches in one region were randomly assigned to either an experimental group (which received training in transformational leadership) or a control group (which did not receive training). The training program familiarized participants with the meaning of transformational leadership and explained how it could be implemented in the managers' branches. It also provided one-on-one "booster" sessions where a trainer met individually with each of the managers to go over the latter's leadership

Turning Continental Airlines Around

Continental Airlines
www.continental.com

When he became CEO of Continental Airlines in the mid-1990s, Gordon Bethune faced a daunting task. Continental was close to bankruptcy. In terms of industry-wide standards like "on-time departures," his firm was a perpetual also-ran. Bethune knew he had to jump-start Continental's performance. But what could he do—quickly—to get the firm's 35 000-plus employees to buy in to the need to improve and also get them on board as far as actually doing it?

One of his first moves was to install a new incentive plan for all of Continental's non-managerial employees. The plan was simple: Any month Continental ranked among the top five airlines in terms of on-time departures, every employee would get a $65 cash bonus. Some experts predicted the plan would never work, arguing that if everyone got $65, "free riders" would just slack off and let their harder-working colleagues carry the brunt of the increased load. It turned out that everyone pitched in. By 1997, the firm was profitable again. The plan was successful because it had the following key characteristics.

1. *The right performance measure.* Continental could easily measure "on-time departures" and compare their performance to that of the competition. It was also a measure that crew members and airport staff could definitely affect.
2. *Mutual monitoring.* Although the firm had more than 35 000 employees, most of them worked locally in very small teams, so the team members helped to keep each other's performance in line.
3. *Visible rewards.* Management was careful not to "hide" the monthly $65 bonus in each employee's paycheque. Each worker got a separate monthly check for the full $65.
4. *Kick start the program.* Bethune "kick-started" the program by immediately modifying the firm's flight schedules to make on-time performance easier to achieve. This virtually guaranteed that employees would get their bonuses in the first month (which they did). This provided immediate reinforcement for the employees' increased efforts.

style and to develop personal action plans for the manager to become more of a transformational leader. The results of this study clearly indicate that managers can be trained to be transformational leaders. For example, the subordinates of the managers who received the training subsequently perceived their mangers as higher on intellectual stimulation, charisma, and individual consideration than did subordinates of managers who received no training.[63]

The Level 5 Leadership Style

Is there one style of leadership that the can make a good company great? That is one of the questions researchers Jim Collins and Jerry Porras pursue in their book *Built to Last: Successful Habits of Visionary Companies*.[64] Collins and Porras focused on 11 companies that had started out years earlier as "good" companies (competent, but nothing spectacular) and then ended up in the mid-1990s as "great" companies. The market values of these "good to great" companies grew eight to nine times faster than did the stock market as a whole.

How to Be a Transformational Leader[65]

☑ Articulate a clear and appealing vision.

☑ Explain how the vision can be attained.

☑ Act confident and optimistic.

☑ Express confidence in followers.

☑ Provide opportunities for early successes.

☑ Celebrate successes.

☑ Use dramatic, symbolic actions to emphasize key values.

☑ Lead by example.

☑ Empower people to achieve the vision.

What sort of leaders led these "good-to-great" companies? Collins and Porras found that most good-to-great companies were led by CEOs that exhibited what Collins calls the **Level 5 Leadership Style**. Figure 11.2 summarizes the main behaviours associated with this style. As you can see, Level 5 leadership is a unique blend of personal humility and professional will. On the one hand, Level 5 leaders are modest, calm, and willing to take the blame when things go wrong. At the same time, they demonstrate an unwavering resolve to do whatever must be done to produce the best long-term results; they not only set high standards, but they also settle for nothing less.

That seems to be the style that epitomizes Dieter Zetsche, the executive DaimlerChrysler sent from Germany to turn around its Chrysler unit. A recent article about him notes that he is tactful ("I would rather talk about what I like than criticize something"), avoids executive airs ("I eat in the employees' cafeteria"), is responsive, not aloof ("my style is talking to people and listening…"), and likes "schmoozing" (he joked with a small group of reporters for hours).[66] At the same time, Mr. Zetsche is no pushover. He has driven Chrysler to slash costs and introduce new, more competitive models.

level 5 leadership style
A unique blend of personal humility and professional will.

Personal Humility	Professional Will
Demonstrates a compelling modesty, shunning public adulation; is never boastful.	Creates superb results, a clear catalyst in the transition from good to great.
Acts with quiet, calm determination; relies principally on inspired standards, not inspiring charisma, to motivate.	Demonstrates an unwavering resolve to do whatever must be done to produce the best long-term results, no matter how difficult.
Channels ambition into the company not the self; sets up successors for even more greatness in the next generation.	Sets the standard of building an enduring, great company; will settle for nothing less.
Looks in the mirror, not out the window, to apportion responsibility for poor results, never blaming other people, external factors, or bad luck.	Looks out the window, not in the mirror, to apportion credit for the success of the company—to other people, external factors, and good luck.

FIGURE 11.2
The Main Behaviours of Level 5

Leadership Styles and Emotional Intelligence

emotional intelligence
A rating that reflects the underlying emotional intelligence traits of self-confidence, trustworthiness, the need to achieve, cross-cultural sensitivity, and persuasiveness.

A person's **emotional intelligence** reflects his or her unique mix of the underlying emotional intelligence traits, namely self-confidence, trustworthiness, the need to achieve, cross-cultural sensitivity, and persuasiveness. People who score high on emotional intelligence usually act self-confidently, are trustworthy, strive to achieve, are culturally sensitive, and are very persuasive. Those scoring low act quite the opposite.

Emotional intelligence seems to reveal itself in distinctive leadership styles. Researchers from the consulting firm Hay/McBer studied a sample of 3810 executives. They concluded that these executives typically used one or more of six leadership styles in trying to influence their followers. Figure 11.3 summarizes the styles. They include coercive, authoritative, affiliative, democratic, pacesetting, and coaching. The figure also provides a snapshot of how each type of leader behaves. For example, the coercive leader is a "do what I tell you" leader. The democratic leader might approach the problem with the phrase "what do you think?" Each style has a basis in the leader's level of emotional intelligence.

The researchers came to two conclusions. First, leaders who are most effective use several of these styles on a regular basis.[67] Second, the best style for one situation might not work for another. To the Hay/McBer researchers, the six leader styles are akin to the clubs in a golf pro's bag. "Over the course of a game, the pro picks and chooses clubs based on the demands of the shot."[68] A golfer wouldn't use a driver to make a putt. You need to fit the style to the situation.

Situational Theories of Leadership

Pepsi
www.pepsico.com

Yum! Brands
www.yum.com

It is clear from the research on leadership traits and styles that the traits, skills, or styles that might be best for one situation might not work so well in another situation. Sometimes close supervision is good, sometimes not. Sometimes participative leadership is good, sometimes not. Good managers need to know when to use each style.

It also seems apparent that people can use several styles simultaneously. This was one conclusion of the Hay/McBer study. Everyday experience also supports the idea that most managers are (or can be) "multi-styled." During the time Andy Pearson ran PepsiCo Inc., he increased revenues from U.S.$1 billion to more than U.S.$8 billion. He did this through what one writer describes as "fear, surprise, and a fanatical devotion to the numbers."[69] Pearson is now running Yum! Brands, which owns KFC, Pizza Hut, Long John Silver's, A&W, and Taco Bell. In his current position, he faces a different set of circumstances and has adapted his leadership style as a result. At one meeting, someone suggested opening an all-night restaurant. Pearson had doubts about the idea, but didn't say so, at least directly. He offers what he sees as "the challenge." He says, "For Kinko's, being open all-night is a

	Coercive	Authoritative
The leader's distinctive behaviour	Demands immediate compliance	Mobilizes people toward a vision
The style in a phrase	"Do what I tell you."	"Come with me."
Underlying emotional intelligence traits	Drive to achieve, initiative, self-control	Self-confidence, empathy, change catalyst
When the style works best	In a crisis, to kick-start a turnaround, or with problem employees	When changes require a new vision, or when a clear direction is needed
Overall impact on climate	Negative	Most strongly positive

FIGURE 11.3
Six Leadership Styles at a Glance

big thing. But we would have to pre-empt the [restaurant] category. You can't share it."[70] What Pearson is doing now is sharing the decision making. Same person, different style.

Of course, the key questions are these: When and under what conditions do I use one style or another? When should I be people-oriented, and when should I "clamp down"? When should I let my subordinates participate, and when should I make the decisions myself? Managers obviously must have answers to questions like these. Several models have been proposed to help managers decide how to fit their leadership style to the situation.

Fiedler's Contingency Theory of Leadership

Fred E. Fiedler and his team originally sought to determine whether a leader who was lenient in evaluating associates was more or less likely to have a high-producing group than a leader who was demanding and discriminating.[71] He measured leadership style with his Least Preferred Co-Worker (LPC) scale. Leaders who describe their least preferred co-worker favourably (pleasant, smart, and so on) are "high LPC" and are more people-oriented. Leaders who describe their least preferred co-worker less favourably are "Low LPCs" and are less people-oriented and more task-oriented. Figure 11.4 presents Fiedler's LPC scale.

According to Fiedler's theory, three situational factors combine to determine whether the high-LPC or the low-LPC style is appropriate.

1. *Position power.* The degree to which the position itself enables the leader to get group members to comply with and accept his or her decisions and leadership.

2. *Task structure.* How routine and predictable the work group's task is.

3. *Leader–member relations.* The extent to which the leader gets along with workers and the extent to which they have confidence in and are loyal to the leader.

Fiedler found that where the situation is either favourable or unfavourable for the leader (that is, where leader–member relationships, task structure, and leader position power are all either very high or very low), a more task-oriented, low-LPC leader is appropriate. In favourable situations, the leader could get away with just focusing on the task. In unfavourable situations, the leader basically had no choice but to focus on the task. In situations that were intermediate in favourableness (that is, where these factors are more mixed and the task is not as clear-cut), a more people-oriented, high-LPC leader is appropriate.

Of the three situational factors, Fiedler wrote that leader–member relations seems to be the key. He says, "A leader who is liked, accepted, and trusted by his [or her] members will find it easy to make his [or her] influence felt."[72] Figure 11.5 summarizes the relationships involved and how to apply Fiedler's model. Many subsequent research findings produced mixed results,[73] and the usefulness of Fiedler's theory remains in some dispute.[74]

Affiliative	Democratic	Pacesetting	Coaching
Creates harmony and builds emotional bonds	Forges consensus through participation	Sets high standards for performance	Develops people for the future
"People come first."	"What do you think?"	"Do as I do, now."	"Try this."
Empathy, building relationships, communication	Collaboration, team leadership, communication	Conscientiousness, drive to achieve, initiative	Developing others, empathy, self-awareness
To heal rifts in a team or to motivate people during stressful circumstances	To build buy-in or consensus, or to get input from valuable employees	To get quick results from a highly motivated and competent team	To help an employee improve performance or develop long-term strengths
Positive	Positive	Negative	Positive

Look at the words at both ends of the line before you put In your "X." Please remember that there are *no right or wrong answers.* Work rapidly; your first answer is likely to be the best. Please do not omit any items, and mark each item only once.

LPC
Think of the person *with whom you can work least well.* It may be someone you work with now, or someone you knew in the past.

It does not have to be the person you like least well, but it should be the person with whom you had the most difficulty in getting a job done. Describe this person as he or she appears to you.

Pleasant	`:___:___:___:___:___:___:___:` 8 7 6 5 4 3 2 1	Unpleasant
Friendly	`:___:___:___:___:___:___:___:` 8 7 6 5 4 3 2 1	Unfriendly
Rejecting	`:___:___:___:___:___:___:___:` 1 2 3 4 5 6 7 8	Accepting
Helpful	`:___:___:___:___:___:___:___:` 8 7 6 5 4 3 2 1	Frustrating
Unenthusiastic	`:___:___:___:___:___:___:___:` 1 2 3 4 5 6 7 8	Enthusiastic
Tense	`:___:___:___:___:___:___:___:` 1 2 3 4 5 6 7 8	Relaxed
Distant	`:___:___:___:___:___:___:___:` 1 2 3 4 5 6 7 8	Close
Cold	`:___:___:___:___:___:___:___:` 1 2 3 4 5 6 7 8	Warm
Co-operative	`:___:___:___:___:___:___:___:` 8 7 6 5 4 3 2 1	Unco-operative
Supportive	`:___:___:___:___:___:___:___:` 8 7 6 5 4 3 2 1	Hostile
Boring	`:___:___:___:___:___:___:___:` 1 2 3 4 5 6 7 8	Interesting
Quarrelsome	`:___:___:___:___:___:___:___:` 1 2 3 4 5 6 7 8	Harmonious
Self-assured	`:___:___:___:___:___:___:___:` 8 7 6 5 4 3 2 1	Hesitant
Efficient	`:___:___:___:___:___:___:___:` 8 7 6 5 4 3 2 1	Inefficient
Gloomy	`:___:___:___:___:___:___:___:` 1 2 3 4 5 6 7 8	Cheerful
Open	`:___:___:___:___:___:___:___:` 8 7 6 5 4 3 2 1	Guarded

FIGURE 11.4
Fiedler's LPC Leadership Scale

Path–Goal Leadership Theory

path–goal leadership theory
The leader's job is to increase the personal rewards subordinates receive for attaining goals and to make the path to these goals easier to follow by reducing roadblocks, setting goals, explaining what needs to be done, and organizing the work.

Path–goal leadership theory says that the leader's job is to increase the personal rewards subordinates receive for attaining goals and to make the path to these goals easier to follow by reducing roadblocks, setting goals, explaining what needs to be done, and organizing the work.[75] Stripped to its essentials, path–goal theory makes these suggestions: If the job is ambiguous, structure it. If it is demoralizing or the employees lack confidence, be supportive and considerate. And, always make it clear how employee effort on the job will lead to rewards.

Path–goal theory originally focused on two leader styles, the Ohio State LBDQ leader dimensions of Consideration and Initiating Structure,[76] but today it has expanded to focus on four leadership styles: directive leadership, supportive leadership, participative leadership, and achievement-oriented leadership. *Directive leaders* let subordinates know what is expected of them, give specific guidance as to what should be done and how it should be done, and schedule the work to be done. *Supportive leaders* are friendly and ap-

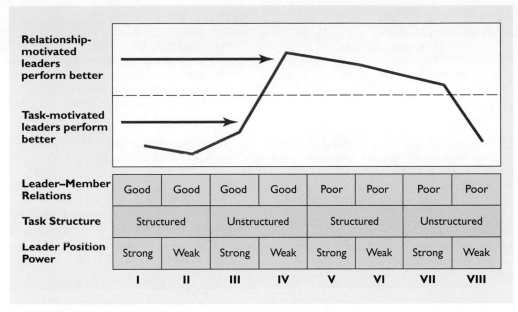

Leader–Member Relations	Good	Good	Good	Good	Poor	Poor	Poor	Poor
Task Structure	Structured		Unstructured		Structured		Unstructured	
Leader Position Power	Strong	Weak	Strong	Weak	Strong	Weak	Strong	Weak
	I	II	III	IV	V	VI	VII	VIII

FIGURE 11.5
How Style of Effective Leadership Varies with Situation.

proachable and show concern for their followers' status and well-being. *Participating leaders* consult with subordinates and solicit their suggestions. *Achievement-oriented leaders* "set challenging goals, expect subordinates to perform at their highest level, continuously seek improvement in performance, and show a high degree of confidence that the subordinates will assume responsibility."[77]

The path–goal theory says that the "right" style of leadership depends on the nature of the task and on the capabilities of the followers. Under this theory, the preferred leadership style therefore depends on the structure of the task, the employee's self-confidence, and the morale of the employees. For example, if subordinates lack confidence in their ability to do the job, they may need more consideration and support. Or, if subordinates aren't clear about what to do or how to do it, the leader should provide structure (in terms of task instructions), as required. The idea is that if people don't know what to do, or think they can't do it, or don't see how effort leads to rewards, they won't do the job. The theory thus makes a good deal of intuitive sense.

In ambiguous, unstructured situations directive leaders have a motivational effect on their followers by clarifying the situation and thus make their followers see that effort will lead to performance and to rewards. For subordinates dealing with frustrating or demoralizing tasks, supportive leaders increase self-confidence and make the task more bearable. For challenging but ambiguous tasks, participative leaders can help clarify expectations and reduce ambiguity, (at least for employees who are not overly frightened by unstructured tasks). Finally, achievement-oriented leadership boosts employee confidence by clarifying goals when the task is ambiguous and challenging. These ideas are sumarized in Table 11.3.

Research regarding the path–goal theory has yielded mixed results.[78] Although supportive leadership behaviour tends to have a positive relationship with morale, regardless of the task, most of the evidence regarding fitting directive leadership behaviour to the task did not support the theory. "Not enough studies were available to provide an adequate test of hypotheses about situational moderators of participative and achievement oriented leadership."[79]

Substitutes for Leadership

The path–goal theory basically suggests that the leader's role is to in some way "substitute" for the nature of the situation. Robert House (who developed the theory) essentially says this: If the task is already so routine and structured that it's clear how to do the task, then leaders who use a high-initiating structure style will trigger worker resentment. Similarly, the

TABLE 11.3 *Fitting the Style to the Situation with Path–Goal Theory*

LEADER BEHAVIOUR	SITUATIONAL FACTORS	MOTIVATIONAL EFFECTS
Directive	Ambiguous, unstructured	Reduces role ambiguity; increases follower beliefs that effort will result in good performance and that performance will be rewarded.
Supportive	Frustrating, routine, stressful, or dissatisfying tasks. Employees may lack self-confidence.	Increases self-confidence; increases the personal value of job-related effort.
Participative	Ambiguous, non-repetitive, challenging	Reduces ambiguity, clarifies expectations, increases consistency of subordinate and organizational goals, increases involvement with and commitment to organizational goals.
Achievement-oriented	Ambiguous, non-repetitive, challenging	Increases subordinate confidence and the personal value of goal-directed effort.

more satisfying the task already is, the less important it is for the leader to be highly considerate and supportive.[80] So, leadership (and, in particular, the specific leadership style) is, to some extent, a substitute for the inherent structure and satisfaction of the task.

Steve Kerr and J. M. Jermier carry this logic even further and argue that there are also substitutes for leadership itself.[81] Their theory focuses on the need for two basic leadership styles—supportive/considerate leadership, and instrumental/initiating structure leadership. They suggest that there are various characteristics of the subordinates, the task, and the organization that may either be a substitute for direct intervention by the leader, or may neutralize the leader's best efforts.

Table 11.4 lists these substitutes and neutralizers, and their likely interplay with each leadership style. For example, if your subordinates are highly professional (you're leading a dedicated team of engineers, for instance) then their professional orientation should substitute for (reduce the need for) either supportive or instrumental leadership. The existence of adequate organizational rules and procedures should make leader structuring less necessary.

This theory suggests that as a leader you can "set the stage" to make your leadership job easier by choosing the right followers and organizing the task properly.[82]

- *Choose the right followers*. If you select and train your followers well, there may be less need to exercise leadership on a daily basis. The greater your subordinates' ability, the greater their experience, the better their training, and the more professional their behaviour, the less direct supervision they will need. Some followers are inherently more effective than others. Choose followers who are co-operative, flexible, and trustworthy, who take initiative, and who are good at solving problems.[83]

- *Organize the task properly*. You may also be able to adjust organizational factors to reduce the need for day-to-day leadership. For example, jobs for which performance standards are clear, or for which there is plenty of built-in feedback, may require less leadership.[84] Similarly, employees engaged in work that is intrinsically satisfying (work they love to do) require less leadership.[85] Cohesive work groups with positive norms also require less leadership (as do, by definition, self-managing teams).

leader–member exchange (LMX) theory
A theory that says that leaders may use different styles with different members of the same work group, based in part on perceived similarities and differences with the leader.

Leader–Member Exchange Theory

Although a leader may have one prevailing style, most leaders don't treat all subordinates the same. The **leader–member exchange (LMX) theory**[86] says that leaders may use

TABLE 11.4 *Specific Substitutes and Neutralizers for Supportive and Instrumental Leadership*

CHARACTERISTICS THAT MAY BE SUBSTITUTE OR NEUTRALIZER	EFFECT ON SUPPORTIVE LEADERSHIP	EFFECT ON INSTRUMENTAL LEADERSHIP
A. Subordinate Characteristics		
1. Experience, ability, training		Substitute
2. Professional orientation	Substitute	Substitute
3. Indifference toward rewards	Neutralizer	Neutralizer
B. Task Characteristics		
1. Structured, routine task		Substitute
2. Feedback provided by task		Substitute
3. Intrinsically satisfying task	Substitute	
C. Organization Characteristics		
1. Cohesive work group	Substitute	Substitute
2. Low position power	Neutralizer	Neutralizer
3. Formalization (roles, procedures)		Substitute
4. Inflexibility (rules, policies)		Neutralizer
5. Dispersed subordinate work sites	Neutralizer	Neutralizer

different styles with different members of the same work group.[87] In this theory, leaders also adapt their styles to the situation, but it is the quality of the relationship between the leader and the subordinate that determines what the situation is.

LMX theory says that leaders tend to divide their subordinates into an "in" group and an "out" group (and you can guess who gets the better treatment!). What determines whether you're part of a leader's "in" or "out" group? The leader usually decides based on very little real information, although perceived leader–member similarities (for example, gender, age, attitudes, etc.) are usually important.[88]

One study is illustrative. Researchers studied nurses and nurse supervisors at a large hospital.[89] The leader's perceptions of two things—similarity of leader–follower attitudes and follower extroversion—seemed to determine the quality of leader–member relations. Leaders assessed the similarity between themselves and their followers in terms of attitudes toward six items: family, money, career strategies, goals in life, education, and overall perspective. Leaders were more favourably inclined toward followers with whom they shared similar attitudes. The extroverted nurses were more likely to have high-quality leader–member exchanges than were the introverts, presumably because they were more outgoing and sociable in general.

This suggests two practical implications. First, members of the in-group tend to perform better than do those in the out-group, so leaders should strive to make the in-group more inclusive. Second, the findings underscore the attraction of being in your leader's in-group and thus of emphasizing similarities rather than differences and of endeavoring to be sociable.

The Vroom-Jago-Yetton Model

Leadership experts Victor Vroom, Arthur Jago, and Philip Yetton focus on participative leadership styles. They have developed a model that enables leaders to analyze a situation and decide how much participation is called for. Their technique consists of three components: (1) a set of management decision styles; (2) a set of diagnostic questions; and (3) a decision tree for identifying how much participation the situation calls for.

The Management Decision Styles As we've seen, there are different degrees of participation. As shown in Figure 11.6, Vroom and his associates propose a continuum of five management decision styles.

At one extreme is style AI, which allows no participation. Here the leader solves the problem and makes the decision without consulting anyone else. At the other extreme is style GII, which allows total participation. Here the leader shares the problem with subordinates and together they reach an agreement. You can see in Figure 11.6 that between these two extremes are styles AII, CI, and CII, each with more participation.

The Diagnostic Questions In this leadership model, the appropriate degree of participation depends on several attributes of the situation. The situational attributes include both the importance of the quality of the decision and the extent to which the leader has enough information to make a high-quality decision alone. The manager can assess the presence or absence of these attributes by asking the following sequence of diagnostic questions.

A. Is there a quality requirement such that one solution is likely to be more rational than another?

B. Do I have sufficient information to make a high-quality decision?

C. Is the problem structured?

D. Is acceptance of the decision by subordinates critical to effective implementation?

E. If you were to make the decision by yourself, is it reasonably certain that it would be accepted by your subordinates?

F. Do subordinates share the organizational goals to be obtained in solving this problem?

G. Is conflict among subordinates likely over preferred outcomes?

The Decision Tree The decision tree in Figure 11.7 puts this all together. This chart enables the leader to quickly choose the appropriate degree of participation. By starting on the left of the chart and answering each sequential diagnostic question with a "yes" or "no," you can work your way across the decision tree and determine which leader style is best. For example, when the problem (1) does not possess a quality requirement (in other words, when the decision doesn't have to be of high quality), and (2) when acceptance of the decision by subordinates is not important for effective implementation, then any of the styles (including the most directive style) would be appropriate. On the other hand, even

---

AI. You solve the problem or make the decision yourself, using information available to you at that time.

AII. You obtain the necessary information from your subordinates, then decide on the solution to the problem yourself. You may or may not tell your subordinates what the problem is when getting the information from them. The role played by your subordinates in making the decision is clearly one of providing the necessary information to you, rather than one of generating or evaluating alternative solutions.

CI. You share the problem with relevant subordinates individually, getting their ideas and suggestions without bringing them together as a group. Then you make the decision, which may or may not reflect your subordinates' influence.

CII. You share the problem with your subordinates as a group, collectively obtaining their ideas and suggestions. Then you make the decision, which may or may not reflect your subordinates' influence.

GII. You share a problem with your subordinates as a group. Together, you generate and evaluate alternatives and attempt to reach agreement (consensus) on a solution. Your role is much like that of a chairperson. You do not try to influence the group to adopt "your" solution, and you are willing to accept and implement any solution that has the support of the entire group.

FIGURE 11.6
Types of Management Decision Styles

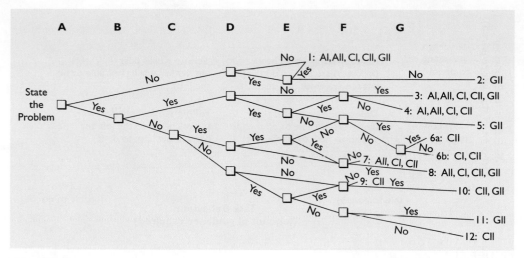

FIGURE 11.7
Vroom and Yetton Decision Process Flow Chart

if there is no particular quality requirement, if acceptance of the decision by subordinates is important for implementation, style GII (sharing the problem with your subordinates as a group) is the way to go.

Studies generally support this model or variations of it. In one study, Vroom and Jago found that there was an average success rate of about 62 percent for decisions made in accordance with the model, versus only 37 percent for those that were not.[90] Remember that this model focuses only participative leadership, but in practice, as we've seen, leaders may have to tap other types of leadership styles, too. For that, other models, like the following one, are available.

The Hersey-Blanchard Situational Leadership Model

The Situational Leadership Model provides a practical way for leaders to decide how to adapt their style to the task.[91] This model focuses on four leadership styles:

- The *delegating leader* lets the members of the group decide what to do.
- The *participating leader* asks the members of the group what to do, but the leader makes the final decisions.
- The *selling leader* makes the decision, but explains the reasons.
- The *telling leader* makes the decision and tells the group what to do.

According to the situational leadership model, each style is appropriate in a specific situation (see Figure 11.8):

- *Delegating* works best where followers are willing to do the job and know how to go about doing it.
- *Participating* works best when followers are able to do the job but are unwilling and so require emotional support.
- *Selling* works best where followers are neither willing nor able to do the job.
- *Telling* works best where followers are willing to do the job but don't know how to do it.

Figure 11.9 provides detailed guidance on what to look for when deciding which style to use.

- *S4.* When followers are "able and willing or confident," a delegating leader who turns over responsibility for decisions and implementation is the style of choice. Delegating leaders encourage autonomy, provide support and resources, and delegate activities.

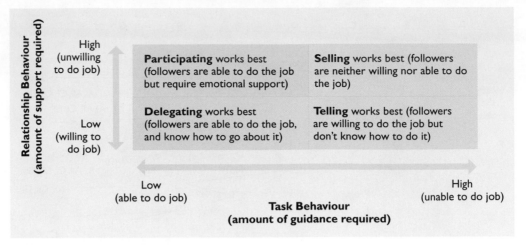

FIGURE 11.8
Summary of Situational Leadership Model

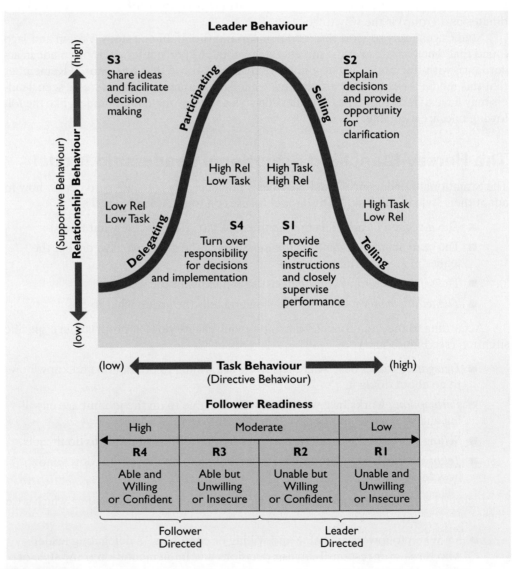

FIGURE 11.9
Applying the Situational Leadership Model

- *S3.* When followers are somewhat less ready to be led—when they are "able but unwilling or insecure," a participating style is best. Participating leaders share ideas and facilitate the decision making. They share responsibility for decision making with their followers, focus on results, and (where necessary) discuss their followers' apprehensions.

- *S2.* When followers are even less ready to be led—where they are "unable but willing or confident," the selling style is best. The selling leader explains decisions, provides opportunity for clarification, and is somewhat less participatory than the previous two leaders. The selling leader seeks to get followers to "buy in" to the decision by persuading them, checks their understanding of the task, encourages questions, explains "why," and emphasizes "how-to."

- *S1.* Finally, you may find that your followers are relatively unprepared for the task at hand because they are both "unable and unwilling, or insecure." This calls for a telling style. Here you provide specific instructions and closely supervise performance. Your main job is structuring what your employees need to do. You therefore provide specific instructions, closely supervise what your followers are doing, positively reinforce small improvements, and consider the possibility of instituting some negative consequences for non-performance.

How to Improve Your Leadership Skills

Being a leader means taking the steps required to boost your effectiveness in the leader's role. No formula can guarantee that you will be a good leader. However, by applying the research presented in this chapter, you can certainly improve the chances that you will be effective in a leadership situation. Doing so requires strengthening your leadership skills.

Skill 1: How to Think Like a Leader

If there is one thing that's clear from what you've read so far in this chapter, it's this: It is important to think before acting. You must understand the problem facing you and to do that you must think through the situation.

Consider this example. Gus owns an engineering company in Vancouver. He's a genius at what he does, and his company now employs about 200 people, including 80 engineers. Though successful, the firm has a persistent problem. An engineering team will work on a project and send off the proposal, but if the client doesn't like the design, the project team will just give up and shelve the project. The team doesn't mention this to Gus, and he is therefore often seen storming around the office yelling, "Why didn't you tell me we didn't get that deal!" Unfortunately, all this is getting Gus nowhere. His engineers still avoid telling him when they lose a job, and morale is starting to slip as well. Gus has turned to you for advice: "What can I do to make those irresponsible engineers let me know before these projects fall apart?" is how he puts it.

You know Gus faces a leadership crisis. The question is, What is the problem, and how should he solve it? Are his employees actually "irresponsible"? Is Gus lacking in the traits effective leaders should have? Is he less participative then he should be? Is the pay scale so low that the engineers simply don't care? There are many possible explanations, and you don't want to choose the wrong one. For example, being more participative won't help Gus if the problem's not leadership style, but pay. Therefore, the first leadership skill is being able to think though situations like these.

"Thinking like a leader" isn't some mysterious process known to just a few. In fact, it's quite logical and scientific. Look at the leadership situation you're facing, and then (1) identify what is happening, (2) explain why it is happening, and (3) decide what you are going to do about it.[92] Figure 11.10 summarizes the process. Let's see how Gus might apply this three-step process.

What Is Happening Here? In Gus's case, the facts seem clear: For some reason, his engineers appear to be refusing to give him bad news. And when he does discover that they've lost a job, he reacts angrily.

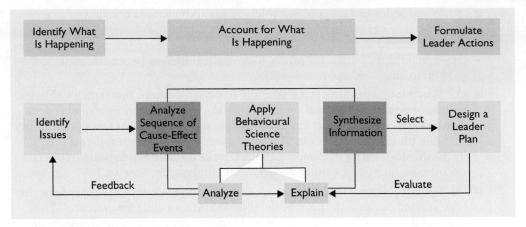

FIGURE 11.10
How to Think Like a Leader

Why Is This Happening? The *what* was simple; the hard part now is explaining *why* this is happening. For years, Gus assumed his engineers were irresponsible. However, he's been reading up on leadership, and now he's not so sure. He sees that thinking like a leader involves understanding "why something is happening." And he knows that answering that question involves applying behavioural science theories and concepts about leadership, motivation, communications, and teamwork to help explain why the engineers refuse to divulge bad news.

Like the engineer he is, Gus needs to formulate a cause-effect relationship between what has occurred and why. For example, "The engineers here refuse to divulge bad news (the effect) because they are punished when they do by having Gus yell at them (the cause)." In figuring out "why is it happening," don't miss the forest for the trees. Try to identify the *root cause* of the situation. View the situation as a coherent whole, while at the same time looking for logical connections. Look at the whole situation, and be analytical: Do the engineers know they're doing something wrong? Are they simply irresponsible? What typically happens when they tell Gus they may have lost the job? How does he react? Are they just reacting to Gus's habit of responding quickly and harshly to any negative news? How does Gus's apparent leadership style enter into the equation?

You may discover that more than one of the leadership or behavioural science concepts covered in this and the next few chapters applies. For example, perhaps the engineers actually are a bit irresponsible. Or, they may be dissatisfied with their pay. Or, Gus may have inadvertently created a blame-oriented culture in which his employees know they'll get dumped on when they bring him negative news. Don't be put off if more than one theory or concept in this and the next few chapters helps to explain the problem. That is really quite normal. You may combine several possible explanations or choose the one you'll take action on first.

What Should I Do About It? Determining what you should do about a problem means applying your knowledge of behavioural science techniques from this and the next four chapters. This will involve such things as choosing the right leadership style for the situation, motivating employees, or resolving inter-group conflict. What actions would you take to resolve Gus's problem? After discussing the situation with you, Gus comes to several conclusions. No doubt, he's been too explosive when people bring him bad news. The engineers are afraid to give him bad news, because they know he'll yell at them. So, that's something that, at a minimum, he will have to address. Good possibilities for leadership action here include the following:

- Get some counselling to deal with the "emotional intelligence" needs that seem to be driving Gus to behave this way. A leader's emotional intelligence—the ability to interact in a healthy manner—with subordinates manifests itself in one or more of these leadership styles: coercive, authoritative, affiliative, democratic, pacesetting, and coaching. Gus's apparent overuse of the coercive, punitive style isn't working.

- Decide what leadership style is best for this situation. What do the situational leadership theories tell us about the style Gus should use? Path–goal and substitutes for leadership theory tell us these people are professionals and should be able to manage themselves, with little extra prodding or "structuring" on Gus's part. Hersey-Blanchard's situational leadership theory suggests that Gus and his engineers are in an "S3"-type situation. The engineers seem "able but unwilling or insecure" about doing their jobs. This model therefore suggests using a "participating" leader style. Gus should "share ideas and facilitate decision making" (for instance, by giving the engineers an opportunity to tap his considerable expertise when they're doing or reworking their proposals.)
- Meet with the engineers to explain that things are going to be different, and then behave consistently like a high-emotional intelligence manager.
- Commence a new profit-sharing plan that rewards engineers in part based on the number of new projects the company sells.

Remember not to limit the behavioural science knowledge you apply to just the material in this chapter. You'll need to apply what you learn in subsequent chapters on motivation, groups, conflict, and change. Fit that knowledge into your assessment of the situation as you account for what is happening and formulate a response. Don't be overwhelmed by the number of theories and concepts that might apply; think of them as tools in your leadership toolkit. There may well be more than one way to solve the problem.

Skill 2: How to Know What Leadership Style to Use

Most people have one prevailing leadership style, but good leaders can usually alter their style to fit the situation. A great football coach won't treat a mistake by a new player the same way he will treat the same blunder by a 10-year veteran (at least, not the first time). Remember that leader styles are like those clubs in the golf-pro's bag.

In picking the right style, there are several situational leadership theories to choose from and apply (as you did for Gus above). Review the path–goal and leadership substitutes theories above to get a sense of whether the situation is already sufficiently structured and/or satisfying that it doesn't warrant additional leader structure and/or support. Ask yourself whether (in line with LMX) you are treating one or two favoured employees differently from the rest. If the leadership question seems to be "to what extent should I let my subordinates participate in making the decision?" apply the Vroom-Jago-Yetton model. If the situation seems to call for a more varied range of leader styles, apply the Hersey-Blanchard model.

Skill 3: How to Pick the Right Leadership Situation

What do you do if you will have difficulty adapting your style to different situations? (Let us hope the autocratic Gus does not fit in that category). One solution is to focus on situations that fit your prevailing leadership style. To do this, use the situational leadership models to choose the right situations for you (rather than to choose a style). For example, suppose you're a more authoritarian, "telling"-type leader. Then, a tough turnaround situation where your employees can't or won't do their jobs may be right for you. If you tend to be very participatory and to prefer delegating most decisions, then unstructured situations with employees who tend to have the right answers may be best for you. Fiedler, in fact, suggests recruiting and hiring managers based on the types of situations in which they're expected to lead: "The organization must then be aware of the type of leadership situations into which the individual should be successively guided..."[93]

Skill 4: How to Build Your Power Base

Remember that a powerless leader is not a leader at all. Therefore, strengthen the foundation of your leadership by enhancing your authority. How much power do you have, and how can you accumulate more? Table 11.5 suggests some specific actions that can be taken for five of the seven types of power outlined in Table 11.2.

TABLE 11.5 *Manager's Bases of Power*

Reward Power

1. Increase pay levels.

2. Influence getting a raise.

3. Provide specific benefits.

4. Influence getting a promotion.

Coercive Power (ethically questionable)

5. Give undesirable work assignments.

6. Make work difficult.

7. Make things unpleasant.

8. Influence getting a promotion.

Legitimate Power

9. Make others feel they have commitments to meet.

10. Make others feel they should satisfy job requirements.

11. Give the feeling that others have responsibilities to fulfill.

12. Make others recognize that they have tasks to accomplish.

Expert Power

13. Give good technical suggestions.

14. Share considerable experience and/or training.

15. Provide sound job-related advice.

16. Provide needed technical knowledge.

Referent Power

17. Make employees feel valued.

18. Make employees feel that you approve of them.

19. Make employees feel personally accepted.

20. Make employees feel important.

Skill 5: How to Exercise Better Judgment

No one wants to be led by someone who keeps making bad decisions. You therefore have to exercise good judgment when making decisions. In Chapter 5, we described several steps that can be taken to improve your judgment. Review those.

Skill 6: How to Develop Your Other Leadership Traits and Skills

Leaders have traits that distinguish them from non-leaders. To some extent, those wanting to be leaders can develop and cultivate these traits. For example, leaders exhibit self-confidence. Although developing self-confidence is a lifelong process, you can enhance yours in several ways. Gravitate toward situations in which you're already more self-confident, such as those in which you are an expert. A stamp collector, for example, would likely exhibit more self-confidence as president of a stamp club than in coaching a baseball team. Act like a leader by exhibiting self-confidence—by making decisions and sticking with them, and by acting somewhat reserved. Exercise honesty and integrity, applying high ethical standards to everything you do.

Your knowledge of the business is probably the easiest trait to modify. Immerse yourself in the details of your new job, and learn as much about the business as you can, as fast as you can. Experiential Exercise #4 provides a quick test of your leadership readiness.

SKILLS AND STUDY MATERIAL

SUMMARY

1. Leadership means influencing others to work willingly toward achieving objectives. Being a leader requires more than having a command of leadership theories. It also means managing organizational culture; motivating employees; managing groups, teams, and conflict; and facilitating organizational change.

2. Thinking like a leader means reviewing a leadership situation and identifying what is happening, accounting for what is happening (in terms of leadership and other behavioural science theories and concepts), and formulating leader actions.

3. The leader must provide a direction for followers. This direction may be a statement of vision, mission, or objectives, depending largely on what the leader wants to achieve and the level at which the leader is acting.

4. To be a leader one must also have the potential to be a leader. Having the right stuff (in terms of personality traits) is a foundation component. Some traits on which leaders differ from non-leaders include drive, the de-

sire to lead, honesty and integrity, self-confidence, cognitive ability, and knowledge of the business.

5. Legitimate power and authority are also elements in the foundation of leadership, because a leader without power is not a leader at all. Sources of leader power include position, rewards, coercion, expertise, and referent power or personal magnetism.

6. Leadership style or behaviours include structuring and considerate styles; participative and autocratic styles; employee-centred and production-centred styles; close and general styles; and transformational behaviour.

7. Although there are some differences in the way men and women lead, they do not account for the slower career progress of most women managers. Institutional biases such as the glass ceiling and persistent, inaccurate, stereotypes are contributing factors.

8. Situational leadership theories and the leader–member exchange theory underscore the importance of fitting the leader's style to the situation.

CRITICAL THINKING EXERCISES

1. The November 22, 1999, issue of *Fortune* was devoted to tracing the concept of leadership during each decade of the twentieth century. The article mentions things like the "captains of industry" in the early twentieth century, government regulation of monopolies, the union movement, the rebuilding of Europe after the Second World War, the "company men" of the 1950s, and high-profile managers of the boom-times during the 1990s. Read the article, and then think about what leadership will be like in 2010, 2020, 2030, 2040, and 2050. Base your thinking on what the chapter presents as well as the ideas from the *Fortune* article.

2. Guidance, vision, culture, empowerment, personality, power, influence, charisma, the "right stuff," revolutionizing the behaviour of others: These seem to be evolving elements of leadership today. Rather than lifelong work in one company, we are also increasingly becoming independent workers or contractors, tied more

to our own profession and skills than to any one company, or country for that matter. Using the research presented in this chapter, develop a profile for the types of leaders needed for the following companies or leadership positions:

Prime Minister of Canada

CEO of Microsoft

Coach of an NHL team

Owner of a small business

CEO of Ford Motor Company in Brazil

Director of Consumer and Corporate Affairs

Director of the United Way

Be prepared to compare your profiles with those of your class members.

3. Compare the perspectives noted below regarding leadership. What concepts from the chapter would help you to understand the various perspectives? Which sentiment do you like best and why?

- "You can't succeed as a leader unless you're more concerned about people's performance than about their feelings. You must focus on people's output, not on their attitude toward their work. Reward the employees who get results, and don't pay much attention to employees who are sincere but incompetent."

- "A leader must subscribe to the view that workers should share in the economic value they help to create. Stock options are a good way to do this, yet many business leaders do not make them available to their workers. When you decide to share the wealth with workers, you give them an incentive to succeed, so it is surprising that more companies don't do this."

- "Leaders must have an overarching vision for their firm, but they must also have a clear understanding of where the company is now and how far it has to go to achieve its vision."

- "The importance of leadership has been overstated. The leaders of business firms and other kinds of organizations make mistakes just like everybody else, and the ones who are successful just happen to be a little luckier than the ones who aren't."

EXPERIENTIAL EXERCISES

1. Leaders come in all sizes, shapes, genders, and races. Research five of the following people and then write a brief analysis of what makes or made them leaders. After you have completed that portion of the task, explain what you think an "ideal" leader is and identify someone you think fits that profile best. Write no more than two pages of analysis.

   The leaders are Jean Chrétien, prime minister of Canada; Golda Meir, former leader of Israel; Bill Clinton, former president of the United States; Mao Zedong, the late communist leader of China; Bill Gates, chairman of Microsoft; Louis Gerstner, former CEO of IBM; Helmut Kohl, former chancellor of Germany; Jesus Christ, religious leader; Paul Tellier, CEO of Bombardier; and Larry Walker, professional baseball player.

2. The world has clearly changed in the last few decades. Many people argue that for families to maintain a decent standard of living, it is necessary for women to enter the labour market and stay there for many years. If Canada is to remain competitive on the international scene, the mixture of work and family is an issue we should address as a nation.

   In groups of four to six, including men and women, discuss the following questions.

   What type of leadership do you think is needed in today's highly competitive workplace?

   Are men and women using the same leadership styles? Should they?

   Can women take their place in leadership positions under the current situation?

3. In their book entitled *The New Global Leaders*, Mansfried F. R. Kets de Vries and Elizabeth Florent-Treacy select Richard Branson of Virgin Atlantic Airlines, Percy Barnevik of ASEA Brown Boveri, and David Simon of British Petroleum as the models for global leadership. Research each of these companies on the internet or obtain a copy of *The New Global Leaders* from the library. Then write a comparative analysis of these individuals' leadership styles and why they are seen as models for the global marketplace.

4. The following self-assessment exercise can give you a feel for your readiness and inclination to assume a leadership role.

   Instructions. Indicate the extent to which you agree with each of the following statements, using the following scale: (1) disagree strongly; (2) disagree; (3) neutral; (4) agree; (5) agree strongly.

1. It is enjoyable having people count on me for ideas and suggestions.	1	2	3	4	5
2. It would be accurate to say that I have inspired other people.	1	2	3	4	5
3. It's a good practice to ask people provocative questions about their work.	1	2	3	4	5
4. It's easy for me to compliment others.	1	2	3	4	5
5. I like to cheer people up even when my own spirits are down.	1	2	3	4	5
6. What my team accomplishes is more important than my personal glory.	1	2	3	4	5
7. Many people imitate my ideas.	1	2	3	4	5
8. Building team spirit is important to me.	1	2	3	4	5
9. I would enjoy coaching other members of the team.	1	2	3	4	5
10. It is important to me to recognize others for their accomplishments.	1	2	3	4	5
11. I would enjoy entertaining visitors to my firm even if it interfered with my completing a report.	1	2	3	4	5
12. It would be fun for me to represent my team at gatherings outside our department.	1	2	3	4	5
13. The problems of my teammates are my problems, too.	1	2	3	4	5
14. Resolving conflict is an activity I enjoy.	1	2	3	4	5
15. I would co-operate with another unit in the organization even if I disagreed with the position taken by its members.	1	2	3	4	5
16. I am an idea generator on the job.	1	2	3	4	5
17. It's fun for me to bargain whenever I have the opportunity.	1	2	3	4	5
18. Team members listen to me when I speak.	1	2	3	4	5
19. People have asked me to assume leadership of an activity several times in my life.	1	2	3	4	5
20. I've always been a convincing person.	1	2	3	4	5

Total score: _____

Scoring and Interpretation. Calculate your total score by adding the numbers circled. A tentative interpretation of the scoring is as follows:

90–100: high readiness for the leadership role

60–89: moderate readiness for the leadership role

40–59: some uneasiness with the leadership role

39 or less: low readiness for the leadership role

If you are already a successful leader and you scored low on this questionnaire, ignore your score. If you scored surprisingly low and you are not yet a leader or are currently performing poorly as a leader, study the statements carefully. Consider changing your attitude or your behaviour so that you can legitimately answer more of the statements with a 4 or a 5.[94]

5. The following self-assessment exercise can give you a better feel for the steps you can take to enhance your power.

Directions. Circle the appropriate number of your answer, using the following scale: (1) disagree strongly; (2) disagree; (3) neutral; (4) agree; (5) agree strongly.

As a manager, I can (or, if I'm not a manager now, my manager can or former manager could) ...

Reward Power

1. Increase pay levels.	1	2	3	4	5
2. Influence getting a raise.	1	2	3	4	5
3. Provide specific benefits.	1	2	3	4	5
4. Influence getting a promotion.	1	2	3	4	5

Coercive Power (ethically questionable)

5. Give undesirable work assignments.	1	2	3	4	5
6. Make work difficult.	1	2	3	4	5
7. Make things unpleasant.	1	2	3	4	5
8. Influence getting a promotion.	1	2	3	4	5

Legitimate Power

9. Make others feel they have commitments to meet.	1	2	3	4	5
10. Make others feel they should satisfy job requirements.	1	2	3	4	5
11. Give the feeling that others have responsibilities to fulfill.	1	2	3	4	5
12. Make others recognize that they have tasks to accomplish.	1	2	3	4	5

Expert Power

13. Give good technical suggestions.	1	2	3	4	5
14. Share considerable experience and/or training.	1	2	3	4	5
15. Provide sound job-related advice.	1	2	3	4	5
16. Provide needed technical knowledge.	1	2	3	4	5

Referent Power

17. Make employees feel valued.	1	2	3	4	5
18. Make employees feel that I approve of them.	1	2	3	4	5
19. Make employees feel personally accepted.	1	2	3	4	5
20. Make employees feel important.	1	2	3	4	5

Total score: _____

Scoring and Interpretation. Add all the circled numbers to calculate your total score. You can make a tentative interpretation of the score as follows:

90+: high power

70–89: moderate power

below 70: low power

Also, see whether you rated much higher on one type of power than on the others.

What's Your Emotional Intelligence at Work?

DIRECTIONS

For each of the following items, rate how well you are able to display the ability described. Before responding, try to think of actual situations in which you have had the opportunity to use the ability.

Minimal Ability 1	Very slight Ability 2	Slight Ability 3	Moderate Ability 4	Very Good Ability 5

_____ 1. Associate different internal physiological cues with different emotions.

_____ 2. Relax when under pressure in situations.

_____ 3. "Gear up" at will for a task.

_____ 4. Know the impact that your behaviour has on others.

_____ 5. Initiate successful resolution of conflict with others.

_____ 6. Calm yourself quickly when angry.

_____ 7. Know when you are becoming angry.

_____ 8. Regroup quickly after a setback.

_____ 9. Recognize when others are distressed.

_____ 10. Build consensus with others.

_____ 11. Know what senses you are currently using.

_____ 12. Use internal "talk" to change your emotional state.

_____ 13. Produce motivation when doing uninteresting work.

_____ 14. Help others manage their emotions.

_____ 15. Make others feel good.

_____ 16. Identify when you experience mood shifts.

_____ 17. Stay calm when you are the target of anger from others.

_____ 18. Stop or change an ineffective habit.

_____ 19. Show empathy to others.

_____ 20. Provide advice and emotional support to others as needed.

_____ 21. Know when you become defensive.

_____ 22. Know when you are thinking negatively and head it off.

_____ 23. Follow your words with actions.

_____ 24. Engage in intimate conversations with others.

_____ 25. Accurately reflect people's feelings back to them.

SCORING

Sum your responses to the 25 questions to obtain your overall emotional intelligence score. Your score for *self-awareness* is the total of questions 1, 6, 11, 16, and 21. Your score for *managing emotions* is the total of questions 2, 7, 12, 17, and 22. Your score for *motivating yourself* is the sum of questions 3, 8, 13, 18, and 23. Your score for *empathy* is the sum of questions 4, 9, 14, 19, and 24. Your score for *social skills* is the sum of questions 5, 10, 15, 20, and 25.

INTERPRETATION

This questionnaire provides an indication of your emotional intelligence. If you received a total score of 100 or more, you have high emotional intelligence. A score from 50 to 100 means you have a good platform of emotional intelligence from which to develop your managerial capability. A score below 50 indicates that you realize that you are probably below average in emotional intelligence. For each of the five components of emotional intelligence—self-awareness, managing emotions, motivating one's self, empathy, and social skill—a score above 20 is considered high, while a score below 10 is considered low.

Managers who are attuned to their own feelings and the feelings of others can use their understanding to enhance the performance of themselves and others in their organizations. The five basic components of emotional intelligence that are most important for managers are discussed here.[95] Review the following discussion of the five components of emotional intelligence and think about what you might do to develop those areas in which you scored low.

- *Self-awareness.* This component provides the basis for all the other components of emotional intelligence. Self-awareness means being aware of what you are feeling, being conscious of the emotions within yourself. People who are in touch with their emotions are better able to guide their own lives. Managers need to be in touch with their emotions to interact effectively and appreciate emotions in others. Managers with high levels of self-awareness learn to trust their "gut feelings" and realize that these feelings can provide useful information about difficult decisions. Answers are not always clear about who is at fault when problems arise, or when to let an employee go, reorganize a business, or revise job responsibilities. In these situations, managers have to rely on their own feelings and intuition.

- *Managing emotions.* The second key component of emotional intelligence is managing emotions. Operationally it means the manager is able to balance his or her own moods so that worry, anxiety, fear, or anger do not get in the way of what needs to be done. Managers who can manage their emotions perform better because they are able to think clearly. Managing emotions does not mean suppressing or denying them but understanding them and using that understanding to deal with situations productively.[96] Managers should first recognize a mood or feeling, think about what it means and how it affects them, and then choose how to act.

- *Motivating oneself.* This ability to be hopeful and optimistic despite obstacles, setbacks, or even outright failure is crucial for pursuing long-term goals in life or in business. A classic example of self-motivation occurred when the MetLife insurance company hired a special group of job applicants who tested high on optimism but failed the normal sales aptitude test. Compared to salespeople who passed the regular aptitude test but scored high on pessimism, the "optimistic" group made 21 percent more sales in their first year and 57 percent more in the second.[97]

- *Empathy.* The fourth component is empathy, which means being able to put yourself in someone else's shoes—to recognize what others are feeling without them needing to tell you. Most of the time people don't tell us what they feel in words but rather in tone of voice, body language, and facial expression. Empathy is built from self-awareness; being attuned to one's own emotions makes it easier to read and understand the feelings of others.

- *Social skill.* The ability to connect to others, build positive relationships, respond to the emotions of others, and influence others is the final component of emotional intelligence. Managers need social skills to understand interpersonal relationships, handle disagreements, resolve conflicts, and pull people together for a common purpose.

INTERNET EXERCISES

As companies evolve and their leadership changes, so does the culture of the company. Leaders have their own leadership styles. These styles aren't right or wrong, they are just different.

1. Compare the leadership styles of Steve Ballmer and Bill Gates at Microsoft Corporation (**www.microsoft.com**).

Access the menu selections About Microsoft/Corporate Information/Company Fast Facts.

2. Did Bill Gates's leadership style in the 1990s affect Microsoft's potential to be innovative and competitive?

3. Has Steve Ballmer's leadership style changed Microsoft's corporate culture?

CASE STUDY 11-1

Leadership in the Canadian Forces

In 1993, soldiers of the Canadian Airborne Regiment who had been sent to Somalia on a United Nations humanitarian mission tortured and killed a teenaged Somali boy. Over the next few months, there was increasing publicity about the case, with most of it focusing on allegations that documents relating to the murder were tampered with and destroyed.

Colonel Geof Haswell, the only person actually charged with document tampering, claimed that General Jean Boyle, Chief of Defence Staff for the →

Canadian forces, knew that the documents had been tampered with before they were released in response to the CBC's access-to-information requests. Several other officers and civilian employees of the Defence Department supported this claim. Boyle denied that he had any knowledge of the document alteration. He did, however, admit that he had broken the spirit of the access-to-information law by failing to disclose certain other documents.

At an inquiry held during the summer of 1996, General Boyle said that he took responsibility for what happened in Somalia but that he would not resign as Chief of Defence. When asked by members of the Somalia Inquiry Board if he was responsible for what he did and what his subordinates did, Boyle said "yes" but added that his responsibility for his subordinates' actions depended on whether he knew about them. One commissioner said that the answer sounded like Boyle was trying to shift the blame onto his subordinates.

Boyle claimed that dishonest and cowardly subordinates conspired to betray him by altering documents relating to the Somalia incident. He therefore felt that he should not have to take responsibility for their actions. He also said that if Chiefs of Defence resigned every time a subordinate made an error, there would never be any leadership in the Canadian Forces.

Boyle was unable to explain how he could be unaware of document tampering while so many other people in the military knew about it. Observers felt that Boyle came across as not willing to accept responsibility for what happened.

As the inquiry progressed, General Boyle hinted that he might consider resigning if he thought that his leadership capability was damaged in the eyes of his subordinates. On October 8, 1996, General Boyle did resign as Chief of Defence Staff. He said that the mili-

tary deserved a leader who was not the focus of attention as he had been during the inquiry.

Observers of the case have varied opinions about what happened and who was responsible for what. A military historian who closely followed Boyle's testimony felt that General Boyle was the victim of a witch hunt. But several retired military officers said that Boyle was unfit to continue in his position, and that, because of the controversy, military personnel were ashamed to wear their uniforms in public. One general noted that there had been misconduct in Canadian troops in both Bosnia and Somalia, which he considered a result of leadership failure in the Canadian Forces. A 1995 survey of Canadian Forces personnel showed that only 17 percent had confidence in the most senior levels in the Department of Defence.

Questions

1. To what extent is a leader responsible for what his or her subordinates do? In this case, how responsible was Boyle?

2. How does a leader ensure that subordinates trust the leader? How effective was Boyle in generating trust and pride among his subordinates? Defend your answer.

3. Assuming that Boyle did not know that documents had been tampered with, should he have been held responsible for the actions of his subordinates? Defend your answer.

Canadian Forces
www.dnd.ca

The Importance of Leadership: Scott vs. Amundsen

How important is leadership? In certain situations, it can mean the difference between life and death. Consider the race between the British and the

Norwegians in 1911–1912 to see who could reach the South Pole first. In his book *The Last Place on Earth*, author Roland Huntford observed that →

For the privilege of being the first to tread this useless yet so desirable spot, both men were prepared to…face any extremity of suffering and danger. The poles of the earth had become an obsession of Western man…. Since the obsession was there, it had to be exorcised, and the sooner the better.[98]

To achieve the goal, each man had to first secure financial support to pay for such a major expedition. The appropriate ships had to be acquired, and tonnes of supplies and animals had to be taken to the starting point on the continent of Antarctica. Once there, a base camp had to be set up and men and equipment readied for the trek to the South Pole.

The trip to the Pole was made in conditions that are hard to imagine. On foot or on skis, the explorers made their way across 1200 km of ice and snow, through –40°C temperatures and over mountains nearly 3000 m high. Once at the Pole, they had to turn around and fight their way back to the coast through the same conditions.

The Norwegians were led by Roald Amundsen, a man who was not only a meticulous planner, but also a great leader. He realized that planning was absolutely essential for a successful expedition to the Pole because he had spent years familiarizing himself with conditions at both the North and South Poles. In the crucial areas of food and fuel, Amundsen developed a system for laying out supply depots so that they could be found even in a raging blizzard. This ensured that the Norwegians had enough supplies to make it safely back to their base camp after they reached the Pole. By studying polar conditions, he knew that sled dogs were the best animals to haul supplies. He also knew that going to the Pole on skis was far superior to walking.

Amundsen carefully selected the four men who would accompany him and with whom he would live in very close quarters during the three-month trip to the Pole and back. Amundsen's men had complete confidence in his abilities, and he, in turn, allowed them to participate in many of the important decisions that had to be made during the expedition.

Robert Scott, the leader of the British expedition, was a sharp contrast to Amundsen. Because he left the planning of important details of the expedition to the last minute, major mistakes were made in decisions about animals and equipment. For example, Scott decided to rely on ponies for hauling supplies, but this decision ignored the obvious fact that ponies were inferior to huskies for hauling supplies in bitter cold weather. Scott did take skis along, but few people in his party knew how to use them properly. They therefore wasted precious energy and covered fewer kilometres each day than they might have.

Scott's planning of supply depots was also haphazard, and insufficient care was taken in the storage of fuel. In the extreme cold of the Antarctic, much of the fuel that Scott had stored in supply depots evaporated. On his return trip, therefore, he consistently ran short of fuel. (Amundsen had no such problems because he had designed an airtight seal for his fuel containers.)

Scott's leadership ability was also questionable. There was dissension in the ranks because of poor communication, conflicting orders, and interpersonal disagreements. Scott did not inspire confidence in his men, and he did not allow them to participate in important decisions.

Who won the race? Although both men managed to reach the Pole, Amundsen beat Scott to the prize by a full month. In the end, Scott's men paid dearly for their leader's shortcomings: they all died of starvation and exposure as they attempted to get back to their base camp on the coast.

Questions

1. Leadership is defined in the chapter as "influencing others to work willingly to achieve the firm's objectives." To what extent were Amundsen and Scott leaders, and how good were they as leaders? Explain.

2. Compare the leadership ability of Scott and Amundsen in terms of the six traits that are thought to distinguish leaders from non-leaders.

3. Compare Scott and Amundsen in terms of the various sources of power described in Table 11.2. What does this imply about their likely leadership success?

4. Use any one of the contingency leadership theories discussed in the chapter to analyze the appropriateness of the leadership styles used by Scott and Amundsen. Were they using the right style? Explain.

Leadership at JetBlue

It is probably not necessary to ask whether David Neeleman is an effective leader. You don't start and manage three very successful airline businesses before you're 40 if you don't have leadership skills. Particularly during the start-up period, it's the leader, by force of his or her personality and vision, who keeps the firm's employees focused. Neeleman has done this not once, but three times. As one person who knows him says, "he's low-key, and he's totally directed." One business writer, watching him make a presentation, said: "The man can be completely, utterly riveting."

However, Neeleman does not just have a "just decide and give orders" directive style. For example, at an employee orientation for new baggage handlers, he carefully explained JetBlue's philosophy, including how JetBlue can make money when the big airlines don't. He shared details about the company's plans, and answered personal questions. He spends most of his time when he flies JetBlue talking to customers and crew. He talks to flight attendants and passengers to find out their concerns and comments, and he spends time walking through the cabin helping to serve snacks. He spends time in the cockpit with the pilots, and when he is at the airport he works with the baggage handlers throwing bags.

An incident after 9/11 provides insight into Neeleman's leadership approach. He had to decide what his first response should be with respect to communicating with the flying public. Neeleman's first reaction was to draft a personal letter from him and run it as a full-page ad. However, his team thought the message was a bit too personal. Other airlines were placing ads that basically tried to convince the flying public that it was patriotic to fly and important to show that "we're not afraid to fly." Neeleman's feeling was that his personal letter was the way to go and that this was the perfect time to publicize JetBlue's low price fares. But as driven as he is as an entrepreneur, Neeleman went with his team's advice. As he says, "I'm being patient because I think the situation demands it. I have to trust the instincts of the people around me."[99]

Assignment

You and your team are consultants to Mr. Neeleman, who is depending on your management expertise to help navigate the launch and management of JetBlue. Here's what he wants to know from you:

1. Do you think I have the traits and skills to be a leader? Specifically, why or why not?

2. What leadership style did I use with respect to the decision to make our first response after 9/11? Do you think I used the right style? Use one or more of the leadership theories in this chapter to explain why you think I did or did not use the right style.

3. What do some of the other incidents in the case tell you about the other leadership styles I typically use? What you think my prevailing style is? Why?

Influencing Individual Behaviour and Motivation

Motivation at Maple Leaf Sports & Entertainment

One of the most interesting organizations in Canada is Maple Leaf Sports & Entertainment Ltd., the company that owns two professional sports franchises—the Toronto Raptors basketball team and the Toronto Maple Leafs hockey team. At Maple Leaf Sports, great emphasis is placed on motivating employees.

One way this is done is through (appropriately enough) a "training camp" that is required attendance for all 1500 employees. This includes everybody from hot-dog vendors through Zamboni drivers to accountants. At the training camp, employees take part in various sessions, including one on "positive psychology" that is conducted by the Toronto Maple Leafs' player development coach, Paul Dennis. Other sessions cover stress management, conflict management, and work-life balance. The training camp is designed to keep employees motivated and in top form.

The sports analogy is evident everywhere. The company receives more than 12 000 résumés every year from people who hope to work at the company. Most of the people who are hired are at entry-level positions. The company focuses a lot of attention on student internship programs to get new talent. Mardi Walker, vice president of the people department, says, "We hire for attitude and train for skill. Our vision is all about creating champions."

Walker says it is important to keep employees "enthusiastic and energized." The company achieves this by rewarding its employees in many different ways, including the following:

- During a garbage workers' strike in Toronto, the employees were told by the company that they could bring their garbage to work for private disposal.

- During the slower summer season, employees can take Friday afternoon off.

- When either the Leafs or Raptors make the first round of the playoffs, each employee receives a free T-shirt; if either team makes it to the second round, every employee gets to go to a road play-off game on a jet the company charters.

■ The company promotes exceptional performance by giving awards for "player of the month" and "coach of the year."

Sefu Bernard is one of the employees at Maple Leaf Sports who is pumped up about working at the company. During the 2001–2002 hockey season, he went on two road trips with the Maple Leafs. He says the experience was a "great team-building exercise," and it helped him get to know many other people in the organization. Bernard has one other perk in his job: His office is close to the food and beverage department, so he gets to "taste-test" the products.

The Importance of Motivation

Planning and organizing are useless if your employees won't do their jobs, or won't do them well. Managers thus need motivational skills. Motivation is the intensity of a person's desire to engage in some activity. Extrinsic motivation exists when a person works hard at a task because of the promise that some tangible reward will be given if the job is done well. Intrinsic motivation, on the other hand, exists if the person performs a task in the absence of any tangible reward. A salesperson who works hard to earn a large monetary bonus is likely to be extrinsically motivated, while a person working on a volunteer basis for the United Way is likely to be intrinsically motivated.

The "Challenge of Change" box illustrates the importance of motivation to organizations.

How Do You Motivate People?

This is not a simple question, but if you think about it, you already have some insights into the area of motivation. Consider the following points.

1. *You know what motivates you.* What are the things you are driven to do, just because you want to do them? For example, are you one of thousands of people who are sitting in the stands watching a CFL football game on a cold October day? If so, chances are you're there because you want to be there—you're motivated to be there. Things like hobbies, sporting events, and the job you love are things you gladly do for hours each day, even if you are not being paid to do them.

2. *You know why you are motivated.* Most people don't sit around asking themselves why they're doing the things they love, they just do them. But if you did ask why you do the things you love, you'd probably say it's because of the feedback you get from doing them. It may be the built-in feedback you get from doing the task, or the feedback you get from your peers. In any case, these activities motivate you because doing them makes you feel good. The feedback you get from doing them helps to satisfy your needs.

3. *You know that different things motivate different people.* Different people have different needs, and so it takes different things to satisfy different people. John might happily work nights for an extra $2000, while Karen thinks nothing of forgoing twice that amount to pursue her favourite hobby.

4. *You know how to motivate people.* Here are some of the things about motivation that you already know.

motivation
The intensity of a person's desire to engage in some activity.

extrinsic motivation
When a person works hard at a task because of the promise that some tangible reward will be given if the job is done well.

intrinsic motivation
When a person performs a task in the absence of any tangible reward.

Herman Miller—Can a Company's Values Motivate Employees?

Herman Miller
www.hermanmiller.com

Herman Miller is a multinational company that produces office, health care, and residential furniture, as well as furniture management services. The source of its vitality has always been its belief systems and its employees. The company is a "community of people who firmly believe that doing the right thing and succeeding as a business must be pursued with equal enthusiasm." Top management believes that the company will be successful only if it defines how it is different from other companies, not just in products but also in the way the company gives meaning to its work.

The company focuses on three key values: good design, participative management, and environmental responsibility. Can a company outperform its competitors because of these values?

The company's executives believe that the answer is "Yes," because having a meaningful place to work will unleash creativity and commitment. The company should then be able to deliver better products and services and build longer and stronger relationships with its customers.

To create a more meaningful place to work, the firm tries to create a sense of community. It has a very high level of employee stock ownership. The company began its employee stock ownership plan in 1983, and today all Herman Miller employees with more than one year of service own stock in the company. The company thinks that owners make better employees because employees and shareholders then have the same interests and goals.

The firm also concentrates on fostering a participative environment. The Herman Miller philosophy has been well articulated in two best-selling books, *Leadership Is an Art* and *Leadership Jazz*, by former Herman Miller CEO and son of its founder, Max DePree. To reinforce its values, the company uses an economic value added (EVA) accounting system. EVA links operating and financial performance to incentive compensation for every employee.

Perhaps the most innovative value held by Herman Miller is its concept of environmental stewardship. The company sees itself as needing to act with great responsibility in regard to the natural environment. High-level teams work to set environmentally responsible strategies for the present and future operations of the company, while continuous improvement teams attempt to meet and exceed the challenges of being environmentally responsible. Herman Miller executives believe this value has helped the company recruit talented, environmentally responsible employees.

- People like getting rewards, but they don't like being punished.
- People like the feedback that comes from doing something well.
- People feel good when they are doing something they like.
- People generally won't even bother trying to do things that they know (or believe) they can't do.
- You have to appeal to a person's needs if you want to motivate that person.
- Needs differ across people.

In summary, you already know some important things about motivation. The rest of this chapter will help you build on what you already know; it will also provide much more information about motivation and its importance to managers. As you read this chapter, don't miss the forest for the trees. Use this chapter to deepen your understanding of what you already know. Think in terms of applying your knowledge and motivating others.

What Managers Should Know About Individual Behaviour

A given stimulus—an order from the boss, an offer of a raise, or the threat of getting fired—doesn't have the same effect on everyone. Jane might emerge from training with excellent skills, while John might learn nothing. One employee jumps whenever the boss gives orders, while another seems uninterested. These different responses to the same stimulus occur as a result of the **law of individual differences**, that is, people differ in personalities, abilities, values, perceptions, self-concept, and needs. As illustrated in Figure 12.1, these factors act much like filters; they add to, detract from, and often distort the effect of any stimulus.

law of individual differences
People differ in personalities, abilities, values, perceptions, self-concept, and needs.

Personality and Behaviour

Personality is probably the first thing that most people think about when they are trying to figure out what determines behaviour. We tend to classify people as introverted, dominant, mature, or paranoid, for instance, and these labels invoke images of particular kinds of behaviour.

Personality Defined **Personality** refers to the characteristic and distinctive traits of an individual and the way these traits interact to help or hinder the adjustment of the person to other people and situations. Raymond Cattell used observations and questionnaires to identify 16 primary personality traits, which he then expressed in pairs of words, such as reserved/outgoing, submissive/dominant, and trusting/suspicious.[1] Based on this work, Cattell and his colleagues developed a questionnaire that produced a personality profile for individuals. Figure 12.2 shows the average personality profiles for people in two sample occupational groups: airline pilots and business executives.

personality
The characteristic and distinctive traits of an individual and the way these traits interact to help or hinder the adjustment of the person to other people and situations.

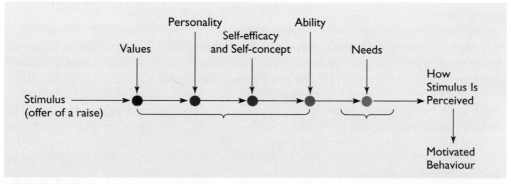

FIGURE 12.1
Some Individual Determinants of Behaviour
A particular stimulus may evoke different behaviours among individuals, because each person's perceptions, personality, abilities, and needs will influence how he or she reacts to the stimulus.

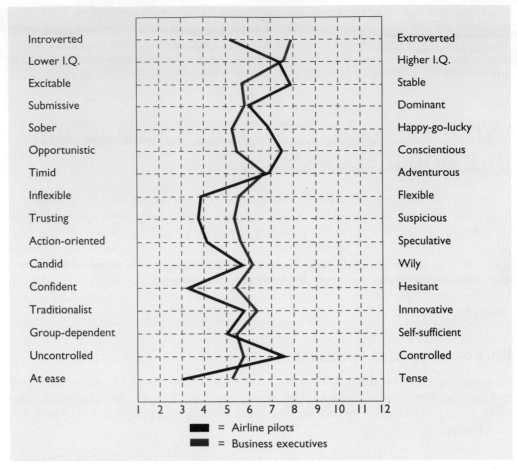

FIGURE 12.2
Cattell's Sixteen Personality Factors
The personalities of various people and even various groups of people are characterized by particular packages of traits such as introverted, dominant, excitable, and innovative.

At work, you will encounter many unique personalities. For example, the authoritarian personality is rigid, intolerant of ambiguity, tends to stereotype people as good or bad, and conforms to the requirements of authority, perhaps while being dictatorial to subordinates. The Machiavellian personality (the name refers to the writings of the sixteenth-century political adviser Niccolò Machiavelli) tends to be oriented toward manipulation and control, with a low sensitivity to the needs of others.[2]

Industrial psychologists often emphasize the "big five" personality dimensions as they apply to behaviour at work: extroversion, emotional stability, agreeableness, conscientiousness, and openness to experience.[3] The particular mix of these traits influences such things as the person's "emotional intelligence" (as we discussed in Chapter 11). If you have the right mix, you may be emotionally intelligent. And they influence behaviour in other ways. For example, in one study of police officers, professionals, managers, sales workers, and unskilled and semiskilled workers, conscientiousness showed a consistent relationship with all job performance criteria for all occupations. Extroversion was tied to performance for managers and sales employees, which of course are two occupations involving a lot of social interaction.[4]

Measuring Personality The Myers-Briggs Type Indicator (MBTI) is one popular tool for measuring personality, particularly in the work setting. The MBTI classifies people as extroverted or introverted (E or I), sensing or intuitive (S or N), thinking or feeling (T or F), and perceiving or judging (P or J). The person's answers to a questionnaire are classified

Myers-Briggs Type Indicator
www.keirsey.com/keirsey.html

into 16 different personality types; these 16 types are in turn classified into one of four cognitive (thinking or problem-solving) styles:

Sensation-Thinking (ST)   Sensation-Feeling (SF

Intuition-Thinking (NT)   Intuition-Feeling (NF)

Classifying personality types and cognitive styles in this way has several applications. Some employers match the MBTI styles to particular occupations. This is illustrated in Figure 12.3. For example, people with the ST approach to problem solving are often well suited to occupations like auditor and safety engineer.

Abilities and Behaviour

Individual differences in abilities also influence how we behave and perform.[5] Even the most highly motivated people will not perform well unless they also have the ability to do the job. Conversely, people with high ability will not perform well if they are not motivated. These important ideas are captured in the following formula:

$$\text{Performance} = \text{Ability} \times \text{Motivation.}$$

There are several types of abilities. *Mental*, cognitive, or "thinking" abilities include intelligence and its building blocks, such as memory, inductive reasoning, and verbal comprehension. *Mechanical* ability, for example, is important for mechanical engineers or machinists. *Psychomotor* abilities include dexterity, manipulative ability, eye-hand coordination, and motor ability. Such abilities are important for employees who put together delicate computer components or who work as dealers in Las Vegas. People also differ in their *visual skills*—for example, in their ability to discriminate between colours and between black and white detail.

In addition to these general abilities, people also have *specific abilities* learned through training, experience, or education. Companies test for these abilities when they are interested in determining a candidate's proficiency on a job such as computer programmer, word processor, or chemical engineer.

Self-Concept and Behaviour

Psychologists like Carl Rogers emphasize the role of **self-concept** in personality. Who we are and how we behave is largely driven, say humanist psychologists, by perceptions we have of who we are and how we relate to other people and things. Psychologist Saul

self-concept
Perceptions of who we are and how we relate to other people and things.

	Thinking Style	Feeling Style
Sensation Style	People with this combined thinking/sensation style tend to be *thorough*, *logical*, and *practical* and to make good *CAs* or *safety engineers*.	People with this combined sensation/feeling style tend to be *conscientious* and *responsible* and to make *good social workers* and *drug supervisors*.
Intuitive Style	People with this combined intuitive/thinking style tend to be *creative*, *independent*, and *critical* and to make good *systems analysts, professors,* and *lawyers*.	People with this combined intuitive/feeling style tend to be *people-oriented, sociable*, and often *charismatic* and to make good *human resource managers, public relations directors,* and *politicians*.

FIGURE 12.3
Four Examples of MBTI Styles and Some Corresponding Occupations

Gellerman says that we are all driven in a constant quest to be ourselves, or the kinds of people we think we should be.[6]

Some people have rigid self-concepts and can't modify how they view themselves.[7] For example, a person who is turned down for a raise may attribute it to office politics or the boss's incompetence, even though the real reason is that the person simply wasn't doing the job properly. To some degree, we all try to protect our self-concept. However, "people with healthy self-concepts can allow new experiences into their lives and can accept or reject them."[8]

One part of this self-concept is **self-efficacy**—a person's belief about his or her capacity to perform a task.[9] Self-efficacy affects how people perform a job and even whether they even try to do well. Research shows that self-efficacy is positively associated with work performance in a wide range of settings: life insurance sales, faculty research productivity, career choice, learning and achievement, and adaptability to new technology, to name just a few.[10]

Perception and Behaviour

We all react to stimuli that reach us via our sense organs. How we define or perceive these stimuli reflects our experiences, our needs, and our personalities.[11] In other words, our behaviour is not just motivated by raw stimuli; it is influenced by the way our personalities and experiences cause us to interpret the stimuli.

Perception affects how we "see" inanimate objects. When we look down a row of arches, as in Figure 12.4, the farthest one looks smaller than the closest one, and its perspective size is in fact smaller (because it is farthest away). Based on experience, however, we know that the arches are actually equal in size. Therefore, what we perceive is a compromise between the perspective size of the arch and its actual size. In the photo, the nearest arch seems about three times the size of the farthest arch. But if you measure the arches, you will see that it is actually more than four times the size of the farthest arch. Our desire to see objects as we expect them to be causes us to perceive things as we expect them to be.

The same phenomenon applies to relationships at work. Some people associate characteristics like industriousness and honesty with certain socio-economic classes, but not with others, a process called **stereotyping**. We tend to stereotype people according to age, gender, race, or national origin. We then attribute the characteristics of this stereotype to everyone we meet who is of that age, gender, race, or national origin.[12]

Perceptions depend on many things, including the following:

- *Personality and needs*. For example, an insecure employee might think an upcoming meeting with the boss will be the one where he gets fired, but the meeting actually concerns vacation schedules.

self-efficacy
A person's belief about his or her capacity to perform a task.

perception
The unique way that each person sees and interprets things.

stereotyping
Associating certain characteristics with certain socio-economic classes but not with others.

FIGURE 12.4
Perception Affects How We "See" the Arches' Sizes
The farthest arch looks to be about one-third the size of the closest, but we know they're actually the same size.

- *Self-efficacy and abilities*. People who have strong beliefs about their abilities perceive even negative occurrences as opportunities. The coach who spends half-time exhorting a losing team that "you can do anything" is acting based on this perception.

- *Values*. Someone with a strong code of ethics might be horrified at the suggestion of taking a bribe, while another person might not attach too much significance to it.

- *Stress*. People who are under stress tend to perceive things less objectively than those who are not. In one experiment, employment interviewers who were under pressure to hire someone perceived candidates' qualifications as being much higher than did interviewers who were not under pressure to hire anyone.

- *Experience*. We learn to associate certain results with certain actions (e.g., "If I call a meeting Friday at 5 p.m., no one shows up"). If your boss calls a meeting at 5 p.m., you might then perceive such a meeting as misguided.

- *Position*. A manager's primary focus influences their perceptions of problems. For example, production managers tend to see problems as production problems, and sales managers tend to see them as sales problems.

Attitudes and Behaviour

When people say things like "I like my job" or "I don't care about my job," they are expressing attitudes. An **attitude** is a predisposition to respond to objects, people, or events in either a positive or negative way.[13] Attitudes are important because they often influence the way people behave on the job.

Job satisfaction—an evaluative judgment about one's job—is probably the most familiar example of attitudes at work.[14] One popular job satisfaction survey, the Job Descriptive Index, measures the following five aspects of job satisfaction.

1. *Pay*. How much pay is received and is it perceived as equitable?

2. *Job.* Are tasks interesting? Are opportunities provided for learning and for accepting responsibility?

3. *Promotional opportunities*. Are promotions and opportunities to advance available and fair?

4. *Supervisor*. Does the supervisor demonstrate interest in and concern about employees?

5. *Co-workers.* Are co-workers friendly, competent, and supportive?[15]

Good (or bad) attitudes can, but do not necessarily, translate into good (or bad) performance.[16] For example, dissatisfied engineers may continue to do their best, because their performance may be governed by their professional standards.

Keep this knowledge about individual differences in mind as we now examine three main approaches to studying motivation: need-based, process-based, and learning or reinforcement-based approaches. Understanding these basic approaches is an important first step in being able to understand how to actually motivate others.

Need-Based Approaches to Motivation

Motives play a central role in both our personal and professional lives. A **motive** is something that incites the person to action or that sustains and gives direction to action.[17] When we ask why a defendant in a court case did what he did, or why a football player works to stay in shape all year, or why a sales manager maintains a gruelling travel schedule to meet with a customer, we are asking about motives.

attitude
A predisposition to respond to objects, people, or events in either a positive or negative way.

job satisfaction
An evaluative judgment about one's job.

motive
Something that incites the person to action or that sustains and gives direction to action.

needs
Motives that remain
unaroused until the proper
conditions bring them
forth.

A motive can be aroused or dormant. Everyone carries within them motivational dispositions or **needs**—motives that, like seeds in winter, remain dormant until the proper conditions bring them forth. You may have a motivational disposition to enjoy yourself at the movies, but that motive is dormant until Saturday night, when you can put your studies aside. Aroused motives are motives that express themselves in behaviour.[18] When the conditions are right—when studies are over, the quiz is done, and the weekend arrives—the movie-attendance motive is aroused, and you may be off to your favourite flick.

Need-based approaches to motivating focus on how needs (or motivational dispositions) drive people to do what they do. Which needs or motivational dispositions are most important? How and under what conditions do they become aroused and transformed into behaviour? These are the sorts of questions studied by psychologists like Abraham Maslow, Clay Alderfer, Frederick Herzberg, David McClelland, and John Atkinson.

Maslow's Needs-Hierarchy Theory

Abraham Maslow argued that people have a hierarchy of five increasingly higher-level needs: physiological, security, social, self-esteem, and self-actualization. People are motivated first to satisfy the lower-order needs and then, in sequence, each of the higher-order needs.[19] Most people envision Maslow's hierarchy as a stepladder, as in Figure 12.5. The lower-level needs, once largely satisfied, trigger the emergence of higher-order needs.[20] In other words, the higher-level needs won't be important in motivating behaviour unless the lower-level needs are pretty well satisfied. The five needs are as follows.

- *Physiological needs.* These are the most basic needs, including the needs for food, water, and shelter.
- *Security needs.* When the physiological needs are largely satisfied, the security, or safety, needs become aroused. If you are in the middle of a desert with nothing to drink, the lower-level need for water will drive your behaviour. You might even risk your life and safety by pursuing that need. But once you have enough to drink, personal safety and security start to motivate your behaviour.
- *Social needs.* These are the needs to give and receive affection, and to have friends. Once your physiological and security needs are largely satisfied, social needs begin to emerge and drive your behaviour.
- *Self-esteem needs.* These include the need for self-confidence, independence, achievement, competence, knowledge, status, recognition, appreciation, and the respect of others.[21]
- *Self-actualization needs.* This refers to the need we all have to become the person we feel we have the potential for becoming. These needs begin to dominate behaviour once all lower-level needs have been satisfied.

In general, lower-level needs (physiological, security, and to some extent social needs) can be quickly satisfied by extrinsic factors like good pay and supervision. Higher-level needs, which are more difficult to satisfy, are more influenced by factors that are intrinsic to the job (like challenging work and responsibility).

There is (unfortunately) not much research supporting the idea that needs fall into a neat hierarchy. What Maslow wanted to do was emphasize that people have different needs and that, quite possibly, as they go grow older, new, "higher-level," needs become more important as people satisfy their lower-level needs.[22] The stepladder idea may make the whole process seem more inflexible than Maslow meant it to be. Later in his career, Maslow actually suggested it might be useful to think of needs as comprising just a two-step hierarchy.[23]

existence needs
Human needs similar to
Maslow's physiological
needs and to the physical
components of Maslow's
security needs.

Existence-Relatedness-Growth (ERG) Theory

Clay Alderfer developed a theory of human needs that refines Maslow's ideas. Alderfer focuses on three needs—existence, relatedness, and growth. **Existence needs** are similar to Maslow's physiological needs and to the physical components of Maslow's security needs.

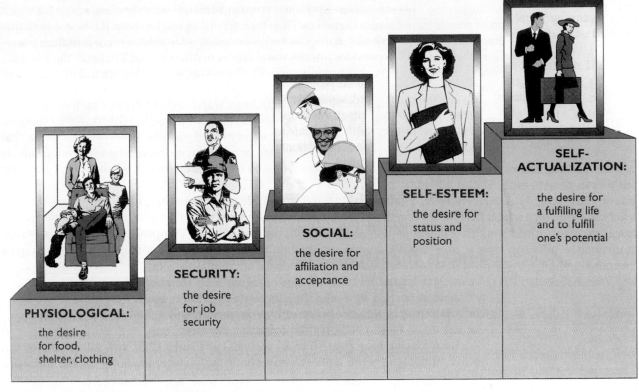

FIGURE 12.5
Maslow's Hierarchy of Needs

(such as concern for losing your job). **Relatedness needs** are those that require interpersonal interaction to satisfy what Maslow would call the needs for things like prestige and esteem from others. **Growth needs** are similar to Maslow's needs for self-esteem and self-actualization. Alderfer says that existence, relatedness, and growth needs are all active simultaneously.[24]

Herzberg's Hygiene–Motivator ("Two-Factor") Theory

After reviewing various studies on job satisfaction, Frederick Herzberg concluded that there was a relationship between job satisfaction and certain types of work conditions (such as challenging work and more responsibility), and also a relationship between job dissatisfaction and another set of work conditions (like inadequate pay). Herzberg's hygiene–motivator theory divides Maslow's hierarchy into lower-level (physiological, safety, social) and higher-level (ego, self-actualization) needs. Herzberg says that the best way to motivate someone is to arrange their job so that it helps them satisfy their higher-level needs (the needs that are insatiable). Herzberg called the two factors at the heart of his theory *hygienes* and *motivators*.

Herzberg says the factors that satisfy lower level needs (hygienes) are different from those that satisfy, or partially satisfy, higher-level needs (motivators). If hygiene factors (factors outside the job itself, such as pay, working conditions, and supervision) are inadequate, employees become dissatisfied. But adding more of these hygiene factors to the job is not an effective way to motivate someone, because lower-level needs are quickly satisfied. Soon the person says, in effect, "What have you done for me lately? I want another raise."

Job content, or motivator, factors are different. First, factors like opportunities for achievement, recognition, responsibility, and more challenge are intrinsic to the work itself. With factors like these, it's the sense of enjoyment and accomplishing the work that provides the motivation, not some extrinsic element like pay or supervision. Furthermore,

relatedness needs
Those needs that require interpersonal interaction to satisfy, such as prestige and esteem from others.

growth needs
Similar to Maslow's needs for self-esteem.

the motivation people get from factors like these goes on and on. This is because it appeals to the person's higher-level needs for achievement and self-actualization, needs for which most people have an infinite craving. Therefore, according to Herzberg, the best way to motivate employees is to build challenges and opportunities for achievement into their jobs—to make sure the job provides intrinsic motivation, in other words. That way the job itself turns the employee on, much as the thought of working on a favourite hobby may motivate you.

Figure 12.6 summarizes Herzberg's findings. Herzberg's motivator factors ranged in importance from getting a sense of achievement from doing the job, down to recognition, the work itself, responsibility, advancement, and growth. The hygiene factors that caused dissatisfaction (when poorly designed or administered) ranged down from company policy and administration, to supervision and relationship with supervisor, salary, and relationship with peers.

Herzberg popularized two important ideas: that intrinsic motivation—motivation that comes from within the person—is very important for keeping employees motivated, and that the nature of the job is important. Much of today's emphasis on enriching jobs (discussed later in this chapter) and on organizing work around empowered, self-managing teams flows from this thinking.

Needs for Achievement, Power, and Affiliation

David McClelland and John Atkinson agree with Herzberg that managers should appeal to employees' higher-level needs. They focus on three needs they believe are especially important—the needs for affiliation, power, and achievement. To understand the nature of these needs, take a quick look (10 to 15 seconds) at Figure 12.7. Then take 5 minutes to write

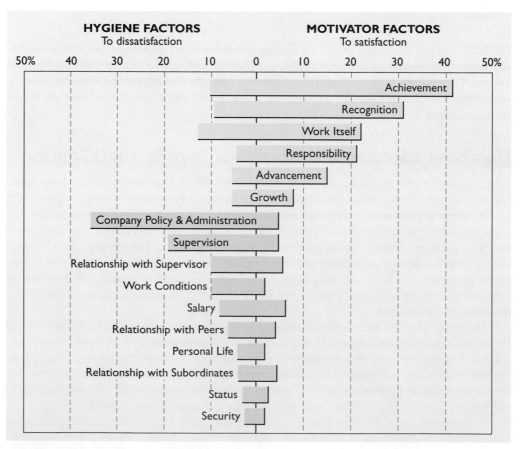

FIGURE 12.6
Summary of Herzberg's Hygiene–Motivator Findings

FIGURE 12.7
What's Happening Here?
Who are the people? What has led up to this situation? What is being thought? What is
wanted? By whom? What will happen?

a short essay about the picture, using the questions below as a guide. (The questions are
only guides, so don't just answer each one. Instead, make your story continuous and let your
imagination roam. Once you have finished writing, resume reading the text.)

1. What is happening? Who are the people?

2. What has led up to this situation? That is, what happened in the past?

3. What is being thought? What is wanted? By whom?

4. What will happen? What will be done?

The picture is from a test called the Thematic Apperception Test. McClelland and
his associates use the TAT to identify a person's needs. The picture is intentionally ambiguous, so when you wrote your essay, you were probably reading into the picture ideas
that reflected your own needs and drives. McClelland says the test is useful for identifying the level of a person's achievement, power, and affiliation needs.[25] This exercise represents only one of several pictures that constitute the Thematic Apperception Test, so it
provides only the most tentative impressions about your needs.

The Need for Achievement Achievement motivation is present in your essay when any
one of the following three things occurs.

1. Someone in your story is concerned about a standard of excellence; for example,
   he wants to win or do well in a competition, or has a self-imposed standard for

good performance. You can infer standards of excellence from the use of words such as good or better to evaluate performance.

2. Someone in the story is involved in a unique accomplishment, such as an invention or an artistic creation.

3. Someone in the story is focused on a long-term goal, such as having a specific career or being a success in life.

People high in the need to achieve have a predisposition to strive for success. They are highly motivated to obtain the satisfaction that comes from accomplishing a challenging task or goal. They prefer tasks for which there is a reasonable chance for success. They avoid those that are too easy or too difficult. They prefer specific, timely feedback about their performance.

The Need for Power Power motivation is present in your essay when any of the following three things occurs.

1. Someone in the story is emotionally concerned about getting or maintaining control or influencing another person. Wanting to win a point, to show dominance, to convince someone, or to gain a position of control, as well as wanting to avoid weakness or humiliation are examples.[26]

2. Someone is actually doing something to get or keep control of the means of influence, such as arguing, demanding or forcing, giving a command, trying to convince, or punishing.

3. The story involves an interpersonal relationship that is culturally defined as one in which a superior has control of the means of influencing a subordinate. For example, a boss is giving orders to a subordinate, or a parent is ordering a child to shape up.

People with a strong need for power want to influence others directly by making suggestions, giving their opinions and evaluations, and trying to talk others into things. They enjoy roles requiring persuasion, such as teaching and public speaking, as well as positions as leaders and members of the clergy. McClelland believed that "a good manager is motivated by a regimented and regulated concern for influencing others," in other words, good managers have a need for power, but one that is under control.[27]

The Need for Affiliation. Affiliation motivation is present in your essay when one of the following three things occurs.

1. Someone in the story is concerned about establishing, maintaining, or restoring a positive emotional relationship with another person. Friendship is the most basic example, such as when your story emphasizes that the individuals are friends. Other relationships, such as father-son, reflect affiliation motivation only if they have the warm, compassionate quality implied by the need for affiliation.

2. One person likes or wants to be liked by someone else. Affiliation motivation is also present if someone is expressing sorrow or grief about a broken relationship.

3. Affiliation activities are taking place, such as parties, reunions, visits, or relaxed small talk. Friendly actions such as consoling or being concerned about the well-being or happiness of another person usually reflect a need for affiliation.

People with a strong need for affiliation are highly motivated to maintain strong, warm relationships with friends and relatives. In group meetings they try to establish friendly relationships, often by being agreeable or giving emotional support.[28]

Employee Needs in Practice

Our needs also drive our career choices, often in ways we don't even notice. For example, psychologist Edgar Schein found that peoples' needs (what he called "career anchors") drove their occupational choices. Some people had a strong technical/functional career anchor. They made decisions that enabled them to remain in their chosen technical or functional fields. Some had managerial competence as a career anchor. They showed a strong motivation to become managers. Some needed to express their creativity. Many of these went on to be successful entrepreneurs. For some, autonomy and independence drove their career decisions. These people seemed driven by the need to be on their own, free of the dependence that arises when a person elects to work in a large organization. Finally, some were mostly concerned with long-run career stability and job security; they did what was required to maintain job security, a decent income, and a stable future, including a good retirement program and benefits.[29]

Process Approaches to Motivation

Process approaches explain motivation not in terms of specific needs, but in terms of the decision-making process individuals use to decide how hard they are going to work. We'll focus on three process approaches here: equity theory, goal theory, and expectancy theory.

Equity Theory

Equity theory assumes that people have a need for fairness at work and that they are motivated to maintain a balance between what they perceive as their inputs or contributions and their rewards.[30] Equity theory states that if a person perceives an inequity, a tension or drive will develop in the person's mind, and the person will be motivated to reduce or eliminate the tension and perceived inequity. For example, the directors of MacMillan-Bloedel were embarrassed to read in the newspaper that their CEO was receiving substantially less compensation than other CEOs in the industry, so they raised his salary by 60 percent.[31]

Research regarding underpayment is consistent with equity theory. People paid on a piece-rate basis typically boost quantity and reduce quality when they believe they are not earning enough. Those paid an hourly rate tend to reduce both quantity and quality when they think they're underpaid. Overpayment inequity does not seem to have the positive effects on either quantity or quality that equity theory predicts.[32] These results are summarized in Figure 12.8.

> **equity theory**
> The theory that people have a need for fairness at work and that they are motivated to maintain a balance between what they perceive as their inputs or contributions and their rewards.

> **goal theory**
> The theory that people regulate their behaviour in such a way as to achieve their goals.

The Goal Theory of Motivation

Goal theory assumes that people regulate their behaviour in such a way as to achieve their goals.[33] Edwin Locke and his colleagues contend that goals provide the mechanism through which unsatisfied needs are translated into action.[34] In other words, unsatisfied needs prompt the person to seek ways to satisfy those needs; the person then formulates goals that prompt action.[35] For example, Laura needs to self-actualize and wants to be an artist. To do so, she must go to university for a fine arts degree, so she sets the goal of graduating from McGill University's fine arts program. That goal (which is prompted by her need) then motivates her behaviour.

The goal-setting literature is voluminous and has "generally been far more rigorous and free of methodological error than that conducted on any of the other theories and ap-

© 1996 Randy Glasbergen

ACCIDENTALLY LISTENED TO MY MOTIVATION TAPES BACKWARDS AND BECAME A FAILURE. PLEASE HELP

	Employee thinks he or she is underpaid	Employee thinks he or she is overpaid
Piece-rate Basis	Quality down Quantity the same or up	Quantity the same or down Quality up
Salary Basis	Quantity or quality should go down	Quantity or quality should go up

FIGURE 12.8
How a Perceived Inequity Affects Performance
According to equity theory, how a person reacts to under-or overpayment depends on whether he or she is paid on a piece-rate or salary basis.

Campbell Soup
www.campbellsoup.com

proaches…"[36] For example, at Campbell Soup's Toronto plant, 120 000 cases of defective soup were sitting in the warehouse at one point in time. Employees set a goal to cut that number in half within three months. The inventory was reduced to only 20 000 cases by the target date. Another goal was to reduce costs to the level of the most efficient Campbell's plant in the United States. At that time, it cost $3.87 more to produce a case of soup in Ontario than it did in Campbell's North Carolina plant. Within one year, the difference had dropped to only 32 cents.[37]

Overall, the research suggests that setting goals is a simple, effective way to motivate employees. Goal-setting-theory research shows that specific, challenging goals lead to higher task performance than specific, unchallenging goals, vague goals, or no goals. This is especially true when there is feedback showing progress in relation to the goals, when individuals possess adequate ability to do the task, and when individuals are committed to the goal.[38] The most straightforward way to motivate employees is to make sure they adopt a specific, challenging goal.

Expectancy Theory

Like equity theory and goal setting theory, expectancy theory views people as "conscious agents." It assumes people are continually sizing up situations in terms of their perceived needs, and then acting in accordance with these perceptions. They will not pursue rewards they find unattractive, or tasks on which the odds of success are very low. **Expectancy theory** says that a person's motivation to exert some level of effort is a function of three things:[39] (1) the person's expectancy (the perceived probability that effort will lead to performance); (2) **instrumentality** (the perceived relationship between successful performance and obtaining a reward); and (3) **valence** (the perceived value the person attaches to the reward).[40]

expectancy theory
A theory that a person's motivation to exert some level of effort is a function of the person's expectancy, instrumentality, and valence.

In expectancy theory, motivation is result of these three interacting factors, expressed as follows:

$$\text{Motivation} = E \times I \times V$$

where E represents expectancy, I instrumentality, and V valence.

Consider, for example, what might happen in a course that you are not interested in but are forced to take as part of your curriculum. There may not be many desired outcomes for you in such a course (valence is low or negative). In addition, assume that you have heard that former students could not see any relationship between the amount of time they spent studying for exams in the course and the grade they got on exams (expectancy is low). This leads them to conclude that there is no connection between performance and rewards (low instrumentality). In this situation, it is very likely that you will not be motivated to work hard in the course.

Expectancy theory was developed to try to better understand and explain vocational choice—why people choose the jobs they do.[41] However, studies of the expectancy approach also provide moderate to strong support for its usefulness in explaining and predicting other types of work motivation.[42] Expectancy theory has some clear implications for how managers motivate employees. First, without an **expectancy** that effort will lead to performance, no motivation will exist. Managers therefore must ensure that their employees have the skills to do the job and know they can do the job. In other words, not all motivation problems are "won't do" problems. Some are "can't do" problems. Training, job descriptions, confidence building, and support are important.

Second, employees must see that successful performance will in fact lead to getting the reward (**instrumentality**). Managers can ensure this by creating easy-to-understand incentive plans and by communicating success stories. Third, managers should think through how to boost the perceived value (**valence**) their subordinates attach to the rewards that are available. Two extra days off may be more important to one person, while another prefers two days' extra pay.

expectancy
In motivation, the probability that a person's efforts will lead to performance.

instrumentality
The perceived correlation between successful performance and obtaining the reward.

valence
In motivation, the perceived value a person ascribes to the reward for certain efforts.

Learning/Reinforcement Approaches to Motivation

Learning refers to the relatively permanent change in a person that occurs as a result of experience.[43] For example, we learn as children that being courteous is rewarded by our parents, and we thus may be motivated to be courteous throughout our lives. Motivation like this tends to be instinctual, and few people consciously think about having been "programmed" to be courteous when they behave in a courteous way.

There are several theories about how people learn, but in this section we'll focus on what may be called learning/reinforcement approaches to motivating employees. These deal with how consequences mould behaviour.

learning
The relatively permanent change in a person that occurs as a result of experience.

B. F. Skinner and Operant Behaviour

B. F. Skinner's findings provide the foundation for much of what we know about learning. Consider an example. Suppose you wanted to train your dog to roll over. How would you do it? You'd probably encourage the dog to roll over (perhaps by gently nudging it down and rolling it over) and then reward it with some treat. Your dog would soon come to associate rolling over with the treat. It would learn that if it wanted a treat, it would have to roll over.

In Skinner's theory, the dog's rolling over is called **operant behaviour**, because it operates on its environment, specifically by causing its owner to give it a treat. The process (training the dog to roll over in return for a treat) is operant conditioning, and the main question is how to strengthen the association between the contingent reward (in this case the treat) and the operant behaviour.[44]

operant behaviour
Behaviour that appears to operate on or to have an influence on the subject's environment.

Behaviour Modification

The principles of operant conditioning are applied at work through behaviour modification. **Behaviour modification** means changing or modifying behaviour through the use of contingent rewards or punishment. It is built on two principles: (1) behaviour that appears to lead to a positive consequence (reward) tends to be repeated, whereas behaviour that appears to lead to a negative consequence (punishment) tends not to be repeated; and (2) by providing the properly scheduled rewards, it is possible to get a person to learn to change his or her behaviour.[45] There are two elements in behaviour modification: the *types* of reinforcement (reward or punishment) and the *schedules* of reinforcement.

behaviour modification
Changing or modifying behaviour through the use of contingent rewards or punishment.

Types of Reinforcement There are several types of reinforcement. **Positive reinforcement** occurs when a pleasant stimulus is presented to a person. It increases the likelihood that a

positive reinforcement
When a pleasant stimulus is presented to a person, the desired behaviour is likely to be repeated.

behaviour will be repeated. For example, if an employee does a job well and is complimented on it by the boss, the probability that the employee will repeat the behaviour is increased.

Punishment occurs when an unpleasant stimulus is presented to a person. Punishment decreases the likelihood of the behaviour occurring again. For example, when an employee arrives late to work, the boss may berate the employee. This decreases the chance the behaviour will recur in the future. Note that in punishment, an unpleasant stimulus is presented, while in negative reinforcement an unpleasant stimulus is withheld. Punishment discourages certain behaviours, while negative reinforcement encourages certain behaviours.

Negative reinforcement occurs when an unpleasant stimulus is withheld from a person. Negative reinforcement also increases the likelihood that a behaviour will be repeated, but here the individual exhibits the desired behaviour to avoid something unpleasant. Suppose an employee knows that arriving late will cause a reprimand from the boss. The employee arrives on time to avoid the reprimand.

Omission occurs when a pleasant stimulus is withheld from the person. Omission decreases the likelihood that the behaviour will occur in the future. When a manager ignores an employee who spends a lot of time playing practical jokes, omission is occurring. Although this approach involves doing nothing, it does have an effect on behaviour. Since reinforced behaviour has a greater chance of recurring, it follows that not reinforcing behaviour reduces the chance that it will happen again.

Schedules of Reinforcement The *timing* of the above-mentioned reinforcements can also be varied. Two basic schedules can be used: continuous and intermittent. In a **continuous reinforcement schedule**, a reward or a punishment follows each time the behaviour of interest occurs. Thus, a parent may praise a child each time a puzzle is done correctly, or a boss may punish a worker each time an error is made. This type of schedule increases the desired response, but if the schedule is not maintained, the response rate decreases rapidly.

In a **partial**, or **intermittent reinforcement schedule**, the behaviour of interest is rewarded or punished only some of the time. Learning is more enduring in this type of schedule than in continuous schedules. Intermittent schedules of reinforcement are relatively slow in stimulating the desired behaviour, but once established, the behaviour tends to last. They are therefore useful for managers.

In a **fixed interval schedule**, a reinforcement is applied after a certain time period has passed, regardless of the number of responses that have occurred. A manager may visit a certain department once every fifth day, or workers may be paid once every two weeks. In a **variable interval schedule**, a reinforcement is applied after a varying amount of time has passed, regardless of the number of desired responses that have occurred. A manager may visit a certain department once a week, but subordinates don't know which day the visit will take place. Or a manager may praise (or punish) a subordinate only some of the time the person does a good (or poor) job.

In a **fixed ratio schedule**, a reinforcement is applied after a fixed number of desired behavioural responses have occurred, regardless of the time that has passed. For example, the department manager may come to the department and congratulate the members every fourth time they achieve their production quota, or employees may be paid on a piece-rate or commission basis.

In a **variable ratio schedule**, behaviour is reinforced after a varying number of responses have occurred; sometimes a reinforcement occurs after 3 responses, sometimes after 10, sometimes after 50, and so on. A manager following this schedule may come through a department irregularly, without the workers knowing why or when. All they know is that at apparently random times their boss visits and reinforces their behaviour (positively or negatively).

Motivation in Action: Ten Methods for Motivating Employees

As a leader, your knowledge of the three motivation approaches (need-based, process-based, and learning/reinforcement) gives you tools for identifying what is happening, why

punishment
The likelihood that a behaviour will occur in the future is decreased when an unpleasant stimulus is presented to a person.

negative reinforcement
When an unpleasant stimulus is withheld from a person, the desired behaviour will likely be repeated.

omission
The likelihood that a behaviour will occur in the future is decreased when a pleasant stimulus is withheld from the person.

continuous reinforcement schedule
According to this schedule, a reward or a punishment follows each time the behaviour of interest occurs.

partial (intermittent) reinforcement schedule
When the behaviour of interest is rewarded or punished only some of the time.

fixed interval schedule
Reinforcement is applied after a certain time period has passed, regardless of the number of responses that have occurred.

variable interval schedule
Reinforcement is applied after a varying amount of time has passed, regardless of the number of desired responses that have occurred.

fixed ratio schedule
Reinforcement is applied after a fixed number of desired behavioural responses have occurred, regardless of the time that has passed.

variable ratio schedule
Behaviour is reinforced after a varying number of responses have occurred.

it is happening, and what you can do to be effective as a leader. Ten practical methods for motivating people are presented in the next few pages. The material is summarized in Table 12.1 on pages 390–391. For example, empowering employees (column 7) is based in part on what psychologists call self-efficacy—the idea that people differ in their estimates of how well they will perform on a task. Building up their skills and self-confidence by empowering them should bolster their self-efficacy and thus their motivation.

Use Pay for Performance

Most people probably think first of "money" when it comes to motivating employees. **Pay for performance** refers to any compensation method that ties pay to the quantity or quality of work the person produces. Sales commissions are a familiar example. Variable pay plans are pay-for-performance plans that put a portion of the employee's pay at risk. In a plan at the DuPont Company, employees could voluntarily place up to 6 percent of their base pay at risk.[46] If their departments met their earnings projections, the employees would get that 6 percent back, plus additional percentages, depending on how much the department exceeded its earnings projections.

The "People Side of Managing" box on the next page describes various incentive programs that have been instituted at several Canadian companies as a means to motivate employees.

Gainsharing plans are incentive plans that engage many or all employees in a common effort to achieve productivity goals.[47] Implementing a gainsharing plan requires several steps. Managers choose specific performance measures, such as cost per unit produced, and a funding formula, such as "47 percent of savings go to employees." Then management decides how to divide and distribute cost savings between the employees and the company, and among employees. If employees achieve cost savings in line with their performance goals, they share in the resulting gains.[48]

Sometimes the performance pay comes in the form of **stock options**. Stock options are rights to purchase company stock at a discount some time in the future. For example, when Jim Eckel went to his first interview with Starbucks, he didn't pay much attention to the stock option plan (affectionately known within the company as Bean Stock). But today, as manager of a Starbucks on Manhattan's Upper West side, Eckel is reportedly a champion of the plan.[49] Jim and about 30 000 Starbucks partners are actually part of a new movement: Stock options for all employees, not just executives. By letting all or most employees participate in this way, each employee has an opportunity to see how performance and hard work translate into a rising stock price—and thus more rewards for them.

But the motivational power of stock options depends on the price of the company's stock. For years, high-tech companies like Cisco Systems and Sun Microsystems didn't have to pay employees a lot of money. Instead, they gave employees stock options. Employees were motivated to work hard because they knew that as the price of these companies' stock rapidly rose, they would become rich. But then stock prices started falling dramatically, and the value of many stock options went "under water" (meaning that the options are now priced above the current market value of the shares). Thus, employees hold millions of options that are worthless.[50]

Whether it's monthly bonuses, sales commissions, or something else, you need to apply motivation theory to make the pay-for-performance plan successful. For example, expectancy theory says that motivation depends on employees' seeing the link between performance and rewards, and on the value of the reward to the employee. Therefore, make sure that employees

pay for performance
Any compensation method that ties pay to the quantity or quality of work the person produces.

DuPont
www.dupont.com

gainsharing plans
Incentive plans that engage many or all employees in a common effort to achieve productivity goals.

stock options
Rights to purchase company stock at a discount some time in the future.

Starbucks' first retail coffee store in Beijing. The company offers its employees a number of opportunities to participate in its success.

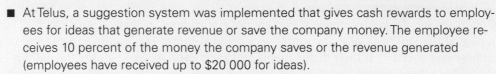

Incentives and Motivation

Canadian companies are realizing that offering incentives beyond the normal benefits can result in creative ideas as well as in large increases in employee productivity. These incentives may be monetary or non-monetary. Consider the following:

Telus
www.telus.com

- At Telus, a suggestion system was implemented that gives cash rewards to employees for ideas that generate revenue or save the company money. The employee receives 10 percent of the money the company saves or the revenue generated (employees have received up to $20 000 for ideas).
- Drexis Inc. flew 12 employees and their families to Disney World as a reward for increasing sales by more than 100 percent in one year.
- Proctor & Redfern Ltd., a consulting engineering firm, lets high achievers serve on committees with senior executives, represent the firm at outside functions, or enrol in development courses where the company pays the bill.
- Avatar Communications Inc. sent employees on a weeklong Outward Bound expedition into the wilderness. The trip had both reward and motivational components.

Pitney Bowes Canada
www.pb.com

- Pitney Bowes Canada Ltd. sent 60 of its top salespeople and their spouses to Hong Kong after they achieved 135 percent of their sales quota (salespeople who achieved 112 percent received a trip to San Diego).
- Manitoba Telephone System instituted a suggestion system called IDEA$PLUS, which gives employees cash awards up to $10 000 for good ideas.

SkyDome
www.skydome.com

- At Toronto's SkyDome, employees are given coupons for exceptional service, such as finding a lost child or repairing a broken seat. The coupons can be used to accumulate points, which can be redeemed for prizes.

Incentives are important for top managers as well. The higher a manager is placed in a firm, the more likely it is that a good chunk of the manager's pay will be performance-based. A Conference Board of Canada study of executive compensation in Canada showed that up to 40 percent of top executives' total compensation comes in the form of incentives. For lower-level managers, the figure was 20 percent, and for other employees it was

value the reward you are giving, can do the job, and can see the link between performance and reward.

Use Merit Pay

merit raise
A salary increase based on individual performance.

A **merit raise** is a salary increase based on individual performance. The theory behind such raises is sound. The prospect of the raise should focus the employee on the link between effort, performance, and rewards, consistent with expectancy theory. Receiving the merit raise should provide reinforcement for a job well done, consistent with learning theory. And it should enable employees to see that their rewards are equitably consistent with their efforts (equity theory).

Unfortunately, merit raises often fail to have the desired effect. One problem is that many supervisors try to avoid bad feelings by awarding raises across the board. This destroys the performance-reward link and cripples the incentive value of the merit pay. Another problem is that merit plans are often based on annual appraisals. But a year is a

Conference Board of
Canada
**www.
conferenceboard.ca**

10 percent. Top managers in the United States often receive up to 60 percent of their total compensation in the form of incentives. Most Canadian companies have set up some type of incentive plan for their senior executives.

Companies are also using technology to improve the effectiveness of their employee incentive programs. For example, new software charts participants' standings and painlessly tallies the final numbers, and email can be used to send reminders and encouragement too—like "10 more days to sell, sell, sell!" or "Think Hawaii!'" Other companies are using their intranets to publicize incentive program rules, award details, prize catalogues, and current status to incentive-plan participants. They offer employees exotic prizes like a trip to Tahiti. Some companies use their intranets to provide links to the destination's internet site.

Software packages help many companies to design and manage employee incentive programs. For example, ASPIRE 1.5 (Automated System Promoting Incentives that Reward Excellence) takes incentive planners through the steps required to design a corporate incentive program. The HR department can use the program to indicate how the winners will be judged (such as percentage of sales growth over past performance) and to choose the rewards from a menu of incentives options (such as travel, gifts, cheques, or even paid time off from the office). Another program, called Motivation Magic, helps incentive planners to custom design corporate award programs; it comes with a database containing suggestions for all types of incentives, as well as a design checklist, a program timeline, and functions for charting results.

Another package—Bob Nelson's Reward Wizard—"keeps performance records for all employees in a department or organization, along with their career objectives, personal preferences, hobbies and family circumstances. Space is also provided to enter their accomplishments, award criteria, time allotted to win an award and individual award preferences." Once it's up and running, Reward Wizard can generate prize suggestions adapted to each employee's needs, such as extra Mondays off for Gary and a bigger computer screen for Jeannine.

long time to wait for a reward, and the passage of time reduces the impact of merit pay.[52]

To make merit raises work as intended, pay attention to the following points. First, clarify performance standards before the measurement period begins. Second, institute a unit-wide performance appraisal system that you can use to systematically and accurately evaluate your employees' performance. Third, train all supervisors to award merit pay based on merit, rather then across the board. Fourth, conduct the award allocations bi-annually, or combine the merit plan with other, more timely financial (and other) rewards such as recognition.

Use Recognition

Recognizing an employee's contribution makes sense in terms of motivation theory. Recognition provides feedback that helps satisfy the Maslow, Alderfer, and McGregor self-esteem needs. Herzberg found that recognition was one of life's big motivators, and studies show that recognition has a positive impact on performance, either alone or in conjunction with financial rewards. In one study of service firms, combining financial

TABLE 12.1 *The Motivational Underpinnings of 10 Motivation Methods*

FOUNDATIONS OF BEHAVIOUR AND MOTIVATION	Pay for Performance	Merit Raises
Self-Concept: People seek to fulfill their potential.		
Self-Efficacy: People differ in their estimates of how they'll perform on a task; self-efficacy influences effort.		
Maslow Needs Hierarchy: High-level needs are never totally satisfied and aren't aroused until lower-level needs are satisfied.		X
Alderfer: All needs may be active, to some degree, at same time.		X
McClelland Ach, Pow, Aff: Needs for achievement, power, affiliation are especially important in work setting.		
Herzberg Dual Factor: Extrinsic factors just prevent dissatisfaction; intrinsic factors motivate workers.		
Vroom Expectancy Approach: Motivation is a function of expectancy that effort leads to performance, performance leads to reward, and reward is valued.	X	X
Locke Goal Setting: People are motivated to achieve goals they consciously set.		
Adams's Equity Theory: People are motivated to maintain balance between their perceived inputs and outputs.		X
Reinforcement: People will continue behaviour that is rewarded and cease behaviour that is punished.	X	X

CHECKLIST 12.1

How to Implement an Incentive Plan

☑ Make sure effort and rewards are directly related. The incentive plan should reward employees in direct proportion to increased productivity or quality.

☑ Make the plan easy to understand. Employee should be able to calculate their rewards for various levels of effort.

☑ Make standards high but reasonable—there should be about a 60 percent to 70 percent chance of success. The goal should also be specific.

☑ View the standard as a contract with your employees. Once the plan is working, use caution before decreasing the size of the incentive.

☑ Get employee support for the plan. Restrictions by peers can undermine the plan.

☑ Use good measurement systems. Make sure the standard and the employees' performance are both easily measured.

☑ Emphasize long-term as well as short-term success. For example, paying plant managers based on yearly productivity may be shortsighted if one or two of them decide to "get around" the requirement by skimping on machine maintenance.

☑ Take the system into account. From the employees' point of view, incentive plans don't exist in isolation. For example, trying to motivate employees with a new incentive plan will likely fail when they don't have the skills to do the job, or are demoralized by unfair supervisors or a lack of respect.[51]

MOTIVATION METHODS							
Spot Rewards	Skill-Based Pay	Recognition Awards	Job Redesign	Empower Employees	Goal Setting	Positive Reinforcement	Lifelong Learning
	X	X	X	X			X
	X			X			X
X		X	X	X			X
X		X	X	X			X
	X	X	X	X			X
			X	X			X
X		X			X		
				X	X		
X		X					
X		X				X	

merit raise
A salary increase based on individual performance.

rewards with non-financial ones (like recognition), produced a 30 percent performance improvement, almost twice the effect of using each reward alone.[53]

Many companies therefore formalize the process of saying "thank you for a job well done." According to one survey, 78 percent of CEOs and 58 percent of HR vice presidents said their firms were using performance recognition programs.[54] At Cloverdale Paint, for example, employees who come up with innovative ideas to improve customer service receive a personal letter from the president and a coffee mug or T-shirt bearing the company logo. The employee who makes the best suggestion of the year receives an engraved plaque, which is presented at a workplace ceremony. Emery Apparel Canada Inc. conducts an annual "Oscar" awards ceremony. With great hoopla, the CEO asks for the envelope with the name of the winner of the top award.

Texas Instruments offers bonuses as well as non-financial recognition, including personalized plaques, parties, movie tickets, golf lessons, team shirts, and jackets. The number of individual Texas Instruments employees recognized in this way jumped by 400 percent in one recent year, from 21 970 to 84 260.[55] Managers at Skandia, which provides insurance and financial planning products and services, regularly evaluate their customer service reps based on specific standards. Those who exceed those standards receive a plaque, a $500 cheque, their photo and story on the firm's internal website, and a dinner for them and their teams.[56]

Cloverdale Paint
www.cloverdalepaint.com

Skandia
www.skandia.com

Use Positive Reinforcement

"Positive reinforcement" is one of the most loosely used terms in management. Every time a manager thanks or recognizes an employee, awards a raise, or gives someone a promotion, the manager probably thinks, "I'm using positive reinforcement." Indeed, as you can see from the illustrative list in Figure 12.9, the variety of potential positive reinforcements (rewards) you can use is considerable. A short list includes salary increases, bonuses, discount airline tickets, promotions, job rotation, department parties, compliments, encouragement, and a bigger desk.

Spot Awards

spot award
An award you give literally "on the spot" as soon as you observe the good performance.

In learning theory, the best reinforcement usually comes immediately. A **spot award** is one you give literally "on the spot" as soon as you observe the good performance. For example, Thomas J. Watson Sr., founder of IBM, reportedly wrote cheques on the spot to employees doing an outstanding job.[57] FedEx's "Bravo-Zulu" voucher program is another example. It lets managers grant immediate small cash rewards to employees for outstanding performance.[58] Scitor, a systems engineering consulting firm, has a program called Be Our Guest, which gives bonuses from $100 to $300 to employees for doing something beyond the call of duty.[59]

Sometimes giving spot awards can causes problems, even if the awards are not cash. Toronto Hydro Corp. used to give gifts like pen and pencil sets, disc players, video cameras, cellular phones, and leather jackets to unionized employees in recognition of their good performance. But the union filed a grievance against such activity, claiming that the program violated the union's right as exclusive bargaining agent for the employees. The union

Scitor
www.scitor.com

Toronto Hydro
www.torontohydro.com

MONETARY	FOOD AND DINING
Salary increases or bonuses	Business luncheon paid by company
Company-paid vacation trip	Company picnics
Discount coupons	Department parties
Company stock	Holiday turkeys and fruit baskets
Extra paid vacation days	
Profit sharing	SOCIAL AND PRIDE RELATED
Paid personal holiday (such as birthday)	Compliments
Movie or athletic event passes	Encouragement
Free or discount airline tickets	Comradeship with boss
Discounts on company products or services	Access to confidential information
Gift selection from catalogue	Pat on back
	Expression of appreciation in front of others
JOB AND CAREER RELATED	Note of thanks
Empowerment of employee	Employee-of-the-month award
Challenging work assignments	Wall plaque indicating accomplishment
Job security (relatively permanent job)	Special commendation
Favourable performance appraisal	Company recognition plan
Freedom to choose own work activity	
Promotion	STATUS SYMBOLS
Having fun built into work	Bigger desk
More of preferred task	Bigger office or cubicle
Role as boss's stand-in when he or she is away	Exclusive use of fax machine
Role in presentations to top management	Freedom to personalize work area
Job rotation	Private office
Encouragement of learning and continuous improvement	Cellular phone privileges
Being provided with ample encouragement	On-line service privileges
Being allowed to set own goals	

FIGURE 12.9
Positive Reinforcement Rewards

also said the program was divisive. An arbitrator ruled that the company had to stop giving workers the gifts.[60]

Whether it's recognition, a spot award, or some other "positive reinforcement," managers must make sure that what they assume is important to employees is actually important. Table 12.2 illustrates why. In this survey of employees, for example, "full appreciation of work done" was ranked #1 by employees, but only #8 by their bosses. Bosses assumed "good wages" were most important, while the employees themselves ranked wages as #5.[61]

Use Behaviour Management

As shown in Figure 12.10, modifying behaviour is like balancing a scale. Suppose wearing a safety helmet is the desired behaviour, and not wearing it is the undesired behaviour. One way to increase the desired behaviour is to add a positive consequence—for example, by praising the worker each time he or she wears the hat. Another option is to remove the negative consequences of wearing the hat—by keeping the plant cooler, or by making the hat less cumbersome. It's best to focus on improving desirable behaviours rather than on decreasing undesirable ones.

The Basic Procedure To a behaviour management expert, any behaviour is a product of its consequences. If the person comes to work late all the time, you are not providing the right consequences for coming to work on time, or you are inadvertently reinforcing coming in late. The way to motivate the right behaviour is to identify the desired behaviours and then carefully reward them. The process involves four steps:[62]

1. Pinpoint behaviour. Identify and define the specific behaviour(s) you want to change.

2. Record. Count the occurrence of the pinpoint behaviour.

3. Change consequences. Analyze the consequences of the behaviour as they are now, and arrange for new or improved consequences to follow the behaviour.

4. Evaluate. Ask, "Did the behaviour improve, and if so, how much?"

TABLE 12.2 *Order of Importance of Various Job Factors*		
JOB FACTORS	SURVEY OF EMPLOYEES	SURVEY OF BOSSES
Full Appreciation of Work Done	1	8
Feeling of Being in on Things	2	10
Sympathetic Help on Personal Problems	3	9
Job Security	4	2
Good Wages	5	1
Interesting Work	6	5
Promotional Growth in Organization	7	3
Personal Loyalty to Employees	8	6
Good Working Conditions	9	4
Tactful Disciplining	10	7

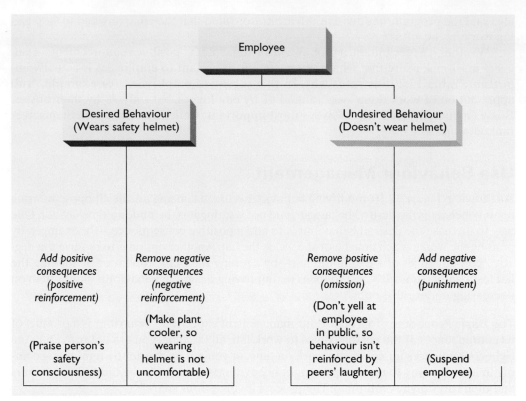

FIGURE 12.10
Options for Modifying Behaviour with Reinforcement

An Example Figure 12.11 provides a summary of how to apply and use this approach. Here, the general problem was that the accounting department was making too many payroll errors. The consultants pinpointed the behaviours (the number of errors reported back to them by department managers) and counted and recorded the reported errors. They then formulated consequences for the behavioural change. In this case, the consequences included the feedback the bookkeepers got from keeping graphs of their errors and feedback from the managers.

Behaviour Modification Programs at Work In one company, a behaviour management program was used to reduce absenteeism. Each day that an employee came to work on time, he or she received a playing card. At the end of the week, the highest poker hand received $20. Over a three-month period, the absenteeism rate decreased 18 percent.[63]

A telephone company identified several desirable behaviours among its operators and embarked on a behaviour management program to increase these behaviours. Praise and recognition were the main reinforcers that were used. Attendance improved 50 percent and productivity and efficiency levels rose above past standards.[64]

In a study involving a city transit company, behaviour management methods were applied to improve the safety record of bus drivers. The system reduced accident rates by nearly 25 percent.[65] At SAS Airlines, agents were trained to sell seats to customers who had simply called in for information. By the end of the program, agents had capitalized on 84 percent of the potential-offer opportunities, compared to only 34 percent at the beginning of the program.[66]

empowerment
Making it possible for people to attain some degree of control over their jobs and to employ suitable power to make their work lives effective.

Empower Employees

Psychologists like Maslow and Herzberg argue that the satisfaction one gets from doing a job and doing it well is highly motivating and that empowering employees is one way to motivate them. **Empowerment** means making it possible for people to attain some degree of control over their jobs and to employ suitable power to make their work lives effective.[67] Empowerment boosts feelings of self-efficacy, and enables employees to use their potential. In the process, it appeals to their higher-level needs for achievement, recognition, and self-actualization. Table 12.3 suggests actions managers can take to empower employees.[68]

1. General Statement of Problem

The accounting department was making too many payroll errors. This increased cost by taking up managers' time and accounting time. It also caused a lot of frustration on the part of employees.

2. Pinpointed Behaviours

The accounting department was instructed to count the number of errors reported back to it by department managers.

3. Count and Record

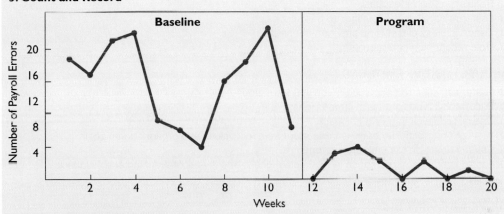

4. Consequences for Behaviour Changes

Each bookkeeper in the accounting department started keeping a graph of the number of errors for which he or she was responsible. The accounting manager discussed each error with the bookkeepers and assigned responsibility. The manager verbally reinforced those bookkeepers who showed improvement on their graphs or who displayed low rates of error to begin with.

5. What Changes Occurred

The number of errors dropped from an average 11.6 errors per week to 1.17 errors per week.

FIGURE 12.11
Performance Improvement Project Worksheet

TABLE 12.3 *Practical Suggestions for Empowering Others*

ARTICULATE A CLEAR VISION AND GOALS

❑ Create a picture of a desired future.
❑ Use word pictures and emotional language to describe the vision.
❑ Identify specific actions and strategies that will lead to the vision.
❑ Establish SMART goals.
❑ Associate the vision and goals with personal values.

(continued)

TABLE 12.3 *(continued)*

FOSTER PERSONAL MASTERY EXPERIENCES

❑ Break apart large tasks and assign one part at a time.
❑ Assign simple tasks before difficult tasks.
❑ Highlight and celebrate small wins.
❑ Incrementally expand job responsibilities.
❑ Give increasingly more responsibility to solve problems.

MODEL SUCCESSFUL BEHAVIOURS

❑ Demonstrate successful task accomplishment.
❑ Point out other people who have succeeded.
❑ Facilitate interaction with other role models.
❑ Find a coach.
❑ Establish a mentor relationship.

PROVIDE SUPPORT

❑ Praise, encourage, express approval for, and reassure.
❑ Send letters or notes of praise to family members of co-workers.
❑ Regularly provide feedback.
❑ Foster informal social activities to build cohesion.
❑ Supervise less closely and provide time slack.
❑ Hold recognition ceremonies.

AROUSE POSITIVE EMOTIONS

❑ Foster activities to encourage friendship formation.
❑ Periodically send lighthearted messages.
❑ Use superlatives in giving feedback.
❑ Highlight compatibility between important personal values and organizational goals.
❑ Clarify impact on the ultimate customer.
❑ Foster attributes of recreation in work: clear goals, effective scorekeeping and feedback systems, and out-of-bounds behaviour.

PROVIDE INFORMATION

❑ Provide all task-relevant information.
❑ Continually provide technical information and objective data.
❑ Pass along relevant cross-unit and cross-functional information.
❑ Provide access to information or people with senior responsibility.
❑ Provide access to information from its source.
❑ Clarify effects of actions on customers.

PROVIDE RESOURCES

❑ Provide training and development experiences.
❑ Provide technical and administrative support.
❑ Provide needed time, space, or equipment.
❑ Ensure access to relevant information networks.
❑ Provide more discretion to commit resources.

CONNECT TO OUTCOMES

❑ Provide a chance to interact directly with those receiving the service or output.
❑ Provide authority to resolve problems on the spot.
❑ Provide immediate, unfiltered, direct feedback on results.
❑ Create task identity or the opportunity to accomplish a complete task.
❑ Clarify and measure effects as well as direct outcomes.

CREATE CONFIDENCE

❑ Exhibit reliability and consistency.
❑ Exhibit fairness and equity.
❑ Exhibit caring and personal concern.
❑ Exhibit openness and honesty.
❑ Exhibit competence and expertise.

Use Job Redesign

Job redesign is the process of altering the nature and structure of jobs with the purpose of increasing employee satisfaction, motivation, and productivity. Many job redesign strategies have been tried, including job enlargement and job rotation, job enrichment, flextime, the compressed workweek, and job sharing.

Job Enlargement and Job Rotation Initial attempts at job redesign centred on job enlargement and job rotation. **Job enlargement** assigns workers additional same-level tasks to increase the number of tasks they have to perform. For example, if the work is assembling chairs, the worker who previously only bolted the seat to the legs might take on the additional tasks of assembling the legs and attaching the back. **Job rotation** systematically moves workers from job to job. Thus, on an auto assembly line, a worker might spend an hour fitting doors, the next hour installing head lamps, the next hour fitting bumpers, and so on. At Abitibi-Price, lateral rotation of employees is done on a case-by-case basis. For example, a communication specialist might move temporarily into marketing or a human resources staff member might move into administration.[69]

Job Enrichment **Job enrichment** means building motivators into a job by making it more interesting and challenging. Managers often accomplish this by giving the worker more autonomy and allowing the person to do much of the planning and inspection normally done by the person's supervisor. Job enrichment is the method Herzberg recommends for applying his hygiene–motivator approach to motivation.

Successfully applying this approach requires understanding several things. First, how does one know if a job is "ripe" for this approach? There is no guaranteed answer to this question, but Figure 12.12 provides a start. It is a form for evaluating the appropriateness of job enrichment.

A lower rating (1.0–1.9) indicates that a job is a prime candidate for enrichment, and if properly implemented has a high expected return on investment. A job enrichment rating of 2.0–3.9 identifies jobs that can be enriched that may have a marginal return on investment in terms of productivity measures. A high rating (4.0–5.0) identifies jobs that for all practical purposes cannot be enriched at the present time.[70]

Second, what specific actions can managers take that will "enrich" an employee's job? Managers enrich jobs in several ways:[71]

1. *Form natural workgroups.* For example, put a team in charge of an identifiable body of work, such as building an entire engine.

2. *Combine tasks.* Let one person assemble a product from start to finish, instead of having it go through separate operations performed by different people.

3. *Establish client relationships.* Let the worker have contact as often as possible with the people who actually use the product the worker made.

4. *Vertically load the job.* Have the worker, rather the supervisor, plan, schedule, troubleshoot, and control his or her job.

5. *Open feedback channels.* Find more and better ways for the worker to get quick feedback on performance.

Many firms have used this approach. At Saturn Corporation, for instance, empowered, self-managing work teams do much of the factory's work, such as maintaining machines and installing dashboard systems. These teams have enriched jobs. Figure 12.13 lists some specific things that make their jobs enriched.

Flextime **Flextime** is a system that allows workers increased discretion in deciding when they will be at their place of work. Technically, flextime does not involve changing the content of the job, but it does change the context. Management decides which hours of the day are "core hours" (times when it is absolutely essential that workers be

job redesign
The process of altering the nature and structure of jobs with the purpose of increasing employee satisfaction, motivation, and productivity.

job enlargement
Assigns workers additional same-level tasks to increase the number of tasks they have to perform.

job rotation
Systematically moves workers from job to job.

job enrichment
Building motivators into a job by making it more interesting and challenging.

flextime
A system that allows workers increased discretion in deciding when they will be at their place of work.

The Job Itself

1. Quality is important and attributable to the worker	/1/2/3/4/5/	Quality is not too important and/or is not controllable by the worker.
2. Flexibility is a major contributor to job efficiency.	/1/2/3/4/5/	Flexibility is not a major consideration.
3. The job requires the coordination of tasks or activities among several workers.	/1/2/3/4/5/	The job is performed by one worker acting independently of others.
4. The benefits of job enrichment will compensate for the efficiencies of task specialization.	/1/2/3/4/5/	Job enrichment will eliminate substantial efficiencies realized from specialization.
5. The conversion and one-time set-up costs involved in job enrichment can be recovered in a reasonable period of time.	/1/2/3/4/5/	Training and other costs associated with job enrichment are estimated to be much greater than expected results.
6. The wage payment plan is not based solely on output.	/1/2/3/4/5/	Workers are under a straight piece-work wage plan.
7. Due to the worker's ability to affect output, an increase in job satisfaction can be expected to increase productivity.	/1/2/3/4/5/	Due to the dominance of technology, an increase in job satisfaction is unlikely to significantly affect productivity.

Technology

8. Changes in job content would not necessitate a large investment in equipment and technology	/1/2/3/4/5/	The huge investment in equipment and technology overrides all other considerations.
9. Employees are accustomed to change and respond favourably to it.	/1/2/3/4/5/	Employees are set in their ways and prefer the status quo.
10. Employees feel secure in their jobs; employment has been stable.	/1/2/3/4/5/	Layoffs are frequent, many employees are concerned about the permanency of employment.
11. Employees are dissatisfied with their jobs and would welcome changes in job content and work relationships.	/1/2/3/4/5/	Employees are satisfied with their present jobs and general work situation.
12. Employees are highly skilled blue- and white-collar workers, professionals, and supervisors.	/1/2/3/4/5/	Employees are semi- and unskilled blue- and white-collar workers.
13. Employees are well educated, with most having college or university degrees.	/1/2/3/4/5/	The average employee has less than a high school education.
14. Employees are from a small town and rural environment.	/1/2/3/4/5/	The company is located in a large, highly industrialized metropolitan area.
15. The history of union–management (if no union, worker–management) relations has been one of co-operation and mutual support.	/1/2/3/4/5/	Union–management (worker–management) relations are strained, and the two parties are antagonistic to each other.

Management

16. Managers are committed to job enrichment and are anxious to participate in its implementation.	/1/2/3/4/5/	Managers show little interest in job enrichment and even less interest in having it implemented in their departments.
17. Managers have attended seminars, workshops, and so forth; are quite knowledgeable of the concept; and have had experience in implementing it.	/1/2/3/4/5/	Managers lack the training and experience necessary to develop and implement job enrichment projects.
18. Management realizes that substantial payoffs from job enrichment usually take one to three years to materialize.	/1/2/3/4/5/	Management expects immediate results (within six months) from job enrichment projects

Total Score _____ ÷ 18 = _____

Job Enrichment Rating

FIGURE 12.12
A Job Enrichment Evaluation Form

National Cash Register
www.ncr.com

compressed workweek
Employees work fewer days per week, but more hours on the days they do work.

on the job). In many firms these core hours are 10 a.m. to 2 p.m. Workers can then decide when to work the remaining number of required hours. 3M Canada and National Cash Register are among the companies that have adopted some form of flextime. A survey of 1600 Canadian companies showed that nearly half of them had some type of flextime program.[72]

The Compressed Workweek In a **compressed workweek**, employees work fewer days per week, but more hours on the days they do work. The most popular compressed workweek is 4 days, 10 hours per day. Tellers at the Bank of Montreal in Oakville Place work long days (up to 14 hours), but enjoy a short workweek. Some tellers work 7 a.m. to 9 p.m. on Thursdays and Fridays, and 7:30 a.m. to 5:30 p.m. on Saturdays.[73]

EACH SATURN TEAM WILL:

1. *Use consensus decision making:* No formal leader [will be] apparent in the process. . . All members of the work unit that reaches consensus must be at least 70% comfortable with the decision and 100% committed to its implementation.

3. *Make their own job assignments:* A work unit . . . ensures safe, effective, efficient, and equal distribution of the work unit tasks to all its members.

5. *Plan their own work:* The work unit assigns timely resources for the accomplishment of its purpose to its customers while meeting the needs of the people within the work unit.

6. *Design their own jobs:* This should provide the optimum balance between people and technology and include the effective use of manpower, ergonomics, machine utilization, quality, cost, job-task analysis, and continuous improvement.

8. *Control their own material and inventory:* Work directly in a coordinated manner with suppliers, partners, customers, and indirect/product material resource team members to develop and maintain necessary work unit inventory.

9. *Perform their own equipment maintenance:* Perform those tasks that can be defined as safe and those they have the expertise, ability, and knowledge to perform effectively.

13. *Make selection decisions of new members into the work unit:* A work unit operating in a steady state has responsibility for determining total manpower requirements, and selection and movement of qualified new members from a candidate pool will be in accordance with the established Saturn selection process.

14. *Constantly seek improvement in quality, cost, and the work environment:* The work unit is responsible for involving all work unit members in improving quality, cost, and the work environment in concert with Saturn's quality system.

18. *Determine their own methods:* The work unit is responsible for designing the jobs of its team members consistent with the requirements of the Saturn production system and comprehending the necessary resources and work breakdown required.

21. *Provide their own absentee replacements:* The work unit is responsible for the attendance of its members. . . The work unit will be required to plan for and provide its own absentee coverage.

22. *Perform their own repairs:* The work unit will have the ultimate responsibility for producing a world-class product that meets the needs and requirements of the customer. In the event a job leaves the work unit with a known or unknown nonconformance to specification, the originating work unit will be accountable for corrective action and repair.

FIGURE 12.13
Sample of Saturn Work Team's Functions

Job Sharing As the name suggests, **job sharing** allows two people to share one full-time job. As staff lawyers at NOVA Corp. in Calgary, Kim Sarjeant and Loraine Champion shared a position advising the human resources department. Sarjeant worked Monday through Wednesday, and Champion worked Wednesday through Friday.[74]

To what extent do Canadian firms actually use job redesign concepts (and other ideas) for motivating workers? Aon Consulting interviewed more than 2000 Canadian workers and asked them about the kinds of programs their firms had introduced to improve the work-life harmony of workers.[75] They found that flextime was most commonly mentioned (by 51 percent of the respondents). Other items most frequently mentioned were paid time off bank (50 percent), discount program (42 percent), job sharing (33 percent), work from home program (23 percent), child care (12 percent), and elder care (8 percent). In terms of motivating workers, there is much room for improvement here, particularly in the child care and elder care areas.

job sharing
An arrangement that allows two people to share one full-time job.

Use Skill-Based Pay

Asking employees to work on self-managing, enriched-work-type teams presents a dilemma as far as paying them is concerned. In most firms employees get paid based on their specific jobs. Presidents make more than vice presidents, sales managers make more than assistant sales managers, and so forth. How do you pay workers when you want to encourage them to move from one job to another, when the jobs may involve considerably different skill levels?

Skill-based pay is one solution. With **skill-based pay**, employees are compensated for the range, depth, and types of skills and knowledge they can use, rather than for the jobs they currently hold.[76] A General Mills plant boosted the flexibility and skill level of its factory workforce by implementing a pay plan that encouraged employees to develop a wider range of skills.[77] The plan paid workers based on attained skill levels. For each of the several types of jobs in the plant, workers could attain three levels of skill: limited ability (ability to perform simple tasks without direction); partial proficiency (ability to apply more advanced principles on the job); and full competence (ability to analyze and solve problems associated with that job).

After starting a job, workers were periodically tested to see whether they had earned certification at the next higher skill level. If they had, they received higher pay even though they kept the same job. The plant's overall skill level increased, as did its ability to switch employees from job to job.

Provide Lifelong Learning

Programs like job enrichment and building self-managing teams (as at Saturn) obviously demand a higher level of knowledge and skills from employees. Hiring team members, analyzing quality problems, and checking to see how the client liked the work requires both school-type learning and on-the-job training. For employees to work effectively, lifelong learning is therefore required. **Lifelong learning** is a formal program that provides employees with the skills they need—from remedial skills through decision-making techniques to advanced degrees—to work effectively throughout their careers. Programs range from ongoing in-house training, through making community college courses available at the plant's facility, to providing tuition reimbursement for relevant college or university coursework.

Lifelong learning is inherently motivational. It enables employees to develop and to see an enhanced possibility of fulfilling their potential; it boosts employees' sense of self-efficacy; and it provides an enhanced opportunity for the employee to self-actualize and gain the sense of achievement that psychologists argue is so important.

Lifelong learning is not the sort of tool (like incentives or merit pay) that springs to mind when you think about motivating employees. However, the motivational effect of giving employees an opportunity to develop their skills and to self-actualize appears to be considerable. One study concluded that "productivity improvements, greater workforce flexibility, reduced material and capital costs, a better motivated work force, and improved quality of the final product or service are all identified as advantages [of lifelong learning] for commercial enterprises."[78]

How to Analyze Performance-Motivation Problems

Assume that one of your employees is not performing up to par, and you want to correct the problem. The model in Figure 12.14 will be useful. It assumes that inadequate performance may be caused by one of three things: (1) the employee does not know what to do; (2) the employee could not do the job even if he or she wanted to; (3) the employee is not motivated to do the job. Follow the steps in the model and you will be able to analyze and solve the performance-motivation problem.

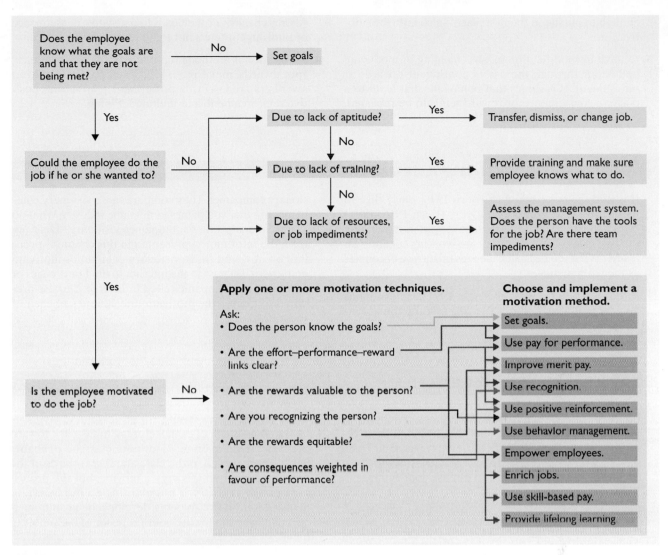

FIGURE 12.14
How to Analyze Performance-Motivation Problems

SKILLS AND STUDY MATERIAL

SUMMARY

1. Motivation is the intensity of a person's desire to engage in some activity. Need-based approaches to motivating employees—such as those of Maslow, Herzberg, and McClelland—emphasize the role played by motivational dispositions or needs such as the need for achievement and for self-actualization.

2. An employee's thought process also influences motivation. People want to be treated equitably. Having decided to pursue a goal, they regulate their behaviour to try to ensure that a goal is reached. Their expectations—that effort will lead to performance, that performance will lead to reward, and that the reward is valuable

enough to pursue in the first place—also influence motivation.

3. Behaviour modification means changing or modifying behaviour through the use of contingent rewards or punishment. It assumes that behaviour that leads to a positive consequence or reward tends to be repeated, whereas behaviour that leads to a negative consequence or punishment tends not to be repeated.

4. Motivational methods include pay for performance, spot awards, merit pay, skill-based pay, recognition awards, job redesign, empowerment, goal setting, positive reinforcement, and lifelong learning.

CRITICAL THINKING EXERCISES

1. It is said the baby boomers (born 1946–1964) "live to work" and that Generation Xers (born 1965–1981) "work to live." What are the challenges in motivating the two groups? What if they are working together on teams? What job design challenges might you encounter as the team manager?

2. In *Built to Last* (Harper Business, 1994), James Collins and Jerry Porras explore the successful habits of visionary companies. They compare these visionary companies to other companies in the same industry. What do you think makes these companies visionary? Drawing from the information presented in this chapter, speculate on how you think visionary companies motivate employees. Then go to the internet to the home pages of several of the companies cited in *Built to Last*. Be prepared to discuss the motivation techniques of each of these firms.

EXPERIENTIAL EXERCISES

1. Interview four or five friends, workmates, or fellow students about what motivates them. Record their responses. Then assess their responses in terms of how well they fit with what the motivation theories in the chapter are saying. Be prepared to discuss your findings in class.

2. In teams of four to five students, use Figure 12.12 to analyze your professor's job for its enrichment potential. To what extent would you say it is enriched now? Why? What specifically would you do to enrich it more?

3. You like everything about your professor, but he insists on spending much of each lecture with his back toward the class. In an average 75-minute class, he probably has his back turned to the class about two-thirds of the time. Students find this very annoying, but the professor's excuse is that he's busy writing on the board. In teams of four to five students, develop a behaviour management program to cure your professor of his annoying habit.

BUILDING YOUR MANAGEMENT SKILLS

Enriching Your Job

Consider a job that you currently or formerly had. Assess the appropriateness of this job for job enrichment, using the material in Figure 12.12 in the chapter. Then answer the following questions:

1. How "ripe" is the job for enrichment, based on the form you filled out?

2. If the job requires enriching, indicate how you would do it. For each of the suggestions contained in the chapter (e.g., form natural work groups, combine tasks, establish client relationships, etc.) indicate specifically what you would do to enrich the job. Make sure you explain how each enrichment suggestion actually addresses one or more of the key characteristics of enriched jobs.

3. Do you prefer an enriched job or an unenriched job? Why?

People are motivated by a whole range of factors. For some managers, motivation is one of the most difficult tasks of their job. Fortunately there are many resources available. One of these is Dreamcatcher Coaching (**www.employee-motivation-in-the-workplace.com**).

1. Review the employee motivation questionnaire that is a guide to help managers identify which motivation "zappers" are influencing them or their staff. If you are currently working, or have worked in the past, complete the questionnaire to assess your motivation level.

2. What are the ten tips that Dreamcatcher Coaching suggests for designing an employee motivation questionnaire? Which of the tips did you find most surprising? Why?

3. To what extent are you motivated by external factors (salary) or internal factors (pride in doing a job well)? Complete one of the motivational questionnaires at **www.humanlinks.com/motiv.htm**.

CASE STUDY 12-1

Galt Contracting

THE SITUATION

Donald Galt, owner and manager of Galt Contracting, sat in his office in Kelowna, B.C., on a cold and rainy February day, and pondered a serious problem that he was facing. The workers he had hired to plant trees during last summer's planting season had made far too many mistakes as they planted seedling trees. The lumber companies who had given Galt tree-planting contracts had threatened to withhold any more contracts if Galt was unable to solve the quality problem. Galt feared that the survival of his company was at stake, and he wondered what he could do.

BACKGROUND

Galt Contracting is a small B.C.-based company that plants trees for lumber companies like Canfor, Gorman Brothers, and Riverside. In the spring of each year, Galt bids on tree-planting contracts that will be available during the summer. Galt usually visits the block of land that is up for bid and looks it over with a lumber company representative. He then develops a bid and submits it to the lumber company. If he is awarded the job, he then hires tree planters to do the actual planting on the block of land. Galt decides how much he will pay his workers. The amount that Galt receives from the lumber company contracts minus the amount he has to pay his workers determines the profit that Galt Contracting makes each year.

Galt usually hires about 15 university students each summer who are looking for good-paying, short-term jobs. The work is very hard, but tree planters can make very good money because they are paid on a piece-rate system (that is, they are paid a certain amount of money for each tree they plant). Galt has been using this payment system for many years, but recently he has become very concerned about it, because trees are not being planted properly and they die soon after planting. Galt thinks this is happening because workers are stressing quantity at the expense of quality to earn a lot of money. At the end of last year's planting season, Galt was told in no uncertain terms by one lumber company that if he did not improve the quality of his tree planting, he would not get any more jobs. This year he has already lost one contract for 200 000 trees because of poor-quality planting that was done by his workers last year.

The problem is significant enough that Galt has been thinking about dropping the piece-rate pay system and moving toward a "flat rate" system, which would give the workers a fixed amount of pay for each day. Galt thinks that this would cause planters to take more time and care when planting each tree, since they would not have to worry about how much money they were going to make for the day. Before making this important decision, Galt reflects on how the tree-planting business works.

A DAY IN THE LIFE OF A TREE PLANTER

At Donald Galt's company, a typical day for a tree planter goes something like this.

→

Time	Activity
4:45 a.m.	Get up
5:00 a.m.	Leave for storage site where trees are kept
5:30 a.m.	Arrive at storage site and load trees into truck
5:30 a.m. – 7:00 a.m.	Drive truck to planting site; everyone "bags up" (puts trees in planting bags) at the main tree cache
7:00 a.m. – 3:00 p.m.	Plant trees
3:00 p.m. – 4:30 p.m.	Return to storage site in preparation for driving home
4:30 p.m. – 5:30 p.m.	Drive home

Galt pays his tree planters between 16 and 32 cents per tree. The amount varies depending on terrain and the kind of tree being planted. Piece rates go above 16 cents per tree if the land to be planted has any of the following characteristics:

- It is uneven.
- It has rocky soil.
- It is covered with "slash" (branches lying on the ground).
- It is covered with high weeds (making it difficult to see where trees have been planted).
- It was logged more than 10 years ago (and there is new growth of alders and poplar).

When the land is particularly uneven, on some occasions Galt has paid a flat "day rate." He sometimes gets the impression that when he does this, workers don't seem to work as hard, and they take more breaks. Galt knows that workers like the piece-rate system because they can make good money. They also feel that it generates competition among planters to see who can be the most productive. This competition increases the number of trees that are planted. (A tree planter may plant as few as 1000 trees or as many as 2500 trees per day, depending on the terrain and the planter's experience. On an average day, a reasonably experienced tree planter can plant 1300 trees.)

When the piece-rate system is used, there is not much socializing among workers on the site, except when they are "bagging up" at the main cache at various times throughout the day. Tree bags hold about 400 seedlings. Planters do not have a set lunch break; instead, they eat lunch on the run. They usually leave their lunch boxes at the main cache, and eat about halfway through the day on one of their return trips to the cache to pick up more trees. Socializing is generally seen as counterproductive because workers who stand around and talk aren't planting trees, and this reduces the worker's pay.

THE PRODUCTION SYSTEM

Trees are delivered to the planting site in boxes, with 360 trees per box. The seedlings range from 7.5 cm to 30 cm high and are called "plugs." The most common trees are lodgepole pine, spruce, Douglas fir, and larch.

Each planter is assigned a "piece" to plant for the day, usually an area equal in size to a football field, but not necessarily symmetrical. The limits of each planter's area are marked with flags by the planters as they begin planting in the morning. The numbers in Figure 12.15 indicate the order in which trees are planted. Planters leave the main cache and begin planting trees in a straight line. As they plant they "flag a line," which indicates the boundaries of their piece. This involves staking out strips of brightly coloured tape close to the line of trees. The planter on piece 1, for example, would flag a line while planting trees 1 through 100. This line helps each of the planters to determine where their piece begins and ends. Planting is then done in a back-and-forth pattern within each piece as planters work toward the main cache. They monitor the number of trees left in their planting bags so they can end up near the main cache when they run out of trees. So, the planter on piece 1 might plant tree 400 near the main cache, then "bag up" and start the process all over again with tree 401. On non-symmetrical pieces, this process is more complicated.

Trees must be planted in different concentrations on different blocks, and a certain jargon has arisen to describe this activity. For example, if spacing is "2.9," this means that trees must be planted 2.9 m apart; if spacing is "3.1," this means that trees must be planted 3.1 m apart. Planters prefer "2.9 days" over "3.1 days" because they don't have to cover as much ground and can therefore plant more trees (and make more money).

A checker—who works for the lumber company—inspects the work of the planters to ensure that they are planting properly. Checkers use a cord to inscribe a circle on random pieces of ground. On "2.9 days," the checker will ensure that 7 trees are contained in the circle within the cord. The checker also determines whether the trees are planted properly; trees must not have any air pockets around the roots, there must be no "j-rooted" (crooked) roots, and trees must be planted on the south (sunny) side of any obstacles in the piece. Trees must also be planted close to obstacles so that they are not trampled by the cattle that graze in the area. If a planter consistently plants too many or too few trees on a piece, the checker can demand that the piece be replanted. This happens infrequently, but when it does, the planter's pay is sharply reduced.

Galt sometimes checks workers himself, especially if he has reason to believe that they are doing a sloppy job. The biggest problem he has encountered is workers who plant large numbers of trees, but do so very poorly. Planters know that if Galt is following them around for any significant period of time, he is suspicious about the quality of their planting. Planters are very hard on each other in terms of quality. They become very upset if one of their group tries to make more money by planting large numbers of trees by cutting corners. Planters put pressure on each other to do a good job because the reputation of the whole group suffers if one or two planters do poor-quality work. As well, planters resent those among them who make more money simply by planting large numbers of trees in a poor quality way. A planter who is known to do a sloppy job or who is forced to replant an area might be nicknamed "j-root," for example.

Planters do not know when the checker will come by. If a planter "gets in good" with a checker, the checker may go easy when checking the planter's work. The checkers are themselves checked by other lumber company employees to ensure that they are doing reasonable quality control work. In turn, the lumber company is checked by the provincial government to see that trees are planted properly.

There is a real art to planting a tree. An experienced planter will push the shovel into the ground with one foot and hand and wiggle it back and forth to make a slit for the tree, while at the same time using the other hand to extract a tree from the tree bag and drop it into the newly created hole. The shovel is then pulled out, and the area around the newly planted tree is chopped up a bit with the shovel to aerate it. Using

this system, an experienced worker planting trees on flat ground can plant more than 300 trees per hour.

DONALD GALT'S DECISION

As Galt considered all of these facts, he wondered what he should do regarding the payment system he uses for workers.

Questions

1. What are the advantages and disadvantages of paying tree planters on a piece-rate system? On a flat day-rate system?

2. What does each of the motivation theories in the chapter say (or imply) about Galt's idea of dropping the piece-rate system and paying tree planters a flat rate for each day of work?

3. Propose a payment system for the tree planters that minimizes negative consequences. Describe the impact of your proposal on the following: the motivation levels of the planters, the activities of the quality control checkers, the level of quality needed in tree planting, the needs of the lumber companies, and Galt Contracting's need for profit. Be specific.

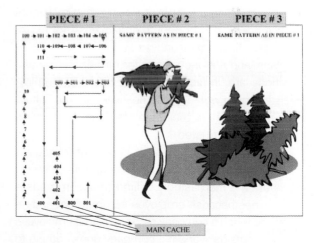

FIGURE 12.15
A Typical Tree Planting Route

A New Era in Employee Perks

Companies are offering more and more perks to both current and prospective employees because they recognize the importance of retaining productive current employees and hiring promising new employees. Emphasizing a richer mix of employee perks makes it necessary for managers to adopt the view that employees can be trusted to do what is beneficial for the company and don't have to be watched all the time to ensure they're doing the right things.

Trimark Investment Management Inc. is just one example of the new era in employee perks. When the company moved from downtown Toronto to the suburbs in 1998, it wanted to make sure it kept valued employees who liked being close to big-city amenities. So it built the Energy Zone, an on-site facility that offers aerobics, self-defence, and yoga classes. It also includes a weight room, massage room, pool tables, a big-screen TV, and an internet café. The Energy Zone gives employees some diversions from work, but it also acts as a place where they can meet and interact with people from other departments. Trimark also has a Recovery Room for employees who feel under the weather while at work.

A study done for *Report on Business Magazine* found that many of the traditional things that managers have assumed are important to employees—for example, fair pay, financial incentives such as share ownership plans, and the opportunity for further training and education—are, in fact, important. However, employees also want to work for a company where the culture values people, where their opinions count, and where their judgment is trusted.

Surveys also show that it is important for today's employees to be able to balance work and life activities. Employers are increasingly willing to accommodate these wishes because employee commitment and retention rise when a company recognizes that employees have a life outside work. If a company does nothing to help employees balance work and life concerns, and if it simply assumes that people are going to be totally devoted to the company, the bottom line is negatively affected because of the stress employees will experience.

A *Canada @ Work* study done by Aon Consulting found that when employers recognize employee needs outside the workplace, the company's employees are more likely to stay with the company and are more likely to recommend the company as a good place to work. Overall, companies need to have a "people-first" attitude about their employees.

Flexible work arrangements such as job sharing, flextime, compressed workweeks, and work-at-home opportunities are examples of "people-first" attitudes. Consider the case of Nicole Black, who returned to her job at the Royal Bank three months after having her first child. She quickly found that she didn't have as much time with her new baby as she wanted. As a result, the bank arranged for a compressed workweek so she could work four days per week. When she became pregnant a second time, she reduced her work hours even further and started job sharing with another employee. She now works only on Mondays and Tuesdays.

A study by Hewitt Associates showed that companies that are recognized on lists such as "The 100 Best Companies to Work For" have almost twice the number of job applications and half the annual turnover as non-ranked companies. A study by the Gallup Organization showed that there was a strong correlation between employee satisfaction and company profitability.

Questions

1. What is the difference between job satisfaction and morale? How do employee perks affect each of these concepts?

2. What do the various motivation factors discussed in this chapter say about the impact on employee satisfaction and motivation of things such as job sharing, compressed workweeks, and flextime?

3. What are the various managerial styles that managers can use? What do the employee perks mentioned above imply about the most effective managerial style?

4. What strategies are available to managers to enhance employee job satisfaction? How are strategies such as compressed workweeks, job sharing, and flextime different from participative management and job enrichment?

5. Are there any potential problems with a company implementing the perks mentioned above? If so, what are they?

JetBlue: Keeping the Troops Happy

One reason JetBlue's costs are low is that it doesn't have labour unions. It can, therefore, "require higher productivity from its 2100 employees while paying them lower wages than unionized airlines."[79]

However, employees are not foolish; they know when they're working harder than their colleagues at other airlines for about the same pay. Yet without that higher productivity, JetBlue would not be as competitive. The question is, "How does JetBlue keep morale and motivation up so that its workers are willing to work harder for the same or less pay?"

JetBlue accomplishes this in several ways. One is by providing very flexible working conditions. For example, its staff of 350 or so reservation agents work from special mini-call-centres in their homes, and so they needn't travel to work.[80] JetBlue also lets its flight attendants decide how many hours they want to work. For example, they have some flight attendants on traditional schedules and some on a more flexible college student flight attendant program. The JetBlue Friend's Crew Program is another example. In this program, JetBlue hires people to share a schedule.[81] Thus, two friends might share one flight attendant's schedule and decide between themselves who flies when.

JetBlue also has several pay and benefits programs aimed at keeping morale and motivation high. Its new, high-tech planes and new systems mean JetBlue can fly with fewer employees per plane. That means pay at JetBlue is quite competitive. Furthermore, JetBlue employees like the company's profit-sharing plan. Asked how the company's profit-sharing plan increases employees productivity, CEO David Neeleman gave the following answer: "One day in December, there were a lot of cancellations in the New York City area, and we operated our flights deep into the night, but we got them all done. I got email from employees who picked up passengers off cancelled flights from all these other carriers from LaGuardia, and they wrote 'profit sharing' in big bold letters."[82]

JetBlue also keeps some employee benefits higher than those at other airlines. For example, rather than wait until a new employee has completed his or her 90-day probationary period, he or she starts getting benefits almost at once. Similarly, whereas most airlines don't pay for new employees benefits (such as hotel expenses) while they're being trained, JetBlue pays them during training.

For much of this, JetBlue can probably thank Ann Rhoades. They hired her as the HR chief from Southwest Airlines, which has a reputation for high morale. However, in that regard, a recent news item might raise some concern for JetBlue's management. Recently, Southwest Airlines has been running into some unexpected turbulence with regard to its employee relations. Its mechanics want a federal mediator to help settle a two-year contract battle. Its flight attendants and reservations agents are demanding new contracts. Ground workers sued the airline because of how Southwest is disciplining its employees. And its pilots were reluctantly voting on a Southwest contract offer that their own pilot union leaders said was insufficient.[83] Since Southwest is, in many respects, the model that David Neeleman used in creating JetBlue, Southwest's recent employee turbulence may be a warning sign. As one writer noted, "Neeleman obsesses over keeping employees happy, and with good reason. Airline watchers say JetBlue's ability to stay union free is critical to its survival as a low-cost carrier."[84] Analysts seem to agree that JetBlue's managers know what it takes to keep employees happy. The question is "Can they do what's necessary to avoid the sorts of problems that Southwest seems to be running into?"

Assignment

You and your team are consultants to Mr. Neeleman, who is depending on your management expertise to help navigate the launch and management of JetBlue. Here's what he wants to know from you:

1. What are the pros and cons of the JetBlue profit-sharing incentive plan? Are there any changes you would recommend?

2. Assume that a consultant has recommended to JetBlue that, if it wants to keep its labour costs down, it should use job enrichment, either for its pilots, mechanics, or flight attendants. Do you agree that JetBlue can substitute "job enrichment" for "pay"—in other words, make the job itself so motivating that people will willingly work hard even if the pay is not as good as it might be at another

airline? Next, choose the pilots', mechanics', or flight attendants' jobs. Ascertain (from what you know about such jobs) if the job is amenable to job enrichment, and explain in detail how you would enrich it.

3. David Neeleman and his managerial colleagues work very hard to make sure they hire sociable, friendly people to be JetBlue employees, because they want to make sure JetBlue's customer service remains among the best in the industry. Assume that you want to develop a behaviour management program for flight attendants. You want to focus on improving "customer service." Define the specific activity you will use to measure customer service, and then develop a behaviour management program for this activity for the flight attendants.

Improving Communication Skills

Store Walking at Home Depot

Home Depot, one of the best known "big box" retailers, operates more than 1500 stores in Canada, the United States, and Puerto Rico. The company employs 300 000 people and its annual sales revenue exceeds $58 billion. Co-founders Bernie Marcus and Arthur Blank (who are no longer with the company) believed that poor communication between managers and employees could sink a company, so they developed a technique—called the store walk—to make sure that managers heard what they needed to hear from employees.

As the term implies, the store walk involves senior store support managers and district managers in a literal walk through Home Depot stores so they can see first-hand what merchandise is being offered, why it is being offered, how it is priced, and what the company expects from the manufacturers who supply the products. After a store walk is completed, the senior manager fields questions from district managers. At these meetings, managers are given "immunity," meaning that they can ask blunt or potentially offensive questions without fear of reprisal. By the time these meetings are over, managers have received clear and direct answers to their questions, and they feel more secure about what they are doing. These meetings also help Home Depot to merchandise products that customers really want, because the local managers know customer needs better than head office managers do.

As part of the store walk, district managers meet with store associates without the store manager being present. The communication that goes on in these meetings can be very interesting. At one Canadian store where an employee stock ownership program (ESOP) had just been introduced, district managers discovered to their dismay that associates didn't know how to participate in the program because no one had explained it to them.

Unannounced store visits are also part of the program to improve communication within Home Depot. These unannounced visits can be made by head office managers or by district managers who walk the aisles, look at how the merchandise is displayed, and

OBJECTIVES

After studying this chapter and the case exercises at the end, you should be able to use the material to:

1. Identify the communications barriers that a manager seems to be ignoring.

2. List and explain the things a manager can do to improve his or her interpersonal communications.

3. Conduct an effective appraisal interview using the facts and roles in a scenario.

4. Persuade a colleague to carry out the task outlined in the scenario.

5. Explain why a manager is not getting good results when trying to encourage upward feedback.

Home Depot
www.homedepot.com

Georgia Pacific
www.gp.com

listen in on conversations between store employees and customers. These activities keep district managers and head office personnel "close to the customer." District managers also conduct announced visits during which they put on orange aprons and wait on customers. They do this to model the proper behaviour for store employees (called associates). This activity effectively flattens the management pyramid and facilitates communication from the very top of the organization to its very bottom.

Home Depot is also using the latest communications technology to communicate more effectively with its suppliers and customers, with the aim of improving everyone's performance. There is nothing unusual about an employee pulling up to a local Home Depot store and using a keypad to log on to a mobile cart that will track and transmit his or her progress as the employee helps shoppers throughout the store's lumberyard. But what is unusual is that this particular employee doesn't work for Home Depot, but for one of its large suppliers.

It's all part of a trial program. Home Depot and Georgia-Pacific want to see whether working together like this can improve their sales and profit performance. This particular program will let Home Depot and Georgia-Pacific compare information from the employee's timecards with data regarding sales and inventory. The firms want to see if this provides insights about what each firm can do to reduce inventories and boost sales in Home Depot's lumber departments.

Just about everything managers do requires communication skills. Studies of managers' communication patterns show that a large amount of time is spent on oral and written communication. An early study by Henry Mintzberg of McGill University showed that CEOs spent 78 percent of their time in oral communication.[1] This took place in situations like scheduled and unscheduled meetings, plant tours, and telephone conversations. A more recent study by other researchers showed that CEOs spent 74 percent of their time in oral communication.[2] In both of these studies, executives spent about half of their time with subordinates and the other half with peers, the board of directors, and people outside the company.

One study of supervisors in a DuPont laboratory found they spent 53 percent of their time in meetings, 5 percent reading and writing, and 9 percent on the phone.[3] Another found that, including meetings, interacting with customers and colleagues, and other ways in which communication takes place, managers spent 60 percent to 80 percent of their time communicating.[4] Communications is also important for employees' peace of mind. One study concluded, for instance that "communication with one's superior was a significant predictor of job satisfaction, irrespective of job level."[5] You simply can't manage or lead if you can't communicate. We'll therefore turn now to communicating and in particular to how to build your communications skills.

The Process of Communications

A man drove up to a gasoline pump to fill his tank. The gas station attendant noticed three penguins in the back seat of the car and, curious, asked about them. "I don't know how they got there," the driver said. "The penguins were there when I took the car out of the garage this morning." The attendant thought for a moment. "Why don't you take them to the zoo?" "Good idea," the driver said, and drove away. The next day, the same man returned to the station. In the back seat were the same three penguins, but now they wore sunglasses. The attendant looked at them in surprise. "I thought you took them to the zoo!" he said. "I did," the driver said, "and they had such a good time that now I'm taking them to the beach."

What Every Manager Should Know About Communicating

"Communication" derives from the Latin verb *communicare*, which means "to make common."[6] How you "communicate"—whether by talking, writing letters, sending emails, or giving lectures—is beside the point. Those are just means to an end and not the heart of what communicating is all about. You are not necessarily communicating when you're telling someone something. You're just conveying information, which may or may not be heard, or understood, or accepted in the way you intend. **Communication** means exchanging information in such a way that you create a common basis of understanding and feeling. The purpose of this chapter is to show you how to do that.

communication
Exchanging information in such a way that you create a common basis of understanding and feeling.

A Model of the Communication Process

What one person says is not always what the other person hears. As you already know from your own experiences, many things—misunderstandings, semantics, or even fear—can distort the meaning of what people think you're trying to say.[7] Barriers like these, left unaddressed, can ruin your management career. They will cripple even your simplest supervisory tasks, such as giving instructions and setting goals, and will make motivating and coaching your employees very difficult.

To better understand how these problems arise, it will help to walk through the **communication process** shown in Figure 13.1. As you can see, the communication process includes five main components, and problems (noise) can arise in any one.[8] Assume you're about to give your subordinate his semi-annual appraisal interview. Where might communication problems arise?

communication process
The series of events that takes place to transfer meaning.

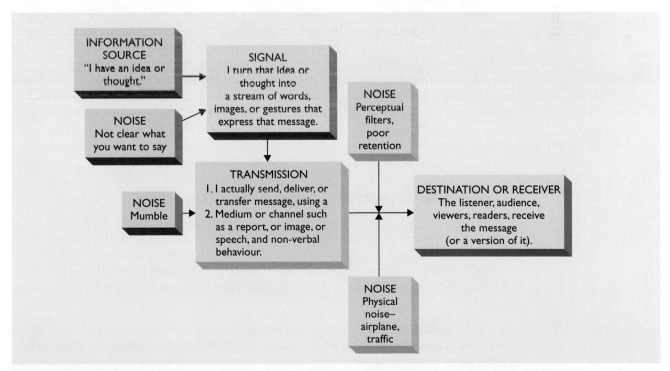

FIGURE 13.1
The Communication Process

The Information Source The **information source** is the message, idea, thought, or fact that you want to communicate. In this case, assume that you have a subordinate (let's call him "Joe") who has not performed well. The basic thought you want to get across to him is this: "Your performance this past six months has been well below par, and if it doesn't improve by the end of the year we're going to have to let you go."

The Signal The **signal** is the stream of words, images, or gestures you use to actually express the message. The signal is what you actually say to Joe when you meet with him, as well as the gestures you use to help communicate your point.

The Transmission Channel or Medium The day of the appraisal interview arrives, and you sit down with Joe. The transmission is the act of actually sending, delivering, or transferring the message to Joe, which you do using a medium or channel, such as a report, speech, TV image, or (in this case) a one-on-one interview.

The Destination or Receiver The destination or **receiver** is the audience, listener, reader, or viewer that you're actually aiming your message at—in this case Joe. The receiver may interact face-to-face with the sender (for example, when a salesperson from the Great Canadian Travel Company tells a customer about a tour package to the Caribbean), or the sender may not be able to see the receiver (for example, when a Canadian Tire television advertisement is aired across Canada).

The Noise Noise is anything that blocks, distorts, or in any way changes the information source (the idea, thought, or fact that you originally started out to communicate) as it makes its way to the destination/receiver. As you can see, noise can arise at each step in the communication process.

Let's assume for the moment that the appraisal interview does not go well. The signal—the stream of words, images, or gestures—that you used to express your message turned out to be muddled. Hoping to set the stage for a positive outcome, you made the mistake of opening the meeting by talking about the local football team's recruiting problems. You sent a mixed signal. Joe, having waited with trepidation for this meeting for two weeks, starts getting agitated and drumming his fingers on the table. The more agitated he gets, the more uptight you get. You're soon mumbling and looking down at your feet.

Annoyed with yourself, you finally make your point (while still looking down) by saying, "Joe, your performance this past six months has been well below par, and if you don't improve by the end of the year we're going to have to let you go." At this point Joe is probably hearing only 10 percent of what you're saying. He hears "... have to let you go" and starts arguing that you can't fire him without warning, especially since he's had such good performance, and besides, his mother is ill. You have not delivered your message, he's missed your point, you're both agitated, and a "common basis of understanding and feeling" has certainly not occurred. There is little likelihood that this meeting will jump-start Joe's performance.

Barriers to Effective Communication

Essentially what you have done is ignored several potential noise/problems/barriers at each step of the communications process. But the situation with Joe did not have to turn out so badly. You could have had a much more productive meeting by (1) keeping the goal of "creating a common basis for understanding and feeling" in mind, and (2) by anticipating the communication problems that could arise.[9] These potential barriers include the following.[10]

Ambiguous, Muddled Messages "Say what you mean, and mean what you say," one expert advises, and that is good advice indeed. Few things cause communications breakdowns more often then ambiguous, muddled messages. *Ambiguity of meaning* causes the person receiving the message to be unsure as to what the person who sent it meant. (Does "We're going to have to let you go" mean immediately or next year?) *Ambiguity of intent* means the words may be clear, but the sender's intentions aren't. ("This is an appraisal interview; why is he talking to me about the football team?") *Ambiguity of effect* means the receiver is uncertain about what the message's consequences might be. (" Is he actually going to fire me?") In any case, the solution is to formulate and send a clear, unambiguous message.

Semantics Words mean different things to different people. The gas station attendant said to "take the penguins to the zoo" but didn't mean as tourists. Telling a hospital administrator that she has "scabs" in her hospital may mean a sign of recuperation to her, but something different to the head of the local union.

Physical Barriers Physical barriers range from obvious to subtle. Street noise, frequent interruptions, and the clattering of machines are obvious distractions. Indecipherable writing and tiny print font are less obvious sources of noise. Even discomfort is a source of noise. A recent ad for a desk chair says, "Think of what your brain could be accomplishing now, if it didn't have to worry about your back."

Loss of Transmission Everyone with satellite TV is familiar with this problem, but "loss of transmission" along the line is not limited to bad weather or cables and wires. People rarely relay messages without subtracting from (or adding to) them in some way. You therefore cannot assume that the message you send will be exactly the one that reaches the destination.

Failing to Communicate Problems like those above assume that you've taken the time to send a message, but failing to communicate at all is a problem in itself. For example, the manager may just assume that "everyone knows" and not follow up by sending a message.

Competition Barriers As professors know, the person you're speaking to is not "yours" alone. The students in the lecture hall may have matters they want to discuss with each other; the employee you're appraising may be preoccupied with a sick mother, and that email you send may simply get lost among two dozen messages your manager has to deal with that day. Many other things are competing for your audience's time and attention. It's therefore usually a mistake to assume that you've got the person's full attention.

Cultural, Linguistic, and Diversity Barriers There is always the potential for a "Tower of Babel" effect in today's diverse and globalized organizations. Words and gestures often mean different things to different ethnic and cultural groups. A survey of managers from 15 countries helps highlight this problem. The managers mentioned "lack of cultural understanding" as the biggest challenge in communicating with people around the world. Other challenges (in order) were "being thorough and very careful with interpretations, careful audience research, keeping communication simple, respecting everyone, using technology as an asset, knowing similarities as well as differences," and "teaching the value of a globally accepted language."[11]

Consider these examples of how cultural and ethnic diversity can impact communications:

- In Canada, winking communicates friendship, but it is considered rude in Australia, Hong Kong, and Malaysia.
- Raising an eyebrow in Tonga means "I agree," but in Peru it means "pay me."
- Circling your ear with your finger means "crazy" in most European countries, but in the Netherlands it means "you have a phone call."
- Waving at someone is a sign of recognition in Canada, but it is considered a severe insult in Nigeria.
- Nodding your head means "yes" in Canada and the United States, but it means "no" in Bulgaria and Sri Lanka. In Turkey,

In Canada, giving a person the "thumbs up" signal is a sign that things are going well; in Bangladesh, it is considered rude.

people say "no" by shutting their eyes, raising their chin, and throwing their head back.

- Slapping a person on the back is inappropriate in Japan because touching is viewed as unacceptable.

Psychological Barriers In addition to these barriers, psychology also plays a role in whether what one person says is the same as what another person hears. Psychological barriers include perception, experiences, emotions, and defences.

Perception

Misperceptions create havoc with communications. This is because (as explained in the previous chapter) people's needs and situations shape how they see things. If you're concerned about losing your job, you may be jumpy if your boss schedules a meeting with you.

Perception problems manifest themselves in several ways. There is the selectivity/exposure filter where you block out unpleasant things that you don't want to hear, or "hear" things that may not have been said. Thus, after buying a new car, people tend to screen out negative data about the car and to be more aware of good news about it. There's also the retention filter: You remember things that feel good, and tend to forget those that are painful.

Experiential Barriers

Similarly, peoples' experiences affect what they hear. For example, most people find it more difficult to understand things they haven't experienced themselves. So, convincing employees who've never been injured at work that it's important to work safely may fall on deaf ears. The converse is that people find it easier to understand things that they can identify with personally. Explaining your point in personal terms can thus improve understanding. The director of one large research lab wanted to make the point to his firm's board of directors that managing research scientists was no easy matter. He made his point by saying that managing the lab "is like trying to herd cats." Although most of the board members had never experienced the difficulties of managing research scientists, they could identify with the difficulty of getting two dozen screaming and independent-minded cats all going in the same direction.

Emotions

Your emotions influence what you say and how you hear things. An angry or frustrated person (like your employee Joe) may be dismissive of even the most persuasive argument, while someone in a good mood may be easily persuaded.

Defensiveness

Defences are adjustments that people make, often without thinking, to avoid acknowledging personal inadequacies that might reduce their self-esteem. Accuse someone of poor performance, and his or her first reaction may well be denial. Denial is a defence mechanism. By denying fault, the person avoids having to question or analyze his or her own competence. People who react this way aren't ignoring what you said. They're simply reacting to it in a way that protects their self esteem. What they are hearing is as real to them as what you're saying is to you.[12]

Non-verbal Communication

You have heard the phrase, "It's not what you say, but how you say it." It has been estimated that in a conversation involving two people, verbal aspects of a message account for less than 5 percent of the meaning, whereas non-verbal aspects of a message account for 95 percent of the meaning."[13] In other words (to use our terms), the channel or medium you use to make your point is not always just the one you consciously choose. People also draw conclusions about who you are and what you mean from your manner of speaking, facial expressions, bodily posture, and so on—in other words, from your non-verbal communication. Here's how an expert interprets some common non-verbal behaviours:

1. Scratching your head indicates confusion or disbelief.

2. Biting your lips signals anxiety.

3. Rubbing the back of your head or neck suggests frustration, impatience.

4. A lowered chin conveys defensiveness or insecurity.

5. Avoiding eye contact conveys insincerity, fear, evasiveness, or (at the very least) lack of interest on what's being discussed.

6. A steady stare suggests a need to control, intimidate, and dominate.

7. Crossing your arms in front of your chest communicates defiance, defensiveness, resistance, aggressiveness, or a closed mind.

8. Hand wringing is a strong sign of anxiety verging on terror.

9. In North America, getting a limp, dead-fish handshake is almost a disappointment.[14]

The non-verbal aspects of communication complicate the task of communicating internationally.[15] For example, a sales manager in Vancouver might email an unsolicited sales pitch to a potential customer in Taiwan and be surprised when the person ignores the message. Yet, to the Taiwanese, ignoring such a message is quite understandable. In Canada, the United States, and northern Europe, the verbal content of a message tends to be more important than the setting in which the message is delivered. In these "low-context" cultures, an email is often accepted as an efficient substitute for an in-person meeting.[16] But in many "high-context" countries, including many in Asia and the Middle East, the context (with its non-verbal cues) can convey far more meaning than the literal words of a given message. Business transactions tend to be ritualistic, and the ritual is all-important. There's more emphasis on face-to-face interaction and on after-hours socializing. You can see why the Vancouver sales manager's efforts failed: The email lacked the non-verbal content and nuances that are so important in doing business in Asia.

Improving Interpersonal Communications

Tasks that require interpersonal communications fill the manager's day. The supervisor disciplines an employee because he broke a rule, shows a new employee how to improve her performance, and tries to convince production to get an order out early. Barriers like ambiguity and defensiveness can cripple a manager's efforts to be understood—and thus the ability to lead.

Methods for Improving Interpersonal Communications

Pay Attention Communication means exchanging information in such a way that you create a common basis of understanding and feeling. You are unlikely to create such a common understanding if you don't make it clear that the person you're communicating with has your full and undivided attention.

Make Yourself Clear Say what you mean and mean what you say. If you mean "immediately," say "immediately," not "as soon as you can." If you are doing an employee appraisal, don't muddy the waters by prefacing your remarks with something irrelevant. Also make sure your tone, expression, and words convey a consistent meaning. Table 13.1 provides guidelines for written and oral work.

Be an Active Listener Communications pioneer Carl Rogers says "active listeners" don't just listen to what the speaker says; they also try to understand and respond to the feelings behind the words.[17] They try to understand the person's point of view and to convey the message that they do understand. Checklist 13.1 presents guidelines for honing your active listening skills.

TABLE 13.1 Guidelines for Written and Oral Work

WRITTEN WORK	ORAL PRESENTATIONS
1. *Make sense.* Express your ideas in a coherent, orderly way.	1. *Speak up.*
2. *Back up your assertions.* Consider the use of examples, anecdotes, citation of authorities, statistics, and other forms of support.	2. *Achieve rapport quickly.* Use the first few moments to orient audience members and show them that you feel comfortable with them.
3. *Write for your audience.* Select language, length, arguments, and evidence that suit your audience.	3. *Look at your listeners.*
4. *Edit and revise.* Eliminate deadwood, provide transitions between ideas, and repair every error in grammar and spelling.	4. *Use gestures to express your ideas.*
5. *Format for readability.* Use word-processing software to create easy-to-read, attractive documents.	5. *Move freely, without pacing.* Use the available space to move naturally.
6. *Write to express, not to impress.* Get to the point.	6. *Use notes (if necessary) as unobtrusively as possible.* Notes function best as "thought triggers."
7. *Prefer common language to difficult verbiage.* Mark Twain vowed "never to write 'metropolis' when I get paid the same for writing 'city.'"	7. *Highlight key ideas.* Use voice volume, pauses, graphic aides, and "headlining" (telling listeners that a point is particularly important) to emphasize key points.
8. *Give credit to your sources.* Ideas, sentences, phrases, and terms that aren't your own must be footnoted.	8. *Channel nervous energy into an enthusiastic delivery.*
9. *Use graphic aids where necessary to capture and highlight ideas.*	9. *Watch your audience for signs of comprehension or misunderstanding.*
10. *Write with energy and conviction.*	10. *End with a bang, not a whimper.* Your concluding words should be memorable.

Don't Attack the Person's Defences Criticizing, arguing, even giving advice can trigger defensiveness, as the other person tries to protect his or her self-image. For example, don't say things like, "You know the reason you're using that excuse is that you can't bear to be blamed for anything." Instead, focus your comments on the act itself ("production levels are too low"). Sometimes it's best to do nothing—postpone action until you both cool down.

Get Feedback It's no coincidence that where life hangs in the balance, feedback is mandatory. In situations like these, communications breakdowns are simply unacceptable. Thus, the operating room nurse repeats "scalpel" when the surgeon says "scalpel." The co-pilot says "wheels down" when the pilot orders "wheels down." However, getting feedback is obviously not limited to life-and-death situations. Asking the person to repeat his or her understanding of your point is always a straightforward way to confirm their understanding of what you said.

How to Be More Persuasive

Many management tasks involve persuading others. The coach who wants to motivate her team, the director who wants to sell his plan to the board, the supervisor who wants a new computer, and the manager who wants to improve employee productivity all need to be persuasive. This is especially true today, when leaders rely more on persuasion than on giving orders. Many managers underestimate the power of and need for persuasive skills in their day-to-day managing. Persuasion is often seen as something that is important only when selling products or closing deals. But managers need to be persuasive in many different situations.

Research provides some insights into what persuasion is and how you can become more persuasive. Persuasion works "by appealing to a limited set of deeply rooted human drives and needs, and it does so in predictable ways. Persuasion, in other words, is governed by basic principles that can be taught, learn, and applied."[18] Most people make several avoidable mistakes when trying to persuade others. These mistakes are as follows:[19]

1. *They attempt to make their case using a "hard sell."* They assume that the way to make a sale is by overwhelming the other party with a barrage of ideas, facts, and figures. This is more often a turn-off and motivates the person you're trying to persuade to resist what you are saying.

2. *They resist compromise.* Persuasion should be a two-way street. By failing to compromise, the manager sends the signal that he or she is not interested in reaching a common basis of understanding.

3. *They think the secret of persuasion lies in presenting great arguments.* Great arguments are important, but they're not everything. The person's credibility, the way in which the proposal is made, and whether the terms satisfy the recipient are all important factors in persuasion.

4. *They assume persuasion is a one-shot effort.* Persuasion is a process, one in which ideas are floated, positions are tested, and new, more "saleable" positions arrived at incrementally.

HERMAN®   by Jim Unger

9-17   © Jim Unger/dist. by United Media, 1999

"Is that your final answer?"

CHECKLIST **13.2**

How to Be More Persuasive

☑ *Establish your credibility.* You probably wouldn't buy an insurance policy from someone you didn't trust. Similarly, it is difficult or impossible to persuade your superiors, colleagues, or subordinates of the wisdom of your recommendation if they think you don't know what you're talking about, or (even worse), don't trust you. Therefore, marshal the facts before you try to persuade someone of something. Learn about the complexities of your position through formal or informal education and conversations with knowledgeable people. If necessary, hire someone, like a consultant, to bolster your expertise. Make a concerted effort to meet one on one with the key people you want to persuade. Finally, take those long-term steps that are required to make sure that your colleagues view you as a person of integrity.

☑ *Frame for common ground.* Communication means arriving at a common understanding, and doing so is particularly important when persuasion is involved. The people you are trying to persuade may not be interested in what you're interested in, but you can be sure they are interested in something. Therefore, you need to find out what that is and then frame your argument in terms that make sense to the person you're trying to persuade.

☑ *Connect emotionally.* A recent ad for a Mitsubishi automobile shows four twenty-something people gliding through a tunnel in their new Mitsubishi, listening to and miming rock lyrics, with the music in the background. Like most ads, this one aims to persuade by connecting emotionally with its audience. Facts, figures, and evidence are certainly important in persuasion, but they're generally of little use if you can't connect emotionally with the interests of the people you're trying to persuade. As in the Mitsubishi ad, couch your presentation in terms that will resonate emotionally with the person you're speaking with.

☑ *Provide evidence.* Once you've established your credibility and framed the opportunities in common terms, "persuasion becomes a matter of presenting evidence."[20] This does not mean overwhelming the person with reams of data. The most effective persuaders supplement numerical data with examples, stories, metaphors, and analogies to make their positions come alive.

☑ *Expose your expertise.* Don't assume it's self-evident. People defer to experts, but don't assume the person or people you're trying to persuade know you're an expert. If they do know, fine. However, if they don't, make it clear that you are an expert and from where your expertise derives.

☑ *Use peer power whenever it's available.* It's easier to persuade someone to do something if you can convince them that others whom they identify with have already done something similar. For example, when researchers went door-to-door soliciting charity donations, they found that displaying a list of neighbours who had already donated substantially helped their cause.[21]

☑ *Have the person make his or her commitment active, public, and voluntary.* As we saw when we discussed goal setting, people align their actions with their commitments. Therefore, having the person make their commitment actively, publicly and voluntarily helps cement their positions.

How to Improve Your Negotiating Skills

Much of what you do can be considered a negotiation. Whether you're buying a car, requesting a raise, asking for a better seat on a plane, or trying to get employees to improve their performance, negotiations are involved. During negotiations, people typically make several big mistakes:[22]

1. *Neglecting the other side's problems.* Like other forms of communication, negotiations usually go best when they aim to achieve a common basis of understanding. However, doing so is not likely if each party is concerned only with its own problems.

2. *Letting price overwhelm other interests.* Some negotiators let the negotiations fall apart over price, when discussing the deal's other terms might have saved the day. For example, a higher price for the new computer system may look less forbidding if the computer maker will finance the purchase.

3. *Searching too hard for common ground.* Sometimes the best way to proceed is to accept that the parties have different agendas. Then, instead of trying to find a common ground (like a price that will satisfy both parties), structure a deal that takes into account these differences. For example, the potential buyer for a small company wants to do the deal but is much less optimistic about the firm's future prospects than is the firm's current owner. Significant differences of opinion thus exist regarding the business's potential. The solution here might take advantage of the parties' differences. For example, negotiate a deal whereby an initial payment is followed by a series of payments contingent on the performance of the business.

4. *Neglecting "BANTRAs."* Some people get so caught up in negotiating a deal that they forget their "Best Alternative to a Negotiated Agreement." In their book *Getting To Yes*, Robert Fisher, Bill Ury, and Bruce Patton stress the importance of knowing your BANTRA. Remember that your best alternative may not be doing the deal, but walking away, approaching another buyer, or making the product in-house. The point is, don't become so wrapped up in negotiating the deal that you forget about your best alternative to a negotiated agreement.

5. *Negotiating tactics.* Experienced negotiators use several tactics to improve their bargaining positions. Leverage refers to the factors that either help or hinder a party in a bargaining situation; you want all the leverage you can muster, of course.[23] Necessity, desire, competition, and time are leveraging factors. The seller who must sell (of necessity) is at a disadvantage. The ability to walk away from a deal (or to look as if you can) wins a negotiator the best terms. That is one reason that having an offer of another job is so persuasive when you're negotiating for a raise. Similarly, the new car may not be a necessity, but if your desire is too obvious, it will undercut your bargaining power. Competition is important, too. There is no more convincing ploy than telling the other party that someone else wants to make the deal. Time (and particularly deadlines) can also tilt the tables, for or against you. This depends on your apparent desire to make the deal.

6. *In negotiations, "knowledge is power."* Going into the negotiation armed with information about the other side and about the situation puts you at a relative advantage (of course, the opposite is also true). Credibility is important. The other side will be trying to decide whether you're bluffing, so convincing them otherwise is an important negotiating skill. Good negotiators also use good judgment. They have "the ability to strike the right balance between gaining advantages and reaching compromises, in the substance as well as in the style of [their] negotiating technique."[24]

Improving Organizational Communications

Organizational communication means exchanging information in such a way that you create a common basis of understanding and feeling among two or more individuals or groups throughout the organization. *Downward communications* go from superior to subordinate and involve issues such as what a job entails, where the firm is heading, and what the firm's required procedures and practices are. *Lateral (horizontal) communications* move between departments or between people in the same department. *Upward communication* (from subordinates to superiors) provides management with insights into the company and its employees and competitors.

organizational communication
Exchanging information in such a way that you create a common basis of understanding and feeling among two or more individuals or groups throughout the organization.

Special Barriers to Organizational Communications

Since people are usually involved, interpersonal barriers like ambiguities, semantics, and perception also affect organizational communication. In addition, however, the nature of organizations means that communications also suffer from some special, organizational communications barriers. For example, managers need to contend with the authority, task, political, and identity boundaries that we discussed in Chapter 9. Thus, subordinates may act deferentially toward their bosses and withhold unwelcome information. Politicking can prompt departments to withhold information from each other as they jockey for power, although the company itself might suffer.

Similarly the organizational cultures of some firms encourage communications better than do others. Even in college and university, some professors set a tone that encourages students to participate, while others prefer a more formal, teacher-oriented arrangement. Differences like these stem from the values the leader projects and sets. Dan Hunt of Nortel Networks uses a monthly videoconference talk show to encourage lower-level employees to speak their minds. He encourages all employees to communicate quickly, openly, and with candour.

We've also seen that some firms have organization structures that are more decentralized and "open" to free-flowing communications than are others. Thus, we saw (in Chapters 8, 9, and 10) that managers create boundaryless organizations to encourage employees to communicate easily and freely with colleagues vertically and laterally throughout the chain of command.

The presence of interpersonal, boundary, cultural, and structural organizational communications barriers means managers need to take some special steps to improve organizational communications in their firms. This means improving upward, downward, lateral, and organization-wide communications flows.

Improving Upward Communication

Encouraging upward communication provides the following benefits:

- It helps management ascertain whether subordinates understand orders and instructions.
- It encourages subordinates to volunteer ideas.
- It provides management with valuable input on which to base decisions.[25]
- It encourages gripes and grievances to surface.[26]
- It cultivates acceptance and commitment by giving employees an opportunity to express ideas and suggestions.[27]
- It helps employees cope with their work problems and strengthens their involvement in their jobs and with the organization.[28]
- It enables managers to see how subordinates feel about their jobs, their superiors, and the organization.

At Imperial Oil, employees were asked to view a planned merger with Texaco Canada as an advantage because the new organization would have more opportunities for promotion. Employees filled out a questionnaire that asked them to indicate what positions they wanted in the new organization. Seventy-nine percent got their first choice, and 93 percent got one of their top three choices.[29]

Robert Glegg, president of Glegg Water Conditioning Inc., lunches regularly with small groups of employees to exchange ideas about projects, people, and problems. In one of these sessions, he heard objections from engineers about a proposed open-office concept and as a result changed the plans to satisfy their needs.[30] At Air Canada, the internal website was used to invite employees to give their opinions about how to improve customer service. One employee suggested that airport employees should use the customer's name at least three times when checking them in for a flight.[31]

Getting upward feedback is more difficult than one might imagine. Some subordinates aren't eager to share bad news with their supervisors, so there's a tendency for bad news to stay under wraps. The common sense solution here is to make sure that bringing bad news does not turn out to be a negative experience for the employee. Don't be defensive, blame others, make excuses, or overreact. Don't "shoot the messenger." Be discreet about your sources of information when you can. Be accessible and approachable. Figure 13.2 summarizes these and other common sense prescriptions. As one expert says, "By far the most effective way of tapping the ideas of subordinates is sympathetic listening in the many day-to-day, informal contacts within the department and outside the workplace."[32]

Other effective methods for fostering upward communication include the following:

1. Social gatherings (including departmental parties, picnics, and recreational events) provide opportunities for informal, casual communication.

2. Union publications can provide useful insights into employee attitudes.

3. Some supervisors schedule formal monthly meetings with their subordinates, in addition to the informal contacts that take place every day.

4. Performance appraisal meetings are good opportunities to seek employees' opinions about their jobs and job attitudes.

5. Grievances provide top management with insights into operational problems.

6. Attitude surveys provide answers to (and help management address) questions like, "Are working hours and shift rotations perceived as reasonable? Do employees feel the boss has favourites?" and "Do employees consider cafeteria prices fair and the quality of the food good?"

7. A suggestion system, even a suggestion box, can encourage upward communication. Figure 13.3 shows one firm's suggestion program.

8. An "open door" policy lets employees express concerns through a channel outside the normal chain of command and can thus act as a safety valve.

9. Indirect measures, including absences, turnover rates, and safety records, are useful indicators of festering problems at the operational level.

Techniques such as suggestion plans can sometimes lead to surprising solutions. For example, the Northern Ireland electric company has about 15 acres of grassy area under the overhead transmission lines that it uses for training its employees. This land has to be mowed and maintained on a regular basis, which is no easy chore given the metal and nuts and bolts that get sprinkled around it.[33] How do you keep those acres mowed? The firm's suggestion program came up with an idea so simple and so obvious that it took top management by surprise. An employee suggested using sheep to graze the land and to keep it neat. The idea at first seemed unusual, however, it has so far saved the company almost U.S.$100 000 over five years.

- Request feedback from people whom you trust and who will be honest with you.

- If the feedback is too general ("You're doing a fine job" or "There's room for improvement"), ask for examples of specific, recent behaviour.

- Don't be defensive, make excuses, or blame others when you hear criticism.

- Do not overreact or underreact to feedback.

- Once the feedback is complete, summarize what the speaker said to make sure that you understand.

- Explain what you are going to do in response to the feedback, do it, evaluate the consequences on performance, and then let the feedback-giver know of the outcome.

- Thank the person for his or her concern and advice.

FIGURE 13.2
Getting Upward Feedback

FIGURE 13.3
Sample Suggestion Program Procedures LearnInMotion.com

Toyota
www.toyota.com

Comprehensive Programs Many firms install formal, comprehensive programs to encourage employees to "speak up." For example, Toyota tells its employees, "Don't spend time worrying about something... Speak up!" The firm has what it refers to as "The Hotline." Employees can pick up any phone, dial the Hotline extension (the number is posted on the plant bulletin board), and deliver their messages to a recorder, 24 hours a day. Toyota guarantees that an HR manager will review and investigate all inquiries and that the process is anonymous. If it's decided that a question would be of interest to other Toyota team members, then the question, with the firm's response, is posted on plant bulletin boards. If the employee wants a personal response, he or she can leave a name.[34]

Upward Appraisals How would you like to appraise your supervisor? How (if at all) do you think knowing he or she will be appraised would influence the way the boss acted? A study sheds some light on this. Researchers collected subordinates' ratings for 238 managers in a large firm at two points in time, six months apart.[35] Subordinates were asked to rate a variety of supervisory behaviours, such as "Regularly challenged me to continuously improve my effectiveness," "Took steps to resolve conflict and disagreement within the team," and "Treated me fairly and with respect."[36]

The prospect of upward appraisals didn't seem to affect the performance of managers whose original appraisals were high; their ratings were about the same six months later. It was a different story with the managers whose initial appraisals were moderate or low. Six months later, their ratings jumped up. The researchers say "this is encouraging, because these are the managers that most need to improve from the organization's (as well as the subordinates') perspective."[37] Interestingly, it didn't seem to matter whether the managers actually got feedback in six months regarding how they were doing. They even improved with no feedback. It seemed that just knowing they'd be appraised was enough to get the bosses to improve their behaviour at work.

Communicating with Your Supervisor The last thing a manager needs is a misunderstanding with his or her own boss. Your boss wants results, expects you to contribute, and may not be an active listener. Therefore, avoid phrases that they may inadvertently signal a lack of responsibility on your part. These include "I'm only human, I'm overworked, It slipped past me, It's not my fault, It's not my problem," and "You don't appreciate me."[38] Similarly, avoid counterproductive body language. Non-verbal mannerisms to avoid include cringing, looking down, slouching in your chair, bringing your hands to your face, mouth, or neck (this suggests anxiety and evasion); and crossing your arms in front of your chest.

Improving Downward Communication

Downward communication includes a variety of essential types of information regarding, for instance, job instructions, rationales for jobs (including how jobs are related to other jobs and positions in the organization), organizational policies and practices, employee appraisal results, and the organization's mission.[39] Much of what happens in companies requires downward communications. Indeed, the whole mechanism of making companies work, including giving orders, training employees, and informing employees about policies and practices and the company's mission, fits under the rubric of "downward communication."[40]

Today's team-based, empowered companies are especially dependent on this type of information. Facilities like Toyota's Camry and GM's Saturn's plants are largely run by knowledgeable and empowered employees, ones who are aware of and committed to the company's vision and strategy. The employees, in essence, are more like partners and as such require more company information than they might in more conventional situations.

Firms like these therefore make heroic efforts to keep their employees informed. At Saturn Corporation, assemblers "get information continuously via the internal television network and from financial documents."[41] The firm also has monthly town-hall meetings, usually with 500 to 700 attendees. The result is that all employees are familiar with Saturn's activities and performance. At Toyota, a television set at each worksite runs continuously, presenting plant-wide information from the in-house Toyota Broadcasting Center. The company sponsors quarterly roundtable discussions between top management and selected non-supervisory staff, as well as an in-house newsletter. The plant's top managers are often on the shop floor fielding questions, providing plant performance information, and ensuring that all team members are "aware of Toyota's goal and where we are heading."[42]

Other firms have introduced *open-book management* programs. Open book management means literally opening the company's books to its employees. The firm shares its financial data, explains its numbers, and rewards workers for improvements in the firm's performance.[43] It is designed to motivate employees to focus on helping the business grow profitably and increasing the return on its human capital.[44] Open-book management fosters trust and commitment among employees by treating them more like partners than employees.

Manco, a manufacturer of industrial products, distributes its financial information to employees in three ways. Every month each department gets four books, designated by colour, with financial information broken down by company, department, product line, and customer. Monthly meetings are held so employees can see whether they're on track to earn their bonuses and what needs to be done to stay on track. Between meetings, management posts daily company-wide sales totals. Employees can take accounting classes to help them understand the numbers.[45]

Communicating with Subordinates There are several things to keep in mind when communicating directly with one or more of your employees. Fairness (and the appearance of fairness), is key. You don't want to undermine your authority by behaving unprofessionally. Do not go into "attack mode," as that will trigger defensiveness on the subordinate's part and bring a halt to constructive discussion. Words to avoid with subordinates include "blame, catastrophe, demand, destroyed, idiotic," and "misguided." Phrases to avoid include "better shape up, don't come to me about it, I don't want to hear it, figure it out for yourself, you don't understand," and "you'd better." In terms of body language, be open and receptive.[46] Maintain eye contact, smile, keep hands away from your face and mouth, use open-handed gestures, and (if you must achieve some subtle domination) direct your glance to the subordinate's forehead, rather than meeting his or her eyes directly.[47]

Toyota employees watch in-house programming during a break from working on the assembly line.

Improving Horizontal Communication

One sure route to managerial oblivion is to fail to get along with your colleagues. You depend on them for help to get your job done, and your career progress and day-to-day peace of mind usually depend, to some extent, on how you get along with your peers. Therefore, belligerent-sounding words like "absurd, bad, can't, crazy, doomed, unworkable," and "are you out of your mind?" are best left unsaid. Mannerisms to avoid include shaking your head no, avoiding eye contact, frowning, and pushing gestures (that is, using the hands as if to push people or things away).[48]

In terms of organizational design issues, we saw in Chapter 9 that managers improve horizontal (interdepartmental) communication in several ways. Review the discussion on abolishing organizational boundaries (pp. 272–274) for additional ideas on how to improve horizontal communication.

Improving Organization-Wide Communication

Many firms superimpose formal, informal, or electronic networks over their existing organizational structures. These essentially let managers from various departments, levels, and geographic areas form into multidisciplinary teams, whose members communicate directly, unencumbered by normal organizational boundaries. Others further encourage such free-flowing communications by stripping away authority, task, identity, and political boundaries that normally inhibit communications. And (recall the Burns and Stalker studies) some firms are more decentralized and thus "open" to free-flowing communications than are others.

Improving Informal Communications

A number of years ago, two consultants, Tom Peters and Robert Waterman, conducted a study of "excellent," highly innovative companies. Their aim was to discover what those firms were doing that caused them to be excellent. One of their more notable findings was that these firms put an enormous amount of effort into fostering informal, almost unorthodox means of communicating. In turn, this wealth of information seemed to enable these firms to be more innovative and responsive and to better manage change.[49] Peters and Waterman's findings regarding the techniques they used to encourage informal communication are worth noting. They found that "excellent" companies do the following things:

1. *They emphasize informality.* At Walt Disney Company, for instance, everyone from the president down wears a name tag with their first name on it. Employees wear these in the parks on a regular basis. At 3M, there are numerous meetings, most of which are characterized by the casual getting together of people from different disciplines who talk about problems in a campus-like, shirt-sleeves atmosphere.

2. *They maintain communication intensity at an extraordinary level.* Meetings and presentations are held at which "the questions are unabashed; the flow is free; everyone is involved; nobody hesitates to cut off the chairman, the president, or board members."[50] In other words, they encourage an open airing of ideas, in which people are blunt and straightforward in going after the issues. Meetings in these companies are not highly formal and politicized. Instead, they are open, informative discussions in which employees feel free to safely air their points of view.

3. *They provide physical support for informal communication.* In one high-tech firm, for instance, all employees from the president down work not in offices, but in 6-foot-high doorless cubicles that encourage openness and interaction among employees. Corning Glass installed escalators rather than elevators in its new engineering building to increase the chance of face-to-face contact.[51] Another firm got rid of its four-person dining room tables and replaced them with long rectangular ones that encourage strangers to come into contact. Blackboards and open

Corning
www.corning.com

offices facilitate and encourage frequent informal interaction. Managers are encouraged to get out of their offices, walk around, and strike up conversations with those both within and outside their departments.

Management by Wandering Around

As the term implies, **management by walking around** means that a manager literally walks around the workplace talking with subordinates to get a better idea of what they are doing in their jobs and the trials and triumphs they have had. As one executive put it, "Go visit the department heads—chat with them, ask them questions, learn what they do for a living. Ask them what is frustrating for them in their business process, and they will talk all day if you let them. You'll learn a great deal about how the cogs mesh..."[52]

For example, the CEO of Marriott Hotels logs more than 250 000 kilometres per year in plane travel, visiting his company's hotels, walking through their lobbies, guest rooms, and kitchens, and speaking with the employees. This not only helps him notice things that may need improvement, but also gives him direct access to what his firm's first-line employees are thinking and doing in all his hotels.

It's useful to keep in mind that wandering around doesn't automatically produce useful information. The communications skill here is not in the wandering but in the interpersonal communications skills you can bring to bear when you're speaking with the employees. These skills include paying attention, making yourself clear, listening actively, and listening sympathetically.

management by walking around
A manager literally walks around the workplace talking with subordinates to get a better idea of what they are doing in their jobs and the trials and triumphs they have had.

Dealing with Rumours and the Grapevine

When it comes to informal organizational communications, rumours and "the grapevine" are critical. The **grapevine** is the informal communications channel that exists in every organization. Rumours are spread by the grapevine, often at great speed.[53] In one study of 100 employees, the researcher found that when management made an important change in the organization, most employees heard the news first through the grapevine. Hearing news from a supervisor and official memorandums ran a poor second and third, respectively.[54] A survey of 393 Canadian companies that had reduced staff revealed that workers had heard the bad news unofficially in nearly half the cases.[55] The website **www.greedyassociates.com** (a big hit with associates at major law firms) announced recently that "I heard [name of major law firm] partners are sacrificing 1 of each 10 associates at midnight during the next full moon." The firm did indeed soon lay off about that many.[56]

Some rumours are accurate and some are not. There are three main reasons rumours get started: Lack of information, insecurity, and conflicts.[57] When employees don't know what's happening, they are likely to speculate about a situation, and a rumour is born. Thus, employees who observe an unscheduled disassembly of a machine may erroneously assume that the firm will soon lay off the machine's operators. Insecure employees are especially likely to react that way. Conflicts—such as between union and management—may trigger rumours, as each side uses propaganda to interpret the situation in a way most favourable to itself.

It is best to release the truth as quickly as possible, since the more the widespread the rumour, the more people will believe it.

grapevine
The informal communications channel that exists in every organization.

Communicating at the Speed of Thought

When many people think about "communicating," they think about technology-based devices like email and the internet. Let's therefore consider how managers use technology to improve communications.

Fitting the Communications Approach to the Task

What can research studies by communications experts tell managers about how to fit the approach they use to communicate to the task? Results from two lines of research—on communications networks and on "media richness"—are informative.

THE COMMUNICATIONS NETWORK STUDIES

What happens when organizational communications are restricted to just a few allowable channels, as in more bureaucratic organizations? Psychologist Harold Leavitt addressed this question. The researchers arranged groups of five persons in one of the "communication networks" shown in Figure 13.4. Each person was in a compartment at a table in such a way that his or her communication was restricted. Each person in the all-channel network could communicate with any other person. People in the wheel network could communicate only with the person in the central position (hub) of the network. This central person could communicate with the four other people in his or her network. (The lines all show two-way linkages.) All each person knew was to whom messages could be sent and from whom messages could be received.

The researchers found that the best communication network depended on the problem they had to solve. Where the problem was simple and amenable to a clear-cut yes or no answer (such as "Is this marble blue?"), the wheel network was best. But for complex, ambiguous problems that required lots of give and take, the all-channel network was best. Here, each person got marbles that were hard to describe. Two people looking at identical marbles could describe them quite differently; what one might view as "greenish-yellow," another might call "aqua." The person in the centre of the wheel network could not himself or herself quickly decide what colour was common to all the marbles. Therefore, the all-channel network, where communications could flow freely to and from everyone, arrived at the fastest decision for ambiguous problems.

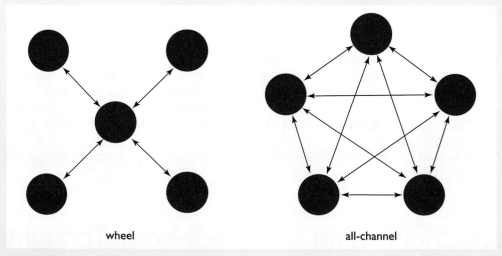

wheel   all-channel

FIGURE 13.4
Two Experimental Communication Networks

THE MEDIA RICHNESS MODEL

If you are an emergency room doctor and have to diagnose a patient who is obviously in difficulty, would you do it face-to-face, or send personal notes back and forth? The question highlights what communications researchers call the media richness model. This line of research says that the communication media or channels used—which may include face-to-face contact, telephone, personally addressed documents, or un-addressed documents, for instance—differ in their "media richness." Figure 13.5 summarizes this idea. Media richness means the capacity of the media to resolve ambiguity. Four aspects of the media—speed of feedback, number of cues and channels employed, personal-ness of the source, and variety of the language used—determine its "richness."

Face-to-face oral communication is the richest medium. As you know from your own experience, it provides instantaneous audio and visual feedback, not just through the person's words, but also through body language and tone as well. At the other extreme, un-addressed documents (like company-wide memos impersonally distributed to all employees) are low in media richness.

Organizations and people often rely more on rich media for addressing ambiguous, fast-changing situations. Face-to-face meeting, videoconferencing, and phone calls often make more sense than memos (especially impersonal memos) in these situations.

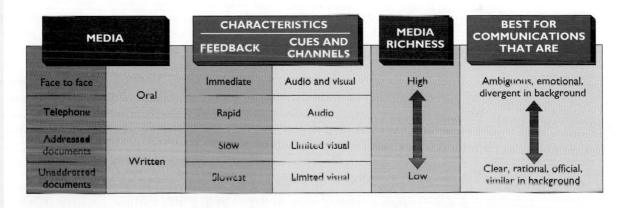

| MEDIA | | CHARACTERISTICS | | MEDIA RICHNESS | BEST FOR COMMUNICATIONS THAT ARE |
		FEEDBACK	CUES AND CHANNELS		
Face to face	Oral	Immediate	Audio and visual	High	Ambiguous, emotional, divergent in background
Telephone		Rapid	Audio		
Addressed documents	Written	Slow	Limited visual		
Unaddressed documents		Slowest	Limited visual	Low	Clear, rational, official, similar in background

FIGURE 13.5
Hierarchy of Media Richness and Managerial Applications

Telecommunications

Telecommunications—the electronic transmission of information—plays a big role in managing organizations today. Consider the network-reliability operations centre of a phone company.[58] The centre's blinking screens let the employees there instantly see how the firm is performing, in terms of phone problems in a given geographic area. The centre's high-tech communications capabilities let its staff provide fast, coordinated responses when emergencies arise. One or more employees from every major technical group (including engineering and repair) are in the room. Large screens alert workers to outages throughout the firm's area of operations.[59] Employees can thus make fast, coordinated decisions and react to problems. For example, when a team monitoring the screens noted a mysterious gridlock in one area, the problem turned out to be the result of thousands of people trying to call one merchant that had just received a shipment of beanie babies.[60]

telecommunications
The electronic transmission of information.

The solution was to put controls on the number of calls into that store's region, so the store's neighbours could start making calls again.

Telecommunications is also crucial for today's technology-based management systems. Levi Strauss uses a sophisticated system to link its own inventory and manufacturing facilities with point-of-sale processing devices at retail stores. Computers analyze sales information instantaneously. Management can then make more accurate inventory and production plan decisions. Retailer J.C. Penney uses telecommunications to manage in-store inventories. Its buyers get instant access to sales information from the stores and can modify their purchasing decisions accordingly. Ford designers at the company's Dearborn, Michigan, headquarters use computers to design new cars. Digitized designs then go electronically to Ford's Turin, Italy, design facility. There the system automatically reproduces the designs and creates styrofoam mock-ups of them.

Videoconferencing

Videoconferencing is a telecommunications-based method that lets group members interact directly with other team members via televised links.[61] The links may be phone- or satellite-based, or use one of the popular PC-based video technologies. Most let users send live video and audio messages, with no more then a few seconds delay.[62] For example, the team developing the Boeing 777 made extensive use of videoconferencing for meetings with engine suppliers and airlines to discuss the new aircraft's design.[63] After 9/11, more firms began substituting videoconferences for on-site meetings.

Electronic Mail

Electronic mail (**email**) is a computerized information system that lets group members electronically create, edit, and communicate messages to one another, using electronic mail boxes. An electronic bulletin board lets one or more group members file messages on various topics, to be picked up later by other group members.

Email systems are not just for messages. The email software Eudora Pro helps one company manage its sales operation. The owner configured a computer to check all customers' accounts every 10 minutes, so he never misses a rush order. It also lets him sort messages based on key words like "brochure" (so requests for his brochures are automatically routed to the person in charge of mailing them).[64]

As email use has proliferated, communications experts have suggested rules governing its use. For example,[65]

1. *Use the right medium for the message.* Dealing with sensitive topics or trying to be persuasive is probably best left to more personal, "rich" media. Email is particularly useful for sending simple messages, for instrumental tasks such as setting up meetings, and, in general for matters that you can cover in a paragraph or so. For more complex matters, consider a phone call or meeting, or (at least) attaching your note as a document.

2. *Think before you hit the "send" key.* Don't send anything that you wouldn't want posted in a public place or that you think you may be sorry about tomorrow.[66] Although just about everyone who uses email knows that it is not a confidential medium, some people seem to be unable to resist the urge to hit the "send" key. To avoid this problem, wait 24 hours before sending any email that you might have second thoughts about.

3. *Be professional.* Among other things, being professional means being concise, clear, respectful, and also sensible about who you add to your distribution list.

Work Group Support Systems

Telecommunications also powers **work group support systems**. These are technology-based systems that make it easier for work groups' members to work together. Team

Levi
www.levi.com

Boeing
www.boeing.com

videoconferencing
A telecommunications-based method that lets group members interact directly with other team members via televised links.

email
A computerized information system that lets group members electronically create, edit, and communicate messages to one another, using electronic mail boxes.

work group support systems
Technology-based systems that make it easier for work groups' members to work together.

members might all be at a single site, or dispersed around the city or the world. In any case, firms increasingly rely on all or most of the following work group support systems to help their employees get their jobs done. Table 13.2 summarizes the more popular digital-based collaboration tools.

Group Decision Support Systems A **decision support system (DSS)** is an interactive, computer-based communications system that facilitates the solution of unstructured problems by a decision-making team.[67] It lets a team get together (often in the same room) and make better and faster decisions and to complete their task more quickly. The DSS (as pictured in Figure 13.6) lets team members interact via their PCs and use several software tools that assist them in decision making and project completion. These software tools include electronic questionnaires, electronic brainstorming tools, idea organizers (to help team members synthesize ideas generated during brainstorming), and tools for voting or setting priorities (so that recommended solutions can be weighted and prioritized).

A DSS can help a group avoid many of the decision-making barriers that often plague traditional face-to-face groups. For example, there's less likelihood that one assertive person will monopolize the meeting, since all the brainstorming and listing of ideas—and the voting—is governed by the computerized programs.

decision support system (DSS)
An interactive, computer-based communications system that facilitates the solution of unstructured problems by a decision-making team.

TABLE 13.2 *Digital Work Group Support and Collaboration Systems*

TOOL	DESCRIPTION	ISSUES
Electronic messaging systems	Messaging infrastructures such as email or instant messenger systems	❏ rules governing use ❏ integration of multiple systems ❏ security
Electronic meeting systems	Real-time conferencing systems that may be managed by either local or remote sources	❏ scheduling ❏ post-meeting follow-up ❏ cost ❏ facilitation ❏ standard systems ❏ number of people who can work on system simultaneously and efficiently
Asynchronous conferencing systems	Content exchange that can occur instantly or over time using such tools as bulletin board systems	❏ facilitation ❏ follow-up on action items ❏ maximizing discussion
Document handling systems	Group document management, storage, and editing tools	❏ security ❏ work flow ❏ data integrity ❏ page mark-up standards ❏ standard systems ❏ ensuring user compatibility
On-line communities	Websites organized by subject matter where members access interactive discussion areas and share content, reference tools, and web links	❏ facilitation ❏ value of shared content ❏ updating of content and resources
Workflow management systems	Project management, process diagramming, and routing tools	❏ establishing work flow standards ❏ making decisions ❏ establishing processes and systems
Group decision-support systems	Tools used to integrate collaboration and team management systems across computer platforms, operating systems, and network architectures	❏ security ❏ updating of systems ❏ customization

FIGURE 13.6
A Decision Support System
The Ventana Corporation demonstrates the features of its GroupSystems for Windows electronic meeting software, which helps people create, share, record, organize, and evaluate ideas in meetings, between offices, or around the world.

collaborative writing systems
Group members can create long written documents (such as proposals) while working simultaneously at a network of interconnected computers.

Other Work Group Support Systems Managers use other such systems to facilitate group work. **Collaborative writing systems** let group members create long written documents (such as proposals) while working simultaneously at a network of interconnected computers. As team members work on different sections of the proposal, each member has automatic access to the rest of the sections and can modify his or her section to be compatible with the rest.

Firms increasingly use instant messaging to support their conference call operations. For example, instant messaging (real-time, interactive email) allows two managers to confer quietly, on the side, as a conference call among several people takes place.[68]

A group scheduling system provides a shared scheduling database. Each group member puts his or her daily schedule into the shared database. This facilitates identifying the most suitable times for meetings. A work flow automation system uses an email-type system to automate the flow of paperwork.[69] For example, if a proposal requires four signatures, the work flow automation system can send it electronically from mail box to mail box for the required signatures.

telecommuting
The substitution of telecommunications and computers for the commute to a central office.

Telecommuting Today, millions of people do much of their work at home and commute with their employers electronically. **Telecommuting** is the substitution of telecommunications and computers for the commute to a central office.[70]

There are three types of telecommuters. Some are not employees at all but are independent entrepreneurs who work out of their homes—perhaps developing new computer applications for consulting clients. The second (and largest) group of telecommuters includes professionals and highly skilled people who work at jobs that involve a great deal of independent thought and action. These employees—for example, computer programmers, regional salespersons, textbook editors, and research specialists—typically work at home most of the time, coming to the office only occasionally, perhaps for monthly meetings.[71] The third telecommuter category includes those who carry out relatively routine and easily monitored jobs like data entry or making reservations.[72]

Telecommuting helps employees avoid driving a long way to work, but they often report feeling isolated and lonely. To avoid this problem, B.C. Tel and Bentall Development Inc. jointly developed a satellite telecommuting office in Langley, B.C. It allows workers who used to have to commute to Burnaby or Vancouver to reduce their travel time considerably and still be able to interact with other workers.[73]

Building Internet-Based Virtual Communities

Managers are increasingly using various forms of internet-based networks to electronically link employees and therefore provide instantaneous communication organization-wide. For example, when PricewaterhouseCoopers accounting manager Rick Richardson arrives at his office each morning, he checks his computer to review the average 20 to 25 email messages he gets in a typical day. PricewaterhouseCoopers also maintains electronic bulletin boards on more than 1000 different jobs. About 18 000 of their employees in 22 countries use these electronic bulletin boards to get updates on matters such as how to handle specialized projects on which they are working.[74]

Other firms are similarly blurring the boundaries between themselves and their customers and suppliers by building "virtual communities." For example, as prime contractor in an effort to win a U.S.$300-million U.S. Navy ship deal, "Lockheed-Martin established a virtual design environment with two major shipbuilders, via a private internet existing entirely outside the firewalls of the three individual companies."[75] Eventually, about 200 suppliers would also be connected to the network via special, secure internet links. This special internet-based network "allows secure transfer of design, project management, and even financial data back and forth among the extended design team via simple browser access, with one homepage as its focal point."[76] Its objective was to substantially increase communication among team members and the customer. They got the contract and built the ship in one-third the time and at one-half the cost of previous contracts.

Lockheed-Martin
www.lockheedmartin. com

More firms are introducing internet-based "virtual community construction kits." Tribal Voice is one example. Its features include instant messaging (sending a message that will pop up on the receivers' screens), text to speech (hearing text as it appears in a window), file transfer (exchanging files), a buddy list (keeping track of regular on-line contacts), a whiteboard (exchanging drawings), and cruising (starting a meeting or conversation with a few people and then directing their web browsers to the pages of your choosing).[77]

Tribal Voice lets a group of employees who share a common interest get together via the internet. For example, says the vice president of marketing for the company that created Tribal Voice, "the sales department could hold forums and share information in an interactive community. A salesperson in a remote location could join this online department and ask for advice on a particular company he wants to call on."[78]

Another company that has used the internet to improve communications is described in the "Challenge of Change" box.

Is There a Company Portal in Your Future?

Although most people today are using portals like Yahoo to surf the net, many are also using their employers' company-based business portals. A business portal is, like other Yahoo-type portals, a window to the internet.[79] But for the companies that are increasingly creating them for their employees, business portals are a great deal more. They are special company and/or function-oriented gateways to internet-based information. Through their business portals, categories of employees—secretaries, engineers, salespeople, and so on— can access all the corporate applications they need to use, as well as "get the tools you need to analyze data inside and outside your company, and see the customized content you need, like industry news and competitive data."[80] Thus, a sales manager could use the portal to access all the information her company has on sales trends, market analyses, and competitors' sales.

Netscape
www.netscape.com

Lucent
www.lucent.com

Many companies are in the business of designing business portals for corporate customers. Netscape (now a division of America Online) has created business portals for employees at FedEx and Lucent. Another firm, Concur Technologies, just installed business portals for Hearst Corporation's 15 000 employees. Thousands of specialized business portals—ranging from benefits portals for letting employees update their benefits, to training portals for letting employees take courses on-line—are also in use at numerous firms. If communication is indeed "the exchange of information and the transmission of meaning," it looks as if a company portal will soon be in most employees' futures. They'll

Concur Technologies
www.concur.com

Electronic Communication at Cushman & Wakefield

Cushman & Wakefield
www.cushman
wakefield.com

Cushman & Wakefield is a commercial real estate broker that manages office buildings, factories, and other commercial properties around the world. With about 2000 employees, keeping the firm's personnel files up-to-date was an expensive logistical nightmare. The internet-based communications system installed by the firm shows how managers can use the internet to communicate today.

Updating each employee's personnel records, benefits, and related legal policies and procedures, and keeping track of all the firm's far-flung offices was a problem. Each time an employee was out sick, took a vacation, completed a college course, got a raise, or changed his or her job, the person's personnel files had to be changed. Keeping track of all this manually and through traditional telecommunications systems was very expensive.

Since virtually all employees already had internet access, Cushman & Wakefield decided to use the internet's low-cost and interactive features to create an internet-based employee communication network. It then turned out that the firm's policies, procedures, and forms were already being stored electronically as Microsoft Word documents, so converting existing documents so they could be displayed on the web was fairly inexpensive. The new system cost the company less than U.S.$10 000 to develop. Then, with all the policies and forms on-line, it was relatively easy for every office to update its files. Managers (or more often the employees themselves) just typed the changes into the web-based documents using Microsoft Word. The company's new software converted these documents and transferred them through the company's new internet-based Employee Resource System.

Cushman & Wakefield soon added other communication applications to its internet system. One uses an internal, internet-based system to calculate employee commissions, so agents and brokers can get the commission data they want. Another, Site Solutions, is a property tracking system that maintains detailed information on thousands of commercial properties worldwide, including available office space. More and more of the company's communications, computations, and record keeping are handled over the net.

help employees zero in on just the information they need to do their jobs and help them to organize and make sense of all the information that's out there.

General Motors calls its employee portal mySocrates, and it's not hard to see why they picked that name. Like other firms' employee internet portals, mySocrates lets GM's 200 000 North American employees take care of many of their routine HR tasks (if they so desire), such as changing their personal data and registering for benefits on-line.

But GM's mySocrates goes well beyond this. If GM gets its way, mySocrates will become the main work and non-work portal for all its employees. At work, mySocrates not only facilitates the sorts of HR activities noted above, but also lets GM employees easily link with hundreds of thousands of other GM websites and information sources to help the employees do their jobs better (assembly workers can get updates on new decision-making methods, for example). When the employee is back home, GM hopes mySocrates will turn out to be a sort of "myYahoo" for all its employees. The aim is to make mySocrates the portal of choice for all its employees—the first thing that opens when they log onto the net. GM thereby hopes to use it as a way to market new products and services (such as financial services from GM's financial services arm) to all its employees.[81]

Personal Digital Assistants

Firms also increasingly using personal digital assistants (PDAs) like PalmPilots to improve their communications. For example, since the consumer markets division of Countrywide Home Loans gave personal digital assistants to all their sales representatives, "I can't go into a restaurant or a grocery store without running into someone who's talking about buying a home" says one manager. And, "now, wherever I am, I pull out my Palm VII, say "how can I help you?" and demonstrate exactly what Countrywide can do for them."

Palm Pilots are an effective way to have information at your fingertips while out of the office.

SKILLS AND STUDY MATERIAL

SUMMARY

1. There are five elements in the communication process: sender, communication channel, noise, receiver, and feedback. Errors can occur in each of these elements.

2. Several interpersonal communication barriers can distort messages and inhibit communication. These barriers include ambiguity, semantics, physical barriers, competition barriers, and psychological barriers.

3. You can improve interpersonal communications by being an active listener, avoiding triggering defensiveness, and clarifying your ideas before communicating.

4. Because organizational communication involves people, it is susceptible to all the problems of interpersonal communication as well as some special problems (including distortion, rumours and the grapevine, information overload, narrow viewpoints, differences in status, organizational culture, structural restrictions, diversity issues, and boundary differences).

5. Upward communication can be encouraged through techniques like social gatherings, union publications, scheduled meetings, and formal suggestion systems.

Downward communication is encouraged through the usual channels (like face-to-face and written messages), as well as techniques like closed-circuit televisions and top managers "walking around."

6. To influence and improve organization-wide communication, a leader can foster informal communication, use networks, encourage boundarylessness, and use electronic networking.

7. Telecommunications and the internet play an important role in managing organizations today. Companies like Levi Strauss use sophisticated telecommunications systems to link their inventory and manufacturing facilities with point-of-sale processing devices at retail stores. Workgroup support systems allow even geographically dispersed employees to interact in real time as teams. Internet-based communications systems let companies use the relatively inexpensive internet to substantially reduce their communications costs. More and more companies are establishing internet-based applications to help them establish their own internet-based virtual communities.

1. English was the international language for the last half of the twentieth century. In the 1980s English was used by at least 750 million people, and barely half of those spoke it as their first language. Today millions of people from every continent and country speak English. Countries such as Taiwan require English as a second language as do many other nations. *The Story of English*, by Robert Crum, William Cran, and Robert MacNeil (1986) is a fascinating analysis of the growth and development of the English language. The book opens with the following:

   > On 5 September 1977, the American spacecraft *Voyager One* blasted off on its historic mission to Jupiter and beyond. On board, scientists, who knew that the Voyager would one day spin through distant star systems, had installed a recorded message greeting from the people of the planet Earth. Preceding a brief message in fifty-five different languages for the people of outer space, the gold-plated disc plays a statement, from the Secretary-General of the United Nations, an Austrian named Kurt Waldheim, speaking on behalf of 147 member states—in English.

   Since then, the world has increasingly embraced English as the language of communications and technology. This is a fine situation for those who use English as a first language, but what happens in an increasingly multi-lingual world? Americans tend to speak one language, but Canadians often speak two, as do many Europeans. Obviously, this is true in many other nations that have adapted to English but still have a native tongue. More and more business is done globally, and increasing numbers of organizations are merging across international borders. What do you think this all means for the English language as a major language of communication? Should we all be learning other languages as the world globalizes to communicate more effectively? What are the costs and benefits of increasing your language base? Can you effectively negotiate if you do not understand the nuances of another person's language?

2. For many of us, communication brings to mind technology. The uses of the computer, from email to the internet, shape our thinking patterns and, consequently, our communication. Everything is speeded up with electronic communication. Where will this electronic revolution take communication in the next 10 years? Will we all be emailing instead of writing letters, banking and shopping from home computers, doing business through our home pages on the internet, and teleconferencing via video computer links? What do you think our patterns of communication will be as technology evolves?

1. Different university presidents have different ways of communicating with their university communities. Form teams of four to five students and answer the following questions: (a) What methods has the president of your college or university used to elicit upward communication from members of the college or university community? (b) What methods does the president use to foster downward communication to the students? (c) What do the president's communication methods tell you about the organizational culture the president is trying to create (or is inadvertently creating) at your school?

2. Like most students, you have probably faced a situation in which you had to speak with a professor about a problem (e.g., you thought your grade should be higher, or you had to miss a test, or you wanted to get into a section that was full). In teams of four to five students, discuss the experiences you have had with various professors along these lines. Then choose a professor, and make a list of what that person did right and wrong with respect to the interpersonal communication skills (how to be an active listener, and so on) described in this chapter. What communication barriers did this person seem to be ignoring?

3. Because actions speak louder than words, non-verbal communication can create confusion. Take international gestures. In Britain, secrecy or confidentiality is conveyed by a tap on one's nose, while in Italy it means a friendly warning. A nod in Bulgaria and Greece signifies "no." In most other countries it means "yes." Placing your fingers in a circle is widely accepted as the "OK" sign, except in Brazil, where it's considered vulgar or obscene.[82]

   Gather 8 to 10 different gestures that mean different things in different nations. Interview classmates, friends, relatives, and co-workers and then come to class ready to discuss what you've discovered. Or brainstorm with a group of four to six classmates, generating a list of 8 to 10 Canadian gestures. Then divide the list and seek out what these gestures communicate in other cultures. Report to the class on your findings.

What Is Your Communication Style?

Think of how you usually communicate with others in everyday situations. For each of the following 18 *pairs*[83] of statements, distribute three points between the two alternatives depending upon which is most characteristic of your style. The point range is from 0–3:0 = Never: 1 = Rarely: 2 = Sometimes: 3 = Always. *The numbers you assign to each pair of statements should add up to 3.*

1A ____ I am open to getting to know people personally and establishing relationships with them.

1B ____ I am not open to getting to know people personally and establishing relationships with them.

2A ____ I react slowly and deliberately.

2B ____ I react quickly and spontaneously.

3A ____ I am open to other people's use of my time.

3B ____ I am not open to other people's use of my time.

4A ____ I introduce myself at social gatherings.

4B ____ I wait for others to introduce themselves to me at social gatherings.

5A ____ I focus my conversations on the interests of the parties involved, even if it means that the conversations stray from the business or subject at hand.

5B ____ I focus my conversations on the tasks, issues, business, or subject at hand.

6A ____ I am not assertive, and I can be patient with a slow pace.

6B ____ I am assertive, and at times I can be impatient with a slow pace.

7A ____ I make decisions based on facts or evidence.

7B ____ I make decisions based on feelings, experiences, or relationships.

8A ____ I contribute frequently to group conversations.

8B ____ I contribute infrequently to group conversations.

9A ____ I prefer to work with and through others, providing support when possible.

9B ____ I prefer to work independently or dictate the conditions in terms of how others are involved.

10A ____ I ask questions or speak more tentatively and indirectly.

10B ____ I make emphatic statements or directly express opinions.

11A ____ I focus primarily on the idea, concept, or results.

11B ____ I focus primarily on the person, interaction, and feelings.

12A ____ I use gestures, facial expressions, and voice intonation to emphasize points.

12B ____ I do not use gestures, facial expressions, and voice intonation to emphasize points.

13A ____ I accept others' points of view (ideas, feelings, and concerns).

13B ____ I do not accept others' point of view (ideas, feelings, and concerns).

14A ____ I respond to risk and change in a cautious or predictable manner.

14B ____ I respond to risk and change in a dynamic or unpredictable manner.

15A ____ I prefer to keep my personal feelings and thoughts to myself, sharing only when I want to do so.

15B ____ I find it natural and easy to share and discuss my feelings with others.

16A ____ I seek out new or different experiences and situations.

16B ____ I choose known or similar situations and relationships.

17A ____ I am responsive to others' agendas, interests, and concerns.

17B ____ I am directed toward my own agendas, interests, and concerns.

18A ____ I respond to conflict slowly and indirectly.

18B ____ I respond to conflict quickly and directly.

SCORING AND INTERPRETATION

People develop habitual ways of communicating with others based on behaviours that were reinforced when growing up. Your communication style can be understood by looking at how open or self-contained you are, and how direct or indirect you are.

To determine your degrees of openness and directness, transfer your scores from the questionnaire to the table below. Then, total each column to get your O, S, D, and I scores.

Communication Style Scoring Sheet

0	S	D	I
1A	1B	2B	2A
3B	3A	4A	4B
5A	5B	6B	6A
7B	7A	8A	8B
9A	9B	10B	10A
11B	11A	12A	12B
13A	13B	14B	14A
15B	15A	16A	16B
17A	17B	18B	18A
O	S	D	I
Total ____	Total ____	Total ____	Total ____

Compare the O and S scores. Which is higher? Write the higher score in the following blank and circle the corresponding letter: ____ **O S**

Compare the D and I scores. Which is higher? Write the higher score in the following blank and circle the corresponding letter: ____ **D I**

Are you more **Open** [higher **O** score] or **Self-Contained** [higher **S** score] when you communicate? When an Open person communicates, he or she is relationship oriented, supportive of others' needs, and shares feelings readily. A Self-Contained person is task oriented, aloof, and not prone to sharing feelings.

Are you more **Direct** [higher **D** score] or **Indirect** [higher **I** score] when you communicate with others? Direct people are extroverted and express their thoughts and feelings quite forcefully. Indirect people hold back and appear more introverted. Direct communicators range from highly assertive to aggressive, while indirect communicators go the other way from moderately assertive to passive.

Four different communication styles can be discerned by how direct and open you are. If your scores are highest on open and direct, you are an assertive and relationship-oriented *Socializer*. If your scores are highest on self-contained and direct, you are an assertive and task-oriented *Director*. If your scores are highest on indirect and self-contained you are a task-oriented and low assertive *Thinker*. If your scores are highest on indirect and open, you are a low assertive and relationship-oriented *Relater*.

Your communication style affects all other aspects of communication discussed in this chapter: what specific communication barriers you face, how you send messages, how you listen to others, how you use nonverbal signals, how you react to diversity or communication styles, and how you approach making formal oral presentations.

INTERNET EXERCISES

Despite technological advancements, it is still essential for today's managers to have fine-tuned verbal, non-verbal, and written communication skills. Access the American Management Association website at **www.amanet.org** and select the Seminars and then the Communication Skills menu option. Review the seminar offerings and content.

1. How would managers benefit from the "Building Better Work Relationships: New Techniques for Results-Oriented Communication" and the "Interpersonal Skills" seminars?

2. What are the key elements of interpersonal skills?

3. How do managers build better working relationships?

4. Access the Canadian Management Centre (a strategic affiliate of AMA International) at **www.cmcamai.org**. Compare and contrast the courses offered by AMA and CMC. Identify the courses that you would be interested in taking.

CASE STUDY 13-1

Should We Go to the Web?

Like most professors who teach the business program's capstone course in strategic management, Cynthia Thomas liked to split her class into groups of five or six students, who then spent the rest of the term analyzing cases and developing a strategic plan for a company in the vicinity of the university.

From the day they got together to analyze their first case and create their presentation, the five members of one group—Maria, Raj, Len, Hal, and Jennifer—seemed to hit it off. During the rest of the semester their friendship grew. Maria was majoring in accounting and planned on earning her CA and then joining an accounting firm. Raj was a finance major whose professors described him as "one of the sharpest students ever." Len was a sales and marketing major with a strong interest in small businesses. Hal was majoring in production and operations management and was also a skilled mathematician. Jennifer's specialty was human resource management, an area in which her intelligence and understanding of people was especially effective.

Something students generally learn in analyzing strategy management cases is that problems and solutions rarely affect only one department in a company. For example, one case this team of students worked on required the development of a new strategy for Kmart, the discount firm that was being battered by the increasingly successful Wal-Mart. When group members thought about changing Kmart's computer systems to make the company more competitive, they immediately found that other departments would also be impacted by the change.

The HR department, for instance, would have to hire new computer people and retrain current employees to use the new systems, and the finance department would have to determine whether buying new computers would be cost-effective. So, having expertise in several areas was a definite plus in solving problems.

In working together, the group also learned the importance of teamwork. As they analyzed company after company, the confidence of these five young business majors grew. By the end of the term they'd decided that after graduation, they wanted to set up a consulting firm together. The idea was to create a consulting firm in which each person on the team would bring his or her expertise to the analysis of client problems. Clients would thus get complete and compre-

hensive top-down solutions. The Business Team, Inc., is the company they formed.

Like many new (as well as large and established) companies, the members of the team are considering whether, and if so how, to use the web to develop their business. One of the more striking examples of how the web is making inroads into business-to-business commerce was the announcement in late February 2000 that General Motors, Ford Motor Company, and DaimlerChrysler had agreed to join forces to create a single automotive exchange on the internet. Basically an enormous new website, the new exchange was to be an independent company that the major auto companies would use to handle their communications with suppliers bidding for the U.S.$240 billion the three companies spend worldwide each year. "All the world is going to the Net for business-to-business communications" is the way Maria put it.

Questions

1. How might the partners use the internet to highlight their multifunction approach to solving business problems?

2. Assuming they decide to "go to the web" and set up their own site, what communication tasks do you think the new site should accomplish for them?

3. Given your answers to questions 1 and 2 above, design the opening page for The Business Team, Inc.'s new website.

4. What concepts and lessons about communications that take place without the use of technology can you apply to internet based communications? How might The Business Team, Inc., take advantage of these lessons?

A Case of Good Intentions

Treeline Paper Ltd. employed 300 people. Management had always prided itself on the good relations that existed between the company and its employees. A strike had never taken place, and relations with the union were good.

The president of Treeline, Alex Kellner, had formed an executive committee that met every Tuesday morning to discuss specific issues facing management. These meetings also served to improve communications between managers since this was the only time they had the opportunity to meet together. At the most recent meeting, the committee was discussing how valuable the meetings had been and suggested that the company should examine ways of improving communication with the employees as well. One manager related an experience that seemed to sum up the lack of communication with employees: He had recently been talking with one employee who did not know who the president of the company was.

After considerable discussion, it was agreed that Treeline would embark on a program to improve communication with employees. Several ideas were put forth, and the executive committee eventually decided to start with a simple campaign that would give employees some basic statistics about the company and its operations. The centrepiece of this campaign would be three time series graphs that would summarize company operations. These graphs would show total sales, inventory levels, and total employment. The graphs would be updated weekly.

A memo was sent to all employees indicating that this decision had been made. Employees were encouraged to consult the graphs and to become better informed about the company they worked for.

After several months, the graphs looked like those in Figure 13.7.

About this time, Kellner had a visit from the president of the union. He was very agitated and said that the union wanted to open up the job security clause of the collective agreement. Several supervisors also reported a noticeable drop in employee morale. One day in the cafeteria several employees confronted Kellner and demanded to speak to him about the rumour they had heard that the plant would be closing soon.

Questions

1. What has gone wrong here?

2. Using concepts introduced in the chapter, make suggestions about what Alex Kellner should do now.

FIGURE 13.7
Treeline's Time Series Graphs

Keeping Communications Open at JetBlue

JetBlue has been built on five values—safety, caring, integrity, fun, and passion—and keeping communications open and transparent is vital for adhering to all of them. Indeed, the company feels so strongly about these values that they appear on all employees' identification cards. Most employees' first exposure to JetBlue's brand of open communication comes during their initial, one-hour orientation when the company's president and CEO explain how JetBlue makes money. The officers go so far as to do the math with the new employees and then show how each of the employees' jobs affects every aspect of the company's expenses and revenues. The basic idea is to get the new employee thinking, "If I do this, then this will happen."

The basic theme is that JetBlue can succeed as a low-cost, high-quality airline only if every employee gives his or her best. Employees therefore have to think of themselves more as partners than as employees. Indeed, there are no "employees" at JetBlue—just "crew members."

JetBlue's monthly "pocket sessions" provide another example of open communications. The pocket sessions are meetings between the company CEO, president, and head of HR with about 200 JetBlue crew members at the company's main crew lounge at JFK airport in New York. These meetings usually involve short presentations by each officer and then a period of frank and open questions and answers between officers and crew members. Given JetBlue's emphasis on open, transparent communication, the officers work hard to answer even the thorniest questions forthrightly. Sometimes these answers aren't what employees want to hear, but the answers do clearly convey what JetBlue's business model involves. For example, at one recent meeting, a flight attendant asked why managers and pilots get stock options, while the flight attendants do not. The answer was that different employees play different roles and that early on management and the board of directors made the decision that only managers, pilots, and others in the company requiring professional licensing and degrees would be eligible for stock options. However, other employees are eligible for profit sharing and other benefits.

Another employee pointed out that because of bad weather, many employees had to work mandatory overtime for three days. This employee objected to mandatory overtime and felt that the supervisor should not have put the order in "mandatory" terms. Management responded that if the supervisor's order was discourteous, they would look into it, but that the bottom line was that everyone joining JetBlue had to understand that on occasion they would have to pitch in and help during periods like these. It was also noted that individuals who were not prepared to work this way might not be well-suited to work at JetBlue.

The company also issues periodic "Blue Notes," which are company-wide emails that cover important news and press releases. However, it does not have some of the trappings of formal communication you might expect from a company this size. For example,

there is no employee manual, although the company is considering publishing one (tentatively titled "The JetBlue Route Map") sometime in the future. New employees do get a "Blue Book," a 13-page pamphlet summarizing major policy issues like equal employment opportunity and sexual harassment. There are also several benefits documents describing matters such as sick leave and vacation pay. The company has disciplinary procedures but does not publicize them or distribute them to employees. JetBlue simply emphasizes that it will treat employees with respect. Then, if there is a problem, employees receive a warning and a description of the progressive disciplinary policy.

The annual employee appraisal at JetBlue (called the "Flight Plan") tends to be an open give-and-take discussion, one in which the employee's commitment to JetBlue looms large. JetBlue also conducts a yearly "Crew Member Experience" survey that monitors employee impressions of various matters ranging from supervision to pay. Generally, according to the company's head of HR, this survey contains few surprises but rather validates things that management already knows. This is because managers—and particularly top managers—spend so much time out in the field (in the terminal, in the aircraft, and so on) talking and interacting with employees and passengers.

Assignment

You and your team are consultants to Mr. Neeleman, who is depending on your management expertise to help navigate the launch and management of JetBlue. Here's what he wants to know from you:

1. Are there any interpersonal or organizational communication barriers that JetBlue seems to be ignoring? If so, how would you suggest they remedy the situation?

2. List and explain the things you would do to improve organizational communication at JetBlue.

3. Make a list of the specific tools that JetBlue is currently using to encourage upward communication, downward communication, and interdepartmental communication. Do you think these are adequate for a company in JetBlue's situation? What would you suggest JetBlue do to improve organizational communication?

Leading Groups and Teams

OBJECTIVES

After studying this chapter and the case exercises at the end, you should be able to use the material to:

1. Analyze a team situation and discuss the reasons why the team does or does not have the necessary building blocks to function effectively.

2. Analyze a team situation, list specific reasons why the team is not performing effectively, and make specific, practical suggestions for improving team performance.

3. List and discuss at least five reasons why you believe a person is (or is not) suited to be a team player.

4. Explain to a manager what organizational characteristics are necessary to adequately support a team environment.

Teams, Teams, Teams

During the past decade, there has been a marked increase in the use of teams in business firms. Consider the following examples.

Willow Manufacturing, a maker of precision components, decided in the mid-1990s to introduce changes that would make the company a better place to work. A team environment was created, which helped to resolve both people problems and production problems. On the people side, the organization was redesigned to remove the traditional status differences between managers and employees by having all employees wear the same uniform. Managers were also given training in how to facilitate teamwork and how to coach employees rather than boss them around. On the production side, work teams were formed to revise production procedures to make them more efficient. The output of one team was then submitted to another team who suggested further refinements. The end result was a more streamlined manufacturing process. Now, employees are consulted before new equipment is purchased, and they are also allowed to decide which hours they will work.

The Shell Canada lubricants factory at Brockville, Ontario, makes oil for automobiles, boats, and industrial applications. The plant's factory floor workers were recently grouped into three teams called "job families." Each team manages one of the plant's three basic activities—blending lubricants, packaging, and warehousing. Each worker must be able to perform all of the jobs allocated to her or his team. Operators are also expected to be knowledgeable about where raw materials come from and where final products are sold. Teams are given the information and authority they need (including the right to talk to suppliers or customers) to make the plant perform up to standard. The plant does not have the traditional supervisors and superintendent who tell people what to do and how to do it. In their place is a system that turns all employees into supervisors by allowing them to tap into the information they need to manage themselves. Teams are responsible for cost control, developing vacation and training schedules, and disciplining nonperforming workers. In essence, the old "command and control" hierarchy has been abandoned and has been replaced by a dynamic organizational structure that runs on worker commitment, enthusiasm, and group cohesiveness.

The emphasis on teams is not restricted to the factory floor. At Steelcase Canada, space for office workers has been reorganized to clearly convey the importance of teamwork. Private offices have for the most part been abolished, and employees work in open spaces. Walls are made of glass, which lets each employees see others in action. The emphasis in office redesign is on teams, not individuals. In the company's new design, space is set up to facilitate interaction of people who need to talk to one another to do their job better. President Jim Mitchell sees a big difference between the teamwork approach and the "military model" that focuses on command and control.

At some companies, team members may not even work in the same city or country, yet they are able to achieve important company goals because their activity is centrally coordinated. Consider the case of Strawberry Frog, an advertising agency that is headquartered in Amsterdam. The company has set up a virtual team of about 50 people worldwide who have expertise in areas that are relevant for various advertising projects. Strawberry Frog has access to all this talent without having to cope with the costs and complications that are associated with a traditional bureaucracy. The idea here is that good advertising campaigns are built on good ideas, not on large bureaucracies.

Willow Manufacturing
www.willowcnc.com

Shell Canada
www.shell.ca

Strawberry Frog
www.strawberryfrog.nl

Teams: Employee Involvement in Action

Anyone who has watched a baseball or football game knows there's a reason why some teams do better then others. Some have better, more committed players. Some have better coaches. Some have better training. And some have higher morale. In this chapter, we'll discuss the methods leaders use to make their teams more effective.

Teamwork Today

Teams, not departments or individuals, do much of the work in North America these days.[1] For example, work teams comprising 40 to 50 workers have been introduced at Imperial Oil's Dartmouth, Nova Scotia, refinery. Each team is responsible for an entire segment of the refinery's operations. The team responsible for first-stage conversion of crude oil into more useful forms is now headed by a single leader. Formerly, the work had been done by a variety of workers representing various trades and skills, each one reporting to a different manager. Under the new team approach, employees have taken on new responsibilities and a layer of supervision has disappeared.[2]

The Center for the Study of Work Teams at the University of North Texas suggests that about 80 percent of the *Fortune* 500 companies have half their employees on teams. Another study by the Hay Group (a

Cohesiveness is essential to the success of many work teams, as much in traditional business settings as in such high-risk work as capping gushing oil wells.

consulting firm) found that 66 percent of the employers surveyed planned to increase the level of employee participation in teams. Reasons given for organizing more work around teams included improving product quality (chosen by 69 percent of the respondents), improving productivity (64 percent), improving employee morale (17 percent), and improving staffing flexibility (13 percent).[3]

Based on a survey of the executives in attendance at one team-building program, cross-functional project groups were by far the most common types of teams, followed by service, marketing, and operations teams. Team size ranged from 3 to 25 members. The average size was about 8 members per team. The most frustrating aspects of teamwork (from most frustrating to least frustrating) were developing/sustaining high motivation, minimizing confusion/coordination problems, managing conflict productively, and managing people problems.[4]

What Is Employee Involvement?

employee involvement program
A formal program that lets employees participate in formulating important work-related decisions or in supervising all or part of their own jobs.

Work teams are examples of employee involvement programs. An **employee involvement program** is any formal program that lets employees participate in formulating important work-related decisions or in supervising all or part of their own jobs.[5] Employee involvement isn't an either-or situation. As shown in Figure 14.1, involvement can range from information sharing (managers make all important operational decisions, inform employees, and then respond to employee questions), through inter-group problem solving (experienced, trained, cross-functional teams meet regularly with managers to solve problems across several organizational units), to total self-direction[6] (every employee belongs to a self-directed team, starting with a high-level executive team).[7] In the last scenario[8] (as we saw in Chapter 9), management arranges its organizational structure and systems around team-based work assignments.[9]

Managers rate involvement programs as their biggest productivity boosters. Several years ago, the editors of *National Productivity Review* found that "increased employee involvement in the generation and implementation of ideas was ranked the highest priority productivity improvement action by the [survey's] respondents." Employee involvement "was similarly ranked number one as the top cause of improvement over the past two years at these firms." The other eight sources of improvement, in descending order, were quality programs, improved process methods, top management, equipment, technology, training, computers, and automation. In this chapter, we'll focus on team-based involvement programs.

It is dangerous to use involvement programs indiscriminately. In one recent study, researchers investigated how worker empowerment affected employee satisfaction in four countries—the United States, Mexico, Poland, and India. Of these four cultures, India

1. *Information sharing:* Managers make decisions on their own, announce them, and then respond to any questions employees may have.

2. Managers usually make the decisions but only after seeking the views of employees.

3. Managers often form temporary employee groups to recommend solutions for specified problems.

4. Managers meet with employee groups regularly—once per week or so—to help them identify problems and recommend solutions.

5. *Intergroup problem solving:* Managers establish and participate in cross-functional employee problem-solving teams.

6. Ongoing work groups assume expanded responsibility for a particular issue, like cost reduction.

7. Employees within an area function full time, with minimal direct supervision.

8. *Total self-direction:* Traditional supervisory roles do not exist; almost all employees participate in self-managing teams.

FIGURE 14.1
Employee Involvement in Your Company: An Informal Checklist

is reportedly the most "vertical," in that "those who are at the top are expected to take charge, to be in control, to give orders, and to know what is right."[10] Worker empowerment programs were not only less successful in India, but "indeed, our results suggest that some practices may in fact be harmful. The negative paths from empowerment to satisfaction in the Indian sample, arguably the most vertical sample, were in stark contrast to the positive paths in the other three samples."[11]

Group Dynamics

All teams are groups, but not all groups are teams. A **group** is defined as two or more persons who are interacting in such a way that each person influences and is influenced by each other person.[12] A work shift or a department's employees may compose a group, since they work together. However, groups like these needn't exhibit a team's unity of purpose. Whether it's a football team, a commando team, or a self-managing work team, a team is always "committed to a common purpose, set of performance goals, and approach for which they hold themselves mutually accountable."[13] Team members usually hold one another accountable for achieving the team's goals.[14] However, because "all teams are groups," much of what we know about team effectiveness comes from research done on small groups. We'll look at this next.

group
Two or more persons who are interacting in such a way that each person influences and is influenced by each other person.

Group Norms

Peer pressure—wanting to look "right" from the point of view of our peers—drives much of what we do, including what we wear and how we behave. It takes a strong-willed person to deliberately go against the grain of what the reference group the person admires is doing. The same is true at work. For example, in a study titled "Monkey See, Monkey Do: The Influence of Workgroups on the Antisocial Behaviour of Employees," two researchers studied how the antisocial behaviour of co-workers influenced individual team members' antisocial behaviour.[15] They found that "... a workgroup was a significant predictor of an individual's antisocial behaviour at work." In fact, the more antisocial the group became, the more it was able to pressure its individual members into taking antisocial actions.[16] Experts on gangs might not be surprised by such findings, but they were something of a surprise in a work setting. In any case, ignoring the group's potential influence can be calamitous.

Groups exert their influence largely through group norms. **Group norms** are "the informal rules that groups adopt to regulate and regularize group members' behavior."[17] They are "rules of behavior, proper ways of acting, which have been accepted as legitimate by members of a group [and that] specify the kind of behaviors that are expected of group members."[18]

group norms
The informal rules that groups adopt to regulate and regularize group members' behaviour.

Group norms may be positive or negative (or neutral) from the company's point of view. At the Toyota Camry plant, positive group norms include "always do your best," and " build these cars as if you own the company." Creating an environment that leads to norms like these can obviously be very beneficial to an employer. We'll look at how to do that later in this chapter. On the other hand, negative group norms like "don't exceed 10 units per hour no matter what the manager says" can inhibit productivity.

It's hard to overestimate the impact of group norms. Studies show that "group norms[19] may have a greater influence on the individual's performance than the knowledge, skills and abilities the individual brings to the work setting."[20] Researchers first stumbled across this fact many years ago during a research project known as the Hawthorne studies. These researchers described, for instance, how production levels that exceeded the group's norms triggered what the workers called "binging," in which the "over-"producer's hand was slapped by other workers.

Group Cohesiveness

The extent to which a group can enforce its norms and influence its members' behaviour depends to some extent on the group's attraction for its members—on the group's

cohesiveness
The extent to which a group can enforce its norms and influence its members' behaviour.

cohesiveness.[21] Members of cohesive teams "sit closer together, focus more attention on one another, shows signs and mutual affection, and display coordinated patterns of behavior."[22] Cohesive groups are also more likely to enforce the group's norms.

Group cohesiveness depends on several things. One is proximity, since geographically dispersed people are less likely to form friendships. Individuals also tend to be attracted to a group because they find its activities or goals attractive, rewarding, or valuable, or because they believe that they can accomplish something through the group that they can't accomplish individually. Agreement regarding goals therefore boosts cohesiveness, while differences reduce it.[23]

Although the old saying "opposites attract" is occasionally true, people generally choose friends based on similarities. Students, for example, tend to choose friends based on similarities such as age, gender, and (to some extent) academic achievement and intelligence.[24] People also tend to choose their friends based on similarities of interest or values. In one study of high school students, most of the friendships were with social class equals.[25] When given a chance to form friendships with any other student, a large percentage of the students tended to choose friendships based on religious similarities. Personality is another factor. In one study, "subjects chose others whom they described as being similar to their own positive traits and rejected those whom they described as being similar to their own negative traits."[26]

Inter-group competition can boost cohesiveness (particularly for the winning group), but intra-group competition tends to undermine it.[27] Similarly, abrasive, antagonistic, or inflexible team members can undermine group cohesiveness. Group cohesiveness also tends to decline as group size increases.[28] Size influences cohesiveness for several reasons. Member satisfaction declines once the size of the group goes beyond five to seven members,[29] and the group's leader has less time to spend communicating with each of the group's members. Larger groups tend to split into two or more, often opposing, subgroups. Based on much small group research, the optimum size seems to be five or six members.[30]

Some firms make formal attempts to develop cohesive work groups because of the increased "energy" that is evident in such groups. For example, at Campbell Soup Canada, the president and six vice presidents went on an Outward Bound program near Lake Superior. The trip included four days of canoeing, spending one day alone in the wilderness, and scaling a sheer granite cliff. After the group returned to work, they spent time discussing what they had learned by working together as a team and how it could be applied to business management.[31] Scarborough-based Honeywell sent a total of 250 of its employees to a team-building program run by a company called Survival in the Bush, which conducts wilderness survival courses for business executives who want to learn leadership skills, self-confidence, and stress management skills.[32]

Outward Bound
Canada
www.outwardbound.ca

How Companies Use Teams at Work

Employers use teams in various ways.[33] We'll look next at the more popular choices.

Suggestion/Problem-Solving Teams and Quality Circles

suggestion team
A temporary team that works on a specific assignment.

problem-solving team
A team formed to identify and solve work-related problems.

quality circle
A team of 6 to 12 specially trained employees that meets regularly to solve problems affecting its work area.

Suggestion teams are temporary teams that work on specific assignments (for example, how to cut costs or raise productivity). **Problem-solving teams** "are somewhat more formal and semi-permanent, and focus on developing effective solutions to work-related problems."[34] They usually consist of the supervisor and five to eight employees from a common work area. No one knows the job as well as the employees do, so employers therefore often wisely ask the employees to analyze work-related problems and to suggest improvements.

Quality circles are one example of problem-solving teams.[35] A **quality circle** (QC) is a team of 6 to 12 specially trained employees that meets regularly, often once a week, to solve problems affecting its work area.[36] It first gets training in problem analysis techniques (including basic statistics). Then it applies the problem analysis process (problem identification, problem selection, problem analysis, solution recommendations, and solution review by top management) to solve problems in its work area.[37]

At Great West Life Assurance Company, quality circles comprise volunteers who meet once a week (on company time) to consider ways to do higher-quality, more effective work. Each group has a leader who has received formal training in how to lead a QC. An agenda is prepared for each meeting. When a group has completed a given project—large projects may take six months or more—a presentation is made to management. All team members are encouraged to take part in these presentations.

Quality circles are now generally more structured and directed than they were some years ago. Many of the original circle programs failed to produce measurable cost savings. Some circles' bottom line goals were too vague. In other firms, having the employees choose and analyze their own problems proved ineffective.[38] In many companies today, quality circle membership is mandatory. The quality circles include most shop floor employees and, in contrast to the bottom-up approach initially practised, the circles work on problems assigned by management.[39]

Great West Life Assurance
www.gwla.com

Project, Development, or Venture Teams

Project teams (also called development or venture teams) are small groups that operate as semi-autonomous units to create and develop new ideas.[40] They often consist of professionals like marketing experts or engineers. They work on specific projects like designing new processes (process design teams), new products (product development teams), or new businesses (venture teams). The classic example is the IBM team organized in Boca Raton, Florida, which developed and introduced IBM's first personal computer. As is usually the case with venture teams, the IBM unit was semi-autonomous. It had its own budget and leader, as well as the freedom to make decisions within broad guidelines.

IBM's venture team experience illustrates the pros and cons of the venture team approach. Working more or less autonomously outside of IBM's usual network of rules and policies, the team created the new personal computer and brought it to market in less than two years. This might have taken IBM years to accomplish under its usual hierarchical, "check with me first" product development approach. However, many believe the venture team's autonomy eventually backfired. Not bound by IBM's traditional policy of using only IBM parts, the team went outside IBM, to Microsoft (for its DOS, or disk operating system) and to Intel (for the computer processor). Unfortunately for IBM, this allowed Intel and Microsoft to sell the same PC parts to any manufacturer and led to the proliferation of IBM clones.[41] The bottom line is that team autonomy can be good but should be tempered by controls.

project teams
Small groups that operate as semi-autonomous units to create and develop new ideas.

Transnational Teams

How do you carry out a project involving activities in several countries at once? Increasingly, managers are solving that problem by creating **transnational teams**, which comprise multinational members whose activities span many countries.[42] Firms use transnational teams in many ways. Fuji-Xerox sent 15 of its most experienced Tokyo engineers to a Xerox Corporation facility in Webster, New York. They worked there for five years with a group of U.S. engineers to develop a "world copier," a product that proved to be a huge success in the global marketplace.[43]

Managers and technical specialists from IBM-Latin America formed a transnational team to market, sell, and distribute personal computers in Latin American countries. A European beverage manufacturer formed a 13-member transnational team called the European Production Task Force, with members from five countries. Its task was to analyze how many factories the firm should operate in Europe, what size they should be, and where they should be placed.[44]

Transnational teams face special challenges.[45] They work on highly complex, important projects. They must operate over vast distances. And they comprise people with dif-

transnational teams
Teams comprise multinational members whose activities span many countries.

Xerox
www.xerox.com

ferent interpersonal styles, languages, and cultures. What can you do to make these transnational teams more effective?

- *Clarify the team's driving goal.* With the distances involved so great, it's especially important for each team member to be able to focus his or her efforts on a crystal-clear common goal.[46]

- *Facilitate communications.* Given the distances involved, the preferred information technology includes videoconferencing as well as telephone, voice mail, email, and fax. Decision support systems—PC-based groupware that permits, for instance, simultaneous computerized discussions of issues—is important, too.

- *Build trust and teamwork.* Fostering group cohesiveness is especially important, given the diverse and multicultural makeup of these groups. "Successful [transnational] teams are characterized by leaders and members who trust each other, are committed to the team's mission, can be counted on to perform their respective tasks, and enjoy working with each other."[47]

- *Demonstrate mutual respect.* Conference times should be rotated so that the members in remote time zones don't always have to do business in the wee hours of the morning. Staff meetings should also be held at various geographic locations. Learn words expressing respect and gratitude in the languages of other team members.[48]

Virtual Teams

Virtual teams are groups of geographically and/or organizationally dispersed co-workers that are assembled to accomplish an organizational task, using a combination of telecommunications and information technologies. These teams may be set up as temporary structures, existing only to accomplish a specific task, or they may be permanent structures, used to address ongoing issues, such as a strategic planning. Team membership is often fluid, evolving according to changing task requirements.[49]

Virtual teams are increasingly popular because of globalization, which demands that work teams communicate continually at great distances, but rarely face to face. As well, the popularity of strategic partnerships and joint ventures means employees of partner companies frequently act together as a team, although they work for different companies and may be in different countries or continents.

Technology and Virtual Teams Virtual teams depend for their existence on several types of information technology. **Desktop videoconferencing systems**—which re-create the face-to-face interactions of conventional groups—are often the core systems around which the firm builds the rest of the virtual team's technologies. Communication among team members can thus include the rich body language and nuances of face-to-face communications.[50] (Some experts wryly contend that the technology most often used by virtual groups is still the jet plane.)

Collaborative software systems (the work group support systems or decision support systems discussed in Chapter 13) further facilitate decision making in virtual teams. For example, one consulting team used a collaborative software system to research and write a proposal for a major project. This enabled each member to access, in real time, the contribution of each other member while inputting his or her own. Microsoft Corp. offers a NetMeeting conference system. When combined with new products like Framework Technologies Corp.'s ActiveProject 5.0, virtual team members can hold live project reviews and discussions and then store the sessions on the project's website.[51]

Other firms use their own intranets. With all the virtual teams' required forms and documents available on internal websites, these Intranets "allow virtual teams to archive text, visual, audio, and numerical data in a user-friendly format, [and] allow virtual teams to keep other organizational members and outside constituents such as suppliers and customers up-to-date on the team's progress."[52] For example, at Intranets.com, in less than three minutes, a company or department can have a central place to keep everyone in a group up-to-date on work, reports, and so on. ScheduleOnline offers a group calendar that lets users schedule events, invite people to meetings, and reserve physical resources, such as conference rooms or equipment.

At I-Many, a Maine-based software company, having an employee meeting is no easy task. Leigh Powell, the firm's chief executive lives in New Jersey. His chief operating officer lives in St. Louis. The customer service vice president lives in Denver. And that vice president's customer service staff is in Portland, Maine. To keep this geographically dispersed team operating, the firm relies heavily on computers, cellphones, and instant messaging. As Powell says, "we're constantly bouncing ideas off each other.... We talk about everything. Ultimately, the people in this company have a lot of authority to make decisions. But very often we're making decisions in a highly collaborative way."[53]

I-Many
www.imany.com

As a marketing manager in consulting firm Accenture's human performance group, Joanne McMorrow has had a similar experience. When she was a consultant, her usual schedule involved flying off Sunday night to be with clients Monday morning. But now, as a marketing manager on the human performance team, she has had to readjust her activities to work harmoniously with her virtual team. Accenture's technology support helps her do this. She uses its Knowledge eXchange to share documents and check project progress.[54] She uses NetMeeting and her phone to participate in team meetings. She's careful to tell team members when she's stepping away for a brief break during a long virtual meeting. She uses **www.mylearning.com** to take courses, and, once a quarter, she and her team get together to renew acquaintances.

Accenture
www.accenture.com

Leadership and Trust Technology notwithstanding, several other factors contribute to a virtual team's success. For one thing, given the lack of proximity and opportunities for personal interaction, fostering trust among team members is a challenge. One study concluded that virtual teams with the highest levels of trust had three characteristics. First, team members began their projects by introducing themselves and providing some personal background, rather than immediately focusing on the team's task.[55] Second, they made sure that each member had a specific task and role. Third, high-trust virtual teams had the right attitude. The team members "consistently displayed eagerness, enthusiasm, and an intense action orientation in all their messages."

It helps if virtual team members keep cultural differences in mind. One expert therefore suggests removing cultural idioms (like "apples to oranges") from communications and using multiple channels (such as videoconferencing and email) to build in redundancy to ensure that both verbal and non-verbal messages are understood.[56]

There is nothing like experience, so many firms rotate team leadership across countries and divisions. As one person who has studied transnational teams said, "by rotating and diffusing team leadership across countries, managers in several subsidiaries gain an appreciation for cross-border coordination and learn to iron out conflicts and to use teams to achieve their objectives."[57]

Procter & Gamble uses this approach. As John Pepper, Procter & Gamble's chairperson, put it: "we felt that if each subsidiary manager also had a team, they would come to understand the value and challenge of working on a regional basis. We set up a brand team on Lenor, another on Pampers, another on Pantene, and so on. We assign different country managers to lead these; really wanting to get everybody into the fire, so to speak, experiencing it. What made the teams work was the mutual interdependency that grew."[58]

Self-Directed Work Teams

Many firms use self-managing teams today. A **self-managing/self-directed work team** is "a highly trained group of around eight employees, fully responsible for turning out a well-defined segment of finished work."[59] The "well-defined segment" might be an entire jet engine or a fully processed insurance claim. The distinguishing features of self-directed teams are that they are empowered to direct and do virtually all their own work, and the work results in a singular, well-defined item.

self-managing/self-directed work team
A group of employees empowered to direct and do virtually all their own work, and the work results in a singular, well-defined item.

Firms often organize the work of a whole facility around self-managing teams. The GE aircraft engine plant in Durham, North Carolina, is a self-managing team-based facility. The plant's 170 workers work in teams, all of which report to one boss, the factory manager.[60]

Johnsonville Foods is another good example. Here self-managing teams recruit, hire, evaluate, and (if necessary) fire on their own. Many of the workers have little or no education beyond high school. However, they "train one another, formulate and track their own budgets, make capital investment proposals as needed, handle quality control and inspection, develop their own quantitative standards, improve every process and product, and create prototypes of possible new products."[61]

Such empowerment can be very motivating and can trigger vast improvements in productivity. As the vice president of one consumer goods company said about organizing his firm around teams: "People on the floor were talking about world markets, customer needs, competitors' products, making process improvements—all the things managers are supposed to think about."[62]

Another example of the use of self-managed teams is presented in the "Challenge of Change" box.

The Building Blocks of Productive Teams

Simply requiring several people to work together doesn't make them a team and certainly not a productive one. Let's look at what managers can do to build effective teams.

THE CHALLENGE OF CHANGE

Team Building at Published Image, Inc.

Published Image, Inc. produces shareholder newsletters. Founder Eric Gershman had organized employees into self-managed teams and envisioned the day that his own position would become superfluous. He felt that employees who were capable of preparing their own work schedules, budgets, and bonuses shouldn't have much use for a boss.

With the growth of mutual funds, Gershman had correctly predicted the need for shareholder newsletters. He spent his entire savings getting Published Image off the ground. Eleven clients and U.S.$600 000 in revenue later, things didn't look so good. Turnover was high, morale was low, factual errors were common, and a third of the clients were leaving annually. Gershman came up with a 250-page plan of action to solve these problems. He says he blew up the whole company and completely changed how people thought about their jobs.

Published Image was divided into four independent teams responsible for client relations, sales, editorial content, and production. Everyone had a specialty, but they all shared responsibility for daily deadlines as well. Account executive Shelley Danse says that in the new structure everyone works together like a single unit, and they all do whatever jobs are necessary to get the total job done. Her day can cover everything from research to proofreading to laying out artwork.

Published Image's team approach has fostered a sense of collective ownership of the firm's output. It has also enhanced appreciation of the work of other employees. Planning has become easier, efficiency has improved, and clients are impressed. For example, Peter Herlihy, vice president of mutual funds marketing at Fleet Financial Group, says that at Published Image there is an entire group of people who know all facets of Fleet's projects, and any one of them can be contacted during the process.

Gershman soon got his wish of working himself out of a job. After annual revenues doubled to more than U.S.$4 million, his company was bought out by Standard & Poors.

Does Teamwork Work?

The evidence regarding work team productivity is actually a bit mixed. After Kodak's consumer film finishing division instituted a team-based structure, its division manager reported that unit costs declined by 6 percent per year over six years, and that productivity increased by more than 200 percent, from 383 units per employee to 836.[63] Another research study analyzed the impact of work teams on manufacturing performance in a unionized plant.[64] During a 21-month period, the plant was converted to a team structure. The researchers found that "quality and labor productivity improved over time after the introduction of work teams."[65]

Kodak
www.kodak.com

Yet other programs have failed.[66] One highly publicized failure occurred in the U.S. factories of Levi Strauss. The firm prided itself on its "made in USA" philosophy. However, as competitors with cheaper sources overseas cut into Levi's sales, the firm tried to find a way to keep its U.S. factories going but with higher productivity. The idea it hit on was the Work Team Program. The results are interesting.

At the time, most of the firm's U.S. plants operated on the piecework system. The firm paid each worker a sum for each specialized task (like attaching a belt loop) that he or she finished.[67] The Work Team Program changed that. Now a pair of pants would be constructed entirely by a group of 10 to 35 workers, who would share all the tasks and be paid according to the total number of trousers the group finished each day. The idea was to boost productivity by, among other things, enabling employees to do several jobs instead of one.

Unfortunately, it didn't work out that way. High-performing, faster workers in a group found their wages pulled down by slower-working colleagues (who, conversely, saw their hourly wages rise). Morale fell, arguments ensued, and at some plants, a pair of Dockers that previously cost U.S.$5 to stitch together now cost U.S.$7.50. But the results weren't entirely negative. Teams that were more homogeneous (in terms of work skills) did see their productivity rise. Average turnaround—the time from when an order is received to when the products are shipped to retail stores—improved from nine weeks to seven. Levi Strauss decided to continue the Work Team Program at its remaining U.S. plants, but for 6000 of its U.S. employees, that is now irrelevant. Levi's soon announced it was closing 11 U.S. plants, dismissing one third of its U.S. employees.

The mixed results at Levi's underscores a fact of life with regard to implementing programs like these: They are always (or should be) merely part of a comprehensive set of associated organizational changes. When teams are introduced, companies also flatten the management hierarchy, cut personnel, restructure tasks, change incentive plans and take other steps, all of which need to be consistent with, and make sense in light of, the new team-based organization. At Levi Strauss, for instance, it wasn't necessarily organizing around teams that created the problem, but the team-based incentive plan that the firm implemented with it. Failing to understand the systemic nature of a program like this is probably enough to doom it but is only one of several potential problems.

What Causes Unproductive Teams?

The list of things that can cause teams to be unproductive is unfortunately quite long.

- Teams should harness divergent skills to achieve their aims, but divergent points of view may instead trigger tension and conflict.[68]

- A team member may simply be ignored, thus eliminating a potentially valuable resource.[69]

- Power struggles may cripple the team, as when individual members undermine potentially productive ideas simply because they want to make their own point.

- An intentionally provocative team member may spread turmoil: "One bad apple can spoil the bunch," as the saying goes.[70]

- An unequal distribution of workload among team members and a lack of management support can further undermine the team.[71]

- Groupthink is one phenomenon that can have disastrous results. Just before the explosion of the ill-fated *Challenger* flight in 1986, one engineer reportedly tried to

"No decision. They're still sleeping on it."

tell colleagues and managers about his concerns that the low temperatures surrounding the shuttle could cause the engine's sealing rings to leak hot gas. As he put it, "I received cold stares ...With looks as if to say, 'go away and don't bother us with the facts.' They just would not respond verbally to...me. I felt totally helpless at that moment and that further argument was fruitless, so I, too, stopped pressing my case."[72]

Many of the problems noted above stem from inadequate leadership, focus, and/or capability (see Figure 14.2). For example, in some team situations, the *leadership* is absent or ineffectual. Where there is (or should be) an elected or appointed team leader, this person is not providing the direction or vision, or isn't fighting hard enough for the team's resources. Improving the situation may mean changing the leader, or at least getting him or her to provide the necessary direction.

Sometimes it's a lack of *focus*. If you spoke with the team members, they'd articulate a lack of clarity about the team's purpose, roles, strategy, and goals. Comments here might include, "Why are we organized this way, and what are we supposed to be doing?" The solution here is to clarify the team's charter or mission, as well as team members' roles.

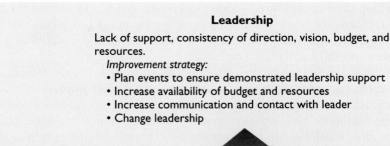

Leadership

Lack of support, consistency of direction, vision, budget, and resources.

Improvement strategy:
- Plan events to ensure demonstrated leadership support
- Increase availability of budget and resources
- Increase communication and contact with leader
- Change leadership

Focus

Lack of clarity about team purpose, roles, strategy, and goals.

Improvement strategy:
- Establish and clarify team charter
- Clarify boundary conditions
- Ensure open channels for communications and information transfer
- Clarify team member roles
- Establish regular team meetings

Capability

Lack of critical skill sets, knowledge, ongoing learning, and development.

Improvement strategy:
- Provide appropriate education and training
- Establish a team development plan
- Establish individual development plans
- Reflect on how group process can be improved
- Regularly assess team effectiveness

FIGURE 14.2
Why Teams Fail: The Leadership, Focus, and Capability Pyramid
Each of three factors—leadership, focus, and capability—requires a different improvement strategy to overcome traps that lead to declines in team effectiveness.

Some teams lack the motivation or *capability*. Here employees may lack critical skills or may not have the knowledge they need to do their jobs. Successful team-based facilities like GE's Durham engine plant therefore devote enormous resources to training employees. Eliminating this problem requires staffing the teams with the right employees, providing appropriate education and training, and establishing an incentive plan for the team and its members

Symptoms of Unproductive Teams

Managers don't have to wait for programs to fail before knowing something is wrong. Various early warning signs indicate that there's an unproductive team. Here's what to look for.[73]

- *Non-accomplishment of goals.* The team should have specific goals and milestones. If these aren't met, the program is not working.

- *Cautious, guarded communication.* When team members fear ridicule or a negative reaction, they may say nothing or be cautious in what they say.

- *Lack of disagreement.* Lack of disagreement among team members may reflect an unwillingness to share true feelings and ideas.

- *Malfunctioning meetings.* Unproductive teams often have meetings characterized by boredom, lack of enthusiastic participation, failure to make decisions, or dominance by one or two people.

- *Conflict within the team.* A suspicious, combative environment and personalized conflict among team members may signal problems in the team.

Characteristics of Productive Teams

Experienced managers who have worked successfully with teams have very clear ideas about what makes teams successful. For example, H. David Aycock, the former chairman, CEO, and president of steel maker Nucor Corp. says successful teams have seven key ingredients:

Nucor
www.nucor.com

1. The mission must be clearly defined and articulated, and everybody has to understand it. That includes an understanding of the project purpose.

2. All team members have to be positive thinkers.

3. Selfish people spell doom for a team effort.

4. Each team member must have enough self-confidence and self-respect to respect other team members.

5. The team leader must always be on the lookout for distractions, tensions, and unproductive or ancillary issues. If the leader spots the project going astray, it is [his or her] responsibility to get it back on track—fast.

6. Each member trusts the motives of the other members.

7. The team has to be as small as possible. If you have more people that are absolutely necessary on a team, members will start functioning like a committee.[74]

What It Takes to Be a Team Player

Whether at school, work, or sports, we've all served on teams with people who did more harm then good. These people weren't team players. They would not

Team members at Rodel, Inc., a manufacturing firm, after completing a rigourous leadership-training program aimed at building trust, teamwork, and leadership.

CHECKLIST **14.1**

How to Build a Productive Team

Research is fairly consistent with respect to what makes teams successful. The building blocks include:[75]

☑ *A clear mission/purpose.* Teams like those that build the Saturn have a clear, broad mission or purpose, such as "Build a world-class quality car."

☑ *Commitment to a mission.* One study found that "the essence of a team is a common commitment. Without it, groups perform as individuals; with it, they become a powerful unit of collective performance."[76] Members believe "we are all in this together" and "we all have to hold ourselves accountable for doing whatever is needed to help the team achieve its mission."[77] Productive teams then develop their own definition of what management wants the team to do: "The best teams invest a tremendous amount of time and effort exploring, shaping, and agreeing on a purpose that belongs to them both collectively and individually."[78]

☑ *Specific performance goals.* Productive teams then translate their common purpose (such as "build world-class quality cars") into specific team goals (such as "reduce new-car defects to no more than four per vehicle"). In fact, "transforming broad directives into specific and measurable performance goals is the surest first step for a team trying to shape a purpose meaningful to its members."[79]

☑ *Right size, right mix.* High-performing teams generally (but not always) have fewer than 25 people, and usually between 7 and 14. Team members' skills should also complement each other in terms of technical expertise, problem solving, decision making, and interpersonal relationships. Getting along is important, too: Teams comprising agreeable and conscientious employees received higher supervisory ratings and better objective measures of team accuracy and completion than did those with less agreeable and conscientious employees.[80]

☑ *An agreed-upon structure appropriate to the task.* Productive teams agree on how they will work together. For example, team members agree about who does particular jobs; how schedules are set and followed; what skills need to be developed; what members have to do to earn continuing membership in the team; and how to make decisions.

☑ *The authority to make the decisions needed, given their mission.*

☑ *Access to or control of the resources needed to complete their mission.*

☑ *A mix of group and individual rewards.*

☑ *Longevity and stability of team membership.*

---

put the team's needs above their own; they would not do their share of the work; and their argumentative nature often caused turmoil and grief. As one writer put it, "some people...find it difficult to subordinate their inner drive to that of their team members. Like it or not, they end up being labelled as not team players and may have hurt their career potential because of their behavior."[81] Managers and prospective managers should therefore ask themselves whether they have the personality and skills to be team players.

Personality Experienced managers (as noted above) know what they're looking for when it comes to hiring team players. Nucor's David Aycock wants "positive thinkers." He says "selfish people spell doom for a team effort," that each team member must have enough "self-confidence and self-respect to respect other team members," and that "each member must trust the motives of the other members." Big Apple Circus's Paul Binder looks for "a certain kind of flexibility—a willingness to work outside their own conceptions of what has to be" (see the "People Side of Managing" box on page 454).

To some extent, your propensity to be a team player reflects your tendency to be "individualistic" or "collectivist" in how you approach tasks and people. Individualists tend to prefer to work alone, while collectivists prefer working with others. Figure 14.3 provides a rough and ready measure of the extent to which these labels fit you. Add your answers

Circle the answer that most closely resembles your attitude.

	Strongly Disagree				Strongly Agree		
1. Only those who depend on themselves get ahead in life.	7	6	5	4	3	2	1
2. To be superior, a person must stand alone.	7	6	5	4	3	2	1
3. If you want something done right, you must do it yourself.	7	6	5	4	3	2	1
4. What happens to me is my own doing.	7	6	5	4	3	2	1
5. In the long run, the only person you can count on is yourself.	7	6	5	4	3	2	1
6. Winning is everything.	7	6	5	4	3	2	1
7. I feel that winning is important in both work and games.	7	6	5	4	3	2	1
8. Success is the most important thing in life.	7	6	5	4	3	2	1
9. It annoys me when other people perform better than I do.	7	6	5	4	3	2	1
10. Doing your best is not enough; it is important to win.	7	6	5	4	3	2	1
11. I prefer to work with others in a group rather than work alone.	7	6	5	4	3	2	1
12. Given a choice, I would rather do a job where I can work alone rather than doing a job where I have to work with others in a group.	7	6	5	4	3	2	1
13. Working with a group is better than working alone.	7	6	5	4	3	2	1
14. People should be made aware that if they are going to be part of a group, then they are sometimes going to have to do things they do not want to do.	7	6	5	4	3	2	1
15. People who belong to a group should realize that they are not always going to get what they personally want.	7	6	5	4	3	2	1
16. People in a group should realize that they sometimes are going to have to make sacrifices for the sake of the group as a whole.	7	6	5	4	3	2	1
17. People in a group should be willing to make sacrifices for the sake of the group's well-being.	7	6	5	4	3	2	1
18. A group is most productive when its members do what *they* want to do rather than what the group wants to do.	7	6	5	4	3	2	1
19. A group is most efficient when its members do what *they* think is best rather than do what the group wants them to do.	7	6	5	4	3	2	1
20. A group is most productive when its members follow their own interests and concerns.	7	6	5	4	3	2	1

Add your answers to calculate your score. The higher your score, the higher your collectivist orientation, so high scores are more compatible with being a team player.

FIGURE 14.3
Do You Have a Team Mentality?

to arrive at your score. In one study of 492 undergraduate students, their average score was about 89. Scores below 65 to 70 suggest a preference for working alone, while scores above 110 indicate a preference for collaborating with others.[82]

Skills Personality is important, but studies show that you also need specific interpersonal and self-management knowledge, skills, and abilities to work effectively in teams.[83] *Interpersonally*, for instance, team members need effective conflict resolution, collaborative problem solving, and communication skills. In terms of *conflict resolution*, team members need (1) the ability to recognize and encourage desirable (but discourage undesirable) team conflict; (2) to recognize the type and source of conflict and implement appropriate resolution strategies; and (3) the ability to use integrative, rather than disruptive approaches to negotiation.

In terms of *collaborative problem solving skills*, team members need (1) the ability to match the proper degree of participation for the problem; and (2) to be able to recognize obstacles to collaborative problem solving and then implement appropriate corrective actions.

In terms of *communication skills*, they need (1) the ability to recognize and utilize decentralized means of communicating (so that everyone can interact); (2) to communicate openly and supportively; (3) to listen non-evaluatively and to use active listening; and (4) to engage in "small talk" and ritual greetings.

Since many teams manage themselves, team members also need various *self-management skills*. These include goal setting and performance management skills, specifically (1) the ability to help establish specific, challenging, and accepted team goals; and (2) to monitor, evaluate, and provide feedback on performance. Team players also need planning and task coordination self-management skills, in particular (1) the ability to coordinate and synchronize activities, information, and tasks among team members; and (2) the ability to help establish task and role assignments for individual team members and ensure proper balancing of workloads.

Consultants who have worked with top management teams say top managers sometimes make the worst team players. Says one, "CEOs often have team-averse personality types. In a way, the problem is too much talent at the table...You get a CEO running a team composed essentially of five other CEOs—the heads of divisions of businesses—and there is a natural tendency to wonder, who is really the boss here? These are super accelerators, ambitious people, and there is only one step higher than the one they're now occupying: the top job.... You would be amazed at the level of threats some executives perceive from one another."[84]

THE **PEOPLE** SIDE OF **MANAGING**

Getting Along at the Circus

Big Apple Circus
www.bigapplecircus.org

Paul Binder, founder and artistic director of the Big Apple Circus, faces an interesting challenge when he staffs and organizes his shows. This travelling circus is famous for the skills of its artists, as well as for their ability to work together as a team in the show. Working together collegially to present a seamless show is no easy matter when you consider how diverse the team is. In a typical year, for instance "the Circus is made up of 25 performers, including Chinese acrobats, Russian and Polish aerialists, elephant trainers from the United States, a French clown, the Danish equestrian, and a bird trainer from England."

How does Big Apple's founder and artistic director put together a troop that is both diverse and collaborative? He says that it is important to pick the right people. "They are talented, of course. Because they travel together and work together, they must be people who can get along well with others and be able to engage each other."

How does he select his performers? When he finds out about potential acts for the Circus, he visits with them and watches them. He's looking for skill. They have to be a great act; they have to bring something dazzling to the audience. But along with that, he tries to spend quite a bit of time talking with them. What he's listening for is a certain kind of flexibility—a willingness to work outside their own conceptions of what "has to be." For instance, Binder might say to them, "You know, I think we might want to change your costumes or music. How do you feel about that?" He wants to hear openness in their answer, and he wants to get a sense that they're willing to create something bigger than their individual act.

Leading Productive Teams

In many respects, "team leadership" is the example that springs to mind when most of us think of leading. We think of the captain leading her team, the soldier leading his squad, or the scientist leading a research team that makes some brilliant discovery. To a large extent, team leadership is what leading is about, and, therefore, the leadership techniques from Chapter 11 are applicable to team leadership situations. For example, you can use the situational leadership model to help decide the style (telling, selling, participating, or delegating) that's best for your team's situation.

Team Leader Skills

Leading productive teams often presents some special challenges. For example, it often requires a lot more emphasis on coaching and much less emphasis on "being the boss." It also therefore frequently requires being able to surrender some of the trappings of supervisory authority. This is particularly the case when the team is supposed to manage itself. In these situations, three underlying skills characterize team leaders. First, they coach, they don't boss. The coach's main role is to help people develop their skills. It is not their job to tell people what to do or to sell their own ideas, but to help others define, analyze, and solve problems.[85] Team leaders also need to stimulate employee initiative and autonomy by raising questions, helping team members identify alternatives, providing general direction, encouraging employees to contribute their own ideas, and supplying feedback.[86] Second, they encourage participation. They solicit input into decisions, share decision-making responsibility, and delegate specifically identified decisions to the team. Third, they are facilitators.[87] They give the other team members the self-confidence, authority, information, and tools they need to get their jobs done.

What Are Team Leader Values?

Skills and behaviours like these don't come easily to some people. For instance, not everyone is philosophically prepared to surrender the trappings of "being a boss." This is not at all like running a traditional assembly line. Leaders like these therefore need to be able to commit to the values described below.

People Deserve Respect Effective team leaders have respect for the individual. At Saturn, for instance, team members carry a card that lists the firm's values, one of which is: "We have nothing of greater value than our people. We believe that demonstrating respect for the uniqueness of every individual builds a team of confident, creative members possessing a high degree of initiative, self-respect, and self-discipline."[88]

Saturn
www.saturn.com

Toyota, long known for its exemplary team approach, also reflects this "people first" philosophy. Here's how one manager puts it: "In all our meetings and in every way, all Toyota top managers continually express their trust in human nature. Mr. Cho [the chief executive of the company] continually reminds us that the team members must come first and that every other action we take and decision we make must be adapted to that basic idea; I must manage around that core idea."[89]

Team Members Can Be Trusted Good team leaders believe that people like to work, have self-control, can motivate themselves, and are smart. They trust team members to do their best. They believe team members can and want to do a good job, and they focus much of their attention on ensuring that team members have what they need to do their jobs.

Teamwork Comes First Team leaders believe in stripping away the barriers that can undermine teamwork. For example, they are willing to minimize status differences, since such differences build barriers to team member relations. At Toyota Manufacturing in Lexington, Kentucky, none of the managers—not even the president—have private offices or even executive parking spaces.

Typical Leader Transition Problems

Moving from being a traditional, in-charge supervisor to a facilitator/coach isn't easy. As one former executive put it: "Working...under the autocratic system was a lot easier, particularly when you want something done quickly and you are convinced you know the right way to do it. It is a lot easier to say, 'OK, we're going to Toronto tomorrow,' rather than sit down and say, 'All right, first of all, do we want to go out of town? And where do we want to go—east or west?'"[90]

The following factors make it hard to transition from "boss" to "coach."

Perceived Loss of Power or Status Moving from supervisor to team leader often involves a loss of power or status.[91] One day you're the boss, with the authority to give orders and have others obey. The next day the pyramid is upside-down. Now you're a facilitator/coach, trying to make sure your team members have what they need to do their jobs—to a large extent, without you.

Unclear Team Leader Roles Some companies make the mistake of overemphasizing what the former supervisor (now team leader) is *not*. You're not the boss, you are not to control or direct any more, you are not to make all the hiring decisions any more. All of this can leave the person with the very real question, "What exactly am I supposed to be doing?" In fact, team leaders do have important duties—for instance, as coaches, facilitators, and boundary managers. Management's job is to ensure that the team leaders understand what their new duties are and how they can do their new jobs effectively.

Job Security Concerns Telling former supervisors/new team leaders they're not in charge anymore understandably undermines their sense of security. After all, it's not unreasonable for someone to ask, "Just how secure is the job of managing a self-managing team?" For example, General Mills claims much of the productivity improvement from its self-directed work teams came from eliminating middle managers.

Companies handle this problem in several ways. Many of the new teams still need a facilitator/coach, so some supervisors will find new jobs as team leaders. When chemical firm Rohm and Haas changed over to self-directing work teams at one of its plants, the redundant supervisors were turned into training coordinators. The firm made them responsible for managing the continuing educational requirements of the plant's new teams.[92]

Rohm & Haas
www.rohmhaas.com

The Double Standard Problem Some supervisors will feel that the company is treating them as second-class citizens compared with the employees who are being trained to be team members. The smart way to proceed is to create and implement a development and transition plan for the supervisors too—one that clarifies their new duties and identifies the training they'll receive as they make the transition from supervisor to team leader.

Steps in Becoming a Functioning, Self-Managing Team

Working as part of a self-managing team can be unnerving to those who haven't done so before. Employees who are used to having the boss plan the work and make most decisions can feel somewhat adrift. Those leading such teams therefore need to be able to anticipate the problems that can arise and react accordingly. Consultants and others who work with teams often describe the team development process in terms of five main stages: forming, storming, norming, performing, and adjourning. We'll look at these as part of the larger context of the typical team-development sequence.

Startup An executive steering committee (often with employee input) analyzes the feasibility of a team-based structure and then takes steps to implement such a program. The committee identifies measurable goals, chooses the initial sites for the team-based program, and makes an initial division of work among teams.

Forming Toward the end of this start-up phase, the committee announces plans for the teams' membership and structure. The teams and their leaders then begin working out their specific roles. During this forming stage, team members work on building friendships and working out issues they may have regarding the team's purpose, structure, and leadership.[93]

Training At about this point, team members suddenly find themselves requiring a great deal of training. They have to learn how to communicate and how to listen, how to use administrative procedures and budgets, and how to develop other skills. Supervisors must learn how to become facilitators and coaches rather than top-down supervisors.[94]

Storming In this stage, questions typically arise regarding who is leading the team and what the team's structure and purpose should be. Now the initial enthusiasm has worn off, and the employees in the newly team-based plant or office may enter a period of confusion. Team members may become concerned about whether their new higher work standards may backfire at compensation time and whether they'll be able to manage themselves. Supervisors may also become increasingly concerned about their apparently shrinking role in day-to-day operations.

Slipping Into Leader-Centred Teams Ideally, the team's confidence grows as members master their new skills and find better ways to accomplish their work. The chief danger now is that the teams become too reliant on leaders. Rather than remaining self-directed, some may slip into the habit of letting an elected team member carry out the former supervisor's role. Rather than making decisions by consensus and letting all team members contribute to the team's direction, they allow someone—perhaps one of their own—to supervise them. One way to avoid this is "to make sure everyone continues to learn and eventually exercise leadership skills...[and] allow anyone to exercise leadership functions as needed."[95]

Norming Co-operation and mutual support characterize this stage. At this point, the team members have already agreed on matters like purpose, structure, and leadership and are prepared to start really working. Misplaced loyalty is one potential danger at this stage. The team's newfound cohesiveness and norms can prompt team members to "cover for" poorly performing members out of a sense of misguided loyalty. Management's job here is to emphasize the need for the team to temper intra-team co-operation with its responsibility to supervise its own members. The organization can then move to what one researcher calls "the period of true self-direction."[96]

Performing The performing stage is a period of productivity, achievement, and pride as the team members work together to get their job done.

Adjourning With some teams (such as temporary project teams) there may be an adjourning stage, as the team wraps up its work. The team members will face the mixed emotions of both separation and satisfaction over a job well done.

How to Improve Team Performance

We saw that productive teams require certain building blocks (for example, "a clear mission or purpose" and "right size, right mix"). Team leaders can take certain actions to put these features in place:

- *Start with employee input.* Participation fosters acceptance. Management can institute team structures unilaterally, but it's probably best to start with a committee of employees.

- *Select members for skill and teamwork.* Teams don't just require technically competent employees. They need people who are able to work together collegially and learn new skills. Choose people both for their existing skills and for their potential to improve existing skills and learn new ones. Recruit and select employees who have a history of preferring to work in teams and of being good team members.

- *Keep size small.* Create teams with the smallest number of employees required to do the work. Large size reduces interaction and involvement and increases the need for extra coordination.[97]

- *Establish challenging performance standards.* All team members need to believe the team has urgent and worthwhile goals. They also need to know what their performance standards are. Provide intermediate milestones.

- *Emphasize the task's importance.* Team members need to know that what they're doing is important for the company. Emphasize the task's importance in terms of customers, other employees, the organization's mission, and the company's overall results.

- *Assign whole tasks.* Try to make the team responsible for a discrete piece of work, such as an entire product, project, or segment of the business. This can boost team members' sense of responsibility and ownership.

- *Send the right signals.* Management has to "walk the talk" by demonstrating that it's committed to the team approach. When potential teams first gather, everyone monitors the signals to confirm, suspend, or dispel concerns about management's commitment to the team approach. If a senior executive leaves the team kickoff meeting "to take a phone call" and then never returns, the message is that he or she doesn't care about the team. Similarly, there are many ways to recognize team performance besides money. They include having a senior executive speak directly to the team about the urgency of its mission and using praise to recognize contributions.

- *Encourage social support.* Teams are more effective when members support each other. A manager should set a good example by being supportive and taking concrete steps to encourage and reinforce positive interactions and cohesiveness within the team.

- *Make sure there are unambiguous team rules.* The most critical rules pertain to attendance (for example, "no interruptions to take phone calls"); discussion ("no sacred cows"); confidentiality ("the only things to leave this room are what we agree on"); analytic approach ("facts are friendly"); end-product orientation ("everyone gets assignments and does them"); constructive confrontation ("no finger pointing"); and contributions ("everyone does real work").

- *Challenge the group with fresh facts and information.* New information—about performance or new competitors—causes a team to redefine and enrich its understanding of the challenges it faces. It also helps the team reshape its common purpose and refine its goals.

- *Train and cross-train.* Training should be extensive and ongoing. It should embrace topics such as the philosophy of doing work through teams, how teams make decisions, interpersonal and communications skills for team members, and the technical skills required to perform their jobs. To boost flexibility and reduce absenteeism-related disruptions, cross-train employees to learn other team member's jobs. The training program for one of BMW's new auto plants included sessions on problem solving, communication, and how to deal with conflict within and between teams. Workers received more than 80 hours of team skills training on topics like problem analysis. As the HR director for BMW Manufacturing put it, training employees about technical matters is straightforward; teaching them how to work well with others is much harder.[98]

BMW
www.bmw.com

- *Provide the necessary tools and material support.* Training and support are futile if the teams don't have the tools and infrastructure they need to do their jobs. One study found such support to "be more important than [just] ensuring group members are cohesive."[99] The researchers found that material support should include timely information, resources, and rewards that encourage group, rather than individual, performance. The findings also suggest that "...organizations should determine if the necessary support resources are available before creating teams."[100]

- *Encourage "emotionally intelligent" team behaviour.* For example, acknowledge and discuss group moods; communicate your sense of what is transpiring in the team; tell your teammates what you're thinking and how you are feeling; ask whether everyone agrees with the decision; ask quiet members what they think; "call" members on their errant behaviour; support members and volunteer to help them if need be; protect members from attack; and never be derogatory or demeaning.[101]

Design the Organization to Support Teams

We saw above (in discussing teams at Levi Strauss) that the context of the team program is quite important.[102] There's more to a successful team program than organizing the teams and telling them to "go at it." Even setting clear missions, providing support, and encouraging emotionally intelligent behaviour won't work if the whole company, including its policies and systems, isn't compatible with the team approach. Experience suggests that the firm must have the right philosophy, structure, systems, policies, and employee skills in order to properly support teams (see Figure 14.4).

Organizational Philosophy Organizing self-managing teams and then showing employees you don't trust them is clearly self-defeating. The team approach therefore calls for a new mindset on management's part. They have to make it clear by word and deed that they're sincere about involving and trusting employees.

Organizational Structure In team-based companies, teams are the basic work units. The teams carry out supervisory tasks ranging from scheduling overtime to actually doing the work. These firms have flat hierarchies with relatively few supervisors and have delegated much decision-making authority to the work teams.

Organizational Systems Every company depends on standard operating systems to make sure that everything goes smoothly. These range from performance appraisal and incentives systems to the systems used to gather marketing data and to monitor sales and production levels.

Organizing around teams means thinking through how to make the firm's systems compatible with the team approach. For example, managers will want to pay financial incentives to the team as a whole, rather than to individual employees. Similarly, they may institute a "360-degree appraisal system" that captures feedback from all the worker's teammates, not just the facility's managers.

Organizational Policies Every company uses organizational policies (such as "we only use fresh ingredients") to guide their employees' decisions. Team-based firms need team-friendly policies. For example, organizing around self-managing teams requires some stability. It hardly pays to spend years building self-managing teams if the firm lays off

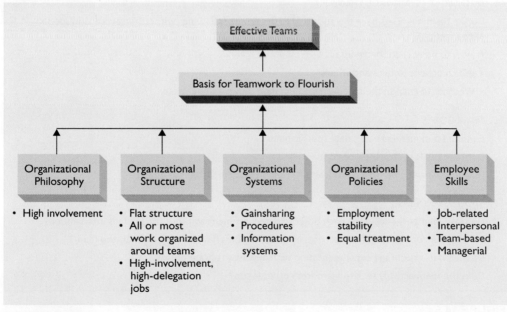

FIGURE 14.4
Designing Organizations to Manage Teams

employees at the first sign of a slowdown. Employment stability is thus one policy firms like these try to adhere to. At Toyota, for instance, slack demand might mean that more employees spend time training to develop new skills, rather than being laid off.

Employee Skills Work teams typically have wide-ranging responsibilities (such as scheduling their own time, hiring team members, and managing their own quality). It's therefore essential that all team members have a wide range of skills. These include (1) the skills to actually do the job, (2) the interpersonal skills to work effectively with other team members, (3) team skills (such as problem solving), and (4) management skills (planning, leading, and controlling).

Figure 14.5 provides diagnostic questions team leaders can use to see whether they're doing what's necessary to address critical factors for a team's success (such as setting a clear direction and formulating an effective team rewards program).

---

1. CLEAR DIRECTION

   Can team members articulate a clear direction, shared by all members, of the basic purpose that the team exists to achieve?

2. A REAL TEAM TASK

   Is the team assigned collective responsibility for all of the team's customers and major outputs?

   Is the team required to make collective decisions about work strategies (rather than leaving it to individuals)?

   Are members cross-trained, able to help each other?

   Does the team get team-level data and feedback about its performance?

   Is the team required to meet frequently, and does it do so?

3. TEAM REWARDS

   Counting all reward dollars available, are more than 80 percent available to teams only and not to individuals?

4. BASIC MATERIAL RESOURCES

   Does the team have its own meeting space?

   Can the team easily get basic materials needed for the work?

5. AUTHORITY TO MANAGE THE WORK

   Do the team members have the authority to decide the following (without first receiving special authorization)?

   • How to meet client demands.

   • Which actions to take and when.

   • Whether to change their work strategies when they deem necessary.

6. TEAM GOALS

   Can the team members articulate specific goals?

   Do these goals stretch their performance?

   Have they specified a time by which they intend to accomplish these goals?

7. STRATEGY NORMS

   Do team members encourage each other to detect problems without the leader's intervention?

   Do members openly discuss differences in what members have to contribute to the team?

   Do members encourage experimentation with new ways of operating?

   Does the team actively seek to learn from other teams?

FIGURE 14.5
Critical Success Factors: Diagnostic Questions for Team Leaders

SKILLS AND STUDY MATERIAL

SUMMARY

1. Work teams are examples of employee involvement programs, which let employees participate in formulating important work decisions or in supervising all or most of their work activities. Managers rank such programs as their biggest productivity boosters.

2. Several aspects of group dynamics are especially important for leaders grappling with how to build more effective teams. Group norms are important because they're the rules groups use to control their members. Group cohesiveness determines the attraction of the group for its members and is influenced by things like proximity, interpersonal attractiveness, homogeneity of interests or goals, and inter-group competition.

3. Leaders can use four general types of teams in organizations: suggestion teams, problem-solving teams, semi-autonomous teams, and self-managing teams. Specific examples of teams include quality circles; project, development, or venture teams; transnational teams; and self-directed work teams.

4. Symptoms of unproductive teams include cautious or guarded communication, lack of disagreement, use of personal criticism, malfunctioning meetings, unclear goals, low commitment, and conflict within the team. Characteristics of productive teams include commitment to a mission, specific performance goals, the right size and mix, a common approach, and mutual accountability.

5. How can a leader go about building a high-performing team? Guidelines include establishing demanding performance standards; selecting members for skill and skill potential; setting clear rules of behaviour; moving from "boss" to "coach"; choosing people who like teamwork; training team members; assigning whole tasks; and encouraging social support. When teams do not succeed, the problem often lies in one of three factors: leadership, focus, or capability.

6. Team leaders have special duties. They coach, encourage participation, are boundary managers, and facilitate. Moving from boss to team leader can therefore cause transition problems stemming from the perceived loss of power or status, unclear team–leader roles, job security concerns, and problems with double standards.

7. Not everyone is cut out to be an effective leader of self-managing teams. A successful team leader must adhere to the right values, including putting team members first, trusting team members to do their best, helping team members to self-actualize, developing team members' capabilities, emphasizing teamwork, delegating, and eliminating barriers to success.

CRITICAL THINKING EXERCISES

1. In many of the exercises throughout this book, you have been working in teams. Compare team cohesiveness as the term has progressed. Has it increased or decreased? What accounts for this? What group norms have evolved? Explain why your team does or does not have the necessary building blocks to be a highly effective team.

2. One of the keys to effective teams is to assemble what Jennifer James in *Thinking in the Future Tense* (Simon & Schuster, 1996) calls thinking skills. She discusses a number of approaches, including evaluating and identifying your thinking (pp. 190–206). Many of her points can be directly applied to teams. Using Edward De Bono's Hat analysis, she gives us an easy way to understand what approach to thinking people take by relating them to imaginary hats they are wearing. This is a condensed version of his guide:

White hat—the white-hat thinker is mainly concerned with facts and figures.

Red hat—the red hat thinker operates from an emotional source.

Black hat—the black-hat thinker dwells on why something cannot be done.

Yellow hat—the yellow-hat thinker is optimistic.

Green hat—the green-hat thinker is creative and open to new ideas.

Blue hat—the blue-hat thinker is concerned with control.

Which hat do you wear at school, work, home, or with friends? Does the same hat always apply? If a team had one each of these hat types, how do you think it would solve problems such as downsizing a company, deciding to merge with another company, or working together on day-to-day projects? What would happen if only green, yellow, and black hats were on a team? Be prepared to discuss and debate these questions in class.

1. You have undoubtedly worked on teams at school, at work, or socially with someone who did not have what it takes to be a team player. In teams of four to five students, discuss your nominees for "the worst team player I ever worked with" (no names, please), including what the person did to win your nomination. List five reasons why you believe the person is not suited to be a team player.

2. Your class has just been appointed by the university administration to form teams to help address racial tensions and discrimination against minorities. Your goal is to create a plan to promote cultural awareness among the student body and to make positive links with the surrounding ethnically diverse community.

The administration prefers that each team consist of students from several constituencies. Assume that those represented are to include the Asian Honour Society, the Aboriginal Outreach Group, the Students with Disabilities Coalition, the Gay and Lesbian Alliance, Christian Outreach, the Muslim Society, the Young Conservatives, and the Older Students Awareness Association.

Form groups of five and select a team leader for each group. Then have each remaining member role-play as a representative of one of the groups listed above. Now create the plan requested by the administration.

BUILDING YOUR MANAGEMENT SKILLS

Analyze Your Team

Most people belong to multiple groups or teams. It might be a volunteer group in the community, a student group at school, a church group, or a work group at your place of employment. Pick any team that you are a member of, and analyze how well it functions. Using the chapter material, answer the following questions:

1. What kind of team is it?

2. How cohesive is the team? How do you know?

3. What are the characteristics of productive teams? To what extent does your team display these characteristics? Be specific and give examples.

4. What are the characteristics of unproductive teams? To what extent does your team display these characteristics? Be specific, and give examples.

5. Make suggestions for improving your team's performance. Address each of the suggestions made in the chapter under the heading "How to Improve Team Performance." Indicate what each of the suggestions would mean in practical terms for your group. For example, for the "start with employee input" suggestion, indicate how that would work in your team and what results it might yield.

Some organizations have implemented self-managed teams (SMTs). To learn more about these teams and the role of the manager, go to R. V. Armstrong & Associates' website at **www.rvarmstrong.com**.

1. Explain the concept of a self-managed team.

2. List the cultural and behavioural differences between traditional work groups and self-managed teams.

3. Identify the downsides of SMTs.

4. Should a self-managed team have a team leader? Explain your answer.

Merging Teams at Canadian National Railways

Over the last decade, the railway industry has been consolidating. There are fewer and fewer small companies as large companies have acquired more and more firms. There was a clear message in the industry: Unless you were large or had a large partner, you were a likely target for a takeover of your firm. Canadian National Railways (CN) understood the market forces clearly. To grow in a consolidating industry, CN would need to acquire other railroads. CN had developed a strong team culture under the leadership of CEO Paul Tellier. Would CN be able to absorb another large railroad and still keep its team-oriented management style? If managers at newly acquired railroads feared for their jobs, would CN be able to get past this fear and build a single team?

The test came in 1998. First, CN merged with the Illinois Central (IC) Railroad. Then, the newly merged firm formed a marketing alliance with the Kansas City Southern Railroad. In the early stages of planning for mergers, Tellier had strong concerns. Regardless of industry forces, Tellier wanted all stakeholders to have a shared vision. He understood that the IC provided a perfect complement to CN (because of their complementary assets) at the perfect time (NAFTA was increasing north–south rail traffic). Communicating this shared vision was the first step.

The second step that Tellier took in building a team was to seek high levels of commitment from top level managers. It was not enough for Tellier to envision the future of CN; the other senior executives also needed to be highly involved. The management team at CN also used proactive communication methods with their stakeholders. Within the first 48 hours of the CN–IC merger, Tellier's team made conference calls to employees in both organizations. They also installed a 1-800 number to handle employee questions about the merger. CN was very careful to establish communication early and to maintain it. CN was also proactive in eliciting commitment to a shared vision.

Although post-acquisition integration can take years, it was apparent from company results that the two formerly separate companies were functioning well as a unit. In 1998, CN announced that it had won the Carrier of the Year award for 1998 from Occidental Chemical Corporation for the third consecutive year. CN had been rated first in performance, ranking ahead of eight other Class 1 railroads.

Questions

1. What concerns might IC managers have about forming teams with their new partner?

2. What steps did Tellier take to build his team?

3. What additional steps would you recommend be taken in the future?

Team Building at the Colorado Symphony Orchestra

Anyone checking the website of the Colorado Symphony Orchestra (CSO) a few years ago would have been greeted by a friendly message that the weekend concert series was sold out. A first-time visitor to the site would not realize that this orchestra, both artistically and financially successful, largely comprised the same group of musicians who watched their Denver Symphony Orchestra (DSO) declare bankruptcy in the late 1980s. The group then decided to change its style and create a new team approach to orchestra management and a new orchestra. The CSO was then founded in 1989. →

Leading Organizational Change

Changing Nissan's Fortunes

OBJECTIVES

After studying this chapter and the case exercises at the end, you should be able to use the material to:

1. Decide whether a company should reorganize and, if so, what the new structure should look like.

2. "Read" a company's organization culture and make specific recommendations regarding how the manager can improve it.

3. Tell a manager what he or she did wrong in implementing the change and how you would rectify the situation.

4. Decide what conflict resolution style is right for a situation, and explain whether your own basic style would be appropriate.

When Renault Car Company executive Carlos Ghosn accepted the job of saving Japan's Nissan Motors, the company faced huge obstacles. In 1999 alone, Nissan had lost U.S.$5.7 billion and had debts of at least U.S.$11.2 billion. It was utilizing just 53 percent of its auto-producing capacity, it was losing U.S.$1000 on every car it sold, and purchasing costs were 15 percent to 25 percent higher than at Renault. As a French citizen flying in to save a famous Japanese company, Ghosn faced a dilemma: How could he implement the widespread cuts and changes he knew were required when doing so might trigger resentment and resistance on the part of the firm's thousands of workers?

The approach used by Carlos Ghosn in his dramatic turnaround of Nissan Motors illustrates how a manager can use his firm's employees to devise and implement the change. Ghosn knew he had to make big changes and that these changes had to be made fast. Another CEO (especially one with experience in the auto business) might have assumed that the way to go was to force through the changes. However, Ghosn felt that if he did that he would have failed. He decided instead to use cross-functional teams in his turnaround effort.

Figure 15.1 summarizes Ghosn's approach. As you can see, he organized cross-functional teams, each with responsibilities for the main tasks required for Nissan to have a successful turnaround. Ghosn appointed teams for business development, purchasing, manufacturing and logistics, research and development, sales and marketing, general and administrative, financing costs, phase-out of products, and organization (the figure shows five of these teams). Each cross-functional team had a set of executive "leaders," a day-to-day operational "pilot," and specific assignments. Each team consisted of about 10 members, all middle managers with line responsibilities (except for the teams "executive leaders").

Based on recent results, the changes designed and implemented by Nissan's teams were quite successful. For example, net profit rose from a loss of U.S.$5.7 billion in fiscal year 1999 to a profit of about U.S.$2.8 billion in fiscal year 2001. Debt dropped from U.S.$11.2 billion to U.S.$5.8 billion in 2002.

Nissan
www.nissan-global.com

Team	Purchasing	Manufacturing & Logistics	Sales & Marketing	Phaseout of Products & Parts Complexity Management	Organization
CFT Leaders	• executive VP of purchasing • executive VP of engineering	• executive VP of manufacturing • executive VP of product planning	• executive VP of overseas sales & marketing • executive VP of domestic sales & marketing	• executive VP of domestic sales & marketing • executive VP of product planning	• executive VP of finance (CFO) • executive VP of manufacturing
CFT Pilot	• general manager of purchasing	• deputy general manager of manufacturing	• manager of overseas sales & marketing	• manager of product planning	• manager of human resources
Functions Represented	• purchasing • engineering • manufacturing • finance	• manufacturing • logistics • product planning • human resources	• sales & marketing • purchasing	• product planning • sales & marketing • manufacturing • engineering • finance • purchasing	• product planning • sales & marketing • manufacturing • engineering • finance • purchasing
Team Review Focus	• supplier relationships • product specifications and standards	• manufacturing efficiency and cost effectiveness	• advertising structure • distribution structure • dealer organization • incentives	• manufacturing efficiency and cost effectiveness	• organizational structure • employee incentive and pay packages
Objectives Based on Review	• cut number of suppliers in half • reduce costs by 20% over three years	• close three assembly plants in Japan • close two power-train plants in Japan • improve capacity utilization in Japan from 53% in 1999 to 82% in 2002	• move to a single global advertising agency • reduce SG&A costs by 20% • reduce distribution subsidiaries by 20% in Japan • close 10% of retail outlets in Japan	• reduce number of plants in Japan from seven to four by 2002 • reduce number of platforms in Japan from 24 to 15 by 2002 • reduce by 50% the variation in parts (due to differences in engines or cars)	• create a worldwide corporate headquarters • create regional management committees • empower program directors • implement performance-oriented compensation.

FIGURE 15.1
Some of Nissan's Cross-Functional Teams (CFTs)

Leading an organizational change can be treacherous, even for a CEO with lots of clout. The change may require the co-operation of dozens or even hundreds of managers and supervisors; resistance may be considerable; and you'll probably have to complete the change while the firm continues to serve its customer. During 2000–2001, Ford CEO Jacques Nasser tried to press through a series of changes aimed at making Ford "one of the world's best-run companies." He tried to change how the firm produced and marketed its cars, and how it evaluated, trained, and rewarded its employees. As CEO, Nasser had enormous clout. However, it wasn't enough to overcome the resistance of the firm's managers, employees, and dealers. His board forced him out in less than a year.

An Overview of the Organizational Change Process

Organizational changes range from simple to complex. Most changes are relatively limited. For example, you may want to stop two departments from bickering, or install a new computer, or get your employees to be less risk-averse. At the other extreme, major changes like those instituted by Jacques Nasser require changing a vast array of organizational variables. At 3M, CEO Jim McNerney had to cut costs, reduce 3M's workforce by almost 10 percent, institute a new "grade on a curve" appraisal system, change the compensation plan, and change the underlying values of the company.[1]

Whether the required change is simple or complex, the basic model for making the change remains the same. As you can see in Figure 15.2, the change agent (usually the manager leading the change) needs to address three basic questions.

1. *What are the forces acting upon me?* What are the actual internal and external forces instigating the change, such as lacklustre financial performance, inadequate new product development, or new competitors gaining market share? Consider the difficulties that were encountered by Fishery Products International Ltd., Canada's largest fishing company. At one time it employed more than 8000 Newfoundlanders and had revenues well over $300 million per year. But when the government imposed a moratorium on cod fishing, 6000 employees were laid off. However, the company did not give up. It survived by making the painful decision to change its focus from fish harvesting to fish trading and processing. It now processes fish that have been caught in other parts of the world.[2]

2. *What should we change?* Sometimes the firm needs a strategic, organization-wide change. At 3M, this meant reformulating the firm's strategy (what business are we in, and how should we compete?), and changing one or more of the firm's systems—its structure, technology, or people—to support the required strategic change. Often, the required effort can be more limited in scope. Perhaps one department needs reorganizing, or the firm needs to install a new technology.

3. *How should we change it?* The manager's basic concern here is to ensure that the change is both successful and timely. No manager wants the kind of nightmare Mr. Nasser ran into at Ford. Overcoming employee resistance will therefore loom large in the manager's implementation decision. "Should I force through the change, or get the employees involved, and (if the latter) how involved should they be?" We'll see in later in this chapter that the basic approach almost always involves a

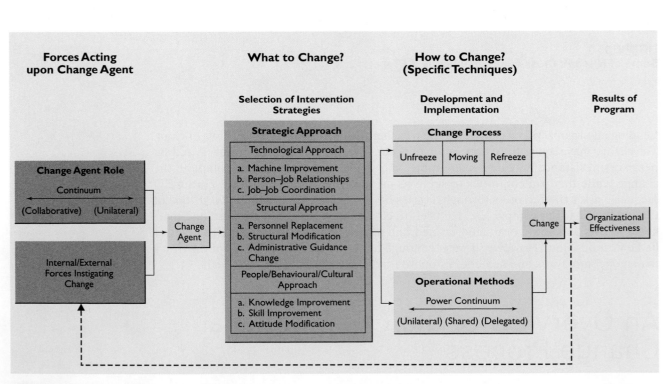

FIGURE 15.2
Model for Planned Organizational Change

process that involves "unfreezing, moving, and refreezing." It underscores the importance of jolting employees out of their traditional ways of doing things.

Deciding What to Change

The change program devised by managers like 3M's Jim McNerney can involve changing the firm's strategy, technology, structure, and people, behaviour, or culture. Let's look at each of these.

Strategic Change

Strategic change involves a shift in the firm's strategy, mission, and vision. Faced with intense competition from Fuji films and from digital cameras, Kodak's former CEO refocused Kodak's strategy. Kodak's operations were streamlined so that it could compete more cost-effectively with Fuji. It simultaneously re-deployed assets to build the firm's competencies in digital photography. Many other firms have changed their strategies in response to market or other environmental changes (for an example, see the "Challenge of Change" box).

strategic change
A shift in the firm's strategy, mission, and vision.

Strategy Change at Home Depot

When the situation changes, wise managers change their strategies. In 2000, Home Depot had nearly 1300 stores worldwide and annual sales revenues of close to $46 billion. But there were only a finite number of communities where home centres could be built, and analysts estimated that Home Depot and its main competitor, Lowe's, would run out of communities in which to build new stores within five years. Newly appointed CEO Robert Nardelli had to decide what to do. Should Home Depot accelerate its expansion in countries like Canada? Should it diversify into new businesses? Should it close less profitable stores and boost Home Depot's operating performance? Many strategies were possible, but Nardelli also knew that choosing the wrong one could spell disaster for his firm.

Home Depot needed a new strategic plan, and CEO Robert Nardelli responded quickly. First, the firm dumped its strategy of growth and adding new stores, and replaced it with a strategy of improving operating performance throughout its system of stores and warehouses. Nardelli says the company is "now more efficient and is rededicating itself to customer service and focusing on neighborhood family friendly stores."

Home Depot's new functional strategies mirror the firm's new competitive emphasis on customer service. Nardelli and his management team revised store management policies to eliminate customer-*un*friendly activities such as stocking the towering shelves during the day. The human resources department also got new orders to boost customer service training for employees.

Home Depot has not entirely written off the need to grow. It continues to expand outside the United States. It is also diversifying and expanding its offerings to provide at-home services for consumers who don't want to do the work themselves. Home improvement is a multi-billion dollar market, and Home Depot currently has barely a 1 percent market share. Home Depot is also experimenting with new types of stores, including flooring specialty shops and the Expo Design Center, an upscale home improvement store.

Strategic changes are risky, and they're often made under crisis conditions that are caused by uncontrollable external events such as deregulation, intensified global competition, and dramatic technological innovations like the internet.[3] They have company-wide implications. They're often made with short time constraints. Even though they are risky, they're often unavoidable.

Strategic change is often vital for survival. This is especially true when the firm faces what researchers call **"discontinuous" change**. This is change of an unexpected nature, as when digital photography suddenly started crowding conventional film off the shelves.

discontinuous change
Change of an unexpected nature.

Technological Change

technological change
Changing the way the company creates and markets its products or services.

Technological change is a second basic approach. Change here might involve (1) installing or modifying the firm's computer systems or machinery, (2) modifying the relationship between the employees and their physical environment, or (3) modifying the interaction of the employees with the technology itself—for instance, improving the work flow or reducing the discomfort caused by bending over a machine.

re-engineering
Introducing major changes in the way business processes are carried out.

Re-engineering means introducing major changes in the way business processes are carried out, with the goal being to cut waste, lower costs, increase quality and service, and maximize the benefits of new information technology. When Novacor Chemicals in Sarnia, Ontario, acquired four different businesses, it had to rethink how it would produce two million tonnes of chemicals. After using re-engineering, it found that it could save millions of dollars by having the four businesses operate in a coordinated fashion rather than as separate entities. For example, when plants were shut down for maintenance, each one used to hire its own maintenance teams. Now, one team is hired and rotated among the four plants.[4]

Structural Change

structural change
Changing one or more aspects of the company's organization structures.

Structural changes can involve several things. For example, managers may reorganize—change the firm's organization chart and structural elements—by moving from a functional to a product departmentalization. Or, they may replace, dismiss, or add personnel. Or, they may change the firm's policies, procedures, and rules (including the firm's performance appraisal system).

Structural changes like these tend to trigger resistance. New structures mean new reporting relationships, and some employees will view the change as a de-facto demotion. New structures may also mean new tasks for employees. For example, Kodak assigned new tasks to its new Digital division employees. Most people prefer predictability and the status quo, and new tasks are not welcomed with open arms.

Reorganizing is a familiar organizational change technique in today's fast-changing times. After laying off thousands of employees, Lucent needed a new organization design. Former CEO Richard McGinn had organized the company around 11 different businesses.[5] When the board of directors dismissed Mr. McGinn, his successor, Harry Schacht, argued that the 11-division structure was too unwieldy, and he chopped the design down to five units. Recently (as Lucent continues to downsize), it announced it was shrinking/reorganizing from five units down to two main units (and laying off more than 80 executives in the process). One unit, Integrated Network Solutions, will handle landline-based businesses, such as optical networks and phone-call switching. The other unit, Mobility Solutions, will focus on Lucent's wireless products.

Reorganizations require the manager to decide whether a new structure is really required and if so, what it should look like.

1. *Is a new structure really required?* An organizational problem doesn't necessarily mean that a dramatic structural overhaul is required. The current structure may simply need a little fine-tuning. Figure 15.3 helps the manager make this determination. For example, fine-tuning may involve refining the allocation of responsibilities, such as by clarifying the manager's responsibilities, or by improving lateral relationships by instituting a new, cross-functional team.

When you identify a problem with your design, first look for ways to fix it without substantially altering it. If that doesn't work, you'll have to make fundamental changes or even reject the design. Here's a step-by-step process for resolving problems.

STEPS NOT INVOLVING MAJOR DESIGN CHANGE

Modify Without Changing the Units.

- Refine the allocation of responsibilities (for example, clarify powers and responsibilities).
- Refine reporting relationships and processes.
- Refine lateral relationships and processes (for example, define coordination mechanisms).
- Refine accountabilities (for example, define more appropriate performance measures).

Redefine Skill Requirements and Incentives.

- Modify criteria for selecting people.
- Redefine skill development needs.
- Develop incentives.

Shape Informal Context.

- Clarify the leadership style needed.
- Define norms of behaviour, values, or social context.

STEPS INVOLVING MAJOR DESIGN CHANGE

Make Substantial Changes in the Units.

- Make major adjustments to unit boundaries.
- Change unit roles (for example, turn functional units into business units or shared services).
- Introduce new units or merge units.

Change the Structure.

- Change reporting lines.
- Create new divisions.

FIGURE 15.3
Is a New Structure Really Required?

2. *What should the new structure look like?* If a totally new structure is required, how does the manager decide what the new structure should look like? Here, the guidelines in Chapters 8 and 9 apply. For example, fast-changing environments require more adaptive, organic, networked "learning organization" structures, while mass production technologies favour mechanistic structures. Consider the firm's strategy and goals. Beyond these general ideas, there are nine specific tests the manager can apply to better gauge what the problem is with the current structure and what the new structure should look like.[6]

The Market Advantage Test Does your design direct sufficient management attention to your sources of competitive advantage in each market? "The first and most fundamental test of a design...is whether it fits your company's market strategy."[7] The firm's strategy must identify the markets in which the company will compete and what the firm's competitive advantages will be. The organization structure must then support that strategy by ensuring that it directs sufficient attention to the firm's chosen markets. For example, if the strategy involves expanding overseas, an organization structure that has no provision for addressing foreign markets should raise a red flag. Two experts who have studied organizations say that the rule of thumb here is this: "if a single unit is dedicated to a single segment, the segment is receiving sufficient attention. If no unit has responsibility for the segment, the design is fatally flawed and needs to be revamped." Smaller firms or those facing other strategic concerns may not be able to afford the duplication inherent in creating a structure that addresses multiple markets. However, the basic test is still, "Does your design direct sufficient management attention to your sources of competitive advantage in each market?"

Hundreds of new Volkswagon Beetles are delivered to an auto port.

Volkswagen recently considered reorganizing its nine brands into three operational divisions—one for premium cars, one for mass-market cars, and one for commercial vehicles.[8] One intent of this reorganization is to enable the firm to better focus on what it increasingly sees as VW's two separate market segments. It would help Volkswagen better distinguish its luxury brands (Audi, Bugatti, Bentley, and Lamborghini) from its mass brand (Volkswagen), and better serve each market.

The Parenting Advantage Test Does your design help the corporate parent add value to the organization? For example, General Electric is a highly diverse conglomerate, and some might therefore ask, "Would it not be more efficient for each of GE's separate divisions to spin off and run themselves, rather than remain as part of GE's overall structure?" GE says "no," arguing that the GE corporate parent brings enormous additional value to each of its subsidiaries. For example, it helps ensure that modern management techniques devised in one unit (such as using the internet to build a boundaryless supply chain) quickly spread to the other divisions. If ensuring that such "sharing of management know-how" is an advantage the parent firm hopes to provide, then the firm's structure should facilitate such knowledge sharing.

The People Test Does your design reflect the strengths, weaknesses, and motivations of your people? The point is that "if an organization is not suited to the skills and attitudes of its members, the problem lies with the design, not the people."[9] The basic question here is whether the organization structure provides the appropriate responsibilities and reporting relationships and wins the commitment of the employees. After PepsiCo purchased Quaker Oats Co, PepsiCo reorganized some business units partly because of the strengths of some of the executives it inherited with the Quaker purchase. For example, Robert Morrison, Quaker's chairman and CEO, quickly assumed responsibility for PepsiCo's Tropicana juice unit while continuing to oversee most of the original Quaker business.

The Feasibility Test Have you take into account all the constraints that may impede the implementation of your design? The basic question here is, "What could stand in the way of successfully implementing the new organization design? Constraints may include government regulations, the interests of the company stakeholders (including its employees and unions), the firm's information systems, and its corporate culture. For example, in terms of culture, "[3M] is a home-grown place with a collegial atmosphere where the emphasis on being nice to each other means issues haven't always surfaced in an honest way," says one 3M senior vice president.[10] That could have meant resistance on the part of employees to making the hard-nosed structural decisions CEO McNerney had to make (including consolidating purchasing units and moving some manufacturing abroad). However, he anticipated the potential constraints and dealt with them successfully.

The Specialist Culture Test Does your design protect units that need distinct cultures? For example, 3M is known for the number of new products its engineers have produced (including Scotch tape and Post-it notes). Reorganizing R&D therefore required addressing their special cultural needs. As McNerney says, "3M people wake up every morning thinking about what new product they can bring to market. Innovation is in their DNA—and if I kill that entrepreneurial spirit I will have failed. My job is to build on that strength, corral it, and focus it."[11]

The Difficult-Links Test Does your design provide coordination solutions for the unit-to-unit links that are likely to be problematic? In other words, have you addressed the hard-to-coordinate relationships? For example, recall from Chapter 9 that Lawrence and Lorsch found that the new product development process in plastics firms required a special coordinated effort. Here managers installed special "independent integrator" departments. These ensured ongoing coordination among the development, sales, and manufacturing departments under rapidly in changing conditions.

The Redundant-Hierarchy Test Does your design have too many parent levels and units? When he first became CEO of General Electric, Jack Welch found that GE had a hierarchy of what he believed were redundant "parent units." There was a corporate headquarters staff, and then below that various group-level executive vice president staffs, and below that business-level groups. One of the first steps Welch took was to eliminate this redundant hierarchy. He pared the corporate staff, eliminated division groupings, and let most of the heads of the largest independent business units report directly to Welch and his team.

The Accountability Test Does your design support effective controls? For example, is the company organized in such a way that if a problem arose for a particular product line (such as a dramatic sales decline), you could quickly identify the manager responsible?

The Flexibility Test Does your design facilitate the development of new strategies and provide the flexibility required to adapt to change? The question here is whether your organization structure "provides ways for a company to pursue innovation and allows for adaptability to changing circumstances."[12] Make sure the organization structure does not actually become an impediment to identifying opportunities and pursuing them. For example, several years ago the magazine publisher Emap saw that new media and internet-based publishing could be a significant future opportunity. Management knew the firm's current magazine-focused business units might not want to risk diluting their own efforts by pursuing new digital opportunities. Emap therefore created a new business function to address these opportunities.

Emap
www.emap.com

People/Cultural Change

Finally, the change effort may have to focus on changing the people. Perhaps employees don't have the skills to do their new jobs This is where managers such as Yellow Freightway's Bill Zollars (see Case Study 15-1) call on training and development techniques like lectures, conferences, and computer-based training to improve employees' skills. At other times, the "people" problems stem from misunderstandings or conflicts. Here "organizational development" interventions or conflict-resolution efforts (like those discussed later in this chapter) may be needed.

Often, however, it's the firm's corporate culture that has to change. Ontario Hydro, for example, had an "engineering" culture for many years, where everything was planned and analyzed down to the last detail before any action was taken. But Ontario Hydro's culture is becoming more consumer-oriented as the company tries to cope with large debt and changes in its markets. The RCMP's culture is also different now than it was in the days when military tradition dominated the organization. It has completed a "visioning process" that resulted in a new mission statement, a new set of core values, and a commitment to the communities in which it works.[13]

Ontario Hydro
www.ontariohydro energy.com

The first step in changing the culture is to understand what the culture looks like at the moment. Checklist 15.1 can be of use here.

The Basics of Changing Culture You know from your own experience that changing someone's values requires a lot more than just talk. When he decided to transform Kodak, for instance, then-CEO George Fisher replaced top executives who weren't performing, and instituted new incentive plans and a new, more-results-oriented appraisal system. The net effect was to send a strong signal to employees throughout the firm. It said, "the values of being efficient, effective, and responsive were a lot more important today then they'd been the week before."

Creating and Sustaining the Right Corporate Culture Suppose you are appointed as CEO of a struggling company that is known for its culture of backbiting, bureaucratic behaviour, and disdain for clients. What steps would you take to change the company's culture? Experts suggest the following broad tactics.[14]

1. *Make it clear to your employees what you pay attention to, measure, and control.* For example, direct the attention of your employees toward controlling costs or serving customers if those are the values you want to emphasize. Management practices send strong signals about what is or is not acceptable. For example, at Toyota, "quality and teamwork" are core values. Therefore, the firm's employee selection and training processes focus on quality and teamwork. The firm selects employees based on careful testing of their quality- and team-orientation. Much of the new employee's initial training revolves around team-building skills and how to solve quality problems.

2. *React appropriately to critical incidents and organizational crises.* Suppose you want to emphasize the value that "we're all in this together." If so, don't react to declining profits by laying off operating employees and middle managers while giving top managers a raise.

3. *Use "signs, symbols, stories, rites, and ceremonies" to signal your values.* At retailer JC Penney, loyalty and tradition are values. To support this, the firm inducts new management employees into the "Penney partnership" at ritualistic conferences. Here they commit to the firm's core values of "honor, confidence, service, and co-operation."

4. *Deliberately model, teach, and coach the values you want to emphasize.* Wal-Mart founder Sam Walton lived the values "hard work, honesty, neighborliness, and thrift" that he wanted Wal-Mart employees to follow. Although he was one of the richest men in the world, he drove a pickup truck. He explained this by saying, "If I drove a Rolls Royce, what would I do with my dog?"

5. *Communicate your priorities by how you allocate rewards.* Leaders communicate their priorities by how they link raises and promotions to particular behaviours. For example, the top management at General Foods decided several years ago to re-orient its strategy from cost control to diversification and sales growth. It therefore revised the firm's pay plan and began to link bonuses to sales volume and to new product development, rather than just to increased earnings.

6. *Make your HR procedures and criteria consistent with the values you espouse.* When he became chairperson and CEO of IBM, Louis Gerstner instituted new appraisal systems and pay plans to reinforce his focus on performance.

Kraft Foods
www.kraft.com

Many of these specific factors can be seen in the steps that Lawrence Weinbach, CEO of Unisys, took to change the culture of the firm, and to focus employees more on performance and execution. As he says,

> ...we've moved to a pay for performance approach, to make sure that we're properly recognizing the people who are doing things right...in some cases, we've needed to tell people to seek opportunities elsewhere where they will be happier...we've invested in training and education and created Unisys University, where employees can find courses and programs on a range of business-related topics. We've also spent a lot of time communicating and educating people about the importance of execution. I think we've done pretty well at getting everyone here to understand what we're good at, what our core competencies are, and then driving home the fact that you have to deliver every single day.[15]

**Unisys University
www.unisys.com
(About/Careers/
Growth &
Development)**

Deciding How to Implement the Change

The second question managers must ask is, "How should the change actually be implemented? Should I force through the change or get the employees involved, and (if the latter) how involved should they be?" As noted above, the manager's basic concern here is to ensure that the change is both successful and timely. Effective implementation of change requires that managers understand the reasons that employees often resist change.

Why Do People Resist Change?

The fact that a change is advisable or even mandatory doesn't mean employees will accept it. In fact, it's often the company's key people—perhaps even top and middle managers—who are the most resistant. They may just prefer the status quo. And it's not just managers who prefer the status quo. Take a personal example. Suppose you've been attending a class in management, with the college's best professor. Several weeks into the term the dean comes in and announces that some students will have to be transferred to another professor and class because the fire marshal says the lecture hall is overcrowded.

You are one of the people who've been asked to move. What would your reaction be? You would very likely object because you're settled in to the class, you like the professor, you have friends in the class, and you fear that moving might adversely affect your grade. Besides, why should you be singled out? It's not fair. So, even though the change makes sense and is fairly simple to make, you don't want to go.

Paul Lawrence says that it's usually not the technical aspects of a change that employees resist, but the changes in human relationships that accompany the change.[16] Thus, they may think the change will reduce their authority and lower their status in the organization. Sometimes it's not fear of the obvious consequences, but rather apprehension about the unknown consequences that produces resistance. For example, how much do you know about the professor who'll be teaching that new class you're being moved to and about your new classmates?

In the book *Beyond the Wall of Resistance*, consultant Rick Maurer says resistance can stem from two main sources. Level 1 resistance stems from a lack of information or an honest disagreement over the facts. Level 2 resistance is more personal and emotional. Here, people are afraid—that the change may cost them their jobs, or that they may lose face, or that it will reduce their control (or in your case, lower your grade). Maurer says treating all resistance as if it were Level 1 (lack of information) can undermine the manager's change efforts. For example, using "slick visual presentations to explain change with nice neat facts, charts, and time lines, when what people really want to hear is 'what does this mean to them?' can be a recipe for disaster."[17]

Some people are inherently more resistant to change than others and seem to be constantly "fighting the system." One research study assessed how managers' personality traits influenced their reactions to change. Three personality traits—tolerance for ambiguity, having a positive self-concept, and being more tolerant of risk—significantly predicted effectiveness in coping with change.[18] Managers with the lowest self-image, least tolerance for ambiguity, and least tolerance for risk were the most resistant to change.

Sometimes employees say they want to change (and may think they mean it), and yet they resist the program. What accounts for this? Two organizational psychologists recently suggested that this resistance may be the result of "competing commitments." Figure 15.4 illustrates this problem. For example, Helen says she is committed to the new initiative. However, she has an unstated competing commitment, "do not upset my relationship with my boss by leaving the mentee role." She's therefore actually not pushing her team to implement the new initiative.

Uncovering competing commitments like these requires a diagnostic process. First, notice and record the person's actual, current behaviour (since it's not what they say they want to do but what they're actually doing that is important to you as a manager). Second, speak with the person and lead them through the process of understanding what their competing commitments really are.

Dealing with Resistance to Change

Kurt Lewin proposed a famous model to summarize the basic process for dealing with resistance to change. To Lewin, all behaviour in organizations was a product of two kinds of forces: those striving to maintain the status quo, and those pushing for change. Implementing change thus meant either reducing the forces for the status quo or building up the forces for change. Lewin's process consists of three steps: unfreezing, moving, and refreezing.

unfreezing
Reducing the forces that favour the status quo.

Unfreezing means reducing the forces that favour the status quo. The usual way to accomplish this is by presenting a provocative problem or event. The goal is to get employees to recognize the need for change and to search for new solutions. Attitude surveys, interview results, or participatory informational meetings often provide such provocative events.

moving
Developing new behaviours, values, and attitudes by applying one or more organizational change techniques.

Once you have employees' attention, you must move them in the desired direction. Lewin's second step, moving, aims to alter the behaviour of the employees. **Moving** means developing new behaviours, values, and attitudes by applying one or more organizational change techniques. We'll discuss these techniques later in this chapter.

Stated commitment I am committed to ...	What am I doing, or not doing, that is keeping my stated commitment from being fully realized?	Competing commitments	Big assumptions
Helen . . . the new initiative.	I don't push for top performance from my team members or myself; I accept mediocre products and thinking too often; I don't prioritize.	I am committed to not upsetting my relationship with my boss by leaving the [mentored] role.	I assume my boss will stop supporting me if I move toward becoming his peer; I assume that I don't have what it takes to successfully carry out a cutting-edge project.
Bill . . . being a team player.	I don't collaborate enough; I make unilateral decisions too often; I don't really take people's input into account.	I am committed to being the one who gets the credit and to avoiding the frustration or conflict that comes with collaboration.	I assume that no one will appreciate me if I am not seen as the source of success; I assume nothing good will come of my being frustrated in conflict.
Jane . . . turning around my department.	Too often, I let things slide; I'm not proactive enough in getting people to follow through with their tasks.	I am committed to not setting full sail until I have a clear map of how we get our department from here to there.	I assume that if I take my group out into deep waters and discover I am unable to get us to the other side, I will be seen as an incompetent leader who is undeserving of trust or responsibility.

FIGURE 15.4
How Immune Is the Person to Change?

Lewin was shrewd enough to know that just making a change is not enough. He knew that people and organizations would tend to revert to their old ways of doing things unless management reinforced the new ways of doing things. Whether it's a new diet, or new saving plan, or a new organizational procedure, Lewin knew you had to reinforce the change. If you don't, you run the risk the change won't be permanent. That's what Lewin meant by **refreezing**. He said you had to institute new systems and procedures that would support and maintain the changes that you made.

The unfreezing-moving-refreezing model is helpful to managers because it suggests that change must be carefully thought out and implemented. But this model is becoming less useful because the rate of organizational change is now so fast. Robbins and Coulter use the metaphor of a ship sailing over calm waters to describe the organizations of the 1950s and 1960s.[19] But many organizations in the twenty-first century are more like a raft hurtling down a whitewater canyon. Managers in these organizations face chaotic situations, and a simple three-step change model may not be very helpful to them.

refreezing
To institute new systems and procedures to support and maintain the changes that you made.

Analyzing Resistance to Change

If managers are to be effective in introducing change, they must have an understanding of the forces that cause resistance to change, as well as the forces that reduce this resistance. **Force field analysis** examines the various forces that operate in organizations to keep the system balanced or unbalanced.[20] Force field analysis proposes that two sets of forces operate in any system: driving forces (those that facilitate change) and resisting forces (those that inhibit change). If the two sets of forces are equal, the system is in equilibrium.

force field analysis
An analysis of the forces that operate in organizations to keep the system balanced or unbalanced.

Figure 15.5 illustrates three possible situations. The length of the arrow for driving forces (D) and resisting forces (R) indicates their relative strength. The numbers along the horizontal axis represent the magnitude of change. In (a), the system is in equilibrium, with the dotted line indicating the system's desired situation. Diagrams (b) and (c) show how the desired situation can be achieved by either increasing the driving forces or decreasing the resisting forces. For example, in (b), driving force #1 has been increased, and a new driving force (#5) has been added. Together, these changes move the system to the new equilibrium. In (c), resisting forces #1 and #3 have been reduced, and resisting force #2 has been removed altogether. This has also led to a new desired equilibrium.

Choosing the Right Tool for Dealing with Resistance

Table 15.1 summarizes tools managers use to deal with resistance and when they use them. For example, "education and communication" are appropriate where inaccurate or missing information is contributing to employee resistance. When Inco Ltd. told 60 office workers (including 30 women) that they had to choose between accepting underground mining work or losing their jobs, the company tried to allay their fears about working underground by conducting mine tours, counselling sessions, and fitness training sessions.[21]

"Participation and involvement" can also be used effectively. At Allen-Bradley Canada, the company wanted to introduce a new automated warehouse and shipping system. It created a team that included shippers, information specialists, and other employees who would be involved in the actual operation of the new facility. The views of all employees who would be affected by the new equipment were carefully considered before any changes were made. Subsequently, the change was introduced successfully. Inventory levels decreased by 34 percent and on-time deliveries to customers improved from 50 percent to 75 percent.[22]

Getting employees to agree to difficult changes in working conditions may be facilitated through education and communication.

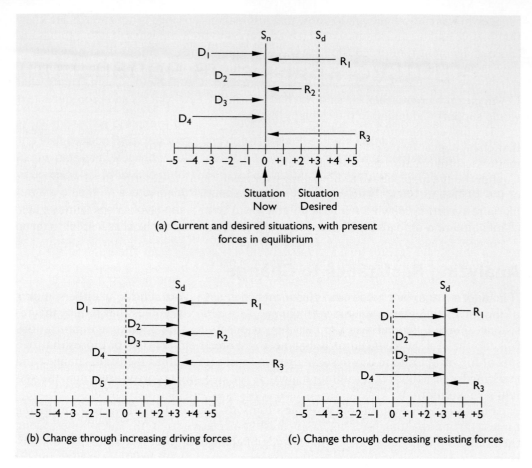

(a) Current and desired situations, with present forces in equilibrium

(b) Change through increasing driving forces

(c) Change through decreasing resisting forces

FIGURE 15.5
Force Field Analysis

A Nine-Step Process for Leading Organizational Change

Lewin's unfreeze-moving-refreeze model provides a powerful framework for making a change, but the devil, of course, is in the details. What exactly should a manager do to carry out a change? The following provides a useful change process for managers.

Create a Sense of Urgency You know something's wrong. What do you do now? Do you just paper over the problems, or do you take remedial action? Most experienced leaders instinctively know that before taking action, they have to unfreeze the old habits. They have to create a sense of urgency.[23] Creating a sense of urgency has a double-barreled benefit. For those who might want to resist the change, it can grab their attention and convince them of the need for the change. And for those who simply don't care, it may jar them out of their complacency. Techniques managers use to create a sense of urgency include the following:[24]

■ Make employees aware of the company's major weaknesses relative to competitors.

■ Eliminate examples of excess such as company-owned country club facilities, aircraft, or gourmet executive dining rooms.

GLASBERGEN

"Your job will be to walk funny and look really cute, so nobody notices how horrible it is to work here."

TABLE 15.1 *Six Methods for Dealing with Resistance to Change*

APPROACH METHOD	COMMONLY USED IN SITUATIONS	ADVANTAGES	DRAWBACKS
Education & communication	Where there is a lack of information or inaccurate information and analysis.	Once persuaded, people will often help with the implementation of the change.	Can be very time consuming if lots of people are involved.
Participation & involvement	Where the initiators do not have all the information they need to design the change, and where others have considerable power to resist.	People who participate will be committed to implementing change, and any relevant information they have will be integrated into the change plan.	Can be very time consuming if participators design an inappropriate change.
Facilitation & support	Where people are resisting because of fear and anxiety.	No other approach works as well with employee adjustment problems.	Can be time consuming, expensive, and still fail.
Negotiation & agreement	Where someone or some group will clearly lose out in a change, and where that group has considerable power to resist.	Sometimes it is a relatively easy way to avoid major resistance.	Can be too expensive in many cases if it prompts others to negotiate.
Manipulation & co-optation	Where other tactics will not work or are too expensive.	It can be a relatively quick and inexpensive solution to resistance problems	Can lead to future problems if people feel manipulated.
Coercion	Where speed is essential and the change initiators possess considerable power.	It is speedy and can overcome any kind of resistance.	Can be risky if it leaves people angry at the initiators.

- Set targets for revenue, income, productivity, customer satisfaction, and product development cycle time so high that they can't be reached by conducting business in the current fashion.

- Send more data about customer satisfaction and financial performance to more employees, especially information that demonstrates weaknesses relative to competitors.

Create a Guiding Coalition and Mobilize Commitment Leading a change is one thing, but trying to do it all yourself is another. Major transformations are often associated with one highly visible leader. But no leader can accomplish a major change alone. That's why most leaders create a guiding coalition of influential people. They become the vanguard—the missionaries and implementers of the change. The coalition should include people with enough power to lead the change effort.

Choose the Right Lieutenants Political support is an important consideration, so the leader has to ensure that there are enough key players on board so that those left out can't easily block progress.[25] The coalition should also have the expertise, credibility, and leadership skills required to explain and implement the change. One option is to create one or more broad, employee-based task forces to diagnose the company's problems. Doing so can produce a shared understanding of, and commitment to, what the company can and must improve.

Develop and Communicate a Shared Vision In addition to the guiding coalition, the firm's other employees also need a vision they can rally around, a signpost on which to focus. As we saw in Chapter 7, a vision is "a general statement of the organization's intended direction that evokes emotional feelings in organization members." When Barry Gibbons became CEO of Spec's Music retail chain, its employees, owners, and bankers required a vision around which to rally. Gibbons's vision of a leaner Spec's offering both concerts and retail music helped to provide the sense of direction they all required.

To transform an organization, a new vision is usually required. For example, when Paul Tellier became CEO of CN he conveyed the vision of CN being a world-class competitor with leading North American railways. Having a vision is useless unless the employees share that vision. Change expert John Kotter says "the real power of a vision is unleashed only when most of those involved in an enterprise or activity have a common understanding of its goals and direction."[26] Key steps in communicating a vision include

- *Keep it simple.* Here is an example of a good statement of vision: "We are going to become faster than anyone else in our industry at satisfying customer needs."
- *Use multiple forums.* Try to use every channel possible—big meetings and small, memos and newspapers, formal and informal interaction—to spread the word.
- *Use repetition.* Ideas sink in deeply only after people have heard them many times.
- *Lead by example.* "Walk the talk" so that your behaviours and decisions are consistent with the vision you advocate.

Empower Employees to Make the Change Some leaders face a dilemma. They need the active assistance of their employees to implement the change. But the employees haven't the tools, skills, authority, or freedom to do what's needed to help. In a study of change in major companies like Sears, Royal Dutch Shell, and the U.S. Army, researchers found that employees were rarely able or willing to do what it took to carry out the change if they thought they lacked the power to do so. Therefore, ask "Do employees believe they can effect organizational performance? Do they believe they have the power to make things happen?"[27] Figure 15.6 explains how to empower employees by removing certain barriers that inhibit their performance.

Generate Short-Term Wins Most people can't wait years before deciding whether they're going in the right direction. The guiding coalition in one company set its sights on producing one highly visible and successful new product about 20 months after the start of its organizational renewal effort.[28] They selected the new product in part because the coalition knew that the introduction was doable. Accomplishing it sent a strong signal that the broader, longer-term change was also doable.

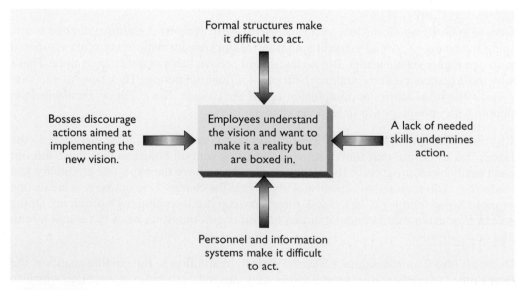

FIGURE 15.6
Barriers to Empowerment

Consolidate Gains and Produce More Change The challenge here is to capitalize on the short-term wins. This is the time to press ahead and to extend your gains. You have increased credibility from the short-term wins. Use it to change all the systems, structures, and policies that don't fit well with the company's new vision.

Anchor the New Ways of Doing Things in the Company Culture As you consolidate and extend the gains, remember you'll need a parallel change in the company's values and culture. You may want a "team-based, quality-oriented, adaptable organization," but that's not going to happen if the firm's shared values still emphasize "selfishness, mediocrity, and bureaucratic behaviour." Changing the culture is therefore crucial. It is one of the manager's most challenging jobs. We'll discuss cultural change later in the chapter.

Monitor Progress and Adjust the Vision as Required Finally, you need to monitor the effectiveness of the change. Continually compare results to goals. One firm appointed an oversight team comprising managers, a union representative, an engineer, and several others. They monitored the functioning of the firm's new self-managing teams. Another firm used morale surveys to monitor employees' reactions to the changes.

Change in Action: Becoming an Ebusiness

Every business is becoming an ebusiness today. As *Fortune* put it, "e or be eaten." Either link your business to the web, or say goodbye to your business. The problem is that "blending old business and e-business—'clicks and mortar'—is an awkward process."[29] The merger of AOL and Time Warner is a striking example. Here Time Warner's more buttoned-down, conservative culture sometimes clashed with AOL's entrepreneurial values. And consider Sears' internet operation. Most Sears headquarters employees are housed in comfortable offices in the Sears Tower in Chicago. Over at their internet division in Hoffman Estates, Illinois, Sears' e-employees, including its former treasurer, have small cubicles.[30]

Sears
www.sears.com

What changes can you expect when moving from a conventional to an internet-based business? "Entering the ecommerce realm is like managing at 90 mph. Ebusiness affects finance, human resources, training, supply-chain management, customer-resource management, and just about every other corporate function. This puts the managers of these departments in a new light," says the chief strategist for one ebusiness.[31]

How to structure the new enterprise is a big issue. For one thing, you'll have to decide whether to blend the new ebusiness into the company's current structure or organize it as a separate entity. If you blend the two entities, how should you structure the ebusiness? Some argue for assigning one manager the job of coming up with an e-strategy. Others say "it's far better to develop an organizational structure that puts the web and ebusiness at the central focus of a cross-departmental business group, rather than merely adding web responsibilities to a pre-existing task list." Greg Rogers heads up Whirlpool Corporation's ecommerce operation. He says that the company's strategy will have to change, too: "internet strategy is really business strategy."[32] The company's new business strategy will have to reflect the fact that the company now embraces ecommerce as part of its competitive advantage.

Whirlpool
www.whirlpool.com

Using Organizational Development to Change Organizations

Organizational development (OD) is a special approach to organizational and cultural change in which the employees formulate and implement the change, usually with the aid of a trained facilitator. OD has three distinguishing characteristics.

organizational development (OD)
An approach to organizational change in which the employees themselves formulate and implement the change that's required, usually with the aid of a trained consultant.

1. It is based on action research. **Action research** means collecting data about a group, department, or organization, and then feeding that data back to the employees. Then the group members analyze the data and develop hypotheses about what the problems in the unit might be.

2. It applies behavioural science knowledge to improve the organization's effectiveness.

3. It changes the organization in a particular direction—toward improved problem solving, responsiveness, quality of work, and effectiveness.[33]

Types of OD Applications

The range of OD applications (also called OD interventions or techniques) has increased substantially over the years. OD got its start with human process interventions. These aimed to help employees better understand and modify their own and others' attitudes, values, and beliefs, and thereby improve the company. Today, OD practitioners aren't just involved in changing participants' attitudes, values, and beliefs (see Table 15.2). Now they also directly alter the firm's structure, practices, strategy, and culture. But OD's distinguishing characteristic has stayed pretty much the same: To have the employees themselves analyze the situation and develop the solutions. Let's look at the four main types of OD interventions: human process, technostructural, HR management, and strategic.

Human Process Applications The goal of **human process applications** is to provide employees with the insight and skills they need to analyze their own and others' behaviour more effectively. With this new insight, they should be able to solve interpersonal and inter-group problems more intelligently. Sensitivity training, team building, and survey research are three classic techniques.

Sensitivity training (also called t-group training) was one of the earliest OD techniques. It aims to increase the participant's insight into his or her own behaviour and the behaviour of others. It accomplishes this by encouraging an open expression of feelings in the training group. Typically, 10 to 15 people meet, usually away from the job. The focus is on the feelings and interactions of the members in the group. T-group training is obviously very personal in nature, so it's not surprising that it is controversial. Its use has diminished markedly.[34]

OD's "action research" emphasis is perhaps most evident in **team building**. This is a special process for improving the effectiveness of a team. The facilitator collects data concerning the team's performance and then feeds it back to the members of the team. The participants examine, explain, and analyze the data. They then develop specific action plans or solutions for solving the team's problems. Before the meeting, the consultant interviews each group member.[35] He or she asks what their problems are, how the group functions, and what obstacles are preventing the group from performing better. The consultant might then categorize the interview data into themes and present the themes to the group at the beginning of the meeting. (Themes like lack of cohesion might be culled from statements like, "I can't get any co-operation around here.") The group then explores and discusses the themes, examines the underlying causes of the problems, and works on solutions.

Some firms use **survey research** to create a sense of urgency. Here the facilitator/consultant has employees throughout the company fill out attitude surveys. The data are then fed back to top management and to the appropriate group or groups. The survey data provide a convenient method for unfreezing an organization's management and employees. It provides a lucid, comparative, graphic illustration of the fact that the organization has problems.

The "People Side of Managing" box describes how OD consultants can help start-up firms deal with a variety of human-related problems.

Technostructural Applications OD practitioners are increasingly involved in efforts to change the structures, methods, and job designs of firms. Compared with human process interventions, **technostructural interventions** (as well as HR management interventions and strategic interventions) focus directly on productivity improvement and efficiency. For example, in a formal structural change program, employees collect data on existing struc-

TABLE 15.2 Examples of OD Interventions and the Organizational Levels They Affect

Interventions	PRIMARY ORGANIZATIONAL LEVEL AFFECTED		
	Individual	Group	Organization
HUMAN PROCESS			
T-groups	X	X	
Process consultation		X	
Third-party intervention	X	X	
Team building		X	
Organizational confrontation meeting		X	X
Intergroup relations		X	X
TECHNOSTRUCTURAL			
Formal structural change			X
Differentiation and integration			X
Cooperative union-management projects	X	X	X
Quality circles	X	X	
Total quality management		X	X
Work design	X	X	
HUMAN RESOURCE MANAGEMENT			
Goal setting	X	X	
Performance appraisal	X	X	
Reward systems	X	X	X
Career planning and development	X		
Managing workforce diversity	X		
Employee wellness	X		
STRATEGIC			
Integrated strategic management			X
Culture change			X
Strategic change			X
Self-designing organizations		X	X

tures and analyze them. The purpose is to jointly redesign and implement new organizational structures. OD practitioners also assist in implementing employee-involvement programs, including quality circles and job redesign.

HR Management Applications OD practitioners also use action research to help employees analyze and change personnel practices. Targets of change include the

Dream Weavers and Start-Ups

Modern start-up companies often have different characteristics than start-ups did a few years ago. In the past, entrepreneurs started their businesses from scratch and then slowly built them, brick by brick and customer by customer. Because the process was relatively slow and continuous, the entrepreneur was usually able to nurture his or her company's vision and to put all the values and systems in place that were needed to help the employees implement that vision.

Today, many start-ups are technology-based and often emerge, full-blown, out of large parent companies (or with the enormous financial backing of venture capital firms). As a result, a start-up firm—say, one born to create a new internet portal—may begin life with millions of dollars of cash and hundreds of employees, but without the traditions and values that normally go along with growing a business from scratch.

OD consultants often play the role of what one calls "dream weavers." They are asked to take all the necessary elements for success that are already in place and help pull them together into a smoothly functioning whole by working with the entrepreneur and his or her employees as a facilitator/transition agent. How exactly can OD consultants help? Here are some examples:

■ *Establish a new identity.* When a giant company spins off a new start-up, OD consultants can help the new entity establish an independent identity by working with the new team to help clarify value, vision, and mission statements.

■ *Build teams.* The new company may be staffed with people who haven't worked together before or who have little or no experience in building effective teams. The OD consultants can use their facilitation skills to create a smoothly functioning team. For example, one start-up was having a serious interpersonal communications problem. In this case, the new company's software engineers complained about each other to third parties and did poorly in one-on-one interactions. The OD consultant worked with the people involved during staff meetings to identify and address the counterproductive behaviour and facilitate teamwork.

■ *Manage cultural change.* Sometimes a new spinoff company's culture may reflect the culture of the parent firm. In one start-up, for instance, the fear of challenging the system was so ingrained that true creativity was thwarted. In this case the OD consultant was able to work with the team to help instill—through a new core value statement, new leadership and management practices, and new signs and symbols—a more risk-oriented and creative set of values.

---

performance appraisal system and reward system. Another typical effort involves using action research to institute workforce diversity programs. These aim at boosting co-operation among a firm's diverse employees.

strategic interventions
Company-wide OD programs aimed at achieving a better fit among a firm's strategy, structure, culture, and external environment.

Strategic Applications **Strategic interventions** are company-wide OD programs aimed at achieving a better fit among a firm's strategy, structure, culture, and external environment. *Integrated strategic management* is one example. It involves four steps:

1. *Analyze current strategy and organizational design.* Senior managers and other employees utilize models such as the SWOT matrix (explained in Chapter 7) to analyze the firm's current strategy and organizational design.

2. *Choose a desired strategy and organizational design.* Based on the analysis, senior management formulates a strategic vision, objectives, and plan, and an organizational structure for implementing them.

3. *Design a strategic change plan.* The group designs a strategic change plan. This is "an action plan for moving the organization from its current strategy and organizational design to the desired future strategy and design."[36] The plan explains how management will implement the strategic change. It includes specific activities as well as the costs and budgets associated with them.

4. *Implement the strategic change plan.* The final step is to implement a strategic change plan, and measure and review the results.[37]

Managing Conflict

Conflict can be either a cause or a result of organizational change. Sometimes conflict makes the need for change apparent, as when two departments resist working cooperatively to achieve some goal. Sometimes an organizational change (like a new strategy) may trigger conflict, as two or more managers or units see in the change an opportunity or need to get more power or resources for themselves. In either case, conflict management is an important aspect of leading organizational change.

Conflict: Pros and Cons

Conflict occurs when individuals or groups have incompatible goals, and these individuals or groups can block each other's goal attainment. Conflict can have dysfunctional effects on the organization and its employees. Opposing parties in conflicts tend to put their own aims above those of the organization, and the organization's effectiveness suffers. Time that could have been used productively is wasted as people hide valuable information and jockey for position. Opponents can become so personally involved in the tensions produced by conflict that they undermine their emotional and physical well-being. Perhaps the most insidious effect of conflict is that it doesn't remain organization-bound for long. Its effects are observed by customers and stockholders and are "taken home" by the opponents, whose families are caught in the fallout.

Despite its adverse effects, conflict is potentially useful because it can, if properly channelled, be an engine of innovation and change. This view explicitly encourages a certain amount of controlled conflict in organizations. The basic case is that a lack of active debate can permit the status quo or mediocre ideas to prevail.

Individual, Interpersonal, and Inter-group Organizational Conflict

Three types of conflict—individual, interpersonal, and inter-group—exist in organizations.

Individual Conflict **Role conflict** is a familiar example of conflict "within" the individual. It occurs when a person is faced with conflicting orders, such that compliance with one would make it difficult or impossible to comply with the other. Sometimes role conflict arises out of obviously conflicting orders, as when a corporal receives orders from a captain that would force her to disobey an order from her sergeant.

Sometimes, however, the role conflict's source is not so obvious: Obeying an order might force a person to violate his or her own cherished values and sense of right and wrong. In any case, role conflict is a serious problem in organizations, one that can be stressful to the people involved and can adversely affect morale and performance.[38]

Interpersonal Conflict **Interpersonal conflicts** in organizations occur between individuals or between individuals and groups. Sometimes, of course, such conflicts arise from

conflict
A condition that occurs when individuals or groups have incompatible goals, and these individuals or groups can block each other's goal attainment.

role conflict
When a person is faced with conflicting orders, such that compliance with one would make it difficult or impossible to comply with the other.

interpersonal conflict
Conflict that occurs between individuals or between individuals and groups.

legitimate sources, as when real differences in goals or objectives exist between the parties involved. Often, however, they arise not from legitimate differences but from personality clashes. Some people are more aggressive and prone to conflict than others, and some are so hypersensitive that every comment is viewed as an insult that demands a response.

McCain Foods, the Canadian French fry giant, has experienced an ongoing interpersonal conflict between two of the founders of the firm, Wallace and Harrison McCain. In 1993, the board of directors voted to oust Wallace from his position as co-chair of the company. He took the company to court and was successful in blocking the board's move. The two brothers then tried to end their feud but were unsuccessful. In 2001, both brothers were given a leadership award at a black tie dinner, but Wallace said that the relationship with his brother had not improved in the intervening eight years.[39]

McCain Foods
www.mccain.com

inter-group conflict
Conflict between groups.

Inter-group Conflict **Inter-group conflicts** occur, for example, between line and staff units or between production and sales departments. Effectively managing inter-group conflict is especially crucial today as firms increasingly try to manage change by moving toward boundaryless organizations.

Techniques for Managing Conflict

The many techniques for managing or resolving conflicts fall into one of two categories: structural approaches and interpersonal approaches.

Structural Approaches Various conflict-management methods are based on using the organization's structure (See Table 15.3). For example, the most frequent way of resolving

TABLE 15.3 *Structural Conflict Resolution Techniques*

TECHNIQUE	DESCRIPTION	EXAMPLE
1. Procedural changes	Work procedures are changed to resolve conflict.	A sales manager argues that a credit manager is cancelling too many deals for credit reasons. The dispute is resolved by involving the credit manager earlier in the process of selling.
2. Personnel changes	Individuals are transferred into or out of a department in order to resolve personality clashes.	A personality clash between two high-performing workers is disrupting departmental productivity. One of the workers is transferred to another department, and both workers are now able to make a positive contribution to the organization.
3. Authority changes	Authority lines are changed or clarified to reduce conflict.	The head of industrial engineering complains that production managers do not listen to his advice about new high-tech machinery. The head of industrial engineering is given functional authority over the production managers on the issue of new machinery procedures.
4. Layout changes	The work space is rearranged to resolve conflict.	Two work groups harass each other continually. A wall is built between the two groups so they can no longer interact.
5. Resource changes	Resources are expanded so that the disputing parties can each have what they want.	The dean of a business school gets a commitment from the provincial government for funds to hire additional faculty members. This reduces the dispute between department heads because they each get to hire two more faculty members.

TABLE 15.4 *Interpersonal Conflict Resolution Techniques*

TECHNIQUE	DESCRIPTION	EXAMPLE
1. Forcing	Managerial authority is used to compel a resolution of the conflict.	A manager orders two disputing subordinates to stop their interpersonal conflict on company time because it is disrupting the work of the department.
2. Smoothing	The manager tries to convince the disputing parties that they really don't have anything to fight about.	A manager tries to calm two disputing subordinates by pointing out all the areas where they are in agreement and down-playing the one area in which they disagree.
3. Avoidance	The conflicting parties avoid each other.	Two managers who are trying to increase the budget for their respective departments begin avoiding each other because every time they meet they get into an argument.
4. Compromise	Each side gives up some of what it wants in order to resolve the conflict.	During collective bargaining, the union demands a 10 percent increase while management offers only 2 percent. Eventually they agree on a 6 percent increase.
5. Mediation	A neutral third party tries to help the disputing parties work out a resolution of the conflict.	During a strike, a mediator is called in to help labour and management reach a settlement. The mediator has no authority to force a settlement.
6. Arbitration	A neutral third party imposes a binding resolution on the disputing parties.	An arbitrator imposes a new collective agreement on a company where there has been a major labour–management dispute. The arbitrator's decision is binding on both parties in the dispute.
7. Superordinate goal	An agreed upon goal by the disputing parties is used to override the conflict.	Arab states in the Middle East may not see eye to eye on many issues, but they join OPEC to achieve a superordinate goal of high oil prices.
8. Majority rule	The side with the most votes gets its way.	At a committee meeting, a motion to resolve a dispute is passed by a vote of 8–7.
9. Confrontation	The opposing sides openly state their views to each other.	In a marriage counselling session, the husband and wife state how they really feel about each other. Each spouse is likely to hear things they have never heard before.
10. Integration	The disputing parties try to find solutions that generate both their desires so that a "win-win" solution can be developed.	The board of directors of a church resolves a dispute about musical style by having two worship services, one with traditional music, and one with contemporary music.
11. Consensus	The disputing parties must attempt to reach a consensus on what should be done to resolve conflict.	At a meeting of the new product committee, seven new product ideas are prioritized in order of importance after a three-hour discussion where each person indicates his or her preferences.
12. Accommodation	One side gives in to the other side.	The manager of one department agrees to do some paperwork for the manager of another department after a conflict develops over who is responsible for the paperwork.

disagreements between departments is still to refer them to a common superior. If the vice presidents for sales and finance cannot reach agreement on some point, they would typically refer their disagreement to the president for a binding decision.

Another structural way to reduce the potential for conflict is to reduce the interdependencies or the need to compete for scarce resources. Sometimes the changes are as simple as separating the units physically, so that the members of one group no longer have to confront members of the other group each day. Another change is to increase the available resources so that both groups can get what they want. Lawrence and Lorsch found that many companies reduced interdepartmental conflict by setting up special liaisons between warring departments. In the high-tech plastics industry, for example, successful companies set up special "integrator" new-product development departments, whose job was to coordinate the work of the research, sales, and manufacturing departments.

Interpersonal Approaches There are many different ways to settle an argument. For example, having both parties meet to establish the facts and develop a solution is usually more effective than simply hiding the conflict by changing its environment. Popular interpersonal conflict-resolution styles are described in Table 15.4.

Choosing a Conflict-Resolution Technique

Many conflicts require the manager's personal intervention. It is at this point that the manager must become something of a diplomat. He or she must size up the situation and decide what conflict-resolution style to use. Every diplomat knows that there are different ways ("conflict-resolution styles") to settle an argument, and that some are better than others, depending on the situation. For example, having both parties meet to resolve the conflict is usually better than simply "smoothing over" the conflict. Yet, there are undoubtedly times when letting things just cool down is advisable. Knowing which approach to use when is something of an art.

We can think of conflict resolution styles in terms of a "dual concern model."[40] This approach views conflict resolution styles as based on two things—the individual's concern for his or her own outcomes, and the individual's concerns for the outcomes of others. The matrix shown in Figure 15.7 shows four styles that can be used. *Accommodators* are high in concern for others and low in concern for self. They tend to sacrifice their own goals and satisfy the needs of others. *Avoiders* are low in concern for both self and others. They let conflicts go unresolved or wait for others to take responsibility for solving the problem.[41] *Competitors* maximize their own outcomes while disregarding the effects on others. For them, conflict is always a win-lose situation. *Collaborators* pursue a win-win style. They are high in their concern for self and for others. They "...try to integrate the needs of both parties into a solution that will maximize the interests of both."[42]

Figure 15.8 provides a self-assessment exercise for sizing up your own conflict-resolution style.

Remember that many people are capable of adapting their style to the situation, and of using several styles at once.[43] A study of supervisors and subordinates illustrates this. The researchers studied how supervisors used seven possible conflict-resolution styles: forcing, confronting, process controlling, problem solving, compromising, accommodating, and avoiding. The researchers' basic question was this: "Is some combination of these styles more effective at resolving conflicts than are others?" They analyzed videotapes of 116 male police sergeants handling a standardized, scripted conflict with either a subordinate or a superior. The possible styles in this study were the following.

- *Confrontation.* "In recent meetings we have had a thrashing around about our needs. At first we did not have much agreement, but we finally agreed on the best solution." Confronting the issue head-on is often the best approach. This is especially so when the parties are willing to confront and air their differences in a civil, problem-solving manner.

- *Forcing.* "If I want something very badly and I am confronted by a roadblock, I go to top management for the backing I need to get the decision made. If

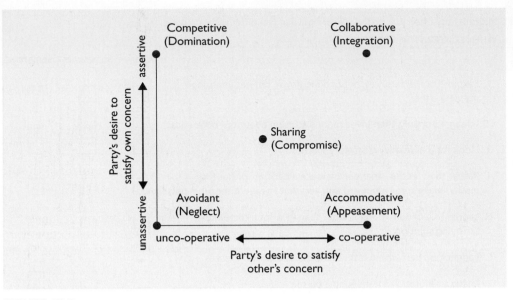

FIGURE 15.7
Conflict-Handling Styles

there is a conflict, then I take the decision to somebody higher up."[44] Forcing can be effective, as a brute show of power. However, remember the old saying, "The person convinced against his will is of the same opinion still." Forcing compliance can backfire if the person you're forcing can wiggle out of the deal later.

- *Avoidance.* "I'm not going to discuss that with you." Avoidance or smoothing over usually won't resolve a conflict. In fact, doing so may actually make it worse if bad feelings fester. However, some problems—especially small ones—sometimes do go away by themselves. And avoidance may be your only option if one party or both parties are highly emotional.

- *Competition.* "We should have gotten that assignment, not you." Letting the parties "fight it out" may be the style of choice when it's okay to resolve the conflict with a clear winner or loser. That works in sports. But if the parties need to continue working together, this approach may leave a residue of ill will.

- *Compromise and collaboration.* "I'm sure we can figure out a way to solve this together. We're all in the same boat." Compromise means each person gives up something in return for reaching agreement. This approach can work well. However, it assumes a high level of maturity and willingness on both parties' parts. And it can leave one or both parties feeling that they could have done better if they had bargained harder.

- *Accommodation.* "Calm down so we can work this out."[45] Accommodation can help calm an opponent who is not uncontrollably irate. However, this is a stop-gap measure. You'll have to take up the issue again later, since the matter remains unresolved.

It was obvious to the researchers that to resolve the conflict the sergeant had to use several styles simultaneously. For example, problem solving tended to enhance the sergeant's effectiveness, especially if he or she combined it with some forcing. However, controlling the process—dominating the conflict-resolution process to one's own advantage, for instance, by not letting the conversation stray off track—was even more effective. It was superior to trying to force the issue by insisting that the adversary follow orders.

Indicate how often you do the following when you differ with someone.

WHEN I DIFFER WITH SOMEONE:

	Usually	Sometimes	Seldom
1. I explore our differences, not backing down, but not imposing my view either.	☐	☐	☐
2. I disagree openly, then invite more discussion about our differences.	☐	☐	☐
3. I look for a mutually satisfactory solution.	☐	☐	☐
4. Rather than let the other person make a decision without my input, I make sure I am heard and also that I hear out the other person.	☐	☐	☐
5. I agree to a middle ground rather than look for a completely satisfying solution.	☐	☐	☐
6. I admit I am half wrong rather than explore our differences.	☐	☐	☐
7. I have a reputation for meeting a person halfway.	☐	☐	☐
8. I expect to get out about half of what I really want to say.	☐	☐	☐
9. I give in totally rather than try to change another's opinion.	☐	☐	☐
10. I put aside any controversial aspects of an issue.	☐	☐	☐
11. I agree early on rather than argue about a point.	☐	☐	☐
12. I give in as soon as the other party gets emotional about an issue.	☐	☐	☐
13. I try to win the other person over.	☐	☐	☐
14. I work to come out victorious, no matter what.	☐	☐	☐
15. I never back away from a good argument.	☐	☐	☐
16. I would rather win than end up compromising.	☐	☐	☐

Scoring Key and Interpretation

Total your choices as follows: Give yourself 5 points for "Usually"; 3 points for "Sometimes"; and 1 point for "Seldom." Then total them for each set of statements, grouped as follows:

Set A: items 13–16	Set C: items 5–8
Set B: items 9–12	Set D: items 1–4

Treat each set separately.

A score of 17 or above on any set is considered high.

Scores of 8 to 16 are moderate.

Scores of 7 or less are considered low.

Sets A, B, C, and D represent conflict-resolution strategies:

A = Forcing/domination. I win, you lose.

B = Accommodation. I lose, you win.

C = Compromise. Both win some, lose some.

D = Collaboration. I win, you win.

Everyone has a basic or underlying conflict-handling style. Your scores on this exercise indicate the strategies you rely upon most.

FIGURE 15.8
Your Conflict-Resolution Style

Some sergeants also boosted their conflict-management effectiveness by being somewhat accommodating.

The bottom line seems to be this: At least for these police sergeants, using three styles together—problem solving while being moderately accommodating and still maintaining a strong hand in controlling the conflict-resolution process—was an especially effective combination.

SKILLS AND STUDY MATERIAL

SUMMARY

1. Thinking like a leader involves reviewing a leadership situation and identifying what is happening, accounting for what is happening (in terms of leadership and other behavioural science theories and concepts), and formulating leader actions. Knowledge of organizational change and development can be useful tools.

2. Managers in their leadership roles can focus on various change targets. They can change the strategy, culture, structure, tasks, technologies, or attitudes and skills of the people in the organization.

3. The hardest part of leading a change is overcoming resistance. Resistance stems from several sources: habit, resource limitations, threats to power and influence, fear of the unknown, and altering employees' personal compacts.

4. Methods of dealing with resistance include education and communication, facilitation and support, participation and involvement, negotiation and agreement, manipulation and co-optation, and coercion. Kurt Lewin suggests unfreezing the situation, perhaps by using a dramatic event to get people to recognize the need for change.

5. Implementing a change is basically like solving any problem: The manager must recognize that there's a problem, diagnose the problem, and then formulate and implement a solution.

6. A nine-step process for actually leading organizational change includes creating a sense of urgency; creating a guiding coalition and mobilizing commitment to change through joint diagnosis of business problems; developing and then communicating a shared vision; removing barriers to the change and empowering employees; generating short-term wins; consolidating gains and producing more change; anchoring the new ways of doing things in the company's culture; and monitoring progress and adjusting the vision as required.

7. Organizational development is a special approach to organizational change that involves letting the employees themselves formulate and implement the change that's required, often with the assistance of a trained consultant. Types of OD applications include human process applications, technostructural interventions, HR management applications, and strategic applications.

8. Conflict can have dysfunctional effects on an organization and its people, although it can be a positive force as well. At least three types of conflict can be identified in organizations: individual, interpersonal, and intergroup. Conflict resolution techniques include structural approaches (which involve changing the organization's structure to help resolve the conflict) and interpersonal approaches (which involve changing the way people interact with each other).

CRITICAL THINKING EXERCISES

1. Lester Thurow is well known for his views on the economics of change and economic changes. *Rethinking the Future*, edited by Rowan Gibson (Nicholas Breakely, 1998), includes an article by Thurow, "Changing the Nature of Capitalism." Causing the change are what he terms five economic tectonic plates that are driving all

the economic changes and fundamentally remaking the economic surface of the earth: the end of Communism; the movement from natural resource-based industries to human-created brainpower industries; the world's population growth, movement, and aging; the new global economy; and the fact that the world does not have one dominant economic, political, or military power. He argues that these changes are shaking the foundations of twenty-first century capitalism because technology and ideology are moving apart. He says, "We know the forces that are going to determine the future of capitalism. But what we don't know is the exact shape of the future, because that's not determined by the stars; it's determined by what we do." What do you think of Thurow's analysis? What sorts of organizational changes do you think they will trigger for companies?

2. One change that many authors have identified is the change from a brawn-based economy to a brain- and knowledge-based economy. In Peter Drucker's *The New Realities* (1989) he noted that only one of the nineteenth-century business-builders had any advanced schooling: That was J. P. Morgan, and he was a college dropout. Since the latter part of the twentieth century knowledge has become the capital of a developed economy. This has occurred in one generation. What are the implications for leadership in this new world of knowledge capital? How will those trained and educated in the 1980s and 1990s survive the changes of today? What techniques discussed in this chapter may help leaders find their way and influence others to change?

EXPERIENTIAL EXERCISES

1. In *Owning the Future* (Houghton-Mifflin, 1999) Seth Shulman warns that freely shared knowledge is fast becoming a valuable asset. We face imminent threats from new monopolies that concentrate vital information in the hands of a few. Shulman writes of today's battles for control over the intangible new assets—genes, software, databases, and scientific information—that make up the lifeblood of our new economy. What do you think of his warnings? Interview five people who are involved in one of these subjects (genes, software, databases, or scientific information), and be prepared to discuss what you find in class.

2. Working in teams of four to five students, explain specifically how you would apply each of the three steps in Lewin's change process to overcome resistance to change in the following situations: (a) Your brother is 100 pounds overweight; how would you get him to eat more healthfully? (b) Your professor gave you a B+ instead of an A because your course marks totalled 79.6 instead of 80; how would you convince her to change your grade to an A? (c) You have just applied for a job as a marketing manager for a local department store, but you have been told that you don't have enough experience; how would you convince the store to hire you?

BUILDING YOUR MANAGEMENT SKILLS

Introducing a Change

Think of an organization that you are part of (e.g., a student group, a volunteer group in the community, a sports club, a hobby group, a church group, or the place you work). Then decide which one of those organizations should make a change in the way they do things to be more effective. The change can deal with any aspect of the organization. Choose a situation that you feel very strongly about, that is, one where you feel the organization really needs to make a change. Then write a one-page description of the situation and why you feel the change is necessary.

Once you have done that, answer the following questions:

1. Develop a plan for implementing the change using the section in the chapter entitled "A Nine-Step Process for Leading Organizational Change." For each step in the process, indicate specifically what you would

do. For example, for the "create a sense of urgency" step, describe specifically what you would do and explain how you would convince others that there actually is an urgent need to introduce a change. Make sure you have specific suggestions for all nine steps.

2. If you have difficulty making specific suggestions for any of the nine steps, what might that mean?

3. Make plans to present your proposed plan for change to the person or group in the organization that would have to give approval for such a change. When doing your planning, carefully consider how you will deal with any resistance to your ideas that might arise. Consult the section in the chapter entitled "Choosing the Right Tool for Dealing with Resistance" as you do your planning. Which of the approaches in Table 15.1 would work in your situation?

As you have read in this chapter, leading organizational change can be one of the most rewarding or frustrating experiences for a manager. Access the website of the Vancouver International Society for Performance Improvement, Spectrum Spring 2002 (**www.ispi-van.org**). Read the article entitled "Leading Organizational Change" by Alex Wray.

1. Define "fair process" and identify its three essential elements.
2. What are the results of observing fair process?
3. List three consequences of violating fair process.

CASE STUDY 15-1

Introducing Change at Yellow Freightways

When Bill Zollars became CEO at Yellow Freightways, the firm had just finished a terrible year. It lost about U.S.$30 million, laid off workers, and had a Teamsters union strike. When he was senior vice president at Ryder Corp., Bill Zollars had built their high-tech integrated logistics unit into a U.S.$1.5 billion business. He therefore knew that saving Yellow Freightways was going to involve considerable technological change.

One of the biggest changes involved upgrading the firm's technology. Yellow has spent more than U.S.$80 million per year in the past few years on new integrated information systems. Now, when customers call 1-800-go-yellow, the service representative automatically sees the profile corresponding to that caller's phone number. That tells the sales representative where the customer's company is located, what kind of shipments it typically makes, what sort of loading dock it has, and the firm's previous shipping destinations. This dramatically reduces the time for processing an order, to as little as 15 seconds in many cases.

Zollars and his team also equipped each dock worker with a wireless "mobile data terminal." Now, even before the truck arrives, the worker can see what's on board and where it's pulling into the dock. And if the worker is not unloading a truck as fast as the system estimates it should take, an alert is sent to the worker's mobile data terminal. This system allows managers back at headquarters to monitor progress and to send in additional employees if help is required.

Simply changing the technology without changing the people is futile. Before making the changes, Zollars explained his plan to all of his employees. With 25 000 employees in hundreds of locations around the country, Zollars spent over a year going from terminal to terminal, standing on loading docks and explaining the changes that were in the works. Although the new technology gives the employees the information they need to solve problems quickly, it also means that management has to make sure that the employees get the additional authority they require, as well as training on the new equipment.

All of these changes have led to a change in Yellow's culture, including an increased sense of urgency. Linking employees in with the new technology, and giving them the authority to make fast, on-the-spot decisions (empowering them) helped to win their commitment and dedication to getting the job done fast.

Questions

1. Analyze the situation facing Bill Zollars by addressing the three questions in the basic change model. (What are the forces acting on me? What should we change? and How should we change it?)

2. What are the four general areas where management can decide to introduce a change? Describe the areas that Bill Zollars focused on when he decided to introduce change at Yellow Freightways.

3. In general terms, why do employees resist change? Why might employees at Yellow Freightways have resisted the changes that Bill Zollars wanted to introduce? Why didn't they resist the change?

4. Review the nine-step process for successfully introducing change. Based on the information provided in the case, identify the actions that Bill Zollars took to increase the chance that the change would be successful.

Yellow Freightways
www.yellowcorp.com

Conflict and Change at Parallax Systems

Janet Palica was the assistant to the president of Parallax Systems Ltd. In this staff position Palica worked on a variety of projects for the president. Recently she had been asked to draw up plans for renovations to the company's administrative offices. The president stressed how important it was that the renovations proceed efficiently and on time. Palica was looking forward to this project because one of the outcomes would be a new office for her.

Because Palica wanted to make a good impression on the president, she immediately put the project at the top of her priority list. She gave considerable thought to what should be included in the renovations and then contacted a local architect and had him draw up renovation plans. When the blueprints were ready, she circulated a memo to all those who would be affected by the renovations and invited them to a meeting to announce the changes that would be made.

At the meeting, everything went wrong. Several secretaries who were going to have to move their workstations as a result of the renovations were very upset. After they had received Palica's memo, they had met (on their own time) and drawn up an alternate plan. Palica saw that their plan was better than hers, but she said nothing at the meeting. The secretaries argued that the renovations should be delayed until everyone had a chance to comment on them.

Several other groups were also upset. The drafting department members complained that their proposed new quarters were unacceptable and that no one had consulted them about the specialized type of space they needed. The marketing people complained that there was no area where sales meetings could be held. They reminded Palica that the president had promised that a large meeting room would be included when renovations were made. By the end of the meeting, Palica was exhausted. She was concerned that the president would hear about the negative tone of the meeting and that it would reflect badly on her management skills. She also felt obliged to consult with several of the groups that had been very vocal at the meeting. She realized that the renovation project could not possibly be completed by the time the president wanted. Palica thought to herself, "If only I had talked to some of these people before I had the renovation plans drawn up!"

Questions

1. Why has the problem arisen for Janet Palica?
2. Why did some groups react so vigorously to the proposed changes?
3. What should Palica do now?

Managing Culture at JetBlue

Anyone who's flown in the past few years (including the industry's most experienced, "elite-status" flyers) knows how frustrating flying can be, with long security lines, testy employees, and (when you finally get on the plane), no food. It hasn't been pleasant, and David Neeleman knew that building JetBlue meant putting "pleasant" back into flying. He knows there's more to building a great airline than buying brand-new planes and offering low fares and seatback TV's (although that certainly helps). Great companies have great cultures, values, and expected behaviours that guide everything employees do. As he says in his "Welcome from our CEO" memo to passengers on JetBlue's website, "...we set out to bring humanity back to air travel and to make traveling more enjoyable". That's why Neeleman and his team have worked so hard to create the right culture at JetBlue.

In building the right culture, he and his team have taken several tangible steps. The "Culture" page on the website lays out the company's five values: safety, caring, integrity, fun, and passion. The "Diversity" page follows up with the company's commitment to "encourage a diverse environment where teamwork prevails over cultural or ethnic differences." Creating the right culture means hiring people who have the sorts of values and behaviour patterns JetBlue is looking for. You will therefore find, if you browse through JetBlue's on-line job listings, numerous references to values and behaviour. For example, a Customer Service Crew needs to be "able to demonstrate a passion for taking care of customers with integrity while having fun and doing it all safely." In other words, they should "find a way to 'YES' the customer."

Other job listings—such as that for the Manager, Operations—similarly stress the need to exhibit a pas-

sion for the work required in that position. JetBlue's on-line employment application form requires applicants to "Tell us your 'shining moment' story," when you've "gone out of your way to meet the needs of a customer or fellow employees." It also asks the applicant to describe an instance when he or she had "FUN on the job."

Neeleman and his team also take other culture-building steps. For example, you will often find him or members of his top-management team on the planes, speaking with passengers and crew to judge the level of service. They also pitch in with the ground crews, helping them load and unload planes and sort baggage.

Assignment

You and your team are consultants to Mr. Neeleman, who is depending on your management expertise to help navigate the launch and management of JetBlue. Here's what he wants to know from you:

1. Develop a form we can use to "read" how employees see our culture now. Could we use the same form to measure our passengers' perceptions of our culture? Tell us how we should go about doing the latter.

2. Write a brief (one-paragraph) summary of the sort of culture we are shooting for now. Then, tell us how you would fine-tune that target culture, how you would delete the aspects you think are unwise, and how you would add aspects you believe are necessary. Explain your changes, please.

3. Based on everything you know about JetBlue, list at least five other tangible things the company does (other than those in the case above) to create its culture.

Changing the Way We Drive: How Long Will It Take?

There are 600 million automobiles in the world, and almost all of them are powered by the internal combustion engine. Developed in the late nineteenth century, the engine is now well-entrenched because it is powerful, reliable, convenient, and efficient. Unfortunately, the internal combustion engine also pollutes the air, so there is a great deal of interest in finding an alternative source of power. In recent years, the hydrogen fuel cell has been touted as the wave of the future. The fuel cell creates electric power while producing virtually no pollution, just water vapour.

But North American drivers are unlikely to change to fuel cells unless it can be shown that they are much better than the internal combustion engine. A group called the California Fuel Cell Partnership is plotting a campaign to accomplish the change. It brings together executives from oil companies and car makers, as well as scientists and government officials. The Partnership wants to triple the number of fuel-cell cars (from 20 to 60) in the near future.

There are two key problems. First, fuel-cell cars can only go about 160 miles before they need refueling. Developers think that they will have to achieve at least 300 miles before the general public is interested. Second, there are virtually no hydrogen-refueling stations in existence that would make it convenient for customers to fuel up. There is a reluctance to build hydrogen-refueling stations until the fuel cell has been perfected for use in cars. But the development of the fuel cell for use in cars is hindered by the lack of fueling stations. This chicken-and-egg problem is a big one for fuel-cell developers.

Two Canadian companies are working to solve these two major problems. Stuart Energy is the world leader in building hydrogen-refueling stations. Jon Slangerup, CEO of Stuart, says the company currently has nine such stations and is building more. He admits that changing the world is going to take a long time, but his company is making a start. Ballard Power Systems is the second company. It received a great deal of publicity in the 1990s about its hydrogen fuel-cell development efforts. However, its star has fallen because results have been slow to come and the investment community has become disillusioned. Fuel-cell testing continues, but the optimistic predictions of just a few years ago have been abandoned.

Frustrated proponents of the fuel cell claim that car companies have been holding back on research-and-development spending on fuel cells because they are too focused on making profits out of the existing internal combustion technology. They say that many billions of dollars must be invested in research and development before the fuel cell will come into wide use. DaimlerChrysler is the first car company to get serious about hydrogen fuel cells. But Ferdinand Panik, a senior advisor at the company, says it will take a long time (somewhere between 20 and 50 years) to change the automobile industry.

The world may want hydrogen fuel cells, but the internal combustion engine still rules as king of the road.

Questions

1. Using Figure 15.1 as a guide, assess the attempts to change from the internal combustion engine to the hydrogen fuel cell. In conducting your assessment, be sure to identify who the change agents are, the forces that are facilitating or inhibiting the change, the type(s) of change that is needed, and the change process.

2. In Chapter 15, several specific suggestions are made for changing an organization's culture. How might these suggestions be applied to an entire society with regard to the issue of hydrogen fuel cells? Be specific. What difficulties might be encountered when trying to apply these suggestions? Be specific.

3. List the reasons why people resist change. How are these reasons relevant to the issue of the adoption of the hydrogen fuel cell as a new idea?

4. Use force field analysis to analyze the hydrogen fuel-cell issue.

Source: "Powering the Future," *Venture* #869, (March 2, 2003).

You've Got Mail!

There are nearly half a billion email messages written every day in North America. People have been claiming for some time that they are overwhelmed by too much email, but now a new problem has arisen: managers are finding that they must be very careful what they say in email, because the content may be used against them later. At the centre of most corporate scandals is an incriminating email that some manager wrote and thought it was erased from the system. But computer technicians have ways of extracting information from hard drives and finding that one email that can be restored and used against the person who wrote it.

Unfortunately, many managers haven't yet learned that they must be careful when sending email. For some reason, people will say almost anything in email they send, and they don't think clearly when they reply to other people's email. At Merrill Lynch, for example, analysts called questionable stocks they were promoting to the general public "pieces of crap," and hoped that investors wouldn't know what they were talking about. Even Microsoft's Bill Gates was caught when he offered a favour if another company would switch to Microsoft software.

An entire industry is now developing that searches for email indiscretions, and it is changing the way lawsuits work. Kroll Consulting (which is expanding its business into Canada) recently purchased an e-evidence company that looks for evidence for important court cases. In one case, a diet drug was alleged to have nasty side effects. Emails were recovered from computers at the company that showed employees talking about consumers who were afraid of some "silly lung problem." Once that email was found, the offending company settled out of court. This case is not an isolated one. These recovered emails can suddenly turn up in court, increasing the risk to companies.

Here's the problem: the "delete" key on your computer is misleading because emails actually stay on your hard drive until the computer needs the space. Only then are they are overwritten (erased). Some messages that you thought you deleted can stay in your computer for as long as two years. At KPMG's forensics lab in Toronto, Rene Hamel shows how he can find almost anything. He first writes an email, then deletes it. It looks like it is gone, but when he begins searching for it, he finds it in *four* different places.

Lawyers in both Canada and the United States who are looking for evidence increasingly search both hard drives and internet provider systems because they know that just one bad email can blow apart the other side's case. Judges and juries want to know what defendants said then, not what they're claiming now.

Teresa Dufort of McMillan Binch warns companies about careless email because they can be used to target companies for litigation. The obvious solution is for employees to think before they send email. Companies are also beginning to use sophisticated "wiping" programs that really do delete what isn't needed. Once a lawsuit is underway, it is too late to be erasing tapes (even if it is innocently done) because it makes you *look* guilty. But if you erase old email in the normal course of business, your company is probably OK.

If employees are scattered around the country and are constantly communicating with customers, it is quite possible that some questionable email will be sent. In some firms, the management team meets with lawyers to assess the risk of employees saying something unreasonable in their email. Even "good" email can get a company in trouble. When two companies start a legal battle, for example, lawyers looking for mischief ask for lots of evidence as they try to wear down the other side. If you're asked to provide massive files of information and you accidentally delete some documents, you can look guilty.

Questions

1. Explain the essential feature of each of the barriers to communication that are noted in Chapter 13. Which barriers are most relevant to the issue of email?

2. What is "the grapevine?" Does email facilitate or inhibit the grapevine? Explain.

3. List and briefly describe the four factors that determine media richness. Where does email fit into this model? When is email most appropriate?

4. What suggestions would you make for resolving the kinds of problems mentioned in this case? (Make sure the suggestions are consistent with the continued productivity of employees.)

Video Resource: "E-mail Alert," *Venture* #851 (October 27, 2002).

PART 5 Controlling

Part 5: Controlling provides an overview of the controlling process and the techniques that managers use to ensure that what is supposed to happen actually *does* happen.

In **Chapter 16, Controlling and Building Commitment**, we begin by noting the important place of control in the management process and explain why managers need to control inputs, processes, and output. We explain the key steps in the traditional control process and describe three main types of traditional control systems. Typical negative human reactions to the traditional approach are noted. An alternative—commitment-based control—is presented, and the advantages of this type of system are noted.

Controlling and Building Commitment

A Failure of Control

OBJECTIVES

After studying this chapter and the case exercises at the end, you should be able to use the material to:

1. Rate the adequacy of a manager's control system.

2. Recommend specific feed-forward, concurrent, and feedback controls a manager should use to control the activity.

3. Write a simple budget for a manager.

4. Specify a "strategic ratio" a manager should have employees focus on.

5. List 10 measures a manager can use to build a "balanced scorecard."

In 2001, Enron was one of the largest companies in the world, and Arthur Andersen (its auditor) was one of the world's "big five" accounting firms. One year later, Enron was in bankruptcy, and Andersen was fighting to stay alive after the firm was found guilty of shredding documents dealing with Enron. In violation of its own ethical policies, Enron allowed some executives to set up special "off the books" partnerships, which were then used by Enron to hide costs and artificially inflate revenues.

Although Andersen had controls in place that challenged these dubious accounting practices, the partners who questioned Enron's accounting practices were shunted off to other jobs, apparently in an attempt to keep Enron as a client. This was not the first time this had happened at Andersen. It has faced several allegations of impropriety over the past five years, and in 2001 was fined U.S.$7 million by the SEC for failing to spot accounting fraud at Waste Management Inc.

Andersen is now facing billion-dollar lawsuits from people who invested in Enron. And investors are not the only people who got hurt. When Enron went bankrupt, thousands of employees at both Enron and Andersen lost their jobs. Most of these employees had nothing to do with the fraud, but they also became victims because they lost their jobs and their retirement money.

The Enron case is just one of the many problems that popped up during the stock market excesses of the late 1990s. The economic boom, and the ever-increasing expectations that went with it, caused many managers to be under intense pressure to show impressive gains in corporate revenues and profits. This led some companies to engage in unethical practices as they tried to artificially inflate financial gains. In June 2002, for example, Xerox announced that it had overstated revenues by billions of dollars. It was fined U.S.$10 million by the U.S. Securities and Exchange Commission. Other companies—including Tyco and WorldCom—also succumbed to the temptation to inflate revenue and profit numbers.

How did all these things happen when the companies' financial statements were audited by accounting firms that are supposed to give an independent opinion about the appropriateness of a company's accounting statements? The answer is that accounting firms sometimes looked the other way when carrying out their auditing activities. But why would accounting firms not point out questionable accounting practices when they found them? One reason is that many accounting firms also do management consulting for the firms they are auditing. Management consulting fees are lucrative, often exceeding the fees the accounting firm receives for its auditing services. Managers in these accounting firms fear that clients will be upset if they question certain accounting practices, and if the clients get upset enough, they may not give the accounting firm any management consulting contracts. If that happens, the accounting firm loses revenue.

One obvious solution to this problem is to prohibit accounting firms from doing both auditing and management consulting for a given client. This solution was resisted by the accounting profession for many years, but the magnitude of the Enron problem has suddenly made this idea more palatable. In 2002, for example, the Canadian Imperial Bank of Commerce (CIBC) announced that it would no longer allow its auditors to do any management consulting for CIBC. Other Canadian companies are also scrambling to reassure their investors that everything is in order. For example, in 2001 TransAlta Corp. made it clear that its auditors did not provide them with any consulting services.

Canada's accounting profession issued new rules in August 2002, which will limit the use of off-balance-sheet entities like the kind that Enron used, and this should also help to reduce Enron-type problems. The new standards will force companies to include the financial impact of special purpose entities (SPEs) on the parent company's balance sheet. Canadian companies that were keeping SPEs off the balance sheet will now be forced to change that practice.

Another major development is that Canada's six largest accounting firms will now be supervised, inspected, and disciplined by a new Canadian Public Accountability Board (CPAB). The accounting firms will have to get CPAB clearance before their clients' financial statements are accepted. In short, the auditors are going to be audited.

Canadian Public
Accountability Board
www.cpab-ccrc.ca

The Enron case is dramatic, but it is only one example of what happens when managers fail to properly carry out the controlling function. Sometimes being "out of control" isn't catastrophic, as when your cleaner is "only" an hour late delivering your blouse. Often, though, the consequences are severe, as they were at Enron. For example, inadequate management controls at toy maker Mattel meant that in one recent Christmas season, stores received barely half of what they ordered on time. Retail customers were not very happy with Mattel's excuse that "this is the toy business," says Mattel's head of worldwide operations.[1]

Control: A Central Issue in Management

control
The task of ensuring that activities are providing the desired results.

Control is the task of ensuring that activities are providing the desired results. All control systems collect, store, and transmit information on profits, sales, or some other metric. And, all control systems try to influence behaviour. This is one reason why "controlling" someone often has negative overtones. Control also requires that targets, standards, or goals be set. This is why managers often use the word "planning" along with the word "control." Enron is just one example of what happens when things get out of control. As one experts says, "The goal [of the control system] is to have no unpleasant surprises in the future."[2]

If you could be sure that every plan you made and every task you assigned would be perfectly executed, you really wouldn't need to "control." All results would occur as planned. There would be no surprises. Unfortunately, things rarely go this smoothly. People often fail to execute plans, and they vary widely in their abilities, motivation, and ethics. A further problem is that plans can suddenly become outdated. (Imagine the scrambling that the big accounting firms had to do when Arthur Andersen began to fall apart). Managers aren't paid just to put a plan in place and then to leave things to chance. They are, ultimately, paid for results. But there's no way to be sure you're progressing toward those results unless you are in control.

Many people associate "control" with large, company-wide accounting systems, but those systems are just part of what control is all about. Control actually applies to every task—large and small—that you delegate. Some tasks may be so unimportant (or your subordinates so able) that you don't need to bother with controls. However, most managers know that abdication like this is a risky way to manage. Effective managers delegate all that they can to subordinates. They also establish sufficient checkpoints so that they know the work has been performed. For every task you delegate, you'll need to establish some formal or informal control mechanism. We'll see how to do that in this chapter.

The Role of Control in the Management Process

Strictly speaking, managers decide "where we're going" (Planning, Chapters 5–7), "who will do what" (Organizing, Chapters 8–10), and "how to motivate people" (Leading, Chapters 11–15). Then, (Chapter 16), they make sure things are under control. The fact is, however, that controlling isn't something managers just think about once they're finished planning, organizing, and leading. For one thing, in practice, managing isn't so sequential. Imagine, for instance that you've just taken over as editor-in-chief of your college or university paper. You would probably want to quickly determine how much money is in your account and what debts you have to your suppliers. Would you really want to start planning your next edition before making sure you wouldn't run out of funds by the end of the month?

Furthermore, it's not so easy to separate control from the other three management functions. Indeed there's a control side to everything managers do. Control always requires that some desirable outcomes (like targets, standards, or goals) be set. That is why managers often use the word "planning" along with the word control. Similarly, control is always an issue in how managers organize. For example, we saw that self-contained, autonomous divisions can easily overspend and spin out of control. Decentralizing therefore always requires thinking through how top management will control the division's results. Leadership similarly relates to control. Leading effectively can dramatically reduce the amount of control the manager must exercise. This is because motivated and committed employees are more likely to exercise self-control. And (as some employees at Andersen and Enron discovered), there's often no practical way to exercise control when an employee is absolutely intent on bending the ethical rules. Figure 16.1 summarizes what control is and its role in the management process.

The Importance of a Timely Response

Managers use three types of controls to ensure that their responses are timely enough for the situation: steering, concurrent, and feedback.

steering control
Controls that predict results and let the manager take corrective action before the operation or project is completed.

Steering Control **Steering control** (also called "feedforward" control) lets the manager take corrective action before the operation or project is completed.[3] For example, on a flight to Mars, you would not want to find out after the fact that you missed your mark. Engineers

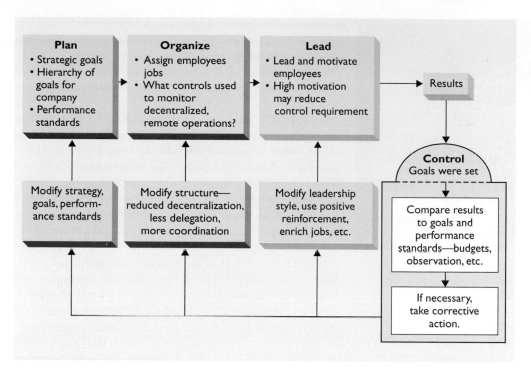

FIGURE 16.1
Management and the Control Process
Note the control aspects (last bulleted item in first row of chart) of each of the management functions.

therefore track the flight path continuously. They can then adjust its trajectory in time to reach the target. Managers use steering controls all the time. For example, managers set intermediate milestones and thus check progress long before the project is complete. They put in place procedures to reject defective raw materials, and to test and screen out candidates who may be problematic.

Consider how steering controls work at UPS, the world's largest air and ground package distribution company. It delivers nearly three billion parcels and documents each year in more than 185 countries. Critical to its success has been the U.S.$1.8 billion UPS invested in the mid-1990s in information technology. Each UPS driver uses a hand-held computer called a Delivery Information Acquisition Device to capture customers' signatures along with pick-up, delivery, and time card information and automatically transmit this information to headquarters via a cellular telephone network.

Through TotalTrack, its automated package-tracking system, UPS can control packages throughout the delivery process. And with its own global communication network called UPSnet, UPS not only tracks its packages, but electronically transmits documentation on each shipment directly to customs officials prior to arrival. Shipments are therefore either cleared for shipment or flagged for inspection when they arrive.

UPS uses the internet to help it and its customers monitor and control the progress of all those millions and millions of packages. The UPS internet-based tracking system lets a customer store up to 25 tracking numbers and then monitor the progress of each package. That not only lets the customer (and UPS) keep on top of each package's progress, but it is also a "value added" feature for the customer, which can easily keep its own customers informed about the progress of the ultimate customer's package.

Another example of a steering control is the **just-in-time (JIT) inventory system**, where inventory is scheduled to arrive just in time to be used in the production process. This system, which was pioneered by Toyota, is based on the idea that very little inventory is actually necessary if it is scheduled to arrive at precisely the time it is needed. Properly managed, the JIT system saves the company considerable money because inventory

United Parcel Service
www.ups.com

just-in-time (JIT) inventory system
A type of steering control where inventory is scheduled to arrive just in time to be used in the production process.

Mount Sinai Hospital uses a JIT system by storing its inventory at a nearby facility. Orders are delivered once a day, as well as in emergency situations.

levels can be drastically reduced. In addition, all of the risks normally associated with inventory—obsolescence, theft, deterioration, or damage—can be avoided.

Mount Sinai Hospital, in downtown Toronto, uses a JIT system. Here's how it works. Individual suppliers no longer come to Mount Sinai to deliver their items. Instead, all suppliers deliver their products to Livingston Healthcare Services Inc. in Oakville, Ontario. Livingston stores these items and fills Mount Sinai's orders once a day. The orders are put into plastic boxes that are delivered to specific nursing stations at the hospital.

The new system is highly computerized. Clerks carry scanners as they tour the stockrooms of each nursing station. Each product has a bar code, and the computer indicates how many of each item are in stock. If more product is needed, that information is transmitted to the hospital's central computer. The computer assembles data from all of the nursing stations and transmits a blanket order to Livingston's warehouse and distribution centre. If there is a crisis, Livingston can deliver within one hour.

Mount Sinai Hospital
www.mtsinai.on.ca

concurrent control
A control system in which the manager exercises control as the activity takes place, and the work may not proceed until or unless it is acceptable.

Concurrent Control With **concurrent control** (also called "yes/no" control), the manager exercises control as the activity takes place. The work may not proceed until or unless it is acceptable. These controls are often in the form of policies and rules. For example, most companies have rules forbidding employees from entering into contracts unless the firm's legal staff approves the agreements. Direct supervision—having the supervisor at a Cheesecake Factory restaurant walk the aisles to make sure all the customers are content—is concurrent control. A quality control chart that lets you plot rejects per minute and repair the machine when the trend is ominous is another example. New computerized controls (like the computerized scorecard discussed below) let managers exercise concurrent control of their operations.

The "Challenge of Change" box describes how one company uses the internet to facilitate concurrent control.

feedback control
A control where results are compared to the standard after the project is complete.

Feedback Control With **feedback control** (also called "post-action" control), results are compared to the standard after the project is complete. The final inspection on a car assembly line is an example. Budgets are also examples, as are the end-of-term grades students receive. The problem with post-action controls is that you usually can't do much to remedy the situation once the results are in. That's why managers (and professors) try to inject an element of timeliness into their controls. Instead of just a final exam, they give a mid-term, too. Instead of just an end-of-year budget, the manager gets monthly budgets, too. Increasing the frequency of a post-action control this way makes it function more like a steering control. The main difference lies in how often you check the intermediate results.

quality control
The activities that are carried out to ensure that the quality level of all goods and services meets the standards required by customers.

Quality control refers to the activities that are carried out to ensure that the quality level of all goods and services meets the standards required by customers. Quality control is an immensely important part of modern management activity. Serious difficulties arise when companies do not properly control output. In 1999, for example, Coca-Cola received very bad publicity when people in Europe became ill after drinking Coke. The Belgian health minister banned Coke products until the problem could be resolved. Coke was eventually forced to recall 14 million cases of Coke, and its profits were reduced by U.S.$35 million. It was later discovered that quality control procedures were inadequate, and that this lapse meant that Coke products had become contaminated during the production process.[4]

Coca-Cola
www.coca-cola.com

In the years following the Second World War, a U.S. consultant named W. Edwards Deming tried to convince U.S. firms of the value of high-quality products. He was not successful in the United States, but he did convince the Japanese. His work there trans-

Controlling on Internet Time

As you can imagine, the internet has improved managers' abilities to make timely mid-course corrections if they see activities trending out of control. Boeing's use of the web is a good example. Boeing has an internet-based network used by 1000 other companies, including aluminum supplier Alcoa, Inc. To gain access to this network, external users (including most of Boeing's suppliers and customers) receive "digital certificates" from Boeing, with passwords authorizing them to access the network.

Boeing's web program managers say that the network allows Boeing and its suppliers to maintain better and more timely control by reducing misunderstandings with business partners and customers.

Access to the e-network means suppliers can continually get real-time updates regarding required delivery dates and schedule changes, and can make course corrections if these are required. And since Boeing's ecommerce system is linked to tracking tools supplied by delivery services such as FedEx, customers can view the status of their orders at any time over the web. Delivery surprises are thus kept to a minimum.

Boeing's internet-based system has improved the timeliness of the company's control system in many other ways because employees can use the system to monitor production lines. For example, the web is used to keep track of shortages on airplane production lines, and that way everyone in the organization (not just managers) knows where the trouble spots are.

The system also makes it easier to control activities in specific areas, such as training. For example, as soon as each instructor was required to publish his or her course lists on the internet-based system, the training department realized that different instructors were sometimes teaching the same thing. This allowed the training department to eliminate redundant courses and to better control the costs of the courses the company makes available to its employees.

---

formed the phrase "Made in Japan" from a synonym for shoddy merchandise into a hallmark of reliability and quality. Now, Japan's highest award for industrial achievement is the Deming Award for Quality.

Deming developed 14 points on how to improve quality, including these:[5]

Deming Award for Quality
www.deming.org/demingprize/prizeinfo.html

1. Make a long-term commitment to improving quality.

2. Reduce dependence on inspection after the product is produced; instead, build quality into the product.

3. Minimize total cost by constantly improving the production system.

4. Be concerned about quality.

5. If you are a leader, help workers do a better job.

Deming's ideas gained prominence in Canada and the United States during the economic troubles of the 1970s and 1980s. In Canada, the Awards for Business Excellence acknowledge those businesses that increase Canada's competitiveness in international business. The Gold Plant Quality Award was given to the workers of Toyota's Cambridge, Ontario, plant in 1991 and 1995. This award honours the plant as the top-quality producer of automobiles in North America.

The **total quality management (TQM)** concept is based on the idea that no defects are tolerable and that employees are responsible for maintaining quality standards.[6] Traditionally, organizations formed separate departments (quality control) and set up specific jobs (quality-control inspector) to monitor quality levels. The workers' responsibility was to make the product, and the quality-control department's responsibility was to check the work.

TQM does away with this distinction and makes each worker responsible for achieving high-quality standards. For example,

- At Standard Aero in Winnipeg, the impetus to submit a bid to the U.S. Air Force for aircraft overhaul work came from employees, not managers. Standard Aero got the contract. The only definition of quality that really counts at Standard Aero is "what the customer wants."[7]
- At Toyota's Cambridge, Ontario, plant, workers can push a button or pull a rope to stop the production line when something is not up to standard.[8]
- Motorola has achieved a level of "six-sigma quality," which translates into just over three defects per million parts produced.
- When Levi Strauss introduced an "alternative work styles" program, it required workers to inspect their own output. Since the program began, there has been a 50 percent decline in defective pieces.[9]

Effective Control Systems

Timeliness is certainly crucial, but it's not the only basis on which to judge the usefulness of control systems. Checklist 16.1 summarizes 10 important requirements.

Two Approaches to Maintaining Control

Assume that you have just taken over as editor-in chief of your college or university's student paper. What are some of the things you'd want to control? A short list would include advertising revenues, expenses, deadlines for articles, each article's length and quality, and the format for each issue. How will you make sure things "stay under control"? You have two basic options: you can use the traditional control process or you can use a commitment-based process. **Traditional control systems** are based on setting standards and then monitoring performance. In contrast, **commitment-based control systems** rely on employees' self-control to do the right things. In the following pages we examine these basic alternatives in depth.

The Traditional Control Process

The control process traditionally includes five steps (see Figure 16.2).

Identify the Areas That Need to be Controlled

The controlling process starts with a clear understanding of the tasks that are being performed and an acceptance of the basic idea that some sort of control must be exercised over the people who do these tasks. To do this step properly, managers must focus not only on the obvious things that must be controlled, but also on all aspects of a task from start to finish.

total quality management (TQM)
A control concept based on the idea that no defects are tolerable and that employees are responsible for maintaining quality standards.

traditional control systems
Based on setting standards and then monitoring performance.

commitment-based control systems
Rely on employees' self-control to do the right things.

CHECKLIST 16.1

Ten Requirements of Adequate Controls[10]

☑ *Controls should reflect the nature and needs of the activity.* In other words, institute controls that make sense in terms of what you're trying to control. For example, you might use a budget to control expenses and a daily log to control whether your salespeople are using their time effectively.

☑ *Controls should report deviations promptly.* Whether it's steering, concurrent, or feedback control, it is useless if it can't report deviations quickly enough for you to do something about them. That is why managers rarely rely on just quarterly reports. Most managers also get monthly and even weekly budget reports.

☑ *Controls should be forward-looking.* The information provided by the control should signal the manager that a trend is evident. For example, by plotting defects per hour, a quality control chart lets the manager visualize a trend and to take corrective action before quality reaches unacceptable limits. Similarly, managers review budgets on a comparative basis, so as to better identify trends.

☑ *Controls should point out exceptions at strategic points.* The "principal of exception" as applied to controls is that the control system should not flood the manager with data that may simply be distracting. It should focus instead on significant matters. Thus, a sales manager would be more concerned about being 30 percent over budget for her department's $1 million travel expenses than she would be about being 60 percent over in the $500 budgeted for pencils.

☑ *Controls should be objective.* To the greatest extent possible, the manager should try to use objective, measurable standards rather than subjective ones.

☑ *Controls should be flexible.* For example, it might be counterproductive to have a salesperson compile the usual, time-consuming weekly report during the week she's working round-the-clock to win a big account.

☑ *Controls should reflect the organization structure.* A lack of clarity about who is responsible for what can lead to finger-pointing and a breakdown in the control system.

☑ *Controls should be economical.* The amount of time and resources the manager puts into controlling activities needs to make sense in terms of the magnitude of those activities and the benefits derived from those controls.

☑ *Controls should be understandable.* Some control systems are so complex as to be unusable. Sometimes the standards are too complex or hard to compute. Sometimes the control forms are too complex. Controls like these breed errors and employee resistance. Ideally, the control should be simple and understandable.

☑ *Controls should indicate corrective action.* Identifying deviations is a useful function of any control system. In addition, however, "an adequate system should disclose where failures are occurring, who is responsible for them, and what should be done about them."[11]

Siebel Systems
www.siebel.com

This understanding of the total task system is necessary if the manager hopes to develop efficient and effective controls. However, such understanding may not be easy, particularly when new initiatives are started and the organization has no expertise or understanding of how to do the work. For example, when Samsung first started making microwave ovens, no one in the company knew much about them. It took several years before Samsung finally became successful in that market. Along the way, identifying the

Samsung
www.samsung.com

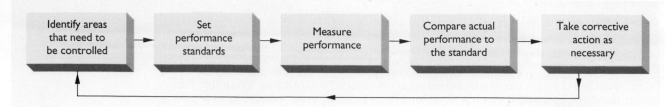

FIGURE 16.2
The Traditional Control Process

things that needed to be controlled was one of the many difficulties that managers had to cope with.

Set Performance Standards

standards
Criteria for evaluating the quality and quantity of the products or services produced by employees.

AMP of Canada
www.amp.com

To be effective, both managers and workers must know what is expected of them. Standards convey these expectations. **Standards** are criteria for evaluating the quality and quantity of the products or services produced by employees. Ideally, standards are set and communicated to employees during the planning process. Standards are most helpful in directing employee behaviour when they are stated in quantitative terms. A standard of "20 sales calls each week" guides behaviour much more specifically than a standard of "maximize sales calls each week." Quantitative standards give clear, objective guidance to employees and allow management to assess performance accurately. AMP of Canada Ltd. produces electrical interconnection devices. In this highly competitive market, it is imperative that the company find out what customers want and then give it to them. To achieve this, standards of performance have been set for all marketing jobs.[12] McDonald's is legendary for its adherence to standards. The company's training manual, for example, sets standards on hundreds of activities, ranging from the cooking time for french fries to the cleanliness of the restrooms.

time standards
Standards that state the length of time it should take to complete a task.

American Express of Canada
www.americanexpress. com

Many types of standards are used in organizations. **Time standards** state the length of time it should take to complete a task. At American Express of Canada Inc., customer contact personnel are required to respond to customer inquiries within 24 hours.[13] Time standards are relevant for many other types of workers, including auto mechanics (time standards for tune-ups, engine scope checks, engine rebuilding, and other repairs), airline pilots (time standards for trips between various cities), and production workers (time standards for the work they do and for the length of time they can spend on a coffee break). Setting time standards can result in significant increases in profitability. Hewlett-Packard discovered that when a new product was late getting to the market, it lost 30 percent of its profitability over the product's life. In contrast, a 50 percent cost overrun in research and development led to only a 3 percent loss.[14]

output standards
Standards that state the quantity of the product or service that employees should be producing.

Output standards state the quantity of the product or service that employees should be producing. At a General Motors Canada plant, for example, the overall output standard might be 60 compact cars per hour. At a McDonald's outlet, the standard might be no more than four people standing in any line waiting to be served.

cost standards
Standards that state the maximum cost that should be incurred in the course of producing goods and services.

Cost standards state the maximum cost that should be incurred in the course of producing goods and services. A customer who buys stock from a broker will normally state the maximum price per share he or she is willing to pay. A volunteer organization will state the maximum salary it is willing to pay its executive director. A manufacturing firm will state the maximum price it is willing to pay for raw materials.

Quality standards define the level of quality that is to be maintained in the production of goods and services. McDonald's sets quality standards for the meat it buys. Asics sets quality standards for the material it uses in its "Gel" running shoe. Legal and accounting firms set quality standards for the services they provide to their clients. At American Express of Canada Inc., quality standards are high: Customer-contact employees are to provide information that is 100 percent accurate.[15]

Behavioural standards state the types of behaviour that are acceptable for employees. Most organizations have standards dealing with smoking, employee dress, use of foul language in front of customers, and so forth.

Measure Performance

The goal of this phase of the controlling process is to measure accurately the output that has resulted from employees' efforts. In many situations, such a measurement is simple. The number of letters typed, the number of hamburgers cooked, the number of automobiles produced, and the number of income tax forms processed can be determined with a high degree of accuracy. But measuring employee output in certain other situations may be problematic. Determining the output level of a psychoanalyst, a university professor, a management consultant, or a researcher in a laboratory may be difficult because of the nature of the work these people are doing. For example, measuring the effect of psychotherapy is difficult because improvements may not be attributable solely to the therapy; other factors, such as the person's home situation, also influence the person's life.

Managers can measure output in various ways. One is through personal observation of the performance of subordinates. At American Express of Canada, for example, supervisors tap into the calls of customer-contact employees 20 times per month to determine whether they are dealing properly with customers. Monthly evaluations of customer complaints are also carried out.[16] Personal observation gives the manager first hand information about subordinates. However, it is not always practical or advisable for a manager to use this approach, since it is very time-consuming. A second approach is to use written reports of employee performance. For example, a manager may require an annual report of activity from an employee. This approach gives the manager a permanent record of employee performance, but it has the disadvantage of requiring the employee to do additional work. A third approach is for the manager to require oral reports from subordinates about their performance. This has the advantage of getting the manager and subordinate together for a face-to-face meeting, but problems may develop if the subordinate feels intimidated by the boss. Because each approach has both strong and weak points, it is best to use them in combination.

If standards have been clearly stated, the measurement of performance is much easier. However, even if standards are explicitly defined, management cannot simply assume that the reported performance has actually occurred. Employees might have made honest errors when reporting their performance, output might have been at the expense of quality standards, or employees might have deliberately falsified reports of their performance.

Compare Performance with Standards

In this step, the manager essentially compares "what is" with "what should be." Since the performance of human beings varies, it is necessary for the manager to determine control tolerances. **Control tolerances** state the degree of deviation from the standard that is permissible. Only if performance is outside the acceptable range of deviation does the manager take further action. If the preceding steps in the control process have been carried out properly, the comparison of performance with standards is straightforward. Comparison is also easier if quantitative standards have been set.

quality standards
Standards that define the level of quality that is to be maintained in the production of goods and services.

behavioural standards
Standards that state the types of behaviour that are acceptable for employees.

Asics
www.asicstiger.com

control tolerances
State the degree of deviation from the standard that is permissible.

Take Corrective Action as Necessary

The final phase in the controlling process requires the manager to decide what corrective action (if any) is required. When making this decision, the manager must ensure that the real cause of the deviation from the standard is identified. For example, if the output of a certain product is below standard, it must be determined whether the cause is human failure or machine failure. The corrective action that is necessary will depend on the cause of the deviation.

When comparing performance with the standard, the manager will find that it exceeds, meets, or falls short of the standard. If performance exceeds the standard, the manager must first ensure that the standard is actually reasonable. If the standard is too low, it must be revised. But if the standard is reasonable, the employee should be praised. If performance meets the standard, no further action needs to be taken.

When performance falls short of the standard, the manager must decide whether the shortfall is significant enough to demand corrective action. For example, if instructors in a college or university must achieve at least a 3.0 out of 5.0 on student evaluations and an instructor receives a 2.9 out of 5.0, the department head will have to decide whether this deviation is significant enough to warrant a talk with the instructor. This process is simplified if control tolerances have already been stated.

immediate corrective action
Actions that solve the problem immediately and get output back to the desired level.

When performance is not up to standard, managers can choose one of the following actions: (1) take corrective action, (2) change the standard, or (3) do nothing and hope things will improve. If the manager decides to take corrective action, two alternatives are available—immediate and long-term. **Immediate corrective action** solves the problem immediately and gets output back to the desired level. If management discovers that a major project is behind schedule and is therefore going to hold up other high-priority projects, immediate corrective action is taken. The top priority is getting the project back on schedule, rather than attaching blame for its lateness. Actions such as adding more personnel to the project, authorizing overtime, giving priority in the secretarial pool for project typing needs, and assigning an expediter to speed up the project are all examples of such action.

long-term corrective action
Determines why deviations occur and what can be done to prevent the problem from happening in the future.

Long-term corrective action determines why deviations occur and what can be done to prevent the problem from happening in the future. Many managers focus too much of their effort on immediate responses and not enough on long-term corrective action. Consider this example: A manager of a department with high turnover finds that she is spending a great deal of her time recruiting new members for the department (immediate corrective action). But the manager never stops to figure out why so many people are leaving the department (long-term corrective action). Unless long-term corrective action is taken, this manager will continually be trying to cope with problems she does not understand.

The Traditional Controlling Process in Action: An Example

Here is how the five steps in the controlling process usually unfold in a classroom setting in a university or community college.

1. *Identify the areas that need to be controlled.* Your instructors do not try to control every aspect of your life (although sometimes it may seem that they do). Certain important elements of the learning process remain under your control: You decide whether to cram for an exam or keep up with your readings, whether to use a highlighter or take written notes, whether to belong to a study group or work on your own, and so on. But instructors do implement controls to ensure that you do certain things, like reading the assigned chapters, because they have identified these things as definitely needing to be controlled.

2. *Set performance standards.* Your instructors typically want you to demonstrate that you can do several things: think critically, understand the course material, apply the material to real-world management situations, and so on. These skills are crucial for your success as a manager, and that is why standards are in place.

3. *Measure performance.* Your performance is measured through assignments, exams, class participation, and group projects.

4. *Compare actual performance to the standard.* Once the instructor has observed your performance, he or she must determine whether you have met the performance standard. This may appear to be a very subjective process if the instructor does not clearly state the standard. For example, consider the comment of one instructor who said, "When I was a student, I never could quite see how a professor could distinguish a B paper from a C+ paper, but now that I'm grading papers, the distinction is crystal clear." The instructor must convey that distinction to students.

5. *Take corrective action as necessary.* Feedback to students in the form of grades provides a clear signal regarding the acceptability of their performance in relation to the standard. The extreme corrective action is requiring the student to take the course over again because the deviation from the standard is unacceptable.

Many people think that the controlling process is a rather mechanical series of steps that managers work through, like following a cookbook recipe when baking a cake. But this example shows that the controlling process (like the decision-making process discussed in Chapter 5) is not so simple. At each step, numerous things can go wrong, and the people who are being controlled can become very upset.

Traditional Control Systems

There are three main types of traditional control systems: diagnostic control systems, boundary control systems, and interactive control systems.

Diagnostic Control Systems

When people think of controls, they are usually thinking of **diagnostic control systems**. Budgets, production reports, and performance reviews are all examples of diagnostic control systems. Diagnostic controls are formal, pre-planned, methodical systems that help managers zero in on discrepancies. As such, they reduce the need for managers to continually and personally monitor everything.[17] Once targets are set, managers can (at least in theory) leave the employees to pursue the goals. Supposedly, management can be secure in the knowledge that if the goals aren't met, the deviations will show up as red flags in the performance reports.

This idea is at the heart of what managers call the principle of exception. The **principle of exception** (or "management by exception") says that to conserve managers' time, only significant deviations from the standard should be brought to the manager's attention.[18]

Managers have many things to control. For our newspaper editor, these include advertising revenues, expenses, deadlines for articles, each article's length and quality, and the format for each issue. Yet, from a practical point of view, there's no doubt that it's usually the financial aspects—the "bottom line"—that's first among equals when it comes to control. Management control systems therefore emphasize budgets, but other diagnostic systems are also used, including ratio analysis, financial responsibility centres, activity-based costing, the balanced scorecard, and enterprise resource planning. We discuss each of these below.

Budgets and Performance Reports **Budgets** are formal financial expressions of a manager's plans. They show targets for things such as sales, cost of materials, production levels, and profit, expressed in dollars. These planned targets are the standards against which the manager compares and controls the unit's actual performance. The first step in budgeting is generally to develop a sales forecast and sales budget. The **sales budget** shows the planned sales activity for each period (usually in units per month) and the revenue expected from the sales. The manager can then produce various operating budgets. **Operating budgets** show the expected sales and/or expenses for each of the company's departments for the planning period in question. For example, take the production and materials budget (or plan).

diagnostic control systems
Formal, pre-planned, methodical systems that help managers zero in on discrepancies.

principle of exception
To conserve managers' time, only significant deviations or exceptions from the standard should be brought to the manager's attention.

budgets
Formal financial expressions of a manager's plans.

sales budget
A budget that shows the planned sales activity for each period (usually in units per month) and the revenue expected from the sales.

operating budget
A budget that shows the expected sales and/or expenses for each of the company's departments for the planning period in question.

This shows what the company plans to spend for materials, labour, administration, and so forth to fulfill the requirements of the sales budget.

The next step is to combine all these departmental budgets into a profit plan for the coming year. This profit plan is the **budgeted income statement** or "pro forma income statement." It shows expected sales, expected expenses, and expected income or profit for the year. In practice, cash from sales usually doesn't flow into the firm in such a way as to coincide precisely with cash disbursements. (Some customers may take 35 days to pay their bills, for instance, but employees expect paycheques every week). The **cash budget** or plan shows, for each month, the amount of cash the company can expect to receive and the amount it can expect to disperse. The manager can use it to anticipate cash needs, and to arrange for short-term loans, if need be.

The company will also have a budgeted balance sheet. The **budgeted balance sheet** shows managers, owners, and creditors what the company's projected financial picture should be at the end of the year. It shows assets (such as cash and equipment), liabilities (such as long-term debt), and net worth (the excess of assets over other liabilities).

Budgets are the most widely used traditional control device. Each manager, from first-line supervisor to company president, usually has an operating budget to use as a standard of comparison (see the example in Figure 16.3). Remember, however, that creating the budget is just the standard-setting step in the control process. You must still compare the actual and the budgeted figures and take corrective action if necessary.

The firm's accountants compile the financial information and feed it back to the appropriate managers. As shown in Figure 16.4, the performance report shows budgeted or planned targets. Next to these numbers, it shows the department's actual performance. Variances show the differences between budgeted and actual amounts. The report may provide a space for the manager to explain any variances. After reviewing the performance report, management can take corrective action.

The firm's accountants will also periodically audit the firm's financial statements. An **audit** is a systematic process that involves three steps: (1) objectively obtain and evaluate evidence regarding important aspects of the firm's performance; (2) judge the accuracy and validity of the data; and (3) communicate the results to interested users, such as the board of directors and the company's banks.[19] The purpose of the audit is to certify that the firm's financial statements accurately reflect its performance.

Ratio Analysis and Return on Investment Managers also use financial ratio analysis to maintain control. **Financial ratios** compare one financial indicator on a financial statement to another. The rate of return on investment (ROI) is one such ratio. ROI equals net profit divided by total investment, and is a measure of overall company performance. Rather than measuring net profit as an absolute figure, it shows profit in relation to the total investment in the business. For example, a $1 million profit is more impressive with a $10 million investment than with a $100 million investment. Figure 16.5 presents some commonly used financial ratios.

Examining financial ratios helps managers analyze their firm's performance. Figure 16.6 illustrates this. For example, suppose the firm didn't meet its net income target. Ratio

---

budgeted income statement
A control that shows the company's expected sales, expected expenses, and expected income or profit for the year.

cash budget
A control that shows, for each month, the amount of cash the company can expect to receive and the amount it can expect to disperse.

budgeted balance sheet
A control that shows managers, owners, and creditors what the company's projected financial picture should be at the end of the year.

audit
A systematic process of objectively obtaining and evaluating evidence regarding important aspects of the firm's performance, judging the accuracy and validity of the data, and communicating the results to interested users.

financial ratios
Calculations that compare one financial indicator on a financial statement to another.

BUDGET FOR MACHINERY DEPARTMENT, JUNE 2003

Budgeted Expenses	Budget
Direct Labour	$2107
Supplies	$3826
Repairs	$ 402
Overhead (electricity, etc.)	$ 500
TOTAL EXPENSES	$6835

FIGURE 16.3
Example of a Budget

PERFORMANCE REPORT FOR MACHINERY DEPARTMENT, JUNE 2003

	Budget	Actual	Variance	Explanation
Direct Labour	$2107	$2480	$373 over	Had to put workers on overtime.
Supplies	$3826	$4200	$374 over	Wasted two crates of material.
Repairs	$ 402	$ 150	$252 under	
Overhead (electricity, etc.)	$ 500	$ 500	0	
TOTAL	$6835	$7330	$495 over	

FIGURE 16.4
Example of a Performance Report

NAME OF RATIO	FORMULA	INDUSTRY NORM (ASSUMED MERELY AS ILLUSTRATION)
1. Liquidity Ratios (measuring the ability of the firm to meet its short-term obligations)		
Current ratio	$\dfrac{\text{Current assets}}{\text{Current liabilities}}$	2.6
Acid-test ratio	$\dfrac{\text{Cash and equivalent}}{\text{Current liability}}$	1.0
Cash velocity	$\dfrac{\text{Sales}}{\text{Cash and equivalent}}$	12 times
Inventory to net working capital	$\dfrac{\text{Inventory}}{\text{Current assets} - \text{Current liabilities}}$	85%
2. Leverage Ratios (measure the contributions of financing by owners compared with financing provided by creditors)		
Debt to equity	$\dfrac{\text{Total debt}}{\text{Net worth}}$	56%
Coverage of fixed charges	$\dfrac{\text{Net profit before fixed charges}}{\text{Fixed charges}}$	6 times
Current liability to net worth	$\dfrac{\text{Current liability}}{\text{Net worth}}$	32%
Fixed assets to net worth	$\dfrac{\text{Fixed assets}}{\text{Net worth}}$	60%
3. Activities Ratios (measuring the effectiveness of the employment of resources)		
Inventory turnover	$\dfrac{\text{Sales}}{\text{Inventory}}$	7 times
Net working capital turnover	$\dfrac{\text{Sales}}{\text{Net working capital}}$	5 times
Fixed-assets turnover	$\dfrac{\text{Sales}}{\text{Fixed assets}}$	6 times
Average collection period	$\dfrac{\text{Receivables}}{\text{Average sales per day}}$	20 days
Equity capital turnover	$\dfrac{\text{Sales}}{\text{Net worth}}$	3 times
Total capital turnover	$\dfrac{\text{Sales}}{\text{Total assets}}$	2 times

(continued)

FIGURE 16.5
Widely Used Financial Ratios

NAME OF RATIO	FORMULA	INDUSTRY NORM
4. Profitability Ratios (indicating degree of success of achieving desired profit levels)		
Gross operating margin	$\dfrac{\text{Gross operating profit}}{\text{Sales}}$	30%
Net operating margin	$\dfrac{\text{Net operating profit}}{\text{Sales}}$	6.5%
Sales margin	$\dfrac{\text{Net profit after taxes}}{\text{Sales}}$	3.2%
Productivity of assets	$\dfrac{\text{Gross income less taxes}}{\text{Total assets}}$	10%
Return on investment	$\dfrac{\text{Net profit after taxes}}{\text{Total investment}}$	7.5%
Net profit on working capital	$\dfrac{\text{Net operating profit}}{\text{Net working capital}}$	14.5%

FIGURE 16.5
(Continued)

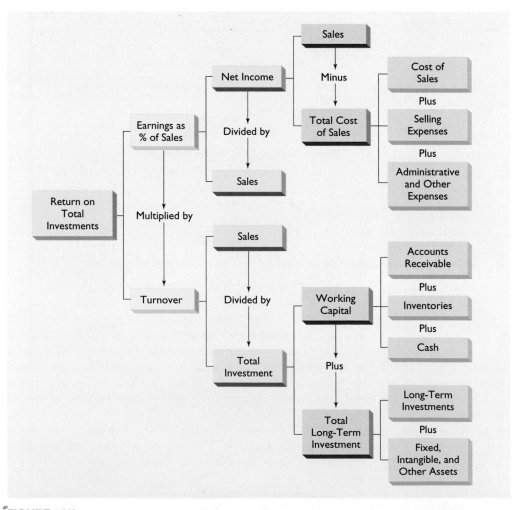

FIGURE 16.6
Relationship of Factors Affecting Return on Investment
The firm's overall profitability—its return on total investments—can be better understood by analyzing its components, including earnings as a percentage of sales and turnover.

analysis shows that low sales or high sales costs may account for this. Similarly, earnings divided by sales (the profit margin) reflects management's success or failure in maintaining satisfactory cost controls. As another example, too much investment may help account for a low ROI. In turn, too much investment might reflect inadequate inventory control, too many accounts receivable, or too much cash.[20]

In his book *Good to Great*, Jim Collins says that one of the things that distinguished companies that went from good to great was that they were able to identify one simple ratio that summed up what their strategy was all about.[21] For example, Gillette bases its strategy in part on selling multiple products repeatedly to customers. They therefore focus on "profit per customer" rather than "profit per division" as other consumer companies do.

Gillette
www.gillette.com

Financial Responsibility Centres In most firms, managers are responsible for specific sets of financial targets. This makes it easier for top management to evaluate each manager's performance. It also makes it easier for the manager to see how the firm will evaluate his or her performance. When the manager has an operating budget tied to specific financial performance targets, we say the manager is in charge of a financial responsibility centre. **Financial responsibility centres** are units that are responsible for, and measured on, a specific set of financial activities.

There are several types of financial responsibility centres. **Profit centres** are responsibility centres whose managers the company holds accountable for profit. **Profit** is the difference between the revenues generated and the cost of generating those revenues.[22] The Saturn division of General Motors is a profit centre. GM holds the division's head responsible for the profitability of that division. GM controls that manager's performance partly by monitoring whether the division makes its profit goals. **Revenue centres** are responsibility centres whose managers are accountable for generating revenues. Thus, firms generally measure sales managers in terms of the sales produced by their revenue centre/departments.

Activity-Based Costing Traditional accounting systems can produce misleading results. Most accounting today and is based on what accountants call "absorption costing." Basically, this means that as a product moves through the production process, it "absorbs" costs at each step of the process, for instance for raw materials, or the amount of labour required to produce it.[23]

The problem with this is that it can cause distortions in what managers think each product really costs. For example, it may not accurately account for "factory overhead"—the cost of heating and lighting the factory, running its cafeteria, and paying its managers and supervisors. The budget may just list these as a plant-wide monthly expense. Similarly, if there's one sales and distribution department for all the firm's products, the budget may also show these as an overall monthly expense. The actual cost of selling a particular product, or distributing it does not get "absorbed" into the product's calculated "cost." So, when a manager asks, "what's the cost of this product?" he or she may well get a misleading answer. The calculated costs usually only includes the actual, absorbed, direct, production costs.

Activity-based costing (or ABC) is a method for allocating costs to products and services that takes all the product's costs (including production, marketing, distribution, and sales activities) into account in calculating the actual cost of each product or service. Introducing an ABC system may not be easy. When Reichhold, Inc. decided to switch to an ABC system, it established an ABC steering committee. The committee included someone from senior management, as well as operational managers from the divisional, manufacturing, and financial units.[24] At Reichhold, the traditional accounting system absorbed raw materials and labour costs into each product based on each product's processing time. It turned out that this produced misleading results. After switching to ABC, it became apparent that processing time was only one of the activities that drove product costs. The operating managers on the committee noticed that product cost also depended on filtration time and waste disposal.[25]

The Balanced Scorecard The **balanced scorecard** gives the firm's managers an integrated and instantaneous way to determine the extent to which the firm is addressing its strategic responsibilities. The "balanced scorecard" itself is typically 15 to 25 interrelated measures, all chosen because they provide insight into the question, "Is the company doing what it needs to do to achieve its strategic objectives?"[26] The "scorecard" itself is

financial responsibility centres
Units that are responsible for, and measured based on, a specific set of financial activities.

profit centres
Responsibility centres whose managers the company holds accountable for profit.

profit
A measure of the difference between the revenues generated and the cost of generating those revenues.

revenue centres
Responsibility centres whose managers are accountable for generating revenues.

activity-based costing
A method for allocating costs to products and services that takes all the product's costs (including production, marketing, distribution, and sales activities) into account.

balanced scorecard
A management tool, usually a computerized model, that traces a multitude of performance measures simultaneously and shows their interactions.

usually a computerized picture of how the firm is doing on those 15–25 measures and what it all means for the firm's strategic success.

The important thing is to choose scorecard measures that make sense in terms of the firm's strategic objectives. For example, consider how Dell Computer could use a balanced scorecard. The firm's mission statement (see its website) is "to be the most successful computer company in the world at delivering the best customer experience in markets we serve." Given this mission, Chairman Michael Dell has been quoted as saying that looking for "value shifts" in his company's customer base is his most important leadership responsibility. He wants to focus his employees' attention on staying in close contact with the customers and making sure that in everything they do Dell is addressing its customers' needs. Therefore, Dell's balanced scorecard should use measures that reflect this need to stay customer-focused. These balanced scorecard measures might therefore include

- Training dollars spent per full-time employee, by customer segment. This would help ensure that well-educated business segment managers provide state-of-the-art advice to customers.

- Percentage of total hours spent in contact with the customer.

- Number of customer-initiated product innovations.[27]

For Dell, 15 to 25 measures like these would provide the main components of an effective balanced scorecard. The measures reflect hypothetical cause-and-effect relationships that link results from specific activities with the firm's strategic objectives.

Enterprise Resource Planning Systems (ERP) Corporate scorecards are often components of more comprehensive systems known as **enterprise resource planning systems**. These are company-wide integrated computer control systems. They integrate a firm's individual control systems (such as order processing, production control, and accounting). The aim is to give managers real-time, instantaneous information regarding the costs and status of every activity and project in the business.[28] By linking all the company's control systems, "managers will now be able to receive daily on-line reports about the costs of specific business processes, for example, and on the real-time profitability of individual products and customers."[29]

The cheque-printing company Deluxe Paper Payment Systems used its ERP to "get a clearer picture of which of its customers were profitable and which were not."[30] Its enterprise resource planning system helped it discover that orders for cheques from banks were much more profitable when they arrived via electronic ordering. Deluxe then launched a campaign to increase electronic ordering—particularly by its 18 000 bank and small-business customers. The number of cheques ordered electronically jumped from 48 percent to 62 percent in just a few months. This dramatically improved profits.

Kohler Co. uses its ERP "to analyze outbound shipments, on-time deliveries, first-time sales, monthly sales trends, and backlog data."[31] "You can drill down and see where in the process things are going wrong," says one Kohler manager.[32]

Boundary Control Systems

Boundary control systems—the second type of diagnostic control system—"establish the rules of the game and identify actions and pitfalls that employees must avoid."[33] They set the boundaries within which the firm expects employees to operate. Boundary control systems include ethics standards, codes of conduct, and strategic policies. It's hard to overestimate the importance of boundary control systems like these in keeping things under control. Asked recently if there's anything he loses sleep over, Jeff Immelt, GE's CEO, said that he worries about an ethical lapse on the part of some employee.

Johnson & Johnson's "Credo" (see Figure 16.7) is a classic example of a boundary control. The Credo contains the firm's code of conduct guidelines (such as, "We believe our first responsibility is to the doctors, nurses, and patients...who use our products."). These provide the boundaries within which Johnson & Johnson employees are expected to operate. Selling a product that might be harmful would obviously be out of bounds. When several bottles of poisoned Tylenol were found some years back, Johnson & Johnson quickly recalled the entire stock of the product.

enterprise resource planning systems
Company-wide integrated computer control systems.

Deluxe Paper Payments Systems
www.deluxeforms.com

boundary control systems
Systems that set the boundaries within which the firm expects employees to operate, including ethics standards, codes of conduct, and strategic policies.

Our Credo

We believe our first responsibility is to the doctors, nurses and patients,
to mothers and fathers and all others who use our products and services.
In meeting their needs, everything we do must be of high quality.
We must constantly strive to reduce our costs
in order to maintain reasonable prices.
Customers' orders must be serviced promptly and accurately.
Our suppliers and distributors must have an opportunity
to make a fair profit.

We are responsible to our employees,
the men and women who work with us throughout the world.
Everyone must be considered as an individual.
We must respect their dignity and recognize their merit.
They must have a sense of security in their jobs.
Compensation must be fair and adequate
and working conditions clean, orderly and safe.
We must be mindful of ways to help our employees fulfill
their family responsibilities.
Employees must feel free to make suggestions and complaints.
There must be equal opportunity for employment, development
and advancement for those qualified.
We must provide competent management,
and their actions must be just and ethical.

We are responsible to the communities in which we live and work
and to the world community as well.
We must be good citizens   support good works and charities
and bear our fair share of taxes.
We must encourage civic improvements and better health and education.
We must maintain in good order
the property we are privileged to use,
protecting the environment and natural resources.

Our final responsibility is to our stockholders.
Business must make a sound profit.
We must experiment with new ideas.
Research must be carried on, innovative programs developed
and mistakes paid for.
New equipment must be purchased, new facilities provided
and new products launched.
Reserves must be created to provide for adverse times.
When we operate according to these principles,
the stockholders should realize a fair return.

Johnson & Johnson

FIGURE 16.7
Johnson & Johnson's Corporate Credo

Johnson & Johnson was therefore shocked when, recently, armed federal agents came in and briefly closed down the firm's LifeScan unit's headquarters. Among other things, LifeScan makes a diabetes diagnostic device. Some J&J employees had failed to report that a software glitch made some units show the wrong diagnosis. How could that happen in a company where all 100 000 employees are supposed to be committed to a strong code of ethics? "Mistakes were made in the LifeScan situation... They were errors in judgment. We did too little, too late," is how the firm's CEO put it.[34]

Codes of conduct are useless unless they trigger action when the boundaries are breached. Employees therefore must understand that the firm takes the boundaries seriously and will monitor results. There's more to establishing boundary controls than just drawing up guidelines. Steps include the following:

1. Emphasize top management's commitment.

2. Publish a code.

3. Establish compliance mechanisms.

4. Measure results.

Johnson & Johnson
www.jnj.com

Boundary controls aren't limited to ethics or codes of conduct. The company's policies also lay out crucial boundaries. For example, "strategic boundaries focus on ensuring that people steer clear of opportunities that could diminish the business's competitive position."[35] Managers at Automatic Data Processing (ADP) use a "strategic boundary list" that lays out the types of business opportunities ADP managers should avoid. One large Netherlands-based multinational has a strategic policy of discouraging its executives from forming joint ventures with firms in the United States, because of the greater possibility of litigation in U.S. courts.

Interactive Control Systems

interactive control system
A system that maintains control by personally monitoring how everyone is doing.

The third type of diagnostic control system—the **interactive control system**—maintains control by personally monitoring how everyone is doing. This is the most basic traditional way to stay in control. With regard to this system, the typical small, entrepreneurial company has one control advantage over its big multinational competitors—managers can talk face-to-face with almost everyone in the firm. This is why large firms are turning to this approach and dividing up a business into smaller units.

But interactive control systems can be effective even in large firms. Senior managers at the newspaper *USA Today* use interactive control.[36] The process starts each Friday morning when they get three weekly reports. These provide an overview of how they have done in the previous week and what they may expect in the next few weeks. This "Friday packet" includes information ranging from advertising sales figures to information about particular advertisers.

Weekly face-to-face meetings among senior managers and key subordinates help apply this information. Regular topics include advertising volume compared to plan and new business by type of client. Senior managers don't just look for unexpected shortfalls. They also look for unexpected successes. These might suggest putting more emphasis on particular areas, such as trying to get more software suppliers to advertise, or instituting a new market-survey service for automotive clients.

How Do People React to Traditional Controls?

Every manager needs a way to ensure that his or her employees are performing as planned. It may be CEO Jeffrey Immelt trying to control GE's Asia operations, or it may be a GE sales manager in Vancouver asking, "How can I make sure Marie files her sales reports on time?" Both managers would use the traditional controls we have described above (diagnostic, boundary, or interactive) to accomplish what they want. In other words, they both would depend to some extent on things like budgets, policies, or close supervision to keep performance in line. Unfortunately, there's a downside to these traditional control approaches.

The Negative Side of Control

If controlling employees' behaviour were the only way to ensure effective performance, we could disregard much of this book. For example, we wouldn't need to know much about what motivates people. Nor would managers have to care so much about what leadership style is best, or how to foster employee commitment. Managers could just set goals and then control employees' work. But the fact is that managers can't rely just on controls for keeping employees in line. For one thing, it's impossible to have a system of rules and controls so complete that you can track everything employees say or do. There's no practical way, for instance, to control how the front-desk clerk is greeting guests every minute of the day. For another, employees often short-circuit the controls, sometimes with ingenious tactics.

Employees may use several tactics to evade controls. One expert classifies these tactics as behavioural displacement, gamesmanship, operating delays, and negative attitudes.[37]

Behavioural Displacement **Behavioural displacement** occurs when controls encourage behaviours that are inconsistent with what the company actually wants to accomplish. A famous management truism is, "you get what you measure." Setting performance targets does tend to focus employees' efforts on those targets. The problem arises when the employees focus just on what you're measuring and disregard the company's more important goals.

The problem stems mostly from limiting what you measure to just one or two control standards. For example, Nordstrom set up a policy of measuring employees in terms of sales per hour of performance.[38] Unfortunately, tracking its salespeople's performance by simply monitoring "sales per hour" backfired. Without other performance measures, the sales-per-hour system didn't work. Some employees claimed their supervisors were pressuring them to underreport hours on the job to boost reported sales per hour.

Gamesmanship **Gamesmanship** refers to management actions that improve the manager's performance in terms of the control system, without producing any economic benefits for the firm. For example, one manager depleted his stocks of spare parts and heating oil at year's end. He knew these stocks would have to be replenished shortly thereafter at higher prices. But by reducing his stocks, the manager reduced his expenses for the year and made his end-of-year results look better. However, in the longer run the company spent more than it had to.[39] Another manager over-shipped products to distributors at year-end. The aim was to ensure that management would meet its budgeted sales targets. It did, but then it had to deal with excess returns the following year.[40]

Operating Delays Managers also must watch for control systems that cause operating delays and thus unnecessarily slow things down. For example, a "yes-no" control policy that prohibits signing agreements without the company lawyer's approval can help keep the firm out of trouble. However, it may also mean losing a good project if a competitor can move faster to make an agreement. GE's former CEO Jack Welch found that it sometimes took a year or more for division managers to get approval to introduce new products; the problem was the long list of approvals required by GE's control system. Streamlining the approval process helped solve this problem.

Negative Attitudes Most people react negatively to efforts to control them. It's therefore not surprising that traditional control systems frequently trigger negative employee attitudes. One study focused on first-line supervisors' reactions to budgets. It found that the employees saw the budgets as pressure devices. In reaction to this perceived pressure, they formed anti-management groups. Their supervisors then reacted by increasing their compliance efforts.[41]

The "People Side of Managing" box describes some of the difficulties that have been encountered as managers use technology to monitor employee activities.

Using Commitment-Based Control Systems

It is clear that traditional control systems (whether diagnostic, boundary, or interactive) have some deficiencies. And it's not practical to have a system of rules and controls that's so complete that you can track everything employees say or do. At some point, the manager must rely on the employees' self-control. This is particularly true today. Globalized, empowered, team-based organizations complicate the task of keeping everything under control. Distance makes monitoring what your employees are doing day-to-day much more difficult. And imposing too much control on self-managing teams is obviously counterproductive. How can you feel empowered if someone else is controlling everything you do?

behavioural displacement
When controls encourage behaviours that are inconsistent with what the company actually wants to accomplish.

Nordstrom
www.nordstrom.com

gamesmanship
Management actions that improve the manager's performance in terms of the control system, without producing any economic benefits for the firm.

The Keystroke Cops

Recent developments in computer surveillance have made it possible for bosses to monitor employees without their knowledge. The latest innovations allow for the monitoring of every keystroke employees make while working at their computers. These silent monitoring programs—with names like Spy, Peek, Silent Watch, and Investigator—cost as little as U.S.$99. Some companies display an on-screen notice that employees' work is being monitored. This acts as a deterrent, even if monitoring is not actually being done.

The Investigator program does not appear as an icon on the computer screen, and it is hard to find among computer files even when someone searches for it. It is usually installed on a worker's computer after-hours. The program allows a manager to choose "alert" words such as "boss" or "union." Any time these words appear in the text of an email, a copy is automatically sent to the employee's supervisor.

One company bought the Silent Watch program after concerns developed about what a computer programmer was actually doing on the job. The program was installed on the worker's computer, and within a few days it became clear that he was spending considerable time visiting pornographic websites. The worker was immediately fired.

These monitoring programs are very effective at intercepting all work that employees do, even work that is erased by the employee before it is sent. Suppose that you type a nasty letter to your boss on your computer while at work. After you calm down, you decide not to send the letter and erase it. Can your boss find out what you wrote? Yes. Your boss can read your unsent draft because it has been intercepted and stored in the computer's memory.

Companies do not restrict their monitoring to keystrokes. They also use other types of monitoring, including listening in on employee conversations with customers to see how well the employee is performing. This monitoring can improve the effectiveness of employees, but it can also increase their stress levels, because they don't know exactly when the boss is listening in on their conversations.

The employer's desire for more information may conflict with the employee's need for privacy. Some studies show that computer monitoring has a negative effect on employee health. A study of telephone operators, for example, showed that those who were monitored had more headaches, back pain, severe fatigue, shoulder soreness, anxiety, and sore wrists than those who were not monitored.

An increasing number of lawsuits are being brought against companies by employees who charge that the firms overstepped the bounds of decency when they monitored their work. The most extensive case is the one against Nortel Networks. The employees' union claims that Nortel installed telephone bugs and hidden microphones in one of its plants and used them to spy on employees over a period of 13 years.

There is, therefore, a growing need to supplement traditional control efforts with efforts aimed at getting employees to control themselves. Management guru Tom Peters explains this well:

> You are out of control when you are "in control." You are in control when you are "out of control." [The executive] who knows everything and who is surrounded by layers of staffers and inundated with thousands of pages of analyses from below may be "in control" in the classic sense but in fact really only has the illusion of

control. The manager has tons of after-the-fact reports on everything, but (almost) invariably a control system and organization that's so ponderous that it's virtually impossible to respond fast enough even if a deviation is finally detected... In fact, you really are in control when thousands upon thousands of people, unbeknownst to you, are taking initiatives, going beyond job descriptions and the constraints of their box on the organization chart, to serve the customer better, improve the process, [or] work quickly with a supplier to nullify a defect.[42]

Managers use three basic techniques to achieve commitment-based control: motivation techniques, belief systems, and commitment-building systems. Obviously, motivated employees are more likely to exercise self-control and to do their jobs right. We have already discussed motivation at length (see Chapter 12). In the remainder of this chapter, therefore, we'll look at how managers use belief systems and commitment-building systems to encourage and foster employee self-control.[43]

Using Belief Systems, Culture, and Values to Foster Self-Control

People tend to behave based on what they value and believe. People who value hard work work harder than those who do not. Those who value consensus and teamwork will probably be more team-oriented than those who do not. Because one's values have a powerful influence on controlling one's behaviour, managers endeavour to instill the right values in their employees. They recognize that by doing so, the company is more likely to obtain the sort of behaviour that it seeks. Instilling values is a powerful way to foster self-control.

Managers cannot control the many lateral relationships that spontaneously develop in organizations. But the company will benefit from these relationships if employees are highly motivated and committed to doing the things that will make the organization effective.

Indeed, doing so helps to explain the relative success of many long-lived companies. James Collins and Jerry Porras studied firms like these and reported their findings in their book *Built to Last*. In it, they describe how firms like Boeing, Disney, GE, Merck, and Motorola put enormous effort into creating shared values. These values answer questions such as "What are we trying to achieve together?" and "What does this organization stand for?"[44] Collins and Porras conclude that

> More than at any time in the past companies will not be able to hold themselves together with the traditional methods of control: hierarchy, systems, budgets, and the like. Even "going into the office" will become less relevant as technology enables people to work from remote sites. The bonding glue will increasingly become ideological.[45]

This is a powerful concept. Collins and Porras emphasize that a strong set of shared values "allows for coordination without control, adaptation without chaos."[46] In other words, employees who buy into the company's values don't need to be coaxed, prodded, or controlled into doing the right thing. Management can be relatively sure these employees will do the right thing, because they believe it's the right thing to do. They'll control themselves.

This helps to explain why companies work hard to create a culture that is consistent with what the company wants to achieve. At Toyota, quality and teamwork are crucial, and its managers therefore steep employees in the culture and values of quality and teamwork. The superior quality of the Toyota Camry, for example, is not just a consequence of technology (since all auto plants have similar machines). Nor is it just a consequence of traditional controls, like final inspection. It is largely a product of employee self-control. It reflects the fact that Toyota invested heavily in gaining its employees' dedication to the handful of core values that drive their behaviour.

Using Commitment-Building Systems to Foster Self-Control

Several years ago, Viacom agreed to sell its Prentice Hall publishing operations to Pearson PLC, for U.S.$4.6 billion. In announcing the sale, Prentice Hall's president thanked its employees for their "past hard work and dedication." And he reminded them that during the transition, "It's more important than ever to focus on our individual responsibilities to ensure that our company performs at the highest levels."[47] His message highlights a management dilemma. All companies want and need employee commitment—an employee's identification with and agreement to pursue the company's mission. But, how does a manager elicit this kind of commitment in the face of today's downsizings, mergers, and change?[48] How do you get employees to exercise self-control and do their jobs as if they own the company when loyalty seems to be going out of style?

Research findings provide some answers. The evidence suggests that earning employees' commitment requires a comprehensive, multifaceted management system. This system draws on all the managers' planning, organizing, leading, and controlling skills. It requires an integrated package of concrete managerial actions. These actions include the following: foster people-first values, guarantee organizational justice, build a sense of community, use value-based hiring, communicate your vision, give financial rewards, and encourage personal development and self-actualization.

Foster People-First Values. People-first values mean that managers trust their employees, assume their employees are crucial assets, respect their employees as individuals and treat them fairly, and are committed to each employee's welfare. Saturn works hard to foster such people-first values. They emphasize these values in much of what they do. For example, all Saturn employees carry a card that lists the firm's values, one of which is

> Trust and respect for the individual: We have nothing of greater value than our people. We believe that demonstrating respect for the uniqueness of every individual builds a team of confident, creative members possessing a high degree of initiative, self-respect, and self-discipline.[49]

Guarantee Organizational Justice. Commitment assumes there's a climate of trust, and that in turn assumes that employees are treated fairly. Managers in firms like Saturn and FedEx don't just talk about being willing "to hear and be heard." They back up that philosophy with action. They institute programs that guarantee the firm will treat employees fairly. Programs include guaranteed fair treatment programs for filing grievances and complaints, "speak up" programs for voicing concerns and making inquiries, periodic survey programs for expressing opinions, and various top-down programs for keeping employees informed.

Self-managing work teams at Saturn have a great deal of discretion. They plan their own work schedules, decide which new members will be added to the team, determine job assignments of team members, and resolve any conflicts within the team.

Build a Sense of Shared Fate and Community. It's also easier to foster commitment when employees genuinely feel that "we're all in this together." Rosabeth Moss Kanter found that leaders build a sense of community in several ways.[50] For example, they minimize status differences. At Hewlett-Packard, managers and employees share one large space, with movable cubicles, and managers shun status symbols such as executive washrooms. Other firms foster "community" by encouraging joint effort and communal work. At Saturn, all employees are on teams, and all teams work on projects together. Other firms emphasize "we're all in this together" by bringing individual employees into regular contact with the group as a whole.[51]

Thanks to the internet, employees don't have to be at the same location to feel that they're part of a close-knit community. Internet-based group communication systems such as Tribal Voice allow companies to build virtual communities by letting employees communicate easily and in real-time, even if they are dispersed around the globe.[52] As one expert puts it, "The sales department could hold forums and share information in an interactive community." Said another, "When people interact in a virtual community, there is an exchange of ideas and information, which becomes powerful and generates excitement."[53]

Use Value-Based Hiring Kanter also found that commitment is higher when employees share the same basic values. High-commitment firms therefore practise **value-based hiring.** They don't just look for job-related skills. They try to get a sense of the applicant's personal values. They look for common experiences and values that may signal the applicant's fit with the firm.

value-based hiring
Looking for common experiences and values that may signal the applicant's fit with the firm.

Communicate Your Vision Committed employees need something to be committed to, preferably a mission that they feel "is bigger than we are." Employees at organizations like the Salvation Army and Saturn become, to some extent, soldiers in a crusade. Through their employment, they redefine themselves and their goals in terms of the mission. The employee, says Kanter, "finds himself anew in something larger and greater."[54] Employee commitment thus derives in part from the power of the firm's mission. It derives from the willingness of the employees to submit, if need be, to the needs of the firm for the good of achieving its mission.

Use Financial Rewards and Profit Sharing There's obviously more to building commitment then what you pay. However, it's also futile to try to build commitment without good financial rewards. High-commitment firms generally provide above-average pay and incentives. FedEx, for instance, provides various types of incentive awards. One is a "Bravo-Zulu" award that a manager can give on the spot.

Encourage Employee Development and Self-Actualization Employees are not foolish. Most understand that becoming committed to their employer is risky in a time of continuing mergers and mass layoffs. They want and need a sign that their employers are committed to them. One strong signal is to show employees that the company is committed to their personal development. Being the best at what one does provides the best job security, whether or not the person stays with the firm. Abraham Maslow emphasized that people need to self-actualize, "to become...everything that one is capable of becoming." There are many ways to help employees self-actualize: train employees to expand their skills and to solve problems; enrich their jobs; empower them; provide career-oriented interviews; and help them to continue their education and to grow.

The results can be dramatic. At FedEx, one manager described his experience as follows:

> At Federal Express, the best I can be is what I can be here. I have been allowed to grow with Federal Express. For the people at Federal Express, it's not the money that draws us to the firm. The biggest benefit is that Federal Express...gave me the confidence and self-esteem to become the person I had the potential to become."[55]

A Final Thought on Management

In this book, we have talked about the management process—planning, organizing, leading, and controlling. Since this is a textbook, we covered the topics sequentially, one at a time. But as you now know, that's not the way managers really manage. You generally won't have the luxury to spend Monday planning, Tuesday organizing, Wednesday and Thursday leading, and Friday controlling. Instead, you'll be doing all these tasks simultaneously. For example, as part of your planning function you'll be sitting with your subordinates trying to formulate goals and to motivate employees to accept them. You may be monitoring and controlling the progress of a project, only to discover that the people staffing the project are not up to the job, or that the milestones you set when the project was planned are no longer valid. Management is really an integrated, "tying it altogether" process.

That fact is particularly evident when it comes to controlling and building commitment, the subject of this last chapter. Planning and controlling are two sides of the same coin: what you control and how you're doing depends entirely on where you want to go, so that deciding where planning leaves off and controlling begins is bound to be somewhat arbitrary.

Similarly, effectively controlling your organization will demand all the people skills you can muster. Employees can be enormously creative when it comes to getting around control systems, and getting them to not want to get around those systems is therefore a very demanding task. Also, and perhaps more important, controlling someone is usually not the best way to stay in control. You can lower your "control costs"—not to mention your aggravation level—enormously by getting your employees to want to do a great job. Doing this of course is essentially a behavioural, not a technical, process.

When you ask most people how they maintain control, their first reaction might be "we use budgets," or "we use time clocks," or "we watch what our people are doing." But getting employees to want to do a great job is in many respects the best way to keep your firm under control, and doing so, as we have seen, relies on behavioural activities like fostering people-first values and building a sense of shared fate and community. And it's just such an integration of the people side of managing into all that they do that managers do best.

SKILLS AND STUDY MATERIAL

SUMMARY

1. Control is the task of ensuring that activities are actually leading to the desired results. In its most general sense, controlling therefore means setting a target, measuring performance, and taking corrective action. Experts distinguish between feedforward controls, concurrent controls, and feedback controls.

2. As companies expand worldwide and compete in fast-changing markets, the problems of relying on a traditional control system (set standards, compare actual to standard, and take corrective action) have become increasingly apparent. Employees have had to become more empowered to be more responsive.

3. There are three types of traditional control methods. Diagnostic control systems like budgets and performance reports are intended to ensure that goals are being achieved and that variances, if any, are explained. Boundary control systems establish the rules of the game and identify actions and pitfalls employees must avoid. Interactive control systems are real-time, usually face-to-face

methods of monitoring both a plan's effectiveness and the underlying assumptions on which the plan was built.

4. Budgets and ratio analysis are among the most widely used diagnostic control tools. Budgets are formal financial expressions of a manager's plan and show targets for yardsticks such as revenues, cost of materials, and profits, usually expressed in dollars. Most managers also achieve control by monitoring various financial ratios.

5. Traditional controls can lead to unintended, undesirable, and often harmful employee reactions, such as behavioural displacement, gamesmanship, operating delays, negative attitudes, and reduced empowerment.

6. Achieving control in an age of empowerment means relying on employees' self-control. Motivation techniques and building value systems are two important ways to tap such self-control. Another powerful way is to get employees to think of the company's goals as their own—to earn their commitment.

1. The budget is a traditional means of control, usually established by top management. Now think about establishing a budget for a company by using committed and empowered employees to develop it. Who would be involved and why? How would your approach differ from traditional budgeting?

2. We are increasingly dependent on technology and the flow of information provided by means such as the internet. Yet there is ongoing debate about the control and privacy aspects of both the internet and intranets. What do you think about using electronic monitoring technology as a control device? What about the privacy issues? Should our boss be able to monitor us and our use of computers?

EXPERIENTIAL EXERCISES

1. You are one of the founding engineers in your six-month-old firm, and you brought to the firm values of environmental awareness, quality, and excellence. These values have united the original members, but you are concerned that they might change with the addition of 50 new people needed by your fast-growing company to meet demand. In teams of four to five students, answer the question, "What type of control system would you develop to ensure your values are adhered to, based on the concepts in this chapter?"

2. There is nothing quite like eating at a restaurant where things are out of control. Visit two or three local restaurants and make a list of the things you see that might suggest that things are out of control. Then meet in teams of four to five students, compare notes, and create a checklist for assessing the adequacy of a restaurant's control mechanisms.

3. Students deal with professors all the time, but they may not realize how difficult it is for administrators to control what faculty members do. The typical professor has a number of responsibilities, including teaching classes, writing research articles, and serving on various committees. The dean wants to make sure that faculty members are conducting themselves professionally when they interact with students, and knowing that you are a management student, the dean has asked you to develop a control package for professors. The package must include a list of the things that you want to control and a description of how you plan to control them. In teams of four to five students, develop a package for the dean.

BUILDING YOUR MANAGEMENT SKILLS

Understanding Control Systems

Interview five of your fellow students and ask them to think about a job that they currently have or formerly had. Ask them the following questions as they keep that job in mind:

1. How was their work controlled?

2. What, if anything, did they dislike about the way they were controlled?

Take careful notes from each of your interviews. When you have completed all five interviews, analyze the responses to each question.

For question #1, determine what basic kind of control system each student worked under (traditional or commitment-based), based on their comments. Was there a pattern in their responses? (For example, did most students work under a traditional system or a commitment-based system?) Why do you think you got the results you did? For students who worked under a traditional system, also determine whether it was a diagnostic, boundary control, or interactive control system. Was there a pattern evident here as well? Why might the pattern exist?

For question #2, identify each of the distinct complaints that were mentioned, and then do a frequency count that shows which complaints were most and least common. How do the responses of your interviewees give you a better understanding of the problems in the controlling process? Suggest ways to reduce the most common complaints, using as your guide the checklist in the chapter dealing with the characteristics of effective control systems.

Developing the culture and values of a company acts as a form of control. In large organizations such as Honeywell, Molex, and Alcan, managers have developed programs and controls that reflect the vision and values of the company. The programs and controls also establish boundaries within which the firm expects employees to operate.

1. Access Honeywell International's website at **www. honeywell.com** and select the *About Us* section. Which program reflects Honeywell's vision and values? What is at the core of this program? Are there any other boundary-control systems?

2. Molex operates on six continents and has more than 16 000 employees (**www.molex.com**). Identify the main elements of its Code of Conduct. If you were a manager at Molex, what would be your responsibility regarding the Code of Conduct? Are there any other boundary-control systems at Molex?

3. Alcan Inc. operates in many countries around the world. Review the *Overview* section of its website at **www.alcan.com**. Compare its Worldwide Code of Employee and Business Conduct to that of Molex. Which company has the most detailed boundary-control systems? Explain your answer.

CASE STUDY 16-1

Where the Rubber Meets the Road

In the summer of 2000, Bridgestone/Firestone Inc. announced that it was recalling 6.5 million Wilderness AT and Firestone ATX tires. Most of these had been installed as original equipment on Ford Explorer SUVs. Hints that there were problems with Firestone tires began cropping up in the early 1990s. There was often a pattern: the tread of a rear tire on a heavily loaded Explorer travelling at high speed separated, and the vehicle swerved out of control and flipped over. These reports generally came from warmer parts of the United States (California, Arizona, Texas, and Florida) and from Venezuela and the Persian Gulf. The investigation revealed that about 100 people had been killed in these kinds of accidents in the United States, and about 50 people had been killed overseas.

Transport Canada launched a probe to determine whether there were similar problems in Canada, but no hard evidence of tire defects was found, even though as many as 500 000 of these tires are on vehicles in Canada. One million Firestone tires were eventually recalled in Canada.

Both Ford and Firestone tested the suspect tires, but no particular problems were found. In public, the two companies portrayed themselves as working together to solve the mystery, but there was tension behind the scenes. Ford noted that it didn't have any problem with blown tires or rollovers with any of its vehicles except Explorers, and those vehicles had the suspect Firestone tires on them. Firestone, on the other hand, accused Ford of contributing to the problem by recommending tire pressures of only 26 pounds

when Firestone recommended 30 pounds of pressure. (Lower tire pressure improves the ride of a vehicle, but underinflation leads to heat build-up and an increased chance of tire failure.) Firestone also claimed that Ford had made design changes in the Explorer that increased the chance that rear tires would fail. Firestone noted that the suspect tires were on other types of vehicles and that the tires on those vehicles had not failed.

What was the problem? Experts thought there were several possibilities: (1) the quality of the material that was used to make the glue that held the tire's steel belts together wasn't up to standard; (2) the raw materials that were used to make the glue weren't sufficiently well mixed; (3) the steel wires that form the belts may have rusted because of high humidity during manufacturing; (4) the tire wasn't properly cured (vulcanized); (5) too much adhesive was used to bond the steel belts to the rubber, and this actually made the treads more likely to separate.

After a four-month investigation, Bridgestone/ Firestone finally concluded that there were quality problems at its plant in Decatur, Illinois. Apparently, that plant did not properly process the rubber that was used to make the tires. However, Firestone also put some of the blame on the Ford Explorer, arguing that higher load limits and lower inflation pressures were part of the problem.

Firestone spent U.S.$450 million recalling the problem tires. In the aftermath of the crisis, Firestone's sales plummeted 40 percent, and its stock lost half its value. →

What is Bridgestone/Firestone doing now to recover its public image? Several steps have been taken, including the appointment of a new senior vice president with a mandate to impose strict production standards and fix operating problems at the company's U.S. unit.

In May 2001, Bridgestone/Firestone abruptly ended its 100-year relationship as a tire supplier to Ford, business that had been worth about U.S.$350 million a year to Firestone. But Firestone is not taking all the blame. It accused Ford of refusing to acknowledge safety concerns about the Ford Explorer and provided evidence showing that Ford Explorers were 10 times more likely to roll over after a tread separation than were Ford Rangers, even though both vehicles were equipped with the same Firestone tires. Ford countered by saying that the Ford Explorer has been near the top of the vehicle safety rankings for years and that Ford Explorers equipped with Goodyear tires haven't had any tread-separation problems.

The loss of business with Ford means that Firestone will have to rebuild the market share it has lost. It may abandon the original equipment market and focus instead on the retail tire replacement market.

It will also launch a racing-oriented image campaign with race-car drivers serving as spokespeople for the company.

A new method of examining product performance data will be introduced to address the criticism that the company was unaware it had quality problems with its tires.

U.S. factories will be brought more into line with the higher standards of Bridgestone's Japanese operation. Quality assurance controls will be introduced that will make it easier for information about tire failures to be shared throughout the company.

Questions

1. What is total quality management? To what extent was total quality management pursued at Bridgestone/Firestone? at Ford?

2. What are the various tools for quality assurance that are available? Which ones are appropriate for helping to resolve this problem?

3. How is quality a competitive tool?

4. Can Firestone get its quality image back? How?

CASE STUDY 16-2

Controlling Quality with Committed Employees at the Ritz-Carlton

The elegant Ritz-Carlton hotel in Montreal opened its doors on December 31, 1912, and has spent the last 90 years contributing to the cosmopolitan reputation of Montreal. Its famous guests have included Mary Pickford and Douglas Fairbanks; Elizabeth Taylor; Richard Burton; Winston Churchill; Charles de Gaulle; Mick Jagger and the Rolling Stones; John Wayne; and members of royalty from other countries around the world. It is now getting an $11.5 million dollar facelift.

Many people think that hotels simply offer a generic service—a safe, clean, comfortable room in a city away from home. Ritz-Carlton Hotel Company views its business differently. Targeting industry executives, meeting and corporate travel planners, and affluent travellers, the Ritz-Carlton manages 25 luxury hotels that pursue the goal of being the very best in each market. Ritz-Carlton has succeeded with more than just business travellers. It was awarded the Malcolm Baldrige National Quality Award. Given a mission of true excellence in service, what types of control systems did Ritz-Carlton need to achieve its goals?

In the presentation of the Baldrige award, the committee commended Ritz-Carlton for a management program that included participatory leadership, thorough information gathering, coordinated planning and execution, and a trained workforce empowered "to move heaven and earth" to satisfy customers. Of all the elements in the system, Ritz-Carlton felt the most important control mechanism was committed employees.

All employees are trained in the company's "Gold Standards," which set out Ritz-Carlton's service credo and the basics of premium service. The company has translated key product and service requirements into a credo, and 20 "Ritz-Carlton Basics." Each employee is expected to understand and adhere to these standards, which describe processes for solving any problem guests may have.

The corporate motto is "ladies and gentlemen serving ladies and gentlemen." Like many companies, Ritz-Carlton gives new employees an orientation followed by on-the-job training. Unlike other hotel firms, Ritz-Carlton then "certifies" employees. Corporate values are reinforced continually by daily "line ups," frequent recognition for extraordinary achievement, and a performance appraisal based on expectations explained during the orientation, training, and certification processes.

All workers are required to take action at the first sign of a problem, regardless of the type of problem or customer complaint. Employees are empowered to do whatever it takes to provide "instant pacification." Other employees must assist if a co-worker requests aid in responding to a guest's complaint or wish. There is no excuse for not solving a customer problem. Responsibility for ensuring high-quality guest services and accommodations rests largely with employees. All employees are surveyed annually to determine their understanding of quality standards and their personal satisfaction as Ritz-Carlton employees. In one case, 96 percent of all employees surveyed singled out excellence in guest services as the key priority.

Questions

1. What steps does Ritz-Carlton take to control the quality of its service?

2. What does Ritz-Carlton do to foster its employees' high level of commitment?

3. How does the company's value system foster employee self-control?

Ritz-Carlton
www.ritzcarlton.com

JetBlue Stays in Control

A recent *Wall Street Journal* article helps illustrate why maintaining control is important for airlines like JetBlue.[56] It compares the efficiency of JetBlue's Flight 112 with United Airlines Flight 235, both of which fly from Dulles International Airport to Oakland California, non-stop. Both fly the same number of miles (2415), both have six crew members (two pilots and four flight attendants), and both use the same aircraft, the Airbus A320. However, United spends about U.S.$23 690 to fly its flight one-way, whereas JetBlue spends U.S.$14 546 to fly Flight 112. How is it that with the same aircraft and number of crew members, United spends more than 50 percent more to operate its flight? By controlling costs in dozens of ways—from lower salaries to not offering meals to quicker turnarounds at the gate—JetBlue maintains its strategy to be the country's premier low-cost airline.

As an airline competing in an environment filled with numerous safety and customer service regulations, controlling its costs is only one of the many areas in which JetBlue has to maintain control. Because the airline industry is governed by various U.S. Department of Transportation (DOT) regulations, JetBlue and other airlines must address at least four main operational metrics: completion factors (did you fly the flight?), on-time performance within 14 minutes; consumer complaints; and baggage delayed, misplaced, or lost. Airlines monitor completion factors and on-time performance on a daily basis, and they monitor consumer complaints and baggage delays monthly.

Airlines also have numerous internal operating measures that they follow closely. For example, all airlines carefully monitor their load factors—in other words, the percentage of filled seats on their aircraft. JetBlue monitors what it calls its "blue turn"—in other words, its target of turning around an aircraft within 35 minutes from the time it first reaches the gate and then takes off again. All airlines also have full budgeting processes to plan for and control their expenses. Many of the expense factors are uncontrollable. For example, airlines like JetBlue don't have a great deal of flexibility with regard to what they have to pay for fuel. For JetBlue, the biggest controllable expenses are personnel related, including salaries, bonuses, and benefits.

The DOT and/or the FAA mandate many of the systems to actually control activities like these. For example, the DOT has its own rules for how airlines are to measure and report activities like on-time performance. At JetBlue, cost-centre managers are usually individually responsible for monitoring many of these activities within their own areas. There is a general manager or director for each city; if a flight doesn't leave on time or arrive on time, he or she has to fill out a clarification report and file it via email with his or her superiors at JetBlue. Similarly, the Federal Aviation Administration (FAA) has issued numerous security directives that airlines are to follow—for instance, with respect to processing passengers and with regard to aircraft parts inspections and acceptability of vendors. JetBlue must also have systems in place to comply with these rules.

For example, when cabin attendants explain the use of safety equipment before the plane takes off and then check to see that everyone's seatback is up, they are enforcing FAA safety regulations. How does the FAA know that the airlines are complying with its regulations? Airlines have their own internal auditors checking selected flights, staffed by people from (in JetBlue's case) their own quality department and safety department. The FAA also has its own inspectors anonymously flying selected flights to ensure that its rules are obeyed.

Although controlling activities with inspectors is certainly essential, there is often no substitute for employee motivation and commitment in ensuring that things are going as planned. JetBlue therefore puts an enormous amount of effort into winning its employees' commitment, starting with a comprehensive orientation with presentations by JetBlue's top management and extending to flexible work rules and profit-sharing plans.

Assignment

You and your team are consultants to Mr. Neeleman, who is depending on your management expertise to help navigate the launch and management of JetBlue. Here's what he wants to know from you:

1. Recommend specific feedforward, concurrent, and feedback controls that JetBlue could use to control any five of the activities mentioned in the case.

2. Specify a specific strategic ratio that JetBlue's CEO David Neeleman should have his employees focus on.

3. List 10 measures David Neeleman could use to build a balanced scorecard for JetBlue.

Forensic Accounting

We've just gotten over the Livent scandal and then along comes Cinar, the Quebec animation house, with all of its various problems. Who's watching the numbers? Is anyone trying to do something? As it turns out, someone *is*. It is Al Rosen, Canada's leading forensic accountant (also known as "The Enforcer"). He has been busy ferreting out fast and loose accounting practices that make a company look better than it actually is. He is working hard to alert the world to these scam artists. Rosen is a frequent expert witness in court cases, and he has given so much information about questionable accounting practices at various firms to *Canadian Business* magazine that he is now on their masthead.

People have described Rosen as hard-nosed, a corporate muckraker, tough, arrogant, bitter, dark, and gloomy. He isn't deterred, he says, because these people haven't seen the evidence he has seen. If a client is caught playing fast and loose with accounting rules, lawyers rush to Rosen's office for advice.

Rosen is an expert at explaining how a company can play with numbers to make its dismal financial statement glow. Rosen's concern is that this can be easily achieved using Generally Accepted Accounting Principles (GAAP), the accountant's "Bible." He says that "crooked" companies look at GAAP and say, "Wow, I can use this stuff to make my company look good."

Rosen wants to blow the whistle on suspicious accounting, and one of the ways he is doing so is by writing a monthly exposé for mutual fund managers. So far he has examined 20 companies in detail. He gives an opinion on whether a given company is on the level, whether it should be watched carefully, or whether it is already a disaster. In the early 1990s, he offered the view that the accounting numbers generated by Cott Corp., the generic cola maker, were not telling the whole story, and the company was not as strong as it appeared. Cott, which was then a stock-market darling, blasted Rosen for his views, but time has proved Rosen right. Cott's stock dropped from nearly $40 per share in 1994 to just $10 per share in 1999. Another company that's unhappy with Rosen is ski-resort operator Interwest. The company complained that Rosen's newsletter caused its stock to drop by 20 percent. It claims it was rock-solid, but that it was "bushwacked" by Rosen, simply because Rosen has a vendetta against

standard accounting practices. Rosen's mutual fund clients seek his advice regarding which companies are good and which ones are questionable. And, indeed, Rosen says that there are many strong Canadian companies that are perfectly good investments. Still, he will continue to do everything he can to make sure that people receive his message that accounting numbers may not be what they seem. At York University, he tells aspiring accountants not to "play the game." He suggests thinking beyond the numbers, and encourages them to think in non-traditional ways about accounting. He warns that a business deal can easily fall prey to slippery accounting practices.

Rosen is keen to be a source for the media. One of his favourite words in describing manipulators is "scumbag." He recognizes that many people think that his perspective is too negative, but he says there are plenty of cheerleaders for companies and someone needs to do serious analyses of their soundness. He says there are 1000 cheerleaders, but no one (except him) is taking care of the other side.

So, corporate Canada beware: The Enforcer is watching.

Questions

1. What are the steps in the controlling process of management? What role does accounting play in this process?

2. At what stage of the production process (inputs, process, output) is accounting important?

3. What are the three main types of traditional control systems? In which of these three systems is accounting activity most obvious?

4. "As companies expand worldwide and compete in fast-changing markets, the problems of relying on traditional control systems have become apparent. Since accounting is very much a traditional system, the former emphasis on accounting should be replaced with a greater emphasis on methods of gaining employee commitment to the organization." Comment.

Video Resource: "On the Case with Al Rosen," *Venture* #745 (March 28, 2000).

Controlling Bad Corporate Behaviour

How do you feel about business leaders today? What will it take to rebuild your trust in them?

The Enron case is illustrative. When Enron went bankrupt, many individuals suffered large financial losses. Charles Presswood, an Enron employee, once had a pension worth $1.3 million; it is now worth $8000. As someone said, "Enron robbed the bank, and its auditing firm, Arthur Andersen, provided the getaway car." As Enron's auditing firm, Arthur Andersen was supposed to make sure that Enron's financial statements accurately conveyed the condition of the company. Unfortunately, the auditors had a "cozy" arrangement with Enron. They not only audited the books, but they also made millions of dollars in management consulting fees. These fees apparently caused Andersen to lose its objectivity in their auditing activities.

At the Wharton School, future managers are getting a lecture from Howard Schilit, one of the harshest critics of business ethics. He has written a book entitled *Financial Shenanigans* that describes various accounting gimmicks that are designed to make a company's financial statements look better than they really are. He says that managers behave badly because they are rewarded for aggressive accounting.

Schilit says it's hard to be objective when you know that a big source of your revenue is coming from consulting, and the revenue from that activity might be at risk if you ask too many questions about the firm's accounting methods. Some progress is being made in this area: recently, Disney and CIBC announced that they will only hire auditors that don't consult for their company.

At a recent Conference Board of Canada seminar, there was a lot of soul searching about these issues. No wonder executives are worried: investors are supersensitive, wondering whether history is going to repeat the great stock market crash of 1929. Then, as now, trust was broken and insiders had great advantages over the average person who was investing.

Just how safe is your money if you invest in the stock market? There have been numerous disturbing cases in the last few years where investors lost millions of dollars because of illegal behaviour by managers:

- YBM collapsed after connections to the Russian mob became known.
- Michael Cowpland was charged with insider trading.
- Employees of RT Capital were involved in a stock manipulation scandal.

- The head of Yorkton Securities was banned from trading after he improperly promoted small companies to investors without disclosing to them that Yorkton was the main player in those companies.

All of this wrongdoing has resulted in dozens of class action suits. These cases will be in the courts for years. Although the Ontario Securities Commission (OSC) is investigating many such cases, critics think the OSC isn't doing enough (it is sometimes called the "Occasional Securities Commission"). The suspicion is that the bad guys too often get off scot-free. Until a few years ago the OSC didn't have the resources to properly investigate wrongdoing. Now, there is enough money to use a sophisticated computer tracking systems to go after financial manipulators.

Critics like Al Rosen say the OSC is simply missing important targets for investigation. He argues that Canada's accounting rules are so soft that major corporations can easily "cook the books." He says that financial statements are just a joke and that an Enron case could happen anywhere.

Questions

1. What is involved in the controlling function of management? Explain the goal of the controlling function in terms of the activities of the OSC.

2. Briefly describe the five steps in the traditional control process. What would these five steps involve when a corporation's financial condition was being assessed? What can go wrong at each step?

3. What is the difference between traditional control systems and commitment-based control systems? How might a commitment-based control system overcome some of the problems that are described above? Be specific.

4. Read the section in Chapter 16 entitled "How Do People React to Traditional Controls?" How do the points made in that section help us understand the problems that arose at Enron and other companies?

Video Resources: "Trust," *Venture* #817 (March 3, 2002); also "OSC," *Venture* #818 (March 10, 2002); also "Enron," *Venture* #812 (January 27, 2002).

Glossary

Note: The number in brackets indicates the chapter in which the term is first defined.

360-degree feedback An appraisal system where the employee's peers, supervisors, subordinates, and customers complete appraisal surveys, which are compiled into individualized reports for the ratee. (10)

A

action research The process of collecting data from employees about a system in need of change, and then feeding that data back to the employees so that they can analyze it, identify problems, develop solutions, and take action themselves. (15)

activity-based costing A method for allocating costs to products and services that takes all the product's costs (including production, marketing, distribution, and sales activities) into account. (16)

advisory staff Employees who advise line managers in areas where these staff have particular expertise. (8)

anchoring Unconsciously giving disproportionate weight to the first information you hear. (5)

application form A form that requests information such as education, work history, and hobbies from a job candidate as a means of quickly collecting verifiable historical data. (10)

assessment centre An approach to selection in which candidates spend two or three days performing realistic management tasks under the observation of expert appraisers. (10)

attitude A predisposition to respond to objects, people, or events in either a positive or negative way. (12)

audit A systematic process of objectively obtaining and evaluating evidence regarding important aspects of the firm's performance, judging the accuracy and validity of the data, and communicating the results to interested users. (16)

authority A person's legal right or power. (8)

authority boundary The boundary at which superiors and subordinates always meet. (9)

B

balanced scorecard A management tool, usually a computerized model, that traces a multitude of performance measures simultaneously and shows their interactions. (16)

behaviour-based interviewing Assesses how an applicant reacted to difficult and/or important job situations in the past, and assumes that these are a good indicator of how you will react to similar job situations in the future. (10)

behaviour modification Changing or modifying behaviour through the use of contingent rewards or punishment. (12)

behavioural displacement When controls encourage behaviours that are inconsistent with what the company actually wants to accomplish. (16)

behavioural standards Standards that state the types of behaviour that are acceptable for employees. (16)

benchmarking The process through which a company learns how to become the best in some area by carefully analyzing the practices of other companies that already excel in that area. (7)

bona fide occupational requirement When an employer may choose one applicant over another based on overriding characteristics of the job. (10)

bonus A one-time financial payment. (10)

boundary control systems Systems that set the boundaries within which the firm expects employees to operate, including ethics standards, codes of conduct, and strategic policies. (16)

boundaryless organization An organization that encourages free-flowing interdepartmental communication unhampered by the usual departmental boundaries. (1)

bounded rationality Managers' decisions are only as rational as their unique values, capabilities, and limited capacity for processing information permit them to be. (5)

brainstorming A group problem-solving technique whereby group members introduce all possible solutions before evaluating any of them. (5)

break-even analysis A decision-making aid that enables a manager to determine whether a particular volume of sales will result in losses or profits. (A5)

break-even chart A graph that shows whether a particular volume of sales will result in profits or losses. (A5)

break-even point The point at which the total-revenues line crosses the total-costs line. (A5)

budget A financial plan that shows financial expectations for a specific period. (6)

budgeted balance sheet A control that shows managers, owners, and creditors what the company's projected financial picture should be at the end of the year. (16)

budgeted income statement A control that shows the company's expected sales, expected expenses, and expected income or profit for the year. (16)

budgets Formal financial expressions of a manager's plans. (16)

business plan A planning tool that lays out what the business is, where it is heading, and how it plans to get there. (4)

C

cafeteria benefits Benefit plans that provide a set dollar amount in benefits and allow employees to pick among alternatives. (10)

Canada Labour Code A comprehensive piece of legislation that applies to the labour practices of firms operating under the legislative authority of Parliament. (10)

Canadian Human Rights Act Ensures that any individual who want to obtain a job has an equal opportunity to apply for it. (10)

Canadian Human Rights Commission The organization that enforces the Canadian Human Rights Act. (10)

cash budget A control that shows, for each month, the amount of cash the company can expect to receive and the amount it can expect to disperse. (16)

causal forecasting Estimating a company factor (such as sales) based on other influencing factors (such as advertising expenditures or unemployment levels). (6)

causal methods Forecasting techniques that develop projections based on the mathematical relationship between a company factor and the variables believed to influence or explain that factor. (6)

cellular organization A structure in which independent companies or self-managing teams (cells) are self-sufficient and perform specialized functions. Each cell contributes to the overall functioning of the company. (8)

centralization When top management makes all key decisions and lower level managers and workers do what is required to ensure that top-level decisions are followed. (9)

certainty Knowing in advance the outcome of the decision. (A5)

chain of command The path that a directive and/or answer or request should take through each level of an organization; also called a scalar chain or the line of authority. (8)

close supervision A leadership style involving close, hands-on monitoring of subordinates and their work. (11)

cohesiveness The attraction of the group for its members. (5)

collaborative software systems Computer-based work group support systems that facilitate decision making in virtual teams. (14)

collaborative writing systems Group members can create long written documents (such as proposals) while working simultaneously at a network of interconnected computers. (13)

commission A financial reward in proportion to the items or services an employee sells. (10)

commitment-based control systems Rely on employees' self-control to do the right things. (16)

common market A system in which no barriers to trade exist among members countries, and a common external trade policy is in force that governs trade with non-members; factors of production, such as labour, capital, and technology, move freely among members. (2)

communication Exchanging information in such a way that you create a common basis of understanding and feeling. (13)

communication process The series of events that takes place to transfer meaning. (13)

comparable worth A legal concept that aims at paying equal wages for jobs that are of comparable value to the employer. (10)

compensation All work-related pay or rewards that go to employees. (10)

competitive advantage The basis for superiority over competitors and thus for hoping to claim certain customers. (7)

competitive intelligence (CI) A systematic way to obtain and analyze public information about competitors. (6)

competitive profile matrix A tool to assess the strengths and weaknesses of potential competitors. (4)

competitive strategy A strategy that identifies how to build and strengthen the business's long-term competitive position in the marketplace. (7)

compressed workweek Employees work fewer days per week, but more hours on the days they do work. (12)

concentration The degree to which an industry or the entire economy is dominated by a few large firms. (2)

concentration strategy The firm offers one product or product line, usually in one market. (2)

conceptual skills The ability to think analytically and logically, and to reason inductively and deductively. (1)

concurrent control A control system in which the manager exercises control as the activity takes place, and the work may not proceed until or unless it is acceptable. (16)

conflict A condition that occurs when individuals or groups have incompatible goals, and these individuals or groups can block each other's goal attainment. (15)

conglomerate diversification Diversifying into other products or markets that are not related to a firm's present businesses. (7)

contingency planning Identifying possible future outcomes and then developing a plan for coping with them. (6)

contingency (situational) theories Theories that assume that different individuals and situations require different management practices. (A1)

contingent (or temporary) worker A temporary worker hired by an employer to fill short-term needs; not a permanent full-time or part-time employee. (10)

continuous reinforcement schedule According to this schedule, a reward or a punishment follows each time the behaviour of interest occurs. (12)

control The task of ensuring that activities are providing the desired results. (16)

control staff Staff who are responsible for controlling some aspect of the organization, such as quality control. (8)

control tolerances State the degree of deviation from the standard that is permissible. (16)

coordination The process of achieving unity of action among interdependent activities. (9)

core competencies The collective learning in the organization, especially the knowledge of how to coordinate diverse design and production skills and integrate multiple streams of technologies. (7)

corporate-level strategy A plan that identifies the portfolio of businesses that compose a corporation and how they relate to each other. (7)

corporate social audit A rating system used to evaluate a corporation's performance with regard to meeting its social obligations. (3)

corporation A legally chartered organization that is a separate legal entity apart from its owners. (4)

cost leadership strategy A strategy to be the low-cost leader in an industry. (7)

cost standards Standards that state the maximum cost that should be incurred in the course of producing goods and services. (16)

creativity The process of developing original, novel responses to a problem. (5)

customer departmentalization Generally self-contained departments are organized to serve the needs of specific groups of customers. (8)

customs union Members dismantle trade barriers among themselves while establishing a common trade policy with respect to non-members. (2)

D

decentralization When the right to make decisions is pushed down to the middle and lower levels of the management hierarchy. (9)

decision A choice from among the available alternatives. (5)

decision making The process of developing and analyzing alternatives and making a choice. (5)

decision support system (DSS) An interactive, computer-based communications system that facilitates the solution of unstructured problems by a decision-making team. (13)

decision tree A technique for making a decision under conditions of risk in which an expected value can be calculated for each alternative. (A5)

delegation The act of pushing down authority from supervisor to subordinate. (9)

departmentalization The process by which the manager groups the enterprise's activities together and assigns them to subordinates. (8)

deregulation A reduction in the number of laws affecting business activity and in the powers of government enforcement agencies. (1)

descriptive plan A plan that states what is to be achieved and how. (6)

desktop videoconferencing systems Computer-based systems that re-create the face-to-face interactions of conventional groups. (14)

diagnostic control systems Formal, pre-planned, methodical systems that help managers zero in on discrepancies. (16)

differentiation The degree to which there are differences in the structures, interpersonal orientations, goals, and time orientations of employees in different departments. (9)

differentiation strategy A firm picks one or more attributes of a product or service that its buyers perceive as important and then positions itself to meet those needs better than its competitors. (7)

discipline Applying a penalty to subordinates, usually when they violate a rule. (10)

discontinuous change Change of an unexpected nature. (15)

discrimination A behavioural bias toward or against a person based on the group to which the person belongs. (3)

dismissal The involuntary termination of an employee's employment with the firm. (10)

diverse Describes a workforce comprising two or more groups, each of which can be identified by demographic or other characteristics. (3)

diversification A strategy of expanding into related or unrelated products or market segments. (7)

divestment Selling the individual businesses of a larger company. (7)

divisionalized structure A form of organization in which the firm's major departments are organized so that each one can manage all or most of the activities needed to develop, manufacture, and sell a particular product or product line. (8)

downsizing Dramatically reducing the size of a company's workforce. (9)

E

economic integration Two or more nations obtain the advantages of free trade by minimizing trade restrictions. (2)

effective To achieve goals that have been set. (1)

efficiency Achieving the greatest possible output with a given amount of input. (1)

electronic brainstorming A form of brainstorming in which group members type ideas into a computer. (5)

electronic networking Networking through technology-supported devices such as email, videoconferencing, and collaborative computing software. (8)

email A computerized information system that lets group members electronically create, edit, and communicate messages to one another, using electronic mail boxes. (13)

emotional intelligence A rating that reflects the underlying emotional intelligence traits of self-confidence, trustworthiness, the need to achieve, cross-cultural sensitivity, and persuasiveness. (11)

employee-oriented leaders Leaders who focus on the individuality and personality needs of their employees and emphasize building good interpersonal relationships. (11)

employee benefits Supplements to pay based on working for the organization. (10)

employee involvement program A formal program that lets employees participate in formulating important work-related decisions or in supervising all or part of their own jobs. (14)

employment agency An intermediary whose business is to match applicants with jobs. (10)

Employment Equity Act Federal legislation that designates four groups as employment disadvantaged: women, visible minorities, Aboriginal people, and people with disabilities. (10)

employment insurance A benefit paid to workers who lose their jobs through no fault of their own; the funds come from a tax on the employer's payroll. (10)

empowerment Making it possible for people to attain some degree of control over their jobs and to employ suitable power to make their work lives effective. (12)

enterprise resource planning systems Company-wide integrated computer control systems. (16)

entrepreneur Someone who creates new businesses for the purpose of gain or growth under conditions of risk and uncertainty. (4)

entrepreneurship The creation of a business for the purpose of gain or growth under conditions of risk and uncertainty. (4)

environmental scanning The process of gathering and compiling information about environmental forces that might be relevant to the firm's strategic planners. (7)

equity theory The theory that people have a need for fairness at work and that they are motivated to maintain a balance between what they perceive as their inputs or contributions and their rewards. (12)

escalation of commitment The situation in which a manager becomes increasingly committed to a previously chosen course of action even though it has been shown to be ineffective. (5)

ethics The principles of conduct governing an individual or a group. (3)

ethnocentrism A tendency to view members of one's own group as the centre of the universe and to view other social groups less favourably than one's own. (3)

exchange rate The rate at which someone can exchange one country's currency for another's. (2)

executive recruiter An agency retained by employers to seek out top management talent. (10)

executive The firm's top level of management. (1)

existence needs Human needs similar to Maslow's physiological needs and to the physical components of Maslow's security needs. (12)

expectancy In motivation, the probability that a person's efforts will lead to performance. (12)

expectancy theory A theory that a person's motivation to exert some level of effort is a function of the person's expectancy, instrumentality, and valence. (12)

expected value The probability of the outcome multiplied by the benefit or cost of that outcome. (A5)

exporting Selling abroad, either directly to customers, or indirectly through sales agents and distributors. (2)

extrinsic motivation When a person works hard at a task because of the promise that some tangible reward will be given if the job is done well. (12)

F

federal organization An organization in which power is distributed among a central unit and a number of constituents, but the central unit's authority is intentionally limited. (8)

feedback control A control where results are compared to the standard after the project is complete. (16)

financial incentive Any financial reward that is contingent on performance. (10)

financial plan The document that combines the various individual financial plans required to manage the business. (6)

financial ratios Calculations that compare one financial indicator on a financial statement to another. (16)

financial responsibility centres Units that are responsible for, and measured based on, a specific set of financial activities. (16)

first-line managers Managers on the lowest rung of the management ladder. (1)

fixed interval schedule Reinforcement is applied after a certain time period has passed, regardless of the number of responses that have occurred. (12)

fixed ratio schedule Reinforcement is applied after a fixed number of desired behavioural responses have occurred, regardless of the time that has passed. (12)

fixed salary Compensation based on an agreed rate for a set period of time. (10)

flextime A system that allows workers increased discretion in deciding when they will be at their place of work. (12)

focus strategy A strategy in which a business selects a narrow market segment and builds its strategy on serving those in its target market better or more cheaply than its generalist competitors. (7)

force field analysis An analysis of the forces that operate in organizations to keep the system balanced or unbalanced. (15)

forecast To estimate or calculate in advance or to predict. (6)

foreign direct investment Operations in one country controlled by entities in a foreign country. (2)

formal organizational network A recognized group of managers or other employees assembled by the CEO and the other senior executive team, drawn from across the company's functions, business units, geography, and levels. (8)

franchise A licence to use a company's business ideas and procedures and to sell its goods or services. (4)

franchisee A firm that obtains a licence to use a franchiser's business ideas and procedures, and that may get an exclusive right to sell the franchiser's goods or services in a specific territory. (4)

franchiser A firm that licenses other firms to use its business idea and procedures and to sell its goods or services in return for royalty and other types of payments. (4)

franchising agreement A document that lays out the relationship between the franchiser and franchisee. (4)

franchising The granting of a right by a parent company to another firm to do business in a prescribed manner. (2)

free trade All trade barriers among participating countries are removed. (2)

functional authority Staff managers can issue orders to line managers within the very narrow limits of the staff manager's special expertise. (8)

functional departmentalization Grouping activities around the enterprise's core functions. (8)

functional strategy The overall course(s) of action and basic policies that each department is to follow in helping the business accomplish its strategic goals. (7)

G

gain-sharing plan An incentive program in which employees receive a bonus if the firm's costs are reduced because of greater worker efficiency and/or productivity. (10)

gamesmanship Management actions that improve the manager's performance in terms of the control system, without producing any economic benefits for the firm. (16)

Gantt chart A production scheduling chart that plots time on a horizontal scale and generally shows, for each product or project, the start and stop times of each operation. (6)

gender-role stereotypes The tendency to associate women with certain (i.e., non-managerial) jobs. (3)

general leader A leader who takes a middle-ground approach between close supervision and laissez-faire leadership. (11)

geographic (territorial) departmentalization An arrangement in which managers establish separate departments for each of the territories in which the firm does business. (8)

geographic expansion A strategic growth alternative of aggressively expanding into new domestic and/or overseas markets. (7)

global integration strategy Taking a centralized, integrated view of where to design and produce the company's product or service. (2)

globalization The tendency of firms to extend their sales, ownership, or manufacturing to new markets abroad. (1)

goal A specific result to be achieved; the end result of a plan. (6)

goal-setting studies Organizational behaviour research that provides useful insights into how to set effective goals. (6)

goal theory The theory that people regulate their behaviour in such a way as to achieve their goals. (12)

grapevine The informal communications channel that exists in every organization. (13)

graphic plan A plan that shows graphically or in charts what is to be achieved and when. (6)

grievance A complaint an employee lodges against an employer. (10)

gross domestic product (GDP) The market value of all goods and services that have been bought for final use during a period of time, and, therefore, the basic measure of a nation's economic activity. (2)

group Two or more persons who interact together for some purpose and in such a manner that each person influences and is influenced by each other person. (5)

group norms The informal rules that groups adopt to regulate and regularize group members' behaviour. (13)

groupthink Occurs when members of a group voluntarily suspend their critical-thinking abilities and repress any conflict and disagreement that could challenge group solidarity. (5)

growth needs Similar to Maslow's needs for self-esteem. (12)

H

health and safety programs Programs that help to reduce absenteeism and turnover, raise productivity, and boost morale by making jobs safer and more healthful. (10)

heuristics Decision-making shortcuts. (5)

horizontal corporation A structure that is organized around customer- oriented processes performed by multidisciplinary cross-functional teams rather than by formal functional departments. (8)

horizontal integration Acquiring ownership or control of competitors who are competing in the same or similar markets with the same or similar products. (7)

host country focus strategy The company gives each market its own autonomous subsidiary with headquarters providing overall coordination. (2)

hourly wage Compensation based on a set hourly pay rate for work performed. (10)

human capital The knowledge, education, training, skills, and expertise of a firm's workers. (1)

human process applications Organizational change techniques aimed at enabling employees to develop a better understanding of their own and others' behaviours for the purpose of improving that behaviour such that the organization benefits. (15)

human resources management (HRM) All the activities that are necessary to acquire, train, appraise, and pay the organization's employees. (10)

human resources plan A plan that projects personnel needs based on sales projections. (6)

hybrid international strategy Blending the efficiencies that come from integrating global production with the ability to provide each country with specialized products or services. (2)

I

identity boundary The boundary identifying those who share values and experiences from those who do not. (9)

immediate corrective action Actions that solve the problem immediately and get output back to the desired level. (16)

incentive program Any program in which a company offers its workers additional pay over and above the normal wage or salary level to motivate them to perform at a higher-than-normal level. (10)

independent integrator An individual or group that coordinates the activities of several interdependent departments but is independent of them. (9)

informal organization The network of interpersonal relationships and the informal way of doing things that inevitably develops in organizations. (8)

informal organizational network Informal relationships between workers that help get work accomplished. (8)

information source The message, idea, thought, or fact that you want to communicate. (13)

instrumentality The perceived correlation between successful performance and obtaining the reward. (12)

integration The process of achieving unity of effort among the various subsystems in accomplishing the organization's tasks. (9)

inter-group conflict Conflict between groups. (15)

interactive control system A system that maintains control by personally monitoring how everyone is doing. (16)

international business Any firm that engages in international trade or investment. (2)

international management The performance of the management functions of planning, organizing, leading, and controlling across national borders. (2)

international trade The export or import of goods or services to consumers in another country. (2)

interpersonal conflict Conflict that occurs between individuals or between individuals and groups. (15)

interview A selection device involving a meeting between the applicant and representatives of the firm. (10)

intrapreneurship The development, within a large corporation, of internal markets and relatively small autonomous or semi-autonomous business units that produce products, services, or technologies that employ the firm's resources in a unique way. (4)

intrinsic motivation When a person performs a task in the absence of any tangible reward. (12)

intuition A cognitive process whereby a person instinctively makes a decision based on his or her accumulated knowledge and experience. (5)

J

job analysis The procedure through which managers determine the duties of the job, and the kinds of people (in terms of skills and experience) that should be hired for the job. (10)

job analysis questionnaire A form used by managers to determine the duties and functions of a job through a series of questions that employees answer. (10)

job-centred leaders Leaders who focus on production and the job's technical aspects. (11)

job description A list of duties showing what the job entails. (10)

job enlargement Assigns workers additional same-level tasks to increase the number of tasks they have to perform. (12)

job enrichment Building motivators into a job by making it more interesting and challenging. (12)

job posting Publicizing the open job to employees and listing the job's attributes. (10)

job redesign The process of altering the nature and structure of jobs with the purpose of increasing employee satisfaction, motivation, and productivity. (12)

job rotation Systematically moves workers from job to job. (12)

job satisfaction An evaluative judgment about one's job. (12)

job sharing An arrangement that allows two people to share one full-time job. (12)

job specification A list of the skills and aptitudes sought in people hired for the job. (10)

joint venture The participation of two or more companies jointly in an enterprise in which each party contributes assets, owns the entity to some degree, and shares risk. (2)

jury of executive opinion A qualitative forecasting technique in which executives are given pertinent data and asked to make independent sales forecasts, which are then reconciled in an executive meeting or by the company president. (6)

just-in-time (JIT) inventory system A type of steering control where inventory is scheduled to arrive just in time to be used in the production process. (16)

L

labour unions Groups of individuals working together to achieve job-related goals such as higher pay, shorter working hours, and better working conditions. (10)

laissez-faire leader A leader who follows a completely hands-off policy with subordinates. (11)

law of individual differences People differ in personalities, abilities, values, perceptions, self-concept, and needs. (12)

leader—member exchange (LMX) theory A theory that says that leaders may use different styles with different members of the same work group, based in part on perceived similarities and differences with the leader. (11)

leadership Influencing others to work willingly to achieve the firm's objectives. (11)

learning The relatively permanent change in a person that occurs as a result of experience. (12)

learning organizations Organizations that learn from their own experiences and change their activities to be more effective. (9)

level 5 leadership style A unique blend of personal humility and professional will. (11)

leveraging resources To gain a competitive edge by concentrating a company's resources on key strategic goals or competencies. (13)

lifelong learning A formal program that provides employees with the skills they need to work effectively throughout their careers. (12)

line-and-staff organization An organization with both line and staff managers. (8)

line manager A manager who is (1) in charge of essential activities such as sales and (2) authorized to issue orders to subordinates down the chain of command. (8)

line–staff conflict Disagreements between a line manager and the staff manager who is giving him or her advice. (9)

linear programming A mathematical method used to solve resource allocation problems. (A5)

long-term corrective action Determines why deviations occur and what can be done to prevent the problem from happening in the future. (16)

M

management The process of planning, organizing, leading, and controlling other people so that organizational objectives are achieved. (1)

management by objectives (MBO) A technique in which the supervisor and subordinate jointly set goals for the latter and periodically assess progress toward those goals. (6)

management by walking around A manager literally walks around the workplace talking with subordinates to get a better idea of what they are doing in their jobs and the trials and triumphs they have had. (7)

management process The four key functions of management: planning, organizing, leading, and controlling. (1)

manager Someone who is responsible for accomplishing an organizational unit's goals, and who accomplishes those goals by planning, organizing, leading, and controlling the efforts of other people. (1)

managing diversity Planning and implementing organizational systems and practices to manage people so that the potential advantages of diversity are maximized while its potential disadvantages are minimized. (7)

market penetration A growth strategy to boost sales of present products by more aggressively permeating the organization's current markets. (8)

marketing-channel departmentalization An arrangement in which departments of an organization focus on particular marketing channels, such as drugstores or grocery stores. (8)

marketing channel A conduit through which a manufacturer distributes its products to its ultimate customers. (8)

marketing plan A plan that specifies the nature of your product or service, as well as the approaches you plan to take with respect to pricing, promotion, and place. (6)

marketing research The procedures used to develop and analyze current customer-related information to help managers make decisions. (6)

matrix organization An organization structure in which employees are permanently attached to one department but simultaneously have on-going assignments to project, customer, product, or geographic unit heads. (8)

mechanistic organization An organization structure characterized by close adherence to the established chain of command, highly specialized jobs, and vertical communications. (9)

megaproject A large-scale, costly construction or engineering project. (2)

mentoring A relationship between two people in which the more experienced member provides support, guidance, and counselling to enhance the proteges success at work and in other areas of life. (3)

merit pay A salary increase awarded to an employee based on individual performance. (10)

merit raise A salary increase based on individual performance. (12)

microenterprise A business that operates from the entrepreneur's home while the entrepreneur continues to work as a regular employee of another organization. (4)

middle manager Managers immediately below the top level of managers and above lower-level managers. (1)

mission A broad outline of the firm's purpose that communicates "who the organization is, what it does, and where it's headed." (7)

mixed economy Some sectors of the economy have private ownership and free market mechanisms, while others are owned and managed by the government. (2)

moral minimum The theory that states that the purpose of the corporation is to maximize profits so long as it commits no harm. (3)

morality A society's accepted norms of behaviour. (3)

motivation The intensity of a person's desire to engage in some activity. (12)

motive Something that incites the person to action or that sustains and gives direction to action. (12)

moving Developing new behaviours, values, and attitudes by applying one or more organizational change techniques. (15)

multinational corporation A firm that operates manufacturing and marketing facilities in two or more countries. (2)

mutual adjustment Achieving coordination through face-to-face interpersonal interaction. (9)

N

needs Motives that remain unaroused until the proper conditions bring them forth. (12)

negative reinforcement When an unpleasant stimulus is withheld from a person, the desired behaviour will likely be repeated. (12)

noise Anything that blocks, distorts, or in any way changes the information source as it makes its way to the destination/receiver. (13)

non-programmed decision A unique and novel decision that relies on judgment. (5)

normative judgment A judgment that implies that something is good or bad, right or wrong, better or worse. (3)

norms The informal rules that groups adopt to regulate and regularize members' behaviour. (5)

O

objective A specific result toward which effort is directed. (6)

off-the-job training Training that is performed at a location away from the work site. (10)

omission The likelihood that a behaviour will occur in the future is decreased when a pleasant stimulus is withheld from the person. (12)

on-the-job training Training in which a person learns a job while her or she is working at it. (10)

operant behaviour Behaviour that appears to operate on or to have an influence on the subject's environment. (12)

operating budget A budget that shows the expected sales and/or expenses for each of the company's departments for the planning period in question. (16)

operational plan A short-term plan that shows the detailed daily steps of business operations. (6)

organic organization An organizational structure characterized by flexible lines of authority, less specialized jobs, and decentralized decisions. (9)

organization A group of people with formally assigned roles who work together to achieve stated goals. (1)

organization chart A chart that shows the structure of the organization including the title of each manager's position and, by means of connecting lines, who is accountable to whom and who has authority for each area. (8)

organizational communication Exchanging information in such a way that you create a common basis of understanding and feeling among two or more individuals or groups throughout the organization. (13)

organizational culture The characteristic values, traditions, and behaviours a company's employees share. (3)

organizational development (OD) An approach to organizational change in which the employees themselves formulate and implement the change that's required, usually with the aid of a trained consultant. (15)

organizational network A system of interconnected or co-operating individuals. (8)

organizational politics The activities that individuals in organizations pursue as they try to achieve their own desired outcomes. (5)

organizational structure The pattern of formal relationships that exists among groups and individuals in an organization. (8)

organizing Arranging activities in such a way that they systematically contribute to the company's goals. (8)

orientation Providing new employees with basic information on things like work rules and vacation policies. (10)

output standards Standards that state the quantity of the product or service that employees should be producing. (16)

P

partial (intermittent) reinforcement schedule When the behaviour of interest is rewarded or punished only some of the time. (12)

partnership An association of two or more persons to carry on as co-owners of a business for profit. (4)

partnership agreement An oral or written contract between the owners of a partnership. (4)

path–goal leadership theory The leader's job is to increase the personal rewards subordinates receive for attaining goals and to make the path to these goals easier to follow by reducing roadblocks, setting goals, explaining what needs to be done, and organizing the work. (11)

patterns of behaviour The ceremonial events, written and spoken comments, and actual behaviours of an organization's members that contribute to creating the organizational culture. (3)

pay for performance Any compensation method that ties pay to the quantity or quality of work the person produces. (12)

perception The selection and interpretation of information we receive through our senses and the meaning we give to the information. (5)

performance appraisal Evaluating an employee's current or past performance in relation to the performance standards for the position. (10)

personal harassment Activities like verbal assaults, bullying, ridiculing, or any other actions that make the workplace stressful for the target of the harassment. (10)

personal staff Employees who assist specific line managers but lack the authority to act for them in their absence. (8)

personality The characteristic and distinctive traits of an individual and the way these traits interact to help or hinder the adjustment of the person to other people and situations. (12)

personnel planning The process of determining the organization's future personnel needs, as well as the methods to be used to fill those needs. (10)

personnel replacement charts Company records showing present performance and promotability of inside candidates for the most important positions. (10)

physical manifestations Observable features of a company's culture such as written rules, office layouts, organizational structure, and dress codes. (3)

piecework A standard sum for each item the worker produces. (10)

plan A method for doing or making something, consisting of a goal and a course of action. (6)

planning The process of setting goals and courses of action, developing rules and procedures, and forecasting future outcomes. (6)

policy A standing plan that sets broad guidelines for the enterprise. (6)

political boundary The boundary defining what different departments want, based on who will benefit from an activity and who will not. (9)

pooled interdependence Departments in an organization can each work separately on their contribution to organizational effectiveness. (9)

population ecology An approach arguing that an organization succeeds based on factors in the organization's external environment, not its internal management practices. (A1)

positive reinforcement When a pleasant stimulus is presented to a person, the desired behaviour is likely to be repeated. (12)

prejudice A bias that results from prejudging someone on the basis of that person's particular trait or traits. (3)

primary data Information specifically collected to solve a current problem. (6)

principle of exception To conserve managers' time, only significant deviations or exceptions from the standard should be brought to the manager's attention. (16)

private corporation One whose stock is held by only a few people and is generally not available for sale. (4)

privatization The process of turning formerly government-owned organizations into publicly traded businesses that pursue a profit. (1)

problem-solving team A team formed to identify and solve work-related problems. (14)

procedure A plan that specifies how to proceed in specific situations that routinely arise. (6)

product departmentalization The firm's departments are organized around the company's products or services. (8)

product development The strategy of improving products for current markets to maintain or boost growth. (7)

production plan A plan that shows how projected manufacturing needs will be supported. (6)

profit A measure of the difference between the revenues generated and the cost of generating those revenues. (16)

profit centres Responsibility centres whose managers the company holds accountable for profit. (16)

profit-sharing plan An incentive program in which employees receive a bonus depending on the firm's profits. (10)

programmed decision A decision that is repetitive and routine and that can be solved through mechanical procedures such as by applying rules. (5)

project teams Small groups that operate as semi-autonomous units to create and develop new ideas. (14)

public corporation One whose stock is widely held and is available for sale to the general public. (4)

punishment The likelihood that a behaviour will occur in the future is decreased when an unpleasant stimulus is presented to a person. (12)

Q

qualitative forecasting Predictive techniques that emphasize human judgment. (6)

quality circle A team of 6 to 12 specially trained employees that meets regularly to solve problems affecting its work area. (14)

quality control The activities that are carried out to ensure that the quality level of all goods and services meets the standards required by customers. (16)

quality standards Standards that define the level of quality that is to be maintained in the production of goods and services. (16)

quantitative forecasting A type of forecasting in which statistical methods are used to examine data and find underlying patterns and relationships; includes time-series methods and causal models. (6)

quota A legal restriction on the import of specific goods. (2)

R

re-engineering Introducing major changes in the way business processes are carried out. (15)

receiver The audience, listener, reader, or viewer that you're aiming your message at. (13)

reciprocal interdependence The highest level of interdependence, when work continually flows back and forth until the job is completed. (9)

recruiting Attracting a pool of viable job applicants. (10)

reengineering Combining several specialized jobs into more enlarged jobs, and giving employees added authority to perform these newly enlarged jobs. (8)

refreezing To institute new systems and procedures to support and maintain the changes that you made. (15)

related diversification A strategy of expanding into other industries or markets related to a company's current business lines, so that the firm's lines of business still have some kind of fit. (7)

relatedness needs Those needs that require interpersonal interaction to satisfy, such as prestige and esteem from others. (12)

retrenchment The reduction of activities or operations. (7)

revenue centres Responsibility centres whose managers are accountable for generating revenues. (16)

risk Being able to assign probabilities to each outcome. (A5)

role conflict When a person is faced with conflicting orders, such that compliance with one would make it difficult or impossible to comply with the other. (15)

rule A highly specific guide to action. (6)

S

sales budget A budget that shows the planned sales activity for each period (usually in units per month) and the revenue expected from the sales. (16)

sales force estimation method A forecasting technique that gathers and combines the opinions of the salespeople on what they predict sales will be in the forthcoming period. (6)

satisfice To look for solutions until a satisfactory one is found. (5)

scenario planning A hypothetical sequence of events constructed for the purpose of focusing attention on causal processes and decision points and thereby helping the manager anticipate events and thus create plans for them. (7)

secondary data Information that is already collected or published. (6)

self-concept Perceptions of who we are and how we relate to other people and things. (12)

self-efficacy A person's belief about his or her capacity to perform a task. (12)

self-managing/self-directed work team A group of employees empowered to direct and do virtually all their own work, and the work results in a singular, well-defined item. (14)

sensitivity training Also called t-group training, the aim of this organizational development technique is to increase the participant's insight into his or her own behaviour and the behaviour of others by encouraging an open expression of feelings in a trainer-guided group. (15)

sequential interdependence The output of one individual or department becomes the input for another individual or department. (9)

service staff Staff who provide specific services to line managers, such as interviewing new applicants. (8)

sexual harassment Unwelcome sexual advances, requests for sexual favours, and other verbal or physical conduct of a sexual nature. (10)

signal The stream of words, images, or gestures you use to actually express the message. (13)

single-use plan A plan made to be used once. (6)

skills The ability to carry out some task in an efficient manner. (11)

skill-based pay Employees are compensated for the range, depth, and types of skills and knowledge they can use, rather than for the jobs they currently hold. (12)

social responsibility The extent to which companies should and do channel resources toward improving one or more segments of society other than the firm's owners. (3)

sole proprietorship A business owned by one person. (4)

span of control The number of subordinates reporting directly to a supervisor. (8)

spot award An award you give literally "on the spot" as soon as you observe the good performance. (12)

staff manager A manager without the authority to give orders down the chain of command (except in his or her own department); generally can only assist and advise line managers in specialized areas such as human resources management. (8)

staffing Filling a firm's open positions. (10)

standards Criteria for evaluating the quality and quantity of the products or services produced by employees. (16)

standing plan A plan established to be used repeatedly, as the need arises. (6)

statistical decision theory techniques Decision-making techniques used to solve problems for which information is incomplete or uncertain. (A5)

steering control Controls that predict results and let the manager take corrective action before the operation or project is completed. (16)

stereotyping Associating certain characteristics with certain groups classes but not with others. (3)

stock options Rights to purchase company stock at a discount some time in the future. (12)

strategic alliance An agreement between potential or actual competitors to achieve common objectives. (7)

strategic change A shift in the firm's strategy, mission, and vision. (15)

strategic choice theory Suggests that managers must decide what niche or industry the company will compete in, how the organization will be designed, and what performance standards will be applied. (A1)

strategic human resource management The process of aligning the firm's human resource management goals and policies with the strategic goals of the enterprise to improve business performance. (10)

strategic interventions Company-wide OD programs aimed at achieving a better fit among a firm's strategy, structure, culture, and external environment. (15)

strategic management The process of identifying and executing the organization's mission by matching the organization's capabilities with the demands of its environment. (7)

strategic planning Identifying the current business of a firm, the business it wants for the future, and the course of action or strategy it will pursue. (6)

strategic, or long-term, goals Goals that specify exactly what the mission means in terms of how many and what specific types of actions need to be taken. (7)

strategy A comprehensive and integrated plan that states how the organization will use its resources in the pursuit of its mission and objectives. (7)

strategy implementation Translating the strategy into actions and results. (7)

structural change Changing one or more aspects of the company's organization structures. (15)

subsidies A direct payment a county makes to support a domestic producer. (2)

suggestion team A temporary team that works on a specific assignment. (14)

supply chain All the production facilities, distribution centres, retail outlets, employees, and information that must work together to get goods and services from producers to consumers. (6)

supply chain management The integration of the activities that procure materials, transform them into intermediate goods and final products, and deliver them to customers. (6)

survey research The process of collecting data from attitude surveys filled out by employees of an organization, then feeding the data back to workgroups to provide a basis for problem analysis and action planning. (15)

SWOT analysis A strategic planning tool for analyzing a company's strengths, weaknesses, opportunities, and threats. (7)

T

tactical plan A plan that shows how top management's plans are to be carried out at the departmental, short-term level. (6)

tariffs Taxes levied on goods shipped internationally. (2)

task boundary The boundary defining how employees from different departments feel about "who does what" as the necessary work is divided up. (9)

team A group of people who work together and share a common work objective. (8)

team building The process of improving the effectiveness of a team through action research or other techniques. (15)

technical skills Those skills specific to an area of expertise. (1)

technological change Changing the way the company creates and markets its products or services. (15)

technology transfer The transfer, often to another country, of systematic knowledge for the manufacturing of a product, for the application of a process, or for the rendering of a service; it does not extend to the mere sale or lease of goods. (2)

technostructural intervention Changes in the structures, methods, and job designs of firms that are intended to improve its efficiency and effectiveness. (15)

telecommunications The electronic transmission of information. (13)

telecommuting The substitution of telecommunications and computers for the commute to a central office. (13)

test A sample of a person's behaviour. (10)

time series A set of observations taken at specific times, usually at equal intervals, to identify fundamental patterns. (6)

time standards Standards that state the length of time it should take to complete a task. (16)

tokenism Appointing a small number of minority-group members to high-profile positions instead of more aggressively seeking full representation for that group. (3)

total quality management (TQM) A control concept based on the idea that no defects are tolerable and that employees are responsible for maintaining quality standards. (16)

TOWS matrix A strategic planning tool that presents possible strategies for addressing the firm's strengths, weaknesses, opportunities, and threats. (7)

trade barriers Governmental influences aimed at reducing the competitiveness of imported products or services. (2)

traditional control systems Based on setting standards and then monitoring performance. (16)

training program The process of providing new employees with information they need to do their jobs satisfactorily. (10)

traits More or less unchanging characteristics of the person that predispose them to act in a particular way. (11)

transactional behaviours Leadership actions that focus on accomplishing the tasks at hand and on maintaining good working relationships by exchanging promises of rewards for performance. (11)

transformational leadership The leadership process that involves influencing major changes in the attitudes and assumptions of organization members and building commitment for the organization's mission, objectives, and strategies. (11)

transnational teams Teams comprise multinational members whose activities span many countries. (14)

U

uncertainty Being unable to even assign probabilities to the likelihood of the various outcomes. (A5)

unfreezing Reducing the forces that favour the status quo. (15)

universalist theories Theories that propose that there is "one best way" to manage organizations and people. (A1)

unlimited liability The business owner is responsible for any claims against the firm that go beyond what the owner has invested in the business. (4)

V

valence In motivation, the perceived value a person ascribes to the reward for certain efforts. (12)

value-based hiring Looking for common experiences and values that may signal the applicant's fit with the firm. (16)

values Basic beliefs we hold about what is good or bad, important or unimportant. (2)

variable interval schedule Reinforcement is applied after a varying amount of time has passed, regardless of the number of desired responses that have occurred. (12)

variable ratio schedule Behaviour is reinforced after a varying number of responses have occurred. (12)

vertical integration A growth strategy in which a company owns or controls the inputs to its processes and/or its distribution channels. (7)

video assessment An approach to selection that involves showing job applicants videos of realistic work situations and then asking the applicants to choose a course of action. (10)

videoconferencing A telecommunications-based method that lets group members interact directly with other team members via televised links. (13)

virtual corporation A temporary network of independent companies linked by information technology to share skills, costs, and access to one another's markets. (7)

virtual teams Groups of geographically and/or organizationally dispersed co-workers that are assembled to accomplish an organizational task, using a combination of telecommunications and information technologies. (14)

vision A general statement of an organization's intended direction that evokes emotional feelings in its members. (7)

W

waiting-line/queuing techniques Mathematical decision-making techniques for solving waiting-line problems. (A5)

whistle-blowing The activities of employees who try to report organizational wrongdoing. (3)

wholly owned subsidiary A company owned 100 percent by a foreign firm. (2)

work group support systems Technology-based systems that make it easier for work groups' members to work together. (13)

worker empowerment Giving front-line employees the authority they need to do their jobs so they can respond quickly to customer needs. (1)

workers' compensation A payment aimed at providing income and medical benefits to victims of work-related accidents or their dependents, regardless of fault. (10)

Sources

Chapter 1

Avon Products Summarized from Katrina Brooker, "It Took a Lady to Save Avon," *Fortune* (October 15, 2001): 203–208; also "The Best (and Worst) Managers," *Business Week* (January 13, 2003). **The Challenge of Change** Summarized from Claudia H. Deutsch, "A Hands-on-the-Helm Leader," *The New York Times,* 13 June 1999, Money and Business Section, p. 2; also Noel Tichy and Ram Charan, "The CEO as Coach: An Interview with Allied-Signal's Lawrence A. Bossidy," *Harvard Business Review* (March–April 1995): 69–78. **The People Side of Managing** Summarized from Henry Mintzbert, *The Nature of Managerial Work* (New York: Harper and Row, 1973), Chapter 3. **Figure 1.3** *Harvard Business Review* (March–April 1998): 82.Copyright © 1998 by the President and Fellows of Harvard College. All rights reserved. **Case Study 1-1** Simon Tuck, "Nortel Faces Investors' Wrath," *The Globe and Mail,* 26 April 2002, sec. B, pp. 1, 4; also Fabrice Taylor, "The Story Behind Nortel's Fall," *The Globe and Mail,* 17 November 2001, sec. B, pp. 1, 4; also Linda Rosborough, "Rise & Fall of Nortel," *The Winnipeg Free Press,* 16 October 2001, sec. B, pp. 3, 7; also Dave Ebner, "A Black Day for Nortel," *The Globe and Mail,* 16 June 2001, sec. B, pp. 1, 6. **Case Study 1-2** Pierre LeBrun, "For a Brief Moment, Jays Fans Revel in Gillick-Mania Again," *The Winnipeg Free Press,* 9 August 2002, p. D4; also "A Message from Mudville," *Canadian Business* (March, 1996): 36–37; also Scott Tayler, "Baseball Develops Class Systems," *The Winnipeg Free Press,* 15 December 1996, sec. A, p. 8; also David Napier, "Beeston Plays Hardball," *The Financial Post Magazine* (September, 1992): 28–32.

Chapter 1 Appendix

Figure A1.1 Thomas A. Stewart, "The All-Time Greatest Hits of Managing," *Fortune* (March 29, 1999): 192. **Figure A1.2** John Usher, "Exploring the Effects of Niche Crowding on Rates of Organizational Change and Failure," Working Paper, Memorial University of Newfoundland. Reprinted by permission of Dr. John M. Usher, Dean, Faculty of Management, University of Lethbridge.

Chapter 2

Making a Splash in International Waters Nelson Wyatt, "Tellier Moves to Bombardier," *The Winnipeg Free Press,* 14 December 2002, sec. B, p. 5; also Bertrand Marotte, "Bombardier Stuns Markets," *The Globe and Mail,* 24 August 2002, sec. B, pp. 1, 5; also Bertrand Marotte, "Bombardier Wins Big Order," *The Globe and Mail,* 12 March 2002, sec. B, pp. 1–2; also Steven Chase, "Harsher Jet Ruling Revealed," *The Globe and Mail,* 12 November 2001, sec. B, pp. 1, 5; also Heather Scoffield and Shawn McCarthy, "WTO Backs Canada in Jet Market Dogfight with Brazil," *The Globe and Mail,* 1 April 2000, sec. B, pp. 1, 5; also Konrad Yakabuski and Heather Scoffield, "Canada, Brazil Claim Victory Over Decision," *The Globe and Mail,* 3 August 1999, sec. B, pp. 1, 4; also Konrad Yakabuski, "Bombardier Soars on Jet Orders, But Turbulence May Loom Ahead," *The Globe and Mail,* 22 February 1999, sec. B, pp. 1, 5; also Heather Scoffield, "Bombardier-Embraer Dog Fight Heats Up," *The Globe and Mail,* 15 February 1999, sec. B, pp. 1, 6. **The Challenge of Change** Sandra Cordon, "Canada Wins Round 1," *The Winnipeg Free Press,* 27 July 2002, sec. B, p. 1; also Peter Kennedy, "Huge Setback Seen for Industry," *The Globe and Mail,* 23 March 2002, sec. B, p. 5; also Wendy Stueck, "Fallout From Softwood War Leaves B. C. Forestry Workers at Loose Ends," *The Globe and Mail,* 23 March 2002, sec. B, p. 4; also Barrie McKenna and Steven Chase, "Canada Vows to Fight Duty," *The Globe and Mail,* 23 March 2002, sec. B, pp. 1, 4; also Barrie McKenna, Peter Kennedy, and Steven Chase, "Canada Quits Lumber Talks," *The Globe and Mail,* 20 March 2002, sec. B, pp. 1, 6; also Barrie McKenna and Steven Chase, "Softwood Lumber Deal in Sight," *The Globe and Mail,* 8 March 2002, sec., B, pp. 1, 6; also Peter Kennedy, "Lumber Duties Could Hit $1.5 Billion," *The Globe and Mail,* 2 November 2001, sec. B, pp. 1, 12. **The People Side of Managing** Summarized from Geoffrey York, "Russians Accuse McDonald's of Union Bashing," *The Globe and Mail,* 14 June 1999, sec. A, p. 17; Geoffrey York, "Beeg Maks on a Roll," *The Globe and Mail,* 12 September 1996, sec. B, pp. 1, 17; Peter Foster, "McDonald's Excellent Soviet Venture?" *Canadian Business* (May 1991): 51–64. **Figure 2.5** "Survey of Europe," *The Economist* (October 23, 1999).The Economist Newspaper Group, Inc. www.economist.com. Reprinted with permission. Further reproduction prohibited. **Figure 2.7** Adapted from Pankaj Ghemawat, "Distance Still Matters," *Harvard Business Review* (September, 2001): 140. **Figure 2.8** Adapted from Pankaj Ghemawat, "Distance Still Matters," *Harvard Business Review* (September, 2001): 142–143. **Figure 2.9** Adapted from Figures 2 and 5 and discussion in Sumantra Ghoshal and Nitin Nohria, reprinted from John Daniels and Lee Radebaugh, *International Business* (Upper Saddle River, NJ: Prentice Hall, 2001): 529. "Horses for Courses: Organizational Forma for Multinational Corporations," *Sloan Management Review* (Winter 1993): 23–36. **Figure 2.11** Adapted from G. Hofstede, *Culture's Consequences* (Beverly Hills, CA: Sage Publications, 1984). **Table 2.2** C. Hampden-Turner and A. Trompenaars, *The Seven Cultures of Capitalism* (New York: Doubleday, 1993). Adapted from Helen Deresky, *International Management,* 2nd ed. (New York: Addison Wesley Longman, 1997), Exh 11-5, p. 402. **Table 2.3** Adapted from Kamal Fatehi, *International Management* (Upper Saddle River, NJ: Prentice Hall 1996), Table 6.1, p. 194.

Chapter 3

The Latest Flap at Cinar Corp. Bertrand Marotte, "Cinar Founders' Trustee Stages Coup," *The Globe and Mail,* 30 April 2002, sec. B, pp. 1, 10; also Bertrand Marotte, "Cinar Settlement $2 Million," *The Globe and Mail,* 16 March 2002, sec. B, pp. 1–2; also Susanne Craig, John Partridge, and Bertrand Marotte,

"Cinar Co-Founder Okayed Investment," *The Globe and Mail,* 22 March 2000, sec. B, pp. 1, 4; also Susanne Craig, "Cinar Co-Founder Pushed Out," *The Globe and Mail,* 15 March 2000, sec. B, pp. 1, 9; also Susanne Craig and Bertrand Marotte, "Cinar to Take Hit Following Probe," *The Globe and Mail,* 21 February 2000, sec. B, pp. 1, 3. **Table 3.1** O. C. Ferrell and John Fraedrich, *Business Ethics,* 3rd ed. (New York: Houghton Mifflin, 1997), 54. **Figure 3.1** Michael Boylan, *Business Ethics* (Upper Saddle River, NJ: Prentice Hall, 2001), 110. **Figure 3.2** Stephen P. Robbins, *Self-Assessment Library: Insights into Your Skills, Abilities and Interests* (Upper Saddle River, NJ: Prentice Hall, 2002), 36–37. Adapted from A. Reichel and Y. Neumann, *Journal of Instructional Psychology* (March 1998): 25–53. With permission of the authors. **Table 3.2** O. C. Ferrell and John Fraedrich, *Business Ethics,* 3rd ed. (New York: Houghton Mifflin, 1997), 28. Adapted from Rebecca Goodell, *Ethics in American Business: Policies, Programs, and Perceptions* (1994), p. 54. Permission provided courtesy of the Ethics Resource Center, 1120 6th Street, NW, Washington, DC, 20005. **Figure 3.3** O. C. Ferrell and John Fraedrich, *Business Ethics,* 3rd ed. (New York: Houghton Mifflin, 1997), 176. Adapted from Walter W. Manley II, *The Handbook of Good Business Practice* (London" Routledge, 1992), 16. **Figure 3.4** Susan Wells, "Turn Employees into Saints," *HRMagazine* (December 1999): 52. **The People Side of Managing** Summarized from Michael J. McCarthy, "Virtual Morality: A New Workplace Quandary," *Wall Street Journal,* 21 October 1999, sec. B, pp. 1, 4; Marina Strauss, "E-Tailers Mix Alcohol with Internet," *The Globe and Mail,* 21 July 2000, sec. M, p. 1. **The Challenge of Change** Ronald Alsop, "Perils of Corporate Philanthropy," *The Wall Street Journal,* 16 January 2002, sec. B, pp. 1, 4; also Alix M. Freedman, "As Unicef Battles Baby-Formula Makers, Africa Infants Sicken," *The Wall Street Journal,* 5 December 2000, sec. A, pp. 1, 18; also Theresa Ebden and Dawn Walton, "Walkerton Recipient of New-Style Corporate Giving," *The Globe and Mail,* 3 June 2000, sec. B, pp. 1, 6. Also Tom Kierans, "Charity Begins at Work," *Report on Business Magazine* (June 1990): 23. **Figure 3.6** Reprinted with permission of the publisher. From *Cultural Diversity in Organizations: Theory, Research and Practice,* copyright © 1993 by Taylor Cox, Jr. Berrett-Koehler Publishers, Inc., San Francisco, CA. All rights reserved, www.bkconnection.com **Case 3-1** Summarized from Terence Corcoran, "Corporate Ungiving," *The National Post,* 1 April 2000, sec. D, p. 5; "Nortel's New Style of Giving," *The National Post,* 1 April 2000, sec. D, p. 5.

Chapter 4

The Urge to Start a New Business Summarized from Murray McNeill, "Patience Pays off for Native Owner," *The Winnipeg Free Press,* 6 November 2002, sec. B, p. 3; also Sarah Kennedy, "Self-Styled Pioneer Aims to Alter Face of Fashion," *The Globe and Mail,* July 1, 2002, p. B12; also Tahl Raz, "This Hip House," *Inc.* (October 2002): 36; see also Sandy Olkowski, "Martha Stewart goes street: An interview with indie Mag dynamo, Shoshana Berger," www. withitgirl. com/life/profile1.htm. **Figure 4.1** Mary Coulter, *Entrepreneurship in Action* (Upper Saddle River, NJ: Prentice Hall, 2001), 4; based on W. B. Gartner, "What Are We Talking About When We Talk about Entrepreneurship?" *Journal of Business Venturing* 5 (1990):

15–28. **Table 4.1** Copyright 2003, The Heritage Foundation, 214 Massachusetts Ave. NE, Washington, D. C. 20002-4999, at **www. heritage. org**. **Figure 4.2** Based on T. S. Batemen and J. M. Crant, "The Proactive Component of Organizational Behavior: A Measure and Correlates," *Journal of Organizational Behavior* (March 1993): 103–118; and J. M. Crant, "The Proactive Personality Scale as a Predictor of Entrepreneurial Intentions," *Journal of Small Business Management* (July 1996): 42–49. **Checklist 4.1** From "The U.S. Small Business Administration's Small Business Start-Up Kit," **www. sba. gov/starting/ask. html,** downloaded May 12, 2002. **The People Side of Managing** Summarized from Gordon Pitts, "The Cuddy Situation is an Extreme Case of Family Company Dysfunctionality," *The Globe and Mail,* 17 April 2000, sec. B, p. 9; David Berman, "Carving Up Cuddy," *Canadian Business* (March 27, 1998): 39–44. Data on various aspects of small business in Canada were provided by Robert W. Sexty of Memorial University. **Figure 4.4** *Franchise Opportunities Handbook* (Washington, D.C. : U.S. Government Printing Office, 1988). **Table 4.2** Fred R. David, *Strategic Management* (Upper Saddle River, NJ: Prentice Hall, 2001), 115. **Figure 4.5** William F. Schoell, Gary Dessler, and John A. Reinecke, *Introduction to Business* (Boston: Allyn & Bacon, 1993), 176. **Figure 4.6** Peggy Lambing and Charles R. Kuehl, *Entrepreneurship* (Upper Saddle River, NJ: Prentice Hall, 2000), 44. **Figure 4.7** Reprinted with permission of *Inc. Magazine* from "First Aide," by Nancy Austin, September 1999, copyright © 1999. Permission conveyed through Copyright Clearance Center, Inc. **Figure 4.8** Adapted from J. Cornwall and B. Perlman, *Organizational Entrepreneurship* (Homewood, IL: Irwin, 1990). **Case Study 4-1** Summarized from Peter Verburg, "Table Talk," *Canadian Business* (May 27, 2002): 49–52. **Case Study 4-2** Marc Dollinger, *Entrepreneurship* (Upper Saddle River, NJ: Prentice Hall, 2003), 37; (adapted from Meera Louis, "Pooled Savings Help Jamaicans Build Business," *The Wall Street Journal,* 17 Oct. 2000, sec. B, pp. 1–2).

Chapter 5

Decision Time at BCE Summarized from Jacquie McNish and Paul Waldie, "BCE Reacquiring 20% Stake in Bell Canada," *The Globe and Mail,* 29 June 2002, sec. B, pp. 1, 4; Karen Howlett and John Saunders, "Teleglobe to Abandon Huge Internet Investment, *The Globe asnd Mail,* 16 May 2002, sec. B, pp. 1, 11; Ian Austen, "On the Hook," *Canadian Business* (May 13, 2002): 35–39; Bertrand Marotte, "Sabia: BCE Committed to Emergis," *The Globe and Mail,* 8 May 2002, sec. B, p. 5; Eric Reguly, "Decision Time for BCE Boss is Now," *The Globe and Mail,* 22 March 2002, sec. B, pp. 1–2; Gordon Pitts, "Monty Ends 28 Years with a Clean Break," *The Globe and Mail,* 25 April 2002, sec. B, p. 3. **Table 5.1** *Management,* 5th ed. by Robbins/Coulter, © 1996 Reprinted by permission of Pearson Education, Inc., Upper Saddle River, NJ. **Figure 5.1** *Management,* 5th ed., by Robbins/Coulter, ©. Reprinted by permission of Pearson Education Inc., Upper Saddle River, NJ. **The Challenge of Change** Summarized from Cathy Olafson, "So Many Decisions, So Little Time," *Fast Company* (October, 1999): 62. **Figure 5.4** Lester A. Lefton and Laura Valvatine, *Mastering Psychology,* 4th ed, © 1992 by Allyn & Bacon, Boston, MA. © by Pearson Education. Reprinted by permission of the publisher. **Figure 5.5** Max H. Bazerman, *Judgment in Managerial Decision*

Making. Copyright © 1994 by John Wiley & Sons, Inc., p. 93. This material is used by permission of John Wiley & Sons, Inc. **The People Side of Managing** Frederick A. Starke and Robert W. Sexty, *Contemporary Management*, 3rd ed. (Scarborough: Prentice Hall Canada, 1998), 266. **Figure 5.6** *Applied Human Relations*, 4th ed. by Benton/Halloran, © 1991. Reprinted by permission of Prentice Hall, Inc., Upper Saddle River, NJ. **Figure 5.7** These items are taken from a 30-item Personal Style Inventory (PSI) assessment of preferences for Rational and Intuitive Behaviour created by professor William Taggert. Log on to www.the-intuitive-self.org to take the complete PSI. Personal Style Inventory copyright 2000 by William Taggert, Ph.D. **Tables 5.4 and 5.5** Irving L. Janis, *Victims of Groupthink*, First Edition. Copyright © 1972 by Houghton Mifflin Company. Adapted with permission. **Case Study 5-1** Murray McNeill, "Inco Deal Delights Thompson," *The Winnipeg Free Press*, 12 June 2002, sec. B, p. 4; Michael McDonald, "$3B Voisey's Bay to Go Ahead," *The Winnipeg Free Press*, 11 June 2002, sec. B, p. 8; Michael MacDonald, "Aboriginals Support Nickel Mine Project," *The Winnipeg Free Press*, 25 May 2002, sec. B, p. 5; Allan Robinson, "Inco Has Hopes For Deal Soon on Voisey's," *The Globe and Mail*, 18 April 2002, sec. B, pp. 1, 10; Paula Arab, "Voisey's Bay Deal Soon: Inco," *The Winnipeg Free Press*, 18 April 2002, sec. B, p. 6; Allan Robinson, "Inco, Province Inch Toward Deal on Voisey's Bay, *The Globe and Mail*, 12 October 2001, sec. B, p. 3; James Stevenson, "Inco Grilled Despite Impressive Rebound," *The Winnipeg Free Press*, 20 April 2000, sec. B, p. 7; "Giant Newfoundland Nickel Project May Soon Proceed," *The Winnipeg Free Press*, 23 November 1999, sec. B, p. 8; Allan Robinson, "Inco to Halt Voisey's Bay Work," *The Globe and Mail*, 28 July 1998, sec. B, pp. 1, 6. **Case Study 5-2** Information provided by Gary Veak of the Southern Alberta Institute of Technology.

Chapter 6

Ups and Downs at Lions Gate Entertainment Corp. Keith Damsell, "Lions Gate Gets Makeover After Mauling," *The Globe and Mail*, 7 February 2001, p. M1; also John Gray, "California Dreamin'," *Canadian Business* (June 25, 2001): 46–49. **Figure 6.3** Adapted from Philip Kotler and Gary Armstrong, *Principles of Marketing* (Upper Saddle River, NJ: Prentice Hall, 2001), 70. **Figure 6.4** Business Plan Pro, Palo Alto Software, Palo Alto, CA. **Figure 6.5** Business Plan Pro, Palo Alto Software, Palo Alto, CA. **Figure 6.6** Business Plan Pro, Palo Alto Software, Palo Alto, CA. **Figure 6.9** Business Plan Pro, Palo Alto Software, Palo Alto, CA. **Tables 6.1 and 6.2** *A Guide to Long-Range Planning*, by George L. Morrissey. Copyright 1996. This material is used by permission of John Wiley & Sons, Inc. **Table 6.3** *A Guide to Tactical Planning*, by George L. Morrissey. Copyright 1996. This material is used by permission of John Wiley & Sons, Inc. **The Challenge of Change** Kenneth Laudon and Jane Laudon, *Management Information Systems* (Upper Saddle River, NJ: Prentice Hall, 2001), 598. See also "Wal-Mart to Triple Size of a Warehouse," *TechWeb*, February 10, 1999, http://192.215.17.45/news-flash/nf617/0210-st6.htm. **The People Side of Managing** Summarized from Christopher Bartlett and Sumantra Ghoshal, "Changing the Role of Top Management: Beyond Systems to People," *Harvard Business Review* (May–June, 1995): 132–142.

Chapter 7

The French-Canadian Connection: Vivendi and Seagram Summarized from Miro Cernetig, "Messier Blames Bronfman," *The Globe and Mail*, 5 July 2002, sec. B, pp. 1, 4; also Brian Milner, "Bronfman Hands Tied as Messier's Vivendi Unravels," *The Globe and Mail*, 17 May 2002, sec. B, p. 11; also Brian Milner, "Bronfmans Win in Seagram Deal," *The Globe and Mail*, 15 June 2000, sec. B, pp. 1, 17; also Brian Milner, "Seagram Dynasty Down the Hatch," *The Globe and Mail*, 20 June 2000, sec. A, pp. 1, 7; also Brian Milner, "Seagram Snares Polygram," *The Globe and Mail*, 22 May 1998, sec. B, pp. 1, 4; also Brian Milner, "Seagram's Top Gun Shoots for the Stars," *The Globe and Mail*, 6 June 1998, sec. B, pp. 1, 6. **Figure 7.1** Adapted from Fred David, *Strategic Management* (Upper Saddle Reiver, NJ: Prentice Hall, 2001), 77. **Figure 7.2** Arit Gadiesh and James Gilbert, "Frontline Action," *Harvard Business Review* (May 2001): 74. **Checklist 7.1** Adapted from Donald Hambrick and James Frederickson, "Are Your Sure You Have a Strategy?" *Academy of Management Executive* 15, no. 4 (2001), 59. **Figure 7.4** Reprinted with the permission of The Free Press, a division of Simon & Schuster Adult Publishing Group, from *Competitive Strategy: Techniques for Analyzing Industries and Competitors* by Michael E. Porter. Copyright © 1980 by The Free Press. **Figure 7.5** Adapted from Michael Porter, "Strategy and the Internet," *Harvard Business Review* (March 2001), 67. **Figure 7.8** Fred David, *Strategic Management* (Upper Saddle River, NJ: Prentice Hall, 2001), 207. **The People Side of Managing** Summarized from Watson Wyatt, "Work USA 1997," *BNA Bulletin to Management* (September 4, 1997): 281. **Case Study 7-1** Caroline Alphonso, "Street Expects Soaring WestJet to Fly Higher," *The Globe and Mail*, 15 March 2002, sec. B, p. 9; also Keith McArthur, "Travel Agents Gird for Turbulence," *The Globe and Mail*, 30 March 2002, sec. B, pp. 1–2; also Keith McArthur, "Airlines Axing Travel Agents' Fees," *The Globe and Mail*, 20 March 2002, sec. B, p. 9; also Keith McArthur, "Discount Air Battle Heats Up," *The Globe and Mail*, 22 February 2002, sec. B, pp. 1, 7; also Keith McArthur, "Tango Spreading Its Wings in Canada," *The Globe and Mail*, 11 January 2002, sec. B, p. 5; also Bertrand Marotte, "Charter Airline Gears Up for Piece of Market," *The Globe and Mail*, 17 January 2002, sec. B, p. 8; also Keith McArthur, "WestJet's Traffic Rises 54.7%," *The Globe and Mail*, 10 January 2002, sec. B, p. 3; also Patrick Brethour and Keith McArthur, "Air Canada Unveils Zip Discount Carrier," *The Globe and Mail*, 20 April 2002, sec. B, pp. 1, 6; also Geoff Kirbyson, "City Flyers Can Now Go Jetsgo," *The Winnipeg Free Press*, 29 May 2002, sec. B, p. 3; also Stephen Irwin, "No-Frills Airline Ready to Fly," *The Winnipeg Free Press*, 28 May 2002, sec. B, p. 3.

Chapter 8

Product Versus Geographical Departmentation Joann Lublin, "Place vs. Product: It's Tough to Choose a Management Model," *The Wall Street Journal*, 27 June 2001, sec. A, pp. 1, 4. **The People Side of Managing** Summarized from Wilma Bernasco, "Balanced Matrix Structure and New Product Development Process at Texas Instruments Materials and Controls Division," *R&D Management* (April, 1999): 121. **Figure 8.8** Adapted from Montreal Trust, *Annual Report*, 1989. **Figure 8.11** Reprinted by permission of *Harvard Business*

Review, from "How Networks Reshape Organizations—For Results," by Ram Charan (September–October, 1991). Copyright © 1991 by the Harvard Business School Publishing Corporation, all rights reserved. **Figures 8.12 and 8.13** John A. Byrne, "The Horizontal Corporation," *Business Week* (December 20, 1993): 80. **The Challenge of Change** Summarized from Karyn Chan, "Overview—From Top to Bottom: Taking Advantage of On-line Marketplaces Isn't Just About Changing Technology, It's About Changing an Entire Company," *The Wall Street Journal*, 21 May 2001, sec., R, p. 12. **Figure 8.14** Reprinted with permission of the *Academy of Management Executive*, from "Organizing in the Knowledge Age: Anticipating the Cellular Form," Raymond Miles, vol. 11, no. 4, © 1997; permission conveyed through Copyright Clearance Center, Inc.

Chapter 9

Strategy and Structure "Planet Starbucks," *Business Week* (September 9, 2002): 100–110; also Jennifer Reese, "Starbucks: Inside the Coffee Cult," *Fortune* (December 9, 1996): 190–200; also information contained on the Starbucks Web site at www.starbucks.com. **Figure 9.1** Keith Bradsher, "The Reality Behind the Slogan," *The New York Times*, 23 August 2001, sec. C, p. 1; and General Motors. **The Challenge of Change** Summarized from Keith Bradsher, "The Reality Behind the Slogan," *The New York Times*, 23 August 2001. **Figure 9.3** Adapted and reprinted by permission of *Harvard Business Review*, "The Four Organizational Boundaries that Matter," from "The New Boundaries of the 'Boundaryless' Company," by Larry Hirschorn and Thomas Gilmore, May–June 1992. Copyright © 1992 by the Harvard Business School Publishing Corporation. All rights reserved. **Figure 9.4** Based on James Thompson, *Organizations in Action* (New York: McGraw-Hill, 1967), Chapter 2. **Case Study 9-1** Summarized from Allan Robinson, "Assets Must Pay Their Way: Brascan Boss," *The Globe and Mail*, 27 April 2002, sec. B, p. 4; also Andrew Willis, "History Says Brascan Will Top Up Trilon Bid With Cherry," *The Globe and Mail*, 27 March 2002, sec. B, p. 17; also Jacquie McNish, "Brascan Seeks to Buy Out Rest of Trilon," *The Globe and Mail*, 27 March 2002, sec. B, pp. 1, 8; also Deirdre McMurdy, "At The Top Of His Game," *Canadian Business* (March 4, 2002): 29–30.

Chapter 10

Human Resource Strategy at Signicast Summarized from Ben Nagler, "Recasting Employees Into Teams," *Workforce* (January, 1998): 101–106. **Figure 10.4** www.hrnext.com (accessed July 28, 2001). **Figure 10.6** Application for employment from the Ontario Human Rights Commission, *Employment Application Forms, Interviews* (1992). © Queen's Printer for Ontario, 1997. Reproduced with permission. **Figure 10.7** Courtesy of NYT Permissions. **The People Side of Managing** Celene Adams, "Interview Style Probes Past to Predict Future," *The Globe and Mail*, 29 April 2002, sec. B, p. 16. **Figure 10.10** *UCSD* Healthcare. Used with permission. **The Challenge of Change** Mary Gooderham, "Oil Firm Looks for Clear Path in Leadership Jungle," *The Globe and Mail*, 17 August 1999, sec. B, p. 9; also www.pcp.ca. **Figure 10.12** *Human Resource Management* 7th ed., by Gary Dessler, © Reprinted by permission of Pearson Education, Inc., Upper Saddle River, NJ. **Case Study 10-1** Interview with Ray Sherwood, Chief Financial Officer of Frantic Films, July 15, 2003; Grant Buckler,

"In Tough Times, Contractors Can Fill Key Gaps," *The Globe and Mail*, May 22, 2003, p. B17; Mark Brender, "Free Isn't Easy," *The Globe and Mail*, August 9, 1994, p. B18; Merle MacIsaac, "New Broom Sweeps Schools," *The Globe and Mail*, March 22, 1994, p. B22; Margot Gibb-Clark, "Temps Take on New Tasks," *The Globe and Mail*, December 22, 1993, p. B1; Sally Ritchie, "Rent-A-Manager," *The Globe and Mail*, August 17, 1993, p. B22; Robert Williamson, "Tradition Gives Way to World of Freelancers," *The Globe and Mail*, January 15, 1993, pp. B1, B4.

Chapter 11

Leadership at WestJet Summarized from Caroline Alphonso, "Street Expects Soaring WestJet to Fly Higher," *The Globe and Mail*, 15 March 2002, sec. B, p. 9; also Peter Verburg, "Prepare for Takeoff," *Canadian Business* (December 25, 2000): 95–99. **Table 11.1** Based on Ralph Stogdill, *Handbook of Leadership: A Survey of the Literature* (New York: Free Press, 1974), 237. **Figure 11.1** Gary A. Yukl, *Leadership in Organizations*, 3rd ed. (Upper Saddle River, NJ: Prentice Hall, 1994), 123. **The Challenge of Change** Summarized from Andrew Nikiforuk, "Saint or Sinner?," *Canadian Business* (May 13, 2002): 55–59. **The People Side of Managing** Summarized from Marc Knez and Duncan Simester, "Making Across-the-Board Incentives Work," *Harvard Business Review* (February 2002): 16, 17. **Figure 11.2** Jim Collins, "Level 5 Leadership," *Harvard Business Review* (January 2001): 73. **Figure 11.3** Daniel Goleman, "Leadership that Gets Results," *Harvard Business Review* (March–April 2000): 82–83. **Figure 11.4** Fred E. Fiedler, *A Theory of Leadership Effectiveness* (New York: McGraw Hill, 1967), 41. **Figure 11.5** Adapted and reprinted by permission of the *Harvard Business Review*. "How the Style of Effective Leadership Varies with the Situation" from "Engineer the Job to Fit the Manager" by Fred E. Fiedler, September–October 1965. Copyright © 1965 by the President and Fellows of Harvard College; all rights reserved. **Table 11.3** Adapted from Jon Howell and Dan Costley, *Understanding Behavior for Effective Leadership* (Upper Saddle River, NJ: Prentice Hall, 2001): 43. **Table 11.4** Based on Steve Kerr and J. M. Jermier "Substitutes for Leadership: Their Meaning and Measurement," *Organizational Behavior and Human Performance* 22 (1978); as printed in Gary Yukl, *Leadership in Organizations* (Upper Saddle River, NJ: Prentice Hall, 1998): 274. **Figure 11.7** Adapted from *Leadership and Decisionmaking* by Victor H. Vroom and Philip W. Yetton, by permission of the University of Pittsburgh Press. Copyright © 1973 by University of Pittsburgh Press. **Figure 11.8** Jerald Greenberg, *Managing Behaviour in Organizations: Science in Service* (Upper Saddle River, NJ: Prentice Hall, 1996). Reprinted by permission. **Figure 11.9** Adapted from Paul Hersey, *Situational Selling* (Escondido, CA: Center for Leadership Studies, 1985), 19. Reprinted with permission. **Figure 11.10** Adapted from Jeffrey A. McNally, Stephen J. Gerra, and R. Craig Bollis, Teaching Leadership at the U.S. Military Academy at West Point," *Journal of Applied Behavioral Science* 32, no. 2, p. 178. Copyright © 1996 by Sage Publications. Reprinted by permission of Sage Publications. **Case Study 11-1** Summarized from Jeff Sallot, "Boyle Leaves Defence Post," *The Globe and Mail*, 9 October 1996, sec. A, pp. 1, 5; also Paul Koring, "General's Ejection Inevitable," *The Globe and Mail*, 9 October 1996, sec. A, p. 4; also "Former Military Leaders Criticize Boyle," *The Globe and Mail*, 23 September 1996, sec. A, p. 5; also Murray Campbell, "Boyle

Entwined in 'Ethical Malaise,'" *The Globe and Mail*, 16 September 1996, sec. A, p. 8; also Paul Koring, "Collenette's Praise for General Draws Fire," *The Globe and Mail*, 29 August 1996, sec. A, pp. 1, 3; also Paul Koring, "Boyle Blames his Subordinates," *The Globe and Mail*, 21 August 1996, sec. A, pp. 1, 4; also Paul Koring, "Boyle Admits Breaking 'Spirit' of Law," *The Globe and Mail*, 15 August 1996, sec. A, pp. 1, 4; also Paul Koring, "Boyle Gets Rough Ride at Inquiry," *The Globe and Mail*, 14 August 1996, sec. A, pp.1, 4; also Paul Koring, "Boyle Breaks Somalia Silence," *The Globe and Mail*, 13 August 1996, sec. A, pp. 1, 3.

Chapter 12

Motivation at Maple Leaf Sports & Entertainment Summarized from Virginia Galt, "Maple Leaf Sports Psyches Up Staff," *The Globe and Mail*, 29 July 2002, sec. B, p. 9. **Figure 12.2** Adapted from Gregory Northcraft and Margaret Neale, *Organizational Behavior* (Fort Worth, TX: The Dryden Press, 1994), 87. **Figure 12.6** Adapted from Frederick Herzberg, "One More Time: How Do You Motivate Employees," *Harvard Business Review* (January–February 1968). **Figure 12.7** *Organizational Psychology: An Experiential Approach* by Kolb/Rubin/McIntyre, © 1971, reprinted by permission of Pearson Education, Inc., Upper Saddle River, NJ. **Table 12.1** Copyright © 1997 by Gary Dessler, Ph. D. **The People Side of Managing** Summarized from Sarah Braley, "Getting Technical: The Incentive Business Gets Wired Slowly," *Meetings and Conventions* (October, 1997), 43; also Bruce McDougall," Perks with Pizzazz," *Canadian Business* (June, 1990): 78–79; also Don Champion, "Quality—A Way of Life at BC Tel," *Candian Business Review* (Spring, 1990): 33; also Margot Gibb-Clark, "Companies Find Merit in Using Pay as a Carrot," *The Globe and Mail*, 10 August 1990, sec. B, p. 5; also Peter Matthews, "Just Rewards—The Lure of Pay for Performance," *Canadian Business* (February, 1990): 78–79; also Bud Jorgensen, "Do Bonuses Unscrupulous Brokers Make?", *The Globe and Mail,* 28 May 1990, sec. B, p. 5; also David Evans, "The Myth of Customer Service," *Canadian Business* (March, 1991): 34–39; also Ian Allaby, "Just Rewards," *Canadian Business* (May 1990): 39; also Wayne Gooding, "Ownership Is the Best Motivator," *Canadian Business* (March 1990): 6; also Neal Templin, "Ford Giving Every Worker a Purpose," *The Globe and Mail,* 28 December 1992, sec. B, p. 6. **Figure 12.9** Several items under the job-and career-related category are from Dean R. Spitzer, "Power Rewards: Rewards that Really Motivate," *Management Review* (May 1996): 48. **Table 12.2** A. I. LeDue, Jr., *Motivation of Programmers* (1980) **Figure 12.11** Lawrence Miller, *Behavior Management: The New Science of Managing People at Work* (New York: John Wiley, 1978), 18. **Table 12.3** David A. Whetton and Kim S. Cameron, *Developing Management Skills* (Upper Saddle River, NJ: Prentice Hall, 2002), 426–427. **Figure 12.12** Theodore T. Herbert, *Organizational Behavior: Readings and Cases* (New York: MacMillan Publishing Co., Inc., 1976), 344–345. **Figure 12.13** Reprinted with permission from *Saturn Work Team Functions*, a training document. **Figure 12.14** Copyright Gary Dessler, PhD. Suggested in part by "Performance Diagnosis Model," Devid Whetton and Kim Cameron, *Developing Management Skills* (Upper Saddle River, NJ: Prentice Hall, 2001), 339. **Case Study 12-2** Anne Howland, "There's No Place Like Work," *CGA Magazine* (July–August 2000): 21–25.

Chapter 13

Store Walking at Home Depot Summarized from Paul McDougall, "Collaborative Business," *Information Week,* no. 36 (May 7, 2001): 42–86; also Arthur Blank, "They Sweat the Small Stuff," *Canadian Business* (May 28, 1999): 51–55. **Figure 13.1** © Garry Dessler, Ph. D. **Table 13.1** Adapted from Arthur H. Bell and Dayle M. Smith, *Management Communication* (New York: Wiley, 1999), 14. **Checklist 13.1** Adapted from Paula J. Caprioni, *The Practical Coach: Management Skills for Everyday Life* (Upper Saddle River, NJ: Prentice Hall, 2001): 86. **Figure 13.2** Adapted from Paula J. Caproni, *The Practical Coach* (Upper Saddle River, NJ: Prentice Hall, 2001), 21. **Figure 13.3** *Business Plan Pro*, Palo Alto Software, Palo Alto, CA. **The People Side of Managing** Harold Leavitt, "Some Effects of Certain Communication Patterns on Group Performance," *Journal of Abnormal and Social Psychology* 46 (1972): 38–50. **Figure 13.5** Adapted from Richard L. Daft and Robert H. Lengel, "Information Richness: A New Approach to Managerial Information Processing and Organization Design," in Barry Staw and Larry L. Cummings, eds, *Research in Organizational Behaviour*, Vol. 6 (Greenwich, CT: JAI Press, 1984), 191–233. Reprinted from R. Daft and R. Steers, *Organizations: A Micro/Macro Approach* (Glenview, IL: Scott, Foresman, 1986), 532. **Table 13.2** Adapted from Jennifer Salopek, "Digital Collaboration," *Training and Development* 54, no. 6 (June 2000): 38. **The Challenge of Change** Summarized from Kenneth Laudon and Jane Laudon, *Management Information Systems* (Upper Saddle River, NJ: Prentice Hall, 1998), 128. **Case Study 13-2** Frederick A. Starke and Robert W. Sexty, *Contemporary Management*, 3rd ed. (Scarborough: Prentice Hall Canada, 1998), 532–533.

Chapter 14

Teams, Teams, Teams C. McLean, "Reinventing a Clean, Lean Manufacturing Machine: Willow Pulls Together as a Team to Survive in the Competitive Metal Working Industry," *Plant* (September 27, 1999): 13; also Bruce Little, "How to Make a Small, Smart Factory," *The Globe and Mail,* 2 February 1993, sec. B, p. 24; also K. Rude, "Retrofitting a Community of Spaces: When Steelcase Canada Moved Its Toronto-Area Operations Under One Roof, Quadrangle Architects Provided a Renovated Facility in Markham that Showcases the Latest Workplace Strategies," *Canadian Interiors* (January/February, 2001): 42–45; also S. Ellison, "Ad Firm Strawberry Frog in Amsterdam Thinks Big But Wants to Stay Small," *Wall Street Journal*, 3 April 2000, p. A43D. **Figure 14.1** Adapted from Jack Osborn et al., *Self-Directed Work Teams* (Homewood, IL: Business One Irwin, 1990), 30. **The Challenge of Change** Summarized from Michael Selz, "Testing Self-Managing Teams, Entrepreneur Hopes to Lose Job," *Wall Street Journal*, 11 January 1994, sec. B, p. 1; also Sally Goll Beatty, "Standard & Poors Acquires Published Image, Inc. "*Wall Street Journal*, 2 July 1997, sec. B, p. 7. **Figure 14.2** Adapted from Steven Rayner, "Team Traps: What They Are, How to Avoid Them," *National Productivity Review* (Summer 1996): 107. Reprinted by permission of John Wiley & Sons, Inc. **Figure 14.3** Adapted from J. A. Wagner III, "Studies of Individualism–Collectivism: Effects on Cooperation in Groups," *Academy of Management Journal* (February, 1995): 162. **The People Side of Managing** Summarized from "Under the Big Top," *Harvard Business Review* (September–October 1999):

17. **Figure 14.4** Adapted from James H. Shonk, *Team-Based Organizations* (Homewood, IL: Irwin, 1997), 36. **Figure 14.5** Ruth Wageman, *Organizational Dynamics* (Summer 1997): 49–61.

Chapter 15

Changing Nissan's Fortunes Summarized from Carlos Ghosn, "Saving the Business Without Losing the Company," *Harvard Business Review* (January 2002): 40–41. **Figure 15.1** Adapted from Carlos Ghosn, "Saving the Business Without Losing the Company," *Harvard Business Review* (January 2002): 40–41. **Figure 15.2** Adapted from Larry Short, "Planned Organizational Change," *MSU Business Topics* (Autumn 1973): 53–61; ed. Theodore Herbert, *Organizational Behavior: Readings and Cases* (New York: McMillan, 1976), 351. **The Challenge of Change** Summarized from Debbie Howell, "The Super Growth Leaders—The Home Depot: Diversification Builds Bridge to the Future," *DSN Retailing Today* 40, no. 23 (December 10, 2001): 17–18. **Figure 15.3** Adapted from Michael Goold and Andrew Campbell, "Do You Have a Well-Designed Organization?" *Harvard Business Review* (March 2002): 124. **Checklist 15.1** Philip Hunsaker, *Training in Management Skills* (Upper Saddle River, NJ: Prentice Hall, 2001), 323. **Figure 15.4** Robert Kegan and Lisa Lahey, "The Real Reason People Won't Change," *Harvard Business Review* (November 2001): 89. **Figure 15.5** Kurt Lewin, "Frontiers in Group Dynamics," *Human Relations* 1 (1947), Plenum Publishing Corporation. Used with permission. **Table 15.1** Reprinted by permission of *Harvard Business Review*, "Six Methods for Dealing with Change," from "Choosing Strategies for Change," by John P. Kotter and Leonard A. Schlesinger, March–April 1979. Copyright © 1979 by the Harvard Business School Publishing Corporation; all rights reserved. **Figure 15.6** Reprinted by permission of Harvard Business School Press. From John P. Kotter, *Leading Change* (Boston: 1996), 102. Copyright © 1996 by John P. Kotter; all rights reserved. **The People Side of Managing** Summarized from Wendell French and Cecil Bell, Jr., *Organization Development* (Upper Saddle River, NJ: Prentice Hall, 1995), 171–193. **Figure 15.7** Kenneth W. Thomas, "Organizational Conflict," ed., Steven Kerr, *Organizational Behavior* (Columbus, OH: Grid Publishing, 1979), in Andrew DuBrin, *Applying Psychology* (Upper Saddle River, NJ: Prentice Hall, 2000), 223. **Figure 15.8** Thomas J. Von de Embse, *Supervision: Managerial Skills for a New Era* (New York: MacMillen Publishing Company, 1987), in Stephen Robbins and Philip Hunsaker, *Training in Interpersonal Skills* (Upper Saddle River, NJ: Prentice Hall, 1996), 217–219. **Case Study 15-1** Summarized from Chuck Salter, "On the Road Again," *Fast Company* (January, 2002): 51–58. **Case Study 15-2** Frederick A. Starke and Robert W. Sexty, *Contemporary Management*, 3rd ed. (Scarborough: Prentice Hall Canada, 1998), 569.

Chapter 16

Accounting Fraud Summarized from Marcy Gordon, "Earnings Inflated $9 Billion; WorldCom Charges Grow," *The Winnipeg Free Press*, 6 November 2002, sec. B, p. 3; also Richard Blackwell, "Auditing Firms Get Tighter Rules," *The Globe and Mail,* 18 July 2002, sec. B, pp. 1, 4; also John Christoffersen, "Xerox Overstated Revenue by Billions of Dollars," *The Winnipeg Free Press*, 29 June 2002, sec. B, p. 3; also John Partridge and Karen Howlett, "CIBC Restricts Its Auditors," *The Globe and Mail,* 1 March 2002, sec. B, pp. 1, 4; also Lily Nguyen, "Accountants Primed For Change," *The Globe and Mail,* 4 February 2002, sec. B, p. 9; also Barrie McKenna, "Enron Disclosure Corrodes Andersen Credibility," *The Globe and Mail,* 15 January 2002, sec., B, pp. 1, 4; also Richard Blackwell, "Accountants to Issue New Rules," *The Globe and Mail,* 28 March 2002, sec. B, pp. 1, 7; also "Andersen Set to Name Interim Worldwide CEO," *The Globe and Mail,* 28 March 2002, sec. B, p. 7. **Figure 16.1** © Gary Dessler, Ph. D. **The Challenge of Change** Summarized from Kristina Sullivan, "Boeing Achieves Internet Liftoff," *PC Week* (May 10, 1999): 67. **Figure 16.8** Courtesy of Johnson & Johnson. **The People Side of Managing** Summarized from Michael J. McCarthy, "You Assumed 'Erase' Wiped Out That Rant Against the Boss? Nope," *The Wall Street Journal*, 7 March 2000, sec. A, pp. 1, 16; G. Bylinsky, "How Companies Spy on Employees," *Fortune* (November 4, 1991): 131–140.

Endnotes

Chapter 1

1. www.dofasco.ca/news (November, 1999).

2. David Kirkpatrick, "IBM: from Blue Dinosaur to E-Business Animal," *Fortune* (April 26, 1999): 119–125.

3. Joan Magretta, "The Power of Virtual Integration: An Interview with Dell Computer's Michael Dell," *Harvard Business Review* (March–April 1998): 73–84.

4. G. Hanson, "Determinants of Firm Performance: An Integration of Economic and Organizational Factors," (Ph.D diss., University of Michigan Business School, 1986).

5. M. A. Huselid, "The Impact of Human Resource Management Practices on Turnover, Productivity, and Corporate Financial Performance," *Academy of Management Journal* (1995): 647; J. Pfeffer and J. Vega, "Putting People First for Organizational Success," *Academy of Management Executive* 13 (1999): 37–48.

6. Peter Drucker, *An Introductory View of Management* (New York: Harper's College Press, 1977), 15.

7. Christina Cheddar, "Boardroom That Move to Power Technology—Sector Has Shed Founders Who Thrived in Labs as Skill Needs Change," *The Wall Street Journal*, 11 September 2001, sec. B, p. 8.

8. Susan Carey, "Costly Race in the Sky," *The Wall Street Journal*, 9 September 2002, sec. B, pp. 1, 3.

9. Henry Mintzberg, "The Manager's Job: Folklore and Fact," *Harvard Business Review* (July–August 1975): 489–561.

10. Liz Simpson, "Fostering Creativity," *Training* 38, no. 12 (December 2001): 54–57.

11. Sumatra Ghoshal and Christopher Bartlett, "Changing the Role of Top Management: Beyond Structure to Processes," *Harvard Business Review* (January–February 1995): 86–96.

12. Sumatra Ghoshal and Christopher Bartlett, "Changing the Role of Top Management: Beyond Structure to Processes," *Harvard Business Review* (January–February 1995): 88.

13. Sumatra Ghoshal and Christopher Bartlett, "Changing the Role of Top Management: Beyond Structure to Processes," *Harvard Business Review* (January–February 1995): 91.

14. Sumatra Ghoshal and Christopher Bartlett, "Changing the Role of Top Management: Beyond Structure to Processes," *Harvard Business Review* (January–February 1995): 96.

15. Sumatra Ghoshal and Christopher Bartlett, "Changing the Role of Top Management: Beyond Structure to Processes," *Harvard Business Review* (January–February 1995): 94.

16. Peter Wilson, "Canadian Execs Don't See the Value of the Internet," *The Vancouver Sun*, 7 October 1999, sec. E, p. E4.

17. Henry Mintzberg, "The Manager's Job: Folklore and Fact," *Harvard Business Review* (July–August 1975): 489–561.

18. See, for example, Henry Mintzberg, "The Manager's Job: Folklore and Fact," *Harvard Business Review* (July–August 1975),; George Copeman, *The Chief Executive* (London: Leviathan House, 1971), 271. See also George Weathersby, "Facing Today's Sea Changes," *Management Review* (June 1999): 5; David Kirkpatrick, "The Second Coming of Apple," *Fortune* (November 9, 1998): 86–104; and Jenny McCune, "The Changemakers," *Management Review* (May 1999): 16–22.

19. John Holland, *Making Vocational Choices: A Theory of Careers* (Upper Saddle River, NJ: Prentice Hall, 1973); see also John Holland, *Assessment Booklet: A Guide to Educational and Career Planning* (Odessa, FL: Psychological Assessment Resources, Inc., 1990).

20. Edgar Schein, *Career Dynamics: Matching Individual and Organizational Needs* (Reading, MA: Addison-Wesley, 1978), 128–129.

21. A. Howard and D. W. Bray, *Managerial Lives in Transition: Advancing Age and Changing Times* (New York: Guilford, 1988), discussed in Dwayne Schultz and Sydney Ellen Schultz, *Psychology and Work Today* (New York: Macmillan Publishing Co., 1994), 103–104.

22. Dwayne Schultz and Sydney Ellen Schultz, *Psychology and Work Today* (New York: Macmillan Publishing Co., 1994), 104.

23. Dwayne Schultz and Sydney Ellen Schultz, *Psychology and Work Today* (New York: Macmillan Publishing Co., 1994), 104.

24. Unless otherwise noted, the following is based on Gary Yukl, *Leadership in Organizations* (Upper Saddle River, NJ: Prentice Hall, 1998), 251–255.

25. Bruce Orwall, "Why Disney CEO Can Be Found in the Trenches," *The Wall Street Journal*, 7 November 2001, sec. B, pp. 1, 4.

26. Gary Yukl, *Leadership in Organizations* (Upper Saddle River, NJ: Prentice Hall, 1998), 252.

27. Joan Lloyd, "Derailing Your Career," *Baltimore Business Journal* 19 (October 19, 2000): 21, 33.

28. Phillip Crowley, "The Executive View," *The Globe and Mail*, 27 October 1999, sec. E, p. 2.

29. Shelley Kirkpatrick and Edwin Locke, "Leadership: The Traits Matter?" *Academy of Management Executive* (May 1991): 49.

30. Gary Yukl, *Leadership in Organizations* (Upper Saddle River, NJ: Prentice Hall, 1998), 253.

31. Quoted in William Holstein, "Why Big Ideas Often Fall Flat," *The New York Times*, 26 May 2002, sec. BU, p. 5, see also Judith Chapman, "The Work of Managers in New Organizational Context," *Journal of Management Development* 20, no. 1 (January 2001): 55.

32. Address by Al Flood, www.cibc.com, October 8, 1990.

33. Daniel Stoffman, "Poor Little Rich Bank," *Canadian Business* (May, 1996): 44–48, 65–70.

34. Richard Crawford, *In the Era of Human Capital* (New York: Harper, 1991), 10.

35. This discussion is based on Gary Dessler, *Management Fundamentals* (Reston, VA: Reston, 1977), 2; and William Berliner and William McClarney, *Management Practice and Training* (Burr Ridge, IL: McGraw-Hill, 1974), 11.

36. Rachel Moskowitz and Drew Warwick, "The 1994–2005 Job Outlook in Brief," *Occupational Outlook Quarterly* 40, no. 1 (Spring 1996): 2–41. See also Mahlon Apgar, IV, "The Alternative Workplace: Changing Where and How People Work," *Harvard Business Review* (May–June 1998): 121–136.

37. Richard Crawford, *In the Era of Human Capital* (New York: Harper, 1991), 26.

38. Peter Drucker, "The Coming of the New Organization," *Harvard Business Review* (January–February 1988): 45. See also Richard Cappelli, "Rethinking the Nature of Work: A Look at the Research Evidence," *Compensation & Benefits Review* (July/August 1997): 50–59.

39. Geoffrey York, "Russian Miner Sees Privatization Payoff," *The Globe and Mail*, 23 July 2001, sec. B, pp. 1, 4.

40. Lily Nguyen and Dave Ebner, "Do Privatizations Mean Big Payoff?" *The Globe and Mail*, 14 December 2001, sec. B, pp. 1, 4.

41. "Mac Attack Goes Global in Battle for Burgers," *The Globe and Mail*, 5 July 1996, sec. B, p. 4.

42. Dianne Cyr, "Organizational Transformation at Skoda in the Czech Republic: An HRM Perspective," in *Readings and Cases in International Human Resource Management*, 3rd ed., eds. M. Mendenhall and G. Oddou (Mason, OH: South-Western College Publishing, 2000), 379–393.

43. Dianne Cyr, "Organizational Transformation at Skoda in the Czech Republic: An HRM Perspective," In M. Mendenhall and G. Oddou (eds.), *Readings and Cases in International Human Resource Management*, 3rd ed. (Mason, OH: South-Western College Publishing, 2000), 379–393.

44. www.nortelnetworks.com.

45. www.bombardier.com.

46. Gerald Ferris, Dwight Frank, and M. Carmen Galang, "Diversity in the Workplace: The Human Resources Management Challenge," *Human Resource Planning* 16, no. 1, pp. 41–51.

47. Thomas Peters and Robert Waterman, Jr., "In Search of Excellence," in *The Manager's Bookshelf*, 5th ed., Jon Pierce and John Newstrom (Upper Saddle River, NJ: Prentice Hall, 2000), 45.

48. Rosabeth Moss Kantor, *When Giants Learn to Dance* (New York: Touchstone, 1989).

49. James Brian Quinn, *Intelligent Enterprises* (New York: The Free Press, 1992).

50. Peter Senge, *The Fifth Discipline* (New York: Currency Doubleday, 1994), 3.

51. Bryan Dumaine, "What the Leaders of Tomorrow See," *Fortune* (July 3, 1989): 58. See also George Weathersby, "Facing Today's Sea Changes," *Management Review* (June 1999): 5. See also Gary Hamel and Jeff Sampler, "The eCorp: Building a New Industrial," *Fortune* (December 7, 1998): 80–112.

52. Tom Peters, *Liberation Management* (New York: Alfred Knopf, 1992), 9.

53. These are based on Walter Kiechel III, "How We Will Work in the Year 2000," *Fortune* (May 17, 1993): 79.

54. Karl Albrecht, *At America's Service: How Corporations Can Revolutionize the Way They Treat Their Customers* (Homewood, IL: Dow-Jones Irwin, 1998).

55. Bryan Dumaine, "What the Leaders of Tomorrow See," *Fortune* (July 3, 1989): 51.

56. Rosabeth Moss Kanter, "The New Managerial Work," *Harvard Business Review* (November–December 1989): 88.

57. Rosabeth Moss Kanter, "The New Managerial Work," *Harvard Business Review* (November–December 1989): 88.

58. Peter Drucker, "The Coming of the New Organization," *Harvard Business Review* (January–February 1988): 45.

59. Tom Peters, *Liberation Management* (New York: Alfred Knopf, 1992).

60. Bryan Dumaine, "The New Non-Managers," *Fortune* (February 22, 1993): 81. See also David Kirkpatrick, "IBM: From Big Blue Dinosaur to e–Business Animal," *Fortune* (April 26, 1999): 116–127. See also Jenny McCune, "The Changemakers," *Management Review* (May 1999): 16–22. See also Brent Schlender, "Larry Ellison: Oracle at Web Speed," *Fortune* (May 24, 1999): 128–137.

61. Peter Drucker, "The Coming of the New Organization," *Harvard Business Review* (January–February 1988): 43.

62. Stratford Sherman, "A Master Class in Radical Change," *Fortune* (December 13, 1993): 82. See also Jenny McCune, "The Changemakers," *Management Review* (May 1999): 16–22.

63. Eryn Brown, "Nine Ways to Win on the Web," *Fortune* (May 24, 1999): 125.

64. Eryn Brown, "Nine Ways to Win on the Web," *Fortune* (May 24, 1999): 125.

65. Mary Janigan, "Going E-Postal," *Maclean's* (September 13, 1999): 34–36.

66. Carlta Vitzthum, "Just in Time Fashion," *The Wall Street Journal*, 18 May 2001, sec. B, p. 1.

67. Joan Magretta, "The Power of a Virtual Integration: An Interview with Dell Computers Michael Dell," *Harvard Business Review* (March–April 1998): 73–84.

68. Joan Magretta, "The Power of a Virtual Integration: An Interview with Dell Computers Michael Dell," *Harvard Business Review* (March–April 1998): 74.

69. Joan Magretta, "The Power of a Virtual Integration: An Interview with Dell Computers Michael Dell," *Harvard Business Review* (March–April 1998): 82.

70. Joan Magretta, "The Power of a Virtual Integration: An Interview with Dell Computers Michael Dell," *Harvard Business Review* (March–April 1998): 82.

71. Joan Magretta, "The Power of a Virtual Integration: An Interview with Dell Computers Michael Dell," *Harvard Business Review* (March–April 1998): 76.

72. Joan Magretta, "The Power of a Virtual Integration: An Interview with Dell Computers Michael Dell," *Harvard Business Review* (March–April 1998): 75.

73. "JetBlue," *Fortune* (Small Business, 1 March 2001, p. 92; "Fort Lauderdale, Florida-Based Discount Airlines Survives Turbulence," *Knight Ridder/Tribune*, 11 March 2001, item 01070000; Harvey Mackay, "Customer Service from the Ground up Really Flies," *Tampa Bay Business Journal* (November 23, 2001): 36; "JetBlue Scores Top Awards for Onboard Service," JetBlue press release, 23 January 2002; Bill Saporito, "Lessons Learned: Air Travel," *Time* (December 31, 2001): 128–129; Catherine Yung, "Collapse of Two Start Up Carriers Puts Focus on Frontier, JetBlue Airlines," *Knight Ridder/Tribune* News, 24 December 2000, item 003 6 000 a.

74. Catherine Yung, "Collapse of Two Start Up Carriers Puts Focus on Frontier, JetBlue Airlines," *Knight Ridder/Tribune* News, 24 December 2000, item 003 6 000 a.

Chapter 1 Appendix

1. Alvin Toeffler, *Future Shock* (New York: Bantam Books, 1971), 43.

2. Adam Smith, *An Inquiry into the Nature and Causes of Wealth of Nations*, 4th ed., ed. Edward Cannan (London: Methuen, 1925). Published originally in 1776.

3. Alfred Chandler, *Strategy and Structure* (Cambridge, MA: MIT Press, 1990); see also Daniel Wren, *The Evolution of Management Thought* (New York: John Wiley, 1979).

4. D.S. Pugh, *Organization Theory* (Baltimore: Penguin, 1971), 126–127.

5. Claude George, Jr., *The History of Management Thought* (Upper Saddle River, NJ: Prentice Hall, 1972), 99–101.

6. Richard Hopeman, *Production* (Columbus, OH: Charles Merrill, 1965), 478–485.

7. Henri Fayol, *General and Industrial Management*, trans. Constance Storrs (London: Sir Isaac Pitman, 1949), 42–43.

8. Based on Richard Hall, "Intra–Organizational Structural Variation: Application of the Bureaucratic Model," *Administrative Science Quarterly* 7, no. 3 (December 1962): 295–308.

9. William Scott, *Organization Theory* (Homewood, IL: Richard D. Irwin, 1967).

10. F.L. Roethlisberger and William Dickson, *Management and Worker* (Boston: Graduate School of Business, Harvard University, 1947), 21.

11. Alfred Chandler, *Strategy and Structure* (Cambridge, MA: MIT Press, 1990), 19–51.

12. Warren G. Bennis, "Organizational Development and the Fate of Bureaucracy." Address at the Division of Industrial and Business Psychology, American Psychological Association, September 5, 1964. Reprinted in L.L. Cummings and W.E. Scott, Jr., *Organizational Behavior and Human Performance* (Homewood, IL: Richard D. Irwin and Dorsey, 1969), 436.

13. Douglas McGregor, "The Human Side of Enterprise," in *Readings in Industrial and Organizational Psychology*, eds.

Edward Deci, B. Von Haller Gilmer, and Harry Kairn (New York: McGraw-Hill, 1972), 123.

14. Rensis Likert, *New Patterns of Management* (New York: McGraw-Hill, 1961), 6.

15. Rensis Likert, *New Patterns of Management* (New York: McGraw-Hill, 1961), 103.

16. Chris Argyris, *Integrating the Individual and the Organization* (New York: John Wiley, 1964).

17. Rensis Likert, *New Patterns of Management* (New York: McGraw-Hill, 1961), 91.

18. Rensis Likert, *New Patterns of Management* (New York: McGraw-Hill, 1961), 100.

19. Rensis Likert, *New Patterns of Management* (New York: McGraw-Hill, 1961), 100.

20. Rensis Likert, *New Patterns of Management* (New York: McGraw-Hill, 1961), 100.

21. Chester Barnard, *The Functions of the Executive* (Cambridge: Harvard University Press, 1968), 84.

22. Chester Barnard, *The Functions of the Executive* (Cambridge: Harvard University Press, 1968), 167.

23. Chester Barnard, *The Functions of the Executive* (Cambridge: Harvard University Press, 1968), 143.

24. Herbert A. Simon, *Administrative Behavior* (New York: Free Press, 1976), 11.

25. C. West Churchman, Russell Ackoff, and E. Linard Arnoff, *Introduction to Operations Research* (New York: John Wiley, 1957), 18.

26. Daniel Wren, *The Evolution of Management Thought* (New York: John Wiley, 1979), 512.

27. C. West Churchman, *The Systems Approach* (New York: Delta, 1968).

28. Peter Frost and Carolyn Egri, "The Political Process of Innovation," in L.L. Cummings and B.M. Staw (eds.), *Research in Organizational Behavior*, Vol. 13 (1991), 229–295.

29. John Usher, "Exploring the Effects of Niche Crowding on Rates of Organizational Change and Failure," Working Paper, Memorial University of Newfoundland.

30. Bruno Dyck, "Build in Sustainable Development and they Will Come: A Vegetable Field of Dreams," *Journal of Organizational Change Management* 7, no. 4 (1994): 47–63.

Chapter 2

1. "High-Tech Sector Discovers the Wonders of Rural Newfoundland," *The Financial Post*, 30 September 1999, sec C, p. 5.

2. *Corporations and Labour Unions Returns Act, Part I—Corporations*, Ottawa: Statistics Canada Catalogue Number 61–210 and 61–220.

3. Heather Scoffield, "Canada Rates Last in Survey of G7 Countries," *The Globe and Mail*, 1 August 2001, sec. B, pp. 1, 4.

4. Harvey Enchin, "Canada Urged to Stop Living off Fat of the Land," *The Globe and Mail*, 25 October 1991, sec. B, pp. 1, 6.

5. Dianne Cyr, *The Human Resource Challenge of International Joint Ventures* (Westport, CT: Quorum Books, 1995).

6. Arnaldo Camuffo et al., "Back to the Future: Benetton Transforms Its Global Network," *MIT Sloan Management Review* 43, no. 1 (Fall 2001): 46–52.

7. Charles Hill, *International Business* (Bun Ridge, IL: Irwin, 1994), 4; Dawn Anfuso, "Colgate's Global HR United Under One Strategy," *Personnel Journal* (October 1995): 44ff; See also Marlene Piturro, "What Are You Doing About the New Global Realities?" *Management Review* (March 1999): 16–22; and Maureen Minehan, "Changing Conditions in Emerging Markets," *HR Magazine* (January 1998): 160.

8. For a discussion see Arvind Phatak, *International Dimensions of Management* (Boston: PWS-Kent, 1989), 2.

9. Theodore Levitt, "The Globalization of Markets," *Harvard Business Review* (May–June 1983): 92–102; For an example see Thomas Stewart, "See Jack. See Jack Run Europe," *Fortune* (September 27, 1999): 124–127.

10. Frederick A. Starke and Robert Sexty, *Contemporary Management in Canada*, 3rd ed. (Scarborough, Ontario: Prentice Hall, 1998), 150; also www.labatt.com.

11. Ted Rakstis, "Going Global," *Kiwanis Magazine* (October 1981), 39–43.

12. www.eicon.com.

13. Barrie McKenna, "Canada Jumps in Ranking on Globalization," *The Globe and Mail*, 10 January 2002, sec. B, p. 8.

14. Charles Hill, *International Business* (Bun Ridge, IL: Irwin, 1994), 402.

15. Art Garcia, "It's in the Mail," *World Trade* (April 1992): 56–62.

16. See, for example, John Daniels and Lee Radebaugh, *International Business* (Reading, MA: Addison-Wesley, 1994), 544.

17. "In Hot Pursuit of International Markets," *Innovation* (Summer 1990): 11–13.

18. David Jordan, "Creo Battles Asian Partner," *Business in Vancouver* (September 28–October 4, 1999): 1, 8, 9.

19. Michael Czinkota, Pietra Rivoli, and Ilka Ronkinen, *International Business* (Fort Worth: The Dryden Press, 1992), 278.

20. Katherine Rudie Harrigan, "Joint Ventures and Global Strategies," *Columbia Journal of World Business* (Summer 1984): 7–16; Michael Czinkota, Pietra Rivoli, and Ilka Ronkinen, *International Business* (Fort Worth: The Dryden Press, 1992), 320.

21. Saritha Rai, "India Company Reaches Deal with AOL for Programming," *The New York Times*, 14 December 2001, p. 1.

22. Wilfred Vanhonacker, "Entering China: An Unconventional Approach," *Harvard Business Review* (March–April 1997): 130–140.

23. Charles Hill, *International Business* (Bun Ridge, IL: Irwin, 1994), 411.

24. Barry James, "Air France and Delta Pave the Way for the Third Alliance," *International Herald Tribune*, 23 June 1999, p. 1.

25. Gregory White, "In Asia, GM Pins Hope on a Delicate Web of Alliances," *The Wall Street Journal*, 23 October 2001, sec. A, p. 23.

26. Aaron Lucchetti, "Pioneer Group Blazes Trail After Purchase by Milan Bank," *The Wall Street Journal*, 9 July 2001, sec. R, p. 1.

27. Robert Neff, "Guess Who's Selling Barbies in Japan Now?" *Business Week* (December 1991): 72, 74, 76; See also Jeffrey Garten, "Troubles Ahead in Emerging Markets," *Harvard Business Review* (May–June 1997): 38–50 and Yagang Pan and Peter Chi, "Financial Performance and Survival of Multinational Corporations in China," *Strategic Management Journal* (April 1999): 359.

28. Note that there are few, if any, "pure" market economies or command economies anymore. For example, much of the French banking system is still under government control. And it was only several years ago that the government of England privatized (sold to private investors) British Airways.

29. "Countries with Highest Gross Domestic Product and Per-Capita GDP," *The World Almanac and Book of Facts*, 1998 (Mahwah, NJ: K-III Reference Corporation, 1997), 112.

30. David Kemme, "The World Economic Outlook for 1999," *Business Perspectives* (January 1999): 6–9.

31. John Daniels and Lee Radebaugh, *International Business* (Reading, MA: Addison-Wesley, 1994), 138.

32. Michael Czinkota, Pietra Rivoli, and Ilka Ronkinen, *International Business* (Fort Worth: The Dryden Press, 1992), 640.

33. For a discussion see, for example, Michael Czinkota, Pietra Rivoli, and Ilka Ronkinen, *International Business* (Fort Worth: The Dryden Press, 1992), Chapter 2; James Flanigan, "Asian Crisis Could Bring New Threat: Protectionism," *Los Angeles Times*, 3 February 1999, p. N1.

34. Michael Czinkota, Pietra Rivoli, and Ilka Ronkinen, *International Business* (Fort Worth: The Dryden Press, 1992), 116.

35. John Daniels and Lee Radebaugh, *International Business* (Reading, MA: Addison-Wesley, 1994), 409.

36. Molly O'Meara, "Riding the Dragon," *World Watch* (March/April 1997): 8–18.

37. This is based on John Daniels and Lee Radebaugh, *International Business* (Upper Saddle River, NJ: Prentice Hall, 2001), 217–219.

38. John Daniels and Lee Radebaugh, *International Business* (Upper Saddle River, NJ: Prentice Hall, 2001), 218.

39. Andrew Tanzer, "Chinese Walls," *Forbes* 168 (November 12, 2001): 74–75.

40. See, for example, Susan Lee, "Are We Building New Berlin Walls?" *Forbes* (January 1991): 86–89; Tom Reilly, "The Harmonization of Standards in the European Union and the Impact on U.S. Business," *Business Horizons* (March–April 1995).

41. Laura Pincus and James Belohlav, "Legal Issues in Multinational Business Strategy: To Play the Game, You Have to Know the Rules," *Academy of Management Executive* (November 1996): 52–61.

42. Laura Pincus and James Belohlav, "Legal Issues in Multinational Business Strategy: To Play the Game, You Have to Know the Rules," *Academy of Management Executive* (November 1996): 53–54.

43. Laura Pincus and James Belohlav, "Legal Issues in Multinational Business Strategy: To Play the Game, You Have to Know the Rules," *Academy of Management Executive* (November 1996): 53.

44. Richard Behar, "China's Phony War on Fakes," *Fortune* (October 30, 2000): 206; see also Derek Dessler, "China's Intellectual Property Protection: Prospects for Achieving International Standards," *Fordham International Law Journal* 181 (1995).

45. Steve Levine and Betsy McKay, "Coke Finds Mixing Marriage and Businesses Tricky in Tashkent," *The Wall Street Journal*, 21 August 2001, sec. A, p. 1.

46. Paul Waldie, "Manulife Indonesia Ruling Toppled," *The Globe and Mail*, 9 July 2002, sec. B, p. 5; also "Jakarta Wants Judges Fired Over Manulife," *The Globe and Mail*, 8 August 2002, sec. B, p. 9.

47. Catherine Tinsley, "Models of Conflict Resolution in Japanese, German, and American Cultures," *Journal of Applied Psychology* (April 1998): 316–322.

48. In John Tagliabue, "In the French Factory, Culture is a Two–Way Street," *The New York Times*, 25 February 2001, sec BU, p. 4.

49. Ken Belson, "As Starbucks Grows, Japan, Too, Is Awash," *The New York Times*, 21 October 2001, sec. BU, p. 5.

50. United Nations, *Draft International Code of Conduct on the Transfer of Technology* (New York: United Nations, 1981), 3; quoted in Michael Czinkota, Pietra Rivoli, and Ilka Ronkinen, *International Business* (Fort Worth: The Dryden Press, 1992), 313.

51. Michael Czinkota, Pietra Rivoli, and Ilka Ronkinen, *International Business* (Fort Worth: The Dryden Press, 1992), 314.

52. www.wal-mart.com/newsroom/firstquarter99.html.

53. Charles Hill, *International Business* (Bun Ridge, IL: Irwin, 1994), 5–6.

54. Gayle MacDonald, "Purdy's Test Asia's Sweet Tooth," *The Globe and Mail*, 9 June 1997, sec. B, p. 7.

55. Kenneth Laudon and Jane Laudon, *Management Information Systems* (Upper Saddle River, NJ: Prentice Hall 1998), 6; and Michael McGrath and Richard Hoole, "Manufacturing's New Economies of Scale," *Harvard Business Review* (May–June 1992): 94; See also Thomas Kochan and Russell Lansbury, "Lean Production and Changing Employment Relations in the International Auto Industry," *Economic and Industrial Democracy* (November 1997): 597–620; and John Sheridan, "Bridging the Enterprise," *Industry Week* (April 5, 1999): 17.

56. Michael McGrath and Richard Hoole, "Manufacturing's New Economies of Scale," *Harvard Business Review* (May–June 1992): 94–102.

57. Kenneth Laudon and Jane Laudon, *Management Information Systems* (Upper Saddle River, NJ: Prentice Hall 1998), 348.

58. Based on Brian O'Reilly, "Your New Global Workforce," *Fortune* (December 1992): 52–66, See also Charlene Solomon, "Don't Get Burned by Hot New Markets," *Global Workforce*, a supplement to *Workforce* (January 1998): 12.

59. David Woodruff, "Distractions Make Global Manager a Difficult Role," *The Wall Street Journal*, 21 November 2000, sec. B, p. 1.

60. David Woodruff, "Distractions Make Global Manager a Difficult Role," *The Wall Street Journal*, 21 November 2000, sec. B, p. 18.

61. David Woodruff, "Distractions Make Global Manager a Difficult Role," *The Wall Street Journal*, 21 November 2000, sec. B, p. 18.

62. Philip Harris and Robert Moran, *Managing Cultural Differences* (Houston: Gulf Publishing Company, 1979), 1.

63. Gail Dutton, "Building a Global Brain," *Management Review* (May 1999): 34–38.

64. Gail Dutton, "Building a Global Brain," *Management Review* (May 1999): 35.

65. Gretchen Spreitzer, Morgan McCall, Jr., and Joan Mahoney, "Early Identification of International Executive Potential," *Journal of Applied Psychology* (February 1997): 6–29.

66. Gary Anthes, "Think Globally, Act Locally," *ComputerWorld* 35, no. 22 (May 28, 2001): 36–37.

67. Kamal Fatehi, *International Management* (Upper Saddle River, NJ: Prentice Hall, 1996), 41.

68. Anant Negandhi, *International Management* (Newton, MA: Allyn & Bacon, Inc. (1987), 61. See also Keith W. Glaister and Peter J. Buckley, "Strategic Motives for International Alliance Formation," *Journal of Management Studies* (May 1996): 301–322.

69. Richard Tomlinson, "Who's Afraid of Wal-Mart?" *Fortune* (June 26, 2000): 196.

70. Richard Tomlinson, "Who's Afraid of Wal-Mart?" *Fortune* (June 26, 2000): 196.

71. Clifford Krause, "Selling to Argentina—as Translated by the French," *The New York Times*, 5 December 1999, sec. BU, p. 7.

72. See, for example, Wendy Zellner, et al., "How Well Does Wal-Mart Travel?" *Business Week* (September 3, 2001): 82–84.

73. Richard D. Robinson, *Internationalization of Business: An Introduction* (Hillsdale, IL: The Dryden Press, 1984), 227–228; See also "Organizing for Europe," *International Journal of Retail and Distribution Management* (Winter 1993), 15–16.

74. PR Newswire, "Reynolds Metal Announces Organizational and Management Changes," 27 March 1997.

75. See, for example, S. M. Davis, "Managing and Organizing Multinational Corporations," in C. A. Bartlett and S. Ghoshal, eds. *Transnational Management* (Homewood, IL: Richard D. Irwin, 1992).

76. This is based on Kamal Fatehi, *International Management* (Upper Saddle River, NJ: Prentice Hall, 1996), 89–91.

77. See also Thomas Malnight, "Emerging Structural Patterns Within Multinational Corporations: Toward Processed Database Structures," *Academy of Management Journal* 44, no. 6 (2001): 1187–1216.

78. Discussed in Kamal Fatehi, *International Management* (Upper Saddle River, NJ: Prentice Hall, 1996), 123.

79. Kamal Fatehi, *International Management* (Upper Saddle River, NJ: Prentice Hall, 1996), 123.

80. Ken Siegmann, "*Workforce*," Profit (November 1999): 47.

81. John Daniels and Lee Radebaugh, *International Business* (Reading, MA: Addison-Wesley, 1994), 529.

82. Kamal Fatehi, *International Management* (Upper Saddle River, NJ: Prentice Hall, 1996), 129.

83. See, for example, Kamal Fatehi, *International Management* (Upper Saddle River, NJ: Prentice Hall, 1996), 230.

84. Kamal Fatehi, *International Management* (Upper Saddle River, NJ: Prentice Hall, 1996), 230.

85. R. G. D'Andrade and C. Strauss, *Human Motives and Cultural Models* (Cambridge: Cambridge University Press, 1992), 4.

86. Geert Hofstede, "Cultural Dimensions in People Management," in Vladimir Pucik, Noel Tichy, and Carole Barnett, eds., *Globalizing Management* (New York: John Wiley & Sons, Inc. (1992), 139–158.

87. Geert Hofstede, "Cultural Dimensions in People Management," in Vladimir Pucik, Noel Tichy, and Carole Barnett, eds., *Globalizing Management* (New York: John Wiley & Sons, Inc. (1992), 143.

88. Geert Hofstede, "Cultural Dimensions in People Management," in Vladimir Pucik, Noel Tichy, and Carole Barnett, eds., *Globalizing Management* (New York: John Wiley & Sons, Inc. (1992), 143.

89. Geert Hofstede, "Cultural Dimensions in People Management," in Vladimir Pucik, Noel Tichy, and Carole Barnett, eds., *Globalizing Management* (New York: John Wiley & Sons, Inc. (1992), 147.

90. Geert Hofstede, "Cultural Constraints and Management Theories," *Academy of Management Review* 7, no. 1 (1993): 81–93; reprinted in Joyce Osland, David Kolb, and Irwin Rubin, *The Organizational Behavior Reader* (Upper Saddle River, NJ: Prentice Hall, 2001), 345–356.

91. Kamal Fatehi, *International Management* (Upper Saddle River, NJ: Prentice Hall, 1996), 279.

92. Discussed in Helen Deresky, *International Management* (Reading, MA: Addison-Wesley, 1997), 401–402.

93. E. C. Nevis, "Using an American Perspective in Understanding Another Culture: Toward a Hierarchy of Needs for the People's Republic of China," *The Journal of Applied Behavioral Science* 19, no. 3 (1983): 249–264; discussed in Kamal Fatehi, *International Management* (Upper Saddle River, NJ: Prentice Hall, 1996), 240.

94. D. C. McClelland and D. G. Winter, *Motivating Economic Achievement* (New York: Free Press, 1969).

95. L. Copland and L. Griggs, *Going International: How to Make Friends and Deal Effectively in the Global Marketplace* (New York: Random House, 1985), 14; discussed in Kamal Fatehi, *International Management* (Upper Saddle River, NJ: Prentice Hall, 1996), 251.

96. Michael Czinkota, Pietra Rivoli, and Ilka Ronkinen, *International Business* (Fort Worth: The Dryden Press, 1992), 205.

97. Frances Fiorino, "JetBlue Pursues Growth While Staying Small," *Aviation Week & Space Technology* 156, no. 23 (June 10, 2002): 41.

98. Joan Feldman, "JetBlue Loves New York," *Air Transport World* 38, no. 6 (June 2001): 78.

Chapter 3

1. Manuel Velasquez, *Business Ethics: Concepts and Cases* (Upper Saddle River, NJ: Prentice Hall, 1992), 9; Kate Walter, "Ethics Hot Lines Tap into More Than Wrongdoing," *HRMagazine* (September 1995): 79–85. See also Skip Kaltenheuser, "Bribery Is Being Outlawed Virtually Worldwide," *Business Ethics* (May 1998): 11.

2. The following, except as noted, is based on Manuel Velasquez, *Business Ethics: Concepts and Cases* (Upper Saddle River, NJ: Prentice Hall, 1992), 9–12.

3. Manuel Velasquez, *Business Ethics: Concepts and Cases* (Upper Saddle River, NJ: Prentice Hall, 1992), 9.

4. This is based on Manuel Velasquez, *Business Ethics: Concepts and Cases* (Upper Saddle River, NJ: Prentice Hall, 1992), 12–14.

5. Manuel Velasquez, *Business Ethics: Concepts and Cases* (Upper Saddle River, NJ: Prentice Hall, 1992), 12. For further discussion see Kurt Baier, *Moral Point of View*, abbr. ed. (New York: Random House, 1965), 88. See also Milton Bordwin, "The 3 R's of Ethics," *Management Review* (June 1998): 59–61.

6. For further discussion of ethics and morality see Tom Beauchamp and Norman Bowie, *Ethical Theory and Business* (Upper Saddle River, NJ: Prentice Hall, 1993), 1–19.

7. See, for example, S. E. Frost, Jr., *Basic Teachings of the Great Philosophers* (New York: Doubleday, 1962): 80–99.

8. S. E. Frost, Jr., *Basic Teachings of the Great Philosophers* (New York: Doubleday, 1962): 81.

9. S. E. Frost, Jr., *Basic Teachings of the Great Philosophers* (New York: Doubleday, 1962): 81.

10. Based on S. E. Frost, Jr., *Basic Teachings of the Great Philosophers* (New York: Doubleday, 1962): 81.

11. S. Morris Engel, *The Study of Philosophy* (San Diego, CA: Collegiate Press, 1987), 52.

12. O. C. Ferrell and John Fraedrich, *Business Ethics* (Boston: Houghton Mifflin, 1997), 55.

13. Example quoted from Michael Boylan, *Business Ethics* (Upper Saddle River, NJ: Prentice Hall, 2001), 37–38.

14. Michael Boylan, *Business Ethics* (Upper Saddle River, NJ: Prentice Hall, 2001), 118.

15. Michael Boylan, *Business Ethics* (Upper Saddle River, NJ: Prentice Hall, 2001), 118.

16. Michael Boylan, *Business Ethics* (Upper Saddle River, NJ: Prentice Hall, 2001), 119.

17. J. Fraedrich et al., "Assessing the Application of Cognitive Moral Development Theory to Business Ethics," *Journal of Business Ethics* 13 (1994): 829–838.

18. M. T. Hegarty and H. P. Sims, Jr., "Organizational Philosophy, Policies, and Objectives Related to Unethical Decision Behavior: A Laboratory Experiment," *Journal of Applied Psychology* 64 (1979): 331–338.

19. Janet Adams et al., "Code of Ethics as Signals for Ethical Behavior," *Journal of Business Ethics* 29, no. 3 (February 2001): 199–211.

20. Sara Morris et al., "A Test of Environmental, Situational, and Personal Influences on the Ethical Intentions of CEOs," *Business and Society* (August 1995): 119–147.

21. Justin Longnecker, Joseph McKinney, and Carlos Moore, "The Generation Gap in Business Ethics," *Business Horizons* (September–October 1989): 9–14.

22. CMA Canada survey, *CMA Magazine*.

23. Thomas Tyson, "Does Believing That Everyone Else is Less Ethical Have an Impact on Work Behavior?" *Journal of Business Ethics* 11 (1992): 707–717. See also Basil Orsini and Diane McDougall, "Fraud Busting Ethics," *CMA 1973* (June 1999): 18–21.

24. Floyd Norris and Diana Henriques, "Three Admit Guilty and Falsifying CUC's Books," *The New York Times*, 15 June 2000, sec. 6, p. C1.

25. "Back to Basics," *The Economist* (March 9, 2002), A Survey of Management, 9

26. "Back to Basics," *The Economist* (March 9, 2002), A Survey of Management, 9.

27. R. Craig Copetas, "Olympic Investigations Sprawl Far Abroad, Vexing a Stressed IOC," *The Wall Street Journal*, 3 March 1999, sec. A, pp. 1, 6; also Craig Copetas and Roger Thurow, "Torch and Burn, or Behind the Scenes at the IOC Meeting," *The Wall Street Journal*, 4 February 1999, sec. A, pp. 1, 16; also Craig Copetas, "A Preliminary Report on Salt Lake Scandal Certain to Rile the IOC," *The Wall Street Journal*, 20 January 1999, sec. A, pp. 1, 8; also Stephen Moore, "For the Olympics, Worrisome Clouds over its Lofty Image," *The Wall Street Journal*, 6 January 1999, sec. a, pp. 1, 10.

28. Leanne Yohemas-Hayes, "Defence Admits Records Purged," *The Winnipeg Free Press*, 23 July 1999, sec. B, p. 1.

29. Julian Barnes, "Unilever Wants P&G Placed Under Monitor and Spikes," *The New York Times*, 1 September 2001, sec. B, p. 1.

30. "Enron Chief Went Online to Urge Stock Purchases," *The New York Times*, 19 January 2002, sec. B, p. 1.

31. For a discussion, see Steen Brenner and Earl Molander, "Is the Ethics of Business Changing?" *Harvard Business Review* (January–February 1977): 57–71; Robert Jackyll, "Moral Mazes: Bureaucracy and Managerial Work," *Harvard Business Review* (September–October 1983): 118–130. See also Ishmael P. Akaah, "The Influence of Organizational Rank and Role of Marketing Professionals' Ethical Judgments," *Journal of Business Ethics* (June 1996): 605–614.

32. Discussed in Samuel Greengard, "Cheating and Stealing," *Workforce* (October 1997): 45–53.

33. From Guy Brumback, "Managing Above the Bottom Line of Ethics," *Supervisory Management* (December 1993): 12.

34. Deon Nel, Leyland Pitt, and Richard Watson, "Business Ethics: Defining the Twilight Zone," *Journal of Business Ethics* 8 (1989): 781; Sten Brenner and Earl Molander, "Is the Ethics of Business Changing?" *Harvard Business Review* (January–February 1977): 57–71; See also Daniel Glasner, "Past Mistakes Present Future Challenges," *Workforce* (May 1998): 117.

35. Quoted in Tom Beauchamp and Norman Bowie, *Ethical Theory and Business* (Upper Saddle River, NJ: Prentice Hall, 1993), 109.

36. Mark Schwartz, "Heat's on to Get an Effective Code," *The Globe and Mail*, 27 November 1997, sec. B, p. 2.

37. Heather Scoffield, "Canadian CEOs Plan Ethics Code," *The Globe and Mail*, 9 July 2002, sec. B, p. 4.

38. James Kunen, "Enron Division (and Values), Thing," *The New York Times*, 19 January 2002, sec. A, p. 19.

39. Janet Adams et al., "Code of Ethics as Signals for Ethical Behavior," *Journal of Business Ethics* 29, no. 3 (February 2001): 199–211.

40. Janet Adams et al., "Code of Ethics as Signals for Ethical Behavior," *Journal of Business Ethics* 29, no. 3 (February 2001): 199–211.

41. Janet Adams et al., "Code of Ethics as Signals for Ethical Behavior," *Journal of Business Ethics* 29, no. 3 (February 2001): 199–211.

42. www.transparency.org.

43. Dawn Walton, "Builders Most Likely to Bribe, Report Finds," *The Globe and Mail*, 21 January 2000, sec. B, p. 5.

44. "Corruption Perceptions Index," www.transparency.org.

45. Nicholas Bray, "OECD Ministers Agree to Ban Bribery as Means for Companies to Win Business," *The Wall Street Journal*, 27 May 1997, sec. A, p. 2.

46. Amy Zuckerman, "Managing Business Ethics in a World of Pay All," *World Trade* 14, no. 12 (December 2001): 38–39.

47. "A Global War Against Bribery," *The Economist* (January 16, 1999): 22–24.

48. Daniel Pearl and Steve Stecklow, "Pushing Pills," *The Wall Street Journal*, 16 August 2001, sec. A, p. 1.

49. Marcia Miceli and Janet Near, "Ethical Issues in the Management of Human Resources," *Human Resource Management Review* 11, no. 1: 1–10.

50. For a discussion see, for example, Alan Rowe et al., *Strategic Management: A Methodological Approach* (Reading, MA: Addison-Wesley Publishing Co., 1994), 101.

51. Alan Rowe et al., *Strategic Management: A Methodological Approach* (Reading, MA: Addison-Wesley Publishing Co., 1994), 6.

52. Dayton Fandray, "The Ethical Company," *Workforce* 79, no. 12 (December 2000): 74–77.

53. Kate Walter, "Ethics Hot Lines Tap into More Than Wrongdoing," *HRMagazine* (September 1995): 79–85.

54. Alan Rowe et al., *Strategic Management: A Methodological Approach* (Reading, MA: Addison-Wesley Publishing Co., 1994), 7; see also John J. Quinn, "The Role of 'Good Conversation' in Strategic Control," *Journal of Management Studies* (May 1996): 381–395.

55. Alan Rowe et al., *Strategic Management: A Methodological Approach* (Reading, MA: Addison-Wesley Publishing Co., 1994), 9.

56. Sandra Gray, "Audit Your Ethics," *Association Management* (September 1996): 188.

57. Michael McCarthy, "Now the Boss Knows Where You're Clicking," *The Wall Street Journal*, 21 October 1999, sec. B, p. 1.

58. "Study Says Employers Monitor One-Third of Employee E-Mail, Internet Use," *Knight/Tribune Business News*, 01191038.

59. Cynthia Kemper, "Big Brother," *Communication World* 18, no. 1 (December 2000/January 2001): 8–12).

60. Rosi Lombardi, "Web Monitoring: Who's in Control at the Office?" *Computing Canada* (November 26, 1999): 28–29.

61. Michael J. McCarthy, "How One Firm Attracts Ethics Electronically," *The Wall Street Journal*, 21 October 1999, sec. B, pp 1.

62. Michael J. McCarthy, "How One Firm Attracts Ethics Electronically," *The Wall Street Journal*, 21 October 1999, sec. B, pp 1.

63. www.ethics.ubc.ca/resources/business.

64. John Emshwiller and Rebecca Smith, "Behind Enron's Fall, A Culture of Operating Outside the Public's View," *The Wall Street Journal*, 5 December 2001, sec. A, pp. 1, 10.

65. Anita Raghavan, Kathryn Kranhold, and Alexei Barrionuevo, "How Enron Bosses Created a Culture of Pushing Limits," *The Wall Street Journal*, 26 August 2002, sec. A, pp. 1, 7.

66. James G. Hunt, Leadership (Newbury Park, CA: Sage Publications, 1991), 220–224. One somewhat tongue-in-cheek writer describes culture as a sort of "organizational DNA," since "it's the stuff, mostly intangible, that determines the basic character of a business." See James Moore, "How Companies Have Sex," *Fast Company* (October–November 1997): 66–68.

67. Ricky Griffin, Ronald Ebert, and Frederick Starke, Business, 3rd Can. ed. (Scarborough: Prentice Hall Canada, 1999), 186.

68. James G. Hunt, *Leadership* (Newbury Park, CA: Sage Publications, 1991), 221. For a discussion of types of cultures see, for example, "A Quadrant of Corporate Cultures," *Management Decision* (September 1996): 37–40.

69. For example, see O.C. Ferrell and John Fraedrich, *Business Ethics*, 3rd ed. (Boston: Houghton Mifflin, 1997), 117.

70. Daniel Stoffman, "Great Workplaces and How They Got That Way," *Canadian Business* (September, 1984): 30–33, 34, 36, 38.

71. Keith McArthur, "Air Canada Tells Employees to Crack a Smile More Often," *The Globe and Mail*, 14 March 2002, sec. B, pp. 1–2.

72. Ric Dolphin, "Magna Force," *Canadian Business* (May, 1988).

73. Max Messmer, "Capitalizing on Corporate Culture," *The Internal Auditor* 58, no. 5 (October 2001): 38–45.

74. Curtis Verschoor, "Why Do Unfortunate Things Happen to Good Corporate Citizens?" *Strategic Finance* 83, no. 5 (November 2001): 20, 22.

75. Milton Friedman, *Capitalism and Freedom* (Chicago: University of Chicago Press, 1962), 133. See also Charles Handy, "A Better Capitalism," *Across the Board* (April 1998): 16–22. See also Robert Reich, "The New Meaning of Corporate Social Responsibility," *California Management Review* (Winter 1998): 8–17. Reich also believes that because of pressure from investors, non-owner stakeholders are being neglected and that the government should step in to protect them.

76. Tom Beauchamp and Norman Bowie, *Ethical Theory and Business* (Upper Saddle River, NJ: Prentice Hall, 1993), 49–52. See also Marjorie Kelly, "Do Stockholders 'Own' Corporations?" *Business Ethics* (June 1999): 4–5.

77. Tom Beauchamp and Norman Bowie, *Ethical Theory and Business* (Upper Saddle River, NJ: Prentice Hall, 1993), 79.

78. Tom Beauchamp and Norman Bowie, *Ethical Theory and Business* (Upper Saddle River, NJ: Prentice Hall, 1993), 60.

79. John Simon, Charles Powers, and John Gunnermann, "The Responsibilities of Corporations and Their Owners," *The Ethical Investor: Universities and Corporate Responsibilitya* (New Haven, CT: Yale University Press, 1972); reprinted in Tom Beauchamp and Norman Bowie, *Ethical Theory and Business* (Upper Saddle River, NJ: Prentice Hall, 1993), 60–65. See also Roger Kaufman et al., "The Changing Corporate Mind: Organizations, Vision, Missions, Purposes, and Indicators on the Move Toward Societal Payoffs," *Performance Improvement Quarterly* 11, no. 3 (1998): 32–44.

80. "Sweatshop Wars," *The Economist* (February 27, 1999), 62–63.

81. Charles Hess and Kenneth Hey, "Good Doesn't Always Mean Right," *Across the Board* 38, no. 4 (July/August 2001): 61–64.

82. Thea Singer, "Can Business Still Save the World?" *Inc.* 23, no. 5 (April 30, 2001): 58–71.

83. Jo-Ann Johnston, "Social Auditors: The New Breed of Expert," *Business Ethics* (March 1996), p. 27.

84. Karen Paul and Steven Ludenberg, "Applications of Corporate Social Monitoring Systems: Types, Dimensions and Goals," *Journal of Business Ethics* 11 (1992): 1–10.

85. Karen Paul, "Corporate Social Monitoring in South Africa: A Decade of Achievement, An Uncertain Future," *Journal of Business Ethics* 8 (1989): 464. See also Bernadette Ruf et al., "The Development of a Systematic, Aggregate Measure of Corporate Social Performance," *Journal of Management* 24, no. 1 (1998): 119–133.

86. Karen Paul, "Corporate Social Monitoring in South Africa: A Decade of Achievement, An Uncertain Future," *Journal of Business Ethics* 8 (1989): 464. See also John S. North, "Living Under a Social Code of Ethics: Eli Lilly in South Africa Operating Under the Sullivan Principles," *Business and the Contemporary World* 8, no. 1 (1996): 168–180; and S. Prakash Sethi, "Working With International Codes of Conduct: Experience of U.S. Companies Operating in South Africa Under the Sullivan Principles," *Business and the Contemporary World* 8, no. 1 (1996): 129–150. Standards similar to the international quality standards that have been used for some time have been put in place for social accountability areas such as child labour and health and safety. See Ruth Thaler-Carter, "Social Accountability 8000: A Social Guide for Companies or Another Layer of Bureaucracy?" *HRMagazine* (June 1999): 106–108.

07. www.bombardier.com

88. Janet Near, "Whistle-Blowing: Encourage It!" *Business Horizons* (January–February, 1989): 5. See also Robert J. Paul and James B. Townsend, "Don't Kill the Messenger! Whistle-Blowing in America: A Review with Recommendations," *Employee Responsibilities and Rights* (June 1996): 149–161. Nick Perry, "Indecent Exposures: Theorizing Whistle Blowing," *Organization Studies* 19, no. 2 (1998): 235–257.

89. Janet Near, "Whistle-Blowing: Encourage It!" *Business Horizons* (January–February, 1989): 5. See also Fraser Younson, "Spilling the Beans," *People Management* (June 11, 1998): 25–26.

90. Janet Near, "Whistle-Blowing: Encourage It!" *Business Horizons* (January–February, 1989): 6. See also David Lewis, "Whistle Blowing at Work: Ingredients for an Effective Procedure," *Human Resource Management Journal* 7, no. 4 (1997): 5–11.

91. "The Importance of Business Ethics," *HR Focus* 78, no. 7 (July 2001): 1, 13.

92. Government of Canada publications at www.canada.gc.ca/publications/publication_e.html.

93. See, for example, Taylor Cox, Jr., *Cultural Diversity in Organizations* (San Francisco: Berrett-Koehler Publishers, Inc. (1993), 3.

94. Taylor Cox, Jr., *Cultural Diversity in Organizations* (San Francisco: Berrett-Koehler Publishers, Inc. (1993), 3.

95. Taylor Cox, Jr., *Cultural Diversity in Organizations* (San Francisco: Berrett-Koehler Publishers, Inc. (1993), 3–4.

96. Taylor Cox, Jr., *Cultural Diversity in Organizations* (San Francisco: Berrett-Koehler Publishers, Inc. (1993), 11.

97. Richard Orlando, "Racial Diversity, Business Strategy, and Firm Performance: A Resource Based View," *Academy of Management Journal* 43, no. 2 (2000): 164–177.

98. G. Pascal Zachary, "Mighty is the Mongrel," *Fast Company* (July 2000): 272–276.

99. G. Pascal Zachary, "Mighty is the Mongrel," *Fast Company* (July 2000): 278.

100. Patricia Digh, "Creating a New Balance Sheet: The Need for Better Diversity Metrics," *Mosaics* (September–October 1999): 1.

101. Michael Carrell, Daniel Jennings, and Christina Heavrin, *Fundamentals of Organizational Behavior* (Upper Saddle River, NJ: Prentice Hall, 1997), 282–283.

102. Michael Carrell, Daniel Jennings, and Christina Heavrin, *Fundamentals of Organizational Behavior* (Upper Saddle River, NJ: Prentice Hall, 1997), 282–283.

103. Vivian Smith, "Breaking Down the Barriers," *The Globe and Mail*, 17 November 1992, sec. B, p. 24.

104. George Kronenberger, "Out of the Closet," *Personnel Journal* (June, 1991): 40–44.

105. Taylor Cox, Jr., *Cultural Diversity in Organizations* (San Francisco: Berrett-Koehler Publishers, Inc. (1993), 88.

106. Taylor Cox, Jr., *Cultural Diversity in Organizations* (San Francisco: Berrett-Koehler Publishers, Inc. (1993), 89.

107. J. H. Greenhaus and S. Parasuraman, "Job Performance Attributions and Career Advancement Prospects: An Examination of Gender and Race Affects," *Organizational Behavior and Human Decision Processes* 55 (July 1993): 273–298.

108. Adapted from Taylor Cox, Jr., *Cultural Diversity in Organizations* (San Francisco: Berrett-Koehler Publishers, Inc. (1993), 64.

109. Taylor Cox, Jr., *Cultural Diversity in Organizations* (San Francisco: Berrett-Koehler Publishers, Inc. (1993), 179–180.

110. Madeleine Heilmann and Lewis Saruwatari, "When Beauty is Beastly: The Effects of Appearance and Sex on Evaluation of Job Applicants for Managerial and Nonmanagerial Jobs," *Organizational Behavior and Human Performance* (June 1979): 360–372; see also Tracy McDonald and Milton Hakel, "Effects of Applicant Race, Sex, Suitability, and Answers on Interviewer's Questioning Strategy and Ratings," *Personnel Psychology* (Summer 1985): 321–334.

111. Francis Milliken and Luis Martins, "Searching for Common Threads: Understanding the Multiple Effects of Diversity in Organizational Groups," *Academy of Management Review* 21, no. 2 (1996): 415; see also Patricia Nemetz and Sandra Christenson, "The Challenge of Cultural Diversity: Harnessing a Diversity of Views to Understand Multiculturalism," *Academy of Management Review* (July 21, 1996): 434–462.

112. Patricia Digh, "Coming to Terms with Diversity," *HRMagazine* (November 1998): 119.

113. Jeremy Kahn, "Diversity Trumps the Downturn," *Fortune* (144, no. 1 (July 9, 2001): 114–116.

114. Taylor Cox, Jr., *Cultural Diversity in Organizations* (San Francisco: Berrett-Koehler Publishers, Inc. (1993), 236.

115. Patricia Digh, "Coming to Terms with Diversity," *HRMagazine* (November 1998): 119.

116. Danny Hakim "Ford Motor Workers Get On the Job Training in Religious Tolerance," *The New York Times*, 19 November 2001, sec. B, p. 6.

117. Michelle Conlon and Wendy Zellner, "Is Wal-Mart Hostile to Women?" *Business Week* (July 16, 2001): 58–59.

118. Jules Oliver, "Seeking Greater Diversity Connectivity: A Canadian Experience," *Diversity Factor* (Winter, 1999).

119. Jules Oliver, "Seeking Greater Diversity Connectivity: A Canadian Experience," *Diversity Factor* (Winter 1999).

120. K. Kram, Mentoring at Work (Glenview, IL: Scott Foresman, 1985); Taylor Cox, Jr., *Cultural Diversity in Organizations* (San Francisco: Berrett-Koehler Publishers, Inc. (1993), 198. See also Ian Cunningham and Linda Honold, "Everyone Can Be a Coach," *HRMagazine* (June 1998): 63–66.

121. See, for example, G. F. Dreher and R. A. Ash, "A Comparative Study of Mentoring among Men and Women in Managerial, Professional, and Technical Positions," *Journal of Applied Psychology* 75, no. 5 (1990): 1–8.

122. Benjamin Hoff, *The Tao of Pooh* (New York: Dutton, 1992), 109–110.

123. Benjamin Hoff, *The Tao of Pooh* (New York: Dutton, 1992), 109–110.

124. "Morgan Stanley Bans the Rules," *Investment Dealers Digest* 4 (March 2002), item 02063001.

Chapter 4

1. Adapted from Marc Dollinger, *Entrepreneurship: Strategies and Resources* (Upper Saddle River, NJ: Prentice Hall, 2003), 5.

2. Jeffrey Timmons, "The Entrepreneurial Mind," *Success* (April 1994): p. 48.

3. Jeffrey Timmons, "The Entrepreneurial Mind," *Success* (April 1994): p. 48.

4. This is based on Marc Dollinger, *Entrepreneurship: Strategies and Resources* (Upper Saddle River, NJ: Prentice Hall, 2003), 7–8.

5. Amy Kover, "Manufacturing's Hidden Assets: Workers," *Fortune* (November 10, 1997): 28–29.

6. W. Gartner, "The Conceptual Framework for Describing the Phenomenon of New Venture Creation," *Academy of Management Review* 10, (1985): 696–706, in Marc Dollinger, *Entrepreneurship: Strategies and Resources* (Upper Saddle River, NJ: Prentice Hall, 2003), 19.

7. Natalie Southworth, "Canada Get Top-Tier Ranking," *The Globe and Mail*, 14 November 2000, sec. B, p. 9.

8. Strategis, Industry Canada, www.strategis.ic.gc.ca.

9. Statistics Canada, CANSIM, Matrix 3451, Series D986059, 986061, (1999).

10. R. J. Arend, "The Emergence of Entrepreneurs Following Exogenous Technological Change," *Strategic Management Journal* 20, no. 1 (1999): 31–47, discussed in Mary Coulter, *Entrepreneurship in Action* (Upper Saddle River, NJ: Prentice Hall, 2001), 4.

11. Mary Coulter, *Entrepreneurship in Action* (Upper Saddle River, NJ: Prentice Hall, 2001), 18.

12. C. R. Brockhaus, "The Psychology of the Entrepreneur," in C. Kent, D. Sexton, and K. Verspers, eds, *Encyclopedia of Entrepreneurship* (Upper Saddle River, NJ: Prentice Hall, 1982), 39–71, discussed in Marc Dollinger, *Entrepreneurship: Strategies and Resources* (Upper Saddle River, NJ: Prentice Hall, 2003), 38.

13. Richard Becherer and John Maurer, "The Proactive Personality Disposition and Entrepreneurial Behavior Among Small Company Presidents," *Journal of Small Business Management* 37, no. 1 (January 1999): 28–37.

14. Richard Becherer and John Maurer, "The Proactive Personality Disposition and Entrepreneurial Behavior Among Small Company Presidents," *Journal of Small Business Management* 37, no. 1 (January 1999): 28–37.

15. Jill Kickul and Lisa Gundry, "Prospective for Strategic Advantage: The Proactive Entrepreneurial Personality and Small Firm Innovation," *Journal of Small Business Management* 40, no. 2 (April 2002): 85–98.

16. S. D. McKenna, "The Darker Side of the Entrepreneur," *Leadership and Organization Development Journal* 17, no. 6 (November 1996): 41–46.

17. S. D. McKenna, "The Darker Side of the Entrepreneur," *Leadership and Organization Development Journal* 17, no. 6 (November 1996): 41–46.

18. Julie Rose, "The New Risk Takers," *Fortune Small Business* 12, no. 2 (March 2002): 28–34.

19. Julie Rose, "The New Risk Takers," *Fortune Small Business* 12, no. 2 (March 2002): 28–34.

20. Arlene Weintraub, "Can Boingo Wireless, From the Founder of EarthLink, Turn Hot Spots into Money?" *Business Week* Issue 3780 (April 29, 2002): 106.

21. Gayle MacDonald, "War Stories from the World's Top Female Owners," *The Globe and Mail*, 2 May 1997, sec. B, p. 9.

22. Murray McNeill, "Women Step Out on Their Own," *The Winnipeg Free Press*, 8 December 1994, sec. C, p. 10.

23. From "The U.S. Small Business Administration's Small Business Start-Up Kit," downloaded 12 May 2002, www.sba.gov/starting/ask.html.

24. Adapted from R. Nielsen, M. Peters, and R. Hisrich, "Intrapreneurship Strategy for Internal Markets: Corporate, Nonprofit Anti-Government Institution Cases," *Strategic Management Journal* 6 (April–June 1985): 181–189, quoted in Marc Dollinger, *Entrepreneurship: Strategies and Resources* (Upper Saddle River, NJ: Prentice Hall, 2003), 333.

25. Marc Dollinger, *Entrepreneurship: Strategies and Resources* (Upper Saddle River, NJ: Prentice Hall, 2003), 333.

26. Marc Dollinger, *Entrepreneurship: Strategies and Resources* (Upper Saddle River, NJ: Prentice Hall, 2003), 335.

27. This is based on Dean Takahashi, "Reinventing the Intrapreneur," *Red Herring* (September 2000): 189–196.

28. A. Bhide, "How Entrepreneurs Craft Strategies That Work," *Harvard Business Review* (March–April 1994): 150–161, and John Case, "The Origins of Entrepreneurship," *Inc.* (June, 1989): 51–62.

29. Peggy Lambing and Charles Kuehl, *Entrepreneurship* (Upper Saddle River, NJ: Prentice Hall, 2000), 90.

30. Peggy Lambing and Charles Kuehl, *Entrepreneurship* (Upper Saddle River, NJ: Prentice Hall, 2000), 91.

31. Stewart Brown, "A Sweet Triumph," *Fortune Small Business* 12, (April 2002): 45–54.

32. Norma Scarborough and Thomas Zimmerer, *Effective Small Business Management* (Upper Saddle River, NJ: Prentice Hall, 2002), 21.

33. Geoff Kirbyson, "Pride in Ownership Fuels Firm," *The Winnipeg Free Press*, 17 August 2002, sec. B, pp. 3–4.

34. Peggy Lambing and Charles Kuehl, *Entrepreneurship* (Upper Saddle River, NJ: Prentice Hall, 2000), 35.

35. Barbara Marsh, "When Owners of Family Businesses Died, Survivors Often Feel Unsuited to Fill the Void," *The Wall Street Journal*, 7 May 1990, sec. B, pp. 1–2, discussed in William Schoell, Gary Dessler, and John Reinecke, *Introduction to Business* (Boston: Allyn and Bacon, 1993), 173.

36. Peggy Lambing and Charles Kuehl, *Entrepreneurship* (Upper Saddle River, NJ: Prentice Hall, 2000), 38.

37. Steps 1–4 from "First Steps: How to Start a Small Business," Small Business Administration, www.sba.gov/starting/in-dexsteps.html, downloaded May 12, 2002.

38. William Schoell, Gary Dessler, and John Reinecke, *Introduction to Business* (Boston: Allyn and Bacon, 1993), 178–179.

39. "Small Business Frequently Asked Questions," U.S. Small Business Administration, www.sba.gov/addl/stats/spfaq.txt, downloaded May 12, 2002.

40. Michael E. Porter, "What Is Strategy?" *Harvard Business Review* (November–December 1996): 61–80.

41. Bill Frskics-Warren, "Tapping an Audience With an Ear to the Ground," *The New York Times*, 17 March 2002, pp. 2, 33.

42. Bill Frskics-Warren, "Tapping an Audience With an Ear to the Ground," *The New York Times*, 17 March 2002, pp. 2, 33.

43. Bill Frskics-Warren, "Tapping an Audience With an Ear to the Ground," *The New York Times*, 17 March 2002, pp. 2, 33.

44. Bill Frskics-Warren, "Tapping an Audience With an Ear to the Ground," *The New York Times*, 17 March 2002, pp. 2, 33.

45. Ross Kerber, "'.coms May be Dead, But Small Businesses are Still Using the Internet," *The Boston Globe*, 15 April 2002, sec. C, p. 1.

46. Ross Kerber, "'.coms May be Dead, But Small Businesses are Still Using the Internet," *The Boston Globe*, 15 April 2002, sec. C, p. 1.

47. This is adapted from John Vinturella, *The Entrepreneur's Field Book* (Upper Saddle River, NJ: Prentice Hall, 1999), 64–65.

48. W. Keith Schilit, *The Entrepreneurs' Guide to Preparing a Winning Business Plan and Raising Venture Capital* (Upper Saddle River, NJ: Prentice Hall, 1990), 4–6.

49. W. Keith Schilit, *The Entrepreneurs' Guide to Preparing a Winning Business Plan and Raising Venture Capital* (Upper Saddle River, NJ: Prentice Hall, 1990), 5.

50. This is based on Marc Dollinger, *Entrepreneurship: Strategies and Resources* (Upper Saddle River, NJ: Prentice Hall, 2003), 313–316.

51. David Yoffie, "Building a Company on Internet Time: Lessons from Netscape," *California Management Review* (Spring 1999): 8.

52. David Yoffie, "Building a Company on Internet Time: Lessons from Netscape," *California Management Review* (Spring 1999): 8.

53. Nancy Austin, "First Aide," *Inc.* (September 1999), 78.

54. Nancy Austin, "First Aide," *Inc.* (September 1999), 72.

55. "Internships Provide Workplace Snapshot," *BNA Bulletin to Management* (May 22, 1997): 168.

56. Gary Dessler, "How to Earn Your Employees Commitment," *Academy of Management Executive* 13, no. 2 (1999): 58–67.

57. Source: Michael Selz, "Testing Self-Managing Teams, Entrepreneur Hopes to Lose Job," *The Wall Street Journal*, 11 January 1994, sec. B, p. 1; and Sally Goll Beatty, "Standard & Poors Acquires Published Image, Inc.," *The Wall Street Journal*, 2 July 1997, sec. B, p. 7.

58. Following is based on "Management Issues for the Growing Business," www.spa.gov/shainfo/manage-8-business/man.txt.

Chapter 5

1. Max Bazerman, *Judgment in Managerial Decision Making* (New York: John Wiley & Sons, Inc. 1994), 3.

2. See, for example, Herbert Simon, *The New Science of Management Decision* (Upper Saddle River, NJ: Prentice Hall, 1971), 45–47.

3. Larry Long and Nancy Long, *Computers* (Upper Saddle River, NJ: Prentice Hall, 1996), M-7.

4. Mairead Browne, *Organizational Decision Making and Information* (Norwood, NJ: Ablex Publishing Corporation, 1993), 6.

5. Max Bazerman, *Judgment in Managerial Decision Making* (New York: John Wiley & Sons, Inc. 1994), 5.

6. Herbert Simon, *Administrative Behavior* (New York: The Free Press, 1977).

7. George Lowenstein, "The Creative Destruction of Decision Research," *Journal of Consumer Research* 00, no. 4 (December 2001): 499–505.

8. See, for example, Max Bazerman, *Judgment in Managerial Decision Making* (New York: John Wiley & Sons, Inc. 1994), 5.

9. James March and Herbert Simon, *Organizations* (New York: John Wiley, 1958), 140–141.

10. For a discussion see, for example, Max Bazerman, *Judgment in Managerial Decision Making* (New York: John Wiley & Sons, Inc. 1994), 4–5.

11. Max Bazerman, *Judgment in Managerial Decision Making* (New York: John Wiley & Sons, Inc. 1994), 4.

12. John Hammond, Ralph Keeney, and Howard Raiffa, *Smart Choices* (Boston: Harvard Business School Press, 1999), 19–30.

13. Of course, this also assumes that Harold wants to stay in marketing.

14. Except as noted, the titles of the steps and the ideas for this section are based on John Hammond, Ralph Keeney, and Howard Raiffa, *Smart Choices* (Boston: Harvard Business School Press, 1999), 35–41.

15. John Hammond, Ralph Keeney, and Howard Raiffa, *Smart Choices* (Boston: Harvard Business School Press, 1999), 47.

16. Max Bazerman, *Judgment in Managerial Decision Making* (New York: John Wiley & Sons, Inc. 1994), 4.

17. Based on John Hammond, Ralph Keeney, and Howard Raiffa, *Smart Choices* (Boston: Harvard Business School Press, 1999), 67–72.

18. Max Bazerman, *Judgment in Managerial Decision Making* (New York: John Wiley & Sons, Inc. 1994), 93.

19. Max Bazerman, *Judgment in Managerial Decision Making* (New York: John Wiley & Sons, Inc. 1994), 105–106.

20. Max Bazerman, *Judgment in Managerial Decision Making* (New York: John Wiley & Sons, Inc. 1994), 108.

21. For an additional perspective, see, for example Ruth Weiss, "How to Foster Creativity at Work," *Training & Development* (February 2001): 61–67; and A. Muoio, "Where Do Great Ideas Come From?" *Fast Company* (January–February 2000): 149–164; Charles Fishman, "Creative Tension," *Fast Company* (November 2000): 359–368; Andrew Hargadon and Robert Sutton, "Building an Innovation Factory," *Harvard Business Review* (May–June 2000): 157–166; Michael Michalko, "Jumpstart Your Company's Creativity," *Supervision* 62, no. 1 (January 2001): 14; and Liz Sampson, "Fostering Creativity: Companies Enhance the Bottom Line by Building Corporate Cultures that Encourage Employee Innovation," *Training* 38, no. 12 (December 2001): 54–58.

22. Prased Padmanabhan, "Decision Specific Experience in Foreign Ownership and Establishment Strategies: Evidence from Japanese Firms," *Journal of International Studies* (Spring 1999): 25–27.

23. This anecdote is quoted and paraphrased from Bill Breen, "What's Your Intuition?" *Fast Company* (September 2000): 294–295.

24. Bill Breen, "What's Your Intuition?" *Fast Company* (September 2000): 296.

25. Kenneth Laudon and Jane Laudon, *Management Information Systems* (Upper Saddle River, NJ: Prentice Hall, 1996), 125. See also Bob F. Holder, "Intuitive Decision Making," *CMA* (October 1995): 6.

26. Joan Johnson et al, "Vigilant and Hypervigilant Decision Making," *Journal of Applied Psychology* 82, no. 4, pp. 614–622.

27. Studies indicate that you can adjust your style and that decision styles are more preferences than set in stone. See Dorothy Leonard and Susan Straus, "Putting Your Company's Whole Brain to Work," *Harvard Business Review* (July–August 1997): 111–121.

28. Dorothy Leonard and Susan Straus, "Putting Your Company's Whole Brain to Work," *Harvard Business Review* (July–August 1997): 111–121. See also, Theodore Rubin, *Overcoming Indecisiveness: The Eight Stages of Effective Decision Making* (New York: Avon Books, 1985). See also John Hammond, Ralph Keeney, and Howard Raiffa, *Smart Choices* (Boston: Harvard Business School Press, 1999).

29. Quoted in Robert L. Heilbroner, "How to Make an Intelligent Decision," *Think* (December 1990): 2–4.

30. Thomas Stewart, "Making Decisions in Real-Time," *Fortune* (June 26, 2000): 332.

31. Michael Hickins, "Xerox Shares Its Knowledge," *Management Review* (September 1999): 42.

32. Robert Cross and Susan Brodt, "How Assumptions of Consensus Undermined Decision-Making," *MIT Sloan Management Review* 42, no. 2 (Winter 2001): 86.

33. See, for example, William Taggart and Enzo Valenzi, "Assessing Rational and Intuitive Styles: A Human Information Processing Metaphor," *Journal of Management Studies* (March 1990): 150–171; Christopher W. Allinson and John Hayes, "The Cognitive Style Index: A Measure of Intuition–Analysis for Organizational Research," *Journal of Management Studies* (January 1996): 119–135.

34. This and the following guidelines are from Robert L. Heilbroner, "How to Make an Intelligent Decision," *Think* (December 1990): 2–4.

35. Max Bazerman, *Judgment in Managerial Decision Making* (New York: John Wiley & Sons, Inc. 1994), 6–8.

36. Michael Roberto, "Making Difficult Decisions in Turbulent Times," *Ivey Business Journal* 66, no. 3, Jan/Feb 2002, pp. 14–20.

37. George Lowenstein, "The Creative Destruction of Decision Research," *Journal of Consumer Research* 38, no. 4 (December 2001): 499–505.

38. Dewitt Dearborn and Herbort A. Simon, "Selective Perception: A Note on the Departmental Identification of Executives," *Sociometry* 21 (1958): 140–144. For a recent study of this phenomenon, see Mary Waller, George Huber, and William Glick, "Functional Background as a Determinant of Executives' Selective Perception," *Academy of Management Journal* (August 1995): 943–994. While not completely supporting the Dearborn findings, these researchers did also conclude that managers' functional backgrounds affected how they perceived organizational changes. See also Paul Gamble and Duncan Gibson, "Executive Values and Decision Making: The Relationship of Culture and Information Flows," *Journal of Management Studies* (March 1999): 217–240.

39. John Hammond, Ralph Keeney, and Howard Raiffa, *Smart Choices* (Boston: *Harvard Business School Press*, 1999), 19–30.

40. Lester Lefton and Laura Valvatne, *Mastering Psychology* (Boston: Allyn and Bacon, 1992), 248–249. See also Daphne Main and Joyce Lambert, "Improving Your Decision Making," Business and Economic Review (April 1998): 9–12.

41. Harvey Enchin, "Consensus Management? Not for Bombardier's CEO," *The Globe and Mail*, 16 April 1990), sec. B, p. 1.

42. Fred Moody, "No Ordinary Ambassador," *Canadian Transportation* (August 1990): 13.

43. James Bowditsch and Anthony Buono, *A Primer on Organizational Behavior* (New York: John Wiley & Sons Inc., 1994), 171–172.

44. Michael Carrell, Daniel Jennings, and Christine Heavrin, *Fundamentals of Organization Behavior* (Upper Saddle River, NJ: Prentice Hall, 1997), 346.

45. For a discussion of these and the following points see, for example, Michael Carrell, Daniel Jennings, and Christine Heavrin, *Fundamentals of Organizational Behavior* (Upper Saddle River, NJ: Prentice Hall, 1997), 346.

46. I. Janis, *Victims of GroupThink* (Boston: Houghton–Mifflin, 1972); for an alternate view of decision-making problems in groups, see Glen Whyte, "Group-Think Reconsidered," *Academy of Management Review* 14 (1989): 40–56.

47. For an additional perspective on many of these see Randy Hirokawa and Marshall Scott Poole, *Communication and Group Decision Making* (Thousand Oaks, CA: Sage Publications, Inc. 1996), 354–364. See also John O. Whitney and E. Kirby Warren, "Action Forums: How General Electric and Other Firms Have Learned to Make Better Decisions," *Columbia Journal of World Business* 30, no. 4 (Winter 1995): 18–27; Steven G. Rogelberg and Steven M. Rumery, "Gender Diversity, Team Decision Quality, Time on Task, and Interpersonal Cohesion," *Small Group Research* 27, no. 1 (February 1996): 79–90; Beatrice Shultz, Sandra M. Ketrow, and Daphne M. Urban, "Improving Decision Quality in the Small Group: The Role of the Reminder," *Small Group Research* 26, no. 4 (November 1995): 521–41.

48. See, for example, Lester Lefton and Laura Valvatne, *Mastering Psychology* (Boston: Allyn and Bacon, 1992), 249.

49. Jerald Greenberg and Robert Baron, *Behavior in Organizations* (Englewood Cliffs, NJ: Prentice Hall, 1995), 393.

50. See Ron Zemke, "In Search of Good Ideas," *Training* (January 1993): 46–52; R. Brent Gallupe, Lana Bastianutti, and William Cooper, "Unblocking Brainstorms," *Journal of Applied Psychology* (January 1991), 137–142.

51. Gerry Blackwell, "You, Too, Can Be an Einstein," *Canadian Business* (May 1993): 66–69.

52. See, for example, Jerald Greenberg and Robert Baron, *Behavior in Organizations* (Englewood Cliffs, NJ: Prentice Hall, 1995), 399–400.

53. See S. G. Rogelberg, J. L. Barnes–Farrell, and C. A. Lowe, "The Stepladder Technique: An Alternative Group Structure Facilitating Effective Group Decision Making," *Journal of Applied Psychology* 57 (1992): 730–737.

54. Norman R. F. Maier and E. P. McRay, "Increasing Innovation in Change Situations Through Leadership Skills," *Psychological Reports* 31 (1972): 30–43.

Chapter 5 Appendix

1. The break-even point is also sometimes defined more technically as the quantity of output or sales that will result in a zero level of earnings before interest or taxes. See for example J. William Petty et al., *Basic Financial Management* (Upper Saddle River, NJ: Prentice Hall 1993), 932.

2. Jay Heizer and Barry Render, *Production and Operations Management* (Upper Saddle River, NJ: Prentice Hall, 1996), 240–250.

Chapter 6

1. George L. Morrisey, *A Guide to Tactical Planning* (San Francisco: Jossey-Bass, 1996), 61.

2. Leonard Goodstein, Timothy Nolan, and Jay William Pfeiffer, *Applied Strategic Planning* (New York: McGraw-Hill, Inc. 1993), 3.

3. R. R. Donnelley and Sons Company Web site, www.rrdonnelley.com, November 10, 1999.

4. Ronald Henkoff, "How to Plan for 1995" *Fortune* (December 31, 1990): 74.

5. Peter Drucker, "Long Range Planning," *Management Science* 5 (1959), 238–49. See also Bristol Voss, "Cover to Cover Drucker," *Journal of Business Strategy* (May–June 1999, Fall 1991): 1–9.

6. Leonard Goodstein, Timothy Nolan, and Jay William Pfeiffer, *Applied Strategic Planning* (New York: McGraw-Hill, Inc. 1993), 170.

7. Leslie Brokow, "One-Page Company Game Plan," *Inc.* (June 1993): 111–113.

8. Arthur Little, *Global Strategic Planning* (New York: Business International Corporation, 1991), 3.

9. This is from George Morrisey, *A Guide to Long-Range Planning* (San Francisco: Jossey-Bass, 1996), 72–73.

10. For a discussion, see Peter Wright, Mark Kroll, and John Parnell, *Strategic Management Concepts* (Upper Saddle River, NJ: Prentice Hall, 1996), 224–225.

11. Peter Wright, Mark Kroll, and John Parnell, *Strategic Management Concepts* (Upper Saddle River, NJ: Prentice Hall, 1996), 224–225.

12. Peter Wright, Mark Kroll, and John Parnell, *Strategic Management Concepts* (Upper Saddle River, NJ: Prentice Hall, 1996), 225.

13. Karen Howlett, "CIBC Regroups After September 11 Devastation," *The Globe and Mail*, 21 December 2001, sec. B, pp. 1, 5.

14. Harvey Kahalas, "A Look at Planning and Its Components," *Managerial Planning* (January–February 1982): 13–16; reprinted in Phillip DuBose, *Readings in Management* (Upper Saddle River, NJ: Prentice Hall 1988), 49–50. See also Mary M. Crossan, Henry W. Lane, Roderick E. White, and Leo Klus, "The Improvising Organization: Where Planning Meets Opportunity," *Organization Dynamics* (Spring 1996): 20–35.

15. Gayle MacDonald, "The Eye of the Storm," *The Globe and Mail*, 11 January 1996, sec. B, p. 13.

16. Martin Cash, "MTS Locks in Clients in Face of Deregulation," *The Winnipeg Free Press*, 20 November 1990, p. 17.

17. Peter F. Drucker, *The Effective Executive* (New York: Harper & Row, 1966); quoted in Keith Curtis, *From Management Goal Setting to Organizational Results* (Westport, CT: Quorum Books, 1994), 101.

18. "Setting Departmental Goals You Can Actually Achieve," *Info-Tech Advisor Newsletter* (January 22, 2002).

19. Peter F. Drucker, *The Practice of Management* (New York: Harper & Row, 1954), 65–83, 100.

20. George Morrisey, *A Guide to Long-Range Planning* (San Francisco: Jossey-Bass, 1996), 25.

21. Gary Latham and J. James Baldes, "The Practical Significance of Locke's Theory of Goal Setting," *Journal of Applied Psychology* (February 1975). See also Gary Latham, "The Effects of Proximal and Distal Goals on Performance on a Moderately Complex Task," *Journal of Organizational Behavior* (July 1999): 421–430.

22. See, for example, Gary Latham and Gary Yukl, "A Review of Research on the Application of Goal Setting in Organizations," *Academy of Management Journal* 18, no. 4 (1964): 824; Gary Latham and Terrance A. Mitchell, "Importance of Participative Goal Setting and Anticipated Rewards on Goal Difficulty and Job Performance," *Journal of Applied Psychology* 63, (1978): 163–171; and Sondra Hart, William Moncrief, and A. Parasuraman, "An Empirical Investigation of Sales People's Performance, Effort, and Selling Method During a Sales Contest," *Journal of the Academy of Marketing Science* (Winter 1989): 29–39. See also, Theresa Libby, "The Influence of Voice and Explanation on Performance in a Participative Budget Setting," *Accounting, Organizations, and Society* (February 1999): 125.

23. The rest of this section, except as noted, is based on Gary Yukl, *Skills for Managers and Leaders* (Upper Saddle River, NJ: Prentice Hall, 1991), 132–33. See also Gary Latham, "Cognitive and Motivational Effects of Participation: A Mediator Study," *Journal of Organizational Behavior* (January 1994): 49–64.

24. Gary Yukl, *Skills for Managers and Leaders* (Upper Saddle River, NJ: Prentice Hall, 1991), 133; and Miriam Erez, Daniel Gopher, and Nira Arzi, "Effects of Goal Difficulty, Self-Set Goals, and Monetary Rewards on Dual Task Performance," *Organizational Behavior & Human Decision Processes* (December 1990): 247–269. See also Thomas Lee, "Explaining the Assigned Gold-Incentive Interaction: The Role of Self-Efficacy and Personal Goals," *Journal of Management* (July–August 1997): 541–550.

25. See, for example, Stephan Schiffman and Michele Reisner, "New Sales Resolutions," *Sales & Marketing* (January 1992): 15–16; and Steve Rosenstock, "Your Agent's Success," *Manager's Magazine* (September 1991): 21–23.

26. Gary Yukl, *Skills for Managers and Leaders* (Upper Saddle River, NJ: Prentice Hall, 1991), 133.

27. Gary Latham and Lise Saari, "The Effects of Holding Goal Difficulty Constant on Assigned and Participatively Set Goals," *Academy of Management Journal* 22 (1979): 163–68; and Mark Tubbs and Steven Ekeberg, "The Role of Intentions in Work Motivation: Implications for Goal Setting Theory and Research," *Academy of Management Review* (January 1991), pp. 180–199. See also Cathy Durham, "Effects of Leader Role, Team Set Goal Difficulty, Efficacy, and Tactics on Keying Effectiveness," *Organizational Behavior & Human Decision Processes* (November 1997): 203–232.

28. Gary Latham and Lise Saari, "The Effects of Holding Goal Difficulty Constant on Assigned and Participatively Set Goals," *Academy of Management Journal* 22 (1979): 163–168.

29. Gary Latham, Terence Mitchell, and Denise Dorsett, "Importance of Participative Goal Setting and Anticipated Rewards on Goal Difficulty and Job Performance," *Journal of Applied Psychology* 63, (1978): 170. See also John Wagner III, "Cognitive and Motivational Frameworks in U.S. Research on Participation: A Meta Analysis of Primary Effects," *Journal of Organizational Behavior* (January 1997): 49–66.

30. See, for example, Anthony Mento, Norman Cartledge, and Edwin Locke, "Maryland Versus Michigan Versus Minnesota: Another Look at the Relationship of Expectancy and Goal Difficulty to Task Performance," *Organizational Behavior and Human Performance* (June 1980): 419–440. See also Robert Renn, "Further Examination of the Measurement Properties of Leifer & McGannons 1986 Goal Acceptance and Gold Commitment Scales," *Journal of Occupational and Organizational Psychology* (March 1999): 107–114.

31. William Werther, "Workshops Aid in Goal Setting," *Personnel Journal* (November 1989): 32–38; See also Kenneth Thompson, et al, "Stretch Targets: What Makes Them Effective?" *Academy of Management Review* 11, no. 3 (1997): 48–60. See also Theresa Libby, "The Influence of Voice and Explanation on Performance in a Participative Budget Setting," *Accounting, Organizations, and Society* (February 1999): 125.

32. Based on interviews with Sterling McLeod and Wayne Walker, vice presidents of sales at Investors Group.

33. Steven Carroll and Henry Tosi, *Management by Objectives* (New York: Macmillan, 1973).

34. Mark McConkie, "A Clarification of the Goal Setting and Appraisal Processes in MBO," *Academy of Management Review*, (December 1991): 29–40. See also Dawn Winters, "The Effects of Learning vs. Outcome Goals on a Simple vs. a Complex Task," *Group and Organization Management* (June 1996): 236–251.

35. *Webster's Collegiate Dictionary of American English* (New York: Simon & Schuster, Inc. 1988).

36. Rona Maynard, "The Pain Threshold," *Canadian Business* (February, 1993): 24.

37. Murray R. Spiegel, *Statistics* (New York: Schaum Publishing, 1961), 283.

38. George Kress, *Practical Techniques of Business Forecasting* (Westport, CT: Quorum Books, 1985), 13. See also Diane Painter, "The Business Economist at Work: Mobil Corp.," *Business Economics* (April 1999): 52–55.

39. See, for example, Thomas Moore, *Handbook of Business Forecasting* (New York: Harper & Row, 1989), 5.

40. Connie Robbins Gentry, "Smart Moves," *Chain Store Age* 78, no. 1 (January 2002): 127–130.

41. Chuck Moozakis, "Silver Bullet Brewer Turns to Web System to Track Orders and Forecast," *Internet Weeks* (July 23, 2001): 14, 46.

42. Jim Chris Better, "Execs at Siebel Systems Know Trouble was Brewing so They Put a Cost-Cutting Plan into Action—Fast," *Business Week* (August 27, 2001): 112.

43. John Chambers, Santinder Mullick, and Donald Smith, "How to Choose the Right Forecasting Technique," *Harvard Business Review* (July–August 1971): 45–74; and Moore, *Handbook of Business Forecasting*, 265–290. See also John Mentzer, et al., "Benchmarking Sales Forecasting Management, *Business Horizons* (May–June 1999): 48–57. This study of 20 leading U.S. firms found widespread dissatisfaction regarding their current sales forecasting techniques.

44. A. Chairncross, quoted in Thomas Milne, *Business Forecasting. A Managerial Approach* (New York: Longman, 1975).

45. Alan Cowell, "In Shift, British Airways Looks to Coach," *The New York Times*, 14 February 2002, p. W–1.

46. Dennis Berman, "Lousy Sales Forecasts Helped Fuel the Telecom Mess," *The Wall Street Journal*, 9 July 2001, sec. B, p. 1.

47. Bolaji Ojo, "Cisco Getting Its House in Order After Gross Miscalculation," *EBN*, (October 1, 2001): 38.

48. Philip Kotler, *Marketing Management* (Upper Saddle River, NJ: Prentice Hall, 1997), 113.

49. Gina Mallet, "Greatest Romance on Earth," *Canadian Business* (August, 1993): 19–23.

50. E. Jerome McCarthy and William Perreault, Jr., *Basic Marketing* (Homewood, IL: Irwin, 1990), 131–132.

51. Susan Warren, "I-Spy: Getting the Lowdown on Your Competition is Just a Few Clicks Away," *The Wall Street Journal*, 14 January 2002, p. 14.

52. Susan Warren, "I-Spy: Getting the Lowdown on Your Competition is Just a Few Clicks Away," *The Wall Street Journal*, 14 January 2002, p. 14.

53. Andy Serwer, "P&G's Covert Operation," *Fortune* (September 17, 2001): 42–44.

54. Andrew Campbell, "Tailored, Not Benchmarked: A Fresh Look at Corporate Planning," *Harvard Business Review* (March–April 1999), 41–50.

55. Andrew Campbell, "Tailored, Not Benchmarked: A Fresh Look at Corporate Planning," *Harvard Business Review* (March–April 1999), 42.

56. Andrew Campbell, "Tailored, Not Benchmarked: A Fresh Look at Corporate Planning," *Harvard Business Review* (March–April 1999), 42.

57. Andrew Campbell, "Tailored, Not Benchmarked: A Fresh Look at Corporate Planning," *Harvard Business Review* (March–April 1999), 43.

58. Eric Matson, "Now that We Have Your Complete Attention," *Fast Company* (February–March 1997).

Chapter 7

1. Peter Drucker, Management: Tasks, Responsibilities, Practices (New York: Harper & Row, 1974), 611. For an interesting point of view on strategic management, see Daniel W. Greening and Richard A. Johnson, "Do Managers and Strategies Matter? A Study in Crisis," *Journal of Management Studies* (January 1996): 25–52.

2. Andrew Campbell and Marchus Alexander, "What's Wrong with Strategy?" *Harvard Business Review* (November–December 1977): 42.

3. Andrew Campbell and Marchus Alexander, "What's Wrong with Strategy?" *Harvard Business Review* (November–December 1977): 48.

4. See for example, Allan J. Rowe, Richard O. Mason, Carl E. Dickel, Richard B. Mann, and Robert J. Mockler, *Strategic Management* (Reading, MA: Addison-Wesley Publishing Co., 1989), 2; James Higgins and Julian Vincze, *Strategic Management* (Fort Worth, TX: The Dryden Press, 1993), 5; Peter Wright, Mark Kroll, and John Parnell, *Strategic Management Concepts* (Upper Saddle River, NJ: Prentice Hall, 1996), 1–15.

5. Arthur Thompson and A. J. Strickland, *Strategic Management* (Homewood, IL: Irwin, 1992), 4; Fred R. David, *Concepts of Strategic Management* (Upper Saddle River, NJ: Prentice Hall, 1997), 1–27. See also Bob Dust, "Making Mission Statements Meaningful," *Training & Development Journal* (June 1996): 53.

6. James Higgins and Julian Vincze, *Strategic Management* (Fort Worth, TX: The Dryden Press, 1993), 5.

7. Melanie Warner, "The Young and the Loaded," *Fortune* (September 27, 1999): 78–118.

8. Scott Kilman and Thomas Burton, "Monsanto Boss's Vision of Life Sciences Firm Now Confronts Reality," *The Wall Street Journal*, 21 December 1999, sec. A, p. 1.

9. Arthur Thompson and A. J. Strickland, *Strategic Management* (Homewood, IL: Irwin, 1992), 4. See also George Morrisey, *A Guide to Strategic Planning* (San Francisco: Jossey-Bass, 1996), 7.

10. Andrew Willis, "New CEO Pledges to Redefine B of M," *The Globe and Mail*, 24 February 1999, sec. B, p. 7.

11. David Berman, "Hold the Fries," *Canadian Business* (January 30, 1998): 32–34.

12. Susanne Craig, "Hunkin Takes Charge of CIBC Renovation," *The Globe and Mail*, 28 June 1999, sec. B, pp. 1, 4.

13. David Pringle, "Nokia Is the CEO, Marking a Decade, Faces Struggling, Quickly Changing Industry," *The Wall Street Journal*, 23 January 2002, sec. B, p. 70.

14. Danny Hakim, "With Hughes Sale, GM Buries a Discarded Strategy," *The New York Times*, 30 October 2001, sec. C, p. 8.

15. Julian Barnes, "Proctor Plans to Jettison Jif and Crisco," *The New York Times*, 26 April 2001, sec. C, p. 1.

16. This is quoted from, and this section is based on, Allan J. Rowe, Richard O. Mason, Carl E. Dickel, Richard B. Mann, and Robert J. Mockler, *Strategic Management* (Reading, MA: Addison-Wesley Publishing Co., 1989), 114–116; and Stephen George and Arnold Weimerskirch, *Total Quality Management* (New York: Wiley, 1994), 207–221. See also Jeffrey Sampler and James Short, "Strategy in Dynamic Information–Intensive Environments," *Journal of Management Studies* (July 1998): 429–436.

17. Oliver Bertin, "Rail Deal Makes Shipping Giant," *The Globe and Mail*, 20 December 1999, sec. B, p. 1.

18. This is based on James Higgins and Julian Vincze, *Strategic Management* (Fort Worth, TX: The Dryden Press, 1993), 200–204.

19. "Tricon Adds A & W, Long John Silver's to its Chain Gang," *The Globe and Mail*, 13 March 2002, sec. B, p. 7.

20. Jim Carbone, "Contract Manufacture is Moved to Vertical Integration," *Purchasing* 130, no. 20 (October 18, 2001): 33–35.

21. Allan J. Rowe, Richard O. Mason, Carl E. Dickel, Richard B. Mann, and Robert J. Mockler, *Strategic Management* (Reading, MA: Addison-Wesley Publishing Co., 1989), 246–247.

22. Arthur Thompson and A. J. Strickland, *Strategic Management* (Homewood, IL: Irwin, 1992), 169. See also Michael Lubatkin and Sayan Chatterjee, "Extending Portfolio Theory into the Domain of Corporate Diversification: Does It Apply?" *Academy of Management Journal* (February 1994): 109–136.

23. Suzanne Kapner, "Strategy Shift Puts Pictures With Words," *The New York Times*, 2 November 2001, p. W1.

24. "Amazon.com in Movie Service Deal with Disney," *The New York Times*, 19 May 2001, sec. B, p. 3.

25. Emily Waizer, "Remodeling the Middle," *Sporting Good Business* 35, no. 1 (January 2002): 44–45.

26. Peter Henig, "Revenge of the Bricks," *Red Herring* (August 2000): 121–133.

27. John Byrne, Richard Brandt, and Otis Port, "The Virtual Corporation," *Business Week* 8 (February 1993): 99. See also Keith Hammonds, "This Virtual Agency Has Big Ideas," *Fast Company* (November 1999), 70–74.

28. See also J. Carlos Jarillo, "On Strategic Networks," *Strategic Management Journal* 9 (1988): 31–41; and William Davidow and Michael Malone, "The Virtual Corporation," *California Business Review* 12 (November 1992): 34–42. See also Keith Hammonds, "This Virtual Agency Has Big Ideas," *Fast Company* (November 1999), 70–74.

29. John Byrne, Richard Brandt, and Otis Port, "The Virtual Corporation," *Business Week* 8 (February 1993): 99.

30. Virtual corporations should not be confused with the Japanese Keiretsus strategy. Keiretsus are tightly knit groups of firms governed by a supra-board of directors concerned with establishing the long-term survivability of the Keiretsus organization. Interlocking boards of directors and shared ownership help distinguish Keiretsus from other forms of strategic alliances, including virtual corporations. See, for example, John Byrne, Richard Brandt, and Otis Port, "The Virtual Corporation," *Business Week* 8 (February 1993): 101; Arthur Thompson and A. J. Strickland, *Strategic Management* (Homewood, IL: Irwin, 1992), 216; and Kenichi Ohmae, "The Global Logic of Strategic Alliances," *Harvard Business Review* (March–April 1989): 143–154. See also Richard Oliver, "Killer Keiretsu," *Management Review* (September 1999): 10–11.

31. Katherine Mieszkowski, "The Elance Economy," *Fast Company* (November 1999): 66–68.

32. Unless otherwise noted, the following is based on Michael E. Porter, *Competitive Strategy: Techniques for Analyzing Industries and Competitions* (New York: The Free Press, 1980); and Michael E. Porter, *Competitive Advantage* (New York: The Free Press, 1985).

33. In Christina Binkley, "Marriott to Turn Renaissance Units into Eclectic, Surprising Hotels," *The Wall Street Journal*, 27 August 2001, sec. B, p. 2.

34. Not everyone agrees that the only ways to compete are differentiation, low-cost, and focus. For example, one recent *Harvard Business Review* article argues that "managers competing in a business can choose among three distinct ways to fight. They can build a fortress and defend it; they can nurture and leverage unique resources; or they can flexibly pursue fleeting opportunities within simple rules." Kathleen Eisenhardt and Donald Sull, "Strategy as Simple Rules," *Harvard Business Review* (January 2001): 109.

35. Michael E. Porter, *Competitive Advantage* (New York: The Free Press, 1985), 14.

36. Michael E. Porter, *Competitive Advantage* (New York: The Free Press, 1985).

37. Michael E. Porter, *Competitive Strategy: Techniques for Analyzing Industries and Competitions* (New York: The Free Press, 1980), 17.

38. Gary Hamel, "Killer Strategies That Make Shareholders Rich," *Fortune* (June 23, 1997): 83.

39. Clayton Christensen, "Making Strategy: Learning by Doing," *Harvard Business Review* (November–December 1997): 141–156.

40. Clayton Christensen, "Making Strategy: Learning by Doing," *Harvard Business Review* (November–December 1997): 69.

41. Margot Gibb-Clark, "Hospital Managers Gain Tool to Compare Noties," *The Globe and Mail*, 9 September 1996, sec. B, p. 9.

42. Adrienne Carter, "Kodak's Promising Development," *Money* 31, no. 2 (February 2002): 39.

43. Herman Kahn and Anthony Weiner, *The Year 2000: A Framework for Speculation on the Next Thirty-Three Years* (New York: Macmillan, 1967), 6; quoted in George A. Steiner, *Strategic Planning: What Every Manager Must Know* (New York: The Free Press, 1979), 237; and Nicholas Georgantzas and William Acar, *Scenario-Driven Planning* (Westport, CT: Quorum Books, 1995). See also Diann Painter, "The Business Economist at Work. Mobil Corporation," *Business Economics* (April 1999): 52–55. See also Peter Bartram, "Prophet Making," *Director* 54, no. 12 (July 2001): 76–79.

44. "The Next Big Surprise," *The Economist* (October 13, 2001): 60.

45. Adam Kahane, "Scenarios for Energy: Sustainable World vs. Global Mercantilism," *Long-Range Planning* 25, no. 4 (1992): 38–46.

46. Kerry Tucker, "Scenario Planning: Visualizing a Broader World of Possibilities Can Help Associations Anticipate and Prepare for Change," *Association Management* (April 1999): 70–77.

47. Gil Ringland, *Scenario Planning: Managing the Future* (New York: Wiley, 1998).

48. Liam Fahey, "Scenario Learning," *Management Review* (March 2000): 30.

49. Michael E. Porter, "What Is Strategy?" *Harvard Business Review* (November–December 1996): 61–80.

50. Interprovincial Pipeline System Inc. 1992 Annual Report, 4–6.

51. Peer Verburg, "Reach for the Bottom," *Canadian Business* (March 6, 2000): 43–47.

52. Gary Hamel and C.K. Prahalad, "Strategy as Stretch and Leverage," *Harvard Business Review* (March–April 1993): 75–84.

53. Gary Hamel and C.K. Prahalad, "Strategy as Stretch and Leverage," *Harvard Business Review* (March–April 1993): 77.

54. Gary Hamel and C.K. Prahalad, "Strategy as Stretch and Leverage," *Harvard Business Review* (March–April 1993): 78.

55. Marlene Piturro, "CarMax: A Cautionary Tale," *Management Review* (September 1999): 30.

56. Shirley Leung, "Upper Crust: Fast Food Chains Fight to Carve Out Empire in Pricey Sandwiches," *The Wall Street Journal*, 5 February 2002, sec. A, p. A1.

57. C. K. Prahalad and Gary Hamel, "The Core Competence of a Corporation" *Harvard Business Review* (May–June 1990): 82.

58. C. K. Prahalad and Gary Hamel, "The Core Competence of a Corporation" *Harvard Business Review* (May–June 1990): 82.

59. Alan D. Gray, "Arrow Takes Aim," *The Montreal Gazette*, 5 September 1995, sec. C, pp. 3–4.

Chapter 8

1. James P. Sterba, "At the Met Opera, It's Not Over Till the Fat Man Folds," *The Wall Street Journal*, 5 January 1998, pp. 1, 6.

2. J. V. Gandz and V. V. Murray, "The Experience of Workplace Politics," *Academy of Management Journal* 23 (1980): 237–251.

3. "How Can Big Companies Keep the Entrepreneurial Spirit Alive?" *Harvard Business Review* (November–December 1995): 188–189. See also Mary Jo Hatch, "Exploring the Empty Spaces of Organizing: How Improvisational Jazz Helps Redescribe Organizational Structure," *Organization Studies* 20, no. 1 (1999): 75–100.

4. Ernest Dale, *Organization* (New York: AMA, 1967), 109. See also Ed Clark, "The Adoption of the Multidivisional Form in Large Czech Enterprises: The Role of Economics, Institutional and Strategic Choice Factors," *Journal of Management Studies* (July 1999): 535–537; and Tom Peters, "Destruction Is Cool" *Forbes* 23 (February 1998): 128.

5. Mark Dale Franco, "Synergies 250 Years in the Making," *Catalog Age* 18, no. 4 (March 15, 2001): 47–48.

6. Daniel Stoffman, "Mr. Clean," *Canadian Business* (June, 1996): 59–65.

7. Rekha Bach, "Heinz's Johnson to Divest Operations, Scrap Management of Firm by Region," *The Wall Street Journal*, 8 December 1997, sec. B, pp.10, 12.

8. Jana Parker-Pope and Joann Lublin, "P&G Will Make Jager CEO Ahead of Schedule," *The Wall Street Journal*, 10 September 1998, sec. B, pp. 1, 8.

9. Richard Blackwell, "New CIBC Boss Promises Shakeup," *The Globe and Mail*, 2 April 1999, sec. B, pp. 1, 4.

10. Chris Adams, "INS Is Retooling to Cast Agency as to Bureaus," *The Wall Street Journal*, 15 November 2001, sec. A, p. 18.

11. See, for example, Lawton Burns and Douglas Wholey, "Adoption and Abandonment of Matrix Management Programs: Effects of Organizational Characteristics and Interorganizational Networks," *Academy of Management Journal* (February 1993): 106–138.

12. Interview with Tom Ward, operations manager for Vancouver Shipyards Ltd.

13. *Organizing for International Competitiveness* (New York: Business International Corp., 1985), 117.

14. John Barham, "The Morgan Matrix," *Latin Finance*, Issue 126 (April 2001): 18.

15. Lawton Burns and Douglas Wholey, "Adoption and Abandonment of Matrix Management Programs: Effects of Organizational Characteristics and Interorganizational Networks," *Academy of Management Journal* (February 1993): 106.

16. For a discussion of this type of organization and its problems, see Stanley Davis and Paul Lawrence, *Matrix* (Reading, MA: Addison-Wesley, 1967); and Stanley Davis and Paul Lawrence, "Problems of Matrix Organizations," *Harvard Business Review* (May–June 1978): 131–142. See also Wilma Bernasco, "Balanced Matrix Structure and New Product Development Process at Texas Instruments Materials and Controls Division," *R&D Management* (April 1999): 121.

17. John Hunt, "Is Matrix Management a Recipe for Chaos?" *Financial Times* (January 1990): 14.

18. See, for example, Henri Fayol, *General and Industrial Management*, trans. Constance Storrs (London: Sir Isaac Putnam, 1949).

19. For a discussion of the contingencies affecting span of control (task uncertainty, professionalism, and interdependence), see, for example, Daniel Robey, *Designing Organizations*, 3rd ed. (Homewood, IL: Irwin, 1991), 258–259.

20. Judith H. Dobrzynski, "Jack Welch: How Good a Manager?" *Business Week* 14 (December 1987): 94. See also Thomas Stewart, "Brain Power," *Fortune* (March 17, 1997): 105–110.

21. *Webster's New World Dictionary*, 3rd college ed. (New York: Simon and Schuster, Inc., 1988), 911. For a discussion of networked organizations, see James Brian Quinn, *Intelligent Enterprise* (New York: Free Press, 1992), 213–240.

22. See, for example, John Child and Rita Gunther McGrath, "Organizations Unfettered: Organizational Form in an Information-Intensive Economy," *Academy of Management Journal* 44, no. 6 (2001): 1135–1148.

23. Paul Evans, Yves Doz, and Andre Laurent, *Human Resource Management in International Firms* (London: Macmillan, 1989), 123.

24. Ram Charan, "How Networks Reshape Organizations—For Results," *Harvard Business Review* (September–October 1991): 104–115.

25. Ram Charan, "How Networks Reshape Organizations—For Results," *Harvard Business Review* (September–October 1991): 108.

26. Christopher Bartlett and Sumantra Ghoshal, "What Is a Global Manager?" *Harvard Business Review* (September–October 1992): 62–74.

27. Cyrus Freidheim, Jr., "The Battle of the Alliances," *Management Review* (September 1999): 46–51.

28. David Kilpatrick, "Groupware Goes Boom," *Fortune* (December 27, 1993): 99–101.

29. Kenneth Laudon and Jane Laudon, Essentials of *Management Information Systems* (Upper Saddle River, NJ: Prentice Hall, 1997), 413–416.

30. Bob Underwood, "Transforming with Collaborative Computing," *AS/400 Systems Management* (March 1999), 59.

31. "Product Development Tool Gets Revamped with Java; IP Team Integrates Suppliers and Contractors," *Computer World* (May 24, 1999), 16.

32. Douglas Johnson, "Discuss Changing Models in Real Time," *Design News* (May 3, 1999): 96.

33. Tom Peters, *Thriving on Chaos* (New York: Harper & Row, 1987), 256.

34. Gordon Pitts, "The Cheese Plant Nobody Wanted," *The Globe and Mail*, 16 February 1993, sec. B, p. 24.

35. Charles Fishman, "Engines of Democracy," *Fast Company* (October 1999): 174–202.

36. Except as noted, the remainder of this section is based on James Shonk, *Team-Based Organizations* (Chicago: Irwin, 1997).

37. Tom Peters, *Liberation Management* (New York: Alfred Knopf, 1992), 238.

38. William H. Miller, "Chesebrough-Ponds at a Glance," *Industry Week* (October 19, 1992): 14–15.

39. Michael Hammer and John Champy, *Reengineering the Corporation* (New York: Harper Business, 1992), 32.

40. Michael Hammer and Steven Stanton, "How Process Enterprise is Really Work," *Harvard Business Review* (November–December 1999): 108–118.

41. Except as noted, this section is based on John A. Byrne, "The Horizontal Corporation," *Business Week* (December 20, 1993): 76–81.

42. See for example *Webster's New Collegiate Dictionary* (Springfield, MA: G&C Miriam Company, 1973), 420.

43. For a discussion of how modularity contributes to flexibility, see, for example, Melissa Schilling and H. Kevin Steensma, "The Use of Modular Organizational Forms: An Industry Level Analysis," *Academy of Management Journal* 44, no. 6 (2001): 1149–1168.

44. Raymond Miles, et al, "Organizing in the Knowledge Age: Anticipating the Cellular Form," *Academy of Management Executive* 1997): 7–24.

45. Raymond Miles et al, "Organizing in the Knowledge Age: Anticipating the Cellular Form," *Academy of Management Executive* 1997): 13.

46. Raymond Miles et al, "Organizing in the Knowledge Age: Anticipating the Cellular Form," *Academy of Management Executive* 1997): 13.

47. John Byrne, Richard Brandt, and Otis Port, "The Virtual Corporation," *Business Week* (February 8, 1993): 99.

48. Marie-Claude Boudreau et al, "Going Global: Using Information Technology to Advance the Competitiveness of the Virtual Transnational Organization," *Academy of Management Executive* (1998): 121–122.

49. Marie-Claude Boudreau et al, "Going Global: Using Information Technology to Advance the Competitiveness of the Virtual Transnational Organization," *Academy of Management Executive* (1998): 122.

50. See for example Gail Dutton, "The New Consortiums," *Management Review* (January 1999): 46–50.

Chapter 9

1. Tom Peters, *Liberation Management* (New York: Alfred Knopf, 1992), 310; see also, Peter Dujardin, "Motivational Speaker Jump-Starts Norfolk Virginia Audience," *Knight-Ridder/Tribune Business News* (September 30, 1999), 6.

2. Tom Burns and G. M. Stalker, *The Management of Innovation* (London: Tavistock, 1961), 1.

3. Emery and Trist, two other British researchers, referred to this innovative environment as a "turbulent field" environment because changes often come not from a firm's traditional competitors, but from out of the blue. Often, in fact, the changes seem to "arise from the field itself," in that they result from interaction between parts of the environment. The very "texture" of a firm's environment changes because previously unrelated or (from the point of view of the firm), irrelevant elements in its environment become interconnected. F. E. Emery and E. C. Trist, "The Causal Texture of Organizational Environments," *Human Relations* (August 1965): 20–26. As an example, after 1970 (when digital watches were introduced), calculator firms like Texas Instruments suddenly and unexpectedly became competitors in the watch industry.

4. How can we explain the fact that an organization's environment and technology influence its structure? One plausible explanation is that some environments and technologies require managers to handle more unforeseen problems and decisions than do others. And since each person's capacity for juggling problems and making decisions is limited, an overabundance of problems forces managers to respond—often by reorganizing. Thus, when a manager finds himself or herself becoming overloaded with problems, one reasonable response is to give subordinates more autonomy, to decentralize (thus letting employees handle more problems among themselves), and to reorganize around self-contained divisions. By reorganizing in these ways, the manager may surrender some direct control, but at least the organization avoids becoming unresponsive, as might otherwise have been the case.

5. Steve Lohr, "He Loves to Win. At IBM, He Did," *The New York Times*, 10 March 2002, sec. Business, p. 11.

6. Joann Lublin, "Price vs. Product: It's Tough to Choose a Management Model," *The Wall Street Journal*, 27 June 2001, sec. A, p. 1.

7. Peter Senge, *The Fifth Discipline: The Art and Practice of the Learning Organizations* (New York: Currency Doubleday, 1994), 3.

8. Peter Senge, *The Fifth Discipline: The Art and Practice of the Learning Organizations* (New York: Currency Doubleday, 1994), 4.

9. Robert Rowden, "The Learning organization and Strategic Change," *SAM Advanced Management Journal* 66, no. 3 (Summer 2001): 11.

10. Peter Senge, *The Fifth Discipline: The Art and Practice of the Learning Organizations* (New York: Currency Doubleday, 1994), 8-10, 139–301.

11. Justin Fox, "Nokia's Secret Code," *Fortune* (May 1, 2000): 170.

12. Mary Anne Devanna and Noel Tichy, "Creating the Competitive Organization of the 21st Century: The Boundaryless Corporation," *Human Resource Management* (Winter 1990): 455–471.

13. This is based on Lary Hirschhorn and Thomas Gilmore, "The New Boundaries of the 'Boundaryless' Company," *Harvard Business Review* (May–June, 1992): 104–108.

14. Lary Hirschhorn and Thomas Gilmore, "The New Boundaries of the 'Boundaryless' Company," *Harvard Business Review* (May–June, 1992): 107.

15. Lary Hirschhorn and Thomas Gilmore, "The New Boundaries of the 'Boundaryless' Company," *Harvard Business Review* (May–June, 1992): 108.

16. Lary Hirschhorn and Thomas Gilmore, "The New Boundaries of the 'Boundaryless' Company," *Harvard Business Review* (May–June, 1992): 109.

17. Luc Hatlestad, "New Shades of Blue," *Red Herring* (November 1999): 126.

18. Except as noted, this section is based on Tom Peters, *Thriving on Chaos* (New York: Harper & Row, 1987), 425–438; and Tom Peters, *Liberation Management* (New York: Alfred Knopf, 1992), 90–95.

19. "How Can Big Companies Keep the Entrepreneurial Spirit Alive?" *Harvard Business Review* (November–December 1996): 188–189.

20. Rob Walker, "Down on the Farm" *Fast Company* (February – March, 1997): 112–122.

21. The following points are based on Robert Rowden, "The Learning Organization and Strategic Change," *SAM Advanced Management Journal* 66, no. 3 (Summer 2001): 11.

22. Robert Hercz, "Shooting for Profits," *Canadian Business* (June 12, 1998): 71–73.

23. John Partridge, "Abitibi Dares to Digest Another Deal," *The Globe and Mail*, 27 February 1998, sec. B, p. 27.

24. Jay Galbraith, "Organizational Design: An Information Processing View," *Interfaces* 4, no. 3, (1974): 28–36; and Jay Galbraith, *Organizational Design* (Reading, MA: Addison-Wesley, 1977). See also Ranjay Gulati, "The Architecture of Co-operation: Managing Coordination Costs and Appropriation Concerns in Strategic Alliances," *Administrative Science Quarterly* (December 1998): 781–784.

25. Henry Mintzberg, *Structure in Fives: Designing Effective Organizations* (Upper Saddle River, NJ: Prentice Hall, 1983), 4–9. Cliff McGoon, "Cutting-Edge Companies Use Integrated Marketing Communication," *Communication World* (December 1998): 15–20.

26. Henry Mintzberg, *Structure in Fives: Designing Effective Organizations* (Upper Saddle River, NJ: Prentice Hall, 1983), 6.

27. Christopher A. Bartlett and Sumantra Ghoshal, "Matrix Management: Not a Structure, a Frame of Mind," *Harvard Business Review* (July–August 1990): 138–145. See also K. Simon-Elorz, "Information Technology for Organizational Systems: Some Evidence with Case Studies," *International Journal of Information Management* (February 1999): 75; and Alexander Gerybadz, "Globalization of R&D: Recent Changes in The Management of Innovation in Transnational Corporations," *Research Policy* (March 1999): 251–253.

28. Henry Mintzberg, *Structure in Fives: Designing Effective Organizations* (Upper Saddle River, NJ: Prentice Hall, 1983), 4.

29. Paul Lawrence and Jay Lorsch, *Organization and Environment* (Cambridge, MA: Harvard University Press, 1967). See also Frank Mueller and Romano Dyerson, "Expert Humans or Expert Organizations?" *Organization Studies* 20, no. 2, (1999): 225–256. Some companies today practise concurrent engineering to improve production coordination, which basically means having all the departments—design, production, and marketing, for instance—work together to develop the product so that its production and marketing are more easily coordinated once the item goes into production. See Hassan Abdalla, "Concurrent Engineering for Global Manufacturing," *International Journal of Production Economics* (April 20, 1999): 251.

30. Paul Lawrence and Jay Lorsch, *Organization and Environment* (Boston: Division of Research, Graduate School of Business Administration, Harvard University, 1967), 1.

31. Alan Church and Janine Waclawski, "Hold the Line: An Examination of Line vs. Staff Differences," *Human Resource Management* 40, no. I (Spring 2001): 21–34.

32. Gary Dessler, *Organization Theory* (Englewood Cliffs, NJ: Prentice Hall, 1980), 333–336.

33. Ross Stagner, "Conflict in the Executive Suite," in *American Bureaucracy*, ed. Warren Ennis (Chicago: Aldine, 1970), 85–95.

34. James Thompson, *Organizations in Action* (New York: McGraw-Hill, 1967).

35. Louis Stern, Brian Sternthal, and C. Samuel Craig, "Strategies for Managing Interorganizational Conflict: A Laboratory Paradigm," *Journal of Applied Psychology* 60, no. 4 (August 1975): 472–482.

36. These are based on Stephen Robbins and Philip Hunsaker, *Training in Interpersonal Skills* (Upper Saddle River, NJ: Prentice Hall, 1996), 91–95; and David Whetter and Kim Cameron, *Developing Management Skills* (Upper Saddle River, NJ: Prentice Hall, 2002), 435–435.

37. Roger Crockett, "Can Chris Galvin Save His Family's Legacy?" *Business Week* Issue 3741, pp. 72–78.

38. Larry Bossidy, "The Job No CEO Should Delegate" *Harvard Business Review* (March 2001): 47–49.

39. Ann Gibbon, "CN's New Boss Takes Hard Line," *The Globe and Mail*, 8 February 1993, sec. B, pp. 1–2.

40. A. Ross, "BMO's Big Bang," *Canadian Business* (January, 1994): 58–63.

41. Tom Hamburger et al., "Auditor Who Questioned Accounting for Enron Speaks to Investigators," *The Wall Street Journal*, 1 April 2001, sec. C, p. 1.

42. The foundation study for this conclusion is Alfred Chandler, *Strategy and Structure* (Cambridge: MIT Press, 1962); for a recent literature review and test of the strategy–structure link see Terry Amburgey and Tina Dacin, "As the Left Foot Follows the Right? The Dynamics of Strategic and Structural Change," *Academy of Management Journal* 37, no. 6, (1994): 1427–1452.

43. Alfred Chandler, *Strategy and Structure* (Cambridge: MIT Press, 1962), 14.

44. Alfred Chandler, *Strategy and Structure* (Cambridge: MIT Press, 1962), 366.

45. Jared Sandberg, "New AOL and Unit Will Promote Marketing Across Multiple Media," *The Wall Street Journal*, 20 August 2002, sec. B, p. 7.

46. Kenneth MacKenzie, *Organizational Structure* (Arlington Heights, OH: AHM 1978), 198–230.

47. John Case, "The Open Book Management Revolution," *Inc.* (June 1995): 26–43.

Chapter 10

1. Peter Boxall, "Placing HR Strategy at the Heart of Business Success," *Personnel Management* 26, no. 7 (July 1994): 32–34.

2. See also James Clifford, "Manage Work Better to Better Manage Human Resources: A Comparative Study of Two Approaches to Job Analysis," *Public Personnel Management* (Spring 1996): 89–103.

3. Gary Dessler, *Human Resource Management*, 9th ed. (Upper Saddle River, NJ: Prentice Hall, 2003), 64–76.

4. Arthur R. Pell, *Recruiting and Selecting Personnel* (New York: Regents, 1969), 10–12; see also Katherine Tyler, "Employees Can Help Recruiting New Talent," *HRMagazine* (September 1996): 57–61.

5. Arthur R. Pell, *Recruiting and Selecting Personnel* (New York: Regents, 1969), 11.

6. Gary Dessler, *Human Resource Management*, 9th ed. (Upper Saddle River, NJ: Prentice Hall, 2003), 112.

7. Allison Thompson, "The Contingent Workforce," *Occupational Outlook Quarterly* (Spring 1995): 45.

8. Gary Dessler, *Human Resource Management*, 9th ed. (Upper Saddle River, NJ: Prentice Hall, 2003), 104.

9. "Search and Destroy," *The Economist* (June 27, 1998): 63.

10. "Search and Destroy," *The Economist* (June 27, 1998): 63.

11. "High-Stakes Recruiting in High-Tech," *BNA Bulletin to Management* (February 12, 1998): 48.

12. Sara Rynes, Marc Orlitzky, and Robert Bretz, Jr., "Experienced Hiring versus College Recruiting: Practices and Emerging Trends," *Personnel Psychology* 50 (1997): 309–339.

13. This compares with 21.5% for black job seekers and 23.9% for white job seekers. Michelle Harrison Ports, "Trends in Job Search Methods, 1990–92," *Monthly Labor Review* (October 1993): 64.

14. "Workplace Testing and Monitoring," *Management Review* (October 1998): 31–42.

15. "Workplace Testing and Monitoring," *Management Review* (October 1998): 31–42.

16. Mel Kleiman, "Employee Testing Essential to Hiring Effectively in the '90s," *Houston Business Journal* (February 8, 1993): 31; and Gerald L. Borofsky, "Pre-Employment Psychological Screening," *Risk Management* (January 1993): 47; See also Christina Ron Quist, "Pre-Employment Testing: Making It Work for You," *Occupational Hazards* (December 1997): 38–40.

17. Louis Olivas, "Using Assessment Centers for Individual and Organizational Development," *Personnel* (May–June 1980): 63–67; Tim Payne, Neil Anderson, and Tom Smith, "Assessment Centers, Selection Systems and Cost–Effectiveness: An Evaluative Case Study," *Personnel Review* (Fall 1992): 48; and Roger Mottram, "Assessment Centers Are Not Only for Selection: The Assessment Center as a Development Workshop," *Journal of Managerial Psychology* (January 1992): A1; Charles Woodruffe, "Going Back a Generation," *People Management* (February 20, 1997): 32–35.

18. Rose Fisher, "Screen Test," *Canadian Business* (May, 1992): 62–64.

19. Neal Schmitt et al., "Computer–Based Testing Applied to Selection of Secretarial Candidates," *Personnel Psychology* 46, no. 19, pp. 149–165.

20. For a full discussion of this, see Gary Dessler, *Human Resource Management*, 8th ed. (Upper Saddle River, NJ: Prentice Hall, 2000), Chapter 6.

21. R. E. Carlson, "Selection Interview Decisions: The Effects of Interviewer Experience, Relative Quota Situation, and Applicant Sample on Interview Decisions," *Personnel Psychology* 20 (1967): 259–280; See also Linda Thornburgh, "Computer-Assisted Interviewing Shortens Hiring Cycle," *HRMagazine* (February 1998): 73–76.

22. Pamela Paul, "Interviewing is Your Business," *Association Management* (November 1992): 29.

23. William Tullar, Terry Mullins, and Sharon Caldwell, "Effects of Interview Length and Applicant Quality on Interview Decision Time," *Journal of Applied Psychology* (December 1979): 669–674; See also Jennifer Burnett et. al. "Interview Notes and Validity," *Personnel Psychology* (Summer 1998): 375–396.

24. Gary Dessler, *Human Resource Management*, 7th ed. (Upper Saddle River, NJ: Prentice Hall, 1997), 242–243.

25. See, for example, George Burgnoli, James Campion, and Jeffrey Bisen, "Racial Bias in the Use of Work Samples for Personnel Selection," *Journal of Applied Psychology* (April 1979): 119–123.

26. Wayne F. Cascio and Val Silbey, "Utility of the Assessment Center as a Selection Device," *Journal of Applied Psychology* (April 1979): 107–118. See also Paul R. Sackett, "Assessment Centers and Content Validity: Some Neglected Issues," *Personnel Psychology* 40 (Spring 1981): 55–64.

27. John Jones and William Terris, "Post-Polygraph Selection Techniques," *Recruitment Today* (May–June 1989): 25–31.

28. These are based on Commerce Clearing House, *Ideas and Trends* (December 29, 1998): 222–223. See also "Divining Integrity Through Interviews," *BNA Bulletin to Management* (June 4, 1987): 184.

29. Gary Dessler, *Human Resource Management*, 9th ed. (Upper Saddle River, NJ: Prentice Hall, 2003), 150–151.

30. Malcolm McKillip, "An Employer's Guide to Drug Testing," *The Globe and Mail*, 9 April 1998, sec. B, p. 13.

31. Margot Gibb-Clark, "Ruling Narrows Options for Drug Testing," *The Globe and Mail*, 28 July 1998, sec. B, p. 11.

32. William Berliner and William McLarney, *Management Practice and Training* (Burr Ridge, IL: McGraw-Hill, 1974), 442–443. See also Stephen Wehrenberg, "Supervisors as Trainees: The Long–Term Gains of OJT," *Personnel Journal* 66, no. 4 (April 1987): 48–51.

33. Bruce Little, "A Factory Learns to Survive," *The Globe and Mail*, 18 May 1993, sec. B, p. 22.

34. Scott Feschuk, "Phi Beta Cuppa," *The Globe and Mail*, 6 March 1993, sec. B, pp. 1, 4.

35. Gordon Pitts, "Stepping on the Quality Ladder," *The Globe and Mail*, 30 June 1992, sec. B, p. 20.

36. Jane Allen, "Literacy at Work," *Canadian Business* (February, 1991): 70–73.

37. Harvey Enchin, "Employee Training a Must," *The Globe and Mail*, 15 May 1991, sec. B, p. 6.

38. "Industry Report 1999" *Training* (October 1999): 37–60.

39. Jennifer Reese, "Starbuck," *Fortune* (December 9, 1996): 190–200.

40. Shari Caudron, "Your Learning Technology Primer," *Personnel Journal* (June 1996): 120–136.

41. "Creating Portals to Effective Learning," *Training* 538, no. 1 (January 2001): 41–42.

42. Del Jones, "More Firms Cut Workers Ranked at Bottom to Make Way for Talent," *USA Today*, 30 May 2001, sec. BU, p. 1.

43. Kenneth Nowack, "360-Degree Feedback: The Whole Story," *Training and Development* (January 1993): 69. For a description of some of the problems involved in implementing 360-degree feedback, see Matthew Budman, "The Rating Game," *Across the Board* (February 1994): 35–38.

44. Katherine Romano, "Fear of Feedback," *Management Review* (December 1993): 39.

45. See, for instance, Gerry Rich, "Group Reviews—Are You Up to It?" *CMA Magazine* (March 1993): 5.

46. Katherine Romano, "Fear of Feedback," *Management Review* (December 1993).

47. "360-Degree Feedback on the Rise, Survey Finds," *BNA Bulletin to Management* (January 23, 1997): 31; see also Kenneth Nowack et al., "How to Evaluate Your 360-Degree Feedback Efforts," *Training and Development Journal* (April 1999): 48–53.

48. Tom Davis and Michael Landa, "Pat or Slap: Do Appraisals Work?" *CMA Management* (March, 1999), 24–26.

49. This is based on Gary Dessler, *Human Resource Management*, 8th ed. (Upper Saddle River, NJ: Prentice Hall, 2000), 321–323.

50. Janet McFarland, "CEO Pay Fails to Mimic Profits," *The Globe and Mail*, 23 April 2002, sec. B, pp. 1, 7.

51. Andrew Willis, "Canadians Don't Trust Executives, Survey Says," *The Globe and Mail*, 2 July 2002, sec. B, p. 5.

52. "How the CEOs Ranked in 2001" *The Globe and Mail*, 23 April 2002, sec. B, p. 6; also "More Big Winners," *The Globe and Mail*, 23 April 2002, sec. B, p. 7.

53. Canada @Work, *Workforce Commitment Report*, 2000, 17.

54. David Roberts," A Long Way from Cambodia," *The Globe and Mail*, 5 July 1994, sec. B, p. 18.

55. Canada @Work, *Workforce Commitment Report*, 2000, 18.

56. Bruce McDougall, "The Thinking Man's Assembly Line," *Canadian Business* (November, 1991): 40.

57. Terrence Belford, "Flex Plans Now Offer What Employees Really Want: Cash," *The Globe and Mail*, 13 May 1998, sec. B, p. 27.

58. Canada @Work, *Workforce Commitment Report*, 2000, 18.

59. "Canadians Are Retiring Earlier," *The Winnipeg Free Press*, 12 June 1997, sec. B, p. 12.

60. Michael Moss, '"For Older Employees, On-the-Job Injuries Are More Often Deadly," *The Wall Street Journal*, 17 June 1991, sec. A, pp. 1, 10.

61. Thomas Claridge, "Fired Jumbo Boss Awarded $226,000" *The Globe and Mail*, 31 May 1995, sec. B, p. 5.

62. Dianne Forrest, "Guess Who You Can't Fire," *Canadian Business* (November, 1991): 97–100.

63. John Partridge, "B of M Lauded for Promoting Women's Careers," *The Globe and Mail*, 7 January 1994, sec. B, p. 3.

64. Vivian Smith, "Breaking Down the Barriers," *The Globe and Mail*, 17 November 1992, sec. B, p. 24.

65. Bob Cox, "Women Gaining on Men's Wages," *The Globe and Mail*, 18 January 1994, sec. B, p. 4.

66. Statistics Canada, *Survey of Labour and Income Dynamics: Moving Out of Low-Paid Work, 1993–1995*.

67. Kirk Makin, "Workplace Harassment is a Dangerous Game," *The Globe and Mail*, 22 April 2002, sec. B, p. 10.

68. Margot Gibb-Clark, "Harassment Cases Can Also Hurt Employers," *The Globe and Mail*, 16 September 1991, sec. B, p. 24.

69. Ted Kennedy, "Beware of Health and Safety Law: It Could Bite You," *Canadian Business* (December, 1990): 19.

70. Moira Farr," Work that Wounds and How to Cure It," *Canadian Business* (December, 1991): 90; also "Industrial Workers Learn to Stretch and Save, *Canadian Business* (October, 1991): 16.

71. Gary Dessler, *Human Resource Management*, 7th ed. (Upper Saddle River, NJ: Prentice Hall, 1997), 632–633.

72. John Aram, *Presumed Superior* (Upper Saddle River, NJ: Prentice Hall, 1993).

73. See Paul Judge, "How Might Your Company Adapt?" *Fast Company*, no. 53 (December 2001): 128–139.

74. Deze Khasru, "JetBlue Hopes to Fly Through Tough Times," *Fairfield County Business Journal* 40, no. 41 (October 8, 2001): 7.

75. "JetBlue," *Fortune Small Business* 11, no. 2 (March 1, 2001): 92.

76. "JetBlue," *Fortune Small Business* 11, no. 2 (March 1, 2001): 92.

77. Amy Kottier, "The Skies Are JetBlue," *Workforce* 80, no. 9 (September 2001): 22.

Chapter 11

1. Jeffrey McNally, Stephen Gerras, and R. Craig Bullis, "Teaching Leadership at the U.S. Military Academy at West Point," *Journal of Applied Behavioral Science* (June 1996): 181.

2. See David Waldman, Gabriel Ramirez, Robert J. House, and Phanish Puranam, "Does Leadership Matter? CEO Leadership Attributes and Profitability Under Conditions of Perceived Incremental Uncertainty," *Academy of Management Journal* 44, no. 1 (2001): 134–143.

3. Gary Yukl, *Leadership in Organizations* (Upper Saddle River, NJ: Prentice Hall, 1998), 235.

4. Ralph Stogdill, *Handbook of Leadership: A Survey of the Literature* (New York: Free Press, 1974), 81, quoted in Gary Yukl, *Leadership in Organizations* (Upper Saddle River, NJ: Prentice Hall, 1998), 236.

5. Shelley Kirkpatrick and Edwin Locke, "Leadership: The Traits Matter?" *Academy of Management Executive* (May 1991): 49.

6. Shelley Kirkpatrick and Edwin Locke, "Leadership: The Traits Matter?" *Academy of Management Executive* (May 1991): 50.

7. Kim-Yin Chan and Fritz Drasgow, "Toward a Theory of Individual Differences and Leadership: Understanding the Motivation to Lead," *Journal of Applied Psychology* 86, no. 3 (2001): 481–498.

8. Shelley Kirkpatrick and Edwin Locke, "Leadership: The Traits Matter?" *Academy of Management Executive* (May 1991): 53.

9. Jerry Useem, "What It Takes" *Fortune* (November 12, 2001): 130.

10. Jerry Useem, "What It Takes" *Fortune* (November 12, 2001): 55.

11. Jerry Useem, "What It Takes" *Fortune* (November 12, 2001): 5–6.

12. Chester Barnard, *The Functions of the Executive* (Cambridge, MA: Harvard University Press, 1938). See also Roger Dawson, *Secrets of Power Persuasion* (Upper Saddle River, NJ: Prentice Hall, 1992); Sydney Finkelstein, "Power in Top Management Teams: Dimensions, Measurement, and Validation," *Academy of Management Journal* (August 1992); and Jeffrey Pfeffer, *Managing with Power: Politics and Influence in Organizations* (Boston: Harvard Business School Press, 1992).

13. Eli Cohen and Noel Tichy, "Operation: Leadership," *Fast Company* (September 1999), 280.

14. Eli Cohen and Noel Tichy, "Operation: Leadership," *Fast Company* (September 1999), 280.

15. See, for example, Shelley Kirkpatrick and Edwin Locke, "Leadership: The Traits Matter?" *Academy of Management Executive* (May 1991): 49.

16. Shelley Kirkpatrick and Edwin Locke, "Leadership: The Traits Matter?" *Academy of Management Executive* (May 1991): 56.

17. See John Kotter, "What Leaders Really Do," *Harvard Business Review* (December 2001): 86–95.

18. Ralph Stogdill, *Managers, Employees, Organizations* (Columbus: Bureau of Business Research, Ohio State University, 1965).

19. Ralph Stogdill and A. E. Koonz, *Leader Behavior: Its Description and Measurement* (Columbus: Bureau of Business Research, Ohio State University, 1957). See also Bernard M. Bass, *Bass & Stogdill's Handbook of Leadership: Theory, Research, & Managerial Applications* 3rd ed. (New York: The Free Press, 1990).

20. Gary Yukl, "Towards a Behavioral Theory of Leadership," *Organizational Behavior and Human Performance* (July 1971): 414–440. See also Gary A. Yukl, *Leadership in Organizations*, 3rd ed. (Upper Saddle River, NJ: Prentice Hall, 1994).

21. Chester Schriesheim, Robert J. House, and Steven Kerr, "Leader Initiating Structure: A Reconciliation of Discrepant Research Results and Some Empirical Tests," *Organizational Behavior and Human Performance* (April 1976). See also Bernard M. Bass, *Bass & Stogdill's Handbook of Leadership: Theory, Research, & Managerial Applications*, 3rd ed. (New York: The Free Press, 1990).

22. Robert Blake and Jane Mouton, *The Managerial Grid* (Houston: Gulf Pub., 1994).

23. Rensis Likert, *New Patterns of Management* (New York: McGraw-Hill, 1961).

24. Robert Day and Robert Hamblin, "Some Effects of Close and Punitive Styles of Leadership," *American Journal of Psychology* 69 (1964): 499–510.

25. See for example, Nancy Morse, *Satisfaction in the White Collar Job* (Ann Arbor, MI: Survey Research Center, University of Michigan, 1953).

26. Rachel Silverman and Chris Maher, "Bosses Challenge: So the Workers Get the Job Done," *The Wall Street Journal*, 23 October 2001, sec. B, p. 1.

27. "Prada Faces Shaky Future with Slowing Economy," *The Wall Street Journal*, 8 November 2001, sec. B, p. 12.

28. Victor Vroom and Arthur Jago, "On the Validity of the Vroom-Yetton Model," *Journal of Applied Psychology* 63, no. 2 (1978): 151–162; Madeleine Heilman et al, "Reactions to Prescribed Leader Behavior as a Function of Role Perspective: The Case of Vroom-Yetton Model," *Journal of Applied Psychology* (February 1984): 50–60. See also Donna Brown, "Why Participative Management Won't Work Here" *Management Review* (June 1992).

29. Harvey Enchin, "Consensus Management? Not for Bombardier's CEO," *The Globe and Mail*, 16 April 1990, sec. B, p. 1.

30. Michael Stern, "New Tory Chief Must Motivate by Leading," *The Globe and Mail*, 29 March 1993, sec. B, p. 4.

31. M. Love, "Let's Forget Tradition," *Winnipeg Business People* (August–September, 1990): 11.

32. See, for example, Mark Tubbs and Steven Akeberg, "The Role of Intentions in Work Motivation: Implications for Goal Setting Theory and Research," *Academy of Management Review* (January 1991): 180–199.

33. Carol Hymowitz, "In Times of Trouble, the Best of Leaders Listen to Dissenters," *The Wall Street Journal*, 13 November 2001, sec. B, p. 1.

34. C. M. Solomon, "Careers Under Glass," *Personnel Journal* 69, no. 4 (1990): 96–105.

35. Gordon Pitts, "Men, Women Don't Manage Differently After All, Study Finds," *The Globe and Mail*, 27 May 2002, sec. B, pp. 1, 5.

36. See, for example, James Bowditch and Anthony Buono, *A Primer on Organizational Behavior* (New York: John Wiley, 1994), 238.

37. Russell Kent and Sherry Moss, "Effects of Sex and Gender Role on Leader Emergence," *Academy of Management Journal* 37, no. 5 (1994): 1335–1346; Jane Baack, Norma Carr–Ruffino, and Monica Pelletier, "Making It to the Top: Specific Leadership Skills," *Women in Management Review* 8, no. 2 (1993): 17–23.

38. S. M. Donnel and J. Hall, "Men and Women as Managers: A Significant Case of No Significant Difference," *Organizational Dynamics* 8 (1980): 60–77. See also Jennifer L. Berdahl, "Gender and Leadership in Work Groups: Six Alternative Models," *Leadership Quarterly* (Spring 1996): 21–40.

39. M. A. Hatcher, "The Corporate Woman of the 1990s: Maverick or Innovator?" *Psychology of Women Quarterly* 5 (1991): 251–259.

40. D. G. Winter, *The Power Motive* (New York: The Free Press, 1975).

41. L. McFarland Shore and G. C. Thornton, "Effects of Gender on Self and Supervisory Ratings," *Academy of Management Journal* 29, no. 1 (1986): 115–129; quoted in James Bowditch and Anthony Buono, *A Primer on Organizational Behavior* (New York: John Wiley, 1994), 238.

42. G. H. Dobbins and S. J. Paltz, "Sex Differences in Leadership: How Real Are They?" *Academy of Management Review* 11 (1986): 118–127; R. Drazin and E. R. Auster, "Wage Differences Between Men and Women: Performance Appraisal Ratings versus Salary Allocation as the Locus of Bias," *Human Resource Management* 26 (1987): 157–168. See also Nancy DiTomaso and Robert Hooijberg, "Diversity and the Demands of Leadership," *Leadership Quarterly* (Summer 1996): 163–187 and Chao C. Chen and Ellen Van Velsor, "New Directions for Research and Practice in Diversity Leadership," *Leadership Quarterly* (Summer 1996): 285–302.

43. M. Jelinek and N. J. Alder, "Women: World-Class Managers for Global Competition," *Academy of Management Executive* 2, no. 1 (1988), 11–19; J. Grant, "Women as Managers: What Can They Offer to Organizations?" *Organizational Dynamics* 16, no. 3 (1988): 56–63. On the other hand, one author suggests that women should be more Machiavellian: "War favors the dangerous woman. Women may love peace and seek stability, but these conditions seldom serve them." Harriet Rubin, *The Princessa: Machiavelli for Women* (New York: Doubleday/Currenly, 1997), quoted in Anne Fisher, "What Women Can Learn from Machiavelli," *Fortune* (April 1997): 162.

44. J. M. Burns, *Leadership* (New York: Harper, 1978).

45. For a discussion, see Ronald Deluga, "Relationship of Transformational and Transactional Leadership with Employee Influencing Strategies," *Group and Organizational Studies* (December 1988): 457–458. See also Philip M. Podsakoff, Scott B. MacKenzie, and William H. Bommer, "Transformational Leader Behaviors as Determinants of Employee Satisfaction, Commitment, Trust, and Organizational Citizenship Behaviors," *Journal of Management* 22, no. 2 (1996): 259–298.

46. Joseph Seltzer and Bernard Bass, "Transformational Leadership: Beyond Initiation and Consideration," *Journal of Management* 4 (1990): 694. See also Bernard M. Bass, "Theory of Transformational Leadership Redux," *Leadership Quarterly* (Winter 1995): 463–478.

47. Gary A. Yukl, *Leadership in Organizations,* 3rd ed. (Upper Saddle River, NJ: Prentice Hall, 1994) 269.

48. N. M. Tichy and M. A. Devanna, *The Transformational Leader* (New York: Wiley 1986).

49. Joseph Seltzer and Bernard Bass, "Transformational Leadership: Beyond Initiation and Consideration," *Journal of Management* 4 (1990): 694.

50. Ronald Deluga, "Relationship of Transformational and Transactional Leadership with Employee Influencing Strategies," *Group and Organizational Studies* (December 1988): 457.

51. Frances Yamarino and Bernard Bass, "Transformational Leadership and Multiple Levels of Analysis," *Human Relations* 43, no. 10 (1990): 976; See also David Walman, "CEO Charismatic Leadership: Levels of Management and Levels of Analysis Effects," *Academy of Management Review* (April 1999), 266–268.

52. Brent Jang, "Nova's Newall a $6.3 million Dollar Man," *The Globe and Mail*, 20 March 1997, sec. B, pp. 1, 6.

53. Andrew Nikiforuk, "Saint or Sinner?" *Canadian Business* (May 13, 2002): 55–59.

54. Bernard Bass, *Leadership and Performance Beyond Expectations* (New York: The Free Press, 1985); and Ronald Deluga, "Relationship of Transformational and Transactional Leadership with Employee Influencing Strategies," *Group and Organizational Studies* (December 1988): 457–458; See also Boas Shamir, "Correlates of Charismatic Leader Behavior in Military Units: Subordinates Attitudes, Unit of Characteristics, and Superiors Appraisals of Leader Performance," *Academy of Management Journal* (August 1998): 387–410.

55. Gary A. Yukl, *Leadership in Organizations,* 3rd ed. (Upper Saddle River, NJ: Prentice Hall, 1994), 298–299.

56. Ronald Deluga, "Relationship of Transformational and Transactional Leadership with Employee Influencing Strategies," *Group and Organizational Studies* (December 1988): 457.

57. Frances Yamarino and Bernard Bass, "Transformational Leadership and Multiple Levels of Analysis," *Human Relations* 43, no. 10 (1990): 981.

58. Frances Yamarino and Bernard Bass, "Transformational Leadership and Multiple Levels of Analysis," *Human Relations* 43, no. 10 (1990): 981.

59. J. M. Howell and C. A. Higgins, "Champions of Technological Innovation," *Administrative Science Quarterly* 35 (1990): 317–341.

60. For a review, see Robert Keller, "Transformational Leadership and the Performance of Research and Development Project Groups," *Journal of Management* 18, no. 3 (1992): 489–501.

61. J. J. Hater and Bernard Bass, "Superiors' Evaluations and Subordinates' Perceptions of Transformational and Transactional Leadership," *Journal of Applied Psychology* 73 (1988): 695–702.

62. Frances Yamarino and Bernard Bass, "Transformational Leadership and Multiple Levels of Analysis," *Human Relations* 43, no. 10 (1990): 981.

63. Julian Barling, Tom Weber, and E. Kevin Kelloway, "Effects of Transformational Leadership *Training* on Attitudinal and Financial Outcomes: A Field Experiment," *Journal of Applied Psychology* (December, 1996): 827–832.

64. Jim Collins, "Level 5 Leadership," *Harvard Business Review* (January 2001): 67–76.

65. Gary A. Yukl, *Leadership in Organizations,* 3rd ed. (Upper Saddle River, NJ: Prentice Hall, 1994), 342.

66. James Healey and David Kiley, "Surprise: Chrysler Loves Its German Boss: 'Car Guy' Eats in the Cafeteria, Hangs Out with Union Members," *USA Today*, 3 May 2001, p. B01.

67. Daniel Goleman, "Leadership That Gets Results" *Harvard Business Review* (March–April 2000): 78, 90.

68. Daniel Goleman, "Leadership That Gets Results" *Harvard Business Review* (March–April 2000): 80.

69. David Dorsey, "Andy Pearson Finds Love," *Fast Company* (August 2001): 78–86.

70. David Dorsey, "Andy Pearson Finds Love," *Fast Company* (August 2001): 78–86.

71. Frederick E. Fiedler, *A Theory of Leadership Effectiveness* (New York: McGraw-Hill, 1967), 147; See also David Stauffer, "Once a Leader, Always a Leader?" *Across the Board* (April 1999): 14–19.

72. Frederick E. Fiedler, *A Theory of Leadership Effectiveness* (New York: McGraw-Hill, 1967), 143.

73. See, for example, Robert J. House and J.V. Singh, "Organizational Behavior: Some New Directions for I/O Psychology," *Annual Review of Psychology* 38 (1987): 669–718; L.H. Peters, D.D. Hartke, and J.T. Pohlmann, "Fiedler's Contingency Theory of Leadership: An Application of the Meta-Analytic Procedures of Schmidt and Hunter," *Psychological Bulletin* 97 (1985): 274–285.

74. Fred Fiedler and J. E. Garcia, *New Approaches to Effective Leadership: Cognitive Resources and Organizational Performance* (New York: John Wiley & Sons, 1987); and Robert T. Vecchio, "Theoretical and Empirical Examination of Cognitive Resource Theory," *Journal of Applied Psychology* (April 1990), 141–147. See also Robert Vecchio, "Cognitive Resource

Theory: Issues for Specifying a Test of Theory" *Journal of Applied Psychology* (June 1992).

75. Robert J. House and Terrence Mitchell, "Path-Goal Theory of Leadership," *Contemporary Business* 3 (1974): 81–98; and Abraham Sagie and Meni Koslowsky, "Organizational Attitudes and Behaviors as a Function of Participation in Strategic and Tactical Change Decisions: An Application of Path-Goal Theory," *Journal of Organizational Behavior* (January 1994): 37–48.

76. Gary Dessler, "An Investigation of a Path-Goal Theory of Leadership" (Ph.D. diss., City University of New York, 1972).

77. Robert J. House and Terence Mitchell, "Path-Goal Theory of Leadership," *Journal of Contemporary Business* (Autumn 1984): 81–97; reprinted in Donald White, *Contemporary Perspectives in Organizational Behavior* (Boston: Allyn and Bacon, 1982), 228–235.

78. Gary A. Yukl, *Leadership in Organizations,* 3rd ed. (Upper Saddle River, NJ: Prentice Hall, 1994), 268–270.

79. Gary A. Yukl, *Leadership in Organizations,* 3rd ed. (Upper Saddle River, NJ: Prentice Hall, 1994).

80. Robert J. House, "A Path-Goal Theory of Leader Effectiveness," *Administrative Science Quarterly* 16, no. 3 (September 1971), reprinted in Henry Tosi and W. Clay Hammer, *Organizational Behavior and Management* (Chicago: St. Clair Press, 1974), 462–463.

81. Steve Kerr and J. M. Jermier, "Substitutes for Leadership: Their Meaning and Measurement," *Organizational Behavior and Human Performance* 22, pp. 374–403.

82. Steve Kerr and J. M. Jermier, "Substitutes for Leadership: Their Meaning and Measurement," *Organizational Behavior and Human Performance* 22 (1978): 375–403. See also Philip M. Podsakoff and Scott B. MacKenzie, "An Examination of Substitutes for Leadership Within a Levels-of-Analysis Framework," *Leadership Quarterly* (Fall 1995): 289–328.

83. David Alcorn, "Dynamic Followership: Empowerment at Work," *Management Quarterly* (Spring 1992): 11–13.

84. Jon Howell, David Bowen, Peter Dorfman, Steven Kerr, and Philip Podsakoff, "Substitutes for Leadership: Effective Alternatives to Ineffective Leadership," *Organizational Dynamics* (Summer 1990): 23.

85. Jon Howell, David Bowen, Peter Dorfman, Steven Kerr, and Philip Podsakoff, "Substitutes for Leadership: Effective Alternatives to Ineffective Leadership," *Organizational Dynamics* (Summer 1990): 23.

86. G. B. Graen and T. A. Scandura, "Toward a Psychology of Daidic Organizing," L. L. Cummings and B. M. Staw (eds.), *Research in Organizational Behavior,* vol. 9 (Greenwich, CT: J.A.I. Press, 1987), 208; See also David Schneider and Charles Goldwasser, "Be a Model Leader of Change," *Management Review* (March 1998): 41–48.

87. Antoinette Phillips and Arthur Bedeian, "Leader-Follower Exchange Quality: The Role of Personal and Interpersonal Attributes," *Academy of Management Journal* 37, no. 4 (1994): 990–1001; see also Nancy Boyd and Robert Taylor, "A Developmental Approach to the Examination of Friendship in Leader and Follower Relationships," *Leadership Quarterly* 9, no. 1 (1998): 1–25; Jaesub Lee, "Leader Member Exchange: The 'Pelz Effect' and Co-operative Communication Between Group Members," *Management Communications Quarterly* (November 1997): 266–287; and Christopher Avery, "All Power to You: Collaborative Leadership Works," *Journal for Quality and Participation* (March–April 1999): 36–41.

88. Jerald Greenberg, Managing *Behavior in Organizations* (Upper Saddle River, NJ: Prentice Hall, 1996), 215.

89. Antoinette Phillips and Arthur Bedeian, "Leader-Follower Exchange Quality: The Role of Personal and Interpersonal Attributes," *Academy of Management Journal* 37, no. 4 (1994): 990–1001.

90. Gary A. Yukl, *Leadership in Organizations,* 3rd ed. (Upper Saddle River, NJ: Prentice Hall, 1994), 132.

91. See Robert P. Vecchio, "Situational Leadership Theory: An Examination of a Prescriptive Theory," *Journal of Applied Psychology* (August 1987): 444–451; and Jerald Greenberg, *Managing Behavior in Organizations* (Upper Saddle River, NJ: Prentice Hall, 1996), 226.

92. Jeffrey McNally, Stephen Gerras, and R. Craig Bullis, "Teaching Leadership at the U.S. Military Academy at West Point," *Journal of Applied Behavioral Science* (June 1996): 178.

93. Frederick E. Fiedler, *A Theory of Leadership Effectiveness* (New York: McGraw-Hill, 1967), 250.

94. Andrew DuBrin, *Leadership: Research Findings, Practice, and Skills* (Boston: Houghton-Mifflin, 1995), 10–11.

95. This discussion is based on B. Burray, "Does Emotional Intelligence Matter in the Workplace?" *APA Monitor* (July 1998): 21; A. Fisher, "Success Secret: A High Emotional IQ," *Fortune* (October 26, 1998): 293–298; D. Goleman, *Working with Emotional Intelligence* (New York: Bantam Books, 1998); R. Daft, *Leadership: Theory and Practice* (Fort Worth, The Dryden Press, 1999): 346–347.

96. H. Weisinger, *Emotional Intelligence at Work* (San Francisco: Jossey-Bass, 1998): 214–215.

97. N. Gibbs, "The EQ Factor," *Time* (October 2, 1995): 65.

98. Roland Huntford, *The Last Place on Earth* (New York: Atheneum, 1985), 17.

99. Summarized from Eryn Brown, "A Smokeless Herb," *Fortune* 143, Issue 11 (May 28, 2001): 78–79; also "JetBlue," *Fortune Small Business* 11, no. 2 (March 1, 2001): 92.

Chapter 12

1. R. Cattel, *The Scientific Analysis of Personality* (Baltimore, Penguin Books, 1965). See also G. Northcraft and M. Neale, *Organizational Behavior* (Hinsdale, IL: Dryden Press, 1994), 64–240.

2. James Bowditch and Anthony Buono, *A Primer on Organizational Behavior* (New York: John Wiley, 1994), 115.

3. See for example, Jesus Delgado, "The Five Factor Model of Personality and Job Performance in the European Community," *Journal of Applied Psychology* 82, no. 1 (1997): 30–43.

4. Murray Barrick and Michael Mount, "The Big Five Personality Dimension and Job Performance: A Meta-Analysis," *Personal Psychology* (Spring 1991): 1–26.

5. Based on Ernest J. McCormick and Joseph Tiffin, *Industrial Psychology* (Upper Saddle River, NJ: Prentice Hall, 1974) 136–174. See also Marilyn Gist and Terence Mitchell, "Self-Efficacy: A Theoretical Analysis of its Determinants and Malleability," *Academy of Management Review* (April 1992): 183–202.

6. Saul Gellerman, *Motivation and Productivity* (New York: AMA-COM, 1963).

7. Lester Lefton and Laura Valvatne, *Mastering Psychology* (Boston: Allyn and Bacon, 1992), 412.

8. Lester Lefton and Laura Valvatne, *Mastering Psychology* (Boston: Allyn and Bacon, 1992).

9. Marilyn Gist and Terence Mitchell, "Self-Efficacy: A Theoretical Analysis of Its Determinants and Malleability," *Academy of Management Review* (April 1992): 183.

10. For a review and listing of these studies, see Marilyn Gist and Terence Mitchell, "Self-Efficacy: A Theoretical Analysis of its Determinants and Malleability," *Academy of Management Review* (April 1992): 183–211.

11. Ernest R. Hilgard, *Introduction to Psychology* (New York: Harcourt Brace and World, 1962), 86.

12. Benson Rosen and Thomas Jerdee, "The Influence of Age Stereotypes on Managerial Decisions," *Journal of Applied Psychology* (August 1976): 428–432.

13. Martin Fishbein and Icek Ajzen, *Attitude, Intention and Behavior: An Introduction to Theory and Research* (Reading, MA: Addison-Wesley, 1975).

14. Craig Pinter, *Work Motivation in Organizational Behavior* (Upper Saddle River, NJ: Prentice Hall, 1998), 245.

15. The Job Descriptive Index is copyrighted by Bowling Green State University, and can be obtained from Dr. Patricia C. Smith, Department of Psychology, Bowling Green State University, Bowling Green, Ohio, 43403.

16. See, for example, M. T. Iaffaldano and M. P. Muchinsky, "Job Satisfaction and Job Performance: A Meta-Analysis," *Psychological Bulletin* (March 1985): 251–273.

17. Ernest R. Hilgard, *Introduction to Psychology* (New York: Harcourt Brace and World, 1962), 124–125.

18. Ernest R. Hilgard, *Introduction to Psychology* (New York: Harcourt Brace and World, 1962), 124.

19. See, for instance, R. Kanfer, "Motivation Theory," in *Handbook of Industrial and Organizational Psychology*, eds. Marvin Dunnette and L. M. Nough (Palo Alto: Consulting Psychologists Press, 1990). See also Robert Hersey, "A Practitioner's View of Motivation," *Journal of Managerial Psychology* (May 1993): 110–115, and Kenneth Kovatch, "Employee Motivation: Addressing a Crucial Factor in Your Organization's Performance," *Employment Relations Today* (Summer 1995): 93–107.

20. See Douglas M. McGregor, "The Human Side of Enterprise," in *Management Classics*, eds. Michael Matteson and John M. Ivancevich (Santa Monica, CA: Goodyear, 1977), 43–49; See also Ewart Woolridge, "Time to Stand Maslow's Hierarchy on Its Head?" *People Management* 21 (December 1995): 17.

21. Douglas M. McGregor, "The Human Side of Enterprise," in *Management Classics*, eds. Michael Matteson and John M. Ivancevich (Santa Monica, CA: Goodyear, 1977), 45.

22. See for example Clay Alderfer, "Theories Reflecting My Personal Experience and Life Development," *Journal of Applied Behavioral Science* (November 1989): 351–366.

23. Abraham Maslow, *Toward a Psychology of Being*, 2nd ed. (New York: Van Nostrand Reinhold, 1968).

24. For a discussion, see, for example, Craig Pinder, *Work Motivation and Organizational Behavior* (Upper Saddle River, NJ: Prentice Hall, 1998), 64–66.

25. This is based on David Kolb, Irwin Rubin, and James McIntyre, *Organizational Psychology: An Experiential Approach* (Upper Saddle River, NJ: Prentice Hall, 1971), 65–69.

26. These are all from David Kolb, Irwin Rubin, and James McIntyre, *Organizational Psychology: An Experiential Approach* (Upper Saddle River, NJ: Prentice Hall, 1971).

27. David McClelland and David Burnham, "Power Is the Great Motivator," *Harvard Business Review* (January–February 1995): 126–136.

28. George Litwin and Robert Stringer, Jr., *Motivation and Organizational Climate* (Boston: Harvard University, 1968), 20–24.

29. Edgar Schein, *Career Dynamics: Matching Individual and Organizational Needs* (Reading, MA: Addison-Wesley, 1978); and Thomas Barth, "Career Anchor Theory," *Review of Public Personnel Administration* 13, no. 4 (1993): 27–42; see also Jeffrey Colvin, "Looking to Hire the Very Best? Ask the Right Questions, Lots of Them," *Fortune* (June 21, 1999): 19–21.

30. R. Kanfer, "Motivation Theory," in *Handbook of Industrial and Organizational Psychology*, eds. Marvin Dunnette and L. M. Nough (Palo Alto: Consulting Psychologists Press, 1990), 102. See also Robert Bretz and Steven Thomas, "Perceived Equity, Motivation, and Final-Offer Arbitration in Major League Baseball," *Journal of Applied Psychology* (June 1992): 280–289; see also Chao Chan, "Deciding on Equity or Parity: A Test of Situational, Cultural, and Individual Factors," *Journal of Organizational Behavior* (March 1998): 115–130.

31. Patricia Lush, "Bargain MacBlo Chief Got Big Raise," *The Globe and Mail*, 21 March 1996, sec. B, pp. 1, 6.

32. See, for example, J. Greenberg, "A Taxonomy of Organizational Justice Theories," *Academy of Management Review* 12 (1987): 9–22; See also Armin Falk, "Intrinsic Motivation and Extrinsic Incentives in a Repeated Game with Incomplete Contracts," *Journal of Economic Psychology* (June 1999): 251–254.

33. For a discussion, see R. Kanfer, "Motivation Theory," in *Handbook of Industrial and Organizational Psychology*, eds. Marvin Dunnette and L.M. Nough (Palo Alto: Consulting Psychologists Press, 1990), 124.

34. Edwin A. Locke and D. Henne, "Work Motivation Theories," in *International Review of Industrial and Organizational Psychology*, eds. C. L. Cooper and I. Robertson (Chichester, England: Wiley, 1986), 1–35; see also Maureen Ambrose, "Old Friends, New Faces: Motivation Research in the 1990s," *Journal of Management* (May–June 1999): 231–237.

35. R. Kanfer, "Motivation Theory," in *Handbook of Industrial and Organizational Psychology*, eds. Marvin Dunnette and L.M. Nough (Palo Alto: Consulting Psychologists Press, 1990), 125.

36. Craig Pinder, *Work Motivation and Organizational Behavior* (Upper Saddle River, NJ: Prentice Hall, 1998), 377.

37. Wendy Trueman, "Alternate Visions," *Canadian Business* (March 1991): 29–33.

38. Edwin Locke et al., "The Effects of Intra-Individual Goal Conflict on Performance," *Journal of Management* 20 (1994): 67–91; see discussion in Craig Pinder, *Work Motivation and Organizational Behavior* (Upper Saddle River, NJ: Prentice Hall, 1998), 383.

39. R. Kanfer, "Motivation Theory," in *Handbook of Industrial and Organizational Psychology*, eds. Marvin Dunnette and L.M. Nough (Palo Alto: Consulting Psychologists Press, 1990), 113.

40. For a discussion, see John P. Campbell and Robert Pritchard, "Motivation Theory in Industrial and Organizational Psychology," in *Industrial and Organizational Psychology*, ed. Marvin Dunnette (1976), 74–75; and R. Kanfer, "Motivation Theory," in *Handbook of Industrial and Organizational Psychology*, eds. Marvin Dunnette and L. M. Nough (Palo Alto: Consulting Psychologists Press, 1990), 115–116.

41. Peter Foreman, "Work Values and Expectancies in Occupational Rehabilitation: The Role of Cognitive Values in the Return to Work Process," *Journal of Rehabilitation* (July–September 1996): 44–49.

42. Mark Tubbs, Donna Boehne, and James Dahl, "Expectancy, Valence, and Motivational Force Functions in Goal Setting Research: An Empirical Test," *Journal of Applied Psychology* (June 1993): 361–373; Wendelien Van Eerde and Hank Thierry, "Vroom's Expectancy Model and Work-Related Criteria: A Meta-Analysis," *Journal of Applied Psychology* (October 1996): 575–586; see also Robert Fudge and John Schlacter, "Motivating Employees to Act Ethically: An Expectancies Theory Approach," *Journal of Business Ethics* (February 1999): 295; see also Barbara Caska, "The Search for Employment: Motivation to Engage in a Coping Behavior," *Journal of Applied Social Psychology* 1 (February 1998): 206–225.

43. For a definition of learning, see Lester Lefton and Laura Valvatne, *Mastering Psychology* (Boston: Allyn and Bacon, 1992), 161.

44. For a review of operant conditioning, see Fred Luthans and R. Kreitner, *Organizational Behavior Modification and Beyond: An Operant and Social Learning Approach* (Glenview, IL: Scott, Foresman, 1985); See also Nancy Chase, "You Get What You Reward," *Quality* (June 1999): 104.

45. W Clay Hamner, "Reinforcement Theory in Management and Organizational Settings," in *Organizational Behaviour and Management: A Contingency Approach*, eds. Henry Tosi and W. Clay Hamner (Chicago: Saint Claire, 1974), 86–112. See also Donald J. Campbell, "The Effects of Goal Contingent Payment on the Performance of a Complex Task," *Personnel Psychology* 37, no. 1 (Spring, 1984): 23–40.

46. Robert McNutt "Sharing Across the Board: DuPont's Achievement Sharing Program," *Compensation & Benefits Review* (July–August 1990): 17–24.

47. Barry Thomas and Madeline Hess Olson, "Gainsharing: The Design Guarantees Success," *Personnel Journal* (May 1988): 73–9. One of the most well known and well-established plans of this type is in place at the Lincoln Electric Company. See, for example, Kenneth Chilton, "Lincoln Electric's Incentive System: A Reservoir of Trust," *Compensation and Benefits Review* (November 1994): 29–34.

48. See, for example, William Atkinson, "Incentive Pay Programs That Work in Textiles," *Textile World* 151, no. 2 (February 2001): 55–57.

49. James Lardner, "Okay Here Are Your Options," *U.S. News and World Report* (March 1, 1999): 44.

50. Rebecca Buckman and David Bank, "For Silicon Valley, Stocks' Fall Upsets Culture of Options," *The Wall Street Journal*, 18 July 2002, sec. A, pp. 1, 6.

51. Adapted from Gary Dessler, *Human Resource Management* (Upper Saddle River, NJ: Prentice Hall, 2003), p. 356.

52. James Brinks, "Is There Merit in Merit Increases?" *Personnel Administrator* (May 1980): 60. See also Atul Migra et al., "The Case of the Invisible Merit Raise: How People See Their Pay Raises," *Compensation & Benefits Review* (May 1995): 71–76.

53. Cheryl Comeau-Kirschner, "Improving Productivity Doesn't Cost a Dime," *Management Review* (January 1999): 7.

54. Scot Hays, "Pros and Cons of Pay for Performance," *Workforce* (February 1999): 69–74.

55. Scot Hays, "Pros and Cons of Pay for Performance," *Workforce* (February 1999): 70.

56. Leslie Yerkes, "Motivating Workers in Tough Times," *Incentive* 75, no. 10 (October 2001): 120.

57. Bob Nelson, *1001 Ways to Reward Employees* (New York: Workmen Publishing, 1994), 47.

58. Federal Express Corporation, "Blueprints for Service Quality," pp. 34–35.

59. Cora Daniels, "Thank You Is Nice, But This Is Better," *Fortune* (November 22, 1999): 370.

60. Virginia Galt, "No More Freebies for Hydro Staff: Arbitrator," *The Globe and Mail*, 16 February 2002, sec. B, p. 3.

61. In David Whetten and Kim Cameron, *Developing Management Skills* (Upper Saddle River, NJ: Prentice Hall, 2002), 324.

62. The following is based on Thomas Connellan, *How to Improve Human Performance: Behaviorism in Business* (New York: Harper and Rowe, 1978); and Lawrence Miller, *Behavior Management: The New Science of Managing People at Work* (New York: Wiley, 1978), 253.

63. Ed Podalinoa and Victor Gamboa, "Behaviour Modification and Absenteeism, *Journal of Applied Psychology* (1974): 694–698.

64. W. Clay Hamner and Ellen P. Hamner, "Behaviour Modification and the Bottom Line," *Organizational Dynamics* 4 (1976): 12.

65. R. S. Haynes, R. C. Pine, and H. G. Fitch, "Reducing Accident Rates with Organizational Behaviour Modification," *Academy of Management Journal* 25 (1982): 407–416.

66. E. J. Feeney, J. R. Staelin, R. M. O'Brien, and A. M. Dickinson, "Increasing Sales Performance Among Airline Reservation Personnel, in *Industrial Behaviour Modification*, eds. Richard O'Brien, Alyce Dickinson, and Michael Rosow (New York : Pergamon Press, 1982), 141–158.

67. Adapted from Craig Pinder, *Work Motivation and Organizational Behavior* (Upper Saddle River, NJ: Prentice Hall, 1998), 203.

68. David Whetten and Kim Cameron, *Developing Management Skills* (Upper Saddle River, NJ: Prentice Hall, 2002), 420–421.

69. Wendy Cuthbert, "Corporate Life After Downsizing," *The Financial Post*, 20 March 1993, p. 8.

70. Quoted in Theodore Herbert, *Organizational Behavior: Readings and Cases* (New York: MacMillan, 1976), 344–345.

71. See, for example, J. Richard Hackman et al., "A New Strategy for Job Enrichment," *California Management Review* 17, pp. 57–71.

72. J. McBride-King and H. Paris, "Balancing Work and Family Responsibilities," *Canadian Business Review* (Autumn, 1989): 21.

73. Margot Gibb-Clark, "Banks' Short Work Week Improves Service," *The Globe and Mail*, 23 September 1991, sec. B, p. 4.

74. "Slaves of the New Economy," *Canadian Business* (April 1996): 86–92.

75. Canada @Work, *Workforce Commitment Report*, 2000, 24.

76. Gerald Ledford, Jr., "Three Case Studies on Skill-Based Pay: An Overview," *Compensation & Benefits Review* 23 (March–April 1991): 11–23.

77. Gerald Ledford, Jr., and Gary Bergel, "Skill-Based Pay Case no. 1: General Mills," *Compensation & Benefits Review* 23, (March–April 1991): 24–38.

78. "The Benefits of Lifelong Learning," *Journal of European Industrial Training* (February–March 1997): 3.

79. Lawrence Zuckerman, "JetBlue, Exception Among Airlines, Is Likely to Post a Profit, ' *The New York Times*, 7 November 2001, sec. C, p. 3.

80. Amy Rottier, "The Skies Are JetBlue," *Workforce* 80, no. 9 (September 2001): 22.

81. Amy Rottier, "The Skies Are JetBlue," *Workforce* 80, no. 9 (September 2001): 22.

82. "JetBlue: Odds Are You Won't Start Two Airlines, Revolutionize Your Industry, or Talk George Soros into Investing in Your Company Anytime Soon," *Fortune Small Business* 11, no. 2, p. 92.

83. Michelle Maynard, "Southwest, Without the Stunts," *The New York Times*, 7 July 2002, sec. BU, p. 2.

84. Sally Donnelly, "Blue Skies," *Time* 158 (July 2001): 24–27.

Chapter 13

1. Henry Mintzberg, *The Nature of Managerial Work* (New York: Harper & Row, 1973).

2. L.B. Kurke and H. Aldrich, "Mintzberg Was Right! A Replication and Extension of the Nature of Managerial Work," *Management Science* 29 (1983): 979.

3. George Miller, *Language and Communication* (New York: McGraw-Hill, 1951), 10, discussed in Gary Hunt, *Communication Skills in the Organization*, 2nd ed. (Upper Saddle River, NJ: Prentice Hall, 1989), 29.

4. This is discussed in and based on Fred Luthans and Janet Larsen, "How Managers Really Communicate," *Human Relations*, (1986): 162.

5. Edward Miles et al., "Job Level as a Variable in Predicting the Relationship Between Supervisory Communication and Job Satisfaction," *Journal of Occupational and Organizational Psychology* 69, no. 3 (September 1996): 277–293.

6. Arthur Bell and Dayle Smith, *Management Communication* (New York: John Wiley, 1999), 19.

7. Daniel Katz and Robert Kahn, *The Social Psychology of Organizations* (New York: Wiley, 1966).

8. This is based on Arthur Bell and Dayle Smith, *Management Communication* (New York: John Wiley, 1999), 22–24.

9. This section on dealing with communication barriers is based on R. Wayne Pace and Don Faules, *Organizational Communication* (Upper Saddle River, NJ: Prentice Hall, 1989), 150–162, unless otherwise noted. See also Tom Geddie, "Leap Over Communications Barriers," *Communication World* (April 1994): 12–17.

10. See, for example, Arthur Bell and Dayle Smith, *Management Communication* (New York: John Wiley, 1999), 36–39.

11. Tom Geddie, "Moving Communication Across Cultures," *Communication World* 16, no. 5 (April-May 1998): 37–41.

12. See Holly Weeks, "Taking the Stress Out of Stressful Conversations," *Harvard Business Review* (July–August 2001): 112–119.

13. R. Wayne Pace and Don Faules, *Organizational Communication* (Upper Saddle River, NJ: Prentice Hall, 1989), 153.

14. Jack Griffin, *How to Say It at Work* (Paramus, NJ: Prentice Hall Press, 1998), 26–28.

15. Ernest Gundling, "How to Communicate Globally," *Training and Development* (June 1999): 28–32.

16. Ernest Gundling, "How to Communicate Globally," *Training and Development* (June 1999): 29.

17. Jay Conger, "The Necessary Art of Persuasion," *Harvard Business Review* (May–June 1998): 85–95, reprinted in Joyce Osland, David Kolb, and Irwin Rubin, *The Organizational Behavior Reader* (Upper Saddle River, NJ: Prentice Hall, 2001), 469–478.

18. Robert Cialdini, "Harnessing the Science of Persuasion," *Harvard Business Review* (October 2001): 72–81.

19. Jay Conger, "The Necessary Art of Persuasion," *Harvard Business Review* (May–June 1998).

20. Jay Conger, "The Necessary Art of Persuasion," *Harvard Business Review* (May–June 1998): 85–95, reprinted in Joyce Osland, David Kolb, and Irwin Rubin, *The Organizational Behavior Reader* (Upper Saddle River, NJ: Prentice Hall, 2001), 458.

21. Robert Cialdini, "Harnessing the Science of Persuasion," *Harvard Business Review* (October 2001): 75.

22. James Sebenius, "Six Habits of Merely Effective Negotiators," *Harvard Business Review* (April 2001): 87–95.

23. James C. Freund, *Smart Negotiating* (New York: Simon & Schuster, 1992), 42–46.

24. James C. Freund, *Smart Negotiating* (New York: Simon & Schuster, 1992), 33.

25. Jitendra Sharma, "Organizational Communications: A Linking Process," *The Personnel Administrator* (July 1979): 35–43. See also Victor Callan, "Subordinate–Manager Communication in Different Sex Dyads: Consequences for Job Satisfaction," *Journal of Occupational and Organizational Psychology* (March 1993): 13–28.

26. William Convoy, *Working Together—Communication in a Healthy Organization* (Columbus, OH: Charles Merrill, 1976). See also David Johnson et al. "Differences Between Formal and Informal Communication Channels," *Journal of Business Communication* (April 1994): 111–124.

27. Gary Dessler, *Winning Commitment: How to Build and Keep a Competitive Workforce* (New York: McGraw-Hill, 1993).

28. R. Wayne Pace and Don Faules, *Organizational Communication* (Upper Saddle River, NJ: Prentice Hall, 1989), 105–106. See also Joanne Yates and Wanda Orlinkowski, "Genres of Organizational Communication: A Structurational Approach to Studying Communication and Media," *Academy of Management Review* (April 1992): 299–327.

29. Joanne Sisto, "Onward and—Oops!" *Canadian Business* (July, 1990): 70–71.

30. Ian Allaby, "The Search for Quality," *Canadian Business* (May, 1990): 75.

31. Keith McArthur, "Air Canada Tells Employees to Crack a Smile More Often," *The Globe and Mail*, 14 March 2002, sec. B, pp. 1–2.

32. Earl Plenty and William Machaner, "Stimulating Upward Communication," in *Readings in Organizational Behaviour*, eds. Jerry Gray and Frederick Starke (Columbus: Merrill, 1977), 229–240. See also R. Wayne Pace and Don Faules, *Organizational Communication* (Upper Saddle River, NJ: Prentice Hall, 1989), 153–160.

33. Alison Coleman, "Open to Suggestions," *Director* 54, no. 12 (July 2001): 27–28.

34. Toyota Motor Manufacturing, USA, Team-Member Handbook (February 1988), 52–53.

35. For a recent review and a discussion see James Smither et al., "An Examination of the Effects of an Upward Feedback Program Over Time," *Personnel Psychology* 48 (1995): 1–34.

36. James Smither et al., "An Examination of the Effects of an Upward Feedback Program Over Time," *Personnel Psychology* 48 (1995): 10–11.

37. James Smither et al., "An Examination of the Effects of an Upward Feedback Program Over Time," *Personnel Psychology* 48 (1995): 27.

38. Jack Griffin, *How to Say It at Work* (Paramus, NJ: Prentice Hall Press, 1998), 86–220.

39. See, for example, R. Wayne Pace and Don Faules, *Organizational Communication* (Upper Saddle River, NJ: Prentice Hall, 1989), 99–100.

40. R. Wayne Pace and Don Faules, *Organizational Communication* (Upper Saddle River, NJ: Prentice Hall, 1989), 99–100.

41. Personal interview (March 1992).

42. Personal interview (March 1992).

43. "Employers Profit from Opening the Books," Bureau of National Affairs Bulletin to Management 5 (September 1999): 288.

44. Rai Aggarwal and Betty Simkins, "Open Book Management—Optimizing Human Capital," *Business Horizons* 44, no. 5, pp. 5–13.

45. Rai Aggarwal and Betty Simkins, "Open Book Management—Optimizing Human Capital," *Business Horizons* 44, no. 5, pp. 5–13.

46. Jack Griffin, *How to Say It at Work* (Paramus, NJ: Prentice Hall Press, 1998), 178.

47. Jack Griffin, *How to Say It at Work* (Paramus, NJ: Prentice Hall Press, 1998).

48. Jack Griffin, *How to Say It at Work* (Paramus, NJ: Prentice Hall Press, 1998).

49. This is based on Tom Peters and Robert Waterman, *In Search of Excellence* (New York: Harper & Row), 119–218.

50. Tom Peters and Robert Waterman, *In Search of Excellence* (New York: Harper & Row), 219.

51. Tom Peters and Robert Waterman, *In Search of Excellence* (New York: Harper & Row), 22.

52. Greg Saltzman, "Managing By Walking Around," *PC Week* 15, no. 20 (May 18, 1998): 94.

53. Bob Smith, "Care and Feeding of the Office Grapevine," *Management Review* (February 1996): 6.

54. Eugene Walton, "How Efficient Is the Grapevine?" *Personnel* (March/April 1961): 45–49, reprinted in Keith Davis, *Organizational Behavior, A Book of Readings* (New York: McGraw-Hill, 1974).

55. Margot Gibb-Clark, "Most Job Losers Find Out Second-Hand," *The Globe and Mail*, 14 April 1993, sec. B, pp. 1, 4.

56. Laura Manserus, "Wall Street Lays Off Lawyers as Deals Drop," *The New York Times*, 9 November 2001, sec. D, p. 1.

57. Keith Davis, "Cut Those Rumors Down to Size," *Supervisory Management* (June 1975): 206.

58. Ron Lieber, "Information Is Everything," *Fast Company* (November 1999): 246–254.

59. Ron Lieber, "Information Is Everything," *Fast Company* (November 1999): 253.

60. Ron Lieber, "Information Is Everything," *Fast Company* (November 1999).

61. See, for example, Cathleen Moore, "Videoconferencing Takes Control," *InfoWorld* 23, no. 37 (September 10, 2001): 40–41.

62. Stephen Loudermilk, "Desktop Video Conferencing Getting Prime Time," *PC Week* 19 (October 1992): 81.

63. Paul Saffo, "The Future of Travel," *Fortune* (Autumn 1993): 119.

64. Sarah Schafer, "E–mail Grows Up," *Inc.* Technology 1 (1997): 87–88.

65. Paula Caproni, *The Practical Coach* (Upper Saddle River, NJ: Prentice Hall, 2001), 106–108.

66. For instance, see Andrea Poe, "Don't Touch That Send Button," *HR Magazine* 46, no. 7 (July 2001): 74–80.

67. Kenneth Laudon and Jane Laudon, *Essentials of Management Information Systems* (Upper Saddle River, NJ: Prentice Hall, 1997), 413.

68. Amy Joyce, "And Maybe IM or Maybe IM Not," *The Washington Post*, 3 March 2002: p. 6.

69. David Kroenke and Richard Hatch, *Management Information Systems* (New York: McGraw-Hill, 1994), 359.

70. Robert Ford and Michael Butts, "Is Your Organization Ready for Telecommuting?" *SAM Advanced Management Journal* (Autumn 1991): p. 19; and Kenneth Laudon and Jane Laudon, *Essentials of Management Information Systems* (Upper Saddle River, NJ: Prentice Hall, 1997), 413–416.

71. Robert Ford and Michael Butts, "Is Your Organization Ready for Telecommuting?" *SAM Advanced Management Journal* (Autumn 1991): p. 19.

72. See Sandra Atchison, "The Care and Feeding of Loan Eagles," *Business Week* (November 15, 1993): 58.

73. Margot Gibb-Clark, "Satellite Office a Hit With Staff," *The Globe and Mail*, 8 November 1991, sec. B, p. 4.

74. David Kirkpatrick, "Groupware Goes Boom," *Fortune* (December 27, 1993): 99–100.

75. Tim Stevens, "Internet-Aided Design," *Industry Week* 23 (June 1997): 50–55.

76. Tim Stevens, "Internet-Aided Design," *Industry Week* 23 (June 1997): 50–55.

77. Joann Davy, "Online at the Office: Virtual Communities Go to Work," *Managing Office Technology* (July–August 1998): 9–11.

78. Joann Davy, "Online at the Office: Virtual Communities Go to Work," *Managing Office Technology* (July–August 1998): 9–11.

79. David Kirkpatrick, "The Portal of the Future? Your Boss Will Run It," *Fortune* (August 2, 1999): 222–227.

80. David Kirkpatrick, "The Portal of the Future? Your Boss Will Run It," *Fortune* (August 2, 1999): 222–227.

81. Martin Piszczalski, "GM's Smart New Portal," *Automotive Design & Production* 114, no. 2 (February 2002): 14–15.

82. Roger E. Axtell (ed.), *Do's and Taboos Around the World* (New York: John Wiley & Sons, Inc. 1985), 37–48.

83. Adapted from T. Alessandra and M. J. O'Connor, *Behavioral Profiles: Self-Assessment* (San Diego: Pfeiffer & Company, 1994). Permission granted from the author.

Chapter 14

1. Carla Johnson, "Teams at Work," *HRMagazine* (May 1999): 30.

2. Merle MacIsaac, "Born-Again Basket Case," *Canadian Business* (May, 1993): 38–44.

3. "Outlook on Teams," *National Affairs Bulletin to Management* 20 (March 1997): 92–93.

4. Leigh Thompson, *Making the Team: A Guide for Managers* (Upper Saddle River, NJ: Prentice Hall, 2000): 11–14.

5. For employee involvement survey data, see Lee Towe, "Survey Finds Employee Involvement a Priority for Necessary Innovation," *National Productivity Review* (Winter 1999–00): 3–15. See also Bradley Kirkman and Benson Rosen, "Beyond Self-Management: Antecedents and Consequences of Team Empowerment," *Academy of Management Journal* (February 1999): 58–74.

6. Jack Osburn, Linda Moran, Ed Musselwhite, John Zenger, and Craig Perrin, *Self-Directed Work Teams: The New American Challenge* (Homewood, IL: Business One Irwin, 1990), 33. See also Bradley Kirkman, "Beyond Self-Management: Antecedents and Consequences of Team Empowerment," *Academy of Management Journal* (February 1999): 58–74.

7. Jack Osburn, Linda Moran, Ed Musselwhite, John Zenger, and Craig Perrin, *Self-Directed Work Teams: The New American Challenge* (Homewood, IL: Business One Irwin, 1990), 33.

8. See, for example, John Katzenbach and Douglas Smith, "The Discipline of Teams," *Harvard Business Review* (March–April 1993): 112–113. Note that many researchers do not, however, distinguish between groups and teams. See, for example, Gary Coleman and Eileen M. VanAken, "Applying Small-Group Behavior Dynamics to Improve Action-Team Performance," *Employment Relations Today* (Autumn 1991): 343–353.

9. Jack Osburn, Linda Moran, Ed Musselwhite, John Zenger, and Craig Perrin, *Self-Directed Work Teams: The New American Challenge* (Homewood, IL: Business One Irwin, 1990), 34. See also Charles Manz, "Self-Leading Work Teams: Moving Beyond Self-Management Myths," *Human Relations* 45, no. 11 (1992): 1119–1141.

10. Christopher Robert et al., "Empowerment and Continuous Improvement in the United States, Mexico, Poland, and India: Predicting Fit on the Basis of the Dimensions of Power Distance and Individuals," *Journal of Applied Psychology* 85, no. 5 (2000): 643–658.

11. Christopher Robert et al., "Empowerment and Continuous Improvement in the United States, Mexico, Poland, and India: Predicting Fit on the Basis of the Dimensions of Power Distance and Individuals," *Journal of Applied Psychology* 85, no. 5 (2000): 655.

12. These definitions are from Marvin E. Shaw, *Self-Directed Work Teams: The New American Challenge* (New York: McGraw-Hill, 1976), 11.

13. Jack Osburn, Linda Moran, Ed Musselwhite, John Zenger, and Craig Perrin, *Self-Directed Work Teams: The New American Challenge* (Homewood, IL: Business One Irwin, 1990), 34. See also Charles Manz, "Self-Leading Work Teams: Moving Beyond Self-Management Myths," *Human Relations* 45, no. 11 (1992).

14. Jon Katzenbach and Jason Santamaria, "Firing Up the Front Line," *Harvard Business Review* (May–June 1999): 114.

15. Sandra Robinson and Ann O'Leary-Kelly, "Monkey See, Monkey Do: The Influence of Workgroups on the Antisocial Behavior of Employees," *Academy of Management Journal* 41, no. 6 (1988): 658–672.

16. Sandra Robinson and Ann O'Leary-Kelly, "Monkey See, Monkey Do: The Influence of Workgroups on the Antisocial Behavior of Employees," *Academy of Management Journal* 41, no. 6 (1988): 667.

17. Daniel Feldman, "The Development and Enforcement of Group Norms," *Academy of Management Review* 9, no. 1 (1984): 47–53.

18. A. P. Hare, *Handbook of Small Group Research* (New York: The Free Press, 1962), 24. See also S. Barr and E. Conlon, "Effects of Distribution of Feedback in Work Groups," *Academy of Management Journal* (June 1994): 641–656.

19. See Stephen Worchel, Wendy Wood, and Jeffrey Simpson, *Group Process and Productivity* (Newbury Park, CA: Sage Publications, 1992), 45–50.

20. Stephen Worchel, Wendy Wood, and Jeffrey Simpson, *Group Process and Productivity* (Newbury Park, CA: Sage Publications, 1992), 245.

21. For a discussion of the difficulty of measuring and defining cohesiveness, see Peter Mudrack, "Group Cohesiveness and Productivity: A Closer Look," *Human Relations* 42, no. 9 (1989)" 771–786. See also R. Saavedra et al., "Complex Interdependence in Task-Performing Groups," *Journal of Applied Psychology* (February 1993): 61–73.

22. Leigh Thompson, *Making the Team: A Guide for Managers* (Upper Saddle River, NJ: Prentice Hall, 2000): 79.

23. John R. P. French, Jr., "The Disruption and Cohesion of Groups," *Journal of Abnormal and Social Psychology* 36 (1941): 361–377.

24. A. Paul Hare, *Small Group Research* (New York: The Free Press, 1962), 244.

25. A. Paul Hare, *Small Group Research* (New York: The Free Press, 1962), 157–158.

26. A. Paul Hare, *Small Group Research* (New York: The Free Press, 1962), 161.

27. Robert Blake and Jane Mouton, "Reactions to Inter-Group Competition under Win-Lose Conditions," *Management Science* 7 (1961): 432.

28. Stanley C. Seashore, *Group Cohesiveness in the Industry Work Group* (Ann Arbor, MI: Survey Research Center, University of Michigan, 1954), 90–5; Joseph Litterer, *The Analysis of Organizations* (New York: Wiley, 1965), 91–101; and J. Haleblian and S. Finkelstein, "Top Management Team Size, CEO Dominance, and Firm Performance: The Moderating Roles of Environmental Turbulence and Discretion," *Academy of Management Journal* (August 1993): 844–864.

29. A. Paul Hare, *Small Group Research* (New York: The Free Press, 1962), 244.

30. A. Paul Hare, *Small Group Research* (New York: The Free Press, 1962), 245.

31. Dorothy Lipovenko, "One Way to Cut Management Flab," *The Globe and Mail*, 1 January 1987, sec. B, pp. 1, 2.

32. Kira Vermond, "Survival Tips for Corporate Jungle," *The Globe and Mail*, 24 December 2001, sec. B, p. 7.

33. This material is based on James H. Shonk, *Team-Based Organizations* (Chicago: Irwin, 1997), 27–33.

34. James H. Shonk, *Team-Based Organizations* (Chicago: Irwin, 1997), 28.

35. John Katzenbach and Douglas Smith, "The Discipline of Teams," *Harvard Business Review* (March–April 1993): 116–118.

36. Everett Adams, Jr., "Quality Circle Performance," *Journal of Management* 17, no. 1 (1991): 25–39.

37. Everett Adams, Jr., "Quality Circle Performance," *Journal of Management* 17, no. 1 (1991).

38. See, for example, Everett Adams, Jr., "Quality Circle Performance," *Journal of Management* 17, no. 1 (1991); and Gilbert Fuchsberg, "Quality Programs Show Shoddy Results," *The Wall Street Journal*, 14 May 1992, sec. B, pp. 1, 4.

39. Gopal Pati, Robert Salitore, and Saundra Brady, "What Went Wrong with Quality Circles?" *Personnel Journal* (December 1987): 83–89.

40. Philip Olson, "Choices for Innovation Minded Corporations," *Journal of Business Strategy* (January–February 1990): 86–90.

41. In many firms, the concept of a venture team is taken to what may be its natural conclusion in that new-venture units and new-venture divisions are established. These are separate divisions devoted to new-product development. See, for example, Christopher Bart, "New Venture Units: Use Them Wisely to Manage Innovation," *MIT Sloan Management Review* (Summer 1988): 35–43; and Robert Burgelman, "Managing the New Venture Division: Research Findings and Implications for Strategic Management," *Strategic Management Journal* 6 (1985): 39–54.

42. Charles Snow, Scott Snell, Sue Canney Davison, and Donald Hambrick, "Use Transnational Teams to Globalize Your Company," *Organizational Dynamics* (Spring 1996): 50–67.

43. Charles Snow, Scott Snell, Sue Canney Davison, and Donald Hambrick, "Use Transnational Teams to Globalize Your Company," *Organizational Dynamics* (Spring 1996): 50.

44. Charles Snow, Scott Snell, Sue Canney Davison, and Donald Hambrick, "Use Transnational Teams to Globalize Your Company," *Organizational Dynamics* (Spring 1996).

45. Charles Snow, Scott Snell, Sue Canney Davison, and Donald Hambrick, "Use Transnational Teams to Globalize Your Company," *Organizational Dynamics* (Spring 1996): 53–57.

46. Lynda McDermott, Bill Waite, and Nolan Brawley, "Putting Together a World-Class Team," *Training and Development* (January 1999): 48.

47. Charles Snow, Scott Snell, Sue Canney Davison, and Donald Hambrick, "Use Transnational Teams to Globalize Your Company," *Organizational Dynamics* (Spring 1996): 61.

48. Based on suggestions by David Armstrong, "Making Dispersed Teams Work," *Bureau of National Affairs Bulletin to Management* 23 (May 1996): 168.

49. Anthony Townsend, Samuel DiMarie, and Anthony Hendrickson, "Virtual Teams: Technology and the Workplace of the Future," *Academy of Management Executive* 12, no. 3 (1998): 17–29.

50. Anthony Townsend, Samuel DiMarie, and Anthony Hendrickson, "Virtual Teams: Technology and the Workplace of the Future," *Academy of Management Executive* 12, no. 3 (1998): 20.

51. Christa Degnan, "ActiveProject Aids Teamwork," *PC Week* (May 31, 1999): 35.

52. Christa Degnan, "ActiveProject Aids Teamwork," *PC Week* (May 31, 1999): 21–22.

53. Michael Rosenwald, "Long Distance Team Worked as Virtual Offices Spread, Managers and Their Staffs are learning to Adapt to New Cultures," *Boston Globe*, 29 April 2001, sec. J, p. 1.

54. Allison Overhault, "Virtually There," *Fast Company*, Issue 56, pp. 108–114.

55. Diane Coutu, "Trust in Virtual Teams," *Harvard Business Review* 76, no. 3 (May–June 1998): 20–22.

56. Rochelle Garner, "Round-the-World Teamwork," *ComputerWorld* 24 (May 1999): 46.

57. Vijay Govindarajan and Anil Gupta, "Building an Effective Global Business Team," *MIT Sloan Management Review* 42, no. 4 (Summer 2001): 63–71.

58. Vijay Govindarajan and Anil Gupta, "Building an Effective Global Business Team," *MIT Sloan Management Review* 42, no. 4 (Summer 2001).

59. Jack Orsburn, Linda Moran, Ed Musselwhite, John Zenger, and Craig Perrin, *Self-Directed Work Teams: The New American Challenge* (Homewood, IL: Business One Irwin, 1990): 8.

60. Charles Fishman, "Engines of Democracy," *Fast Company* (Oct. 1999): 173–202.

61. Tom Peters, *Liberation Management* (New York: Alfred Knopf, 1992), 238–239.

62. Jack Orsburn, Linda Moran, Ed Musselwhite, John Zenger, and Craig Perrin, *Self-Directed Work Teams: The New American Challenge* (Homewood, IL: Business One Irwin, 1990): 22–23.

63. "Kodak's Team Structure Is Picture Perfect," *Bureau of National Affairs Bulletin to Management* 15 (August 1996): 264.

64. Rojiv Banker, Roger Schroeder, and Kingshuk Sinha, "Impact of Work Teams on Manufacturing Performance: A Longitudinal Field Study," *Academy of Management Journal* 39, no. 4 (1996): 867–888.

65. Rojiv Banker, Roger Schroeder, and Kingshuk Sinha, "Impact of Work Teams on Manufacturing Performance: A Longitudinal Field Study," *Academy of Management Journal* 39, no. 4 (1996): 887–888.

66. Rojiv Banker, Roger Schroeder, and Kingshuk Sinha, "Impact of Work Teams on Manufacturing Performance: A Longitudinal Field Study," *Academy of Management Journal* 39, no. 4 (1996): 870. After reviewing the evidence, one writer recently suggested that self-managing teams may turn out to have been a management fad and that proponents overstated the benefits firms derived from them. Jane Gibson and Dana Testone, "Management Fad: Emergence, Evolution, and Implications for Managers," *Academy of Management Executive* 15, no. 4, pp. 122–133.

67. Ralph King, Jr., "Levi's Factory Workers are Assigned to Teams, and Morale Has Taken a Hit," *The Wall Street Journal*, 20 May 1998, sec. A, pp. 1, 6.

68. Based on Erin Neurick, "Facilitating Effective Work Teams," *SAM Advanced Management Journal* (Winter 1993): 22–26. See also Margarita Alegria, "Building Effective Research Teams When Conducting Drug Prevention Research with Minority Populations," *Drugs & Society* 14, NO. 1–2 (1999): 227–245. George Neuman and Julie Wright, "Team Effectiveness: Beyond Skills and Cognitive Ability," *Journal of Applied Psychology* (June 1999): 376–389.

69. Erin Neurick, "Facilitating Effective Work Teams," *SAM Advanced Management Journal* (Winter 1993): 23.

70. Joann Keyton, "Analyzing Interaction Patterns in Dysfunctional Teams," *Small Group Research* (August 1999): 491–518.

71. Suchitra Mouly and Jayaram Sankaran, "Barriers to the Cohesiveness and Effectiveness of Indian R&D Project Groups: Insights from Four Federal R&D Organizations," in *Advances in Qualitative Organization Research*, vol. 2, John Wagner et al., (Stanford, CT: A.I. Press, 1999), 221–243.

72. Discussed in Paul Mulvey, John Veiga, and Priscilla Elsass, "When Teammates Raise the White Flag," *Academy of Management Executive* 10, no. 1 (1996): 40. See also Richard Hackman, "Why Teams Don't Work," in *Theory and Research on Small Groups: Social Psychological Applications in Social Issues*, vol. 4, R. Tindale et al. (Plenum Press, New York, 1998), 245–267.

73. The following, except as noted, is based on Glenn H. Varney, *Building Productive Teams: An Action Guide and Resource Book* (San Francisco: Jossey-Bass Publishers, 1989), 11–18. See also

P. Bernthal and C. Insko, "Cohesiveness without Group Think: The Interactive Effects of Social and Task Cohesion," *Group and Organization Management* (March 1993): 66–88; and Vanessa Druskat, "The Antecedents of Team Competence: Toward a Fine-Grained Model of Self-Managing Team Effectiveness," *Research on Managing Groups and Teams: Groups in Context*, vol. 2 (Stamford, CT: Jai Press, 1999), 201–231.

74. Quoted or paraphrased from Regina Maruca, "What Makes Teams Work?" *Fast Company* (November 2000): 128.

75. See, for example, Drew Harris, "Seven Principles for Sustainable Social System: Lessons from Teams, Organizations and Communities," *Competitiveness Review* 10, no. 2 (Summer–Fall 2000): 169–173.

76. John Katzenbach and Douglas Smith, "The Discipline of Teams," *Harvard Business Review* (March–April 1993): 112. See also C. Meyer, "How the Right Measures Help Teams Excel," *Harvard Business Review* (May–June 1994): 112.

77. Erin Neurick, "Facilitating Effective Work Teams," *SAM Advanced Management Journal* (Winter 1993): 23.

78. John Katzenbach and Douglas Smith, "The Discipline of Teams," *Harvard Business Review* (March–April 1993): 113.

79. John Katzenbach and Douglas Smith, "The Discipline of Teams," *Harvard Business Review* (March–April 1993). The evaluation process is important as well. See R. Saavedra and S. Kwun, "Peer Evaluation in Self-Managing Work Groups," *Journal of Applied Psychology* (June 1993): 450–463.

80. George Neuman and Julie Wright, "Team Effectiveness: Beyond Skills and Cognitive Ability," *Journal of Applied Psychology* (June 1999): 376–389.

81. Sal Divita, "Being a Team Player is Essential to Your Career," *Marketing News* 30, no. 19 (September 9, 1996): 8.

82. Philip Hunsaker, *Training in Management Skills* (Upper Saddle River, NJ: Prentice Hall, 2001), 286.

83. Michael Stevens and Michael Campion, "Staffing Work Teams: Development and Validation of a Selection Test for Teamwork Settings," *Journal of Management* 25, no. 2 (March–April 1999): 207–225.

84. Michael Finley, "All for One, But None for All?" *Across the Board* 39, no. 1 (January/February 2002): 45–48.

85. See James H. Shonk, *Team-Based Organizations* (Chicago: Irwin, 1997), 133–138; Andrew DuBrin, *Leadership: Research Findings, Practice and Skills* (Boston: Houghton-Mifflin, 1995), 224–227.

86. James H. Shonk, *Team-Based Organizations* (Chicago: Irwin, 1997), 133.

87. Kimball Fisher, *Leading Self-Directed Work Teams* (New York: McGraw-Hill, 1993), 151–153.

88. Gary Dessler, *Winning Commitment* (New York: McGraw-Hill, 1992), 28.

89. Gary Dessler, *Winning Commitment* (New York: McGraw-Hill, 1992), 30.

90. Gary Dessler, *Winning Commitment* (New York: McGraw-Hill, 1992), 44.

91. These are based on Kimball Fisher, *Leading Self-Directed Work Teams* (New York: McGraw-Hill, 1993), 48–56.

92. Kimball Fisher, *Leading Self-Directed Work Teams* (New York: McGraw-Hill, 1993), 53.

93. This is based on Philip Hunsaker, *Training in Management Skills* (Upper Saddle River, NJ: Prentice Hall, 2001), 293–296.

94. Jack Orsburn, Linda Moran, Ed Musselwhite, John Zenger, and Craig Perrin, *Self-Directed Work Teams: The New American Challenge* (Homewood, IL: Business One Irwin, 1990): 20–27.

95. Jack Orsburn, Linda Moran, Ed Musselwhite, John Zenger, and Craig Perrin, *Self-Directed Work Teams: The New American Challenge* (Homewood, IL: Business One Irwin, 1990): 21.

96. Jack Orsburn, Linda Moran, Ed Musselwhite, John Zenger, and Craig Perrin, *Self-Directed Work Teams: The New American Challenge* (Homewood, IL: Business One Irwin, 1990): 22.

97. The remaining items in this section, except as noted, are quoted from or based on Michael A. Campion and A. Catherine Higgs, "Design Work Teams to Increase Productivity and Satisfaction," *HR Magazine* (October 1995): 101–7. See also Steven G. Rogelberg and Steven M. Rumery, "Gender Diversity, Team Decision Quality, Time on Task, and Interpersonal Cohesion," *Small Group Research* (February 1996): 79–90; Steven E. Gross and Jeffrey Blair, "Reinforcing Team Effectiveness Through Pay," *Compensation & Benefits Review* (September 1995): 34–38; and Joan M. Glaman, Allan P. Jones, and Richard M. Rozelle, "The Effects of Co-Worker Similarity on the Emergence of Affect in Work Teams," *Group and Organization Management* (June 1996): 192–215.

98. "Getting the Most from Employee Teams," *Bureau of National Affairs Bulletin to Management*, 20 (March 1997): 96.

99. David Hyatt and Thomas Ruddy, "An Examination of the Relationship Between Workgroup Characteristics and Performance: Once More into the Breach," *Personnel Psychology* (1997). 577.

100. David Hyatt and Thomas Ruddy, "An Examination of the Relationship Between Workgroup Characteristics and Performance: Once More into the Breach," *Personnel Psychology* (1997). 578.

101. Vanessa Druskat and Steven Wolff, "Building the Emotional Intelligence of Groups," *Harvard Business Review* (March 2001): 87.

102. James H. Shonk, *Team-Based Organizations* (Chicago: Irwin, 1997).

Chapter 15

1. Carol Hymowitz, "How a Leader at 3M Got His Employees to Back Big Changes," *The Wall Street Journal*, 23 April 2002, sec. B, p. 1.

2. Kevin Cox, "Sea Change," *The Globe and Mail*, 17 May 1994, sec. B, p. 24.

3. Based on David Nadler and Michael Tushman, "Beyond the Charismatic Leader: Leadership and Organizational Change," *California Management Review* (Winter 1990): 80; and Alfred Marcus, "Responses to Externally Induced Innovation: To Their Effects on Organizational Performance," *Strategic Management Journal* 9 (1988), 194–202. See also Steve Crom, "Change Leadership: the Virtues of Obedience," *Leadership & Organization Development Journal* (March–June 1999): 162–168.

4. Cathryn Motherwell, "How to Fix a Model of a Muddle," *The Globe and Mail*, 22 November 1994, sec. B, p. 30.

5. Dennis Berman, "Lucent's Latest Revamped to Split Five Businesses into Two Units," *The Wall Street Journal*, 11 July 2001, sec. B, p. 7.

6. Michael Goold and Andrew Campbell, "Do You Have a Well-Designed Organization?" *Harvard Business Review* (March 2002): 117–124.

7. Michael Goold and Andrew Campbell, "Do You Have a Well-Designed Organization?" *Harvard Business Review* (March 2002): 118.

8. Scott Miller, "Volkswagen Ways to Reorganizing Itself into Three Divisions," *The Wall Street Journal*, 26 June 2001, p. 18.

9. Michael Goold and Andrew Campbell, "Do You Have a Well-Designed Organization?" *Harvard Business Review* (March 2002): 120.

10. Carol Hymowitz, "How a Leader at 3M Got His Employees to Back Big Changes," *The Wall Street Journal*, 23 April 2002, sec. B, p. 1.

11. Carol Hymowitz, "How a Leader at 3M Got His Employees to Back Big Changes," *The Wall Street Journal*, 23 April 2002, sec. B, p. 1.

12. Michael Goold and Andrew Campbell, "Do You Have a Well-Designed Organization?" *Harvard Business Review* (March 2002): 123.

13. Doug Nairne, "Mounties Riding the Vision Thing," *The Winnipeg Free Press* 16 September 1996, sec. A, p. 5.

14. See, for example, John Rizzo, Robert J. House, and Sydney I. Lirtzinan, "Role Conflict and Ambiguity in Complex Organizations," *Administrative Science Quarterly* 15 (June 1970): 150–163. For additional views on sources of conflict, see Patricia A. Gwartney-Gibbs and Denise H. Lach, "Gender Differences in Clerical Workers' Disputes Over Tasks," *Human Relations*, (June 1994): 611–640; and Kevin J. Williams and George Alliger, "Role Stressors, Mood Spillover, and Perceptions of Work-Family Conflict in Employed Parents," *Academy of Management Journal* (August 1994): 837–869.

15. Peter N. Haapaniemi, "How Companies Transformed Themselves," *Chief Executive* (November 2001): 2–5.

16. Paul Lawrence, "How to Deal with Resistance to Change," *Harvard Business Review* (May–June, 1954. See also Andrew W. Schwartz, "Eight Guidelines for Managing Change," *Supervisory Management* (July 1994): 3–5; Thomas J. Werner and Robert F. Lynch, "Challenges of a Change Agent" *Journal for Quality and Participation* (June 1994): 50–54; Larry Reynolds, "Understand Employees' Resistance to Change," *HR Focus* (June 1994): 17–18; Kenneth E. Hultman, "Scaling the Wall of Resistance," *Training & Development Journal* (October 1995): 15–18; and Eric Dent, "Challenging Resistance to Change," *Journal of Applied Behavioral Science* (March 1999): 25.

17. John Mariotti, "The Challenge of Change," *Industry Week* (April 6, 1998): 140.

18. Timothy Judge et al., "Managerial Coping with Organizational Change: A Dispositional Perspective," *Journal of Applied Psychology* 84, no. 1 (1999): 107–122.

19. Stephen Robbins and Mary Coulter, *Management* (Englewood Cliffs, NJ: Prentice Hall, 1996), 423–425.

20. Kurt Lewin, "Frontiers in Group Dynamics," *Human Relations* 1 (1947): 5–42.

21. "30 Women Opt to Become Miners," *The Globe and Mail*, 24 February 1993, sec. B, p. 1.

22. Peter Larson, "Winning Strategies," *Canadian Business* Review (Summer, 1989): 41–42.

23. John P. Kotter, *Leading Change* (Boston: Harvard Business School Press, 1996), 40–41. See also Gary Hamel, "Waking up IBM," *Harvard Business Review* (July–August 2000): 137–146.

24. John P. Kotter, *Leading Change* (Boston: Harvard Business School Press, 1996), 44.

25. John P. Kotter, *Leading Change* (Boston: Harvard Business School Press, 1996), 90–91.

26. Richard Pascale et al., "Changing the Way We Change," *Harvard Business Review* (November–December 1997): 129.

27. Richard Pascale et al., "Changing the Way We Change," *Harvard Business Review* (November–December 1997): 65.

28. Richard Pascale et al., "Changing the Way We Change," *Harvard Business Review* (November–December 1997): 91.

29. Richard Pascale et al., "Changing the Way We Change," *Harvard Business Review* (November–December 1997).

30. David Baum, "Running the Rapids," *Profit Magazine* (November 1999): 54.

31. David Baum, "Running the Rapids," *Profit Magazine* (November 1999).

32. Stewart Alsop, "E or Be Eaten," *Fortune* (November 8, 1999): 94–95.

33. Thomas Cummings and Christopher Worley, *Organization Development and Change* (Minneapolis: West Publishing Company, 1993), 3.

34. Robert J. House, *Management Development* (Ann Arbor, MI: Bureau of Industrial Relations, University of Michigan, 1967), 71; Louis White and Kevin Wooten, "Ethical Dilemmas in Various Stages of Organizational Development," *Academy of Management Review* 8, no. 4 (1983): 690–697.

35. Wendell French and Cecil Bell, Jr., *Organization Development* (Upper Saddle River, NJ: Prentice Hall, 1995), 171–193.

36. Thomas Cummings and Christopher Worley, *Organization Development and Change* (Minneapolis: West Publishing Company, 1993), 501.

37. For a description of how to make OD a part of organizational strategy, see Aubrey Mendelow and S. Jay Liebowitz, "Difficulties in Making OD a Part of Organizational Strategy," *Human Resource Planning* 12, no. 4 (1995): 317–329.

38. See, for example, John Rizzo, Robert J. House, and Sydney I. Lirtzman, "Role Conflict and Ambiguity in Complex Organizations," *Administrative Science Quarterly* (June, 1970): 150–163.

39. Gordon Pitts, "McCain Brothers Unlikely to End Feud," *The Globe and Mail*, 24 December 2001, sec. B, pp. 1, 4.

40. Christina Gabrielidis et al., "Preferred Styles of Conflict Revolution: Mexico and United States," *Journal of Cross-Cultural Psychology* 28, no. 6 (November 1997): 667–678.

41. Christina Gabrielidis et al., "Preferred Styles of Conflict Revolution: Mexico and United States," *Journal of Cross-Cultural Psychology* 28, no. 6 (November 1997).

42. Christina Gabrielidis et al., "Preferred Styles of Conflict Revolution: Mexico and United States," *Journal of Cross-Cultural Psychology* 28, no. 6 (November 1997).

43. This section is based on Evert Van De Vliert, Martin Euwema, and Sipke Huismans, "Managing Conflict with a Subordinate or a Superior: Effectiveness of Conglomerated Behavior," *Journal of Applied Psychology* (April 1995): 271–281.

44. Paul Lawrence and Jay Lorsch, *Organization and Environment* (Boston: Division of Research, Graduate School of Business Administration, Harvard University, 1967), 74–75.

45. Kenneth Thomas, "Conflict and Conflict Management," in *Handbook of Industrial and Organizational Psychology*, Marvin Dunnette (Chicago: Rand McNally, 1976), 900–902; and Michael Carrell, Daniel Jennings, and Christina Heavrin, *Fundamentals of Organizational Behavior* (Upper Saddle River, NJ: Prentice Hall, 1997), 505–509.

Chapter 16

1. Lisa Bannon, "New Playbook: Taking To Use from GE, Mattel's CEO Wants Toymaker to Grow Up," *The Wall Street Journal*, 14 November 2001, sec. A, p. 1.

2. Kenneth Merchant, "The Control Function of Management," *MIT Sloan Management Review* (Summer 1982): 44.

3. This section is based on William Newman, *Constructive Control* (Upper Saddle River, NJ: Prentice Hall, 1995), 6–9.

4. "Anatomy of a Recall: How Coke's Controls Fizzled Out in Europe," *The Wall Street Journal*, 29 June 1999, sec. A, pp. 1, 5.

5. W. Edwards Deming, *Out of the Crisis* (Cambridge, MA: Center for Advanced Engineering Study, 1986).

6. W. Edwards Deming, *Out of the Crisis* (Cambridge, MA: Center for Advanced Engineering Study, 1986).

7. Ted Wakefield, "No Pain, No Gain," *Canadian Business* (January 1993): 50–54.

8. Richard J. Schonberger, "Production Workers Bear Major Quality Responsibility in Japanese Industry," *Industrial Engineering* (December, 1982): 34–40.

9. Bruce McDougall, "The Thinking Man's Assembly Line," *Canadian Business* (November, 1991): 40.

10. The ten specific requirements are quoted from Harold Koontz and Cyril O'Donnell, *Principles of Management* (New York: McGraw-Hill Book Co., 1964), 541–544.

11. Harold Koontz and Cyril O'Donnell, *Principles of Management* (New York: McGraw-Hill Book Co., 1964), 544.

12. Barrie Whittaker, "Increasing Market Share Through Marketing Excellence," *Canadian Business* Review (Spring, 1990): 35–37.

13. Eva Kiess-Moser, "Customer Satisfaction," *Canadian Business* Review (Summer, 1989): 44–45.

14. John Gilks, "Total Quality: A Strategy for Organizational Transformation," *Canadian Manager* (Summer, 1990): 19–21.

15. Eva Kiess-Moser, "Customer Satisfaction," *Canadian Business Review* (Summer, 1989): 44.

16. Eva Kiess-Moser, "Customer Satisfaction," *Canadian Business Review* (Summer, 1989): 44.

17. For example, see Robert Simons, *Levers of Control: How Managers Use Innovative Control Systems to Drive Strategic Renewal* (Boston: Harvard Business School Press, 1995), 82.

18. Daniel Wren, *The Evolution of Management Thought* (John Wiley & Sons, 1994), 115.

19. Based on Kenneth Merchant, *Modern Management Control Systems* (Upper Saddle River, NJ: Prentice Hall, 1998), 642.

20. For a discussion, see Kenneth Merchant, *Modern Management Control Systems* (Upper Saddle River, NJ: Prentice Hall, 1998), 542–545.

21. Bill Motley, "Picking the Right Ratio to Measure Performance," *Bank Marketing* 34, Issue 1 (January/February 2002): 44.

22. Kenneth Merchant, *Modern Management Control Systems* (Upper Saddle River, NJ: Prentice Hall, 1998), 304.

23. Sydney Baxendale, "Activity Based Costing for the Small Business: A Primer," *Business Horizons* 44, no. 1 (January 2001): 61.

24. Edward Blocher, et al., "Making Bottom-Up ABC Work and Right Show Link," *Strategic Finance* 83, no. 10 (April 2002): 51–56.

25. See also John Lere, "Selling Activity Based Costing," *The CPA Journal* 72, no. 3 (March 2002): 54–56.

26. Peter Brewer, "Putting Strategy into the Balanced Scorecard," *Strategic Finance* 83, no. 7 (January 2002): 44–52.

27. Examples from Peter Brewer, "Putting Strategy into the Balanced Scorecard," *Strategic Finance* 83, no. 7 (January 2002).

28. See for example Matt Hicks, "Tuning to the Big Picture for a Better Business," *PC Week*, (July 15, 1999): 69.

29. Robin Cooper and Robert Kaplan, "The Promise and Peril of Integrated Costs Systems," *Harvard Business Review* (July–August 1998). 109.

30. Matt Hicks, "Tuning to the Big Picture for a Better Business," *PC Week*, (July 15, 1999): 69.

31. Doug Bartholomew, "Maximizing ERP," *Industry Week* 251, Issue 3 (March 2002): 58.

32. See also Mark Cross, "Decision Support Systems: Using Technology for Successful Management," *CMA Management* 75, no. 8 (December 2001): 48–50.

33. Robert Simons, *Levers of Control: How Managers Use Innovative Control Systems to Drive Strategic Renewal* (Boston: Harvard Business School Press, 1995), 81.

34. Jeffrey Seglin, "A Company Credo, as Applied or Not," *The New York Times*, 15 July 2001, 3–4.

35. Robert Simons, *Levers of Control: How Managers Use Innovative Control Systems to Drive Strategic Renewal* (Boston: Harvard Business School Press, 1995), 86.

36. This discussion is based on Robert Simons, *Levers of Control: How Managers Use Innovative Control Systems to Drive Strategic Renewal* (Boston: Harvard Business School Press, 1995), 87–88.

37. The following, except as noted, is based on Kenneth Merchant, *Control in Business Organizations* (Boston: Pitman, 1985), 71–120. See also Robert Kaplan, "New Systems for Measurement and Control," *The Engineering Economist* (Spring 1991): 201–218.

38. This is based on Robert Simons, *Levers of Control: How Managers Use Innovative Control Systems to Drive Strategic Renewal* (Boston: Harvard Business School Press, 1995), 81–82.

39. Kenneth Merchant, *Control in Business Organizations* (Boston: Pitman, 1985), 98.

40. "Did Warner-Lambert Make a $468 Million Mistake?" *Business Week* 21 (November 1983), 123; quoted in Kenneth Merchant, *Control in Business Organizations* (Boston: Pitman, 1985), 98–99.

41. Chris Argyris, "Human Problems with Budgets," *Harvard Business Review* (January–February 1953), 97–110.

42. Tom Peters, *Liberation Management* (New York: Alfred A. Knopf, 1992), 465–466.

43. See also Eric Krell, "Greener Pastures," *Training* 38, no. 11, pp. 54–59.

44. Tom Burns and G. M. Stalker, *The Management of Innovation* (London: Tavistock, 1961), 119.

45. This quote is based on William Taylor, "Control in an Age of Chaos," *Harvard Business Review* (November–December 1994): 70–71. James Collins and Jerry Porras, *Built to Last: Successful Habits of Visionary Companies* (New York: Harper and Row, 1994).

46. William Taylor, "Control in an Age of Chaos," *Harvard Business Review* (November–December 1994): 71.

47. J. Newcomb, 1008 letter to employees, May 17, 1999.

48. Gary Dessler, "How to Earn Your Employees Commitment," *Academy of Management Executive* 13, no. 2 (1999): 58–67.

49. Personal interview. See Gary Dessler, *Winning Commitment: How to Build and Keep a Competitive Workforce* (New York: McGraw-Hill, 1993), 27–28.

50. Rosabeth Moss Kantor, *Commitment and Community* (Cambridge, MA: Harvard University Press, 1972), 24–25.

51. See Gary Dessler, "How to Earn Your Employees Commitment," *Academy of Management Executive* 13, no. 2 (1999): 64.

52. JoAnn Davy, "Online at the Office: Virtual Communities Go to Work," *Managing Office Technology* (July–August 1998): 9–11.

53. JoAnn Davy, "Online at the Office: Virtual Communities Go to Work," *Managing Office Technology* (July–August 1998). 9–11.

54. Gary Dessler, "How to Earn Your Employees Commitment," *Academy of Management Executive* 13, no. 2 (1999): 69.

55. Personal interview, March 1992.

56. Susan Carey, "Costly Race in the Sky," *The Wall Street Journal*, 9 September 2002, sec. B, p. 1.

Name Index

Subject Index

360 degree feedback, 315

A

abilities, and behaviour, 375
absenteeism, 331
absorption costing, 515
accommodators, 488
accountability test, 473
accounting fraud, 500–501
achievement motivation, 381–382
achievement-oriented leaders, 351
achievements, 10–11
action research, 482
active listening, 415–417
activity based costing, 515
administrative approach to decision making, 137
advertising, for recruitment, 299
advisory staff, 235
affiliation motivation, 382
aging of the population, 301
Algeria, and foreign sellers, 54
ambiguity, 412–413
analytical competence, 10
anchoring, 151
angels, 114
application forms, 301, 302
artificial intelligence, 529
Asia Pacific Economic Cooperation (APEC), 51
assessment centres, 303–304
assistant managers, 9
Association of Southeast Asian Nations (ASEAN), 51
attitudes, 377
audit, 512
Australia, and Individualism, 64
Austria, and "masculinity," 64
authority
    defined, 28, 235
    delegation. See delegation
    functional authority, 235
    line authority, 235
    sources of, 280
    staff authority, 235
authority boundary, 272–273
autocratic style of leadership, 340–342
avoiders, 488

B

background investigations, 308
balanced scorecard, 515–516
BANTRAs, 419
BCG matrix, 215–217
behaviour. See individual behaviour
behaviour-based interviewing, 304, 305
behaviour management
    basic procedure, 393
    example, 393–394
    work programs, 394
behaviour modification
    defined, 385
    negative reinforcement, 386

omission, 386
    positive reinforcement, 386
    punishment, 386
    schedules of reinforcement, 386
    types of reinforcement, 385–386
behavioural displacement, 519
behavioural school of management
    behaviouralist prescriptions, 31–32
    changing environment, 30–31
    decentralization, 31
    diversification stage, 30
    employee-centred organization, 31
    gaining compliance, 32–33
    Hawthorne studies, 29–30
    increased diversity, 30–31
    the mature individual, 31
    Theory X, 31
    Theory Y, 31
    zone of indifference, 32
behavioural standards, 509
belief systems, 521
benchmarking, 215
Bennett Test of Mechanical Comprehension, 301, 304
bona fide occupational requirement, 321
bonus, 318
border security, 129
boundary control systems, 516–518
boundaryless organization, 17, 272
bounded rationality, 137
brainstorming, 155
break-even analysis, 162–163
break-even charts, 162
break-even formula, 162–163
break-even point, 162
Bribe Payers Index, 81
bribery, 81
budgeted balance sheet, 512
budgeted income statement, 512
budgets
    budgeted balance sheet, 512
    budgeted income statement, 512
    cash budget, 512
    defined, 180, 511
    operating budgets, 512
    sales budget, 511
bureaucratic organization theory, 28–29
Burns and Stalker study, 266–268
business ownership, forms of. See forms of business ownership
business plan
    components of, 172–176
    defined, 173
    entrepreneurs and, 117–118
    financial plan, 176
    human resources plan, 174
    importance of, 172
    marketing plan, 173–174
    personnel/management plan, 174–175
    production/operations plan, 175–176
    production plans, 174
business planning software, 118
business start-up
    business ownership, forms of, 111–114
    debt, 115
    equity, 114
    existing business, purchase of, 108–111

family-owned business, 108
    franchise, 111, 112
    funding, 114–115
    the idea, 107–108
    methods, 108–111
    microenterprise, 110
    new business, 109–110

C

cafeteria benefits, 319
Canada
    legal system in, 54
    mixed economy in, 50
Canada Labour Code, 320, 325
Canadian economy
    characteristics of, 40–41
    foreign ownership, 41
    megaprojects, influence of, 40
    one-company towns, 40
    resource-based economy, 40
    services, emphasis on, 40
Canadian Human Rights Act, 321, 323
Canadian Human Rights Commission, 321
Canadian management environment
    Canadian economy, characteristics of, 40–41
    competition, 42
    environmental factors, 39–40
    government, role of, 42
    industrial concentration, 42
    innovation, 43
    ownership of business firms, 41
    research and development (R&D), 43
    societal trends, 43
    technology, 43
    workforce, 42–43
capability pyramid, 450
capitalist system, 50
case studies
    "A Case of Good Intentions," 437–440
    "CEO Succession Planning at American Express," 329
    "Conflict and Change at Parallax Systems," 494
    "Controlling Quality with Committed Employees at the Ritz-Carlton," 527–528
    "Finally! A Decision on Voisey's Bay," 159
    "Ford's Response to Global Changes," 70–71
    "Freelancing," 327
    "Galt Contracting," 403–405
    "Getting by with a Little Help from His Mother's Friends," 127
    "The Importance of Leadership: Scott vs. Amundsen," 367–368
    "Introducing Change at Yellow Freightways," 493
    "It's a 'Good Thing' to Have a Well-Known Brand Name," 225–226
    "Jersak Holdings Ltd.," 260–261
    "Leadership in the Canadian Forces," 366–367
    "Merging Teams at Canadian National Railways," 463

gender-role stereotypes, 93
glass ceiling, 342
and leadership, 342
and "old boy's network," 342
Woodward studies, 268
work, nature of, 14–15
work group support systems
collaborative writing systems, 430
defined, 429
digital work group support and collaboration systems, 429
group decision support systems, 429

online work group support systems, 429–430
worker empowerment, 17–18
workers' compensation, 319
workforce
in Canadian management environment, 42–43
diverse, 90, 92, 300–301
see also managing diversity
in modern management environment, 16
stress, 331

World Trade Organization (WTO), 37–38, 46, 51–54

Y

yes/no control, 504

Z

zone of indifference, 32

Photo Credits

Chapter 1

p. 1 Alan Levenson; **p. 2** Mario Tamo/Getty Images Inc.—Liaison; **p. 14** Courtesy of Seagull Pewter Inc.; **p. 15** John Dakers/Eye Ubiquitous; **p. 16** Michael Newman/PhotoEdit.

Chapter 2

p. 37 Image courtesy of Bombardier Inc.; **p. 42** Labatt Breweries of Canada; **p. 55** (top and bottom) AP/Wide World Photos.

Chapter 3

p. 73 Pearson Education/PH College, **p. 79** Fabrice Coffrini/Associated Press; **p. 85** Courtesy of www.ethics.ubc.ca/resources/business; **p. 92** Alan Levenson.

Chapter 4

p. 101 CP Photo/Wayne Hiebert.

Chapter 5

p. 131 Masterfile Corporation; **p. 132** Dick Loek/Toronto Star; **p. 143** Masterfile Corporation; **p. 152** Michael Newman/PhotoEdit.

Chapter 6

p. 166 Dick Hemingway; **p. 187** SMAILES ALEX/Corbis/Sygma; **p. 189** Spencer Grant/PhotoEdit.

Chapter 7

p. 198 Paul Chiasson/Canapress; **p. 209** Jim Whitmer/Jim Whitmer Photography; **p. 217** AFP PHOTO EPA/DPA/Rainer Jenson/CORBIS.

Chapter 8

p. 231 John Abbott Photography; **p. 232** Exide Technologies; **p. 244** Washington Marine Group; **p. 246** Photo courtesy of Manitoba Hydro Corporation.

Chapter 9

p. 464 Jon Anderson for Black Star; **p. 266** John Abbott Photography; **p. 267** John Abbott Photography; **p. 279** SIU BioMedical/Custom Medical Stock Photo; **p. 284** "O": Duo Trapeze. Photo: Veronique Vial. Costumes: Dominique Lemieux. Cirque du Soleil Inc.

Chapter 10

p. 291 Signicast Corporation; **p. 300** Michael Newman/PhotoEdit; **p. 310** (top) Internal and External Communication, Inc.; **p. 310** (bottom) Frank Gunn/Canapress.

Chapter 11

p. 333 Steve Lehman/SABA Press Photos, Inc.; **p. 334** WestJet; **p. 345** Suncor Energy Inc.

Chapter 12

p. 370 Maple Leaf Sports & Entertainment Ltd.; **p. 376** David Norton/ImageState/International Stock Photography Ltd.; **p. 387** AP/World Wide Photos.

Chapter 13

p. 409 The Home Depot Canada; **p. 413** Dick Hemingway; **p. 423** Toyota Motor Manufacturing, Kentucky, Inc.; **p. 430** Ventana Corporation Group Systems; **p. 433** Rommel/Masterfile Corporation.

Chapter 14

p. 440 Shell Canada Limited; **p. 441** Steve Lehman/SABA Press Photos, Inc.; **p. 451** James Wasserman/James Wasserman Photography.

Chapter 15

p. 466 Koichi Kamoshida/Getty Images, Inc.—Liaison; **p. 472** AP/Wide World Photos; **p. 477** Richard Heinzen/SuperStock.

Chapter 16

p. 499 Courtesy of Saturn Corporation; **p. 500** CP Photo/Jeff McIntosh; **p. 504** Dick Hemingway; **p. 521** www.comstock.com; **p. 522** Courtesy of Saturn Corporation.

MANAGEMENT Principles and Practices for Tomorrow's Leaders

Dear Students:

For most people, the best way to learn how to do something is by actually doing it. The question is, how to build that kind of practical component into a textbook. What we've done in Management: Principles and Practices for Tomorrow's Leaders is create a portfolio of opportunities for you to use your newly acquired knowledge.

The Manager's Portfolio has three parts:

1. LEARN IT

Each chapter has 15 fill-in questions to help you review key concepts.

2. PRACTICE IT

A CD-ROM filled with realistic business scenarios challenges you to practice your new skills. You watch the scenario, read the discussion questions in this Manager's Portfolio, and then apply the principles and practices you learned in each chapter to solve the problems presented in the video.

Each video depicts a decision-making situation at CanGo, a startup company that sells a variety of products and services, ranging from books and videos to (eventually) providing online video games. Each of Chapters 2–17 will have one video. Chapter 1 has two. The video segments are pretty much independent of one another. Therefore, you and your professor may decide to use only, say, the videos from Chapters 5, 8, and 16 (or some others) without losing any continuity.

MORE PRACTICE

The CD-ROM also contains interactive exercises using tables and figures from the text. All are tied to the video situation, and you can use them to help solve the decision-making problem the video presents. You can also test yourself.

3. APPLY IT

Few decisions managers make involve just one management function (such as planning). Special Apply It Manager's Portfolio questions help you analyze selected CanGo scenarios in an integrated, multi-functional way.

Managing in the Twenty-First Century

LEARN IT

Test Your Understanding

1. In our club we have people with formally assigned roles, all of whom must work together in order to achieve our goals. It is clear that our club meets the definition of a(n) _____.

2. Someone who plans, organizes, leads, and controls the people and the work of the organization in such a way that the organization reaches its goals is a(n) _____.

3. Anil is a top manager. He spends most of his time _____ and setting goals.

4. When Lourdes spends time setting quality standards for her manufacturing team, she is _____.

5. Henrietta supervises the workers who actually produce the cookies for which her organization is known. She is a(n) _____.

6. Mei is an ambitious and assertive manager who believes that she is a good public speaker and feels that she has the reputation of being able to deal with difficult people. She exhibits the _____ personality orientation.

7. As a sales manager, George has always been competent at developing quarterly sales forecasts, setting realistic sales quotas for the team's commissioned sales reps, and hiring exceptional sales people. He gets high marks for his _____ skills.

8. Yet, George has been criticized by some of his sales reps as exhibiting favouritism towards his friends on the sales team and being overly harsh to new hires. For this reason, he is attending a workshop to improve his _____ skills.

9. An executive at the top headhunting firm, Savanah is best known for her excellent _____ skills, which enable her to cut through drawn-out discussions on the details and present the big picture.

10. Toyota, a Japanese company, manufactures its Camry in Kentucky for sales in Canada, the United States, and Mexico. It is part of a growing trend toward _____.

11. The huge increase in service jobs means that there is a growing emphasis on _____ the knowledge, education, training, skills, and expertise of a firm's workers.

12. In the _____ organization, employees reach across the company to interact with whomever they must to get the job done. This speeds decision-making immensely.

13. When Ritz-Carlton allows a front-line hotel employee to spend up to $2000 to resolve a customer problem—all without consulting his or her supervisor—the company is exhibiting _____.

14. Many employees and supervisors have been affected by the change from a pyramid-shaped organization with many levels to a(n) _____ organization with subordinates who have more _____.

15. By training and coaching employees, sharing information with them, and giving them the resources they need to do their job well, Chantal is using a(n) _____ approach to management.

PRACTICE IT

Videos for The Environment and Foundations of Modern Management.

Video 1 The introductory video shows Elizabeth, CanGo's founder, as she introduces her management and employee team. Here's some background information on Elizabeth, and on each of the people you'll meet:

Elizabeth is CanGo's founder. She's a smart, enthusiastic, and driven CEO. She can be intimidating to some employees, but evokes a great deal of admiration from them as well. She's a visionary with a magnetic personality.

Andrew is director of marketing. He is enthusiastic and creative, and keeps his focus on what the competition is doing. He loves coming up with new ideas, and as far as CanGo is concerned, he's always thinking, "What are we going to do tomorrow?"

Ethel is director of accounting. She is a very detail-oriented and meticulous person. Elizabeth and the company depend on her to consider the potential costs of all the new ideas managers and employees at CanGo are coming up with. You can count on her to raise important issues and to help shape profitable projects.

Warren is director of operations. He's been at CanGo since its inception. Warren is a realist, and his colleagues count on him to help make their new ideas become realities. He's also a sports buff: CanGo employees usually refer to him as "coach."

Maria is a director of human resources. Like a good HR manager, she's a real "people person" who has to make many of the hard decisions regarding hiring and firing at CanGo. Many employees also turn to her to discuss personnel issues. Elizabeth leans heavily on her to provide advice and feedback.

Clark is director of finance. He's a realist, and whenever new ideas emerge within CanGo, you can count on him to ask, "Are we making our shareholders more money with this idea?" He adds an air of respectability to the young firm and is always the one to ask, "How does this new idea add value to the firm?"

Gail is a senior staff member. She's a perfectionist by nature and is very serious about her work at CanGo. She is quick to volunteer and is willing to work extra hours to get the job done. Her CanGo peers like and respect her.

Nick is also a senior staff member. He's a recent college graduate who is best known for his sense of humour. He is inexperienced, but anxious to please. The other staff members generally tolerate his good-natured antics.

Whitney, another staff member, is a single mother who enjoys her job at CanGo. She was attracted to the company by Elizabeth's concern for her employees and her desire to build an employee-friendly firm.

Debbie, another senior staff member, is a teacher by training. She likes the teamwork at CanGo and enjoys the fast-paced ebusiness environment CanGo operates within.

Video 2 In the second video clip, a difficult Christmas has just passed and CEO Elizabeth has called a meeting to compare last year's performance with this year's performance. Warren, director of operations, is obviously in the hot seat. He has asked Jack, a consulting operations system engineer, to accompany him to the meeting to offer suggestions on how to correct the problems the company experienced over the past 12 months. As you watch this video, pay particular attention to Elizabeth's management skills and to the techniques she uses to try to get to the bottom of the problem, and to get her team started down the road toward a solution.

Watch the videos, and answer the following questions:

1. In terms of what we discussed in Chapter 1 about what managers do, list the specific management tasks Elizabeth seems to be demonstrating in this scenario. If you were watching this video and hadn't been told ahead of time who is in charge, how could you identify the person who is the head of the management team? Is there anyone else in the scenario who seems to be eligible to fill that role? Why?

2. While this and the preceding video in this chapter obviously don't give a lot of detail about Elizabeth, do your best to answer the following question: Do you think she has the traits and competencies to be a manager? Why or why not?

3. Chapter 1 focuses on the four basic functions of management, namely, planning, organizing, leading, and controlling. This video provides you with realistic examples of what managing is really like in practice. (For example, Warren seems to be getting a little defensive when Elizabeth challenges him, a situation that will require Elizabeth to use her leadership and communication skills.) Based on what you see in this video, list other specific examples of what managers do or should do, and categorize the examples under the topics planning, organizing or leading, or controlling.

CHAPTER 2

The Environment of Management: Canadian and Global

LEARN IT

Test Your Understanding

1. After several successful years of retail carpet sales, Julie is planning to expand her chain of stores into the United States. If she does so, her business could be characterized as a(n) _____ business.

2. Shell is a giant petroleum company that basically sells the same things in the same ways everywhere. Shell, evidently, is a(n) _____.

3. NAFTA eliminated all barriers to trade among its member countries. In doing so it created a(n) _____ _____ _____ in which goods are freely traded among member nations.

4. Companies usually go global in order to expand _____, but they may also seek to reduce _____ _____.

5. We've just decided to sell our toys and games to markets in England, Australia, and the United States. By _____ over the internet, we may avoid _____, costly government taxes on imports.

6. Brun Corporation decided to start its international operations through _____ by granting a Swedish firm the right to utilize one of its patents for three years in return for certain royalties.

7. Several Japanese auto manufacturers have built manufacturing plants in the United States. For the Japanese firms, these efforts are examples of _____ _____ _____.

8. A large U.S. paper manufacturing company has decided to share the costs of developing very sophisticated lumbering technology with a Canadian company. It is in the interest of both companies to pursue this project. This strategic alliance is actually a(n) _____ _____.

9. Having a(n) _____ _____ is a relatively costly strategy for expanding into foreign markets in which the company makes the entire investment itself.

10. Philip, an expatriate manager in our China plant, made a drastic mistake when he assumed that the Chinese employees would be motivated by the same _____ as our Canadian employees.

11. Our CEO is only comfortable internationalizing our operations into countries that are democratic in nature. He wants to limit our operations to a few individual foreign markets. It appears that he has a(n) _____ managerial philosophy.

12. The best global managers are flexible enough to accept that their own ways of doing things are not always the best, and they are willing to solve problems using the best solutions from different systems. We can say these managers have a(n) _____ _____.

13. By teaching local managers in foreign markets how to both use and adapt their sophisticated information technology, many Canadian computer companies have achieved a successful _____.

14. To take advantage of economies of scale, most automakers produce a standardized "world car" and then fine-tune it for subtle differences in national tastes. They are pursuing a(n) _____ strategy.

15. The institutionalization of inequality in India is very high. According to Hofstede, India would rank high in the area of _____.

PRACTICE IT

Video for The Environment of Management: Canadian and Global

This video illustrates a common situation facing companies. Before the video opened, Andrew suggested that CanGo should expand abroad and begin aggressively marketing its services in other countries. In the video, Liz is not entirely convinced of the wisdom of expanding abroad. After all, CanGo's stock and financial performance have not satisfied the Board of Directors, and Liz barely managed to avoid being booted. She rightfully points out that going global could involve more time, energy, and resources than CanGo can spare at the moment. Furthermore, as the consultant points out, international expansion might require expertise none of the CanGo team possesses. It looks like the management team at CanGo lacks strong experience and expertise in doing business abroad. As you watch this video, ask yourself whether you think this team at this juncture should be following up on Andrew's big opportunity and expanding abroad.

Watch the video, and answer the following questions:

1. In Chapter 2 we listed erroneous assumptions managers make in expanding abroad. Based on this video and what you know about CanGo, which of these erroneous assumptions seems to apply to its management team?

2. Before this video opened, Andrew has mentioned to Liz that the country he is particularly interested in expanding to is Japan. Using the principles and practices you learned in Chapter 2, explain to Liz's management team why CanGo is (or is not) a suitable candidate for expanding into Japan, based on the cultural, administrative, geographic, and economic "distance" between Japan and Canada.

APPLY IT

As is often the case, few decisions that managers have to make involve a single function. This is certainly the case when it comes to expanding your firm abroad. In fact, in the case of CanGo, some people might find it just a little mind-boggling that with the company's deteriorating financial situation and Elizabeth's precarious situation with the Board of Directors, CanGo is even considering expanding abroad at this time. In any case, assume for a minute that Liz has agreed to go to the Board of Directors and tell them that she wants to expand abroad. She knows that the Board is going to ask her many questions about how she plans to do this. One thing they're going to want to know is the five main tasks she thinks she and the company will have to address with respect to planning, organizing, leading, and controlling before CanGo can embark on international expansion. In teams of three or four students, put together those lists of tasks so that Elizabeth can take them to her board.

CHAPTER 3

Ethics, Social Responsibility, and Diversity

LEARN IT

Test Your Understanding

1. Antonella believes that any employee theft is wrong. This is a(n) _____.

2. Josh is about to go for a job interview. In deciding whether to admit that he never completed his MBA or falsify his resume, Josh is making a(n) _____ decision.

3. The pressure to meet unrealistic business expectations led Enron employees to fudge accounting figures and hide liabilities off the balance sheet. This is an example of how _____ _____ influence(s) ethics.

4. Product managers at The Body Shop would purchase a cosmetic ingredient that has *not* been tested on animals over a less expensive one that has been tested on animals. The Body Shop is an example of a(n) _____ _____ company.

5. As a toy manufacturer, Mihir's company is careful not to produce products that are potentially harmful for its customers, but also believes that profit maximization is a worthy goal. Apparently this company has adopted the _____ view.

6. As part of their Moral Minimum approach to social responsibility, Lashawna's company encourages employees to report organizational wrongdoing. They are encouraging _____ _____.

7. As the composition of our workforce changes dramatically, it is becoming increasingly important that we _____ _____, which means that we need to plan and implement systems and practices so that the potential advantages of diversity are maximized while its disadvantages are minimized.

8. Jim thinks that all women are poor drivers. This is a(n) _____. Jennifer is a woman, so Jim thinks that she is a bad driver. This is an example of _____.

9. _____ is the tendency to view members of one's own group as the centre of the universe and other social groups less favourably.

10. Maria is a Chicana woman who sued the company for _____ when her boss repeatedly refused to promote her even though she brought in more sales than the white male managers in less senior positions.

11. We have 500 employees, and we recently hired three women vice-presidents even though we only have 100 women employees. This is an example of _____.

12. By admitting that the company hires too few visible minorities, and by resolving to hire more minorities, the CEO of our company is using strong _____ to manage diversity.

13. In the heavily male chemistry department, the University has assigned _____ to all female scientists in order to provide them with the support, guidance, and counselling that they do not get informally.

14. A written code of conduct or _____ _____ will signal that top management is serious about ethics, but the organizational culture must support it and "walk the talk."

PRACTICE IT

Video for Ethics, Social Responsibility, and Diversity In this video, after some introductory small talk, the head of classicartwork.com suggests that Liz and CanGo sell his firm personal information about CanGo's customers. CanGo could make a tidy profit from the sale of this information, and it's not likely that CanGo's customers would find out where classicartwork.com got its contact list. Furthermore, there is no privacy guarantee on CanGo's website. Liz is considering the offer, but she's obviously somewhat uncomfortable with it. Her CFO seems to be leaning toward accepting. As you watch this video, ask yourself, "What is the right thing to do in this situation?"

Watch the video, and answer the following questions:

1. Go to several popular websites, and read and compare their privacy statements. What kind of information about their users do these ecommerce companies gather? Will they sell your personal information?

2. Based on what the three people in the video have done so far, identify actions or comments that are ethical and unethical.

3. Based on how this chapter defined the meaning of ethics, what do you think is the ethical thing for Liz to do in this case, and why?

CHAPTER 4

Managing Entrepreneurial Organizations

LEARN IT

Test Your Understanding

1. David turned his stint at teaching business English to Japanese businesspeople into a flourishing business. He formed a team of business English consultants who charge top dollar for their seminars and one-on-one sessions with businesspeople from a wide variety of countries. Because he created a valuable business from nothing, David is a classic example of a(n) _____.

2. David's brother Hank, who owns and runs the family deli, is considered a(n) _____ _____ _____. Yet both he and David, who started a business from scratch, must be well versed in _____ _____ _____, the art of planning, organizing, leading, and controlling a small business.

3. _____ is not just for startups but for all companies that want to stimulate innovation and create new businesses. When corporations create radically new products or services using internal markets and relatively small autonomous or semi-autonomous business units, we call the process _____ _____.

4. Entrepreneurship typically flourishes in regions where there is greater _____ rather than in countries, like Cuba or North Korea, where there are governmental and bureaucratic obstacles to starting, financing, and growing a business.

5. Mica has struggled for years to get her line of silk-screened greeting cards on the shelves not only of local stationery stores but also of national venues like Indigo. She has trekked all over the country, showing her wares to buyers, some of who laughed in her face! Mica certainly possesses _____, a common trait of entrepreneurs.

6. Wendy's, McDonald's, and KFC are all examples of restaurant _____, firms that license other firms or individuals to use their business ideas and procedures and sell their goods in return for royalties or other payments.

7. Gabi had always liked being a(n) _____ _____ of her own publishing house because she owns all her business's profits (or losses) outright. However, she came up against a major disadvantage when she was sued by an author's estate over a copyright issue. Her _____ _____ meant that she was solely responsible for the claim against the firm and was forced to use her personal savings to settle the case.

8. Tad wants the freedom and adventure of starting a new business without taking on so much of the risk. He decided that a good option for him would be to open up a Second Cup store in his neighbourhood. By becoming a(n) _____, he gets much of the startup, preparatory work done by Second Cup and also gets a business that is based on a proven business model.

9. With a winning idea, Michelle was able to fund her internet startup with _____ from wealthy private investors, known as _____, and also from _____ _____, professionals who specialize in evaluating new venture opportunities and funding those they deem worthy.

10. In 1994 two Cornell students came up with a business idea to create an online community— TheGlobe.com— where participants would go to find news, discussion forums, and stuff to buy. They recruited employees in the student lounge, paid them with Dominoes pizzas, drained bank accounts, and lived off credit cards. Four years later TheGlobe.com sold stock to outsiders and netted $27 million in a(n) _____ _____ _____, and the former dorm buddies became joint CEOs.

11. The two Cornell students who started TheGlobe.com may have had a(n) _____ _____, in which they were liable for the firm's debts only to the extent of their financial investment in the firm.

12. When Eileen finally quit Air Canada to start her own travel agency geared toward group tours for singles, her first step was to conduct a(n) _____ _____. She studied the market, customers, industry, and competition to see whether her idea had a reasonable chance of success.

13. The chances that Patrice will get financing for his startup are practically nil without a solid _____ _____. I urged him to sit down today and outline what business he is in, where it is headed, and how he plans to take it there!

14. General Motors, Eli Lilly, and Dupont are examples of _____. Each is a separate legal entity with shareholders that own a part interest in that entity. These shareholder owners also have _____ _____ _____ because the most a shareholder can lose is what he or she paid for the shares.

15. In addition to getting startup funding from their own bank accounts or from family and friends, entrepreneurs are likely to use borrowed capital, or _____, to finance their businesses.

PRACTICE IT

Video for Managing Entrepreneurial Organizations In this video, Liz is in trouble with her Board of Directors' executive committee, and she knows it. By hiring a consultant, the executive committee has demonstrated their lack of faith in Liz's ability to lead CanGo and to make it a powerhouse in ecommerce. As you can see in the video, the consultant will identify areas of strength in the firm, and shortcomings in Elizabeth's management style. These representatives of the company's Board of Directors (who probably represent the financial companies that helped CanGo raise money through a sale of stock) understandably seem to be more concerned with Liz's shortcomings, insofar as they may prove fatal for the firm. All this is not unusual for a young, fast-growing entrepreneurial firm. As we saw in Chapter 4, entrepreneurs supply the spark that gets firms off the ground. Inevitably, though, they reach a point where everyone (including the entrepreneur) has to ask whether the capabilities and strengths of the company's founder are suitable for expanding the company's success as the firm matures. As you watch the video, listen to what the consultant has to say and to the board members' obvious concerns.

Watch the video, and answer the following questions:

1. Chapter 4 lists a number of activity areas for which a new business owner should establish controls. In teams of three or four students, review this list and use it to provide specific examples of controls you believe Liz should have but did not implement for CanGo.

2. Elizabeth is an entrepreneur, and yet the consultant says her main management flaw is that she micromanages too much. Watch the other videos. Do you agree? Assuming for a moment that the consultant is right, do you think it's possible for a person to be both entrepreneurial and a micromanager? Do the two usually go together (based on what you learned in Chapter 4), or do they tend to be mutually exclusive?

APPLY IT

As is often the case, few decisions that managers have to make involve a single function only. This is particularly the case with respect to the situation Elizabeth finds herself in now with the Board of Directors. Chances are, she didn't just get into this situation by micromanaging. Instead, she exhibited definite shortcomings with respect to planning, organizing, leading, and controlling the people and resources at CanGo. Watch the other videos, form teams of three or four students, and list five specific planning, organizing, leading, and controlling management principles and practices where Liz has fallen down on the job. Then (assuming the board is going to let her continue for now) develop a one-page summary telling her what you think she should do next in order to institute a more effective management system at CanGo.

CHAPTER 5

Decision Making

LEARN IT

Test Your Understanding

1. Charlie had established the monthly sales goal of $15 000. Last month his unit only sold $10 000. Charlie is looking at a(n) _____.

2. Nalini owns and manages a small, but growing, real estate firm. She is considering expanding her operations into two neighbouring towns. This is a(n) _____ decision.

3. Decisions that rely upon rules, are procedural in nature, and have well-defined information and decision criteria are _____ decisions.

4. Marisa uses the rule of thumb "never give a perfect score" on a performance appraisal when making her decision as to what score to assign one of her employees. This decision-making shortcut is know as a(n) _____.

5. When choosing a location for a new manufacturing plant, Javier is concerned with several things: the distance from the company's major markets, the location of raw material, the quality and availability of the labour supply. Before making this decision, Javier needs to make his _____ clear.

6. Marsha's department has an extremely high turnover rate. When asked by her boss what she is going to do about it, she simply said, "Well, if they don't like working here, that is fine with me," instead of generating possible solutions. This rigid strategy or point of view is called Marsha's _____.

7. I wanted to eliminate tardiness in my department because it significantly impacts on customer service. After thinking about it, I decided to implement attendance incentives. This has greatly reduced tardiness, but has not eliminated it. I guess that I will settle for that. I have decided to _____.

8. K.J. uses a trial-and-error approach to decision-making, bouncing from one alternative to another to get a feel for what works best. K.J. has a(n) _____ decision-making style.

9. Lois is the leader of a very cohesive group. There is a strong need and desire among the group members to get along well with each other, and to present a unified front to non-group members. _____ is a very real possibility in this situation.

10. When trying to think up a title for their new imprint, the editorial staff held a(n) _____ session in which they all contributed their ideas with one condition: no comments or judgments until all their ideas had been aired.

11. Avram tends to take a logical, structured, step-by-step approach to solving problems. We can say that he has a(n) _____ decision style.

12. The first candidate Kareem interviewed for the programmer position said that the job seemed to demand a lot of night and weekend time. He then found himself grilling subsequent applicants about whether they were comfortable working after hours—even though the position had never required it! Kareem has fallen into the _____ trap.

13. You want to resign from your job to start a new business, but before you make your decision you project yourself into the future and imagine what your days are like without your old colleagues, 9–5 hours, and a steady source of income. You are analyzing the _____ of your decision.

14. Adeline gets paralyzed with fear whenever she has to make a decision, with the result that she misses deadlines and just got low marks on her performance review. Adeline's mistake is that she overemphasizes the _____ of each decision.

PRACTICE IT

Video for Decision Making This video follows a decision made by Elizabeth (with some help from her employees and managers) to expand CanGo from a company that just offers books and related media over the internet to one that also offers an opportunity for its users to play online games. After playing several video-type games—often with competing players in other countries—Liz came away very impressed with the prospects for offering opportunities for online games, and she and her team made the decision to get into this business. The video clip picks up at this point, and you see Andrew, Clark, and Warren discussing the pros and cons of this decision, which the company has already made. Andrew and Warren get into a heated discussion about whether or not CanGo's decision to enter the online gaming market is a good one. What sorts of things do you think are influencing them to take their positions?

Watch the video, and answer the following questions:

1. Based on what you read in Chapter 5, what would you suggest to improve the quality of Andrew's and Warren's evaluations of CanGo's decision to enter the online gaming market?

2. How valid is Clark's argument that since CanGo has sunk a "ton of money" into online gaming, the company is compelled to stick with this decision? Are there any decision-making biases underlying his view?

3. In making this decision, Elizabeth and her team defined the problem as "Should we get into online gaming, or not?" Name several ways in which the team could have defined the problem. What do you think actually triggered the problem in this situation?

The Planning Process

LEARN IT

Test Your Understanding

1. Joni wants to graduate in two years with a degree in Journalism. This is a(n) _____.

2. At the recent management retreat, we determined our firm's _____ by answering the question, "What business are we in?" Then, we produced a(n) _____ _____ outlining what business we will be in during the next 3–5 years and the steps we must take to accomplish this.

3. Our software company plans to shift its focus from technology to customer relationships, so now managers in the human resource department are developing _____ (or _____) plans that spell out how hiring, training, and other department activities can help accomplish this shift.

4. Anjana's message to the sales force, "Do your best and I'll be happy," is not an effective goal because it is neither _____ nor _____.

5. A key characteristic of a(n) _____ is that the plans and goals of each subordinate unit contribute to achieving the goals of the next higher unit's plans— and all contribute to the company-wide plans and goals.

6. One of the best ways to ensure that employees are motivated to achieve goals is through their _____ in setting them. _____ is a technique in which supervisor and subordinate jointly set goals for the latter and periodically assess progress toward those goals.

7. In order to best forecast sales of our new Robopuppy toy, our company is using _____ forecasting methods, such as gathering the opinion of our seasoned sales force, and _____ forecasting methods, in which we use statistical methods to examine data and find underlying patterns.

8. Abdub is responsible for inventory control at his store. He has decided that the best way to approach this responsibility is to take a series of biweekly observations of his inventory. He is using the _____ forecasting method.

9. Katrina is certain there is a relationship between sales in her department and the country-wide unemployment rate. As she tracks the unemployment rate, she makes her sales predictions. Katrina is doing _____ forecasting.

10. While we were developing the Robomaster prototype, we went on the internet to get sales reports from toy companies with similar products. After analyzing this _____ data, we then gleaned _____ data by observing 5–7-year-old boys—our target market—playing with similar robotic toys.

11. We think that it is very important for our planning premises that we know and understand the competition. We "shop" their stores, hire their workers, and question their customers in order to gain information about them. These practices are known as _____ _____.

12. Even when thinking about your own career, a big first step in the planning process is defining your _____.

13. As most companies are moving away from having plans developed in large planning departments to having plans developed by product and divisional managers, we can say that planning is becoming more _____.

14. At our school we provide every student with a written plan of study that contains the courses that must be taken in order to graduate with a certain degree. This plan of study can be described as a(n) _____ plan.

15. The economy was in a severe slump when Angus, a sales manager for a floundering computer company, told his department that they were to achieve a 50% increase in sales over the next two quarters. The sales reps were demoralized because this goal was not _____.

PRACTICE IT

Video for The Planning Process In this video, Warren, the company's operations manager, is telling one of his employees, Nick, that Nick has to develop a plan for the implementation of CanGo's new online gaming business, and that he has to do so as soon as possible. It seems obvious to Nick and his colleagues (but not to Warren) that Nick doesn't even know where to start regarding developing a plan for getting the new business off the ground. He and the team should use a number of planning tools. As you watch this video, consider what you'd tell Nick, and where you think Warren may have fallen down on his job.

Watch the video, and answer the following questions:

1. Explain what Warren did right and did wrong with respect to setting goals for Nick.

2. Create a Gantt chart for Nick that he can use as the basis for the plan he has to develop for Warren.

3. Are there any other types of plans that you think Nick should be using in order to provide Warren with the documentation that he wants, and if so what are they?

4. In this video, Nick's colleagues seem to be making the point that organizing and planning have something in common, since they say Nick won't be able to develop his plan until he gets organized. What do they mean by that? Can a company be organized without a plan? Can a company have a plan if the company is not organized?

APPLY IT

As is often the case, few decisions that managers have to make involve a single function only. In this video, you saw Warren giving an assignment to Nick. Based on what you know about management, how would you rate Warren's managerial skills in this video, with specific reference to his ability to plan, organize, lead, and control?

Strategic Management

LEARN IT

Test Your Understanding

1. The process of identifying and pursuing the organization's mission by aligning the organization's internal capabilities with the external demands of its environment is _____.

2. Tim Hortons plans to boost sales in its existing United States units before opening more restaurants there. This growth strategy is called _____ _____.

3. Nestlè purchasing Hershey's would be an example of the growth strategy known as _____ _____, whereas when Levi's or Nike opened their own retail stores, they were pursuing the growth strategy of _____ _____.

4. Many companies have downsized their operations in an attempt to remain competitive. This reduction in operations is also known as _____.

5. A temporary network of independent companies linked by information technology to share skills, costs, and access to one another's markets is a(n) _____ _____.

6. Network TV stations must now struggle to win their audiences' attention away from cable stations, DVDs, computer games, and other forms of home entertainment. In order to establish a profitable and sustainable position in the industry, each network station needs a(n) _____ strategy.

7. A local electronic and small appliance chain advertises "We will NEVER be undersold." This competitive strategy is known as _____.

8. Cataloguer Garnet Hill emphasizes the relationship between cost and quality. Its uniquely designed natural fibre clothes and linens may cost a bit more, but their quality is much higher. Garnet Hill has adopted the competitive strategy known as _____.

9. In SWOT analysis, strengths and weaknesses are _____, while opportunities and threats are _____.

10. As a result of a recent SWOT analysis, we know that one of our weaknesses is that we have extensive management turnover. We have identified a competitor who is the best in our industry at attracting, developing, and retaining management talent, and are carefully analyzing how he accomplishes this, so that we can improve our operations. This process is known as _____.

11. The pizza business in our region is saturated. Marco owns a small chain of pizza stores. He has low market share and the market is not growing. In terms of the BCG matrix, this business would be characterized as a(n) _____.

12. The collective learning and skills in the organization that often cut across departmental lines are known as _____.

13. Some companies do not utilize forecasting for their strategic planning. Instead, they develop "stories" about alternative possible futures. This approach to strategic planning is called _____ planning.

14. Effective implementation of any strategic plan requires _____, which is developing functional plans so that all the firm's activities contribute in an orderly and coordinated way to what the company wants to achieve.

15. Hamel and Prahalad argue that rather than align the strategic plan with current resources, companies should supplement what they have and do more with what they have. In other words, they should _____ _____ for future growth.

PRACTICE IT

Video for Strategic Management One of the things this chapter stresses is the importance of having clear-cut strategy and strategic plan. As the chapter notes, top managers need a strategy so that "they can know what mail to throw out in the morning." In other words, if you don't have a clear idea of what business you're in, you can't really evaluate proposals to enter new businesses (like the one that Ethel has brought to the management team in this video). The video actually illustrates something that's not uncommon in management: a proposal for forming a joint venture or entering a new business that just comes in unsolicited. In this case, Ethel gets a phone call from an old friend who's now the CEO of the new Radiojustforme.com. He wants to do business with CanGo. As you watch this video, ask yourself if this opportunity really fits with CanGo's strategy. Try to assess the extent to which the management team here is applying the principles and practices of strategic planning.

Watch the video, and answer the following questions:

1. Based on what you read in Chapter 7 and what you know about CanGo, what business is CanGo in now? What are its current corporate and business-level strategies?

2. Liz and the management team are thinking about spinning off the proposed venture with Radiojustforme.com (to offer jazz and swing MP3s), and to commit their own resources for web page development, logistics, product distribution, and sales for doing so. That would seem to suggest CanGo would actually have to set up a separate subsidiary to run this spinoff. Does creating a separate business and division like this fit the way CanGo management has defined the business now? Why or why not?

3. Compare and contrast the strategy of (1) going into online games and (2) forming a joint venture with Radiojustforme.com. How well does each strategy fit with the business CanGo is in now (assuming it is not offering games at the moment)? Why do you say that, based on Chapter 7's discussion of corporate strategy?

4. Based on what you know about CanGo's current definition of its business, develop a vision and mission statement for the company.

APPLY IT

As is often the case, few decisions that managers have to make involve a single function only. In this video, you saw CanGo presented with a business opportunity. Try to assess the extent to which the opportunity really fits with CanGo's strategy. To do this, you need to consider CanGo's business plan, as well as the opportunities and threats in its environment. Form teams of three or four students and size up CanGo's opportunities and threats. Then use that information to explain whether or not CanGo should pursue the suggested new business.

Fundamentals of Organizing

LEARN IT

Test Your Understanding

1. If you want to see the structure of the organization, who is in charge of what area, and who is accountable to whom, you would look at a(n) _____ _____.

2. When Serge, who works in claims, wants to find out what is happening in the underwriting department, he calls Altagracia, who works in that department, instead of going through the chain of command. This is an example of the _____ organization.

3. In our automobile dealership we have a sales department, a finance department, and a service department. While this _____ departmentalization is logical and efficient, it also reduces our dealership's sensitivity to customers and produces fewer generalists.

4. Our publishing company realizes that colleges, high schools, and elementary schools are, in fact, different customers. We have separate divisions serving each of those different customers. We have adopted a _____ form of departmentalization.

5. Like IBM, our company has a(n) _____ structure in which employees are allocated permanently to one special functional department but simultaneously have ongoing assignments to project, custom, product, or geographic unit heads.

6. Philippa is a market researcher on my software development team and complains that she often doesn't know whether to report to me or the company's marketing manager. Hence, a big drawback to our matrix organization structure is _____.

7. All product and operational decisions for our apparel company are made at the headquarters level. Don Li, who is the local manager of our Beijing plant, complains he lacks _____ to make decisions affecting his employees. This is one of the drawbacks of a(n) _____ organizational structure.

8. Manuel is one of the production managers at our plant, and since production is very essential to our business, he would be considered a(n) _____ manager.

9. We have a very extensive legal department in our corporation. As the head of that department, Mr. Nessing has the ability to tell his subordinates what to do, but no ability to order anyone in sales to do or not to do something. He can only advise sales personnel. Within his own department we can say that he has _____ _____.

10. One of my responsibilities is effective inventory control for my department. I have a very capable subordinate who is looking for new challenges, so I have decided to assign her the authority and the responsibility for effective inventory control. This is _____.

11. Advances in interactive communication technology have helped lead to the creation of _____ organizations, which link employees from different functions, departments, levels, and geographic areas, so they can have free-flowing communication and get their jobs done more effectively.

12. Our biotech start-up is a(n) _____ organization in which our 35 employees are all members of small, self-managing teams, and there's only one manager. We have no traditional organizational hierarchy or chain of command.

13. Marina only has three people reporting directly to her. This number of people reflects a relatively narrow _____ _____ _____.

14. Our company recently underwent some moderate downsizing. The resulting _____ organization gave the remaining managers a wider span of control, and it _____ workers to do their jobs without having to get managerial approval for every decision they need to make.

15. Most human resource managers are considered _____ managers because they can only advise line managers, but cannot issue orders down the chain of command.

PRACTICE IT

Video for Fundamentals of Organizing CanGo is at a crucial point, because it is preparing to go public. Issuing an IPO (an initial public offering of its stock) will bring a greater degree of outside scrutiny as potential investors try to assess the company's strengths, weaknesses, and future potential. Liz is obviously convinced that CanGo is not where it needs to be to issue an IPO, at least organizationally. CanGo's CEO seems to know the broad types of organizational changes she wants to make. However, she's obviously faced with the problem of convincing her managers that organizational change is required. In some sense, it's easy, watching the video, to understand her managers' concerns. After all, CanGo now seems to have just the sort of informal, network organization structure that encourages employees to freely "cross over." Things thus get done quickly. What could be wrong with that?

Watch the video, and answer the following questions:

1. Draw the company's current organization chart, as best you can, and list its pros and cons. Now, based on what you've seen in this video clip and what you've learned about CanGo from the previous seven chapters, develop a new, preferred organization chart for the company. Include the specific recommendations in this video, such as Liz's desire to move customer service into Warren's department. Make sure it's clear what type of departmentalization you are proposing.

2. It's clear from the video that at least part of the managers' reluctance to reorganize seems to stem from their desire to avoid doing things more bureaucratically. Is it possible that her managers are correct, and that Liz might actually be doing more harm than good by formalizing things at CanGo? Why or why not?

3. What exactly are the pros and cons of hiring two new assistants, as suggested in this video. Might the idea backfire, and if so how?

APPLY IT

As is often the case, few decisions managers have to make involve a single function only. For example, to some extent, Liz's problem here is not just organizational; she has to motivate her managers to implement the change. Similarly, Warren's insistence that his own employees want to deal directly with him could raise the question of whether Warren is ready for broader managerial responsibilities. Watch this video clip, and list and briefly explain five specific examples from it that illustrate the fact that the problem Liz and her team face also involves planning, leading, and controlling.

Designing Organizational Structures

LEARN IT

Test Your Understanding

1. Our former CEO was forever tinkering with the organizational chart, but, fortunately, our new CEO understands that _____ drive the organization!

2. Last year our company let go of 325 of the company's 575 employees. The reduction in the workforce affected every level in the organization. This dramatic reduction in workforce is also known as _____.

3. When we shifted to purchasing supplies online, we decentralized our purchasing department to allow lower-level employees in all divisions to make quick purchasing decisions. Our company's ability to adapt quickly to new situations is one reason why we consider ourselves a(n) _____ organization.

4. One of the most important, but difficult, tasks in designing organizations to manage change is _____, the process of achieving unity of action among interdependent activities.

5. Every two months everyone in our whole company meets to go over the company values, mission statement, and strategic plan for the coming year. We're using _____ to achieve coordination.

6. In order to streamline our bank and make every division more entrepreneurial, the president split the company up into _____.

7. Anish is working for a service organization in which he is encouraged to remain open to criticism, and be willing to accept "orders" from lower-ranking employees with expertise in certain areas. Anish is working for an organization that is attempting to pierce the _____ boundary.

8. If you look at our organization chart, it appears the responsibilities are separated into various "smoke-stacks." We have a production smokestack, a sales smokestack, and a finance smokestack. We are still operating in an environment with a(n) _____ boundary.

9. Our sales department is very cohesive. We all identify with "our" department, all the way from company athletic teams to issues with the production department. In terms of boundaries, we all have a(n) _____ boundary.

10. At our magazine, the marketing and editorial employees are in constant conflict since marketing is trying to cut back on the space devoted to content. Then, our publisher had a brainstorm and decided that the marketing and editorial staff should switch places for one day. This really helped us reduce _____.

11. A grant writer for a nonprofit, Mira was struggling with a grant proposal and couldn't finish it. She came into the development director's office and said, "Jonah, I just can't get the summary right." "Here, hand it to me and I'll finish it," sighed Jonah, who has just become a victim of _____ _____.

12. This morning our product manager handed me a two-inch thick stack of papers and said, "Here are the reviewers' comments on the alpha version of the software. Now run with it!" And, with that he left to go on a business trip. I feel lost. In order to delegate more effectively, our product manager needs to _____ the assignment.

13. In practice, you can't decentralize everything. Decentralization must always represent a balance between delegated _____ and _____ _____ of essential functions.

14. Tanya works in a factory. Her job is very specialized, and she is expected to follow and use the chain of command to resolve issues. Her organization can probably be characterized as being _____.

15. An organic organization uses _____ decision-making with a(n) _____ type of departmentalization.

PRACTICE IT

Video for Designing Organizational Structures There is an ancient Chinese saying, "Be careful what you wish for, you are liable to get it." As you can see in this video, Elizabeth successfully imposed a much more formal organization structure on her company, and her company is now a long way from its days as a brash startup. The atmosphere is now more professional, more structured, and more formal. These developments were certainly necessary for CanGo to prepare for its planned IPO, which requires a more professional image and formal procedures. So, the changes had the intended benefits. However, as you'll see in this video, one unintended (but not entirely unexpected) outcome was that CanGo seems to be less fun. In other words, in changing its structure and procedures, Liz also changed CanGo's corporate culture, and in some respects not for the better. Watching the video, one has to wonder whether Liz didn't swing too far from an organic to a mechanistic type of organizational approach.

Watch the video, and answer the following questions:

1. Based on what you know about CanGo's industry and environment and its management team, explain (using what you learned in Chapter 9) what the situation calls for, in terms of organizing CanGo's lines of authority; departmentalization; degree of specialization of jobs; delegation and decentralization; and span of control. Do you think Elizabeth was right to impose a more formal organization on the company? Why or why not?

2. Based on what you know about the company, write a short (1/2-page) explanation of how you would reorganize CanGo from its current structure to that of a learning organization.

APPLY IT

As is often the case, few decisions that managers have to make involve a single function only. In this video, Elizabeth almost seems to be more concerned with non-organizational issues than with organizational ones; morale ("It used to be fun," as she puts it) is one example. Give several examples of planning, leading, or controlling issues she seems to be concerned about, and briefly explain how you would address them if you were Elizabeth.

Staffing and Human Resource Management

LEARN IT

Test Your Understanding

1. If an organization has men and women performing the same or similar work, they must be paid equal pay according to the _____.

2. _____ _____ is now an important staffing tool for speeding the recruitment process, generating job descriptions, and facilitating training sessions.

3. Our employer feels that after the employee has been recruited and selected, the applicant should go through a(n) _____ program in which we cover such topics as safety rules, information about working conditions, and how to get on the payroll.

4. Yvonne must develop complete and accurate job descriptions for her organization. In order to do so she must first conduct a(n) _____ _____.

5. Jennifer is trying to fill an opening in her department. She is looking for someone who is a university graduate, with at least three years' experience in the field, and with excellent computer skills. These requirements are _____ _____.

6. When Raymundo interviewed me for the web designer job, he asked me, "If you could change the design of our current corporate website, how would you do it?" Fortunately, I was prepared to answer this _____ question, and I aced the interview!

7. Suzanne is very upset. The office where she works is not only male dominated but also prominently displays sexually suggestive posters and calendars that make her feel very uncomfortable. She is experiencing _____.

8. Many companies use a variety of _____ _____ to screen for suitable job candidates, though they must pay attention to legal and ethical constraints. In addition, one can't use them to tell whether a prospective employee is likely to remain _____, an increasingly important consideration given today's uncertain economic climate.

9. Manuel owns a construction company that has several government contracts. He must make extra effort to hire and promote women and minorities according to his _____ _____ plan.

10. As a first-line supervisor, Marika must evaluate the job performance of her 15 employees over the last year. Her company uses the _____ _____ method in which several job characteristics are listed, and she must rate each employee from poor to excellent on each of those characteristics.

11. Al, a project manager, hates using his company's performance appraisal method since he must give at least 10% of his employees a "poor" rating. This _____ _____ method places predetermined percentages of employees into performance categories. In recent years, Ford and other companies have come under fire for using it.

12. Avivah's company has recently adopted a program by which an employee first gets an oral warning for breaking company rules, then a written warning, then a paid one-day "decision-making leave" for the next occurrence. This paid decision-making technique is known as _____ _____ _____.

13. Na'il feels that he has been discriminated against because of his race and colour. If he chooses, he may file a complaint with the _____, which will investigate the charges.

14. Most fast-food organizations must ensure that they are paying their employees at least the minimum wage, and are not violating rules concerning the employment of minors. Both of these issues are regulated by the _____ _____ Act.

PRACTICE IT

Video for Staffing and Human Resource Management In this video, the CanGo management team gets a short presentation from Ethel, the company's accountant, regarding the results of the performance appraisals they did for each of their subordinates. As she explains it, the main problem seems to be that the managers are not discriminating very well among employees in terms of performance. Instead, they are rating all or most employees high, which means all are in line for merit raises and promotions. As you watch this video, consider the alternatives the management team proposes.

Watch the video, and answer the following questions:

1. Clark is clearly having a problem with the present system. What kind of error is he making? What can be done to lessen or eliminate this problem?

2. Evaluate Clark's suggestion that managers should rank, not rate, employees. Do you think that ranking generally works well? Will it work well at CanGo? Why or why not?

APPLY IT

As is often the case, few decisions that managers have to make involve a single function only. In this video, for instance, you might ask whether Liz and her HR managers really did their jobs in terms of training the management team in how to use the performance appraisal form, and therefore avoid the problems Ethel is talking about now. Based on what you read in this chapter, what other staffing techniques might have helped Liz and the HR manager avoid the problems that are surfacing now? What could Liz have done in terms of planning, leading, or controlling that might have helped avoid these problems?

Being a Leader

LEARN IT

Test Your Understanding

1. Jay is somewhat eccentric but he does a good job of influencing us to work willingly toward organizational objectives. This can also be called _____ ___.

2. Natasha's leadership _____ include drive, integrity, and self-confidence, but she also possesses important _____, such as know-how and creativity, that spur us on to achieve our departmental goals.

3. Our team leader, Ranu, is modest, calm, and always willing to take the blame when things go wrong, but, at the same time, he sets high standards and will settle for nothing less than the best—whatever gets the job done, he'll do. Ranu exhibits __ _____ leadership.

4. As a recently hired manager, Oliver knows that power is important to leadership, and that a good degree of his power will stem from his _____ as manager.

5. Even though Ivan is not the manager of his department, he is recognized throughout the company when it comes to meeting ISO quality standards. Normally, if he says that something needs to happen in order to meet the latest quality standards, it happens. In this regard, Ivan is a(n) _____ __.

6. Tamiko always lets her subordinates know what she expects of them, gives them specific guidance as to what should be done, how it should be done, and when it should be finished. According to the Ohio State University studies, Tamiko is exhibiting _____ leadership.

7. Colleen is a very _____ leader in that when there is a need to make a decision, she makes the decision herself, rather than involving her subordinates.

8. My son works as a store manager for a retail hardware chain. His approach to leadership appears to be focusing upon accomplishing goals while maintaining good working relationships with his employees. He is a(n) _____ leader.

9. The educational environment is changing rapidly with the accessibility of the internet and the move toward distance learning. Many of us at this college feel that we need a(n) _____ leader, which is someone who can bring about change and innovation, and build employee commitment to those changes.

10. As a government agency that deals with people in extreme crisis, we feel that it is important that we choose a leader who will be a role model of patience, build effective relationships internally and externally, have a high degree of social sensitivity, and be a good communicator. The high scores in these areas have mostly been _____.

11. David took an LPC test and, much to his surprise, found out that he had a very low LPC score. According to Fiedler, this means that he would be a(n) _____ oriented leader.

12. I recently hired several young workers who seem to be willing to do the job but don't know how to do it. According to the Situational Leadership Theory, I should use the _____ style of leadership with these workers and a(n) _____ style for those who are clearly able to do the job but are unwilling to do it.

13. Tamara is a supervisor with 10 highly skilled educated subordinates. It is clear to even the most casual observer that she has an "in" group and an "out" group. According to the _____ _____ _____ theory, the "in" group members will be treated better and perform better than their "out" group counterparts.

14. Rebecca tends to give unreasonable work assignments and make the job difficult or unpleasant. She also frequently disciplines her staff for minor infractions and has even fired some of her employees. She speaks of these incidents as "setting an example." In terms of power, Rebecca appears to be exercising her _____ power.

15. Our new president is excellent! She shows me how to think about problems in new ways. In terms of being a transformational leader, she is providing _____.

PRACTICE IT

Video for Being a Leader In this video scenario, CanGo CEO Elizabeth has decided to take her online book company into a new business—providing users with the ability to engage in real time online games like chess with people who may be thousands of miles away. As you'll see from the first scenario in this video, she's enormously enthusiastic about the business's potential. However, she knows she can't get this new business off the ground by herself. Her first order of business is to use her leadership skills to get her management team and employees to help her develop the plans CanGo needs to start this new business. As we saw in Chapter 11, the leader always has a variety of tools in his or her leadership toolbox. The video shows the leadership style Elizabeth uses, first with her management team (scenario one), and then with her employees (scenario two). The third scenario raises an interesting question: Since Liz is the same person in both scenarios, why is it she seems to have succeeded with the managers, but struck out with her employees?

Watch the video, and answer the following questions:

1. As a quick first approximation, why do you think she struck out with her employees? (Use what you learned in this chapter to answer.)

2. If you had been in Liz's spot, what two leadership models that you learned how to use in this chapter would you use in these scenario situations, and why?

3. Apply those models in each scenario and explain where you think Elizabeth went wrong and what she should do about it now.

APPLY IT

As is often the case, few decisions that managers have to make involve a single function only. In the situations in this video, how will Liz's leadership style(s) influence her ability to get her plans for CanGo implemented? If her employees don't want to or can't do what she asks of them here, what tools do you think she will have to use to *control* their progress and final results?

CHAPTER 12

Influencing Individual Behaviour and Motivation

LEARN IT

Test Your Understanding

1. Many students enter college with doubts about their ability or capacity to do well in college. In other words their _____ _____ is low.

2. Jillian just won the lottery, so she doesn't have any money worries. She continues to work because she needs to be recognized and appreciated for what she does. In Maslow's terms, it appears that she is motivated to fulfill her _____ needs.

3. I agree with Herzberg: I think that in the workplace _____ factors such as salary and working conditions are dissatisfiers, in that if they are not present or not adequate they will produce dissatisfaction, but if they are adequate they will not motivate the employee.

4. According to McClelland, most teachers would have a strong need to influence or persuade others. He calls this need a need for _____.

5. Kristalee is a financial advisor for a new investment dot com. Her CEO believes that employees will be more motivated if they have a portion of their pay at risk, with the opportunity to earn additional pay. This year, Kristalee brought in so many new clients that she not only got back her 5% at risk but also earned an additional 10%. Kristalee's company is using a(n) _____ _____ to motivate employees.

6. I am an assistant art director at the ad agency where I work now, and my boss, Lucy, knows I would really like to be an art director. She and I have worked together to outline specific, challenging goals I need to achieve before I can be moved up to the art director position. We could say that Lucy is using _____ _____ _____.

7. I feel that I am working harder than Kieran and yet we are getting the same salary. I don't think that this is fair, so according to _____ theory I will be motivated to achieve a level of fairness.

8. Cyrus was happy to move into the project manager position and pleased that his boss, the vice president of research and development, had such confidence in his abilities. However, with no prior managerial experience and no training, Cyrus soon felt overwhelmed and unmotivated. According to Vroom's theory, Cyrus does not have the _____ that his effort will lead to performance.

9. I think that if you truly want to motivate someone to do something, then you need to apply contingent rewards or punishment to their behaviour. This is the basis of _____ _____.

10. I know that many of our employees are bored. I have decided to change their jobs from being fairly specialized and only revolving around two or three tasks, to being responsible for doing four or five tasks on the same level. This horizontal loading of a job is called _____.

11. Manny works for a company in which he changes jobs every nine months in order to increase worker flexibility and alleviate boredom. His company has adopted the practice of _____.

12. Joyce has several customer service people working for her. She frequently observes them "doing something right," but she gives them positive reinforcement only at intervals because she knows that this is the most powerful method of sustaining behaviour. She is using _____.

13. We always get prompt feedback on our work when we do it and praise for extraordinary performance at the monthly staff meetings. The leadership at our company knows that _____ is an inexpensive but extremely effective motivator.

14. If our department increases productivity over the next year, a portion of that gain in productivity will come back to us. This incentive plan is known as a(n) _____ plan.

15. A grant writer for an environmental group, Igor was feeling increasingly bored with his work. After a discussion with his boss, the two realized that Igor needed more contact with the donors to whom the proposals were directed. The nonprofit redesigned Igor's job so that he would meet with major donors and solicit information directly from them. This is an example of using _____ _____ to build motivators, such as opportunities for achievement and recognition, into a job.

PRACTICE IT

Video for Influencing Individual Behaviour and Motivation In this video, you'll see an uncomfortable meeting in which Liz is talking with Andrew about weaknesses in his department's performance. Andrew, in turn, is trying to get his subordinates to create a new logo quickly. Andrew says he's not clear why his staff is not producing the logo as he's told them to. As you watch this video, pay particular attention to how Andrew responds to Liz, and what you think he does wrong or what he fails to do in his attempts to motivate his staff to come up with the new logo.

Watch the video, and answer the following questions:

1. Are you surprised that Andrew's group hasn't accomplished anything on the logo assignment? Why?

2. Whitney clearly feels that her work arrangement is unfair. She feels others in her group have less work to do than she does. How would you use Equity Theory to explain how this situation is leading to decreased motivation on her part?

3. Andrew seems to be under the impression that he is going to motivate his subordinates with a sort of pay for performance incentive plan ("I'll make you marketer of the month," or "We'll go to dinner"). However, judging from his subordinates' reactions, his approach seems to be not just ineffective, but counterproductive. Why do you think they're reacting this way? If you were in Andrew's position, how would you handle his task now?

4. Do you think it would help if Andrew created a behaviour management program for this particular project (developing a new logo)? Why or why not? Assuming you did decide to go ahead with a behaviour management program, analyze the performance problem and recommend how to solve it, including a sample of the forms you might use.

APPLY IT

As is often the case, few decisions that managers have to make involve a single function only. In this video, watching Andrew might cause someone to question his managerial abilities in several areas. For example, watch very carefully how he responds to Liz (about how surprised he is that his employees haven't created the logo yet), and then how (in the video) he seems to be presenting them with the assignment for the first time. There seems to be a disconnect, one that might raise a question about Andrew's forthrightness. Beyond that, the whole situation—whether or not he set goals for completing the task, for instance, and how he controls progress and follows up—raises many questions about his management ability. Watch the video carefully and list the ways in which it raises questions about Andrew's managerial capabilities with respect to ethics, planning, organizing, leading, and controlling. Be specific.

Improving Communication Skills

LEARN IT

Test Your Understanding

1. Jennifer is preparing a sales presentation for tomorrow, and she wants to urge the sales reps to emphasize one particular feature of the new software package. This central idea is the _____ in the communication process. Jennifer's actual speech is the _____ and the face-to-face sales presentation is the communication _____.

2. In today's world of multi-tasking and information overload, one of the most important techniques to improve communication is actually one of the hardest to do: _____.

3. During my conversation with Mitra over the sales projections, I noticed that she was standing with her arms crossed. This sign of defiance or defensiveness is a form of _____ communication.

4. Sanjay indicated that getting the Henderson account out was "Top Priority." Does this mean that I am supposed to drop the work I am doing for all my customers and work on the Henderson account? This is an example of the interpersonal communication barrier of ambiguity of _____.

5. If I do drop everything else and work on the Henderson account, as the boss told me, what is going to happen when all the other customers start demanding their orders? This interpersonal communication barrier is known as ambiguity of _____.

6. When a manager argues with, criticizes, or even gives advice to a subordinate, the manager is running the risk of triggering _____ mechanisms.

7. I am in the process of privately selling my car. I have three people who are very interested in purchasing it. I can use this competition to my advantage in negotiations. This knowledge is known as _____.

8. Anita is trying to persuade Shelly, the human resources manager, to support an initiative for a new on-site day care centre. She knows Shelly has no children of her own but is very fond of her niece Keisha, who is in the day care. Shelly says, "Just think how wonderful it would be for your sister if she could have Keisha near her during the day and could look in on her and know that she is safe!" Anita is trying to persuade Shelly by seeking _____.

9. At monthly meetings our firm shares financial data, explains the numbers, and rewards employees for performance improvements. In addition, sales data are posted weekly on company bulletin boards throughout headquarters. This method of fostering trust and commitment is called _____ _____ _____.

10. Social gatherings, attitude surveys, formal suggestion systems, and "open-door" policies are all mechanisms of encouraging _____ communication.

11. Toyota's top managers are often found on the shop floor, fielding questions, providing performance information, and ensuring that all employees are aware of their goals and direction. This practice is known as management by _____ _____.

12. In order to coordinate order processing for our company, which manufactures fleece tops, vests, and jackets, our catalogue and retail sales managers have offices right on the factory floor. This is one way in which we seek to improve _____ communication.

13. As a manager, I would not send a memo or email in order to reprimand one of my staff members for poor performance because these forms of communication are too _____ in _____.

14. In our company we use electronic questionnaires, electronic brainstorming tools, and tools for voting or setting priorities as part of an interactive computer-based system that facilitates the solution of unstructured problems by a team of decision makers. This technique is known as a _____ _____ _____ system.

15. We find that it is helpful to use a _____ _____ system that lets each group member put his or her own daily schedule into a shared database to identify the most suitable times for meetings.

PRACTICE IT

Video for Improving Communication Skills This video raises further concerns about Andrew's managerial abilities. You'll see how Andrew's questionable communication skills confuse the situation with George, a new employee. It not only leaves George uncertain about what his work schedule is going to be, but actually triggers a round of rumours among other CanGo employees. As you watch the video, think about what Andrew could have done to avoid giving George a false impression.

Watch the video, and answer the following questions:

1. Based on what you read in Chapter 13, identify the communication barriers Andrew seems to be ignoring in this video.

2. If you were a consultant watching this interaction between Andrew and George, what exactly would you tell Andrew to do to improve his interpersonal communications, based on the principles and practices in Chapter 13?

3. What does this situation tell you about how rumours get started? Given that the rumour is now widespread around CanGo, what do you think Andrew (or some other manager) should do to clarify the situation?

APPLY IT

As is often the case, few decisions that managers have to make involve a single function only. In this video, Andrew seems to be exhibiting a number of traits and inadequacies that could raise further doubts about his abilities as a manager. Drawing on what you know to this point about individual behaviour and motivation and about planning, organizing, leading, and controlling, how would you size up Andrew's managerial skills in this video? If you were advising Liz, what would you advise her to do about Andrew at this point?

Leading Groups and Teams

LEARN IT

Test Your Understanding

1. I was surprised to learn that many managers rate _____ _____ programs as their biggest productivity boosters.

2. A(n) _____ is distinguished by the fact that its members are committed to a common purpose or set of performance goals, while a(n) _____ is two or more persons who are interacting with one another in such a manner that each person influences and is influenced by each other person.

3. Members of our work group always "cover" for each other when someone is having a bad day, but members of Chaz's group tend to stick to more rigidly defined roles. The behaviour of either group could be labelled a group _____.

4. _____ competition, such as bowling tournaments between teams, tend to boost cohesiveness, whereas _____ competition among team members tends to undermine it.

5. Our work team has a lot of influence in the activities in our own work area, such as setting our own goals and scheduling our work, but we know that Aylin is still the supervisor. We are a(n) _____ team.

6. Five of us have been assigned to the task of identifying workable alternatives for increasing productivity by 15 percent. We could be called a(n) _____ team.

7. I wish that I were a member of Farah's team. They set their own work schedule, establish their own goals, hire and train team members, and deal with vendors on their own. They are obviously a(n) _____ _____ team.

8. A semi-autonomous unit that is given the task of developing new and creative ideas and that has its own budget and leader, as well as the freedom to make decisions within broad guidelines, is a(n) _____ team.

9. In today's world of global activities and demands, it is often very useful to utilize _____ teams whose members rarely, if ever, meet face-to-face. Instead, they rely upon information technology for their very existence.

10. Our team, which is spread out across several divisions, kicked off with a cocktail party at which we all introduced ourselves and spoke about our backgrounds and expectations for the team. I'm pleased that each team member has a specific task and role and is enthusiastic about our goal. All of these things contribute to creating high level of _____.

11. It's a few weeks into our shift to self-managed teams, and members of our team are notably less enthusiastic. There is also considerable confusion about whom to report to on a daily basis. Yet our team leader says, "Not to worry, we're just in the _____ stage of team creation."

12. Alistair has decided to avoid some of the possible disadvantages of group decision-making by soliciting experts' opinions via questionnaires. He is using the _____ _____.

13. One or two members of Lisa's group will inevitably try to dominate a group. Lisa has decided that in order to avoid this situation, she will appoint one person to defend the proposed group solution, and another person to argue against the proposed solution. Lisa is using the _____ _____ _____.

14. Our organization discovered the hard way that although social support is important, _____ _____ such as timely information, resources, and rewards that encourage group, rather than individual, performance are more important in ensuring cohesiveness.

15. Perhaps the most important determinant in producing cohesive and effective teams isn't demographic similarity, but creating teams whose members share _____ _____.

PRACTICE IT

Video for Leading Groups and Teams CanGo is preparing for an IPO. If the IPO is successful, CanGo will have the funds it needs to expand. Before an IPO can happen, it is important that potential investors have a good understanding of what CanGo does and why it will be successful as a publicly owned company. The video revolves around an early stage in the process of taking CanGo public. It involves developing a presentation which makes the case that CanGo is ready for an IPO. Management needs to provide detailed information about all aspects of the business. This is a huge and immensely important task, because if the presentation fails, so may CanGo's IPO. It is not a project for just one person. The task is too big, the timing is too tight, and it requires integrating different areas of expertise. It calls for the work of a cohesive team. The video is focused on the formation of a work team to develop CanGo's presentation. As you watch, pay close attention to how the team is formed and to the directions and guidance the team gets.

Watch the video, and answer the following questions:

1. Based on what you learned in Chapter 14, analyze this team situation and discuss at least eight reasons why the team does or does not have the necessary building blocks to function effectively.

2. List at least six reasons why the team is not performing effectively.

3. List and discuss at least five reasons why you believe Nick (as usual, the funny man at CanGo) is or is not a team player.

4. Use the checklist in Chapter 14, How to Build a Productive Team, and the list on How to Improve Team Performance to suggest how you would improve the CanGo team's performance.

APPLY IT

As is often the case, few decisions that managers have to make involve a single function. The manager's actions in this video, for example, seem to reflect widespread inadequacies in how she plans, organizes, and gives orders. Pinpoint at least four non-teamwork-related managerial principles or practices she seems to be failing to apply effectively.

Leading Organizational Change

LEARN IT

Test Your Understanding

1. It is imperative that James implements a change in the work flow at his company as speedily as possible. Because speed is essential, he might consider using _____ as his primary method of overcoming resistance to change. However, the risk here is that influential employees will undermine the change.

2. In Paulette's company, everyone has heard rumours that the organization will soon be undergoing a "reorganization." In the past, this term has been a euphemism for downsizing. Paulette and her co-workers are afraid they will lose their jobs. They are experiencing _____ _____ _____ resistance.

3. Benjamin has decided to distribute an attitude survey to all employees and then hold participatory informational meetings to discuss the results in order to get people to recognize the need for change. In Lewin's model, Benjamin is in the _____ step of the change process.

4. A key point to remember about business reengineering is that its purpose is to reengineer a business _____.

5. A local insurance company has recently decided to send every employee the latest customer satisfaction data, which shows the company ranking fourth out of five companies in customer satisfaction. Management is distributing this information in order to create a(n) _____ _____ _____ _____.

6. The deregulation of the telecommunications industry and the subsequent increase in competition forced our telecom company to undergo a(n) _____ change.

7. While the business press is full of stories singing the praises of visionary change leaders such as IBM's former CEO Lou Gerstner, the truth is that most leaders effect change by creating a _____ _____.

8. We have decided to use action research to help our employees analyze and change various personnel practices such as our performance appraisal system and our reward system. These targets are evidence of the _____ _____ _____ management application or intervention.

9. A medical supply company that had recently been lambasted for the poor quality of its products decided to overhaul the entire company to focus on product quality. To keep employees motivated and give them feedback on the change process, the CEO decided to first use business process engineering on one easily fixed aspect of the production process. This company is creating _____ _____ _____.

10. Now that our company has reorganized into teams, Ellen has dug her heels in and absolutely refuses to take on her new responsibilities as team member. She continues to try to maintain control over her little marketing fiefdom. Yet, when other team members or I complain to Saud, the team leader, he just shrugs our complaints off and says, "Ellen will come around. Give her time." In the meantime, we pick up her slack! Saud's conflict resolution style is that of _____.

11. Ryan has discovered that even if both sides differ widely in their approaches, if they trust each other and can discuss their differences in a civil, problem-solving manner, the best conflict-resolution style is often _____.

12. Most labour-management contract negotiations are characterized by both sides giving up on certain issues in order to achieve gains in other areas. This conflict-resolution style is known as _____.

13. Our CEO and company vice presidents tried to make our organization more "open" by sharing information with all employees and even changing the layout of our offices so that everyone—even the CEO—sits in a cubicle. However, within a matter of months, the top managers were still holding meetings away from headquarters and sending out company newsletters with misleading information. This company is in danger of _____.

14. A special approach to organizational and cultural change in which the employees themselves formulate and implement changes that are required (sometimes with the assistance of a trained facilitator) is called _____ _____.

15. When we made the shift from a hierarchical organization to a team-based one, our progress was often halted by conflicts over our roles and responsibilities. Fortunately, our company used a human process application technique called _____ _____ in which data concerning the team's performance was collected and then fed back to the members of the group, to be examined, explained, and analyzed. Then specific action plans were recommended.

PRACTICE IT

Video for Leading Organizational Change In this video, Liz and Warren have a discussion about the sorts of challenges Warren thinks he'll have in convincing his subordinates to go along with CanGo's new organizational structure (which, you may recall, includes bringing in two new assistants). It seems clear that CanGo's management team has now accepted the need for change, and is comfortable with the new structure and procedures. Managers are one thing, however, and employees are another. Warren is especially concerned about how the change will affect his team. He knows the change is necessary, and he knows that he has to get his team to accept the new way of doing things. The question is, how? Pay careful attention to Warren's concerns as you watch this video.

Watch the video, and answer the following questions:

1. Warren's point about his employees not "being focused on the big picture" is a good one. It's important that all of CanGo's employees have a clear idea of where the company is going and why their efforts matter if you want them to buy into the change. What would you do to show them the big picture?

2. We saw in Chapter 15 that changes in reporting relationships and work assignments that result from organizational restructuring are often a source of employee anxiety and concern. What approach should Warren use in explaining to his team that some of them will now be reporting to a different manager and will be performing new tasks?

3. Chapter 15 contains several useful tools, including a model for analyzing what needs to be changed, and a form for analyzing the need for (and how to) reorganizing. Use these two tools to size up the wisdom of the organizational changes CanGo has made to this point, and to make a recommendation to Elizabeth regarding what still needs to be changed at CanGo.

4. Based on the principles and practices in Chapter 15 and what you know about CanGo from this and the other videos, size up the company's organizational culture and make specific recommendations regarding how Elizabeth and her team can improve it.

APPLY IT

As is often the case, few decisions that managers have to make involve a single function only. In this video, Warren is concerned about getting his team to accept change. Give several examples of planning, leading, or controlling issues Warren should address in this attempt to manage change.

Controlling and Building Commitment

LEARN IT

Test Your Understanding

1. In an effort to make his end-of-year performance results look better than they actually were in terms of expenses, Sam ran low on inventory even though he knew that the inventory would have to be purchased in January at a higher price. This is known as _____ .

2. June has established a target of an A grade in her college course. The course has four exams, one paper, and a final exam. After each exam she checks her progress against her goal and takes whatever corrective action is required. June is using the various exams and papers in the course as _____ _____.

3. Our goal this year was to increase profit by 10 percent over last year. Our income statement shows that we increased profits by only 5 percent. In this case the income statement serves as a _____ _____.

4. Our company uses performance reviews as a method for establishing targets and goals for the coming year. They also serve as an excellent tool for identifying performance discrepancies. We use performance reviews as a _____ _____ system.

5. Angelo is so busy that he has stipulated to his employees that only exceptionally good or bad performance should be brought to his attention. Angelo evidently believes in the _____ _____.

6. _____ _____ comprise the heart of the basic management control system.

7. _____ control systems involve setting standards and then monitoring performance through some kind of external monitoring process, whereas _____ control systems rely on getting employees to want to do things right—to exercise self-control.

8. One traditional way to monitor performance and maintain control is to use _____ ratios, such as return on investments (ROI), which compare one financial measure on a financial statement to another. Another way is to use _____ ratios, such as profit per customer or profit per customer visit, to sum up a strategy and monitor whether the company is on target in meeting its strategic goals.

9. When companies use computers to get data on the amount of orders an employee processes or other performance measures, they often _____ employees' feelings of personal control. For this reason _____ _____ _____, while popular, is often controversial.

10. My law firm relies upon a reputation of trust and dependability that I have developed over the years. I am insistent upon every employee knowing and following our code of ethics. Our ethics code is a good example of a(n) _____ control system.

11. Every Friday morning, I meet with all four department heads to discuss circulation numbers and revenues from advertising and to look at our strategies and the assumptions they are based upon. These face-to-face meetings could also be described as a(n) _____ control system.

12. A large local restaurant has decided that one of its goals over the next three months is to increase the sale of desserts by 50 percent. Sales targets were established for the servers, and incentives for reaching the targets were determined. After the end of the month we were surprised to find out that although dessert sales had increased by 75 percent, there had also been a 30 percent rise in customer complaints over the same period. Most of the complaints concerned "pushy" servers. This is an example of _____.

13. Company-wide integrated computer control systems, known now as _____ _____ _____, aim to give managers real-time, instantaneous information regarding the costs and status of every activity and project in the business.

14. Shakim's organization desires to build employee commitment and reduce the need for strict written traditional controls. Building employee commitment usually starts with establishing a sound foundation of _____ _____ values.

15. At our internet startup it's important that everyone—from the CEO to the administrative assistants—be happy to wear many hats and think in terms of "company first" rather than their own little areas. We also seek people who value creativity and risk-taking over security and playing it safe. Hence, when we interview job candidates, we use _____ _____ hiring practices.

PRACTICE IT

Video for Controlling and Building Commitment Prior to the start of the scenario in this video, Elizabeth has gotten some very bad news from her CEO and her accountant. The bad news is that the CanGo financials look terrible. The company is running at a loss, revenues exceed expenses, and many of the important financial ratios suggest that, financially at least, the company is out of control. Elizabeth understandably does not want to take these results to the Board—or, to be more precise, she does not want to take these results to the Board unless she has a plan in place to correct the problem.

As the video opens, Liz's management team has obviously heard the bad news about the financial results, and they're concerned that one or more of them are liable to take the brunt of the blame. Instead, as you can see in the video, Liz comes in and takes the blame herself, saying that she should have kept her eye on the ball. Considering the gravity of the situation, Liz actually doesn't seem as concerned as you might expect her to be. As you watch the video, consider what you would do if you were in Liz's place and just received those horrendous financial results?

Watch the video, and answer the following questions:

1. In the video, Liz admits to the team that she has not used proper control techniques. Exactly which control techniques should she have been using?

2. Liz says she wants a list of the managers' key success factors (KSFs) for their departments, including those for product quality, customer service, employee morale, and competition. Describe one measurable performance standard for each of the KSFs.

3. Based on what you've seen in this video and in the others, rate the adequacy of CanGo's control system, using the checklist in Chapter 16.

APPLY IT

As is often the case, few decisions that managers have to make involve a single function only. This particularly true when it comes to the control function. In this and the preceding chapters, we've talked about the management process—namely, planning, organizing, leading, and controlling. Since this is a textbook, we necessarily cover the topic sequentially, one topic at a time. But as you can probably imagine, that's not the way mangers really manage day-to-day. In other words, you generally won't have the luxury to spend Monday planning, Tuesday organizing, Wednesday and Thursday leading, and Friday controlling. Instead, you'll be doing all these tasks simultaneously. For example, as part of your planning function you'll be sitting with your subordinates trying to formulate goals and motivate them to accept them.

"AS IS" LICENSE AGREEMENT AND LIMITED WARRANTY

READ THIS LICENSE CAREFULLY BEFORE OPENING THIS PACKAGE. BY OPENING THIS PACKAGE, YOU ARE AGREEING TO THE TERMS AND CONDITIONS OF THIS LICENSE. IF YOU DO NOT AGREE, DO NOT OPEN THE PACKAGE. PROMPTLY RETURN THE UNOPENED PACKAGE AND ALL ACCOMPANYING ITEMS TO THE PLACE YOU OBTAINED THEM. *THESE TERMS APPLY TO ALL LICENSED SOFTWARE ON THE DISK EXCEPT THAT THE TERMS FOR USE OF ANY SHAREWARE OR FREEWARE ON THE DISKETTES ARE AS SET FORTH IN THE ELECTRONIC LICENSE LOCATED ON THE DISK:*

1. **GRANT OF LICENSE and OWNERSHIP:** The enclosed computer programs <<and any data>> ("Software") are licensed, not sold, to you by Pearson Education Canada Inc. ("We" or the "Company") in consideration of your adoption of the accompanying Company textbooks and/or other materials, and your agreement to these terms. You own only the disk(s) but we and/or our licensors own the Software itself. This license allows instructors and students enrolled in the course using the Company textbook that accompanies this Software (the "Course") to use and display the enclosed copy of the Software for academic use only, so long as you comply with the terms of this Agreement. You may make one copy for back up only. We reserve any rights not granted to you.

2. **USE RESTRICTIONS:** You may not sell or license copies of the Software or the Documentation to others. You may not transfer, distribute or make available the Software or the Documentation, except to instructors and students in your school who are users of the adopted Company textbook that accompanies this Software in connection with the course for which the textbook was adopted. You may not reverse engineer, disassemble, decompile, modify, adapt, translate or create derivative works based on the Software or the Documentation. You may be held legally responsible for any copying or copyright infringement which is caused by your failure to abide by the terms of these restrictions.

3. **TERMINATION:** This license is effective until terminated. This license will terminate automatically without notice from the Company if you fail to comply with any provisions or limitations of this license. Upon termination, you shall destroy the Documentation and all copies of the Software. All provisions of this Agreement as to limitation and disclaimer of warranties, limitation of liability, remedies or damages, and our ownership rights shall survive termination.

4. **DISCLAIMER OF WARRANTY: THE COMPANY AND ITS LICENSORS MAKE NO WARRANTIES ABOUT THE SOFTWARE, WHICH IS PROVIDED "AS-IS." IF THE DISK IS DEFECTIVE IN MATERIALS OR WORKMANSHIP, YOUR ONLY REMEDY IS TO RETURN IT TO THE COMPANY WITHIN 30 DAYS FOR REPLACEMENT UNLESS THE COMPANY DETERMINES IN GOOD FAITH THAT THE DISK HAS BEEN MISUSED OR IMPROPERLY INSTALLED, REPAIRED, ALTERED OR DAMAGED. THE COMPANY DISCLAIMS ALL WARRANTIES, EXPRESS OR IMPLIED, INCLUDING WITHOUT LIMITATION, THE IMPLIED WARRANTIES OF MERCHANTABILITY AND FITNESS FOR A PARTICULAR PURPOSE. THE COMPANY DOES NOT WARRANT, GUARANTEE OR MAKE ANY REPRESENTATION REGARDING THE ACCURACY, RELIABILITY, CURRENTNESS, USE, OR RESULTS OF USE, OF THE SOFTWARE.**

5. **LIMITATION OF REMEDIES AND DAMAGES: IN NO EVENT, SHALL THE COMPANY OR ITS EMPLOYEES, AGENTS, LICENSORS OR CONTRACTORS BE LIABLE FOR ANY INCIDENTAL, INDIRECT, SPECIAL OR CONSEQUENTIAL DAMAGES ARISING OUT OF OR IN CONNECTION WITH THIS LICENSE OR THE SOFTWARE, INCLUDING, WITHOUT LIMITATION, LOSS OF USE, LOSS OF DATA, LOSS OF INCOME OR PROFIT, OR OTHER LOSSES SUSTAINED AS A RESULT OF INJURY TO ANY PERSON, OR LOSS OF OR DAMAGE TO PROPERTY, OR CLAIMS OF THIRD PARTIES, EVEN IF THE COMPANY OR AN AUTHORIZED REPRESENTATIVE OF THE COMPANY HAS BEEN ADVISED OF THE POSSIBILITY OF SUCH DAMAGES.** SOME JURISDICTIONS DO NOT ALLOW THE LIMITATION OF DAMAGES IN CERTAIN CIRCUMSTANCES, SO THE ABOVE LIMITATIONS MAY NOT ALWAYS APPLY.

6. **GENERAL:** THIS AGREEMENT SHALL BE CONSTRUED AND INTERPRETED ACCORDING TO THE LAWS OF THE PROVINCE OF ONTARIO. This Agreement is the complete and exclusive statement of the agreement between you and the Company and supersedes all proposals, prior agreements, oral or written, and any other communications between you and the company or any of its representatives relating to the subject matter.

Should you have any questions concerning this agreement or if you wish to contact the Company for any reason, please contact in writing: Editorial Manager, Pearson Education Canada, 26 Prince Andrew Place, Don Mills, Ontario, M3C 2T8.

This integrative process is particularly evident when it comes to controlling and building commitment. For one thing, planning and controlling are merely two sides of the same coin: what you control and how you're doing depends entirely on where you want to go, so that deciding where planning leaves off and controlling begins is bound to be somewhat arbitrary. Form teams of three or four students and use Figure 14.1 to present at least five examples showing at what stages in the management process you think CanGo's current "control" problems got their start.